W9-BUY-426

Keats, Shelley, Byron, Hunt, and Their Circles

Keats, Shelley, Byron, Hunt, and Their Circles

A Bibliography: July 1, 1962–December 31, 1974

Edited by

Robert A. Hartley

Compiled by David Bonnell Green, Robert A. Hartley, Robert G. Kirkpatrick, Rae Ann Nager, G. Curtis Olsen, Robert M. Ryan, Lewis M. Schwartz, and Edwin Graves Wilson

UNIVERSITY OF NEBRASKA PRESS
Lincoln and London

Manufactured in the United States of America

Library of Congress Cataloging in Publication Data
Main entry under title:

Keats, Shelley, Byron, Hunt, and their circles.

A collection of the annual bibliographies which appeared in v. 13–25 of the Keats-Shelley journal.
Includes index.
1. English literature—19th century—Bibliography. 2. Romanticism—England—Bibliography. 3. Keats, John, 1795–1821—Bibliography. 4. Shelley, Percy Bysshe, 1792–1822—Bibliography. 5. Byron, George Gordon Noël Byron, Baron, 1788–1824—Bibliography. 6. Hunt, Leigh, 1784–1859—Bibliography. I. Hartley, Robert A., 1940– II. Green, David Bonnell, 1922– III. Keats-Shelley journal.
Z2013.K42 [PR457] 016.821'7'09 78–16118
ISBN 0–8032–0960–6

Contents

Acknowledgments

THE COMPILATION of a reference work such as this requires the cooperation of many individuals.

Over the years, these scholars and librarians have contributed to the annual bibliographies which compose this volume: D. H. Borchardt, Margaret Dalziel, Nils Erik Enkvist, Albert Gérard, H. W. Häusermann, B. L. Kandel, Anna Katona, Siegfried Korninger, Ranka Kuić, Jean de Palacio, Jaime Rest, J. G. Riewald, Takeshi Saito, and Helmut Viebrock. Also: Williston R. Benedict, P. Bogomolva, A. Bose, Arthur Efron, Doucet D. Fischer, Louise M. Hall, Masao Hirai, Mrs. G. Louis-Dreyfus, Mrs. Kenneth McIntyre, Marsha M. Manns, L. Nikitina, Estuardo Nuñez, Witold Ostrowski, A. C. Partridge, Barbara E. Rooke, Donald J. Ryan, Edvige Schulte, Aloys Skoumal, Torbjörn Söderholm, Karel Štěpaník, K. Szymanowski, Magdi Wahba, Zofia Walczy, and Helena Więckowska.

Assistance was provided by the library staffs of Boston University, Columbia University, Duke University, Harvard University, Hunter College, Kingsborough Community College, Lehman College, Library of Congress, New York Public Library, University of North Carolina at Chapel Hill, University of Notre Dame, University of Pennsylvania, Rutgers University–Camden, Saint Mary's College, and Wake Forest University.

Hubert F. Babinski, Istvan Deak, Mihai H. Handrea, Mrs. Evro Layton, and Mrs. Kisia Trolle translated many foreign-language entries.

The bibliographies were compiled by David Bonnell Green, Robert A. Hartley, Robert G. Kirkpatrick, Rae Ann Nager, G. Curtis Olsen, Robert M. Ryan, Lewis M. Schwartz, and Edwin Graves Wilson, with the assistance of Clement Dunbar and Gerald B. Kauvar.

Carl Woodring and Donald H. Reiman supplied the organizational initiative that allowed the bibliography to survive the death of David Bonnell Green, and they frequently have been helpful in other ways.

I am grateful to Helen Manheim Hartley, who devoted a substantial amount of time to help in proofreading.

The composition of the index was facilitated through the use of a computer. I owe a special debt of gratitude to Peter Smith, Department of Mathematics, Saint Mary's College (Notre Dame, Indiana), who programed the computer specifically for this project. His consistently helpful participation was a model for cooperative efforts between the sciences and the humanities. I am also grateful to Saint Mary's College for the use of their data processing and duplicating facilities.

How to Use This Book

Contents

This book reprints in chronological order the annual bibliographies originally published with Volumes XIII, XIV, XV, XVI, XVII, XVIII, XIX, XX, XXI–XXII, and XXIII–XXV of the *Keats-Shelley Journal.* Thus, it lists items published during the period July 1962 through December 1974, and forms a companion volume to *Keats, Shelley, Byron, Hunt, and Their Circles—A Bibliography: July 1, 1950–June 30, 1962*, edited by David Bonnell Green and Edwin Graves Wilson and published by the University of Nebraska Press (Lincoln, 1964), which collected the annual bibliographies published with the first twelve volumes of the *Journal.*

Over the years the annual issues have been compiled by various people, but the guiding principle of all has been thoroughness. With the exception of textbooks, the bibliography lists all publications by or about Keats, Shelley, Byron, Hunt, and members of their circles that the compilers were able to discover. Even works on other subjects are included if they contain significant reference to a relevant figure. For example, an edition of George Bernard Shaw's letters is listed because it contains a number of comments on Shelley. Readers interested in the relevant figures can be confident that they are using the most complete listing available for the specified period. The descriptive annotations, which accompany most items, should also contribute to the usefulness of the bibliography.

Clearly the bibliography lists publications dealing with Keats, Shelley, Byron, and Hunt. But who are the members of their circles also covered? It must be admitted that over the years the identification of circle members has varied somewhat according to the compiler. All of the compilers, however, have regarded the following as circle members and thus treated them with the same fullness accorded to Keats, Shelley, Byron, and Hunt: William Godwin, Benjamin Robert Haydon, William Hazlitt, John Cam Hobhouse, Thomas Hood, Thomas Love Peacock, John Hamilton Reynolds, Horace Smith, Mary Shelley, Edward John Trelawny, and Mary Wollstonecraft. Compilers of the early issues collected here appear to have given full treatment to the artist Peter De Wint, who was an acquaintance of Keats's. Thomas Moore and Matthew Gregory ("Monk") Lewis, on the other hand, are given full treatment, as members of Byron's circle, only in Volumes XXI–XXII and XXIII–XXV. Judging by the listings, John Clare appears to have been considered a member of the Keats circle by all the compilers, but with no recorded statements on this we cannot be certain that he has been treated fully through the whole period.

Arrangement

Each of the bibliographies reprinted here is divided into the following sections and subsections:

I. General
  Current Bibliographies
  Books and Articles Relating to English Romanticism
II. Byron
  Works
  Books and Articles Relating to Byron and His Circle
III. Hunt
  Works
  Books and Articles Relating to Hunt
IV. Keats
  Works
  Books and Articles Relating to Keats and His Circle
V. Shelley
  Works
  Books and Articles Relating to Shelley and His Circle
VI. Phonograph Records (omitted after 1972)

In each volume, items are arranged alphabetically within each subsection but are numbered consecutively through the whole issue.

Cross-references

The annual bibliographies collected in this volume contain numerous cross-references. Cross-references such as "See No. 36," "Also see No. 15," and "See Nos. 648, 650a, 813" point to items within the same issue. Cross-references to previous issues take two forms. In Volumes XIII through XIX cross-reference is to the page number of the previous issue in question: for example, if the cross-reference reads "See K-SJ, XVI (1967), 126," the reader should first turn to the part of the book designated Volume XVI (the volume number appears at the top of each right-hand page) and then within that volume to page 126, using the original pagination appearing at the *top* of each page. Beginning with Volume XX, cross-reference is to item number, not page number: if the cross reference reads "See K-SJ, 18 (1969), No. 178" the reader once again turns to the volume number, in this case XVIII (within the bibliography, Roman numerals for volume numbers of periodicals were replaced by Arabic beginning with Volume XX) and then to the item number, in this case No. 178. No confusion between these two systems will arise because the second system always includes the abbreviation "No." or "Nos." to indicate that the reference is to item number, not page.

Index

A single comprehensive index provides access to all the annual bibliographies collected in this book. This index includes (1) authors, editors, compilers, etc., of items listed in the bibliographies; (2) authors of book reviews; (3) figures whose names or works are included in titles of books and articles or are mentioned in annotations.

In addition, the index includes titles of works by Keats, Shelley, Byron, Hunt, and members of their circles when they appear as, or in, titles of items, or when they are mentioned in annotations. "Hidden" references are not indexed: if, for example, a book includes a discussion of *Endymion,* a reference to the book is included in the index under "*Endymion*" only if the poem is mentioned in the annotation to the entry for the book. Thus, though *John Keats* by Walter Jackson Bate contains a discussion of *Endymion* (and numerous other works by Keats), the index listing for *Endymion* does not refer the reader to Bate's book.

Since the present volume photographically reprints in sequence Volumes XIII through XXIII–XXV of the bibliographies originally published with the *Keats-Shelley Journal,* the index refers the reader first (in boldface Roman numerals) to the volume in which the item appears, and second (in Arabic numerals) to the item number within that volume. A sample from the index will demonstrate the arrangement. To find **XXI–XXII**, 121, the reader should first turn to the part of the book designated Volume XXI–XXII (the volume number is printed at the top of each right-hand page). He will then quickly pick up the sequence of entries in numerical order and readily locate item 121.

Errata

An errata list follows the index. The editor would appreciate being notified of additional errors discovered by readers. Please write to him in care of the University of Nebraska Press, 318 Nebraska Hall, Lincoln, Nebraska, 68588.

Trends in Scholarship

Judging by the numbers of items alone, some general conclusions may be drawn regarding the relative interest in Keats, Shelley, and Byron over the period covered by this volume, mid-1962 through 1974. The year-to-year figures show that interest in Byron grew slowly but quite steadily until 1974, the 150th anniversary of Byron's death, when the number of items was almost double that for the previous year, far surpassing those for Shelley and Keats. (Data for 1975 and 1976 indicate that the very high level of interest in Byron was maintained.) Until the Byron anniversary, interest in Shelley and Keats grew at a faster rate, but less uniformly, than interest in Byron, and interest in Shelley increased more rapidly than interest in Keats during the full period of mid-1962 through 1974.[1]

Of course, the numbers by themselves suggest only the most general trends. If we consider the notable works published during this period, a much more detailed and revealing picture emerges, and what stands out most is the number of significant works on Shelley. An astonishing number of these represent a new effort to transmit accurately the Shelley canon. Among these were a collected edition of the letters edited by Frederick L. Jones, editions of the Esdaile notebook of early poems by Kenneth Neill Cameron and Neville Rogers, a reediting of "The Triumph of Life" by Donald H. Reiman, Lawrence John Zillman's edition of *Prometheus Unbound,* Irving Massey's *Posthumous Poems of Shelley,* new versions of major Shelley lyrics from Judith Chernaik, the first volume in Rogers's edition of the complete poetry, and other texts edited by R. B. Woodings, Joseph Raben, and Timothy Webb. Deserving of special mention is The Carl H. Pforzheimer Library's continuing series *Shelley and his Circle, 1773–1822,* Vols. III and IV edited by Kenneth Neill Cameron, V and VI edited by Donald H. Reiman, whose wealth of textual and biographical material, not only on Shelley, remains to be fully assimilated. A book that does make use of this material is Cameron's essential critical and biographical study of Shelley's mature years (1814–1822), *Shelley: The Golden Years.* A full biographical treatment, *Shelley: The Pursuit*, came from Richard Holmes. Of critical works, there is general recognition that Earl R. Wasserman's *Shelley's "Prometheus Unbound": A Critical Reading* and *Shelley: A Critical Reading* have had great influence. Also significant are Stuart Curran's study of *The Cenci*, Gerald McNiece's book on Shelley and revolution, and the chapter on Shelley in Carl Woodring's *Politics in English Romantic Poetry*.

1. Data for these comparisons were derived from the bibliographies collected here and from the *MLA International Bibliography*.

Interest in Byron during this period remained strongly biographical and (less strongly) critical. Exceptions include new editions, with critical commentary, of *Cain* and *Hebrew Melodies* by Truman Guy Steffan and Thomas L. Ashton, respectively, and concordances by Ione Dodson Young and (to *Don Juan*) by Charles W. Hagelman, Jr., and Robert J. Barnes. A most ambitious project got under way with the publication of the first three volumes of Leslie Marchand's edition of *Byron's Letter and Journals*, a source of nourishment for Byronists for years to come. Important biographical works include new editions of the "conversations" of Byron recorded by Thomas Medwin and Lady Blessington, both edited by Ernest J. Lovell, Jr., Doris Langley Moore's *Lord Byron: Accounts Rendered,* and Malcolm Elwin's *Lord Byron's Wife.* Critical studies were published by Robert F. Gleckner, Jerome J. McGann, Michael G. Cooke, and W. Paul Elledge. A new periodical, *Byron Journal,* made its appearance in 1973.

The major event in Keats scholarship was the publication of Walter Jackson Bate's *John Keats,* a literary biography that was accepted by many as the standard life. It was followed by two other biographies of note, *John Keats: The Making of a Poet* by Aileen Ward and *John Keats* by Robert Gittings. A book that opened new perspectives was Ian Jack's study of Keats's debt to the fine arts, *Keats and the Mirror of Art.* But most of the activity in Keats scholarship was critical. Whereas there were a modest number of critical books on Byron's poetry and few on Shelley's, there were numerous ones on Keats's.[2] Among them were those written by Walter Evert, Mario L. D'Avanzo, Norman Talbot, M. A. Goldberg, John Jones, Gerald B. Kauvar, Charles I. Patterson, Morris Dickstein, Stuart M. Sperry, and Christopher Ricks. For the most part, these studies used H. W. Garrod's edition (1939; slightly revised, 1958), but Jack Stillinger's study, *The Texts of Keats's Poems* (1974), heralds for Keats a renewed concern for textual accuracy, which has been preoccupying Shelleyans and is beginning to preoccupy Byronists.

Though important works were published on Hunt, Hazlitt, Godwin, and Peacock during this period, the numbers indicate a more or less constant level of interest. On the other hand, interest in Mary Wollstonecraft and Mary Shelley definitely increased. For both mother and daughter this was evidenced by reprintings of their works (some long unavailable) and more books and articles about them.

It remains to note some works of Romantic scholarship relevant to more than one of our authors. Three works that combine, in diverse ways, history and literary criticism are M. H. Abrams's *Natural Supernaturalism,* with considerable discussion of Shelley and some of Keats, Ian Jack's *English Literature, 1815–1832* (Oxford History of English Literature), and Carl

2. We are dealing here with general critical studies. Numerous articles, and some books, on specific poems by all three writers continued to be published. These can be located by looking in the index under the titles of the subject poems.

Woodring's *Politics in English Romantic Poetry,* already mentioned for its chapter on Shelley but also containing an important chapter on Byron and some treatment of Keats. A noticeable concentration of attention, consistent with Abrams's approach, was the relationship between the Romantics and Milton, a subject treated by Joseph Anthony Wittreich, Jr., Stuart Curran, Luther L. Scales, Jr., and Leslie Brisman. The subject of contemporary reviews of the Romantics received a great deal of attention, with studies, collections, and listings by John O. Hayden, Donald H. Reiman, William S. Ward, Theodore Redpath, and Lewis M. Schwartz. Last, but in a sense first, were some useful bibliographies: Ian Jack's *English Literature, 1815–1832; The New Cambridge Bibliography of English Literature,* Vol. III, *1800–1900,* edited by George Watson; a new edition of the MLA's *The English Romantic Poets: A Review of Research and Criticism,* edited by Frank Jordan, Jr.; and *Keats, Shelley, Byron, Hunt, and Their Circles–A Bibliography: July 1, 1950–June 30 1962,* which brings us up to the present volume.

Abbreviations and Symbols

ABC	American Book Collector
AL	American Literature
AN&Q	American Notes and Queries
ASNS	Archiv für das Studium der neueren Sprachen
AUMLA	AUMLA: Journal of the Australasian Universities Language and Literature Association
BA	Books Abroad
BC	Book Collector
BJ	Byron Journal
BNYPL	Bulletin of the New York Public Library
CE	College English
CL	Comparative Literature
CLB	Charles Lamb Bulletin
CLSB	C. L. S. Bulletin (Charles Lamb Society)
CR	Contemporary Review
DA	Dissertation Abstracts
DAI	Dissertation Abstracts International
EA	Etudes anglaises
EC	Essays in Criticism
ELH	ELH. Journal of English Literary History
ELN	English Language Notes
ES	English Studies
Exp	Explicator
HLQ	Huntington Library Quarterly
ICS	L'Italia che scrive
ILN	Illustrated London News
JAAC	Journal of Aesthetics and Art Criticism
JEGP	Journal of English and Germanic Philology
JHI	Journal of the History of Ideas
KR	Kenyon Review
K-SJ	Keats-Shelley Journal
KSMB	Keats-Shelley Memorial Bulletin
LC	Library Chronicle

Li	Listener
LJ	Library Journal
MLN	Modern Language Notes
MLQ	Modern Language Quarterly
MLR	Modern Language Review
MP	Modern Philology
MWN	Mary Wollstonecraft Newsletter, *and successor,* Mary Wollstonecraft Journal
N&Q	Notes and Queries
NS	New Statesman
NYHT	New York Herald Tribune Book Review
NYRB	New York Review of Books
NYT	New York Times Book Review
PBSA	PBSA: Papers of the Bibliographical Society of America
PMLA	PMLA: Publications of the Modern Language Association of America
PQ	Philological Quarterly
PR	Partisan Review
QQ	Queen's Quarterly
RES	Review of English Studies
RLC	Revue de littérature comparée
SAQ	South Atlantic Quarterly
SatR	Saturday Review
SEL	Studies in English Literature 1500–1900
SIR	Studies in Romanticism
SP	Studies in Philology
Spec	Spectator
SR	Sewanee Review
T&T	Time and Tide
TC	Twentieth Century
TLS	Times Literary Supplement
UES	Unisa English Studies
UTQ	University of Toronto Quarterly
VQR	Virginia Quarterly Review
WC	Wordsworth Circle
*	Item not seen by compiler
†	Item abstracted in *Abstracts of English Studies*
‡	Item abstracted in *MLA Abstracts*

Bibliography for July 1, 1962–June 30, 1963

VOLUME XIII

Compiled by DAVID BONNELL GREEN and EDWIN GRAVES WILSON

THIS BIBLIOGRAPHY, a regular department of the *Keats-Shelley Journal,* is a register of the literary interest in Keats, Shelley, Byron, Hunt, and their circles from (approximately) July 1962 through June 1963.

The compilers are indeed grateful, for their generous assistance, to Professors Nils Erik Enkvist, Åbo Akademi; Albert Gérard, University of Wisconsin; H. W. Häusermann, the University of Geneva; Dr. Siegfried Korninger, Universität, Wien; Ranka Kuić, the University of Belgrade; Estuardo Nuñez, Universidad de San Marcos, Lima; Jaime Rest, Universidad Nacional del Sur, Bahia Blanca; Takeshi Saito, International Christian University, Emeritus Professor of Tokyo University; Dr. Helmut Viebrock, Johann Wolfgang Goethe Universität, Frankfurt am Main; Drs. Margaret Dalziel, University of Otago, Dunedin; J. G. Riewald, University of Groningen; Barbara E. Rooke, University of Hong Kong; Miss Zofia Walczy, M.A., Biblioteka Jagiellońska in Krákow; D. H. Borchardt, the University of Tasmania; B. L. Kandel, the M. E. Saltykov-Schedrin State Public Library in Leningrad; Aloys Skoumal, formerly of Prague University Library; and the library staffs of Boston University, Duke University, Harvard University, and Wake Forest College.

We wish to thank Mrs. Kisia Trolle, of the Harvard College Library, for her gracious help with the Russian entries, and Mrs. Evro Layton, also of the Harvard College Library staff, for her kind assistance with the Greek entries.

Each item that we have not seen is marked by an asterisk. Entries which have been abstracted in *Abstracts of English Studies* are marked with a dagger, but entries in previous bibliographies which were abstracted too late for notice have not been repeated.

ABBREVIATIONS

ABC	American Book Collector
AL	American Literature
ASNS	Archiv für das Studium der Neueren Sprachen
BA	Books Abroad
BC	Book Collector
BNYPL	Bulletin of the New York Public Library
CE	College English
CL	Comparative Literature
CLSB	C. L. S. Bulletin (Charles Lamb Society)

CR	Contemporary Review
DA	Dissertation Abstracts
EA	Etudes Anglaises
EC	Essays in Criticism
ELH	Journal of English Literary History
ES	English Studies
Exp	Explicator
HLQ	Huntington Library Quarterly
ICS	L'Italia Che Scrive
ILN	Illustrated London News
JAAC	Journal of Aesthetics and Art Criticism
JEGP	Journal of English and Germanic Philology
JHI	Journal of the History of Ideas
KR	Kenyon Review
K-SJ	Keats-Shelley Journal
KSMB	Keats-Shelley Memorial Bulletin
Li	The Listener
MLN	Modern Language Notes
MLQ	Modern Language Quarterly
MLR	Modern Language Review
MP	Modern Philology
N&Q	Notes and Queries
NS	New Statesman
NYHT	New York Herald Tribune Book Review
NYT	New York Times Book Review
PBSA	Papers of the Bibliographical Society of America
PMLA	Publications of the Modern Language Association of America
PQ	Philological Quarterly
PR	Partisan Review
QQ	Queen's Quarterly
RES	Review of English Studies
RLC	Revue de Littérature Comparée
SAQ	South Atlantic Quarterly
SatR	Saturday Review
SEL	Studies in English Literature 1500-1900
SIR	Studies in Romanticism
SP	Studies in Philology
Spec	Spectator
SR	Sewanee Review
T&T	Time & Tide/ John o'London's Weekly
TC	Twentieth Century
TLS	Times Literary Supplement
VQR	Virginia Quarterly Review

I. GENERAL

Current Bibliographies

1. [Carpenter, Hazen C.] *A Selective Annotated Bibliography of the Major English Writers, 1798-1832.* Special Bibliography Series No. 6. [Colorado Springs:] U. S. Air Force Academy Library, 1959.
2. Erdman, David V., *et al.* "The Romantic Movement: A Selective and Critical Bibliography for the Year 1961," PQ, XLI (Oct. 1962), 649-729.
3. Friedman, Arthur, *et al. English Literature, 1660-1800: A Bibliography of Modern Studies, Founded by Ronald S. Crane,* ed. Gwin J. Kolb and Curt A. Zimansky. Vols. III and IV. Princeton: Princeton Univ., 1962.
4. Gilbert, Judson Bennett. *Disease and Destiny: A Bibliography of Medical References to the Famous.* With Additions and an Introduction by Gordon E. Mestler. London: Dawsons, 1962.
   Byron, Keats, Shelley, and others are included.
5. Green, David Bonnell, and Edwin Graves Wilson. "Current Bibliography," K-SJ, XII (1963), 121-156.
6. Kuntz, Joseph M. *Poetry Explication: A Checklist of Interpretation since 1925 of British and American Poems Past and Present.* Revised Edition. Denver: Alan Swallow, 1962.
   Includes poems by Byron, Hunt, Keats, Peacock, and Shelley.
7. Mish, Charles C., *et al.* "Nineteenth Century [English]" in "1962 Annual Bibliography," ed. Paul A. Brown *et al.*, PMLA, LXXVIII (May 1963), 155-165.
8. Nilon, Charles, and Marjory Rigby, eds. "Nineteenth Century," *Annual Bibliography of English Language and Literature,* XXXIV (1962 [for 1959]), 195-259.
9. Rigby, Marjory, and Charles Nilon, eds. "Nineteenth Century," *Annual Bibliography of English Language and Literature,* XXXV (1963 [for 1960]), 191-261.
10. Saito, Takeshi, comp. "A Blunden Bibliography," *Today's Japan,* V (March-Apr. 1960), 63-68.
    Contains items about Byron, Godwin, Haydon, Hunt, Keats, Shelley, and Mary Shelley.
11. Stratman, Carl J. *A Bibliography of British Dramatic Periodicals 1720-1960.* New York: New York Public Library, 1962.
12. Yarker, P. M., and Sheila M. Smith. "The Nineteenth Century," in *The*

Year's Work in English Studies, ed. Beatrice White and T. S. Dorsch, XLI (1963 [for 1960]), 217-241.

BOOKS AND ARTICLES RELATING TO ENGLISH ROMANTICISM

13. Amarasinghe, Upali. *Dryden and Pope in the Early Nineteenth Century: A Study of Changing Literary Taste 1800-1830.* Cambridge: Cambridge Univ., 1962.

Rev. by K[enneth]. H[opkins]. in *Books and Bookmen,* VIII (Dec. 1962), 46; by I[rène]. S[imon]. in *Revue des langues vivantes,* XXIX (1963), 186-187; by William Kean Seymour in CR, CCIII (Feb. 1963), 109; in TLS, Feb. 1, 1963, p. 78; by G. D. Klingopulos in MLR, LVIII (Apr. 1963), 245-246; by Emerson Robert Loomis in *American Notes & Queries,* I (Apr. 1963), 126-127; by P. K. Elkin in *Aumla,* No. 19 (May 1963), pp. 151-152; by Geoffrey Bullough in *English,* XIV (Summer 1963), 202; by John Butt in *Durham University Journal,* LV (June 1963), 154-155.

14. Artz, Frederick B. *From the Renaissance to Romanticism: Trends in Style in Art, Literature, and Music, 1300-1830.* Chicago: Univ. of Chicago, 1962.

Chapter VI (pp. 219-282) is on "Neo-Classicism and Romanticism 1750-1830."

15. Ashley, L. R. N. "A Guide Right Through the Romantic Movement," CE, XXIV (Nov. 1962), 140.

A poem.

16. Auden, W. H., and Louis Kronenberger, eds. *The Viking Book of Aphorisms: A Personal Selection.* New York: Viking, 1962.

Byron, Hazlitt, Keats, Peacock, and Shelley are among those selected.

17. Barzun, Jacques. *Classic, Romantic and Modern.* See K-SJ, XI (1962), 109.

Now available in an English edition (London: Secker and Warburg, 1962).

Rev. in TLS, Oct. 26, 1962, p. 826.

18. Beach, Joseph Warren. *English Literature of the 19th and the Early 20th Centuries, 1798 to the First World War.* New York: Collier, 1962.

A paper-bound reprint of Vol. IV of *A History of English Literature,* ed. Hardin Craig, which was first published in 1950.

19. Blackstone, Bernard. *The Lost Travellers: A Romantic Theme with Variations.* London: Longmans, 1962.

An analysis of "various travel patterns in early-nineteenth-century verse." Byron, Keats, Shelley, and other Romantics are discussed at length.

Rev. by A. O. J. Cockshut in *Tablet,* CCXVI (July 14, 1962), 666; by G. M. Matthews in Spec, July 27, 1962, p. 123; in TLS, Aug. 3, 1962, p. 558; by John Gross in NS, LXIV (Aug. 17, 1962), 202-203; by Mario Praz in MLR, LVIII (Jan. 1963), 107-108.

20. Bloom, Harold, ed. *English Romantic Poetry: An Anthology.* 2 vols. Garden City: Doubleday, 1963. "Anchor Books."

An expanded edition of a work first published in 1961. See K-SJ, XII (1963), 123.

21. Bloom, Harold. *The Visionary Company: A Reading of English Romantic Poetry.* See K-SJ, XII (1963), 123.

Rev. by *Joanna Richardson in *Punch,* CCXLII (May 2, 1962), 699; in *Economist,* CCIII (May 12, 1962), 553; by John Gross in NS, LXIV (Aug. 17, 1962), 202-203; by Gilbert Thomas in *English,* XIV (Autumn 1962), 110; by J[ames]. V. L[ogan]. in PQ, XLI (Oct. 1962), 655; by Carlos Baker in K-SJ, XII (1963), 113-115; by H. A. Smith in MLR, LVIII (Jan. 1963), 108-109; by James Benziger in *Criticism,* V (Spring 1963), 185-188; by J. W. R. Purser in RES, N.S., XIV (May 1963), 209-211; by C. S. Lewis in *Encounter,* XX (June 1963), 74, 76. See also No. 73.

22. Brand, C. P. *Italy and the English Romantics: The Italianate Fashion in Early Nineteenth-Century England.* See K-SJ, VIII (1959), 53, IX (1960), 49, XII (1963), 123.

Rev. by R. Pouilliart in *Lettres Romanes,* XVII (1963), 96-101; by Jean de Palacio in RLC, XXXVII (Jan.-March 1963), 119-121.

23. * Brinton, Crane. *The Political Ideas of the English Romanticists.* New York: Russell & Russell, 1962.

A reprint of a book first published in 1926.

24. * Brugger, Ilse M. de. *Breve historia del teatro inglés.* Buenos Aires: Editorial Nova, 1959.

Includes (pp. 142-144) a survey of drama in the Romantic age.

25. Bullough, Geoffrey. *Mirror of Minds: Changing Psychological Beliefs in Eng-*

lish Poetry. London: Athlone, 1962.

Discusses Byron (pp. 138-139), Keats (pp. 139-143), and Shelley (pp. 152-157); makes occasional other references to these poets and their contemporaries.

Rev. by Gilbert Thomas in *English*, XIV (Autumn 1962), 110-111.

26. Bush, Douglas. *English Poetry: The Main Currents from Chaucer to the Present*. London: Methuen, 1961; *New York: Oxford (A Galaxy Book), 1963.

A reprint of the 1952 edition. See K-SJ, III (1954), 113.

27. Bush, Douglas. *Mythology and the Romantic Tradition in English Poetry*. New York: Norton, 1963.

A paper-bound reprint of a book first published in 1937.

28. Cecchi, Emilio. *I grandi romantici inglesi*. See K-SJ, XII (1963), 123.

Rev. by Augusto Guidi in *Lettere Italiane*, XIV (Apr.-June 1962), 234-238.

29. * Craig, Hardin, ed. *Dějiny anglické literatury*. [*A History of English Literature*.] Vols. I and II. Prague: SKNLU, 1963.

Supplemented by a detailed bibliography of Czech translations in book form. Useful bibliographical information is also to be found in Zdeněk Vančura's commentary.

30. * Dąbrowski, Jan. *Polacy w Anglii i o Anglii*. Cracow: Wydawnictwo Literackie, 1962.

Includes discussion of the relationship between Polish and English Romantic poets.

31. Daiches, David. *A Critical History of English Literature*. See K-SJ, XI (1962), 109.

Rev. by J. G. Riewald in ES, XLIV (Feb. 1963), 42-45.

32. Davies, Hugh Sykes. *The Poets and Their Critics*. Vol. II: *Blake to Browning*. London: Hutchinson, 1962.

Has sections on Byron (pp. 101-144), Shelley (pp. 145-195), and Keats (pp. 196-242); also has material on Hazlitt, Hunt, and Peacock.

Rev. in TLS, July 13, 1962, p. 510; by G. M. Matthews in Spec, July 27, 1962, p. 123; in *English*, XIV (Autumn 1962), 120.

33. * D'iakonova, N. "Novella Bokachcho v stikhotvornoi obrabotke angliiskikh romantikov," in *Problemy mezhdunarodnykh literaturnykh sviazei* [*Problems of Comparative Literature*] (Leningrad: Leningrad State Univ., 1962), pp. 69-90.

34. * Earle, Peter G. *Unamuno and English Literature*. New York: Hispanic Institute, 1960.

Rev. by J. M. Alberich in *Hispanic Review*, XXX (Jan. 1962), 59-62; by Geoffrey Ribbans in *Bulletin of Hispanic Studies*, XXXIX (Oct. 1962), 252-253; by Oscar Borgers in *Lettres Romanes*, XVII (1963), 191-193.

35. Evans, Sir [Benjamin] Ifor. *English Literature: Values and Traditions*. London: Allen & Unwin; New York: Barnes & Noble (1962).

A revised edition of a work first published in 1942.

Has references to Byron, Keats, and Shelley.

Rev. in TLS, March 8, 1963, p. 170.

36. Fairchild, Hoxie Neale. *Religious Trends in English Poetry*. Vol. V: *1880-1920, Gods of a Changing Poetry*. New York: Columbia Univ., 1962.

Discusses the influence of Byron, Keats, and Shelley on a number of the poets of the period.

37. Fletcher, Richard McClurg. "English Romantic Drama: 1795-1843. A Critical and Historical Study" [Doctoral dissertation, Pennsylvania, 1962], DA, XXIII (Oct. 1962), 1364.

38. Foerster, Donald M. *The Fortunes of Epic Poetry: A Study in English and American Criticism 1750-1950*. Washington: Catholic Univ., 1962.

Discusses English Romantic concepts of the epic.

39. Ford, Boris, ed. *From Blake to Byron*. See K-SJ, VIII (1959), 53, IX (1960), 50, X (1961), 73, XI (1962), 110, XII (1963), 124.

Rev. by William Kean Seymour in CR, CCII (Sept. 1962), 160.

40. Freeman, John. *Literature & Locality: The Literary Topography of Britain and Ireland*. London: Cassell, 1963.

Discusses places associated with Byron, Hazlitt, Hood, Hunt, Keats, Peacock, and the Shelleys.

41. Gleckner, Robert F., and Gerald E. Enscoe, eds. *Romanticism: Points of View*. See K-SJ, XII (1963), 124.

Rev. in *Creative Writing*, XIII (Oct. 1962), 33.

42. Gottfried, Leon. *Matthew Arnold and*

the Romantics. London: Routledge, 1963.
Rev. by Kenneth Allott in Li, LXIX (March 14, 1963), 469; by K[enneth]. H[opkins]. in *Books and Bookmen*, VIII (Apr. 1963), 29; in TLS, May 24, 1963, p. 372.

43. Hartman, Geoffrey H. "Romanticism and 'Anti-Self-Consciousness,'" *Centennial Review of Arts & Science*, VI (1962), 553-565.

44. Hobsbawm, E. J. *The Age of Revolution 1789-1848*. Cleveland: World, 1962.
Devotes a chapter to "The Arts" (pp. 253-276).

45. * Hussain, Imdad. "Oriental Elements in English Poetry, 1784-1859," *Venture*, I (June 1960), 156-165.†

46. James, D. G. *Matthew Arnold and the Decline of English Romanticism*. See K-SJ, XI (1962), 110, XII (1963), 124.
Rev. by J. Hillis Miller in CE, XXIV (Oct. 1962), 71; by Robert Langbaum in MP, LX (May 1963), 298-300.

47. * Jechová, Hana. "Quelques remarques sur le style de la poésie romantique polonaise," *Acta Universitatis Palackianae Olomucensis, Fac. Philos.*, XIII, *Philologica*, VIII, in *Studie o literatuře a překladatelství* (1962), pp. 45-54.
Discusses the relationship of some Polish Romantic poets to the style and philosophy of English Romanticism.

48. * Jerschina, S., Z. Libera, and E. Sawrymowicz. *Historia literatury polskiej okresu romantyzmn*. Warsaw: Państw. Zakład Wydawnictw Szkolnych, 1960.
Includes discussion of English Romantic literature.

49. *Keats-Shelley Memorial Bulletin*, XII (1961). See K-SJ, XII (1963), 124.
Rev. by Prema Nandakumar in *Aryan Path*, XXXIII (Sept. 1962), 422-423.

50. *Keats-Shelley Memorial Bulletin*, XIII (1962).
Rev. in CLSB, No. 170 (March 1963), p. 404; in TLS, March 29, 1963, p. 222.

51. Kroeber, Karl. *Romantic Narrative Art*. See K-SJ, XI (1962), 110, XII (1963), 124.
Rev. by C. J. Rawson in N&Q, CCVII (Nov. 1962), 429-430; by Paul Goetsch in *Neueren Sprachen*, Jan. 1963, pp. 39-40. See also No. 73.

52. Laski, Marghanita. *Ecstasy: A Study of Some Secular and Religious Experiences*. Bloomington: Indiana Univ., 1961.
Uses material from Byron, Haydon, Keats, and Shelley.

53. * Lewik, Włodzimierz. "Translations from the English," *Polish Perspectives* (Warsaw), No. 11 (1960), pp. 72-76.
Deals in part with the translations of English Romantic writings.

54. Lister, Raymond. *Great Craftsmen*. London: G. Bell, 1962.
Includes chapter on James and William Tassie, modellers (pp. 125-132); mentions Byron's and Shelley's interest in their work.

55. Mitchell, Stanley. "Romanticism and Socialism," *New Left Review*, No. 19 (March-Apr. 1963), pp. 56-68.
Looks back to the Romantics as "natural forbears" of modern socialist poets.

56. Moore, John [Cecil]. *You English Words*. London: Collins, 1961.
Uses illustrations from the poetry of Byron, Keats, and Shelley.

57. Munby, A. N. L. *The Cult of the Autograph Letter in England*. London: Athlone, 1962.
Has references to Byron, Keats, Shelley, and others.

58. Newton, Eric. *The Romantic Rebellion*. New York: St Martin's, 1963.
A study of Romanticism in the visual arts.
Rev. in TLS, March 1, 1963, p. 148.

59. Nikoliukin, A. N. *Massovaia Poeziia v Anglii, kontsa XVIII nachala XIX vekov*. Moscow: Akad. Nauk. SSSR, 1961.
Includes discussion of Byron, Keats, Shelley, Godwin, and other Romantics.

60. Nowottny, Winifred. *The Language Poets Use*. New York: Oxford Univ.; London: Athlone (1962).
Makes use of passages from Byron, Keats, and Shelley.
Rev. in TLS, May 4, 1962, p. 311; by M. C. Bradbrook in *British Journal of Aesthetics*, III (Apr. 1963), 183-184.

61. Pearson, Gabriel. "Romanticism and Contemporary Poetry," *New Left Review*, No. 16 (July-Aug. 1962), pp. 47-69.
Makes frequent critical use of the poetry of the major Romantics.

62. Peyre, Henri. *Literature and Sincerity*. New Haven: Yale Univ., 1963.

Includes discussion of Byron, Keats, Shelley, and other Romantics.

63. Phelps, Gilbert. *A Short History of English Literature*. London: Folio Society, 1962.
Chapter 5 (pp. 101-127) is on "The Romantic Revival."
Rev. in TLS, March 8, 1963, p. 170.

64. Piper, H[erbert]. W[alter]. *The Active Universe: Pantheism and the Concept of Imagination in the English Romantic Poets*. London: Athlone, 1962.
Rev. in TLS, Apr. 19, 1963, p. 266; by Derek Stanford in *English*, XIV (Summer 1963), 202.

65. *Price, Lawrence Marsden. *Die Aufnahme englischer Literatur in Deutschland 1500-1960*. Bern: Francke, 1961.
A translation of *English Literature in Germany* (1953).
Rev. by Th. C. van Stockum in ES, XLIV (Feb. 1963), 51-53. See also No. 74.

66. Reeves, James. *A Short History of English Poetry*. See K-SJ, XII (1963), 124-125.
Rev. by John Wright in *Aumla*, No. 18 (Nov. 1962), pp. 263-265.

67. Renwick, W[illiam]. L[indsay]. *English Literature 1789-1815*. Oxford: Clarendon, 1963. "The Oxford History of English Literature, Vol. IX."
Includes discussion of Godwin, references to the younger Romantics.
Rev. in TLS, March 1, 1963, p. 154.

68. * Rowland, John Carter. "The Reputation of Dr. Samuel Johnson in England, 1779-1835." (Doctoral dissertation, Western Reserve, 1962.)

69. Roy, G. Ross. *Le sentiment de la nature dans la poésie canadienne anglaise 1867-1918*. Paris: Nizet, 1961.
Notes influence of Byron, Keats, and Shelley.
Rev. in *Bulletin critique du livre français*, XVII (Dec. 1962), 903.

70. Sampson, George. *The Concise Cambridge History of English Literature*. Second Edition. Cambridge: Cambridge Univ., 1961.
Chapter XII (pp. 620-694), "The Nineteenth Century. Part I," is on Byron, Keats, Shelley, and their contemporaries.

71. * Schlauch, Margaret. *Zarys wersyfikacji angielskiej*. Wrocław: Zakład Narodowy im. Ossolińskich, 1958.
Includes discussion of English Romantic poetry.

72. Spender, Stephen, and Donald Hall, eds. *The Concise Encyclopedia of English and American Poets and Poetry*. New York: Hawthorn, 1963.
Includes sections on Byron (pp. 65-66), Hunt (p. 154), Keats (pp. 182-184), and Shelley (pp. 288, 305-306).

73. Stillinger, Jack. "Recent Studies in Nineteenth-Century English Literature," SEL, II (Autumn 1962), 509-528.†
An omnibus review. See K-SJ, XI (1962), 125, No. 316, XII (1963), 123, No. 18, 124, No. 41, 130, No. 153, 132, Nos. 170 and 183, 137, No. 262, 144, No. 404. Also see Nos. 21, 51, 197, 211, 223, and 454.

74. Voisine, J[acques]. "La littérature anglaise en Allemagne au cours des siècles," *Etudes Germaniques*, XVIII (Apr.-June 1963), 217-220.
A review article on *Die Aufnahme englischer Literatur in Deutschland 1500-1960*. See No. 65.

75. Wellek, René. *Concepts of Criticism*. Ed. Stephen G. Nichols, Jr. New Haven: Yale Univ., 1963.
Includes "The Concept of Romanticism in Literary History" (pp. 128-198) and "Romanticism Re-examined" (pp. 199-221). The former is reprinted from CL (1949).

76. Whartenby, Harry Allen, Jr. "Western Mediterranean Islands in English, French, and German Romantic Literature" [Doctoral dissertation, North Carolina, 1962], DA, XXIII (June 1963), 4679.

77. Woodward, Sir Llewellyn. *The Age of Reform 1815-1870*. Second Edition. Oxford: Clarendon, 1962. "The Oxford History of England, Vol. XIII."

II. BYRON

Works: Selected, Single, Translated

78. * "Bajron: More," [translated by] Ivana Anžek, *Smotra* (Belgrade), No. 1 (1962), p. 3. [In Serbo-Croatian.]
Translation of a Byron poem.

79. * *Bajron: Parisina*. [Translated by] Janez Menart. Državna založba Slovenije, 1963. [In Slovenian.]

80. * "Bajron: Proštalna pesma na Čajld Harold," *Razvigor* (Skopje), No. 6 (1963), p. 2. [In Macedonian.]

81. Barnet, Sylvan, *et al.*, eds. *The Genius of the Later English Theater.* New York: New American Library, 1962. "A Mentor Book."
   Includes *Cain* (pp. 186-245).
82. Bush, Eric Wheler, ed. *The Flowers of the Sea: An Anthology of Quotations, Poems and Prose.* London: Allen & Unwin, 1962.
   Includes passages from Byron.
83. *Byron.* Ed. George R. Creeger. New York: Dell, 1962. "Laurel Poetry Series."
84. * *Caim.* [*Cain.*] [Translated by] Manuel Bandeira. Rio de Janeiro: Serviço Nacional de Teatro, 1961.
85. De Selincourt, Aubrey, ed. *The Book of the Sea.* London: Eyre & Spottiswoode, 1961; New York: Norton, 1963.
   Includes passages from Byron, Keats, and Shelley.
86. Gregory, Horace, and Marya Zaturenska, comps. *The Crystal Cabinet: An Invitation to Poetry.* New York: Holt, Rinehart and Winston, 1962.
   Includes poems by Byron (p. 191) and Keats (pp. 115-117).
87. Hall, Donald. ed. *A Poetry Sampler.* New York: Franklin Watts, 1962.
   Includes two poems by Byron and four each by Keats and Shelley.
88. Head, Joseph, and S. L. Cranston, comps. *Reincarnation: An East-West Anthology.* New York: Julian, 1961.
   Includes selections from Byron and Shelley (pp. 128-130).
89. Heinz, W. C., ed. *The Fireside Book of Boxing.* New York: Simon and Schuster, 1961.
   Includes passages from Byron's letters and journal (pp. 64-65), Hazlitt's "The Fight" (pp. 171-178), and two poems by John Hamilton Reynolds (pp. 328-329).
90. Hollander, John, and Harold Bloom, eds. *The Wind and the Rain: An Anthology of Poems for Young People.* Garden City: Doubleday, 1961.
   Includes one poem by Byron, two by Keats, three by Peacock, and four by Shelley.
91. * *Izbrannoe.* [*Selected Poems.*] Ed. Ia. Semezhonova. Preface by Iu. Gavriuk. Minsk: Gosizdat BSSR, 1963. [In White Russian.]
92. Kauffman, Donald T., comp. *The Treasury of Religious Verse.* Westwood, N. J.: Fleming H. Revell, 1962.
   Includes selections from Byron (p. 76), Hunt (p. 206), and Keats (p. 6).
93. Keyes, Frances Parkinson, comp. *A Treasury of Favorite Poems.* New York: Hawthorn, 1963.
   Includes two selections from Byron and four from Keats.
94. * *Lirika. Shil'onskii. Manfred.* [*Lyric Poetry. The Prisoner of Chillon. Manfred.*] [Translated by] A. Khurginas. Preface by D. Iudeliavichus. Second Edition. Kaunas: Gos. izd. ped. literatury, 1962. [In Lithuanian.]
95. Mayer, Tony, ed. and trans. *L'Humour Anglais.* Paris: Julliard, 1961.
   Includes excerpts from Byron and Hazlitt.
96. Nash, Ogden, comp. *Everybody Ought to Know.* Philadelphia: Lippincott, 1961.
   Includes two selections from Byron and one each from Peacock and Hunt.
97. * *Opere alese.* [*Works.*] [Translated by] Virgil Teodorescu. [Preface by] Dan Grigorescu. Bucharest: Editura pentru literatură universală, 1961.
98. * "Palomnichestvo Chail'd Garol'da" [*Childe Harold's Pilgrimage*], (Otryvok iz poemy) [Fragment of the poem], [translated by] G. Sevan, *Grakan tert,* March 30, 1962. [In Armenian.]
99. Canceled.
100. * "Senakheribovo porazhenie" (Stikhi) ["The Destruction of Sennacherib"], [translated by] D. Palamarchuk, *Vsesvyt,* No. 7 (1961), p. 25. [In Ukrainian.]
101. Sutherland, Alistair, and Patrick Anderson, eds. *Eros. An Anthology of Male Friendship.* New York: Citadel, 1963
   Includes selections from Byron (pp. 212-226), Keats (pp. 226-227), Shelley (p. 416), and Hunt (p. 417).
102. * *Tan'damaly šygarmalar.* [*Selected Works.*] Vol. I. [Translated by] Ġ. Qajyrbekov *et al.* Alma-Ata: Kazgoslitizdat, 1960. [In Kazakh.]
103. Untermeyer, Louis, ed. *Collins Albatross Book of Verse: English and American Poetry from the Thirteenth Century to the Present Day.* Revised and Enlarged Edition. London: Collins, 1960.
   Includes poetry by Hunt (p. 346), Byron (pp. 346-352), Shelley (pp. 352-366), and Keats (pp. 369-388).
104. * *When We Two Parted.* Leicester: Pandora, 1962.

105. *Wiersze i poematy*. Ed. Juliusz Żuławski. See K-SJ, XII (1963), 126.
Rev. by *Z. Łapiński in *Tygodnik Powszechny* (Cracow), No. 43 (1961), p. 4; by *Grzegorz Sinko in *Nowe Książki* (Warsaw), No. 22 (1961), pp. 1345-1347.

Books and Articles Relating to Byron and his Circle

106. Adams, Percy G. *Travelers and Travel Liars, 1660-1800*. Berkeley: California Univ., 1962.
Includes material on Admiral John Byron.

107. Alekseev, M. P. *From the History of English Literature: Studies, Essays, Investigations*. See K-SJ, XI (1962), 113, XII (1963), 126.
Rev. by C. L. Wrenn in RES, N.S., XIII (Aug. 1962), 322-323. See also No. 184.

108. Alexander, Boyd. *England's Wealthiest Son: A Study of William Beckford*. London: Centaur, 1962.
Discusses Byron's and Hazlitt's relations with Beckford.

109. Allott, Kenneth. "Arnold's *Empedocles on Etna* and Byron's *Manfred*," N&Q, CCVII (Aug. 1962), 300-302.†
"Arnold discovered a structure for *Empedocles on Etna* by simplifying and rearranging some of the materials of *Manfred*."

110. * Almeida, Pires de. *A escola byroniana no Brasil* (Coleçao Textos e Documentos, 5). São Paulo: Comissâo Estadual de Cultura, Comissâo de Literatura. [Reminiscences of Álvares Azevedo, Aureliano Lessa, *et al.*, with translation of poem by Byron, first published in *O Jornal do Comércio*, 1903-1905.]

111. *Anglo-German and American-German Crosscurrents*. Vol. II. Ed. Philip Allison Shelley and Arthur O. Lewis, Jr. See No. 143.
Rev. by Ann C. Weaver in MLR, LVIII (Apr. 1963), 288; by Leslie Bodi in *Aumla*, No. 19 (May 1963), 191-193.

112. "Auction Sales," ABC, XIII (Jan. 1963), 22, 27.
At Parke-Bernet Galleries (Oct. 16, 1962), first editions of *Don Juan* brought $200; a 40-page Byron manuscript, "The Episode of Nisus and Euryalus," brought $3750; first edition of Keats's *Lamia, Isabella, The Eve of St. Agnes, and Other Poems*, $1000.

113. Auden, W. H. *The Dyer's Hand and Other Essays*. New York: Random House, 1962.
Includes essay on *Don Juan* (pp. 386-406).
Rev. by Patrick Cruttwell in *Hudson Review*, XVI (Summer 1963), 316-318; in TLS, June 7, 1963, p. 404.

Auden, W. H., and Louis Kronenberger, eds. See No. 16.

114. Balzac, Honoré de. *Correspondance*. Vol. I: 1809-June 1832. Vol. II: June 1832-1835. Ed. Roger Pierrot. Paris: Editions Garnier Frères, 1960, 1962.
Refers to Byron several times in his letters.

115. Banks, Gordon T. "The Auction Market," *Manuscripts*, XV (Spring 1963), 46-49.
At the Parke-Bernet sale of Feb. 19, 1963, a letter from Carlyle in which he analyzes *Don Juan* brought $130.

116. Barlow, S[amuel]. L. M. *The Astonished Muse*. New York: John Day, 1961.
Chapter 6 on "The Artist in Politics" (pp. 201-274) includes discussion of Godwin, Byron, and Shelley.

117. Barrows, Herbert. "Convention and Novelty in the Romantic Generation's Experience of Italy," BNYPL, LXVII (June 1963), 360-375.
Looks at Shelley's and Byron's sojourn in Italy "in the context of the individual life, with its specific motivations and needs."

118. Beaty, Frederick L. "Byron's Concept of Ideal Love," K-SJ, XII (1963), 37-54.
A "physical and spiritual union requiring innocence, youth, self-sacrifice, intense passion, and independence from social cares." It "by its very nature could not long endure even if achieved."

119. Beaty, Frederick L. "The Placement of Two Rejected Stanzas in *Don Juan*," N&Q, CCVII (Nov. 1962), 422-423.†
They belong more plausibly after stanza 210 of Canto II than after stanza 211.

Blackstone, Bernard. See No. 19.

120. * Bogusławska, Zofia, and Adam Gruchalski. *Literatura polska okresu romantyzmu. Podręcznik dla techników*. Warsaw: Państw. Wydawnictwa Szkolenia Zawodowego, 1961.
Includes a chapter on Byron.

121. Boyd, Elizabeth French. *Byron's Don Juan: A Critical Study*. See K-SJ, IX (1960), 54.
Rev. by John Heath-Stubbs in *Cambridge Review*, LXXX (May 23, 1959), 543.

122. Bradford, Ernle. *The Wind off the Island*. New York: Harcourt, Brace, 1960.
When in Palermo (pp. 159-160) saw letter written by Byron to great-grandfather of Giulio, a Sicilian friend. There were "several more" there.
Rev. by Charles Poore in *New York Times*, March 18, 1961, p. 21.

123. Britton, Karl. "J. S. Mill: A Debating Speech on Wordsworth, 1829," *Cambridge Review*, LXXIX (March 8, 1958), 418-420, 423.
Discusses Mill's notes for the speech, including his remarks on Byron.

124. Broca, Brito. "L'Italia e i poeti romantici brasiliani," *Letterature moderne*, XII (Jan.-Feb. 1962), 61-67.
Includes discussion of Byron.

125. Bruce, Ian. *Lavalette Bruce, His Adventures and Intrigues before and after Waterloo*. London: Hamish Hamilton, 1953.
The life of Michael Bruce. Includes discussion of his relationship with Lady Caroline Lamb, who took him "into her confidence over her affair with Lord Byron."

Bullough, Geoffrey. See No. 25.

126. * Calin, Vera. *Byron*. Bucharest: Editura tineretului, 1961.

127. Calland, Fred. "Revival of 'Manfred' at Mershon [Auditorium] Is a Memorable Experience," *Citizen-Journal* (Columbus, Ohio), Apr. 6, 1963.
A review of Schumann's work, which was revived as part of the Fifth Conference on the Humanities at Ohio State University.

128. Canaday, John. "Revered, Detested, Romantic Rebel," *New York Times Magazine*, May 5, 1963, pp. 62-63.
About Eugène Delacroix. Reproduces his "Greece Lamenting on the Ruins of Missolonghi."

129. Childers, William C. "A Note on the Dedication to *Don Juan*," K-SJ, XII (1963), 9.
The spelling *pye* in the last line of stanza i probably alludes to a pun by George Steevens on the name of the poet laureate Henry James Pye.

130. * Chudakov, S. V. "O nekotorykh khudozhestvenno—stilisticheskikh osobennostiakh liriki Bairona," *Nauchnye doklady vyssh. shkoly. Filol. nauki*, No. 4 (1962), pp. 145-157.
Discusses style in Byron's poetry.

Clifford, James L., ed. See No. 456.

131. Conrad, Barnaby. *Famous Last Words*. Garden City: Doubleday, 1961.
Includes Byron's, Haydon's, Hazlitt's, Keats's, Peacock's, and Mary Wollstonecraft's.

132. * Cooke, Michael George. "Byron and the Restoration." (Doctoral dissertation, California, 1962.)

133. Courthion, Pierre. *Romanticism*. Translated by Stuart Gilbert. [Lausanne:] Skira, 1961.
Discusses Delacroix's admiration for Byron (pp. 32-34) and reproduces two paintings inspired by the poet.

134. Curtis, Myra. *"Lord Byron's Wife,"* TLS, Dec. 21, 1962, p. 989.
Suggests a fourth course, "to accept Lushington's statements at their face value without supposing that they cover a more sensational revelation than their words convey." See Nos. 140, 146, 149-152, 172, 173, 180-182, 198, and 240.

135. Davies, H. M. P. "The King's School, Canterbury," EA, XVI (Jan.-March 1963), 59-62.
Its Hugh Walpole Collection includes two Byron items.

Davies, Hugh Sykes. See No. 32.

136. de Beer, Gavin. "Byron on the Burning of Shelley," KSMB, XIII (1962), 8-11.
Asserts that a third-hand account recorded by John Carne "represents fairly faithfully what Byron told Hobhouse."

137. de Beer, Gavin. "Meshes of the Byronic Net in Switzerland," ES, XLIII (Oct. 1962), 384-395.†
Relations connecting Byron with Switzerland.

138. de Beer, G[avin]. R. "Mrs. Yosy, A Friend of Switzerland," *Hesperia*, II (Jan. 1951), 104-107.
An account of Anne Cope Yosy, on whose behalf Byron wrote to John Murray.

139. "Le Deuxième Congrès de la Société des Anglicistes de l'Enseignement Supérieur (Lyon, 27-28-29 avril 1962)," EA, XV (Oct.-Dec. 1962), 399-415.

Includes (pp. 408-411) section by F. Natter on "Les Héroïnes Byroniennes (Les femmes dans l'œuvre de Lord Byron)."

140. Dickins, F. *"Lord Byron's Wife,"* TLS, Jan. 11, 1963, p. 32.
Asks for "an end to all this muckraking over Lord and Lady Byron *et al.*" See Nos. 134, 146, 149-152, 172, 173, 180-182, 198, and 240.

141. * Dobree, Bonamy. *Byron's Dramas.* Byron Foundation Lecture 1962. [Nottingham: Univ. of Nottingham, 1962.]

142. Donker, Anthonie. *Ben ik mijn broeders hoeder? Verbeeldingen van Kaïn en Abel.* Amsterdam: Em. Querido's Uitgeversmij N. V., 1960.
Contains an analysis of *Cain* (pp. 92-104) and, in the appendix, an extract from it.
Rev. by Walter Thys in CL, XIV (Fall 1962), 391-392.

143. Dowden, Wilfred S. "Byron through Austrian Eyes," in *Anglo-German and American-German Grosscurrents,* ed. Philip Allison Shelley and Arthur O. Lewis, Jr. (Chapel Hill: Univ. of North Carolina, 1962), II, 175-224.
Examines attitude of Austrian government toward Byron and nature of surveillance placed upon him.
See No. 111.

144. * Dreierström, Else-Marie. "Den sköne lorden," *Växjöbladet,* Feb. 8, 1963.
On Byron.

145. Du Bos, Charles. *Journal IX: Avril 1934-Février 1939.* Paris: La Colombe, 1961.
Mentions Byron and Keats several times.

146. Eaton, Peter. *"Lord Byron's Wife,"* TLS, Jan. 4, 1963, p. 9.
Suggests a "'comic' opera" on the Byron controversy. See Nos. 134, 140, 149-152, 172, 173, 180-182, 198, and 240.

147. Edel, Leon. *Henry James, 1882-1895: The Middle Years.* Philadelphia: Lippincott, 1962.
Discusses James's interest in Byron and Shelley.

148. * Edschmid, Kasimir. *Lord Byron: Roman e Leidenschaft.* Frankfort am Main: Ullstein, 1962.
A reprint of a book first published in 1929.

149. Elwin, Malcolm. *Lord Byron's Wife.* London: Macdonald, 1962; New York: Harcourt, Brace, 1963.
Rev. by Richard Whittington-Egan in *Books and Bookmen,* VIII (Nov. 1962), 25 [see No. 153]; in TLS, Nov. 23, 1962, p. 890; by Peter Quennell in *Observer,* Nov. 25, 1962, p. 26; by John D. Jump in *Manchester Guardian Weekly,* LXXXVII (Nov. 29, 1962), 11; in *The Times,* London, Nov. 29, 1962, p. 15; by Cyril Connolly in *Sunday Times,* Dec. 2, 1962, p. 31; by the Earl of Lytton in T&T, LIII (Dec. 6-13, 1962), 19; by Sylvia Plath in NS, LXIV (Dec. 7, 1962), 828-829; by Edward Lucie-Smith in Li, LXVIII (Dec. 13, 1962), 1019; by B. S. Johnson in Spec, Dec. 14, 1962, p. 938; by Sir Charles Petrie in ILN, CCXLI (Dec. 22, 1962), 1011; in TC, CLXXI (Winter 1962-63), 174; by Orville Prescott in *New York Times,* Apr. 24, 1963, p. 37; by Peter Quennell in NYT, Apr. 28, 1963, pp. 6, 14; in *Time,* May 3, 1963, p. 110; by DeLancey Ferguson in NYHT, May 5, 1963, pp. 6, 11; by Harry T. Moore in SatR, May 11, 1963, pp. 29-30; in *New Yorker,* XXXIX (May 11, 1963), 180-181; by John A. M. Rillie in *Library Review,* Summer 1963, p. 85; by Rosemary Neiswender in *Library Journal,* LXXXVIII (June 15, 1963), 2506.

150. Elwin, Malcolm. *"Lord Byron's Wife,"* TLS, Dec. 14, 1962, p. 973.
Supports his views of Stephen Lushington's accuracy. See Nos. 134, 140, 146, 149, 151, 152, 172, 173, 180-182, 198, and 240.

151. Elwin, Malcolm. *"Lord Byron's Wife,"* TLS, Jan. 4, 1963, p. 9.
Defends his interpretation of Lushington's conduct and his accuracy as a transcriber. See Nos. 134, 140, 146, 149, 150, 152, 172, 173, 180-182, 198, and 240.

152. Elwin, Malcolm. *"Lord Byron's Wife,"* TLS, Jan. 18, 1963, p. 41.
Defends the importance of the subject and his handling of it. See Nos. 134, 140, 146, 149-151, 172, 173, 180-182, 198, and 240.

153. Elwin, Malcolm. "Pre-Strachey View of Biography," *Books and Bookmen,* VIII (Jan. 1963), 11.
In a response to a review of his book by Richard Whittington-Egan (see No. 149), defends his omission of his own personal views about Byron's marriage.

154. Emden, Cecil S. *Poets in Their Letters.* See K-SJ, IX (1960), 55, X (1961), 77, XI (1962), 115, XII (1963), 128.
Rev. by J. G. Ritz in EA, XVI (Jan.-March 1963), 105.

155. Émery, Léon. *L'Age romantique.* Lyon: Cahiers Libres [1958].
Includes discussion of Byron and Shelley.
Rev. by S.-M. Vergnaud in RLC, XXXIII (July-Sept. 1959), 448-451; by Henri Peyre in *French Review,* XXXIV (Apr. 1961), 501.

156. Erlich, Victor. "Krasiński and the Romantic Concept of the Poet," SIR, I (Summer 1962), 193-208.
Compares Keats and Byron to Krasiński.

157. Escarpit, Robert. "Byron et Venise," in *Venezia nelle Letterature moderne, Atti del Primo Congresso dell' Associazione Internazionale di Letteratura Comparata (Venezia, 25-30 settembre 1955),* ed. Carlo Pellegrini (Venice: Istituto per la Collaborazione Culturale, 1961), pp. 107-114.
Discusses "le rôle exact qu'a joué le séjour de Venise dans la vie psychologique de notre poète et dans l'histoire de la maturation de son talent." See No. 213.

Evans, Sir Benjamin Ifor. See No. 35.

Fairchild, Hoxie Neale. See No. 36.

158. "A Filtered Picture: China's Foreign Reading before—and after the Revolution," TLS, Sept. 21, 1962, pp. 740-741.
Mentions Chinese interest in Byron and Shelley.

159. Fisher, John. *Eighteen Fifteen: An End and a Beginning.* London: Cassell; New York: Harper (1963).
Recounts the events of Byron's wedding day (pp. 16-25).
Rev. by E. D. O'Brien in ILN, CCXLII (Feb. 16, 1963), 246; by Robert R. Rea in *Library Journal,* LXXXVIII (May 1, 1963), 1878; by Charles Poore in *New York Times,* May 25, 1963, p. 23.

Freeman, John. See No. 40.

160. Friis, Oluf. *Hjortens Flugt: Bidrag til studiet af Christian Winthers digtning.* Copenhagen: Huschsprung, 1961.
Discusses Byron's influence on Winther.

161. Gianascian, P. Mesrop. "Lord Byron à St. Lazare," in *Venezia nelle Letterature moderne, Atti del Primo Congresso dell' Associazione Internazionale di Letteratura Comparata (Venezia, 25-30 settembre 1955),* ed. Carlo Pellegrini (Venice: Istituto per la Collaborazione Culturale, 1961), pp. 115-126.
Reviews Byron's relationship with the monastery of St. Lazare and traces his influence on modern Armenian literature. See No. 213.

Gilbert, Judson Bennett. See No. 4.

162. Graves, Robert. "Pretense on Parnassus," *Horizon,* V (May 1963), 81-85.
About "vulgarity" in English poetry, with Byron as a central target. Keats's instinct for poetry was "genuine."

163. Green, David Bonnell. "Byron's Cousin Trevanion," ES, XLIV (Apr. 1963), 119-121.
Concerns John Trevanion Purnell Bettesworth Trevanion.

164. * Harmon, Maurice. "Little Chandler and Byron's 'First Poem,'" *Threshold,* No. 17 (1962), pp. 59-61.

165. "The Heart of a Poet," Li, LXIX (May 2, 1963), 741.
Describes an exhumation of Byron that took place in 1938.

166. Highet, Gilbert. *The Anatomy of Satire.* Princeton: Princeton Univ., 1962.
Includes discussion of Byron, especially *The Vision of Judgment* (pp. 83-89), Shelley, Peacock, and James and Horace Smith.

167. Hudson, Derek. *The Forgotten King and Other Essays.* London: Constable, 1960.
Includes "John Murray II: A Great Publisher" (pp. 98-103).

168. * Hussain, Imdad. "Beckford, Wainewright, De Quincey, and Oriental Exoticism," *Venture,* I (Sept. 1960), 234-248.†
Includes discussion of Byron.

169. Jerman, B. R. "Nineteenth-Century Holdings at the Folger," *Victorian Newsletter,* No. 22 (Fall 1962), p. 23.
Notes books or manuscripts of Byron, the Cowden Clarkes, and Shelley.

170. Johnston, Johanna. *Runaway to Heaven: The Story of Harriet Beecher Stowe.* Garden City: Doubleday, 1963.
Relates her role in the Byron controversy.
Rev. by Iola Haverstick in NYT, Apr. 28, 1963, pp. 6, 30.

171. Jovanovich, William. *Now, Barabbas.* New York: Harcourt, Brace, 1960.
Remarks on publishing prompted by John Murray's handling of Byron's literary properties.

172. Joyce, Michael. *"Lord Byron's Wife,"* TLS, Dec. 14, 1962, p. 973.
Supports his view that the separation was caused by Byron's having successfully "made an unnatural attempt on his wife." See Nos. 134, 140, 146, 149-152, 173, 180-182, 198, and 240.

173. Joyce, Michael. *"Lord Byron's Wife,"* TLS, Jan. 11, 1963, p. 32.
Reiterates his "'unnatural attempt' explanation." See Nos. 134, 140, 146, 149-152, 172, 180-182, 198, and 240.

174. Juden, B., and J. Richer. "L'Entente Cordiale au Théatre: Macready et *Hamlet* à Paris en 1844," *Revue des lettres modernes,* Nos. 74-75 (1962-63), pp. 1-35.
Discusses briefly the reception of *Werner* in Paris.

175. * Jungblutt, Gertrud. "Studien zum literarischen Charakter des Briefes der englischen Hochromantik: Byron, Shelley und Keats." (Doctoral dissertation, Marburg, 1963.)

Kaser, David, ed. See No. 252.

176. Knight, G. Wilson. "Byron and Hamlet," *Bulletin of the John Rylands Library,* XLV (Sept. 1962), 115-147.†
Points out connections and resemblances in life and character between Byron and Shakespeare's hero. See No. 177.

177. * Knight, G. Wilson. *Byron and Hamlet.* Manchester: John Rylands Library, 1962.
See No. 176.
Rev. in TLS, March 8, 1963, p. 174.

178. Knight, G. Wilson. *The Christian Renaissance, with Interpretations of Dante, Shakespeare and Goethe and New Discussions of Oscar Wilde and the Gospel of Thomas.* London: Methuen; New York: Norton (1962).
A revised edition of a work first published in 1933. Has numerous references to Byron, Keats, and Shelley.
Rev. in TLS, May 18, 1962, p. 360.

179. Knight, G. Wilson. *The Golden Labyrinth: A Study of British Drama.* See K-SJ, XII (1963), 129.
Rev. by Timothy Rogers in *English,* XIV (Autumn 1962), 108-109.

180. Knight, G. Wilson. *"Lord Byron's Wife,"* TLS, Dec. 7, 1962, p. 955.
Declares that the cause of Byron's separation from his wife has not yet been determined but that it was not incest. See Nos. 134, 140, 146, 149-152, 172, 173, 181, 182, 198, and 240.

181. Knight, G. Wilson. *"Lord Byron's Wife,"* TLS, Dec. 21, 1962. p. 989.
Discusses the nature of Lushington's statement and questions the transcription of a passage in the Bathurst statement. See Nos. 134, 140, 146, 149-152, 172, 173, 180, 182, 198, and 240.

182. Knight, G. Wilson. *"Lord Byron's Wife,"* TLS, Jan. 11, 1963, p. 32.
Pleads for "an uninhibited treatment of Byron's life" and defends Lushington's character. See Nos. 134, 140, 146, 149-152, 172, 173, 180, 181, 198, and 240.

183. Korg, Jacob. "Reply," CE, XXIV (Nov. 1962), 155.
Acknowledges Robert S. Phillips' correction. See No. 214.

Kuntz, Joseph M. See No. 6.

Laski, Marghanita. See No. 52.

184. Lewin, J. "Das sowjetische Akademiemitglied Michael Alekseev und sein Buch über die englische Literatur," *Zeitschrift für Anglistik und Amerikanistik,* XI (1963), 189-194.
A review, with considerable discussion of the Byron articles, of a German translation, *Aus der Geschichte der englischen Literatur,* of Alekseev's book (see No. 107). The translation is by Hans Heidrich.

Lister, Raymond. See No. 54.

185. Livermore, Anne Lapraik. "Byron and Emily Brontë," *Quarterly Review,* July 1962, pp. 337-344.
Discusses Byron's influence on *Wuthering Heights,* on Anne Brontë's novels, and on the Gondal series; touches also on Shelley's influence on Emily's poetry.

186. Lloyd, Quentin. "Famous Publishing Houses—3, Where Byron Met Sir Walter Scott," T&T, XLIII (Nov. 15-22, 1962), 24-25.
Byron's relations with John Murray are touched upon.

187. Logan, John. *Ghosts of the Heart: New Poems.* Chicago: Univ. of Chicago, 1960.
Includes "Byron at Shelley's Burning" (p. 41). See K-SJ, IX (1960), 57.

188. Loomis, Emerson Robert. "The Turn-

ing Point in Pope's Reputation: A Dispute Which Preceded the Bowles-Byron Controversy," PQ, XLII (Apr. 1963), 242-248.

Godwin and Mary Wollstonecraft were among those attacked in the controversy between T. J. Mathias and William Burdon.

189. * "Lord Byron: Ende in Versen," *Spiegel* (Hamburg), XVI (1962), 71-76.

190. Lovell, Ernest J., Jr. *Captain Medwin: Friend of Byron and Shelley*. Austin: Univ. of Texas, 1962.

Rev. by Ben W. Fuson in *Library Journal*, LXXXVIII (Feb. 15, 1963), 773-774; in *Nineteenth-Century Fiction*, XVIII (June 1963), 101; by Harry T. Moore in SatR, June 15, 1963, pp. 36, 42.

191. Lytton, Earl of. "The Lovelace Papers," Li, LXVIII (Sept. 27, 1962), 465-466.

A short account of their origin.

192. McCullough, Norman Verrle. *The Negro in English Literature: A Critical Introduction*. Ilfracombe: Arthur H. Stockwell, 1962.

Discusses references to the Negro in Byron (pp. 107-110) and Shelley (pp. 145-146).

193. Magarshack, David. *Stanislavsky, A Life*. London: MacGibbon & Kee; *New York: Chanticleer (1950).

Describes (pp. 353-354) Stanislavsky's production of *Cain*.

194. Marjarum, Edward Wayne. *Byron as Skeptic and Believer*. New York: Russell & Russell, 1962.

A reprint of a book first published in 1938.

195. Marshall, William H. *The Structure of Byron's Major Poems*. Philadelphia: Univ. of Pennsylvania, 1962.

196. May, Frederick. "Ugo Foscolo's 'Parallel between Dante and Petrarch' in Two Literary Periodicals of 1821," in *Italian Studies Presented to E. R. Vincent*, ed. C. P. Brand *et al.* (Cambridge: Heffer, 1962), pp. 219-225.

A review of Byron's *The Prophecy of Dante* in the June 1821 *New Monthly Magazine* was derived from this essay of Foscolo's.

197. Moore, Doris Langley. *The Late Lord Byron: Posthumous Dramas*. See K-SJ, XII (1963), 130-131.

Rev. by Frederick T. Wood in ES, XLIII (Aug. 1962), 272; by E[dward]. E. B[ostetter]. in PQ, XLI (Oct. 1962), 661-662; by Karl Heinz Göller in ASNS, CXCIX (Oct. 1962), 258-260; by David Bonnell Green in K-SJ, XII (1963), 115-116. See also No. 73.

198. Moore, Doris Langley. *"Lord Byron's Wife,"* TLS, Dec. 14, 1962, p. 973.

Protests G. Wilson Knight's misinterpretation of her position. See Nos. 134, 140, 146, 149-152, 172, 173, 180-182, and 240.

Moore, John Cecil. See No. 56.

199. Müller, Joachim. *Der Augenblick ist Ewigkeit: Goethestudien*. Leipzig: Koehler & Amelang, 1960.

One study is "Goethes Byrondenkmal" (pp. 107-122).

Rev. by J. F. A. Ricci in *Etudes Germaniques*, XVII (July-Sept. 1962), 300-301.

Munby, A. N. L. See No. 57.

200. * Nakaoka, Hiroshi. "Emily Brontë and Byron," *English Literature* (Waseda Univ. English Literary Society), No. 22 (Nov. 1962), pp. 23-33. [In Japanese.]

201. "New Acquisitions on View in British Art Galleries," ILN, CCXLII (Jan. 19, 1963), 93.

Reproduces Richard Westall's "A Portrait of Lord Byron."

202. Newell, Kenneth B. "Paul Elmer More on Byron," K-SJ, XII (1963), 67-74.

Shows how More's judgments of Byron stem from and are to be interpreted in terms of "his Neo-Humanist doctrine."

Nikoliukin, A. N. See No. 59.

203. "Notes on Sales in England—and America," TLS, May 31, 1963, p. 396.

At Parke-Bernet Galleries on Feb. 19, "a letter from Horace Smith to J. Reading of Colburn and Co., written from Versailles, February 26, 1822, . . . with interesting references to Byron, Shelley, Leigh Hunt and others" brought $375.

Nowottny, Winifred. See No. 60.

204. Núñez, Estuardo. "El magisterio de José Joaquín de Mora en América del Sur," *Cuadernos Americanos*, XX (Sept.-Oct. 1961), 167-177.

Discusses Mora's interest in Byron.

205. Núñez, Estuardo. *Nuevos Estudios Ingleses*. Lima, 1958.

The first of three studies, "Gonzalez Prada y la cultura inglesa," originally in *Letras*, No. 61 (1958). Includes discussion of Byron.

206. Origo, Iris. *The Last Attachment.* See K-SJ, XII (1963), 131.
Rev. by Godfrey Harrison in *Books and Bookmen,* VII (July 1962), 61.

207. Osborn, James M. "Travel Literature and the Rise of Neo-Hellenism in England," BNYPL, LXVII (May 1963), 279-300.
Discusses (pp. 295-298) the role of Byron in the development of Romantic Hellenism and Philhellenism in England.

208. Paden, W. D. "Swinburne, the *Spectator* in 1862, and Walter Bagehot," in *Six Studies in Nineteenth-Century English Literature and Thought,* ed. Harold Orel and George J. Worth, University of Kansas Humanistic Studies, No. 35 (1962), pp. 91-115.
Swinburne may have reviewed a French translation of *Childe Harold.*

209. Partridge, A. C. "Hours in a Florentine Library," *English Studies in Africa,* V (Sept. 1962), 156-165.
Looks at English manuscripts in Biblioteca Nazionale Centrale, among them 26 March 1815 letter of Byron (pp. 159-160) apparently never before published.

210. Partridge, A. C. "Unpublished Wordsworthiana: The Continental Tour of 1820, Described in Mary Wordsworth's Journal," *English Studies in Africa,* VI (March 1963), 1-6.
The journal makes no reference to a meeting with Trelawny in Lausanne.

211. Peck, Louis F. *A Life of Matthew G. Lewis.* See K-SJ, XII (1963), 132.
Rev. by Karl S. Guthke in *Anglia,* LXXX (1962), 216-220; by Curt A. Zimansky in PQ, XLI (July 1962), 606; by William H. Marshall in K-SJ, XII (1963), 116-118. See also No. 73.

212. Peckham, Morse. *Beyond the Tragic Vision.* See K-SJ, XII (1963), 132.
Rev. by George Steiner in NYT, July 1, 1962, p. 5; by Frank E. Manuel in *American Historical Review,* LXVIII (Jan. 1963), 415-416.

213. Pellegrini, Carlo, ed. *Venezia nelle Letterature moderne, Atti del Primo Congresso dell' Associazione Internazionale di Letteratura Comparata (Venezia, 25-30 settembre 1955).* Venice: Istituto per la Collaborazione Culturale, 1961.
See Nos. 157 and 161.
Rev. by Enea Balmas in RLC, XXXVI (Jan.-March 1962), 131-136.

Peters, Robert L. See No. 501.
Peyre, Henri. See No. 62.

214. Phillips, Robert S. "A Note on 'What Aspern Papers? A Hypothesis,'" CE, XXIV (Nov. 1962), 154-155.
Corrects error in preceding article [by Jacob Korg, CE, XXIII (Feb. 1962), 378-381] about identity of "younger woman" living with Claire Clairmont: it was Paula Clairmont. See No. 183.

215. * Poluiakhtova, I. K. "Bairon i romantizm v Italii," *Uchenye Zapiski,* No. 180 (Zarubezhnaia literatura) (1962), pp. 307-332.

216. Poston, M. L. "Contemporary Collectors XXXIV: Bibliotheca Medici," BC, XII (Spring 1963), 44-54.
Mentions his collection of Byron first editions and the Hazlitts and the Hunt in his library.

217. Poulet, Georges. "Timelessness and Romanticism," in *Ideas in Cultural Perspective,* ed. Philip P. Wiener and Aaron Noland (New Brunswick: Rutgers Univ., 1962), pp. 658-677.
Discusses "temporal experiences" felt and observed by the Romantic poets, including Shelley and Byron. Reprinted from JHI, XV [see K-SJ, IV (1955), 112].

Pun, T. W. See No. 382.

218. "Recent Acquisitions," *Yale University Library Gazette,* XXXVII (July 1962), 39-40.
Include the autograph manuscript of Byron's poem beginning "Some bards the Theban feuds recall" and a letter from Augusta Byron Leigh to Mrs. Knight, July 22 [n.y.]

219. "Recent Acquisitions," *Yale University Library Gazette,* XXXVII (Jan. 1963), 119-121.
Include Byron and Keats items.

220. Rehm, Walther. *Europäische Romdichtung.* Revised Edition. Munich: Max Hueber, 1960.
Chapter XIV (pp. 226-238) is on Byron and the Roman motif in poetry.
Rev. by Felix M. Wassermann in CL, XIV (Fall 1962), 397-399.

221. * Richards, B. G. ". . . Lord Byron and Myself: From a Projected Book of Memoirs," *Jewish Affairs* (Johannesburg), XVI (Oct. 1961), 22-26.

222. Ridenour, George M. *The Style of "Don Juan."* See K-SJ, X (1961), 80, XI (1962), 119, XII (1963), 132.

Rev. by Karl Heinz Göller in ASNS, CXCIX (Oct. 1962), 258-260.

Roy, G. Ross. See No. 69.

223. Rutherford, Andrew. *Byron: A Critical Study*. See K-SJ, XI (1962), 119, XII (1963), 132.

Rev. by F[rancis]. C[hristensen]. in *Personalist*, XLIII (Summer 1962), 417-418; by Ernest J. Lovell, Jr., in SAQ, LXI (Summer 1962), 432; by Frederick T. Wood in ES, XLIII (Aug. 1962), 272-273; by J. A. R. in *University of Edinburgh Journal*, XX (Autumn 1962), 323; by E[dward]. E. B[ostetter]. in PQ, XLI (Oct. 1962), 662-663; by Karl Heinz Göller in ASNS, CXCIX (Oct. 1962), 258-260; by J. D. Jump in RES, N.S., XIII (Nov. 1962), 421-422. See also No. 73.

224. * Säfve, Torbjörn. "Gudarnas utvalde. 1-2," *Norrbottens-Kuriren*, Jan. 5 and 8, 1962.

On Byron.

Saito, Takeshi, comp. See No. 10.

Sampson, George. See No. 70.

225. Schirmunski, V. M. "Die Gedichte [illegible]es und Byrons ("Kennst du das [illegible] . . ."—"Know Ye the Land . . .") Versuch einer vergleichenden Stilanalyse," *Weimarer Beiträge, Zeitschrift für Deutsche Literaturgeschichte*, No. 1 (1963), pp. 58-75.

A close stylistic comparison of Goethe's song from *Wilhelm Meister* and the first strophe from *The Bride of Abydos*. This article is translated from the Russian by Ernst Moritz Arndt (see No. 246).

226. * Shepherd, Geoffrey. "Byron's Mastery of Convention," *Venture*, I (Dec. 1960), 298-312.†

227. Simonsen, Peter. "Om 'Hedda Gabler,' 'Lille Eyolf,' og Lord Byron," *Edda Nordisk Tidsskrift for Litteraturforskning*, LXII (1962), 176-184.†

The influence of Byron and Byronism on Ibsen's *Hedda Gabler* and *Little Eyolf*.

Spender, Stephen, and Donald Hall, eds. See No. 72.

228. Stallknecht, Newton P., and Horst Frenz, eds. *Comparative Literature: Method and Perspective*. See K-SJ, XII (1963), 133.

Rev. by R[ené]. W[ellek]. in CL, XIV (Spring 1962), 192-195.

229. * Štěpaník, Karel. "The Return of the Romantics," *Sborník prací filos. fak. brněnské university*, Vol. XI (1962), Ser. D, 9, pp. 226-230.

A review article on reprints of Herbert Read's *Byron*, Stephen Spender's *Shelley*, and Edmund Blunden's *John Keats*. See K-SJ, I (1952), 91, No. 67, III (1954), 123, No. 239, V (1956), 127, No. 167.

230. Stevenson, R. Scott. *Famous Illnesses in History*. London: Eyre & Spottiswoode, 1962.

Includes "The Lameness of Lord Byron" (pp. 117-127).

Rev. in TLS, Nov. 30, 1962, p. 942; by R[ichard]. B[ury]. in *Books and Bookmen*, VIII (Feb. 1963), 32.

Taylor, Robert H. See No. 409.

231. Thomas, Henry, and Dana Lee Thomas. *Living Biographies of Great Poets*. Garden City: Doubleday, 1959.

A reprint of a book first published in 1941.

Has sections on Byron (pp. 123-135), Shelley (pp. 137-151), and Keats (pp. 153-165).

Rev. by Kennedy Williamson in *Poetry Review*, LI (Jan.-March 1960), 39.

232. Thorslev, Peter L., Jr. *The Byronic Hero: Types and Prototypes*. See K-SJ, XII (1963), 133.

Rev. by Charles T. Dougherty in CE, XXIV (Apr. 1963), 588; by Derek Stanford in *English*, XIV (Summer 1963), 202.

233. * Tomlinson, T. B. "Don Juan's Morals," *Melbourne Critical Review*, No. 2 (1959), pp. 47-56.

An assessment of critical work on Byron.

234. Treneer, Anne. *The Mercurial Chemist: A Life of Sir Humphry Davy*. London: Methuen, 1963.

Discusses Davy's relations with Byron.

Rev. in TLS, Apr. 5, 1963, p. 236.

235. Trueblood, Paul Graham. *The Flowering of Byron's Genius: Studies in Byron's "Don Juan."* New York: Russell & Russell, 1962.

A reprint of a book first published in 1945.

236. * Uesugi, Fumio. "Vitality of Poison—Byron's Resistance and Pilgrimage," *Hiroshima Studies in English Language and Literature* (English Literature Association, Hiroshima Univ.), Vol. VI, Nos. 1-2 (1963), pp. 30-44. [In Japanese.]

237. * Ujejski, Józef. *Romantycy.* Warsaw: Państw. Wydawnictwo Naukowe, 1962.
Includes "Giaur w przekładzie Mickiewicza" (pp. 59-69), on Mickiewicz's translation of *The Giaour,* and "Byronizm i Skotyzm w Konradzie Wallenrodzie" (pp. 23-54), on Byron's and Scott's influence on Mickiewicz's poem "Konrad Wallenrod."

238. Van Tieghem, Philippe. *Les influences étrangères sur la littérature française (1550-1880).* Paris: Presses Universitaires de France, 1961.
Discusses the influence of Byron and Byronism (pp. 181-189) and of Shelley (pp. 189-191).
Rev. in *Bulletin critique du livre français,* XVII (Feb. 1962), 99-100.

Watson, George. See No. 417.

239. Wellek, René. "Italian Criticism in the Thirties and Forties: from Scalvini to Tenca," *Italian Quarterly,* VI (Summer 1962), 3-25.
Mentions the evaluation of Byron by critics of the period.

240. Whiting, F. A. *"Lord Byron's Wife,"* TLS, Jan. 18, 1963, p. 41.
Hopes the correspondence on the subject will continue. See Nos. 134, 140, 146, 149-152, 172, 173, 180-182, and 198.

241. Whittemore, Reed. *The Fascination of the Abomination: Poems, Stories, and Essays.* New York: Macmillan, 1963.
Includes (pp. 306-312) "Childe Byron," a review of *His Very Self and Voice* [see K-SJ, VI (1957), 136, No. 117]; also discusses Shelley in essay on "Robert Browning" (pp. 184-204).

242. Wilde, Oscar. *The Letters of Oscar Wilde.* Ed. Rupert Hart-Davis. London: Rupert Hart-Davis, 1962.
Contains references to Byron, Keats, and Shelley.

243. Wilson, Angus. "Evil in the English Novel," *Books and Bookmen,* VIII (June 1963), 3-6, 39-43.
Discusses briefly the influence of the Byronic hero; also discusses *Caleb Williams.*

244. Woods, Ralph L. *Famous Poems and the Little-Known Stories behind Them.* New York: Hawthorn, 1961.
Gives the background for five of Byron's poems (pp. 21-29), four of Keats's (pp. 111-117), and three of Shelley's (pp. 203-221).

245. Young, Stark. "The Magic World of Stark Young 1881-1963," *New Republic,* CXLVIII (Jan. 26, 1963), 21-23.
Reprints some comments on "Byron's Letters" from a Sept. 27, 1922 article.

246. * Zhirmunskii, V. M. "Stikhotvoreniia Gete i Bairona 'Ty znaesh' Krai?'" in *Problemy mezhdunarodnykh literaturnykh sviazei* [*Problems of Comparative Literature*] (Leningrad: Leningrad State Univ., 1962), pp. 48-68.
See No. 225.

III. HUNT

Works: Selected, Single

Kauffman, Donald T., comp. See No. 92.

247. *Leigh Hunt's Dramatic Criticism, 1808-1831,* ed. Lawrence H. Houtchens and Carolyn W. Houtchens. See K-SJ, I (1952), 92, III (1954), 117.
Rev. by Willard Thorp in *Educational Theatre Journal,* II (Dec. 1950), 361-365.

248. *Leigh Hunt's Political and Occasional Essays.* Ed. Lawrence Huston Houtchens and Carolyn Washburn Houtchens. With an Introduction by Carl R. Woodring. New York: Columbia Univ., 1962.
Rev. by Robert R. Rea in *Library Journal,* LXXXVIII (Jan. 1, 1963), 103; in *New Yorker,* XXXVIII (Feb. 9, 1963), 146.

Nash, Ogden, comp. See No. 96.

Sutherland, Alistair, and Patrick Anderson, eds. See No. 101.

Untermeyer, Louis, ed. See No. 103.

249. Woodring, Carl R., ed. *Prose of the Romantic Period.* See K-SJ, XII (1963), 134.
Rev. by D[avid]. V. E[rdman]. in PQ, XLI (Oct. 1962), 656; by Charles I. Patterson in K-SJ, XII (1963), 118-120.

Books and Articles Relating to Hunt

Bill, Alfred Hoyt. See No. 445.

Davies, Hugh Sykes. See No. 32.

250. Fadiman, Clifton. *Enter, Conversing.* Cleveland: World, 1962.
Recalls Hunt's place in English literature (pp. 15-16).

Freeman, John. See No. 40.

251. Gaunt, William. *Kensington.* London: Batsford, 1958.
Refers frequently to Hunt and his writings.

252. Kaser, David, ed. *The Cost Book of*

Carey & Lea 1825-1838. Philadelphia: Pennsylvania Univ., 1963.
Gives figures for their edition (1828) of *Lord Byron and Some of His Contemporaries*.

Kuntz, Joseph M. See No. 6.

253. Lowenthal, Leo. *Literature, Popular Culture, and Society*. Englewood Cliffs, N. J.: Prentice-Hall, 1961. "A Spectrum Book."
Summarizes (pp. 33-35) attitude of Hazlitt and Hunt toward the "popular culture" of their day.

254. Mayo, Robert D. *The English Novel in the Magazines 1740-1815, with a Catalogue of 1375 Magazine Novels and Novelettes*. Evanston: Northwestern Univ.; London: Oxford Univ. (1962).
Includes discussion of Hunt's *Classic Tales*.

"Notes on Sales. . . ." See No. 203.

255. Nowell-Smith, Simon. "Leigh Hunt's *The Descent of Liberty*," *Library*, 5th Series, XVII (Sept. 1962), 238-240.
Suggests that "a prototype with a Cawthorn title-page" of *The Descent of Liberty* existed but that Cawthorn's imprint was "cancelled before publication."

Poston, M. L. See No. 216.

256. Prance, C. A. "A Charles Lamb Library," *Private Library*, IV (Jan. 1962), 2-10.
Includes books by Hunt, Hood, Hazlitt, and others.
Reprinted in CLSB, No. 166 (July 1962), pp. 375-378, No. 167 (Sept. 1962), pp. 384-385.

Saito, Takeshi, comp. See No. 10.

257. Sanders, Charles Richard. "The Correspondence and Friendship of Thomas Carlyle and Leigh Hunt: The Early Years," *Bulletin of the John Rylands Library*, XLV (March 1963), 439-485.
Prints thirty letters of Carlyle and Hunt revealing the early course of "a friendship of a very rare and high quality which reflected great credit on the humanity of both men."

Spender, Stephen, and Donald Hall, eds. See No. 72.

258. Stillians, Bruce Moore. "Leigh Hunt: The Political Response of a Literary Radical" [Doctoral dissertation, Iowa, 1962], DA, XXIII (Feb. 1963), 2906.

259. Watson, Melvin R. *Magazine Serials and the Essay Tradition, 1746-1820*. See K-SJ, VII (1958), 121, VIII (1959), 66, IX (1960), 61, X (1961), 84.
Rev. by Frederick T. Wood in ES, XLIV (Feb. 1963), 57-58.

IV. KEATS

Works: Collected, Selected, Single, Translated

260. Beckson, Karl, ed. *Great Theories in Literary Criticism*. New York: Farrar, Straus, 1963.
Includes (pp. 284-289) selections from Keats's letters.

De Selincourt, Aubrey, ed. See No. 85.

Gregory, Horace, and Marya Zaturenska, comps. See No. 86.

Hall, Donald, ed. See No. 87.

261. Herbert, David, comp. *Comic Verse*. London: Vista, 1962.
Includes Keats's "The Gadfly" (pp. 44-45).

Hollander, John, and Harold Bloom, eds. See No. 90.

262. **John Keats versei*. [*Poems of John Keats*.] Ed. László Kardos and László Kéry. Budapest: Magyar Helikon Publishers, 1962.
Rev. by Lenke Bizám in *New Hungarian Quarterly*, IV (Apr.-June 1963), 204-206.

Kauffman, Donald T., comp. See No. 92.

263. *Keats: Poems and Selected Letters*. Ed. Carlos Baker. See K-SJ, XII (1963), 135.
Rev. by Charles I. Patterson in K-SJ, XII (1963), 118-120.

Keyes, Frances Parkinson, comp. See No. 93.

264. *The Letters of John Keats 1814-1821*. Ed. Hyder Edward Rollins. See K-SJ, IX (1960), 61, X (1961), 84, XI (1962), 123, XII (1963), 135.
Rev. by Mario Praz in ES, XLIV (Apr. 1963), 151-153.

265. "Ode à l'automne (To Autumn)," [translated by Jean Grosjean], *Nouvelle revue française*, X (July 1962), 179-180.

266. "On a Leander Which Miss Reynolds My Kind Friend Gave Me," K-SJ, XII (1963), 36.
"From the transcript by Richard Woodhouse in the Harvard College Library."

267. *The Poetical Works of John Keats*. Ed. H. W. Garrod. Second Edition. See K-SJ, VIII (1959), 67, IX (1960), 62, X (1961), 84.

Rev. by Mario Praz in ES, XLIV (Apr. 1963), 151-153.

268. * *Poezje Wybrane*. Ed. Jerzy Żuławski. Warsaw: Pánstw. Instytut Wydawniczy, 1962.

269. Skelton, Robin, ed. *Viewpoint: An Anthology of Poetry*. London: Hutchinson, 1962.
Includes one poem each by Keats (pp. 121-122) and by Peacock (pp. 82-83).

270. * "Sonet. Piosenka z nienapisanej opery. Podwieczorek kochanków," [translated by] Jerzy Żuławski, *Twórczość* (Warsaw), No. 2 (1962), pp. 86-87.
Translations of a Sonnet; "A Party of Lovers"; and Song from "Extracts from an Opera."

271. "Sonnet" ("If by dull rhymes"), K-SJ, XII (1963), 94.

Sutherland, Alistair, and Patrick Anderson, eds. See No. 101.

Untermeyer, Louis, ed. See No. 103.

272. * " 'Vvek ne umret poeziia zemli . . .'; 'Osen,' " [translated by] G. Kochur and D. Palamarchuk, *Vsesvyt,* No. 7 (1961). [In Ukrainian.]
Literal translations of "On the Grasshopper and Cricket" and "To Autumn."

Books and Articles Relating to Keats and His Circle

273. * Abrahams, B-Z. "Jewish Associations of John Keats," *Jewish Affairs* (Johannesburg), XVI (July 1961), 21-23.

274. Albrecht, W. P. "Hazlitt on Wordsworth; or The Poetry of Paradox," in *Six Studies in Nineteenth-Century English Literature and Thought,* ed. Harold Orel and George J. Worth, University of Kansas Humanistic Studies, No. 35 (1962), pp. 1-21.
Discusses Hazlitt's criticism of Wordsworth, particularly of the leveling and egotistical elements in his poetry which prevent it from achieving "the dramatic invention that the greatest poetry requires."

Alexander, Boyd. See No. 108.

275. Altick, Richard D. "Memo to the Next Annotator of Browning," *Victorian Poetry,* I (Jan. 1963), 61-68.
Doubts that Keats is the poet referred to in "Popularity," though that is not "to deny that there is a strain of Keatsian suggestion" in the poem.

276. Anderson, Valborg, and George Steiner. "Hazlitt," *Reporter,* XXVIII (Feb. 28, 1963), 8, 10, 12.
A letter criticizing Steiner's review; Steiner's rejoinder. See No. 280.

277. Antal, Frederick. *Hogarth and His Place in European Art*. London: Routledge; *New York: Basic Books (1962).
Includes discussion of Hogarth's influence on Haydon.

"Auction Sales." See No. 112.

278. Auden, W. H. "Keats in His Letters," in *The Partisan Review Anthology,* ed. William Phillips and Philip Rahv (New York: Holt, Rinehart and Winston, 1962), pp. 428-432.
Reprinted from PR. See K-SJ, III (1954), 118.

Auden, W. H., and Louis Kronenberger, eds. See No. 16.

279. Bagehot, Walter. "Tennyson's *Idylls,*" with an Introduction by Norman St. John-Stevas, in *The Wind and the Rain: An Easter Book for 1962,* ed. Neville Braybrooke (London: Secker & Warburg, 1962), pp. 156-189.
An uncollected Bagehot essay from *The National Review* of Oct. 1859 in which Tennyson is compared with Shelley and Keats.

280. Baker, Herschel. *William Hazlitt*. See K-SJ, XII (1963), 136.
Also available in an English edition (London: Oxford Univ., 1962).
Rev. by *C. T. Houpt in *Christian Science Monitor,* May 31, 1962, p. 7; by Peter Quennell in NYT, July 1, 1962, pp. 6, 17; by D[eLancey]. F[erguson]. in NYHT, July 8, 1962, pp. 8-9; in *New Yorker,* XXXVIII (Aug. 18, 1962), 99-100; by William C. DeVane in *Yale Review,* LII (Autumn 1962), 112-118; in TC, CLXXII (Autumn 1962), 143; in *Times (London) Weekly Review,* Sept. 13, 1962, p. 10; by Harold Clurman in *Nation,* CXCV (Sept. 15, 1962), 134; by *R. W. L. in *San Francisco Sunday Chronicle "This World" Magazine,* XXVI (Sept. 30, 1962), 35; in TLS, Oct. 5, 1962, pp. 769-770; by Robert Greacen in Li, LXVIII (Oct. 11, 1962), 570; in *Economist,* CCV (Oct. 27, 1962), 356; by W. P. Albrecht in K-SJ, XII (1963), 110-112; in *Quarterly Review,* Jan. 1963, pp. 119-120; by George Steiner in *Reporter,* XXVIII (Jan. 17, 1963), 50-51 [also see No. 276]; by Margaret Willy in *Eng-*

lish, XIV (Spring 1963), 154-155; by C. A. Prance in CLSB, No. 170 (March 1963), pp. 403-404; by John Gross in NS, LXV (Apr. 12, 1963), 521-522.

281. * Baldini, Gabriele. "La conchiglia di Keats," *Messaggero* (Rome), Oct. 19, 1962.

282. Ball, Patricia M. "Tennyson and the Romantics," *Victorian Poetry,* I (Jan. 1963), 7-16.†

Briefly discusses Keats's poetic theory.

283. Balslev, Thora. *Keats and Wordsworth: A Comparative Study.* Copenhagen: Munksgaard, 1962.

Rev. by Ralph Lawrence in *English,* XIV (Spring 1963), 160.

284. Barron, David B. "*Endymion:* The Quest for Beauty," *American Imago,* XX (Spring 1963), 27-47.

A psychoanalytic interpretation of the poem.

285. Benoit, Ray. "Emerson on Plato: The Fire's Center," AL, XXXIV (Jan. 1963), 487-498.

Uses Keats's "Ode on a Grecian Urn" to help explain Emerson's mystical synthesis of matter and spirit.

286. Benziger, James. *Images of Eternity: Studies in the Poetry of Religious Vision from Wordsworth to T. S. Eliot.* Carbondale: Southern Illinois Univ., 1962.

Includes chapters on Shelley (pp. 72-102) and Keats (pp. 103-137).

287. Bevington, Helen. *When Found, Make a Verse Of.* New York: Simon and Schuster, 1961.

Includes "Keats's Three Trees" (pp. 106-107) and "On Gusto" (pp. 135-136), short essays inspired by Keats and Hazlitt respectively.

288. Bhattacherje, M. M. "Pictorial Poetry," *Research Bulletin (Arts) of the University of the Panjab,* Series No. XIV (1954), Vol. II.

Includes (pp. 47-73) a lecture on "Keats and Tennyson."

289. Blackstone, Bernard. "Caverns Measureless to Man," *Epistēmonikē epetēris tēs Philosophikēs Scholēs tou Panepistēmiou Athēnōn,* Series II, XI (1960-61), 347-360.

Discusses images of the cave in Keats and Shelley.

290. Blackstone, Bernard. "Keats and the Tetraktys," *Epistēmonikē epetēris tēs Philosophikēs Scholēs tou Panepistēmiou Athēnōn,* Series II, IV (1953-54), 330-344.

Discusses the possible influence of Dacier's *Life of Pythagoras, with His Symbols and Golden Verses* on Keats, who was "concerned to get back behind all human traditions to the primeval doctrine literally handed down, not from man to man, but from God to Man, in the first age of the world."

Blackstone, Bernard. See No. 19.

291. Blunden, Edmund. *A Hong Kong House: Poems 1951-1961.* London: Collins, 1962.

"To a British Jar Containing Stephens' Ink" (pp. 76-77) refers to Keats's friend, Henry Stephens.

Rev. in TLS, Nov. 16, 1962, p. 874.

292. Blunden, Edmund. "Thoughts on Kirke White," *Renaissance and Modern Studies,* VI (1962), 147-151.†

Touches on the appeal of Kirke White to Keats and Shelley.

293. Bracker, Jon. "The Christopher Morley Collection," *American Oxonian,* L (Jan. 1963), 1-14.

This collection at the University of Texas includes "worn and marked copies" of books by Keats; Hazlitt is also represented in the library.

294. * Broughton, L. N., *et al. A Concordance to the Poems of John Keats.* Tokyo: Senjo-shobo, 1963.

A reproduction of the original edition (1917).

295. Brown, Calvin S. "Toward a Definition of Romanticism," in *Varieties of Literary Experience: Eighteen Essays in World Literature,* ed. Stanley Burnshaw (New York: New York Univ., 1962), pp. 115-135.

Includes discussion of Keats and Shelley.

Bullough, Geoffrey. See No. 25.

296. Cacciatore, Vera. "A Note from the Keats House in Rome," K-SJ, XII (1963), 10.

A copy of *Marmion* in the Keats House, Rome, was probably bought by Keats for his brother Tom, "T. K.," not as has been assumed for "T. H."

297. Chaudhury, Pravas Jivan. "Keats and the Indian Ideal of Life Poetry," *Personalist,* XLIII (Summer 1962), 352-359.†

Contrasts "the ideal of life and poetry that Keats held with that which we find in Indian tradition."

298. Chen, David Ying. "Li Ho and Keats: A Comparative Study of Two Poets" [Doctoral dissertation, Indiana, 1962], DA, XXIII (Feb. 1963), 2941.

299. Church, Richard. "Posterity and Poet. Who Fished the Murex Up: What Porridge Had John Keats," *The Times*, London, March 6, 1962, p. 14.
Speculates on collateral descendants of Keats.

Clifford, James L., ed. See No. 456.

300. Clubbe, John. [In] "Information, Please," TLS, Dec. 21, 1962, p. 994.
Asks for letters or other papers for a biography of Hood.

301. Cohn, Robert Greer. "The A B C's of Poetry," CL, XIV (Spring 1962), 187-191.
Mentions Keats's playing (seriously) with letters in his Odes.

Conrad, Barnaby. See No. 131.

302. Coolidge, Archibald C., Jr. "Dickens's Use of Hazlitt's Principle of the Sympathetic Imagination," *Mississippi Quarterly*, XV (Spring 1962), 68-73.†
"Dickens's method of creating characters was to follow Hazlitt's principle."

303. Cunningham, J[ames]. V[incent]. *Tradition and Poetic Structure*. Denver: Alan Swallow, 1960.
One essay—"Classical and Medieval: Statius, *On Sleep*," pp. 25-39—discusses Keats's sonnet to Sleep and others of his sonnets.

304. "Curiosities of the Judgment of Solomon: Haydon's Masterpiece Restored," *The Times*, London, Apr. 16, 1962, p. 14.
An account from a correspondent of the restoration of the painting, which is reproduced.

305. Dale, Patricia. "Conrad: A Borrowing from Hazlitt's Father," N&Q, CCVIII (Apr. 1963), 146.
Conrad quotes in *Lord Jim* a sentence from a letter of the Rev. William Hazlitt to his son William.

306. Darbishire, Helen. *Somerville College Chapel Addresses and Other Papers, with a List of Her Published Writings 1908-1961*. London: [Privately Printed,] 1962.
"Didactic Poetry in English Literature" (pp. 78-93) concerns Coleridge, Wordsworth, Shelley, and Keats as didactic poets.
Rev. in TLS, Aug. 31, 1962, p. 658.

307. Dasgupta, H. "The Nightingale in English Poetry," *Calcutta Review*, CLXIII (May 1962), 137-140.
Discusses Keats's "Ode" as the greatest of the poems on the nightingale.

Davies, Hugh Sykes. See No. 32.

308. Doubleday, F. N. "John Keats and the Borough Hospitals," KSMB, XIII (1962), 12-17.
A sketch of Keats as a medical student and of his surroundings.

309. Dowden, Wilfred S. "Thomas Moore and the Review of *Christabel*," MP, LX (Aug. 1962), 47-50.
New letters of Moore, here published, indicate that he was not the author of the article in the *Edinburgh Review* attributed also to Jeffrey and Hazlitt.

310. * Downer, A. C. *The Odes of Keats*. [Translated by] Ryo Okachi. Tokyo: Sunshu-sha, 1963.

311. "Drawings and Water-Colours at Two London Exhibitions," ILN, CCXLI (Oct. 13, 1962), 567.
Reproduces Peter De Wint's "Gloucester Cathedral with the Ruins of St. Catherine's Church in the Foreground."

Du Bos, Charles. See No. 145.

312. Elliott, Eugene Clinton. "Reynolds and Hazlitt," JAAC, XXI (Fall 1962), 73-79.
Compares and analyzes the art aesthetic of the two men.

313. * Elmen, Paul. "The Fame of Jeremy Taylor," *Anglican Theological Review*, XLIV (Oct. 1962), 389-403.†
Refers to Keats's interest in Taylor.

314. "English and Continental Drawings in a London Exhibition," ILN, CCXLII (March 30, 1963), 471.
Includes De Wint's "Lowther Castle," here reproduced.

Erlich, Victor. See No. 156.

Evans, Sir Benjamin Ifor. See No. 35.

315. ["Extensive View of Windsor, Showing Castle and River in Foreground" and "A View of Holme Fen, Hunts. 1841,"] *Apollo*, LXXVII (March 1963), xxxiv-xxxv.
These De Wint water-colors are reproduced with an announcement of an exhibition at Appleby Brothers'.

Fairchild, Hoxie Neale. See No. 36.

316. Finney, Claude Lee. *The Evolution of*

Keats's Poetry. 2 vols. New York: Russell & Russell, 1963.

A reprint of a work first published in 1936.

317. Flesch-Brunningen, H. "The Physician and the Pen. John Keats—Physician and Patient," *Ciba Symposium,* X (1962), 33-37.

A brief sketch of Keats's career.

318. Fogle, Richard Harter. *The Imagery of Keats and Shelley: A Comparative Study*. Hamden, Conn.: Archon, 1962.

A reprint of a book first published in 1949.

319. Ford, George H. *Keats and the Victorians: A Study of His Influence and Rise to Fame 1821-1895*. Hamden, Conn.: Archon, 1962.

A reprint of a book first published in 1944.

320. "Forum on Poetry," TLS, Apr. 12, 1963, p. 249.

Summarizes comments on Keats made by Francis Berry and William Empson at Universities Poetry Conference.

Freeman, John. See No. 40.

321. * Friedman, Martin Boris. "William Hazlitt and the Development of Evocative Criticism." (Doctoral dissertation, Yale, 1962.)

322. Gaunt, William. "A Book of Drawings by Benjamin Robert Haydon," *Connoisseur,* CLIII (June 1963), 106-110.

Describes a book of studies and sketches by Haydon at the Royal Academy of Arts and reproduces four of them.

323. Gibson, Alan. "Dinner with Mr Hazlitt," Li, LXIX (Apr. 11, 1963), 628.

Retails Haydon's account of Hazlitt's christening party for his son.

324. * Cidwani, M. A. *John Keats*. Delhi: Kitab Mahal, 1962. [In English.]

Gilbert, Judson Bennett. See No. 4.

325. Gittings, Robert. "Great Writers—5: John Keats," T&T, XLIV (Jan. 31-Feb. 6, 1963), 22-23.

One of a series.

326. Gittings, Robert. *John Keats: The Living Year*. See K-SJ, XII (1963), 137.

Rev. by Godfrey Harrison in *Books and Bookmen,* VII (July 1962), 61.

327. Gittings, Robert. *The Mask of Keats: A Study of Problems*. See K-SJ, VII (1958), 124, VIII (1959), 69, IX (1960), 64.

Rev. by David Ward in *Cambridge Review,* LXXVIII (Feb. 9, 1957), 367.

328. Gittings, Robert, and Jo Manton. *The Story of John Keats*. See K-SJ, XII (1963), 137.

Rev. by Mabel A. E. Steele in *Horn Book Magazine,* XXXIX (June 1963), 294.

329. Goodin, George Vincent. "The Comic Theories of Hazlitt, Lamb, and Coleridge" [Doctoral dissertation, Illinois, 1962], DA, XXIII (Aug. 1962), 632.

330. Grant, Douglas. "An Address on 'Hazlitt and Lamb,'" CLSB, No. 170 (March 1963), pp. 399-400.

Reviews briefly the relationship of the two men.

Graves, Robert. See No. 162.

331. Guidi, Augusto. "Linguaggio e figura nella poesia di John Keats," *Annali, Sezione Germanica* (Istituto Universitario Orientale), Naples, IV (1961), 137-148.

332. Häusermann, H. W. "The Australian Strain in the Work of W. J. Turner," ES, XLIII (Oct. 1962), 413-419.

Notes influence of Keats on this Australian poet.

333. Halpern, Martin. "Keats's Grecian Urn and the Singular 'Ye,'" CE, XXIV (Jan. 1963), 284-288.

Argues for the urn itself as the addressee of the concluding line-and-a-half of the Ode.

334. Haresnape, G. "The Poet's Active and Passive Attributes," *English Studies in Africa,* V (Sept. 1962), 166-170.

Keats and Shelley are partly responsible for the popular image of the "delicate, suffering poet"; in contrast, Blake and Milton are active and masculine.

335. Haydon, Benjamin Robert. *The Diary of Benjamin Robert Haydon*. Ed. Willard Bissell Pope. Vols. I and II. See K-SJ, X (1961), 87, XI (1962), 125-126, XII (1963), 138.

Rev. by Marcia Allentuck in *Art Bulletin,* XLV (March 1963), 74-77.

336. ["Haymaking near Tewkesbury,"] *Apollo,* LXXVII (Apr. 1963), lxxiii.

This De Wint water-color is reproduced with an announcement of an exhibition at The Fine Art Society.

337. Haynes, Jean. "John Jennings: Keats's Grandfather," KSMB, XIII (1962), 18-23.

Gives information to be found "in the records of the Worshipful Company of Innholders."

Heinz, W. C., ed. See No. 89.

338. Herrmann, Luke. "From Marco Zoppo to Claude Monet: Pictures from the Collection of the Earl of Inchcape," *Connoisseur,* CXLVIII (Oct. 1961), 151-154.

De Wint's water-color "Partridge Shooting" (one of a pair) is reproduced here.

339. Hertz, Neil H. "Poetry in an Age of Prose: Arnold and Gray," in *In Defense of Reading: A Reader's Approach to Literary Criticism,* ed. Reuben A. Brower and Richard Poirier (New York: Dutton, 1962), pp. 57-75.

Considers Arnold's indebtedness to Keats.

340. Holloway, John. *The Charted Mirror: Literary and Critical Essays.* See K-SJ, X (1961), 87, XI (1962), 126, XII (1963), 138.

Rev. by Marvin Mudrick in *Hudson Review,* XV (Autumn 1962), 446-450.

341. Holthusen, Hans Egon. *Das Schöne und das Wahre: Neue Studien zur modernen Literatur.* See K-SJ, X (1961), 88.

Rev. by Frank Wood in CL, XIV (Spring 1962), 198-199.

342. * Hoshino, Nobuo. "On Keats's Poverty and Money-Affairs—An Investigation Based on His Letters," *Studies in English Language and Literature* (Kansai Univ., Suita), No. 6 (June 1962), pp. 14-37. [In Japanese.]

343. Hummel, William C. "Liber Amoris: Hazlitt's Napoleon," *Kansas Magazine,* 1963, pp. 73-81.†

Sees the *Life of Napoleon* "as one of the most elaborate restatements of eighteenth-century radicalism."

344. * Jarcho, Saul. "Auenbrugger, Laennec, and John Keats: Some Notes on the Early History of Percussion and Auscultation," *Medical History,* V (1961), 167-172.

Jerman, B. R. See No. 169.

345. Johnson, Mary Lynn. "Two Views of the Romantic Hero: Myth in the Poetry of Wordsworth and Keats" [Doctoral dissertation, Tulane, 1962], DA, XXIII (Jan. 1963), 2528-2529.

Jungblutt, Gertrud. See No. 175.

346. * Kamijima, Kenkichi. "Explorers of the Inane (IV)—Keats," *Essays* (Tokyo, The Essay Society), XIV (June 1962), 14-37. [In Japanese.]

347. Kaufman, Paul. "The Leigh Browne Collection at the Keats Museum," *Library,* 5th Series, XVII (Sept. 1962), 246-250.

"An inventory of the items, as a preliminary to a comprehensive editing of this significant contribution to our knowledge of the Keats circle."

348. Kendall, Lyle H., Jr. "John Murray to J. W. Croker: An Unpublished Letter on Keats," K-SJ, XII (1963), 8-9.

Probably dated April 1818 and concerning Croker's review of Keats.

349. Kenyon, Katharine M. R. "When Did Keats and Fanny Brawne Become Engaged?" KSMB, XIII (1962), 4-7.

Suggests May 1, 1819.

350. * Kikuchi, Wataru. "Keats's Letter to P. B. Shelley, August 16, 1820," *Hitotsubashi Journal of Arts and Sciences,* II (1962), 1-14.

351. * Kikuchi, Wataru. "On the 'Ode to a Nightingale,'" *Studies in the Humanities and Natural Sciences* (Hitotsubashi Univ., Tokyo), No. 4 (March 1962), pp. 81-110. [In Japanese.]

352. Kilgour, Norman. "Mrs. Jennings' Will," KSMB, XIII (1962), 24-27.

An account of the provisions of Alice Jennings' will and Richard Abbey's handling of it.

353. * Kinugasa, Umejiro. "A Survey of 'Hakumeiki' [*Record of an Ill-Starred Life*] Written by Tokuboku Hirata," *Studies in Humanities* (Doshisha Univ., Kyoto), No. 60 (July 1962), pp. 83-103. [In Japanese.]

An essay on the article on Keats's love for Fanny Brawne which was printed in *Bungakukai (Literary World),* published in Tokyo in 1894.

Knight, G. Wilson. See No. 178.

354. Kroeber, Karl. "The New Humanism of Keats's Odes," *Proceedings of the American Philosophical Society,* CVII (June 19, 1963), 263-271.

Interprets the odes "as the celebration of a new 'humanism,' which strives to define the unity of mankind in terms of the vitality of each man's unique and personal experience."

355. * Kudō, Naotarō. "The Ideas of Color in Keats and Shelley," *English Literature* (Waseda English Literary Society, Tokyo), No. 22 (Nov. 1962), pp. 100-113.

Kuntz, Joseph M. See No. 6.

Laski, Marghanita. See No. 52.

356. LeFanu, William. *A Catalogue of the Portraits and Other Paintings Draw-*

ings and Sculpture in the Royal College of Surgeons of England. Edinburgh and London: E. & S. Livingstone, 1960.

Includes reproduction of portrait of Sir Astley Cooper by Sir Thomas Lawrence and portrait of Thomas Alcock by B. R. Haydon.

357. "List of Acquisitions," *British Museum Quarterly,* XXV (June 1962), 103-110.

Includes "letters from Vincent Novello to T. Severn; 1841, 1846."

358. * Lombardo, Agostino. *La poesia di John Keats.* Milan: La goliardica, 1961.

Lowenthal, Leo. See No. 253.

359. Mahoney, John L. "Theme and Image in a Keats Sonnet on Fame," *Creative Writing,* XIII (Nov. 1962), 25-26.

Reprinted from *English Record.* See No. 360.

360. Mahoney, John L. "Theme and Image in a Keats Sonnet on Fame," *English Record,* XII (Fall 1961), 24-25.†

Notes "striking similarity" between theme and image in sonnet ("How fever'd is the man, who cannot look").

361. Maiorana, Maria Teresa. "Un conte de Bocace repris par Keats et Anatole France," RLC, XXXVII (Jan.-March 1963), 50-67.

Compares the handling of a common source by Keats in *Isabella* and France in *Le Basilic.*

362. Mann, Phyllis G. "Keats's Reading," KSMB, XIII (1962), 39-47.

Suggests G. L. Way's translations of J. B. Legrand D'Aussy's selections from twelfth and thirteenth century tales and Joseph Warton's *History of English Poetry* as sources for some of Keats's poetry.

363. Mann, Phyllis G. "More Keatsiana," KSMB, XIII (1962), 37-38.

Gives details concerning Keats as a medical student and George Keats's marriage. See K-SJ, XII (1963), 135, No. 233.

364. * Marilla, E. L. *Three Odes of Keats.* Copenhagen: Munksgaard, 1962.

365. Marshall, William H. "'Pulpit Oratory,' I-III: Essays by John Hamilton Reynolds in Imitation of William Hazlitt," *Library Chronicle,* XXVIII (Spring 1962), 88-105.

Introduces and reprints the three essays.

366. Martin, Robert Bernard. *Enter Rumour: Four Early Victorian Scandals.* London: Faber; *New York: Norton (1962).

Includes material on Sir James Clark, Keats's physician.

367. Martz, Louis L. "The Teaching of Poetry," in *Essays on the Teaching of English: Reports of the Yale Conferences on the Teaching of English,* ed. Edward J. Gordon and Edward S. Noyes (New York: Appleton-Century-Crofts, 1960), pp. 244-260.

Discusses Keats's "On First Looking into Chapman's Homer" (pp. 252-253).

368. *Mary Baker Eddy Mentioned Them.* Boston: Christian Science Publishing Society, 1961.

Includes a section on Keats (pp. 127-128).

369. Mason, Eudo C. *Rilke, Europe, and the English-Speaking World.* Cambridge: Cambridge Univ., 1961.

Discusses Rilke's interest in Keats and Shelley.

Rev. by Geneviève Bianquis in *Etudes Germaniques,* XVII (July-Sept. 1962), 307; by H. Wiemann in *Aumla,* No. 18 (Nov. 1962), pp. 272-275; by H. F. Peters in *German Quarterly,* XXXVI (May 1963), 299-301.

370. Maurice, Robert R. *Au coeur de l'enchantement romantique.* Paris: Editions du Scorpion, 1961.

Contains essays on Keats (pp. 77-97) and on Shelley (pp. 99-155).

Rev. in *Bulletin critique du livre français,* XVII (Oct. 1962), 716.

Mayer, Tony, ed. See No. 95.

371. Michelis, Euralio De. "Un Poeta d'Autunno," *Nuova Antologia,* XCVIII (March 1963), 323-331.

Includes discussion of Keats.

372. Miles, Josephine. "Reading Poems," *English Journal,* LII (March 1963), 157-164; (Apr. 1963), 243-246.

Makes use of "Ozymandias" and "On Seeing the Elgin Marbles."

373. Monteiro, George. "Melville and Keats," *Emerson Society Quarterly,* No. 31 (2nd quarter 1963), p. 55.

A parallel between *Billy Budd* and a Keats letter suggests the latter as a possible source for Melville.

Moore, John Cecil. See No. 56.

Munby, A. N. L. See No. 57.

374. Murry, John Middleton. *Selected Criticism, 1916-1957.* Ed. Richard Rees. See K-SJ, X (1961), 88-89, XI (1962), 128, XII (1963), 140.

Rev. by H. W. Häusermann in *Anglia,* LXXX (1962), 358-359.

Nikoliukin, A. N. See No. 59.

375. "Notes on Sales," TLS, Aug. 3, 1962, p. 564.

At Christie's, May 30, "a copy of the first edition of Keats's *Poems,* 1817, presented jointly by Keats and his brother George, and inscribed by George Keats to his future wife, Georgiana Wylie, brought £780."

376. Nowell-Smith, Simon. [In] "Information, Please," TLS, Oct. 12, 1962, p. 798.

Asks about presentation copies of Keats's *Poems,* 1817.

Nowottny, Winifred. See No. 60.

377. * O'Hara, James Donald. "William Hazlitt and the Fine Arts." (Doctoral dissertation, Harvard, 1963.)

378. Olney, Clarke. "Wodehouse and the Poets," *Georgia Review,* XVI (Winter 1962), 392-399.†

Allusions in his works to Keats, Shelley, and others.

379. Owen, Harold H., Jr., *et al.* "Some General Remarks on Poetry: Report of the Committee on the Teaching of Poetry," in *Essays on the Teaching of English: Reports of the Yale Conferences on the Teaching of English,* ed. Edward J. Gordon and Edward S. Noyes (New York: Appleton-Century-Crofts, 1960), pp. 270-319.

Includes "teaching plans" for "Ode on a Grecian Urn" (pp. 298-300) and for "Ozymandias" (p. 313).

380. Pearson, Norman Holmes. "The American Writer and the Feeling for Community," ES, XLIII (Oct. 1962), 403-412.

Notes parallels between *Light in August* and "Ode on a Grecian Urn."

381. Perkins, David. *The Quest for Permanence: The Symbolism of Wordsworth, Shelley and Keats.* See K-SJ, X (1961), 89, XI (1962), 129, XII (1963), 140.

Rev. by Frederic Ewen in *Science & Society,* XXVI (Fall 1962), 447-453.

Peters, Robert L. See No. 501.

Peyre, Henri. See No. 62.

Poston, M. L. See No. 216.

Prance, C. A. See No. 256.

382. * Pun, T. W. "Keats and His Contemporaries: A Study of the Poetry of Keats in Relation to Wordsworth, Coleridge, Scott and Byron." (Doctoral dissertation, London, 1961.)

383. Quennell, Peter. "In the Glow of the Perfect Patron," *Horizon,* V (March 1963), 62-71.

Haydon is quoted at some length in this article on the third Earl of Egremont.

384. "Reality of Keats," *The Times,* London, March 22, 1962, p. 17.

Reports on John Bayley's Chatterton lecture at the British Academy.

"Recent Acquisitions." See No. 219.

385. Richardson, Joanna. "John Taylor, 1781-1864 and James Augustus Hessey, 1785-1870: A Centenary Address," CLSB, No. 171 (May 1963), pp. 408-409.

386. Ridley, M[aurice]. R[oy]. *Keats' Craftsmanship: A Study in Poetic Development.* New York: Russell & Russell, 1962.

A reprint of a book first published in 1933.

387. Robinson, Dwight E. "Ode on a 'New Etrurian' Urn: A Reflection of Wedgwood Ware in the Poetic Imagery of John Keats," K-SJ, XII (1963), 11-35.

Suggests Wedgwood ware as a major source of inspiration for the "Ode on a Grecian Urn": "Winckelmann's aesthetics, Wedgwood's entrepreneurship, and Keats's ode form an unbreakable chain."

388. [Rogers, Neville.] "Miss Elsa Forman," K-SJ, XII (1963), 4.

Gives a brief account of Miss Forman (d. 1962), niece of Harry Buxton Forman and former Secretary of the Keats-Shelley Memorial Association.

Roy, G. Ross. See No. 69.

389. ["St. Mary's Church, Beverley,"] *Apollo,* LXXVII (Feb. 1963), xvii.

This De Wint water-color is reproduced in an Agnew advertisement.

Saito, Takeshi, comp. See No. 10.

390. * Sakata, Shozo. "On the 'Ode to a Nightingale,'" *Studies and Essays* (Miyagi-Gakuin Women's College), No. 19 (Dec. 1961), pp. 127-145. [In Japanese.]

Sampson, George. See No. 70.

391. * Sanminiatelli, Bino. "Il canto dell'uomo,'" *Resto del Carlino* (Bologna), Dec. 9, 1962.

Discusses Keats and Shakespeare.

392. Scarlett, E. P. "John Keats: Medical

Student," *Archives of Internal Medicine,* CX (Oct. 1962), 535-541.
"An account of Keats's connection with medicine."

393. "A Season of American Sales," TLS, Aug. 24, 1962, p. 648.
At Parke-Bernet Galleries on Nov. 29-30, 1961, Keats's 1817 *Poems* brought $950; *Lamia, etc.,* 1820, $2500; Shelley's *Adonais,* 1821, $2500. Also sold "during season" was "autograph manuscript of Hazlitt's essay *On Coffee House Politicians,* 1821, $1700."
See K-SJ, XII (1963), 135, No. 234.

394. Sen Gupta, D. P. "Keats's Poetic Theory and the Cult of Sincerity," *Patna University Journal,* XIV (1961), 36-47.
Examines Keats's poetic theory in the light of his "continuous search for sincerity of poetic utterance."

395. *Shakespeare-Jahrbuch,* XCVII (1961). See K-SJ, XII (1963), 142, No. 360.
Rev. by Kurt Otten in *Neueren Sprachen,* June 1962, pp. 290-292.

396. Sitwell, [Sir] Osbert. *Pound Wise.* London: Hutchinson, 1963.
Blames critics for Keats's death (pp. 11-12); alludes elsewhere to Keats and to Haydon.

Spender, Stephen, and Donald Hall, eds. See No. 72.

397. Spender, Stephen. *The Imagination in the Modern World.* Washington: Library of Congress, 1962.
Alludes frequently to Keats and Shelley. See No. 398.

398. Spender, Stephen. *The Struggle of the Modern.* London: Hamish Hamilton, 1963.
Based in part on the Library of Congress lectures. See No. 397.

399. Spender, Stephen. "Tendencies in Modern Poetry," in *The Quest for Truth,* comp. Martha Boaz (New York: Scarecrow, 1961), pp. 21-38.
Discusses influence of Keats on Wilfred Owen and other poets of the First World War.

400. Sperry, Stuart M., Jr. "The Allegory of *Endymion,*" SIR, II (Autumn 1962), 38-53.
Considers *Endymion* "as a reflection of Keats's concern with visionary experience. . . . an integral part of that larger allegory that was Keats's life and achievement, possessing something of the same incompleteness and contradiction."

401. Sperry, Stuart M., Jr. "Keats's Skepticism and Voltaire," K-SJ, XII (1963), 75-93.
Keats's "vein of skepticism," his "distrust of formalized religion," and his view of history were all significantly influenced by Voltaire.

402. Spitzer, Leo. *Essays on English and American Literature.* Ed. Anna Hatcher. Princeton: Princeton Univ., 1962.
Includes (pp. 67-97) "The 'Ode on a Grecian Urn,' or Content *vs.* Metagrammar." See K-SJ, VI (1957), 145.

403. Štěpaník, Karel. "The Idea of Progress in Keats's *Hyperion,*" *Philologica Pragensia,* VI (1963), 35-48.
Keats did not intend to represent allegorically the French Revolution but rather the *"general revolutionary idea* of the infinite progress of human society."

Štěpaník, Karel. See No. 229.

404. Stillinger, Jack. "The Text of 'The Eve of St. Agnes,'" *Studies in Bibliography,* XVI (1963), 207-212.†
Proposes revision of the text of the poem in accordance with Keats's wishes. Future editors "should restore the *Ew* version of lines 314-322 and the additional stanza between VI and VII."
See No. 405.

405. *Studies in Bibliography,* XVI (1963). See No. 404.
Rev. by Ralph Lawrence in *English,* XIV (Summer 1963), 208; in TLS, June 28, 1963, p. 484.

406. Swallow, Alan. *An Editor's Essays of Two Decades.* Seattle: Experiment, 1962.
"A Reading of the Romantic Odes" (pp. 62-75) includes discussion of Keats and Shelley.

407. * Tabuchi, Mikio. "Aspects of Conflict in Keats's Odes," *Hiroshima Studies in English Language and Literature* (English Literary Association, Hiroshima Univ.), Vol. VI, Nos. 1-2 (1963), pp. 18-29.

408. * Takeda, Miyoko. "A Study of John Keats's Sonnets—Mainly through His Letters (5)," *Journal of Baiku Junior College* (Toyonaka), XI (Dec. 1962), 28-41. [In Japanese.]

409. Taylor, Robert H. "Contemporary Collectors XXXV: Henry Bradley Martin," BC, XII (Summer 1963), 184-193.
Collection includes Keats, Shelley, Byron, and Godwin items.

Thomas, Henry, and Dana Lee Thomas. See No. 231.

410. Thomas, Roy. *How to Read a Poem.* London: Univ. of London, 1961.

Includes commentary on "Ode to the West Wind" (pp. 85-91) and "Ode on a Grecian Urn" (pp. 92-96), as well as other observations on Keats and Shelley.

411. Tillotson, Geoffrey. *Augustan Studies.* See K-SJ, XII (1963), 142.

Rev. by Jacques Golliet in EA, XVI (Jan.-March 1963), 82-83.

412. Trawick, Leonard M., III. "Sources of Hazlitt's 'Metaphysical Discovery,'" PQ, XLII (Apr. 1963), 277-282.

In Adam Smith, Hume, Priestley, Kames, Bishop Butler, James Usher, and George Campbell.

413. Trías, Manuel B. "La Estética de Keats," *Boletin de la Academia Argentina de Letras,* XXIV (Jan.-June 1959), 111-132.

414. "Two Centuries of English Water-Colours and Drawings, at Agnew's," ILN, CCXLII (Jan. 26, 1963), 129.

Includes reproduction of "Waltham Abbey" by De Wint.

415. Wais, Kurt. *An den Grenzen der Nationalliteraturen, Vergleichende Aufsätze.* Berlin: De Gruyter, 1958.

Includes (pp. 155-168) "Mallarmé's Neuschöpfung eines Gedichtes von Keats."

416. * Watanabe, Jun. "Love and Death in Keats's Poetry," *Bulletin of the Kyoto Gakugei University,* No. 20 (March 1962), pp. 1-6. [In Japanese.]

417. Watson, George. *The Literary Critics: A Study of English Descriptive Criticism.* [Harmondsworth:] Penguin, 1962.

Discusses Hazlitt's criticism (pp. 135-139); also touches upon Byron, Keats, and Shelley.

418. Welsh, Alexander. *The Hero of the Waverley Novels.* New Haven: Yale Univ., 1963.

Discusses Hazlitt's criticism of the novels.

419. Whiting, George W. "Charlotte Smith, Keats, and the Nightingale," K-SJ, XII (1963), 4-8.

Suggests that the last stanza of "Ode to a Nightingale" was influenced by Miss Smith's sonnet "Farewell to the Nightingale" and other similar poems.

Wilde, Oscar. See No. 242.

420. Will, Frederic. "A Confrontation of Kierkegaard and Keats," *Personalist,* XLIII (Summer 1962), 338-351.†

Keats is seen as a type of Kierkegaard's "aesthetic man" and therefore a failure, but "the aesthetic existence" may have its own values. We are left with a dilemma.

421. Williams, Joseph M. "Caliban and Ariel Meet Trager and Smith or Descriptive Linguistics and Teaching Literature," CE, XXIV (Nov. 1962), 121-126.

Contrasts Dell Hymes's phonemic analysis of Keats's poetry with W. J. Bate's. See K-SJ, XI (1962), 126, No. 336, IX (1960), 62, No. 276.

422. Wolpers, Theodor. "Zur Struktur der Bildlichkeit bei Keats," *Anglia,* LXXX (1962), 89-110.

Woods, Ralph L. See No. 244.

423. Yost, George, Jr. "Keats's Early Religious Phraseology," SP, LIX (July 1962), 579-591.

"Keats's Christian phraseology and his mode of intensity seem to originate in the teachings of his mother. His pagan phraseology seems to originate in his revulsion at her death and possibly also at the events that preceded it."

424. * Żuławski, Jerzy. "John Keats," *Twórczość* (Warsaw), No. 2 (1962), p. 88.

V. SHELLEY

Works: Selected, Single, Translated

425. * *A megszabaditott Prometheus.* [*Prometheus Unbound.*] [Translated by] Sándor Weöres. Budapest: Móra Kiadó, 1961.

426. * *Beatrice Cenci.* [*The Cenci.*] [Translated by] Stanislav Blaho. Bratislava: DILIZA, 1960.

De Selincourt, Aubrey, ed. See No. 85.

427. * "Filosofie lásky" ["Love's Philosophy"], [translated by] J. Zunar, *Lidová demokracie,* Aug. 5, 1962, p. 5.

428. "From *Prometheus Unbound,*" K-SJ, XII (1963), 66.

Reprints Act II, Scene 1, lines 1-12.

Hall, Donald, ed. See No. 87.

Head, Joseph, and S. L. Cranston, comps. See No. 88.

Hollander, John, and Harold Bloom, eds. See No. 90.

429. * *Izbrannoe.* [*Selected Poems.*] [Translated and edited by] Vs. Rozhdestvenskii. [Preface by] B. Kolesnikova. Moscow: Goslitizdat, 1962.
Verses, poems, and dramas.

430. Knight, Margaret, comp. *Humanist Anthology: From Confucius to Bertrand Russell.* London: Barrie & Rockliff, 1961.
Includes selection from *A Refutation of Deism* (pp. 64-65).

431. * *Lirika.* [Translated by] Imants Ziedonis *et al.* Riga: Latgosizdat, 1961. [In Latvian.]

432. * *Lirika (Izbrannoe).* [*Lyric Poetry (Selections).*] [Compiled and with a Preface by] A. Kruklis. See K-SJ, XII (1963), 143.
Rev. by V. Velshevitsa in *Karogs* (Znamia), No. 5 (1962), pp. 139-140 [in Latvian].

433. * *"Osvobozhdennyi Prometei: Liricheskaia drama v 4-kh d. D. 1"* [*Prometheus Unbound*], [translated by] Z. Gamsakhurdia, *Tsiskari* (Zaria), No. 1 (1962), pp. 90-100. [In Georgian.]

434. * "Ozymandias," [translated by] Vladimír Holan, in *Cestou* (Prague: SNKLU, 1962), p. 296.
Based on an earlier translation by Jaroslav Vrchlický.

434a. * *Poezje Wybrane.* Ed. Juliusz Żuławski. See K-SJ, XII (1963), 143.
Rev. by *Grzegorz Sinko in *Nowe Ksiażki* (Warsaw), No. 16 (1961), pp. 977-979.

435. * "Šeli: Askin Serendi, Askin Felsefesi," *Birlik* (Skopje), XI (1962), No. 1, p. 497. [In Turkish.]

436. * *Shelley's Poems.* [Translated by] Kiyoshi Sato. Tokyo: Apollon-sha, 1962.

437. *Shelley's Prometheus Unbound: A Variorum Edition.* Ed. Lawrence John Zillman. See K-SJ, IX (1960), 70, X (1961), 91, XI (1962), 133, XII (1963), 143.
Rev. by Frederic Ewen in *Science & Society,* XXVI (Fall 1962), 447-453.

Sutherland, Alistair, and Patrick Anderson, eds. See No. 101.

Untermeyer, Louis, ed. See No. 103.

438. Villiers, Alan, comp. *Of Ships and Men: A Personal Anthology.* London: Newnes, 1962.
Includes a selection from Shelley (p. 35).

Books and Articles Relating to Shelley and His Circle

439. Angeli, Helen Rossetti. "Two Early Drawings by Shelley," KSMB, XIII (1962), 28-29.
These are reproduced.

Auden, W. H., and Louis Kronenberger, eds. See No. 16.

Bagehot, Walter. See No. 279.

440. Barber, R. W. *Arthur of Albion: An Introduction to the Arthurian Literature and Legends of England.* New York: Barnes & Noble, 1961.
Touches upon Peacock's use of Arthurian materials.

Barlow, Samuel L. M. See No. 116.

Barrows, Herbert. See No. 117.

Benziger, James. See No. 286.

441. Berry, Francis. *Poetry and the Physical Voice.* See K-SJ, XII (1963), 144.
Rev. by Herbert Bluen in *Aryan Path,* XXXIII (Aug. 1962), 375-376; by V. de S. Pinto in *Critical Quarterly,* IV (Autumn 1962), 265-267; by M. C. Bradbrook in *British Journal of Aesthetics,* III (Apr. 1963), 183-184.

442. Berry, Francis. *Poets' Grammar: Person, Time and Mood in Poetry.* See K-SJ, VIII (1959), 67, IX (1960), 63, XI (1962), 124.
Rev. by Herbert Rauter in *Anglia,* LXXX (1962), 136-137.

443. Berry, Francis. "The Poet's Voice," in *The Wind and the Rain: An Easter Book for 1962,* ed. Neville Braybrooke (London: Secker & Warburg, 1962), pp. 190-200.
Discusses Shelley's voice. See K-SJ, XI (1962), 133. Also see No. 441.

444. Bigland, Eileen. *Mary Shelley.* See K-SJ, IX (1960), 71, X (1961), 92.
Rev. by Jean de Palacio in RLC, XXXVII (Jan.-March 1963), 122-123.

445. Bill, Alfred Hoyt. "Long Ago and Far Away," *Princeton University Library Chronicle,* XXII (Summer 1961), 157-162.†
Wilfred Meynell told author how he acquired bust of Shelley done by Mrs. Leigh Hunt.

Blackstone, Bernard. See Nos. 19 and 289.

446. Bloom, Harold. *Shelley's Mythmaking.* See K-SJ, IX (1960), 71, X (1961), 92, XI (1962), 133, XII (1963), 144.
Rev. by John Heath-Stubbs in *Cambridge Review,* LXXXI (Feb. 6, 1960), 325; by Frederic Ewen in *Science &*

Society, XXVI (Fall 1962), 447-453.

447. Blunden, Edmund. "George Edward Shelley, M. B. E.," KSMB, XIII (1962), 2-3.

A cousin of Shelley's who died in 1961 and was a poet in his own right.

Blunden, Edmund. See No. 292.

448. Boas, Louise Schutz. *Harriet Shelley: Five Long Years.* See K-SJ, XII (1963), 144.

Rev. by *Frederic E. Faverty in *Chicago Sunday Tribune Magazine of Books,* March 25, 1962, p. 8; in *New Yorker,* XXXVIII (Apr. 21, 1962), 182-183; by P. H. Butter in MLR, LVII (Oct. 1962), 633; by Donald H. Reiman in JEGP, LXI (Oct. 1962), 933-935; by Richard Harter Fogle in K-SJ, XII (1963), 109-110.

449. Bolton, Guy. *The Olympians.* New York: New American Library, 1962. "A Signet Book."

A paper-bound reprint. See K-SJ, XI (1962), 133, XII (1963), 144.

Rev. by C[olin]. S[tanden]. in *Books and Bookmen,* VIII (June 1963), XI.

450. Brooks, Roger L. "Some Unaccomplished Projects of Matthew Arnold," *Studies in Bibliography,* XVI (1963), 213-216.

They included "a purely literary essay on the poetry of Shelley."

451. Brooks, Van Wyck. *Fenellosa and His Circle, with Other Essays in Biography.* New York: Dutton, 1962.

Describes Fanny Wright's relations with Mary Shelley (pp. 92-94) and includes description of Frederick Catherwood's relations with John Lloyd Stephens.

Brown, Calvin S. See No. 295.

452. *Bulletin of the New York Public Library,* LXVII (Jan. 1963). See Nos. 466 and 487.

Rev. in TLS, May 17, 1963, p. 364.

Bullough, Geoffrey. See No. 25.

453. Butler, Samuel. *The Family Letters of Samuel Butler 1841-1886.* Ed. Arnold Silver. Stanford: Stanford Univ., 1962.

Butler's grandfather visited Lerici a few days after Shelley's death.

454. Cameron, Kenneth Neill, ed. *The Carl H. Pforzheimer Library: Shelley and His Circle 1773-1822.* Vols. I and II. See K-SJ, XI (1962), 133, XII (1963), 144.

Rev. in *The Times,* London, Oct. 12, 1961, p. 16; by R. Glynn Grylls in *Library,* 5th Series, XVII (June 1962), 166-168; by P. H. Butter in MLR, LVII (July 1962), 423-424; by Frederick T. Wood in ES, XLIII (Aug. 1962), 271-272; by Frederic Ewen in *Science & Society,* XXVI (Fall 1962), 447-453; by D[avid]. V. E[rdman]. in PQ, XLI (Oct. 1962), 673-674; by Neville Rogers in RES, N.S., XIV (May 1963), 206-209. See also No. 73.

455. Casey, Bill Harris. "The Misanthrope in English Literature of the Eighteenth Century" [Doctoral dissertation, Texas, 1962], DA, XXIII (Nov. 1962), 1683-1684.

Includes discussion of Godwin's *St. Leon.*

456. Clifford, James L., ed. *Biography as an Art: Selected Criticism 1560-1960.* New York: Oxford Univ., 1962. "A Galaxy Book."

Includes (p. 94) passage from Peacock's "Memoirs of Percy B. Shelley" *(Frazer's Magazine).* There are also references to Byron, Keats, and Shelley in other excerpts in this anthology.

457. "Commentary," BC, XI (Autumn 1962), 277-293.

Reports (pp. 292-293) sale of "Esdaile Notebook" at Sotheby's on July 2, 1962. See Nos. 495, 513, and 528.

Conrad, Barnaby. See No. 131.

458. Corrigan, Beatrice. "Giovanni Ruffini's Letters to Vernon Lee, 1875-1879," *English Miscellany,* XIII (1962), 179-240.

Includes material on Cornelia Turner.

Darbishire, Helen. See No. 306.

Davies, Hugh Sykes. See No. 32.

de Beer, Gavin. See No. 136.

459. Drew, Philip. "Browning's *Essay on Shelley,*" *Victorian Poetry,* I (Jan. 1963), 1-6.†

Includes discussion of Browning's attitude toward Shelley, "a poet who combines the powers of the objective and the subjective poet."

460. Duerksen, Roland A. "Shelley and Shaw," PMLA, LXXVIII (March 1963), 114-127.

"Essentially, Shelley's way of thinking about social concerns appealed to Shaw, and he sought to extend and perfect the ideas Shelley had offered."

Edel, Leon. See No. 147.

461. Eltzbacher, Paul. *Anarchism: Exponents of the Anarchist Philosophy.* Trans. Steven T. Byington. Ed. James

J. Martin. New York: Libertarian Book Club, 1960.

Discusses Godwin as an anarchist (pp. 24-40).

Émery, Léon. See No. 155.

462. England, Martha Winburn. "Further Discussion of Godwin's *Imogen:* Felix Culpa," BNYPL, LXVII (Feb. 1963), 115-118.†

A critical evaluation of the novel. See Nos. 466, 487, 503, and 504.

Evans, Sir Benjamin Ifor. See No. 35.

Fairchild, Hoxie Neale. See No. 36.

"A Filtered Picture. . . ." See No. 158.

Fogle, Richard Harter. See No. 318.

463. Ford, George H. "Shelley or Schiller? A Note on D. H. Lawrence at Work," *Texas Studies in Literature and Language,* IV (Summer 1962), 154-156.

Explains a reference to Shelley in *Women in Love.*

Freeman, John. See No. 40.

464. Gaer, Joseph. *The Legend of the Wandering Jew.* New York: New American Library, 1961. "A Mentor Book."

Discusses Shelley's use of the legend (pp. 118-121).

Gilbert, Judson Bennett. See No. 4.

465. * Godwin, William. *Caleb Williams oder Die Dinge, wie sie sind.* Trans. Rudolf Rocker. With an Introduction by Joachim Krehayn. Leipzig: Reclam, 1962.

466. Godwin, William. "Imogen: A Pastoral Romance from the Ancient British," BNYPL, LXVII (Jan. 1963), 17-32; (Feb. 1963), 119-134; (March 1963), 191-202; (Apr. 1963), 261-270; (May 1963), 328-340; (June 1963), 395-410.†

The text of the novel. See No. 452. Also see Nos. 462, 487, 503, and 504.

467. * Godwin, William. *Kaleb Uil'jams.* [Translated by] A. M. Karnauhova. Moscow: Goslitizdat, 1961.

468. Grayburn, William F. "George Borrow's German Interests," in *Anglo-German and American-German Crosscurrents,* ed. Philip Allison Shelley and Arthur O. Lewis, Jr. (Chapel Hill: Univ. of North Carolina, 1962), II, 225-256.

Compares Borrow's translation of scene from *Faust* with Shelley's version ("The limits of the sphere of dream").

469. Guzzo, Augusto. *Scritti critici e studi d'arte religiosa.* Turin: Edizioni di "Filosofia," 1959.

Includes (pp. 57-61) an article on *Hellas.*

Rev. by Johannes A. Gaertner in BA, XXXV (Winter 1961), 82.

470. Hancock, Sir [William] Keith. *Smuts: The Sanguine Years, 1870-1919.* Vol. I. Cambridge: Cambridge Univ., 1962.

Discusses Smuts's admiration of Shelley.

Haresnape, G. See No. 334.

471. Harper, George Mills. "Mary Wollstonecraft's Residence with Thomas Taylor the Platonist," N&Q, CCVII (Dec. 1962), 461-463.†

Probably occurred during 1782.

472. * Hibbard, E. L. "Shelley's Farewell to the World—A Study of 'The Triumph of Life,'" *Bulletin of the Doshisha Women's College,* XIII (Dec. 1962).

Highet, Gilbert. See No. 166.

473. Hodgart, Matthew. "Politics and Prose Style in the Late Eighteenth Century: The Radicals," BNYPL, LXVI (Sept. 1962), 464-469.†

In one of three papers in the *Bulletin* on "non-subjects," a case is made for Paine's *The Rights of Man* and Godwin's *Political Justice* as representing "different radical styles" and as deriving much from the genius of Burke.

474. Hogan, Robert. "With a Surly Nod to Shelley," *University of Kansas City Review,* XXIX (Dec. 1962), 113.

A poem.

475. Hughes, D. J. "Potentiality in *Prometheus Unbound,*" SIR, II (Winter 1963), 107-126.

Studies Act IV, lines 180-318, and II, scenes ii, iii, and v, which "define the characteristic movement of mind in the poem; the cleansing of the actual that a new potential may emerge."

Jerman, B. R. See No. 169.

Jungblutt, Gertrud. See No. 175.

476. Kaymer, Günter. *Der gesellschaftliche Optimismus William Godwins in seiner literarischen Darlegung.* Cologne: [University of Cologne,] 1958.

477. Kendall, Kenneth E. "Some Words in the Poetry of Shelley and Wordsworth," N&Q, CCVII (Nov. 1962), 423-424.†

Corrects entries in the OED.

Kikuchi, Wataru. See No. 350.

478. King-Hele, Desmond. "The Influence of Erasmus Darwin on Shelley," KSMB, XIII (1962), 30-36.

Finds echoes of Darwin in Shelley's thought and poetry.

479. * King-Hele, Desmond. *Shelley: His Thought and Work.* London: Macmillan, 1963.

A paper-bound reprint. See K-SJ, X (1961), 93.

Knight, G. Wilson. See No. 178.

480. * Kolesnikova, B. *Revoliutsionnaia estetika P. V. Shelli.* Moscow: Vysshaia shkola, 1963. "V pomoshch' studentu-filologu."

481. * Komatsu, Fumio. "Shelley's 'Epipsychidion,'" *Literary Wagon* (Ryukoku Univ., Tokyo), I (Dec. 1962). [In Japanese.]

Kudō, Naotarō. See No. 355.

Kuntz, Joseph M. See No. 6.

Laski, Marghanita. See No. 52.

482. Lemaitre, Hélène. *Shelley, Poète des Eléments.* See K-SJ, XII (1963), 146.

Rev. in TLS, Sept. 21, 1962, p. 728; by Henri Peyre in K-SJ, XII (1963), 107-109; by P. H. Butter in MLR, LVIII (Apr. 1963), 249-250.

483. Levin, Richard. "Shelley's 'Indian Serenade': A Re-Revaluation," CE, XXIV (Jan. 1963), 305-307.

The poem deserves to be taken seriously and is "invulnerable to the charge of sentimentality."

Lister, Raymond. See No. 54.

Livermore, Anne Lapraik. See No. 185.

Logan, John. See No. 187.

484. Loomis, Emerson Robert. "The New Philosophy Satirized in American Fiction," *American Quarterly,* XIV (Fall 1962), 490-495.

American attacks on the ideas of Godwin and his followers were usually in non-fiction or verse; the one satirical novel was Benjamin Silliman's *Letters of Shahcoolen. . . .* (1802). See Nos. 485 and 523.

Loomis, Emerson Robert. See No. 188.

Lovell, Ernest J., Jr. See No. 190.

485. McClary, Ben Harris. "A Note on *Letters of Shahcoolen,*" *Nineteenth-Century Fiction,* XVII (Dec. 1962), 288.

The work is by Benjamin Silliman. See K-SJ, XII (1963), 146, No. 430. See also Nos. 484 and 523.

McCullough, Norman Verrle. See No. 192.

486. Macpherson, Jay. "Narcissus: Some Uncertain Reflections, or, From 'Lycidas' to *Donovan's Brain,*" *Alphabet,* No. 2 (July 1961), pp. 65-71.

Includes discussion of *Alastor.*

487. Marken, Jack W. "Godwin's *Imogen* Rediscovered," BNYPL, LXVII (Jan. 1963), 7-16.†

About a recently discovered two-volume novel by Godwin, published anonymously in 1784. See Nos. 452, 462, 466, 503, and 504.

Mason, Eudo C. See No. 369.

488. Massey, Irving. "Mary Shelley, Walter Scott, and 'Maga,'" N&Q, CCVII (Nov. 1962), 420-421.†

Prints Mary's letter of June 14, 1818, to Scott and her letter of March 21, 1831, to William Blackwood.

489. Massey, Irving. "Shelley's 'Time': An Unpublished Sequel," SIR, II (Autumn 1962), 57-60.

Prints Shelley's holograph version, which suggests a different meaning for the poem.

490. Mathewson, George. "The Search for Coherence: T. S. Eliot and the Christian Tradition in English Poetry" [Doctoral dissertation, Princeton, 1961], DA, XXIII (July 1962), 225-226.

Clarifies Eliot's attitude towards romanticism by reviewing his comments on Shelley.

Maurice, Robert R. See No. 370.

491. Maxwell, D[esmond]. E. S. *American Fiction: The Intellectual Background.* New York: Columbia Univ.; London: Routledge (1963).

Discusses Shelley's *Alastor* (pp. 83-90).

492. Merriman, James Douglas. "The Flower of Kings: A Study of the Arthurian Legend in England between 1485 and 1835" [Doctoral dissertation, Columbia, 1962], DA, XXIII (March 1963), 3354-3355.

Includes discussion of Peacock and other writers of the period.

Miles, Josephine. See No. 372.

Moore, John Cecil. See No. 56.

Munby, A. N. L. See No. 57.

Nash, Ogden, comp. See No. 96.

493. Nelson, Lowry, Jr. "Night Thoughts on the Gothic Novel," *Yale Review,* LII (Winter 1963), 236-257.

Analyzes *Frankenstein.*

Nikoliukin, A. N. See No. 59.

494. Nomad, Max. *Political Heretics: From Plato to Mao Tse-tung.* Ann Arbor: Univ. of Michigan, 1963.

Discusses Godwin briefly (pp. 152-153).

495. "Notes on Sales," TLS, Oct. 5, 1962, p. 784.

"The earliest known poetical notebook of Shelley . . . was sold at Sotheby's . . . on July 2-3 for £10,000." [See Nos. 457, 513, and 528.] A series of 87 letters from Moore to Mary Shelley, 1827-41, brought £900. Lady Shelley's privately printed *Shelley and Mary,* 3 vols., 1882, made £140.

496. "Notes on Sales," TLS, March 15, 1963, p. 192.

At Sotheby's, Dec. 17-19, *Caleb Williams,* "uncut copy in original boards," 3 vols., 1794, brought £120.

"Notes on Sales. . . ." See No. 203.

Nowottny, Winifred. See No. 60.

Olney, Clarke. See No. 378.

497. Owen, A. L. *The Famous Druids: A Survey of Three Centuries of English Literature on the Druids.* Oxford: Clarendon, 1962.

Peacock, "who liked little in Druidism," nevertheless defended the Druids.

Owen, Harold H., Jr., *et al.* See No. 379.

498. Palacio, Jean de. "Shelley Traducteur de Dante: Le Chant XXVIII du *Purgatoire,*" RLC, XXXVI (Oct.-Dec. 1963), 571-578.

Presents Shelley's text, with a discussion of his methods as a translator.

499. Palmer, D. J., and R. E. Dowse. "*Frankenstein:* a Moral Fable," Li, LXVIII (Aug. 23, 1962), 281, 284.

Sees the novel in terms "of the conflicting authorities of reason and feeling in modern man."

500. * Peacock, Thomas Love. *The Complete Novels of Thomas Love Peacock.* Ed. David Garnett. 2 vols. London: Hart-Davis, 1963. "Harvest Books."

A paper-bound reprint.

501. Peters, Robert L. "Swinburne's Idea of Form," *Criticism,* V (Winter 1963), 45-63.

Discusses some of the relationships between Swinburne's principles and those of Shelley; Keats and Byron are also mentioned.

Peyre, Henri. See No. 62.

502. Pollin, Burton Ralph. *Education and Enlightenment in the Works of William Godwin.* See K-SJ, XII (1963), 147.

Rev. in TLS, Jan. 4, 1963, p. 11; by Francis Golffing in BA, XXXVII (Spring 1963), 202-203; by Ralph M. Wardle in CE, XXIV (May 1963), 662-663; by David Fleisher in *Nineteenth-Century Fiction,* XVIII (June 1963), 95-97.

503. Pollin, Burton Ralph. "Primitivism in *Imogen,*" BNYPL, LXVII (March 1963), 186-190.

See Nos. 462, 466, 487, and 504.

Poulet, Georges. See No. 217.

504. Primer, Irwin. "Further Discussion of Godwin's *Imogen:* Some Implications of Irony," BNYPL, LXVII (Apr. 1963), 257-260.

See Nos. 462, 466, 487, and 503.

505. Prouteau, Gilbert. *Les dieux meurent le matin.* Paris: Bernard Grasset, 1962.

One section, "Chronique du malheur" (pp. 83-116), is on Shelley.

Rev. in *Annales,* LXX (June 1963), 63.

506. Pulos, C. E. *The Deep Truth: A Study of Shelley's Scepticism.* See K-SJ, XII (1963), 147.

Rev. by Donald H. Reiman in SAQ, LXI (Autumn 1962), 571; by B[ernice]. S[lote]. in *Personalist,* XLIV (Winter 1963), 121-122; by Donald H. Reiman in CE, XXIV (Apr. 1963), 588.

507. Raben, Joseph. "Milton's Influence on Shelley's Translation of Dante's 'Matilda Gathering Flowers,'" RES, N.S., XIV (May 1963), 142-156.

Traces Milton's influence in Shelley's rendering of an excerpt from the *Purgatorio.* The changes he made in Dante "reflect a conscious effort by Shelley to learn from Milton the poetic skills needed to re-create Dante in English."

508. Raben, Joseph. "Shelley's *Prometheus Unbound:* Why the Indian Caucasus?" K-SJ, XII (1963), 95-106.

"Shelley found in the Prometheus myth three truths: historical, that man had known a golden age in the mountains of central Asia and had perhaps already acted out there the enslavement and emancipation that foreshadowed the universal freedom; physical, that the rule of change is cyclical, like the seasons, the ice-ages, the vast patterns of the universe; and moral, that the regeneration of mankind is as inevitable as these physical examples."

509. Raymond, William O. "Browning and the Harriet Westbrook Shelley Letters," *University of Toronto Quarterly,* XXXII (Jan. 1963), 184-192.†

Browning saw the letters in "1858 or

thereabouts," not 1851 as some critics have contended.

510. Reiman, Donald H. "Shelley in the Encyclopedias," K-SJ, XII (1963), 55-65.

Traces Shelley's reputation in English encyclopedias of the nineteenth century and finds "that one of the factors contributing to the stability and growth of the poet's reputation among middle-class readers was the presence of eloquent defences of him in the general reference works of the day."

511. Reiman, Donald H. "Structure, Symbol, and Theme in 'Lines Written among the Euganean Hills,'" PMLA, LXXVII (Sept. 1962), 404-413.

"Shelley has created a symbolic universe that skillfully embodies and reverberates his theme: although it is ordinarily man's fate to be the slave and victim of forces beyond his conscious control (a situation so intolerable that death and oblivion are preferable to it), there come to the man of imagination moments in which his soul becomes one with the universe, in which he is able to see . . . clearly and vitally . . . the values and end of human existence; such moments, in which a divine infusion of love and reason breaks through the clouds of mortality, have their own kind of inevitability but one that gives their recipient true moral freedom; such moments, if cultivated and trusted, might break the harsh chain of provocation and retribution."

Renwick, William Lindsay. See No. 67.

512. * Rieger, James Henry. "The Gnostic Prometheus: A Study of Godwin and the Shelleys." (Doctoral dissertation, Harvard, 1963.)

513. Rogers, Neville. "The Esdaile Notebook," TLS, July 6, 1962, p. 500.

Describes and summarizes the importance of this Shelley notebook. See Nos. 457, 495, and 528.

514. Rogers, Neville. "A Portrait of Elizabeth Shelley," KSMB, XIII (1962), 1.

Shelley's sister, whom he greatly resembled. The portrait is reproduced in color as a frontispiece.

515. Rogers, Neville. *Shelley at Work: A Critical Inquiry*. See K-SJ, VII (1958), 131, VIII (1959), 77, IX (1960), 74, X (1961), 95.

Rev. by John Beer in *Cambridge Review*, LXXVIII (Apr. 27, 1957), 515, 517.

516. Rountree, Thomas Jefferson. "Wordsworth's Theme of Benevolent Necessity" [Doctoral dissertation, Tulane, 1962], DA, XXIII (May 1963), 4364-4365.

Discusses Godwin's influence on the poet.

Roy, G. Ross. See No. 69.

Saito, Takeshi, comp. See No. 10.

Sampson, George. See No. 70.

517. Schulze, Earl John. "Shelley's Theory of Poetry: A Reappraisal" [Doctoral dissertation, Northwestern, 1962], DA, XXIII (June 1963), 4689.

"A Season of American Sales." See No. 393.

518. Seiden, Morton Irving. *William Butler Yeats: The Poet as a Mythmaker 1865-1939*. [East Lansing:] Michigan State Univ., 1962.

Discusses Shelley's influence on Yeats.

519. Sharrock, Roger. "Godwin on Milton's Satan," N&Q, CCVII (Dec. 1962), 463-465.†

His views resemble Blake's; possible influences are suggested.

520. * "Shaw on Shelley," *Independent Shavian*, I (Oct. 1962), 3-5.†

Shaw's review of a production of *The Cenci*.

521. * Shelley, Mary Wollstonecraft. *Frankenštajn ili moderni Prometej*. [Translated by] Slavka Stevović. Belgrade: Mlado pokolenje, 1960.

522. * Shelley, Mary Wollstonecraft. *Frankenstein*. [Translated by] Mazharul Haq Alvi. Lucknow: Nasim Book Depot [n.d.]. [In Urdu.]

523. [Silliman, Benjamin.] *The Letters of Shahcoolen (1802)*. Ed. Ben Harris McClary. Gainesville: Scholars' Facsimiles & Reprints, 1962.

The introduction discusses the attack on Mary Wollstonecraft. See Nos. 484 and 485.

524. * Sitaramayya, K. B. "The Fugitives: A Lyrical Ballad by Shelley," *Report of the Proceedings of the All India English Teachers' Conference* (Madras, 1959), pp. 158-163.

Skelton, Robin, ed. See No. 269.

Spender, Stephen, and Donald Hall, eds. See No. 72.

Spender, Stephen. See Nos. 397 and 398.

525. Stafford, William. "Ozymandias's Brother," *Carleton Miscellany*, IV (Summer 1963), 91.

A poem.

Štěpaník, Karel. See No. 229.

526. Stewart, J. I. M. *Thomas Love Peacock*. London: Longmans, for the British Council, 1963. "Writers and Their Work No. 156."

Swallow, Alan. See No. 406.

527. * Takenami, Yoshikazu. "Shelley's 'Defence of Poetry,'" *Memoirs of the Osaka Institute of Technology*, V (March 1960), 39-46. [In Japanese.]

Taylor, Robert H. See No. 409.

528. "£10,000 for Earliest Shelley Notebook: Verse That Was Never Published," *The Times*, London, July 3, 1962, p. 5.
See Nos. 457, 495, and 513.

Thomas, Henry, and Dana Lee Thomas. See No. 231.

Thomas, Roy. See No. 410.

529. Thurber, James. "The Future, if Any, of Comedy or, Where Do We Non-Go from Here?" *Harper's Magazine*, CCXXIII (Dec. 1961), 40-45.
A humorous conversation with a literary critic which includes some thoughts on Shelley as a scientist.

530. Tillyard, E. M. W. *Essays Literary & Educational*. London: Chatto & Windus; New York: Barnes & Noble (1962).
Includes "Shelley's 'Ozymandias'" (pp. 108-113) and "Thomas Love Peacock" (pp. 114-129).
Rev. in TLS, July 13, 1962, p. 510; by J. B. Beer in NS, LXIV (Aug. 24, 1962), 235-236.

531. Tschumi, Raymond. *A Philosophy of Literature*. London: Linden, 1961.
Discusses Shelley's "To a Skylark" (pp. 173-179).

Van Tieghem, Philippe. See No. 238.

532. * Vančura, Zdeněk. *Anglická literatura od převratu r. 1688 k období francouzské revoluce*. [*English Literature from the Revolution of 1688 to the Period of the French Revolution*.] Revised Edition. Prague: SPN, 1962.
Includes discussion of Godwin.

533. * Vlajčić, Milan. "Šeli, Odbrana poezije," *Razlog* (Zagreb), VIII (1962), 639-647.

Watson, George. See No. 417.

Whittemore, Reed. See No. 241.

Wilde, Oscar. See No. 242.

Wilson, Angus. See No. 243.

534. Wilson, Milton. *Shelley's Later Poetry: A Study of His Prophetic Imagination*. See K-SJ, IX (1960), 75, X (1961), 97, XI (1962), 138, XII (1963), 148.
Rev. by Frederic Ewen in *Science & Society*, XXVI (Fall 1962), 447-453.

535. Wojcik, Manfred. "In Defense of Shelley," *Zeitschrift für Anglistik und Amerikanistik*, XI (1963), 143-188.
"Shelley's revolutionary spirit and prophetic genius enabled him to go beyond the reality of bourgeois society, to forecast the victory of a truly human order of society, to anticipate communism which is now being built by a third of mankind. This is his greatest achievement, an achievement that makes him a poet whose personality and work will live for ages to come."

Woods, Ralph L. See No. 244.

536. * Yamaguchi, Tetsuo. "Some Aspects of Serpent in the Works of Shelley," *Hiroshima Studies in English Language and Literature* (English Literary Association of Hiroshima Univ.), Vol. VI, Nos. 1-2 (1963), pp. 11-17. [In Japanese.]

VI. PHONOGRAPH RECORDINGS

Byron, Keats, Shelley

537. * *English Romantic Poetry*. Read by John S. Martin. Folkways FL 9883.
Includes selections from Keats and Shelley.
Rev. in *English Journal*, LII (Feb. 1963), 153-154; by Thomas Lask in *New York Times*, May 26, 1963, p. 17X.

538. * *A Treasury of Great Poetry*. Based on the Anthology by Louis Untermeyer. Read by Alexander Scourby, Bramwell Fletcher, and Nancy Wickwire. Libraphone A 1626. 3 records. 7-in. 16 RPM.
Includes three poems by Byron, five by Shelley, and three by Keats.
Rev. by John Muri in *English Journal*, LI (Oct. 1962), 501-502; by Thomas Lask in *New York Times*, May 26, 1963, p. 17X.

Bibliography for July 1, 1963–June 30, 1964

VOLUME XIV

Compiled by David Bonnell Green and Edwin Graves Wilson

This bibliography, a regular department of the *Keats-Shelley Journal,* is a register of the literary interest in Keats, Shelley, Byron, Hunt, and their circles from (approximately) July 1963 through June 1964.

The compilers are most grateful, for their kind assistance, to Professors Nils Erik Enkvist, Åbo Akademi; H. W. Häusermann, the University of Geneva; Dr. Siegfried Korninger, Universität Wien; Ranka Kuić, the University of Belgrade; A. C. Partridge, University of the Witwatersrand; Jaime Rest, Universidad Nacional del Sur, Bahia Blanca; Takeshi Saito, International Christian University, Emeritus Professor of Tokyo University; Dr. Helmut Viebrock, Johann Wolfgang Goethe Universität, Frankfurt am Main; Magdi Wahba, Cairo University; Drs. Anna Katona, University of Debrecen; J. G. Riewald, University of Groningen; D. H. Borchardt, the University of Tasmania; B. L. Kandel, the M. E. Saltykov-Schedrin State Public Library in Leningrad; Aloys Skoumal, formerly of Prague University Library; and the library staffs of Boston University, Duke University, Harvard University, and Wake Forest College.

We wish to thank Mrs. Kisia Trolle, of the Harvard College Library, for her generous help with the Russian entries.

Each item that we have not seen is marked by an asterisk. Entries which have been abstracted in *Abstracts of English Studies* are marked with a dagger, but entries in previous bibliographies which were abstracted too late for notice have not been repeated.

ABBREVIATIONS

ABC	American Book Collector
AL	American Literature
ASNS	Archiv für das Studium der Neueren Sprachen
BA	Books Abroad
BC	Book Collector
BYNPL	Bulletin of the New York Public Library
CE	College English
CL	Comparative Literature
CLSB	C. L. S. Bulletin (Charles Lamb Society)
CR	Contemporary Review
DA	Dissertation Abstracts
EA	Etudes Anglaises
EC	Essays in Criticism
ELH	Journal of English Literary History
ES	English Studies
Exp	Explicator

HLQ	Huntington Library Quarterly
ICS	L'Italia Che Scrive
ILN	Illustrated London News
JAAC	Journal of Aesthetics and Art Criticism
JEGP	Journal of English and Germanic Philology
JHI	Journal of the History of Ideas
KR	Kenyon Review
K-SJ	Keats-Shelley Journal
KSMB	Keats-Shelley Memorial Bulletin
Li	The Listener
MLN	Modern Language Notes
MLQ	Modern Language Quarterly
MLR	Modern Language Review
MP	Modern Philology
N&Q	Notes and Queries
NS	New Statesman
NYHT	New York Herald Tribune Book Week
NYT	New York Times Book Review
PBSA	Papers of the Bibliographical Society of America
PMLA	Publications of the Modern Language Association of America
PQ	Philological Quarterly
PR	Partisan Review
QQ	Queen's Quarterly
RES	Review of English Studies
RLC	Revue de Littérature Comparée
SAQ	South Atlantic Quarterly
SatR	Saturday Review
SEL	Studies in English Literature 1500-1900
SIR	Studies in Romanticism
SP	Studies in Philology
Spec	Spectator
SR	Sewanee Review
T&T	Time & Tide / John o'London's Weekly
TC	Twentieth Century
TLS	Times Literary Supplement
VQR	Virginia Quarterly Review

I. GENERAL

Current Bibliographies

1. Allen, Robert V. "Slavica: USSR—Bibliographies and Other Reference Works," *Library of Congress Quarterly Journal of Current Acquisitions,* XX (June 1963), 200-209.

   Records (p. 208) the fifth volume of *Trudy* (Transactions) of the Lenin State Library that contains "a bibliography of Russian language works of criticism and literary history concerning Lord Byron, which lists 973 items published between 1815 and 1960." See No. 166.
2. Derby, J. Raymond, ed. "The Romantic Movement: A Selective and Critical Bibliography for the Year 1951," PQ, XXXI (Apr. 1952), 97-155.
3. Erdman, David V., *et al.* "The Romantic Movement: A Selective and Critical Bibliography for the Year 1962," PQ, XLII (Oct. 1963), 433-524.
4. Green, David Bonnell, and Edwin Graves Wilson. "Current Bibliography," K-SJ, XIII (1964), 119-159.
5. Hirsch, Rudolf, and Howell J. Heaney. "A Selective Check List of Bibliographical Scholarship for 1962," *Studies in Bibliography,* XVII (1964), 229-252.
6. Kiell, Norman, ed. *Psychoanalysis, Psychology, and Literature: A Bibliography.* Madison: Wisconsin Univ., 1963.

   Lists items pertaining to Byron, Hazlitt, Hood, Keats, and Shelley.
7. Lang, Cecil Y. "Current Bibliography," K-SJ, I (1952), 87-102.
8. Read, Bill. "Thomas Love Peacock: An Enumerative Bibliography," *Bulletin of Bibliography,* XXIV (Sept.-Dec. 1963), 32-34; (Jan.-Apr. 1964), 70-72.
9. Woodring, Carl R. "Current Bibliography," K-SJ, III (1954), 111-127.
10. Yarker, P. M., and Sheila M. Smith. "The Nineteenth Century," in *The Year's Work in English Studies,* ed. Beatrice White and T. S. Dorsch, XLII (1963 [for 1961]), 223-244.

Books and Articles Relating to English Romanticism

11. * Abdullah, Adel Mohammed. "The Arabian Nights in English Literature to 1900." (Doctoral dissertation, Cambridge, 1963.)
12. * Bandaranaike, Malini Yasmine Dias. "English Literature in Ceylon and the Development of an Anglo-Ceylonese Literature, 1815-78." (Doctoral dissertation, Cambridge, 1963.)
13. Bentman, Raymond. "The Romantic Poets and Critics on Robert Burns," *Texas Studies in Literature and Language,* VI (Spring 1964), 104-118.

    Discusses the attitude towards Burns of—among others—Hazlitt, Byron, Hunt, Shelley, and Keats.

14. Bernhardt-Kabisch, Ernst Karl-Heinz Reinhold. "Poet Agonistes: A Study of the Poet as Hero in Romantic Poetry, with Particular Emphasis on Wordsworth" [Doctoral dissertation, California, Berkeley, 1962], DA, XXIV (May 1964), 4691.

15. Blackstone, Bernard. *The Lost Travellers: A Romantic Theme with Variations.* See K-SJ, XIII (1964), 121.

Rev. by F. T. Wood in ES, XLIV (Aug. 1963), 311; by Louis James in *Critical Quarterly,* V (Autumn 1963), 276-277; by C[arl]. W[oodring]. in PQ, XLII (Oct. 1963), 444; by P. H. Butter in RES, N.S., XIV (Nov. 1963), 419-420.

16. Bloom, Harold. *The Visionary Company: A Reading of English Romantic Poetry.* See K-SJ, XII (1963), 123, XIII (1964), 121.

Rev. by F. T. Wood in ES, XLIV (Aug. 1963), 311; by Louis James in *Critical Quarterly,* V (Autumn 1963), 276-277; by W[alter]. M. C[rittenden]. in *Personalist,* XLV (Spring 1964), 281.

17. Bostetter, Edward E. *The Romantic Ventriloquists: Wordsworth, Coleridge, Keats, Shelley, Byron.* Seattle: Washington Univ., 1963.

Rev. by Marius Bewley in *Hudson Review,* XVII (Spring 1964), 124-131.

18. Bowra, C. M. *The Romantic Imagination.* See K-SJ, I (1952), 88, II (1953), 100, III (1954), 112, XI (1962), 109.

Rev. by Michèle S. Plaisant in *Langues modernes,* LVII (Nov.-Dec. 1963), 58-59.

19. * Cowell, R. "The Concern with the Problems of Contemporary Society in English Romantic Literature, with Particular Reference to Wordsworth and Coleridge." (Doctoral dissertation, Bristol, 1962.)

20. Foakes, R. A. *The Romantic Assertion.* See K-SJ, IX (1960), 49-50, X (1961), 73, XI (1962), 109-110, XII (1963), 124.

Rev. by Edward Carney in *Moderna Språk,* LIII (1959), 97-98.

21. Frye, Northrop, ed. *Romanticism Reconsidered: Selected Papers from the English Institute.* New York: Columbia Univ., 1963.

Contains Frye's "The Drunken Boat: The Revolutionary Element in Romanticism" (pp. 1-25), M. H. Abrams' "English Romanticism: The Spirit of the Age" (pp. 26-72), Lionel Trilling's "The Fate of Pleasure: Wordsworth to Dostoevsky" (pp. 73-106), and René Wellek's "Romanticism Re-examined" (pp. 107-133). See K-SJ, XIII (1964), 124, No. 75. Also see Nos. 218 and 351.

Rev. by Marius Bewley in *Hudson Review,* XVII (Spring 1964), 124-131.

22. Gottfried, Leon. *Matthew Arnold and the Romantics.* Lincoln: Nebraska Univ., 1963. See K-SJ, XIII (1964), 122-123.

Rev. by Basil Willey in *Critical Quarterly,* V (Autumn 1963), 274-275; by William A. Jamison in K-SJ, XIII (1964), 116-117; by Clyde de L. Ryals in SAQ, LXIII (Spring 1964), 248-249; by Nicholas A. Salerno in CE, XXV (March 1964), 475-476.

23. * Halpé, A. "Poetry and the Theatre, 1800-1850: A Study of the Place of Dramatic Poetry in the English Theatre during the First Half of the Nineteenth Century, with Particular Reference to the Verse Drama of the Period." (Doctoral dissertation, Bristol, 1962.)

24. Hübner, Walter. *Das englische Literaturwerk: Theorie und Praxis der Interpretation.* Heidelberg: Quelle & Meyer, 1963.

Byron, Hazlitt, Hunt, Keats, and Shelley are discussed.

25. Jack, Ian. *English Literature 1815-1832.* Oxford: Clarendon, 1963. "The Oxford History of English Literature, Vol. X."

Rev. by Kenneth Allott in Li, LXX (Oct. 24, 1963), 664; in TLS, Oct. 25, 1963, p. 852; by C. D. Klingopulos in Spec, Nov. 8, 1963, p. 601; in *Books and Bookmen,* IX (Dec. 1963), v; by Donald Davie in NS, LXVI (Dec. 6, 1963), 845-846; by Walter Jackson Bate in NYHT, Jan. 5, 1964, pp. 5, 8; by * E. Frykman in *Göteborgs Handels- och Sjöfartstidning,* Feb. 27, 1964; by Marius Bewley in *Hudson Review,* XVII (Spring 1964), 124-131; by Hermann Peschmann in *English,* XV (Spring 1964), 26-27; by Steven Marcus in *New York Review of Books,* II (Apr. 2, 1964), 10.

26. *Keats-Shelley Memorial Bulletin,* XIII (1962). See K-SJ, XIII (1964), 123.

Rev. by K. R. Srinivasa Iyengar in *Aryan Path,* XXXV (Apr. 1964), 184-185.

27. *Keats-Shelley Memorial Bulletin,* XIV (1963).
Rev. in TLS, Apr. 23, 1964, p. 348.

28. Keiser, Robert. *Die Aufnahme englischen Schrifttums in der deutschen Schweiz von 1830 bis 1860.* Zurich: Juris, 1962. "Zürcher Beiträge zur vergleichenden Literaturgeschichte, X."
Includes discussion of Godwin, Mary Wollstonecraft, Hazlitt, Byron, Keats, Shelley, Hunt, and others.

29. Kreutz, Christian. *Das Prometheussymbol in der englischen Romantik.* Göttingen: Vandenhoek & Ruprecht, 1963.

30. Marshall, William H., ed. *The Major English Romantics: An Anthology.* New York: Washington Square Press, 1963.
Byron, Keats, and Shelley are included.

31. Nowottny, Winifred. *The Language Poets Use.* See K-SJ, XIII (1964), 123.
Rev. by Kenneth Muir in RES, N.S., XIV (Nov. 1963), 432-434.

32. Peckham, Morse. "Recent Studies in Nineteenth-Century English Literature," SEL, III (Autumn 1963), 595-611.
An omnibus review. See K-SJ, XII (1963), 124, No. 31, 132, No. 171, 133, No. 188, 136, No. 237, 145, No. 411, XIII (1964), 121, Nos. 13 and 14, 122, No. 36, 124, No. 64, 131, Nos. 190 and 195, 137, No. 286. See also Nos. 34, 120, 122, 143, 164, 207, and 211.

33. Pellegrini, Carlo, ed. *Storia delle letterature moderne d'Europa e d'America.* 6 vols. Milan: Vallardi, 1958-60.
Vol. III contains "Letteratura inglese" by Sergio Baldi.

34. Piper, H[erbert]. W[alter]. *The Active Universe: Pantheism and the Concept of the Imagination in the English Romantic Poets.* See K-SJ, XIII (1964), 124.
Rev. by H. A. Smith in MLR, LVIII (July 1963), 414-415; by Jack Stillinger in JEGP, LXII (July 1963), 690-692. See also No. 32.

35. Raysor, Thomas M., ed. *The English Romantic Poets: A Review of Research.* See K-SJ, I (1952), 89, III (1954), 114, IV (1955), 113, V (1956), 120.
Rev. by R[ichard]. D. A[ltick]. in PQ, XXX (Apr. 1951), 100-101; by Edith C. Batho in MLR, XLVI (July-Oct. 1951), 547-548.

36. Reeves, James. *A Short History of English Poetry 1340-1940.* * New York: Dutton, 1962. See K-SJ, XII (1963), 124-125, XIII (1964), 124.
Rev. by Paull F. Baum in SAQ, LXII (Summer 1963), 455-456.

37. Riquer, Martín de, and José María Valverde. *Historia de la Literatura Universal.* 3 vols. Barcelona: Noguer, 1957-59.
Vol. III, "Del Romanticismo a Nuestros Días," is by Valverde.

38. Rodway, Allan. *The Romantic Conflict.* London: Chatto, 1963.
Has chapters on Byron, Keats, and Shelley.
Rev. by Donald Davie in NS, LXVI (Dec. 6, 1963), 845-846; in TLS, Jan. 9, 1964, p. 22; by Kenneth Allott in EC, XIV (Apr. 1964), 189-193.

39. * Stokoe, Frank W. *German Influence in the English Romantic Period, 1788-1818; with Special Reference to Scott, Coleridge, Shelley, and Byron.* New York: Russell & Russell, 1963.
A reprint of a book first published in 1926.

40. White, R. J. *Life in Regency England.* London: Batsford; New York: Putnam's (1963). "English Life Series."
Byron, Haydon, Hazlitt, Hunt, Keats, Shelley, and others are included.

II. BYRON

Works: Collected, Selected, Single, Translated

41. Brown, Ivor, ed. *A Book of Marriage.* London: Hamish Hamilton, 1963.
Includes selections from Byron, Shelley, Keats, Peacock, and Hazlitt.

42. *Byron's Poems.* Ed. V. de Sola Pinto. 3 vols. London: Dent, 1963. "Everyman's Library."
Rev. by Thomas Foster in T&T, XLIV (July 4-10, 1963), 26; by Kenneth Muir in MLR, LIX (Jan. 1964), 119-120.

43. Cole, William, ed. *Erotic Poetry: The Lyrics, Ballads, Idyls and Epics of Love—Classical to Contemporary.* Foreword by Stephen Spender. New York: Random House, 1963.
Includes selections from Byron and Keats.

44. **Dnevniki.—Pis'ma.* [*Journals, Letters.*] Ed. Z. E. Aleksandrova *et al.* Moscow:

Akad. nauk SSSR., 1963. (Lit. pamiatniki.)

Includes a bibliography of contemporary references and opinions by A. N. Nikoliukin (pp. 418-423) and a commentary "Dnevniki i pis'ma Bairona" by A. A. Elistratova (pp. 341-358).

45. Grigson, Geoffrey, ed. *The Cherry-Tree: A Collection of Poems.* London: Phoenix, 1959.

An anthology for children that includes poems by Byron, Hood, Hunt, Keats, and Shelley.

46. **Izbrannoe.* [*Selections.*] Minsk: Gosizdat BSSR, 1963. [In White Russian.]

Rev. by *Ia. Khelemskii in *Druzhba narodov,* No. 8 (1963), pp. 280-283; by A. Zaritskii in *Belarus'* (Minsk), No. 6 (1963), p. 29; by U. Karatkevich in *Polymia* (Minsk), No. 10 (1963), pp. 186-190.

47. *"Khotel by ia byt' vol'nym rebenkom," [translated by] S. Asanov, *Zhuldyz* (Alma-Ata), No. 1 (1963), pp. 82-83. [In Kazakh.]

48. **Lord Byron: Selections from His Poetry and Prose.* Ed. Ian Gregor and Andrew Rutherford. London: Chatto, 1963. "Queen's Classics."

Marshall, William H., ed. See No. 30.

49. Meister, Robert, ed. *A Literary Guide to Seduction.* Introduction by Leslie A. Fiedler. New York: Stern and Day, 1963.

Includes selections from *Don Juan.*

50. *"Oda avtoram billia protiv razrushitelei stankov.—Na begstvo Napoleona s ostrova El'by.—Nadpis' na oborote razvodnogo akta v aprele 1816 g. Iz Martsiala.—Na samoubiistvo britanskogo ministri Kestleri," [translated by] S. Shavly, *Ialav* (Cheboksary), No. 3 (1963), p. 26. [In Chuvash.]

51. **Parizina.* [*Parisina.*] [*Translated by*] Janez Menart. Ljubljana: Država založha Slovenije, 1963. [In Slovenian.]

52. *"Pesn'ludditov.—'Esli ne smozhesh' borot'sia za krai svoi rodnoi . . .'—Ty okonchil svoi zhiznennyi put.—'Ne budem bluzhdat' po stepi . . .'—Stansy," [translated by] Iu. Barzhanskii, *Nistrul* (Kishinev), No. 1 (1963), pp. 124-125. [In Moldavian.]

53. *"Proštalna Pasna Na Čajld Harold," *Razvigor,* No. 6 (1963). [In Macedonian.]

54. **Selections from Byron's Poetry.* Ed. Ksenija Anastasijević. Belgrade: Naućna Knjiga, 1963.

55. Untermeyer, Louis, ed. *An Uninhibited Treasury of Erotic Poetry.* New York: Dial, 1963.

Includes poems by Byron, Keats, and Shelley.

Books and Articles Relating to Byron and His Circle

56. Ades, John Irvine. "Charles Lamb as a Literary Critic" [Doctoral dissertation, Cincinnati, 1963], DA, XXIV (June 1964), 5378.

"An appendix includes speculations on Lamb's categorical rejections of both Byron and Shelley."

Allen, Robert V. See No. 1.

57. Anderson, George K. "The Legend of the Wandering Jew," *Books at Brown,* XIX (May 1963), 143-159.

Touches upon Byron, Godwin, and Shelley.

58. André, P. "Sur les pas de Byron à travers les Préalpes vaudoises et l'Oferland bernois," *Vie et langage* (Paris), No. 125 (Aug. 1962), pp. 416-421.

Recounts Byron's trip through the Vaudois to Berne.

59. *Anglo-German and American-German Crosscurrents.* Vol. II. Ed. Philip Allison Shelley and Arthur O. Lewis, Jr. See K-SJ, XIII (1964), 126.

Rev. by Karl J. R. Arndt in JEGP, LXII (Oct. 1963), 821-822.

60. Auden, W. H. *The Dyer's Hand and Other Essays.* See K-SJ, XIII (1964), 126.

Rev. by Aaron Rosen in KR, XXV (Autumn 1963), 739-743.

61. Baker, Paul R. *The Fortunate Pilgrims: Americans in Italy, 1800-1860.* Cambridge, Mass.: Harvard Univ., 1964.

Includes discussion of Byron.

62. Baker, Paul R. "Lord Byron and the Americans in Italy," K-SJ, XIII (1964), 61-75.

Reviews the meetings of Byron with Americans and traces his influence on American visitors to Italy in the quarter century after his death.

Bentman, Raymond. See No. 13.

63. Berenson, Bernard. *Sunset and Twilight. From the Diaries of 1947-1958.* Ed. Nicky Mariano. Introduction by Iris Origo. New York: Harcourt, Brace,

1963; *London: Hamish Hamilton, 1964.
Includes comment on Byron.

64. Beyer, Werner W. *The Enchanted Forest.* New York: Barnes & Noble, 1963.
Appendix VI is entitled "Byron and Sotheby, and Wieland's Eroticism"; Appendix VII, "The Case of T. L. Peacock's 'Rhododaphne.' "

65. *Bo, C. "Byron e il secolo," *La Stampa,* 23, IX, 1958.

66. Borrow, K. T., and Dorothy Hewlett. "Byron: A Link with Australia," KSMB, XIV (1963), 17-20.
An account of Marshall MacDermott, who met Byron in 1823, and of a carriage of Lord Byron's that was sent to Australia.

67. Bose, Amalendu. *Chroniclers of Life: Studies in Early Victorian Poetry.* Bombay: Orient Longmans, 1962.
Discusses the influence of Byron and Shelley on early Victorian poetry and includes an appendix on "Admiration for Milton and Shelley."

Bostetter, Edward E. See No. 17.

68. Brown, Calvin S. "Monosyllables in English Verse," SEL, III (Autumn 1963), 473-491.
Monosyllabic lines are to be found in Keats, Shelley, and Byron, as well as in most other great English poets.

69. *Brownstein, Rachel Mayer. *"Don Juan:* The Absurd Point of View." (Doctoral dissertation, Yale, 1963.)

70. *Brusiloff, Constant. "Washington, Bolivar y Byron," *Revista de la Sociedad Bolivariana de Venezuela,* XVIII, No. 58 (1959), pp. 58-65.

71. Butler, Maria Hogan. "An Examination of Byron's Revision of *Manfred,* Act III," SP, LX (Oct. 1963), 627-636.
Byron's revision "seems to indicate that the drama is intended to represent the full cycle of man's eternal struggle for a 'way out' which is not devoid of hope, even for the 'lost' man."

72. Byrne, Clifford Michael. "Lord Byron: His Classical Republicanism, Cyclical View of History, and Their Influence on His Work" [Doctoral dissertation, Vanderbilt, 1963], DA, XXIV (July 1963), 282.

73. * Byron, John. *El naufragio de la fragata Wager.* Santiago de Chile: Empresa Editora Zig-Zag, 1955.
Rev. by A[lvaro]. J[aru]. in *Revista de Historia de América* (Mexico), No. 42 (1956), 570.

74. * *Byron in seinen Briefen und Tagebüchern.* Ed. Cordula Gigon. Zürich: Artemis, 1963.
Rev. by Hans Georg Peters in *Neue Deutsche Hefte,* No. 94 (July-Aug. 1963), pp. 120-124.

75. "Byron's Life in Music," *The Times,* London, June 7, 1962, p. 15.
Describes the first performance of a Byron Symphony by Alan Bush. Mentions the earlier symphonic portrait *Lord Byron* by Richard Arnell.

76. Carb, Nathan R. E., Jr. "The 'Leon'—'Noel' Anagram," N&Q, CCIX (Jan. 1964), 25.†
"Leon" in *Don Leon* and *Leon to Annabella* may be an anagram of "Noel."

77. Chatterton, Roylance Wayne. "Lord Byron's Dramas: An Attempt to Reform the English Stage" [Doctoral dissertation, Utah, 1963], DA, XXIV (Nov. 1963), 2029-2030.

78. * Chudakov, S. B. "Poeziia Bairona v otsenke angliiskoi esteticheskoi kritiki" ["Byron's Poetry at the Bar of English Esthetic Criticism"], *Uchenye zapiski* (Khabarovsk Gos. ped. In-t.), Filol. seriia, X (1963), 3-39.

79. * Chudakov, S. B. "Romanticheskaia problematika 'Vostochnykh povestei' Bairona" ["Problems of Romanticism in Byron's 'Oriental Tales' "], *Uchenye zapiski* (Khabarovsk Gos. ped. In-t.), Filol. seriia, X (1963), 111-126.

80. *Cialfi, Mario. "Byron e il titanismo," *Osservatore politico letterario,* IX, vii (1963), 69-78.

Clare, John. See No. 223.

81. Cogswell, Fred. "Scott-Byron," *Studies in Scottish Literature,* I (Oct. 1963), 131-132.
Prints from the manuscript an incomplete sketch of Scott and Byron by John Galt.

82. Cohen, Ralph. *The Art of Discrimination: Thomson's "The Seasons" and the Language of Criticism.* Berkeley: California Univ., 1964.
The attitudes of Byron, Hazlitt, Keats, and Shelley are discussed.

83. * Comorovski, Cornelia. "Pe marginea traducerilor romînşti din operele lui Byron si Shelley. (Probleme de măiestrie artistică şi traducere.)," *Revista de*

filologie romanicà și germanicà, VI (1962), 153-168.

84. Cooper, Douglas. *Great Private Collections.* Introduction by Kenneth Clark. New York: Macmillan, 1963.
Reproduces (p. 220) Delacroix's "The Death of Hassan," an episode from *The Giaour.*

85. Downs, Brian W. "Anglo-Norwegian Literary Relations 1867-1900," MLR, XLVII (Oct. 1952), 449-494.
Includes discussion of criticism and translations of Byron, Keats, and Shelley.

86. Ehrsam, Theodore G. *Major Byron: The Incredible Career of a Literary Forger.* See K-SJ, I (1952), 90, II (1953), 101.
Rev. by John Bakeless in PBSA, LV (1951), 272.

Eliot, George, *pseud.* See No. 389.

87. Elwin, Malcolm. *Lord Byron's Wife.* See K-SJ, XIII (1964), 128.
Rev. by * Knut Hagberg in *Svenska Dagbladet,* March 2, 1963; by Carl Woodring in VQR, XXXIX (Summer 1963), 506-509; by E[dward]. E. B[ostetter]. in PQ, XLII (Oct. 1963), 451-452; by F. T. Wood in ES, XLIV (Oct. 1963), 385-386; by Ernest J. Lovell, Jr., in K-SJ, XIII (1964), 105-107.

88. Enkvist, Nils Erik. *British and American Literary Letters in Scandinavian Public Collections.* Acta Academiae Aboensis, Humaniora, Vol. XXVII, No. 3. Åbo: Åbo Akademi, 1964.
Prints letters of Byron, Hobhouse, Hunt, and Mary Shelley; lists letters of Charles Cowden Clarke, Charles Wentworth Dilke, Hobhouse, Tom Moore (to John Hunt), and Horace Smith.

Erlich, Victor. See No. 237.

89. Eversole, Richard L. "What Did Jeffrey Mean by 'Elaborate'?: A Note on Two Byron Letters," N&Q, CCIX (Jan. 1964), 26.†
Byron referred to a different passage of Jeffrey's from that suggested by Prothero.

90. Frye, Northrop. *Fables of Identity: Studies in Poetic Mythology.* New York: Harcourt, Brace, 1963.
Includes (pp. 168-189) "Lord Byron," reprinted from *Major British Writers* (1959).
Rev. by Ben W. Fuson in *Library Journal,* LXXXIX (Feb. 1, 1964), 631-632.

91. Ghosh, R. N. "Malthus on Emigration and Colonization: Letters to Wilmot-Horton," *Economica,* N.S., XXX (Feb. 1963), 45-62.
Letters to Sir Robert John Wilmot-Horton, Byron's cousin.

92. * Glas, Norbert. *Byrons Schicksalsrätsel.* Stuttgart: Freies Geistesleben, 1962.

93. Goff, Frederick R. "Rare Books," *Library of Congress Quarterly Journal of Current Acquisitions,* XX (June 1963), 193-199.
Records the acquisition of eight first editions of the works of Byron.

94. * Golovashenko, Iu. "Na stsene-Bairon" ["Byron on the Stage"], *Teatr,* No. 8 (1963), pp. 16-18.
On the production of the poem *Don Juan* at the Leningrad Comic Theatre.

95. Gotlieb, Howard B. *William Beckford of Fonthill: Writer, Traveller, Collector, Caliph, 1760-1844: A Brief Narrative and Catalogue of an Exhibition to Mark the Two Hundredth Anniversary of Beckford's Birth.* New Haven: Yale Univ. Library, 1960.
Exhibited were Beckford's copies, with his annotations, of *Frankenstein,* Hobhouse's *A Journey through Albania . . .,* Galt's *The Life of Lord Byron,* Moore's *Letters and Journals of Lord Byron,* and Hogg's *Memoirs of Prince Alexey Haimatoff.*

96. Green, David Bonnell. "Hanson's Partner, John Birch," K-SJ, XIII (1964), 5-6.
Supplies information about Birch and includes a letter to him from Mrs. Byron.

97. Gregory, L. F. "English Romantics at a Swiss Castle," *Country Life,* CXXXV (Feb. 6, 1964), 262-263.
Byron and Shelley at Chillon.

98. Grylls, Rosalie Glynn. *Trelawny.* See K-SJ, I (1952), 90.
Rev. by A. L. Rowse in T&T, XXXI (July 8, 1950), 678.

99. * Hachiya, Akio. "Byron's *Cain* and the Bible," *Foreign Literary Studies of Osaka Women's College,* No. 15 (Feb. 1963), pp. 1-10.

100. Heath-Stubbs, John. *The Darkling Plain: A Study of the Later Fortunes of Romanticism in English Poetry from George Darley to W. B. Yeats.* London: Eyre & Spottiswoode, 1950.
Includes frequent references to Byron, Keats, and Shelley.

Rev. by Ralph Abercrombie in T&T, XXXI (Nov. 4, 1950), 1110-1111.

101. Horn, András. *Byron's "Don Juan" and the Eighteenth-Century English Novel.* See K-SJ, XII (1963), 128.

Rev. by D[avid]. V. E[rdman]. in PQ, XLII (Oct. 1963), 452; by A. H. Elliott in RES, N.S., XV (Feb. 1964), 118-119.

102. Hough, Graham, *Reflections on a Literary Revolution.* See K-SJ, X (1961), 78, XII (1963), 128.

Rev. by Monroe C. Beardsley in JAAC, XXI (Summer 1963), 497-498.

103. Houghton, Walter E. *The Poetry of Clough: An Essay in Revaluation.* New Haven: Yale Univ., 1963.

Discusses Clough's interest in Byron; also touches upon Keats and Shelley.

104. Howarth, Herbert. *Notes on Some Figures behind T. S. Eliot.* Boston: Houghton Mifflin, 1964.

Discusses Byron's influence on Eliot.

105. Hudson, Frederick. "A Catalogue of the Works of Charles Villiers Stanford (1852-1924)," *Music Review,* XXV (Feb. 1964), 44-57.

Lists songs written to poems by Byron, Keats, and Shelley.

Hübner, Walter. See No. 24.

106. Huyghe, René, *et al. Delacroix.* Paris: Hachette; * New York: Abrams; * London: Thames and Hudson (1963).

Includes frequent discussion of Byron and reproductions of paintings based on his works.

107. "In the Sale Room," TLS, Apr. 9, 1964, p. 300.

On Feb. 10, 1964, at Sotheby's, letters of Lady Byron to Mrs. Henry Siddons made £300, and "a fine series of letters from Robert Southey to Anna Eliza Bray," which made £300, "included an uncompromising description of the origins of *Liber Amoris.*"

108. James, Louis. *Fiction for the Working Man 1830-1850: A Study of the Literature Produced for the Working Classes in Early Victorian Urban England.* London: Oxford Univ., 1963.

Touches upon the influence and reprintings—often in fictionalized form—of Byron and Shelley.

109. Johnson, Lee. "The Delacroix Centenary in France—I," *Burlington Magazine,* CV (July 1963), 297-305.

Reproduces a "Study for the Executioner in 'Marino Faliero.' "

110. Johnson, Lee. "The Delacroix Centenary in France—II," *Burlington Magazine,* CVI (June 1964), 259-267.

Reproduces Delacroix's "The Giaour Contemplating the Dead Hassan."

111. * Joseph, M[ichael]. K[ennedy]. *Byron the Poet.* London: Gollancz, 1964.

Rev. by Graham Hough in Li, LXXI (Apr. 16, 1964), 642; by Raymond Mortimer in *Sunday Times,* Apr. 19, 1964, p. 34; by Geoffrey Grigson in *Country Life,* CXXXV (Apr. 30, 1964), 1080-1081; by Stephen Haskell in Spec, May 8, 1964, p. 639; by Francis Hope in NS, LXVII (May 8, 1964), 731-732; by E. D. O'Brien in ILN, CCXLIV (May 16, 1964), 796; in TLS, May 28, 1964, p. 448.

Keiser, Robert. See No. 28.

Kiell, Norman, ed. See No. 6.

112. King-Hele, Desmond. *Erasmus Darwin.* London: Macmillan; New York: St Martin's (1963).

Includes discussion of Darwin's influence on Byron, Keats, and Shelley. Godwin and Peacock are touched upon.

Rev. in TLS, Dec. 19, 1963, p. 1046.

113. * Klimenko, E. I. "Inoskazatel'nyi smysl 'Moria' v poezii Bairona" ["Allegorical Meanings of 'Sea' in Byron's Poetry"], *Vestnik Leningrad University,* No. 8 (1963), pp. 164-167. (Seriia literatury, istorii, iazyka, vyp. 2.)

114. Knight, G. Wilson. *Lord Byron's Marriage: The Evidence of Asterisks.* See K-SJ, VII (1958), 117, VIII (1959), 60, IX (1960), 56, XII (1963), 129.

Rev. in *University of Leeds Review,* V (June 1957), 322-323.

115. Kuhn, Christoph. " 'Mein Geist ist ein Fragment': Aus Lord Byrons Briefen und Tagebüchern," *Du, Kulturelle Monatsschift* (Zürich), XXIII (June 1963), 56-58.

116. Lentricchia, Frank, Jr. "Byron in Boston," *Emerson Society Quarterly,* No. 37, Part 2 (1964), pp. 73-74.

Describes a controversy arising from a review of Henley's edition of Byron's letters in the Boston *Literary World,* Apr. 3, 1897.

117. Leslie, Doris. *This for Caroline.* London: Heinemann, 1964.

"The true life story of one of the most dynamic personalities of the early nineteenth century: Lady Caroline Lamb."

118. Losh, James. *The Diaries and Correspondence of James Losh*. Ed. Edward Hughes. Vol. I: Diary, 1811-1823. Vol. II: Diary 1824-1833; Letters to Charles, 2nd Earl Grey and Henry Brougham. Durham: Andrews & Co.; London: Quaritch (1962, 1963). "Publications of the Surtees Society, Vols. CLXXI and CLXXIV."
Includes material on Byron.
Rev. in TLS, Feb. 13, 1964, p. 125.

119. Lovell, Ernest J., Jr. *Byron, the Record of a Quest: Studies in a Poet's Concept and Treatment of Nature*. See K-SJ, I (1952), 90, II (1953), 101.
Rev. by D[avid]. V. E[rdman]. in PQ, XXX (Apr. 1951), 109-110; by J. M. S. Tompkins in MLR, XLVI (Apr. 1951), 265-266.

120. Lovell, Ernest J., Jr. *Captain Medwin: Friend of Byron and Shelley*. * London: Macdonald, 1963. See K-SJ, XIII (1964), 131.
Rev. in TLS, Aug. 9, 1963, p. 610; by Peter Quennell in *Observer*, Aug. 18, 1963, p. 20; by John D. Jump in *Manchester Guardian Weekly*, LXXXIX (Sept. 5, 1963), 10; in *Books and Bookmen*, IX (Oct. 1963), ii; by K[enneth]. N[eill]. C[ameron]. in PQ, XLII (Oct. 1963), 463; by Martin Dodsworth in NS, LXVI (Oct. 18, 1963), 534; by William H. Marshall in K-SJ, XIII (1964), 113-116; in *Quarterly Review*, Jan. 1964, p. 114. See also No. 32.

121. Luke, Hugh J., Jr. "Drams for the Vulgar: A Study of Some Radical Publishers and Publications of Early Nineteenth-Century London" [Doctoral dissertation, Texas, 1963], DA, XXIV (Jan. 1964), 2893.
Discusses piratical editions of Byron and Shelley.

122. Marshall, William H. *The Structure of Byron's Major Poems*. See K-SJ, XIII (1964), 131.
Rev. by Carl Woodring in VQR, XXXIX (Summer 1963), 506-509; by E[dward]. E. B[ostetter]. in PQ, XLII (Oct. 1963), 453; by Leslie A. Marchand in K-SJ, XIII (1964), 104-105; by James V. Baker in *Criticism*, VI (Spring 1964), 187-189; by T. G. Steffan in JEGP, LXIII (Apr. 1964), 376-378; by Paul West in MLR, LIX (Apr. 1964), 280-281. See also No. 32.

123. Martin, L. C. *Byron's Lyrics*. Byron Foundation Lecture 1948. [Nottingham: Nottingham Univ., 1948.]
Rev. by W. D. Thomas in RES, N.S., II (July 1951), 298-299.

124. Martini, Stelio. "San Giorgio e Inghilterra sulle Rive del Tevere," *Capitolium*, XXXVIII (Apr. 1963), 192-197.
Includes discussion of Byron, Keats, and Shelley.

125. Merritt, James Douglas. "The Novels of Benjamin Disraeli: A Study" [Doctoral dissertation, Wisconsin, 1964], DA, XXIV (May 1964), 4702.
Discusses Byron's influence on Disraeli.

126. Mill, John Stuart. *The Earlier Letters of John Stuart Mill, 1812-1848*. Ed. Francis E. Mineka. Vols. I and II. (Vols. XII and XIII of *Collected Works of John Stuart Mill*.) Toronto: Toronto Univ.; London: Routledge (1963).
Has material on Byron, Hunt, Peacock, and Shelley.

127. * Miyamoto, Masato. "Methods of Studies in Byron," *Bulletin of the English Society* (Osaka Gakugei College), No. 9 (March 1964), pp. 104-113. [In Japanese.]

128. Moore, Doris Langley. *The Late Lord Byron*. See K-SJ, XII (1963), 130-131, XIII (1964), 131.
Rev. by *V. Zakharov in *Voprosy literatury*, No. 4 (1963), pp. 222-225.

129. Morokoff, Gene Emerson. "A Critical Study of Byron's *Manfred*" [Doctoral dissertation, Illinois, 1963], DA, XXIV (Apr. 1964), 4193-4194.

130. Mortenson, Robert. "Another Continuation of *Don Juan*," SIR, II (Summer 1963), 244-247.†
Described and excerpted, doubtless as a literary hoax, in the Jan. 1822 issue of the *Newcastle Magazine*.

131. * Mukoyama, Yasuko. "A Study of Lord Byron," *Bulletin of Aoyama Women's Junior College* (Tokyo), No. 16 (1963).

132. * Negreeva, G. "Pevets svobody" ["Singer of Freedom"], *Lit. Azerbaidzhan*, No. 1 (1963), pp. 154-155.

133. "Newstead Abbey in the 1720s," *Country Life*, CX (July 27, 1951), 283.
Reproduces two views of Newstead

Abbey painted by Pieter Tillemans about 1725.

134. "Notes on Sales," TLS, March 12, 1964, p. 224.

At Sotheby's, Dec. 16-17, 1963, "two letters from Mary Wollstonecraft Godwin concerning her novel *The Wrongs of Women, or Maria,* [made] £120. A collection of letters and documents, almost all unpublished, from the papers of Edward John Trelawny, mainly covering the last days of Shelley and Byron were sold . . . for £2,100. They included letters from Edward E. Williams, Captain Daniel Roberts (concerning the salvaging of Shelley's boat the Don Juan), Leigh Hunt and Mary Shelley."

135. Orel, Harold. "Lord Byron's Debt to the Enlightenment," *Studies in Voltaire and the Eighteenth Century,* XXIV-XXVII (1963), 1275-1290.

Traces the influence of Pope, Rousseau, Voltaire, and Gibbon on Byron.

136. Origo, Iris. *The Last Attachment.* See K-SJ, I (1952), 90-91, XII (1963), 131, XIII (1964), 132.

Rev. by Paul Graham Trueblood in K-SJ, I (1952), 115-116.

137. Owen, W. J. B. "A Byronic Shipwreck in the Pacific," N&Q, CCVIII (July 1963), 265-267.†

Finds echoes of Canto II of *Don Juan* in Charles Reade's novel *Foul Play.*

138. Parks, Edd Winfield. *Ante-Bellum Southern Literary Critics.* Athens: Georgia Univ., 1962.

Byron, Keats, Shelley, Godwin, and others are discussed.

139. Parsons, C. R. "Eugène Delacroix and Literary Inspiration," *University of Toronto Quarterly,* XXXIII (Jan. 1964), 164-177.

Discusses Delacroix's interest in Byron.

140. Partridge, A. C. "Byron and Italy," *English Studies in Africa,* VII (March 1964), 1-12.

Reviews Byron's associations with Italy.

141. Partridge, Monica. "Slavonic Themes in English Poetry of the 19th Century," *Slavonic and East European Review,* XLI (June 1963), 420-441.

Discusses the relevant work of Byron, Hunt, and Keats.

142. Peck, Louis F. *A Life of Matthew G. Lewis.* See K-SJ, XII (1963), 132, XIII (1964), 132.

Rev. by Lloyd W. Griffin in *Library Journal,* LXXXVI (Nov. 1, 1961), 3785.

143. Peckham, Morse. *Beyond the Tragic Vision.* See K-SJ, XII (1963), 132, XIII (1964), 132.

Rev. by M[artin]. K. N[urmi]. in PQ, XLII (Oct. 1963), 437-438. See also No. 32.

144. Perkins, David. *Wordsworth and the Poetry of Sincerity.* Cambridge, Mass.: Harvard Univ., 1964.

Includes discussion of Byron, Keats, Shelley, and others.

145. Praz, Mario. *Macchiavelli in Inghilterra ed altre saggi sui rapporti letterari anglo-italiani.* Second Edition. Florence: Sansoni, 1962.

Has references to Byron, Hazlitt, Hunt, Keats, and Shelley.

146. Rawson, C. J. " 'Beppo' and 'Absalom and Achitophel'; A Parallel," N&Q, CCIX (Jan. 1964), 25.†

147. "Recent Acquisitions," *Library Notes: A Bulletin Issued for the Friends of the Duke University Library,* No. 36 (Dec. 1962), pp. 20-26.

Include a first edition of *Marino Faliero.*

148. "Revival of *Manfred,*" K-SJ, XIII (1964), 4.

Describes the production of Schumann's version in Columbus, Ohio. See K-SJ, XIII (1964), 127, No. 127.

Roberts, Cecil. See No. 443.

Rodway, Allan. See No. 38.

149. Rutherford, Andrew. *Byron: A Critical Study.* See K-SJ, XI (1962), 119, XII (1963), 132, XIII (1964), 133.

Rev. by Kathleen Valmai Richardson in *Poetry Review,* LII (Oct.-Dec. 1961), 234-235; by H. S. Whittier in *Dalhousie Review,* XLII (Summer 1962), 254-256.

150. Ryals, Clyde de L. *Theme and Symbol in Tennyson's Poems to 1850.* Philadelphia: Pennsylvania Univ., 1964.

Discusses the influence on Tennyson of Byron, Keats, and Shelley.

151. Sanders, Charles Richard. "The Byron Closed in *Sartor Resartus,*" SIR, III (Winter 1964), 77-108.

Traces the attitude of Carlyle and of Jane Welsh Carlyle to Byron.

152. Shahane, V. A. "Rabindranath Tagore:

A Study in Romanticism," SIR, III (Autumn 1963), 53-64.†

Includes discussion of the influence of Keats, Shelley, and Byron on Tagore.

153. Smith, S[tephen]. R[eginald]. B[irt]. *Balzac et l'Angleterre: Essai sur l'influence de l'Angleterre sur l'œuvre et la pensée de Balzac.* London: Williams, Lea, 1953.

Has extensive discussion of Byron's influence; touches upon Shelley and Mary Shelley.

154. Sofer, Johann. "Claudels Stellung zu England," *Neueren Sprachen,* Feb. 1962, pp. 65-78.†

Discusses Claudel's attitude toward Byron, Keats, and Shelley.

155. * Sokolets, F. B. "Tema natsional'no-osvoboditelnoi bor'by v zakliuchitel'-noi pesne *Chail'd-Gorol'da* Dzh. G. Bairona" ["The Theme of the Fight for National Liberation in Byron's *Childe Harold's Pilgrimage*"], *Vistnyk Kyivs'k University,* No. 5 (1962), pp. 59-71. (Seriia Filolohii ta zhurnalistyky, vyp. 2.) [In Ukrainian.]

156. * Šorm, Gustav. "Gorge Gordon Byron," *Stadión* (Prague), XI, No. 6 (1963), p. 5.

Mainly on Byron's sportsmanship.

157. Souffrin, Eileen. "Le Byronisme de Théodore de Banville," RLC, XXXVII (Oct.-Dec. 1963), 497-512.

Finds Byron's influence on Banville more lasting and pervasive than has been supposed.

158. Spears, Monroe K. *The Poetry of W. H. Auden: The Disenchanted Island.* New York: Oxford Univ., 1963.

Discusses Byron's influence on Auden.

159. Staël-Holstein, Madame de. *Madame de Staël et le duc de Wellington, correspondance inédite, 1815-1817.* Ed. Victor de Pange. Paris: Gallimard, 1962.

Byron is referred to in the correspondence.

160. Stavrou, C. N. "Religion in Byron's *Don Juan,*" SEL, III (Autumn 1963), 567-594.†

Emphasizes Byron's scepticism, "the considered conviction that traditional religious beliefs are disintegrating and that humanity's cause can best be served by expediting rather than attempting to deter this disintegration."

Stokoe, Frank W. See No. 39.

161. Straumann, Heinrich. *Byron and Switzerland.* Byron Foundation Lecture 1948-49. [Nottingham: Nottingham Univ., 1949.]

Rev. by W. D. Thomas in RES, N.S., II (July 1951), 298-299.

162. Swanson, Roy Arthur. "Nostrigods Gaggin Bananafishygods: Thirteen Innings of Criticism," *Minnesota Review,* III (Summer 1963), 499-514.

An omnibus review that includes discussion of Peter L. Thorslev, Jr.'s *The Byronic Hero.* See K-SJ, XII (1963), 133, XIII (1964), 133. See also Nos. 32 and 164.

163. Swiggart, Peter. "Faulkner's *The Sound and the Fury,*" Exp, XXII (Dec. 1963), Item 31.†

Byron's "wish" in Faulkner's novel alludes to *Don Juan,* VI, xxvii.

164. Thorslev, Peter L., Jr. *The Byronic Hero: Types and Prototypes.* See K-SJ, XII (1963), 133, XIII (1964), 133.

Rev. by E[dward]. E. B[ostetter]. in PQ, XLII (Oct. 1963), 153-151; by Paul West in MLR, LVIII (Oct. 1963), 567-568; by C. T. P. in ABC, XIV (Nov. 1963), 3-4; by Barbara Hardy in *British Journal of Aesthetics,* IV (Jan. 1964), 83-84; by J. D. Jump in RES, N.S., XV (Feb. 1964), 100-101. See also Nos. 32 and 162.

165. Thorslev, Peter L., Jr. "The Romantic Mind Is Its Own Place," CL, XV (Summer 1963), 250-268.

Discusses the "Romantic Satanism" of Byron and Shelley.

166. Tiulina, N. I. "Bairon v Russkoi Kritike i Literaturovedenii," *Trudy, Gosudarstvennai ordena Lenina Biblioteka SSSR* (Moscow), V (1961), 269-320.

A bibliography of Russian-language works of criticism and literary history concerning Byron which lists 973 items published between 1815 and 1960. See No. 1.

Uesugi, Fumiyo. See No. 457.

167. VanDerBeets, Richard. "A Note on Dramatic Necessity and the Incest Motif in *Manfred,*" N&Q, CCIX (Jan. 1964), 26-28.†

The motif "satisfies the particular dramatic needs arising from both the Gothic tradition and the Faust legend as Byron uses them."

168. Vickery, W. N. "Parallelizm v Litera-

turnom Razvitii Bairona i Pushkina," *American Contributions to the Fifth International Congress of Slavists, Sofia, September 1963*, II, 371-401. The Hague: Mouton, 1963. [In Russian.]

169. Vincent, E. R. P. *Byron, Hobhouse and Foscolo.* See K-SJ, I (1952), 91.

Rev. by John Purves in RES, N.S., II (Oct. 1951), 391-394; by Paul Graham Trueblood in MLQ, XII (Dec. 1951), 502-503.

170. Wain, John. *Essays on Literature and Ideas.* London: Macmillan, 1963.

Includes (pp. 85-102) "Byron: The Search for Identity." See K-SJ, IX (1960), 59.

Rev. by Richard Ellmann in *Encounter*, XXI (Dec. 1963), 88-89.

171. * Wallen, Gunnar. "Byrons simmarfärd vid Hellesponten," *Upsala Nya Tidning*, June 1, 1963.

172. Wellek, René. *Essays on Czech Literature.* Introduction by Peter Demetz. The Hague: Mouton, 1964.

Includes (pp. 148-178) "Mácha and English Literature," which deals with the influence of Byron.

Rev. in TLS, May 21, 1964, p. 436.

*173. West, Paul, ed. *Byron: A Collection of Critical Essays.* Englewood Cliffs: Prentice-Hall, 1963. "Twentieth Century Views."

Reprints essays by G. Wilson Knight. Bernard Blackstone, Mario Praz, Paul West, Guy Steffan, F. R. Leavis, W. W. Robson, Helen Gardner, George M. Ridenour, Edmund Wilson, Gilbert Highet, Bertrand Russell, and John Wain. See K-SJ, III (1954), 117, Nos. 108 and 110; V (1956), 122, No. 83; VII (1958), 114, 126, Nos. 75 and 323; VIII (1959), 63, No. 216; IX (1960), 55, 59, Nos. 143 and 221; X (1961), 80, No. 168; XI (1962), 114, 121, Nos. 117 and 255.

174. West, Paul. *Byron and the Spoiler's Art.* See K-SJ, XI (1962), 121, XII (1963), 133.

Rev. by H. S. Whittier in *Dalhousie Review*, XLII (Summer 1962), 254-256.

White, R. J. See No. 40.

175. Wind, Edgar. *Art and Anarchy: The Reith Lectures 1960.* Revised and Enlarged. London: Faber, 1963.

Comments on Byron and Keats.

176. Wright, Nathalia. *Horatio Greenough: The First American Sculptor.* Philadelphia: Pennsylvania Univ., 1964.

Discusses Greenough's statue of the dead Medora from "The Corsair"; a photograph of it is included. Greenough also executed a bust of Byron.

177. Zayed, Georges. *La Formation littéraire de Verlaine (avec des documents inédits).* Geneva: Droz; Paris: Minard (1962).

Mentions the influence of Byron and Shelley.

III. HUNT

Works: Selected, Single

Grigson, Geoffrey, ed. See No. 45.

178. Kiell, Norman. *The Universal Experience of Adolescence.* New York: International Universities Press, 1964.

Includes selections from Haydon, Hazlitt, and Hunt.

179. *Leigh Hunt's Dramatic Criticism.* Ed. Lawrence Huston Houtchens and Carolyn Washburn Houtchens. See K-SJ, I (1952), 92, III (1954), 117, XIII (1964), 134.

Rev. by E[lisabeth]. S[chneider]. in PQ, XXX (Apr. 1951), 115.

180. *Leigh Hunt's Political and Occasional Essays.* Ed. Lawrence Huston Houtchens and Carolyn Washburn Houtchens. See K-SJ, XIII (1964), 134.

Rev. in TLS, Aug. 16, 1963, p. 618; by David V. Erdman in CE, XXV (Oct. 1963), 59; by S[tephen]. F. F[ogle]. in PQ, XLII (Oct. 1963), 460-461; by Stephen F. Fogle in K-SJ, XIII (1964), 108-110; by Harry W. Rudman in BA, XXXVIII (Spring 1964), 193-194; by Leslie A. Marchand in *English Language Notes*, I (March 1964), 233-236; by Geoffrey Carnall in JEGP, LXIII (Apr. 1964), 373-376; by Derek Roper in N&Q, CCIX (May 1964), 198-199; by F. T. Wood in ES, XLV (June 1964), 264.

181. "Sonnet, To Hampstead," K-SJ, XIII (1964), 76.

Books and Articles Relating to Hunt

182. Ball, Patricia M. "Sincerity: The Rise and Fall of a Critical Term," MLR, LIX (Jan. 1964), 1-11.

Discusses Hunt's use of the term.

Bentman, Raymond. See No. 13.

183. Blunden, Edmund. "Critics Who Have Influenced Taste—IX. Leigh Hunt,"

The Times, London, May 30, 1963, p. 16.
"At once an independent and an intimate critic."

Enkvist, Nils Erik. See No. 88.

184. Fisher, Walt. "Leigh Hunt as Friend and Critic of Keats: 1816-1859," *Lock Haven Bulletin,* Ser. 1, No. 5 (1963), pp. 27-42.†
Traces Hunt's devotion to Keats both as man and poet.

Green, David Bonnell. See No. 254.

185. Gross, John, and Gabriel Pearson, eds. *Dickens and the Twentieth Century.* Toronto: Toronto Univ.; * London: Routledge (1962).
Includes "Sketches by Boz" (pp. 19-34), an essay by Robert Browning which discusses Hunt's influence on Dickens.

186. Howell, A. C. "Milton's Mortal Remains and Their Literary Echoes," *Ball State Teachers College Forum,* IV (Autumn 1963), 17-30.
Discusses Hunt's lock of Milton's hair and his and Keats's poems on it.

Hübner, Walter. See No. 24.

Keiser, Robert. See No. 28.

187. Killham, John. *Tennyson and the Princess: Reflections of an Age.* London: Athlone, 1958.
Touches upon Hunt and Mary Wollstonecraft.

Mill, John Stuart. See No. 126.

"Notes on Sales." See Nos. 134 and 302.

Partridge, Monica. See No. 141.

Praz, Mario. See No. 145.

188. Sanders, Charles Richard. "The Correspondence and Friendship of Thomas Carlyle and Leigh Hunt: The Later Years," *Bulletin of the John Rylands Library,* XLVI (Sept. 1963), 179-216.
Continues and concludes the account of their relationship. See K-SJ, XIII (1964), 135.

189. Smith, Michael A. "The Charles Swain Collection," *Manchester Review,* IX (Autumn 1962), 323-332.
Prints a portion of a letter from Hunt to Samuel Carter Hall.

White, R. J. See No. 40.

IV. KEATS

Works: Selected, Single, Translated

Brown, Ivor, ed. See No. 41.

Cole, William, ed. See No. 43.

Grigson, Geoffrey, ed. See No. 45.

190. *The Letters of John Keats.* Ed. Maurice Buxton Forman. Fourth Edition. See K-SJ, II (1953), 102.
Rev. by J[oanna]. R[ichardson]. in Spec, July 11, 1952, p. 80.

Marshall, William H., ed. See No. 30.

191. * " 'On Peace,' 'After Dark Vapours,' 'To . . .,' " [translated by Noboru Matsuura], *Shikai* (Bulletin of the Japan Poets' Club, Tokyo), No. 70 (March 1963), pp. 20-21. [In Japanese.]

192. "On Sitting Down to Read King Lear Once Again," K-SJ, XIII (1964), 42.

193. * *Poems.* Comp. David Herbert. London: Vista, 1963.

194. *Selected Letters.* Ed. Lionel Trilling. See K-SJ, I (1952), 93, III (1954), 118, No. 135, IV (1955), 118, V (1956), 127, VI (1957), 140.
Rev. by Marvin B. Perry, Jr., in K-SJ, I (1952), 106-107.

195. *Selected Poems and Letters.* Ed. Roger Sharrock. London: Oxford Univ., 1964. "New Oxford English Series."

196. "Sonnet," K-SJ, XIII (1964), 96.
"How many bards gild the lapses of time!"

197. * " 'To My Brother George,' 'On Sitting Down to Read King Lear Once Again,' 'On a Picture of Leander,' " [translated by Noboru Matsuura], *Shikai* (Bulletin of the Japan Poets' Club, Tokyo), No. 72 (Nov. 1963), pp. 13-14. [In Japanese.]

Untermeyer, Louis, ed. See No. 55.

198. * *Versei.* [Translated by] Mihály Babits, István Bernáth, *et al.* Budapest: Euröpa, 1962.

199. * " 'Why Did I Laugh Tonight?' 'Oh! How I Love . . .!' 'To Sleep,' " *Shikai* (Bulletin of the Japan Poets' Club, Tokyo), No. 73 (March 1964), pp. 13-14. [In Japanese.]

Books and Articles Relating to Keats and His Circle

200. Adams, Richard P. "The Apprenticeship of William Faulkner," *Tulane Studies in English,* XII (1962), 113-156.
Discusses Faulkner's reading and use of Keats. Faulkner also read Shelley.

201. * Ahlström, Stellan. "Keatsminnen i Rom," *Sydsvenska Dagbladet Snällposten,* Aug. 3, 1963.

202. Albrecht, William P. *William Hazlitt and the Malthusian Controversy.* University of New Mexico Publications in

Language and Literature No. 4. Albuquerque: New Mexico Univ., 1950.

Rev. in TLS, Aug. 18, 1950, p. 522; by E[lisabeth]. S[chneider]. in PQ, XXX (Apr. 1951), 114.

203. Altick, Richard D. *The Cowden Clarkes.* See K-SJ, I (1952), 93.

Rev. by R. W. King in RES, N.S., I (Oct. 1950), 372-373.

204. * Aoyama, Fujio. "On *The Eve of St. Agnes*," *Thought Currents in English Literature* (Aoyama Gakuin Univ., Tokyo), XXXVI (Dec. 1963), 83-102.

205. Ashford, E. Bright. *Lisson Green: A Domesday Village in St. Marylebone.* St. Marylebone Society Publication No. 3 (1960).

Includes some account of Haydon's residence there.

206. Austin, Allen: "Keats's Grecian Urn and the Truth of Eternity," CE, XXV (March 1964), 434-436.

The urn "gives promise that earthly beauty is the truth of eternity and that the truth of eternity is beauty. This is all that man knows of eternity and all that he needs to know."

207. Baker, Herschel. *William Hazlitt.* See K-SJ, XII (1963), 136, XIII (1964), 136-137.

Rev. by John Kinnaird in PR, XXX (Summer 1963), 302-306; by Royal A. Gettmann in JEGP, LXII (July 1963), 692-695; by F. T. Wood in ES, XLIV (Aug. 1963), 314; by S[tephen]. F. F[ogle]. in PQ, XLII (Oct. 1963), 459-460; by L[ouis]. Bonnerot in EA, XVII (Apr.-June 1964), 194-195; by Geoffrey Carnall in RES, N.S., XV (May 1964), 210-212. See also No. 32.

208. Bate, Walter Jackson. *John Keats.* Cambridge, Mass.: Harvard Univ., 1963.

Rev. by Stephen Spender in NYHT, Sept. 22, 1963, p. 3; by *C. T. Houpt in *Christian Science Monitor,* Oct. 17, 1963, p. 11; by A. Alvarez in *New York Review of Books,* I (Oct. 31, 1963), 20-21; by John R. Willingham in *Library Journal,* LXXXVIII (Nov. 1, 1963), 4205; by Charles Alva Hoyt in SatR, XLVI (Nov. 2, 1963), 22; in *New Yorker,* XXXIX (Dec. 7, 1963), 245; by Howard Moss in NYT, Dec. 29, 1963, p. 5; by Denis Donoghue in *Hudson Review,* XVI (Winter 1963-64), 617-623; by Marvin B. Perry, Jr., in VQR, XL (Winter 1964), 150-154; by David Perkins in K-SJ, XIII (1964), 97-100; by Frederick A. Pottle in *Yale Review,* LIII (Winter 1964), 276-279; by John G. Rideout in *American Oxonian,* LI (Jan. 1964), 39-41; by Robert Gittings in Li, LXXI (Jan. 30, 1964), 203-204; by M. R. Ridley in Spec, Feb. 7, 1964, p. 185; by John Press in *Sunday Times,* Feb. 9, 1964, p. 37; by Christopher Ricks in NS, LXVII (Feb. 21, 1964), 298; by John Gross in *Encounter,* XXII (March 1964), 81-83; in TLS, March 5, 1964, p. 196; by F. A. Reid in *Manchester Guardian Weekly,* XC (March 12, 1964), 11; by Edward Weeks in *Atlantic Monthly,* CCXIII (Apr. 1964), 139-140; by Naomi Lewis in *Observer,* Apr. 19, 1964, p. 28; by Dudley Fitts in *American Scholar,* XXXIII (Summer 1964), 462, 464; by Ernest J. Lovell, Jr., in *English Language Notes,* I (June 1964), 303-306.

209. Bayley, John. "Keats and Reality," *Proceedings of the British Academy,* XLVIII (1962), 91-125.

The most decisive ingredient in Keats's poetry is vulgarity, "but vulgarity in the heroic sense in which Antony and Cleopatra are vulgar."

210. Benjamin, Adrian. "'Ode to a Nightingale,'" TLS, Feb. 6, 1964, p. 112.

Alleges Shakespearean echoes in "Ode on a Grecian Urn." See Nos. 213, 224, 270, 285, 312, 339, and 341.

Bentman, Raymond. See No. 13.

211. Benziger, James. *Images of Eternity.* See K-SJ, XIII (1964), 137.

Rev. by K[arl]. K[roeber]. in PQ, XLII (Oct. 1963), 443-444; by Max F. Schulz in JEGP, LXII (Oct. 1963), 810-813. See also No. 32.

212. Bernard, F. V. "Some Hazlitt Quotations and Their Sources," N&Q, CCIX (Jan. 1964), 24-25.†

In Burke, Shakespeare, Cowper, Pope, and Boswell.

213. Bevan, Jack. "'Ode to a Nightingale,'" TLS, Feb. 13, 1964, p. 132.

Emphasizes Keats's feeling. See Nos. 210, 224, 270, 285, 312, 339, and 341.

214. Bhalla, M. M. "Keats and the Concept of Space," *Indian Journal of English Studies,* III (1962), 78-88.

For Keats, space "is an obstacle in the apprehension of the unity of existences and, consequently, in the discovery of vital, as opposed to dead, knowledge about life."

215. Blunden, Edmund. "Barry Cornwall and Keats," KSMB, XIV (1963), 4-7.
Suggests Keats's influence on Procter.

216. Blunden, Edmund. *A Selection of His Poetry and Prose.* Comp. Kenneth Hopkins. New York: Horizon, 1961.
Includes (pp. 175-179) "The Cowden Clarkes."

Bostetter, Edward E. See No. 17.

217. Brander, Laurence. *Thomas Hood.* London: Longmans, for the British Council, 1963. "Writers and Their Work No. 159."
Rev. by J. M. Cohen in Spec, Sept. 20, 1963, p. 360; in TLS, Oct. 4, 1963, p. 782; by K. H. in *Books and Bookmen,* IX (Nov. 1963), x.

Brown, Calvin S. See No. 68.

218. Camden, Carroll, ed. *Literary Views: Critical and Historical Essays.* Chicago: Chicago Univ., 1964.
Reprints Lionel Trilling's "The Fate of Pleasure: Wordsworth to Dostoevsky," pp. 93-114. See Nos. 21 and 351.

219. Chalke, H. D. "The Impact of Tuberculosis on History, Literature and Art," *Medical History,* VI (Oct. 1962), 301-318.
Keats, Hood, Shelley and others are touched upon.

220. Chayes, Irene H. "Little Girls Lost: Problems of a Romantic Archetype," BNYPL, LXVII (Nov. 1963), 579-593.†
Discusses Madeline and "The Eve of St. Agnes."

221. Chayes, Irene H. "Rhetoric as Drama: An Approach to the Romantic Ode," PMLA, LXXIX (March 1964), 67-79.
Traces the rhetorical-dramatic structure, in terms of Aristotle's *Rhetoric* and *Poetics,* in "Dejection," "Ode to the West Wind," and "Ode to a Nightingale."

222. Clare, John. *The Letters of John Clare.* Ed. J. W. Tibble and Anne Tibble. London: Routledge, 1951.
Includes letters to Taylor, Hessey, and De Wint, references to Keats and Reynolds.

223. Clare, John. *The Prose of John Clare.* Ed. J. W. Tibble and Anne Tibble. London: Routledge, 1951.
Contains material on Byron, De Wint, Hazlitt, Hessey, Elizabeth Kent, Keats, Reynolds, and Taylor.

224. Clayton, Thomas. "'Ode to a Nightingale,'" TLS, Apr. 16, 1964, p. 317.
The last two lines of "Ode on a Grecian Urn" are probably said by the speaker to the Urn. See Nos. 210, 213, 270, 285, 312, 339, and 341.

Cohen, Ralph. See No. 82.

225. Connolly, Cyril. *Previous Convictions.* London: Hamish Hamilton, 1963.
Reprints a review of *Liber Amoris.* See K-SJ, IX (1960), 65, No. 322.

226. Cummings, Frederick. "B. R. Haydon and His School," *Journal of the Warburg and Courtauld Institutes,* XXVI (1963), 367-380.
"Haydon's 'school' was the first private art school in the London area in the nineteenth century, and in a more direct way than has heretofore been supposed, it was responsible for the superb draughtsmanship of the later nineteenth century English painters, the Pre-Raphaelites in particular." With it "a new phase in art education in England began."

227. Cummings, Frederick. "Charles Bell and *The Anatomy of Expression,*" *Art Bulletin,* XLVI (June 1964), 191-203.
Discusses the work "which served as the basis" for the acquaintance of Bell and Haydon.

228. Cummings, Frederick. "Nature and the Antique in B. R. Haydon's 'Assassination of Dentatus,'" *Journal of the Warburg and Courtauld Institutes,* XXV (Jan.-June 1962), 147-157.
Discusses in connection with the painting Haydon's "methods, models, relationships with his master, Fuseli, and his later assessment of his own works in the *Autobiography.*"

229. D'Avanzo, Mario Louis. "Recurrent Metaphors for Poetry in John Keats's Works" [Doctoral dissertation, Brown, 1963], DA, XXIV (March 1964), 3745.

230. Day Lewis, C. *The Grand Manner.* Byron Foundation Lecture 1952. [Nottingham: Nottingham Univ., 1952.]
Includes discussion of Keats.

231. Devoto, Daniel. "Quelques Notes au Sujet du 'Pot de Basilic,'" RLC, XXXVII (July-Sept. 1963), 430-436.
Points out other treatments of the theme, especially in folklore. See K-SJ, XIII (1964), 141, No. 361.

232. *D'iakonova, N. "Esteticheskie vzgliady Kitsa" ["Keats's Esthetics"], *Voprosy literatury,* No. 8 (1963), pp. 91-103.

233. Donner, H. W. "Echoes of Beddoesian Rambles, Edgeworthstown to Zürich,"

Studia Neophilologica, XXXIII (1961), 219-264.

Prints a letter from Beddoes to Procter, Nov. 5, 1823, in which he discusses Keats and Shelley.

234. Douglass, Kathryn Floyd. "William Hazlitt: Romantic Theorist of the Imagination" [Doctoral dissertation, Illinois, 1963], DA, XXIV (Aug. 1963), 740-741.

Downs, Brian W. See No. 85.

235. Empson, William. "Argufying in Poetry," Li, LXX (Aug. 22, 1963), 277, 290.

Discusses briefly the "muscular imagery" in "To Autumn."

Enkvist, Nils Erik. See No. 88.

236. Enscoe, Gerald Eugene. "Eros and the Romantics: Sexual Love as a Theme in Coleridge, Shelley and Keats" [Doctoral dissertation, Washington, 1962], DA, XXIV (July 1963), 296-297.

237. Erlich, Victor. *The Double Image: Concepts of the Poet in Slavic Literatures.* Baltimore: Johns Hopkins Univ., 1964.

Compares Keats and Krasiński; touches on Byron. See K-SJ, XIII (1964), 129.

238. "An Error Corrected," K-SJ, XIII (1964), 3-4.

Keats's age at death has been corrected from 26 to 25 on the memorial tablet on the Keats House, Rome.

239. Fairclough, G. Thomas. "Hazlitt, Shadwell and a Figure of Speech," N&Q, CCIX (Jan. 1964), 24.†

A probable allusion in *Table-Talk* to Shadwell's *The Sullen Lovers.*

240. Faulkner, William. *William Faulkner: Early Prose and Poetry.* Ed. Carvel Collins. Boston: Little, Brown, 1962.

Includes discussion of Keats and Shelley.

Fisher, Walt. See No. 184.

241. Fitzgerald, F. Scott. *The Letters of F. Scott Fitzgerald.* Ed. Andrew Turnbull. New York: Scribner's, 1963.

Includes remarks on Keats and Shelley.

242. Fogle, Richard Harter. *The Imagery of Keats and Shelley.* See K-SJ, I (1952), 93, XIII (1964), 139.

Rev. by Cleanth Brooks in K-SJ, I (1952), 113-114.

243. *Fukuda, Tamio. "*Ode on a Grecian Urn*—On the Meaning of the Aphorism in Context," *Studies in Foreign Literature* (Hiroshima Univ.), IX (Feb. 1963), 1-12. [In Japanese.]

244. Ganz, A. W. *Berlioz in London.* London: Quality Press, 1950.

Includes references to Edward Holmes and reprints portions of his *Fraser's Magazine* article on Berlioz.

245. Garrod, H. W. *The Study of Good Letters.* Ed. John Jones. Oxford: Clarendon, 1963.

Includes (pp. 1-19) "The Place of Hazlitt in English Criticism."

246. Gilmour, J[ohn]. S. L. "Some Uncollected Authors VII: Thomas Hood," BC, IV (Autumn 1955), 239-248.

A brief bibliography.

247. Gittings, Robert. "Mr. Keats's Origin," TLS, March 5, 1964, p. 200.

Traces Keats's maternal ancestry. See Nos. 248 and 290.

248. Gittings, Robert. "Mr. Keats's Origin," TLS, March 19, 1964, p. 238.

Feels that he sufficiently acknowledged the sources of information in his article. See Nos. 247 and 290.

249. Gittings, Robert. "The Psyche Unchained," Spec, Feb. 14, 1964, p. 212.

Disagrees with M. R. Ridley over the relative merits of the biographies by W. J. Bate and Aileen Ward. Asserts that Abbey did not know of the "Chancery Fund." See Nos. 250 and 277. See also Nos. 208 and 355.

250. Gittings, Robert. "The Psyche Unchained," Spec, March 13, 1964, p. 343.

Says that Abbey did not know of the fund set up Feb. 13, 1810. See Nos. 249 and 277. See also Nos. 208 and 355.

251. Gittings, Robert, and Jo Manton. *The Story of John Keats.* See K-SJ, XII (1963), 137, XIII (1964), 139.

Rev. by Ellen Rudin in *Library Journal,* LXXXVIII (Apr. 15, 1963), 1776-1777; by *M. S. Libby in NYHT, May 12, 1963, p. 23.

252. Glover, Kenneth. "An Unidentified De Wint," *Country Life,* CVIII (Aug. 18, 1950), 514.

The picture, a "water-colour of a water-mill," is reproduced.

253. Grant, Douglas. "Critics Who Have Influenced Taste—VII. Hazlitt," *The Times,* London, May 16, 1963, p. 15.

"He interpreted a work within the terms of his own sympathies. . . . His criticisms were coherent and deliberate, not whimsical or simply impressionistic."

254. Green, David Bonnell. "Three New Letters of Charles Lamb," HLQ, XXVII (Nov. 1963), 83-86.
One, in which Hunt is mentioned, is to Charles Cowden Clarke.

255. Gross, George Clayburn. "Keats's 'Presider': The Influence of Shakespeare on Keats" [Doctoral dissertation, Southern California, 1963], DA, XXIV (Aug. 1963), 726.

256. Guy, E. F. "Keats's Use of 'Luxury': A Note on Meaning," K-SJ, XIII (1964), 87-95.
"*Luxury* at its most significant use in Keats is to be understood as descriptive of, or equating a pleasure to a delight in, sensual activation."

257. Harmsworth, Geoffrey. "The Centenary of Peter De Wint," *Country Life,* CVI (July 1, 1949), 32-34.
With nine illustrations.

258. Haydon, Benjamin Robert. *The Diary of Benjamin Robert Haydon*. Ed. Willard Bissell Pope. Vols. III, IV, and V. Cambridge, Mass.: Harvard Univ., 1963. See K-SJ, X (1961), 87.
Rev. by *C. T. Houpt in *Christian Science Monitor,* Aug. 8, 1963, p. 11; in NYHT, Sept. 1, 1963, p. 8; in TLS, Dec. 5, 1963, p. 1012; by Martin Dodsworth in NS, LXVI (Dec. 20, 1963), 913-914; by Howard Mumford Jones in K-SJ, XIII (1964), 110-113.

259. "Haydon's 'Christ's Entry into Jerusalem,'" K-SJ, XIII (1964), 4.
The picture is now hung at The Athenaeum of Ohio, Saint Gregory's Seminary, Cincinnati.

260. Haynes, Jean. "A Coroner's Inquest, 3 April, 1804," KSMB, XIV (1963), 46.
On the death of Thomas Keats, Sr.

261. *Hazlitt, William. *Muhimmat al-Nāqid. [The Role of the Critic.]* [Translated by] Nazmi Khalīl. Cairo: al-Dār al Qawmiyyah, 1962.

Heath-Stubbs, John. See No. 100.

262. Hewlett, Dorothy. *Life of John Keats.* Second Edition. See K-SJ, I (1952), 94, IV (1955), 119.
Rev. by C[larence]. D. T[horpe]. in PQ, XXX (Apr. 1951), 117; by David Bonnell Green in K-SJ, I (1952), 112-113.

263. Hewlett, Dorothy. "Some Thoughts on 'The Fall of Hyperion,'" *Aryan Path,* XXXIV (Oct. 1964), 462-466.
In recasting "Hyperion" "it would seem as if Keats was applying the ancient myth to himself; that it is the making of a poet, not of a god, which now occupied his mind."

264. Hobson, Alan. *Symbols of Transformation in Poetry.* London: Guild of Pastoral Psychology, 1963.
Keats and Wordsworth are discussed.

265. Hood, Thomas. "Sonnet Written in a Volume of Shakespeare," K-SJ, XIII (1964), 12.

266. Hoshino, Nobuo. "Keats' Water-Imagery in *Endymion,*" *Anglica,* V (June 1963), 62-74.
An analysis.

267. *Hoshino, Nobuo. "On Water-Imagery in the Works of Keats," *Essays in English Language and Literature* (Kansai Univ. Suita), Special number in memory of Prof. Matsutaro Yamada (1963). [In Japanese.]

Houghton, Walter E. See No. 103.

Howell, A. C. See No. 186.

Hudson, Frederick. See No. 105.

Hübner, Walter. See No. 24.

268. Hutchings, Richard John. *Keats, Morland and Morton at Eglantine Cottage, Shanklin.* Shanklin: Clarendon Bookshop, 1963. "Famous Isle of Wight Homes Series."

269. *Imanishi, Nobuya. "The Moon and John Keats," *Bulletin of the English Society* (Osaka Gakugei College), No. 9 (March 1964), pp. 45-52.

"In the Sale Room." See No. 107.

270. James, G. Ingli. "'Ode to a Nightingale,'" TLS, Feb. 20, 1964, p. 154.
Believes that the last lines of the "Ode on a Grecian Urn" are addressed to the Urn itself. See Nos. 210, 213, 224, 285, 312, 339, and 341.

271. Jarvis, William A. W. "A Cousin of John Keats," KSMB, XIV (1963), 37-42.
Midgley John Jennings (1806-1857), son of Keats's maternal uncle.

272. Jones, Stanley. "Hazlitt in Edinburgh: An Evening with Mr. Ritchie of *The Scotsman,*" EA, XVII (Jan.-March 1964), 9-20; (Apr.-June 1964), 113-127.
Gives an account of those present and of the evening.

273. Jones, Stanley. "An Unidentified Shakespearean Allusion in Hazlitt," ES, XLV (Apr. 1964), 126-129.
To *Cymbeline* in an 1820 article on the drama.

274. Jordan, R. Furneaux. "The Creative Act in Architecture and Literature,"

University of Leeds Review, VII (June 1961), 214-234.

Includes discussion of Keats.

Keiser, Robert. See No. 28.

275. Kenyon, Katharine M. R. "Keats and the Countryside," KSMB, XIV (1963), 24-29.

Keats had a countryman's knowledge, and it is reflected in his poetry.

Kiell, Norman. See Nos. 6 and 178.

276. Kilgour, Norman. "Keats and the Abbey Cocks 'Account,'" KSMB, XIV (1963), 35-36.

Blame for Keats's financial distress "must certainly also be laid upon Richard Abbey."

277. Kilgour, Norman. "The Psyche Unchained," Spec, March 6, 1963, p. 312.

Asserts that Abbey "must have known of the 'Chancery Fund.'" See Nos. 249 and 250. See also Nos. 208 and 355.

King-Hele, Desmond. See No. 112.

278. *Kodama, Sanechika. "D. G. Rossetti and J. Keats," *Studies in the Humanities* (Literary Association, Doshisha Univ., Kyoto), No. 67 (Nov. 1963), pp. 62-75.

279. *Krishna, Daya. "*Endymion* and Keats' Later Work," *Literary Criterion,* IV (Summer 1961), 23-26.

280. Kroeber, Karl. "The Commemorative Prophecy of *Hyperion*," *Transactions of the Wisconsin Academy of Sciences, Arts and Letters,* LII (1963), 189-204.

"Hyperion" is principally characterized by "the intensity with which a commemorative, traditionalistic impulse interacts with a prophetic, progressive impulse. Keats fabricates a new 'personal' mythology out of old religion and traditional literature. . . . The old is not to be obliterated but absorbed into a more complicated and comprehensive unity. . . . *The Fall of Hyperion* . . . even more than the earlier version . . . speaks in two voices, one commemorative, one prophetic."

281. Kudo, Naotaro. "What a Japanese Thinks of Keats and Shelley," KSMB, XIV (1963), 8-16.

Explains the appeal of these poets to the Japanese.

282. *Kumar, Jatendra. *Mahākavi Keats Ka Kāvya-Loka.* [*The World of Poetry of the Great Poet Keats.*] Delhi: Atma Ram & Sons, 1962.

Contains translations into Hindi verse of "Isabella," "Hyperion," "Lamia," the Odes, "The Fall of Hyperion," "Sleep and Poetry," and a number of sonnets and shorter poems; translations of twenty-five letters of Keats; and essays on Keats the man and Keats the poet.

283. Lane, William G. "A Chord in Melancholy: Hood's Last Years," K-SJ, XIII (1964), 43-60.

Prints eight new letters by Hood and six about him and his family; establishes the relationship between Hood and Barham, and between these two writers and Colburn and Bentley.

284. Langer, Susanne K. "Abstraction in Art," JAAC, XXII (Summer 1964), 379-392.

Includes analysis of a line from "Ode to a Nightingale."

285. Laski, Marghanita. "'Ode to a Nightingale,'" TLS, Jan. 2, 1964, p. 16.

Suggests a new interpretation for the last six lines of the first stanza. See Nos. 210, 213, 224, 270, 312, 339, and 341.

286. Lerner, Laurence. "Love and Gossip: or, How Moral Is Literature?" EC, XIV (Apr. 1964), 126-147.

Discusses Keats.

287. McFarland, G. F. "The Early Literary Career of Julius Charles Hare," *Bulletin of the John Rylands Library,* XLVI (Sept. 1963), 42-83.

Has information on Hare's relationships with John Taylor and the Olliers.

288. MacGillivray, J. R. *John Keats: A Bibliography and Reference Guide, 1816-1946.* See K-SJ, I (1952), 94, III (1954), 119.

Rev. by Frederick Page in RES, N.S., II (Oct. 1951), 404.

289. Mahoney, John L. "Keats and the Metaphor of Fame," ES, XLIV (Oct. 1963), 355-357.

Through the medium of his two sonnets on fame "Keats reveals most graphically the idea of Fame that was ever before him."

290. Mann, Phyllis G. "Mr. Keats's Origin," TLS, March 12, 1964, p. 215.

Rebukes and corrects Robert Gittings. See Nos. 247 and 248.

291. Marchand, Leslie A. "A First Edition of *Endymion*," *Journal of the Rutgers*

University Library, XXVI (June 1963), 58-59.
Acquired by Rutgers.

Martini, Stelio. See No. 124.

292. Maxwell, J. C. "Hazlitt and Fielding," N&Q, CCIX (Jan. 1964), 25.†
An allusion to *Joseph Andrews* in *The Spirit of the Age*.

293. Miles, Josephine. "Toward a Theory of Style and Change," JAAC, XXII (Fall 1963), 63-67.
Discusses Keats.

294. *Miyazaki, Yuko. "On Keats's Odes," *Bulletin of Musashi Univ.* (Tokyo), No. 1 (1964). [In Japanese.]

295. *Mizushima, Kanji. "*Hyperion:* An Appreciation," *Kyoto University Bulletin of Foreign Studies,* No. 4 (1964).

296. Morgan, Peter F. "Corrections in Some Letters of Thomas Hood," N&Q, CCVIII (July 1963), 261-262.†
In the *Letters of Thomas Hood . . .* (1945).

297. Morgan, P. "A Whimsical Letter of Thomas Hood," N&Q, CCVIII (Oct. 1963), 385.
Identifies Mary Elliot, dates the letter. See No. 335.

298. Moyne, Ernest J. "The Reverend William Hazlitt: A Friend of Liberty in Ireland during the American Revolution," *William and Mary Quarterly,* 3rd Series, XXI (Apr. 1964), 288-297.
Describes the stay of Hazlitt and his family in Ireland and his efforts on behalf of American prisoners.

299. Murry, John Middleton. *Mystery of Keats.* See K-SJ, I (1952), 94.
Rev. by Gilbert Dunklin in *Thought,* XXVI (Autumn 1951), 468-469; by C[larence]. D. T[horpe]. in PQ, XXX (Oct. 1951), 118.

300. *Die Musik in Geschichte und Gegenwart: Allgemeine Enzyklopädie der Musik.* Ed. Friedrich Blume. Kassel: Bärenreiter, 1949- .
Vol. VI contains an article on Edward Holmes by Charles Cudworth; Vol. VII on Keats by Helmut Viebrock; Vol. IX on Vincent Novello by Charles Humphries.

301. Nethery, Wallace. "Robert Balmanno, Father-in-Love," ABC, XIV (Oct. 1963), 15-21; (Nov. 1963), 15-20.
Recounts Balamanno's friendship with the Cowden Clarkes.

302. "Notes on Sales," TLS, Aug. 9, 1963, p. 616.
A letter from De Quincey to John Wilson, Nov. 27, 1820, "virulently attacking the 'Cockney School,'" made £150 at Sotheby's, Apr. 8-9, 1963.

303. "Notes on Sales," TLS, Feb. 6, 1964, p. 116.
At Sotheby's on Nov. 12, 1963, "a fragment of fourteen lines from the autograph manuscript of . . . *Otho* . . . brought £450."

304. Noxon, James. "Hazlitt as Moral Philosopher," *Ethics,* LXXIII (July 1963), 279-283.
Examines Hazlitt's treatment of "the metaphysical issue underlying the ethical controversy between proponents of self-interest and of benevolence" and finds that he handles "this problem in an original and provocative way."

305. *Ogata, Takao. "John Keats: *To Autumn,*" *Bulletin of the Second Faculty of Technology, General Education* (Nihon Univ., Tokyo), No. 4 (1963). [In Japanese.]

306. *Okachi, Ryo. "On *Ode on a Grecian Urn,*" *Studies in English Language and Literature* (Chuo Univ., Tokyo), No. 3 (1963). [In Japanese.]

Parks, Edd Winfield. See No. 138.

Partridge, Monica. See No. 141.

307. *Pastalosky, Rosa. *Testimonio social de los románticos ingleses.* Santa Fe: Castellvi, 1963.
Discusses the social ideas of Keats, Shelley, and others.
Rev. by *Raquel Saúl in *Sur* (Buenos Aires), No. 281 (Apr.-May 1963), pp. 77-79; by *Aníbal César Goñi in *La Prensa* (Buenos Aires), Oct. 13, 1963.

308. Perkins, David. *The Quest for Permanence: The Symbolism of Wordsworth, Shelley and Keats.* See K-SJ, X (1961), 89, XI (1962), 129, XII (1963), 140, XIII (1964), 142.
Rev. by Neville Rogers in MLR, LIX (Jan. 1964), 118-119.

Perkins, David. See No. 144.

309. Pettet, E. C. *On the Poetry of Keats.* See K-SJ, VII (1958), 126, VIII (1959), 72, IX (1960), 67, X (1961), 89, XI (1962), 129.
Rev. by S. Korninger in ES, XLIV (Aug. 1963), 315-316.

Praz, Mario. See No. 145.

310. Praz, Mario. *The Romantic Agony.* Trans. Angus Davidson. See K-SJ, VII (1958), 126, XI (1962), 129.
Rev. by George Whalley in QQ,

LIX (Spring 1952), 126-129; by Renato Poggioli in JAAC, X (June 1952), 373-374.

311. Reid, J[ohn]. C[owie]. *Thomas Hood.* London: Routledge, 1963.

Rev. by Elizabeth Jennings in Li, L.XX (Aug 29, 1963), 320; by V. S. Pritchett in NS, LXVI (Aug. 30, 1963), 255-256; by J. M. Cohen in Spec, Sept. 20, 1963, p. 360; in TLS, Oct. 4, 1963, p. 782; by C. A. Prance in CLSB, No. 174. (Nov. 1963), pp. 427-428; by Naomi Lewis in *Encounter,* XXII (Jan. 1964), 72-74.

312. Rhydderch, William. " 'Ode to a Nightingale,' " TLS, March 5, 1964, p. 199.

The dictum of the Urn "should extend to the whole of the last two lines." See Nos. 210, 213, 224, 270, 285, 339, and 341.

313. Ribman, Ronald Burt. "John Keats: The Woman and the Vision" [Doctoral dissertation, Pittsburgh, 1962], DA, XXIV (Nov. 1963), 2019.

314. Richardson, Joanna. "The Critic and the Public," *Essays by Divers Hands, Being the Transactions of the Royal Society of Literature,* XXII (1963), 99-111.

Reprints Keats's letter of Oct. 8, 1818, to J. A. Hessey.

315. Richardson, Joanna. *The Everlasting Spell: A Study of Keats and His Friends.* London: Cape, 1963.

Rev. by Robert Gittings in Li, LXX (Sept. 5, 1963), 355; in TLS, Sept. 13, 1963, p. 690; by Richard Church in *Country Life,* CXXXIV (Sept. 26, 1963), 772-773; by Martin Dodsworth in NS, LXVI (Oct. 18, 1963), 534.

Richmond, Hugh M. See No. 441.

316. Ridley, M. R. *Keats' Craftsmanship: A Study in Poetic Development.* Lincoln: Nebraska Univ.; *London: Methuen (1963).

Paperback reprints of a book first published in 1933. See K-SJ, XIII (1964), 142.

317. Riga, Frank P. [In] "Information, Please," TLS, Feb. 13, 1964, p. 133.

Asks "about doubtful ascriptions, for an edition" of John Hamilton Reynolds' poetical works. See No. 318.

318. Riga, Frank P. "John Hamilton Reynolds: The Canon," N&Q, CCIX (Apr. 1964), 151.

Asks for information on doubtful ascriptions. See No. 317.

319. Roberts, Keith. "Current and Forthcoming Exhibitions," *Burlington Magazine,* CV (Dec. 1963), 573-578.

Includes discussion of "two quite important studies" by Haydon for a picture exhibited in 1842, "Mary Queen of Scots. . . ." One drawing is illustrated.

320. Robinson, Eric, and Geoffrey Summerfield. "John Taylor's Editing of Clare's *The Shepherd's Calendar,*" RES, N.S., XIV (Nov. 1963), 359-369.

Because of his pruning and censorship of Clare's poetry, "Taylor cannot be judged a consistently reliable editor."

Rodway, Allan. See No. 38.

321. Rogers, Neville. "Donna Nerina Medici di Marignano," KSMB, XIV (1963), vi.

An obituary notice.

322. Rollins, Hyder Edward, and Stephen Maxfield Parrish, eds. *Keats and the Bostonians.* See K-SJ, I (1952), 94-95, II (1953), 104, III (1954), 120.

Rev. by Eleanor E. Murdock in *New England Quarterly,* XXIV (Sept. 1951), 404-406; by H. W. Garrod in Spec, Oct. 5, 1951, pp. 447-448; by R[osalie]. G[lynn]. G[rylls]. in T&T, XXXII (Oct. 13, 1951), 994.

323. Ruotolo, Lucio P. "Keats and Kierkegaard: The Tragedy of Two Worlds," *Renascence,* XVI (Summer 1964), 175-190.

An existentialist reading of Keats's poetry.

Ryals, Clyde de L. See No. 150.

324. St. John-Stevas, Norman. "Walter Bagehot as a Writer," *Wiseman Review,* No. 495 (Spring 1963), pp. 38-65.

Includes discussion of Bagehot's attitude toward Shelley and Keats.

325. *Sakata, Katsuzo. "The Relation between Joy and Pain in Keats's Poetry," *Studies in English Literature* (English Literature Society of Japan, Tokyo), XXXIX (Nov. 1963), 173-194. [In Japanese.]

326. Sallé, J.-C. "Hazlitt the Associationist," RES, N.S. XV (Feb. 1964), 38-51.

Analyzes Hazlitt's theory of the associative imagination and his "conception of the relationship between the complex mesh of reality and the 'diffusive,' yet 'self-centred,' mind."

327. Sansom, Clive. "Keats's Accent," KSMB, XIV (1963), 43-45.
Although "one of the world's worst spellers," Keats did not have a Cockney accent.

328. Sayers, Dorothy L. *The Poetry of Search and the Poetry of Statement and Other Posthumous Essays on Literature, Religion and Language.* London: Gollancz, 1963.
Discusses Keats as "a typical poet of Search."
Rev. by Joanna Richardson in Li, LXX (Sept. 12, 1963), 393; by Elizabeth Jennings in *Sunday Times,* Sept. 22, 1963, p. 36.

329. Schulte, Edvige. "Henry Crabb Robinson, Goethe e l'*Hyperion* di Keats," *Annali, Sezioni Germanica* (Istituto Universitario Orientale), VI (Dec. 1963), 65-82.

330. Scott, Wilbur Stewart, ed. *Five Approaches of Literary Criticism: An Arrangement of Contemporary Critical Essays.* New York: Macmillan, 1962.
Reprints Cleanth Brooks's "Keats's Sylvan Historian: History without Footnotes," pp. 231-244. See K-SJ, I (1952), 88, No. 5.

331. *Seetaraman, M. V. "Keats's 'Hyperion,'" *Sri Aurobindo Circle* (Pondicherry), No. 17 (1961), pp. 101-117.

332. Sen Gupta, D. P. "The Unconventional Sonnets of Keats," *Visvabharati Quarterly,* XXVIII (1962-63), 139-148.
Stresses "the individuality, richness and technical innovations of the sonnets."

333. Sen Gupta, S. C. *Towards a Theory of the Imagination.* Calcutta: Oxford Univ., 1959.
Refers to Keats and Shelley.

Shahane, V. A. See No. 152.

334. Shapiro, Karl. "A Malebolge of 1400 Books, Six Lectures," *Carleton Miscellany,* V (Summer 1964), 3-135.
Keats is among those discussed.

335. Shuman, R. Baird. "A Whimsical Letter of Thomas Hood," N&Q, CCVIII (July 1963), 262-263.†
To Mary Elliot. See No. 297.

336. *Singh, Yoginder. "John Keats," *Trend* (Bombay), July 1963, pp. 31-33.

337. *Skutches, Peter. "Keats's Grecian Urn and Myth," *Iowa English Yearbook,* No. 8 (Fall 1963), pp. 45-51.†

338. Smith, L. E. W. *Twelve Poems Considered.* London: Methuen, 1963.
"Ode to the West Wind" and "Ode on a Grecian Urn" are two of those considered.

Sofer, Johann. See No. 154.

339. Southall, Raymond. "'Ode to a Nightingale,'" TLS, March 5, 1964, p. 199.
This and the "Ode on a Grecian Urn" conclude after the "pathetic recognition of the inadequacies of Nightingale and Urn." The "easily coined diction . . . expresses a slackening of attention." See Nos. 210, 213, 224, 270, 285, 312, and 341.

340. Sparshott, Francis Edward. *The Structure of Aesthetics.* Toronto: Toronto Univ., 1963.
Compares Keats and Edgar Guest.

341. Stahl, E. L. "'Ode to a Nightingale,'" TLS, March 19, 1964, p. 238.
Suggests similarities in thought between Schiller's *Die Künstler* and "Ode on a Grecian Urn." See Nos. 210, 213, 224, 270, 285, 312, and 339.

342. Sutton, Walter. *Modern American Criticism.* Englewood Cliffs: Prentice-Hall, 1963.
Discusses the criticism of Keats and Shelley.

343. Swaminathan, S. R. "Hazlitt, Lamb and Fielding," N&Q, CCIX (May 1964), 180.
Lamb echoes the same phrases from Fielding as Hazlitt.

344. Szudra, Klaus Udo. "Grundlagen und Formen der sozialen Kritik bei Elizabeth Inchbald," *Zeitschrift für Anglistik und Amerikanistik,* XI (1963), 341-376.
Discusses Hazlitt's criticism of, and Godwin's influence on, her novel *Nature and Art.*

345. * Tabuchi, Mikio. "An Essay on *Lamia*—Its Dramatic Viewpoint," *Studies in Foreign Literature* (Hiroshima Univ.), IX (Feb. 1963), 13-24. [In Japanese.]

346. * Takeda, Miyoko. "A Study of John Keats's Sonnets—Mainly through His Letters (6)," *Journal of Baika Junior College* (Toyonaka), Vol. XII (1963). [In Japanese.]

347. * Tamura, Einosuke. "On *The Eve of St. Agnes,*" *Studies in English Language and Literature* (Chuo Univ., Tokyo), No. 3 (1963). [In Japanese.]

348. * Tanabe, Michiyo. "On the Characteristic Imagery of Keats's Poems,"

Journal of the Society of English and American Literature (Kwansei Gakuin Univ.), VIII (Feb. 1964), 50-61. [In Japanese.]

349. Thaxter, Rosamond. *Sandpiper: The Life & Letters of Celia Thaxter and Her Home in the Isles of Shoals, Her Family, Friends & Favorite Poems.* Revised Edition. Francestown, N. H.: Marshall Jones, 1963.

Includes account of a visit to Mary Cowden Clarke.

350. Tillotson, Geoffrey. *Augustan Studies.* See K-SJ, XII (1963), 142, XIII (1964), 144.

Rev. by C. J. Rawson in N&Q, CCVIII (Sept. 1963), 358-359.

351. Trilling, Lionel. "The Fate of Pleasure: Wordsworth to Dostoevsky," PR, XXX (Summer 1963), 167-191.

Includes discussion of Keats and of "that dialectic of pleasure which is the characteristic intellectual element of Keats's poetry." See Nos. 21 and 218.

352. * Tsukano, Ko. "An Essay on *The Fall of Hyperion*—'I Want to Compose without This Fever,'" *Bulletin of the English Society* (Osaka Gakugei College), No. 9 (March 1964), pp. 114-125. [In Japanese.]

353. Valentine, Alan, ed. *Fathers to Sons: Advice without Consent.* Norman: Oklahoma Univ., 1963.

Includes a letter from Hazlitt to his son and one from Sir Timothy Shelley to Shelley.

Rev. by Simon Raven in *New York Review of Books,* II (March 5, 1964), 17-18.

354. Wagner, Robert D. "Keats: 'Ode to Psyche' and the Second 'Hyperion,'" K-SJ, XIII (1964), 29-41.

Sees these poems as expressing Keats's anti-romanticism: "he alone among the Romantics points the way through sickness, through romanticism to the life of the imagination."

355. Ward, Aileen. *John Keats: The Making of a Poet.* New York: Viking; * London: Secker & Warburg (1963).

Rev. by Carlos Baker in NYT, Sept. 8, 1963, pp. 7, 40; by Stephen Spender in NYHT, Sept. 22, 1963, p. 3; by Benjamin DeMott in *Harper's Magazine,* CCXXVII (Oct. 1963), 102, 104-105; by John R. Willingham in *Library Journal,* LXXXVIII (Oct. 1, 1963), 3608; by Richard McLaughlin in *Commonweal,* LXXIX (Oct. 18, 1963), 113-115; by A. Alvarez in *New York Review of Books,* I (Oct. 31, 1963), 20-21; by Charles Alva Hoyt in SatR, XLVI (Nov. 2, 1963), 22; by John Press in *Sunday Times,* Nov. 3, 1963, p. 35; by Robert Gittings in Li, LXX (Nov. 7, 1963), 750; by Anthony Burgess in *Country Life,* CXXXIV (Nov. 14, 1963), 1289; in TLS, Dec. 12, 1963, p. 1032; by Denis Donoghue in *Hudson Review,* XVI (Winter 1963-64), 617-623; by Jack Stillinger in K-SJ, XIII (1964), 100-104; by Marvin B. Perry, Jr., in VQR, XL (Winter 1964), 150-154; by Frederick A. Pottle in *Yale Review,* LIII (Winter 1964), 276-279; by M. R. Ridley in Spec, Feb. 7, 1964, p. 185; by Christopher Ricks in NS, LXVII (Feb. 21, 1964), 298; by John Gross in *Encounter,* XXII (March 1964), 81-83; by F. A. Reid in *Manchester Guardian Weekly,* XC (March 12, 1964), 11; by David Bonnell Green in CE, XXV (May 1964), 636.

356. Waters, Edward N. "Music," *Library of Congress Quarterly Journal of Current Acquisitions,* XX (Dec. 1962), 30-67.

Lists the acquisition of the holograph of the full orchestrated score of Edward MacDowell's third symphonic poem, *Lamia,* "which was inspired by Keats and composed in 1887."

357. Watson, Tommy G. "Johnson and Hazlitt on the Imagination in Milton," *Southern Quarterly,* II (Jan. 1964), 123-133.†

Johnson's analysis of Milton has "certain affinities with Hazlitt's analysis" and clearly looks forward to it.

White, R. J. See No. 40.

Wind, Edgar. See No. 175.

358. Woodroofe, Kenneth S. "Keats and the Principle of Beauty in All Things," *Visvabharati Quarterly,* XXVIII (1962), 34-47.

"The sense of Beauty . . . is not only the sense of the Beauty of particular things but the sense of the Beauty in all things."

359. "Works Printed, Designed, or Illustrated by T. M. Cleland, A Checklist of These Works in the Collections of the Library of Congress," *Library of Congress Quarterly Journal of Current Acquisitions,* XX (June 1963), 170-173.

The "Hampstead" Keats was designed by Cleland, and his design for the binding is illustrated.

360. *Yamane, Yoshio. "Keats's Poetic Mind—with Reference to His Letters," *Academia* (Nanzan Univ., Nagoya), No. 37 (1963).

361. Yost, George, Jr. "The Poetic Drive in the Early Keats," *Texas Studies in Literature and Language,* V (Winter 1964), 555-566.

"Keats's interest in sleep . . . originates as overmastering drive to poetic attainment, which governs not only his sleep but his choice and tenure of friendships and locality and even, to some extent, his interest in death."

V. SHELLEY

Works: Selected, Single, Translated

Brown, Ivor, ed. See No. 41.

362. *The Esdaile Notebook: A Volume of Early Poems.* Ed. Kenneth Neill Cameron. New York: Knopf, 1964.

Rev. by Graham Hough in NYHT, Apr. 26, 1964, pp. 6, 23; by G. M. Matthews in *New York Review of Books,* II (May 28, 1964), 18-19; by Ben W. Fuson in *Library Journal,* LXXXIX (June 15, 1964), 2623.

363. "Fragments," K-SJ, XIII (1964), 86.

"Rain," "A Tale Untold," and "To Italy."

Grigson, Geoffrey, ed. See No. 45.

364. Grigson, Geoffrey, ed. *O Rare Mankind! A Short Collection of Great Prose.* London: Phoenix, 1963.

Has selections from Shelley.

365. **Izbrannye stroki.* [*Selected Passages.*] [Translated by] E. Avagian. Erevan: Aipetrat, 1963. [In Armenian.]

366. *The Letters of Percy Bysshe Shelley.* Ed. Frederick L. Jones. 2 vols. Oxford: Clarendon, 1964.

Rev. by Raymond Mortimer in *Sunday Times,* Feb. 16, 1964, p. 35; by Christopher Ricks in *Manchester Guardian Weekly,* XC (Feb. 27, 1964), 11; by John Bayley in Spec, March 6, 1964, p. 317; by Geoffrey Grigson in NS, LXVII (March 6, 1964), 366; by John Wain in *Observer,* March 8, 1964, p. 26; by Herbert Read in Li, LXXI (March 19, 1964), 486-487; in TLS, Apr. 16, 1964, p. 313; by Carlos Baker in *English Language Notes,* I (June 1964), 306-308; by Ben W. Fuson in *Library Journal,* LXXXIX (June 15, 1964), 2623.

Marshall, William H., ed. See No. 30.

367. **Persi Biš Šeli, Poezija.* [*Selected Poems of Percy Bysshe Shelley.*] [Translated by] Ranka Kuić, with an introduction and notes. Belgrade: Zavod za udž benike, 1964. [In Serbo-Croatian.]

Also includes translation of *A Defence of Poetry* and *A Letter to Lord Ellenborough.*

368. **Poesie. Compreso il saggio Difesa della poesia, di Percy Bysshe Shelley.* Ed. Rodolfo Quadrelli. Milan: E. Dall' Oglio, 1963.

369. *Selected Poems and Prose.* Ed. G. M. Matthews. London: Oxford Univ., 1964. "New Oxford English Series."

Untermeyer, Louis, ed. See No. 55.

Books and Articles Relating to Shelley and His Circle

Adams, Richard P. See No. 200.

Ades, John Irvine. See No. 56.

Anderson, George K. See No. 57.

370. Anscomb, Kathleen. "Literary Circles: A Shrine for Shelley?" T&T, XLV (Jan. 23-29, 1964), 39.

Report of a proposal to establish a "shrine" in Hampstead, from the bequest of Mrs. Freda Shelley to the Keats-Shelley Memorial Association.

371. "Author's Query," NYT, Apr. 5, 1964, p. 42.

Joseph L. Fant asks information on Gilbert Imlay.

372. Baxter, B. M. *Albert Verwey's Translations from Shelley's Poetical Works: A Study of Their Style and Rhythm and a Consideration of Their Value as Translations.* Leiden: Leiden Univ., 1963.

Bentman, Raymond. See No. 13.

373. Berry, Francis. *Poetry and the Physical Voice.* See K-SJ, XII (1963), 144, XIII (1964), 145.

Rev. by Esther L. Schwerman in SAQ, LXII (Summer 1963), 457; by Charles Tomlinson in *Poetry,* CII (Aug. 1963), 341-345; by F. T. Wood in ES, XLIV (Aug. 1963), 310.

Beyer, Werner W. See No. 64.

374. Boas, Louise Schutz. *Harriet Shelley: Five Long Years.* See K-SJ, XII (1963), 144, XIII (1964), 146.

Rev. by K[enneth]. N[eill]. C[ameron]. in PQ, XLII (Oct. 1963), 464; by F. T. Wood in ES, XLIV (Oct. 1963), 386-387.

375. Boas, Louise Schutz. " 'Shelley and Mary,' " TLS, Nov. 14, 1963, p. 927.

Describes the circumstances surrounding the book. See Nos. 376, 424, and 425.

376. Boas, Louise Schutz. " 'Shelley and Mary,' " TLS, Feb. 20, 1964, p. 153.

Further information on the state of various copies of *Shelley and Mary*. See Nos. 375, 424, and 425.

377. Boas, Louise Schutz. "Shelley: Three Unpublished Lines," N&Q, CCIX (May 1964), 178.

In a copy of *Prometheus Unbound* that Shelley gave to Trelawny on one of the last days of his life.

Bose, Amalendu. See No. 67.

Bostetter, Edward E. See No. 17.

Brown, Calvin S. See No. 68.

378. Brown, Nathaniel Hapgood. "Shelley's Theory of Erotic Love" [Doctoral dissertation, Columbia, 1963], DA, XXIV (May 1964), 4676.

379. Brown, T. J. "Some Shelley Forgeries by 'Major Byron,' " KSMB, XIV (1963), 47-54.

Lists and describes the forged Shelley letters that came to the Keats-Shelley Memorial Association from the estate of Sir John C. E. Shelley-Rolls, 6th Bart.

380. Cameron, Kenneth Neill. *The Young Shelley: Genesis of a Radical.* See K-SJ, I (1952), 96, II (1953), 105, III (1954), 122, XII (1963), 145.

Rev. by Frederick L. Jones in PQ, XXX (Apr. 1951), 120-121; by Sylva Norman in Spec, Nov. 23, 1951, p. 716.

381. *Cecchi, Emilio. "Percy Bysshe Shelley, analisi e confronti," *Osservatore politico letterario,* VIII (1962), iv, 41-50.

Chalke, H. D. See No. 219.

382. Chatterjee, Kalyan. "Shelley and Modern Thought," *Calcutta Review,* CLXVI (March 1963), 252-256.

"Shelley's poetry . . . is a serious attempt at offering a characteristic vision of life."

Chayes, Irene H. See No. 221.

383. *Cialfi, Mario. "Shelley o la sanità del frammento," *Osservatore politico letterario,* IX (1963), x, 100-110.

384. Clemens, Samuel L. *The Complete Essays of Mark Twain.* Ed. Charles Neider. Garden City: Doubleday, 1963.

Reprints "In Defense of Harriet Shelley," pp. 119-155.

Cohen, Ralph. See No. 82.

385. Collins, Thomas J. "Browning's *Essay on Shelley:* In Context," *Victorian Poetry,* II (Spring 1964), 119-124.

"If Browning did think of Shelley as a 'whole poet' by 1851, it was only after a youthful emphasis on, and mistrust of, Shelley's subjective element."

Comorovski, Cornelia. See No. 83.

386. Davies, Rosemary Reeves. "Charles Brockden Brown's *Ormond:* A Possible Influence upon Shelley's Conduct," PQ, XLIII (Jan. 1964), 133-137.

Ormond, known to Shelley, "contains an important episode which bears a striking similarity to the Harriet-Mary-Shelley triangle."

387. *Dibella, Francisco. "Shelley: el poeta de las predicciones," *La Nación* (Buenos Aires), July 8, 1962, p. 6.

Donner, H. W. See No. 233.

Downs, Brian W. See No. 85.

388. Dunleavy, Gareth W. "Two New Mary Shelley Letters and the 'Irish' Chapters of *Perkin Warbeck,*" K-SJ, XIII (1964), 6-10.

The letters, to T. Crofton Croker, indicate that Mrs. Shelley was more careful in working up the background of her historical novels than has been supposed.

389. Eliot, George, *pseud. Essays of George Eliot.* Ed. Thomas Pinney. London: Routledge; *New York: Columbia Univ. (1963).

Reprints "Margaret Fuller and Mary Wollstonecraft" (pp. 199-209). Byron is referred to in other essays.

390. *Ellis, F. S. *A Lexical Concordance to the Poetical Works of Percy Bysshe Shelley.* With an Appendix by Takeshi Saito. Tokyo: Senjo Publishing Co., 1963.

A reprint of a volume first published in 1892.

Enkvist, Nils Erik. See No. 88.

Enscoe, Gerald Eugene. See No. 236.

Faulkner, William. See No. 240.

Fitzgerald, F. Scott. See No. 241.

391. Fleisher, David. *William Godwin: A Study in Liberalism.* See K-SJ, I (1952), 97.

Rev. by Maurice Cranston in Spec, May 11, 1951, p. 628.

392. Gardiner, Leslie. "At the Riviera's

End," *Blackwood's Magazine,* CCXCV (May 1964), 395-408.

Includes description of Shelley and Lerici.

393. Gilenson, Boris. "Shelley in Russian," *Soviet Literature,* No. 3 (1963), pp. 171-172.†

A review of recent Russian scholarship on Shelley, and especially of the *Selected Poems* (1962), which includes Boris Pasternak's translation of "Ode to the West Wind." See K-SJ, XIII (1964), 145, No. 429.

394. *Gilinskii, I. N. "Stilisticheskii analiz stikhotvoreniia P. B. Shelli 'Pesnia k liudiam Anglii,'" ["A Stylistic Analysis of Shelley's 'Song to the Men of England'"], *Trudy* (Leningrad Gos. bibliotech In-t.), Vol. X (1963), pp. 109-123.

395. Godwin, William. *Imogen, A Pastoral Romance from the Ancient British.* Introduction by Jack W. Marken. New York: New York Public Library, 1963.

See K-SJ, XIII (1964), 147.

396. Göller, Karl Heinz. "Shelleys Bilderwelt," *Germanisch-Romanisch Monatsschrift,* XLIV (Oct. 1963), 380-397.

Shelley's imagery reflects his interpretation of the "unreality" of the visible world, his vision of it as process masking reality.

Gotlieb, Howard B. See No. 95.

397. Grabo, Carl H. *Shelley's Eccentricities.* See K-SJ, I (1952), 97, IV (1955), 122-123.

Rev. by K[enneth]. N[eill]. C[ameron]. in PQ, XXX (Apr. 1951), 122.

398. Graves, Robert. "Poetry's False Face," *Horizon,* V (Nov. 1963), 42-47.†

Includes discussion of "To a Skylark," "among the shoddiest poems ever wished on us as the product of genius."

399. Green, Roger Lancelyn. *Authors & Places: A Literary Pilgrimage.* London: Batsford, 1963.

Has material on Peacock and Shelley.

Gregory, L. F. See No. 97.

400. Guinn, John Pollard, Jr. "Shelley's Political Thought" [Doctoral dissertation, Texas, 1963], DA, XXIV (Nov. 1963), 2012.

401. *Gummerus, E. R. "Diktaren och dubbelgångaren," *Hufvudstadsbladet* (Helsinki), Oct. 13, 1963.

402. *Gusmanov, I. G. "Nekotorye osobennosti obraza Prometeia v liricheskoi drame P. B. Shelli *Raskovannyi Prometei*" ["Some Peculiarities of the Image of Prometheus in P. B. Shelley's Lyric Drama *Prometheus Unbound*"], *Uchenye zapiski* (Moskva Gos. ped. In-t. im V. I. Lenina), No. 203, Zarubezhnaia literatura (1963), pp. 3-22.

403. Harding, D. W. *Experience into Words: Essays on Poetry.* London: Chatto, 1963.

Reprints "The Hinterland of Thought" (pp. 175-197). See K-SJ, XI (1962), 134.

Heath-Stubbs, John. See No. 100.

Houghton, Walter E. See No. 103.

404. "The Houghton Library," TLS, Apr. 2, 1964, p. 280.

Godwin's *Dramas for Children* was among the 1962-63 accessions.

Hudson, Frederick. See No. 105.

Hübner, Walter. See No. 24.

405. Hughes, Daniel. "Kindling and Dwindling: The Poetic Process in Shelley," K-SJ, XIII (1964), 13-28.

Discusses the word kindle "as pointing to Shelley's poetic strategies, with particular reference to his image of the fading coal as the condition of the poetic act, and all that act implies."

406. Huscher, Herbert. "A New Viviani Letter," KSMB, XIV (1963), 30-33.

Prints a letter of May 1821 from Teresa Viviani to Shelley.

407. Imlay, Gilbert, and Mary Wollstonecraft. *The Emigrants (1793).* Introduction by Robert R. Hare. Gainesville, Fla.: Scholars' Facsimiles and Reprints, 1964.

A facsimile reproduction of the Dublin edition (1794).

408. Jackson, MacD. P. "Entangled by locks—entangled by looks: An Addendum," ES, XLV (Feb. 1964), 43-44.

Comments on *Prometheus Unbound,* II, v, 48-53.

James, Louis. See No. 108.

409. Jones, Frederick L. "Hogg's Peep at Elizabeth Shelley," PQ, XXIX (Oct. 1950), 422-426.

An 1811 letter presented as Shelley's in *New Shelley Letters* is really by Hogg.

410. *Kamijima, Kenkichi. "The Explorers of the Inane: Part V, Shelley," *Essays,* No. 17 (1963), pp. 11-34. [In Japanese.]

411. *Kato, Takashi. "Shelley and Didacticism," *Shiron, Essays* (Tohoku Univ.,

Sendai), No. 5 (1963). [In Japanese.]

Keiser, Robert. See No. 28.

Kiell, Norman, ed. See No. 6.

Killham, John. See No. 187.

King-Hele, Desmond. See No. 112.

412. King-Hele, Desmond. "Shelley, An Address," CLSB, No. 176 (March 1964), pp. 441-442.

413. Kosok, Heinz. *Die Bedeutung der Gothic Novel für das Erzählwerk Herman Melvilles.* Hamburg: Cram, de Gruyter, 1963. (Britannica et Americana, Vol. XII.)

Discusses the influence of Godwin, Shelley, and Mary Shelley.

Kudo, Naotaro. See No. 281.

414. * Kuić, Ranka. "Šelijeva Poetike" ["Shelley's Poetry"] in *Veliki pesnici o poeziji* [*Great Poets on Poetry*] (Belgrade: Kolavčev narodni universitet, 1964), pp. 79-100.

415. Laird, John. *Philosophical Incursions into English Literature.* New York: Russell & Russell, 1962.

A reprint of a book first published in 1946. Contains "Shelley's Metaphysics," pp. 116-135.

416. Lemaitre, Hélène. *Shelley, Poète des Eléments.* See K-SJ, XII (1963), 146, XIII (1964), 148.

Rev. by P. M.-M. in *Revue des langues vivantes,* XXIX (1963), 380-381; by C. E. Nelson in BA, XXXVII (Autumn 1963), 411; by K[enneth]. N[eill]. C[ameron]. in PQ, XLII (Oct. 1963), 465; by Joan Rees in RES, N.S., XIV (Nov. 1963), 421-422.

417. Linebarger, James M. "Yeats's 'Among School Children' and Shelley's *Defence of Poetry,*" N&Q, CCVIII (Oct. 1963), 375-377.†

"Yeats derived several of the major images and ideas of "Among School Children' directly from *A Defence of Poetry.*"

Luke, Hugh J., Jr. See No. 121.

418. Lund, Mary Graham. "Shelley as Frankenstein," *Forum,* IV (Fall 1963), 28-31.†

Sees *Frankenstein* "as Mary Godwin's own story of her tragic love, of her suprahuman poet lover!"

419. McGann, Jerome J. "James Thomson (B. V.): The Woven Hymns of Night and Day," SEL, III (Autumn 1963), 493-507.

Discusses Shelley's influence on Thomson.

420. Marken, Jack W. "Joseph Bevan and William Godwin," *Georgia Historical Quarterly,* XLIII (Sept. 1959), 302-318.

Prints Godwin's letters to Bevan, the man to whom *Letters of Advice to a Young American* . . . was addressed, and a selection of Bevan's to Godwin.

Martini, Stelio. See No. 124.

421. Matthews, G. M. "'Julian and Maddalo': the Draft and the Meaning," *Studia Neophilologica,* XXXV (1963), 57-84.†

Argues that the structure of the poem and the evidence of the draft, along with other factors, "confirm that *Julian and Maddalo* was conceived and written as a dramatic experiment, suggested—but only suggested—by Tasso's madness."

422. Maxwell, J. C. "A Shelley Letter: An Unrecorded Printing," N&Q, CCIX (May 1964), 178-179.

In *Englische Studien,* LI (1917-18).

423. Mertens, Helmut. "Entsprechung von Form und Gehalt in Shelleys Gedicht 'To Jane: "The Keen Stars Were Twinkling,"'" *Neueren Sprachen,* May 1964, pp. 229-233.

An analysis of the relationship of verse form and content.

424. Michell, Anne Lee. "'Shelley and Mary,'" TLS, Dec. 12, 1963, p. 1038.

Describes her copy; discusses Lady Shelley's attitude toward the work. See Nos. 375, 376, and 425.

425. Michell, Anne Lee. "'Shelley and Mary,'" TLS, March 12, 1964, p. 220.

Laments misrepresentation of Harriet Shelley and her descendants. See Nos. 375, 376, and 424.

Mill, John Stuart. See No. 126.

426. * Nagai, Makoto. "Structure and Meaning in Shelley's 'Lines Written among the Euganean Hills,'" *Bulletin of Aichi Women's College* (Nagoya), No. 14 (Feb. 1964), pp. 1-16.

427. Nares, Gordon. "Field Place, Sussex—I and II, The Home of Mrs. G. N. Charrington," *Country Life,* CXVIII (Oct. 6 and 13, 1955), 724-727, 788-791.

Describes and gives the history of Shelley's birthplace. Twenty illustrations.

428. Norman, Sylva. "Critics Who Have Influenced Taste—XVIII. Percy B. Shelley," *The Times,* London, Aug. 1, 1963, p. 13.

"Poetry . . . is to Shelley a divine

essence that should interpenetrate moral, political and historical wisdom, scientific and economic knowledge alike."

429. "Notes on Sales," TLS, Oct. 11, 1963, p. 815.
"The Kelmscott Shelley, three volumes, 1895, made £45" at a miscellaneous sale at Hodgson's, June 20-21, 1963.

"Notes on Sales." See No. 134.

Parks, Edd Winfield. See No. 138.

Pastalosky, Rosa. See No. 307.

430. Peacock, Thomas Love. *The Complete Novels of Thomas Love Peacock.* See K-SJ, XIII (1964), 149.
Rev. by Nicholas Armour in T&T, XLIV (July 25-31, 1963), 24; by Olivia Manning in Spec, Sept. 6, 1963, p. 293.

431. Peacock, Thomas Love. *Nightmare Abbey and Crotchet Castle.* Introduction by J. B. Priestley. New York: Capricorn, 1964.
A paperback edition.

432. * Peake, Charles. "*Cards of Identity,* An Intellectual Satire," *Literary Half-Yearly,* I (July 1960), 49-57.†
Discusses Peacock's influence on Nigel Dennis.

Perkins, David. See No. 144.

433. Peter, Mary. "A Portrait of Mary Wollstonecraft Godwin by John Opie in the Tate Gallery," KSMB, XIV (1963), 1-3.
Analyzes the portrait.

434. Pollin, Burton R. "William Godwin's 'Fragment of a Romance,'" CL, XVI (Winter 1964), 40-54.
A tale with a Spanish setting that appeared in the *New Monthly Magazine* (1833): "it mirrors significant themes and concerns in the works of Godwin and other literary men of the early nineteenth century."

435. Pottle, Frederick A. "'Lost' Articles—Information Given and Requested," K-SJ, XIII (1964), 10-11.
Suggests that attention be called "to good articles of past years which have failed to get into the standard bibliographies"; cites Melvin M. Rader's "Shelley's Theory of Evil Misunderstood" as an outstanding example.

Praz, Mario. See No. 145.

Read, Bill. See No. 8.

436. Read, Herbert. "The Poet and His Muse," *British Journal of Aesthetics,* IV (Apr. 1964), 99-108.
Discusses Shelley.

437. Read, Herbert. "The Poet and His Muse," *Eranos-Jahrbuch,* XXXI (1963 for 1962), 217-248.
Includes discussion of Shelley.

438. Read, Herbert. *Selected Writings: Poetry and Criticism.* Foreword by Allen Tate. London: Faber, 1963; New York: Horizon, 1964.
Reprints "In Defence of Shelley." See K-SJ, III (1954), 114.
Rev. by Stephen Spender in NYT, March 15, 1964, pp. 5, 45.

439. Rees, Joan. "'But for such Faith': A Shelley Crux," RES, N.S., XV (May 1964), 185-186.
Interprets the phrase as meaning "for the sake of such a faith alone," a reading which significantly alters our interpretation of the following portion of the poem.

440. Reiman, Donald H. "Shelley's 'The Triumph of Life': The Biographical Problem," PMLA, LXXVIII (Dec. 1963), 536-550.
Contests G. M. Matthews' view of Jane Williams' importance to the poem, suggesting instead that the work was influenced by Rousseau's *Nouvelle Héloïse* and by Shelley's "feeling that his writings were unread and exerted no influence." See K-SJ, XI (1962), 135, No. 498, XII (1963), 146, No. 434.

441. Richmond, H[ugh]. M. *The School of Love: The Evolution of the Stuart Love Lyric.* Princeton: Princeton Univ., 1964.
Discusses Shelley; touches on Keats.

442. Rieger, James. "Dr. Polidori and the Genesis of *Frankenstein,*" SEL, III (Autumn 1963), 461-472.
Asserts that the received account is inaccurate and that Polidori's role is much more important than has been recognized.

443. Roberts, Cecil. "Shelley and Mr. Roberts," KSMB, XIV (1963), 21-23.
The "Mr. Roberts" of a sketch attributed to Shelley was the Rev. William Roberts, Vice Provost of Eton. A cousin, William Roberts, was editor of the *British Review* and quarreled with Byron.

Rodway, Allan. See No. 38.

444. * Rovinazzi, Renzo. *La poesia dram-*

matica di Percy Bysshe Shelley. Rimini: Tip. Giusti, 1962.

Ryals, Clyde de L. See No. 150.

St. John-Stevas, Norman. See No. 324.

445. * Sato, Masaji. "Shelley and the Wandering Jew," *English Literature and Language, 1963* (Sophia Univ., Tokyo), Nov. 1963, pp. 112-124. [In Japanese.]

446. * Saviane, S. "I due romanzi di Shelley," *Il Mondo*, 29, IV, 1958.

Sen Gupta, S. C. See No. 333.

447. * Serdiukov, A. I. "Esteticheskie vzgliady P. B. Shelli" ["Shelley's Esthetics"], *Uchenye zapiski* (Azerbaidzhi Univ.), Istoriia i filosofiia, No. 5 (1963), pp. 65-72.

Shahane, V. A. See No. 152.

448. "Shelley Bequest," *Bodleian Library Record*, VII (July 1963), 60.

A brief description of the collection that came to the Bodleian on the death of Lady Shelley-Rolls in 1961.

Smith, L. E. W. See No. 338.

449. Smith, Paul. "Restless Casuistry: Shelley's Composition of *The Cenci*," K-SJ, XIII (1964), 77-85.

Outlines "the rather complicated creative process that was involved in the writing of this play."

Smith, Stephen Reginald Birt. See No. 153.

Sofer, Johann. See No. 154.

450. * Solve, Melvin T. *Shelley: His Theory of Poetry*. New York: Russell & Russell, 1964.

Reprint of a book first published in 1927.

451. Spark, Muriel. *Child of Light: A Reassessment of Mary Wollstonecraft Shelley*. See K-SJ, II (1953), 106, III (1954), 123, VII (1958), 132.

Rev. by Sylva Norman in Spec, Nov. 23, 1951, p. 716.

452. Steensma, Robert C. "Shelley and the New Critics," *Proceedings of the Utah Academy of Sciences, Arts, and Letters*, Vol. XL, Part 2 (1963), pp. 146-153.

Surveys and examines "what the New Critics have said about Shelley's poetry."

453. Stemmler, Theo. "W. B. Yeats' *Song of the Happy Shepherd* und Shelleys *Defence of Poetry*," *Neophilologus*, XLVII (July 1963), 221-225.

Discusses Yeats's indebtedness to Shelley.

454. Stevens, F. Bentham. "Field Place, Warnham," *Sussex Notes and Queries*, XIV (Nov. 1956), 189-192.

Shelley's birthplace came into the possession of the family by Edward Shelley's purchase, probably in 1704, not through Mary Catherine Michell.

Stokoe, Frank W. See No. 39.

Sutton, Walter. See No. 342.

Szudra, Klaus Udo. See No. 344.

455. * Tamai, Yasushiko. "On Shelley's Description of Nature," *Bulletin of the Defence Academy* (Yokosuka), No. 6 (1963). [In Japanese.]

Thorslev, Peter L., Jr. See No. 165.

456. Tillyard, E. M. W. *Essays Literary and Educational*. See K-SJ, XIII (1964), 151.

Rev. by Allan Rodway in N&Q, CCVIII (Aug. 1963), 320.

457. * Uesugi, Fumiyo. "Byron and P. B. Shelley," *Hiroshima Studies in English Language and Literature* (The English Literary Association, Hiroshima Univ.), X (June 1964), 58-71. [In Japanese.]

Valentine, Alan, ed. See No. 353.

458. Wardle, Ralph M. *Mary Wollstonecraft: A Critical Biography*. Lawrence: Kansas Univ., 1951; * London: Richards Press, 1952.

Rev. in *Nation*, CLXXIII (Oct. 13, 1951), 313; in *New Yorker*, XXVII (Nov. 3, 1951), 143; in VQR, XXVIII (Winter 1952), xviii; by K[enneth]. N[eill]. C[ameron]. in PQ, XXXI (Apr. 1952), 128; in TLS, Sept. 5, 1952, p. 582; by Angus Wilson in NSN, XLIV (Oct. 4, 1952), 382, 384.

459. Ware, Malcolm. *Sublimity in the Novels of Ann Radcliffe: A Study of the Influence upon Her Craft of Edmund Burke's "Enquiry into the Origin of Our Ideas of the Sublime and Beautiful."* Upsala: A. B. Lundequistska, 1963. (Essays and Studies in English Language and Literature, XXV.)

Includes discussion of Burke's influence on Mary Shelley.

460. Wasserman, Earl R. *The Subtler Language: Critical Readings of Neoclassic and Romantic Poems.* See K-SJ, IX (1960), 75, X (1961), 96, XI (1962), 138, XII (1963), 148.

Rev. by Richard Harter Fogle in CL, XV (Fall 1963), 373-374.

461. Wedgwood, C. V. "On Historic Birthplaces," Li, LXX (Dec. 26, 1963), 1066-1067, 1086.

Describes visit to Lerici.

462. White, Newman I., *et al. An Examina-*

tion of the Shelley Legend. See K-SJ, I (1952), 98, III (1954), 124.

Rev. by Willis W. Pratt in K-SJ, I (1952), 103-104.

White, R. J. See No. 40.

463. Whittington-Egan, Richard, and Geoffrey Smerdon. *The Quest of the Golden Boy: The Life and Letters of Richard Le Gallienne*. London: Unicorn Press, 1960.

Describes the 1892 Shelley centenary celebrations.

464. Wilson, Milton. *Shelley's Later Poetry: A Study of His Prophetic Imagination*. See K-SJ, IX (1960), 75, X (1961), 97, XI (1962), 138, XII (1963), 148, XIII (1964), 151.

Rev. by Helmut Viebrock in *Anglia*, LXXXI (1963), 256-258.

465. Woodcock, George. *Anarchism: A History of Libertarian Ideas and Movements*. Cleveland: World, 1962.

Includes extensive treatment of Godwin.

466. Woodman, Ross Greig. *The Apocalyptic Vision in the Poetry of Shelley*. Toronto: Toronto Univ., 1964.

467. * Yamada, Chiyoshi. "On *Alastor*," *Studies in English Language and Literature* (The English Literary Society, Kumamoto Univ.), No. 7 (Dec. 1963), pp. 23-50. [In Japanese.]

Zayed, Georges. See No. 177.

Bibliography for July 1, 1964–June 30, 1965

VOLUME XV

Compiled by DAVID BONNELL GREEN and EDWIN GRAVES WILSON

THIS BIBLIOGRAPHY, a regular department of the *Keats-Shelley Journal*, is a register of the literary interest in Keats, Shelley, Byron, Hunt, and their circles from (approximately) July 1964 through June 1965.

The compilers are indeed grateful, for their generous assistance, to Professors A. Bose, University of Calcutta; Nils Erik Enkvist, Åbo Akademi; H. W. Häusermann, the University of Geneva; Dr. Siegfried Korninger, Universität, Wien; Ranka Kuić, the University of Belgrade; Jaime Rest, Universidad Nacional del Sur, Bahia Blanca; Takeshi Saito, Emeritus, Tokyo University; Dr. Helmut Viebrock, Johann Wolfgang Goethe Universität, Frankfurt am Main; Drs. Margaret Dalziel, University of Otago, Dunedin; Albert Gérard, Seraing, Belgium; Anna Katona, the University of Debrecen; J. G. Riewald, University of Groningen; D. H. Borchardt, Chief Librarian, La Trobe University, Melbourne; B. L. Kandel, the M. E. Saltykov-Schedrin State Public Library, Leningrad; Torbjörn Söderholm, Åbo Akademi Library; and the library staffs of Boston University, Duke University, Harvard University, and Wake Forest College.

We wish to thank Mrs. Kisia Trolle, of the Harvard College Library, for her kind help with the Russian entries.

Each item that we have not seen is marked by an asterisk. Entries which have been abstracted in *Abstracts of English Studies* are marked with a dagger, but entries in previous bibliographies which were abstracted too late for notice have not been repeated.

ABBREVIATIONS

ABC	American Book Collector
AL	American Literature
ASNS	Archiv für das Studium der neueren Sprachen
BA	Books Abroad
BC	Book Collector
BNYPL	Bulletin of the New York Public Library
CE	College English
CL	Comparative Literature
CLSB	C. L. S. Bulletin (Charles Lamb Society)
CR	Contemporary Review
DA	Dissertation Abstracts
EA	Etudes Anglaises
EC	Essays in Criticism
ELH	Journal of English Literary History
ELN	English Language Notes
ES	English Studies

Exp	Explicator
HLQ	Huntington Library Quarterly
ILN	Illustrated London News
JAAC	Journal of Aesthetics and Art Criticism
JEGP	Journal of English and Germanic Philology
JHI	Journal of the History of Ideas
KR	Kenyon Review
K-SJ	Keats-Shelley Journal
KSMB	Keats-Shelley Memorial Bulletin
Li	Listener
MLN	Modern Language Notes
MLQ	Modern Language Quarterly
MLR	Modern Language Review
MP	Modern Philology
N&Q	Notes and Queries
NS	New Statesman
NYHT	New York Herald Tribune Book Week
NYT	New York Times Book Review
PBSA	Papers of the Bibliographical Society of America
PMLA	Publications of the Modern Language Association of America
PQ	Philological Quarterly
PR	Partisan Review
QQ	Queen's Quarterly
RES	Review of English Studies
RLC	Revue de Littérature Comparée
SAQ	South Atlantic Quarterly
SatR	Saturday Review
SEL	Studies in English Literature 1500-1900
SIR	Studies in Romanticism
SP	Studies in Philology
Spec	Spectator
SR	Sewanee Review
T&T	Time & Tide
TC	Twentieth Century
TLS	Times Literary Supplement
VQR	Virginia Quarterly Review

I. GENERAL

Current Bibliographies

1. Benítez, Rubén. *Ensayo de bibliografía razonada de Gustavo Adolfo Bécquer.* Buenos Aires: Universidad de Buenos Aires, 1961.

   Includes section on "Bécquer y Byron" (pp. 78-79).

   Rev. by Edmund L. King in *Hispanic Review,* XXXII (July 1964), 273-276.

2. Bentley, G. E., Jr., and Martin K. Nurmi. *A Blake Bibliography: Annotated Lists of Works, Studies, and Blakeana.* Minneapolis: Minnesota Univ., 1964.

   Includes references to Byron, Godwin, Hunt, Keats, Shelley, and others.

3. Chester, Allan G., and M. A. Shaaber. "Nineteenth Century [English]" in "American Bibliography for 1951," ed. Paul A. Brown *et al.,* PMLA, LXVII (Apr. 1952), 126-133.

4. Green, David Bonnell, and Edwin Graves Wilson. "Current Bibliography," K-SJ, XIV (1965), 105-140.

5. Green, David Bonnell, and Edwin Graves Wilson, eds. *Keats, Shelley, Byron, Hunt, and Their Circles. A Bibliography: July 1, 1950-June 30, 1962.* Lincoln: Nebraska Univ., 1964.

   Rev. by Lloyd W. Griffin in *Library Journal,* LXXXIX (Nov. 15, 1964), 4510; in TLS, Dec. 3, 1964, p. 1114; by B[ernice]. D. S[lote]. in CE, XXVI (Feb. 1965), 418; in *English,* XV (Spring 1965), 160.

Hem, Day. See No. 408.

6. Lang, Cecil Y. "Current Bibliography," K-SJ, II (1953), 99-108.

7. Read, Bill. "Thomas Love Peacock: An Enumerative Bibliography," *Bulletin of Bibliography,* XXIV (May-Aug. 1964), 88-91.

   Continues and completes the listings. See K-SJ, XIV (1965), 106.

8. Rigby, Marjory, and Charles Nilon, eds. "Nineteenth Century," *Annual Bibliography of English Language and Literature,* XXXVI (1964 [for 1961]), 207-285.

9. Rigby, Marjory, and Charles Nilon, eds. "Nineteenth Century," *Annual Bibliography of English Language and Literature,* XXXVII (1965 [for 1962]), 228-312.

10. Watson, George, ed. *The Concise Cambridge Bibliography of English Literature.* Second Edition. Cambridge: Cambridge Univ., 1965.

    See K-SJ, IX (1960), 48.

11. *Wise, Thomas James. *A Bibliography of George Gordon Noel Baron Byron.* 2 vols. London: Dawsons of Pall Mall, 1964.

    A reprint of a work first published in 1932-33. See No. 99.

12. Woodring, Carl R. "Current Bibliography," K-SJ, IV (1955), 109-130.

13. Wright, Austin, ed. "Victorian Bibliography for 1951," MP, XLIX (May 1952), 248-273.

14. Yarker, P. M., and Brian Lee. "The Nineteenth Century," in *The Year's Work in English Studies,* ed. Beatrice White and T. S. Dorsch, XLIII (1964 [for 1962]), 225-252.

Books and Articles Relating to English Romanticism

15. Barnett, George L. *Charles Lamb: The Evolution of Elia.* Indiana University Humanities Series, No. 53. Bloomington: Indiana Univ., 1964.
Includes discussion of Byron, Godwin, Hazlitt, Hood, Hunt, Peacock, Shelley, and others.
Rev. by C. A. Prance in CLSB, No. 179 (Sept. 1964), pp. 462-463.

16. Blackstone, Bernard. *The Lost Travellers: A Romantic Theme with Variations.* See K-SJ, XIII (1964), 121, XIV (1965), 107.
Rev. in *Osmania Journal of English Studies,* No. 3 (1963), pp. 78-79.

17. Bostetter, Edward E. *The Romantic Ventriloquists: Wordsworth, Coleridge, Keats, Shelley, Byron.* See K-SJ, XIV (1965), 107.
Rev. by H. A. Smith in MLR, LIX (July 1964), 465-466; in TLS, July 2, 1964, p. 572; by William E. Coles, Jr., in CE, XXVI (Oct. 1964), 63; by A[lbert]. J. K[uhn]. in PQ, XLIII (Oct. 1964), 443; by John E. Grant in K-SJ, XIV (1965), 93-96; by James V. Baker in *Criticism,* VII (Spring 1965), 199-200; by J. W. R. Purser in RES, N.S., XVI (May 1965), 214-215. Also see No. 47.

18. Brand, C. P. *Italy and the English Romantics: The Italianate Fashion in Early Nineteenth-Century England.* See K-SJ, VIII (1959), 53, IX (1960), 49, XII (1963), 123, XIII (1964), 121.
Rev. by Éva Zentai in *Filologiai Közlöny,* VIII (June 1962), 223-226.

19. Collins, Philip. "Dickens's Reading," *Dickensian,* LX (Sept. 1964), 136-151.
Discusses Dickens's familiarity with the Romantics: he was more fully acquainted with the prose writers than with the poets.

20. Crawley, C. W., ed. *The New Cambridge Modern History: Volume IX: War and Peace in an Age of Upheaval 1793-1830.* Cambridge: Cambridge Univ., 1965.
Includes brief discussion of Byron, Hunt, and Shelley.

21. Creeger, George R., and Joseph W. Reed, Jr., eds. *Selected Prose and Poetry of the Romantic Period.* New York: Holt, 1964.
Includes selections from Hunt, Hazlitt, Peacock, Hood, Reynolds, and others.

22. Forsyth, R. A. "The Myth of Nature and the Victorian Compromise of the Imagination," ELH, XXXI (June 1964), 213-240.
Discusses the Romantic attitude toward nature (pp. 215-220).

23. Frye, Northrop, ed. *Romanticism Reconsidered: Selected Papers from the English Institute.* See K-SJ, XIV (1965), 107.
Rev. by William Blissett in *University of Toronto Quarterly,* XXXIII (July 1964), 401-408; in TLS, Aug. 27, 1964, pp. 757-758; by M[artin]. K. N[urmi]. in PQ, XLIII (Oct. 1964), 436-437; by Mark Roberts in EC, XV (Jan. 1965), 118-130. Also see Nos. 47 and 236.

24. Gottfried, Leon. *Matthew Arnold and the Romantics.* See K-SJ, XIII (1964), 122-123, XIV (1965), 107.
Rev. by W. Stacy Johnson in *Western Humanities Review,* XVIII (Summer 1964), 280-281; by Donald H. Reiman in JEGP, LXIII (July 1964), 532-534; by Frederick T. Wood in ES, XLV (Aug. 1964), 343-344; by J. D. Jump in RES, N.S., XVI (Feb. 1965), 97-98; by Fraser Neiman in MP, LXII (Feb. 1965), 274-276; by J. P. Curgenven in *Victorian Studies,* VIII (June 1965), 369-370.

25. Grigson, Geoffrey, comp. *The Romantics: An Anthology of English Prose and Poetry.* Cleveland: World, 1962. "Meridian Books."
Includes selections from Byron, Haydon, Hood, Hunt, Keats, Shelley, and Mary Shelley.

26. Gros Louis, Kenneth Richard Russell. "The Myth of Orpheus and Eurydice in English Literature to 1900" [Doctoral dissertation, Wisconsin, 1964], DA, XXV (Oct. 1964), 2488.

Discusses treatment of the myth by the Romantic poets.

27. Hayward, John, ed. *The Oxford Book of Nineteenth-Century English Verse.* Oxford: Clarendon, 1964.

Includes selections from Byron, Keats, Shelley, Hunt, Peacock, Hood, Reynolds, and others.

Rev. by Raymond Mortimer in *Sunday Times,* June 21, 1964, p. 35; in TLS, June 25, 1964, p. 550; by Graham Hough in Spec, July 10, 1964, p. 53; by Aileen Ward in NYT, Aug. 16, 1964, pp. 1, 28; by Kenneth Allott in MLR, LX (Jan. 1965), 99-101; by A. Norman Jeffares in *Durham University Journal,* LVII (June 1965), 178-180.

28. Hewlett, Dorothy. "On the Romantic Movement in English Poetry," *Aryan Path,* XXXV (Nov. 1964), 498-501.

29. Hilles, Frederick W., and Harold Bloom, eds. *From Sensibility to Romanticism: Essays Presented to Frederick A. Pottle.* New York: Oxford Univ., 1965.

Includes George M. Ridenour's "Byron in 1816: Four Poems from Diodati" (pp. 453-465), E. D. Hirsch, Jr.'s "Byron and the Terrestrial Paradise" (pp. 467-486), Earl R. Wasserman's "Shelley's Last Poetics: A Reconsideration" (pp. 487-511), Harold Bloom's "Keats and the Embarrassments of Poetic Tradition" (pp. 513-526), and M. H. Abrams' "Structure and Style in the Greater Romantic Lyric" (pp. 527-560). Also includes references to Hazlitt.

30. Hodgart, Patricia, and Theodore Redpath, eds. *Romantic Perspectives: The Work of Crabbe, Blake, Wordsworth, and Coleridge as Seen by Their Contemporaries and by Themselves.* London: Harrap; *New York: Barnes & Noble (1964).

Includes selections from Keats, Hazlitt, Peacock, and Shelley.

Rev. in TLS, Aug. 27, 1964, pp. 757-758.

31. Hoffman, Daniel G., and Samuel Hynes, eds. *English Literary Criticism: Romantic and Victorian.* New York: Appleton-Century-Crofts, 1963. "Goldentree Books."

Has selections from Byron, Keats, Hazlitt, Peacock, and Shelley.

32. Hopkins, Kenneth. *English Poetry: A Short History.* Philadelphia: Lippincott, 1962.

Discusses Byron, Keats, Shelley, and their contemporaries (pp. 341-366).

33. *Hutchings, Richard John. *Landfalls of the Romantic Poets: A Book for G.C.E. Students.* Bath: Brodie, 1964.

Includes Byron, Keats, and Shelley.

34. Izzo, Carlo. *Storia della Letteratura Inglese.* 2 vols. Milan: Nuova Accademia Editrice, 1961-1963.

Vol. II includes sections on Byron, Keats, Shelley, Hunt, Hazlitt, and Peacock.

35. Jack, Ian. *English Literature 1815-1832.* See K-SJ, XIV (1965), 107.

Rev. in *Economist,* CCIX (Nov. 9, 1963), 573-574; in *Revue des langues vivantes,* XXX (1964), 404-405; by H. W. Donner in *Studia Neophilologica,* XXXVI (1964), 195-199; by Allan Rodway in *Cambridge Review,* LXXXV (March 7, 1964), 336; by M. K. Joseph in *Aumla,* No. 21 (May 1964), pp. 115-116; by Geoffrey Carnall in EC, XIV (July 1964), 310-318; by Frederick T. Wood in ES, XLV (Aug. 1964), 336; by J[ames]. A. M[ichie]. in *Aberdeen University Review,* XL (Autumn 1964), 363-364; by R. W. King in MLR, LIX (Oct. 1964), 643-645; by J. B. Beer in *Critical Quarterly,* VI (Winter 1964), 382-384; by Harold Bloom in MLQ, XXV (Dec. 1964), 479-485; by Bruce King in SR, LXXIII (Winter 1965), 125-129; by Donald H. Reiman in JEGP, LXIV (Apr. 1965), 325-332. See also No. 47.

36. James, D. G. *The Romantic Comedy: An Essay on English Romanticism.* London: Oxford Univ., 1963. "Oxford Paperbacks."

A reprint of a work first published in 1948. See No. 240.

37. *Kudo, Naotaro. "The Romantics and Nature Poetry," *English Literature* (Waseda Univ. English Literary Society, Tokyo), No. 26 (March 1965), pp. 1-15.

38. Marshall, William H., ed. *The Major English Romantics: An Anthology.* See K-SJ, XIV (1965), 108.

Rev. by R. S. Woof in N&Q, CCX (June 1965), 240.

39. Mencher, Samuel. "The Influence of Romanticism on Nineteenth-Century

British Social Work," *Social Service Review,* XXXVIII (June 1964), 174-190.

40. Piper, Herbert Walter. *The Active Universe: Pantheism and the Concept of Imagination in the English Romantic Poets.* See K-SJ, XIII (1964), 124, XIV (1965), 108.
Rev. by Roger Sharrock in RES, N.S., XVI (Feb. 1965), 84-86.

41. Ray, Gordon N. "Contemporary Collectors XXXVII: A 19th-Century Collection," BC, XIII (Spring 1964), 33-44; (Summer 1964), 171-184.
The collection includes most of the major Romantic writers.

42. Renwick, William Lindsay. *English Literature 1789-1815.* See K-SJ, XIII (1964), 124.
Rev. by R. W. King in MLR, LIX (Oct. 1964), 643-645. See also No. 47.

43. Rodway, Allan. *The Romantic Conflict.* See K-SJ, XIV (1965), 108.
Rev. by J. B. Beer in *Critical Quarterly,* VI (Winter 1964), 382-384; by R. A. Foakes in *Durham University Journal,* LVII (Dec. 1964), 54-55; by J. W. R. Purser in RES, N.S., XVI (May 1965), 214-215.

44. Roy, G. Ross. *Le sentiment de la nature dans la poésie canadienne anglaise 1867-1918.* See K-SJ, XIII (1964), 124.
Rev. by Earle Birney in CL, XVI (Spring 1964), 188-189.

45. Schubel, Friedrich. *Englische Literaturgeschichte, III: Romantik und Viktorianismus.* Berlin: De Gruyter, 1960.
Pages 9-84 cover the Romantic period.

46. Strout, Alan Lang. *A Bibliography of Articles in "Blackwood's Magazine," 1817-1825.* See K-SJ, X (1961), 75.
Rev. by H. Teyssandier in EA, XVIII (Jan.-March 1965), 86-87.

47. Super, R. H. "Recent Studies in Nineteenth-Century English Literature," SEL, IV (Autumn 1964), 663-685.
An omnibus review. See K-SJ, XIII (1964), 124, No. 67, 128, No. 149, 141, No. 364, XIV (1965), 107, Nos. 17, 21, and 25, 118, No. 208, 126, No. 355, 127, No. 366. Also see Nos. 17, 23, 35, 42, 112, 239, 313, 347, and 361.

48. Sypher, Wylie. *Loss of the Self in Modern Literature and Art.* New York: Random House, 1962.
Chapters Two and Three discuss, respectively, "The Romantic Self" and "The Romantic Touch in Painting."

49. Thorpe, Clarence D., Carlos Baker, and Bennett Weaver, eds. *The Major English Romantic Poets: A Symposium in Reappraisal.* Carbondale: Southern Illinois Univ., 1964.
A paperback reprint of a book first published in 1957. See K-SJ, VII (1958), 113.

50. *Tosswill, T. D., ed. *Seven Romantic Poets.* London: George Bell, 1964.
Includes selections from Byron, Keats, and Shelley.

51. Vitoux, Pierre. *L'Œuvre de Walter Savage Landor.* Paris: Presses Universitaires de France, 1964. (Publications de la Faculté des Lettres et Sciences Humaines de l'Université de Montpellier, XXI.)
Has discussion of Byron, Hazlitt, Keats, and Shelley. Hunt and others are touched upon.

52. Wasserman, Earl R. "The English Romantics: The Grounds of Knowledge," SIR, IV (Autumn 1964), 17-34.
Wordsworth, Coleridge, Keats, and Shelley "all face the central need to find a significant relationship between the subjective and objective worlds."

53. Wilkie, Brian. *Romantic Poets and Epic Tradition.* Madison: Univ. of Wisconsin, 1965.
Has a chapter each on Shelley, Keats, and Byron.

II. BYRON

WORKS: SELECTED, SINGLE, TRANSLATED

54. Astre, Georges-Albert. *La poésie anglaise.* Paris: Seghers, 1964.
Includes translations from the work of Byron, Keats, and Shelley.

55. **Le chevalier Harold.* [Introduction, translation, and notes by] Roger Martin. New Edition. Paris: Editions Montaigne [n.d.]. "Collection bilingue des classiques étrangers."

56. **Dnevniki. Pis'ma.* [*Journals. Letters.*] Moscow, 1963.
Rev. by *M. S., "S pylom i strast' iu boitsa" ["With the ardor and passion of a warrior"], *Znamia,* No. 5 (1964), p. 245.

57. **Don Juan.* Abridged Edition. London: Oxford Univ., in association with

British Council, 1964. "English Poets, Chaucer to Yeats Series."

58. **Don Juan*. [Translated by] E. Ábrányi, [revised by] G. Görgey, [with introduction by] G. Hegedüs. Budapest: Európa, 1964.

59. **Don-Zhuan*. [Translated by] T. Gnedich. [Introduction and commentary by] N. D'iakonova. Moscow and Leningrad: Khudozh literatura, 1964.

60. Grafe, Felix. *Dichtungen*. Ed. Joseph Strelka. Vienna: Bergland, 1961.
Includes (pp. 207-211) translations of Byron's "Darkness" and Shelley's "Ode to the West Wind."
Rev. by Herbert Lederer in *German Quarterly*, XXXVI (Nov. 1963), 477-479.

Grigson, Geoffrey, comp. See No. 25.

61. Grisenthwaite, N[ora]., comp. *Pegasus: An Anthology of Verse. Senior Two*. Huddersfield: Schofield & Sims, 1962.
Includes poems by Byron and Peacock.

62. Harding, Gilbert, comp. *A Book of Happiness*. London: Michael Joseph, 1959.
Includes selections from Byron, Hazlitt, Hood, Hunt, Keats, Peacock, and Shelley.

Hayward, John, ed. See No. 27.

63. Hilditch, Neville, comp. *In Praise of Beauty: An Anthology of Taste*. London: Frederick Muller, 1959.
Includes selections from Byron, Keats, and Shelley.

Hoffman, Daniel G., and Samuel Hynes, eds. See No. 31.

64. Hürlimann, Martin, comp. *Venedig*. Zurich: Atlantis, 1963.
Includes excerpts from *Childe Harold's Pilgrimage* and Byron's letters.

65. **Izbrannoe*. [*Selections*.] [Introduction and commentary by] Iu. Kondrat'ev. Moscow: Detskaia literatura, 1964. "Shkol'naia biblioteka."

66. *Komlós, Aladár. *Külföldi versek könyve*. [*A Book of Foreign Poems*.] Budapest: Móra kiadó, 1964.
Includes translations of poems by Byron, Moore, Keats, and Shelley.

67. Macbeth, George, ed. *The Penguin Book of Sick Verse*. [Harmondsworth:] Penguin, 1963.
Includes one selection each from Byron and Shelley and three each from Hood and Keats.

68. Maloff, Saul, ed. *The Young Readers' Treasury of British and American Verse*. New York: Avon, 1963.
Includes selections from Byron, Shelley, and Keats.

69. Maud, Ralph N., and Aneirin Talfan Davies, eds. *The Colour of Saying: An Anthology of Verse Spoken by Dylan Thomas*. London: Dent, 1963. [Published in New York (New Directions, 1963) as *Dylan Thomas's Choice*.]
Includes one poem each by Byron and Hood.

70. Meister, Robert, ed. *A Literary Guide to Seduction*. See K-SJ, XIV (1965), 109.
Now available in an English edition (London: Elek, 1964).
Rev. in TLS, July 9, 1964, p. 614.

71. Pound, Ezra, and Marcella Spann, eds. *Confucius to Cummings: An Anthology of Poetry*. New York: New Directions, 1964.
Includes selections from Byron and Keats.

72. Schneider, Isidor, ed. *The World of Love*. 2 vols. New York: Braziller, 1964.
Vol. I includes passage from *Liber Amoris* and selections from Shelley and from Byron's letters.

73. **Selected Poems of Byron*. Ed. Robin Skelton. London: Heinemann, 1964. "Poetry Bookshelf Series."

74. *Szabó, Lórinc. *Örök barátaink*. [*Eternal Friends*.] Budapest: Szépirodalmi Kiadó, 1964.
An anthology of Szabó's translations that includes poems by Byron, Keats, Shelley, and Moore.

75. Thomas, R. S., ed. *The Penguin Book of Religious Verse*. [Harmondsworth:] Penguin, 1963.
Includes passages from Byron, Keats, and Shelley.

76. "To Thomas Moore," K-SJ, XIV (1965), 88.

Tosswill, T. D., ed. See No. 50.

77. *Tóth, Árpád. *Összes müvei*. [*Works*.] [Edited by] L. Kardos. Budapest: Akadémiai Kiadó, 1964.
Vol. II (Translations) includes excerpts from *Childe Harold's Pilgrimage* and poems by Shelley and Keats.

78. **Vybranae*. [*Selected Works*.] [Trans-

lated by] Ja. Semjažon *et al.* Minsk: Gosizdat BSSR, 1963. [In Byelorussian.]

79. Wallace, Robert, and James G. Taaffe, eds. *Poems on Poetry: The Mirror's Garland.* New York: Dutton, 1965.
A paperback anthology that includes selections from Byron, Hunt, Keats, and Shelley.

80. Williams, Oscar, ed. *The Mentor Book of Major British Poets from William Blake to Dylan Thomas.* New York: New American Library, 1963.
Includes Byron, Shelley, and Keats.

Books and Articles Relating to Byron and His Circle

81. Adams, Hazard. *The Contexts of Poetry.* Boston: Little, Brown, 1963.
Contains extended discussion of poems by Byron, Keats, and Shelley.

82. Ades, John I. "Charles Lamb's Judgment of Byron and Shelley," *Papers on English Language & Literature,* I (Winter 1965), 31-38.
"Shelley's visionary views offended Lamb's common sense; and Byron's satire, in its apparent lack of human sympathy, made him uncomfortable—and angry. . . ."

83. *Anglo-German and American-German Crosscurrents.* Vol. II. Ed. Philip Allison Shelley and Arthur O. Lewis, Jr. See K-SJ, XIII (1964), 126, XIV (1965), 109.
Rev. by Harry Tucker, Jr., in MLN, LXXIX (Oct. 1964), 472-473.

84. Auden, W. H. *The Dyer's Hand and Other Essays.* See K-SJ, XIII (1964), 120, XIV (1965), 109.
Rev. by Hermann Peschmann in *English,* XIV (Autumn 1963), 240-241.

85. Balestreri, Leonida. "Sui giornali dell'emigrazione italiana in Grecia durante il periodo del risorgimento," *Rassegna Storica del Risorgimento,* XLI (1954), 258-263.
Mentions Byron's attitude towards the *Telegrafo greco* which appeared in Missolonghi in 1824.

Barnett, George L. See No. 15.

86. *Bartholomew, James Reece. "Byron's *Sardanapalus:* A Manuscript Edition." (Doctoral dissertation, Texas, 1964.)

87. Bayley, John. "Vulgarity," *British Journal of Aesthetics,* IV (Oct. 1964), 298-304.
Touches upon Keats and Byron.

88. Beebe, Maurice. *Ivory Towers and Sacred Founts: The Artist as Hero in Fiction from Goethe to Joyce.* New York: New York Univ., 1964.
Discusses Byron and Shelley. Keats and Hazlitt are touched upon.

Benítez, Rubén. See No. 1.

Bentley, G. E., Jr., and Martin K. Nurmi. See No. 2.

89. Benton, Richard P. "Is Poe's 'The Assignation' a Hoax?" *Nineteenth-Century Fiction,* XVIII (Sept. 1963), 193-197.†
Attempts to demonstrate in part that Poe's "The Assignation" was "indeed inspired by the Byron-Guiccioli romance."

90. Berveiller, Michel. *L'Eternel Don Juan.* Paris: Hachette, 1961.
Discusses Byron's *Don Juan* (pp. 151-153).

91. Beyer, Werner W. *The Enchanted Forest.* See K-SJ, XIV (1965), 110.
Also available in an English edition (Oxford: Blackwell, 1963).
Rev. by Derek Van Abbé in *Cambridge Review,* LXXXV (March 7, 1964), 341-342.

92. *Breitholtz, Lennart, ed. *Västerlandets litteraturhistoria.* Vol. II. Stockholm: Almqvist & Wiksell, 1964.
A chapter by Bernhard Tarschys, "Engelsk romantik," includes discussion of Byron, Shelley, and Keats (pp. 248-254).

93. Bundy, Murray W. "John Drinkwater and 'The Cats,'" *Research Studies,* XXXIII (June 1965), 37-55.
Discusses Drinkwater's annotations in his copy of the second edition of *Astarte* and their relation to the opening chapter of his biography of Byron, *The Pilgrim of Eternity.*

94. "Byron's Ghost Would Walk Uneasily Here," *The Times,* London, Aug. 10, 1964, p. 10.
Touches upon Byron's associations with Ouchy. See Nos. 119 and 130.

95. "Byron's Writing Desk Sold for £867," *The Times,* London, Apr. 11, 1964, p. 5.
Said to have belonged to Byron. Sold at auction sale of furnishings of the Labia Palace, Venice, at Milan, Apr. 9, 1964.

96. Campbell, N. "The Whereabouts of a Portrait," *Country Life,* CXI (May 9, 1952), 1403.

Reproduces photograph of a portrait by Lawrence of Emily Beauclerk, who knew Byron and Shelley at Pisa in 1821-22.

97. Chew, Samuel C., Jr. *The Dramas of Lord Byron: A Critical Study.* New York: Russell & Russell, 1964.

A reprint of a work first published in 1915.

98. *Ciampini, Raffaele. *Il primo amante di Teresa Guiccioli.* Florence: Barbera, 1963.

Her first lover was Cristoforo Ferri.

Rev. by C. P[ellegrini]. in *Rivista di letterature moderne e comparate,* XVII (March 1964), 79-80.

99. "Commentary," BC, XIII (Summer 1964), 143-160.

Mentions acquisition by Morgan Library of 41 letters from Coleridge to Godwin. Also reviews reprint of T. J. Wise's *Bibliography of Byron* (see No. 11).

100. Cooke, M. G.'"The Restoration Ethos of Byron's Classical Plays," PMLA, LXXIX (Dec. 1964), 569-578.†

"It is clear that what Byron derived from *All for Love* in the way of language, incidents, attitudes, characters, and themes has gotten into the innermost substance of *Sardanapalus.*" *Marino Faliero* is indebted to *Venice Preserved.*

Crawley, C. W., ed. See No. 20.

101. Delattre, Geneviève. *Les Opinions littéraires de Balzac.* Paris: Presses Universitaires de France, 1961.

Balzac's opinions of Byron and Godwin are discussed. See K-SJ, XI (1962), 115.

102. Deslandres, Yvonne. *Delacroix: A Pictorial Biography.* New York: Viking, 1963.

Alludes to Byron; reproduces paintings inspired by Byron's poetry.

103. De Sua, William J. *Dante into English: A Study of the Translation of the "Divine Comedy" in Britain and America.* University of North Carolina Studies in Comparative Literature, No. 32. Chapel Hill: Univ. of North Carolina, 1964.

Discusses Byron's translation from it.

104. *D'iakonova, N. Ia. "Iz istorii poemy Bairona *Don Zhuan* (K voprosy o razvitii romantizma v Anglii)" ["From the history of Byron's *Don Juan* (In relation to the problem of the development of romanticism in England)"] in *Voprosy tvorcheskoi istorii literaturnogo proizvedeniia* [*Problems in the Creative History of Literary Work*] (Leningrad: Leningrad un-t, 1964), pp. 112-140.

Dickens, Charles. See No. 216.

105. *Diller, Hans-Jürgen. "Aspekte der poetischen Technik Lord Byrons." (Doctoral dissertation, Munich, 1963.)

106. *Dombrovskaia, E. Ia. "Bairon—poet, chelovek, i grazhdanin (1807-1816)" ["Byron—poet, person, and citizen (1807-1816)"], *Uchenye zapiski* (Mosk. obl. ped. in-t im. N. K. Krupskoi), CXXX, Zarubezhnaia literatura, No. 8 (1963), 93-152.

107. Drew, Elizabeth. *The Literature of Gossip: Nine English Letterwriters.* New York: Norton, 1964.

Byron is one of the nine.

Rev. by W. K. Rose in *American Scholar,* XXXIV (Spring 1965), 300, 302-303.

108. *Dubashinskii, I. "Avtobiograficheskii roman Bairona" ["Byron's Autobiographical Novel"], *Voprosy literatury,* No. 8 (1964), pp. 237-239.

109. Dyer, Marie. [In] "Readers' Forum," *English Studies in Africa,* VIII (March 1965), 90-97.

Responds to A. C. Partridge [see K-SJ, XIV (1965), 114]: questions whether *Beppo* represents an acceptance by Byron of Italian life and manners.

110. Eaton, Vincent L. "The American Academy of Arts and Letters Collection," *Library of Congress Quarterly Journal of Current Acquisitions,* X (Aug. 1953), 190-193.

Describes the manuscript collection deposited in the Library of Congress that includes letters or manuscripts of Byron, Hunt, Keats, and Shelley. See Nos. 131 and 259.

111. *Ehrstine, John W. "An Analysis of Byron's Plays." (Doctoral dissertation, Wayne State, 1964.)

112. Elwin, Malcolm. *Lord Byron's Wife.* See K-SJ, XIII (1964), 128, XIV (1965), 111.

Rev. by M. Bellasis in *Tablet,* CCXVI (Dec. 8, 1962), 1194; in *Economist,* CCV (Dec. 22, 1962), 1196-1197; by Richard Church in *Country Life,* CXXXIII (Jan. 3, 1963), 36-37; by Keith Walker in *Cambridge Review,* LXXXIV (Feb. 9, 1963), 263; by Norman Podhoretz in *Show,* III (July 1963), 38, 40. See also No. 47.

113. Emerson, Ralph Waldo. *The Journals and Miscellaneous Notebooks of Ralph Waldo Emerson.* Ed. William H. Gilman *et al.* Vols. III, IV, and V. Cambridge, Mass.: Harvard Univ., 1963-1965.

Includes references to Byron and, in Vol. V, to Keats and Shelley. See K-SJ, XI (1962), 115, XII (1963), 128.

114. Escholier, Raymond. *Eugène Delacroix.* Paris: Editions Cercle d'Art, 1963.

Reproduces and discusses pictures based on subjects from Byron's poetry.

115. Feinberg, Leonard. *The Satirist: His Temperament, Motivation, and Influence.* Ames: Iowa State Univ., 1963.

Gives some attention to Byron.

116. Fiess, Edward. "Byron and Byronism in the Mind and Art of Herman Melville" [Doctoral dissertation, Yale, 1951], DA, XXV (Jan. 1965), 4145. See K-SJ, I (1952), 91, II (1953), 101.

117. Frye, Northrop. *Fables of Identity: Studies in Poetic Mythology.* See K-SJ, XIV (1965), 111.

Rev. by William Blissett in *University of Toronto Quarterly,* XXXIII (July 1964), 401-408; by Robin Skelton in *Canadian Literature,* No. 24 (Spring 1965), pp. 63-66.

118. Fuess, Claude M. *Lord Byron as a Satirist in Verse.* New York: Russell & Russell, 1964.

A reprint of a work first published in 1912.

119. Galway, G. Leslie. "Byron at Ouchy," *The Times,* London, Aug. 17, 1964, p. 9.

Says "The Prisoner of Chillon" is "one of the most moving poems ever written." See Nos. 94 and 130.

120. Gauthier, Maximilien. *Delacroix.* Paris: Larousse, 1963.

Reproduces paintings based on subjects from Byron's poetry.

121. Ghosh, R. N. "The Colonization Controversy: R. J. Wilmot-Horton and the Classical Economists," *Economica,* XXXI (Nov. 1964), 385-400.

Outlines Horton's role in the struggle with E. G. Wakefield.

122. Gray, Denis. *Spencer Perceval, 1762-1812: The Evangelical Prime Minister.* Manchester: Manchester Univ., 1963.

Prints excerpts from the letters to Perceval of Mrs. Catherine Byron.

Green, David Bonnell, and Edwin Graves Wilson, eds. See No. 5.

123. "Halnaby Hall," *Country Life,* CXI (May 23, 1952), 1582.

The hall where Byron and his wife spent their honeymoon is threatened with demolition. A photograph of the north front is reproduced.

124. Hardy, S. M. "Wilmot-Horton's Government of Ceylon, 1831-1837," *University of Birmingham Historical Journal,* VII (1960), 181-199.

Describes his policies and activities as governor.

125. Hassall, Christopher, arranger. *Ambrosia and Small Beer: The Record of a Correspondence between Edward Marsh and Christopher Hassall.* London: Longmans, 1964.

Includes passing comments on Byron, Haydon, Keats, Peacock, and Shelley.

126. Hassler, Donald M. "*Marino Faliero,* the Byronic Hero, and *Don Juan,*" K-SJ, XIV (1965), 55-64.

"Cantos Ten through Sixteen of *Don Juan* are the most bitterly satiric, and they were all written before *Marino Faliero.* The expression of the ideas in the play . . . helped Byron to write the later satire. For his disgust with hypocrisy and his belief in the reality of the heroic posture and the timelessness of ideals became part of the positive position for his later satire."

127. *Hegedüs, Géza. *Byron.* Budapest: Gondolat, 1961.

Hilles, Frederick W., and Harold Bloom, eds. See No. 29.

128. Hocke, Gustav René. *Das europäische Tagebuch.* Wiesbaden: Limes, 1964.

Includes discussion of Byron and Haydon.

Rev. in TLS, May 14, 1964, pp. 405-406.

Hopkins, Kenneth. See No. 32.

129. Horn, András. *Byron's "Don Juan" and the Eighteenth-Century English Novel.* See K-SJ, XII (1963), 128, XIV (1965), 112.
Rev. by Kaspar Spinner in ES, XLV (Aug. 1964), 326-327.

130. Hudson, Derek. "Byron at Ouchy," *The Times*, London, Aug. 14, 1964, p. 9.
Says "The Prisoner of Chillon" "is not at all a good poem." See Nos. 94 and 119.

Hutchings, Richard John. See No. 33.

131. "In the Sale Rooms," *The Times*, London, Nov. 13, 1963, p. 6.
At the sale of the Archer M. Huntington Collection, the property of the American Academy of Arts and Letters, at Sotheby's, Nov. 12, 1963, an autograph fragment of *Otho the Great* brought £450, a letter from Shelley (1812) £290, and a letter from Byron £190. See Nos. 110 and 259.

Izzo, Carlo. See No. 34.

132. Johnson, Lee. *Delacroix.* London: Weidenfeld and Nicolson, 1963.
Reproduces and discusses pictures based on subjects from Byron's poetry.

133. Joseph, Michael Kennedy. *Byron the Poet.* See K-SJ, XIV (1965), 112.
Rev. by William Kean Seymour in CR, CCV (July 1964), 389-390; by Gilbert Thomas in *English*, XV (Autumn 1964), 109; by Ian Jack in *Landfall*, XIX (March 1965), 89-91; by Andrew Rutherford in MLR, LX (Apr. 1965), 260-261.

134. Kahn, Arthur David. "The Horatian and Juvenalian Traditions of Verse Satire in Byron's *Don Juan*" [Doctoral dissertation, New York, 1963], DA, XXV (July 1964), 451.

135. *Klimenko, E. I. "Liriko-epicheskaia poema Bairona (Osnovy zhanra)" ["Lyric-epic poems of Byron (Fundamentals of genre)"], in *Sbornik statei k 70-letiiu V. M. Zhirmunskogo [Problems of Comparative Philology, Studies in Honor of the 70th Birthday of V. M. Zhirmunskii]* (Moscow and Leningrad: Akad. nauk SSSR Otd-nie literatury i iazyka, 1964), pp. 393-400.

136. Knight, G. Wilson. *The Golden Labyrinth: A Study of British Drama.* See K-SJ, XII (1963), 129, XIII (1964), 130.
Rev. by A. J. Farmer in *Erasmus*, XV (1963), 614-616; by Bruce King in *Drama Survey*, III (Fall 1963), 315-316; by R. J. Kaufmann in *Educational Theatre Journal*, XV (Dec. 1963), 366-373.

137. Knight, G. Wilson. "Lord Byron," NSN, XLIV (Dec. 20, 1952), 757.
Replies to Helen Gardner's review of *Lord Byron: Christian Virtues.* See K-SJ, III (1954), 116.

138. Lacretelle, Jacques de. "La Galerie des amants II: de Keats à d'Annunzio," *Revue de Deux Mondes*, Aug. 15, 1963, pp. 492-506.
Byron and Keats are among the lovers discussed.

139. *Lehtonen, Maija. *L'expression imagée dans l'œuvre de Chateaubriand.* "Mémoires de la Société neophilologique de Helsinki," No. 26. Helsinki, 1964.
Discusses—at some length and with a number of quotations—Byron's influence on Chateaubriand.

140. Leslie, Doris. *This for Caroline.* See K-SJ, XIV (1965), 112-113.
Rev. by Anne Britton in *Books and Bookmen*, IX (March 1964), 28.

141. Letzring, Madonna Marie. "The Influence of Camoens in English Literature" [Doctoral dissertation, Maryland, 1962], DA, XXV (Sept. 1964), 1915-1916.
Notes interest of Byron and other Romantics in Camoens.

142. Levitt, John, and Joan Levitt. *The Spell of Words.* London: Darwen Finlayson, 1959.
Gives origins of surnames of some English poets, including Byron, Hunt, Keats, and Shelley (p. 91).

143. Lovell, Ernest J., Jr. *Byron, the Record of a Quest: Studies in a Poet's Concept and Treatment of Nature.* See K-SJ, I (1952), 90, II (1953), 101, XIV (1965), 113.
Rev. by Willis W. Pratt in *Library Chronicle of the University of Texas*, IV (Fall 1950), 48-50.

144. Lovell, Ernest J., Jr. "Byron, Mary Shelley, and Madame de Staël," K-SJ, XIV (1965), 13.
Material on Byron in Mary Shelley's article on Madame de Staël in the Cabinet Cyclopaedia is based entirely on printed sources.

145. Lovell, Ernest J., Jr. *Captain Medwin: Friend of Byron and Shelley.* See K-SJ, XIII (1964), 131, XIV (1965), 113.

Rev. by Frederick T. Wood in ES, XLV (Aug. 1964), 341.

146. Luke, Hugh J., Jr. "The Publishing of Byron's *Don Juan*," PMLA, LXXX (June 1965), 199-209.

The hostile reception of *Don Juan* was "undoubtedly owing to the piratical editions . . . by the London radicals" with whom as politically dangerous Byron came to be grouped by the Tories.

147. Marshall, William H. *The Structure of Byron's Major Poems.* See K-SJ, XIII (1964), 131, XIV (1965), 113.

Rev. by Ralph Lawrence in *English,* XIV (Autumn 1963), 247; by Andrew Rutherford in RES, N.S., XVI (Feb. 1965), 89-90.

148. Mason, Eudo C. *Deutsche und englische Romantik: Eine Gegenüberstellung.* See K-SJ, X (1961), 79, XI (1962), 118, XII (1963), 130.

Rev. by Roland Hoermann in CL, XVI (Fall 1964), 361-362.

149. Mattheisen, Paul F. "Gosse's Candid 'Snapshots,'" *Victorian Studies,* VIII (June 1965), 329-354.

Prints selections from Gosse's unpublished sketches and notes that include references to Byron, Keats, Fanny Brawne, Hazlitt, Mary Shelley, and others.

150. Maurois, André. *Byron.* New York: Frederick Ungar, 1964.

A reprint of a book first published in English in 1930.

151. May, Frederick. "Callirroe e Ifianco (Work in Progress on the 'English' Period of Ugo Foscolo)," *Italica,* XLI (March 1964), 63-73.

152. Mayfield, John S. "To Whom Was It Written? Note on a Byron Letter," *Manuscripts,* XVII (Winter 1965), 3-4.

Prints a Byron letter of May 20, 1812.

153. *Mellon, John Paul. "Byron's *Manfred* and the Critics: A Review of Sources and Ideas." (Doctoral dissertation, Pittsburgh, 1964.)

154. *Mickiewicz, Adam. "Goethe und Byron," *Mickiewicz-Blätter für das Mickiewicz-Gremium der Deutschen Bundesrepublik* (Heidelberg), VIII (1959), 75-81.

155. Montoro, Antonio. *El romanticismo literario europeo (60 nombres·biografia·antologia·critica).* Madrid: Biblioteca Nueva, 1959.

Includes sketches of Byron, Shelley, and Keats.

156. Moore, L. Hugh, Jr. "*The Sunny South* and Its Literature," *Georgia Review,* XIX (Summer 1965), 176-185.

Mentions attitude of this nineteenth-century Atlanta magazine toward Byron and Shelley.

157. Moore, Thomas. *The Journal of Thomas Moore 1818-1841.* Ed. Peter Quennell. New York: Macmillan; *London: Batsford (1964).

Rev. by Geoffrey Grigson in *Country Life,* CXXXV (Apr. 16, 1964), 945; by Ellen Moers in *New York Review of Books,* III (Jan. 14, 1965), 16-18.

158. Moore, Thomas. *The Letters of Thomas Moore.* Ed. Wilfred S. Dowden. 2 vols. Oxford: Clarendon, 1964.

Includes letters to Byron, Leigh Hunt, John Cam Hobhouse, John Hunt, Mary Shelley, Haydon, and others; references to Godwin, Countess Guiccioli, Horace Smith, and others.

Rev. by Raymond Mortimer in *Sunday Times,* Feb. 14, 1965, p. 47; by Joanna Richardson in Li, LXXIII (Feb. 25, 1965), 306, 309; in TLS, Feb. 25, 1965, p. 146; by Peter Quennell in Spec, March 5, 1965, p. 304; by Christopher Ricks in NS, LXIX (March 5, 1965), 363; by Naomi Lewis in *Observer,* March 14, 1965, p. 27.

159. Mortenson, Robert Lawrence. "Lord Byron's *Cain, A Mystery:* A Variorum Edition" [Doctoral dissertation, Pennsylvania, 1964], DA, XXV (Sept. 1964), 1894-1895.

160. Moseley, Maboth. *Irascible Genius: A Life of Charles Babbage, Inventor.* London: Hutchinson, 1964.

Includes frequent discussion of Byron's daughter, Augusta Ada, Countess of Lovelace.

Rev. by W. H. Chaloner in *Manchester Guardian Weekly,* XCI (July 2, 1964), 11; in TLS, Aug. 13, 1964, p. 722.

161. Mynors, R. A. B., comp. *Catalogue of the Manuscripts of Balliol College Oxford.* Oxford: Clarendon, 1963.

Lists manuscripts of Byron and Shelley.

162. Nemerov, Howard. *Poetry and Fic-*

tion: Essays. New Brunswick: Rutgers Univ., 1963.

Includes (pp. 34-41) "Poetry and Life: Lord Byron," reprinted from *Hudson Review.* See K-SJ, IV (1955), 114, No. 75, 115-116, No. 104.

163. Nowell-Smith, Simon. "Contemporary Collectors XLI: The Ewelme Collection," BC, XIV (Summer 1965), 185-193.

In the collection are Byron, Hunt, Keats, and Shelley items.

164. O'Daniel, Therman B. "Emerson as a Literary Critic," *CLA Journal,* VIII (Sept. 1964), 21-43; (Dec. 1964), 157-189; (March 1965), 246-276.

Notes briefly his attitude toward Hunt, Shelley, and Byron.

165. Oldham, Ellen M. "Lord Byron and Mr Coolidge of Boston," BC, XIII (Summer 1964), 211-213.†

Discusses Joseph Coolidge's interview with Byron and the copy of *Marino Faliero* which the poet gave him.

166. Ostrowski, Witold. "Juliusz Słowacki i Walter Scott," *Żesyty Naukowe Uniwersytetu Łódzkiego, Nauki Humanistyczno-Społeczne,* Series I, No. 36 (1964), pp. 131-142. [English summary.]

Byron is also discussed.

167. Ostrowski, Witold. "Walter Scott in Poland, Part I: Warsaw and Vilno," *Studies in Scottish Literature,* II (Oct. 1964), 87-95.

Also touches upon Byron's reputation in Poland.

168. Ostrowski, Witold. "Walter Scott w Polsce 1816-1830," *Zesyty Naukowe Uniwersytetu Łódzkiego, Nauki Humanistyczno-Społeczne,* Series I, No. 29 (1963), pp. 115-132. [English summary.]

Includes discussion of Byron and Poland.

169. Paolucci, Anne. "Dante's Satan and Milton's 'Byronic Hero,'" *Italica,* XLI (June 1964), 139-149.

An understanding of Milton's Satan heightens one's insight into Dante's representation of the Devil.

170. Parks, Edd Winfield. *Edgar Allan Poe as Literary Critic.* Athens: Georgia Univ., 1964.

Includes comments on Poe and Byron, Keats, and Shelley.

171. Pearsall, Ronald. "A Letter from Byron," *Books and Bookmen,* X (March 1965), 46.

About the discovery of a Byron letter that turned out to be one of many replicas of a probably destroyed original.

172. Peters, Robert L. *Swinburne's Principles of Literature and Art: The Crowns of Apollo. A Study in Victorian Criticism and Aesthetics.* Detroit: Wayne State Univ., 1965.

Includes discussion of Byron, Keats, Shelley, and Hazlitt.

173. Pinto, V. de S. "To Lord Byron: On Editing His Poems, 1963," *English,* XV (Summer 1964), 57.

A poem.

174. Pohle, Almut. *Das Gedicht "Quaïn" von Leconte de Lisle: Eine literarhistorische Interpretation.* Hamburger Romanistisches Studien, Series A, Vol. XLVII. Hamburg: Cram, De Gruyter, 1964.

Includes discussion of *Cain.*

Rev. by Rainer Hess in *Romanische Forschungen,* LXXVI (1964), 474-476.

175. Pósa, Péter. "Burns és az angol romantika költészetének néhány kérdése," *Acta Universitatis Szegediensis,* Sectio Litteraria, IV, No. 2 (1959), 55-73.

Includes discussion of Byron, Keats, and Shelley.

176. Pritchard, John Paul. *Literary Wise Men of Gotham: Criticism in New York, 1815-1860.* [Baton Rouge:] Louisiana State Univ., 1963.

Refers briefly to Byron, Hazlitt, Keats, and Shelley.

177. Pushkin, Alexander. *The Letters of Alexander Pushkin.* Trans. J. Thomas Shaw. 3 vols. Bloomington: Indiana Univ.; Philadelphia: Univ. of Pennsylvania (1963).

Contains numerous references to Byron.

Rev. by Ernest J. Simmons in SatR, XLVII (May 30, 1964), 34-35.

178. *Read, Sir Herbert. *Lord Byron at the Opera: A Play for Broadcasting.* North Harrow: Philip Ward, 1963. "Herbert Read Series No. 2."

179. Ridenour, George M. "The Mode of Byron's *Don Juan,*" PMLA, LXXIX (Sept. 1964), 442-446.†

The poem is essentially comic rather than ironic or satiric.

180. Rieger, James. "Lord Byron as 'Albè,'" K-SJ, XIV (1965), 6-7.
The soubriquet comes from the title of Sophie Cottin's novel, *Claire d'Albe.*

181. Ritz, Jean-Georges. *Le Poète Gérard Manley Hopkins, S.J., 1844-1889: L'Homme et l'œuvre.* Paris: Didier, 1964.
Discusses influence of Byron, Keats, and Shelley on Hopkins' poetry.

182. *Roemer-Hoffmann, H. E. "Seine Lordschaft, der allerromantischste Patient: George Byron und seine Ärzte," *Ärztliche Mitteilungen* (Cologne), LX (1963), 500-506.

183. Roppen, Georg, and Richard Sommer. *Strangers and Pilgrims: An Essay on the Metaphor of Journey.* Norwegian Studies in English No. 11. New York: Humanities Press; Oslo: Norwegian Universities Press (1964).
Includes chapter on "Byron's Pilgrimage" (pp. 209-283).

184. Rowland, Benjamin, Jr. *The Classical Tradition in Western Art.* Cambridge, Mass.: Harvard Univ., 1963.
Has allusions to Byron, Haydon, Keats, and Shelley.

185. Saunders, J. W. *The Profession of English Letters.* London: Routledge; Toronto: Toronto Univ. (1964).
Includes discussion of Byron, Keats, and Shelley; Godwin, Hazlitt, Hunt, Peacock, and others are referred to.

186. Sinclair, Alexander R. "English Poetry in Hungarian Translation: The Hungarian Language as a Translating Instrument—an English Viewpoint," *New Hungarian Quarterly,* VI (Summer 1965), 47-53.
Discusses Hungarian translations of Byron, Keats, and Shelley.

187. Stamm, Rudolf. *Zwischen Vision und Wirklichkeit: Zehn Essays über Shakespeare, Lord Byron, Bernard Shaw, William Butler Yeats, Thomas Stearns Eliot, Eugene O'Neill und Christopher Fry.* Berne and Munich: Francke, 1964.
Includes "Lord Byron's *Cain:* Mysterium der Versuchung" (pp. 85-98).
Rev. by W. J. M. Bronzwaer in *Neophilologus,* XLIX (Apr. 1965), 193-194.

188. Stendhal, *pseud.* [Henri Beyle.] *Correspondance I: 1800-1821.* Ed. Henri Martineau and V. del Litto. Paris: Gallimard, 1962.
Refers to Byron, Godwin, Hazlitt, and Mary Wollstonecraft.

189. Stevens, Harold Ray. "Byron and the Bible: A Study of Poetic and Philosophic Development" [Doctoral dissertation, Pennsylvania, 1964], DA, XXV (March 1965), 5286-5287.

190. Swinburne, Algernon Charles. *New Writings by Swinburne, or Miscellanea Nova et Curiosa, Being a Medley of Poems, Critical Essays, Hoaxes and Burlesques.* Ed. Cecil Y. Lang. Syracuse: Syracuse Univ., 1964.
Includes comments on Byron, Keats, and Shelley.

191. Thompson, James Roy. "Studies in the Drama of Lord Byron" [Doctoral dissertation, Cincinnati, 1964], DA, XXV (Jan. 1965), 4130-4131.

192. Thorslev, Peter L., Jr. *The Byronic Hero: Types and Prototypes.* See K-SJ, XII (1963), 133, XIII (1964), 133, XIV (1965), 115.
Rev. by James D. Merritt in BA, XXXVII (Summer 1963), 336; by Wolfgang Bernard Fleischmann in *Comparative Literature Studies,* I (1964), 73-75; by Andrew Rutherford in JEGP, LXIII (Oct. 1964), 814-817.

193. Thorslev, Peter L., Jr. "Incest as Romantic Symbol," *Comparative Literature Studies,* II (1965), 41-58.
Centers on Byron and Shelley.

194. Trousson, Raymond. *Le thème de Prométhée dans la littérature européenne.* 2 vols. Geneva: Droz, 1964.
Byron, Shelley, and Mary Shelley are among those discussed.
Rev. by J. Seznec in *French Studies,* XIX (Jan. 1965), 51-53.

195. Verey, David. "Busts of Byron," *Country Life,* CXV (Jan. 14, 1954), 102.
Reproduces a "plaster copy of a bust of Byron by Lawrence Gahagan."

Vitoux, Pierre. See No. 51.

196. Voisine, Jacques-René. *J.-J. Rousseau en Angleterre à l'époque romantique: Les écrits autobiographiques et la légende.* See K-SJ, VI (1957), 138, VII (1958), 120, VIII (1959), 64, IX (1960), 59, X (1961), 82, XII (1963), 133.
Rev. by P. I. Maguire in *Erasmus,* XVI (1964), 396-398.

197. Wagenknecht, Edward. *Harriet Beecher Stowe: The Known and the Unknown.* New York: Oxford Univ., 1965.

Discusses Mrs. Stowe's relationship with Lady Byron.

198. Wain, John. *Essays on Literature and Ideas*. See K-SJ, XIV (1965), 116.
Rev. by R. G. Cox in *Critical Quarterly*, VI (Summer 1964), 183-184.

199. Walton, Francis R. "Portrait of a Bibliophile XII: Joannes Gennadius, 1844-1932," BC, XIII (Autumn 1964), 305-326.
Discusses his "significant collection of Byroniana."

200. Warner, Oliver. *English Literature: A Portrait Gallery*. London: Chatto, 1964.
Includes portraits of Byron, Keats, Peacock, and Shelley.

201. Wellek, René. *Confrontations: Studies in the Intellectual and Literary Relations between Germany, England, and the United States during the Nineteenth Century*. Princeton: Princeton Univ., 1965.
Includes "German and English Romanticism: A Confrontation" (pp. 3-33). See No. 202.

202. Wellek, René. "German and English Romanticism: A Confrontation," SIR, IV (Autumn 1964), 35-56.
Byron, Keats, and Shelley are among those discussed. See No. 201.

203. *Wells, Nannie Katharin. *Byron Comments on the 20th Century*. Old Castle, Slains, Collieston (Aberdeenshire): Michael Slains, 1962.

204. *Wells, Nannie Katharin. *George Gordon, Lord Byron: A Scottish Genius*. Old Castle, Slains, Collieston (Aberdeenshire): Michael Slains, 1962.
A reprint of a book first published in 1960. See K-SJ, XI (1962), 121.

205. West, Paul, ed. *Byron: A Collection of Critical Essays*. See K-SJ, XIV (1965), 116.
Rev. by Ernest J. Lovell, Jr., in K-SJ, XIV (1965), 89-91; by Carl H. Ketcham in *Arizona Quarterly*, XXI (Spring 1965), 89-90.

206. Whipple, A[ddison]. B[eecher]. C[olvin]. *The Fatal Gift of Beauty: The Final Years of Byron and Shelley*. New York: Harper & Row, 1964.
Rev. by Doris Langley Moore in NYT, Nov. 29, 1964, pp. 36, 38; by G. M. Matthews in *New York Review of Books*, III (Dec. 3, 1964), 28.

Wilkie, Brian. See No. 53.

Wise, Thomas James. See No. 11.

207. Woodring, Carl. "Lord Byron's Widow, 1825," *Columbia Library Columns*, XIV (May 1965), 11-20.
Publishes and discusses a letter sent by Lady Byron to Mrs. Augusta Leigh on June 4, 1825, which bears upon the burning of Byron's memoirs.

208. Worth, George. *James Hannay: His Life and Works*. University of Kansas Publications, Humanistic Studies, No. 37. Lawrence: Kansas Univ., 1964.
Touches on Hannay's estimates of Hunt and Byron.

209. *Yakushigawa, Koichi. "The Loneliness of Byron," *Studies in Foreign Literature* (Ritsumeikan Univ., Kyoto), No. 9 (Dec. 1964), pp. 23-41.

210. Żuławski, Juliusz. *Byron Nieupozowany*. [Warsaw:] Państwowy Instytut Wydawniczy, 1964.

III. HUNT

Works: Selected, Single

211. Cole, William, comp. *The Birds and the Beasts Were There: Animal Poems*. Cleveland: World, 1963.
Includes one poem by Hunt and three by Keats.

Creeger, George R., and Joseph W. Reed, Jr., eds. See No. 21.

Grigson, Geoffrey, comp. See No. 25.

212. Grisenthwaite, N[ora]., comp. *Pegasus: An Anthology of Verse. Senior One*. Huddersfield: Schofield & Sims, 1962.
Includes poems by Hood, Hunt, and Shelley.

Harding, Gilbert, comp. See No. 62.

Hayward, John, ed. See No. 27.

213. *Leigh Hunt: Musical Evenings*. Ed. David R. Cheney. Columbia: Missouri Univ., 1964.

214. *Leigh Hunt's Political and Occasional Essays*. Ed. Lawrence Huston Houtchens and Carolyn Washburn Houtchens. See K-SJ, XIII (1964), 134, XIV (1965), 116.
Rev. by Frederick T. Wood in ES, XLV (June 1964), 264; by G. D. Stout in MP, LXII (Nov. 1964), 172-174.

Wallace, Robert, and James G. Taaffe, eds. See No. 79.

Books and Articles Relating to Hunt

Barnett, George L. See No. 15.

Bentley, G. E., Jr., and Martin K. Nurmi. See No. 2.

215. Brewer, Luther A. "Leigh Hunt Association Books," *Books at Iowa,* No. 1 (Oct. 1964), pp. 4-10.
In an excerpt from his unpublished "Huntiana and Association Books" describes and quotes from books owned, marked, and annotated by Hunt.

Crawley, C. W., ed. See No. 20.

216. Dickens, Charles. *The Letters of Charles Dickens. Volume One: 1820-1839.* Ed. Madeline House and Graham Storey. Oxford: Clarendon, 1965.
Prints a letter from Hunt to Dickens and two from Dickens to Hunt; includes references to Dilke, Medwin, and Reynolds.

Duerksen, Roland A. See No. 392.

Eaton, Vincent L. See No. 110.

217. Fogle, Stephen F. "Leigh Hunt, Thomas Powell, and the *Florentine Tales,*" K-SJ, XIV (1965), 79-87.
"The evidence, internal and circumstantial, suggests that Hunt is the most likely author" of *Florentine Tales,* a work often attributed to Thomas Powell.

Green, David Bonnell, and Edwin Graves Wilson, eds. See No. 5.

Hayter, Alethea. See No. 288.

218. Holme, Thea. *The Carlyles at Home.* London: Oxford Univ., 1965.
Includes references to Hunt and his wife.
Rev. by V. S. Pritchett in NS, LXIX (May 28, 1965), 843.

219. "Index Benefactorum," *Colby Library Quarterly,* VI (Dec. 1963), 369-370.
Records acquisition for library of copy of essays of Lamb, Hazlitt, and Hunt inscribed by Edwin Arlington Robinson.

Izzo, Carlo. See No. 34.

Levitt, John, and Joan Levitt. See No. 142.

Moore, Thomas. See No. 158.

Nowell-Smith, Simon. See No. 163.

O'Daniel, Therman B. See No. 164.

Palacio, Jean de. See No. 435.

220. Pasmore, H. Stephen. "The Story of a London Square," *Country Life,* CXVI (Dec. 23, 1954), 2252-2254.
Edwardes-Square, where Hunt lived from 1840 to 1851. A picture of his house is included.

221. San Juan, E., Jr. "Material Versus Totality of Literary Devices: A Formalist-Contrastive Analysis of Two Poems," *Discourse,* VII (Summer 1964), 295-302.†
The poems are those by Keats and Hunt on the grasshopper and the cricket.

Saunders, J. W. See No. 185.

222. Turner, E[rnest]. S[ackville]. *What the Butler Saw: Two Hundred and Fifty Years of the Servant Problem.* New York: St Martin's, 1963.
Summarizes (pp. 101-103) Hunt's picture of a "cheerful maidservant in one of the new town houses."

Vitoux, Pierre. See No. 51.

Worth, George. See No. 208.

IV. KEATS

Works: Selected, Single, Translated

Astre, Georges-Albert. See No. 54.

223. Blishen, Edward, comp. *Oxford Book of Poetry for Children.* New York: Franklin Watts, 1963.
Includes selections by Hood, Keats, and Shelley.

Cole, William, comp. See No. 211.

224. Eastman, A. M., and G. B. Harrison, eds. *Shakespeare's Critics. From Jonson to Auden: A Medley of Judgments.* Ann Arbor: Univ. of Michigan, 1964.
Includes passages from Hazlitt, Keats, and Mary Cowden Clarke.

225. Fremantle, Anne, ed. *The Protestant Mystics.* Boston: Little, Brown; *London: Weidenfeld and Nicolson (1964).
Has a selection from Keats.

Grigson, Geoffrey, comp. See No. 25.

Harding, Gilbert, comp. See No. 62.

Hayward, John, ed. See No. 27.

Hilditch, Neville, comp. See No. 63.

Hodgart, Patricia, and Theodore Redpath, eds. See No. 30.

Hoffman, Daniel G., and Samuel Hynes, eds. See No. 31.

226. **Isabella o il vaso di basilico.* [Translated by] Pasquale Maffeo. Milan: Ceschina, 1963. [In Italian.]
Includes a critical essay.

Komlós, Aladár. See No. 66.

227. *Letters of John Keats.* Selected by Frederick Page. See K-SJ, V (1956), 127.
Rev. by Howard Spring in *Country Life,* CXVI (Sept. 16, 1954), 921-922.

Macbeth, George, ed. See No. 67.

Maloff, Saul, ed. See No. 68.

228. *The Naughty Boy*. New York: Viking, 1965.
An edition of "There was a naughty Boy" for children, with illustrations by Ezra Jack Keats.

229. "Ode on a Grecian Urn," *Greek Heritage,* I, No. 3 (1964), pp. 64-65.

230. "On First Looking into Chapman's Homer," K-SJ, XIV (1965), 14.

231. *Poems. [Translated by] Ryo Okachi. Tokyo: Bunshudo, 1965. [In Japanese.]

232. *Poems of John Keats.* Comp. Stanley Kunitz. New York: Crowell, 1964.
Rev. by Walker Gibson in NYT, Nov. 1, 1964, Part II, p. 57; by Alice Dalgliesh in SatR, XLVII (Nov. 7, 1964), p. 56; by R. H. V. in *Horn Book,* XL (Dec. 1964), 629; by K. M. Harris in *Library Journal,* XC (Feb. 15, 1965), 966.

Pound, Ezra, and Marcella Spann, eds. See No. 71.

233. **Selected Poems.* Ed. Augusto Guidi. Milan: U. Mursia-A. P. E. Corticelli, 1962.

Szabó, Lórinc. See No. 74.

Thomas, R. S., ed. See No. 75.

Tosswill, T. D., ed. See No. 50.

Tóth, Árpád. See No. 77.

Wallace, Robert, and James G. Taaffe, eds. See No. 79.

Williams, Oscar, ed. See No. 80.

Books and Articles Relating to Keats and His Circle

Adams, Hazard. See No. 81.

234. *Arrieta, Rafael Alberto. "Dos sonetos ingleses sobre el soneto," *La Prensa* (Buenos Aires), Apr. 18, 1965.
On "Scorn not the sonnet" by Wordsworth and "If by dull rhymes" by Keats.

235. Baker, Herschel. *William Hazlitt.* See K-SJ, XII (1963), 136, XIII (1964), 136-137, XIV (1965), 118.
Rev. by A. Owen Aldridge in *Modern Language Journal,* XLVI (Nov. 1962), 330; by John W. Bilsland in *Dalhousie Review,* XLIV (Autumn 1964), 355-359.

236. Baker, J. "Poets of Their Time," TLS, Sept. 10, 1964, p. 845.
Suggests a source for "To Autumn" in the Book of Ruth. See No. 23.

237. Baldwin, Dane Lewis, *et al.,* eds. *A Concordance to the Poems of John Keats.* Gloucester, Mass.: Peter Smith, 1963.
A reprint of a work first published in 1917.

238. Balslev, Thora. *Keats and Wordsworth: A Comparative Study.* See K-SJ, XIII (1964), 137.
Rev. by Mary Lynn Johnson Woolley in JEGP, LXIII (July 1964), 527-528.

Barnett, George L. See No. 15.

239. Bate, Walter Jackson. *John Keats.* See K-SJ, XIV (1965), 118.
Rev. in *Time,* LXXXII (Oct. 25, 1963), 106, 109; by Thomas Lask in *New York Times,* Jan. 13, 1964, p. 33; in *The Times,* London, Feb. 6, 1964, p. 15; in *Economist,* CCX (Feb. 8, 1964), 518; by M. L. Rosenthal in *Reporter,* XXX (Feb. 13, 1964), 52-54; by Richard Whittington-Egan in *Books and Bookmen,* IX (March 1964), 19; by William Heath in *Massachusetts Review,* V (Summer 1964), 784-788; by Gilbert Thomas in *English,* XV (Summer 1964), 64; by Ian Gregor in *Month,* CCXVIII (July-Aug. 1964), 83-85; by Dorothy Hewlett in *Aryan Path,* XXXV (Aug. 1964), 368-369; by Carl H. Ketcham in *Arizona Quarterly,* XX (Autumn 1964), 269-271; by Garry Wills in *Modern Age,* VIII (Fall 1964), 430-432; by Miriam Allott in MLR, LIX (Oct. 1964), 646-647; by Barbara Hardy in *British Journal of Aesthetics,* IV (Oct. 1964), 379-380; by Jack Stillinger in JEGP, LXIII (Oct. 1964), 811-813; by Malcolm R. Ware in *Cithara,* IV (Nov. 1964), 72-74; by Harold Bloom in MLQ, XXV (Dec. 1964), 479-485; by A. E. Rodway in RES, N.S., XVI (Feb. 1965), 90-92; by E[dith]. C[opeland]. in BA, XXXIX (Spring 1965), 227; by Bonamy Dobrée in *Critical Quarterly,* VII (Spring 1965), 94-96; by Edward E. Bostetter in MP, LXII (May 1965), 363-366. See also Nos. 47 and 241.

240. Bate, Walter Jackson, ed. *Keats: A Collection of Essays.* Englewood Cliffs: Prentice-Hall, 1964. "Twentieth Century Views."
Reprints essays by T. S. Eliot, Douglas Bush, Richard Harter Fogle, Walter Jackson Bate, Jack Stillinger, Harold Bloom, David Perkins, Earl Wasserman, and D. G. James. See K-SJ, I

(1952), 93, No. 151; III (1954), 121, No. 184; X (1961), 89, No. 332; XII (1963), 123, No. 18, 142, No. 349; XIII (1964), 122, No. 27; XIV (1965), 118, No. 208. See also No. 36.

241. Bate, Walter Jackson. "The Ode to Autumn," *Harvard Today*, Autumn 1963, pp. 22-25.
An excerpt from his *John Keats*. See No. 239.

242. Bayley, John. *Keats and Reality*. Chatterton Lecture on an English Poet, British Academy, 1962. London: Oxford Univ. [n.d.]
Reprinted from *Proceedings of the British Academy*. See K-SJ, XIV (1965), 118.
Rev. by Kenneth Muir in MLR, LIX (July 1964), 466.

Bayley, John. See No. 87.

Beebe, Maurice. See No. 88.

243. Bell, Quentin. *The Schools of Design*. London: Routledge and Kegan Paul, 1963.
Includes material on Haydon and Severn.
Rev. in TLS, Nov. 1, 1963, p. 880; by E. L. in *Manchester Review*, X (Winter 1963-64), 92-96; by Winslow Ames in *Victorian Studies*, VIII (March 1965), 295-296.

Bentley, G. E., Jr., and Martin K. Nurmi. See No. 2.

244. Benziger, James. *Images of Eternity: Studies in the Poetry of Religious Vision from Wordsworth to T. S. Eliot*. See K-SJ, XIII (1964), 137, XIV (1965), 118.
Rev. by Edward E. Bostetter in SR, LXXII (Summer 1964), 545-548; in TLS, May 6, 1965, p. 355.

245. Bernhardt-Kabisch, Ernest. "Wordsworth's Expostulator: Taylor or Hazlitt?" ELN, II (Dec. 1964), 102-105.
Suggests that "The Tables Turned" could describe an incident "between an older Wordsworth and young Hazlitt."

246. *Blanco Amores de Pagella, Ángela. "Sombra de Keats, en Roma," *La Prensa* (Buenos Aires), Apr. 4, 1965.

247. Blunden, Edmund. *Chaucer to "B. V." with an Additional Paper on Herman Melville: A Selection of Lectures Given Chiefly at Tokyo University*. Tokyo: Kenkyusha, 1950.
Includes a chapter on Hood (pp. 180-193).

248. Blunden, Edmund. "John Taylor, 1781-1864," KSMB, XV (1964), 21-24.
A centenary appreciation.

249. "A Book That May Have Helped Keats," *The Times*, London, Dec. 3, 1963, p. 14.
Discusses Keats's and Brown's markings in Burton's *Anatomy of Melancholy;* asserts that "Brown had believed there was something here which might help Keats." See No. 277.

250. Borges, Jorge Luis. *Other Inquisitions*. [Translated by] Ruth L. C. Simms. Austin: Texas Univ., 1964.
Includes (pp. 121-124) "The Nightingale of Keats." See K-SJ, IX (1960), 63.

Breitholtz, Lennart, ed. See No. 92.

251. Brown, Lynda. "Image and Idea," *Carnegie Technical*, XXIX (Oct. 1964), 33-35.
Contrasts the handling of the relationship between image and idea in Keats and Donne.

252. Brydon, Robert. "Keats Was Homeward Bound," VQR, XLI (Winter 1965), 76.
A poem.

253. Burgess, C .F. " 'The Eve of St. Agnes': One Way to the Poem," *English Journal*, LIV (May 1965), 389-394.
An approach which correlates "poetic technique, structure, and theme."

254. Burgess, C. F. "Keats' 'Ode on a Grecian Urn, 2,' " Exp, XXIII (Dec. 1964), Item 30.†
Discusses why Keats calls the Urn the "foster-child" of silence and time.

255. Burke, Kenneth. *Perspectives by Incongruity / Terms for Order*. Ed. Stanley Edgar Hyman, with the assistance of Barbara Karmiller. Bloomington: Indiana Univ., 1964.
Reprints "Symbolic Action in a Poem by Keats." See K-SJ, VII (1958), 124, No. 283.

256. Cain, Roy E. "David Hume and Adam Smith as Sources of the Concept of Sympathy in Hazlitt," *Papers on English Language & Literature*, I (Spring 1965), 133-140.
The influence of the thought of Hume and Smith on Hazlitt's *Essay on the Principles of Human Action* and

through Hazlitt on Keats is greater than has been realized.

257. Calder-Marshall, Arthur. "The Spoken Word: Discussing Keats," Li, LXXII (Oct. 1, 1964), 528.

Brief account of a broadcast in which Robert Gittings discussed *John Keats: The Making of a Poet* with Aileen Ward. See No. 347.

258. *Chatterjee, Bhabatosh. "Keats on Shakespeare," *Essays on Shakespeare*, ed. Bhabatosh Chatterjee (Calcutta: Orient Longmans for the University of Burdwan, 1965), pp. 169-230.

259. "Commentary," BC, XIII (Spring 1964), 7-22.

Mentions sale at Sotheby's in Nov. 1963 of autograph fragment of "Otho the Great" for £450. See K-SJ, XIV (1965), 123, No. 303. See also Nos. 110 and 131.

Creeger, George R., and Joseph W. Reed, Jr., eds. See No. 21.

260. Cummings, Frederick. "Phidias in Bloomsbury: B. R. Haydon's Drawings of the Elgin Marbles," *Burlington Magazine*, CVI (July 1964), 322-328.

Provides a basis for dating the drawings, classifies them, indicates the purposes for which they were executed, and outlines "the development of Haydon's drawing before the sculptures."

261. Cutting, Vivien. "The Theology of the Grecian Urn," Li, LXXIII (Jan. 14, 1965), 61.

Asks Erich Heller to "modify his comments as far as Keats . . . is concerned." See No. 290.

262. Day Lewis, C[ecil]. *The Lyric Impulse*. Cambridge, Mass.: Harvard Univ.; *London: Chatto (1965).

Discusses Keats.

263. De Silva, K. M. *Social Policy and Missionary Organizations in Ceylon 1840-1855*. London: Longmans, 1965. (Published for the Royal Commonwealth Society.)

Includes material on Benjamin Bailey.

Dickens, Charles. See No. 216.

264. Doubleday, F. N. "A Note on the Operating Theatre in Old St. Thomas's Hospital," KSMB, XV (1964), 35-36.

The theatre has been restored to a condition approximating what it was in Keats's day.

Eaton, Vincent L. See No. 110.

Emerson, Ralph Waldo. See No. 113.

265. Enzensberger, Christian. "Die Fortentwicklung der Romantik am englischen Beispiel: Thomas Hood," *Deutsche Vierteljahrsschrift für Literaturwissenschaft und Geistesgeschichte*, XXXVIII (Dec. 1964), 534-560.

266. Evert, Walter H. *Aesthetic and Myth in the Poetry of Keats*. Princeton: Princeton Univ., 1965.

267. Felperin, Howard. "Keats and Shakespeare: Two New Sources," ELN, II (Dec. 1964), 105-109.

Finds sources for "Ode on a Grecian Urn" and "Ode to a Nightingale" in "The Phoenix and the Turtle" and "The Passionate Pilgrim" respectively.

268. Fielding, K. J. "The Misfortunes of Hood: 1841," N&Q, CXCVIII (Dec. 1953), 534-536.

Hood did apply, in a letter here printed, for the grant awarded by the Royal Literary Fund which he had at first refused.

269. *Fischer, Hermann. *Die romantische Verserzählung in England: Versuch einer Gattungsgeschichte*. Tübingen: Max Niemeyer, 1964.

Includes discussion of Keats (pp. 202-228) and Shelley (pp. 229-243).

270. Gannan, G. A. "Early English Watercolours in the National Gallery of Victoria, Melbourne," *Connoisseur Year Book, 1960*, pp. 89-98.

Reproduces De Wint's "Lincoln Cathedral" (p. 94).

271. Garrett, William. "Hazlitt's Debt to C. W. Dilke," KSMB, XV (1964), 37-42.

Suggests Hazlitt's indebtedness in *Lectures Chiefly on the Dramatic Literature of the Age of Elizabeth* to Dilke's Introduction to his continuation of Dodsley's *Old English Plays*.

272. ["Gatton, Huntingdon,"] *Apollo*, LXXVIII (Oct. 1963), lvi.

This De Wint watercolor is reproduced with an announcement of an exhibition at Appleby Brothers'.

273. Gaull, Marilyn S. "Keats and Wordsworth: Their Historical and Literary Relationship" [Doctoral dissertation, Indiana, 1964], DA, XXV (Nov. 1964), 2957-2958.

274. Gaunt, William. *A Concise History of English Painting*. New York: Frederick

A. Praeger; *London: Thames and Hudson (1964).

Haydon is touched upon and one of his paintings reproduced.

275. *Gidwani, M. A. *John Keats (with Selected Poems).* A. Probsthain, 1964. "Masters of English Literature."

See K-SJ, XIII (1964), 139.

276. Gittings, Robert. *The Keats Inheritance.* London: Heinemann, 1964.

Rev. by R. J. White in Li, LXXII (Oct. 29, 1964), 686, 688; in TLS, Nov. 5, 1964, p. 1000; by Alec Reid in *Manchester Guardian Weekly,* XCI (Nov. 19, 1964), 10; by Martin Dodsworth in NS, LXVIII (Dec. 18, 1964), 969-970; by Bonamy Dobrée in *Critical Quarterly,* VII (Spring 1965), 94-96; by Gilbert Thomas in *English,* XV (Spring 1965), 145-146.

277. Gittings, Robert. "Keats's Markings," *The Times,* London, Dec. 6, 1963, p. 13.

Suggests that "Keats had a very precise system of marking." See No. 249.

278. Gittings, Robert. "Poverty in Ignorance," Li, LXXII (Oct. 22, 1964), 631-632.

Gives an account of the funds from John Jennings' estate which were tied up in Chancery and of which Keats was apparently ignorant.

279. Gordan, John D. "Doctors as Men of Letters: English and American Writers of Medical Background. An Exhibition in the Berg Collection," BNYPL, LXVIII (Nov. 1964), 574-601.†

Shelley and Keats are included.

280. Grant, Maurice Harold. *A Dictionary of British Landscape Painters: From the 16th Century to the Early 20th Century.* Leigh-on-Sea: F. Lewis, 1952.

De Wint, "one of the first English Masters both in oil and water-colour," is included.

281. Gray, Donald Joseph. "Victorian Verse Humor: 1830-1870" [Doctoral dissertation, Ohio State, 1956], DA, XVII (May 1957), 1083.

Hood is among those treated.

Green, David Bonnell, and Edwin Graves Wilson, eds. See No. 5.

Grisenthwaite, Nora, comp. See No. 212.

282. Gross, Barry Edward. *"The Eve of St. Agnes* and *Lamia:* Paradise Won, Paradise Lost," *Bucknell Review,* XIII (May 1965), 47-57.

"Lamia" is "the record of our experience"; "The Eve of St. Agnes" is "the record of what we seek to achieve."

Grosskurth, Phyllis. See No. 405.

283. Hall, Douglas. "The Tabley House Papers," *The Walpole Society,* XXXVIII (1960-62), 59-122.

These include letters of Haydon to Sir John Leicester, which are printed; also lists letters of Hilton.

284. Hartman, Geoffrey H. *Wordworth's Poetry 1787-1814.* New Haven: Yale Univ., 1964.

Includes discussion of Keats and Shelley.

Hassall, Christopher, arranger. See No. 125.

285. Haworth, Helen Ellis. "Keats and Nature" [Doctoral dissertation, Illinois, 1964], DA, XXV (Feb. 1965), 4699-4700.

286. Haydon, Benjamin Robert. *The Diary of Benjamin Robert Haydon.* Ed. Willard Bissell Pope. See K-SJ, X (1961), 87, XI (1962), 125-126, XII (1963), 138, XIII (1964), 139, XIV (1965), 121.

Rev. in *The Times* (London), Oct. 31, 1963, p. 15; by John Lawlor in MLR, LIX (July 1964), 466-467; by Graham Reynolds in *Apollo,* LXXX (July 1964), 78-80.

287. Haynes, Jean. "Keats's Paternal Relatives," KSMB, XV (1964), 27-28.

Tradespeople in London.

288. Hayter, Alethea. *A Sultry Month: Scenes of London Literary Life in 1846.* London: Faber, 1965.

Includes extensive treatment of Haydon; Keats, Hunt, and others are also discussed.

Rev. by John Daniel in *Manchester Guardian Weekly,* XCII (Apr. 15, 1965), 11; by Peter Quennell in Spec, Apr. 30, 1965, p. 567; in TLS, May 20, 1965, p. 392; by V. S. Pritchett in NS, LXIX (May 28, 1965), 843.

289. *Hazlitt, William. *Essays.* Ed. Rosalind Vallance and John Hampden. London: Folio Society, 1964.

290. Heller, Erich. "From Hegel to Hamlet —I: The Theology of the Grecian Urn," Li, LXXII (Dec. 31, 1964), 1037-1039.

Touches on "Ode on a Grecian Urn." See No. 261.

291. Hennig, John. "The Literary Relations between Goethe and Thomas

Hood," MLQ, XII (March 1951), 57-66.

Goethe, in his review of *Whims and Oddities,* gave one of the "fairest and most comprehensive appreciations of Hood's qualities and shortcomings"; but Hood knew and used Goethe's work only in imperfect fashion.

292. Hewlett, Dorothy. "Keats and Shakespeare," *Aryan Path,* XXXV (June 1964), 257-261.

Hilles, Frederick W., and Harold Bloom, eds. See No. 29.

293. Hobsbaum, Philip. "The 'Philosophy' of the Grecian Urn: A Consensus of Readings," KSMB, XV (1964), 1-7.

Concludes that "the variations of reading are not so bewildering as they have been made out to be."

Hocke, Gustav René. See No. 128.

294. Honigmann, E. A. J. *The Stability of Shakespeare's Text.* London: Arnold, 1965.

Discusses Keats's text.

Hopkins, Kenneth. See No. 32.

Hutchings, Richard John. See No. 33.

295. Hutchison, Sidney C. "The Royal Academy Schools, 1768-1830," *The Walpole Society,* XXXVIII (1960-62), 123-191.

A register of students admitted. Haydon, Hilton, De Wint, and others are listed.

296. Huxley, Aldous. *Literature and Science.* New York: Harper & Row, 1963.

Refers several times to Keats.

"In the Sale Rooms." See No. 131.

297. *Inada, Katsuhiko. "'La Belle Dame sans Merci'—Keats's Love-Patterns," *Research Bulletin of the Faculty of Liberal Arts, Kagawa University,* No. 18 (Aug. 1964), pp. 1-45. [In Japanese.]

"Index Benefactorum." See No. 219.

Izzo, Carlo. See No. 34.

298. *Jinbo, Nagao. "The Meaning of *Sleep and Poetry,*" *Studies in Foreign Literature* (Ritsumeikan Univ., Kyoto), No. 10 (March 1965), pp. 96-130. [In Japanese.]

299. *Jones, Stanley. "William Hazlitt at Renton House," *College Courant* (Glasgow University), XVI, xxxi (1963), 15-20.

300. Kallich, Martin. "John Keats's Dispassionate Star: A Contextual Analysis," *Ball State Teachers College Forum,* V (Winter 1964), 11-16.†

A defense of "Bright Star . . .": suggests that "the ideas and images of the sonnet are organically integrated."

301. Kiely, Robert. *Robert Louis Stevenson and the Fiction of Adventure.* Cambridge, Mass.: Harvard Univ., 1964.

Includes extensive comparison of Keats and Stevenson.

302. *Kikuchi, Wataru. "Some Notes on 'Ode on a Grecian Urn' and 'To Autumn,'" *Journal of Humanistic Studies* (Hitotsubashi University, Tokyo), No. 7 (March 1965), pp. 93-139. [In Japanese.]

303. Kinnaird, John. "'Philo' and Prudence: A New Hazlitt Criticism of Malthus," BNYPL, LXIX (March 1965), 153-163.

A letter signed "Philo" in the Apr. 1809 *Monthly Magazine* was the original text of Hazlitt's "Queries Relating to the Essay on Population."

304. Kroeber, Karl. *The Artifice of Reality: Poetic Style in Wordsworth, Foscolo, Keats, and Leopardi.* Madison: Wisconsin Univ., 1964.

Rev. in TLS, Nov. 26, 1964, p. 1090; by Gilbert Thomas in *English,* XV (Spring 1965), 146.

Lacretelle, Jacques de. See No. 138.

305. "Landmarks of English Literature," *Princeton University Library Chronicle,* XXVI (Winter 1965), 109-110.

An exhibition that included the presentation copy to Wordsworth of Keats's *Poems* and the copy of *Adonais* containing lines in Shelley's hand, both from the library of Robert H. Taylor.

Levitt, John, and Joan Levitt. See No. 142.

306. Lewis, Hanna Ballin. "English and American Influences on Hugo von Hofmannsthal" [Doctoral dissertation, Rice, 1964], DA, XXV (Sept. 1964), 1916.

Keats and Shelley were among the English writers who influenced Hofmannsthal.

307. Lucie-Smith, Edward. "Avant-garde or Academic," *The Times,* London, Jan. 14, 1964, p. 12.

Includes discussion of Haydon, whose sketch "The immortal B. R. H. painting his 'Solomon'" is reproduced.

308. McFarland, G. F. "Julius Charles Hare: Coleridge, De Quincey, and German Literature," *Bulletin of the John Rylands Library,* XLVII (Sept. 1964), 165-197.

Touches upon Hare's relations with John Taylor. See K-SJ, XIV (1965), 122, No. 287.

309. Mackerness, E. D. "Edward Holmes (1797-1859)," *Music & Letters,* XLV (July 1964), 213-227.
An evaluation of his achievement as a writer on music.

310. Maidment, Wm. R. "Preservation of the Keats Relics," KSMB, XV (1964), 25-26.
Details the steps taken for this purpose.

311. Mann, Phyllis G. "Death of a London Bookseller," KSMB, XV (1964), 8-12.
Describes the will of Joseph Johnson, who died in 1809. An appended "Keats Note" suggests the story of Robert Emmet and Sarah Curran as a possible source for "Isabella."

312. Mann, Phyllis G. "Keats's Maternal Relations," KSMB, XV (1964), 32-34.
Details about the Jennings and Sweetenburgh families.

313. Marilla, E. L. *Three Odes of Keats.* See K-SJ, XIII (1964), 141.
Rev. by S. B. Liljegren in ASNS, CCI (Nov. 1964), 297. See also No. 47.

314. *Matsushita, Senkichi. "On 'The Fall of Hyperion,'" *Review of English Literature* (English Dept., College of Liberal Arts, Kyoto Univ.), XVI (Oct. 1964), 68-105. [In Japanese.]

315. *Matsuura, Cho. "Keats's Sonnet Pattern," *Journal of Nagoya College of Commerce,* IX (Oct. 1964), 1-23. [In Japanese.]

Matthiessen, Paul F. See No. 149.

Maud, Ralph N., and Aneirin Talfan Davies, eds. See No. 69.

316. Miller, Bruce E. "The Allusion to *Paradise Lost* in Keats's Letter on Imagination," N&Q, CCIX (Nov. 1964), 423.†
The allusion is to Book VIII, ll. 283-311, not ll. 450-490. See No. 342.

317. Miller, Bruce E. "On the Incompleteness of Keats' *Hyperion,*" *CLA Journal,* VIII (March 1965), 234-239.
Perhaps Keats did not finish the poem because it expressed "a philosophical problem which he could not solve."

318. Miller, Bruce E. "On the Meaning of Keats's *Endymion,*" K-SJ, XIV (1965), 33-54.
"*Endymion* is a poem about love and reality, about love as a guide to the fullest reality."

319. Mitchell, Adrian. "John Keats Eats His Porridge Up," NS, LXIX (June 18, 1965), 960.
A poem.

Montoro, Antonio, See No. 155.

Moore, Thomas. See No. 158.

320. Morgan, Peter F. "Charles Lamb and Thomas Hood: Records of a Friendship," *Tennessee Studies in Literature,* IX (1964), 71-85.
Aims "to give an unvarnished factual account of the friendship" between Lamb and Hood.

321. *Nagasawa, Jiro. "On the Circumstances of the Composition of Keats's *Hyperion,*" *Research Bulletin of the Faculty of Liberal Arts, Oita University,* II, No. 4 (Sept. 1964), 75-90. [In Japanese.]

322. *Nonaka, Ryo. "The Autumn of Keats," *English Literature* (Waseda Univ. English Literary Society, Tokyo), No. 26 (March 1965), pp. 24-43. [In Japanese.]

Nowell-Smith, Simon. See No. 163.

323. *Painting in England 1700-1850: Collection of Mr & Mrs Paul Mellon.* Introduction by Basil Taylor. 2 vols. Richmond: Virginia Museum of Fine Arts, 1963.
De Wint is among the artists represented.

Palacio, Jean de. See No. 435.

Parks, Edd Winfield. See No. 170.

324. Pelles, Geraldine. *Art, Artists & Society: Origins of a Modern Dilemma. Painting in England and France 1750-1850.* Englewood Cliffs: Prentice-Hall, 1963.
Refers frequently to Haydon.

Peters, Robert L. See No. 172.

325. Philbrick, Charles. "On Prester John of Hampstead (John Keats, 1795-1821)," *Western Humanities Review,* XIX (Spring 1965), 132-134.
A poem.

326. Polgar, Mirko. "The Setting of 'The Eve of St. Agnes,'" KSMB, XV (1964), 29-31.
"The setting of the poem . . . is simply human."

Pollin, Burton Ralph. See No. 442.

327. Pope, Willard Bissell. "Haydon on Shelley," KSMB, XV (1964), 45-48.
Outlines Haydon's views on Shelley,

especially his loathing for the latter's ideas about free love.

328. Pope, Willard B[issell]. [In] "Information, Please," TLS, Dec. 10, 1964, p. 1132.

Requests information about letters of Elizabeth Barrett to Haydon (outside the Wellesley College Library) for an edition.

Pósa, Péter. See No. 175.

329. Poulet, Georges. "La pensée critique de Charles du Bos," *Critique,* XXI (June 1965), 491-516.

This review article on works by Du Bos mentions his observations on Keats and Shelley.

330. Prance, Claude A. *Peppercorn Papers: A Miscellany on Books and Book-Collecting.* Cambridge: Golden Head Press, 1964.

Includes chapters on the first fourteen months of the *London Magazine* (pp. 118-131) and on the death of John Scott (pp. 132-151). Reprints "A Charles Lamb Library" (pp. 50-63) and "Some Association Books" (pp. 80-87). See K-SJ, XIII (1964), 135, No. 256.

Pritchard, John Paul. See No. 176.

331. Raymond, Ernest. *Two Gentlemen of Rome.* See K-SJ, II (1953), 104, III (1954), 120, IV (1955), 120.

Rev. by Howard Spring in *Country Life,* CXII (July 25, 1952), 279, 281.

332. Reid, John Cowie. *Thomas Hood.* See K-SJ, XIV (1965), 124.

Now available in an American edition (New York: Hillary House, 1964).

Rev. by Frederick T. Wood in ES, XLV (Aug. 1964), 342; by Lionel Stevenson in SAQ, LXIII (Autumn 1964), 601-602; by Alvin Whitley in *Victorian Studies,* VIII (Dec. 1964), 196-198.

333. Richardson, Joanna. *The Everlasting Spell: A Study of Keats and His Friends.* See K-SJ, XIV (1965), 124.

Rev. by David Williams in *Punch,* CCXLV (Sept. 25, 1963), 470; by Frederick T. Wood in ES, XLV (Aug. 1964), 341.

Ritz, Jean-Georges. See No. 181.

334. Robinson, Dwight E. "Keats' Ode on a Wedgwood Urn," *Greek Heritage,* I, No. 3 (1964), pp. 66-71.

Reprints a revised version of an article that first appeared in K-SJ. See K-SJ, XIII (1964), 142.

335. Rollins, Hyder Edward, ed. *The Keats Circle: Letters and Papers and More Letters and Poems of the Keats Circle.* Second Edition. 2 vols. Cambridge, Mass.: Harvard Univ., 1965.

Rowland, Benjamin, Jr. See No. 184.

336. Saly, John. "Keats's Answer to Dante: *The Fall of Hyperion,*" K-SJ, XIV (1965), 65-78.

Suggests the influence of the *Divine Comedy* in the original Italian on Keats's poem, and sees *The Fall* as an answer to Dante's views on salvation.

San Juan, E., Jr. See No. 221.

Saunders, J. W. See No. 185.

Schneider, Isidor, ed. See No. 72.

337. Seaton, Esta. "Message to Tennyson, et al.," *English Journal,* LIII (Apr. 1964), 265.

A poem about Keats: "Others wrote and are unread. / His voice stayed bold."

338. Sewell, Elizabeth. *The Human Metaphor.* [Notre Dame:] Notre Dame Univ., 1964.

Discusses Keats and Shelley.

339. Shmiefsky, Marvel. *"Principle in Art* as Criticism in the Mainstream," *Victorian Newsletter,* No. 26 (Fall 1964), pp. 28-32.

Includes discussion of Patmore's criticism of Keats.

Sinclair, Alexander R. See No. 186.

340. Sinclair, J. M. "When Is a Poem like a Sunset?" *Review of English Literature,* VI (Apr. 1965), 76-91.

Uses "La Belle Dame sans Merci" as an experiment designed to reveal the shortcomings of orally transmitted poetry.

341. Singh, Satyanarain. "Changing Perspectives of Taste in Eighteenth Century England," *Osmania Journal of English Studies,* No. 3 (1963), pp. 21-31.

Discusses Keats's relationship to David Hume. Godwin is touched upon.

Stendhal, *pseud.* See No. 188.

342. Swaminathan, S. R. "The Allusion to *Paradise Lost* in Keats's Letter on the Imagination (ccix. 423)," N&Q, CCX (May 1965), 195-197.

Supports the view that Keats is alluding to the second dream (VIII, 452-490) rather than the first. See No. 316.

Swinburne, Algernon Charles. See No. 190.

343. Thorpe, Clarence DeWitt. *The Mind*

of *John Keats*. New York: Russell & Russell, 1964.

A reprint of a book first published in 1926.

344. *Toriumi, Hisayoshi. "Arnold and Keats," *English and American Studies* (Wayo Women's University, Ichikawa), No. 2 (Dec. 1964), pp. 55-67. [In Japanese.]

Vitoux, Pierre. See No. 51.

345. Vivante, Leone. *English Poetry and Its Contribution to the Knowledge of a Creative Principle*. *Carbondale: Southern Illinois Univ., 1963.

First American edition of a book published in England in 1950. Has chapters on Keats and Shelley.

346. *Vogler, Thomas Allen. "Preludes to Vision: The Epic Venture in Blake, Wordsworth, Keats and Hart Crane." (Doctoral dissertation, Yale, 1964.)

347. Ward, Aileen. *John Keats: The Making of a Poet*. See K-SJ, XIV (1965), 126.

Rev. by Orville Prescott in *New York Times*, Sept. 6, 1963, p. 31; in *Time*, LXXXII (Oct. 25, 1963), 106, 109; in *The Times*, London, Nov. 21, 1963, p. 18; by M. L. Rosenthal in *Reporter*, XXX (Feb. 13, 1964), 52-54; by William Heath in *Massachusetts Review*, V (Summer 1964), 784-788; by L[eonard]. F. M[anheim]. in *Literature and Psychology*, XIV (Summer-Fall 1964), 137-138; by Frederick T. Wood in ES, XLV (Aug. 1964), 341; by Garry Wills in *Modern Age*, VIII (Fall 1964), 430-432; by Edward E. Bostetter in MP, LXII (May 1965), 363-366. See also Nos. 47 and 257.

Warner, Oliver. See No. 200.

Wasserman, Earl R. See No. 52.

348. *Watanabe, Jun. "A Comment on Keats's Sonnets," *Bulletin of the Kyoto Gakugei University*, Series A, No. 25 (Oct. 1964), pp. 1-6. [In Japanese.]

349. Watkins, Vernon. *Affinities: Poems*. New York: New Directions, 1962.

Includes "The Death of Keats" (p. 52). See K-SJ, V (1956), 131.

Wellek, René. See No. 202.

350. Wheelock, John Hall. *What Is Poetry?* New York: Scribner's, 1963.

Has allusions to Keats and Shelley.

351. Whitley, Alvin. "Hood and Dickens: Some New Letters," HLQ, XIV (Aug. 1951), 385-413.

Reviews the relationship of the two men and prints twenty letters from Hood to Dickens.

352. Whitley, Alvin. "Thomas Hood as a Dramatist," *University of Texas Studies in English*, XXX (1951), 184-201.

Enumerates and evaluates "the facts of his dramatic and theatrical associations."

Wilkie, Brian. See No. 53.

353. *Williams, Richard J. "The Principles of Hazlitt's Critical Thinking." (Doctoral dissertation, Chicago, 1964.)

354. Wilson, Katharine M. *The Nightingale and the Hawk: A Psychological Study of Keats' Ode*. London: Allen and Unwin; *New York: Barnes & Noble (1964).

Rev. in TLS, Oct. 15, 1964, p. 940; by Martin Dodsworth in NS, LXVIII (Dec. 18, 1964), 969-970; by Herbert Read in Li, LXXIII (Jan. 7, 1965), 26; by Gilbert Thomas in *English*, XV (Spring 1965), 146.

355. Woodring, Carl. "On Looking into Keats's Voyagers," K-SJ, XIV (1965), 15-22.

The Chapman's Homer sonnet "demonstrates, even while we explore its workings, that the discovery of every new world, large or small, actual or imaginary, of matter or of spirit, can be wondrous, and all discoveries wondrously akin. Vehicle and tenor interchange and coalesce in a root experience, discovery of land and sky from the sea and of sea and sky from the land, all 'one wide expanse' of the mind's encompassment."

356. Woodward, John. *A Picture History of British Painting*. London: Vista, 1962.

Reproduces (p. 127) Haydon's "Curtius leaping into the Gulf" and Millais' "Lorenzo and Isabella."

357. *Yamane, Yoshio. "An Interpretation of 'The Eve of St. Agnes,'" *Academia* (Nanzan Univ., Nagoya), XLV-XLVI (Dec. 1964), 1-46.

358. Zall, P. M. "Wordsworth on Disinterestedness and on Michelangelo," BNYPL, LXIX (Feb. 1965), 131-134.

Summarizes chapter in William Bewick's memoirs about a meeting at

Haydon's between Wordsworth and Foscolo.

V. SHELLEY

Works: Collected, Selected, Single, Translated

Astre, Georges-Albert. See No. 54.

Blishen, Edward, comp. See No. 223.

359. *The Complete Works of Percy Bysshe Shelley*. Ed. Roger Ingpen and Walter E. Peck. 10 vols. New York: Gordian; London: Ernest Benn (1965).

A reprint of the Julian Edition, first published in 1926-1930.

360. *The Esdaile Notebook: A Volume of Early Poems*. Ed. Kenneth Neill Cameron. See K-SJ, XIV (1965), 127.

Also available in an English edition (London: Faber, 1964).

Rev. by Frederick L. Jones in NYT, May 31, 1964, pp. 5, 20; by Phoebe Adams in *Atlantic Monthly*, CCXIII (June 1964), 139; by *Godfrey John in *Christian Science Monitor*, June 19, 1964, p. 9; by Richard Harter Fogle in *Key Reporter*, XXX (Autumn 1964), 5; by Richard Harter Fogle in VQR, XL (Autumn 1964), 665-668; in *Yale Review*, LIV (Autumn 1964), xxxviii, xliv; by James Rieger in EC, XIV (Oct. 1964), 401-409; in *The Times*, London, Oct. 1, 1964, p. 16; in TLS, Oct. 15, 1964, p. 940; by John Holloway in Spec, Oct. 16, 1964, p. 514; by Donald Davie in NS, LXVIII (Nov. 27, 1964), 840-841; in *Science and Society*, XXIX (Winter 1965), 123; in *Twentieth Century*, CLXXIII (Winter 1964-65), 154; by Richard Harter Fogle in K-SJ, XIV (1965), 91-93; by Joseph Raben in JEGP, LXIV (Jan. 1965), 185-186; in *Quarterly Review*, CCCIII (Jan. 1965), 114-115; by Gilbert Thomas in *English*, XV (Spring 1965), 146-147; by Donald H. Reiman in MLQ, XXVI (June 1965), 341-344. See also Nos. 383, 425, and 449.

Grafe, Felix, See No. 60.

Grigson, Geoffrey, comp. See No. 25.

Grisenthwaite, Nora, comp. See No. 212.

Harding, Gilbert, comp. See No. 62.

Hayward, John, ed. See No. 27.

Hilditch, Neville, comp. See No. 63.

Hodgart, Patricia, and Theodore Redpath, eds. See No. 30.

Hoffman, Daniel G., and Samuel Hynes, eds. See No. 31.

Komlós, Aladár. See No. 66.

361. *The Letters of Percy Bysshe Shelley*. Ed. Frederick L. Jones. See K-SJ, XIV (1965), 127.

Rev. by Carlos Baker in NYT, May 31, 1964, p. 5; by Richard Harter Fogle in VQR, XL (Autumn 1964), 665-668; by Donald H. Reiman in SAQ, LXIII (Autumn 1964), 583-585; by P. H. Butter in MLR, LIX (Oct. 1964), 645-646; by Stewart C. Wilcox in K-SJ, XIV (1965), 96-98; by Hugh J. Luke in CE, XXVI (Feb. 1965), 418. See also No. 47.

Macbeth, George, ed. See No. 67.

Maloff, Saul, ed. See No. 68.

362. *Prometheus Unbound, A Lyrical Drama in Four Acts*. Ed. Nitish Kumar Basu. Second Edition. Calcutta: Bookland Private Ltd., 1963.

The first edition was published in 1961. See K-SJ, XII (1963), 144.

Schneider, Isidor, ed. See No. 72.

363. **Selected Poems*. London: Oxford Univ., in association with British Council, 1964. "English Poets, Chaucer to Yeats Series."

364. *Selected Poems and Prose*. Ed. G. M. Matthews. See K-SJ, XIV (1965), 127.

Rev. in TLS, July 2, 1964, p. 572.

365. *Shelley's Prometheus Unbound: A Variorum Edition*. Ed. Lawrence John Zillman. See K-SJ, IX (1960), 70, X (1961), 91, XI (1962), 133, XII (1963), 143, XIII (1964), 145.

Rev. by A. A. Prins in ES, XLVI (June 1965), 272-274.

366. **Shelley versei*. Ed. László Kardos and László Kéry. Budapest: Magyar Helikon, 1963.

A representative selection of Shelley's poems and dramas, with notes and a summary of the poet's life.

Szabó, Lórinc. See No. 74.

Thomas, R. S., ed. See No. 75.

Tosswill, T D., ed. See No. 50.

Tóth, Árpád. See No. 77.

367. "Untitled Lyric ['Music, when soft voices die']," K-SJ, XIV (1965), 32.

368. **Versei*. [Translated by] Mihály Babits, István Bernáth, *et al.* Budapest: Magyar Helikon, 1963.

Wallace, Robert, and James G. Taaffe, eds. See No. 79.

Williams, Oscar, ed. See No. 80.

Books and Articles Relating to Shelley and His Circle

Adams, Hazard. See No. 81.

Ades, John I. See No. 82.

369. Baker, Joseph E. *Shelley's Platonic Answer to a Platonic Attack on Poetry.* Iowa City: Iowa Univ., 1965. "University of Iowa Monographs."

370. Baker, Sheridan. "The Idea of Romance in the Eighteenth-Century Novel," *Papers of the Michigan Academy of Science, Arts, and Letters,* XLIX (1964 [for 1963]), 507-522.†
Discusses Godwin.

371. Barnard, Ellsworth. *Shelley's Religion.* New York: Russell & Russell, 1964.
A reprint of a book first published in 1937.

Barnett, George L. See No. 15.

372. Baxter, B. M. *Albert Verwey's Translations from Shelley's Poetical Works: A Study of Their Style and Rhythm and a Consideration of Their Value as Translations.* See K-SJ, XIV (1965), 127.
Rev. by. P. K. King in MLR, LIX (July 1964), 493-494.

Beebe, Maurice. See No. 88.

373. Beer, J. B. *The Achievement of E. M. Forster.* London: Chatto, 1962.
Includes brief discussion of Shelley's influence on Forster.
Rev. in TLS, June 22, 1962, p. 460.

Bentley, G. E., Jr., and Martin K. Nurmi. See No. 2.

374. *Bhalla, M. M. "*Adonais.* A Note," *English Miscellany* (Delhi), No. 2 (1963), pp. 12-22.

375. *Bhalla, M. M. "*Alastor or The Spirit of Solitude:* an Interpretation," *Essays Presented to Amy G. Stock,* ed. R. K. Kaul (Jaipur: Rajasthan, 1965), pp. 68-77.

376. Bilder, John Raban. "The Minor Tradition in English Prose Fiction: The Novel of Ideas" [Doctoral dissertation, Pennsylvania, 1964], DA, XXV (Dec. 1964), 3565.
Peacock is among those included.

377. Boas, L[ouise]. S[chutz]. "Edward Dowden, the Esdailes, and the Shelleys," N&Q, CCX (May 1965), 163-166; (June 1965), 227-231.
Recounts the relationship of Dowden with the Esdailes and with Sir Percy and Lady Shelley in connection with his biography of the poet.

378. Boas, Louise Schutz. "A Letter about *Shelley and Mary,*" HLQ, XXVIII (May 1965), 283-285.
From Frances Power Cobbe to Frederick R. Halsey, dated May 11 [1900].

379. Boas, Louise Schutz. "Shelley and Mary," TLS, July 16, 1964, p. 631.
Prints an important excision, not previously reported, found in the Yale copy of *Shelley and Mary.* See K-SJ, XIV (1965), 128, No. 376.

380. Boulton, James T. *The Language of Politics in the Age of Wilkes and Burke.* London: Routledge; *Toronto: Toronto Univ. (1963).
Includes discussion of Godwin and Mary Wollstonecraft.
Rev. by Donald C. Bryant in PQ, XLIII (July 1964), 321-323: by Carl B. Cone in *American Historical Review,* LXX (Oct. 1964), 231-232; by D[avid]. V. E[rdman] in PQ, XLIII (Oct. 1964), 443-444.

381. Bowra, C. M. *In General and Particular.* Cleveland: World, 1964.
Reprints (pp. 223-240) "The Prophetic Element." See K-SJ, X (1961), 92, XI (1962), 133.

382. Bratcher, James T., and Lyle H. Kendall, Jr. "Two Further Footnotes to an Enquiry," *Texas Studies in Literature and Language,* VII (Spring 1965), 67-75.
The second part of the article deals with "Forman and Wise as Editors of Shelley."

Breitholtz, Lennart, ed. See No. 92.

383. Cameron, Kenneth Neill. "The Esdaile Notebook," *New York Review of Books,* II (July 9, 1964), 21-22.
Replies to G. M. Matthews' review. See K-SJ, XIV (1965), 127, No. 362. See also Nos. 360 and 425.

Campbell, N. See No. 96.

384. Campbell, Olwen W. *Thomas Love Peacock.* See K-SJ, III (1954), 122, IV (1955), 122.
Rev. by Howard Spring in *Country Life,* CXIII (May 1953), 1449, 1451.

385. Chernaik, Judith Sheffield. "The Lyrics of Shelley" [Doctoral dissertation, Yale, 1964], DA, XXV (Feb. 1965), 4683-4684.

386. *Chesser, Eustace. *Shelley and Zas-*

trozzi: Self-Revelations of a Neurotic. London: Gregg Press and Archive Press, 1965.

Rev. in TLS, Apr. 29, 1965, p. 333; by Richard Whittington-Egan in *Books and Bookmen,* X (May 1965), 27.

"Commentary." See No. 99.

387. Cooke, B. Campbell. "Clerks of the Peace for Sussex 1594-1950," *Sussex Notes and Queries,* XIII (Aug. 1951), 145-153.

Timothy Shelley, the poet's great-great-great-grandfather, was clerk 1661-1668.

Crawley, C. W., ed. See No. 20.

Creeger, George R., and Joseph W. Reed, Jr., eds. See No. 21.

388. Daiches, David. *English Literature.* Englewood Cliffs: Prentice-Hall, 1964.

Comments on the sources of antagonism to Shelley in twentieth-century English literary criticism.

Delattre, Geneviève. See No. 101.

389. Deschamps, Paul. *La Formation de la pensée de Coleridge (1772-1804).* Paris: Didier, 1964.

Discusses Godwin's influence on Coleridge.

390. Dickins, Bruce. "The U. L. C. Copy of *Posthumous Fragments of Margaret Nicholson,*" *Transactions of the Cambridge Bibliographical Society,* III (1963), 423-427.

Notes a seventh extant copy in the University Library, Cambridge. Gives data also on the other six copies.

391. Duerksen, Roland A. "Disraeli's Use of Shelley," *Victorian Newsletter,* No. 26 (Fall 1964), pp. 19-22.†

Centers on "the equivocal use made in *Venetia.*"

392. Duerksen, Roland A. "Shelley in *Middlemarch,*" K-SJ, XIV (1965), 23-31.

G. H. Lewes, in part through the influence of Leigh Hunt, was a great admirer of Shelley, and it seems very likely "that Lewes and George Eliot frequently discussed Shelley and that Will Ladislaw, the Shelleyan character in *Middlemarch,* may have evolved largely from Lewes's ideas about Shelley."

393 Duerksen, Roland A. "Shelley's 'Defence' and Whitman's 1855 'Preface': A Comparison," *Walt Whitman Review,* X (Sept. 1964), 51-60.

Discusses Whitman's interest in Shelley and compares the two critical manifestos.

394. Dyson, A. E. *The Crazy Fabric: Studies in Irony.* London: Macmillan, 1965.

Discusses Peacock.

Rev. in TLS, March 18, 1965, p. 216.

Eaton, Vincent L. See No. 110.

395. Edwards, Oliver. "Shelley's Peacock," *The Times,* London, July 30, 1964, p. 13.

An appreciation.

Emerson, Ralph Waldo. See No. 113.

396. *Faure, Georges. "Les Eléments du rythme poétique en anglais moderne, esquisse d'une nouvelle analyse et essai d'application au *Prometheus Unbound* de P. B. Shelley." (Thèse complimentaire, Paris, 1963.)

397. Fennessy, R. R. *Burke, Paine, and the Rights of Man: A Difference of Political Opinion.* The Hague: Nijhoff, 1963. "Université Catholique de Louvain Collection de l'Ecole des Sciences Politiques et Sociales, No. 171."

Discusses Godwin and Mary Wollstonecraft.

Rev. by Donald C. Bryant in PQ, XLIII (July 1964), 321-323.

Fischer, Hermann. See No. 269.

398. Flanders, Wallace Austin. "The Didactic and 'Philosophical' Novel in England, 1792-1805" [Doctoral dissertation, Wisconsin, 1964], DA, XXV (Oct. 1964), 2510.

Among the writers considered are Godwin and Mary Wollstonecraft.

399. Fletcher, Angus. *Allegory: The Theory of a Symbolic Mode.* Ithaca: Cornell Univ., 1964.

Has discussion of Shelley.

400. Galt, John. *The Common Ground.* Denver: Verb Publications, 1964.

A book of poems that includes (p. 20) "Shelley at Lerici."

401. Garlick, Kenneth. "A Catalogue of the Paintings, Drawings and Pastels of Sir Thomas Lawrence," *The Walpole Society,* XXXIX (1962-64), 9-334.

Lists two drawings of Godwin.

402. Godwin, William. *Imogen, A Pastoral Romance from the Ancient British.* See K-SJ, XIV (1965), 129.

Rev. by David Fleisher in *Nineteenth-Century Fiction,* XIX (Dec. 1964), 309-311.

Gordan, John D. See No. 279.

403. Green, David Bonnell. "Oscar Wilde and Gabriel Sarrazin: A New Wilde Letter," EA, XVIII (Apr.-June 1965), 137-138.

Wilde writes Sarrazin that the latter's articles on Shelley and on Rossetti are "admirable."

Green, David Bonnell, and Edwin Graves Wilson, eds. See No. 5.

404. Grigson, Geoffrey. "Lovers Who Meet in Churches (Suggested by Mary Godwin's Letter to Shelley, October 25th, 1814)," TLS, June 11, 1964, p. 512.

A poem.

Grisenthwaite, Nora, comp. See No. 61.

405. Grosskurth, Phyllis. *John Addington Symonds: A Biography*. London: Longmans, 1964.

Discusses Symonds' study of Shelley and touches on his attitude to Keats.

406. Gunn, Peter. *Vernon Lee, Violet Paget, 1856-1935*. London: Oxford Univ., 1964.

Has material on Cornelia Turner.

407. *Gusmanov, I. G. "Tragediia Shelli *Chenchi* (K probleme geroia)" ["Shelley's *The Cenci* (Problems of the Hero)"], *Uchenye zapiski* (Mosk. gos. ped. in-t. im. V. I. Lenina), No. 218, Zarubezhnaia literatura (1964), pp. 61-84.

Hartman, Geoffrey H. See No. 284.

Hassall, Christopher, arranger. See No. 125.

408. Hem, Day. "Quelques remarques bibliographiques sur l'influence de William Godwin en France," *Bulletin of the International Institute of Social History*, X (1955), 5-16.

A bibliography of French translations of Godwin and of French books and articles about him.

409. Hem, Day, ed. *William Godwin (1756-1836): Philosophe de la Justice et de la Liberté*. Paris: Pensée et Action, 1953.

Hilles, Frederick W., and Harold Bloom, eds. See No. 29.

410. Hodgart, Matthew. "Radical Prose in the Late Eighteenth Century," *The English Mind: Studies in the English Moralists Presented to Basil Willey*, ed. Hugh Sykes Davies and George Watson (Cambridge: Cambridge Univ., 1964), pp. 146-152.

Includes discussion of Godwin.

411. Honan, Park. "Browning's Testimony on His Essay on Shelley in 'Shepherd *v.* Francis'," ELN, II (Sept. 1964), 27-31.

The testimony is here reprinted; Browning may have suspected the authenticity of the letters in Moxon's edition before he wrote the *Essay*.

412. *Hondo, Masao. "Abstract Ideas and the Inanimate World in *Prometheus Unbound*," *Eibungaku Shiron [Essays in English Literature], Presented to Professor Kochi Doi* (Tokyo: Kenkyusha, 1964), pp. 85-94. [In Japanese.]

Hopkins, Kenneth. See No. 32.

Hutchings, Richard John. See No. 33.

413. Imlay, Gilbert, and Mary Wollstonecraft. *The Emigrants (1793)*. See K-SJ, XIV (1965), 129.

Rev. by James Walt in BA, XXXVIII (Summer 1964), 312.

"In the Sale Rooms." See No. 131.

Izzo, Carlo. See No. 34.

414. Jones, Frederick L. "Shelley's Letter of 23 June 1811 to Hogg," KSMB, XV (1964), 13-14.

Prints a transcript of the original manuscript.

415. Katope, Christopher G. "West's 'Love, Death, and the Ladies' Drill Team,'" Exp, XXIII (Dec. 1964), Item 27.†

Sees echoes of "Ode to the West Wind" in Jessamyn West's short story.

416. Kenyon, John Garland. "A New Approach to Teaching Explication," *English Journal*, LIII (Sept. 1964), 428-430.

Reports on a classroom experiment with "Ozymandias."

417. *Komatsu, Fumio. "Shelley's *Adonais*," *Literary Wagon* (Ryukoku Univ., Kyoto), No. 2 (Nov. 1964), pp. 32-41. [In Japanese.]

"Landmarks of English Literature." See No. 305.

418. Lemaitre, Hélène. *Shelley, Poète des Eléments*. See K-SJ, XII (1963), 146, XIII (1964), 148, XIV (1965), 130.

Rev. by Herbert Huscher in *Anglia*, LXXXI (1963), 498-504; by Jean de Palacio in RLC, XXXVIII (Oct.-Dec. 1964), 606-610.

Levitt, John, and Joan Levitt. See No. 142.

Lewis, Hanna Ballin. See No. 306.

419. "List of Acquisitions: Department of Manuscripts: Acquisitions, January to June 1964," *British Museum Quar-*

terly, XXIX (Winter 1964-5), 57-58.
Included are "Letters, etc., relating to the death of Shelley: 1822-3."

Lovell, Ernest J., Jr. See No. 144.

420. Luke, Hugh J., Jr. "Sir William Lawrence: Physician to Shelley and Mary," *Papers on English Language & Literature,* I (Spring 1965), 141-152.
Gives an account of Lawrence's career and of his relationship to Shelley and his wife.

421. McAleer, Edward C. "Romantic Letters," TLS, March 25, 1965, p. 240.
Corrects the account of Lady Mount Cashell in the article named. See No. 455.

422. McAleer, Edward C. *The Sensitive Plant: A Life of Lady Mount Cashell.* See K-SJ, IX (1960), 72-73, X (1961), 94, XI (1962), 135.
Rev. by Maureen Wall in *Irish Historical Studies,* XIII (March 1962), 87-88.

423. McCelvey, George Edward, III. "William Godwin's Novels: Theme and Craft" [Doctoral dissertation, Duke, 1964], DA, XXV (Aug. 1964), 1215-1216.

424. Mahony, Patrick J. "An Analysis of Shelley's Craftsmanship in *Adonais,*" SEL, IV (Autumn 1964), 555-568.†
Concludes that probably not since Spenser himself has there been "such consummate artistry with the nine-line stanza."

Mattheisen, Paul F. See No. 149.

425. Matthews, G. M. "The Esdaile Notebook," *New York Review of Books,* II (July 9, 1964), 22.
Replies to Kenneth Neill Cameron's reply. See Nos. 360 and 383. See also K-SJ, XIV (1965), 127, No. 362.

426. May, Frederick. "Mary Wollstonecraft Shelley e il sonetto autoritratto del Foscolo," *Giornale storico della letteratura italiana,* CXLI (3rd quarter 1964), 390-393.
Concerning her sonnet "Portrait of Ugo Foscolo/By Himself."

427. Menen, Aubrey. "The Myth of English Literature," in *Party of Twenty,* ed. Clifton Fadiman (New York: Simon and Schuster, 1963), pp. 183-195.
Describes his experiences in reading Shelley—"as bad a scribbler as Scott."

428. Monte, Alberto del. *Breve storia del romanzo poliziesco.* Bari: Laterza, 1962.
Includes brief discussion of *Caleb Williams.*

Montoro, Antonio. See No. 155.

Moore, L. Hugh, Jr. See No. 156.

Moore, Thomas. See No. 158.

429. *Morita, Masami. "Shelley's Idea of Love and Intellectual Beauty in *Alastor, or The Spirit of Solitude,*" *Tandai Ronso* (Kanto Gakuin Junior College, Yokohama), No. 24 (Dec. 1964), pp. 61-73. [In Japanese.]

430. Mortenson, Peter. "Image and Structure in Shelley's Longer Lyrics," SIR, IV (Winter 1965), 104-110.
Concludes that "a core metaphor frequently becomes an anticipation of the structure and statement of the entire poem" and that the structure suggests "the pattern of the meditative lyrics of the seventeenth century."

431. Moskowitz, Sam. *Explorers of the Infinite: Shapers of Science Fiction.* Cleveland: World, 1963.
Includes (pp. 33-45) a chapter on "The Sons of Frankenstein."

Mynors, R. A. B., comp. See No. 161.

432. Norman, Sylva. *Flight of the Skylark: The Development of Shelley's Reputation.* See K-SJ, IV (1955), 124, V (1956), 134, VI (1957), 149, IX (1960), 73, X (1961), 94.
Rev. by Howard Spring in *Country Life,* CXVII (Jan. 27, 1955), 267, 269.

Nowell-Smith, Simon. See No. 163.

O'Daniel, Therman B. See No. 164.

433. O'Malley, Glenn. *Shelley and Synesthesia.* [Evanston:] Northwestern Univ., 1964.

434. Palacio, Jean de. "Mary Shelley's Latin Studies, Her Unpublished Translation of Apuleius," RLC, XXXVIII (Oct.-Dec. 1964), 564-571.
An evaluation and analysis.

435. Palacio, Jean de. "Music and Musical Themes in Shelley's Poetry," MLR, LIX (July 1964), 345-359.†
His musical development "falls into three main divisions: Shelley before 1817; his increasing interest in music from 1817 onwards; and music as the intimation of something beyond. . . ." The influence of Hunt and Hazlitt on Shelley's interest in music is discussed at length.

Parks, Edd Winfield. See No. 170.

436. *Peacock, Thomas Love. *Crotchet Castle*. With an Introduction by Kenneth Hopkins. London: Folio Society, 1964.

437. *Peacock, Thomas Love. *Nightmare Abbey*. New York: Norton, 1964.
A paperback reprint.

438. Pelletier, Robert R. "*The Revolt of Islam* and *Paradise Lost*," K-SJ, XIV (1965), 7-13.
Points out echoes and parallels.

439. Perry, John Oliver. "The Relationships of Disparate Voices in Poems," EC, XV (Jan. 1965), 49-64.
Briefly discusses "Ode to the West Wind."

Peters, Robert L. See No. 172.

440. *Political Justice: A Poem (Anonymous. 1736)*. Introduction by Burton R. Pollin and John W. Wilkes. Augustan Reprint Society Publication No. 111. Los Angeles: William Andrews Clark Memorial Library, Univ. of California, Los Angeles, 1965.
Godwin is briefly discussed in the introduction.

441. Pollin, Burton Ralph. *Education and Enlightenment in the Works of William Godwin*. See K-SJ, XII (1963), 147, XIII (1964), 149.
Rev. by Roger Sharrock in N&Q, CCX (Jan. 1965), 37-38; by Jack W. Marken in K-SJ, XIV (1965), 98-100.

442. Pollin, Burton R[alph]. "Godwin's *Letters of Verax*," JHI, XXV (July-Sept. 1964), 353-373.
Examines this hitherto undiscussed pamphlet and its background. The pamphlet "links Godwin in 1815 with the radical Whigs and with the few *littérateurs*, such as Hazlitt, who courageously advocated basic political changes."

443. Pollin, Burton R[alph]. "Verse Satires on William Godwin in the Anti-Jacobin Period," *Satire Newsletter*, II (Fall 1964), 31-40.
Reprints and discusses two satirical poems directed against Godwin.

444. Polt, John H. R. "Jovellanos and His English Sources, Economic, Philosophical, and Political Writings," *Transactions of the American Philosophical Society*, N. S., LIV, Part 7 (1964).
Godwin is one of the sources.

Pope, Willard Bissell. See No. 327.

Pósa, Péter. See No. 175.

Poulet, Georges. See No. 329.

445. Praz, Mario. *The Hero in Eclipse in Victorian Fiction*. Translated by Angus Davidson. London: Oxford Univ., 1956.
Contains a chapter on Peacock.

446. Prins, A. A. "Postscript to 'The Religious Background of Shelley's Prometheus Unbound,'" ES, XLVI (June 1965), 253.
See No. 447.

447. *Prins, A. A. "The Religious Background of Shelley's *Prometheus Unbound*," *English Studies Presented to R. W. Zandvoort on the Occasion of His Seventieth Birthday: A Supplement to English Studies*, XLV (1964), 223-234.
The basic features of *Prometheus Unbound* are derived from Zoroastrianism and Gnosticism. See No. 446.

Pritchard, John Paul. See No. 176.

448. Raymond, William O. *The Infinite Moment and Other Essays in Robert Browning*. Second Edition. Toronto: Toronto Univ., 1965.
Reprints (pp. 236-243) "Browning and the Harriet Westbrook Shelley Letters." See K-SJ, XIII (1964), 149-150.

Read, Bill. See No. 7.

449. Read, Herbert. "Poor Old Shelley," NS, LXVIII (Dec. 11, 1964), 924.
A reply to Donald Davie's review of *The Esdaile Notebook*. See No. 360.

450. Reiman, Donald H. *Shelley's "The Triumph of Life": A Critical Study Based on a Text Newly Edited from the Bodleian Manuscript*. Illinois Studies in Language and Literature No. 55. Urbana: Illinois Univ., 1965.

451. Richmond, H. M. *The School of Love: The Evolution of the Stuart Love Lyric*. See K-SJ, XIV (1965), 131.
Rev. in TLS, July 9, 1964, p. 614.

452. Richmond, H. M. "Tradition and the Lyric: An Historical Approach to Value," *Comparative Literature Studies*, I (1964), 119-132.
Discusses Shelley.

453. Rieger, James. "Shelley's Paterin Beatrice," SIR, IV (Spring 1965), 169-184.
Sees *The Cenci* as "a child of the left hand" between the third and fourth acts of *Prometheus Unbound:*

"the satanically vengeful Beatrice" demonstrates the condition of sin that precedes Prometheus' conversion.

Ritz, Jean-Georges. See No. 181.

454. Rogers, Neville. "Justice and Harriet Shelley," KSMB, XV (1964), 13-20.

Finds the evidence insufficient to judge either Harriet or Shelley himself.

455. "Romantic Letters," TLS, Feb. 4, 1965, p. 96.

Gives an account of the Cini sale at Sotheby's, Nov. 10, 1964. See No. 421.

Rowland, Benjamin, Jr. See No. 184.

Saunders, J. W. See No. 185.

Sewell, Elizabeth. See No. 338.

456. *Shelley, Mary Wollstonecraft. *Frankenstein.* London: Corgi, 1964.

A paperback reprint.

457. *Shelley, Mary Wollstonecraft. *Frankenstein.* New York: Dell, 1965. "Laurel Editions."

A paperback reprint.

458. *Shelley, Mary Wollstonecraft. *Frankenstein.* [Translated by] Hannah Betjeman. [Preface and Filmography of *Frankenstein* by] Michel Boujut. Lausanne: Editions Rencontre, 1964.

459. *Shelley, Mary Wollstonecraft. *Frankenstein.* [Translated by] Hannah Betjeman. Paris: Union générale d'éditions, 1965. "Collection Le Monde."

460. *Shelley, Mary Wollstonecraft. *Frankenstein, ou Le Prométhée moderne.* [Translated by] Joe Ceurvost. [Preface by] Jacques Bergier. Verviers Gérard [Belgium], 1964.

461. "Shelley Exposed—by Computer," *The Times,* London, Sept. 12, 1964, p. 8.

"A computer has compared Milton's *Paradise Lost* and Shelley's *Prometheus Unbound* and has concluded that Shelley borrowed heavily from Milton to refute the latter's philosophy."

462. "Shelley Poetry Put to Music," *The Times,* London, Nov. 26, 1963, p. 15.

Gives an account of the performance of four Shelley songs composed by Malcolm Lipkin.

Sinclair, Alexander R. See No. 186.

Singh, Satyanarain. See No. 341.

463. *Spender, Stephen. *Shelley: Etude sur l'écrivain.* [With selected poems and bibliography.] Paris: Seghers, 1964. "Ecrivains d'hier et d'aujourd'hui."

Stendhal, *pseud.* See No. 188.

464. *Suzuki, Hiroshi. "An Essay on Shelley," *English Literature* (Waseda Univ. English Literary Society, Tokyo), No. 26 (March 1965), pp. 14-23. [In Japanese.]

Swinburne, Algernon Charles. See No. 190.

465. *Szobotka, Tibor. *Shelley.* Budapest: Gondolat, 1960.

466. *Takashashi, Noritsune. "Last Phase of Shelley's Theory of Poetry, with Special Reference to His Definition of Poetry as 'the Expression of the Imagination,'" *Journal of the Textile Faculty, Shinshu University* (Ueda), I (Dec. 1964), 23-37.

467. Thomas, James Andrew. "The Philosophical Anarchism of William Godwin: His Philosophy of Man, State and Society" [Doctoral dissertation, Southern California, 1964], DA, XXV (Dec. 1964), 3621.

Thorslev, Peter L., Jr. See No. 193.

Trousson, Raymond. See No. 194.

Vitoux, Pierre. See No. 51.

Vivante, Leone. See No. 345.

Warner, Oliver. See No. 200.

Wasserman, Earl R. See No. 52.

468. Wasserman, Earl R. "Shakespeare and the English Romantic Movement," in *The Persistence of Shakespeare Idolatry: Essays in Honor of Robert W. Babcock,* ed. Herbert M. Schueller (Detroit: Wayne State Univ., 1964), pp. 77-103.

Includes discussion of Shelley: "Like others of this age of post-idolatry, when Shelley looked into the Shakespearean mirror what he saw was himself."

Rev. by Eugene M. Waith in *Criticism,* VII (Spring 1965), 194-195.

469. Wasserman, Earl R. *The Subtler Language: Critical Readings of Neoclassic and Romantic Poems.* See K-SJ, IX (1960), 75, X (1961), 96, XI (1962), 138, XII (1963), 148, XIV (1965), 132.

Rev. by D. R. M. Wilkinson in ES, XLV (Aug. 1964), 324-326.

Wellek, René. See No. 202.

470. Whalley, George. "Revolution and Poetry," *Centennial Review,* VIII (Fall 1964), 371-390.

Discusses Shelley as a revolutionary poet.

Wheelock, John Hall. See No. 350.

Whipple, Addison Beecher Colvin. See No. 206.

Wilkie, Brian. See No. 53.

471. Woodman, Ross Greig. *The Apocalyptic Vision in the Poetry of Shelley*. See K-SJ, XIV (1965), 133.
Rev. by Harold Bloom in *Yale Review,* LIV (Autumn 1964), 143-149; in TLS, Dec. 31, 1964, p. 1182; by Ants Oras in K-SJ, XIV (1965), 100-102; by James Gray in QQ, LXXII (Spring 1965), 210-211; by Gilbert Thomas in *English,* XV (Spring 1965), 146.

472. Zwerdling, Alex. "The Mythographers and the Romantic Revival of Greek Myth," PMLA, LXXIX (Sept. 1964), 447-456.†
Discusses the shift in the attitude towards classical myth during the eighteenth century, and examines the work of Lemprière, Godwin, Richard Payne Knight and others that was in part responsible for it.

VI. PHONOGRAPH RECORDINGS

Byron, Keats

473. **Byron: Don Juan.* Read by Richard Johnson and Peggy Ashcroft. Argo RG 374.
The selections are from Cantos I and II.
Rev. by Margaret Willy in *English,* XV (Summer 1965), 189.

474. **The English Poets, from Chaucer to Yeats.* Recorded in association with the British Council and Oxford University Press. Directed by George Rylands. Argo 12-in. LP.
No. RG 344 in this series is devoted to the poetry of Byron; No. RG 345 to the poetry of Keats.
Rev. by Margaret Willy in *English,* XV (Spring 1964), 19-20.

475. **"Now, What Is Love?"* Devised and Produced by John Barton. Argo RG 370.
Includes passage from Keats letter to Fanny Brawne.
Rev. by Margaret Willy in *English,* XV (Spring 1964), 20-21.

476. **The Pattern of Poetry*. Vols. III and IV. Compiled by William Kean Seymour and John Smith. HMV CLP1736 and CLP1750.
These records contain a reading of "To Autumn" by Dulcie Gray.

477. **Poetry Readings by Robert Speaight: Treasury of Keats.* Read by Robert Speaight and Robert Eddison. Spoken Arts.
Rev. in *English Journal,* LIV (Apr. 1965), 355.

478. **Robert Donat*. Spoken Arts 848.
Reads Keats and others.
Rev. by T[homas]. L[ask]. in *New York Times,* Sept. 15, 1963, p. 13X.

Bibliography for July 1, 1965–June 30, 1966

VOLUME XVI

Compiled by David Bonnell Green and Edwin Graves Wilson

This bibliography, a regular department of the *Keats-Shelley Journal,* is a register of the literary interest in Keats, Shelley, Byron, Hunt, and their circles from (approximately) July 1965 through June 1966.

The compilers are most grateful, for their kind assistance, to Professors H. W. Häusermann, the University of Geneva; Dr. Siegfried Korninger, Universität, Wien; Ranka Kuić, the University of Belgrade; Takeshi Saito, Emeritus, Tokyo University; Edvige Schulte, Istituto Universitario Orientali, Naples; dr. Karel Štěpaník, J. E. Purkyne University, Brno; Dr. Helmut Viebrock, Johann Wolfgang Goethe Universität, Frankfurt am Main; Drs. Margaret Dalziel, University of Otago, Dunedin; Albert Gérard, Seraing, Belgium; Anna Katona, the University of Debrecen; J. G. Riewald, University of Groningen; D. H. Borchardt, Chief Librarian, La Trobe University, Melbourne; B. L. Kandel, the M. E. Saltykov-Schedrin State Public Library, Leningrad; Torbjörn Söderholm, Åbo Akademi Library; and the library staffs of Boston University, Harvard University, and Wake Forest College.

We wish to thank Mrs. Kisia Trolle, of the Harvard College Library, for her very generous help with the Russian entries, and Mrs. Evro Layton, also of the Harvard College Library, for her most gracious assistance with the Greek entries.

Each item that we have not seen is marked by an asterisk. Entries which have been abstracted in *Abstracts of English Studies* are marked with a dagger, but entries in previous bibliographies which were abstracted too late for notice have not been repeated.

ABBREVIATIONS

ABC	American Book Collector
AL	American Literature
ASNS	Archiv für das Studium der neueren Sprachen
BA	Books Abroad
BC	Book Collector
BNYPL	Bulletin of the New York Public Library
CE	College English
CL	Comparative Literature
CLSB	C. L. S. Bulletin (Charles Lamb Society)
CR	Contemporary Review
DA	Dissertation Abstracts
EA	Etudes Anglaises
EC	Essays in Criticism

ELH	Journal of English Literary History
ELN	English Language Notes
ES	English Studies
Exp	Explicator
HLQ	Huntington Library Quarterly
ILN	Illustrated London News
JAAC	Journal of Aesthetics and Art Criticism
JEGP	Journal of English and Germanic Philology
JHI	Journal of the History of Ideas
KR	Kenyon Review
K-SJ	Keats-Shelley Journal
KSMB	Keats-Shelley Memorial Bulletin
Li	Listener
MLN	Modern Language Notes
MLQ	Modern Language Quarterly
MLR	Modern Language Review
MP	Modern Philology
N&Q	Notes and Queries
NS	New Statesman
NYT	New York Times Book Review
PBSA	Papers of the Bibliographical Society of America
PMLA	Publications of the Modern Language Association of America
PQ	Philological Quarterly
PR	Partisan Review
QQ	Queen's Quarterly
RES	Review of English Studies
RLC	Revue de Littérature Comparée
SAQ	South Atlantic Quarterly
SatR	Saturday Review
SEL	Studies in English Literature 1500-1900
SIR	Studies in Romanticism
SP	Studies in Philology
Spec	Spectator
SR	Sewanee Review
TLS	Times Literary Supplement
VQR	Virginia Quarterly Review

I. GENERAL

Current Bibliographies

1. *English Literary Manuscripts in the Boston Public Library: A Checklist.* Boston: Boston Public Library, 1966.

   Byron, Lady Byron, Charles Cowden Clarke, Godwin, Mary Wollstonecraft Godwin, Haydon, Hazlitt, J. A. Hessey, Hobhouse, Hood, Hunt, Charles Ollier, Mary Shelley, and John Taylor are among those listed.

2. Erdman, David V., *et al.* "The Romantic Movement: A Selected and Critical Bibliography for 1964," ELN, III, Supplement (Sept. 1965), 1-149.
3. Erdman, David V., *et al.* "The Romantic Movement: A Selective and Critical Bibliography for the Year 1963," PQ, XLIII (Oct. 1964), 433-525.†
4. Freeman, Ronald E. "Victorian Bibliography for 1965," *Victorian Studies,* IX (June 1966), 429-483.
5. Green, David Bonnell, and Edwin Graves Wilson. "Current Bibliography," K-SJ, XV (1966), 141-178.
6. Green, David Bonnell, and Edwin Graves Wilson, eds. *Keats, Shelley, Byron, Hunt, and Their Circles. A Bibliography: July 1, 1950-June 30, 1962.* See K-SJ, XV (1966), 142.

   Rev. by *Nella Morace in *Annali, Sezioni Germanica* (Istituto Universitario Orientale), VIII (1965), 300-301; by Lawrence S. Thompson in PBSA, LIX (1st quarter 1965), 98-99; in *Choice,* I (Feb. 1965), 545; by M[ax]. F. S[chulz]. in *Personalist,* XLVI (Summer 1965), 409-410; by R[obert]. V[lach]. in BA, XXXIX (Summer 1965), 355; by K[enneth]. N[eill]. C[ameron]. in ELN, III, Supplement (Sept. 1965), 12; by Frederick T. Wood in ES, XLVI (Dec. 1965), 513.

7. Rice, Sister Pio Maria. "John Keats, A Classified Bibliography of Critical Writings on John Keats's Poems Occurring in Periodicals over the Fifteen-Year Period, 1947-1961," *Bulletin of Bibliography,* XXIV (May-Aug. 1965), 167-168; (Sept.-Dec. 1965), 187-192.†

   Adds nothing to the material taken from the *Keats-Shelley Journal* bibliographies except a few standard items from the period before the *Journal* began. The transcriptions and classifications contain numerous errors.

8. Rigby, Marjory, and Charles Nilon, eds. "Nineteenth Century," *Annual Bibliography of English Language and Literature,* XXXVIII (1965 [for 1963]), 183-262.
9. Stuart, Dorothy Margaret. "The Nineteenth Century and After: I," *The Year's Work in English Studies,* ed. Frederick S. Boas, XXIX (1950 [for 1948]), 241-256.
10. Stuart, Dorothy Margaret, and Eliza-

beth Brocklehurst. "The Nineteenth Century and After: I," *The Year's Work in English Studies,* ed. Frederick S. Boas, XXX (1951 [for 1949]), 206-221.

11. Yarker, P. M., and Brian Lee. "The Nineteenth Century," in *The Year's Work in English Studies,* ed. Beatrice White and T. S. Dorsch, XLIV (1965 [for 1963]), 263-301.

Books and Articles Relating to English Romanticism

12. Altick, Richard D. *Lives and Letters: A History of Literary Biography in England and America.* New York: Knopf. 1965.

Byron, Hunt, Keats, Shelley, Godwin, Hazlitt, Peacock, and others are discussed.

13. Anderson, George K. *The Legend of the Wandering Jew.* Providence: Brown Univ., 1965.

Includes discussion of Byron, Godwin, Shelley, and Thomas Medwin.

14. Benoit, Raymond Paul. "Romanticism: A Reinterpretation" [Doctoral dissertation, Oregon, 1965], DA, XXVI (Apr. 1966), 6018.

15. *Bibliotheca Bibliographici: A Catalogue of the Library Formed by . . . Geoffrey Keynes.* London: Trianon Press, 1964.

Books of Byron, Godwin, Haydon, Hazlitt, Hood, Hunt, Peacock, Reynolds, Shelley, and Mary Wollstonecraft are listed, as are letters of Hazlitt and Reynolds.

Rev. by H. Richard Archer in PBSA, LIX (3rd quarter 1965), 334-338.

16. Bostetter, Edward E. *The Romantic Ventriloquists: Wordsworth, Coleridge, Keats, Shelley, Byron.* See K-SJ, XIV (1965), 107, XV (1966), 143.

Rev. by Marshall Suther in *Western Humanities Review,* XVIII (Autumn 1964), 376-377; by Geoffrey H. Hartman in MP, LXIII (Nov. 1965), 165-168; by Donald Weeks in JAAC, XXIV (Winter 1965), 322-323; by Frederick T. Wood in ES, XLVI (Dec. 1965), 510-511. Also see No. 29.

17. Bousquet, Jacques. *Les Thèmes du Rêve dans la Littérature Romantique (France-Angleterre-Allemagne): Essai sur la naissance et l'évolution des images.* Paris: Didier, 1964.

Byron, Keats, and Shelley are discussed.

18. Brand, C. P. *Italy and the English Romantics: The Italianate Fashion in Early Nineteenth-Century England.* See K-SJ, VIII (1959), 53, IX (1960), 49, XII (1963), 123, XIII (1964), 121, XV (1966), 143.

Now reissued (*Cambridge: Cambridge Univ., 1965).

Rev. in *English,* XV (Autumn 1965), 246.

19. Brand, C. P. *Torquato Tasso: A Study of the Poet and of His Contribution to English Literature.* Cambridge: Cambridge Univ., 1965.

Byron, Hunt, Keats, Shelley, Hazlitt, and Peacock are discussed or touched upon.

Rev. by William Kean Seymour in CR, CCVI (May 1965), 279; by Judy Rawson in *Durham University Journal,* LVIII (March 1966), 111-112.

20. Day, Martin S. *History of English Literature 1660-1837.* Garden City: Doubleday, 1963.

21. Ehrstine, John W. "The Drama and Romantic Theory: The Cloudy Symbols of High Romance," *Research Studies,* XXXIV (June 1966), 85-106.

Drama in any traditional sense was impossible to the Romantics: "the whole psychological and poetic orientation of this group of poets was directed inwards, focused on the personal, on the stage of the mind."

22. Fogle, Richard Harter. "Recent Studies in English Romanticism," SEL, V (Autumn 1965), 735-748.

An omnibus review. See K-SJ, XIV (1965), 127, Nos. 362 and 366, 133, No. 466, XV (1966), 144, No. 29, 145, No. 53, 151, No. 158, 154, No. 201, 156, No. 240, 158, No. 266, 159, No. 276, 163, No. 354, 165, No. 369, 168, No. 433, 169, No. 450. Also see Nos. 27, 40, 148, 219, 236, 243, 340, 346, 351, 362, 423, 436, and 478.

23. Frye, Northrop, ed. *Romanticism Reconsidered: Selected Papers from the English Institute.* See K-SJ, XIV (1965), 107, XV (1966), 143.

Rev. by Z. S. Fink in *Western Humanities Review,* XIX (Summer 1965),

273-275; by Frederick T. Wood in ES, XLVI (Dec. 1965), 511.

24. Halsted, John B., ed. *Romanticism: Problems of Definition, Explanation, and Evaluation*. Boston: Heath, 1965. "Problems of European Civilization."

25. Hayden, John Olin. "The Reviewers of British Romantic Literature 1802-24" [Doctoral dissertation, Columbia, 1965], DA, XXVI (Feb. 1966), 4629.

26. Hayward, John, ed. *The Oxford Book of Nineteenth-Century English Verse*. See K-SJ, XV (1966), 144.

Rev. by Harold Bloom in *Victorian Studies,* IX (Sept. 1965), 68-69; by R. V. Johnson in *Southern Review, An Australian Journal of Literary Studies,* I, No. 3 (1965), 92-94.

27. Hilles, Frederick W., and Harold Bloom, eds. *From Sensibility to Romanticism: Essays Presented to Frederick A. Pottle*. See K-SJ, XV (1966), 144.

Rev. in *Choice,* II (July-Aug. 1965), 316; by R. L. Brett in *Critical Quarterly,* VIII (Spring 1966), 95-96; by Hermann Peschmann in *English,* XVI (Spring 1966), 21; by James Walt in BA, XL (Spring 1966), 213; by John L. Mahoney in *Thought,* XLI (Summer 1966), 284-285. See also No. 22.

28. Jack, Ian. *English Literature 1815-1832*. See K-SJ, XIV (1965), 107, XV, (1966), 144.

Rev. by Gerard Meath in *Tablet,* CCXVII (Dec. 7, 1963), 1319-1321; by M. Bryn Davies in *Southern Review, An Australian Journal of Literary Studies,* I, No. 2 (1964), 97-101, 103; by John Jones in RES, N.S., XVI (Aug. 1965), 319-320. See also Nos. 29 and 32.

29. Kostelanetz, Anne. "Romantic Poets and Pontificators," *Minnesota Review,* IV (Summer 1964), 532-543.

An omnibus review. See K-SJ, XIII (1964), 142, No. 386, XIV (1965), 107, Nos. 17 and 25, 118, No. 208, 124, No. 316, 126, No. 355, XV (1966), 143, No. 17, 144, No. 35, 156, No. 239, 163, No. 347. Also see Nos. 16, 28, 218, and 334.

30. Marshall, William H., ed. *The Major English Romantic Poets*. New York: Washington Square, 1966.

A hardcover edition of a work first published in 1963. See K-SJ, XIV (1965), 108, XV (1966), 144.

31. Massey, Irving. "The Romantic Movement: Phrase or Fact?" *Dalhousie Review,* XLIV (Winter 1964-65), 396-412.†

Assembles arguments against the phrase "Romantic Movement."

32. Mills, Howard. "Subject of Curious Speculation," *Delta,* No. 33 (Summer 1964), pp. 16-20.

A review article on W. L. Renwick's *English Literature 1789-1815* and Ian Jack's *English Literature 1815-1832*. [See K-SJ, XIII (1964), 124, XIV (1965), 107. Also see No. 28.] Tests them on Crabbe and Peacock.

33. Peckham, Morse, ed. *Romanticism: The Culture of the Nineteenth Century*. New York: Braziller, 1965.

Includes selections from Byron and Keats.

34. Piper, Herbert Walter. *The Active Universe: Pantheism and the Concept of Imagination in the English Romantic Poets*. See K-SJ, XIII (1964), 124, XIV (1965), 108, XV (1966), 145.

Rev. by Geoffrey Bullough in *Aumla,* No. 24 (Nov. 1965), 305-307.

35. Rodway, Allan. *The Romantic Conflict*. See K-SJ, XIV (1965), 108, XV (1966), 145.

Rev. by Gerard Meath in *Tablet,* CCXVII (Dec. 7, 1963), 1319-1321; in *Choice,* I (Apr. 1964), 63.

36. Saintsbury, George. *A History of English Prose Rhythm*. Bloomington: Indiana Univ., 1965.

A reprint of a book first published in 1912.

Hunt, Hazlitt, Peacock, and Shelley are treated.

37. Stilwell, Robert Lee. "The Long Poem in English Romantic Criticism, 1750-1850" [Doctoral dissertation, Ohio State, 1965], DA, XXVI (May 1966), 6700.

38. Thorslev, Peter L., Jr. "Freedom and Destiny: Romantic Contraries," *Bucknell Review,* XIV (May 1966), 38-45.

39. Wellek, René. *A History of Modern Criticism*. Vol. III: *The Age of Transition*. Vol. IV: *The Later Nineteenth Century*. New Haven: Yale Univ., 1965. See K-SJ, VI (1957), 133.

Includes references to Byron, Hazlitt, Keats, and Shelley.

Rev. by Roger Sale in *Hudson Review,* XIX (Summer 1966), 324-329.

40. Wilkie, Brian. *Romantic Poets and*

Epic Tradition. See K-SJ, XV (1966), 145.

Rev. by William A. Walling in *Commonweal,* LXXXII (Apr. 30, 1965), 197-199; in *Choice,* II (Sept. 1965), 390; by Donald H. Reiman in JEGP, LXIV (Oct. 1965), 747-751; by Ernest Bernhard-Kabisch in ELN, III (Dec. 1965), 142-147; by S[tephen]. M. Parrish in K-SJ, XV (1966), 126-128; by Ralph Lawrence in *English,* XVI (Spring 1966), 28; by John Buxton in RES, N.S., XVII (May 1966), 215-217; by James Scoggins in CE, XXVII (May 1966), 645-646. Also see No. 22.

II. BYRON

Works: Selected, Single, Translated

41. **Anglika tragoudia*. [Translated by] Angelos Doxas, *pseud*. Athens: Difros, 1961.
 Includes translations from the poetry of Byron, Hood, Keats, and Shelley.
42. "Apopse de tha planēthoume," [translated by] Stephanos Tsatsoulas, *Philologike Prōtochronia,* XVII (1960), 277.
 "So we'll go no more a-roving."
43. **Byron shishû*. [*Poetical Works*.] [Translated by] Abe Tomoji. Tokyo: Yayoi shobô, 1963.
44. Charpier, Jacques, and Pierre Seghers, eds. *L'art poétique*. Paris: Seghers, 1956.
 Includes selections from Byron, Keats, and Shelley.
45. *Djurić, Votislav, ed. *Lirika*. [*Lyrics*.] Belgrade: "Zavod za udzbenike," 1965.
 Includes translations by Ranka Kuić of excerpts from *Queen Mab* and Fragments to William Shelley, by Borivoje Nedić of a poem by Keats, by Aleksandar Spasić of a poem by Keats and Byron's sonnet "To Chillon."
46. "Hola gia ton Erōta," "Strophes stēn Augousta," "Stichoi stē gynaika tou," and "Sēmera kleinō ta triantaexē mou chronia," in "30 Anglika tragoudia," [translated by] Angelos Doxas, *pseud., Kainouria Epochē,* No. 20 (1960), pp. 100-105.
47. **Izbrannoe*. [Translated by] A. Blok *et al.* Moscow: Det. lit., 1964.
48. *Kinsley, James, and James T. Boulton, eds. *English Satiric Poetry: Dryden to Byron*. London: Arnold, 1966. "Arnold's English Texts."
49. *Kormos, I., ed. *Uj szerelmes kalendárium* [*A New Love Calendar*.] Budapest: Móra, 1965.
 Includes one poem each by Byron, Keats, and Shelley.
50. *Lator, L., ed. *A világirodalom legszebb versei*. [*The Most Beautiful Poems of World Literature*.] Budapest: Európa, 1966.
 Includes one poem by Byron, eight by Shelley, and nine by Keats.
51. *Lengyel, B., and F. Vincze, eds. *A világirodalom ars poeticái*. [*The Ars Poeticas of World Literature*.] [Introduction by] L. Kardos. Budapest: Gondolat, 1965.
 Includes excerpts from Byron, Keats, and Shelley.
52. **Lirika*. [*Lyrics*.] Tbilisi: Nakaduli, 1965. "Biblioteka mirovoi poezii" ["World Library of Poems"]. [In Georgian.]
53. **Lord Byron: "Childe Harold."* [Translated by] Danko Andelinović. Zagreb: "Zora," Matica Hrvatska, 1965.
54. Meynell, Sir Francis, comp. *Memorable Poetry, Chosen from All Periods*. London: Nonesuch, 1965; New York: Franklin Watts, 1966.
 Includes selections from Byron, Hunt, Keats, and Shelley.

Peckham, Morse, ed. See No. 33.

55. **Poems of Newstead: Poetry Relating to Newstead Abbey and Its Neighbourhood Extracted from the Works of Lord Byron*. Nottingham: Public Library, 1965.
56. **Poezija Vekova*. [*Poetry of the Ages*.] [Translated by] Trifun Dukić. Belgrade: "Kultura," 1965.
 Includes translations of poems by Byron and Shelley.
57. **Sobranie sochinenii*. [*Collected Works*.] [Foreword by] Kh. Dashtents. Erevan: Aiastan, 1965. [In Armenian.]
58. *"U vod vavilonskikh . . . Stroki, napisannye pod viazom . . . K Tirze. Prometei (stikhi)," [translated by] Dzh. Charkviani, *Tsiskari,* No. 4 (1965), pp. 51-55.
59. *Zolder, Anth. *Nostalgies*. Agrinion, 1961.
 Includes translations from Byron's poetry.

Books and Articles Relating to Byron and His Circle

Altick, Richard D. See No. 12.

60. Anderson, Edgar. "A Botanist Looks at Poetry," *Michigan Quarterly Review,* IV (Summer 1965), 177-184.
Byron, Keats, and Shelley appear on a metroglyph.

Anderson, George K. See No. 13.

61. "Auction Sales," ABC, XVI (March 1966), 29-31.
First edition of *English Bards and Scotch Reviewers* sold at Parke-Bernet Galleries for $85.

62. "Auction Sales," ABC, XVI (May 1966), 29, 31.
At Sotheby's a first edition of Byron's *Waltz* brought $3,920.

63. *Babchina, T. "Drama Bairona *Kain* v perevode Rainisa" ["Rainis' Translation of Byron's *Cain*"], *Karogs,* No. 8 (1965), pp. 125-127. [In Latvian.]

Bagehot, Walter. See No. 360.

64. Barr, D. J. "Byron and Johnson," N&Q, CCX (Dec. 1965), 464.
Asks whether a line in *Childe Harold's Pilgrimage* echoes *Idler,* No. 42.

65. Bartel, Roland. "Byron's Respect for Language," *Papers on English Language & Literature,* I (Autumn 1965), 373-378.
"Byron on many occasions expressed a deep respect for the purity and power of precise language properly used."

66. Bartholomew, James Reece. "Byron's *Sardanapalus:* A Manuscript Edition" [Doctoral dissertation, Texas, 1964], DA, XXVI (July 1965), 363.
See K-SJ, XV (1966), 147.

67. Battiscombe, Georgina, and Marghanita Laski, eds. *A Chaplet for Charlotte Yonge.* London: Cresset, 1965.
Includes Kathleen Tillotson's "Charlotte Yonge as a Critic of Literature" (pp. 56-70), which touches upon her attitude towards Byron and Shelley.

68. Beyer, Werner W. *The Enchanted Forest.* See K-SJ, XIV (1965), 110, XV (1966), 147.
Rev. by Horst Oppel in *Anglia,* LXXXIII (1965), 248-250.

Bibliotheca Bibliographici. See No. 15.

69. Blotner, Joseph, comp. *William Faulkner's Library—A Catalogue.* Charlottesville: Virginia Univ., 1964.
It included works of Byron, Keats, and Shelley.

70. Blunt, Wilfrid. *Cockerell: Sydney Carlyle Cockerell, Friend of Ruskin and William Morris and Director of the Fitzwilliam Museum, Cambridge.* New York: Knopf, 1965.
Has material on Baroness Wentworth.

71. Borgini, Alma. "Carlo Bini traduttore," *Rassegna della Letteratura Italiana,* LXVIII (May-Dec. 1964), 382-398.
Discusses his translations of Byron.

Bousquet, Jacques. See No. 17.

72. Brack, O. M., Jr. "Lord Byron, Leigh Hunt and *The Liberal:* Some New Evidence," *Books at Iowa,* No. 4 (Apr. 1966), pp. 36-38.
Prints a letter from Byron to Mary Shelley, Oct. 14, 1822, that suggests he may have disparaged Leigh Hunt in a letter or letters to John Murray earlier than that of Oct. 9, 1822.

73. Braekman, W. "Letters by Robert Southey to Sir John Taylor Coleridge," *Studia Germanica Gandensia,* VI (1964), 103-230.
The letters (1794-1834) include references to Byron, Godwin, Hunt, Keats, and Shelley.

Brand, C. P. See No. 19.

74. Bruffee, Kenneth Allen. "Satan and the Sublime: The Meaning of the Romantic Hero" [Doctoral dissertation, Northwestern, 1964], DA, XXVI (Oct. 1965), 2203-2204.
Is particularly concerned with Byron and the Byronic hero.

75. [Byron, John.] *Byron's Journal of His Circumnavigation 1764-66.* Ed. Robert E. Gallagher. Cambridge: Cambridge Univ., for the Hakluyt Society, 1964.
Rev. in TLS, June 17, 1965, p. 492.

76. Cannon, Garland. "The Literary Place of Sir William Jones (1746-94)," *Journal of the Asiatic Society,* II (1960), 47-61.
Includes discussion of his influence on Byron and Shelley; touches on Hunt and Keats.

77. Capps, Jack L. *Emily Dickinson's Reading 1836-1886.* Cambridge, Mass.: Harvard Univ., 1966.
Keats and Byron were among those read. Severn is touched upon.

78. Carlos, Alberto J. "El *Mal du Siècle* en un Soneto de la Avellaneda," *Ro-*

mance Notes, VII (Spring 1966), 134-138.

Byron's influence is discussed.

79. Chatzēdēmētriou, Iphianassa. "Ho Byrōn kai hoi gynaikes," *Nea Hestia,* No. 814 (1961), pp. 725-728, No. 815 (1961), pp. 784-788.

80. *Chew, Samuel C. *Byron in England: His Fame and After-Fame.* New York: Russell & Russell, 1965.

A reprint of a book first published in 1924.

81. Chew, Samuel C., Jr. *The Dramas of Lord Byron: A Critical Study.* See K-SJ, XV (1966), 148.

Rev. in *Choice,* II (May 1965), 157.

82. Church, Richard. "The English Poets from Chaucer to Yeats," REL, VI (Oct. 1965), 100-106.

Reviews recordings (Marlowe Dramatic Society) of the poetry of Byron, Keats, and Shelley.

83. Coleman, Ronald Gregg. "Cosmic Symbolism in Byron's Dramas" [Doctoral dissertation, Vanderbilt, 1965], DA, XXVI (Oct. 1965), 2206.

84. *De-Logu, P. "Byron carbonaro a Ravenna sotto finte spoglie di 'cavalier servente,'" *Il Messaggero,* i, II, 1957.

85. Derry, Warren. *Dr. Parr: A Portrait of the Whig Dr. Johnson.* Oxford: Clarendon, 1966.

Byron and Godwin are treated; references to T. J. Hogg and Shelley.

86. De Sua, William J. *Dante into English: A Study of the Translation of the "Divine Comedy" in Britain and America.* See K-SJ, XV (1966), 148.

Rev. by Barbara Reynolds in *Forum for Modern Language Studies,* I (Apr. 1965), 117-125; by A. Bartlett Giamatti in *Comparative Literature Studies,* III (1966), 83-87.

87. Diller, Hans-Jürgen. "Form und Funktion der Apostrophen in Byrons *Childe Harold's Pilgrimage,*" *Anglia,* LXXXII (1964), 321-341.

88. Drew, Fraser Bragg. "Search for Lord Byron," *Vermont Historical Society News and Notes,* XVII (Feb. 1966), 42-44.

Describes visits to Newstead, Hucknall Torkard, Cambridge, and Byron's birthplace in London.

89. Elledge, Waymon Paul. "The Enkindled Clay: Imagery and Theme in Byron's Poetry" [Doctoral dissertation, Tulane, 1965], DA, XXVI (Oct. 1965), 2180-2181.

90. Elledge, W[aymon]. Paul. "Imagery and Theme in Byron's *Cain,*" K-SJ, XV (Winter 1966), 49-57.

Byron "strengthens the argument of the play by framing it in a refined and subtle imagistic construct."

91. England, A. B. "An Echo of Prior in *Don Juan,*" N&Q, CCXI (May 1966), 179.

From *Hans Carvel.*

English Literary Manuscripts. See No. 1.

92. Ennis, Julian. "Advanced Level Poet," *Review of English Literature,* VII (Apr. 1966), 74.

A poem on Byron.

93. *Escarpit, Robert. *Byron: Etude sur l'écrivain. Choix de textes de George Byron.* Paris: Seghers, 1965. "Coll. Ecrivains d'hier et d'aujourd'hui."

94. *Euangelatos, Chr[ēstos]. *Ho heortasmos tēs 135ēs epeteiou tēs Exodou kai tēs 137ēs epeteiou tou Byrōnos, tēn 1-2 Apriliou 1961. Prosklēseis-Programma.* Missolonghi, 1961.

95. Euangelatos, Chrēstos. "To Mesolongi Lo. Byrōn, ho Palamas kai ho Mager," *Stereoelladikē Hestia,* Nos. 9-10 (1961), pp. 173-175.

96. Fontane, Theodor. *Aus England und Schottland,* ed. Charlotte Jolles. Vol. XVII of Fontane's *Sämtliche Werke.* Munich: Nymphenburger, 1963.

References to Byron and Shelley.

97. Frykman, Erik. *W. E. Aytoun, Pioneer Professor of English at Edinburgh: A Study of His Literary Opinions and His Contribution to the Development of English as an Academic Discipline.* Gothenburg Studies in English No. 17. Gothenburg: Almqvist & Wiksell, 1963.

Mentions his views on Byron, Keats, Shelley, and others.

Rev. by David Murison in ASNS, CCII (Apr. 1966), 470-471.

98. García Blanco, Manuel. "Unamuno y la cultura inglesa," *Filologia Moderna,* Nos. 19-20 (Apr.-Aug. 1965), 125-157.

Byron, Keats, and Shelley are discussed.

99. George, M. Dorothy. *Catalogue of Political and Personal Satires Preserved in the Department of Prints and Drawings in the British Museum.* Vol. X:

1820-1827. London: British Museum, 1952.
Has material on Byron, Hobhouse, Hunt, Haydon, and Shelley.

100. George, M. Dorothy. *Catalogue of Political and Personal Satires Preserved in the Department of Prints and Drawings in the British Museum.* Vol. XI: *1828-1832*. London: British Museum, 1954.
Includes material on Byron, Hobhouse, and Hunt.

101. Geyl, P[ieter]. *Figuren en problemen.* 2 vols. Amsterdam and Antwerp: Wereldbibliotheek, 1964. "Telstar Pocket."
Has a chapter on Byron (II, 102-110).

102. *Giannakspoulos, Takēs. "Mia paradosi gia to Mesolongi kai ho Lordos Byrōn," *Hellēnikē Periēgētikē Leschē,* No. 15 (1960).

103. Gleckner, Robert F., "Ruskin and Byron," ELN, III (Sept. 1965), 47-51.
Analyzes Ruskin's criticism of a passage from *The Island.*

104. *Goode, Clement Tyson. *Byron as Critic.* New York: Haskell House, 1964.
A reprint of a book first published in 1920.

105. Gordan, John D. "An Anniversary Exhibition: The Henry W. and Albert A. Berg Collection 1940-1965," BNYPL, LXIX (Oct. 1965), 537-554; (Nov. 1965), 597-608; (Dec. 1965), 665-677.
Includes Byron, Shelley, and Keats treasures. See No. 156.

106. Gordon, David J. *D. H. Lawrence as a Literary Critic.* New Haven: Yale Univ., 1966.
References to, and discussions of his criticism of, Byron, Keats, and Shelley.

107. Grigson, Geoffrey. "The Demolishers at Work," *Country Life,* CXXVII (Jan. 28, 1960), 158-159.
Includes photographs of Halnaby Hall as it was in 1933 and during demolition in 1953.

108. Grønbech, Vilhelm. *Religious Currents in the 19th Century.* [Translated by] P. M. Mitchell and W. D. Paden. Lawrence: Kansas Univ., 1964.
Discusses Byron and Shelley.

109. Hauser, Arnold. *The Social History of Art.* 2 vols. London: Routledge, 1951.
Discusses Byron and Shelley. Keats and Hazlitt are touched upon.

110. Hayter, Alethea. "Landscape in English Romantic Poetry and Painting," *Annales de la Faculté des Lettres et Sciences Humaines d'Aix,* XXXVIII, No. 2 (1964), 269-284.
Byron, Keats, and Shelley are among those discussed.

111. Hirst, Wolfe Ze'ev. "Old Testament Influences on the Romantic Hero Figure in England, France, and Germany" [Doctoral dissertation, Washington, 1965], DA, XXVI (Nov. 1965), 2725-2726.
Includes discussion of Byron.

112. Hudson, Gertrude Reese, ed. *Browning to His American Friends: Letters between the Brownings, the Storys, and James Russell Lowell, 1841-1890.* New York: Barnes and Noble, 1965.
References to Byron, Hunt, Keats, Shelley, Severn, and Seymour Kirkup.

113. Hyde, H. Montgomery. *A History of Pornography.* London: Heinemann, 1964.
Includes discussion of *Don Leon.*

114. Joseph, M. K. *Byron the Poet.* See K-SJ, XIV (1965), 112, XV (1966), 150.
Rev. by E. E. B[ostetter]. in ELN, III, Supplement (Sept. 1965), 26; by J. D. Jump in RES, N.S., XVI (Nov. 1965), 438-439; by Frederick T. Wood in ES, XLVI (Dec. 1965), 514; by Frederick L. Beaty in K-SJ, XV (1966), 124-126.

Juel-Jensen, Bent. See No. 269.

115. Kairophylas, Kōstas. "Agapēse Lo. Mpaijron tēn korē tōn Athēnōn?" *Ta Athenaïka,* No. 18 (1961), pp. 1-16.

116. Kernan, Alvin B. *The Plot of Satire.* New Haven: Yale Univ., 1965.
Includes a chapter on *Don Juan.*

117. Kirchner, Sister Mary Evangelista. "The Function of the Persona in the Poetry of Byron" [Doctoral dissertation, Notre Dame, 1965], DA, XXVI (Oct. 1965), 2217.

118. Kotker, Norman, and Howard Nelson. "The Thinking Man's Lake," *Horizon,* VII (Autumn 1965), 65-79.†
Leman: Byron and the Shelleys are included.

119. *Lector. "Il suo amore per l'Italia non fu solo entusiasmo romantico," *Il Messaggero,* 21, IV, 1959.
On Byron.

120. *Lehn, Gertrude Lydia. "The Development of Byron as a Dramatist." (Doctoral dissertation, Harvard, 1966.)

121. Leifer, Walter. *Rhein und Themse fliessen zueinander: Geschichte und Gegenwart der deutsch-englischen Beziehungen.* Herrenalb: Horst Erdmann, 1964.

Goethe's attitude toward Byron is analyzed.

122. Lentricchia, Frank, Jr. "Harriet Beecher Stowe and the Byron Whirlwind," BNYPL, LXX (Apr. 1966), 218-228.

Discusses the reaction to Mrs. Stowe's charges by America's leading literary figures and by the newspapers and periodicals of the day.

123. Leonard, William Ellery. *Byron and Byronism in America.* New York: Gordian, 1965.

A reprint of a book first published in 1907.

124. Lindenberger, Herbert. "On Commentary, Romanticism, and Critical Method: Reflections on Three Recent Books," MLQ, XXVII (June 1966), 212-220.

A review article. Two of the books are *Strangers and Pilgrims* by Roppen and Sommer and Kroeber's *The Artifice of Reality.* See K-SJ, XV (1966), 153, No. 183, 160, No. 304. Also see No. 272.

125. Lombardi, Thomas W. [In] "Information Please," TLS, July 15, 1965, p. 602.

Asks information regarding manuscripts of and other materials on the *Hebrew Melodies.*

126. •Lovell, Ernest J., Jr. *Byron: The Record of a Quest: Studies in a Poet's Concept and Treatment of Nature.* Hamden, Conn.: Archon, 1966. See K-SJ, I (1952), 90, II (1953), 101, XIV (1965), 113, XV (1966), 150.

A reprint of a book first published in 1949.

127. McKemy, Kay. "Lord Byron's Tooth Powder," *Journal of the American Dental Association,* LXXI (Dec. 1965), 1506-1507.

Reviews Byron's efforts to obtain tooth powder.

128. MacNeice, Louis. *Varieties of Parable.* Cambridge: Cambridge Univ., 1965.

Discusses Byron and Shelley.

129. Maitre, Raymond. *Disraeli, Homme de Lettres: La personnalité, la pensée, l'œuvre littéraire.* Paris: Didier, 1963.

Discusses Disraeli's relationships to Byron, Shelley, and Peacock.

130. Marchand, Leslie A. "Byron and Rossini," *Opera News,* XXX (March 19, 1966), 6-7.

Byron during his stay in Venice enjoyed Rossini's operas, the melodies particularly appealing to him; the composer later "honored the poet's memory with a cantata for tenor and mixed chorus."

131. Marchand, Leslie A. *Byron's Poetry: A Critical Introduction.* Boston: Houghton Mifflin; •London: Murray (1965). "Riverside Studies in Literature."

Rev. by Annette Park in CLSB, No. 189 (May 1966), 525-526.

132. Marchand, Leslie A. "The Land of Byron's 'Pilgrimage,'" *Life International,* XXXVIII (Feb. 8, 1965), 66-71.

Summarizes the story of Byron's two voyages to Greece.

133. Marshall, J. F. "Stendhal, Byron et les *Mémoires d'une contemporaine,*" *Stendhal Club,* VII (Apr. 1965), 247-249.

Gives an account of Byron's comments on Stendhal as reported in the *Mémoires* by Elzélina Van Aylde Jonghe, better known as Ida de Saint-Elme.

134. Martinengo, Alessandro. *Polimorfismo nel "Diablo mundo" d'Espronceda.* University of Pisa "Studi di Filologia Moderna," N.S. II. Turin: Bottega d'Erasmo, 1962.

Discusses influence of Byron on Espronceda.

Rev. by Joaquín Casalduero in *Hispanic Review,* XXXIV (Jan. 1966), 84-85.

135. Martins, Heitor. "Byron e *O Guairini,*" *Luso-Brazilian Review,* II (Winter 1965), 69-74.

Considers the influence of Byron on Alencar's work.

136. Medwin, Thomas. *Medwin's "Conversations of Lord Byron," Revised with a New Preface by the Author for a New Edition and Annotated by Lady Byron, John Cam Hobhouse, Sir Walter Scott, Sir Charles Napier, John Murray, John Galt, William Harness, Robert Southey, Lady Caroline Lamb, Leigh Hunt, Mary Shelley, E. J. Trelawny, William Fletcher, Countess Teresa Guiccioli, and Others Who Knew the Poet Personally.* Ed. Ernest

J. Lovell, Jr. Princeton: Princeton Univ., 1966.

Rev. by Robert Halsband in SatR, XLIX (June 11, 1966), 49.

137. Meijer, Hendrik Arnold. *De Boekanier met Inleiding en Aantekeningen Door.* Ed. W. Drop. Zwolle: W. E. J. Tjeenk Willink, 1964.

The introduction includes discussion of Byron's influence on Meijer.

138. Mellon, John Paul. "Byron's *Manfred:* A Study of Sources and Ideas" [Doctoral dissertation, Pittsburgh, 1964], DA, XXVI (Sept. 1965), 1633-1634.

139. Mellown, M. J. "The Development of Lord Byron's Literary Criticism and of the Literary Attitudes Revealed in His Poetry and Prose." (Doctoral dissertation, London, 1965.)

140. Merchant, W. Moelwyn. *Creed and Drama: An Essay in Religious Drama.* London: S.P.C.K., 1965.

Includes (pp. 72-80) a chapter "Lord Byron: *Cain: A Mystery.*"

141. Merimée, Prosper. *Correspondance générale.* Ed. Maurice Parturier *et al.* 18 vols. Paris: Le Divan; Toulouse: Privat (1941-1964). [Vol. XVIII (1964) completes the edition.]

References to Byron and Mary Shelley. Prints a letter of Mary Shelley to Victor Jacquemont.

142. Merritt, James D. "Disraeli as a Byronic Poet," *Victorian Poetry,* III (Spring 1965), 138-139.†

A poem in *Alroy* is derived from "She walks in beauty like the night."

143. Meserole, Harrison T. "Charles Lamb's Reputation and Influence in America to 1835," *Journal of General Education,* XVI (Jan. 1965), 281-308.

Byron, Keats, and Shelley are touched upon.

144. Mills, Carl Henry. "The Intellectual and Literary Background of George Bernard Shaw's *Man and Superman*" [Doctoral dissertation, Nebraska, 1965], DA, XXVI (Nov. 1965), 2727-2728.

Notes influence of Shelley and Byron.

145. Mogan, Joseph J., Jr. "*Pierre* and *Manfred:* Melville's Study of the Byronic Hero," *Papers on English Language & Literature,* I (Summer 1965), 230-240.

"Melville is far more indebted to Byron's *Manfred* for the entire conception of his novel than has been hitherto realized."

146. Moore, Doris Langley. *The Late Lord Byron.* See K-SJ, XII (1963), 130-131, XIII (1964), 131, XIV (1965), 113.

Rev. by Richard Church in *Country Life,* CXXX (July 20, 1961), 159, 161; by *L. Th. Lehrmann in *Litterair paspoort,* Feb. 1962, pp. 26-27.

147. Moore, Thomas. *The Journal of Thomas Moore 1818-1841.* Ed. Peter Quennell. See K-SJ, XV (1966), 151.

Rev. in **Choice,* II (Apr. 1965), 95.

148. Moore, Thomas. *The Letters of Thomas Moore.* Ed. Wilfred S. Dowden. See K-SJ, XV (1966), 151.

Rev. by J. E. P. Thomson in *Aumla,* No. 24 (Nov. 1965), 307-308; by Hoover H. Jordan in K-SJ, XV (1966), 132-135; by William H. Marshall in JEGP, LXV (Jan. 1966), 204-207; by Cecil Price in RES, N.S., XVII (May 1966), 213-215. See also No. 22.

149. Moorman, Mary. *William Wordsworth: A Biography. The Later Years 1803-1850.* Oxford: Oxford Univ., 1965.

Frequent references to Byron, Godwin, Haydon, Hazlitt, Hunt, Keats, Shelley, and others.

150. Moreux, Françoise. *Thomas De Quincey: La Vie—L'Homme—L'OEuvre.* Paris: Presses Universitaires de France, 1964. "Publications de la Faculté des Lettres et Sciences Humaines de Paris, Série 'Recherches,' " Vol. XII.

References to Byron, Godwin, Hazlitt, Hunt, Keats, Shelley, and others.

151. Morgan, Lucretia B. Payne. "Byron's Influence on Villiers de l'Isle-Adam" [Doctoral dissertation, Georgia, 1965], DA, XXVI (Oct. 1965), 2220-2221.

152. Morillo, Marvin. "Faulkner's *The Sound and the Fury,*" Exp, XXIV (Feb. 1966), Item 50.

Mentions Faulkner's use here and in three other works of Byron's "kissing wish."

153. *Mukohyama, Yasuko. "The Theme of the Early Poems of Lord Byron," *Studies in Literature and Arts* (Tsurumi Woman's College, Yokohama), III (Dec. 1965), 47-64. [In Japanese.]

154. *Mukohyama, Yasuko. "Young Byron and Greece," *Thought Currents in English Literature* (Aoyama Gakuin Univ., Tokyo), XXXVIII (Dec. 1965), 161-173. [In Japanese.]

155. Muschg, Walter. "Germanistik? In memoriam Eliza M. Butler," *Euphorion,* LIX (1965), 18-45.
Discusses her *Byron and Goethe.* See K-SJ, VII (1958), 115, VIII (1959), 58, IX (1960), 54, XII (1963), 127.

156. "News and Notes," PBSA, LIX (4th quarter 1965), 442-444.
Mentions exhibitions from Syracuse University and at N. Y. Public Library which included Byron and Keats items respectively. See No. 105.

157. Origo, Iris. *The Last Attachment.* See K-SJ, I (1952), 90-91, XII (1963), 131, XIII (1964), 132, XIV (1965), 114.
Rev. by A[ndré]. Koszul in *Langues modernes,* XLIV (Nov. 1950), 429.

158. Peckham, Morse. "Romanticism: The Present State of Theory," *PCTE Bulletin,* No. 12 (Dec. 1965), pp. 31-53.
Includes discussion of Byron.

159. Piromalli, Antonio. "Momenti della cultura Livornese," *Historica, Rivista Bimestrale di Cultura,* XVI (1963), 106-111.
Byron's influence on Livornese romanticism is discussed.

160. Praz, Mario. "Dante in England," *Forum for Modern Language Studies,* I (Apr. 1965), 99-116.
Discusses the appeal of Dante to Byron and Shelley.

161. Quennell, Peter. "Speaking of Books: Literary Sight-Seeing," NYT, Dec. 12, 1965, pp. 2, 45.
Has several paragraphs on Byron and Newstead Abbey.

162. Raith, Joseph. *Englische Metrik.* Munich: Max Hueber, 1962.
Byron, Keats, Shelley, Hunt, and others are discussed.

163. Rawson, C. J. "Pope Echoes in Byron's 'To Romance' and *Don Juan,* IV. 3," N&Q, CCXI (May 1966), 179.
From the "Epistle to Dr. Arbuthnot" and "Ode to Solitude."

164. Reboul, Pierre. *Le Mythe Anglais dans la Littérature Française sous la Restauration.* Lille: Bibliothèque Universitaire, 1962. (Travaux & Mémoires de l'Université de Lille, Series in -4°-, No. 1.)
Discusses Byron and Godwin.

165. Reed, Joseph W., Jr. *English Biography in the Early Nineteenth Century, 1801-1838.* New Haven: Yale Univ., 1966.
Includes a chapter on Moore's life of Byron.
Rev. in TLS, Apr. 21, 1966, p. 343.

166. Riley, Susan B. "Albert Pike as an American Don Juan," *Arkansas Historical Quarterly,* XIX (Autumn 1960), 207-224.†
Discusses the influence of Keats and Shelley and particularly Byron on his work.

167. Rossetti, Dante Gabriel. *Letters of Dante Gabriel Rossetti.* Ed. Oswald Doughty and John Robert Wahl. Vols. I and II. Oxford: Clarendon, 1965.
Contains references to Keats, Hunt, Severn, Haydon, Byron, and others.

168. Roston, Murray. *Prophet and Poet: The Bible and the Growth of Romanticism.* Evanston: Northwestern Univ.; London: Faber (1965).
Byron and Shelley are discussed.
Rev. by Ralph Lawrence in *English,* XVI (Spring 1966), 28; by James Scoggins in CE, XXVII (May 1966), 645-646.

169. Roumanis, C. "Peri tou theatrou tou Byrōnos," *Paratērētēs,* No. 1 (1960).

170. Ruskin, John. *The Literary Criticism of John Ruskin.* Ed. Harold Bloom. Garden City: Doubleday, 1965. "An Anchor Book."
Reprints three selections on Byron. References to Keats and Shelley.

171. *Rutherford, Andrew. *Byron: A Critical Study.* Edinburgh: Oliver & Boyd, 1966.
A paperback reprint of a book first published in 1961. See K-SJ, XI (1962), 119, XII (1963), 132, XIII (1964), 133, XIV (1965), 114.

172. *Rutherford, Andrew. *Byron the Best-Seller.* Byron Foundation Lecture 1964. [Nottingham: Univ. of Nottingham, 1965.]

173. Ryan, J. S. "Literary Taste—Some Fossilized Preferences," *Names,* XIII (June 1965), 116-124.
Includes a discussion of places in Australia named after Byron or his grandfather. A street in Byron Bay is named after Keats.

174. Sambrook, A. J. "A Romantic Theme: The Last Man," *Forum for Modern Language Studies,* II (Jan. 1966), 25-33.
Discusses its appearance in—among others—Byron, Mary Shelley, and Hood.

175. Serullaz, Maurice. *Mémorial de l'Exposition Eugène Delacroix organisée au Musée du Louvre à l'occasion du centenaire de la mort de l'artiste, Paris 1963*. Paris: Musées Nationaux, 1963.
Reproduces paintings based on subjects taken from Byron's poems.

176. Sherrard, Philip, comp. *The Pursuit of Greece: An Anthology*. London: John Murray, 1964.
Refers to Byron and Shelley; includes two selections from Byron.

177. Southey, Robert. *New Letters of Robert Southey*. Ed. Kenneth Curry. 2 vols. New York: Columbia Univ., 1965.
Has references to Byron, Hunt, Keats, Shelley, Godwin, Haydon, Hazlitt, and others.
Rev. by C. J. Myers in *Dalhousie Review,* XLVI (Spring 1966), 109-111.

178. Steffan, T. G. "Byron's Dramas," N&Q, CCX (July 1965), 278.
Requests information on Byron's manuscripts for a critical book on his dramas. See No. 179.

179. Steffan, T. G. [In] "Information Please," TLS, July 15, 1965, p. 602.
Requests information on the manuscripts and proofs of Byron's dramas. See No. 178.

180. Stevenson, Ronald. "Alan Bush, Committed Composer," *Music Review,* XXV (Nov. 1964), 323-342.
Includes analysis of Bush's *Byron* Symphony, Op. 53.

181. Stock, Ely. "The Biblical Context of 'Ethan Brand,'" AL, XXXVII (May 1965), 115-134.†
Discusses the influence of *Cain: A Mystery* on Hawthorne's story.

182. *Strickland, Geoffrey. "Stendhal, Byron et John Cam Hobhouse," *Stendhal Club,* VII (July 1965), 309-328.

183. Taylor, Robert H. "'Fine Bold Signature,'" *Manuscripts,* XII (Summer 1960), 4-13.
Mentions his copies of works by Byron, Keats, and Shelley.

184. Thorslev, Peter L., Jr. *The Byronic Hero: Types and Prototypes*. See K-SJ, XII (1963), 133, XIII (1964), 133, XIV (1965), 115, XV (1966), 153.
Rev. by Melvin J. Friedman in *Modern Language Journal,* XLVII (May 1963), 216-217.

185. Todd, William B. "London Printers' Imprints, 1800-1840," *Library,* 5th Series, XXI (March 1966), 46-59.
Discusses the imprints of *English Bards and Scotch Reviewers.*

186. Trilling, Lionel. *Beyond Culture: Essays on Literature and Learning.* New York: Viking, 1965.
Reprints (pp. 57-87) "The Fate of Pleasure." See K-SJ, XIV (1965), 107, No. 21, 126, No. 351.

187. Trousson, Raymond. *Le thème de Prométhée dans la littérature européenne.* See K-SJ, XV (1966), 153.
Rev. by Guy Mermier in BA, XL (Winter 1966), 47-48.

Vianu, Tudor. See No. 473.

188. Weinstock, Herbert. *Donizetti and the World of Opera in Italy, Paris, and Vienna in the First Half of the Nineteenth Century.* New York: Pantheon, 1963.
Includes references to Byron.
Rev. by J[ohn]. W. K[lein]. in *Music & Letters,* XLV (Oct. 1964), 377-379.

Wellek, René. See No. 39.

189. Whipple, A. B. C. *The Fatal Gift of Beauty: The Final Years of Byron and Shelley.* See K-SJ, XV (1966), 154.
Rev. by K[enneth]. N[eill]. C[ameron]. in ELN, III, Supplement (Sept. 1965), 27; in *Choice,* I (Jan. 1966), 481.

190. Williams, Gwyn. "The Drowned Man in English Poetry," *Litera,* VIII (1965), 62-90.
Includes discussion of Byron, Keats, and Shelley.

191. Young, Ione Dodson, ed. *A Concordance to the Poetry of Byron.* 4 vols. Austin, Texas: Pemberton Press, 1965.

192. Zegger, Robert Elie. "John Cam Hobhouse at Westminster, 1818-1833" [Doctoral dissertation, Columbia, 1965], DA, XXVI (Oct. 1965), 2153.

III. HUNT

Works: Selected, Single

193. Auden, W. H., ed. *19th Century British Minor Poets.* New York: Delacorte, 1966.
Includes selections from Hunt, Peacock, Hood, and others.

Meynell, Sir Francis, comp. See No. 54.

194. *Musical Evenings.* Ed. David R. Cheney. See K-SJ, XV (1966), 154.
Rev. by [M. A.] M[alkin]. in *Anti-*

quarian Bookman, XXXV (May 31-June 7, 1965), 2362; in *Choice,* II (June 1965), 222; by C[arl]. W[oodring]. in ELN, III, Supplement (Sept. 1965), 33; by Carolyn W. Houtchens in K-SJ, XV (1966), 138-139; by Jean de Palacio in MLR, LXI (Apr. 1966), 294-295.

195. *On Eight Sonnets of Dante: Notes Printed from the Autograph Manuscript in the University of Iowa Library, with Translations of the Sonnets into English by Joseph Garrow, Shelley, and Charles Lyell, a Pencil Drawing of Hunt by Anne Gliddon, and an Editorial Introduction by Rhodes Dunlap.* Iowa City: University of Iowa School of Journalism, 1965.

BOOKS AND ARTICLES RELATING TO HUNT

Altick, Richard D. See No. 12.

196. Barnes, Warner. "Leigh Hunt's Letters in the Luther Brewer Collection: Plans for a New Edition," *Books at Iowa,* I (Nov. 1965), 10-14.
Announces plans for a new edition of the letters in the Brewer collection; prints three letters: to Henry Colburn, July 28, 1827, Anna Mowatt, March 9, 1850, and Alfred Novello, Dec. 28, 1853.

Bibliotheca Bibliographici. See No. 15.

Blunden, Edmund. See No. 367.

Brack, O. M., Jr. See No. 72.

Braekman, W. See No. 73.

Brand, C. P. See No. 19.

197. Butler, Francelia. *The Strange Critical Fortunes of Shakespeare's "Timon of Athens."* Ames: Iowa State Univ., 1966.
Discusses the reactions of Hunt and Hazlitt to the play.

Cannon, Garland. See No. 76.

198. Carter, John Stewart. "Poetry and the Hucksters," *Tri-Quarterly,* Winter 1965, pp. 55-60.
Discusses Hunt's role in popularizing Keats; touches on Shelley and Mary Shelley.

English Literary Manuscripts. See No. 1.

199. Fothergill, Brian. *Mrs. Jordan: Portrait of an Actress.* London: Faber, 1965.
Touches upon Hunt's and Hazlitt's reactions to her.

George, M. Dorothy. See Nos. 99 and 100.

200. "Hayward in the Saleroom," TLS, March 31, 1966, p. 272.
At the John Hayward sale at Sotheby's, March 14-15, 1966, a copy of Hunt's *Foliage* made £48.

Hudson, Gertrude Reese, ed. See No. 112.

201. Hughes, Rosemary. "The Musical Scene in Europe in 1829," *Proceedings of the Royal Musical Association,* LXXX (1953-54), 15-27.
Describes Vincent Novello's tour of the continent in 1829.

202. Kendall, Kenneth Everett. "Leigh Hunt's *Reflector*" [Doctoral dissertation, Florida, 1965], DA, XXVI (May 1966), 6697.

203. Kendall, Lyle H., Jr. "Leigh Hunt on Shelley's Missing Will: An Unpublished Letter," K-SJ, XV (1966), 6-7.
The letter, to John Gisborne, is dated July 23, 1822.

Medwin, Thomas. See No. 136.

Moorman, Mary. See No. 149.

Moreux, Françoise. See No. 150.

Raith, Joseph. See No. 162.

Rossetti, Dante Gabriel. See No. 167.

204. Ryan, A. P., ed. *Critics Who Have Influenced Taste.* London: Bles, 1965.
Reprints essays on Hunt, Hazlitt, and Shelley. See K-SJ, XIV (1965), 116-117, No. 183, 120, No. 253, 130-131, No. 428.

Saintsbury, George. See No. 36.

Southey, Robert. See No. 177.

IV. KEATS

WORKS: SELECTED, SINGLE, TRANSLATED

Anglika tragoudia. See No. 41.

Charpier, Jacques, and Pierre Seghers, eds. See No. 44.

Djurić, Votislav, ed. See No. 45.

205. **Keats's Poems.* [Translated by] Yasuo Deguchi. Tokyo: Yayoi-shobo, 1966.

Kormos, I., ed. See No. 49.

206. *Kosztolányi, Dezsö. *Idegen költök.* [*Foreign Poets.*] Budapest: Kiadó Szépirod, 1966.
His translations include three poems by Keats and eight by Shelley.

Lator, L., ed. See No. 50.

Lengyel, B., and F. Vincze, eds. See No. 51.

207. **Letters of John Keats.* Ed. Stanley Gardner. London: London Univ., 1965.

Meynell, Sir Francis, comp. See No. 54.

208. "Ōdē se mian hydria Hellēnikē," *Kainouria Epochē,* No. 2 (1960), pp. 106-107.

"Ode on a Grecian Urn."

Peckham, Morse, ed. See No. 33.

209. *Poèmes choisis.* [Translated by] Albert Laffay. See K-SJ, III (1954), 118, VI (1957), 145, No. 277.
Rev. by L[ouis]. Cazamian in *Langues modernes,* XLVII (May-June 1953), 300-301.

210. "Se mian Hellēnikē Hydria," [translated by] B. Karamanos, *Kainouria Epochē,* No. 17 (1960), pp. 168-169.
"Ode on a Grecian Urn."

211. "To One Who Has Been Long [in City Pent]," [translated by] Arēs Diktaios, *Philologike Prōtochronia,* XVII (1960), 277.

212. "Written in the Cottage Where Burns Was Born," K-SJ, XV (1966), 58.

Books and Articles Relating to Keats and His Circle

213. *Abdus-Sabour, S. "Nazuk el Mala'ika and Free Verse," *Al Katib,* XXIV (1963), 114-121.
Influence of Shelley and Keats is noted.

214. Albrecht, W. P. *Hazlitt and the Creative Imagination.* Lawrence: Kansas Univ., 1965.
Rev. by Herschel M. Sikes in MLQ, XXVII (June 1966), 228-229.

Altick, Richard D. See No. 12.

Anderson, Edgar. See No. 60.

Auden, W. H., ed. See No. 193.

Bagehot, Walter. See No. 360.

215. Bagg, Robert Ely. "The Sword Upstairs: Essays on the Theory and Historical Development of Autobiographical Poetry" [Doctoral dissertation, Connecticut, 1965], DA, XXVI (March 1966), 5408.
Includes study of Keats's letters.

216. Baker, Herschel. *William Hazlitt.* See K-SJ, XII (1963), 136, XIII (1964), 136-137, XIV (1965), 118, XV (1966), 156.
Rev. in *The Times,* London, Sept. 6, 1962, p. 13; by Peter Stockham in *British Journal of Aesthetics,* V (Oct. 1965), 411-412.

217. *Baldini, Gabriele. *La poesia di John Keats.* Rome: De Santis, 1964. (Pubbli. dell'Università degli studi di Roma. Facoltà di Magistero.)

218. Bate, Walter Jackson. *John Keats.* See K-SJ, XIV (1965), 118, XV (1966), 156.
Rev. by Roger Sharrock in *Tablet,* CCXVIII (May 2, 1964), 498; by *D. J. Gordon in *New Leader,* XLVII (July 20, 1964), 19; by R[ichard]. H[arter]. F[ogle]. in PQ, XLIII (Oct. 1964), 456-457; by David Bonnell Green in *Manuscripta,* IX (July 1965), 117-118; by Milton Wilson in SR, LXXIII (Autumn 1965), 678-685; by Frederick T. Wood in ES, XLVI (Dec. 1965), 515. Also see No. 29.

219. Bate, Walter Jackson, ed. *Keats: A Collection of Essays.* See K-SJ, XV (1966), 156-157.
Rev. by John R. Willingham in *Library Journal,* LXXXIX (Dec. 15, 1964), 4914; in *Choice,* II (June 1965), 224; in TLS, July 1, 1965, p. 565; by Stuart M. Sperry, Jr., in K-SJ, XV (1966), 121-123. Also see No. 22.

220. Baxter, K. M. *Speak What We Feel: A Christian Looks at the Contemporary Theatre.* *London: SCM Press, 1964. [Published in New York (Abingdon [n.d.]) as *Contemporary Theatre and the Christian Faith.*]
Includes discussion of Keats.

Bibliotheca Bibliographici. See No. 15.

221. Birkenhead, Sheila. *Illustrious Friends: The Story of Joseph Severn and His Son Arthur.* London: Hamish Hamilton; *New York: Reynal, in association with William Morrow (1965).
Rev. by Naomi Lewis in *Observer,* Nov. 21, 1965, p. 28; by John Raymond in *Sunday Times,* Dec. 19, 1965, p. 36; by Marghanita Laski in NS, LXXI (Jan. 7, 1966), 22; by William Buchan in Spec, Feb. 11, 1966, p. 173; by Aileen Ward in NYT, May 8, 1966, p. 4.

Blotner, Joseph, comp. See No. 69.

222. Bluhm, Heinz, ed. *Essays in History and Literature: Presented by Fellows of the Newberry Library to Stanley Pargellis.* Chicago: Newberry Library, 1965.
Includes (pp. 179-191) "'The Infernal Hazlitt,' *The New Monthly Magazine* and the *Conversations of James Northcote, R. A.*" by Herschel M. Sikes.
Rev. by Robert O. Dougan in *Library Quarterly,* Apr. 1966, pp. 175-177; by Gordon H. McNeil in *American Historical Review,* LXXI (Apr. 1966), 902-903.

Bousquet, Jacques. See No. 17.

Braekman, W. See No. 73.
Brand, C. P. See No. 19.

223. Brown, Charles Armitage. *The Letters of Charles Armitage Brown*. Ed. Jack Stillinger. Cambridge, Mass.: Harvard Univ., 1966.

Rev. by Arnold Smithline in *Library Journal*, XCI (March 1, 1966), 1225-1226; by Aileen Ward in NYT, Apr. 3, 1966, pp. 4, 14.

224. Brown, Pearl LeBlanc. "The Artistry and Development of Keats's Narrative Verse" [Doctoral dissertation, Arkansas, 1965], DA, XXVI (Feb. 1966), 4652-4653.

225. Brumbaugh, Thomas A. "Artists' Autographs: A Diagnosis," ABC, XVI (Sept. 1965), 16-25.

One of those reproduced is Haydon's.

226. Bush, Douglas. *John Keats: His Life and Writings*. New York: Macmillan, 1966. "Masters of World Literature Series."

Rev. by Elizabeth Nelson in *Library Journal*, XCI (March 15, 1966), 1406; in NYT, Apr. 10, 1966, p. 22; by Jeffrey Hart in *National Review*, XVIII (Apr. 19, 1966), 371-372 [see No. 261].

Butler, Francelia. See No. 197.

227. * Caldwell, James Ralston. *John Keats' Fancy: The Effect on Keats of the Psychology of His Day*. New York: Octagon, 1965.

A reprint of a book first published in 1945.

Cannon, Garland. See No. 76.
Capps, Jack L. See No. 77.
Carter, John Stewart. See No. 198.

228. Chandler, Alice. "'The Eve of St. Agnes' and "Porphyria's Lover,'" *Victorian Poetry*, III (Autumn 1965), 273-274.

Asserts that the poems "are strikingly similar in plot, phrasing, and theme."

229. Chaudhury, Pravas Jivan. "Keats and the Indian Ideal of Life and Poetry," JAAC, XXIV, Supplement (Fall 1965), 207-211.

Reprints an article first published in 1962. See K-SJ, XIII (1964), 137-138.

Church, Richard. See No. 82.

230. Cornforth, John. "Wellington Sketch," *Country Life*, CXXXI (May 3, 1962), 1045.

Reproduces an oil sketch of the Duke of Wellington by Haydon in the United Service Club, London.

231. Davies, R. E. "Thomas Hood as Playwright and Prose Writer," *English Studies in Africa*, II (March 1959), 73-89.

Reviews Hood's drama, fiction, and non-fiction prose.

232. Delasanta, Rodney, and Mario L. D'Avanzo. "Truth and Beauty in *Brideshead Revisited*," *Modern Fiction Studies*, XI (Summer 1965), 140-152.

Points out the relevance of "Ode on a Grecian Urn" to Waugh's novel.

233. Donohue, Joseph W., Jr. "Hazlitt's Sense of the Dramatic: Actor as Tragic Character," SEL, V (Autumn 1965), 705-721.

"The actor as he interprets the role of the tragic hero will succeed in proportion to his ability to convey to his audience an impassioned dramatic moment. . . . Hazlitt's criticism, confined largely by the success or failure of the star actor, is based on the assumption that a play is composed of a series of 'moments,' crises in which the chief character is called upon to respond imaginatively to strong external influences by conceiving, or revising his conception, of some ultimate future good."

234. Duncan-Jones, E. E. "Hazlitt's Mistake," TLS, Jan. 27, 1966, p. 68.

It is Hazlitt who is alluded to in *Middlemarch* as "the most brilliant English critic of the day."

235. Eisner, Janet. "Undergraduate Maiden's Lament to John Keats," CE, XXVII (Feb. 1966), 425.

A poem.

English Literary Manuscripts. See No. 1.

236. Evert, Walter H. *Aesthetic and Myth in the Poetry of Keats*. See K-SJ, XV (1966), 158.

Rev. in *Choice*, II (July-Aug. 1965), 296; by Helen E. Haworth in *Dalhousie Review*, XLV (Autumn 1965), 378-381; in TLS, Sept. 23, 1965, p. 828; by Bernice Slote in K-SJ, XV (1966), 135-138; by Allan Rodway in RES, N.S., XVII (May 1966), 233. See also No. 22.

237. ["Extensive Landscape with Many Buildings and Cattle,"] *Apollo*, LXXXI (June 1965), cxliii.

This De Wint is reproduced with an announcement of an exhibition at Appleby Brothers'.

238. * Ford, Newell F. *The Prefigurative Imagination of John Keats: A Study of the Beauty-Truth Identification and Its Implications.* Hamden, Conn.: Shoe String Press, 1966. "Archon Books." See K-SJ, I (1952), 93, II (1953), 103, III (1954), 119, IV (1955), 119, V (1956), 128.

A reprint of a book first published in 1951.

Fothergill, Brian. See No. 199.

Frykman, Erik. See No. 97.

239. Gál, István. "Keats magyar vonatkozású drámája," *Filológiai Közlöny,* XI (Jan.-June 1965), 70-92.

240. Garber, Fredrick. "Wordsworth and the Romantic Synecdoche," *Bucknell Review,* XIV (March 1966), 33-43.

Compares Wordsworth and Keats.

García Blanco, Manuel. See No. 98.

George, M. Dorothy. See No. 99.

241. Gerber, Richard. "Cybele, Kubla Khan, and Keats: An Essay on Imaginative Transmutation," ES, XLVI (Oct. 1965), 369-389.

Explores "a mysterious echo of the ambiguous dream-alliance between Cublai and Cybele in Keats's 'Endymion.'"

242. Gittings, Robert. *John Keats: The Living Year.* See K-SJ, IV (1955), 119, V (1956), 128, VI (1957), 142, VIII (1959), 69, X (1961), 87, XII (1963), 137, XIII (1964), 139.

Rev. by Sylva Norman in *Britain To-day,* No. 218 (June 1954), pp. 42-43.

243. Gittings, Robert. *The Keats Inheritance.* See K-SJ, XV (1966), 159.

Rev. by *S. A. Belzer in *New York Times,* July 17, 1965, p. 23; by A. H. Elliott in RES, N.S., XVI (Aug. 1965), 334-335; by R[ichard]. H[arter]. F[ogle]. in ELN, III, Supplement (Sept. 1965), 34; by John Rutherford in K-SJ, XV (1966), 117-121. See also No. 22.

244. * Gittings, Robert. *The Mask of Keats: A Study of Problems.* New York: Hillary House, 1966. See K-SJ, VII (1958), 124, VIII (1959), 69, IX (1960), 64, XIII (1964), 139.

A reprint of a book first published in 1956.

245. Gittings, Robert. "A Short Guide to Keats Studies," *Critical Survey,* II (Winter 1964), 47-49.

246. Gleckner, Robert F. "Keats's Odes: The Problems of the Limited Canon," SEL, V (Autumn 1965), 577-585.

If the odes are to be dealt with as a group, "we must take fuller responsibility both for establishing clearly the basis for their sequential arrangements and for the manifold implications of our use of the limited canon for elucidation of Keats's poetry and ideas."

247. Godfrey, D. R. "Keats and the Grecian Urn," *Hermathena,* No. 100 (Summer 1965), pp. 44-53.

What is described in the "Ode on a Grecian Urn" is "the world of classical antiquity, of ancient Greece," "not our world or Keats'," and the last two lines of the ode "are spoken exclusively by the urn and with reference to its own contemporary world."

248. Goldberg, M. A. "John Keats and the Elgin Marbles," *Apollo,* LXXXII (Nov. 1965), 370-377.

Keats was inspired by the Marbles, but his "Classicism is more characteristic of the nineteenth century than of the fifth century B.C. Almost invariably, Keats's concern is with sensations and unbridled passions, with a typical romantic breakthrough from restraint."

Gordan, John D. See No. 105.

249. Gordon, Alistair. "Peter de Wint, the Undramatic Master," *Connoisseur,* CLXI (March 1966), 150-151.

An appreciation based on the exhibition at the Reading Museum and Art Gallery.

Gordon, David J. See No. 106.

250. Gorell, Lord. *John Keats: The Principle of Beauty.* London: Sylvan Press, 1948.

Rev. by Albert Laffay in *Langues modernes,* XLIV (Nov. 1950), 433.

251. * Gotoh, Akio. "'Precariousness' in the Poetry of Keats," *Thought Currents in English Literature* (Aoyama Gakuin Univ., Tokyo), XXXVIII (Dec. 1965), 175-193. [In Japanese.]

252. Graaf, Daniel A. de. "Henry [*sic*] Mercier traducteur de Keats," *Revue des langues vivantes,* XXXII (1966), 327-328.

Suggests that Mercier was the first French translator of Keats and that he used the pseudonyms J.-J. Réthoré and A. Buisson de Berger.

253. Graves, Robert. "Language Levels," *Encounter,* XXVI (May 1966), 49-51.
Briefly discusses the language of Keats's poetry.

254. Grube, John. *"Tender Is the Night:* Keats and Scott Fitzgerald," *Dalhousie Review,* XLIV (Winter 1964-65), 433-441.†
The novel should be approached with the same respect that one brings to the landscape of Keats.

255. Halpern, Martin. "Keats and the 'Spirit that Laughest,'" K-SJ, XV (1966), 69-86.
Considers "the way the spirit of laughter operates in certain poems from early 1818 to the end of Keats's career, with a view to demonstrating how integral it was to his total sensibility and how central a place it came to assume in his mature poetic vision."

256. Harwell, Thomas Meade. "Keats and the Critics, 1848-1900" [Doctoral dissertation, Columbia, 1965], DA, XXVI (Feb. 1966), 4628-4629.

Hauser, Arnold. See No. 109.

257. Haydon, Benjamin Robert. *The Diary of Benjamin Robert Haydon.* Ed. Willard Bissell Pope. See K-SJ, X (1961), 87, XI (1962), 125-126, XII (1963), 138, XIII (1964), 139, XIV (1965), 121, XV (1966), 159.
Rev. by Frederick J. Cummings in *Art Journal,* XXIV (Summer 1965), 396-397; by Marcia Allentuck in *Art Bulletin,* XLVII (Sept. 1965), 395; by Ellis Waterhouse in *Victorian Studies,* IX (Sept. 1965), 72-74; by Norman Gash in *English Historical Review,* LXXX (Oct. 1965), 862-863; by Fred J. Cummings in *Journal of Modern History,* XXXVII (Dec. 1965), 491-492.

Hayter, Alethea. See No. 110.

258. Hayter, Alethea. *A Sultry Month: Scenes of London Literary Life in 1846.* See K-SJ, XV (1966), 159.
Rev. by Ralph Lawrence in *English,* XVI (Spring 1966), 27.

259. Heller, Erich. *The Artist's Journey into the Interior and Other Essays.* New York: Random House, 1966.
Discusses Keats.

260. Hood, Thomas. "To nekriko krebati," *Kainouria Epochē,* No. 2 (1960), pp. 107-108.

261. Howell, Margaret J. "Keats and the Romantics," *National Review,* XVIII (May 31, 1966), 547.
A letter to the editor protesting Jeffrey Hart's slur on the other Romantics. Hart's "A Reply" follows. See No. 226.

Hudson, Gertrude Reese, ed. See No. 112.

262. * Inglis, Fred. *Keats.* London: Evans, 1966. "Literature in Perspective."

263. Jacobs, Roderick A. "A Poem for the Junior High," *English Journal,* LV (Jan. 1966), 98-100.
In analyzing Wilfred Gibson's "The Ice-Cart" makes use of "Ode to a Nightingale."

264. Jennings, Audrey. "Hood's 'Autumn,'" TLS, June 26, 1953, p. 413.
Shows that Hood did not change the gender of Autumn in the poem.

265. Johnson, Richard E. "Architectural Imagery in *The Eve of St. Agnes* and *Lamia,*" *Xavier University Studies,* V (March 1966), 3-11.
"The castle of *The Eve of St. Agnes* and the palace of *Lamia* . . . help to reveal views of the world which are very nearly antithetical."

266. Jones, Frederick L. "Macaulay's Theory of Poetry in *Milton,*" MLQ, XIII (Dec. 1952), 356-362.
Points out the influence of Hazlitt and Peacock on Macaulay's theory.

267. Jones, James Land. "Keats and Yeats: 'Artificers of the Great Moment,'" *Xavier University Studies,* IV (May 1965), 125-150.
Explores "the similarities between the two poets."

268. Jones, Stanley. "Hazlitt and *John Bull:* A Neglected Letter," RES, N.S., XVII (May 1966), 163-170.
Reprints and comments on Hazlitt's letter to Sarah Walker published in the June 22, 1823, number of *John Bull;* suggests that Croker obtained the letter for the journal.

269. Juel-Jensen, Bent. "Contemporary Collectors XLIII," BC, XV (Summer 1966), 152-174.
Collection includes Shelley, Mary Shelley, Keats, Byron, and "practically everything by John Hamilton Reynolds."

270. Juel-Jensen, Bent. "John Hamilton Reynolds," BC, XV (Summer 1966), 210-211.

Corrects two mistakes in earlier article. See K-SJ, V (1956), 129, No. 204.

271. * Kimura, Akiko. "A Study of John Keats—the Evolution of Keats's Idea of Beauty," *Essays and Studies in British and American Literature* (Tokyo Woman's Christian College), XIII (Sept. 1965), 1-33.

272. Kroeber, Karl. *The Artifice of Reality: Poetic Style in Wordsworth, Foscolo, Keats, and Leopardi.* See K-SJ, XV (1966), 160.

Rev. by Lionel Stevenson in SAQ, LXIV (Spring 1965), 276; by Francis Golffing in BA, XXXIX (Summer 1965), 344; by Morse Peckham in JEGP, LXIV (July 1965), 591-593; by Glauco Cambon in *Criticism,* VII (Fall 1965), 382-385; by C[arl]. W[oodring]. in ELN, III, Supplement (Sept. 1965), 9; by Frederick T. Wood in ES, XLVI (Dec. 1965), 513; by Henry Gifford in N&Q, CCXI (May 1966), 195-196. Also see No. 124.

273. * Kumar, Ish. "Keats—The Poet of Sorrow," *Jammu and Kashmir University Review,* VI (July 1963), 29-34.

274. Laski, Marghanita. "The Language of the Nightingale Ode," *Essays and Studies,* XIX (1966), 60-73.

"Almost all the ecstatic states I have been concerned to systematize are in one way or another described in this poem."

275. Leach, Terence R. "Peter De Wint's Birth-Place," *Country Life,* CXXXI (March 15, 1962), 609-610.

A letter giving information about De Wint and William Hilton.

276. Lindsay, Julian I. "Wordsworth and Haydon," N&Q, CCX (Nov. 1965), 416-417.†

Reprints from the *Burlington Free Press* an anecdote concerning the two men.

277. McFarland, George Foster. "The Early Literary Career of Julius Charles Hare from 1818 to 1834" [Doctoral dissertation, Pennsylvania, 1964], DA, XXVI (July 1965), 371.

278. MacGillivray, J. R. *Keats: A Bibliography and Reference Guide, with an Essay on Keats' Reputation.* See K-SJ, I (1952), 94, III (1954), 119.

Rev. by A[lbert]. Laffay in *Langues modernes,* XLIV (Nov. 1950), 432.

279. Machin, Noel. "The Case of the Empty-Handed Maenad," *Observer* [Colour Magazine], Feb. 28, 1965, pp. 11-12.

Suggests engravings in Henry Moses' *A Collection of Antique Vases . . .* (1814) as the source of the Grecian Urn.

280. Madden, J. S. "Melancholy in Medicine and Literature: Some Historical Considerations," *British Journal of Medical Psychology,* XXXIX (June 1966), 125-130.

Briefly discusses Keats's "Ode on Melancholy."

281. Magaw, Malcolm. "Yeats and Keats: The Poetics of Romanticism," *Bucknell Review,* XIII (Dec. 1965), 87-96.

Discusses their similarities and differences, focusing primarily on "Sailing to Byzantium" and the "Nightingale" and "Grecian Urn" poems.

282. Majdiak, Daniel Thomas. "The Prose Style of William Hazlitt" [Doctoral dissertation, Western Reserve, 1965], DA, XXVI (May 1966), 6698-6699.

283. * Matsushita, Senkichi. "Keats and Wordsworth," *Review of English Literature* (Kyoto Univ.), XVIII (Nov. 1965), 82-108. [In Japanese.]

284. * Matsuura, Cho. "Keats's Scotch Tour and *Inferno,*" *Seijo Bungei* (Seijo Univ., Tokyo), No. 40 (Sept. 1965), pp. 1-15. [In Japanese.]

285. * Matsuura, Cho. "Metamorphosis in Keats's Sonnets," *Rising Generation,* CXI (Aug. 1965), 517-519. [In Japanese.]

286. Mayhead, Robin. *Understanding Literature.* Cambridge: Cambridge Univ., 1965.

Includes analysis of "To Autumn."

287. Menascè, Esther. 'Keats traduttore di Ronsard," *English Miscellany,* XVI (1965), 169-181.

Discusses Keats's translation of Ronsard's sonnet "Nature ornant Cassandre, qui devoyt."

Mererole, Harrison T. See No. 143.

288. Meynell, Alice. *The Wares of Autolycus: Selected Literary Essays of Alice Meynell.* Ed. P. M. Fraser. London: Oxford Univ., 1965.

Includes (pp. 70-73) "The Five Odes of Keats."

289. Mills, Mervyn. "Keats Church," *The Times,* London, March 30, 1965, p. 13.

St. Stephen's, Coleman St., where

Keats's father, mother, grandmother, and brother Tom were buried, was destroyed during World War II. Asks that a plaque be placed on the site.

Moorman, Mary. See No. 149.

Moreux, Françoise. See No. 150.

290. Morgan, P. F. "Thomas Hood and *The Times*," TLS, June 7, 1957, p. 349.

Points out Hood's deep awareness of the "involvement of literature with social justice." See No. 337.

291. [Muir, Edwin.] "Some Letters of Edwin Muir," *Encounter*, XXVI (Jan. 1966), 3-10.

Quotes Keats twice approvingly.

292. Munby, A. N. L. *The Libraries of English Men of Letters*. London: The Library Association, 1964. "Arundell Esdaile Memorial Lecture 1964."

Mentions "the sale catalogue of the pictures, engravings and books of Benjamin Robert Haydon, sold by Crook on 11 June 1823."

293. * Munekata, Kuniyoshi. "An Essay on Keats—What Sustained His Existence," *Daito Bunka University Bulletin* (Tokyo), III (Jan. 1965), 41-70.

294. Murry, John Middleton. *Mystery of Keats*. See K-SJ, I (1952), 94, XIV (1965), 123.

Rev. by A[ndré]. Koszul in *Langues modernes*, XLIV (Nov. 1950), 432.

295. * Nagasawa, Jiro. "Keats's Dual Character: Imaginative and Philosophic," *Research Bulletin of the Faculty of Liberal Arts* (Ōita Univ.), II (Sept. 1965), 33-47. [In Japanese.]

"News and Notes." See No. 156.

296. * Notcutt, H[enry]. Clement. *An Interpretation of Keats's Endymion*. New York: Haskell House, 1964.

A reprint of a book first published in 1919.

297. Notopoulos, James A. " 'Truth-Beauty' in the 'Ode on a Grecian Urn' and the Elgin Marbles," MLR, LXI (Apr. 1966), 180-182.

The phrase "truth-beauty," at the time of the composition of the Ode, was intimately associated with the Elgin Marbles. These words constituted the new aesthetics of the Marbles proclaimed by Haydon, who imparted it to Keats.

298. * Oshita, Michi. "On *Hyperion* and *The Fall of Hyperion*," *Shuryu* [*Main Currents*] (Doshisha Univ., Kyoto), No. 27 (Nov. 1965), pp. 68-88. [In Japanese.]

299. * Pla y Beltran, Pascual. "Tres poetas románticos ingleses: Burns-Shelley-Keats," *Revista Shell*, XI (June 1962), 21-27.

300. * Polgar, Mirko. "J. Keats, Profil čovjeka i pjesnika" ["J. Keats, the Profile of Man and Poet"], *Savremenik*, No. 3 (March 1966).

301. * Polgar, Mirko. "Povodom 170. godišnjice rodenja J. Keats-a" ["The 170th Anniversary of Keats's Birth"], *Djakovački Vijesnik*, Nos. 10 and 11 (Oct. and Nov. 1965).

302. * Polgar, Mirko. "Religiozni profil J. Keats-a" ["The Religious Profile of J. Keats"], *Djakovački Vijesnik*, No. 12 (Dec. 1965).

303. Pollin, Burton R. "Keats, Charlotte Smith, and the Nightingale," N&Q, CCXI (May 1966), 180-181.

Claims "that Charlotte Smith should be recorded as one of the definite origins for ideas and diction in Keats's 'To a Nightingale.' "

304. Quinn, Michael. "The Objectivity of Keats's Ode 'To Autumn,' " *Critical Survey*, II (Winter 1965), 146-150.

"Sadness and joy are so interwoven that they are quite inseparable. This would seem to be the experience of reading the poem; and it is an experience, not a 'telling,' and as such is undeniable and hence 'objective.' "

Raith, Joseph. See No. 162.

305. Reese, Jack E. "Keats and Others on Chapman's Homer," *Cithara*, IV (May 1965), 32-42.†

Touches on Keats's and Godwin's attitudes towards Chapman's translation.

Rice, Sister Pio Maria. See No. 7.

306. Richardson, Joanna. *The Everlasting Spell: A Study of Keats and His Friends*. See K-SJ, XIV (1965), 124, XV (1966), 162.

Rev. by Roger Sharrock in *Tablet*, CCXVIII (May 2, 1964), 498.

Riley, Susan B. See No. 166.

307. Riley, Susan B. "An Early Appearance of the Classic-Romantic Ode: Albert Pike's 'Hymns to the Gods,' " *Arkansas Historical Quarterly*, XXII (Winter 1963), 351-364.†

Pike was "imitative of Keats" in these poems.

308. Rilke, Rainer Maria. "John Keats Drawn in Death," [translated by] Neville Rogers, TLS, Feb. 24, 1966, p. 148.

309. Robinson, Dwight E. "A Question of the Impact of Wedgwood in the Longer Poems of Keats," *The Sixth Wedgwood International Seminar [April 20-22, 1961]* (San Francisco: Wedgwood International Seminar, 1965), pp. 101-108.

Suggests the influence of Wedgwood pottery on *The Fall of Hyperion* and *Endymion.*

310. Rollins, Hyder Edward, ed. *The Keats Circle: Letters and Papers and More Letters and Poems of the Keats Circle.* See K-SJ, XV (1966), 162.

Rev. in TLS, Feb. 10, 1966, p. 99; by Royal A. Gettmann in JEGP, LXV (Apr. 1966), 341-342.

Rossetti, Dante Gabriel. See No. 167.

Ruskin, John. See No. 170.

Ryan, A. P., ed. See No. 204.

Ryan, J. S. See No. 173.

Saintsbury, George. See No. 36.

311. Salvesen, Christopher. *The Landscape of Memory: A Study of Wordsworth's Poetry.* London: Arnold; *Lincoln: Nebraska Univ. (1965).

Includes discussion of Hazlitt; Keats is referred to.

Sambrook, A. J. See No. 174.

312. ["Scarborough Castle,"] *Apollo,* LXXXIII (June 1966), liii.

This De Wint is reproduced with an announcement of an exhibition at the Manning Gallery.

313. * Schulze, F. W. "'Vita brevis—ars longa' als Emotions-Ursache und Motiv-Mitte in Keats' Dichtung," in *Literatur, Kultur, Gesellschaft in England und Amerika: Festgabe für Friedrich Schubel,* ed. Gerhard Müller-Schwefe and Konrad Tuzinski (Frankfurt: Diesterweg, 1966), pp. 320-336.

314. Seright, Orin Dale. "Syntactic Structures in Keats' Poetry" [Doctoral dissertation, Indiana, 1964], DA, XXVI (Aug. 1965), 1033-1034.

315. Shivers, Alfred S. "Nursery Stories for Adults IV: Big Toes on a Little Hill," ABC, XVI (March 1966), 8-9.

Inspired by Keats's "I Stood Tip Toe upon a Little Hill."

316. Shuster, George N. *The English Ode from Milton to Keats.* Gloucester, Mass.: Peter Smith, 1964.

A reprint of a book first published in 1940.

317. Siegel, Paul N., ed. *His Infinite Variety: Major Shakespearean Criticism since Johnson.* Philadelphia: Lippincott, 1964.

Includes selection from Hazlitt (pp. 33-43).

318. Singh, G. S. "Better History and Better Criticism: The Significance of F. R. Leavis," *English Miscellany,* XVI (1965), 215-279.

Reviews Leavis' evaluation of Shelley and Keats (pp. 249-251).

319. * Singh, S. "Keats' Conception of Poetry: A Study in the Context of the Romantic Revolution and with Special Reference to His Major Poems." (Doctoral dissertation, Bristol, 1964.)

Southey, Robert. See No. 177.

320. Spandōnidēs, Petros S. "Ho John Keats kai hē poiēsē tēs ousias," *Panathēnaia,* III, Nos. 25-27 (March 1961), 2-3.

321. Spencer, Benjamin T. "Criticism: Centrifugal and Centripetal," *Criticism,* VIII (Spring 1966), 139-154.

Discusses Keats briefly.

322. Sperry, Stuart M., Jr. "Keats's First Published Poem," HLQ, XXIX (Feb. 1966), 191-197.

A study of the sonnet "To Solitude."

323. Starr, Nathan Comfort. "Negative Capability in Keats's Diction," K-SJ, XV (1966), 59-68.

Reflects "a struggle which reveals the extraordinary division of a sensitive, gifted mind, and Keats's realization that try as he might, he could not deny the passion of his inner self."

324. Štěpaník, Karel. *William Hazlitt jako literární kritik.* [*William Hazlitt as Literary Critic.*] See K-SJ, IX (1960), 69.

Rev. by Simeon Potter in MLR, XLVI (Jan. 1951), 137-138.

325. Sutton, Denys. "Wide Range of English Water-Colours," *Country Life,* CXXXI (March 15, 1962), 592-593.

"A View of Chester" by Peter De Wint is reproduced.

326. * Takahashi, Yushiro. "A Study of 'Ode on a Grecian Urn,'" *Annual Reports of Studies* (Jissen Woman's College, Tokyo), IX (March 1966), 1-44. [In Japanese.]

Taylor, Robert H. See No. 183.

327. Teich, Nathaniel. "Criticism and

Keats's *Grecian Urn*," PQ, XLIV (Oct. 1965), 496-502.

Holds that modern critics "take the philosophically incomplete statements of young Keats and unconsciously complete them by adding their own mature philosophical conclusions."

328. Trawick, Leonard M., III. "Hazlitt, Reynolds, and the Ideal," SIR, IV (Summer 1965), 240-247.

Although accepting usable ideas from Reynolds, Hazlitt sets his concept of the ideal "on new metaphysical underpinnings, and, in place of an objective One . . . finds a new unity in the power of the individual mind to impose a valid order on nature's infinite manifestations."

329. Vickery, John B., ed. *Myth and Literature: Contemporary Theory and Practice.* Lincoln: Nebraska Univ., 1966.

Reprints (pp. 229-242) "Symbolism of the Cyclical Myth in *Endymion*" by Robert Harrison. See K-SJ, X (1961), 87.

330. ["View of St. Donat's Castle, Glamorganshire,"] *Apollo,* LXXXIII (March 1966), lxxiii.

This De Wint is reproduced with an announcement of an exhibition at Appleby Brothers'.

331. ["A Village in Norfolk,"] *Country Life,* CXVIII (Dec. 1, 1955), 1329.

This painting of De Wint is reproduced in a Spink & Son advertisement.

332. Visick, Mary. "'Tease us out of thought': Keats's *Epistle to Reynolds* and the Odes," K-SJ, XV (1966), 87-98.

Traces connections of thought and image between his *Epistle* and the "Ode to a Nightingale" and "Ode on a Grecian Urn."

333. Walsh, T. J., comp. *A Tribute to Wilfred Owen.* Birkenhead: Birkenhead Institute, 1964.

Includes (pp. 46-57) Francis Berry's "Vain Citadels: An Essay on the Poetry of Wilfred Owen," which discusses Keats's influence on Owen.

334. Ward, Aileen. *John Keats: The Making of a Poet.* See K-SJ, XIV (1965), 126, XV (1966), 163.

Rev. by Carol Paine in *Punch,* CCXLV (Dec. 18, 1963), 901; by John Colmer in *Southern Review, An Australian Journal of Literary Studies,* I, No. 2 (1964), 106-110; by *D. J. Gordon in *New Leader,* XLVII (July 20, 1964), 19; by R[ichard]. H[arter]. F[ogle]. in PQ, XLIII (Oct. 1964), 457-458; by L[eonard]. F. M[anheim]. in *Literature and Psychology,* XIV (Summer-Fall 1965), 137-138; by Milton Wilson in SR, LXXIII (Autumn 1965), 678-685. See also No. 29.

335. Warncke, Wayne. "Keats' 'Ode on a Grecian Urn,'" Exp, XXIV (Jan. 1966), Item 40.

The significance of the poem is "in the specific relationship between the art work Keats was creating and the already created art work of the urn."

336. Webster, Grant T. "Keats's 'La Belle Dame': A New Source," ELN, III (Sept. 1965), 42-47.

Suggests Thomas Sackville's "Induction" for the *Mirror for Magistrates,* of which Keats probably read excerpts in Thomas Warton's *History of English Poetry.*

Wellek, René. See No. 39.

337. Whitley, Alvin. "Thomas Hood and *The Times*," TLS, May 17, 1957, p. 309.

Discusses his use of police reports in *The Times* as sources for his poetry. See No. 290.

338. Will, Frederic. "Six Poems," *Poetry,* CVII (Nov. 1965), 85-90.

Number three, beginning "Silent upon a peak in Iowa City," is entitled "After Keats."

339. Williams, A. Hyatt. "Keats' 'La Belle Dame sans Merci': The Bad-Breast Mother," *American Imago,* XXIII (Spring 1966), 63-81.

A psychoanalytic interpretation of the poem.

Williams, Gwyn. See No. 190.

340. Wilson, Katharine M. *The Nightingale and the Hawk: A Psychological Study of Keats' Ode.* See K-SJ, XV (1966), 163.

Rev. in *Choice,* II (Sept. 1965), 390; by Frederick T. Wood in ES, XLVI (Dec. 1965), 515; by Miriam Allott in MLR, LXI (Jan. 1966), 114-115. See also No. 22.

341. "With Keats in Galloway," *The Times,* London, Aug. 13, 1965, p. 10.

Describes a tour following Keats's footsteps.

Woodhouse, A.S.P. See No. 477.

342. * Wright, John. "Keats's *Endymion* as

Spenserian Allegory," *Proceedings of the Ninth Congress of the Australasian Universities Languages and Literature Association, 19-26 August 1964,* ed. Marion Adams (Melbourne: Melbourne Univ., 1964), pp. 63-64.

343. *Yamada, Yutaka. "Dream and Reality in Keats's Poetic Vision—Shifts of 'Negative Capability,'" *Ritsumeikan Bungaku* (The Research Institute of Cultural Sciences, Ritsumeikan Univ., Kyoto), No. 244 (Oct. 1965), pp. 33-54. [In Japanese.]

V. SHELLEY

Works: Collected, Selected, Single, Translated

Anglika tragoudia. See No. 41.

Charpier, Jacques, and Pierre Seghers, eds. See No. 44.

344. *The Complete Works of Percy Bysshe Shelley.* Ed. Roger Ingpen and Walter E. Peck. See K-SJ, XV (1966), 164.

Rev. in *Choice,* II (July-Aug. 1965), 300-301.

345. *A Defence of Poetry* [by] Percy Bysshe Shelley/*The Four Ages of Poetry* [by] Thomas Love Peacock. Ed. John E. Jordan. Indianapolis: Bobbs-Merrill, 1965. "The Library of Liberal Arts."

Djurić, Votislav, ed. See No. 45.

346. *The Esdaile Notebook: A Volume of Early Poems.* Ed. Kenneth Neill Cameron. See K-SJ, XIV (1965), 127, XV (1966), 164.

Rev. by *H. Gilroy in *New York Times,* Apr. 18, 1964, p. 27; in *Choice,* I (July 1964), 180-181; in *Quarterly Review,* CCCIV (Jan. 1965), 114-115; by *E. Frykman in *Göteborgs Handels- och Sjöfartstidning,* July 2, 1965; by Frederick T. Wood in ES, XLVI (Aug. 1965), 365; by Neville Rogers in RES, N.S., XVII (Feb. 1966), 97-99. See also No. 22.

347. *The Esdaile Poems: Early Minor Poems from the "Esdaile Notebook."* Ed. Neville Rogers. Oxford: Clarendon, 1966.

348. * *Den Følende Blomst.* [Translated by] Sophus Clausen. Fifth Edition. Copenhagen: Gyldendals, 1965. "Gyldendals Spættebøger 19."

"The Sensitive Plant" in Danish, printed with the English original.

349. "From *Hellas,*" K-SJ, XV (1966), 24.

The concluding stanza.

350. "Hotan hē lampa syntriphtei," *Kainouria Epochē,* No. 20 (1960), pp. 105-106.

"Lines: 'When the lamp is shattered.'"

Kormos, I., ed. See No. 49.

Kosztolányi, Dezsö. See No. 206.

Lator, L., ed. See No. 50.

Lengyel, B., and F. Vincze, eds. See No. 51.

351. *The Letters of Percy Bysshe Shelley.* Ed. Frederick L. Jones. See K-SJ, XIV (1965), 127, XV (1966), 164.

Rev. by R. B. Woodings in *Cambridge Review,* LXXXVI (Oct. 10, 1964), 19; in *Choice,* I (Nov. 1964), 372-373; by Frederick T. Wood in ES, XLVI (Aug. 1965), 365; by K[enneth]. N[eill]. C[ameron]. in ELN, III, Supplement (Sept. 1965), 39-40; by Neville Rogers in RES, N.S., XVI (Nov. 1965), 439-440; by Royal A. Gettmann in JEGP, LXV (Jan. 1966), 207-211. See also No. 22.

Meynell, Sir Francis, comp. See No. 54.

352. *New Shelley Letters.* Ed. W. S. Scott. See K-SJ, I (1952), 96.

Rev. by A[ndré]. Koszul in *Langues modernes,* XLIV (Nov. 1950), 430-431.

Poezija Vekova. See No. 56.

353. "From *Prometheus Unbound,*" K-SJ, XV (1966), 42.

The concluding stanza of Act IV.

354. "The Pursued and the Pursuer," K-SJ, XV (1966), 14.

See K-SJ, XII (1963), 143, No. 380.

355. *Selected Poems and Prose.* Ed. G. M. Matthews. See K-SJ, XIV (1965), 127, XV (1966), 164.

Rev. by K[enneth]. N[eill]. C[ameron]. in ELN, III, Supplement (Sept. 1965), 41.

356. * "Stansy" ["Stanzas"], [translated by] M. Zaalishvili, *Tsiskari,* No. 1 (1965), p. 89. [In Georgian.]

Books and Articles Relating to Shelley and His Circle

Abdus-Sabour, S. See No. 213.

357. Adams, Charles L. "The Structure of *The Cenci,*" *Drama Survey,* IV (1965), 139-147.

Sees the play as "structurally effective in presenting an Iago-like Orsino to initiate action, control pace, and represent a separate kind of evil, in order to present a larger theme parallel to that in *Prometheus Unbound*."

Altick, Richard D. See No. 12.

Anderson, Edgar. See No. 60.

Anderson, George K. See No. 13.

358. Arnold, Donna. "Frankenstein's Monster: Paragon or Paranoic?" *Trace*, No. 54 (Autumn 1964), pp. 285-287.†

"A decent sort as monsters go."

359. Arseniev, Nicholas S. "The Religious Meaning of the Experience of Beauty," *Comparative Literature Studies*, II (1965), 315-322.

Makes use of Shelley's poetry.

Auden, W. H., ed. See No. 193.

360. Bagehot, Walter. *The Collected Works of Walter Bagehot*. Ed. Norman St. John-Stevas. Vols. I and II: *The Literary Essays*. Cambridge, Mass.: Harvard Univ., 1965.

Vol. I contains an essay on Shelley. References in both volumes to Byron, Hazlitt, and Keats.

361. Baine, Rodney M. *Thomas Holcroft and the Revolutionary Novel*. University of Georgia Monographs No. 13. Athens: Georgia Univ., 1965.

Godwin is discussed.

Rev. by Benjamin Boyce in *South Atlantic Bulletin*, XXXI (March 1966), 14; by Lionel Stevenson in *Georgia Review*, XX (Summer 1966), 242-243.

362. Baker, Joseph E. *Shelley's Platonic Answer to a Platonic Attack on Poetry*. See K-SJ, XV (1966), 165.

Rev. by Edwin G. Silverman in K-SJ, XV (1966), 123-124; by E. D. Mackerness in *British Journal of Aesthetics*, VI (Jan. 1966), 87-89. See also No. 22.

363. Barrell, Joseph. *Shelley and the Thought of His Time: A Study in the History of Ideas*. See K-SJ, I (1952), 96.

Rev. by A[ndré]. Koszul in *Langues modernes*, XLIV (Nov. 1951), 430.

Battiscombe, Georgina, and Marghanita Laski, eds. See No. 67.

364. Bessinger, Jess B., Jr., Stephen M. Parrish, and Harry F. Arader, eds. *Literary Data Processing Conference Proceedings, September 9, 10, 11, 1964*. [New York: MLA, 1964.]

Includes (pp. 230-274) "A Computer-Aided Study of Literary Influence: Milton to Shelley" by Joseph Raben.

Bibliotheca Bibliographici. See No. 15.

365. Bloom, Harold. "Frankenstein, or The New Prometheus," *Partisan Review*, XXXII (Fall 1965), 611-618.

"What makes *Frankenstein* an important book, though it is only a strong, flawed, frequently clumsy novel is that it vividly projects a vision of the Romantic mythology of the self."

Blotner, Joseph, comp. See No. 69.

366. *Blunden, Edmund. *Shelley: A Life Story*. London: Oxford Univ., 1965. "Oxford Paperbacks."

A paperback edition of a book first published in 1946.

Rev. by R. V. Adkinson in *Revue des langues vivantes*, XXXII (1966), 108.

367. Blunden, Edmund. "T. J. Hogg's Library," KSMB, XVI (1965), 45-46.

Volumes by Hunt, Peacock, Shelley, and others, sold by Hogg's daughter in 1897, are described.

368. Boulton, James T. *The Language of Politics in the Age of Wilkes and Burke*. See K-SJ, XV (1966), 165.

Rev. by Wilbur Samuel Howell in *William and Mary Quarterly*, 3rd Series, XXII (July 1965), 520-523; by C. W. Parker in *English Historical Review*, LXXX (Oct. 1965), 849-850.

Bousquet, Jacques. See No. 17.

Brack, O. M., Jr. See No. 72.

Braekman, W. See No. 73.

Brand, C. P. See No. 19.

369. Brophy, Brigid. *Mozart the Dramatist: A New View of Mozart, His Operas and His Age*. New York: Harcourt, Brace & World, 1964.

Includes discussion of Peacock; Shelley is touched upon.

370. *Broun, Heywood Hale. "Books: Thomas Love Peacock, A Friend of Shelley's and Mine," *Diplomat and the Arts*, May 1966, pp. 52, 56-57, 62-63.

An appreciation.

371. Bryan, Robert A., *et al.*, eds. *All These to Teach: Essays in Honor of C. A. Robertson*. Gainesville: Florida Univ., 1965.

Includes (pp. 180-189) "Peacock on the Spirit of the Age (1809-1860)" by John T. Fain.

Rev. by Michael Shugrue in CE, XXVII (May 1966), 653-654.

372. Burke, Edmund. *The Correspondence of Edmund Burke*. Vol. V: *July 1782-June 1789*. Ed. Holden Furber with the assistance of P. J. Marshall. Cam-

bridge: Cambridge Univ.; Chicago: Chicago Univ. (1965).

Prints a letter from Godwin to Burke, Jan. 16, 1783.

Cannon, Garland. See No. 76.

Carter, John Stewart. See No. 198.

373. Chandler, Alice. "The Quarrel of the Ancients and Moderns: Peacock and the Medieval Revival," *Bucknell Review,* XIII (Dec. 1965), 39-50.

Peacock was interested in reviving the harmony of the Middle Ages, but he was not doctrinaire and offered "no closed system" for society to follow.

374. Chesser, Eustace. *Shelley and Zastrozzi: Self-Revelations of a Neurotic.* See K-SJ, XV (1966), 165-166.

Rev. by Richard Allan Davison in *Literature and Psychology,* XVI (Winter 1966), 51-55.

Church, Richard. See No. 82.

375. Collins, Thomas J. "Shelley and God in Browning's *Pauline:* Unresolved Problems," *Victorian Poetry,* III (Summer 1965), 151-160.

"At no point in the poem is it clear that Browning is declaring a final allegiance to either Shelley or God. . . . What is clear, however, is that Shelley and God are representative of whole areas of thought which Browning had not yet carefully explored when he wrote *Pauline.*"

376. Cook, Wayne. "Two Letters of William Godwin," K-SJ, XV (1966), 9-13.

To Aaron Burr, Apr. 3, 1809, and, probably, Catherine Wilmot, Apr. 25, 1809.

377. Cooke, Arnold. *Nocturnes: A Cycle of Five Songs for Soprano, Horn, and Piano.* London: Oxford Univ., 1963.

The first is Shelley's "The Moon."

Rev. by A[rthur]. H[utchings]. in *Music & Letters,* XLVI (Jan. 1965), 92.

378. Delasanta, Rodney. "Shelley's 'Sometimes Embarrassing Declarations': A Defence," *Texas Studies in Literature and Language,* VII (Summer 1965), 173-179.

Contends that the lines singled out for criticism by Cleanth Brooks are used by Shelley in a "rhetorically recapitulatory way."

Derry, Warren. See No. 85.

379. Duerksen, Roland A. "Unidentified Shelley Texts in Medwin's *Shelley Papers,*" PQ, XLIV (July 1965), 407-410.

Provides information on their derivation and supports Medwin's accuracy.

380. Eliot, T. S. *To Criticize the Critic, and Other Writings.* London: Faber; New York: Farrar (1965).

Includes (pp. 130-132) discussion of Shelley and Dante.

English Literary Manuscripts. See No. 1.

381. *English Studies Presented to R. W. Zandvoort on the Occasion of His Seventieth Birthday.* Amsterdam: Swets & Zeitlinger, 1964. See K-SJ, XV (1966), 169, No. 447.

Rev. by Herbert Koziol and Pierre Danchin in ES, XLVI (Dec. 1965), 498-503.

382. Flanders, Jane Townend. "Charles Brockden Brown and William Godwin: Parallels and Divergences" [Doctoral dissertation, Wisconsin, 1965], DA, XXVI (Dec. 1965), 3334-3335.

Fontane, Theodor. See No. 96.

Frykman, Erik. See No. 97.

García Blanco, Manuel. See No. 98.

George, M. Dorothy. See No. 99.

383. Gérin, Winifred. "The Montpensier Miniature of Shelley," KSMB, XVI (1965), 1-11.

The drawing presented to the Bodleian by Sir John Shelley-Rolls may "be regarded as an authentic portrait taken from the life."

384. *Godwin, William. *Caleb Williams, or, Things as They Are.* Ed. Ernest A. Baker. London: New English Library, 1966.

385. Godwin, William. *Four Early Pamphlets (1783-1784): A Defence of the Rockingham Party; Instructions to a Statesman; An Account of the Seminary . . . at Epsom; The Herald of Literature.* Ed. Burton R. Pollin. Gainesville, Fla.: Scholars' Facsimiles & Reprints, 1966.

386. Godwin, William. *Italian Letters, or, The History of the Count de St. Julian.* Ed. Burton R. Pollin. Lincoln: Nebraska Univ., 1965.

Gordan, John D. See No. 105.

Gordon, David J. See No. 106.

Grønbech, Vilhelm. See No. 108.

387. Grylls, R. Glynn. *Trelawny.* See K-SJ, I (1952), 90, XIV (1965), 111.

Rev. by Sylva Norman in *Britain*

To-day, No. 173 (Sept. 1950), p. 50; by A[ndré]. Koszul in *Langues modernes*, XLIV (Nov. 1950), 431-432.

388. Grylls, R. Glynn. *William Godwin and His World*. See K-SJ, IV (1955), 123, V (1956), 133.

Rev. by Arnold Palmer in *Britain To-day*, No. 216 (Apr. 1954), pp. 46-47.

389. *Gusmanov, I. G. "Tragediia Shelli *Chenchi* (K probleme geroia)" ["The Problem of the Hero in Shelley's Tragedy *The Cenci*"], *Uchenye zapiski* (Mosk. gos. ped. in-t. m. V. I. Lenina), No. 218 (1964), pp. 61-84.

Hauser, Arnold. See No. 109.

390. *Hayashida, Minoru. "Shelley's View of Poetry—On His *Defence of Poetry*," *Annual Reports of English and American Literature* (Osaka Shoin Women's College), No. 2 (Nov. 1964), pp. 1-15. [In Japanese.]

Hayter, Alethea. See No. 110.

391. Hirsch, David H. "Charles Brockden Brown as a Novelist of Ideas," *Books at Brown*, XX (1965), 165-184.

Discusses Brown's indebtedness to Godwin.

Hudson, Gertrude Reese, ed. See No. 112.

392. Hughes, A. M. D. "The Triumph of Life," KSMB, XVI (1965), 12-20.

An interpretation.

393. Hurt, James R. "*Prometheus Unbound* and Aeschylean Dramaturgy," K-SJ, XV (1966), 43-48.

Considers the poem "as a dramatic trilogy, inspired by the example of Aeschylus."

394. Huscher, Herbert. "Alexander Mavrocordato, Friend of the Shelleys," KSMB, XVI (1965), 29-38.

A biographical sketch.

395. *Inoue, Hatsuno. "Vision of Eternity in Shelley," *Konan Women's College Studies in English Literature* (Kobe), II (Dec. 1965), 29-50. [In Japanese.]

396. Ishikawa, Shigetoshi. "P. B. Shelley's *Demogorgon*," *English Language & Literature* (Korea), XLV-XLVI (Dec. 1964), 147-159. [In Japanese.]

397. Joll, James. *The Anarchists*. London: Eyre and Spottiswoode; Boston: Little, Brown (1964).

Includes discussion of Godwin.

Rev. in TLS, Dec. 24, 1964, pp. 1153-1154.

Jones, Frederick L. See No. 266.

398. Jones, Frederick L. "Trelawny and the Sinking of Shelley's Boat," KSMB, XVI (1965), 42-44.

A letter by Daniel Roberts to Trelawny, recently sold at Sotheby's, does not, as some have suggested, implicate Trelawny as a forger. And it supports the view of the sinking expressed elsewhere by Roberts.

Juel-Jensen, Bent. See No. 269.

399. *Kagarlitskii, Iu. "Roman Meri Shelli" ["Mary Shelley's Novel"], *Inostrannaia literatura*, No. 1 (1966), pp. 262-263.

Kendall, Lyle H., Jr. See No. 203.

400. *King, Francis. "Piquancy of Peacock," *Sunday Telegraph* (London), Jan. 23, 1966.

A centenary tribute.

401. King-Hele, Desmond. "Erasmus Darwin's Influence on Shelley's Early Poems," KSMB, XVI (1965), 26-28.

Points out Darwin's influence on the poems in the Esdaile Notebook.

402. King-Hele, Desmond. "Shelley and Nuclear Disarmament Demonstrations," KSMB, XVI (1965), 39-41.

Traces Shelley's ideas on non-violence in "The Masque of Anarchy" through Lord Russell to recent demonstrations.

403. *Komatsu, Fumio. "Demogorgon in *Prometheus Unbound*," *Journal of Ryukoku University* (Kyoto), No. 380 (March 1966), pp. 2-38. [In Japanese.]

Kotker, Norman, and Howard Nelson. See No. 118.

404. Levine, Paul. "The American Novel Begins," *American Scholar*, XXXV (Winter 1965-66), 134-148.

Discusses influence of Godwin on Charles Brockden Brown.

405. Lewes, George Henry. *Literary Criticism of George Henry Lewes*. Ed. Alice R. Kaminsky. Lincoln: Nebraska Univ., 1964.

Reprints (pp. 72-77) an essay on Shelley.

406. Losh, James. *The Diaries and Correspondence of James Losh*. Ed. Edward Hughes. See K-SJ, XIV (1965), 113.

Rev. by R. S. Woof in N&Q, CCX (Nov. 1965), 433-436. The review identifies and clarifies remarks on *Frankenstein*.

407. Luke, Hugh J., Jr. "*The Last Man*: Mary Shelley's Myth of the Solitary," *Prairie Schooner*, XXXIX (Winter 1965-66), 316-327.

A shortened preliminary version of the introduction to Luke's edition of the novel. See No. 454.

408. Luke, Hugh J., Jr. "An Overlooked Obituary Notice of Shelley," *Papers on Language & Literature,* II (Winter 1966), 38-46.

Reprints and discusses the "long (six full pages), highly laudatory" notice from the Sept. 1822 *Rambler's Magazine.*

409. McGann, Jerome J. "The Secrets of an Elder Day: Shelley after *Hellas,*" K-SJ, XV (1966), 25-41.

Asserts "that after 1822 Shelley no longer sought after death in the natural world; that his development was the result of a growing awareness both of the inadequacy of a divinized (and therefore dehumanized) earth, and of the divisiveness resulting from pure idealism; and that the poetry of 1822, in the very act of denying the myth of Absolute Beauty, found a way of reconciling itself to mortality."

410. Mackerness, E. D. "Thomas Love Peacock's Musical Criticism," *Wind and the Rain,* IV (Winter 1948), 177-187.

"Music was for him . . . an extension of the potentialities of language."

MacNeice, Louis. See No. 128.

411. *McNiece, Gerald Mason. "Shelley and the Revolutionary Idea." (Doctoral dissertation, Harvard, 1966.)

412. *Madariaga, Salvador de. *Shelley and Calderón, and Other Essays on English and Spanish Poetry.* Port Washington, N. Y.: Kennikat, 1965.

A reissue of the 1920 edition.

Maitre, Raymond. See No. 129.

413. Malins, Edward. *English Landscaping and Literature 1660-1840.* London: Oxford Univ., 1966.

Discusses *Headlong Hall.*

414. Mathewson, George. "Shelley's Atheism: An Early Victorian Explanation," K-SJ, XV (1966), 7-9.

By the Rev. Dr. Edward Craven Hawtrey, who "had known Shelley as a boy at Eton."

415. Meaker, M. J. *Sudden Endings.* Garden City: Doubleday, 1964.

One chapter, "The Deserted Wife" (pp. 67-93), is on Harriet Shelley.

Medwin, Thomas. See No. 136.

Merimée, Prosper. See No. 141.

Meserole, Harrison T. See No. 143.

Mills, Carl Henry. See No. 144.

Mills, Howard. See No. 32.

416. *Moeckli, Gustave. "Un Genevois méconnu: Frankenstein," *Musées de Genève,* III (Nov.-Dec. 1962), 10-13.

On the genesis of Mary Shelley's novel and on its Genevese background.

Moorman, Mary. See No. 149.

Moreux, Françoise. See No. 150.

417. *Morita, Masami. "Shelley's Idea of Necessity and Nature's Spirit," *Tandai Ronso* (Kanto Gakuin Junior College, Yokohama), No. 27 (March 1966), pp. 47-58.

418. Murray, Eugene Bernard. "Shelley's Use of the Journey Image" [Doctoral dissertation, Columbia, 1965], DA, XXVI (Feb. 1966), 4636.

419. *Die Musik in Geschichte und Gegenwart: Allgemeine Enzyklopädie der Musik.* Ed. Friedrich Blume. Kassel: Bärenreiter, 1949- . See K-SJ, XIV (1965), 123.

Vol. XII contains an article on Shelley by Percy M. Young.

420. *Newman, David, and Robert Benton. "The Basic Library of Trash," *Esquire,* LXIII (Feb. 1965), 78-79, 126-127.†

One of the volumes picked for this collection is *Frankenstein.*

421. Notopoulos, James A. "New Texts of Shelley's Plato," K-SJ, XV (1966), 99-115.

From the Shelley notebooks in the Bodleian.

422. *Okuda, Heihachiro. "'Ode to the West Wind'—A Revaluation of Shelley," *Essays* (Tokyo), No. 20 (June 1966), pp. 32-41. [In Japanese.]

423. O'Malley, Glenn. *Shelley and Synesthesia.* See K-SJ, XV (1966), 168.

Rev. in *Choice,* I (Dec. 1964), 422; by K[enneth]. N[eill]. C[ameron]. in ELN, III, Supplement (Sept. 1965), 41-42; by Donald Weeks in JAAC, XXIV (Winter 1965), 324; by Newell F. Ford in K-SJ, XV (1966), 130-132; by Lawrence J. Zillman in ELN, III (March 1966), 229-231. See also No. 22.

On Eight Sonnets of Dante. See No. 195.

424. Parry, Bryn R. "Local Archives of Great Britain XXVII. The Caernarvonshire Record Office," *Archives: The Journal of the British Records Association,* VII (Apr. 1965), 34-39.

Collection includes the Ynystowyn

letters, one of which concerns attack on Shelley at Tremadoc in 1813.

425. *Pasternak, Boris. "Zametki perevodchika" ["Translator's Notes"], *Literaturnaia Rossiia,* March 19, 1965, pp. 18-19.

Reprints his Foreword to Shelley's *Poems,* Published in *Znamia* in 1944.

426. *Peacock, Thomas Love. *A Peacock Selection.* Ed. H. L. B. Moody. London: Macmillan; New York: St. Martin's (1966).

Includes a selection of Peacock's poetry and miscellaneous prose.

Pla y Beltran, Pascual. See No. 299.

427. Pollin, Alice and Burton. "In Pursuit of Pearson's Shelley Songs," *Music & Letters,* XLVI (Oct. 1965), 322-331.

An account of the songs and their composer.

428. Pollin, Burton R. "Philosophical and Literary Sources of *Frankenstein,*" CL, XVII (Spring 1965), 97-108.

Among them were works by Mme. de Genlis, Milton, Ovid, Locke, Condillac, and Diderot.

429. Pollin, Burton R. "Poe and Godwin," *Nineteenth-Century Fiction,* XX (Dec. 1965), 237-253.

"Godwin represented to Poe the apex of narrative and stylistic achievement."

430. Pollin, Burton R. " 'Rappacini's Daughter'—Sources and Names," *Names,* XIV (March 1966), 30-35.

Frankenstein and *St. Leon* are two of the sources.

431. * Pottle, Frederick A. *Shelley and Browning: A Myth and Some Facts.* Hamden, Conn.: Archon, 1965.

A reprint of a book first published in 1923.

Rev. in *Choice,* II (Jan. 1966), 773.

432. *Power, Julia. *Shelley in America in the Nineteenth Century: His Relation to American Critical Thought and His Influence.* New York: Haskell House, 1964.

A reprint of a book first published in 1940.

Praz, Mario. See No. 160.

433. Raben, Joseph. "Shelley's 'Invocation to Misery': An Expanded Text," JEGP, LXV (Jan. 1966), 65-74.

Mary Shelley's treatment of the poem follows a "pattern of repression and distortion." The actual fragments of the poem are here transcribed.

Raith, Joseph. See No. 162.

434. Ramos, Charles. "Letters of Robert Southey to John May 1797-1838: Edited from the MSS in the University of Texas Library" [Doctoral dissertation, Texas, 1965], DA, XXVI (Feb. 1966), 4637-4638.

Includes material on Shelley.

435. Raymond, William O. *The Infinite Moment and Other Essays in Robert Browning.* See K-SJ, XV (1966), 169.

Rev. by John Hulcoop in *Canadian Literature,* No. 26 (Autumn 1965), pp. 78-79.

Reboul, Pierre. See No. 164.

Reese, Jack E. See No. 305.

436. Reiman, Donald H. *Shelley's "The Triumph of Life": A Critical Study Based on a Text Newly Edited from the Bodleian Manuscript.* See K-SJ, XV (1966), 169.

Rev. in *Choice,* II (Dec. 1965), 685; in TLS, Jan. 20, 1966, p. 44; by James Rieger in K-SJ, XV (1966), 128-130. See also No. 33.

437. Ridenour, George M., ed. *Shelley: A Collection of Critical Essays.* Englewood Cliffs: Prentice-Hall, 1965. "Twentieth Century Views."

Includes (pp. 1-12) an introductory essay by the editor, "Introduction: Shelley's Optimism," and an original essay by Frederick A. Pottle, "The Role of Asia in the Dramatic Action of Shelley's *Prometheus Unbound"* (pp. 133-143). Reprints essays by Richard Harter Fogle, Leone Vivante, Humphry House, Carlos Baker, Earl R. Wasserman, Melvin M. Rader, G. M. Matthews, G. Wilson Knight, Milton Wilson, and Harold Bloom. See K-SJ, I (1952), 93, No. 151, 96, No. 234, VIII (1959), 76, No. 463, IX (1960), 75, Nos. 500 and 505, X (1961), 88, No. 316, XII (1963), 123, No. 18, XIV (1965), 131, No. 435, XV (1966), 163, No. 345.

Rev. by Harry Halpern in *Library Journal,* XC (Dec. 15, 1965), 5395-5396.

Riley, Susan B. See No. 166.

438. Rivers, Charles. "Robert Browning's *Pauline:* 'The Dim Orb of Self,'" *Northwest Missouri State College Studies,* XXIX (Feb. 1, 1965), 3-19.

Discusses Shelley's influence on the poem.

439. Roe, Ivan. *Shelley: The Last Phase.* See K-SJ, III (1954), 123, IV (1955), 124, V (1956), 134, VI (1957), 150, X (1961), 95.

Rev. by Sylva Norman in *Britain To-day,* No. 208 (Aug. 1953), p. 46.

440. Rogers, Neville. "Shelley's Spelling: Theory and Practice," KSMB, XVI (1965), 21-25.

Warns against " 'system-spinning' with words."

441. *Rogers, Stephen Joseph, Jr. "Classical Greece and the Poetry of Chénier, Shelley, and Leopardi." (Doctoral dissertation, Harvard, 1966.)

442. Rose, Edward J. "Shelley Reconsidered Plain," *Bucknell Review,* XIV (May 1966), 46-65.

Examines Shelley as "a poet who is both a Christian and a Humanist."

Roston, Murray. See No. 168.

443. Rountree, Thomas J. *This Mighty Sum of Things: Wordsworth's Theme of Benevolent Necessity.* University: Alabama Univ., 1965.

One of the chapters is "Hartleian and Godwinian Influence."

Rev. by Carl H. Ketcham in *Arizona Quarterly,* XXII (Summer 1966), 175-176.

Ruskin, John. See No. 170.

Ryan, A. P., ed. See No. 204.

444. St. George, Priscilla P. "The Styles of Good and Evil in 'The Sensitive Plant,' " JEGP, LXIV (July 1965), 479-488.

These are used to describe respectively a nonmaterial reality, "not to be communicated by means of a visual picture," and a more directly material reality that demands "verbal painting almost photographically exact."

Saintsbury, George. See No. 36.

445. *Salama, A. M. "A Study of Shelley's Major Poems in the Light of His Critical Ideas." (Doctoral dissertation, Liverpool, 1963.)

Sambrook, A. J. See No. 174.

446. Schaefer, William David. *James Thomson (B. V.): Beyond "The City."* Berkeley: California Univ., 1965.

Discusses Shelley's influence on Thomson.

447. *Schaubert, Else von. *Shelleys Tragödie "The Cenci" und Marlowes Doppeldrama "Tamburlaine."* Paderborn: Ferdinand Schöningh, 1965.

Rev. by Guy Lambrechts in EA, XIX (Jan.-March 1966), 90.

448. Shaw, [George] Bernard. *Collected Letters 1874-1897.* Ed. Dan H. Laurence. London: Reinhardt, 1965.

Shaw comments on Shelley and others.

449. Shelley, Mary [Wollstonecraft]. *Frankenstein.* With an Introduction by Mary M. Threapleton. New York: Airmont, 1963.

A paperback reprint.

450. *Shelley, Mary Wollstonecraft. *Frankenstein, or, The Modern Prometheus.* Ed. Harold Bloom. New York: New American Library, 1965; London: New English Library, 1966.

A paperback reprint.

451. *Shelley, Mary Wollstonecraft. *Frankenstein oder Der moderne Prometheus.* 1964. [In German.]

452. *Shelley, Mary Wollstonecraft. *Frankenstein.* [Translated and adapted by] Tomáš Korbař. Prague: Práce, 1966. "Knižnice Románové novinky" ["New Novels Library"] Vol. 159.

453. *Shelley, Mary Wollstonecraft. *Frankenstein, ili Sovremennyi Promethei.* [*Frankenstein, or The Modern Prometheus.*] [Translated by] Z. Aleksandrova. [Foreword by] A. Elistratova. Moscow: Khudozhestvennaia literatura, 1965.

454. Shelley, Mary [Wollstonecraft]. *The Last Man.* Ed. Hugh J. Luke, Jr. Lincoln: Nebraska Univ., 1965. "A Bison Book."

A paperback reprint of her novel, first published in 1826.

Rev. by Walter Guzzardi, Jr., in SatR, XLIX (Jan. 8, 1966), 86; by Ernest J. Lovell, Jr., in CE, XXVII (May 1966), 646. Also see No. 407.

Sherrard, Philip, comp. See No. 176.

Singh, G. S. See No. 318.

455. Skipp, Francis E. "Whitman and Shelley: A Possible Source for 'The Sleepers,' " *Walt Whitman Review,* XI (Sept. 1965), 69-74.

"It seems possible that Whitman found in the last twenty-two stanzas of Shelley's 'The Witch of Atlas' a dramatic structure and imagery adaptable to his own poetic intention in 'The Sleepers.' "

456. Smith, Elton Edward, and Esther

Greenwell Smith. *William Godwin.* New York: Twayne, 1966. "Twayne English Authors Series 27."

457. Solve, Melvin T. *Shelley: His Theory of Poetry.* See K-SJ, XIV (1965), 132.
Rev. in *Choice,* I (June 1964), 134-135.

Southey, Robert. See No. 177.

458. Spector, Robert Donald, ed. *Seven Masterpieces of Gothic Horror.* New York: Bantam, 1963.
Includes Mary Shelley's "The Heir of Mondolfo."

459. Spender, Stephen. *Shelley: Etude sur l'écrivain.* See K-SJ, XV (1966), 170.
Rev. by Raymond Bellour in *Nouvelle revue française,* XIII (March 1965), 533.

460. Steeves, Harrison R. *Before Jane Austen: The Shaping of the English Novel in the Eighteenth Century.* New York: Holt, Rinehart, and Winston, 1965.
Includes a chapter devoted mainly to Godwin and Mary Wollstonecraft.

461. Stempel, Daniel. "Shelley and the Ladder of Love," K-SJ, XV (1966), 15-23.
"There is not one *unio mystica* in Shelley's hierarchy of love but two: the oblivion of the flesh at the foot of the ladder and the oblivion of the spirit on a higher level."

462. Swaminathan, S. R. "The Wind and the Leaf," in *Critical Essays on English Literature in Honor of Professor M. S. Doraiswami,* ed. S. Ramaswami (Madras: Orient Longmans, 1965), pp. 57-80.
Traces "the evolution of this symbol in Shelley's major work," and finds that although "the *West Wind* is the cumulative result of Shelley's meditations on the wind and the leaf, and their most powerful expression, the image continues to haunt almost every major poem that follows."

463. *Takahashi, Noritane. "Themes in 'An Exhortation' and 'To a Skylark,'" *Ivy: The Nagoya Review of English Studies* (Nagoya Univ.), V (March 1966), 23-35. [In Japanese.]

464. *Takahashi, Yushiro. "On Keats's Allegory," *Igirisu Bungaku* [*English Literature*], No. 1 (March 1966), pp. 2-8. [In Japanese.]

465. *Takei, Ryokichi. "An Essay on P. B. Shelley," *Daito Bunka University Bulletin* (Tokyo), III (Jan. 1965), 1-17. [In Japanese.]

466. Tate, Allen. "The Unliteral Imagination; Or, I, Too, Dislike It," *Southern Review,* N.S., I (Summer 1965), 530-542.
Includes comment on Shelley.

467. *Tatham, Lewis Charles, Jr. "Shelley and His Twentieth-Century Detractors." (Doctoral dissertation, Florida, 1965.)

Taylor, Robert H. See No. 183.

468. Taylor, Thomas. *A Vindication of the Rights of Brutes (1792).* A Facsimile Reproduction with an Introduction by Louise Schutz Boas. Gainesville, Fla.: Scholars' Facsimiles & Reprints, 1966.
A parody of Mary Wollstonecraft's works by her friend.

469. Thorslev, Peter L., Jr. "Wordsworth's *Borderers* and the Romantic Villain-Hero," SIR, V (Winter 1966), 84-103.
Deprecates Godwin's influence on the play.

470. Thwaite, M. F. *From Primer to Pleasure: An Introduction to the History of Children's Books in England, from the Invention of Printing to 1900, with a Chapter on Some Developments Abroad.* London: Library Association, 1963.
Godwin is discussed.

471. Tillotson, Geoffrey and Kathleen. *Mid-Victorian Studies.* London: Athlone, 1965.
Reprints "Donne's Poetry in the Nineteenth Century" (pp. 278-300), with material on Godwin added. See K-SJ, X (1961), 84, No. 231.

472. Vachot. Charles. *James Thomson (1834-1882).* Paris: Didier, 1964.
Discusses Thomson's poem on Shelley.

473. Vianu, Tudor. *Studii de literatură universală şi comparată.* Second Edition. Bucharest: Academiei Republicii Populare Romîne, 1963.
Prometheus Unbound is discussed; Byron is touched upon.

474. Vowles, Richard. "About Books and Ideas: Mary Wollstonecraft's Scandinavian Letters," *Norseman,* X (Sept.-Oct. 1952), 350-357.
Mary Wollstonecraft "merits attention as perhaps the first sociologist to

visit the Scandinavian countries and make a sensitive record of what she found" (in *Letters Written During a Short Residence in Sweden, Norway, and Denmark* [1796]).

Reprinted in **Bulletin of the American Swedish Institute,* VII (Winter 1952), 22-29, and in **Pacific Coast Viking,* XIX (1953), No. 5, pp. 16-20.

475. Wasserman, Earl R. *Shelley's "Prometheus Unbound": A Critical Reading.* Baltimore: Johns Hopkins Univ., 1965.

Rev. by John R. Willingham in *Library Journal,* XC (Nov. 15, 1965), 4983; by Seymour Reiter in *New Mexico Quarterly,* XXXV (Winter 1965-66), 375-379; in *Creative Writing,* XVIII (Feb. 1966), 12; by Melvin T. Solve in *Arizona Quarterly,* XXII (Summer 1966), 184-186.

Wellek, René. See No. 39.

476. Whitaker, Thomas R. *Swan and Shadow: Yeats's Dialogue with History.* Chapel Hill: North Carolina Univ., 1964.

Touches on Shelley's influence on Yeats.

Williams, Gwyn. See No. 190.

477. Woodhouse, A. S. P. *The Poet and His Faith: Religion and Poetry in England from Spenser to Eliot and Auden.* Chicago: Chicago Univ., 1965.

Discusses Shelley; Keats is referred to.

478. Woodman, Ross Greig. *The Apocalyptic Vision in the Poetry of Shelley.* See K-SJ, XIV (1965), 133, XV (1966), 171.

Rev. in *Choice,* I (May 1964), 100; by Devendra P. Varma in *Dalhousie Review,* XLIV (Winter 1964-65), 511, 513; by Craig W. Miller in *Canadian Literature,* No. 25 (Summer 1965), pp. 59-62; by Richard Harter Fogle in *University of Toronto Quarterly,* XXXIV (July 1965), 387-388; by K[enneth]. N[eill]. C[ameron]. in ELN, III, Supplement (Sept. 1965), 42-43. See also No. 22.

479. *Yoshioka, Nobuo. "*Alastor,* 'Epipsychidion' and 'The Triumph of Life'—On Shelley's Idea of Love, Life and Death, II," *Studies in British and American Literature* (Univ. of Osaka Prefecture), No. 13 (March 1966), pp. 24-39. [In Japanese.]

VI. PHONOGRAPH RECORDINGS

Keats, Shelley

480. *The English Poets, from Chaucer to Yeats.* See K-SJ, XV (1966), 171, No. 474.

Rev. by Ady Mineo in *Lingue straniere,* XV (May-June 1966), 27.

481. **The English Poets: Percy Bysshe Shelley.* Read by Richard Marquand, Patrick Garland, and Gary Watson. Argo RG380.

Rev. by Margaret Willy in *English,* XVI (Spring 1966), 14-15.

482 **Forms of Poetry.* Read by Agnes E. Futterer. Theatre Alumni Association Recordings, State University of New York at Albany.

Includes poems by Shelley and Keats.

Rev. by J[ohn]. R. S[earles]. in *English Journal,* LV (Feb. 1966), 237.

483. **Robert Donat Reads Romantic and Twentieth-Century Poems.* Argo RG-437.

Includes selections from Shelley and Keats.

Rev. by Margaret Willy in *English,* XVI (Spring 1966), 15.

484. **Robert Donat Reads Selected Poetry.* Poetry Recordings, London Records.

Includes selections from Keats and Shelley.

Rev. by J[ohn]. R. S[earles]. in *English Journal,* LV (Apr. 1966), 498-499.

Bibliography for July 1, 1966–June 30, 1967

VOLUME XVII

Compiled by DAVID BONNELL GREEN, ROBERT G. KIRKPATRICK, and EDWIN GRAVES WILSON

THIS BIBLIOGRAPHY, a regular department of the *Keats-Shelley Journal,* is a register of the literary interest in Keats, Shelley, Byron, Hunt, and their circles from (approximately) July 1966 through June 1967. A number of the items were discovered by our friend the late David Bonnell Green. Including him as a complier of this issue of the bibliography is, therefore, more than a deserved tribute to his years of service with the *Journal*; it is a recognition of his actual contribution to the contents of this volume.

We are grateful, as always, to those scholars from overseas who have sent us items for this issue: Professors Jean L. de Palacio, Université de Lille; Jaime Rest, Universidad Nacional del Sur, Bahia Blanca; and Takeshi Saito, Emeritus, Tokyo University; Dr. Helmut Viebrock, Johann Wolfgang Goethe Universität, Frankfurt am Main; Dr. Anna Katona, the University of Debrecen; Dr. J. G. Riewald, University of Groningen; Dr. Witold Ostrowski, University of Lódz; Dr. Helena Wieckowska, Chief Librarian, University of Lódz; D. H. Borchardt, Chief Librarian, La Trobe University, Melbourne; and B. L. Kandel, the M. E. Saltykov-Schedrin State Public Library, Leningrad. We also thank helpful members of the library staffs of Harvard University, the University of North Carolina at Chapel Hill, and Wake Forest University.

Each item that we have not seen is marked by an asterisk. Entries which have been abstracted in *Abstracts of English Studies* are marked with a dagger, but entries in previous bibliographies which were abstracted too late for notice have not been repeated.

ABBREVIATIONS

ABC	American Book Collector
AL	American Literature
ASNS	Archiv für das Studium der neueren Sprachen
BA	Books Abroad
BC	Book Collector
BNYPL	Bulletin of the New York Public Library
CE	College English
CL	Comparative Literature
CLSB	C. L. S. Bulletin (Charles Lamb Society)

CR	Contemporary Review
DA	Dissertation Abstracts
EA	Etudes Anglaises
EC	Essays in Criticism
ELH	Journal of English Literary History
ELN	English Language Notes
ES	English Studies
Exp	Explicator
HLQ	Huntington Library Quarterly
ICS	L'Italia Che Scrive
ILN	Illustrated London News
JAAC	Journal of Aesthetics and Art Criticism
JEGP	Journal of English and Germanic Philology
JHI	Journal of the History of Ideas
KR	Kenyon Review
K-SJ	Keats-Shelley Journal
KSMB	Keats-Shelley Memorial Bulletin
Li	Listener
MLN	Modern Language Notes
MLQ	Modern Language Quarterly
MLR	Modern Language Review
MP	Modern Philology
N&Q	Notes and Queries
NS	New Statesman
NYT	New York Times Book Review
PBSA	Papers of the Bibliographical Society of America
PMLA	Publications of the Modern Language Association of America
PQ	Philological Quarterly
PR	Partisan Review
QQ	Queen's Quarterly
RES	Review of English Studies
RLC	Revue de Littérature Comparée
SAQ	South Atlantic Quarterly
SatR	Saturday Review
SEL	Studies in English Literature 1500-1900
SIR	Studies in Romanticism
SP	Studies in Philology
Spec	Spectator
SR	Sewanee Review
T&T	Time and Tide
TLS	Times Literary Supplement
VQR	Virginia Quarterly Review

I. GENERAL

Current Bibliographies

1. Boyle, Andrew. *An Index to the Annuals.* Vol. I: *The Authors (1820-1850).* Worcester: Andrew Boyle, 1967.

   Lists items by Byron, Clare, Hazlitt, Hood, Hunt, Keats, Shelley, Mary Shelley, and others of their circles.

2. Erdman, David V., *et al.* "The Romantic Movement: A Selective and Critical Bibliography for 1965," ELN, IV, Supplement (Sept. 1966), 1-133.

3. Fogle, Richard Harter, comp. *Romantic Poets and Prose Writers.* New York: Appleton-Century-Crofts, 1967. "Goldentree Bibliographies."

   Includes bibliographies for Byron, Hazlitt, Hunt, Keats, Moore, and Shelley.

4. Freeman, Ronald E. "Victorian Bibliography for 1966," *Victorian Studies,* X (June 1967), 457-517.

5. Green, David Bonnell, and Edwin Graves Wilson. "Current Bibliography," K-SJ, XVI (1967), 113-149.

6. Rigby, Marjory, Charles Nilon, and James B. Misenheimer, Jr., eds. "Nineteenth Century," *Annual Bibliography of English Language and Literature,* XXXIX [1966 (for 1964)], 274-365.

7. Stratman, Carl J. *Bibliography of English Printed Tragedy, 1565-1900.* Carbondale: Southern Illinois Univ., 1966.

   Lists nineteenth-century editions of dramas by Byron and Shelley.

   Rev. by Ifan Kyrle Fletcher in *Theatre Notebook,* XXI (Summer 1967), 190.

8. Watson, George, ed. *The Concise Cambridge Bibliography of English Literature.* Second Edition. See K-SJ, XV (1966), 142.

   Rev. by R. V. Anderson in

Revue des langues vivantes, XXXII (Aug. 1966), 438.

9. Yarker, P. M., and Brian Lee. "The Nineteenth Century," in *The Year's Work in English Studies,* ed. T. S. Dorsch and C. G. Harlow, XLV (1966 [for 1964]), 291-319.

BOOKS AND ARTICLES RELATING TO ENGLISH ROMANTICISM

10. Addison, Agnes. *Romanticism and the Gothic Revival.* New York: Gordian, 1967.
    A reprint of a book first published in 1938.

11. Artz, Frederick B. *From the Renaissance to Romanticism: Trends in Style in Art, Literature, and Music 1300-1830.* See K-SJ, XIII (1964), 121.
    Rev. by R. A. Katz in *Romanic Review,* LVIII (Feb. 1967), 48-49.

12. Ayling, S. E. *The Georgian Century: 1714-1837.* London: Harrap; Mystic, Conn.: Verry (1966).
    Mentions Byron, Godwin, Hunt, Keats, and Shelley.

13. Bate, W[alter]. J[ackson]. "The English Poet and the Burden of the Past, 1660-1820," in *Aspects of the Eighteenth Century,* ed. Earl R. Wasserman (Baltimore: Johns Hopkins, 1965), pp. 245-264.
    Illustrates "the perennial relevance of the eighteenth century."

14. Bateson, F. W. *A Guide to English Literature.* Chicago: Aldine, 1965.
    Chapter VIII (pp. 130-149) is "The Approach to Romanticism," and Chapter IX includes a reading list for the Romantic period.

15. Beach, Joseph Warren. *The Concept of Nature in Nineteenth-Century English Poetry.* New York: Russell and Russell, 1966.
    A reprint of a book first published in 1936.

16. *Beers, Henry Augustin. *A History of English Romanticism in the Nineteenth Century.* New York: Gordian, 1966.
    A reprint of the 1901 edition.

17. Bernhardt-Kabisch, Ernest. "The Epitaph and the Romantic Poets: A Survey," HLQ, XXX (Feb. 1967), 113-146.
    Frames a literary context for the Romantics' interest in inscriptions for monuments.

18. Booth, Michael R. *English Melodrama.* London: Herbert Jenkins, 1965.
    Discusses development of melodrama "from about 1790 to 1900."

19. *Borges, Jorge Luis. *Introducción a la literatura inglesa.* Buenos Aires: Columba, 1965. "Colección Esquemas," No. 64.
    Includes (pp. 32-37) a chapter on Romanticism.

20. Bostetter, Edward E. *The Romantic Ventriloquists: Wordsworth, Coleridge, Keats, Shelley, Byron.* See K-SJ, XIV (1965), 107, XV (1966), 143, XVI (1967), 115.
    Rev. by Richard Harter Fogle in JEGP, LXVI (Jan. 1967), 155-156.

21. Bousquet, Jacques. *Les Thèmes du Rêve dans la Littérature Romantique (France-Angleterre-Allemagne).* See K-SJ, XVI (1967), 115.
    Rev. by J.-B. Barrere in *Revue belge de philologie et d'histoire,* XLV (1967), 155-157.

22. Brand, C. P. *Italy and the English Romantics: The Italianate Fashion in Early Nineteenth-Century England.* See K-SJ, VIII (1959), 53, IX (1960), 49, XII (1963), 123, XIII (1964), 121, XV (1966), 143, XVI (1967), 115.
    Rev. by John D. Jump in N&Q, CCXI (May 1966), 198-199.

23. Brinton, Crane. *The Political Ideas of the English Romanticists.* Ann Arbor: Univ. of Michigan, 1966.
    A paperback reprint of a book first published in 1926.
    Rev. in *Choice,* IV (March 1967), 38.

24. Croce, Benedetto. *Philosophy, Poetry, History: An Anthology of Es-*

says. Trans. Cecil Sprigge. London: Oxford Univ., 1966.

Includes an essay on "Romanticism" (pp. 1100-1113) and other critical writings of general interest.

25. Davy, Charles. *Words in the Mind: Exploring Some Effects of Poetry, English and French*. London: Chatto, 1965.

Includes chapter on "Romantic Feeling" (pp. 43-52).

26. Donohue, Joseph Walter, Jr. "Toward the Romantic Concept of Dramatic Character: *Richard III* and *Macbeth* in Criticism and Performance, 1740-1820" [Doctoral dissertation, Princeton, 1965], DA, XXVI (June 1966), 7314.

Includes discussion of critical views of Hazlitt, Hunt, Byron, and other Romantics.

27. Elwin, Malcolm. *The First Romantics*. New York: Russell and Russell, 1967.

A reprint of a book first published in 1947.

28. Fletcher, Ian, ed. *Romantic Mythologies*. London: Routledge, 1967.

A collection of eight essays, none of them on the major English Romantics.

29. Fletcher, Richard M. *English Romantic Drama 1795-1843: A Critical History*. New York: Exposition, 1966.

30. Fulmer, Oliver Bryan. "The Wandering Jew in English Romantic Poetry" [Doctoral dissertation, Tulane, 1965], DA, XXVII (Aug. 1966), 455-A-456-A.

31. Gilpatric, Mary Ellen Park. "Gothic Elements in English Romantic Poetry" [Doctoral dissertation, Kent State, 1965], DA, XXVII (July 1966), 179-A.

32. Greenwood, E. B. "Poetry and Paradise: A Study in Thematics," EC, XVII (Jan. 1967), 6-25.

A "historical sketch of the theme of paradise" which includes, briefly, the Romantics.

33. Hartman, Geoffrey. "Recent Studies in the Nineteenth Century," SEL, VI (Autumn 1966), 753-782.

An omnibus review. See K-SJ, XV (1966), 162, No. 335, XVI (1967), 116, No. 39, 121, Nos. 131 and 136, 124, No. 177, 127, No. 223, 134, No. 345, 140, No. 454, 142, No. 475. Also see Nos. 69, 183, 190, 319, 336, 420, 586, and 608.

34. Hayward, John, ed. *The Oxford Book of Nineteenth-Century English Verse*. See K-SJ, XV (1966), 144, XVI (1967), 116.

Rev. by Gerhard Müller-Schwefe in *Anglia,* LXXXIV (1966), 470-472.

35. Hilles, Frederick W., and Harold Bloom, eds., *From Sensibility to Romanticism: Essays Presented to Frederick A. Pottle*. See K-SJ, XV (1966), 144, XVI (1967), 116.

Rev. by John D. Jump in RES, N.S., XVII (Aug. 1966), 331-333; by James Kinsley in MLR, LXI (Oct. 1966), 680-683; by B. R. McElderry in *Personalist,* XLVIII (Apr. 1967), 267.

36. Irwin, David. *English Neoclassical Art: Studies in Inspiration and Taste*. Greenwich, Conn.: New York Graphic Society, 1966.

Alludes regularly to English Romanticism and to Romantic writers and artists.

37. *Isoda, Koichi. "English Romanticism in Japan—A Historical Survey," *Studies in English Literature,* XLIII (March 1967), 149-162. [In Japanese.]

38. Jack, Ian. *English Literature 1815-1832*. See K-SJ, XIV (1965), 107, XV (1966), 144, XVI (1967), 116.

Rev. by Herbert Huscher in *Anglia,* LXXXIV (1966), 110-115.

39. Jones, Howard Mumford. *History and the Contemporary: Essays in Nineteenth-Century Literature.* Madison: Univ. of Wisconsin, 1964.

Includes (pp. 23-42) "The Greatness of the Nineteenth Century." See K-SJ, VII (1958), 112, No. 42.

40. *Kamishima, Kenkichi. "Romanticism and the Voice of the Conscious," *Essays,* XX (1966), 42-48. [In Japanese.]

41. Keiser, Robert. *Die Aufnahme englischen Schrifttums in der deutschen Schweiz von 1830 bis 1860.* See K-SJ, XIV (1965), 108.

Rev. by Jacques Voisine in EA, XIX (Apr.-June 1966), 195.

42. Kreutz, Christian. *Das Prometheussymbol in der englischen Romantik.* See K-SJ, XIV (1965), 108.

Rev. by Helmut Viebrock in *Anglia,* LXXXIV (1966), 115-117.

43. Kroeber, Karl. *Romantic Narrative Art.* Madison: Univ. of Wisconsin, 1966.

A paperback reprint of a book first published in 1960. See K-SJ, XI (1962), 110, XII (1963), 124, XIII (1964), 123.

44. Kumar, Shiv K., ed. *British Romantic Poets: Recent Revaluations.* New York: New York Univ.; London: Univ. of London (1966).

Includes two new essays: Bernard Blackstone, "The Mind of Keats in His Art," pp. 257-275, and Shiv K. Kumar, "The Meaning of *Hyperion:* A Reassessment," pp. 305-318. Reprints essays by Morse Peckham, R. A. Foakes, Wilfred S. Dowden, Andrew Rutherford, C. M. Bowra, Richard Harter Fogle, Carlos Baker, Stewart C. Wilcox, Stuart M. Sperry, Jr., and Cleanth Brooks. See K-SJ, I (1952), 88, Nos. 4 and 5, 90, No. 45, 96, No. 234; IX (1960), 49, No. 27; XI (1962), 119, No. 223; XIII (1964), 143, No. 400.

Rev. in *Choice,* IV (June 1967), 422.

45. Logan, James V., John E. Jordan, and Northrop Frye, eds. *Some British Romantics: A Collection of Essays.* Columbus: Ohio State Univ., 1966.

Includes ten essays, of which five are the following: Stephen F. Fogle, "Leigh Hunt and the End of Romantic Criticism," pp. 117-139; Kathleen Coburn, "Hazlitt on the Disinterested Imagination," pp. 167-188; Ian Jack, "Poems of John Clare's Sanity," pp. 189-232; Karl Kroeber, "Trends in Minor Romantic Narrative Poetry," pp. 267-292; William S. Ward, "Periodical Literature," pp. 293-331.

Rev. in TLS, Sept. 15, 1966, p. 860; in *Choice,* IV (March 1967), 41.

46. Malins, Edward. *English Landscaping and Literature 1660-1840.* London: Oxford Univ., 1966.

47. Marshall, William H., ed. *The Major English Romantic Poets.* See K-SJ, XIV (1965), 108, XV (1966), 144, XVI (1967), 116.

Rev. by William D. Templeman in *Personalist,* XLVIII (Apr. 1967), 261-262.

48. *Nagai, Makoto. "New Criticism and Romanticism," *Bulletin* (Faculty of Literature, Univ. of Aichi Prefecture), XVII (1966), 59-69. [In Japanese.]

49. Parreaux, André. *La Société anglaise de 1760 à 1810: Introduction à une étude de la civilisation anglaise au temps de George III.* Paris: Presses Universitaires de France, 1966.

50. Parreaux, André. *La Vie quotidienne en Angleterre au temps de George III.* Paris: Hachette, 1966.

51. Perkins, David, ed. *English Romantic Writers.* New York: Harcourt, Brace & World, 1967.

An anthology with selections from Hazlitt, Moore, Hunt, Peacock, Haydon, Byron, Trelawny, Shelley, Clare, Keats, Clarke, Bailey, and Woodhouse.

52. Peyre, Henri. "L'Œuvre de Louis Cazamian," EA, XIX (Apr.-June 1966), 125-141.

Notes some of Cazamian's comments on the English Romantics.

53. Poulet, Georges. *The Metamor-*

phoses of the Circle. Trans. Carley Dawson and Elliott Coleman. Baltimore: Johns Hopkins, 1966.

Chapter VI (pp. 91-118) is on "Romanticism."

54. *Raysor, T. M., ed. *The English Romantic Poets: A Review of Research*. New York: Kraus, 1966.

A reprint of the revised edition. Adds an index for the first time. See K-SJ, I (1952), 89, III (1954), 114, IV (1955), 113, V (1956), 120, XIV (1965), 108.

55. Rest, Jaime. "Evaluación del Romanticismo," *Cuadernos de Crítica*, Buenos Aires, No. 3 (Aug. 1966), pp. 17-24.

Attempts to demonstrate that English Romanticism, through its influence on Poe and French Symbolism, is the basis of poetic modernism.

56. Rhodes, Jack Lee. "A Study in the Vocabulary of English Romanticism: *Joy* in the Poetry of Blake, Wordsworth, Coleridge, Shelley, Keats, and Byron" [Doctoral dissertation, Texas, 1966], DA, XXVII (Apr. 1967), 3434-A.

57. Rodway, Allan. *The Romantic Conflict*. See K-SJ, XIV (1965), 108, XV (1966), 145, XVI (1967), 116.

Rev. by Mario Praz in ES, XLVII (Oct. 1966), 388-389.

58. Schenk, H. G. *The Mind of the European Romantics: An Essay in Cultural History*. With a Preface by Isaiah Berlin. New York: Ungar, 1967.

Has references to all the major Romantic poets.

Rev. in TLS, June 22, 1967, pp. 549-550.

59. *Stone, Peter William Kirby. "The Art of Poetry, 1750-1820: A Comparison of Neo-Classic and Romantic Theories of Poetic Composition in Their Relation to Traditional Rhetoric." (Doctoral dissertation, Cambridge, 1965.)

60. Stone, P[eter]. W[illiam]. K[irby]. *The Art of Poetry 1750-1820: Theories of Poetic Composition and Style in the Late Neo-Classic and Early Romantic Periods*. London: Routledge, 1967.

61. *Straszewska, M., ed. *Romantyzm Wstęp, wybór materialów i przypisy Marie Straszewska*. Warsaw: Pánstowe Zaklady Wydawnictw Szkolnych, 1964.

The Romantic movement in Poland and Western Europe.

62. *Takahashi, Yasunari. *The Genealogy of Ecstasy*. Kyoto: Apollonsha, 1966. [In Japanese.]

63. *Takahashi, Yasunari. "Tragedy, Nightmare and Nature—From the Romantics to Yeats," *Rising Generation*, CXII (Sept. 1966), 600-602. [In Japanese.]

64. Thorlby, Anthony. *The Romantic Movement*. London: Longmans, 1966. "Problems and Perspectives in History."

A collection of essays and other "select documents."

65. *Tillotson, Geoffrey. *Criticism and the Nineteenth Century*. Hamden, Conn.: Archon, 1967.

A reprint of the 1951 edition.

66. Von Hendy, Andrew. "A Poetics for Demogorgon: Northrop Frye and Contemporary Criticism," *Criticism*, VIII (Fall 1966), 318-335.

Sees Frye's criticism as constituting "a Romantic poetics in a Romantic culture."

67. Warren, Alba Houghton. *English Poetic Theory, 1825-1865*. New York: Octagon, 1966.

A reprint of a book first published in 1950. See K-SJ, II (1953), 102, III (1954), 114.

68. *Welby, Thomas Earle. *The Victorian Romantics*. Hamden, Conn.: Archon, 1966.

A reprint of the 1929 edition.

69. Wellek, René. *A History of Modern Criticism*. Vol. III: *The Age of Transition*. Vol. IV: *The Later Nineteenth Century*. See K-SJ, XVI (1967), 116.

Rev. by John R. Willingham in

Library Journal, XC (Nov. 1, 1965), 4784; by Robie Macauley in NYT, Jan. 2, 1966, p. 6; by Walter J. Ong in *Yale Review,* LV (Summer 1966), 585-589; by John D. Boyd in *Thought,* XLI (Sept. 1966), 459-461; by Lee T. Lemon in JAAC, XXV (Winter 1966), 231-232; by Christopher Ricks in NS, LXXIII (Jan. 6, 1967), 16-17; by G. N. G. Orsini in *Victorian Studies,* X (March 1967), 308-310; by Robert W. Simmons, Jr., in *Slavic and East European Journal,* XI (Summer 1967), 222-224. Also see No. 33.

70. Wilkie, Brian. *Romantic Poets and Epic Tradition.* See K-SJ, XV (1966), 145, XVI (1967), 116-117.

Rev. by Carl F. Keppler in *Arizona Quarterly,* XXI (Autumn 1965), 286-288; by Karl Ludwig Klein in *Anglia,* LXXXIV (1966), 480-483; by K[arl]. K[roeber]. in ELN, IV, Supplement (Sept. 1966), 17; by Frederick T. Wood in ES, XLVII (Oct. 1966), 396-397; by Robert F. Gleckner in *Criticism,* IX (Winter 1967), 93-95; by Stuart M. Sperry, Jr., in MP, LXIV (Feb. 1967), 263-264; by Kirsti Olin in *Neuphilologische Mitteilungen,* LXVIII (March 1967), 104-110.

71. Wimsatt, William K., and Cleanth Brooks. *Literary Criticism: A Short History.* New York: Random House, 1967.

A reprint of a book first published in 1957. See K-SJ, VII (1958), 113, VIII (1959), 55, IX (1960), 52, X (1961), 75.

72. Wittreich, Joseph Anthony, Jr. "'A Power amongst Powers': Milton and His Romantic Critics" [Doctoral dissertation, Western Reserve, 1966], DA, XXVII (Apr. 1967), 3436-A-3437-A.

II. BYRON

Works: Collected, Selected, Single, Translated

73. Bebbington, W. G., comp. *Famous Poems: An Anthology of the Favourite Poems of English Verse.* Huddersfield: Schofield & Sims, 1962.

Byron, Hunt, Keats, Hood, Peacock, and Shelley are represented.

74. Bender, Robert M., and Charles L. Squier, eds. *The Sonnet: A Comprehensive Anthology of British and American Sonnets from the Renaissance to the Present.* New York: Washington Square, 1965.

Includes sonnets by Hunt, Byron, Shelley, Clare, Reynolds, Keats, and Hood.

75. Berg, Leila, comp. *Four Feet and Two and Some with None: An Anthology of Verse.* Harmondsworth: Penguin, 1960.

Includes selections from Byron, Hood, Keats, and Shelley.

76. Bleiler, E. F., ed. *Three Gothic Novels and a Fragment of a Novel by Lord Byron.* New York: Dover, 1966.

Includes Polidori's *The Vampyre* and the "fragment" dated June 17, 1816.

Rev. in TLS, Dec. 8, 1966, p. 1146.

77. **Byron shin-shishu.* [*Poetical Works: Newly Translated*] [Translated by] Miura Itsuo. Tokyo: Nihonbungei-sha, 1966.

78. **Byron shishu.* [*Poetical Works.*] [Translated by] Abe Keio. Tokyo: Kinyen-sha, 1966.

79. *Byron's Poems.* Ed. V. de Sola Pinto. See K-SJ, XIV (1965), 108.

Rev. by L[ouis]. C. B[onnerot]. In EA, XIX (Apr.-June 1966), 200.

80. Cheetham, Anthony, and Derek Parfit, eds. *Eton Microcosm.* London: Sidgwick & Jackson, 1964.

Includes excerpts from Byron and Shelley.

81. Clark, Leonard, comp. *Common Ground: An Anthology for the Young.* London: Faber, 1964.

Includes selections from Byron, Keats, Hood, Peacock, and Shelley.

82. **Don Juan: Cantos I-IV.* Ed. T. S.

Dorsch. Abridged Edition. London: Routledge, 1967. "English Texts."

83. Flint, E. L., and M. K. Flint, comps. *Poetry in Perspective: A Critical Anthology*. London: London Univ., 1963.
   Selections from Byron, Keats, and Shelley are included.

84. Frewin, Leslie, comp. *The Boundary Book: A Lord Taverner's Miscellany of Cricket*. London: Macdonald, 1962.
   Includes a selection from Byron.

85. Frewin, Leslie, comp. *The Poetry of Cricket: An Anthology*. London: Macdonald, 1964.
   Includes selections from Byron and Hood.

86. "From *Don Juan*," K-SJ, XVI (1967), 22.
   Two stanzas from the first canto.

87. Hadfield, John, ed. *A Book of Pleasures: An Anthology of Words and Pictures*. London: Vista, 1960.
   Byron, Hunt, Hazlitt, Peacock, and Shelley are included.

88. Hadfield, John, comp. *Love for Life: An Anthology of Words and Pictures*. London: Book Society, 1961.
   Includes Byron and Shelley.

89. Hadfield, Miles, and John Hadfield, comps. *Gardens of Delight*. London: Cassell, 1964.
   Includes excerpts from Byron and Hood.

90. Hanratty, Jerome, comp. *The Wheel of Poetry: An Anthology*. 4 vols. London: Athlone, 1963.
   Includes selections from Byron, Hunt, Keats, Hood, Peacock, and Shelley.

91. Hope, Ronald, ed. *The Harrap Book of Sea Verse*. London: Harrap, 1960.
   Includes selections from Byron, Hunt, Keats, Hood, and Shelley.

92. Humphreys, Christmas, ed. *Poems I Remember*. London: Michael Joseph, 1960.
   Includes selections from Byron, Hunt, Keats, and Shelley.

93. MacQueen, John, and Tom Scott, comps. *The Oxford Book of Scottish Verse*. Oxford: Clarendon, 1966.
   Includes (pp. 440-442) two poems by Byron.

94. Massingham, Hugh, and Pauline Massingham. *The Englishman Abroad*. London: Phoenix House, 1962.
   Includes selections from Byron, Haydon, Hazlitt, Hobhouse, and Shelley.
   Rev. by E. D. O'Brien in ILN, CCXLI (Sept. 22, 1962), 460; in TLS, Nov. 2, 1962, p. 843; by Robert H. Hill in *Blackwood's Magazine,* CCXCII (Dec. 1962), 570.

95. Massingham, Hugh, and Pauline Massingham, eds. *The London Anthology*. London: Phoenix House, 1950.
   Includes selections from Byron, Haydon, Hazlitt, Hood, and Peacock.

96. Mears, Esmé, comp. *Mood and Rhythm*. 4 vols. London: Black, 1963.
   Includes selections from Byron, Hunt, Keats, Hood, Peacock, and Horace Smith.

97. Morgan, Edwin, ed. *Collins Albatross Book of Longer Poems: English and American Poetry from the Fourteenth Century to the Present Day*. London: Collins, 1963.
   Includes poems by Byron, Keats, Hood, and Shelley.

98. Oehlmann, Werner. *Don Juan*. Frankfurt: Ullstein, 1965.
   Includes translations from Byron (pp. 116-135).
   Rev. by Peter Branscombe in *German Life & Letters,* XX (Apr. 1967), 275-276.

Perkins, David, ed. See No. 51.

99. Pickles, Wilfred, comp. *For Your Delight: A Personal Selection of Poetry for All Occasions*. London: W. H. Allen, 1960.

Selections from Byron, Hunt, Hood, Keats, and Shelley.

100. Pinion, F. B., comp. *A Book of Dramatic Poems*. London: Arnold, 1964.
Includes poems by Byron and Keats.

101. **The Selected Poetry and Prose of Byron*. Ed. W. H. Auden. New York: New American Library, 1966. "Signet Classic Poetry Series."

102. Seymour, William Kean, and John Smith, comps. *The Pattern of Poetry: The Poetry Society Verse-Speaking Anthology*. London: Burke, 1963.
Byron, Keats, Hood, and Shelley are included.

103. Tough, A. J., comp. *Looking beneath the Surface: An Anthology of Narrative Poetry*. London: Arnold, 1962.
Includes selections from Byron and Keats.

104. *Vas, István. *Énekek éneke*. [*Song of Songs*.] Budapest: Európa, 1966.
An anthology of translations that includes poems by Byron, Moore, Shelley, and Keats.

105. Wall, Bernard, ed. *Italy: A Personal Anthology*. London: Newnes, 1964.
Includes selections from Byron and Keats.
Rev. in TLS, Sept. 24, 1964, p. 881.

106. *The Works of Lord Byron. Letters and Journals*, ed. Rowland E. Prothero, 6 vols. *Poetry*, ed. E. H. Coleridge, 7 vols. New York: Octagon, 1966.
A reprint of the "standard edition," first published 1898-1904.

Books and Articles Relating to Byron and His Circle

107. Adams, Robert Martin. *Nil: Episodes in the Literary Conquest of Void during the Nineteenth Century*. New York: Oxford Univ., 1966.
Discusses "Darkness" (pp. 200-201).

Adnitt, Frank W. See No. 467.

108. *Aldao, Martín. "Byron en Venecia," *La Nación*, Buenos Aires, Aug. 8, 1965.
Comments on the residence of Byron in Venice.

109. Angles, Robert. "Commonplace Byron," *Music and Musicians*, X (July 1962), 45.
Reviews the performance, June 6, 1962, by the Kensington Symphony Orchestra, of Alan Bush's *Byron Symphony*, a programmatic work based on Byron's life.

110. *Ara, Guillermo. "Los *Cantos del Peregrino*," *La Nación*, Buenos Aires, Aug. 1, 1965.
Comments on the work of the Argentine poet Esteban Echeverría and the influence of Byron's *Childe Harold*.

111. Auden, W. H. "Byron: The Making of a Comic Poet," *New York Review of Books*, VII (Aug. 18, 1966), 12-18.
An evaluation of Byron, whose "genius was essentially a comic one." "*Don Juan* is the most original poem in English."

Ayling, S. E. See No. 12.

112. *Barbary, James. *The Young Lord Byron*. London: Parrish, 1965; New York: Roy, 1966.
A juvenile adventure.

113. Bartlett, C. J. *Castlereagh*. New York: Scribner's, 1966.
Quotes Byron's and Shelley's attacks on Castlereagh.

Barton, Bernard. See No. 307.

114. Bell, Harry. *The Story of English Literature*. Edinburgh: Chambers, 1964.
A history for children: Byron, Keats, and Shelley are treated.

115. Beyer, Werner W. *The Enchanted Forest*. See K-SJ, XIV (1965), 110, XV (1966), 147, XVI (1967), 118.
Rev. by W. D. Robson-Scott in *German Life & Letters*, XX (Jan. 1967), 150-152.

116. Blackmur, R. P. *A Primer of Ignorance*. Ed. Joseph Frank. New York: Harcourt, Brace & World, 1967.
Contrasts Byron and William Carlos Williams (pp. 52-53).

Boyle, Andrew. See No. 1.

117. Briscoe, Walter A., ed. *Byron, the Poet: A Collection of Addresses and Essays*. New York: Haskell House, 1967.
A reprint of a book first published in 1924.

118. Browning, Robert. *Learned Lady: Letters from Robert Browning to Mrs. Thomas FitzGerald 1876-1889*. Ed. Edward C. McAleer. Cambridge, Mass.: Harvard Univ., 1966.
Letters refer to Byron, Hazlitt, and Shelley.
Rev. in TLS, Oct. 6, 1966, p. 916.

119. Brownstein, Rachel Mayer. "Byron's *Don Juan:* Sóme Reasons for the Rhymes," MLQ, XXVIII (June 1967), 177-191.
The "alogical rhymes" are a part of Byron's experiments with the "nondenotative function of words."

120. Bruffee, Kenneth A. "The Synthetic Hero and the Narrative Structure of *Childe Harold* III," SEL, VI (Autumn 1966), 669-678.†
The experience described in the poem "depends for its importance on the process of identification, on the 'confusion' of narrator and 'hero,' by which a new 'synthetic hero' is introduced."

121. Buckley, Jerome Hamilton. *The Triumph of Time: A Study of the Victorian Concepts of Time, History, Progress, and Decadence*. Cambridge, Mass.: Harvard Univ., 1966.
Alludes to Byron, Hazlitt, Keats, and Shelley.

122. Casey, John. *The Language of Criticism*. London: Methuen, 1966.
Has references to Byron, Keats, and Shelley.

123. Cecchi, Emilio. *Scrittori inglesi e americani*. 2 vols. Milan: Il Saggiatore, 1962, 1964.
Vol. I includes essay, "Ombre byroniane" (pp. 50-55).
Rev. by Fausto Belfiori in ICS, XLVI (Sept.-Oct. 1963), 162.

124. *Cervellati, Alessandro. *Donne e poeti all'arena del Sole*. Bologna: Tamari, 1966.
Includes material on Byron and Teresa Guiccioli.

125. Chatman, Seymour. *A Theory of Meter*. The Hague: Mouton, 1965.
Makes use of lines from Byron, Keats, and Shelley.

126. Clare, John. *The Later Poems of John Clare*. Ed. Eric Robinson and Geoffrey Summerfield. Manchester: Manchester Univ., 1964.
Clare's "Childe Harold" and "Don Juan" are herein printed for the first time. See No. 127.

127. Clare, John. *Selected Poems and Prose of John Clare*. Ed. Eric Robinson and Geoffrey Summerfield. London: Oxford Univ., 1966.
Notes Clare's delusion that he was Byron, a delusion that was in part responsible for some of his poems. See No. 126.

128. Colby, Reginald. *Mayfair: A Town within London*. London: Country Life, 1966.
Discusses the houses Byron knew in Mayfair (pp. 118-120).
Rev. in TLS, July 14, 1966, p. 612.

129. Colby, Robert A. *Fiction with a Purpose: Major and Minor Nineteenth-Century Novels*. Bloomington: Indiana Univ., 1967.
Notes influence of Byron on *Pendennis*. Refers to several of Godwin's novels.

130. Cunningham, Gilbert F. *The Divine Comedy in English: A Critical Bibliography*. 2 vols. New York: Barnes and Noble, 1965, 1967.

Mentions the translations of various passages by Byron, Shelley, and Medwin.

131. Dahlberg, Edward. *Epitaphs of Our Times: The Letters of Edward Dahlberg*. New York: Braziller, 1967.

Comments on Byron, Hazlitt, and Keats.

132. Deen, Leonard W. "Liberty and License in Byron's *Don Juan*," *Texas Studies in Literature and Language*, VIII (Fall 1966), 345-357.

Argues that the terms "liberty and license" suggested to Byron the rhetorical means and the "appropriate form" by which to reflect the disorder of the world he knew.

133. de Ford, Miriam Allen. *Thomas Moore*. New York: Twayne, 1967.

134. Deslandres, Yvonne. "Delacroix and Great Britain," *Scottish Art Review*, IX, No. 4 (1964), pp. 18-21, 32.

Includes discussion of the painter and Byron; reproduces "Self Portrait in Costume of Childe Harold" and "Death of Lara."

Donohue, Joseph Walter, Jr. See No. 26.

135. *Du Bos, Charles. *Lord Byron e la fatalita*. Translated from the French by Francesco Saba Sardi. Milan, 1961.

See K-SJ, VII (1958), 115, VIII (1959), 58.

136. Dutt, Toru. "Toru Dutt's Letters," *Indian Literature*, IX (Apr.-June 1966), 15-23.

Speaks of having read Byron.

137. "1819 Letter, Apparently by Byron, Discovered," *New York Times*, July 9, 1966, p. 24.

At the Univ. of Miami Library: to A. W. Galignani, Apr. 27, 1819.

138. Eliot, C. W. J. "Lord Byron, Early Travelers, and the Monastery at Delphi," *American Journal of Archaeology*, LXXI (1967), 283-291, Plates 85-86.

139. Emerson, Ralph Waldo. *The Journals and Miscellaneous Notebooks of Ralph Waldo Emerson*. Vol. VI: *1824-1838*. Ed. Ralph H. Orth. Cambridge, Mass.: Harvard Univ., 1966.

Contains references to Byron and Hazlitt. See K-SJ, XI (1962), 115, XII (1963), 128, XV (1966), 149.

140. Enkvist, Nils Erik. *British and American Literary Letters in Scandinavian Public Collections*. See K-SJ, XIV (1965), 111.

Rev. by J. C. Maxwell in N&Q, CCXI (Nov. 1966), 440.

141. Fermor, Patrick Leigh. *Roumeli: Travels in Northern Greece*. London: John Murray, 1966.

Makes frequent reference to Byron and to ways in which Greece remembers him.

Rev. by Freya Stark in NYT, Aug. 28, 1966, p. 7.

142. Fiess, Edward. "Byron's Dark Blue Ocean and Melville's Rolling Sea," ELN, III (June 1966), 274-278.†

Melville "saw the ocean with the Romantic vision of Byron and Byron's contemporaries before he attained, or even while he was attaining his own Melvillean vision."

Fogle, Richard Harter, comp. See No. 3.

Fowler, Roger, ed. See No. 340.

143. Friesner, Donald Neil. "Ellis Bell and Israfel," *Brontë Society Transactions*, XIV (1964), 11-18.†

Both Emily Brontë and Poe were influenced by Byron.

144. Fussell, Paul, Jr. *Poetic Meter and Poetic Form*. New York: Random House, 1965.

Uses passages from Byron, Keats, and Shelley for illustrative purposes.

145. "The Gennadius Library," TLS, May 4, 1967, p. 388.

Mentions that the laurel wreath from Byron's coffin is preserved in the Gennadeion in Athens.

146. Gérin, Winifred. "Byron's Influ-

ence on the Brontës," KSMB, XVII (1966), 1-19.

Traces the Byronic experience that "confirmed the Brontës in a poetic disposition to which they were by nature born."

147. Gleckner, Robert F. "Byron in *Finnegans Wake*," in *Twelve and a Tilly: Essays on the Occasion of the 25th Anniversary of Finnegans Wake*, ed. Jack P. Dalton and Clive Hart (London: Faber; Evanston: Northwestern Univ., 1965), pp. 40-51.

Rev. in *Literary Half-Yearly*, VII (July 1966), 134-135.

148. Goethe, Johann Wolfgang von. *Goethe: Conversations and Encounters.* Ed. David Luke and Robert Pick. Chicago: Regnery, 1966.

Includes comments on and allusions to Byron.

Rev. by Burton Feldman in *University of Denver Quarterly*, I (Autumn 1966), 156-158.

149. Gordon, David J. *D. H. Lawrence as a Literary Critic.* See K-SJ, XVI (1967), 120.

Rev. by Richard Wasson in JEGP, LXVI (Jan. 1967), 162-164.

150. Gore, John. "Clio in No Hurry," *Quarterly Review*, CCCIV (Oct. 1966), 414-418.

In discussing the slowness with which facts often come to light in historical research, cites as an example the discovery in 1935 that "When we two parted" had been written to Lady Frances Wedderburn Webster.

151. *Goyena, Pedro. "El gaucho, personaje byroniano," *La Prensa*, Buenos Aires, Oct. 2, 1966.

Extract from an essay written in 1870: the gaucho as Byronian character.

Graves, Robert. See No. 511.

152. Greene, William Chace. *The Choices of Criticism.* Cambridge, Mass.: M.I.T., 1965.

Alludes to "The Isles of Greece" (p. 83).

153. Grønbech, Vilhelm. *Religious Currents in the 19th Century.* See K-SJ, XVI (1967), 120.

Rev. by Lawrence S. Thompson in JEGP, LXV (July 1966), 574-575.

154. Hagelman, Charles W., Jr., and Robert J. Barnes, eds. *A Concordance to Byron's "Don Juan."* Ithaca: Cornell Univ. 1967.

155. Hardy, Thomas. *Thomas Hardy's Personal Writings: Prefaces, Literary Opinions, Reminiscences.* Ed. Harold Orel. Lawrence: Univ. of Kansas, 1966.

Includes comments on Byron and Shelley.

156. Harson, Robert R. "A Profile of John Polidori, with a New Edition of *The Vampyre*" [Doctoral dissertation, Ohio, 1966], DA, XXVII (March 1967), 3010-A.

157. Haslam, G. E., ed. *Wise after the Event: A Catalogue of Books, Pamphlets, Manuscripts and Letters Relating to Thomas James Wise Displayed in an Exhibition in Manchester Central Library September 1964.* Manchester: Manchester Libraries Committee, 1964.

Includes items pertaining to Byron, Keats, and Shelley.

158. Hays, H. R. *The Dangerous Sex: The Myth of Feminine Evil.* New York: Putnam's, 1964.

Has references to Byron and Keats.

159. Holloway, John. *Widening Horizons in English Verse.* Evanston: Northwestern Univ., 1967.

Refers to Byron, Hunt, Keats, and Shelley and to their interest in Islam and in India.

160. Howarth, R. G. *A Pot of Gillyflowers: Studies and Notes.* Cape Town: The Author, 1964.

Includes "Byron as Dramatist" (pp. 46-54).

161. Hudson, Arthur Palmer. "The 'Su-

perstitious' Lord Byron," SP, LXIII (Oct. 1966), 708-721.

Surveys the evidence and concludes that it "seems to prove that Byron *was* superstitious, but also suggests that the degree of his superstitiousness was exaggerated by some reporter[s] and by his habit of mystification."

162. Jeffrey, Lloyd N. "Lord Byron and the Classics," *Classical Outlook,* LXIII (March 1966), 76-78.

Byron "seems to have had a special predilection for classical literature and myth."

163. Joburg, Leon. "Lord Byron's Greece: Glory Reborn," *Mankind,* I (May-June 1967), 40-47, 74-77.

An account of the struggle for Greek independence and of Byron's service to the cause.

164. Joyce, James. *Letters of James Joyce.* Vols. II and III. Ed. Richard Ellmann, London: Faber, 1966.

Has references to Byron and Shelley. See K-SJ, VII (1958), 117.

165. *Katona, Anna. "A byronizmustól a dühöngökig" ["From Byronism to the Angry"], *Alföld,* No. 12 (1966), pp. 61-71.

Traces similarities to Byronic attitudes in Eliot's and Beckett's heroes and in the angry hero of the fifties.

166. *Kaul, Raj Kumar, ed. *Byron's Vision of Judgment.* Jaipur, 1965.

Rev. by Vilmala Rao in *Literary Criterion,* VII (Summer 1966), 88.

167. Kenyon, F. W. *The Absorbing Fire: The Byron Legend.* New York: Dodd, Mead, 1966.

"A story based on the life and loves of Lord Byron."

Rev. by Frederick T. Wood in ES, XLVIII (June 1967), 276.

168. Kernan, Alvin B. *The Plot of Satire.* See K-SJ, XVI (1967), 120.

Rev. by Charles Witke in CL, XVIII (Summer 1966), 277-279; in VQR, XLII (Summer 1966), xcix-c; by Ronald Paulson in JEGP, LXV (July 1966), 602-604; by Marshall Waingrow in *Yale Review,* LVI (Autumn 1966), 138-144; by G. K. Hunter in N&Q, CCXI (Oct. 1966), 395; by Ernest J. Lovell, Jr., in MP, LXIV (May 1967), 380-382.

169. Knight, G. Wilson. *Byron and Shakespeare.* London: Routledge; New York: Barnes & Noble (1966).

Rev. by John Bayley in Spec, Nov. 25, 1966, pp. 690-691; in TLS, Feb. 23, 1967, p. 148.

170. Korisis, Hariton. *Die politischen Parteien Griechenlands: Ein neuer Staat auf dem Weg zur Demokratie 1821-1910.* Nuremberg: Karl Pfeiffer, 1966.

Has material on the years Byron was in Greece.

Rev. in TLS, May 18, 1967, p. 414.

171. Langley, Noël. *An Elegance of Rebels: A Play in Three Acts.* London: Arthur Barker, 1960.

A play "for reading purposes only" on Byron, Hunt, and Shelley, 1822-1824. It is wildly inaccurate.

Rev. by E. Poulenard in EA, XIV (Apr.-June 1961), 168-169.

172. Lemon, Lee T. *The Partial Critics.* New York: Oxford Univ., 1965.

Has critical comments on Byron, Hazlitt, Hunt, Keats, and Shelley.

173. Lindsay, Jack. *J.M.W. Turner: His Life and Work.* Greenwich, Conn.: New York Graphic Society, 1966.

Has references to Byron, Haydon, Hazlitt, and Keats.

174. *Loder, Elizabeth. "Maurice Guest: Some Nineteenth-Century Progenitors," *Southerly,* XXVI (1966), 94-105.

Refers briefly to the Byronic hero.

175. Lombardi, Thomas W. "Hogg to Byron to Davenport: An Unpublished Byron Letter," BNYPL, LXXI (Jan. 1967), 39-46.

The letter is dated February 7, 1815.

176. Lovell, Ernest J., Jr. *Byron: The*

Record of a Quest. See K-SJ, I (1952), 90, II (1953), 101, XIV (1965), 113, XV (1966), 150, XVI (1967), 121.

Rev. in *Choice,* III (Oct. 1966), 644.

177. McClary, Ben Harris. "Another Moore Letter," N&Q, CCXII (Jan. 1967), 24-25.†

Concerns the destruction of Byron's memoirs. See Nos. 179 and 195.

178. McClary, Ben Harris. "Irving's Literary Midwifery: Five Unpublished Letters from British Repositories," PQ, XLVI (Apr. 1967), 277-283.

Letters to Godwin concerning American publishers and to Moore concerning Byron's letters and journals.

179. McClary, Ben Harris. "The Moore-Irving Letter File," N&Q, CCXI (May 1966), 181-182.

Notes three published letters from Moore to Irving not included in W. S. Dowden's edition. See K-SJ, XV (1966), 151, XVI (1967), 122. See also Nos. 177 and 195.

180. McGann, Jerome J. *"Childe Harold's Pilgrimage* and the Poetics of Self-Expression" [Doctoral dissertation, Yale, 1966], DA, XXVII (Feb. 1967), 2503-A.

181. McGann, Jerome. "Childe Harold's Pilgrimage I-II: A Collation and Analysis," KSMB, XVII (1966), 37-54.

Traces the course of Byron's composition of Cantos I and II, supplying "a good deal of new information about when and how the poem was written" and giving "some fruitful insights into the meaning and poetic structure of the early cantos."

182. ["*Manfred* Performed,"] *The Times,* London, Dec. 29, 1966, p. 6.

A review of a performance of *Manfred,* with Schumann's music, at the Rome Opera House.

183. Marchand, Leslie A. *Byron's Poetry: A Critical Introduction.* See K-SJ, XVI (1967), 121.

Rev. by J. B. Caird in *Library Review,* XX (Summer 1966), 429-430; in *Choice,* III (July-Aug. 1966), 411; by Ralph Lawrence in *English,* XVI (Autumn 1966), 115; by E. E. B[ostetter]. in ELN, IV, Supplement (Sept. 1966), 25-26; in TLS, Sept. 15, 1966, p. 855; by W. J. B. Owen in RES, N.S., XVIII (Feb. 1967), 107-108; by M. K. Joseph in *Aumla,* No. 27 (May 1967), 121-122. Also see No. 33.

184. Marshall, William H. "The Byron Collection in Memory of Meyer Davis, Jr.," *Library Chronicle,* XXXIII (Winter 1967), 8-29.

A description of the holdings at the University of Pennsylvania.

185. Marshall, William H. *Byron, Shelley, Hunt, and "The Liberal."* See K-SJ, X (1961), 79, XI (1962), 117, XII (1963), 130.

Rev. by C. A. Bodelsen in ES, XLVIII (Apr. 1967), 175-176.

186. Marshall, William H. "The Byron Will of 1809," *Library Chronicle,* XXXIII (Spring 1967), 97-114.

Prints for the first time a will dated 1809 now in the Davis collection at the University of Pennsylvania.

187. Martin, M. H. Combe. "Byron Trouvaille?" N&Q, CCXII (Jan. 1967), 26.

Prints verses ascribed to Byron.

188. Matthews, Honor. *The Primal Curse: The Myth of Cain and Abel in the Theatre.* New York: Schocken, 1967.

Makes only passing mention of Byron.

189. *A Medical History of Lord Byron.* Norwich, N. Y.: Eaton Laboratories, 1965.

A pamphlet edited from an original manuscript by Benjamin S. Abeshouse, M.D., who collected data on "the influence of genitourinary disease in the lives of famous men and women."

190. Medwin, Thomas. *Medwin's "Conversations of Lord Byron."* Ed. Ernest J. Lovell, Jr. See K-SJ, XVI (1967), 121-122.

Rev. in *The Times,* London, July 21, 1966, p. 16; by Peter Quennell in Spec, Aug. 5, 1966, pp. 178-179†; in TLS, Oct. 6, 1966, p. 916; in *Choice,* III (Nov. 1966), 771; by Peter L. Thorslev, Jr., in K-SJ, XVI (1967), 97-99. Also see No. 33.

191. Melchiori, Barbara. "Browning's Don Juan," EC, XVI (Oct. 1966), 416-440.

A study of *Fifine at the Fair,* with allusions to Byron.

192. Miliband, Marion, ed. *The Observer of the Nineteenth Century: 1791-1901.* Introduced by Asa Briggs. London: Longmans, 1966.

Includes section on "Byron—The Romantic Hero" (pp. 95-98).

193. *Miyamoto, Masato. " 'I awoke one morning'—Byron and Caroline," *Bulletin of the English Society* (Osaka Gakugei Univ.), XII (March 1967), 47-56. [In Japanese.]

194. ["Monument to His Dog,"] *The Times,* London, Nov. 1, 1966, p. 12.

Byron's monument to Boatswain is included in a list of historic buildings and sites.

195. Moore, Thomas. *The Letters of Thomas Moore.* Ed. Wilfred S. Dowden. See K-SJ, XV (1966), 151, XVI (1967), 122.

Rev. by Wolfgang Weiss in *Anglia,* LXXXIV (1966), 117-118; by Robert Brainard Pearsall in ELN, III (June 1966), 310-312; by E. E. B[ostetter]. in ELN, IV, Supplement (Sept. 1966), 35; by Ernest J. Lovell, Jr., in SR, LXXV (Spring 1967), 358-364; by Carlos Baker in MP, LXIV (May 1967), 361-362.

See Nos. 177 and 179.

196. *Moreau, Pierre. *Ames et thèmes romantiques.* Paris: Librairie José Corti, 1965.

Mentions influence of Byron on Chateaubriand's descriptions of nature.

Rev. by Jacques Body in RLC, XL (Apr.-June 1966), 310-312.

197. Moreux, Françoise. *Thomas De Quincey: La Vie—L'Homme—L'Œuvre.* See K-SJ, XVI (1967), 122.

Rev. by John E. Jordan in EA, XVIII (Oct.-Dec. 1965), 422-424.

198. Nabokov, Vladimir. *Notes on Prosody: From the Commentary to His Translation of Pushkin's "Eugene Onegin."* New York: Pantheon, 1964.

Discusses passages from Byron and Keats.

199. Nicolson, Harold. *Diaries and Letters 1930-1939.* Ed. Nigel Nicolson. New York: Atheneum, 1966.

Contains references to Byron.

200. ["Notice of Unveiling a Memorial Plaque,"] *The Times,* London, July 12, 1966, p. 15.

The plaque in Byron's memory overlooks Lake Albano and has lines on it from *Childe Harold's Pilgrimage.*

201. Otten, Terry Ralph. "The Empty Stage: A Comment on the Search for Dramatic Form in the Early Nineteenth Century" [Doctoral dissertation, Ohio, 1966], DA, XXVII (Nov. 1966), 1344-A.

Discusses plays of Byron and Shelley.

202. Pack, S. W. C. *The "Wager" Mutiny.* London: Redman, 1964.

Byron's grandfather was involved.

Rev. in TLS, Feb. 4, 1965, p. 93.

203. Parsons, Coleman O. " 'Pilgrims of Research' in the British Museum: 1820-1826," *Quarterly Review,* CCCV (Jan. 1967), 54-66.

Records show that users of the Reading Room during this period included Moore, Murray, Godwin, Taylor and Hessey, Dilke, Haydon, T. J. Hogg, Peacock, and others.

204. Pedrini, Lura Nancy, and Duilio Thomas Pedrini. *Serpent Imagery*

and Symbolism: A Study of the Major English Romantic Poets. New Haven: College and University Press, 1966.

Includes material on Byron, Shelley, and Keats.

Rev. by Henry Halpern in *Library Journal,* XCI (Nov. 1, 1966), 5401-5402.

205. Pellegrin, Jean. "Commentaire sur 'El Desdichado,'" *Cahiers du Sud,* LIII (1966), 276-295.

Includes discussion of the "Biron" who is mentioned in this poem by Gérard de Nerval.

206. Playfair, Giles. *The Prodigy: A Study of the Strange Life of Master Betty.* London: Secker & Warburg, 1967.

Byron, Godwin, Haydon, Hazlitt, Hunt, and others appear in this biography.

Rev. in TLS, June 8, 1967, p. 511.

207. Potts, Abbie Findlay. *The Elegiac Mode: Poetic Form in Wordsworth and Other Elegists.* Ithaca: Cornell Univ., 1967.

Makes frequency reference to Byron, Keats, and Shelley.

208. Praz, Mario. "Byron and Foscolo," in *Renaissance and Modern Essays: Presented to Vivian de Sola Pinto in Celebration of His Seventieth Birthday,* ed. G. R. Hibbard (New York: Barnes and Noble, 1966), pp. 101-118.

Maintains that in spite of similarities between Byron and Foscolo, Foscolo, like Keats, represents the ultimate development of classicism "reached within the general framework of Romantic sensibility," whereas Byron "lacked the enviable classical qualities of restraint, economy, fastidiousness and the consciousness of limits."

209. *Quennell, Peter. *Byron: The Years of Fame.* London: Collins, 1967.

A reprint of a book first published in 1935. See K-SJ, IV (1955), 116.

210. Radcliff-Umstead, Douglas. "Cainism and Gérard de Nerval," PQ, XLV (Apr. 1966), 395-408.

Includes comparison of the Cains of Byron and Gérard de Nerval.

211. Raizis, Marios Byron. "The Prometheus Theme in British and American Poetry" [Doctoral dissertation, New York, 1966], DA, XXVII (Oct. 1966), 1064-A.

Includes discussion of Byron and Shelley.

212. Ramsey, L. G. G., ed. *The Connoisseur New Guide to English Painting & Sculpture.* London: The Connoisseur, 1962.

Haydon and De Wint are discussed; Severn is referred to. Westall's portrait of Byron is reproduced.

213. *Randi, Aldo. *Lord Byron e la contessa Guiccioli.* Ravenna, 1965.

214. Reed, Joseph W., Jr. *English Biography in the Early Nineteenth Century, 1801-1838.* See K-SJ, XVI (1967), 123.

Rev. by Clarence Tracy in QQ, LXXIII (Autumn 1966), 454-455; in *Choice,* III (Feb. 1967), 1128.

215. Rennes, Jacob Johan van. *Bowles, Byron and the Pope-Controversy.* New York: Haskell House, 1966.

A reprint of a book first published in 1927.

216. Reynolds, Graham. *Victorian Painting.* New York: Macmillan, 1966.

Refers to Haydon, De Wint, Hilton, and Severn. Reproduces Ford Madox Brown's *The Finding of Don Juan by Haidée.*

Rhodes, Jack Lee. See No. 56.

217. Richardson, Joanna. *George the Magnificent: A Portrait of King George IV.* New York: Harcourt, Brace & World, 1966.

Published in Great Britain as *George IV.*

Discusses the Regent's relations with Byron. Other Romantic writers are mentioned more briefly.

218. Roberts, K. S. "The Marquesa De Alorna and the English Poets," *Kentucky Foreign Language Quarterly*, XIII, No. 3 (1966), pp. 147-155.

Notes that this Portugese poetess wrote a poem to Byron, "Soneto dedicando una obra poetica ao Auctor de Childe Harold."

219. Robinson, Forest Elmo. "The Peninsular War in the Political Evolution of Five English Romantic Poets" [Doctoral dissertation, Colorado, 1965], DA, XXVII (Sept. 1966), 782-A.

Byron is one of the five.

220. Robinson, Henry Crabb. *The Diary of Henry Crabb Robinson: An Abridgement*. Ed. Derek Hudson. London: Oxford Univ., 1967.

Refers to Byron, Hunt, Keats, Shelley, and others of their circles.

221. Robson, W. W. *Critical Essays*. London: Routledge, 1966.

Includes "The Romantic Poets" (pp. 115-123) and "Byron as Poet" (pp. 148-188). See K-SJ, VIII (1959), 63, IX (1960), 58.

Rev. by Martin Dodsworth in Li, LXXVI (Dec. 15, 1966), 901-902; in TLS, Apr. 27, 1967, p. 353.

222. Rogers, Katharine M. *The Troublesome Helpmate: A History of Misogyny in Literature*. Seattle: Univ. of Washington, 1966.

Includes material from Byron and Keats.

223. Roston, Murray. *Prophet and Poet: The Bible and the Growth of Romanticism*. See K-SJ, XVI (1967), 123.

Rev. by E. D. Mackerness in MLR, LXI (July 1966), 502-503; by Donald H. Reiman in JEGP, LXV (July 1966), 605-606.

224. Rüdiger, Horst. "Weltliteratur in Goethes *Helena*," *Jahrbuch der Deutschen Schillergesellschaft*, VIII (1964), 172-198.

Byron's role in the work is discussed.

225. Sarkar, Manojkumar. "Voice of the Haunted Ruins," *Calcutta Review*, CLXXV (June 1965), 241-250.

Treats briefly some of the plays of Byron, Shelley, and Keats.

226. Sealts, Merton M., Jr. *Melville's Reading: A Check-List of Books Owned and Borrowed*. Madison: Univ. of Wisconsin, 1966.

Included are books by Byron, Godwin, Haydon, Hazlitt, Hood, Hunt, Keats, Mary Shelley, Shelley, and others.

227. Shipps, Anthony W. "Alaric A. Watts," N&Q, CCXII (March 1967), 105.

Reply to a query: source is *English Bards and Scotch Reviewers*.

228. Shipps, Anthony. [In] "Replies," N&Q, CCXII (Apr. 1967), 145.

Replies to queries: sources wanted are Byron, Keats, and Southey respectively, the last for a quotation in *Cryll Grange*.

229. Shipps, Anthony W. [In] "Replies," N&Q, CCXII (May 1967), 195. Reply to a query: source is Byron's *The Corsair*.

230. Singh, G. *Leopardi and the Theory of Poetry*. Lexington: Univ. of Kentucky, 1964.

Refers to Byron, Hazlitt, Keats, Peacock, and Shelley.

Rev. by R. Ceserani in *Belfagor*, XXI (Jan. 1966), 122-123.

231. Spalding, Philip A. *In the Margin: Being Extracts from a Bookman's Notebook*. 1957.

References to Byron, Hunt, Keats, and Shelley.

232. Stallworthy, Jon. "Poet and Publisher," *Review of English Literature*, VIII (Jan. 1967), 39-49.

Mentions Byron, Keats, and Shelley.

233. Stamm, Rudolf. *Zwischen Vision und Wirklichkeit*. See K-SJ, XV (1966), 153.

Rev. by Jacques Roos in EA, XVIII (Oct.-Dec. 1965), 434; by C. R. Barrett in *Aumla*, No. 25 (May 1966), pp. 134-136; by [R. W.]

Z[andvoort]. in ES, XLVII (Oct. 1966), 404.

234. Steffan, T. G. "A Byron Facsimile," *Library Chronicle* (Texas), VIII (Spring 1966), 3-7.

Concerning the appearance on the market as originals of the facsimiles of the Byron letter included in the Galignani edition of the poems. See No. 235. Also see K-SJ, XV (1966), 152, No. 171.

235. Steffan, T. G. "A Byron Facsimile: A Postscript," *Library Chronicle* (Texas), VIII (Spring 1967), 19-21.

See No. 234.

236. Steffan, T. G. "Byron's Dramas: Three Untraced MSS," BC, XIV (Autumn 1965), 367.

Is looking for the MSS of three plays and the proof sheets of all eight plays.

237. Steffan, T. G. "Some 1813 Byron Letters," K-SJ, XVI (1967), 9-21.

Four letters and two memoranda now at the University of Texas.

Stratman, Carl J. See No. 7.

238. Strich, Fritz. *Goethes Faust*. Bern: Francke, 1964.

Discusses the identity of Euphorion.

239. Tenenbaum, Samuel. *The Incredible Beau Brummell*. South Brunswick, N. J.: A. S. Barnes; London: Yoseloff (1967).

Byron and others appear in their familiar roles.

240. Thomson, P. W. "Byron and Edmund Kean—A Comment," *Theatre Research/Recherches Theatrales,* VIII, No. 1 (1966), pp. 17-19.

Suggests that Byron incorporated a gesture seen in Kean's performance as Richard III in the stage directions for *Werner.*

241. Thorpe, Michael. *Siegfried Sassoon: A Critical Study*. London: Oxford Univ., 1967.

Notes briefly the influence of Byron, Keats, and Shelley.

242. Trease, Geoffrey. *The Grand Tour.* New York: Holt, Rinehart and Winston, 1967.

Byron is one of the travelers who appear.

243. *Tsuji, Chuichi. "Byron in *Cain,*" *Shuryu* [*Main Current*] (Doshisha Univ.), XXIX (Apr. 1967), 72-87. [In Japanese.]

244. *Tuzet, Hélène, *Le Cosmos et l'Imagination.* Paris: Jose Corti, 1965.

"Un essai de psychologie de l'imagination" mentions Byron and Shelley.

245. Uden, Grant, comp. *They Looked like This: An Assembly of Authentic Word-Portraits of Men and Women in English History and Literature over 1900 Years.* Oxford: Basil Blackwell, 1965.

Byron, Haydon, Hazlitt, Hunt, Keats, and Shelley are included.

246. *Walker, Keith McKay. "Byron's Readers: A Study of Attitudes towards Byron 1812-1832." (Doctoral dissertation, Cambridge, 1967.)

247. Walsh, William. *Coleridge: The Work and the Relevance.* New York: Barnes and Noble; London: Chatto (1967).

Has references to Byron, Godwin, Hazlitt, and Keats.

248. Watson, George. *Coleridge the Poet.* London: Routledge, 1966.

Includes discussion of Byron, Keats, Hazlitt, and Shelley.

249. Wellek, René. *Confrontations.* See K-SJ, XV (1966), 154.

Rev. by Lilian R. Furst in MLR, LXI (Oct. 1966), 655-656; by S. Hauch in *Neophilologus,* L (Oct. 1966), 483-484; by Inga-Stina Ewbank in RES, N.S., XVII (Nov. 1966), 442-443.

250. Whipple, A. B. C. "The Italy of Byron and Shelley," *Life International,* XXXIV (Feb. 11, 1963), 3, 67-79; (Feb. 25, 1963), 68-79.

Recounts the story of Byron and Shelley in Italy.

251. "William Beckford in the Saleroom," TLS, Oct. 20, 1966, p. 968.

At Sotheby's July 4-5 Beckford's

annotated copy of Byron's *Sardanapalus* brought £380.

252. Wilson, Angus. "Evil in the English Novel," KR, XXIX (March 1967), 167-194.
References to Godwin's *Caleb Williams* and to the Byronic hero in the novels of the Brontës and others.

253. Wright, Austin. "The Byron of *Don Juan*," in *Six Satirists* (Pittsburgh: Carnegie Institute of Technology, 1965), pp. 69-84.†

254. Yano, Kazumi. "A Note on Modern Japanese Poetry: With Special Reference to English Influence (I)," *Studies in English Liteature* (English Number), 1965, pp. 77-87.
Byron's influence is discussed.

255. Young, Ione Dodson, ed. *A Concordance to the Poetry of Byron*. See K-SJ, XVI (1967), 124.
Rev. by Leslie A. Marchand in K-SJ, XVI (Winter 1967), 96-97

III. HUNT

Works: Selected, Single

Bebbington, W. G., comp. See No. 73.

Bender, Robert M., and Charles L. Squier, eds. See No. 74.

256. Cole, Hubert, ed. *The Bedside Book of Bedrooms*. London: Heinemann, 1962.
Includes selections from Hunt, Keats, and Hood.

257. Daffern, T. G., comp. *Poems for Assemblies*. Oxford: Blackwell, 1963.
Includes selections from Hunt, Keats, Hood, Peacock, and Horace Smith.

258. Gammon, Clive, comp. *The Fisherman's Fireside Book*. London: Heinemann, 1961.
Includes Hunt's "The Fish, the Man, and the Spirit."

259. Goudge, Elizabeth, comp. *A Book of Comfort: An Anthology*. London: Michael Joseph, 1964.
Includes selections from Hunt, Keats, and Shelley.

260. Hadfield, John, comp. *A Book of Joy: An Anthology of Words and Pictures*. London: Vista, 1962.
Includes selections from Hunt.

Hadfield, John, ed. See No. 87.

Hanratty, Jerome, comp. See No. 90.

Hope, Ronald, ed. See No. 91.

Humphreys, Christmas, ed. See No. 92.

261. Manning-Sanders, Ruth. *Birds, Beasts and Fishes*. London: Oxford Univ., 1962.
Poems by Hunt, Keats, and Shelley are included.

Mears, Esmé, comp. See No. 96.

262. *Musical Evenings*. Ed. David R. Cheney. See K-SJ, XV (1966), 154, XVI (1967), 124.
Rev. by Geoffrey Carnall in N&Q, CCXII (Jan. 1967), 34.

263. *On Eight Sonnets of Dante*. See K-SJ, XVI (1967), 125.
Rev. by Carl Woodring in K-SJ, XVI (1967), 107-108.

Perkins, David, ed. See No. 51.

Pickles, Wilfred, comp. See No. 99.

264. Pinion, F. B., ed. *Shorter Narrative Poems*. Second Edition. London: Arnold, 1964.
Includes poems by Hunt, Hood, and Peacock.

265. "To Percy Shelley on the Degrading Notions of Deity," K-SJ, XVI (1967), 50.

266. Verney, John, and Patricia Campbell, comps. *Under the Sun: Stories, Poems, Articles from "Elizabethan" and Other Sources*. London: Constable, 1964.
Includes a poem by Hunt.

267. Woodring, Carl R., ed. *Prose of the Romantic Period*. See K-SJ, XII (1963), 134, XIII (1964), 134.
Rev. by J. Randolph Fisher in *CLA Journal*, IX (Dec. 1965), 196-197.

Books and Articles Relating to Hunt

Ayling, S. E. See No. 12.

Barton, Bernard. See No. 307.

Boyle, Andrew. See No. 1.

Donohue, Joseph Walter, Jr. See No. 26.

268. Dunn, Richard J. "Skimpole and Harthouse: The Dickens Character in Transition," *Dickens Studies,* I (Sept. 1965), 121-128.

A comparative study of characters from *Bleak House* and *Hard Times.*

Fogle, Richard Harter, comp. See No. 3.

269. Gaskell, Elizabeth. *The Letters of Mrs Gaskell.* Ed. J. A. V. Chapple and Arthur Pollard. Cambridge, Mass.: Harvard Univ., 1967.

One letter (p. 131) is addressed to Hunt. There are other allusions to him and to his Romantic contemporaries.

270. Harbage, Alfred. *Conceptions of Shakespeare.* Cambridge, Mass.: Harvard Univ., 1966.

Includes references to Hazlitt, Hunt, and Keats.

Rev. by Oscar James Campbell in NYT, Oct. 16, 1966, p. 32.

271. Haven, R. [In] "Information Please," TLS, Aug. 4, 1966, p. 713.

Asks for material on Robert Balmanno.

Holloway, John. See No. 159.

272. Houtchens, Carolyn Washburn, and Lawrence Huston Houtchens, eds. *The English Romantic Poets & Essayists: A Review of Research and Criticism.* Revised Edition. New York: New York Univ. for MLA; London: Univ. of London (1966).

Includes sections on Hazlitt by Elisabeth W. Schneider (pp. 75-113) and Hunt by the editors (pp. 255-288). See K-SJ, VIII (1959), 66, IX (1960), 60, X (1961), 83, XI (1962), 122.

Rev. by Claude A. Prance in ABC, XVII (Feb. 1967), 5-6.

273. *Kasegawa, Koh. "On *Leigh Hunt's Autobiography: The Earliest Sketches,*" *Shi-to-sanbun* [*Poetry and Prose*], XV (March 1967), 17-19. [In Japanese.]

See K-SJ, X (1961), 82, No. 206, XI (1962), 122.

Langley, Noël. See No. 171.

Lemon, Lee T. See No. 172.

Logan, James V., *et al.,* eds. See No. 45.

274. Norrie, Ian, ed. *The Heathside Book of Hampstead and Highgate.* Hampstead: High Hill Books, 1962.

Includes Hardy's "At a House in Hampstead, Sometime the Dwelling of John Keats" (pp. 32-33), an essay by Ivor Brown on "The Poets" (pp. 119-125), and scattered allusions to Hunt, Keats, and others.

Playfair, Giles. See No. 206.

275. Renier, Anne. *Friendship's Offering: An Essay on the Annuals and Gift Books of the 19th Century.* London: Private Libraries Association, 1964.

Hunt and Hood are touched upon.

276. Riley, Paul E. "John Wilson Croker as a Literary Critic" [Doctoral dissertation, Florida, 1966], DA, XXVII (Nov. 1966), 1345-A.

Discusses his critical remarks on Keats, Hunt, and Shelley.

Robinson, Henry Crabb. See No. 220.

277. Scoggins, James. *Imagination and Fancy: Complementary Modes in the Poetry of Wordsworth.* Lincoln: Univ. of Nebraska, 1966.

Discusses Hunt's *Imagination and Fancy.* Alludes to the other major Romantics.

Sealts, Merton M., Jr. See No. 226.

278. Slater, Joseph, ed. *The Correspondence of Emerson and Carlyle.* New York: Columbia Univ., 1964.

Has allusions to Hunt.

Spalding, Philip A. See No. 231.

Uden, Grant, comp. See No. 245.

IV. KEATS

Works: Selected, Single, Translated

Bebbington, W. G., comp. See No. 73.

Bender, Robert M., and Charles L. Squier, eds. See No. 74.

Berg, Leila, comp. See No. 75.

279. Clark, Leonard. *The Poetry of Nature*. London: Rupert Hart-Davis, 1965.
Includes poems by Keats and Shelley.

Clark, Leonard, comp. See No. 81.

280. *Coffey, Dairine, ed. *The Dark Tower*. New York: Atheneum, 1967.
Includes "The Eve of St. Agnes" and "La Belle Dame sans Merci."
Rev. by Muriel Rukeyser in NYT, May 7, 1967, sec. II, p. 6.

Cole, Hubert, ed. See No. 256.

281. Cunningham, W. T., comp. *Birthright Poetry: A Selection of Poems for Children*. 4 vols. London: Hamish Hamilton, 1963.
Includes selections from Keats.

Daffern, T. G., comp. See No. 257.

282. Ehrenpreis, Anne Henry, ed. *The Literary Ballad*. London: Edward Arnold, 1966.
Includes two Keats poems (pp. 121-123).

283. Engelberg, Edward, ed. *The Symbolist Poem: The Development of the English Tradition*. New York: Dutton, 1967.
Includes selections from Shelley (pp. 66-69) and Keats (pp. 70-71).

284. **English Poetry and Its Appreciation*. [Noted and Translated by] Anzai Shichinosuke. Tokyo: Shinozaki-shorin, 1967.
Includes seven poems by Keats and three by Shelley.

Flint, E. L., and M. K. Flint, comps. See No. 83.

285. *Garai, Gábor. *Szabad-kikötő*. [*Free Port*]. Budapest: Magvető, 1966.
An anthology of translations that includes poems by Shelley and Keats.

286. Gassner, John, and Sidney Thomas, eds. *The Nature of Art*. New York: Crown, 1964.
Has selections from Haydon and Keats.

Goudge, Elizabeth, comp. See No. 259.

287. Hadfield, John, comp. *A Book of Delights: An Anthology of Words and Pictures*. London: Hulton, 1954.
Includes selections from Hazlitt, Hood, Keats, Peacock, and Shelley.

Hanratty, Jerome, comp. See No. 90.

Hope, Ronald, ed. See No. 91.

Humphreys, Christmas, ed. See No. 92.

288. Hunt, Peter, comp. *Eating and Drinking: An Anthology for Epicures*. London: Ebury, 1961.
Includes selections from Keats, Hood, and Peacock.

289. **A Keats Selection*. Ed. Norman Howlings. London: Macmillan; New York: St. Martin's (1966). "English Classics."

Manning-Sanders, Ruth. See No. 261.

Mears, Esmé, comp. See No. 96.

290. "Modern Love," K-SJ, XVI (1967), 78.

Morgan, Edwin, ed. See No. 97.

291. *The Naughty Boy*. See K-SJ, XV (1966), 156.
Now available in an English edition (London: Whiting & Wheaton, 1966).
Rev. in TLS, Nov. 24, 1966, p. 1089.

292. Norman, Charles, ed. *Come Live with Me: Five Centuries of Romantic Poetry*. New York: David McKay, 1966.
Includes poems by Clare, Keats, Peacock, and Shelley.

293. O'Malley, Raymond, and Denys Thompson, comps. *The Key of the Kingdom*. 4 vols. London: Chatto, 1961-1963.
The first volume, *Poetry One*, includes a selection from Peacock; *Poetry Three*, a selection from Hood; and *Poetry Four*, selections from Keats, Peacock, and Shelley.

Perkins, David, ed. See No. 51.

Pickles, Wilfred, comp. See No. 99.

Pinion, F. B., comp. See No. 100.

294. *Poems*. Ed. Aileen Ward. New York: Heritage, 1966.

295. Read, Miss, *pseud*. [Dora Jessie Saint], ed. *Country Bunch: A Col-*

lection by Miss Read. London: Michael Joseph, 1963.
Includes selections from Keats.

296. Scott, A[rthur]. F[inlay]., ed. *Sing to the Sun: A Book of Verse for Children.* London: Max Parrish, 1959.
Includes poems by Keats, Hood, Peacock, Shelley, and Horace Smith.

297. **Selected Poems and Letters of John Keats.* Ed. with an introduction and commentary by Robert Gittings. London: Heinemann, 1966.
Rev. in TLS, Feb. 2, 1967, p. 88.

298. **Selected Poems and Letters of John Keats.* Ed. James Reeves. London: Heinemann, 1967. "Poetry Bookshelf."
Rev. in *English,* XVI (Spring 1967), 161.

299. *The Selected Poetry of Keats.* Ed. Paul de Man. New York: New American Library, 1966. "Signet Classic Poetry Series."

Seymour, William Kean, and John Smith, comps. See No. 102.

Tough, A. J., comp. See No. 103.

300. "Twenty-Four Sonnets," *Saturday Book,* No. 10 (1950), pp. 137-155.
Reprints one by Keats and one by Shelley.

Vas, István. See No. 104.

Wall, Bernard, ed. See No. 105.

301. Williams, Kathleen, and Sidney Denham. *The Cat-Lover's Week-End Book.* London: Seeley, 1961.
Includes Keats's "To a Cat."

Books and Articles Relating to Keats and His Circle

302. *Akikuni, Tadanori. "Sense and Self—on John Keats," *Studies in British & American Literature* (Univ. of Osaka Prefecture), XIV (1967), 54-77. [In Japanese.]

303. Albrecht, W. P. *Hazlitt and the Creative Imagination.* See K-SJ, XVI (1967), 126.
Rev. by Daniel Majdiak in JEGP, LXV (July 1966), 613-617; by J. D. O'Hara in CE, XXVIII (Oct. 1966), 62-65; by Frederick T. Wood in ES, XLVII (Oct. 1966), 399; by Sylvan Barnet in K-SJ, XVI (1967), 106-107; by J. R. de J. Jackson in QQ, LXXIV (Spring 1967), 188; by Harold Pagliaro in ELN, IV (March 1967), 222-225.

304. Appelbe, Jane Lund. "An Inquiry into the Rehabilitation of Certain Seventeenth-Century Poets, 1800-1832" [Doctoral dissertation, Toronto, 1965], DA, XXVII (Dec. 1966), 1777-A-1778-A.
Includes discussion of Hazlitt's role.

305. "Auction Sales," ABC, XVI (Summer 1966), 29-32.
Provides details of the sale of 5 Keats items and 6 Shelley items at Sotheby's.

Ayling, S. E. See No. 12.

306. Barr, D. J. "Reference Wanted," N&Q, CCXII (Jan. 1967), 27.
Reply to query: reference is in Houghton's *Life and Letters of John Keats.*

307. Barton, Bernard. *The Literary Correspondence of Bernard Barton.* Ed. James E. Barcus. Philadelphia: Pennsylvania Univ., 1966.
Includes letters to John Taylor and to Taylor and Hessey. References to Byron, Hazlitt, Hunt, and Shelley.

308. Batchelor, Denzil, ed. *The Boxing Companion.* London: Eyre & Spottiswoode, 1964.
Includes excerpts from Hazlitt.
Rev. by Robert Davenport in T&T, XLV (Nov. 5-11, 1964), 21.

309. Bate, Walter Jackson. *John Keats.* New York: Oxford Univ., 1966. "A Galaxy Book."
A paperback reprint of a book first published in 1963. See K-SJ, XIV (1965), 118, XV (1966), 156, XVI (1967), 126.
Rev. by *María Inés del Río in *La Nación,* Buenos Aires, Dec. 11, 1966.

310. B[ateson]., F. W. "Editorial Postscript," EC, XVI (Oct. 1966), 464-465.
Comments on Mrs. Vendler's review of *Essays on Style and Language*. See No. 340.

311. Bateson, Frederick W. *English Poetry: A Critical Introduction*. New York: Barnes and Noble, 1966.
A revision of the 1950 edition. See K-SJ, III (1954), 118.

312. Beall, Chandler. "Eugenio Montale's *Sarcofaghi*," in *Linguistic and Literary Studies in Honor of Helmut A. Hatzfeld*, ed. Alessandro S. Crisafulli (Washington: Catholic Univ. of America, 1964), pp. 65-78.
Discusses the influence of "Ode on a Grecian Urn."

Bell, Harry. See No. 114.

313. Birkenhead, Sheila. *Illustrious Friends*. See K-SJ, XVI (1967), 126.
Rev. by Iain Hamilton in ILN, CCXLVII (Dec. 4, 1965), 43; by Arthur Minerof in *Library Journal*, XCI (July 1966), 3428; in *Choice*, III (Jan. 1967), 1012-1013.

314. *Blunden, Edmund. *John Keats*. Revised Edition. London: Longmans, for the British Council, 1966. "Writers and Their Work."
See K-SJ, I (1952), 93, V (1956), 127, VI (1957), 141.

315. Blunden, Edmund. *Reprinted Papers, Partly Concerning Some English Romantic Poets*. Tokyo: Kenkyusha, for the English Literary Society of Japan, 1950.
Includes "Free Thoughts on the Biography of Keats" (pp. 1-13), "Coleridge, Shelley and Keats" (pp. 36-96), "A. D. 1827 in English Literature" (partly on Hood) (pp. 124-258), and "Keats's Letters, 1931: Marginalia" (pp. 209-266).

Boyle, Andrew. See No. 1.

316. Bratton, Edward William. "The Substance of Greatness: Hazlitt's Wordsworthian Criticism in Its Personal, Political and Philosophical Context" [Doctoral dissertation, Illinois, 1966], DA, XXVII (Sept. 1966), 766-A-767-A.

317. Briggs, K. M. *The Fairies in Tradition and Literature*. London: Routledge, 1967.
Chapter 19 on "The Poets: The Nineteenth Century and After" (pp. 165-173) looks at Shelley, Keats, and Hood.

318. Brooks, Cleanth. "The Language of Poetry: Some Problem Cases," ASNS, CCIII (Apr. 1967), 401-414.
Discusses Keats's use of the word "fade" in "Ode to a Nightingale."

319. Brown, Charles Armitage. *The Letters of Charles Armitage Brown*. Ed. Jack Stillinger. See K-SJ, XVI (1967), 127.
Rev. in *Choice*, III (July-Aug. 1966), 407; in TLS, Dec. 22, 1966, p. 1190; by Joanna Richardson in K-SJ, XVI (1967), 94-96; by William H. Marshall in JEGP, LXVI (Jan. 1967), 159-162; by Frederick T. Wood in ES, XLVIII (June 1967), 281. Also see No. 33.

Browning, Robert. See No. 118.

320. Bruère, Richard T. "Pliny the Elder, Diaper, and Keats," *Classical Philology*, LXI (Apr. 1966), 107-108.†
Passage in *Endymion* was more likely influenced by a William Diaper eclogue than by Philemon Holland translation of Pliny.

Buckley, Jerome Hamilton. See No. 121.

321. Burke, Kenneth. *Language as Symbolic Action: Essays on Life, Literature, and Method*. Berkeley: Univ. of California, 1966.
"Formalist Criticism: Its Principles and Limits" (pp. 480-506) has discussion of Keats.

322. Bush, Douglas. *John Keats: His Life and Writings*. New York: Collier, 1967.
A paperback reprint of a book first published in 1966. See K-SJ, XVI (1967), 127.
Rev. in *Choice*, III (July-Aug. 1966), 408; by David Perkins in

K-SJ, XVI (1967), 93-94; in TLS, Feb. 2, 1967, p. 88.

323. Bush, Warren V., ed. *The Dialogues of Archibald MacLeish and Mark Van Doren.* New York: Dutton, 1964.
They discuss Keats and Shelley.

324. Carben, Edward. "John Keats: Pioneer of Modern Existentialist Thought," *Trace,* No. 55 (Winter 1964), pp. 322-330.†
Keats is more like twentieth-century existentialists in his thinking than he is his own contemporaries.

Casey, John. See No. 122.

Chatman, Seymour. See No. 125.

325. Chatterjee, Bhabatosh. "Echoes of Cary's Dante in 'Endymion,'" N&Q, CCXII (Jan. 1967), 23.†

326. Chesser, Eustace. *The Cost of Loving.* London: Methuen, 1964.
Includes discussion of Hazlitt's affair with Sarah Walker.

327. *Clare, John. *Selected Poems.* Ed. J. W. Tibble and Anne Tibble. London: Dent, 1965. "Everyman's Library."
Rev. by Frederick T. Wood in ES, XLVII (Aug. 1966), 321.

328. Clubbe, John Louis Edwin. "Victorian Forerunner: The Career of Thomas Hood, 1835-1845" [Doctoral dissertation, Columbia, 1965], DA, XXVI (June 1966), 7295.

329. Cooper, Burton L., ed. *12 Prose Writers.* New York: Holt, Rinehart and Winston, 1967.
Includes (pp. 46-77) section on Hazlitt with four of his essays.

330. Cox-Johnson, Ann. *Handlist of Painters, Sculptors & Architects Associated with St. Marylebone, 1760-1960.* London: Borough of St. Marylebone Public Libraries Committee, 1963.
Haydon, De Wint, Hilton, and others are listed.

331. Crawford, Alexander W. *The Genius of Keats: An Interpretation.* New York: Russell & Russell, 1967.
A reprint of a book first published in 1932.

Dahlberg, Edward. See No. 131.

332. D'Avanzo, Mario L. "Keats's and Vergil's Underworlds: Source and Meaning in Book II of *Endymion,*" K-SJ, XVI (1967), 61-72.
Vergil was Keats's chief mentor.

333. D'Avanzo, Mario L. *Keats's Metaphors for the Poetic Imagination.* Durham: Duke Univ., 1967.

334. Davis, Frank. "The Very English Art of Painting in Watercolour," ILN, CCXLVIII (Feb. 12, 1966), 24-25.
Reproduces three watercolors by De Wint: "Picnic in the Fields," "Gloucester Cathedral from the Meadows," and "Self-Portrait."

335. *Deguchi, Yasuo. "Another Keats," *Journal of General Science* (Waseda Univ.), I (March 1967), 27-50. [In Japanese.]

336. De Quincey, Thomas. *New Essays by De Quincey: His Contributions to the "Edinburgh Saturday Post" and the "Edinburgh Evening Post" 1827-1828.* Ed. Stuart M. Tave. Princeton: Princeton Univ., 1966.
Contains brief comments on Godwin, Hazlitt, John Taylor, and others of their contemporaries.
Rev. in TLS, Nov. 24, 1966, p. 1101. Also see No. 33.

Donohue, Joseph Walter, Jr. See No. 26.

Emerson, Ralph Waldo. See No. 139.

337. Erdman, David V., and Ephim G. Fogel, eds. *Evidence for Authorship: Essays on Problems of Attribution.* Ithaca: Cornell Univ., 1966.
Includes annotated bibliography which lists articles on Hazlitt and Keats. Also reprints articles by Leonidas M. Jones and Hoover H. Jordan. See K-SJ, IV (1955), 119-120, No. 178, VII (1958), 125, No. 287.

338. *Evert, Walter H. *Aesthetic and Myth in the Poetry of Keats.* Princeton: Princeton Univ., 1966.
A paperback reprint of a book

first published in 1965. See K-SJ, XV (1966), 158, XVI (1967), 127.

Rev. by Gilbert Thomas in *English,* XVI (Autumn 1966), 108; by R[ichard]. H[arter]. F[ogle]. in ELN, IV, Supplement (Sept. 1966), 32-33; by Mary Lynn Woolley in JEGP, LXV (Oct. 1966), 730-734; by Miriam Allott in MLR, LXII (Jan. 1967), 118-119.

339. Fausset, Hugh I'Anson. *Keats: A Study in Development.* [Hamden, Conn.:] Archon, 1966.

A reprint of a book first published in 1922.

Rev. in *Choice,* III (Oct. 1966), 636.

Fogle, Richard Harter, comp. See No. 3.

340. Fowler, Roger, ed. *Essays on Style and Language: Linguistic and Critical Approaches to Literary Style.* New York: Humanities, 1966.

Includes "The New Criticism and the Language of Poetry" by Brian Lee (pp. 29-52), which includes comments on poems by Byron and, especially, Keats. There are brief allusions to Keats and Byron in other essays in the book.

Rev. by Helen Hennessy Vendler in EC, XVI (Oct. 1966), 457-463. See No. 310.

341. Fréchet, R. "Yeats's 'Sailing to Byzantium' and Keats's 'Ode to a Nightingale,'" in *W. B. Yeats, 1865-1965: Centenary Essays on the Art of W. B. Yeats,* ed. D. E. S. Maxwell and S. B. Bushrui (Ibadan: Ibadan Univ., 1965), pp. 217-219.

Frewin, Leslie, comp. See No. 85.

342. *Fukuda, Tamio. "Keats's 'To Autumn,'" *Studies in Foreign Language & Literature* (Hiroshima Univ.), XIII (1967), 1-18. [In Japanese.]

343. *Fukuda, Tamio. "The 'Ode to Psyche'—Art and Life," *Studies in Foreign Language & Literature* (Hiroshima Univ.), XII (1966), 71-88. [In Japanese.]

344. *Fukuma, Kinichi. "Keats and the World of 'Uncertainties,'" *Essays in Literature and Thought* (Fukuoka Women's College), XXIX (1966), 83-96. [In Japanese.]

Fussell, Paul, Jr. See No. 144.

345. Gomme, Andor. *Attitudes to Criticism.* With a Preface by Harry T. Moore. Carbondale: Southern Illinois Univ., 1966.

Appendix A, pp. 139-144, "Burke's Method in Action," examines "Symbolic Action in a Poem by Keats." See K-SJ, VII (1958), 124, No. 283, XV (1966), 157, No. 255.

346. Gordon, Ian A. "Keats and the English Pindaric," *Review of English Literature,* VIII (Apr. 1967), 9-23.

Reviews the history and aesthetic of the Pindaric ode in English and argues that Keats's odes are more firmly rooted in that tradition than is usually acknowledged.

347. Goswami, Kanailal. "The Essential Keats," *Calcutta Review,* CLXXVII (Dec. 1965), 223-228.

Graves, Robert. See No. 511.

348. Graves, Robert. *Poetic Craft and Principle: Lectures and Talks.* London: Cassell, 1967.

Discusses Keats (pp. 73-82) and Shelley (pp. 44-45). Also includes essay on "The Word 'Romantic'" (pp. 183-195).

349. Greaves, Margaret. *Regency Patron: Sir George Beaumont.* London: Methuen, 1966.

Explores Beaumont's relations with Haydon. Others of the Keats circle appear more briefly.

Rev. in TLS, Nov. 17, 1966, p. 1049.

350. Green, David Bonnell. "An Early Reprinting of Three Poems from Keats's 1820 Volume," PBSA, LX (3rd quarter 1966), 363.†

In Rivington's *Annual Register* for 1820 (published 1822).

351. Hadfield, John, comp. *A Book of Britain: An Anthology of Words*

and Pictures. London: Hulton, 1956.

Includes selections from Hazlitt and Hood.

Hadfield, John, ed. See No. 87.

Hadfield, Miles, and John Hadfield, comps. See No. 89.

352. Hamilton-Edwards, Gerald. "John Keats and the Hammonds," KSMB, XVII (1966), 31-36.

Traces information on John Hammond and his descendants.

353. Handley, Graham. "Mrs. Gaskell's Reading: Some Notes on Echoes and Epigraphs in 'Mary Barton,'" *Durham University Journal,* LIX (June 1967), 131-138.

Keats's "Hyperion" was an influence.

Harbage, Alfred. See No. 270.

354. Hardie, Martin. *Water-Colour Painting in Britain.* Vol. II: *The Romantic Period.* Ed. Dudley Snelgrove *et al.* London: Batsford, 1967.

Has chapter on De Wint and reproduces eleven of his works. Also contains allusions to Hilton.

355. Harrold, William E. "Keats's 'Lamia' and Peacock's 'Rhododaphne,'" MLR, LXI (Oct. 1966), 579-584.

"A close reading of the two poems seems to indicate . . . that [Keats] had read Peacock's poem before he wrote *Lamia.*"

Haslam, G. E., ed. See No. 157.

356. Hassall, Christopher, comp. *Poems for Children.* London: Nelson, 1963.

Includes a poem by Hood.

Hays, H. R. See No. 158.

357. Hayter, Alethea. *A Sultry Month: Scenes of London Literary Life in 1846.* See K-SJ, XV (1966), 159, XVI (1967), 129.

Rev. by Naomi Lewis in *Encounter,* XXV (Aug. 1965), 78-79; by Willard B. Pope in K-SJ, XVI (1967), 104-105.

358. Hazlitt, William. *Lectures on the English Comic Writers, and Fugitive Writings.* Introduction by Arthur Johnston. London: Dent, 1963. "Everyman's Library."

359. Hill, James Lewis. "Tennyson and Expressive Art: The Relationship between Tennyson's Early Poetry and Nineteenth-Century Esthetic Theory" [Doctoral dissertation, Princeton, 1965], DA, XXVII (Dec. 1966), 1786-A.

Studies the "relationship between Tennyson, Shelley, and Keats."

360. Holloway, John. *The Lion Hunt: A Pursuit of Poetry and Reality.* Hamden, Conn.: Archon, 1964.

Comments about Keats and Shelley.

Holloway, John. See No. 159.

361. *Hooker, Charlotte Schrader. "The Poet and the Dreamer: A Study of Keats's *The Fall of Hyperion,*" *McNeese Review,* XVII (1966), 39-48.

362. *Hoshino, Nobuo. "On the 'Arbour'-Image Revealed in Keats's Poems—Mainly in *Endymion,*" *Studies in English Language and Literature* (Kansai Univ.), XVI (Jan. 1967), 40-55. [In Japanese.]

363. *The Houghton Library 1942-1967: A Selection of Books and Manuscripts in Harvard Collections.* Cambridge, Mass.: Harvard College Library, 1967.

Reproduces page from Shelley holograph notebook (p. 65) and includes section on treasures in the Keats Room (pp. 72-75).

Rev. in TLS, May 18, 1967, p. 428.

Houtchens, Carolyn Washburn, and Lawrence Huston Houtchens, eds. See No. 272.

Howes, Frank. See No. 520.

364. Hudnall, Clayton Edward. "Metaphorical Projection and the Picturesque in the Writings of John Keats" [Doctoral dissertation, Illinois, 1966], DA, XXVII (May 1967), 3841-A-3842-A.

365. Hungerford, Edward B. *Shores*

of Darkness. Cleveland: World, 1963. "Meridian Books."

A paperback reprint of a book first published in 1941.

"A study of the influence of mythology on the Romantic movement in poetry as seen in Blake, Keats, Shelley, and Goethe."

366. "In the Galleries," ILN, CCXLIX (Oct. 22, 1966), 57.

Reproduces De Wint's "Lincoln from the South."

367. Inglis, Fred. *Keats.* See K-SJ, XVI (1967), 129.

Rev. in *Quarterly Review,* CCCIV (Oct. 1966), 469; by William Forbes in *Aberdeen University Review,* XLII (Spring 1967), 58-60.

368. Ireson, Barbara, comp. *Verse That Is Fun.* London: Faber, 1962.

Includes poems by Hood.

369. Jack, Ian. *Keats and the Mirror of Art.* Oxford: Clarendon, 1967.

Rev. in *The Times,* London, Apr. 13, 1967, p. 13; in TLS, May 4, 1967, p. 380.

370. Johnson, Carol. *Reason's Double Agents.* Chapel Hill: Univ. of North Carolina, 1966.

Looks briefly at Keats and Shelley.

371. Johnson, E. D. H., ed. *The Poetry of Earth: A Collection of English Nature Writings.* New York: Atheneum, 1966.

Includes (pp. 167-195) selections from Clare.

372. Jones, Stanley. "Nine New Hazlitt Letters and Some Others," EA, XIX (July-Sept. 1966), 263-277.

From the years 1815-1818, mostly relating to *The Round Table* and to the legal action against William Blackwood.

373. Kauvar, Gerald Bluestone. "Figurative Relationships in the Poetry of Keats" [Doctoral dissertation, Duke, 1966], DA, XXVII (Dec. 1966), 1787-A-1788-A.

374. *Keats House: A Guide to the House and Museum.* Sixth Edition. London, 1966.

375. ["Kenilworth,"] ILN, CCXLIX (Nov. 26, 1966), 47.

This De Wint is reproduced with an announcement of an exhibition at the Leger Galleries.

376. *Kinoshita, Hirotoshi. "Keats: 'La Belle Dame sans Merci'—An Interpretation," *Studies in English Language and Literature* (Seinan Gakuin Univ.), VI, Nos. 1-2 (1966), pp. 115-140. [In Japanese.]

377. Kinsella, Thomas. *Nightwalker and Other Poems.* London: Oxford Univ., 1967.

Includes a poem entitled " 'To Autumn' " on Keats's composition of that ode.

378. Krieger, Murray. "*Ekphrasis* and the Still Movement of Poetry; or Laokoön Revisited," in *The Poet as Critic,* ed. Frederick P. W. McDowell (Evanston: Northwestern Univ., 1967), pp. 2-25.

Discusses "Ode on a Grecian Urn" as an example of the ekphrastic element in Keats's art.

379. Krieger, Murray. *The Play and Place of Criticism.* Baltimore: Johns Hopkins, 1967.

Comments on poems by Keats and Shelley.

380. Kroeber, Karl. *The Artifice of Reality: Poetic Style in Wordsworth, Foscolo, Keats, and Leopardi.* See K-SJ, XV (1966), 160, XVI (1967), 130.

Rev. by Helmut Viebrock in *Anglia,* LXXXV (1967), 113; by Alan Grob in MP, LXIV (Feb. 1967), 264-268.

Kumar, Shiv K., ed. See No. 44.

381. Laughlin, Richard Edward. "The Influence of Eighteenth-Century Associationism on the Criticism of William Hazlitt" [Doctoral dissertation, Tulane, 1966], DA, XXVII (Nov. 1966), 1371-A.

382. Lauter, Paul, ed. *Theories of Comedy.* Garden City: Doubleday, 1964. "Anchor Books."

Includes (pp. 263-294) a selection from Hazlitt.

Lemon, Lee T. See No. 172.

Lindsay, Jack. See No. 173.

383. Little, G. L. "Keats' 'Ode on Melancholy,'" Exp, XXV (Feb. 1967), Item 46.

Proposes an analysis that brings "consistency and unity" to the poem and mitigates the gloom of the last stanza.

Logan, James V., *et al.*, eds. See No. 45.

384. McAleer, John J. "Mary Cowden Clarke: Shakespeare's First Woman Editor," *Shakespeare Newsletter,* XIII (Apr. 1963), 18.†

A "biography in brief."

385. *McAuley, James. "Shaw Neilson's Poetry," *Australian Literary Studies,* II (1966), 235-253.

Refers to influence of Shelley and Keats on Neilson.

386. Maddison, Carol. *Apollo and the Nine: A History of the Ode.* Baltimore: Johns Hopkins, 1960.

Has passing references to Keats.

Rev. by B. M. Baxter in ES, XLVIII (Apr. 1967), 168-169.

387. *Maiorana, María Teresa. "Un cuento de Boccaccio en poemas de Keats y de Anatole France," *Boletín de la Academia Argentina de Letras,* Buenos Aires, XXVIII (July-Dec. 1963), 251-279.

See K-SJ, XIII (1964), 141, No. 361.

388. Mannin, Ethel. *Loneliness: A Study of the Human Condition.* London: Hutchinson, 1966.

Hazlitt and Keats are among the "great lonely ones" discussed.

389. Margetson, Stella. *Journey by Stages: Some Account of the People Who Travelled by Stage-Coach and Mail in the Years between 1660 and 1840.* London: Cassell, 1967.

One chapter (pp. 128-145) is on "Coleridge, Keats & Mary Wordsworth." Hazlitt is mentioned elsewhere.

390. Marquard, N. J. "Keats's 'Ode on a Grecian Urn,'" *Theoria,* No. 6 (1954), pp. 101-105.

Discusses the poem and especially the final lines of the poem: the claim that Keats "makes for this knowledge is not extravagant: the acceptance of the tragedy inescapably bound up with life as a necessity and a condition of beauty is fundamental—the first and last of man's needs."

391. Marshall, Percy. *Masters of English Poetry.* London: Dennis Dobson, 1966.

Includes chapters on Shelley (pp. 131-148) and Keats (pp. 149-166).

Massingham, Hugh, and Pauline Massingham. See No. 94.

Massingham, Hugh, and Pauline Massingham, eds. See No. 95.

392. Maxwell, J. C. "'Hyperion' and 'Rejected Addresses,'" N&Q, CCXII (Jan. 1967), 23.†

Suggests that in "Hyperion" Keats unconsciously recalled two lines from the parody of Crabbe in *Rejected Addresses.*

393. Maxwell, J. C. "Porphyro as 'Famish'd Pilgrim,'" N&Q, CCXII (Jan. 1967), 23.†

Suggests that Carew may have furnished Keats with a line for *The Eve of St. Agnes.*

394. Mayerson, Caroline W. "Keats' 'Ode to a Nightingale,' 31-33," Exp, XXV (Nov. 1966), Item 29.

Suggests that Keats possibly had Pegasus in mind "as a symbol for the poetic imagination."

395. Mayhead, Robin. *Understanding Literature.* See K-SJ, XVI (1967), 130.

Rev. by M. Tarinayya in *Literary Criterion,* VII (Winter 1966), 95-97.

396. *Miyazaki, Yuko. "An Interpretation of 'Lamia,'" *Journal* (Musashi Univ.), IV (Dec. 1966), 40-66. [In Japanese.]

397. Morgan, Peter F. "Principles and Perspectives in Jeffrey's Criticism,"

Studies in Scottish Literature, IV (Jan.-Apr. 1967), 179-193.

Asserts that Jeffrey's views often worked against Wordsworth in favor of Keats.

Nabokov, Vladimir. See No. 198.

398. *Nakabayashi, Mitsuo. "On *Endymion," Essays and Studies* (Hiroshima Jogakuin College), XVI (Dec. 1966), 29-42. [In Japanese.]

Norrie, Ian, ed. See No. 274.

399. O'Hara, J. D. "Hazlitt and the Function of the Imagination," PMLA, LXXXI (Dec. 1966), 552-562.†

Refers to Keats in treating Hazlitt's view of "sympathetic identification."

400. Olney, Clarke. "Keats as John Foster's 'Man of Decision,'" K-SJ, XVI (1967), 6-8.

401. *O'Neill, Judith, comp. *Critics on Keats.* London: Allen & Unwin, 1967. "Readings in Literary Criticism."

402. Ormerod, David. "Nature's Eremite: Keats and the Liturgy of Passion," K-SJ, XVI (1967), 73-77.

A reading of "Bright Star!"

403. Osler, Alan. "Keats and Baldwin's 'Pantheon,'" MLR, LXII (Apr. 1967), 221-225.

Discusses Keats's use of "Edward Baldwin's" (i.e., William Godwin's) mythological handbook for *Endymion* and "Hyperion."

Parsons, Coleman O. See No. 203.

Pedrini, Lura Nancy, and Duilio Thomas Pedrini. See No. 204.

404. Perry, David Scott. "Hazlitt, Lamb, and the Drama" [Doctoral dissertation, Princeton, 1966], DA, XXVII (Oct. 1966), 1035-A-1036-A.

Pinion, F. B., ed. See No. 264.

405. Platt, Polly. "W. H. Auden," *American Scholar,* XXXVI (Spring 1967), 266-270.

In an interview Auden comments briefly on Keats.

Playfair, Giles. See No. 206.

406. Polgar, Mirko. "Keats's Beauty-Truth Identification in the Light of Philosophy," KSMB, XVII (1966), 55-62.

"There are many echoes of harmony in the paganistic creed of the Romantic poet and the mediaeval priest [Aquinas]."

407. Polgar, Mirko. "The Religious Profile of John Keats," *Cithara,* VI (Nov. 1966), 15-31.†

The references to religion in Keats's poetry are natural and convincing.

Potts, Abbie Findlay. See No. 207.

Praz, Mario. See No. 208.

408. Pringle, Patrick. *101 Great Lives.* London, 1963.

"For younger readers." Includes Keats.

409. Purcell, H. D. "The Probable Origin of a Line in Keats's 'Ode to a Nightingale,'" N&Q, CCXII (Jan. 1967), 24.†

In Thomas Heywood's *A Challenge for Beauty.*

Ramsey, L. G. G., ed. See No. 212.

410. Read, Herbert. *Poetry and Experience.* New York: Horizon, 1967.

Chapter 4, "The Definition of Comedy" (pp. 61-70), makes use of Hazlitt.

411. Reck, Rima Drell, ed. *Explorations of Literature.* Baton Rouge: Louisiana State Univ., 1966.

Includes "'Love's Rare Universe': Eros in Shelley's Poetry," by Seraphia Leyda (pp. 43-69), and "*Tender Is the Night* and the 'Ode to a Nightingale,'" by William E. Doherty (pp. 100-114). The former examines "Shelley's concept of eros as defined by its thematic and structural function in several of his love poems." The latter suggests that both works declare an "abandonment of faith in the imagination."

412. *Reid, John Cowie. *Thomas Hood.* London: Routledge, 1967.

A paperback reprint of a book first published in 1963. See K-SJ, XIV (1965), 124, XV (1966), 162.

Renier, Anne. See No. 275.

Reynolds, Graham. See No. 216.

413. Reynolds, John Hamilton. *Selected Prose of John Hamilton Reynolds.* Ed. Leonidas M. Jones. Cambridge, Mass.: Harvard Univ., 1966.

Rev. in TLS, Feb. 23, 1967, p. 148; in *Choice,* IV (June 1967), 424.

Rhodes, Jack Lee. See No. 56.

414. Richardson, Joanna. *The Everlasting Spell: A Study of Keats and His Friends.* See K-SJ, XIV (1965), 124, XV (1966), 162, XVI (1967), 131.

Rev. in *Choice,* III (May 1966), 211.

415. Ridley, M. R. *Keats' Craftsmanship.* See K-SJ, XIII (1964), 142, XIV (1965), 124.

Rev. by Manfred Wojcik in *Zeitschrift für Anglistik und Amerikanistik,* XIV (1966), 302-305.

Riley, Paul E. See No. 276.

416. Robinson, Dwight E. "A Question of the Imprint of Wedgwood in the Longer Poems of Keats," K-SJ, XVI (1967), 23-28.

Notes parallels between "certain of the shapes that inhabit Keats's poetry and those that emboss Wedgwood's pottery." See K-SJ, XVI (1967), 132, No. 309.

Robinson, Henry Crabb. See No. 220.

417. Roche, Alex E. *More Medical and Other Verses.* London: Lewis, 1959.

Includes a sonnet "On Visiting Keats's Home with His Sister's Great Great Grand-daughter" (p. 17).

Rogers, Katharine M. See No. 222.

418. Rogers, Robert. "Keats's Strenuous Tongue: A Study of 'Ode on Melancholy,'" *Literature and Psychology,* XVII (1967), 2-12.

Finding a "strenuous eroticism" in phallic images and overtones of castration, the author thinks the poem suggests a manic-depressive's "orientation to life and love." See Nos. 419 and 448.

419. Rogers, Robert. "Reply," *Literature and Psychology,* XVII (1967), 41-43.

Replies to Aileen Ward and reasserts views set forth in "Keats's Strenuous Tongue." See Nos. 418 and 448.

420. Rollins, Hyder Edward, ed. *The Keats Circle.* Second Edition. See K-SJ, XV (1966), 162, XVI (1967), 132.

Rev. by R[ichard]. H[arter]. F[ogle]. in ELN, IV, Supplement (Sept. 1966), 33-34; by R. W. King in RES, N.S., XVIII (May 1967), 238. Also see No. 33.

421. Russel, Stanley G. "'Self-Destroying' Love in Keats," K-SJ, XVI (1967), 79-91.

Love brought Keats joy but brought also "the loss of his artistic integrity."

Saito, Yuzo. See No. 579.

422. Sallé, J.-C. "Shakespeare's Sonnet 27 and Keats's 'Bright Star!'" N&Q, CCXII (Jan. 1967), 24.†

Finds verbal echoes and a similarity in the fusion of erotic and religious elements.

Sarkar, Manojkumar. See No. 225.

423. Schlüter, Kurt. *Die englische Ode: Studien zu ihrer Entwicklung unter dem Einfluss der antiken Hymne.* Bonn: H. Bouvier, 1964.

Includes sections on Keats (pp. 197-267) and Shelley (pp. 268-282, 290-297).

Rev. by M. D. E. De Leve in *Neophilologus,* LI (Apr. 1967), 210-211.

424. Scholefield, Guy H., ed. *The Richmond-Atkinson Papers.* Vols. I and II. Wellington: R. E. Owen, Government Printer, 1960.

Includes letters by Charles Brown, son of Charles Armitage Brown, as well as a photograph of and many allusions to him.

425. Schwaber, Paul. "Stays against Confusion: The Poems of John

Clare" [Doctoral dissertation, Columbia, 1966], DA, XXVII (Dec. 1966), 1794-A.

Sealts, Merton M., Jr. See No. 226.

426. Severn, Arthur. *The Professor: Arthur Severn's Memoir of John Ruskin.* Ed. James S. Dearden. London: Allen & Unwin, 1967.

Has allusions to Joseph Severn. Rev. in TLS, March 16, 1967, p. 212.

427. Seymour, William Kean. *Cestius and Keats.* Old Alresford, Hampshire: Cygnet Press, c. 1963.

A poem, published as a broadside. See K-SJ, XII (1963), 141.

428. Shephard, Esther. *An Oriental Tale and a Romantic Poet.* Santa Cruz, Calif.: Pacific Rim, 1967.

An ancient story is "coupled with a kind of parallel in the real life, and death, of the poet Keats." The poetry enhances the legend.

Shipps, Anthony. See No. 228.

429. *Shoji, Shin. "The Theme of Dream in Keats's Narrative Poems," *Bulletin* (Faculty of Arts and Sciences, Ibaraki Univ.), XVII (Dec. 1966), 99-110. [In Japanese.]

Singh, G. See No. 230.

430. Smith, Barbara Herrnstein. "'Sorrow's Mysteries': Keats's 'Ode on Melancholy,'" SEL, VI (Autumn 1966), 679-691.†

Sees the poem as a structure of unusually complicated "pretenses" involving the character of the speaker, the nature of his utterance, and his audience.

431. Smith, Julian. "Keats and Hawthorne: A Romantic Bloom in Rappaccini's Garden," *Emerson Society Quarterly,* No. 42 (1st quarter 1966), pp. 8-12.

"Lamia" is another possible source for "Rappaccini's Daughter."

Spalding, Philip A. See No. 231.

432. Spitzer, Leo. *Essays on English and American Literature.* See K-SJ, XIII (1964), 143.

Rev. by T. A. Birrell in *Neophilologus,* L (July 1966), 401-402.

433. Spurgeon, Caroline F. E. *Keats's Shakespeare: A Descriptive Study.* Oxford: Clarendon, 1966.

A reprint of a book first published in 1928.

Stallworthy, Jon. See No. 232.

434. Stevens, Wallace. *Letters of Wallace Stevens.* Ed. Holly Stevens. New York: Knopf, 1966.

Includes references to Keats and Shelley.

435. Story, Patrick L. "William Hazlitt's *The Spirit of the Age,* Third Edition, 1858," BC, XV (Autumn 1966), 356.

Is trying to find a copy of this edition "interleaved with the larger portion of the holograph manuscript."

436. *Tabuchi, Mikio. "An Aspect of Keats's Development," *Studies in Foreign Language & Literature* (Hiroshima Univ.), XIII (1967), 19-32. [In Japanese.]

437. *Takeda, Miyoko. "A Study of 'The Eve of St. Agnes,'" *Study Reports* (Baika Women's College), III (Dec. 1966), 17-42. [In Japanese.]

438. Tanner, Tony. "Lionel Trilling's Uncertainties," *Encounter,* XXVII (Aug. 1966), 72-77.

Discusses Trilling's use of Keats in *The Opposing Self* and elsewhere. See K-SJ, V (1956), 131, No. 235, VI (1957), 146.

439. Thompson, Phyllis Rose. "The 'Haiku Question' and the Reading of Images," *English Journal,* LVI (Apr. 1967), 547-551.

Includes discussion of Keats's "To Autumn."

Thorpe, Michael. See No. 241.

440. *Tsuda, Michio. "Keats's 'The Eve of St. Agnes'—On the Death of a Beadsman," *Ronko* [*Study*] (Kansei Gakuin Univ.), XIII (Sept. 1966), 145-158. [In Japanese.]

441. *Tsukano, Tagayasu. "A Study of a Favourite Word with Keats—

Intellect," *Bulletin of the English Society* (Osaka Gakugei Univ.), XII (March 1967), 57-70. [In Japanese.]

Uden, Grant, comp. See No. 245.

442. Varnhagen von Ense, K. A. *The Letters of Varnhagen von Ense to Richard Monckton Milnes.* Ed. Philip Glander. Heidelberg: Carl Winter, 1965.

Eleven letters and an introduction.

Rev. by Horst Oppel in *Neueren Sprachen,* No. 3 (March 1966), p. 149; by W. D. Robson-Scott in *German Life & Letters,* XX (Apr. 1967), 268-269.

443. Vaughan, Dorothy M., comp. "Celia Thaxter's Library," *Colby Library Quarterly,* VI (Dec. 1964), 536-549.

Included works by Hazlitt and Mary Cowden Clarke.

444. *Viebrock, Helmut. "Arzt, Kranker und Kranhkeit in der englischenschönen Literatur des 19. Jahrhunderts," in *Studien zur Medizingeschichte des 19. Jahrhunderts.* Bd. I: *Der Arzt und der Kranke in der Gesellschaft des 19. Jahrhunderts,* ed. W. Artelt and W. Rüegg (Stuttgart, 1967), pp. 107-115.

Discusses Keats.

445. Villiers, André de. "Hazlitt and 'The Pleasure of Tragedy,'" *English Studies in Africa,* IX (Sept. 1966), 176-183.

To Hazlitt "the real pleasure of tragedy is moral."

446. Villiers, André de. "Hazlitt and Kemble's Retirement," N&Q, CCXII (Jan. 1967), 22-23.†

Hazlitt did not attend the banquet in Kemble's honor.

Walsh, William. See No. 247.

447. Ward, Aileen. *John Keats: The Making of a Poet.* New York: Viking, 1967. "Compass Books."

A paperback reprint of a book first published in 1963. See K-SJ, XIV (1965), 126, XV (1966), 163, XVI (1967), 133.

448. Ward, Aileen. "The Psychoanalytic Theory of Poetic Form: A Comment," *Literature and Psychology,* XVII (1967), 30-37.

Attempts to temper the views expressed by Robert Rogers. See Nos. 418 and 419.

449. Ware, Malcolm. "Keats' 'Stout Cortez': A Deliberate Error," ELN, IV (Dec. 1966), 113-115.

"Cortez in the poem was awed by another person's discovery just as Keats was."

450. Wasserman, Earl R. *The Finer Tone: Keats' Major Poems.* Baltimore: Johns Hopkins, 1967.

A paperback edition of a book first published in 1953. See K-SJ, III (1954), 121, IV (1955), 121, V (1956), 131, VIII (1959), 74.

Watson, George. See No. 248.

451. *Weller, E. V. *Keats and Mary Tighe: The Poems of Mary Tighe with Parallel Passages from the Work of John Keats.* New York: Kraus, 1966.

A reprint of a book first published in 1928.

452. Woolf, Virginia. *Collected Essays.* 4 vols. London: Hogarth, 1966.

Reprints essays on Hazlitt (I, 155-164), Mary Wollstonecraft (III, 193-199), Haydon (IV, 8-12), and Shelley (IV, 20-26).

453. *Yabushita, Takuro. "The Death-Consciousness of Keats," *ALBION* (Kyoto Univ.), X (1966). [In Japanese.]

454. *Yamane, Yoshio. "Imitation and Creation—With Reference to Keats's 'Imitation of Spenser,'" *Academia* (Nanzan Univ.), LVII (March 1967), 21-36. [In Japanese.]

455. Zillman, Lawrence John. *The Art and Craft of Poetry: An Introduction.* New York: Macmillan, 1966.

Contains an analysis of Keats's "On First Looking into Chapman's Homer."

Rev. by Ben W. Fuson in *Library Journal,* XCI (Apr. 1, 1966), 1900.

V. SHELLEY

WORKS: SELECTED, SINGLE, TRANSLATED

456. Ashley, Leonard R. N., ed. *Nineteenth-Century British Drama: An Anthology of Representative Plays.* Glenview, Ill.: Scott, Foresman, 1967.
Includes *The Cenci* (pp. 22-101).

Bebbington, W. G., comp. See No. 73.

Bender, Robert M., and Charles L. Squier, eds. See No. 74.

Berg, Leila, comp. See No. 75.

Cheetham, Anthony, and Derek Parfit, eds. See No. 80.

Clark, Leonard. See No. 279.

Clark, Leonard, comp. See No. 81.

Engelberg, Edward, ed. See No. 283.

English Poetry and Its Appreciation. See No. 284.

457. *The Esdaile Notebook: A Volume of Early Poems.* Ed. Kenneth Neill Cameron. See K-SJ, XIV (1965), 127, XV (1966), 164, XVI (1967), 134.
Rev. by Jean de Palacio in *Langues modernes,* LX (1966), 557-561; by R[ichard]. H[arter]. F[ogle]. in ELN, IV, Supplement (Sept. 1966), 37-38.

458. *The Esdaile Poems: Early Minor Poems from the "Esdaile Notebook."* Ed. Neville Rogers. See K-SJ, XVI (1967), 134.
Rev. in *English,* XVI (Summer 1966), 77; in TLS, July 14, 1966, p. 616; in *Choice,* III (Oct. 1966), 651; by Lawrence J. Zillman in K-SJ, XVI (1967), 102-103; by Anthea Morrison in *Durham University Journal,* LIX (June 1967), 171-172; by Frederick T. Wood in ES, XLVIII (June 1967), 283. Also see No. 574.

Flint, E. L., and M. K. Flint, comps. See No. 83.

Garai, Gábor. See No. 285.

Goudge, Elizabeth, comp. See No. 259.

Hadfield, John, comp. See Nos. 88 and 287.

Hadfield, John, ed. See No. 87.

Hanratty, Jerome, comp. See No. 90.

Hope, Ronald, ed. See No. 91.

Humphreys, Christmas, ed. See No. 92.

459. Lyon, Marjorie, comp. *Where the Golden Apples Grow: An Anthology of Poetry for Speaking and Reading Aloud.* London: Samuel French, 1962.
Includes a poem by Shelley.

Manning-Sanders, Ruth. See No. 261.

Massingham, Hugh, and Pauline Massingham. See No. 94.

460. *Mészöly, Dezsö. *Villon és a többiek.* [*Villon and the Others.*] Budapest: Magvetö, 1966.
An anthology of translations that includes poems by Shelley.

461. Morgan, Edmund Robert. *The Undiscovered Country.* London: Edward Arnold, 1962.
Includes excerpt from *Adonais.*

Morgan, Edwin, ed. See No. 97.

Norman, Charles, ed. See No. 292.

O'Malley, Raymond, and Denys Thompson, comps. See No. 293.

Perkins, David, ed. See No. 51.

Pickles, Wilfred, comp. See No. 99.

462. **Prometheus Bound* by Aeschylus (trans. Rex Warner) and *Prometheus Unbound* by Percy Bysshe Shelley. New York: Heritage, 1966.

463. *Prometheus Unbound.* Ed. Nitish Kumar Basu. See K-SJ, XII (1963), 144, No. 394, XV (1966), 164.
Rev. by K[enneth]. N[eill]. C[ameron]. in ELN, IV, Supplement (Sept. 1966), 37.

Scott, Arthur Finlay, ed. See No. 296.

464. *The Selected Poetry and Prose of Shelley.* Ed. Harold Bloom. New York: New American Library, 1966; London: New English Library, 1967. "Signet Classic Poetry Series."

Seymour, William Kean, and John Smith, comps. See No. 102.

465. **Shelley's Critical Prose.* Ed. B. R. McElderry, Jr. Lincoln: Univ. of Nebraska, 1966. "Regents Critics Series."

466. **Shelley's Prose; or, The Trumpet of a Prophecy.* Ed. David Lee Clark.

Albuquerque: Univ. of New Mexico, 1967.

A reprint of a work first published in 1954. See K-SJ, IV (1955), 121-122, V (1956), 131, VI (1957), 147.

Rev. in TLS, Feb. 23, 1967, p. 148.

"Twenty-Four Sonnets." See No. 300.

Vas, István. See No. 104.

Books and Articles Relating to Shelley and His Circle

467. Adnitt, Frank W. "The Rise of English Radicalism—Part II," CR, CCX (May 1967), 258-272.

Godwin and Hobhouse are included in the section on "Revolution and Reform 1789-1837."

468. Appleyard, J. A. *Coleridge's Philosophy of Literature: The Development of a Concept of Poetry 1791-1819*. Cambridge, Mass.: Harvard Univ., 1965.

References to Godwin.

469. Armens, Sven. *Archetypes of the Family in Literature*. Seattle: Univ. of Washington, 1966.

Comments briefly on "Ozymandias."

470. *Aschenbrenner, J. P. *Shelleys Weltanschauung: Eine Untersuchung über Shelleys Verhältnis zu Holbachs "Système de la Nature."* Tübingen, 1967.

"Auction Sales." See No. 305.

471. "Auction Sales," ABC, XVII (Dec. 1966), 24-27.

Two Shelley first editions brought $250 and $320 respectively at Parke-Bernet.

Ayling, S. E. See No. 12.

472. Baine, Rodney M. *Thomas Holcroft and the Revolutionary Novel.* See K-SJ, XVI (1967), 135.

Rev. by Peter Faulkner in MLR, LXII (Jan. 1967), 117-118.

473. Baker, Carlos. *Shelley's Major Poetry: The Fabric of a Vision.* Princeton: Princeton Univ. [1966].

A paperback reprint of a book first published in 1948. See K-SJ, I (1952), 96.

474. Baker, Joseph E. *Shelley's Platonic Answer to a Platonic Attack on Poetry*. See K-SJ, XV (1966), 165, XVI (1967), 135.

Rev. by K[enneth]. N[eill]. C[ameron]. in ELN, IV, Supplement (Sept. 1966), 37; by Michael Millgate in MLR, LXI (Oct. 1966), 686-687.

Bartlett, C. J. See No. 113.

Barton, Bernard. See No. 307.

475. *Batard, Yvonne. *Dante, Minerve et Apollon*. Paris: Les Belles Lettres, 1952.

Contains (pp. 484-485) "Dante, Shelley et Balzac d'après G. Bachelard."

476. Bateson, F. W. "Exhumations V. Shelley on Wordsworth: Two Unpublished Stanzas from 'Peter Bell the Third,'" EC, XVII (Apr. 1967), 125-129.

The stanzas allude to possible "scandals" in Wordsworth's life.

477. *Baxter, B. M. "Albert Verwey and Shelley," in *Actes: Proceedings of the Fourth Congress of the International Comparative Literature Association,* ed. F. Jost (The Hague: Mouton, 1966), pp. 868-874.

See K-SJ, XIV (1965), 127, XV (1966), 165.

478. Beazley, Elisabeth. *Madocks and the Wonder of Wales*. London: Faber, 1967.

Discusses Shelley's adventures in Wales (pp. 192-197). Also refers to Peacock.

Rev. in TLS, March 2, 1967, p. 160.

Bell, Harry. See No. 114.

Blunden, Edmund. See No. 315.

479. Blunden, Edmund. *Shelley: A Life Story*. See K-SJ, XVI (1967), 135.

Rev. by Manfred Wojcik in *Zeitschrift für Anglistik und Amerikanistik,* XIV (1966), 302-305.

480. Borer, Mary Cathcart. *Women Who*

Made History. London: Warne, 1963.
Mary Wollstonecraft Godwin is one.

481. Bornstein, George Jay. "The Surfeited Alastor: William Butler Yeats's Changing Relation to Percy Bysshe Shelley" [Doctoral dissertation, Princeton, 1966], DA, XXVII (May 1967), 3832-A-3833-A.

Boyle, Andrew. See No. 1.

482. Brain, John Valentine. "A Group of Poems," *Discourse*, X (Winter 1967), 48-53.
One of the six poems is "The Death of Shelley."

Briggs, K. M. See No. 317.

483. Bronowski, Jacob. *The Poet's Defence: The Concept of Poetry from Sidney to Yeats*. Cleveland: World, 1966.
A reprint of the 1939 edition. Considers the poetry and criticism of Shelley.
Rev. by Burton Feldman in *University of Denver Quarterly*, I (Autumn 1966), 154; by Robert L. Enequist in *Library Journal*, XCI (Nov. 15, 1966), 5618-5619.

Browning, Robert. See No. 118.

Buckley, Jerome Hamilton. See No. 121.

Bush, Warren V., ed. See No. 323.

484. Campbell, Olwen Ward. *Shelley and the Unromantics*. New York: Russell and Russell, 1966.
A reprint of the 1924 edition.

Casey, John. See No. 122.

Chatman, Seymour. See No. 125.

485. Chesser, Eustace. *Shelley and Zastrozzi*. See K-SJ, XV (1966), 165-166, XVI (1967), 136.
Rev. by K[enneth]. N[eill]. C[ameron]. in ELN, IV, Supplement (Sept. 1966), 38; by Richard Allan Davison in *Literature and Psychology*, XVI (Winter 1966), 51-55.

486. Chevrillon, Pierre. "André Chevrillon, ou Angleterre, Seconde Patrie," EA, XIX (Oct.-Dec. 1966), 325-345.
Includes references to André Chevrillon's Shelley criticism.

487. Cixous, Hélène. "Vers une lecture détachée du *Prometheus Unbound*," *Langues modernes*, LX (Sept.-Oct. 1966), 582-594.
Rambling considerations on the nature of evil, allegory, Plato, and the essence of lyricism in *Prometheus Unbound.*

488. Clarke, I. F. *Voices Prophesying War 1763-1984*. London: Oxford Univ., 1966.
Frankenstein is one of many works referred to.

489. Cohen, Maurice. "Santayana on Romanticism and Egotism," *Journal of Religion*, XLVI (Apr. 1966), 264-281.
Finds Santayana sympathetic to the platonic side of Shelley's vision.

Colby, Robert A. See No. 129.

490. Crompton, Margaret. *Shelley's Dream Women*. London: Cassell, 1967.
Rev. in TLS, May 25, 1967, p. 436; in T&T, May 4-17, 1967, p. 12.

491. Culler, Jonathan D., ed. *Harvard Advocate Centennial Anthology*. Cambridge: Schenkman, 1966.
Reprints 1869 review of *Frankenstein* (p. 10).

Cunningham, Gilbert F. See No. 130.

Daffern, T. G., comp. See No. 257.

492. Damon, S. Foster. *A Blake Dictionary: The Ideas and Symbols of William Blake*. Providence: Brown Univ., 1965.
Suggests that Bard of Oxford "might well be Shelley."
Rev. by David V. Erdman in JEGP, LXV (July 1966), 606-610.

493. Darring, Walter. "The Rose by Another Name," CE, XXVIII (Apr. 1967), 536-539.
Comments briefly on several Shelley poems.

494. Dawson, Carl. "The Literary Career of Thomas Love Peacock" [Doctoral dissertation, Columbia, 1966], DA, XXVII (Dec. 1966), 1781-A-1782-A.

De Quincey, Thomas. See No. 336.

495. Dowden, Edward. *The Life of Percy Bysshe Shelley*. Preface by Herbert Read. New York: Barnes and Noble, 1966.

A reprint of the 1909 edition with Read's preface of 1950.

Rev. in *Choice,* IV (March 1967), 38.

496. Duerksen, Roland A. *"Caleb Williams, Political Justice,* and *Billy Budd,"* AL, XXXVIII (Nov. 1966), 372-376.

Compares Godwin's and Melville's treatments of "innocence, justice, duty, and virtue."

497. Duerksen, Roland A. *Shelleyan Ideas in Victorian Literature*. The Hague: Mouton, 1966.

Rev. in TLS, July 21, 1966, p. 642.

498. Dumas, D. Gilbert. "Things as They Were: The Original Ending of *Caleb Williams,"* SEL, VI (Summer 1966), 575-597.†

Reports and discusses a canceled first version of the ending of Godwin's novel which is more consistent with its political theme.

499. Duplantis, Stanley. "Shelley and Cosmic Inconsistency," *Xavier University Studies,* V (June 1966), 109-116.

Considers *Alastor* as a warning to fellow poets that the real and the ideal must be seen as irreconcilable.

500. Dyson, A. E. *The Crazy Fabric.* See K-SJ, XV (1966), 166.

Rev. by Juliet Sutton in *Dalhousie Review,* XLVI (Autumn 1966), 391-393; by Marshall Waingrow in *Yale Review,* LVI (Autumn 1966), 138-144.

501. Echeruo, J. C. "Shelley on Wordsworth," *English Studies in Africa,* IX (Sept. 1966), 117-145.

A study of Shelley's changing attitude toward Wordsworth.

502. *English Studies Presented to R. W. Zandvoort on the Occasion of His Seventieth Birthday*. See K-SJ, XV (1966), 169, No. 447, XVI (1967), 136, No. 381.

Rev. by Paul Bacquet in EA, XIX (July-Sept. 1966), 253-260.

503. Faure, G. "Le thème central du *Prométhée Délivré* et son retentissement sur la composition 'musicale' du poème," *Langues modernes,* LX (Sept.-Oct. 1966), 547-556.

Prometheus Unbound is more than a drama or a philosophic poem: it is a triumphant symphony.

504. Findlater, Richard, *pseud.* [Kenneth Bruce Findlater Bain.] *Banned! A Review of Theatrical Censorship in Britain.* London: Macgibbon & Kee, 1967.

Discusses opposition to *The Cenci* (pp. 80-82).

505. Flanders, Wallace Austin. "Godwin and Gothicism: *St. Leon," Texas Studies in Literature and Language,* VIII (Winter 1967), 533-545.

In *St. Leon* Godwin attempts to "unite the manner of Gothic fiction with a serious comment on man's moral life."

506. Fleck, P. D. "Mary Shelley's Notes to Shelley's Poems and *Frankenstein,"* SIR, VI (Summer 1967), 226-254.

Points out Mary's defensive tone in her annotations of Shelley's poems and her inability to accept his idealism. Notes the echoes of *Alastor* in *Frankenstein* but points out the fundamental difference in the attitudes towards their respective heroes.

507. Fleisher, David. *William Godwin: A Study in Liberalism.* See K-SJ, I (1952), 97, XIV (1965), 128.

Rev. in *World Review,* N.S., No. 27 (May 1951), p. 79.

Fogle, Richard Harter, comp. See No. 3.

508. Fuller, John. [In] "Information, Please," TLS, Dec. 8, 1966, p. 1158.

Wants to borrow copy of third edition of *Caleb Williams.*

Fussell, Paul, Jr. See No. 144.

509. *Godwin, William. *The Adventures of Caleb Williams, or, Things as They Are*. Ed. Herbert Van Thal with an Introduction by Walter Allen. London: Cassell, 1966. "First Novel Library."

510. Godwin, William. *Italian Letters, or, The History of the Count de St. Julian*. Ed. Burton R. Pollin. See K-SJ, XVI (1967), 136.

Rev. in *Choice*, III (May 1966), 208; by W[illiam]. H. M[arshall]. in ELN, IV, Supplement (Sept. 1966), 31; in *Nineteenth-Century Fiction*, XXI (Dec. 1966), 297-298; by Peter Faulkner in MLR, LXII (Jan. 1967), 117-118; by Terence Wright in N&Q, CCXII (May 1967), 197.

511. Graves, Robert. *Mammon and the Black Goddess*. London: Cassell, 1965.

Discusses "To a Skylark" (pp. 79-82); also looks at Byron and Keats. See K-SJ, XIII (1964), 129, No. 162, XIV (1965), 129, No. 398.

Graves, Robert. See No. 348.

512. Grob, Alan. "Wordsworth and Godwin: A Reassessment," SIR, VI (Winter 1967), 98-119.

A fresh examination of their complex relationship.

513. Gronow, R. E. *The Reminiscences and Recollections of Captain Gronow, Being Anecdotes of the Camp, Court, Clubs & Society, 1810-1860*. Abridged and with an Introduction by John Raymond. New York: Viking, 1964.

Gronow was at Eton with Shelley, of whom he gives a pleasing picture in the usual role of pugilist.

514. Gross, Harvey. "History as Metaphysical Pathos: Modern Literature and the Idea of History," *University of Denver Quarterly*, I (Autumn 1966), 1-22.

Includes discussion of Shelley's idea of history.

515. Gross, John. "For Love or Money," *Encounter*, XXV (Dec. 1965), 41-43.

Includes review of production at the Royal Court Theatre of Ann Jellicoe's *Shelley*. See Nos. 524 and 600.

516. Grylls, R. Glynn. "New York Public Library," TLS, March 23, 1967, p. 254.

Questions whether Shelley material is still "withheld" by his family. See No. 565.

517. *Guardia, Alfredo de la. "Poesía dramática de Shelley," *La Nación*, Buenos Aires, Dec. 18 and 24, 1966.

518. Haining, Peter, ed. *The Gentlewomen of Evil: An Anthology of Rare Supernatural Stories from the Pens of Victorian Ladies*. London: Robert Hale, 1967.

Includes "Transformation" by Mary Shelley (pp. 15-31).

519. Halliburton, David G. "Shelley's 'Gothic' Novels," K-SJ, XVI (1967), 39-49.

A study of *Zastrozzi* and *St. Irvyne*.

Hardy, Thomas. See No. 155.

Harrold, William E. See No. 355.

Haslam, G. E., ed. See No. 157.

Hill, James Lewis. See No. 359.

Holloway, John. See Nos. 159 and 360.

The Houghton Library 1942-1967. See No. 363.

520. Howes, Frank. *The English Musical Renaissance*. London: Secker & Warburg, 1966.

Discusses Sir Hubert Parry's *Prometheus Unbound* and other musical settings of poetry by Keats and Shelley.

Rev. by Neville Cardus in NYT, Aug. 28, 1966, pp. 6-7, 20, 22.

Hungerford, Edward B. See No. 365.

Hunt, Peter, comp. See No. 288.

521. Hunter, Parks C., Jr. "Textual Differences in the Drafts of Shelley's 'Una Favola,'" SIR, VI (Autumn 1966), 58-64.

The text, and English translation, "most familiar to Shelley readers, probably reflect Shelley's ideas less accurately than" the original text.

522. Igo, John. "A Calendar of Fausts," BNYPL, LXXI (Jan. 1967), 5-24.
Includes Shelley's *Faust* (translation of scenes from Goethe) and Godwin's *Lives of the Necromancers.*

523. *Ishikawa, Shigetoshi. "P. B. Shelley's *Defence of Poetry*—A Comparison with T. S. Eliot," *Review* (Tohoku Gakuin Univ.), XLIX-L (Nov. 1966, 95-120. [In Japanese.]

524. Jellicoe, Ann. *Shelley or The Idealist.* London: Faber, 1966.
A play. See Nos. 515 and 600.
Rev. in TLS, May 4, 1967, p. 380.

Johnson, Carol. See No. 370.

Joyce, James. See No. 164.

525. Kamm, Josephine. *Rapiers and Battleaxes: The Women's Movement and Its Aftermath.* London: Allen & Unwin, 1966.
Discusses Mary Wollstonecraft's role (pp. 18-20).

526. Kaufman, Violet Webber. "Thomas Love Peacock" [Doctoral dissertation, Connecticut, 1965], DA, XXVII (Nov. 1966), 1369-A.

527. Kennedy, William F. "Peacock's Economists: Some Mistaken Identities," *Nineteenth-Century Fiction,* XXI (Sept. 1966), 185-191.
Sees Mr. Fax as a "Benthamite Philosophic Radical"; MacQuedy as a "representative Utilitarian thinker."

528. Klukoff, Philip J. "Shelley's 'Hymn of Apollo' and 'Hymn of Pan': The Displaced Vision," *Neuphilologische Mitteilungen,* LXVII (1966), 290-294.†
Finds that the "Hymn of Apollo" affirms the infinite vision of the artist but denies, ironically, the artist's personality; the "Hymn of Pan" comments on the imaginative vision of the "Hymn of Apollo" and affirms what that poem denies.

Krieger, Murray. See No. 379.

529. Kroese, Irvin Bertus. "The Beauty and the Terror: Shelley's Visionary Women" [Doctoral dissertation, Ohio, 1966], DA, XXVII (Feb. 1967), 2501-A-2502-A.

530. La Cassagnere, Christian. "Une Mystique plotinienne chez Shelley: Essai d'interprétation de l'acte II de *Prometheus Unbound,*" *Langues modernes,* LX (Sept.-Oct. 1966), 562-574.
A neo-platonic reading of the poem.

Langley, Noël. See No. 171.

Lemon, Lee T. See No. 172.

531. Leyda, Seraphia DeVille. "'The Serpent Is Shut Out from Paradise': A Revaluation of Romantic Love in Shelley" [Doctoral dissertation, Tulane, 1965], DA, XXVII (Aug. 1966), 480-A-481-A.

532. Lodge, David. *Language of Fiction: Essays in Criticism and Verbal Analysis of the English Novel.* London: Routledge; New York: Columbia Univ. (1966).
Makes use of Shelley's criticism.

533. London, Jack. *Letters from Jack London, Containing an Unpublished Correspondence between London and Sinclair Lewis.* Ed. King Hendricks and Irving Shepard. New York: Odyssey, 1965.
Has two allusions to Shelley.

534. Luke, Hugh J., Jr. "An Overlooked Obituary Notice of Shelley," *Papers on Language & Literature,* II (Winter 1966), 38-46.
Reprints for the first time a lengthy obituary which appeared in Sept. 1822 in *The Rambler's Magazine; or, Fashionable Emporium of Polite Literature.*

McAuley, James. See No. 385.

McClary, Ben Harris. See No. 178.

535. Margolis, John D. "Shakespeare and Shelley's Sonnet 'England in 1819,'" ELN, IV (June 1967), 276-277.
The opening line about George III echoes Lear's description of himself.

536. Marken, Jack W. "William Godwin's History of the United Prov-

inces," PQ, XLV (Apr. 1966), 379-386.

Identifies his *History of the Internal Affairs of the United Provinces,* published in 1787.

Marshall, Percy. See No. 391.

537. Mason, Stanley. "The Skylark," *Dalhousie Review,* XLVI (Summer 1966), 248.

A poem. Refers to "Shelley's violet-eyed hysteria."

538. Massey, Irving. "The First Edition of Shelley's *Poetical Works* (1839): Some Manuscript Sources," K-SJ, XVI (1967), 29-38.

Massingham, Hugh, and Pauline Massingham, eds. See No. 95.

539. Matthews, G. M. "Accident," *New York Review of Books,* VIII (June 15, 1967), 30.

Answers James Rieger's letter about Matthews' review. See Nos. 571 and 572.

Maxwell, J. C. See No. 392.

Mears, Esmé, comp. See No. 96.

540. Medawar, P. B. "Anglo-Saxon Attitudes," *Encounter,* XXV (Aug. 1965), 52-58.

Makes use of Shelley's observations on science and poetry.

541. Millett, Fred B. "Thomas Love Peacock," in *Minor British Novelists,* ed. Charles Alva Hoyt (Carbondale: Southern Illinois Univ., 1967), pp. 32-58.

542. *Mills, Howard William. "Conservatism and Development in Regency Literature: A Study Centring on Peacock and His Relation to His Period." (Doctoral dissertation, Cambridge, 1967.)

543. Moskowitz, Samuel, and Roger Elwood, eds. *Strange Signposts: An Anthology of the Fantastic.* New York: Holt, 1966.

Includes Mary Shelley's *The Last Man.*

544. Neri, Nicoletta. "Il romanzo di conversazione," in *Friendship's Garland: Essays Presented to Mario Praz on His Seventieth Birthday,* ed. Vittorio Gabrieli (Rome: Edizioni di Storia e Letteratura, 1966), II, 269-330.

Has extended discussion of Peacock.

545. Norman, Sylva. "Twentieth-Century Theories on Shelley," *Texas Studies in Literature and Language,* IX (Summer 1967), 223-237.

Uses Shelley to attack Huxley, Eliot, Leavis, *et al.*

546. Northcote, Sydney. *Byrd to Britten: A Survey of English Song.* London: John Baker, 1966.

Mentions musical settings of poems by Shelley.

547. *Okuda, Heihachiro. "On Shelley's 'Ode to the West Wind'—A Symbolical Interpretation," *Bulletin* (Seisen College), IX (Dec. 1966), 1-14. [In Japanese.]

548. O'Malley, Glenn. *Shelley and Synesthesia.* See K-SJ, XV (1966), 168, XVI (1967), 138.

Rev. by Jean de Palacio in *Langues modernes,* LX (1966), 557-561; by Richard Harter Fogle in JEGP, LXVI (Jan. 1967), 158-159.

549. Orel, Harold. "Wordsworth's Repudiation of Godwinism," *Studies on Voltaire and the Eighteenth Century,* LVII (1967), 1123-1145.

There is a "pattern of consistency" in Wordsworth's concept of Godwinism; he "shared certain assumptions with Godwin and was concerned over many of the same issues independently of Godwin."

Osler, Alan. See No. 403.

Otten, Terry Ralph. See No. 201.

550. Palacio, Jean de. "État Présent des Études godwiniennes," EA, XX (Apr.-June 1967), 149-159.

A review article on Burton Ralph Pollin's *Education and Enlightenment in the Works of William Godwin* and Pollin's edition of Godwin's *Italian Letters.* See K-SJ, XII (1963), 147, XIII (1964), 149, XV (1966), 169, XVI (1967), 136. Also see No. 510.

Parsons, Coleman O. See No. 203.

551. *Peacock, Thomas Love. *Headlong*

Hall and Nightmare Abbey. Introduction by P. M. Yarker. London: Dent, 1966. "Everyman Paperbacks."

A paperback reprint of a volume first published in 1961. See K-SJ, XII (1963), 147.

552. *Peacock, Thomas Love. *Nightmare Abbey*. Introduction and Notes by A. R. Tomkins. London: Blackie, 1966. "Medallion English Texts."

Pedrini, Lura Nancy, and Duilio Thomas Pedrini. See No. 204.

553. Peyre, Henri. "André Chevrillon et les Lettres Anglaises," EA, XIX (Oct.-Dec. 1966), 351-370.

Refers to Chevrillon's Shelley criticism.

554. Piggott, Stuart. "The Roman Camp and Three Authors," *Review of English Literature,* VII (July 1966), 21-28.

Peacock is one. Includes discussion of *Melincourt.*

Pinion, F. B., ed. See No. 264.

Playfair, Giles. See No. 206.

555. Politi, Francesco. *Studi di letteratura tedesca e marginalia*. Bari: Adriatica, 1963.

Includes "Epifanie dello spirito cosmico nella lirica di Shelley" (pp. 201-233).

556. *Political Justice. A Poem. (Anonymous. 1736)*. Introduction by Burton R. Pollin and John W. Wilkes. Los Angeles: William Andrews Clark Memorial Library, UCLA, 1965. "Augustan Reprint Society Publication Number 111."

A reprint of a poem that may have connections with Godwin.

557. Pollin, Burton R. "Fanny Godwin's Suicide Re-examined," EA, XVIII (July-Sept. 1965), 258-268.

Reviews possible motives for her suicide and concludes that her hopeless love for Shelley "is the only one that corresponds to harsh reality."

558. Pollin, Burton R. "A Federalist Farrago," *Satire Newsletter,* IV (Fall 1966), 29-34.

Includes Federalist satire on Godwin and Mary Wollstonecraft.

559. Pollin, Burton R. "Nicholson's Lost Portrait of William Godwin: A Study in Phrenology," K-SJ, XVI (1967), 51-60.

It is Godwin "to the life."

560. Pollin, Burton R. "Poe's 'Von Kempelen and His Discovery'—Sources and Significance," EA, XX (Jan.-March 1967), 12-23.

Godwin's *St. Leon* as one of Poe's sources in the tale.

Potts, Abbie Findlay. See No. 207.

561. *Priestley, John Boynton. *Thomas Love Peacock*. Introduction by J. I. M. Stewart. London: Macmillan; New York: St. Martin's (1966).

A reprint of a book first published in 1927.

562. Raben, Joseph. "Coleridge as the Prototype of the Poet in Shelley's *Alastor*," RES, N.S., XVII (Aug. 1966), 278-292.†

Argues that *Alastor* may be read "as an allegory of Coleridge's actual failure and Shelley's possible duplication of it."

563. Raben, Joseph. "Shelley's 'The Boat on the Serchio': The Evidence of the Manuscript," PQ, XLVI (Jan. 1967), 58-68.

This fresh examination of the manuscripts and printed versions argues that the poem is "an unassimilated composite of manuscript fragments intended for a variety of poems; that these have nothing to do with any drift toward orthodox Christianity; that some of them were probably composed in 1817 and 1818."

564. Rader, Melvin. *Wordsworth: A Philosophical Approach*. Oxford: Clarendon, 1967.

Includes discussion of Godwin's influence.

Raizis, Marios Byron. See No. 211.

565. Randall, David A. "New York

Public Library," TLS, March 9, 1967, p. 202.

Mentions Shelley material "still . . . withheld by his descendants in England." See No. 516.

566. Raymond, William O. *The Infinite Moment and Other Essays in Robert Browning*. See K-SJ, XV (1966), 169, XVI (1967), 139.

Rev. by Frederick T. Wood in ES, XLVII (Oct. 1966), 402.

Reck, Rima Drell, ed. See No. 411.

567. Reiman, Donald H. "Roman Scenes in *Prometheus Unbound* III.iv," PQ, XLVI (Jan. 1967), 69-78.

Argues that the sculptural accuracy of the scenes was based on actual observations made in Rome which were important to Shelley's thought about the lessons taught by past civilizations.

568. Reiman, Donald H. *Shelley's "The Triumph of Life": A Critical Study Based on a Text Newly Edited from the Bodleian Manuscript*. See K-SJ, XV (1966), 169, XVI (1967), 139.

Rev. by K[enneth]. N[eill]. C[ameron]. in ELN, IV, Supplement (Sept. 1966), 39-40; by Kenneth Neill Cameron in *The Library*, XXII (March 1967), 81-84; by P. H. Butter in MLR, LXII (Apr. 1967), 319-320; by R. A. Foakes in RES, N.S., XVIII (May 1967), 216-217.

569. ["Relics to Be Displayed at Hampstead Permanently,"] *The Times*, London, Feb. 2, 1967, p. 12.

Rhodes, Jack Lee. See No. 56.

570. Ridenour, George M., ed. *Shelley: A Collection of Critical Essays*. See K-SJ, XVI (1967), 139.

Rev. by Glenn O'Malley in K-SJ, XVI (1967), 110-112.

571. Rieger, James. "Accident," *New York Review of Books*, VIII (June 15, 1967), 29-30.

Responds to G. M. Matthews' review of his book. See Nos. 539 and 572.

572. Rieger, James. *The Mutiny Within: The Heresies of Percy Bysshe Shelley*. New York: Braziller, 1967.

Rev. by Duane B. Schneider in *Library Journal*, XCII (Jan. 1, 1967), 115-116; by G. M. Matthews in *New York Review of Books*, VIII (Apr. 20, 1967), 21-23. See Nos. 539 and 571.

Riley, Paul E. See No. 276.

Robinson, Henry Crabb. See No. 220.

573. Rogers, Neville. "The Punctuation of Shelley's Syntax," KSMB, XVII (1966), 20-30.

Suggests that simple transcription of what Shelley wrote is not enough: an editor must understand the syntax and punctuate accordingly.

574. Rogers, Neville. "Second to None," TLS, Aug. 25, 1966, p. 770.

Replies to review of his edition of *The Esdaile Poems*. See No. 458.

575. "Romios and Hellene," TLS, July 7, 1966, pp. 585-587.

Briefly discusses Shelley's *Hellas*.

576. Rozenberg, Simone. "Les virtualités du Feu dans *Prometheus Unbound*," *Langues modernes*, LX (Sept.-Oct. 1966), 575-581.

Finds that the imaginative rendering of the elements, particularly that of fire, gives the poem its promethean significance.

577. Sage, Judith Ann. "George Meredith and Thomas Love Peacock: A Note on Literary Influence," ELN, IV (June 1967), 279-283.

A scene in *The Amazing Marriage* is modeled on a comparable scene in *Crotchet Castle*.

578. St. George, Priscilla P. "Romantic Poetry as Wisdom: The Contemplative Metaphor in Wordsworth, Coleridge and Shelley" [Doctoral dissertation, Yale, 1966], DA, XXVII (Feb. 1967), 2544-A.

579. *Saito, Yuzo. "The Tombs of Shelley and Keats, and the Assumed Theory of Shelley's Assassination," *Rising Generation*, CXII (Nov. 1966), 756-759. [In Japanese.]

Sarkar, Manojkumar. See No. 225.

580. Sastri, P. S. "Shelley's Theory of Poetry," *Calcutta Review,* CLXXVI (Sept. 1965), 151-161.

581. Schaefer, William David. *James Thomson (B.V.): Beyond "The City."* See K-SJ, XVI (1967), 140.
Rev. by Dale Kramer in JEGP, LXV (July 1966), 621-623; by Barbara Charlesworth Gelpi in *Victorian Studies,* X (Sept. 1966), 101-103.

Schlüter, Kurt. See No. 423.

582. Schueller, Herbert M., ed. *The Persistence of Shakespeare Idolatry.* See K-SJ, XV (1966), 170, No. 468.
Rev. by M. T. Jones-Davies in EA, XIX (July-Sept. 1966), 298-300.

583. Schulze, Earl J. *Shelley's Theory of Poetry: A Reappraisal.* The Hague: Mouton, 1966.

Sealts, Merton M., Jr. See No. 226.

584. *Séjourné, Philippe. *Aspects généraux du roman féminin en Angleterre de 1740 à 1800.* Gap: Louis-Jean, 1966.
Discusses Mary Wollstonecraft at some length.

585. *Shelley, Mary Wollstonecraft. *Frankenstein.* [Translated by] Eugène Rocart and Georges Cuvelier. Paris: "Club Géant," Les Editions de la Renaissance, 1967.
Contains a brief introductory sketch by Hubert Juin entitled "Au Pays des Monstres."

586. Shelley, Mary Wollstonecraft. *The Last Man.* Ed. Hugh J. Luke, Jr. See K-SJ, XVI (1967), 140.
Rev. by K[enneth]. N[eill]. C[ameron]. in ELN, IV, Supplement (Sept. 1966), 37; in *Choice,* III (Nov. 1966), 773; in *Nineteenth-Century Fiction,* XXI (Dec. 1966), 298; by J. M. S. Tompkins in K-SJ, XVI (1967), 108-109. Also see No. 33.

Shipps, Anthony. See No. 228.

587. Silverman, Edwin Barry. "Poetic Synthesis in *Adonais*" [Doctoral dissertation, Northwestern, 1966], DA, XXVII (Jan. 1967), 2162-A.

Singh, G. See No. 230.

588. Smith, Elton Edward, and Esther Greenwell Smith. *William Godwin.* See K-SJ, XVI (1967), 140-141.
Rev. in *Choice,* III (May 1966), 212; in *Nineteenth-Century Fiction,* XXI (Dec. 1966), 298.

Spalding, Philip A. See No. 231.

Stallworthy, Jon. See No. 232.

589. Steeves, Harrison R. *Before Jane Austen.* See K-SJ, XVI (1967), 141.
Rev. by Derek Hudson in *English,* XVI (Spring 1967), 149.

590. Stempel, Daniel. "Browning's *Sordello:* The Art of the Makers-See," PMLA, LXXX (Dec. 1965), 554-561.†
Refers to the role of Shelley in the poem.

Stevens, Wallace. See No. 434.

Stratman, Carl J. See No. 7.

591. *Suzuki, Hiroshi. "Dream and Reality—Shelley's 'Alastor' and Browning's 'Pauline,'" *Journal of General Science* (Waseda Univ.), I (March 1967), 1-25. [In Japanese.]

592. *Suzuki, Hiroshi. "On Urania in 'Adonais,'" *General Studies* (Waseda Univ.), XXV (Feb. 1967), 65-88. [In Japanese.]

593. *Suzuki, Hiroshi. "Prometheus and Satan—What Stands between Rebel and Hero," *General Studies* (Waseda Univ.), XXVI (June 1967), 21-44. [In Japanese.]

594. Taubman, Howard. "Tool for the Humanist," *New York Times,* June 30, 1967, p. 38.
Concerns computer work on poetry by Milton and Shelley.

595. Taylor, John Chesley. "A Critical History of Miltonic Satanism" [Doctoral dissertation, Tulane, 1966], DA, XXVII (Nov. 1966), 1348-A-1349-A.
Includes "detailed analysis" of Shelley's critical opinions on Milton's Satan.

596. Thompson, Francis. *The Mistress of Vision.* With . . . an Essay on Francis Thompson by Henry Williamson. [Aylesford:] Saint Albert's, 1966.
Shelley is discussed in the Williamson essay.

Rev. in TLS, Dec. 15, 1966, p. 1172.

597. Thompson, William I. "Collapsed Universe and Structured Poem: An Essay in Whiteheadian Criticism," CE, XXVIII (Oct. 1966), 25-39.†

Shelley's "Ode to the West Wind" is one of five poems discussed.

Thorpe, Michael. See No. 241.

598. Thurmond, Margaret E. *Elena Adelaide Shelley as the "Spirit of the Earth" in Shelley's "Prometheus Unbound."* Los Angeles: Lorrin L. Morrison, 1966.

"Even if positive identification is never made for lack of testamentary and documentary evidence, the parallel of the child in the drama and the 'Neapolitan ward' whom Shelley planned to have in his household is an interesting one."

"To Percy Shelley. . . ." See No. 265.

599. Trawick, Leonard M., ed. *Backgrounds of Romanticism: English Philosophical Prose of the Eighteenth Century.* Bloomington: Indiana Univ., 1967.

Includes (pp. 189-221) selections from Godwin's *Enquiry Concerning Political Justice.*

600. Trewin, J. C. "Congreve Revived, Shelley Plain—and Auschwitz," ILN, CCXLVII (Oct. 30, 1965), 40.

Includes review of Royal Court production of *Shelley*. See Nos. 515 and 524.

Tuzet, Hélène. See No. 244.

Uden, Grant, comp. See No. 245.

601. Van Doren, Carl. *The Life of Thomas Love Peacock.* New York: Russell and Russell, 1966.

A reprint of a book first published in 1911.

602. *Viebrock, Helmut. "Der böse Adler und die gute Schlange: Shelleys Abwandlung eines traditionellen Motivs," in *Lebende Antike: Symposion für Rudolf Sühnel,* ed. Horst Meller and Hans-Joachim Zimmermann (Berlin, 1967), pp. 333-347.

603. Wade, Philip Tyree. "Influence and Intent in the Prose Fiction of Percy and Mary Shelley" [Doctoral dissertation, North Carolina, 1966], DA, XXVII (March 1967), 3021-A.

604. Walling, J. J. "Le Sentiment de la Nature chez André Chevrillon," EA, XIX (Oct.-Dec. 1966), 371-380.

Notes Shelley's influence on Chevrillon.

Walsh, William. See No. 247.

605. *Wapnir, Salomón. "La casa en que vivió Shelley," *La Prensa,* Buenos Aires, Nov. 20, 1966.

On the house of Shelley at Rome.

606. Wardle, Ralph M., ed. *Godwin & Mary: Letters of William Godwin and Mary Wollstonecraft.* Lawrence: Univ. of Kansas, 1966.

Rev. by Frederick T. Wood in ES, XLVIII (June 1967), 280; in TLS, June 15, 1967, p. 531.

607. *Wardle, Ralph M. *Mary Wollstonecraft: A Critical Biography.* Lincoln: Univ. of Nebraska, 1966. "Bison Books."

A reprint of a book first published in 1951. See K-SJ, XIV (1965), 132.

Rev. in *Choice,* IV (March 1967), 42.

608. Wasserman, Earl R. *Shelley's "Prometheus Unbound": A Critical Reading.* See K-SJ, XVI (1967), 142.

Rev. by B. R. McElderry, Jr., in *Personalist,* XLVII (Summer 1966), 435; by Ross Woodman in *Dalhousie Review,* XLVI (Summer 1966), 259-260; in TLS, Aug. 4, 1966, p. 702; by Gilbert Thomas in *English,* XVI (Autumn 1966), 107-108; by K[enneth]. N[eill]. C[ameron]. in ELN, IV, Supplement (Sept. 1966), 40-41; by Klaus Hofmann in *Anglia,* LXXXV (1967), 223-227; by Donald H. Reiman in K-SJ, XVI (1967), 99-102; by Carl Woodring in *Criticism,* IX (Winter 1967), 96-98; by Eleanor N. Hutchens in MP, LXIV (May

1967), 364-365; by Harold Bloom in ELN, IV (June 1967), 303-304. Also see No. 33.

Watson, George. See No. 248.

Whipple, A. B. C. See No. 250.

609. White, Newman Ivey. *The Unextinguished Hearth: Shelley and His Contemporary Critics.* New York: Octagon, 1966.

A reprint of a book first published in 1938.

Rev. in *Choice,* III (Oct. 1966), 654.

Wilson, Angus. See No. 252.

610. Wilson, Angus. "The Novels of William Godwin," *World Review,* N.S., No. 28 (June 1951), pp. 37-40.

Asserts "the peculiar psychological and social comprehension of Godwin's novels."

611. Woodcock, George. *Anarchism.* [Harmondsworth:] Penguin, 1963.

A reprint of the 1962 edition. See K-SJ, XIV (1965), 133.

Rev. in TLS, Dec. 24, 1964, pp. 1153-1154.

612. Woodhouse, A. S. P. *The Poet and His Faith.* See K-SJ, XVI (1967), 142.

Rev. by John R. Willingham in *Library Journal,* XCI (Apr. 1966), 1900; by Kenneth Hamilton in QQ, LXXIII (Summer 1966), 298-299; by E. D. Mackerness in MLR, LXI (Oct. 1966), 666-668.

Woolf, Virginia. See No. 452.

613. *Yamaguchi, Tetsuo. "Some Aspects of Shelley and Signs Involved in 'Alastor,'" *Studies in Foreign Language & Literature* (Hiroshima Univ.), XII (1966), 55-69. [In Japanese.]

614. *Yasunaga, Yoshio. "Light and Shadow Images of Shelley," *Reports* (Shizuoka Univ.), II (1966), 83-90. [In Japanese.]

615. *Yoshioka, Nobuo. "A Study of Shelley's 'Alastor,' 'Epipsychidion,' and 'The Triumph of Life'—with Special Reference to His Ideas of Love, Life and Death as Seen in Them," *Studies in British & American Literature* (Univ. of Osaka Prefecture), XIV (Jan. 1967), 100-147. [In Japanese.]

616. *Zillman, Lawrence J. *The Complete Known Drafts of Shelley's "Prometheus Unbound."* Ann Arbor: University Microfilms, 1966. [A xerographic reproduction of the literal transcription.]

VI. PHONOGRAPH RECORDINGS

Byron, Keats, Shelley

617. **Great British Narrative Poems.* Six records with reading scripts and six filmstrips. Encyclopaedia Britannica.

Includes "The Eve of St. Agnes" and "The Prisoner of Chillon."

Rev. by J[ohn]. R. S[earles]. in *English Journal,* LVI (Apr. 1967), 639.

618. **Poems of London.* Argo.

Includes selection from Hood.

Rev. by Margaret Willy in *English,* XVI (Summer 1966), 58.

619. **Poems of the Sea.* Argo.

Includes selections from Keats and Byron.

Rev. by Margaret Willy in *English,* XVI (Summer 1966), 58.

620. **Poetry Records Treasury, Vol. I: Great Poems of the English Language.* Read by David Allen. Poetry Records.

Includes poems by Shelley, Byron, Keats, and Hood.

Rev. by J[ohn]. R. S[earles]. in *English Journal,* LVI (Jan. 1967), 158-159.

621. **Robert Donat Reads Favourite Poetry at Home.* London Records.

Includes several poems by Keats.

Rev. by J[ohn]. R. S[earles]. in *English Journal,* LIV (Sept. 1965), 575.

622. **Treasury of George Gordon, Lord Byron.* Read by Peter Orr. Spoken Arts.

Rev. by J[ohn]. R. S[earles]. in *English Journal,* LVI (March 1967), 487-488.

Bibliography for July 1, 1967–June 30, 1968

VOLUME XVIII

Compiled by EDWIN GRAVES WILSON,
with the assistance of Robert G. Kirkpatrick

THIS bibliography, a regular department of the *Keats-Shelley Journal*, is a register of the literary interest in Keats, Shelley, Byron, Hunt, and their circles from (approximately) July 1967 through June 1968.

The compilers are very grateful for their kind assistance to Professors Jean L. de Palacio, Université de Lille; Jaime Rest, Universidad Nacional del Sur, Bahia Blanca; Masao Hirai, University of Tokyo; and Takeshi Saito, Emeritus, University of Tokyo; Dr. Helmut Viebrock, Johann Wolfgang Goethe Universität, Frankfurt am Main; Dr. Anna Katona, the University of Debrecen; Dr. J. G. Riewald, University of Groningen; Dr. Witold Ostrowski, University of Łódź; Dr. Helena Więckowska, Chief Librarian, University of Łódź; D. H. Borchardt, Chief Librarian, La Trobe University, Melbourne; and B. L. Kandel, the M. E. Saltykov-Schedrin State Public Library, Leningrad. We also thank Mrs. G. Louis-Dreyfus; Miss Louise M. Hall, Mrs. Kenneth McIntyre, and other members of the library staff of the University of North Carolina at Chapel Hill; and the library staffs of Harvard University and Wake Forest University.

Each item that we have not seen is marked by an asterisk. Entries which have been abstracted in *Abstracts of English Studies* are marked with a dagger, but entries in previous bibliographies which were abstracted too late for notice have not been repeated.

ABBREVIATIONS

ABC	American Book Collector
AL	American Literature
ASNS	Archiv für das Studium der neueren Sprachen
BA	Books Abroad
BC	Book Collector
BNYPL	Bulletin of the New York Public Library
CE	College English
CL	Comparative Literature
CLSB	C. L. S. Bulletin (Charles Lamb Society)
CR	Contemporary Review
DA	Dissertation Abstracts
EA	Etudes Anglaises
EC	Essays in Çriticism
ELH	Journal of English Literary History
ELN	English Language Notes
ES	English Studies
Exp	Explicator
HLQ	Huntington Library Quarterly
ICS	L'Italia Che Scrive
ILN	Illustrated London News
JAAC	Journal of Aesthetics and Art Criticism
JEGP	Journal of English and Germanic Philology
JHI	Journal of the History of Ideas
KR	Kenyon Review
K-SJ	Keats-Shelley Journal
KSMB	Keats-Shelley Memorial Bulletin
Li	Listener
MLN	Modern Language Notes
MLQ	Modern Language Quarterly
MLR	Modern Language Review
MP	Modern Philology
N&Q	Notes and Queries
NS	New Statesman
NYT	New York Times Book Review
PBSA	Papers of the Bibliographical Society of America
PMLA	Publications of the Modern Language Association of America
PQ	Philological Quarterly
PR	Partisan Review
QQ	Queen's Quarterly
RES	Review of English Studies
RLC	Revue de Littérature Comparée
SAQ	South Atlantic Quarterly
SatR	Saturday Review
SEL	Studies in English Literature 1500–1900
SIR	Studies in Romanticism
SP	Studies in Philology
Spec	Spectator
SR	Sewanee Review
T&T	Time and Tide
TLS	Times Literary Supplement
VQR	Virginia Quarterly Review

Current Bibliography

I. GENERAL

Current Bibliographies

1. Erdman, David V., *et al.* "The Romantic Movement: A Selective and Critical Bibliography for 1966," ELN, v, Supplement (Sept. 1967), 1–136.
2. Freeman, Ronald E., ed. "Victorian Bibliography for 1967," *Victorian Studies*, xi (June 1968), 555–614.
3. Gerstenberger, Donna, and George Hendrick. *Second Directory of Periodicals Publishing Articles in English and American Literature and Language*. Denver: Alan Swallow, 1965.
4. Green, David Bonnell, and Edwin Graves Wilson, eds. *Keats, Shelley, Byron, Hunt, and Their Circles. A Bibliography: July 1, 1950–June 30, 1962*. See K-SJ, xv (1966), 142, xvi (1967), 114.

   Rev. by L[ouis]. C. B[onnerot]. in EA, xx (July–Sept. 1967), 327; by Janine Renaudineau in *Bulletin des bibliothèques*, 25 Sept. 1967, Item 1492.
5. Houghton, Walter E., ed. *The Wellesley Index to Victorian Periodicals 1824–1900: Tables of Contents and Identification of Contributors with Bibliographies of Their Articles and Stories*. Vol. i. Toronto: Univ. of Toronto; London: Routledge (1966).

   Lists articles by and about Romantic writers.

   Rev. by H. B. de Groot in ES, xlix (Apr. 1968), 175–178.
6. McBurney, William H., and Charlene M. Taylor, comps. *English Prose Fiction 1700–1800 in the University of Illinois Library*. Urbana: Univ. of Illinois, 1965.

   Lists items by Mary Wollstonecraft and William Godwin.
7. Rigby, Marjory, Charles Nilon, and James B. Misenheimer, Jr., eds. "Nineteenth Century," *Annual Bibliography of English Language and Literature*, xl (1967 [for 1965]), 290–394.
8. Rigby, Marjory, Charles Nilon, and James B. Misenheimer, Jr., eds. "Nineteenth Century," *Annual Bibliography of English Language and Literature*, xli (1968 [for 1966]), 291–402.
9. Schulz, H. C. "English Literary Manuscripts in the Huntington Library," HLQ, xxxi (May 1968), 251–302.

   Lists manuscripts by the Countess of Blessington, Byron, Charles and Mary Cowden Clarke, William and Mary Godwin, Haydon, Hazlitt, Hobhouse, Hood, Hunt, Keats, Milnes, Murray, Peacock, Severn, Shelley, and Mary Shelley.
10. Slack, Robert C., ed. *Bibliographies of Studies in Victorian Literature for the Ten Years 1955–1964*. Urbana: Univ. of Illinois, 1967.

    Lists items relevant to the Romantic period.
11. Stratman, Carl J. *Bibliography of English Printed Tragedy, 1565–1900*. See K-SJ, xviii (1968), 2.

    Rev. by Phyllis Hartnoll in N&Q, ccxiii (June 1968), 238–239.
12. Ward, William S. "Contemporary Reviews of Thomas Love Peacock: A Supplementary List for the Years 1805–1820," *Bulletin of Bibliography*, xxv (Jan.–Apr. 1967), 35.

    Supplements the bibliography by Bill Read. See K-SJ, xiv (1965), 106, No. 8, xv (1966), 142, No. 7.
13. Yarker, P. M., and Brian Lee. "The Nineteenth Century," in *The Year's Work in English Studies*, ed. T. S. Dorsch and C. G. Harlow, xlvi (1967 [for 1965]), 253–293.

Books and Articles Relating to English Romanticism

14. Aarsleff, Hans. *The Study of Language in England, 1780–1860*. Princeton: Princeton Univ., 1967.

    Rev. in TLS, 27 July 1967, p. 689.

15. Anderson, George K. *The Legend of the Wandering Jew*. See K-SJ, XVI (1967), 115.

Rev. by P. H. Butter in MLR, LXIII (Jan. 1968), 138–139.

16. Ball, Patricia M. *The Central Self: A Study in Romantic and Victorian Imagination*. London: Univ. of London; New York: Oxford Univ. (1968).

Chapter IV (pp. 103–151) is entitled "Egotistical and Chameleon: Byron, Shelley and Keats."

17. *Barfield, Owen. *Romanticism Comes of Age*. First American Edition. Middletown, Conn.: Wesleyan Univ., 1967.

Rev. by R. H. Ward in *Aryan Path*, XXXVIII (July 1967), 328.

18. Barnes, T. R. *English Verse: Voice and Movement from Wyatt to Yeats*. Cambridge: Cambridge Univ., 1967.

Chapter 5 (pp. 165–227) is on "The Romantics."

19. Bateson, F. W. "The Language of Poetry," TLS, 27 July 1967, pp. 688–689.

Discusses the major movements of poetry since the Middle Ages, including the Romantic and the post-Romantic. See No. 79.

20. Blainey, Ann. *The Farthing Poet: A Biography of Richard Hengist Horne 1802–84, A Lesser Literary Lion*. London: Longmans, 1968.

Has frequent references to Romantic writers, including Byron, Hazlitt, Hunt, Keats, and Shelley.

Rev. by Ian Fletcher in NS, LXXV (12 Apr. 1968), 484, 486.

21. Bostetter, Edward. "Recent Studies in the Nineteenth Century," SEL, VII (Autumn 1967), 741–766.

An omnibus review. See K-SJ, XVII (1968), 4, No. 29, 5, No. 45, 13, No. 169, 24, No. 333, 30, No. 413, 41, No. 572. Also see Nos. 30, 47, 207, 390, 478, and 639.

22. Brett, R. L. "The Philosophy of Romanticism," *Critical Survey*, III (Summer 1968), 235–242.

At its best Romanticism stands for "a mind united with itself and not divided."

23. Burton, Elizabeth. *The Georgians at Home 1714–1830*. London: Longmans, 1967.

Has a few references to the Romantic poets.

The American edition is entitled *The Pageant of Georgian England* (New York: Scribner's, 1968).

Rev. by Paul von Khrum in *Library Journal*, XCIII (15 Apr. 1968), 1626–27.

24. Byrns, Richard H. "Nationalism and Cosmopolitanism in the English Romantic Essay," in *Actes: Proceedings of the IVth Congress of the International Comparative Literature Association*, ed. François Jost (The Hague: Mouton, 1966), I, 467–473.

Hazlitt is one of those discussed.

See Nos. 49 and 487.

25. Cooper, Martin. *Ideas and Music*. London: Barrie and Rockliff, 1965.

Has extended discussions of Romanticism, in poetry as well as in music.

26. *Dean, Dennis Richard. "Geology and English Literature, 1770–1830." (Doctoral dissertation, Wisconsin, 1968.)

27. *Deguchi, Yasuo. "British Periodicals in the Early 19th Century," *Rising Generation*, CXIV (May 1968), 2pp. [In Japanese.]

28. *Deguchi, Yasuo. "A Study of British Periodicals in the Romantic Period," *Studies of Liberal Arts and Sciences* (Waseda Univ.), IV (March 1968), 8pp. [In Japanese.]

29. Fletcher, Ian, ed. *Romantic Mythologies*. See K-SJ, XVII (1968), 4.

Rev. by Graham Hough in Li, LXXVII, (22 June 1967), 827; in TLS, 26 Oct. 1967, p. 1011.

30. Fletcher, Richard M. *English Romantic Drama 1795–1843: A Critical History*. See K-SJ, XVII (1968), 4.

Rev. by Ralph Lawrence in *English*, XVI (Summer 1967), 196–197; in *Yale Review*, LVII (Winter 1968), xvi. Also see No. 21.

31. French, Richard. "Sir Walter Scott and His Literary Contemporaries," *CLA Journal*, XI (March 1968), 248–254.

Discusses Scott's opinions of the other major Romantic writers.

32. Frye, Northrop. *A Study of English Romanticism*. New York: Random House, 1968. "Studies in Language and Literature."

Treats the Romantic movement as

"primarily a change in the language of poetic mythology"; illustrates this thesis by critical discussions of Beddoes' *Death's Jest-Book*, Shelley's *Prometheus Unbound*, and Keats's *Endymion*.

33. Furst, Lilian R. "Romanticism in Historical Perspective," *Comparative Literature Studies*, v (June 1968), 115–143.

A "chronological survey of the emergence of the Romantic movements in England, France, and Germany."

34. Hayward, John, ed. *The Oxford Book of Nineteenth-Century English Verse*. See K-SJ, xv (1966), 144, xvi (1967), 116, xvii (1968), 4.

Rev. by Christopher Ricks in NS, lxviii (3 July 1964), 18–19.†

35. *Hough, Graham. *The Romantic Poets*. Third Edition. London: Hutchinson, 1967. "University Library, English Literature Series."

See K-SJ, iii (1954), 113, iv (1955), 111, vii (1958), 112.

36. *Hutchings, R. J. *Landfalls of the Romantic Poets*. Bath: James Brodie, 1966.

Advertised as a "delightful record of episodes in the lives of Byron, Coleridge, Keats, Shelley and Wordsworth."

37. Jack, Ian. *English Literature 1815–1832*. See K-SJ, xiv (1965), 107, xv (1966), 144, xvi (1967), 116, xvii (1968), 4.

Rev. by *Wanda Krajewska in *Kwartalnik Neofilologiczny*, No. 2 (1964), pp. 187–191; by Helmut Viebrock in ASNS, cciv (March 1968), 463–465.

38. Jennings, Elizabeth. *Christianity and Poetry*. London: Burns & Oates, 1965.

One chapter (pp. 75–91) is on "The Nineteenth Century."

39. *John, B. "The Changing Climate of Taste, as It Affects Literary Aims and Performances, 1815–1845." (Doctoral dissertation, Wales, Bangor, 1968.)

40. *Kolbuszewski, Stanisław. *Romantyzm i modernizm: Studia o literaturze i kulturze*. Katowice: Śląsk, 1959. [In Polish.]

A book on Romanticism and modernism which discusses Byron, Keats, and Shelley.

41. Kozloff, Max. "Art," *Nation*, ccvi (22 Apr. 1968), 549–550.

A review of an exhibition, "Romantic Art in Britain, 1760–1860," at the Philadelphia Museum.

42. Kumar, Shiv K., ed. *British Romantic Poets: Recent Revaluations*. See K-SJ, xvii (1968), 5.

Rev. by D[avid]. V. E[rdman]. in ELN, v, Supplement (Sept. 1967), 18.

43. *Larrabee, Stephen Addison. *English Bards and Grecian Marbles: The Relationship between Sculpture and Poetry, Especially in the Romantic Period*. Port Washington, N.Y.: Kennikat, 1964.

A reprint of a book first published in 1943.

44. Lentricchia, Frank. "Four Types of Nineteenth-Century Poetic," JAAC, xxvi (Spring 1968), 351–366.

One section is on "Romantic Theory: The Idealistic Imagination."

45. Linnér, Sven. "The Structure and Functions of Literary Comparisons," JAAC, xxvi (Winter 1967), 169–179.

Uses examples from Romantic criticism.

46. Locker, Malka. *Les Romantiques: Allemagne, Angleterre, France*. Paris: Presses du temps présent, 1964.

Includes sections on Byron (pp. 186–194), Shelley (pp. 195–204), and Keats (pp. 205–215).

Originally published in Yiddish (New York, 1958), as *Romantiker*.

47. Logan, James V., John E. Jordan, and Northrop Frye, eds. *Some British Romantics: A Collection of Essays*. See K-SJ, xvii (1968), 5.

Rev. by Lawrence H. Houtchens in ELN, v (Sept. 1967), 65–67; by R. W. King in MLR, lxiii (Jan. 1968), 206. Also see No. 21.

48. MacGillivray, J. R. "New Editors and Critics of the English Romantics," *University of Toronto Quarterly*, xxxvii (Apr. 1968), 309–320.

An omnibus review. See K-SJ, xv (1966), 169, No. 450, xvi (1967), 124, No. 177, 127, No. 223, 134, No. 347, 142, No. 475, xvii (1968), 30, No. 413, 41, No. 572, 42, No. 583. See also Nos. 265, 271, 369, 478, 530, 635, 639, 640, 651, and 681.

49. Mahoney, John L. "Imitation and the Quest for Objectivity in English Ro-

mantic Theory," in *Actes: Proceedings of the IVth Congress of the International Comparative Literature Association*, ed. François Jost (The Hague: Mouton, 1966), II, 774–780.

See Nos. 24 and 487.

50. *Mains, J. A. "British Travellers in Switzerland, with Special Reference to Some Women Travellers between 1750 and 1850." (Doctoral dissertation, Edinburgh, 1967.)

51. Malins, Edward. *English Landscaping and Literature 1660–1840*. See K-SJ, XVII (1968), 5.

Rev. by Walter J. Hipple, Jr., in JAAC, XXVI (Summer 1968), 549–550.

52. Marples, Morris. *Romantics at School.* New York: Barnes & Noble, 1967.

Includes chapters on "Byron at Harrow," "Shelley at Eton," and "Keats at Mr. Clarke's School, Enfield."

Rev. in TLS, 28 Dec. 1967, p. 1262; by Robert M. Adams in *New York Review of Books*, X (15 Feb. 1968), 25–27; in *Choice*, V (Apr. 1968), 196.

53. Marshall, William H., ed. *The Major English Romantics: An Anthology*. See K-SJ, XIV (1965), 108, XV (1966), 144, XVI (1967), 116, XVII (1968), 5.

Rev. by George A. Panichas in *Modern Age*, XI (Spring 1967), 216–220.

54. *Meller, Horst, *et al. British and American Classical Poems in Continuation of Herrig's "Classical Authors."* Braunschweig: Georg Westermann, 1966.

Rev. by Rudolf Haas in *Neueren Sprachen*, LXVII (May 1968), 261–262.

55. *Miles, Alfred Henry, *et al.*, eds. *The Poets and the Poetry of the Nineteenth Century*. Revised Edition. 12 vols. New York: AMS, 1968.

A reprint of a series first published in 1905–07.

56. O'Brien, Gordon W. "The Genius and the Mortal Instruments: Mind and Body and the Romantic Imagination," *Minnesota Review*, VI (1966), 316–352.†

The idea of a union of mind and body helped to shape "the world-picture of the Romantics."

57. *Ogawa, Kazuo. *English Poetry—Appreciation and Analysis.* Tokyo: Kenkyusha, 1968. [In Japanese.]

58. *The Oxford Companion to English Literature*. Ed. Sir Paul Harvey. Fourth Edition, Revised by Dorothy Eagle. Oxford: Clarendon, 1967.

Rev. in TLS, 30 Nov. 1967, p. 1168.

59. *Payne, William Morton. *The Greater English Poets of the Nineteenth Century.* Freeport, N.Y.: Books for Libraries, 1967. "Essay Index Reprint Series."

A reprint of a volume first published in 1907.

Includes Keats, Shelley, and Byron.

60. Price, Lawrence Marsden. *Die Aufnahme englischer Literatur in Deutschland 1500–1960*. See K-SJ, XIII (1964), 124.

Rev. by Ralph P. Rosenberg in CL, XIX (Fall 1967), 378–379.

61. Raine, Kathleen. "Thomas Taylor, Plato and the English Romantic Movement," *British Journal of Aesthetics*, VIII (Apr. 1968), 99–123.

Argues that a revival of Platonism was "the most powerful source of inspiration of the Romantic movement"; discusses Taylor's role in this revival. See No. 62.

62. Raine, Kathleen. "Thomas Taylor, Plato, and the English Romantic Movement," SR, LXXVI (Spring 1968), 230–257.

See No. 61.

63. *Read, Herbert. *The True Voice of Feeling: Studies in English Romantic Poetry.* London: Faber, 1968.

A paperback reprint of a book first published in 1953.

64. Riese, Teut Andreas, and Dieter Riesner, eds. *Versdichtung der englischen Romantik: Interpretationen*. Berlin: Erich Schmidt, 1968.

A collection of essays which includes the following: Horst Oppel, "Englische und deutsche Romantik: Gemeinsamkeiten und Unterschiede," pp. 25–44; Hans-Jürgen Diller, "George Noel Gordon, Lord Byron: *So We'll Go No More A-Roving*," pp. 251–262; Desmond King-Hele, "Percy Bysshe Shelley: *Ode to the West Wind*," pp. 263–268; Horst Meller, "Percy Bysshe Shelley: *The Cloud*," pp. 269–293; Roswith Riese-von Freydorf, "Die Gestalt des letzten Hirten—ein Selbstportrait Shelleys? (*Adonais* XXXI–XXXIV)," pp. 294–316; Neville Rogers, "Life, Thought and Effectuality: Shelley,

Goethe, and the Unnoticed Theme of *The Triumph of Life*," pp. 317–333; Dieter Riesner, "John Keats, Benjamin Robert Haydon und die Parthenonskulpturen: Freundschaftsadresse und Kunstanschauung in den 'Elgin-Marbles-Sonetten,'" pp. 334–367; Arno Esch, "John Keats: *Ode to a Nightingale*," pp. 368–382; Rudolf Sühnel, "John Keats: *Ode on a Grecian Urn*," pp. 383–413; Dorothy Hewlett, "Some Thoughts on *The Fall of Hyperion*," pp. 414–419; "Literatur zur englischen Romantik: Eine ausgewählte Bibliographie," pp. 440–448.

65. St. Clair, William. *Lord Elgin and the Marbles*. London: Oxford Univ., 1967.

Rev. by Peter Quennell in Spec, 7 July 1967, p. 18; in TLS, 13 July 1967, p. 620; by Sir Charles Petrie in ILN, CCLI (22 July 1967), 32–33; by Arnold de Montmorency in CR, CCXI (Aug. 1967), 110–111.

66. *Sampson, George. *Historia literatury angielskiej w zarysie: Podręcznik*. [Translated by] Piotr Graff. [Edited by] Irena Dobrzycka. Warsaw: Pánstw. Wydawn. Naukowe, 1966.

A Polish translation of *The Concise Cambridge History of English Literature*, Second Edition. See K-SJ, XIII (1964), 124, No. 70.

67. Schenk, H. G. *The Mind of the European Romantics: An Essay in Cultural History*. See K-SJ, XVII (1968), 6.

Rev. by Edith Lenel in *Library Journal*, XCIII (1 Jan. 1968), 74.

68. Smith, R. J. "Romanticism in English Poetry," *English Studies in Africa*, XI (March 1968), 11–33.

Discusses "common features" shared by writers of the period and demonstrates "what elements are suggested by the historical term 'Romanticism.'"

69. Stone, Peter William Kirby. *The Art of Poetry 1750–1820: Theories of Poetic Composition and Style in the Late Neo-Classic and Early Romantic Periods*. See K-SJ, XVII (1968), 6.

Rev. by H. W. Piper in *Southern Review* (Adelaide), III (1968), 191–193.

70. Stunkel, Kenneth Reagan. "Indian Ideas and Western Thought during the Romantic Age: A Critical Study" [Doctoral dissertation, Maryland, 1966], DA, XXVII (May 1967), 3799-A–3800-A.

71. Szenczi, Nicholas Joseph. "Reality and the English Romantics," HLQ, XXXI (Feb. 1968), 179–198.

The main concern of the Romantics was "to penetrate into the recesses of the human soul, to represent man in interrelation with external nature and with the forces that shape history." It was their intention to explore reality.

72. Talmon, J. L. *Romanticism and Revolt: Europe 1815–1848*. London: Thames and Hudson; New York: Harcourt (1967).

Rev. by George Lichtheim in NS, LXXIV (7 July 1967), 19; by Robert A. Kann in *Western Humanities Review*, XXII (Summer 1968), 273.

73. Thorlby, Anthony. *The Romantic Movement*. See K-SJ, XVII (1968), 6.

Rev. in TLS, 26 Oct. 1967, p. 1011.

74. *Vinge, Louise. *The Narcissus Theme in Western European Literature up to the Early Nineteenth Century*. Lund: Gleerup, 1967.

Rev. by Erich Köhler in *Romanische Forschungen*, LXXX (1968), 444–448.

75. Wali, Obiajunwa. "The Negro in English Literature with Special Reference to the Eighteenth and Early Nineteenth Centuries" [Doctoral dissertation, Northwestern, 1967], DA, XXVIII (March 1968), 3652-A.

76. Wellek, René. *A History of Modern Criticism*. Vol. III: *The Age of Transition*. Vol IV: *The Later Nineteenth Century*. See K-SJ, XVI (1967), 116, XVII (1968), 6–7.

Rev. by Richard Harter Fogle in *Criticism*, IX (Spring 1967), 197–199; by Edward Wasiolek in MP, LXV (Aug. 1967), 91–92; in TLS, 31 Aug. 1967, p. 782; by F. W. J. Hemmings in EC, XVIII (Jan. 1968), 78–86; by George Watson in RES, n.s., XIX (Feb. 1968), 96–98.

77. Whalley, George. "Literary Romanticism," QQ, LXXII (Summer 1965), 232–252.

"What is of first importance about good romantic poetry is not that it is 'romantic' but that it is in its own right poetry."

78. Wilkie, Brian. *Romantic Poets and Epic Tradition*. See K-SJ, XV (1966), 145, XVI (1967), 116–117, XVII (1968), 7.

Rev. by Michael N. Nagler in CL, XIX (Fall 1967), 380–381.

79. Williams, Stanley. "The Language of Poetry," TLS, 3 Aug. 1967, p. 707.

Finds Bateson's definition of romanticism "absurdly crude." See No. 19.

80. Wilshire, Bruce, comp. *Romanticism and Evolution: The Nineteenth Century*. New York: Putnam, 1968.

An anthology of selected texts, including Blake, Coleridge, and Wordsworth. Shelley and Keats are mentioned in the Introduction.

81. Winters, Yvor. *Forms in Discovery: Critical & Historical Essays on the Forms of the Short Poem in English*. [Chicago:] Alan Swallow, 1967.

The major Romantics are dealt with briefly and unsympathetically (pp. 160–180). Byron is dismissed. "The 'Indian Serenade' is Shelley at his worst, but most of Shelley is as bad or almost as bad." Keats is treated little better: " 'Ode to a Nightingale' is a mediocre poem with . . . some of the worst lines of the century."

Rev. by Graham Hough in NS, LXXV (5 Jan. 1968), 15–16; in TLS, 1 Feb. 1968, p. 106; by Denis Donoghue in *New York Review of Books*, X (29 Feb. 1968), 22–24; by Patrick Cruttwell in *Hudson Review*, XXI (Summer 1968), 413–416; by John Goode in PR, XXXV (Summer 1968), 462–466.

82. Wittreich, Joseph Anthony, Jr. "Milton, Man and Thinker: Apotheosis in Romantic Criticism," *Bucknell Review*, XVI (March 1968), 64–84.

Romantic criticism harmonized Milton as man, thinker, and poet; it also "preserved the sophistication and ambiguity" of his poetry.

II. BYRON

Works: Selected, Single, Translated

83. *The Age of the Grand Tour*. [With a Historical Introduction] by Anthony Burgess and an Appreciation of the Art of Europe in the Eighteenth Century by Francis Haskell. New York: Crown, 1967.

Includes selections from Hazlitt, Byron, and Shelley.

Rev. by John Canaday in NYT, 3 Dec. 1967, p. 62; in TLS, 8 Feb. 1968, p. 135.

84. *Ai to kodoku no heureki; Byron no tegami to nikki*. [*Works*.] [Translated by] Nakano Yoshio and Ogawa Kazuo. Tokyo: Kadokawa shoten, 1968. [In Japanese.]

85. Aloian, David. *Poems and Poets*. Foreword by John Crowe Ransom. New York: McGraw-Hill, 1965.

An anthology with some critical remarks on the poetry. Includes poems by Byron, Hunt, Keats, and Shelley.

86. **Antologia liryki angielskiej, 1300–1950*. [Edited and translated by] J. Pietrkiewicz. London: Veritas, 1958.

These bilingual texts (in English and Polish) include poems by Byron, Keats, and Shelley.

87. **Bairon Sijib, Nae Maeum Geunsime Jamgildae*. [*Poems*.] [Translated by] Dong-Il Lee. Seoul: Seongmunsa, 1965. [In Korean.]

88. **Byron shishu*. [*Poetical Works*.] [Translated by] Yoshida Shinichi. Tokyo: Mikasa-shobo, 1967. [In Japanese.]

89. **Byron shishu*. [*Poetical Works*.] [Translated by] Saito Shoji. Tokyo: Kadokawa-shoten, 1967. [In Japanese.]

90. **Byron shishu*. [*Poetical Works*.] [Translated by] Abe Tomoji. Tokyo: Shinchosha, 1968. [In Japanese.]

91. Cole, William. *A Book of Love Poems*. New York: Viking, 1965.

Includes selections from Byron, Clare, Keats, and Shelley.

92. Coleman, Elliott, ed. *Poems by Byron, Keats, and Shelley*. New York: Doubleday, 1968.

Rev. by James A. Phillips in *Library Journal*, XCIII (1 Apr. 1968), 1489.

93. *"Do autora sonetu," [translated by] J. Minkiewicz, *Kalendarz Szpilek* (1958), p. 30. [In Polish.]

"To the Author of a Sonnet."

94. **Don Juan*. [Translated by] A. Espina. Madrid: Mediterráneo, 1966. [In Spanish.]

95. **Evreiskie melodii: Stikhi*. [*Hebrew Melodies: Verses*.] [Translated by] G. Kairbekov. Alma-Ata: Dzhuzuti, 1965. [In Kazakh.]

96. *Evrej sazdary. [Hebrew Melodies.] [Translated by] Ğafu Qajyrbekov. Alma-Ata: Žazušy, 1966. [In Kazakh.]

97. Freedman, Morris, and Paul B. Davis. *Controversy in Literature: Fiction, Drama and Poetry with Related Criticism.* New York: Scribner's, 1968.

Includes selections from Byron, Keats, and Shelley.

98. **Giaur.* [*The Giaour.*] [Translated by] Adam Mickiewicz. Warsaw: P. I. W., 1952. [In Polish.]

99. **Izabrana dela.* [Translated by] Dušan Puvačić. Belgrade: Prosveta, 1968. [In Yugoslavian.]

100. Kelly, T. J. *The Focal Word: An Introduction to Poetry.* Brisbane: Jacaranda, 1966.

Reprints selections from Byron, Shelley, and Keats with accompanying critical remarks of a general nature.

101. Kroeber, Karl, and John O. Lyons. *Studying Poetry: A Critical Anthology of English and American Poems.* New York: Harper & Row, 1965.

Includes selections from Byron, Clare, Hood, Hunt, Keats, Peacock, and Shelley.

102. **Lirika.* [Translated by] Ljuben Ljubenov *et al.* Sofia: Nar. kultura, 1968. [In Bulgarian.]

103. **Lirika.* [Translated by] G. Šengeli *et al.* Moscow and Leningrad: Hudož. lit., 1967. [In Russian.]

104. *"Listy do W. Scotta . . . , H. Beyle . . . , A. Leigh," [translated by] B. Zieliński, *Świat*, No. 5 (1956), pp. 17–23. [In Polish.]

Letters by Byron to Scott, Stendhal, and Augusta Leigh.

105. Lucie-Smith, Edward, ed. *The Penguin Book of Satirical Verse.* [Harmondsworth:] Penguin, 1967.

Includes selections from *English Bards and Scotch Reviewers, The Vision of Judgment, Don Juan,* and "The Mask of Anarchy."

106. *Mickiewicz, Adam. *Dzieła poetyckie.* 2 vols. Warsaw: Czytelnik, 1964–65. [In Polish.]

These volumes of Mickiewicz's works include his translations of some of Byron's poems.

Payne, William Morton. See No. 59.

107. "The Poet and the World," K-SJ, XVII (1968), 112.

Two stanzas from *Childe Harold's Pilgrimage,* Canto III.

108. Simpson, Louis. *An Introduction to Poetry.* New York: St. Martin's, 1967.

Includes selections from Byron, Keats, and Shelley.

109. Stanford, Derek, ed. *The Body of Love: An Anthology of Erotic Verse from Chaucer to Lawrence.* London: Anthony Blond, 1965.

Includes verses from *Don Juan* and *The Revolt of Islam.*

110. Trilling, Lionel. *The Experience of Literature: A Reader with Commentaries.* Garden City, N.Y.: Doubleday, 1967.

Includes selections from Byron, Shelley, and Keats.

Rev. by Irvin Stock in CE, XXIX (Nov. 1967), 160–168.

111. *"Wędrówki Childe Harolda. Spójrz na to miejsce . . . Tu krzyż czerwony," [translated by] J. Kasprowicz, *Argumenty,* No. 2 (1957), p. 3. [In Polish.]

Two stanzas from *Childe Harold's Pilgrimage.*

112. **Wiersze i poematy.* [Translated by] Juliusz Żuławski. Warsaw: P. I. W., 1954. [In Polish.]

113. Wright, David, ed. *The Penguin Book of English Romantic Verse.* [Harmondsworth:] Penguin, 1968.

Includes poems by Peacock, Byron, Shelley, Clare, Keats, and Hood.

114. **Wybór poematów.* [Edited by] Władysław Brodzki. Wrocław: Ossolineum, 1964. [In Polish.]

See K-SJ, VIII (1959), 57, No. 96.

115. **Wybór poematów.* [Edited by] Władysław Brodzki. Wrocław: Ossolineum, 1966. [In Polish.]

The third edition. See No. 114.

116. **Wybór poematów.* Wrocław: Ossolineum, 1967. [In Polish.]

Books and Articles Relating to Byron and his Circle

117. Adams, Robert Martin. *Nil: Episodes in the Literary Conquest of Void during the Nineteenth Century.* See K-SJ, XVII (1968), 9.

Rev. by Louis Harap in *Science & Society*, XXXI (Summer 1967), 368–370; by Julian Moynahan in *New Republic*, CLVI (3 June 1967), 34–36; by Gita May in MP, LXV (Feb. 1968), 280–282.

118. *Andrić, Ivo. "Byron w Sintrze," [translated from Serbian by] Z. Stoberski, *Trybuna Robotnicza*, *Katowice*, No. 298 (1961), p. 6. [In Polish.]

"Byron at Sintra," a story. See No. 119.

119. *Andrić, Ivo. "Byron w Sintrze," [translated by] Z. Stoberski, *Głos Koszaliński*, No. 36 (1962), p. 6. [In Polish.]

See No. 118.

120. "Auction Sales," ABC, XVIII (Nov. 1967), 30.

Volume I of Dante's *La Divina Commedia*, with a 17-line inscription by Byron, brought $625 at Parke-Bernet.

121. *Babchina, T. "Liricheskie zarisovki i opisanie fona v drame Bairona *Kain*" ["The Lyric Sketches and Description of the Background of Byron's Drama *Cain*"], *Uchenye Zapiski* [*Scientific Notes: Latvian State University Philological Science Series*], LXXX (Riga, 1966), 115–145. [In Latvian, with a résumé in Russian.]

122. *Babchina, T. "Tretii akt drame Bairona *Kain* ve prervode Rainisa" ["The Third Act of Byron's Drama *Cain* in the Translation of Rajnis"], *Uchenye Zapiski* [*Scientific Notes: Latvian State University; A Collection of Works by the English Department*], LXXVII (Riga, 1966), 96–112. [In English.]

Ball, Patricia M. See No. 16.

123. *Berkovskii, N. "Lirika Bairona" ["Byron's Lyric Poetry"], *Voprosy Literatury*, No. 6 (1966), pp. 132–143. [In Russian.]

124. Bewley, Marius. "Good Manners," *New York Review of Books*, VIII (18 May 1967), 31–34.

A review article which compares a MacNeice poem with Keats's "To Autumn" and discusses influence of Byron on A. D. Hope.

125. [Beyle, Henri.] Stendhal, *pseud. Correspondance*. 3 vols. Ed. Henri Martineau and V. Del Litto. Paris: Gallimard, 1962–1968.

Includes letter to Byron, 23 June 1823 (II, 16–18) and one from Byron, 29 May 1823 (II, 779–780). Other references to Byron in all three volumes.

126. *Bishai, N. Z. "The Light Thrown on the Poetry of Blake, Byron and Tennyson by the Composers Who Have Set Its Words to Music." (Doctoral dissertation, London, 1968.)

Blainey, Ann. See No. 20.

127. Bo, Carlo. *La Religione di Serra: Saggi e note di lettura*. Florence: Vallecchi, 1967.

Includes essay "Byron e il secolo" (pp. 412–416).

Rev. by Mario Petrucciani in BA, XLII (Spring 1968), 249.

128. Borinski, Ludwig. *Der englische Roman des 18. Jahrhunderts*. Frankfurt am Main: Athenäum, 1968.

Mentions Byron.

129. Brooks, Elmer L. "Two Notes on Byron," N&Q, CCXII (Aug. 1967), 295–297.†

Notes that Byron's coming-of-age party was held at Newstead Abbey, even though he was in London, and that in 1814 he gave financial aid to the Royal Lancasterian Institution, enabling it to continue operations.

130. Brumbaugh, Thomas B. "A Landor Collection," *Library Chronicle* (Texas), VIII (Spring 1966), 23–27.

Contains an epigram on Byron's marriage as well as letters to Lady Blessington.

131. Buxton, John. *Byron and Shelley: A Friendship Renewed.* [Middletown, Conn.:] Wesleyan Univ., 1967. "Monday Evening Papers: Number 11."

132. Buxton, John. *Byron and Shelley: The History of a Friendship*. London: Macmillan; New York: Harcourt (1968).

Rev. in TLS, 30 May 1968, p. 549; in *Blackwood's Magazine*, CCCIII (June 1968), 565–566; by Mary Conroy in *The Times*, London, 15 June 1968, p. 20; by Naomi Lewis in NS, LXXV (28 June 1968), 874–875. See No. 172.

133. Byrne, Clifford M. "Byron's Cyclical Interpretation of History," *McNeese Review*, XVIII (1967), 11–26.

Suggests that Byron's cyclical views of natural processes and of history may be due to his philosophical dualism.

134. "Byron in the Abbey at Last," *The Times*, London, 6 May 1968, p. 8.

The Dean of Westminster is petitioned to allow a memorial plaque for Byron in the Abbey. See No. 135.

135. "Byron Memorial," *The Times*, London, 25 June 1968, p. 11.

The Dean approves the erection of a plaque to Byron in the Poet's Corner. See No. 134.

136. "A Byron Poem for £13,500: MS. with Many Revisions," *The Times*, London, 10 Apr. 1968, p. 12.

First draft of "The Prisoner of Chillon" auctioned at Sotheby's: "22 pages, written on both sides of 11 leaves, in a flaring handwriting with many revisions." Also sold was an A.L.S. from Byron to Count Alborghetti, protesting an insult offered Shelley by the Archbishop of Ravenna in 1821.

137. Cano, José Luis. *El escritor y su aventura.* Barcelona: Plaza & Janes, 1966.

Includes "Recuerdos de Shelley y Byron" (pp. 203–209), "Byron y Teresa Guiccioli" (pp. 211–215), "Keats y España" (pp. 217–229), and "Keats y Fanny Brawne" (pp. 231–241).

138. Carter, Ernest John. "Byron's Historical Imagination: The Poetry of Byron Seen in Relation to Pessimistic Attitudes in Eighteenth-Century History" [Doctoral dissertation, Claremont, 1966], DA, XXVIII (Oct. 1967), 1389-A–1390-A.

139. *Caruthers, Clifford Mack. "A Critical Study of the Plays of Lord Byron." (Doctoral dissertation, Missouri, Columbia, 1968.)

140. Cate, Hollis L. "Emily Dickinson and 'The Prisoner of Chillon,'" *American Notes & Queries*, VI (Sept. 1967), 6–7.

She mentions the poem four times in her letters but does not refer to any other Byron poem.

141. *Chłędowski, Kazimierz. "Lord Byron we Włoszech" ["Lord Byron in Italy"], in *Rokoko we Włoszech* (Warsaw, 1959), pp. 410–458.

142. *Christensen, Allan Conrad. "Heroism in the Age of Reform: Byron, Goethe, and the Novels of Carlyle." (Doctoral dissertation, Princeton, 1968.)

143. Ciampini, Raffaele. *Il primo amante di Teresa Guiccioli.* See K-SJ, XV (1966), 148.

Rev. by T. J. B. Spencer in MLR, LXIII (Apr. 1968), 464.

144. Clark, Alexander P. "Belles Lettres," *Manuscripts*, XX (Winter 1968), 41–44.

Discusses exhibition at the Grolier Club (18 Oct.–10 Dec. 1967) of authorial proof corrections, including an example of Byron's.

145. Clark, Peter. "Henry Hallam Reconsidered," *Quarterly Review*, CCCV (Oct. 1967), 410–419.

Mentions Byron's sarcasm in *English Bards and Scotch Reviewers* and Hallam's publisher, John Murray.

146. Cline, C. L. "Sacrilege at Lucca and the Pisan Circle," *Texas Studies in Literature and Language*, IX (Winter 1968), 503–509.

Recounts the incident of sacrilege in the Church of San Michele in Lucca and the excitement it created in the Byron-Shelley circle at Pisa.

147. Coblentz, Stanton A. *The Poetry Circus.* New York: Hawthorn, 1967.

Makes critical comments on Byron, Keats, and Shelley.

148. Cooke, Michael G. "The Limits of Skepticism: The Byronic Affirmation," K-SJ, XVII (1968), 97–111.

Between skepticism and religion a third option appears: "the peculiar form of humanism and stoicism that may be called counter-heroic."

149. Cooney, Seamus. "Satire without Dogma: Byron's *Don Juan*," *Ball State University Forum*, IX (Spring 1968), 26–30.

150. Culler, A. Dwight. *Imaginative Reason: The Poetry of Matthew Arnold.* New Haven: Yale Univ., 1966.

Has numerous references to Byron, Keats, and Shelley.

Rev. by Robert Langbaum in JEGP, LXVI (July 1967), 470–473; by Robert Alan Donovan in MP, LXV (May 1968), 417–419.

151. Cunningham, Gilbert F. *The Divine Comedy in English: A Critical Bibliography.* See K-SJ, XVII (1968), 10–11.

Rev. in TLS, 21 Dec. 1967, p. 1237.

152. de Ford, Miriam Allen. *Thomas Moore.* See K-SJ, XVII (1968), 11.

Rev. in *Choice*, V (March 1968), 48.

153. Demetz, Peter. *Marx, Engels, and the Poets: Origins of Marxist Literary Criticism.* Trans. Jeffrey L. Sammons. Chicago: Univ. of Chicago, 1967.

Has a few references to Byron and Shelley.

154. *Diakonova, N. Ia. "Russkii epizod ve poeme Bairona *Don-Zhuan*" ["A Russian Episode in Byron's Poem *Don Juan*"], in *Russo-evropeiskie literaturnye sviazi: sbornik statei k 70. letiiu so dnia rozhdeniia akademika M. P. Alekseeva* [*Russian-European Literary Ties: A Collection of Articles Commemorating the Seventieth Birthday of Academician M. P. Alekseyev*], ed. Akademia nauk SSSR. Institut russkoi literatury (Moscow and Leningrad: Nauka, 1966), pp. 256–263.

155. Dobrzycka, Irena. "Byron and Ireland," in *Studies in Language and Literature in Honour of Margaret Schlauch*, ed. Mieczsław Brahmer *et al.* (Warsaw: Państwowe Wydawnictwo Naukowe, 1966), pp. 95–102.

Discusses Byron's interest in Ireland as an "oppressed and rebelling" nation.

156. *Dobrzycka, Irena. *Kształtowanie się twórczości Byrona. Bohater bajroniczny a zagadnienie narodowe.* Wrocław: Zakład Narodowy im. Ossolińskich, 1963.

Two main motifs in Byron's early poetry (the Byronic hero and the struggle of nations for freedom), with a bibliography and an English summary.

157. *Dobrzycka, Irena. "Listy i pamiętniki G. G. Byrona," *Języki Obce w Szkole*, No. 4 (1958), pp. 204–207.

Discusses Byron's letters and journals.

158. Dörken, Hildegard. *Lord Byron's Subjektivismus in seinem Verhalten zur Geschichte: Untersucht an seinem Verserzählungen.* New York: Johnson Reprint, 1967.

A reprint of a book first published in 1929.

159. Doherty, Francis. "An Unpublished Letter of Lady Caroline Lamb to Clare," N&Q, CCXII (Aug. 1967), 297–299.†

The letter, probably written in Dec. 1812 or Jan. 1813, is in the Archives of the University of Keele.

160. **Don Juan* [staged in Teatr Rapsodyczny in Kraków in 1958].

Rev. by *O. Jędrzejczyk in *Gazeta Krakowska*, No. 68 (1958), p. 3; by *T. Kudliński in *Tygodnik Powszechny*, No. 13 (1958), p. 5; by *H. Vogler in *Dziennik Polski*, No. 73 (1958), p. 3; by *J. Zagórski in *Kurier Polski*, No. 102 (1958), p. 4; in **Program Teatru Rapsodycznego*, Kraków (1957–58).

161. **Don Juan* [staged in Leningradzki Teatr Komedii].

Rev. by *Eugeniusz Żytomirski in *Teatr*, No. 1 (1964), p. 11.

162. "The Don Juan Story," *Prairie Schooner*, XXXIX (Summer 1965), 176–185.

A review by Bruce Cutler of Oscar Mandel's *The Theatre of Don Juan*, followed by comments by Mandel, Boyd Carter, James Roberts, and Louis Crompton.

163. Dunn, John Joseph. "The Role of MacPherson's Ossian in the Development of British Romanticism" [Doctoral dissertation, Duke, 1966], DA, XXVII (Aug. 1966), 454-A–455-A.

Byron and Hazlitt were among the Romantics who admired Ossian.

164. Ehrstine, John W. "An Analysis of Byron's Plays" [Doctoral dissertation, Wayne State, 1964], DA, XXVIII (May 1968), 4596-A.

165. *Elektorowicz, L. "Losy pamiętnika G. G. Byrona," *Dziennik Polski Kraków*, No. 302 (1959), p. 7.

The fate of Byron's journal.

166. Ellis, Amanda M. *Rebels and Conservatives: Dorothy and William Wordsworth and Their Circle.* Bloomington: Indiana Univ., 1967.

Byron, Godwin, Hazlitt, Hunt, Keats, the Shelleys, and others appear.

167. Elwin, Malcolm. [In] "Letters to the Editor," TLS, 4 Apr. 1968, p. 357.

Reply to TLS review of *The Noels and the Milbankes*. See No. 168.

168. Elwin, Malcolm. *The Noels and the Milbankes: Their Letters for Twenty-Five Years 1767–1792.* London: Macdonald, 1967.

Rev. in TLS, 21 March 1968, p. 298. See No. 167.

169. Escarpit, Robert. *Byron: Etude sur l'écrivain. Choix de textes de George Byron.* See K-SJ, XVI (1967), 119.

Rev. by Sylvère Monod in EA, xx (July–Sept. 1967), 313.

170. Escarpit, Robert. *L'Humour.* Paris: Presses Universitaires de France, 1963.
Briefly discusses Byron as the successor to Sterne in the art of humorous digression.

171. Eskin, Stanley G. "Revolution and Poetry: Some Political Patterns in the Romantic Tradition and After," *CLA Journal,* xi (March 1968), 189–205.
Discusses the revolutionary impulse in Shelley and Byron.

172. "First Meeting of Two Poets," *The Times,* London, 23 March 1968, p. 17.
Excerpts from John Buxton's book, *Byron and Shelley: The History of a Friendship.* See No. 132.

173. Fuess, Claude M. *Lord Byron as a Satirist in Verse.* See K-SJ, xv (1966), 149.
Rev. in *Choice,* ii (Apr. 1965), 92.

174. Fulford, Roger. *Samuel Whitbread 1764–1815: A Study in Opposition.* London: Macmillan, 1967.
Has passing references to Byron.
Rev. in TLS, 8 June 1967, p. 513.

Gál, István. See No. 580.

175. Garber, Frederick. "Self, Society, Value, and the Romantic Hero," CL, xix (Fall 1967), 321–333.
Discusses, among others, Byron's and Shelley's heroes.

176. Gardner, Helen. *T. S. Eliot and the English Poetic Tradition.* Byron Foundation Lecture 1965. [Nottingham: Univ. of Nottingham, 1965.]
Pays brief tribute to "the genius of Byron."

177. George, M. Dorothy. *Hogarth to Cruikshank: Social Change in Graphic Satire.* New York: Walker, 1967.
Includes references to Byron, Haydon, Hunt, and others.

178. Gleckner, Robert F. *Byron and the Ruins of Paradise.* Baltimore: Johns Hopkins Univ., 1967.
Rev. in *Yale Review,* lvii (Spring 1968), xxxi-xxxii; by Richard Freedman in *Kenyon Review,* xxx (No. 2, 1968), 299–302; by G. M. Matthews in *New York Review of Books,* x (23 May 1968), 23–28.

179. Grant, Judith. *A Pillage of Art.* London: Robert Hale, 1966.
Includes a chapter on the Elgin Marbles (pp. 102–117); refers in this chapter and elsewhere to Byron.

Green, David Bonnell. See No. 408.

180. Gunn, Peter. *My Dearest Augusta: A Biography of Augusta Leigh, Lord Byron's Half-Sister.* New York: Atheneum, 1968.
Rev. by Mary Conroy, *The Times,* London, 15 June 1968, p. 20; by Naomi Lewis in NS, lxxv (28 June 1968), 874–875.

181. Haakonsen, Daniel. *Henrik Ibsens "Peer Gynt."* Oslo: Gyldendal, 1967.
Emphasizes the scene with the strange passenger, maintaining that the passenger is Byron.

182. Hagelman, Charles W., Jr., and Robert J. Barnes, eds. *A Concordance to Byron's "Don Juan."* See K-SJ, xvii (1968), 12.
Rev. by Leslie A. Marchand in K-SJ, xvii (1968), 132–133; in TLS, 25 Apr. 1968, p. 442; in *English,* xvii (Summer 1968), 74.

183. Hamer, Douglas. "Conversation-Notes with Sir Thomas Dyke Acland," N&Q, ccxii (Feb. 1967), 65–66.†
Mentions 1829 debate in Oxford Union on *Shelley v. Byron.*

184. Harding, Walter. *Emerson's Library.* Charlottesville: Univ. of Virginia, 1967.
The library included works by or about Byron, Haydon, Hazlitt, Hunt, Keats, Mary Shelley, and Shelley.

185. *Herdegen, Leszek. "Byron nieznany," *Przekrój,* No. 476 (1954), pp. 9–10.
Byron the Unknown.

186. *Herdegen, Leszek. "Poeta nie tylko miłości i śmierci," *Echo Tygodnia,* No. 4 (1955), p. 1.
The poet not only of love and death.

187. Hibbard, G. R., ed. *Renaissance and Modern Essays.* See K-SJ, xvii (1968), 16, No. 208.
Rev. in *Choice,* iv (July-Aug. 1967), 528.

188. *Hijikawa, Akira. "Lord Byron and the Spirit of Freedom," *Bulletin* (Tamagawa Univ.), viii (Jan. 1968), 43–52. [In Japanese.]

189. Hirsch, E. D., Jr. *Validity in Interpretation.* New Haven: Yale Univ., 1967.

In a chapter on "The Concept of Genre" includes discussion of Byron.

190. Holcomb, Adele Mansfield. "J. M. W. Turner's Illustrations to the Poets" [Doctoral dissertation, California, Los Angeles, 1966], DA, XXVIII (July 1967), 164-A.

Considers Turner's illustration of Byron.

191. Holloway, John. *Widening Horizons in English Verse*. See K-SJ, XVII (1968), 12.

Rev. by Graham Martin in Li, LXXVI (25 Aug. 1966), 282.

192. Howard, John Douglas, Jr. "The Child-Hero in the Poetry of Blake, Shelley, Byron, Coleridge, and Wordsworth" [Doctoral dissertation, Maryland, 1967], DA, XXVIII (Jan. 1968), 2647-A.

193. Hudson, Derek. *Holland House in Kensington*. London: Peter Davies, 1967.

Chapter 7, "Bards and Reviewers," has material on Byron; Chapter 12, "Byron's 'Halting Angel,'" is about Henry Fox, 4th Baron Holland.

Rev. in TLS, 12 Oct. 1967, p. 965.

194. Hume, Robert D. "The Non-Augustan Nature of Byron's Early 'Satires,'" *Revue des langues vivantes*, XXXIV (1968), 495–503.

Denies that Byron ever experienced a period of "early neo-classicism" and suggests why his early work is not discussable in terms of Augustan aims and methods.

Hutchings, R. J. See No. 36.

195. *Jabłkowska, Róża. "Literatura angielska," *Rocznik Literacki* (1958–60), pp. 379–398.

Discusses a Polish edition of the letters and journals of Byron.

196. *Jabłkowska, Róża. "Literatura angielska," *Rocznik Literacki* (1961), pp. 298–314.

Discusses Polish editions of the poems of Byron and selected poems of Shelley.

197. Jansse, Lucien. "Stendhal et la Constitution anglaise," *Stendhal Club*, IX (15 July 1967), 327–348.

Discusses Stendhal's meeting with Hobhouse; mentions Byron.

198. *Jarosz, Irena. "O Angliku, który walczył o wolność Grecji. W 128 rocznicę śmierci Byrona," *Słowo Tygodnia*, No. 8 (1952), p. 2.

"An Englishman who fought for the freedom of Greece: on the 128th anniversary of Byron's death."

199. Joshi, P. C. "Subjectivism in the Nineteenth-Century Poetic Drama," *Literary Criterion*, VIII (Winter 1967), 9–18.

Mentions Byron, Keats, and Shelley.

200. *Jump, John D. *Byron's Don Juan: Poem or Hold-All?* The W. D. Thomas Memorial Lecture Delivered at the University College of Swansea on 6 Feb. 1968. Swansea: Univ. College of Swansea, 1968.

201. Jump, John D. "Byron's Letters," *Essays and Studies*, XXI (1968), 62–79.

His letters, like his *ottava rima* poems, express "a zest for life which is conditioned but not inhibited by a sober sense of what life really is."

202. Jump, John D. "Literary Echoes in Byron's 'Don Juan,'" N&Q, CCXII (Aug. 1967), 302.†

Echoes from Milton, Shakespeare, and Smollett.

Jump, John D., ed. See No. 314.

203. Keenan, Hugh T. "Another 'Hudibras' Allusion in Byron's 'Don Juan,'" N&Q, CCXII (Aug. 1967), 301–302.†

An allusion from the first canto of *Hudibras* in *Don Juan*, VIII, 1103–12.

204. Kemper, Claudette. "Irony Anew, with Occasional Reference to Byron and Browning," SEL, VII (Autumn 1967), 705–719.†

An attempt to establish some general principles about irony. *Don Juan* is quoted.

205. Kenyon, F. W. *The Absorbing Fire: The Byron Legend*. See K-SJ, XVII (1968), 13.

Rev. by Judith Worthy in *Books and Bookmen*, XI (Apr. 1966), 35.

206. Kernan, Alvin B. *The Plot of Satire*. See K-SJ, XVI (1967), 120, XVII (1968), 13.

Rev. by Lilla A. Heston in *Quarterly Journal of Speech*, LIII (Apr. 1967), 197; by D[avid]. V. E[rdman]. in ELN, V, Supplement (Sept. 1967), 25; by P. K. Elkin in AUMLA, No. 28 (Nov. 1967), pp. 248–249.

Kloos, Willem. See No. 600.

207. Knight, G. Wilson. *Byron and Shakespeare*. See K-SJ, XVII (1968), 13.

Rev. in *The Times*, London, 10 Nov.

1966, p. 14; by John D. Jump in *Critical Quarterly*, IX (Spring 1967), 93–94; by Tom Cain in *Cambridge Review*, LXXXIX (20 May 1967), 354–356†; in *Choice*, IV (July-Aug. 1967), 532; by Frederick T. Wood in ES, XLVIII (Aug. 1967), 366; by D[avid]. V. E[rdman]. in ELN, V, Supplement (Sept. 1967), 25. Also see No. 21.

208. Knight, G. Wilson. *Gold-Dust with Other Poetry*. New York: Barnes & Noble, 1968.

Includes (p. 57) a poem called "Chillon Castle."

209. *Knight, G. Wilson. *Lord Byron: Christian Virtues*. New York: Barnes & Noble, 1967.

A reprint of a book first published in 1953. See K-SJ, III (1954), 116, IV (1955), 115–116, V (1956), 123.

210. Knight, G. Wilson. *Poets of Action, Incorporating Essays from "The Burning Oracle."* London: Methuen, 1967.

Includes "Byron: the Poetry" (pp. 179–265), from *The Burning Oracle*, and "Byron's Dramatic Prose" (pp. 266–293), Byron Foundation Lecture 1953 [see K-SJ, IV (1955), 115, No. 102].

Rev. in *English*, XVII (Summer 1968), 73.

211. Knight, G. Wilson. *Shakespeare and Religion: Essays of Forty Years*. London: Routledge, 1967.

Makes frequent reference to Byron and his works.

Kolbuszewski, Stanisław. See No. 40.

212. *Kovalskaia, M. I. "Byron i karbonarskoe dvizhenie" ["Byron and the Carbonari Movement"], *Voprosy istorii*, No. 11 (1966), pp. 213–217. [In Russian.]

213. *Lapidus, N. "Bairon v Vitebske" ["Byron in Vitebsk"], *Belarus*, XXIII, No. 8 (1966), pp. 31ff. [In Belorussian.]

Discusses *Pushkin's Relationship to Byron* by N. D. Tikomirov (Vitebsk, 1899).

214. Lauber, John. "Byron's Concept of Poetry," *Dalhousie Review*, XLVII (Winter 1967–68), 526–534.

For Byron the highest quality of poetry was truth. He thus distrusted the imagination and was suspicious of "systematic thought."

215. Lawrence, D. H. *Phoenix II: Uncollected, Unpublished, and Other Prose Works*. Ed. Warren Roberts and Harry T. Moore. New York: Viking, 1968.

Has brief observations on Byron, Keats, and Shelley.

216. Leppmann, Wolfgang. *Pompeji: Eine Stadt in Literatur und Leben*. Munich: Nymphenburger, 1966.

One chapter, "Die Romantiker" (pp. 117–168), has discussion of Shelley and Byron.

Rev. by Peter Gontrum in CL, XIX (Fall 1967), 369–373.

217. Liebert, Herman W. "The Beinecke Library: Recent Acquisitions," *Yale University Library Gazette*, XLII (Apr. 1968), 171–210.

Comments on Lovelace's *Lady Noel Byron and the Leighs* (1887), a copy of which is now at Yale; reports the acquisition of several valuable Shelley items.

218. Lill, James. "Because It Is There," *Texas Quarterly*, X (Summer 1967), 215–228.

A general survey of the literary image of the mountain, including descriptions by Byron and Shelley.

219. Lim, Pauline Marquez, Jr. "The Style of Byron's Plays" [Doctoral dissertation, California, Los Angeles, 1967], DA, XXVIII (March 1968), 3641-A–3642-A.

Locker, Malka. See No. 46.

220. McDonald, Eva. *Lord Byron's First Love*. London: Robert Hale, 1968.

A novel about Lady Caroline Lamb.

221. McDowell, Robert E. "Tirso, Byron, and the Don Juan Tradition," *Arlington Quarterly*, I (Autumn 1967), 52–68.

Byron did more than take liberties with the tradition; he wrote an "allegory of the self."

222. McGann, Jerome J. "Byron, Teresa, and *Sardanapalus*," KSMB, XVIII (1967), 7–22.

Finds resemblances between Teresa Guiccioli and Myrrha, who, he asserts, is one of Byron's finest female characters because "she lives an independent life in the world of the play."

223. McGann, Jerome. "The Composition, Revision, and Meaning of *Childe Harold's Pilgrimage III*," BNYPL, LXXI (Sept. 1967), 415–430.

224. *Mackiewicz, Stanisław. "Początki ro-

mantyzmu," *Kierunki*, No. 25 (1960), p. 9. [In Polish.]

The beginnings of Romanticism, with facts from Byron's life.

225. Madden, William A. *Matthew Arnold: A Study of the Aesthetic Temperament in Victorian England*. Bloomington: Indiana Univ., 1967.

Has references to Byron, Keats, and Shelley.

Rev. in TLS, 9 Nov. 1967, p. 1058.

226. Marchand, Leslie A. *Byron's Poetry: A Critical Introduction*. See K-SJ, XVI (1967), 121, XVII (1968), 14.

Rev. by Andrew Rutherford in *Cambridge Review*, LXXXIX (4 Feb. 1967), 201; by Frederick T. Wood in ES, XLVIII (Aug. 1967), 366.

227. Mariels, Raymond P. "The Grotesque in Byron's Poetry" [Doctoral dissertation, Oregon, 1967], DA, XXVIII (March 1968), 3643-A–3644-A.

Marples, Morris. See No. 52.

228. Marshall, William H. "The Catalogue for the Sale of Byron's Books," *Library Chronicle* (University of Pennsylvania), XXXIV (Winter 1968), 24–50.

An annotated copy of a catalogue printed by the auctioneer who handled the sale of Byron's books in 1816.

229. Marshall, William H. *The World of the Victorian Novel*. South Brunswick, N.J.: A. S. Barnes, 1967.

Mentions Byron, Hunt, Keats, and Shelley.

Rev. in TLS, 1 Feb. 1968, p. 110.

230. Maxwell, J. C. " 'Academician,' " N&Q, CCXII (Aug. 1967), 303.†

As used in *Don Juan*, ix, 17, it means the same thing as the O.E.D.'s *academist*, "An Academic philosopher; a sceptic."

231. Maxwell, J. C. "More Literary Echoes in 'Don Juan,' " N&Q, CCXII (Aug. 1967), 302–303.†

Echoes from Pope, Goldsmith, *Macbeth*, and Cicero.

232. Medwin, Thomas. *Medwin's "Conversations of Lord Byron."* Ed. Ernest J. Lovell, Jr. See K-SJ, XVI (1967), 121–122, XVII (1968), 15.

Rev. by Muriel J. Mellown in SAQ, LXVI (Spring 1967), 284; by E. E. B[ostetter]. in ELN, v, Supplement (Sept. 1967), 25–26.

233. *Mellown, M. J. "The Development of Lord Byron's Literary Criticism and of the Literary Attitudes Revealed in His Poetry and Prose." (Doctoral dissertation, London, 1965.)

234. Michaels, Leonard. "Hail, Muse! *Et cetera.*—An Essay on Narrative Pattern, Costume, and the Idea of the Self in Byron's *Cain* and His Tales" [Doctoral dissertation, Michigan, 1967], DA, XXVIII (Jan. 1968), 2651-A.

235. Miles, Josephine. *Style and Proportion: The Language of Prose and Poetry*. Boston: Little, Brown, 1967.

Byron, Shelley, Keats, Godwin, and Hazlitt are all included in this study.

236. Miller, Arthur McA. "The Last Man: A Study of the Eschatological Theme in English Poetry and Fiction from 1806 through 1839" [Doctoral dissertation, Duke, 1966], DA, XXVIII (Aug. 1967), 687-A.

Discusses works by Byron, Shelley, Mary Shelley, Hood, and others.

237. Moore, Doris Langley. *The Late Lord Byron: Posthumous Dramas*. See K-SJ, XII (1963), 130–131, XIII (1964), 131, XIV (1965), 113, XVI (1967), 122.

Rev. by *A. Baranowska in *Twórczość*, No. 10 (1962), pp. 160–161.

238. Moreau, Pierre. "Le mythe de Don Juan. IV. Don Juan et le donjuanisme dans la poésie et dans le roman: de Byron à Barrès," *Annales: Revue mensuelle des lettres françaises*, LXXIII (Oct. 1966), 28–36.

Briefly discusses Byron's use of the legend.

239. *Mortenson, Robert. "Byron's Letter to Murray on 'Cain,' " *Library Chronicle*, XXXIV (Spring 1968), 94–99.

240. Mortenson, Robert. [In] "Information, Please," TLS, 29 Feb. 1968, p. 212.

Asks for information about *Cain*.

241. Mras, George P. *Eugène Delacroix's Theory of Art*. Princeton: Princeton Univ., 1966.

Refers to Delacroix's use of Byron's poetry.

242. "News & Comment," BC, XV (Winter 1966), 461–483.

First editions of Keats announced for

sale by Thomas Crowe (p. 469); a copy of Byron's *Sardanapalus* with Beckford's notes sold at Sotheby's for £380. See K-SJ, XVII (1968), 18–19, No. 251.

243. "News & Comment," BC, XVI (Spring 1967), 55–79.

Rhododaphne and "a long run of Byron" sold at Hodgson's 8 Dec. 1966 (pp. 58–59).

244. Nurmi, Martin K. "The Prompt Copy of Charles Kean's 1838 Production of Byron's *Sardanapalus*," *Serif*, V (June 1968), 3–13.

Description of the various deletions and changes made in the prompt copy used for Kean's first production of the play in 1838.

245. *Obrzud, Zdzisław. "Byron dzisiaj: 19 kwietnia 1824–19 kwietnia 1952," *Świat i Życie*, No. 17 (1952), p. 1. [In Polish.]

"Byron Today, 19 April 1824–19 April 1952."

246. Orel, Harold. *The Development of William Butler Yeats: 1885–1900.* University of Kansas Publications, Humanistic Studies No. 39. Lawrence: Univ. of Kansas, 1968.

Mentions Byron, Keats, and Shelley.

247. *Ostrowski, Witold. "Powieść poetycka: Materiały do 'Słownika rodzajów literackich,'" *Zagadnienia Rodzajów Literackich*, VII (1964). [In Polish.]

Discusses the English origins and development of the genre of the poetic tale popularized by Scott and Byron.

Owen, Wilfred. See No. 469.

248. Paananen, Victor Niles. "Byron and Browning: The Aesthetics of Skepticism" [Doctoral dissertation, Wisconsin, 1967], DA, XXVIII (Aug. 1967), 639-A–640-A.

249. Partridge, Monica. "Slavonic Themes in English Poetry of the 19th Century," *Slavonic and East European Review*, XLI (June 1963), 420–441.†

Hunt, Keats, Moore, and Byron are among the English poets considered.

250. Praz, Mario. *Cronache Letterarie Anglosassoni.* Vols. III and IV. Rome: Edizioni di storia e letteratura, 1966.

Includes essays on Byron, Shelley, Keats, and the Romantics generally.

Rev. in TLS, 23 Nov. 1967, p. 1117.

251. Prokosch, Frederic. *The Missolonghi Manuscript.* New York: Farrar, Straus & Giroux; London: W. H. Allen (1968).

A novel about Byron.

Rev. by Harry T. Moore in SatR, LI (13 Jan. 1968), 82; by Iris Origo in NYT, 14 Jan. 1968, pp. 5, 38; by Phoebe Adams in *Atlantic*, CCXXI (Feb. 1968), 142–143; by G. M. Matthews in *New York Review of Books*, X (23 May 1968), 23–28; in TLS, 30 May 1968, p. 549; by J. A. Cuddon in *Books and Bookmen*, XIII (June 1968), 33–34; by Mary Conroy in *The Times*, London, 15 June 1968, p. 20; by Naomi Lewis in NS, LXXV (28 June 1968), 874–875.

252. Quennell, Peter. *Alexander Pope: The Education of Genius 1688–1728.* London: Weidenfeld and Nicolson, 1968.

Mentions Byron and Hazlitt.

253. Quennell, Peter. *Byron: The Years of Fame.* See K-SJ, XVII (1968), 16.

Rev. in *Choice*, IV (Oct. 1967), 834.

254. Reed, Joseph W., Jr. *English Biography in the Early Nineteenth Century, 1801–1838.* See K-SJ, XVI (1967), 123, XVII (1968), 16.

Rev. by Frederick T. Wood in ES, XLVIII (Aug. 1967), 363; by D[avid]. V. E[rdman]. in ELN, V, Supplement (Sept. 1967), 19; by Derek Roper in N&Q, CCXIII (May 1968), 200.

Riese, Teut Andreas, and Dieter Riesner, eds. See No. 64.

255. *Robinson, Charles E. "The Frustrated Dialectic of Byron and Shelley: Their Reciprocal Influences." (Doctoral dissertation, Temple, 1967.)

256. Robinson, Henry Crabb. *The Diary of Henry Crabb Robinson: An Abridgment.* See K-SJ, XVII (1968), 17.

Rev. in *Quarterly Review*, CCCV (Apr. 1967), 231–232.

257. Robinson, Henry Crabb. *The London Theatre 1811–1866: Selections from the Diary of Henry Crabb Robinson.* Ed. Eluned Brown. London: Society for Theatre Research, 1966.

Has references to Byron, Godwin, Hazlitt, and Hunt.

258. Robson, W. W. *Critical Essays.* See K-SJ, XVII (1968), 17.

Rev. by David H. Rawlinson in *Cam-*

bridge Quarterly, II (Autumn 1967), 403–413; by A. D. Nuttall in *Critical Quarterly*, IX (Winter 1967), 383–384; by David G. Halliburton in JAAC, XXVI (Spring 1968), 410.

Rogers, Neville. See No. 484.

259. Roston, Murray. *Biblical Drama in England: From the Middle Ages to the Present Day*. Evanston: Northwestern Univ., 1968.
Includes a section on "Byron's 'Cain' and 'Heaven and Earth' " (pp. 198–215).

260. Roston, Murray. *Prophet and Poet: The Bible and the Growth of Romanticism*. See K-SJ, XVI (1967), 123, XVII (1968), 17.
Rev. by Abraham Avni in *Comparative Literature Studies*, III (Dec. 1966), 468–470.

261. Rothenberg, Jacob. " 'Descensus ad Terram': The Acquisition and Reception of the Elgin Marbles" [Doctoral dissertation, Columbia, 1967], DA, XXVIII (Jan. 1968), 2611-A–2612-A.
Discusses roles played in controversy by Haydon and Byron.

262. Saagpakk, Paul F. "A Survey of Psychopathology in British Literature from Shakespeare to Hardy," *Literature and Psychology*, XVIII (1968), 135–165.
Includes discussion of Godwin, Byron, and the Byronic hero.

263. *Santucho, Oscar José. "A Comprehensive Bibliography of Secondary Materials in English: George Gordon, Lord Byron." (Doctoral dissertation, Baylor, 1968.)

264. *Sawrymowicz, E. [In] *Pamiętnik Biblioteki Kórnickiej*, VI, No. 14 (1958), p. 5.
Quotes from Mickiewicz's translation of *The Giaour*.

Schulz, H. C. See No. 9.

265. Schulz, Max F. *The Poetic Voices of Coleridge: A Study of His Desire for Spontaneity and Passion for Order*. Detroit: Wayne State Univ., 1963.
Has references to Byron, Hunt, Keats, and Shelley.
See No. 48.

266. Sheridan, Richard Brinsley. *The Letters of Richard Brinsley Sheridan*. Ed. Cecil Price. 3 vols. Oxford: Clarendon, 1966.
Mentions Byron several times.
Rev. in TLS, 24 Nov. 1966, p. 1066.

267. *Shirakawa, S. H. M. "Lord Byron's Metrical Romances: A Study in Poetic Development." (Doctoral dissertation, London, 1968.)

268. Sifton, Paul G., ed. "On the European Scene," *Manuscripts*, XX (Spring 1968), 42–44.
Mentions Byron's "Song of the Suliotes" (Ashley MS. 4754) on display at the British Museum as part of a show arranged by T. S. Pattie, "Greeks and Franks—Post Byzantine Greek."

269. Singer, Armand E. *The Don Juan Theme: Versions and Criticism: A Bibliography*. Morgantown, W. Va.: Univ. of West Virginia, 1965.
See K-SJ, V (1956), 124, VI (1957), 138, IX (1960), 59, X (1961), 81. Also see No. 270.
Rev. by A. Nougué in *Bulletin hispanique*, LXIX (July–Dec. 1967), 545–546; by Leo Weinstein in *Hispanic Review*, XXXVI (Apr. 1968), 167–169.

270. Singer, Armand E. "First Supplement to *The Don Juan Theme, Versions and Criticism: A Bibliography* (1965)," *Philological Papers*, XV (June 1966), 76–88.†
See No. 269.

271. Southey, Robert. *New Letters of Robert Southey*. See K-SJ, XVI (1967), 124.
Rev. by R. S. Woof in N&Q, CCXIII (Jan. 1968), 36–38. Also see No. 48.

272. Sperry, Stuart M., Jr. "The *Harolds* of Berlioz and Byron," *Your Musical Cue* (Indiana University), IV (Apr. 1968), 3–8.
Berlioz's *Harold in Italy* is "the finest evocation of the Byronic sensibility in musical literature."

273. Stange, G. Robert. *Matthew Arnold: The Poet as Humanist*. Princeton: Princeton Univ., 1967.
Has references to Byron, Keats, and Shelley.
Rev. in TLS, 6 July 1967, p. 596.

274. Steffan, T. G. "Another Doubtful Byron Letter," N&Q, CCXII (Aug. 1967), 299–301.†
The letter in question, dated 23 Aug. 1813, is at the University of Texas.

275. Sundell, M. G. " 'Tintern Abbey' and 'Resignation,' " *Victorian Poetry*, V (Winter 1967), 255–264.

Includes a brief discussion of lyric and narrative problems in *Childe Harold's Pilgrimage* and *The Giaour.*

Symonds, John Addington. See No. 671.

276. Terry, R. C. "Big Alfred and the Critics," TLS, 15 Feb. 1968, p. 157.

Asserts that Trollope satirized the poetry of Byron and Shelley in *The Eustace Diamonds* far more than he did Tennyson's *Idylls of the King.*

277. Thomas, Clara. *Love and Work Enough: The Life of Anna Jameson.* Toronto: Univ. of Toronto, 1967.

Has references to Lady Byron.

Rev. in TLS, 30 Nov. 1967, p. 1130; in *Choice*, v (March 1968), 54.

278. Thompson, James R. "Byron's Plays and *Don Juan*: Genre and Myth," *Bucknell Review*, xv (Dec. 1967), 22–38.

Drama represented to Byron the "concrete embodiment of belief"; *Don Juan* expresses "faith in the endless vitality of the self."

279. Timko, Michael. *Innocent Victorian: The Satiric Poetry of Arthur Hugh Clough.* Athens, Ohio: Ohio Univ., 1966.

Includes references to Byron, Keats, and Shelley.

280. Trease, Geoffrey. *The Grand Tour.* See K-SJ, xvii (1968), 18.

Rev. by Benjamin Boyce in SAQ, lxvii (Spring 1968), 388.

281. *Treugutt, Stefan. "Nareszcie Byron!" *Przegląd Kulturalny*, No. 25 (1955), p. 5. [In Polish.]

"Byron at Last!" An experimental theatre of suggestions; premiere 3: "Marino Faliero, the Doge of Venice."

282. Trousson, Raymond. *Le thème de Prométhée dans la littérature européenne.* See K-SJ, xv (1966), 153, xvi (1967), 124.

Rev. by Pierre Moreau in RLC, xlii (Apr.-June 1968), 291–296.

283. Viets, Henry R. [In] "Information, Please," TLS, 26 Oct. 1967, p. 1022.

Asks about Countess Breuss, in whose villa Polidori wrote *The Vampyre.*

284. *Walker, K. M. "Byron's Readers: A Study of Attitudes towards Byron, 1812–1832." (Doctoral dissertation, Cambridge, 1967.)

Walsh, John. See No. 677.

285. Webby, Elizabeth. "English Literature in Early Australia: 1820–1829," *Southerly*, xxvii (No. 4, 1967), 266–285.

Byron was among the authors who were widely read.

286. Weinstein, Mark A. *William Edmondstoune Aytoun and the Spasmodic Controversy.* New Haven: Yale Univ., 1968.

Discusses influence of Byron, Keats, and Shelley and makes other references to them.

287. Weinstock, Herbert. *Rossini: A Biography.* New York: Knopf, 1968.

Byron is referred to and quoted.

288. Whitmore, Allen Perry. "The Major Characters of Lord Byron's Dramas" [Doctoral dissertation, Colorado, 1966], DA, xxviii (Oct. 1967), 1412-A.

289. *Williams, Tennessee. "List miłosny lorda Byrona," [translated by] K. Skarżyńska, *Dialog*, No. 2 (1956), pp. 80–84.

A translation into Polish of Williams' *Lord Byron's Love Letter.*

290. Wilson, Joy Lee Clark. "An Edition of Thomas Moore's 'Commonplace Book'" [Doctoral dissertation, Rice, 1967], DA, xxviii (Nov. 1967), 1800-A.

Winters, Yvor. See No. 81.

291. "Wreath for Byron Irks Athens," *The Times*, London, 20 Apr. 1968, p. 10.

Wreath inscribed "I dreamed that Greece might yet be free" placed on Athens monument by a British MP.

292. *Yakushigawa, Koichi. "Byron and His Relation to Nature—On *Childe Harold's Pilgrimage* and *Manfred*," *Studies in Foreign Literature* (Ritsumeikan Univ.), xv (1968), 1–28.

293. *Zgorzelski, A. "A. Z.: Wykłady o Byronie," *Kamena*, No. 9 (1958), p. 7. [In Polish.]

Lectures on Byron by Bolesław Taborski.

294. *Žirmunskij, V[iktor]. [Maksimovič]. "Stichotvorenija Goethe i Byron 'Ty znaeš kraj?'" in *Problemy meždunarodnych literaturnych svjazej* (Leningrad, 1962). [In Polish.]

Method of comparative stylistics exemplified by analysis of Goethe's and Byron's poems.

Rev. by *Małgorzata Książek-Czermińska in *Przegląd Humanistyczny*, No. 2 (1963), pp. 162–167.

295. Żuławski, Juliusz. *Byron Nieupozowany.* See K-SJ, xv (1966), 154.
Rev. by *Henryk Bereza in *Twórczość,* No. 4 (1965), pp. 137–139; by *Zbigniew Florczak in *Nowe Książki,* No. 9 (1965), pp. 394–396; by *Hamilton in *Kultura,* No. 9 (1965), p. 12; by *Jarosław Iwaszkiewicz in *Życie Warszawy,* No. 3 (1965), p. 4; by *Stanisław Rutkowski in *Polonistyka,* No. 2 (1965), pp. 51–52.

296. *Żuławski, Juliusz. *Byron Nieupozowany.* Second Edition. Warsaw: Państw. Instytut Wydawn., 1966.
See No. 295.

297. *Żuławski, Juliusz. "Szkic do portretu lorda Byrona," *Twórczość,* No. 2 (1963), pp. 94–101.
A Sketch for a Portrait of Lord Byron.

III. HUNT

Works: Selected, Single

Aloian, David. See No. 85.

298. Auden, W. H., ed. *19th Century British Minor Poets.* See K-SJ, xvi (1967), 124.
Rev. in TLS, 27 July 1967, p. 670; by Timothy Hilton in NS, lxxiv (28 July 1967), 120; by Anthony Burgess in Spec, 11 Aug. 1967, pp. 161–162; in *Quarterly Review,* cccv (Oct. 1967), 473–474.

299. Bishop, John, comp. *Music and Sweet Poetry: A Verse Anthology.* London: John Baker, 1968.
Includes selections from Hunt and Shelley.

Kroeber, Karl, and John O. Lyons. See No. 101.

300. **The Liberal: Verse and Prose from the South.* Vols. i and ii. Numbers 1–4. *Leigh Hunt's London Journal and the Printing Machine.* Vols. i and ii. Numbers 1–91. *The Companion.* Numbers 1–28. New York: AMS, 1967.
Reprints of Leigh Hunt periodicals of 1822–23, 1834–35, and 1828 respectively.

Books and Articles Relating to Hunt

Blainey, Ann. See No. 20.

301. Blunden, Edmund. *A Few Not Quite Forgotten Writers?* London: Oxford Univ., 1967. "The English Association Presidential Address 1967."
One is Hunt (pp. 12–14).

302. *Blunden, Edmund. *Leigh Hunt's "Examiner" Examined.* With a new introduction by the author. Hamden, Conn.: Archon, 1967.
A reprint of the book first published in 1928.

303. Cary, Richard. "The Library of Edwin Arlington Robinson: Addenda," *Colby Library Quarterly,* vii (March 1967), 398–415.
Included copies of Hazlitt's and Hunt's *Essays.*

304. Chatterjee, Bhabatosh. "Leigh Hunt on Keats's Imagery," N&Q, ccxii (Aug. 1967), 307.†
Asserts that Hunt was the first to perceive that the characteristic quality of Keats's imagery was "movement in repose."

305. Cheney, David R. "Leigh Hunt's Efforts to Encourage an Appreciation of Classical Music," K-SJ, xvii (1968), 89–96.
His attempts, both in the evenings at Novello's and in *Musical Evenings,* were "largely failures."

306. Cheney, David R. "Leigh Hunt's 'Evening the First' of *Musical Evenings,*" KSMB, xviii (1967), 39–42.
Quotes in full the recently discovered table of contents of "Evening the First" and prints the letter Hunt wrote to James Power, who was to publish *Musical Evenings.* Concludes that "Evening the First" probably was completed and that the incomplete ms. at the University of Iowa contains a major portion.
See K-SJ, xv (1966), 154, No. 213, xvi (1967), 124–125, xvii (1968), 19.

307. Davies, James Atterbury. "Leigh Hunt and John Forster," RES, n.s., xix (Feb. 1968), 25–40.
"The friendship with Hunt throws much valuable light on the way Forster conducted his literary relationships . . . and is central to any consideration of Forster's achievements as a critic."

308. Dowson, Ernest. *The Letters of Ernest Dowson.* Ed. Desmond Flower and Henry Maas. Rutherford, N.J.: Fairleigh Dickinson Univ., 1967.

Comments (p. 178) on essays of Hazlitt and Hunt.

309. Eichler, Udi, and Alan Osler. "A Carlyle MS.," TLS, 8 Feb. 1968, p. 141.

Unidentified Carlyle MS. found written on the verso of the title page to an 1820 volume of Hunt's *Indicator*. See No. 322.

Ellis, Amanda M. See No. 166.

310. Fenner, Theodore Lincoln. "Leigh Hunt on Opera: The *Examiner* Years" [Doctoral dissertation, Columbia, 1967], DA, XXVIII (June 1968), 5013-A.

311. Fielding, K. J. "Leigh Hunt and Skimpole: Another Remonstrance," *Dickensian*, LXIV (Jan. 1968), 5–9.

Hunt's manner represented "a survival of artistic bohemianism and irresponsibility" that Dickens opposed.

George, M. Dorothy. See No. 177.

312. Gittings, Robert. "Leigh Hunt's Examiner," TLS, 23 Nov. 1967, p. 1111.

A reexamination by a critic who, preparing a new biography of Keats, has "read almost every word" of *The Examiner*. See No. 403.

Harding, Walter. See No. 184.

313. Houtchens, Carolyn Washburn, and Lawrence Huston Houtchens, eds. *The English Romantic Poets & Essayists: A Review of Research and Criticism*. Revised Edition. See K-SJ, XVII (1968), 20.

Rev. in *Choice*, IV (July–Aug. 1967), 519; by D[avid]. V. E[rdman]. in ELN, V, Supplement (Sept. 1967), 17–18.

314. Jump, John D., ed. *Tennyson: The Critical Heritage*. London: Routledge; New York: Barnes & Noble (1967).

A collection of critical essays, including Hunt's review of *Poems* (1842) in the *Church of England Quarterly Review*. Many references to Byron, Keats, and Shelley are scattered throughout the various essays.

Marshall, William H. See No. 229.

Owen, Wilfred. See No. 469.

Partridge, Monica. See No. 249.

315. "Recent Acquisitions," *Books at Iowa*, No. 6 (Apr. 1967), 36–38.

Announces acquisition of letters and manuscripts for the Leigh Hunt Collection.

316. "Recent Acquisitions," *Books at Iowa*, No. 8 (Apr. 1968), 37–40.

Nine Hunt letters and seven letters addressed to Hunt have been added to the Leigh Hunt Collection.

Robinson, Henry Crabb. See No. 257.

317. "The Royal Literary Fund," TLS, 21 March 1968, p. 300.

An article celebrating the 150th anniversary of a Fund that included among its beneficiaries Peacock, Haydon, Hunt, Clare, and Hood.

318. Salemo, Nicholas A. [In] "Information, Please," TLS, 13 July 1967, p. 624.

Asks for facts about Hunt's life and acquaintances.

Schulz, H. C. See No. 9.

Schulz, Max F. See No. 265.

319. Stewart, John Francis. "An Anatomy of Humor" [Doctoral dissertation, Southern California, 1967], DA, XXVIII (Jan. 1968), 2658-A–2659-A.

Uses criticism of Hazlitt and Hunt.

320. Tatchell, Molly. [In] "Information, Please," TLS, 20 June 1968, p. 659.

Asks for portraits or photographs of certain members of Hunt's family.

321. "When Found—," *Dickensian*, LXII (Sept. 1966), 131–132.

Reports sale at Christie's on 7 June 1966 of a miniature of Hunt with an inscription purportedly in Hunt's hand.

322. Wilson, D. G. "A Carlyle MS.," TLS, 15 Feb. 1968, p. 157.

Identifies Hunt as the object of Carlyle's "generous pleading" in a Carlyle memorandum quoted in an earlier TLS letter. See No. 309.

IV. KEATS

WORKS: SELECTED, SINGLE, TRANSLATED

Aloian, David. See No. 85.

Antologia liryki angielskiej, 1300–1950. See No. 86.

323. Cecchin, Giovanni. *Poetry Appreciation without Tears: Twenty-One English Poems Considered with a Guide to Reading, Hints, and Suggestions*. Turin: G. Giappichelli, 1968.

"When I Have Fears" is one of the group.

324. Coffey, Dairine, ed. *The Dark Tower*. See K-SJ, XVII (1968), 21.
Rev. by Samuel French Morse in *Poetry*, CXI (March 1968), 410–413.

Cole, William. See No. 91.

325. Cole, William, ed. *Eight Lines and Under: An Anthology of Short, Short Poems*. New York: Macmillan, 1967.
Includes "Lines Supposed to Have Been Addressed to Fanny Brawne."

Coleman, Elliott, ed. See No. 92.

326. Ellmann, Richard, and Charles Feidelson, Jr., eds. *The Modern Tradition: Backgrounds of Modern Literature*. New York: Oxford Univ., 1965.
Includes (pp. 70–71) a selection from Keats.

327. Foakes, R. A., ed. *Romantic Criticism 1800–1850*. London: Edward Arnold, 1968. "Arnold's English Texts."
Includes selections from Keats, Hazlitt, and Shelley.

Freedman, Morris, and Paul B. Davis. See No. 97.

328. "From 'To My Brother George,' " K-SJ, XVII (1968), 120.
Some lines from the poem.

329. Goudge, Elizabeth. *A Book of Peace: An Anthology*. London: Michael Joseph, 1967.
Contains selections from Clare and Keats.

330. **John Keats: Lamia*. [Translated by] Shinya Imanishi. Osaka: Kyoiku Tosho, 1968. [In Japanese.]

331. **John Keats: Poetical Works*. Moscow: Progress, 1966. [In English.]
Includes "Jon Kits, ego zhian i poeziia" ["John Keats, His Life and Poetry"] by V. Rogof, pp. 5–21.

332. Kapp, Paul. *Cock-A-Doodle-Doo! Cock-A-Doodle-Dandy! A New Songbook for the Newest Singers*. New York: Harper & Row, 1966.
Includes musical settings for poems by Hood and Keats.

333. **Keats shishû. [Complete Poetical Works.]* [Translated by] Okaji Mine. Tokyo: Bunshûdô, 1965. [In Japanese.]

334. **Keats shishû. [Complete Poetical Works.]* [Translated by] Tamura Einosuke. Tokyo: Shichôsha, 1968. [In Japanese.]

335. **Keats's Sonnets*. [Edited by] Tohru Matsuura. Tokyo: Azuma Shobo, 1966.

Kelly, T. J. See No. 100.

Kroeber, Karl, and John O. Lyons. See No. 101.

336. **Lamia. Isabella. Sei Agnes no yomiya. [Lamia, Isabella, The Eve of St. Agnes, and Other Poems.]* [Translated by] Imanishi Nobuya. Tokyo: Osaka kyôiku tosho, 1968. [In Japanese.]

Payne, William Morton. See No. 59.

337. *"Piosenka z nienapisanej opery, Podwieczorek kochanków, 'Kilka wierszowanych nonsensów' w liście do brata," [translated by] Juliusz Żuławski, *Twórczość*, No. 2 (1962), pp. 86–87.
Translations into Polish.

338. **Poèmes choisis. [Selected Poems.]* [Translated by] Albert Laffay. Paris: Aubier-Flammarion, 1968. [In French.]

339. **Poeziji*. [Translated by] Vasyl Mysyk. Kiev: Dnipro, 1968. [In Ukrainian.]

340. Reeves, James, and Martin Seymour-Smith, eds. *A New Canon of English Poetry*. London: Heinemann, 1967.
Includes selections from Shelley, Clare, and Keats.

341. **Selected Letters & Poems*. Ed. J. H. Walsh. London: Chatto & Windus, 1967.
A paperback edition.

342. *Selected Poems and Letters of John Keats*. Ed. Robert Gittings. See K-SJ, XVII (1968), 22.
Rev. by *Richard Gustafson in *Poet and Critic*, III (1967), 42.

Simpson, Louis. See No. 108.

343. "Sonnet," K-SJ, XVII (1968), 14.
"If by dull rhymes our English must be chain'd."

344. *"Stikhi," [translated into Ukrainian by] V. Misik, *Prapor*, No. 12 (1965), pp. 92–93.
A group of short Keats poems.

Trilling, Lionel. See No. 110.

Wright, David, ed. See No. 113.

Books and Articles Relating to Keats and his Circle

345. ["Account of a soirée to be held in aid of restoration fund of Keats House in Rome,"] *The Times*, London, 2 Nov. 1967, p. 13.

The Age of the Grand Tour. See No. 83.

346. *Akikuni, Tadanori. "Keats' 'Ode on Melancholy,'" *Studies in British and American Literature* (Univ. of Osaka Prefecture), xv (Jan. 1968), 91–115. [In Japanese.]

347. Albrecht, W. P. *Hazlitt and the Creative Imagination*. See K-SJ, xvi (1967), 126, xvii (1968), 22.

Rev. by Stanley Jones in RES, n.s., xviii (Aug. 1967), 346–347; by J[ohn]. E. J[ordan]. in ELN, v, Supplement (Sept. 1967), 32–33; by Richard L. Kowalczyk in *Studies in Burke and His Time*, ix (Spring 1968), 989–993. See Nos. 348 and 464.

348. Albrecht, W. P. "More on Hazlitt and the Functions of the Imagination," PMLA, lxxxiii (March 1968), 151–152, 153–154.

See Nos. 347 and 464.

349. Anderson, Norman A. "'Rappaccini's Daughter': A Keatsian Analogue?" PMLA, lxxxiii (May 1968), 271–283.

Suggests parallels between Hawthorne's story and *Lamia*.

350. Antippas, Andy Peter. "The Burden of Poetic Tradition: A Study in the Works of Keats, Tennyson, Arnold, and Morris" [Doctoral dissertation, Wisconsin, 1968], DA, xxviii (May 1968), 4591-A–4592-A.

351. Arnheim, Rudolf. *Toward a Psychology of Art: Collected Essays*. Berkeley: Univ. of California, 1967.

Discusses revisions Keats made in two poems.

352. "Art News in Pictures," *Connoisseur*, clxv (May 1967), 44–45.

Reproduces De Wint's "Waterloo Bridge."

353. Astre, Georges-Albert. *John Keats: Un tableau synoptique de la vie et des œuvres de John Keats et des événements littéraires, artistiques et historiques de son époque*. Paris: Seghers, 1966. "Ecrivains d'hier et d'aujourd'hui."

Ball, Patricia M. See No. 16.

354. Balslev, Thora. *Keats and Wordsworth: A Comparative Study*. See K-SJ, xiii (1964), 137, xv (1966), 156.

Rev. by Helmut Viebrock in *Anglia*, lxxxvi (1968), 241–242.

355. Barton, Bernard. *The Literary Correspondence of Bernard Barton*. See K-SJ, xvii (1968), 22.

Rev. in TLS, July 27, 1967, p. 675; in *Choice*, iv (Sept. 1967), 671.

356. Bate, Walter Jackson. *John Keats*. See K-SJ, xiv (1965), 118, xv (1966), 156, xvi (1967), 126, xvii (1968), 22.

Rev. by Brendan Kennelly in *Dubliner*, iii (Autumn 1964), 63–64; by Hermann Fischer in ASNS, cciv (March 1968), 461–463.

357. Bates, L. M. *Somerset House: Four Hundred Years of History*. London: Frederick Muller, 1967.

Briefly recounts (pp. 174–175) Haydon's opposition to the Government Schools of Design.

358. *Beaudry, Harry Richard. "The English Theatre and John Keats." (Doctoral dissertation, Duke, 1968.)

359. Bellairs, John. "Variations on a Vase," *Southern Review* (Adelaide), i, No. 4 (1965), pp. 58–68.†

Reviews "distorted" essays by Cleanth Brooks, Earl Wasserman, and Kenneth Burke on "Ode on a Grecian Urn." [See K-SJ, i (1952), 88, No. 5, iii (1954), 114, No. 50, 121, No. 184.] His own reading would "stay a lot closer to the literal level, to what Keats says the poem is about." See Nos. 448 and 518.

360. Benton, Richard P. "Keats and Zen," *Philosophy East and West*, xvi (Jan.–Apr. 1966), 33–47.

"Keats did succeed in achieving a genuine loss of self-identity. He uncovered his universal Self or Buddha nature in a manner closely resembling Zen awakening, or *satori*."

Bewley, Marius. See No. 124.

361. "Bibliophily on the Eastern Seaboard," TLS, 1 Feb. 1968, p. 116.

Article on an exhibition at the J. Pierpont Morgan Library which included Joseph Severn's copy of the first edition of *Adonais*.

Blainey, Ann. See No. 20.

362. Blunden, Edmund. "Random Tributes to British Painters," *Saturday Book*, No. 26 (1966), 10–14.

A poem which mentions De Wint, Hilton, and other Romantic artists.

363. Boggs, W. Arthur. "Permanence & Impermanence: Keatsian Mutability," *Trace*, No. 62 (Fall–Winter 1966), 358–369.

Keats "impregnated" the seven great poems in 1819 with "very complicated configurations of permanence-impermanence."

364. Bolton, W. F., ed. *The English Language: Essays of English and American Men of Letters 1490–1839*. Cambridge: Cambridge Univ., 1966.

Includes (pp. 185–190) an essay by Hazlitt.

365. Bratton, Edward W. "Unidentified Wordsworthian Echoes in Hazlitt," N&Q, CCXIII (Jan. 1968), 25–27.†

Lists sixteen unnoticed quotations from, or allusions to, Wordsworth in Hazlitt's works.

366. Breslin, James E. "Whitman and the Early Development of William Carlos Williams," PMLA, LXXXII (Dec. 1967), 613–621.†

Also discusses the influence of Keats on Williams.

367. Brooke, Rupert. *The Letters of Rupert Brooke*. Ed. Geoffrey Keynes. New York: Harcourt, Brace & World, 1968.

Makes reference to Keats and Shelley.

368. *Brooke, Stopford A. *Studies in Poetry: William Blake, Walter Scott; Shelley, and Keats*. Port Washington, N.Y.: Kennikat, 1967.

A reprint of the volume first published in 1907.

369. Brown, Charles Armitage. *The Letters of Charles Armitage Brown*. Ed. Jack Stillinger. See K-SJ, XVI (1967), 127, XVII (1968), 23.

Rev. by Donald H. Reiman in SAQ, LXVI (Spring 1967), 283–284; by Miriam Allott in N&Q, CCXII (Aug. 1967), 316–318; by R. W. King in RES, n.s., XVIII (Aug. 1967), 347–348; by J. R. MacGillivray in MP, LXV (Nov. 1967), 168–170. See also No. 48.

370. *Burney, E. L. "Peasant Poets, or Peasants, Poetry, Patronage and the Pauper's Pit," *Manchester Review*, XI (1966), 59–72.

A general article on various unlearned poets, including Clare.

371. Bush, Douglas. *John Keats: His Life and Writings*. See K-SJ, XVI (1967), 127, XVII (1968), 23–24.

Rev. by Jeffrey Hart in *National Review*, XVIII (19 Apr. 1966), 371–373; by C. B. Cox in Spec, 3 Feb. 1967, p. 140; by L. M. Wallace in *Books and Bookmen*, XII (Apr. 1967), 42–44.

Byrns, Richard H. See No. 24.

Cano, José Luis. See No. 137.

372. Carter, Paul J., and George K. Smart, eds. *Literature & Society, 1961–1965: A Selective Bibliography*. Coral Gables, Fla.: Univ. of Miami, 1967.

Lists several articles on Keats.

Cary, Richard. See No. 303.

373. ["Cattle Watering in a Farmyard,"] *Apollo*, LXXXIII (Apr. 1966), ci.

This De Wint is reproduced in an announcement by the Fine Art Society.

374. Charlesworth, Barbara. *Dark Passages: The Decadent Consciousness in Victorian Literature*. Madison: Univ. of Wisconsin, 1965.

Refers to Keats and Shelley.

Rev. by Francis Noel Lees in N&Q, CCXI (Sept. 1966), 350–351; by Ian Fletcher in MLR, LXI (Oct. 1966), 693–695; by John M. Munro in MP, LXIV (Feb. 1967), 272–274.

Chatterjee, Bhabatosh. See No. 304.

375. Chayes, Irene H. "Dreamer, Poet, and Poem in *The Fall of Hyperion*," PQ, XLVI (Oct. 1967), 499–515.

A reading of the poem in the context of other dream visions, claiming that it is "Keats's most forthright exploration of the nature of the creative act."

376. *Chwalewik, Witold. "Literatura angielska," in *Rocznik Literacki* (1962), pp. 301–317.

Discusses a Polish edition of selected poems of Keats.

377. Clare, John. *Life and Works of John Clare*. Ed. C. Xenophontos. [London:] C. Nicholls, 1966.

Coblentz, Stanton A. See No. 147.

378. Cockburn, Alexander. "Fun at a Funeral Feast," NS, 21 July 1967, p. 94.

Would Hazlitt's comments about Gifford be thought libelous today?

379. Cohen, Jane Rabb. "Keats's Humor in 'La Belle Dame sans Merci,' " K-SJ, XVII (1968), 10–13.

On the evidence of an original journal letter, attempts to show that laughter was the initial catalyst for the composition of the poem and that both "la belle dame" and the knight are more genial figures than hitherto supposed.

380. Colton, Judith. "The Endymion Myth and Poussin's Detroit Painting," *Journal of the Warburg and Courtauld Institutes*, xxx (1967), 426–431.

"Only in the nineteenth century, at the end of Keats's *Endymion*, do we find a sequel to Poussin's kneeling youth."

381. *Colvin, Sidney. *Keats*. London: Macmillan, 1968. "Macmillan's Pocket Library."

A paperback edition of a book originally published in 1887.

382. "Comment: Keats For Ever," *Critical Survey*, III (Summer 1968), 191–195.

Responds to a silly column in *The Guardian* by Anne Duchene called "Keats in Retrospect" (May 13). She had quoted her goddaughter: "Shelley's all right, but Keats is awful, isn't he?"

383. Coulter, Sara Rivard. "William Hazlitt as an Essayist" [Doctoral dissertation, Colorado, 1966], DA, XXVIII (July 1967), 226-A.

384. Crawford, Alexander W. *The Genius of Keats: An Interpretation*. See K-SJ, XVII (1968), 24.

Rev. in *Choice*, IV (Dec. 1967), 1115.

385. Crombie, Theodore. "First-fruits of the Fall," *Apollo*, LXXXIV (Oct. 1966), 330–331.

Reviews De Wint exhibit at Thomas Agnew & Sons. Reproduces "Landscape with a Wagon."

Culler, A. Dwight. See No. 150.

386. *Cummings, Frederick James. "Benjamin Robert Haydon and the Critical Reception of the Elgin Marbles." (Doctoral dissertation, Chicago, 1967.)

387. Cunningham, J. V. "How Shall the Poem Be Written?" *University of Denver Quarterly*, II (Spring 1967), 45–62.

Uses "La Belle Dame sans Merci" for illustrative purposes.

388. Cusac, Marian Hollingsworth. "Keats as Enchanter: An Organizing Principle of *The Eve of St. Agnes*," K-SJ, XVII (1968), 113–119.

Expands on Keats's role as magician-narrator in the poem and suggests that this role is an organizing principle corollary to the primary concentric structure of the poem.

389. Cutler, Bruce. *At Keats' Grave: The Making of a Poem*. Wichita: Wichita State Univ., 1967. Wichita State University Studies No. 72.

The process of composition by which the author wrote the poem of this name.

390. D'Avanzo, Mario L. *Keats's Metaphors for the Poetic Imagination*. See K-SJ, XVII (1968), 24.

Rev. in *Choice*, IV (Feb. 1968), 1379–1380; by Earl F. Guy in *Dalhousie Review*, XLVIII (Spring 1968), 123–125; by Gilbert Thomas in *English*, XVII (Spring 1968), 26–27. See also No. 21.

391. De Selincourt, Ernest. "Fifty-Year Rule," TLS, 30 Nov. 1967, p. 1171.

Extracts from a review of Sir Sidney Colvin's *John Keats: His Life and Poetry, His Friends, Critics, and After Fame*, published anonymously in TLS on 29 Nov. 1917.

392. Dickstein, Morris. "The Divided Self: A Study of Keats' Poetic Development" [Doctoral dissertation, Yale, 1967], DA, XXVIII (Apr. 1968), 4168-A.

393. Doubleday, F. N. "Keats and the Hammonds," TLS, 9 May 1968, p. 484.

Briefly reviews Keats's medical history, especially as interpreted by William Hale White. See Nos. 403, 405, and 413.

Dowson, Ernest. See No. 308.

Dunn, John Joseph. See No. 163.

Ellis, Amanda M. See No. 166.

394. Enscoe, Gerald E. *Eros and the Romantics: Sexual Love as a Theme in Coleridge, Shelley and Keats*. The Hague: Mouton, 1967.

One chapter is on "The Physical Basis of Love in Shelley's *Alastor* and *Epipsychidion*," and two are entitled "Keats and the Triumph of Eros" and "Keats and the Failure of Eros."

395. ["Extensive Park Scene with Deer,"] *Apollo*, LXXXIV (Oct. 1966), lxvii.

This De Wint is reproduced in an announcement by Appleby Brothers.

396. Farr, Dennis. "The Collection of Mr and Mrs Paul Mellon," *Museums Journal*, LXV (Dec. 1965), 203–216.

Reproduces and briefly discusses Haydon's "Venus and Anchises."

397. Free, William J. "Murray Krieger and the Place of Poetry," *Georgia Review*, XXII (Summer 1968), 236–246.
Mentions Krieger's criticism of Keats.

Frye, Northrop. See No. 32.

398. *Fujihira, Takeaki. "Dialogue Structure in 'Ode on a Grecian Urn,'" *Rising Generation*, CXIV (May 1968), 374–375. [In Japanese.]

399. *Fuller, James A. "Our Debt to Keats," *CEA Critic*, XXVI (Nov. 1963), 3.

400. Gemmett, Robert J. "The Critical Reception of William Beckford's Fonthill," *English Miscellany*, XIX (1968), 133–151.
In spite of Hazlitt's denunciation Fonthill was "received as a dramatic success in its day."

401. *George, Eric. *The Life and Death of Benjamin Robert Haydon, Historical Painter, 1786–1846*. Second Edition, with Additions by Dorothy George. Oxford: Clarendon, 1967.
The first edition appeared in 1948.
Rev. by H. Osborne in *British Journal of Aesthetics*, VIII (Apr. 1968), 202.

George, M. Dorothy. See No. 177.

402. Gérard, Albert S. *English Romantic Poetry: Ethos, Structure, and Symbol in Coleridge, Wordsworth, Shelley, and Keats*. Berkeley: Univ. of California, 1968.

403. Gittings, Robert. *John Keats*. London: Heinemann, 1968.
Rev. by Graham Hough in NS, LXXV (22 March 1968), 382–383; by Martin Seymour-Smith in Spec, 22 March 1968, pp. 370–371; by Dennis Potter in *The Times*, London, 23 March 1968, p. 21; in TLS, 11 Apr. 1968, p. 372. See also Nos. 312, 393, 405, and 413.

404. *Gittings, Robert. *John Keats: The Living Year*. New York: Barnes & Noble, 1968.
A reprint of a book first published in 1954.

405. Gittings, Robert. "Keats and the Hammonds," TLS, 4 Apr. 1968, p. 357.
"It seems that the Hammond 'intemperance,' allied with Keats's notoriously quick temper, may have been a prime factor in the financial distress which Keats eventually suffered." See Nos. 393, 403, and 413.

Gittings, Robert. See No. 312.

406. Gordon, Alastair. "Peter de Wint, the Undramatic Master," *Connoisseur*, CLXI (March 1966), 150–151.
Reviews exhibition at Reading Museum and Art Gallery; reproduces three of De Wint's works.

407. Greaves, Margaret. *Regency Patron: Sir George Beaumont*. See K-SJ, XVII (1968), 25.
Rev. by Geoffrey Grigson in NS, LXXII (30 Sept. 1966), 482.

408. Green, David Bonnell. "New Letters of John Clare to Taylor and Hessey," SP, LXIV (Oct. 1967), 720–734.
Letters include references to Byron, Keats, and Lamb.

409. Green, David Bonnell. "Three Early American Admirers of John Clare," *Bulletin of the John Rylands Library*, L (Spring 1968), 365–386.
Dean Dudley, Romeo Elton, and Benjamin P. Avery.

410. Greene, Balcomb. "A Thing of Beauty," *Art Journal*, XXV (Summer 1966), 364–369, 376.
A painter contemplates his "intellectual affinity" with Keats.

411. Grigson, Geoffrey. *Poets in Their Pride*. London: Phoenix House, 1962.
Includes (pp. 110–123) chapter on Clare.

412. *Groot, H. B. de. "Albert Verwey, Keats en Matthew Arnold," *De Nieuwe Taalgids*, LXI (1968), 36–48.

413. Hamilton-Edwards, Gerald. "Keats and the Hammonds," TLS, 28 March 1968, p. 325.
A "manuscript history of the Heaven family" has some bearing on Keats's relations with Thomas Hammond. See Nos. 393, 403, and 405.

414. Hardie, Martin. *Water-Colour Painting in Britain*. Vol. II: *The Romantic Period*. See K-SJ, XVII (1968), 26.
Rev. in TLS, 16 Nov. 1967, p. 1079; by Luke Herrmann in *Burlington Magazine*, CX (Jan. 1968), 51.

Harding, Walter. See No. 184.

415. Hardwick, Michael, and Molly Hardwick. "Keats House," *Books and Bookmen*, XIII (June 1968), 14–15.

An extract from *Writers' Houses*. See No. 416.

416. Hardwick, Michael, and Mollie Hardwick. *Writers' Houses: A Literary Journey in England*. London: Phoenix House, 1968.

Includes a chapter on "Keats House, Hampstead" (pp. 1–5).

Rev. in TLS, 6 June 1968, p. 604. Also see No. 415.

417. *Hasegawa, Mitsuaki. "The Ritualistic Pattern in 'Ode to a Nightingale' and 'Ode on a Grecian Urn,'" *Hiroshima Studies in English Language and Literature*, XV (1968), 111–122. [In Japanese.]

418. Hawkins, Robert. *Preface to Poetry*. New York: Basic Books, 1965.

Includes one poem by Keats.

419. Haworth, Helen E. "The Redemption of Cynthia," *Humanities Association Bulletin*, XVIII (Fall 1967), 80–91.

A study of *Endymion*.

420. Haynes, Jean. *The Young Keats*. London: Max Parrish; New York: Roy (1967).

A book for young readers.

Rev. in TLS, 30 Nov. 1967, p. 1160.

421. Hazlitt, Margaret. *The Journal of Margaret Hazlitt: Recollections of England, Ireland, and America*. Ed. Ernest J. Moyne. Lawrence: Univ. of Kansas, 1967.

The journal of Hazlitt's sister.

422. *Hazlitt, William. *De l'amour de la vie. De la crainte de la mort*. [*On the Love of Life. On the Fear of Death*.] [Translated by] Yvette Hilaire. Paris: Lettres modernes, 1966. [In French.]

423. *Hazlitt, William. *The Works of William Hazlitt*. The Standard or "Centenary" Edition. Edited by Percival P. Howe after the Edition of A. R. Waller and Arnold Glover. 21 vols. New York: AMS, 1968.

A reprint of the set originally published in 1930–34.

424. Heller, Erich. *The Artist's Journey into the Interior and Other Essays*. New York: Random House, 1965.

Includes discussion of Keats.

Rev. by Michael Hamburger in Spec, 1 July 1966, p. 18.

425. ["Horses Drinking,"] *Apollo*, LXXXIV (Nov. 1966), liii.

This De Wint is reproduced in an announcement by the Manning Gallery.

Hutchings, R. J. See No. 36.

426. Hutchison, Sidney C. *The History of the Royal Academy 1768–1968*. New York: Taplinger, 1968.

Has references to Haydon.

427. Inglis, Fred. *Keats*. See K-SJ, XVI (1967), 129, XVII (1968), 27.

Rev. by Frank McCombie in N&Q, CCXII (Oct. 1967), 399–400.

428. *Ino, Keiko. "Steps to Immortality—A Study of Keats's Development from 'Sleep and Poetry' to 'The Fall of Hyperion,'" *Bulletin* (Seisen College), XVI (1968), 125–144. [In Japanese.]

429. Jack, Ian. *Keats and the Mirror of Art*. See K-SJ, XVII (1968), 27.

Rev. by Christopher Salvesen in *Cambridge Review*, LXXXIX (27 May 1967), 375; by Graham Hough in Li, LXXVII (1 June 1967), 724; in *Choice*, IV (Oct. 1967), 828; by Jack Stillinger in K-SJ, XVII (1968), 121–123; by Noel Machin in *British Journal of Aesthetics*, VIII (Jan. 1968), 82–84; by Patrick Cruttwell in *Hudson Review*, XXI (Spring 1968), 204–205; by Gilbert Thomas in *English*, XVII (Spring 1968), 26–27; by C. A. Bodelsen in ES, XLIX (Apr. 1968), 172–174; by M. M. Mahood in EC, XVIII (Apr. 1968), 193–200; by Allan Rodway in RES, n.s., XIX (May 1968), 220–222.

430. Jäger, Dietrich. "Über Zeit und Raum als Formen lyrischer Welterfahrung, besonders bei Eichendorff und Keats. I," *Literatur in Wissenschaft und Unterricht*, I (1968), 169–189.

The first part of a two-part essay.

431. Jeffrey, Lloyd N. "A Freudian Reading of Keats's *Ode to Psyche*," *Psychoanalytic Review*, LV (Summer 1968), 289–306.

In the ode we see "a conflict between the life and death wishes" and a "commingling" of the forces of love and despair.

432. *Jinbo, Nagao. "Keats's Genius in Poetry," *Studies in Foreign Literature* (Ritsumeikan Univ.), XVI (1968), 23pp. [In Japanese.]

433. Jones, Stanley. "A Hazlitt Quotation," N&Q, CCXIII (Jan. 1968), 27–28.†

The puzzling quotation in *Table Talk*,

"For Kais is fled and our tents are forlorn," was taken from Isaac Brandon's opera *Kais, or Love in the Deserts*, which Hazlitt probably heard about from Lamb.

434. Jones, Stanley. "Isabella Bridgwater: A Charade by Hazlitt?" *Review of English Literature*, VIII (July 1967), 91–95.

Hazlitt, in having Northcote quote specific lines from Pope, "had in mind, not 'the beautiful Lady Bridgewater' whom Jervas had painted . . . but Isabella Bridgwater of the island of Grenada whom Hazlitt was hoping to marry."

Joshi, P. C. See No. 199.

Jump, John D., ed. See No. 314.

435. Kleinschmidt, Hans J. "The Angry Act: The Role of Aggression in Creativity," *American Imago*, XXIV (Spring–Summer 1967), 98–128.

Briefly discusses Keats's longing for death.

436. Kohli, Devindra. "Coleridge, Hazlitt and Keats's Negative Capability," *Literary Criterion*, VIII (Summer 1968), 21–26.

Argues that Coleridge's distinction between Shakespeare and Milton in Chapter XV of *Biographia Literaria* is the source for Hazlitt's observations in his lecture "On Shakespeare and Milton" and for Keats's remarks in his letters of 22 Nov. 1817 and 22 Oct. 1818.

Kolbuszewski, Stanisław. See No. 40.

437. Kotker, Norman. "The Literary Road to Rome," *Horizon*, IX (Summer 1967), 16–31.†

The section on "Death of a Poet" (pp. 24–25) is about Keats in Rome.

438. Kroeber, Karl. *The Artifice of Reality: Poetic Style in Wordsworth, Foscolo, Keats, and Leopardi*. See K-SJ, XV (1966), 160, XVI (1967), 130, XVII (1968), 27.

Rev. by Helmut Viebrock in ASNS, CCIV (May 1967), 59–60.

439. *Kubiak, Zygmunt. "Anioł i Hyperion czyli o potrzebie sztuki," *Tygodnik Powszechny*, No. 40 (1966), p. 3.

"The Angel and Hyperion, or about the Need of Art": an article.

440. *Kubiak, Zygmunt. "Szkice z notatnika: Grób Keatsa: Egzemplarz Homera," *Tygodnik Powszechny*, No. 51 (1965), p. 3.

"Keats's Grave," an essay.

441. *Kume, Ayako. "The 'Still Point' of John Keats," *Bulletin* (Faculty of Literature, Univ. of Aichi Prefecture), XIII (Dec. 1967), 17–31.

442. *Kuriyama, Minoru. "Dream and the Sense of Reality: An Essay on *Endymion*," *Studies in the Humanities* (Osaka City Univ.), XX (Jan. 1968), 60–75. [In Japanese.]

Lawrence, D. H. See No. 215.

443. Leavis, F. R., comp. *A Selection from "Scrutiny."* 2 vols. Cambridge: Cambridge Univ., 1968.

Section 7 of Volume I, "Judgment and Analysis: Notes in the Analysis of Poetry" (pp. 211–257), contains critical comments on poems by Shelley and Keats.

444. *Leoff, Eve. "A Study of John Keats's *Isabella*." (Doctoral dissertation, Columbia, 1968.)

445. Lewis, R. W. B. *The Poetry of Hart Crane: A Critical Study*. Princeton: Princeton Univ., 1967.

Has references to Keats and Shelley.

Rev. by Alan Trachtenberg in *Kenyon Review*, XXIX (Nov. 1967), 712–719,.

Locker, Malka. See No. 46.

446. *Low, Donald Alexander. "A Biographical and Critical Study of John Scott (1784–1821)." (Doctoral dissertation, Cambridge, 1968.)

447. Lozano, Ann. "Phonemic Patterning in Keats's 'Ode on Melancholy,'" K-SJ, XVII (1968), 15–29.

A study of the structural patterns that govern the distribution of individual phonemes throughout the poem. Phonemic transcriptions are used to reveal the poem's internal balance, complementation, and tripartite organization.

448. Mackenzie, Manfred. "A Reply," *Southern Review* (Adelaide), I, No. 4 (1965), 70–73.†

Praises Burke's essay on "Ode on a Grecian Urn." See Nos. 359 and 518.

449. MacLeish, Archibald. *Poetry and Experience*. See K-SJ, XI (1962), 127, XII (1963), 139.

Rev. by Roger Asselineau in EA, XXI (Apr.–June 1968), 212.

Madden, William A. See No. 225.

450. Marks, Arthur S. "David Wilkie's 'Let-

ter of Introduction,'" *Burlington Magazine*, CX (March 1968), 125–133.

Wilkie, an artist, was an early and close friend of Haydon.

Marples, Morris. See No. 52.

Marshall, William H. See No. 229.

451. Maxwell, J. C. "Hazlitt and 'The European Magazine for the Year 1761.'" N&Q, CCXIII (Jan. 1968), 25.†

Points out why Dunster in "On Londoners and Country People" must have owned a copy of the *British Magazine* for 1761 instead of the *European Magazine*.

452. Mayhead, Robin. *John Keats*. Cambridge: Cambridge Univ., 1967. "British Authors: Introductory Critical Studies."

Rev. in TLS, 7 Sept. 1967, p. 801; by Gilbert Thomas in *English*, XVII (Spring 1968), 26–27; by M. I. Leveson in *English Studies in Africa*, XI (March 1968), 76–77; in *Choice*, V (June 1968), 484.

453. Melchiori, Barbara. "A Light-Fingered English Visitor to Italy," *English Miscellany*, XVIII (1967), 257–282.

Robert Gray, who went to Italy in 1821: the second half of his MS. journal is in the Keats-Shelley Memorial Library in Rome.

Miles, Josephine. See No. 235.

Miller, Arthur McA. See No. 236.

454. Milner, Perry Lou. "William Hazlitt on the Genius of Shakespeare," *Southern Quarterly*, V (Oct. 1966), 64–71.†

A discussion of Hazlitt's critical theories in relation to his comments on Shakespeare.

455. *Mitsui, Kiyoshi. "An Aspect of the Diction in 'The Eve of St. Agnes,'" *Studies in English Literature and Language* (Kyushu Univ.), XVIII (March 1968), 61–65. [In Japanese.]

456. *Miura, Ikuyo. "Images of Nature in Keats," *English Literature* (Waseda Univ.), XXXI (1967), 33–41. [In Japanese.]

457. Montgomery, Lyna Lee. "The Prosodic Techniques of Edward Young and John Keats in Heroic Couplets and Blank Verse" [Doctoral dissertation, Arkansas, 1967], DA, XXVIII (July 1967), 199-A–200-A.

458. Moore, Don D. *John Webster and His Critics 1617–1964*. Baton Rouge: Louisiana State Univ., 1966.

Discusses Hazlitt as a critic of Webster (pp. 35–37).

Rev. by S. E. Sprott in *Dalhousie Review*, XLVII (Spring 1967), 94–97.

"News & Comment." See No. 242.

459. "News & Comment," BC, XVI (Summer 1967), 195–222.

A copy of Keats's *Poems*, 1817, is among the treasures of the Library Company of Philadelphia (pp. 202–205).

460. N[icolson]., B[enedict]. "Current and Forthcoming Exhibitions," *Burlington Magazine*, CX (Feb. 1968), 106–107.

Mentions exhibition at Agnew's of watercolors by De Wint and others.

461. *O'Connell, Adelyn, R.S.C.J. "Intensity as Excellence and 'The Eve of St. Agnes,'" *Barat Review* (Lake Forest, Ill.), III (1968), 16–23.

462. Ogden, Hugh Stephen. "Hyperion and the Critics: A Study of Criticism and Scholarship on Keats's *Hyperion, A Fragment* and *The Fall of Hyperion, A Dream*" [Doctoral dissertation, Michigan, 1967], DA, XXVIII (June 1968), 5065-A.

463. Ogden, James. "Hazlitt, Lamb and 'Astrophel and Stella,'" *Trivium* (St. David's College, Wales), II (May 1967), 141–142.

The two friends disagreed in their evaluation of Sidney.

464. O'Hara, J. D. "More on Hazlitt and the Functions of the Imagination," PMLA, LXXXIII (March 1968), 152–153.

See Nos. 347 and 348.

465. O'Neill, Judith, comp. *Critics on Keats*. See K-SJ, XVII (1968), 29.

Rev. by Robin Mayhead in *Durham University Journal*, LX (March 1968), 121–123.

466. *Oobayashi, Teruhiko. "Keats's 'Negative Capability,'" *Research Reports* (Kochi Univ.), XVII (Feb. 1968), 133–139. [In Japanese.]

Orel, Harold. See No. 246.

467. *Osler, A. E. "Keats' Sense of the Past." (Doctoral dissertation, London, 1967.)

468. Otten, Terry. "Porphyro's Feast in *The Eve of St. Agnes*," *Serif*, V (March 1968), 22–24.

Argues that the function of the feast

supports, by its incompleteness, the ambiguous and fragmentary qualities in the poem as a whole.

469. Owen, Wilfred. *Collected Letters.* Ed. Harold Owen and John Bell. London: Oxford Univ., 1967.

Has many references to Keats and Shelley; also alludes to Byron and Hunt.

470. Paradinas, Fernando. "Evidence in Spain," KSMB, XVIII (1967), 23–25.

Reports finding the baptism certificate of Fanny Keats's daughter, Rosa Matilde (b. 1833), showing her as "granddaughter of Mr. Thomas Keats of Land's End, Cornwall." Includes an account of Fanny's husband, Valentín Llanos.

471. *Park, Roy. "Hazlitt's Literary Criticism: Its Foundations in Philosophy and Painting." (Doctoral dissertation, Cambridge, 1968.)

Partridge, Monica. See No. 249.

472. Pearce, Donald. "Flames Begotten of Flame," SR, LXXIV (Summer 1966), 649–668.†

On the continuity of tradition in Horace's "Epode XIV," Keats's "Ode to a Nightingale," and Yeats's "Byzantium" poems.

473. ["Peasants at Dieppe" and "Canterbury,"] *Apollo*, LXXXIV (Oct. 1966), i.

Two of De Wint's paintings are reproduced in this announcement by Thos. Agnew & Sons.

474. Pool, Bernard, ed. *The Croker Papers 1808–1857.* New York: Barnes & Noble, 1967.

Mentions the review of *Endymion.*

Rev. in TLS, 13 Apr. 1967, p. 307.

475. Pratt, Willis W. "*The Eve of St. Agnes* and W. S. Rose's *Partenopex de Blois,*" *Texas Studies in Literature and Language*, X (Spring 1968), 83–90.

Observes "strands of reminiscence" of Rose's translation of the twelfth-century tale (1807) in Keats's poem.

Praz, Mario. See No. 250.

Quennell, Peter. See No. 252.

Raine, Kathleen. See No. 632.

476. Raine, Kathleen. "The Use of the Beautiful," *Southern Review*, II (Apr. 1966), 245–263.†

Includes Keats and Shelley among those poets who "held to the Platonic doctrine."

477. "Recent Acquisitions," *Books at Iowa*, No. 2 (Apr. 1965), 41–42.

Announces acquisition of first edition of Keats's *Poems* (1817).

478. Reynolds, John Hamilton. *Selected Prose of John Hamilton Reynolds.* Ed. Leonidas M. Jones. See K-SJ, XVII (1968), 30.

Rev. by Jack Stillinger in JEGP, LXVI (July 1967), 465–467; by William H. Marshall in K-SJ, XVII (1968), 123–126; by Miriam Allott in N&Q, CCXIII (Jan. 1968), 40. See also Nos. 21 and 48.

479. Richardson, Joanna. *The Everlasting Spell: A Study of Keats and His Friends.* See K-SJ, XIV (1965), 124, XV (1966), 162, XVI (1967), 131, XVII (1968), 30.

Rev. in *Choice*, III (May 1966), 211.

480. Ridley, M. R. *Keats' Craftsmanship.* See K-SJ, XIII (1964), 142, XIV (1965), 124, XVII (1968), 30.

Rev. by R[ichard]. W[hittington].-E[gan]. in *Books and Bookmen*, IX (Sept. 1964), 32–33.

Riese, Teut Andreas, and Dieter Riesner, eds. See No. 64.

481. Riga, Frank Peter. "The Uncollected and Apocryphal Poems of John Hamilton Reynolds" [Doctoral dissertation, Buffalo, 1967], DA, XXVIII (Nov. 1967), 1825-A–1826-A.

482. ["River Landscape with Deer Drinking,"] *Apollo*, LXXXIII (March 1966), lxxii.

This De Wint is reproduced in an announcement by Appleby Brothers.

483. Roberts, Keith. [In] "Current and Forthcoming Exhibitions," *Burlington Magazine*, CVIII (Nov. 1966), 591–596.

Reviews two exhibitions featuring De Wint's works, three of which are reproduced.

Robinson, Henry Crabb. See No. 257.

484. Rogers, Neville. "The Poetic Process: Notes on Some Observations by Keats, Rilke and Others," KSMB, XVIII (1967), 26–35.

Argues that a comparison of the phenomenological perspectives of Rilke and Keats would give us a closer view of the workings of the imagination and the poetic craft. Mentions Byron and Shelley.

485. *Rokuda, Masataka. " 'La Belle Dame sans Merci': Keats' Poetic Self-Portrait," *Journal* (Aichi Gakuin Univ.), XVI (1968), 69–90. [In Japanese.]

486. Rollins, Hyder Edward, ed. *The Keats Circle*. Second Edition. See K-SJ, XV (1966), 162, XVI (1967), 132, XVII (1968), 30.

Rev. by Frederick T. Wood in ES, XLVIII (Aug. 1967), 366.

Rothenberg, Jacob. See No. 261.

"The Royal Literary Fund." See No. 317.

487. Saito, Yuzo. "The Sensibility of Basho and Keats," in *Actes: Proceedings of the IVth Congress of the International Comparative Literature Association*, ed. François Jost (The Hague: Mouton, 1966), pp. 1399–1403.

Compares the "keen and subtle sensibility" of the two poets. See Nos. 24 and 49.

488. *Sakata, Shozo. "Keats's Dilemma," *Rising Generation*, CXIV (Feb. 1968), 10–11. [In Japanese.]

489. Salvesen, Christopher. *The Landscape of Memory: A Study of Wordsworth's Poetry*. Lincoln: Univ. of Nebraska, 1965.

Refers frequently to Hazlitt.

490. *San Juan, Epifanio, Jr. "Keats's 'Ode to a Nightingale': Aesthetic and Myth," *Saint Louis Quarterly* (Baguio City), III (1965), 343–362.

491. ["Scarborough Castle,"] *Apollo*, LXXXIII (June 1966), liii.

This De Wint is reproduced in an announcement by the Manning Gallery.

492. Schlüter, Kurt. *Die englische Ode: Studien zu ihrer Entwicklung unter dem Einfluss der antiken Hymne*. See K-SJ, XVII (1968), 30.

Rev. by Horst Oppel in *Neueren Sprachen*, LXVI (Sept. 1967), 454–455.

Schulz, H. C. See No. 9.

Schulz, Max F. See No. 265.

493. Shakespeare, William. "From *The Tempest*: Act IV, Scene I," K-SJ, XVII (1968), 30.

Lines from a book owned by Keats, "with passages he underlined printed in italics."

494. Sheats, Paul D. "Stylistic Discipline in *The Fall of Hyperion*," K-SJ, XVII (1968), 75–88.

Discusses the fundamental change in imagery in "The Fall of Hyperion," proposing that Keats sought in this poem to repress "intensity" of sensation in order to attain to an ethical and philosophic authority.

495. Siemens, Reynold Gerrard. "One Role of the Woman in the Artist's Development in Certain British Artist-Hero Novels of the Nineteenth and Early Twentieth Centuries" [Doctoral dissertation, Wisconsin, 1966], DA, XXVIII (Sept. 1967), 1059-A–1060-A.

Makes use of *Liber Amoris* and "La Belle Dame sans Merci."

496. *Skwarczyńska, Stefania, ed. *Teoria badán literackich za granicą*. I: *Romantyzm i pozytywizm*. Part 1: *Kierunki romantyczne i przedmarksowska rosyjska szkola realizmu*. Krakow: Wydawnictwo Literackie, 1965.

Includes, in Polish, some of Hazlitt's criticism.

Rev. by Z. Folejewski in BA, XLI (Winter 1967), 99–100.

497. Sperry, Stuart M., Jr. "Richard Woodhouse's Interleaved and Annotated Copy of Keats's *Poems* (1817)," *Literary Monographs*, I (1967), 101–164.

A carefully detailed introduction, followed by a virtually complete text of Woodhouse's annotations. The volume is in the Henry E. Huntington Library.

Rev. in *Choice*, IV (Oct. 1967), 831; by John Pick in MLJ, LI (Dec. 1967), 518–519.

Stange, G. Robert. See No. 273.

498. Stevens, Aretta J. "The Edition of Montaigne Read by Melville," PBSA, LXII (1st quarter 1968), 130–134.

Melville most likely owned William Hazlitt the Younger's edition, either the 1842 or the 1845 impression.

499. Stevenson, John. "Arcadia Re-Settled: Pastoral Poetry and Romantic Theory," SEL, VII (Autumn 1967), 629–638.

Touches briefly on "Ode on a Grecian Urn."

Stewart, John Francis. See No. 319.

500. Stillinger, Jack. "The Meaning of 'Poor Cheated Soul' in Keats's 'The Eve of Saint Mark,' " ELN, V (March 1968), 193–196.

". . . by ignoring the life in the village

outside her room, Bertha is cheating herself of reality."

501. *Story, Patrick Lee. "Hazlitt's *Spirit of the Age*: A Facsimile Edition with Introduction and Textual Collations." (Doctoral dissertation, Northwestern, 1968).

502. Sullivan, G. Brian. "The Alchemy of Art: A Study in the Evolution of the Creative Mind of John Keats" [Doctoral dissertation, Nebraska, 1967], DA, XXVIII (Jan. 1968), 2698-A.

503. Swaminathan, S. R. "Keats's Epistle to John Hamilton Reynolds, Line 14," N&Q, CCXII (Aug. 1967), 306–307.†

"Patent" should read "patient."

504. Swingle, Larry James. "Days That Cannot Die: A Romantic Manner of Thought about Time and Human Value" [Doctoral dissertation, Wisconsin, 1967], DA, XXVIII (Aug. 1967), 646-A.

Discusses the Romantic mind in "The Fall of Hyperion."

Symonds, John Addington. See No. 671.

505. Tabbert, Reinbert. "John Keats' 'Ode on Melancholy' in deutschen Übertragungen: Versuch einer Typologie der dichterischen Übersetzung," *Germanisch-Romanische Monatsschrift*, XLIX (Jan. 1968), 38–58.

506. *Tabuchi, Mikio. " 'A power to see'—An Aspect of Keats's Poetic Character," *Studies in Foreign Language and Literature* (Hiroshima Univ.), XV (1968), 53–70. [In Japanese.]

507. *Takeda, Miyoko. "A Study on 'Lamia' and *Jasei-no-in*," *Study Reports* (Baika Women's College), IV (Dec. 1967), 19–54. [In Japanese.]

508. Talbot, Norman. *The Major Poems of John Keats*. Sydney: Sydney Univ., 1968. "Sydney Studies in Literature."

509. Thomas, W. K. "Keats' 'To Sleep,' " Exp, XXVI (March 1968), Item 55.

Discusses the words "embalmer" and "casket," which have "changed their meaning radically" since 1819.

510. Thorpe, Clarence DeWitt. *The Mind of John Keats*. See K-SJ, XV (1966), 162–163.

Rev. in *Choice*, II (Apr. 1965), 96–97.

Timko, Michael. See No. 279.

511. Ting, Nai-tung. "The Holy Man and the Snake-Woman: A Study of a Lamia Story in Asian and European Literature," *Fabula*, VIII (1966), 145–191.

Includes discussion of Keats.

512. Tomory, P. A. "Two Drawings by Benjamin Robert Haydon," *Burlington Magazine*, CX (March 1968), 144–145.

One is a preparatory sketch for *Alexander's Combat with a Lion*; the other is a drawing of a lion. Both are reproduced.

513. Tschumi, Raymond. "Le génie anglais chez Pierre-Louis Matthey," in *Mélanges offerts à Monsieur Georges Bonnard* (Geneva: Droz, 1966), pp. 87–97.

Discusses Matthey's translations of Keats.

514. Viebrock, Helmut. "Poetische Dialektik bei John Keats," *Anglia*, LXXXVI (1968), 124–142.

515. ["View of St. Donat's Castle, Glamorganshire,"] *Apollo*, LXXXIII (March 1966), lxxiii.

This De Wint is reproduced in an announcement by Appleby Brothers.

516. *Viswanatham, K. "A Note on Keats' Quintuplets," *Triveni*, XXXVI, 15–28.

517. Waldoff, Leon. "The Mythic Basis of Three Major Poems of the Romantic Period" [Doctoral dissertation, Michigan, 1967], DA, XXVIII (Jan. 1968), 2699-A.

The three poems are *Endymion*, *Alastor*, and "The Rime of the Ancient Mariner."

518. Waldron, Philip. "A Reply," *Southern Review* (Adelaide), I, No. 4 (1965), pp. 68–70.†

Says that Bellairs' treatment of Brooks's essay is "miscomprehending and distorted." See Nos. 359 and 448.

519. Wallace, James Peter. "The Political Theory of William Hazlitt" [Doctoral dissertation, California, Los Angeles, 1967], DA, XXVIII (March 1968), 3738-A.

Walsh, John. See No. 677.

Weinstein, Mark A. See No. 286.

520. Wills, Garry. "Classicism in Keats's Chapman Sonnet," EC, XVII (Oct. 1967), 456–460.†

The sestet rescues Homer and the "*whole* Western poetic tradition" from the "oppressive classicism" accepted in the octave.

Wilshire, Bruce, comp. See No. 80.

Winters, Yvor. See No. 81.

521. *Yabushita, Takuro. "On 'Ode to Psyche,'" *Outlook*, IX (Summer 1967), 13–23. [In Japanese.]

522. *Yaho, Tsutomu. "Keats's Aesthetic Consciousness," *Kanazawa English Studies* (Kanazawa Univ.), X (Autumn 1967), 30–50. [In Japanese.]

523. *Yasunaga, Yoshio. "On Keats's 'Ode to a Nightingale,'" *Reports* (Shizuoka Univ.), IV (March 1968), 10pp. [In Japanese.]

524. Young, Percy M. *A History of British Music*. London: Ernest Benn, 1967.

Discusses (pp. 420–422) the Romantic poets' interest in music; also includes brief sections on Edward Holmes and Hubert Parry.

525. Zillman, Lawrence John. *John Keats and the Sonnet Tradition: A Critical and Comparative Study*. New York: Octagon, 1966.

A reprint of a book first published in 1939.

V. SHELLEY

WORKS: SELECTED, SINGLE, TRANSLATED

The Age of the Grand Tour. See No. 83.

Aloian, David. See No. 85.

Antologia liryki angielskiej, 1300–1950. See No. 86.

526. Ashley, Leonard R. N., ed. *Nineteenth-Century British Drama: An Anthology of Representative Plays*. See K-SJ, XVII (1968), 33.

Rev. by Michael R. Booth in *Educational Theatre Journal*, XX (March 1968), 107–108.

Bishop, John, comp. See No. 299.

527. *Les Cenci*. [*The Cenci*.] [Translated by] Maurice Castelain. Second Edition. Paris: les Belles Lettres, 1968. [In French.]

Cole, William. See No. 91.

Coleman, Elliott, ed. See No. 92.

528. "A Dirge," K-SJ, XVII (1968), 74.

"Rough wind, that moanest loud."

529. *The Esdaile Notebook: A Volume of Early Poems*. Ed. Kenneth Neill Cameron. See K-SJ, XIV (1965), 127, XV (1966), 164, XVI (1967), 134, XVII (1968), 33.

Rev. by Newell F. Ford in MP, LXV (May 1968), 408–411.

530. *The Esdaile Poems: Early Minor Poems from the "Esdaile Notebook."* Ed. Neville Rogers. See K-SJ, XVI (1967), 134, XVII (1968), 33.

Rev. by R[ichard]. H[arter]. F[ogle]. in ELN, V, Supplement (Sept. 1967), 39–40; by P. H. Butter in MLR, LXII (Oct. 1967), 711–712; by Roger Sharrock in RES, n.s., XIX (Feb. 1968), 86–87; by Newell F. Ford in MP, LXV (May 1968), 408–411. See also No. 48.

Foakes, R. A., ed. See No. 327.

Freedman, Morris, and Paul B. Davis. See No. 97.

531. *"Indiiskia serenada" ["Indian Serenade"], [translated into Georgian by] M. Zaalishvili, *Tsiskari*, No. 2 (1966), p. 87.

Kelly, T. J. See No. 100.

Kroeber, Karl, and John O. Lyons. See No. 101.

532. *The Letters of Percy Bysshe Shelley*. Ed. Frederick L. Jones. See K-SJ, XIV (1965), 127, XV (1966), 164, XVI (1967), 134.

Rev. by Herbert Huscher in ASNS, CCIV (May 1967), 63–66; by Helmut Viebrock in *Anglia*, LXXXVI (1968), 243–245.

Lucie-Smith, Edward, ed. See No. 105.

533. *Note Books of Percy Bysshe Shelley: From the Originals in the Library of W. K. Bixby*. Ed. H. Buxton Forman. 3 vols. New York: Phaeton, 1968.

A reprint of a set first published in 1911.

534. *Osvoboždennyj Prometej*. [*Prometheus Unbound*.] Erevan: Ajastan, 1968. [In Armenian.]

Payne, William Morton. See No. 59.

535. *"Piosenka," [translated by] Roman Gorzelski, *Odgłosy*, No. 38 (1965), p. 6.

Probably a free translation of "A Dirge."

536. *Prometeu descătuşat şi alte poeme*. [*Prometheus Unbound*.] [Translated by] Petre Solomon. Bucharest: Editura pentru literatură, 1965. [In Romanian.]

537. **Prométhée délivré*. [*Prometheus Unbound*.] [Translated by] Louis Cazamian. Paris: Aubier-Flammarion, 1968. [In French.]

Reeves, James, and Martin Seymour-Smith, eds. See No. 340.

538. *Selected Poetry*. Ed. Neville Rogers. Boston: Houghton Mifflin, 1968. "Riverside Editions."

539. Cancelled.

540. *Shelley's Critical Prose*. Ed. B. R. McElderry, Jr. See K-SJ, XVII (1968), 33.
Rev. in *Choice*, V (June 1968), 487.

541. *Shelley's "Prometheus Unbound": The Text and the Drafts*. Ed. Lawrence John Zillman. New Haven: Yale Univ., 1968.

542. *Shelley's Prose; or, The Trumpet of a Prophecy*. Ed. David Lee Clark. See K-SJ, IV (1955), 121–122, V (1956), 131, VI (1957), 147, XVII (1968), 33–34.
Rev. in *Choice*, IV (July–Aug. 1967), 533.

Simpson, Louis. See No. 108.

Stanford, Derek, ed. See No. 109.

Trilling, Lionel. See No. 110.

Wright, David, ed. See No. 113.

Books and Articles Relating to Shelley and his Circle

543. "Anniversary Gifts to the Houghton Library," *Harvard Library Bulletin*, XV (July 1967), 308–309.
One gift was the manuscript of an unpublished French translation of *Nightmare Abbey*.

544. "Auction Sales," ABC, XVIII (Jan.–Feb. 1968), 45–47.
A first edition of Peacock's *Palmyra and Other Poems* brought $80 at Swann Galleries, 21 Sept. 1967; *The Genius of the Thames* (1810), $65.

545. Bailey, M. H. "Marriage Lines," TLS, 6 July 1967, p. 606.
Responds to TLS review of Wardle's edition of *Godwin and Mary*: reviewer "over-generalizes alarmingly about the two complex protagonists." See Nos. 610, 662, and 679.

546. Baine, Rodney M. *Thomas Holcroft and the Revolutionary Novel*. See K-SJ, XVI (1967), 135, XVII (1968), 34.
Rev. by W[illiam]. H. M[arshall]. in ELN, V, Supplement (Sept. 1967), 33.

Ball, Patricia M. See No. 16.

547. Barton, Wilfrid Converse. "Shelley and the New Criticism: The Anatomy of a Critical Misvaluation" [Doctoral dissertation, Tulane, 1967], DA, XXVIII (June 1968), 5006-A.

548. *Baskiyar, D. D. "Shelley's Theory of Poetry: A Study of the Evolution of His Poetic and of Its Relation to His Creative Practice." (Doctoral dissertation, Leeds, 1966.)

549. Bass, Eben. "The Fourth Element in 'Ode to the West Wind,'" *Papers on Language & Literature*, III (Fall 1967), 327–338.
The three "classical" elements of the opening are completed by the superior fourth, that of fire, in stanza V.

550. Baxter, B. M. *Albert Verwey's Translations from Shelley's Poetical Works*. See K-SJ, XIV (1965), 127, XV (1966), 165.
Rev. by H. B. de Groot in ES, XLIX (June 1968), 263–268.

551. Behar, Rudolph Souvenir. "Heaven's Ever-Changing Shadow: The Reflection Cluster in Shelley's Poetry" [Doctoral dissertation, Oregon, 1967], DA, XXVIII (March 1968), 3631-A.

552. Berthoff, Warner. "Brockden Brown: The Politics of the Man of Letters," *Serif*, III (Dec. 1966), 3–11.†
Discusses influence of Godwin on Brown.

"Bibliophily on the Eastern Seaboard." See No. 361.

Blainey, Ann. See No. 20.

553. Blunden, Edmund. *Shelley: A Life Story*. See K-SJ, XVI (1967), 135, XVII (1968), 34.
Rev. by L[ouis]. C. B[onnerot]. in EA, XX (July–Sept. 1967), 327.

554. Brazell, James Reid. "Shelley and the Concept of Humanity: A Study of His Moral Vision" [Doctoral dissertation, Michigan, 1967], DA, XXVIII (Jan. 1968), 2675-A.

555. Bronowski, Jacob. *The Poet's Defence*. See K-SJ, XVII (1968), 35.
Rev. by Coburn Freer in *Arizona Quarterly*, XXIII (Winter 1967), 357–359.

Brooke, Rupert. See No. 367.

Brooke, Stopford A. See No. 368.

556. Bryan, Robert A., *et al.*, eds. *All These to Teach: Essays in Honor of C. A. Robertson*. See K-SJ, XVI (1967), 135.
Rev. by J. A. Bryant, Jr., in *South Atlantic Bulletin*, XXXII (March 1967), 22–23.

557. Burke, Edmund. *The Correspondence of Edmund Burke*. Vol. V: July 1782–June 1789. Ed. Holden Furber. Cambridge:

Cambridge Univ.; Chicago: Univ. of Chicago (1965).
Includes one letter, 16 Jan. 1783, from Godwin to Burke.

Buxton, John. See Nos. 131 and 132.

"A Byron Poem. . . ." See No. 136.

558. Campbell, Olwen Ward. *Shelley and the Unromantics.* See K-SJ, XVII (1968), 35.
Rev. in *Choice*, v (March 1968), 46.

559. Campbell, William Royce. "The Views of Blake and Shelley on Man in Society" [Doctoral dissertation, Oregon, 1967], DA, XXVIII (March 1968), 3632-A–3633-A.

Cano, José Luis. See No. 137.

560. Chapman, J. A. *Papers on Shelley, Wordsworth & Others.* Freeport, N.Y.: Books for Libraries, 1967.
A reprint of a book first published in 1929.

Charlesworth, Barbara. See No. 374.

Cline, C. L. See No. 146.

Coblentz, Stanton A. See No. 147.

561. Coles, William Eliot, Jr. "Novelist of Style: A Critical Reading of the Novels of Thomas Love Peacock" [Doctoral dissertation, Minnesota, 1967], DA, XXVIII (June 1968), 5012-A.

562. Collins, Thomas J. *Robert Browning's Moral-Aesthetic Theory 1833–1855.* Lincoln: Univ. of Nebraska, 1967.
Includes chapter on "*Pauline* and the Question of Shelley: Unresolved Problems" (pp. 3–16) and also discusses Browning's *Essay on Shelley* (pp. 121–122). See K-SJ, XVI (1967), 136, No. 375.

"Comment: Keats For Ever." See No. 382.

563. Crompton, Margaret. *Shelley's Dream Women.* See K-SJ, XVII (1968), 35.
Rev. by L. M. Wallace in *Books and Bookmen*, XII (July 1967), 42; by Elizabeth Nelson in *Library Journal*, XCIII (1 Jan. 1968), 81.

Culler, A. Dwight. See No. 150.

564. *Curran, Stuart Alan. "Shelley's Tragedy *The Cenci* as Poem and Play." (Doctoral dissertation, Harvard, 1967.)

565. Davison, Richard Allan. "A Websterian Echo in 'The Cenci,'" *American Notes & Queries*, VI (Dec. 1967), 53–54.
Notes similarities with speeches in *The Duchess of Malfi.*

566. Dawson, Carl. *Thomas Love Peacock.* London: Routledge; New York: Humanities (1968). "Profiles in Literature."
Rev. in TLS, 23 May 1968, p. 529.

567. de Beer, Gavin. "Some Blunders on Shelley's Elopement in 1814," KSMB, XVIII (1967), 36–38.
A reexamination of the errors in E.-D. Forgues' review (1848) of Medwin's *Life of Shelley.*

Demetz, Peter. See No. 153.

568. *De Rocco, Joseph. "Shelley's Empiricism." (Doctoral dissertation, Columbia, 1968.)

569. Dodson, Charles Brooks. "*Crotchet Castle*, by Thomas Love Peacock: A Critical Edition" [Doctoral dissertation, Nebraska, 1967], DA, XXVIII (Aug. 1967), 674-A.

570. Donohue, Joseph W., Jr. "Shelley's Beatrice and the Romantic Concept of Tragic Character," K-SJ, XVII (1968), 53–73.
Explores the influence of a portrait, *La Cenci*, and the theatrical style of the Regency actress Eliza O'Neill, on Shelley's concept of tragic character in *The Cenci.*

571. Du Bos, Charles. *Du Spirituel dans l'ordre littéraire.* Preface by Georges Poulet. Paris: José Corti, 1967.
Includes essay on "Milton, Shelley" (pp. 15–52).
Rev. in TLS, 13 June 1968, p. 623.

572. Duerksen, Roland A. *Shelleyan Ideas in Victorian Literature.* See K-SJ, XVII (1968), 36.
Rev. by Frederick T. Wood in ES, XLVIII (Aug. 1967), 367; by K[enneth]. N[eill]. C[ameron]. in ELN, v, Supplement (Sept. 1967), 38; by Jerome H. Buckley in K-SJ, XVII (1968), 126–128; by Alan Grob in JEGP, LXVII (Apr. 1968), 316–319.

573. Eigner, Edwin M. *Robert Louis Stevenson and Romantic Tradition.* Princeton: Princeton Univ., 1966.
Includes discussion of Godwin and the Shelleys; alludes to other Romantics.
Rev. by Karl Kroeber in JEGP, LXVII (Jan. 1968), 170–172; by Andrew Rutherford in RES, n.s., XIX (May 1968), 226–227.

Ellis, Amanda M. See No. 166.

574. Ellis, F. S., comp. *A Lexical Concordance*

to the Poetical Works of Percy Bysshe Shelley. New York: Johnson, 1967.

A reprint of a volume first published in 1892.

Enscoe, Gerald E. See No. 394.

Eskin, Stanley G. See No. 171.

"First Meeting of Two Poets." See No. 172.

575. Fogle, Richard Harter. "Dante and Shelley's *Adonais*," *Bucknell Review*, XV (Dec. 1967), 11–21.

Uses passages from the *Paradiso* to interpret *Adonais*.

576. Fogle, Richard Harter. "John Taaffe's Annotated Copy of *Adonais*," K-SJ, XVII (1968), 31–52.

Reproduces an unpublished commentary by Taaffe on *Adonais* and underscores the significance of his discovery of parallels between *Adonais* and Dante's *The Divine Comedy*.

577. Foxell, Nigel. *Ten Poems Analysed*. London: Pergamon, 1966.

Shelley's "To a Skylark" is reprinted with some useful annotations (pp. 143–163) and a sympathetic introduction which takes issue with F. R. Leavis' judgment in *Revaluation* that Shelley has a "weak grasp of the actual."

578. *French, Roberts W. "Shelley's Vision," *Humanist*, XXVII (July 1967), 132.

Frye, Northrop. See No. 32.

579. Fuller, Jean Overton. *Shelley: A Biography*. London: Jonathan Cape, 1968.

Rev. by Robert Nye in *The Times*, London, 9 March 1968, p. 21; by Mary Gould in *Books and Bookmen*, XIII (Apr. 1968), 20–21; in TLS, 4 Apr. 1968, p. 334.

580. Gál, István. "Shelley Plain," *New Hungarian Quarterly*, VIII (Winter 1967), 184–189.

An account of various Hungarian travelers who met literary figures in nineteenth-century England, including a brief mention of Byron.

581. Gallon, David. "Thomas Love Peacock and Wales: Some Suggestions," *Anglo-Welsh Review*, XVII (Summer 1968), 125–134.

Garber, Frederick. See No. 175.

Gérard, Albert S. See No. 402.

582. Godwin, William. *Four Early Pamphlets (1783–1784)*. See K-SJ, XVI (1967), 136.

Rev. by D[onald]. H. R[eiman]. in ELN, V, Supplement (Sept. 1967), 31–32; by F. E. L. Priestley in *Studies in Burke and His Time*, IX (Spring 1968), 983–986.

583. Godwin, William. *Italian Letters, or, The History of the Count de St. Julian*. See K-SJ, XVI (1967), 136, XVII (1968), 37.

Rev. in *Choice*, III (May 1966), 208; by Frederick W. Hilles in SEL, VI (Autumn 1966), 611; by R. V. Adkinson in *Revue des langues vivantes*, XXXIII (1967), 441–442; by Erik Frykman in *Studia Neophilologica*, XXXIX (1967), 188–189; by A[lfred]. O[wen]. A[ldridge]. in *Comparative Literature Studies*, IV (Dec. 1967), 457.

584. Godwin, William. *Uncollected Writings (1785–1822): Articles in Periodicals and Six Pamphlets, One with Coleridge's Marginalia*. Ed. Jack W. Marken and Burton R. Pollin. Gainesville, Fla.: Scholars' Facsimiles & Reprints, 1968.

585. Grabo, Carl. *Prometheus Unbound: An Interpretation*. New York: Gordian, 1968.

A reprint of a book first published in 1935.

586. Graham, John. "Character Description and Meaning in the Romantic Novel," SIR, V (Summer 1966), 208–218.†

Discusses Godwin's use of physiognomy.

587. *Hachiya, Akio. "Some Observations on Shelley's 'Alastor,'" *Review of English Literature* (Kyoto Univ.), XXII (Jan. 1968), 26–45. [In Japanese.]

588. Hack, Arthur. "The Psychological Pattern of Shelley's *Prometheus Unbound*" [Doctoral dissertation, Wisconsin, 1967], DA, XXVIII (Sept. 1967), 1078-A.

Hamer, Douglas. See No. 183.

Harding, Walter. See No. 184.

589. Hare, Robert Rigby. "Charles Brockden Brown's *Ormond*: The Influence of Rousseau, Godwin, and Mary Wollstonecraft" [Doctoral dissertation, Maryland, 1967], DA, XXVIII (May 1968), 4599-A.

590. *Hayashida, Minoru. "A Study of Shelley's 'Mont Blanc,'" *Annual Reports of English & American Literature* (Osaka Shoin Women's College), V (Dec. 1967), 1–13. [In Japanese.]

591. Hildebrand, William Harry. "An Ana-

gogic Interpretation of Shelley's *Prometheus Unbound*" [Doctoral dissertation, Western Reserve, 1967], DA, XXVIII (July 1967), 197-A.

592. Hill, James L. "Dramatic Structure in Shelley's *Julian and Maddalo*," ELH, XXXV (March 1968), 84–93.

Discusses "the central problem of the poem, the question of meaning rather than identity."

Howard, John Douglas, Jr. See No. 192.

593. Hoyt, Charles Alva, ed. *Minor British Novelists*. See K-SJ, XVII (1968), 39, No. 541.

Rev. in *Prairie Schooner*, XLI (Spring 1967), 93; by E. Wright in *Nineteenth-Century Fiction*, XXII (March 1968), 401–405.

594. Huscher, Herbert. *Studien zu Shelleys Lyrik*. New York: Johnson, 1967.

A reprint of a book first published in 1919.

Hutchings, R. J. See No. 36.

Jabłkowska, Róża. See No. 196.

595. Jellicoe, Ann. *Shelley or The Idealist*. See K-SJ, XVII (1968), 38.

Rev. by Michael Thorpe in ES, XLIX (June 1968), 274.

596. Johnson, Diane. [In] "Information, Please," TLS, 11 Jan. 1968, p. 44.

Asks about Mary Allen Meredith, Peacock's daughter.

597. Jones, A. R. "Robert Browning and the Dramatic Monologue: The Impersonal Art," *Critical Quarterly*, IX (Winter 1967), 301–328.

Discusses influence of Shelley on Browning.

Joshi, P. C. See No. 199.

Jump, John D., ed. See No. 314.

598. Kendall, Lyle H., Jr. "The Not-So-Gentle Art of Puffing: William G. Kingsland and Thomas J. Wise," PBSA, LXII (1st quarter 1968), 25–37.

Recounts Kingsland's promotion in the pages of *Poet Lore* of Wise's books, including several Shelley publications.

599. King-Hele, Desmond. "Shelley and Dr. Lind," KSMB, XVIII (1967), 1–6.

Lind introduced Shelley to Erasmus Darwin's poems, Godwin's *Political Justice*, Plato, and the use of pamphlets printed on a private press.

600. Kloos, Willem. *Willem Kloos 1859–1938: zijn jeugd, zijn leven*. Introduction by Hubert Michaël. The Hague: Bert Bakker, 1965.

Includes Kloos's unfinished translation of Shelley's "Lines Written in the Vale of Chamounix" (pp. 271–274) and his essay "Shelley en Byron" (pp. 276–279).

Rev. in TLS, 14 Sept. 1967, p. 818.

Kolbuszewski, Stanisław. See No. 40.

Lawrence, D. H. See No. 215.

Leavis, F. R., comp. See No. 443.

601. Leed, Jacob, and Robert Hemenway. "Use of the Computer in Some Recent Studies of Literary Style," *Serif*, II (June 1965), 16–20.†

Discusses study by computer of similarity in diction between *Prometheus Unbound* and *Paradise Lost*.

Leppmann, Wolfgang. See No. 216.

Lewis, R. W. B. See No. 445.

Liebert, Herman W. See No. 217.

Lill, James. See No. 218.

Locker, Malka. See No. 46.

602. Lund, Mary Graham. "Shelley's God—Transcendent or Imminent [*sic*]?" *Discourse*, XI (Winter 1968), 55–61.

A "transcendence of Love" such as Shelley dreamed of is still available to "the seeking soul."

McBurney, William H., and Charlene M. Taylor, comps. See No. 6.

603. *McCracken, James David. "Politics and Propaganda in Godwin's Novels." (Doctoral dissertation, Chicago, 1967.)

604. McGill, Mildred Sloan. "The Role of Earth in Shelley's *Prometheus Unbound*," SIR, VII (Winter 1968), 117–128.

Earth's function is "to effect the revitalization of Demeter-Earth's chthonian qualities, and to enlarge and refine the erotic limitations implicit in the Spirit of the Earth."

605. Mackey, Louis H. "On Philosophical Form: A Tear for Adonais," *Thought*, XLII (Summer 1967), 238–260.†

A lecture which derives its title but not its content from Shelley.

606. *McTaggart, William Joseph. "A Textual Study of Percy Bysshe Shelley's 'A Ballad' Followed by a Brief Examination of Certain Sociological Problems Affect-

ing Church and State in Shelley's Day." (Doctoral dissertation, Ohio, 1968.)

607. Madden, J. L. "Gladstone's Reading of Thomas Love Peacock," N&Q, CCXII (Oct. 1967), 384.†

Gladstone's markings in a three-volume edition of Peacock given him by Robert Temple.

608. *Madden, Lionel. *Thomas Love Peacock.* London: Evans Bros., 1967. "Literature in Perspective Series."

Madden, William A. See No. 225.

609. Maniquis, Robert Manuel. "The Human Image in the Poetry of Shelley: A Study of Human Description and Physical Imagery" [Doctoral dissertation, Columbia, 1967], DA, XXVIII (Oct. 1967), 1440-A.

Marples, Morris. See No. 52.

610. "Marriage Lines," TLS, 6 July 1967, p. 606.

Reviewer replies to Bailey's and Small's criticisms. See Nos. 545, 662, and 679.

Marshall, William H. See No. 229.

611. Maurois, André. "Le biographe et ses personnages: vérité et poésie," *Annales: Revue mensuelle des lettres françaises*, LXXIV (Feb. 1967), 5–19.

Recalls writing his biography of Shelley.

Melchiori, Barbara. See No. 453.

612. *Mesterházi, Márton. "Shelley a cenciek c. drámája és ag angol reneszánsz tragédia," *Filológia Közlöny*, XIV (1968), 207–217.

Miles, Josephine. See No. 235.

Miller, Arthur McA. See No. 236.

613. Miller, Milton L. "Manic-Depressive Cycles of the Poet Shelley," *Psychoanalytical Forum*, I (1966), 188–195.

Contends that the facts of Shelley's life and his poetic imagery "epitomize many of the essentials that psychoanalytic theory has outlined regarding manic depressives."

Criticisms of the paper (pp. 195–203) are by George Frumkes, Louis Fraiberg, Maurice Walsh, and Fred Feldman, with a reply by Milton Miller.

614. Moravia, Alberto. *Beatrice Cenci.* Translated by Angus Davidson. London: Secker & Warburg, 1965.

A play.

615. Mullett, Charles F. "*The Bee* (1790–1794): A Tour of Crotchet Castle," SAQ, LXVI (Winter 1967), 70–86.†

Peacock could have found ideas about political economy in *The Bee*, an Edinburgh periodical edited by James Anderson.

616. Nelson, Mary Elizabeth. "Crabbe's Tales and the Theory and Practice of Narrative in the Eighteenth and Early Nineteenth Century" [Doctoral dissertation, California, Berkeley, 1966], DA, XXVIII (July 1967), 238-A–239-A.

Includes comparison of Crabbe's verse tales with Godwin's prose fiction.

"News & Comment." See No. 243.

617. *Nikitas, A. "Peacock's *Nightmare Abbey* Edited with a Critical Introduction and Commentary." (Doctoral dissertation, London, 1967.)

Orel, Harold. See No. 246.

618. *Ostromęcki, Bohdan. "Percy Bysshe Shelley," *Radio i Świat*, No. 11 (1956), p. 6. [In Polish.]

Owen, Wilfred. See No. 469.

619. Palacio, Jean de. "La 'Fortune' de Godwin en France: Le cas d'Elizabeth Hamilton," RLC, XLI (July–Sept. 1967), 321–341.

Full discussion of the little-known novel, *Bridgetina, ou Les Philosophes Modernes* (Paris, 1802), an ostensible satire on Godwinism which may have helped to introduce many of his ideas into France.

620. Palacio, Jean de. "Mary Shelley and the 'Last Man': A Minor Romantic Theme," RLC, XLII (Jan.–March 1968), 37–49.

An examination of the relevance of the sources to the design of the novel, as well as an evaluation of the motif in various Continental and British works.

621. *Peacock, Thomas Love. *Headlong Hall, Nightmare Abbey, The Misfortunes of Elphin, and Crotchet Castle.* Introduction by J. B. Priestley. Notes by Barbara Lloyd-Evans. London: Pan Books, 1967. "Best-sellers of Literature."

622. *Peacock, Thomas Love. *A Peacock Selection.* Ed. H. L. B. Moody. London: Macmillan; New York: St. Martin's (1966). "English Classics, New Series."

623. Peacock, Thomas Love. *The Works of*

Thomas Love Peacock. 10 vols. New York: AMS, 1967.

A reprint of the Halliford Edition, ed. H. F. B. Brett-Smith and C. E. Jones (London, 1924–34).

624. Pollin, Burton R. *Godwin Criticism: A Synoptic Bibliography.* Toronto: Univ. of Toronto, 1967.

The first complete annotated bibliography of Godwin's life and writings.

Rev. in *American Notes & Queries,* VI (Jan. 1968), 75; by Alfred Owen Aldridge in *Comparative Literature Studies,* V (June 1968), 227–228.

625. Pollin, Burton R. "Godwin's Letter to Ogilvie, Friend of Jefferson, and the Federalist Propaganda," JHI, XXVIII (July–Sept. 1967), 432–444.

Text, with commentary, of a Godwin letter pertinent to the "Federalist-Jeffersonian polemics of 1801."

626. Pollin, Burton R. "Mary Shelley as the Parvenue," *Review of English Literature,* VIII (July 1967), 9–21.

Mary Shelley's short story, "The Parvenue" (1836), "provides a provocative insight into the complex psyche and the developing ideas of Shelley's wife."

627. Pollin, Burton R. "'Ozymandias' and the Dormouse," *Dalhousie Review,* XLVII (Autumn 1967), 361–367.

"Glirastes," the pseudonym Shelley used when the poem was first published, was derived in part from the Latin for "dormouse," a word with many associations for the poet.

628. Pollin, Burton R. "'Rappaccini's Daughter'—Sources and Names," *Names,* XIV (March 1966), 30–35.

Suggests that *Frankenstein* and Godwin's *St. Leon* contributed to Hawthorne's story.

629. Poston, Elizabeth. "English Choral," *Musical Times,* CIX (March 1968), 260–261.

A music review that includes comment on Geoffrey Bush's setting for "Ozymandias."

Praz, Mario. See No. 250.

630. Prosen, Anthony J. "Suffering in Aeschylus and Hopkins," *Classical Bulletin,* XLI (Nov. 1964), 11–13.†

Shelley also understood the reason for suffering.

631. Raben, Joseph. "Coleridge and Shelley's *Alastor,*" RES, n.s., XIX (May 1968), 180–181.

Reaffirms that Coleridge is "the most obvious model of the *Alastor*-poet," answering Timothy Webb. See No. 683.

632. Raine, Kathleen. *Defending Ancient Springs.* London: Oxford Univ., 1967.

Includes a chapter (pp. 139–155) entitled "A Defence of Shelley's Poetry." Refers in other chapters to Shelley and to Keats. See No. 633.

Rev. by John Goode in NS, LXXV (2 Feb. 1968), 144–145; by Howard Sergeant in *English,* XVII (Summer 1968), 70.

633. Raine, Kathleen. "A Defense of Shelley's Poetry," *Southern Review,* III (Oct. 1967), 856–873.

"Shelley's work is poetry itself, as Mozart's is music itself." His work "speaks to the soul in its own language and of its native place." See No. 632.

Raine, Kathleen. See No. 476.

634. Reck, Rima Drell, ed. *Explorations of Literature.* See K-SJ, XVII (1968), 29.

Rev. by M[ary]. R. M[ahl]. in *Personalist,* XLVIII (July 1967), 431; by Josephine Z. Knopp in MLJ, LII (Feb. 1968), 132–133.

635. Reiman, Donald H. *Shelley's "The Triumph of Life."* See K-SJ, XV (1966), 169, XVI (1967), 139, XVII (1968), 41.

Rev. by Dietrich Jäger in *Anglia,* LXXXV (1967), 496–499; by G. M. Matthews in JEGP, LXVI (Oct. 1967), 597–605; by Derek Roper in N&Q, CCXIII (Jan. 1968), 38–39. See also No. 48.

636. Reiter, Seymour. "Shelley the Cubist," TLS, 7 March 1968, p. 237.

Questions TLS reviewer's contention that other scholars have demonstrated the "wide range of Shelley's artistry." Reviewer replies. See Nos. 637 and 638.

637. Reiter, Seymour. "Shelley the Cubist," TLS, 18 Apr. 1968, p. 405.

Sees "distortion" in TLS reviewer's answer to his letter. See Nos. 636 and 638.

638. Reiter, Seymour. *A Study of Shelley's Poetry.* [Albuquerque:] Univ. of New Mexico, 1967.

Rev. by Stuart Curran in K-SJ, XVII (1968), 130–132; in *Choice*, IV (Jan. 1968), 1245; in TLS, 22 Feb. 1968, p. 182; by Michael Thorpe in *English*, XVII (Summer 1968), 62–63. See also Nos. 636 and 637.

639. Rieger, James. *The Mutiny Within: The Heresies of Percy Bysshe Shelley*. See K-SJ, XVII (1968), 41.

Rev. in *Choice*, IV (Sept. 1967), 674. See also Nos. 21 and 48.

Riese, Teut Andreas, and Dieter Riesner, eds. See No. 64.

Robinson, Charles E. See No. 255.

Robinson, Henry Crabb. See No. 257.

Rogers, Neville. See No. 484.

640. *Rogers, Neville. *Shelley at Work: A Critical Inquiry*. Second Edition. Oxford: Clarendon, 1967.

Contains "important revisions and additions based on recent researches." See K-SJ, VII (1958), 131, No. 408.

Rev. in *English*, XVI (Autumn 1967), 243; in TLS, 21 Sept. 1967, p. 840; in *Choice*, V (March 1968), 51. See also No. 48.

641. Rosen, Frederick. "Godwin and Holcroft," ELN, V (March 1968), 183–186.

The breach between the two friends in 1805 came about because Holcroft thought that Godwin had used him as a model for a character in *Fleetwood.*

642. Rosenberg, Samuel. "The Horrible Truth about Frankenstein," *Life*, LXIV (15 March 1968), 74B–84.

The "eerie drama" behind the creation of the novel: "What psychic forces drove Mary Shelley to write the most famous of all horror novels?"

643. Rothstein, Eric. "Allusion and Analogy in the Romance of *Caleb Williams*," *University of Toronto Quarterly*, XXXVII (Oct. 1967), 18–30.

Contends that the novel is a skillfully planned and aesthetically unified *Bildungsroman*, in which the hero learns about things as they are "through a flow of actual events and of psychologically symbolic events connected by analogy."

644. Rountree, Thomas J. *This Mighty Sum of Things: Wordsworth's Theme of Benevolent Necessity*. See K-SJ, XVI (1967), 140.

Rev. by Roger Sharrock in N&Q, CCXIII (Jan. 1968), 35–36.

"The Royal Literary Fund." See No. 317.

645. *Ruff, James Lynn. "Image, Theme and Structure in *The Revolt of Islam*." (Doctoral dissertation, Northwestern, 1968.)

646. *Ruksina, K. S. "Meri Uolstonkraft—xudoznik," *Filologiceskie Nauki*, XI, No. 2, pp. 29–40.

Mary Wollstonecraft the artist.

647. Russell, Bertrand. *The Autobiography of Bertrand Russell 1914–1944*. Boston: Little, Brown, 1968.

Briefly compares D. H. Lawrence with Shelley.

Saagpakk, Paul F. See No. 262.

648. St. George, Priscilla P. "Another Look at Two Famous Lyrics in *Prometheus Unbound*," JEGP, LXVII (Apr. 1968), 279–295.

Discusses "Life of Life!" and "My soul is an enchanted boat" as examples of Shelley's mature art.

648a. St. George, Priscilla P. "Cwm Elan and Nangtwillt: Two Vanished Sites," K-SJ, XVII (1968), 7–9.

A reservoir now covers the places Shelley stayed in the summer of 1811 and the spring of 1812.

649. Schaubert, Else von. *Shelleys Tragödie "The Cenci" und Marlowes Doppeldrama "Tamburlaine."* See K-SJ, XVI (1967), 140.

Rev. by Herbert Huscher in ASNS, CCIV (May 1967), 60–62.

650. Schueller, Herbert M., ed. *The Persistence of Shakespeare Idolatry*. See K-SJ, XV (1966), 170, No. 468, XVII (1968), 42.

Rev. by Joseph B. Fort in *Comparative Literature Studies*, V (March 1968), 88–92.

Schulz, H. C. See No. 9.

Schulz, Max F. See No. 265.

651. Schulze, Earl J. *Shelley's Theory of Poetry: A Reappraisal*. See K-SJ, XVII (1968), 42.

Rev. by Joseph DeRocco in K-SJ, XVII (1968), 128–130. Also see No. 48.

652. *Shelley, Mary Wollstonecraft. *El doctor Frankenstein*. [Translated by] Antonio Gobernado. Madrid: Aguilar, 1966. [In Spanish.]

653. *Shelley, Mary Wollstonecraft. *Frankenshtain: ili sovremenyi Prometei*. [*Frankenstein: A Modern Prometheus*.] [Translated

by] E. Aleksandrov. Moscow: Khudozh. Lit-ra, 1965. [In Russian.]

Rev. by *A. Gorvunov in *Novii Mir*, No. 5 (1966), p. 283.

654. *Shelley, Mary Wollstonecraft. *Frankenstein*. [Translated by] Elisabetta Bützeberger. Milan: Corno, 1966. [In Italian.]

655. *Shelley, Mary Wollstonecraft. *Frankenstein*. [Translated by] Kirsten Diemer. Copenhagen: Bülmann & Eriksen, 1966. [In Danish.]

656. *Shelley, Mary Wollstonecraft. *Frankenstein o el moderno Prometeo*. [Translated by] Jorge Ferreiro. Mexico: Novaro, 1967. [In Spanish.]

657. *Shelley, Mary Wollstonecraft. *Frankenstein*. [Translated by] Tomáš Korbař. Prague: Práce, 1966. [In Czech.]

658. *Shelley, Mary Wollstonecraft. *Frankenstein*. [Translated by] Yamamoto Masaki. Tokyo: Kadokawa shoten, 1968. [In Japanese.]

659. *Shelley, Mary Wollstonecraft. *Frankenstein*. Introduction by Robert Donald Spector. New York: Bantam, 1967.

660. *Shelley, Mary Wollstonecraft. *Het monster van Frankenstein*. [Translated by] Else Hoog. Utrecht: Bruna, 1968. [In Dutch.]

661. Shelley, Mary Wollstonecraft. *The Last Man*. Ed. Hugh J. Luke, Jr. See K-SJ, XVI (1967), 140, XVII (1968), 42.

Rev. by R. V. Adkinson in *Revue des langues vivantes*, XXXIII (1967), 441–442.

662. Small, Martin. "Marriage Lines," TLS, 6 July 1967, p. 606.

Questions TLS reviewer's opinion of Godwin's marriage and the influence of his marriage on his later moral philosophy. See Nos. 545, 610, and 679.

663. Smith, Elton Edward, and Esther Greenwell Smith. *William Godwin*. See K-SJ, XVI (1967), 140–141, XVII (1968), 42.

Rev. in *Choice*, III (May 1966), 212.

664. *Smith, Robert Metcalf, *et al. The Shelley Legend*. Port Washington, N.Y.: Kennikat, 1967.

A reprint of the book first published in 1945.

665. *Spanos, William V. "Shelley's 'Ozymandias' and the Problem of the Persona," *CEA Critic*, XXX (Jan. 1968), 14–15.

666. Spurling, Hilary. "Hit and Miss," Spec, 5 Nov. 1965, p. 584.

A review of production at the Royal Court Theatre of Ann Jellicoe's *Shelley*. See K-SJ, XVII (1968), 37, No. 515, 43, No. 600.

Stange, G. Robert. See No. 273.

667. Storch, Rudolf F. "Metaphors of Private Guilt and Social Rebellion in Godwin's *Caleb Williams*," ELH, XXXIV (June 1967), 188–207.

668. *Suzuki, Hiroshi. "Sailing Out into the Boisterous Sea—*The Cenci* and *Macbeth*," *General Studies* (Waseda Univ.), XXVIII (Feb. 1968), 67–90. [In Japanese.]

669. *Swaminathan, S. R. "The Mourners in Shelley's 'Adonais,'" *Indian Journal of English Studies*, IX (1968), 96–108.

670. Swaminathan, S. R. "Shelley's 'Triumph of Life,'" N&Q, CCXII (Aug. 1967), 305–306.†

Argues that the "sacred few" (lines 116–137) may also include the *Avatars of* Indian mythology and *Maya*, or illusion.

671. Symonds, John Addington. *The Letters of John Addington Symonds*. Vol. I: 1844–68. Ed. Herbert M. Schueller and Robert L. Peters. Detroit: Wayne State Univ., 1967.

Has references to Byron, Haydon, Keats, and especially to Shelley.

672. *Symonds, John Addington. *Shelley*. New York: AMS, 1967.

A reprint of a book first published in 1878.

673. *Szenwald, Lucjan. "Życzenia," *Dąbrowszczak. Jednodniówka* (Warsaw, 1956), p. 6. [In Polish.]

"Wishes": an idea from *Hellas*.

674. *Terlecki, T. "The Cenci," *Wiadomości*, No. 24 (London, 1959), p. 4. [In Polish.]

An article about the play.

Terry, R. C. See No. 276.

Timko, Michael. See No. 279.

675. *Tokoo, Tatsuo. "Aerial Shelley," *Outlook*, IX (Summer 1967), 24–43. [In Japanese.]

676. Vitoux, Pierre. "Jupiter's Fatal Child in 'Prometheus Unbound,'" *Criticism*, X (Spring 1968), 115–125.

Examines the episode of Demogorgon's birth and relates it to Shelley's main theme and to his problems as a dramatist.

Waldoff, Leon. See No. 517.

677. Walsh, John. *Strange Harp, Strange Symphony: The Life of Francis Thompson*. New York: Hawthorn, 1967.
Contains numerous references to Shelley; also alludes to Byron and Keats.
Rev. in TLS, 18 Apr. 1968, p. 398.

678. Walsh, William. *A Human Idiom: Literature and Humanity*. New York: Barnes & Noble, 1964.
Briefly discusses Shelley as the "voice of detachment in an age of uncertainty."
Rev. by J. Loiseau in EA, XXI (Jan.–March 1968), 101–102.

Ward, William S. See No. 12.

679. Wardle, Ralph M., ed. *Godwin & Mary: Letters of William Godwin and Mary Wollstonecraft*. See K-SJ, XVII (1968), 43.
Rev. by K[enneth]. N[eill]. C[ameron]. in ELN, V, Supplement (Sept. 1967), 32; by Irwin Primer in *Studies in Burke and His Time*, IX (Spring 1968), 980–983. See also Nos. 545, 610, and 662.

680. Wardle, Ralph M. *Mary Wollstonecraft: A Critical Biography*. See K-SJ, XVII (1968), 43.
Rev. in *Prairie Schooner*, XLI (Spring 1967), 93.

681. Wasserman, Earl R. *Shelley's "Prometheus Unbound": A Critical Reading*. See K-SJ, XVI (1967), 142, XVII (1968), 43–44.
Rev. by Roger Sharrock in RES, n.s., XIX (Feb. 1968), 86–87. See also No. 48.

682. *Weaver, Bennett. *Toward the Understanding of Shelley*. New York: Octagon, 1966.
A reprint of a book first published in 1932.

683. Webb, Timothy. "Coleridge and Shelley's *Alastor*: A Reply," RES, n.s., XVIII (Nov. 1967), 402–411.
Contends that "Coleridge had little or nothing to do with the conception of *Alastor*," in answer to Joseph Raben. See K-SJ, XVII (1968), 40, No. 562. See also No. 631.

Weinstein, Mark A. See No. 286.

684. Welsford, Enid. *Salisbury Plain: A Study in the Development of Wordsworth's Mind and Art*. Oxford: Basil Blackwell, 1966.
Includes an appendix (pp. 145–148) on "Wordsworth and Godwin."

685. Williams, J. Peter. "Aesthetic Ambivalence in the Work of Thomas Love Peacock" [Doctoral dissertation, Michigan, 1966], DA, XXVIII (July 1967), 206-A–207-A.

Wilshire, Bruce, comp. See No. 80.

Winters, Yvor. See No. 81.

686. Woodhouse, A. S. P. *The Poet and His Faith*. See K-SJ, XVI (1967), 142, XVII (1968), 44.
Rev. by Roy W. Battenhouse in SAQ, LXVI (Winter 1967), 126–127.

687. Woodings, R. B. "'A Devil of a Nut to Crack': Shelley's *Charles the First*," *Studia Neophilologica*, XL (1968), 216–237.
A fresh examination of the unfinished work in the light of Shelley's later preoccupation with historical fact and aesthetic design.

688. Woodings, R. B., ed. *Shelley: Modern Judgements*. London: Macmillan, 1968.
A collection of sixteen critical essays on Shelley, with an introduction by the editor.

689. Wyatt, Sybil White. *The English Romantic Novel and Austrian Reaction: A Study in Hapsburg-Metternich Censorship*. New York: Exposition, 1967.
Discusses reasons Mary Shelley's *The Last Man* was among the books censored.

VI. PHONOGRAPH RECORDINGS

Byron, Keats, Shelley

690. *English Lyric Poems and Ballads*. Read by Kathleen Danson Read. See K-SJ, XI (1962), 139, No. 550.
Rev. by J[ohn]. R. S[earles]. in *English Journal*, LVI (Sept. 1967), 909.

691. *The English Poets, from Chaucer to Yeats*. Directed by George Rylands. See K-SJ, XV (1966), 171, No. 474.
Rev. by R. V. Adkinson in *Revue des langues vivantes*, XXXIII (1967), 667; by Klaus Oltmann in *Neueren Sprachen*, LXVI (Sept. 1967), 456–457.

Bibliography for July 1, 1968–June 30, 1969

VOLUME XIX

Compiled by LEWIS M. SCHWARTZ and RAE ANN NAGER,
with the assistance of Gerald B. Kauvar

THIS bibliography, a regular department of the *Keats-Shelley Journal*, is a register of the literary interest in Keats, Shelley, Byron, Hunt, and their circles from (approximately) July 1968 through June 1969.

Where a book has been issued by more than one publisher during the same year, the publication date appears within parentheses at the end of the entry. Each item that the compilers have not seen is marked by an asterisk. Entries which have been abstracted in *Abstracts of English Studies* are marked with a dagger, but entries in previous bibliographies which were abstracted too late for notice have not been repeated.

ABBREVIATIONS

AUMLA Journal of the Australasian Universities Language and Literature Association
BC Book Collector
BNYPL Bulletin of the New York Public Library
CL Comparative Literature
CLSB C. L. S. Bulletin (Charles Lamb Society)
DA Dissertation Abstracts
EC Essays in Criticism
ELH Journal of English Literary History
ELN English Language Notes
ES English Studies
Exp Explicator
ILN Illustrated London News
JAAC Journal of Aesthetics and Art Criticism
JEGP Journal of English and Germanic Philology
JHI Journal of the History of Ideas
KR Kenyon Review
K-SJ Keats-Shelley Journal
KSMB Keats-Shelley Memorial Bulletin
Li Listener
MLN Modern Language Notes
MLQ Modern Language Quarterly
MLR Modern Language Review
MP Modern Philology
N&Q Notes and Queries
NS New Statesman
NYT New York Times Book Review
PBSA Papers of the Bibliographical Society of America
PMLA Publications of the Modern Language Association of America
PQ Philological Quarterly
PR Partisan Review
QQ Queen's Quarterly
RES Review of English Studies
RLC Revue de Littérature Comparée
SAQ South Atlantic Quarterly
SatR Saturday Review
SEL Studies in English Literature 1500–1900
SIR Studies in Romanticism
SP Studies in Philology
Spec Spectator
TLS Times Literary Supplement

Current Bibliography

I. GENERAL

Current Bibliographies

1. Bailey, Richard W., and Dolores M. Burton. *English Stylistics: A Bibliography.* Cambridge, Mass.: M.I.T., 1968.

   Includes the nineteenth century.

   Rev. by Donald McCluskey in *General Linguistics*, IX, No. 3 (1969), 132–134.

1a. Brack, O. M., Jr., and Warner Barnes, eds. *Bibliography and Textual Criticism: English and American Literature, 1700 to the Present.* Chicago: Univ. of Chicago, 1969.

1b. *Clarke, Derek A., and Howell J. Heaney. "A Selective Check List of Bibliographical Scholarship for 1967," *Studies in Bibliography*, XXII (1969), 319–334.†

   Heaney lists 302 items from the later Renaissance to the present.

2. Erdman, David V., *et al.* "The Romantic Movement: A Selective and Critical Bibliography for 1967," ELN, VI, Supplement (Sept. 1968), 1–158.

3. Freeman, Ronald E. "Victorian Bibliography for 1968," *Victorian Studies*, XII (June 1969), 491–553.

3a. Green, David Bonnell, Robert G. Kirkpatrick, and Edwin Graves Wilson. "Current Bibliography," K-SJ, XVII (1968), 1–54.

4. *Lowe, Robert W. *A Bibliographical Account of English Theatrical Literature, From the Earliest Times to the Present Day.* Detroit: Gale Research Company, 1966.

   This reprint of a reference work first published in 1888 has been superseded by the publication in 1970 of a bibliography based on Lowe but extended to 1900 by James Arnott and John Robinson.

   Rev. by Carl J. Stratman in *Restoration and 18th Century Theatre Research*, VII (Nov. 1968), 47.

4a. Park, William, *et al. National Library of Scotland: Catalogue of Manuscripts Acquired Since 1925.* Vol. III: *Blackwood Papers, 1805–1900.* Edinburgh: Her Majesty's Stationery Office, 1968.

   This is a gold mine for those interested in nineteenth-century periodical literature. The catalogue includes correspondence received by *Blackwood's Magazine*, manuscripts, proofs, and contributors' lists (pp. 31–32) which, when consulted at the library, will form a guide to the authors of anonymous articles in *Blackwood's* between 1817–1900. Also catalogued are uncorrected proofs of two apparently unpublished, undated letters from James Hogg to Byron (p. 19) and two unpublished, undated parodies of Hunt by Hogg (p. 15).

5. Rosenberg, Henry, and Sheila Rosenberg. "Proposed Bibliography of Writings on Nineteenth Century Serials," *Victorian Periodicals Newsletter*, No. 3 (Nov. 1968), 5–6.

   More details on the bibliography of materials relating to nineteenth-century serials in progress at the University of Leicester. Published by the University of Leicester Victorian Studies Center.

6. Watson, George, ed. *The New Cambridge Bibliography of English Literature.* Vol III: *1800–1900.* Cambridge: Cambridge Univ., 1969.

7. Yarker, P. M., and Brian Lee. "The Nineteenth Century," in *The Year's Work in English Studies*, ed. T. S. Dorsch and C. G. Harlow, XLVII (1968 [for 1966]), 252–286.

Books and Articles Relating to English Romanticism

8. Anderson, George K. *The Legend of the Wandering Jew.* See K-SJ, XVI (1967), 115, XVIII (1969), 6.

   Rev. by Francis Lee Utley in MP, LXVI (Nov. 1968), 188–193.

8a. *Balduino, Armando. "Il VI Congresso

dell'Associazione internazionale per gli Studi di Lingua e Letteratura italiana sul Romanticismo," *Lettere Italiane*, xx (1968), 91–101.

Includes English Romanticism.

9. Bartlett, C. J. *Castlereagh*. See K-SJ, xvii (1968), 9.

Rev. by Ian R. Christie in *English Historical Review*, lxxxiii (July 1968), 628–629; by Archibald S. Ford in *Journal of Modern History*, xl (Dec. 1968), 614–615.

10. Baugh, Albert C., ed. *The Literary History of England*. Second Edition. New York: Appleton-Century-Crofts; London: Routledge and Kegan Paul (1967).

Includes the Richard D. Altick revision of Samuel Chew's "The Nineteenth Century and After."

Rev. by Jacques Voisine in RLC, xlii (Oct.–Dec. 1968), 603–608; by W. D. Maxwell-Mahon in *Unisa English Studies*, vii (March 1969), 106–107.

10a. Ben-Israel, Hedva. *English Historians on the French Revolution*. Cambridge: Cambridge Univ., 1968.

Includes references to Byron, Godwin, Hazlitt, and Shelley.

11. Bloom, Harold. "The Internalization of Quest Romance," *Yale Review*, lviii (Summer 1969), 526–536.

Maintains that the Romantic poet transposes the patterns of quest romance into his own imaginative life. Allusions are made to Byron, Keats, and Shelley.

12. Booth, Michael R. *English Melodrama*. See K-SJ, xvii (1968), 3.

Rev. by Gary J. Scrimgeour in *Victorian Studies*, xii (Sept. 1968), 91–100.

13. *Brand, Peter. "Romanticismo italiana e Romanticismo inglese," in *Il Romanticismo: Atti del Sesto Congresso dell'Associazione internazionale per gli studi di lingua e letteratura italiana* (Budapest e Venezia, 10–17 Ottobre 1967), ed. Vittore Branca and Tibor Kardos (Budapest: Akadémiai Kiadó, 1968), pp. 361–376.

14. Bush, Douglas. *English Poetry: The Main Currents from Chaucer to the Present*. Second Edition. London: Methuen, 1965.

The second edition of a book first published in 1952. See K-SJ, iii (1954), 113.

Rev. by Geoffrey Watson in MLR, lxiii (July 1968), 671.

15. Bush, Douglas. *Mythology and the Romantic Tradition in English Poetry*. Cambridge, Mass.: Harvard Univ., 1969.

A reissue of the 1937 edition with a new preface.

16. Chew, Samuel, and Richard D. Altick. *The Nineteenth Century and After*. London: Routledge and Kegan Paul, 1968. See Baugh, Albert C., No. 10.

A paperback reprint of Vol. iv of *The Literary History of England*.

17. Churchill, R. C., ed. *Concise Cambridge History of English Literature*. Cambridge: Cambridge Univ., 1968.

18. Clifford, James L., ed. *Man Versus Society in Eighteenth Century Britain: Six Points of View*. Cambridge: Cambridge Univ., 1968.

J. H. Plumb's essay on "Political Man" deals directly with the Romantic period.

Rev. by Kenneth T. Abrams in ELN, vii, Supplement (Sept. 1969), 12; by Donald J. Greene in *Studies in Burke and His Time*, x (Fall 1968), 1049–60; by M. W. Flinn in *Economic History Review*, xxii (Apr. 1968), 135.

19. Darwin, Erasmus. *The Essential Writings of Erasmus Darwin*. Ed. Desmond King-Hele. London: MacGibbon and Kee, 1968.

Devotes a chapter to Darwin's influence on the English Romantic poets, pp. 163–175.

20. Dawson, Leven M. "Melmoth the Wanderer: Paradox and the Gothic Novel," SEL, viii (Autumn 1968), 621–632.

Through paradox Gothic fiction "makes contact with romanticism."

21. Derry, John W. *The Radical Tradition: Tom Paine to Lloyd George*. London: Macmillian; New York: St. Martin's (1967).

Contains a chapter on William Cobbett, pp. 46–79.

Rev. by Kenneth O. Morgan in *History*, liii (Feb. 1968), 138; by Carl B. Cone in *Canadian Journal of History*, iii (1968), 102–103; by F. M. Leventhal in *Victorian Studies*, xii (Dec. 1968), 250–252; by E. A. Smith in *English Historical Review*, lxxxiv (Jan. 1969), 197–198; by J. F. C. Harrison in *Journal of Modern History*, xli (March 1969), 87–89.

22. Ellis, Amanda M. *Rebels and Conservatives*. See K-SJ, XVIII (1969), N. 166.
Rev. by Jenijoy La Belle in KR, XX No. 3, (1968), 426–429; by Kenneth T. Abrams in ELN, VI, Supplement (Sept. 1968), 39; by Ralph J. Mills, Jr., in *Poetry*, CXIII (Jan. 1969), 264; by W. J. B. Owen in RES, XX (Feb. 1969), 101–104.

22a. Fletcher, Ian, ed. *Romantic Mythologies*. See K-SJ, XVII (1968), 4.
Rev. by Leonee Ormand in MLR, LXIV (Apr. 1969), 409–411.

23. Fletcher, Richard M. *English Romantic Drama 1795–1843*. See K-SJ, XVII (1968), 4, XVIII (1969), No. 30.
Rev. by Gary J. Scrimgeour in *Victorian Studies*, XII (Sept. 1968), 91–100.

24. Foltinek, Herbert. *Vorstufen zum viktorianischen Realismus: Der englische Roman von Jane Austen bis Charles Dickens*, in *Wiener Beiträge zur englischen Philologie*, Bd. LXXI (1968).
This monograph includes a survey of the English literary scene from 1815–1837.

25. Fulford, Roger. *The Trial of Queen Caroline*. London: Batsford, 1967; New York: Stein and Day, 1968.

26. Furst, Lilian R. *Romanticism in Perspective: A Comparative Study of Aspects of the Romantic Movements in England, France, and Germany*. London: Macmillian; New York: St. Martin's (1969).
Rev. by Robert Hughes in *Sunday Times*, 23 Feb. 1969, p. 59; in TLS, 15 May 1969, p. 530.

27. Cancelled.

28. Gross, John. *The Rise and Fall of the Man of Letters: English Literary Life Since 1800*. London: Weidenfeld and Nicolson, 1969.
Hazlitt is included.
Rev. by Cyril Connolly in *Sunday Times*, 18 May 1969, p. 60; by V. S. Pritchett in NS, 23 May 1969, pp. 733–734; by John Grass in Spec, 30 May 1969, pp. 723–724.

29. Halsted, John B., ed. *Romanticism*. New York: Walker; New York: Harper and Row (1969).
An anthology of verse and prose which includes Shelley's *Defence*, excerpts from *Childe Harold* and *Manfred*, and a letter of Keats.

30. Harris, R. W. *Romanticism and the Social Order 1780–1830*. London: Blandford; New York: Barnes and Noble (1969).
Rev. in TLS, 15 May 1969, p. 530.

31. Hartman, Geoffrey H. "Romantic Poetry and the Genius Loci," in *The Disciplines of Criticism: Essays in Literary Theory, Interpretation, and History*, ed. Peter Demetz, Thomas Greene, and Lowry Nelson, Jr. (New Haven: Yale Univ., 1968), pp. 289–314.

32. Hawes, Louis. "Recent Exhibitions," *Art Bulletin*, LI (March 1969), 88–90.
Includes discussion of the concept of "Romanticism," 1760–1860.

33. Hayden, John O. *The Romantic Reviewers, 1802–1824: A Study of Literary Reviewing in the Early Nineteenth Century*. Chicago: Univ. of Chicago [c. 1968]; London: Routledge and Kegan Paul, 1969.

34. Hayter, Alethea. *Opium and the Romantic Imagination*. London: Faber; Berkeley: Univ. of California (1968).
In addition to the better-known addicts, there are references to Byron and Keats, who, although not addicted, did take opium on occasions.
Rev. by Cyril Connolly in *Sunday Times*, 10 Nov. 1968, p. 61; by Anthony Starr in NS, 15 Nov. 1968, pp. 674–675; in TLS, 28 Nov. 1968, p. 1343; by Geoffrey Grigson in Li, LXXX (12 Dec. 1968), 798–800; by Patrick Anderson in Spec, 20 Dec. 1968, pp. 880–881; by A. S. Byatt in the *Times* (London), 21 Dec. 1968, p. 19; by Iain Hamilton in ILN, 18 Jan. 1969, p. 28; by Elinor Shaffer in *Cambridge Review*, 31 Jan. 1969, pp. 234–239; by Elaine Bender in *Library Journal*, 1 Feb. 1969, p. 551; by Richard Freedman in *New Republic*, 15 Feb. 1969, pp. 30–31; in *Choice*, XI (Apr. 1969), 214.

35. Hayward, John, ed. *The Oxford Book of Nineteenth-Century English Verse*. See K-SJ, XV (1966), 144, XVI (1967), 116, XVII (1968), 4, XVIII (1969), No. 34.
Rev. by Georg Seehase in *Zeitschrift für Anglistik und Amerikanistik*, XVI, No. 3 (1968), 309–312.

36. Hilles, Frederick W., and Harold Bloom, eds. *From Sensibility to Romanticism; Essays Presented to Frederick A. Pottle*. New York: Oxford Univ., 1969.

A paperback "Galaxy" reprint of a book first published in 1965. See K-SJ, XV (1966), 144, XVI (1967), 116, XVII (1968), 4.

36a. Hollander, John, ed. *Modern Poetry: Essays in Criticism.* London and New York: Oxford Univ., 1968.

A paperback which includes Harold Bloom's "Yeats and the Romantics," pp. 501–520.

37. Kroeber, Karl, comp. *Backgrounds to British Romantic Literature.* San Francisco: Chandler, 1968.

A collection of essays describing the political, social, and cultural conditions in Britain during the Romantic period.

38. Kumar, Shiv K., ed. *British Romantic Poets: Recent Revaluations.* See K-SJ, XVII (1968), 5, XVIII (1969), No. 42.

Rev. in TLS, 12 Dec. 1968, p. 1407; by Vivian de Sola Pinto in *Critical Quarterly,* XI (1969), 90–91.

39. Levine, George, and William Madden, eds. *The Art of Victorian Prose.* New York: Oxford Univ., 1968.

Frequent references in this collection of essays to Byron, Godwin, Hazlitt, Keats, Shelley, and to Romantic prose.

40. *Levy, Maurice. *Le roman "Gothique" anglais, 1764–1824.* Toulouse: Assn. des Pubs. de la Faculté des Letters et Sciences Humaines de Toulouse, 1964.

41. Logan, James V., John E. Jordan, and Northrop Frye, eds. *Some British Romantics: A Collection of Essays.* See K-SJ, XVII (1968), 5, XVIII (1969), No. 47.

Rev. by Geoffrey Carnall in N&Q, CCXIII (Sept. 1968), 352–353; by Peter Hoy in *American Notes and Queries,* VII (Sept. 1968), 16.

42. *Maciejewski, Marian. "Zagadka i tajemnica: Z zagadnień świadomosci literackiej w oknesie przelomu romantycznego," *Roczniki Humanistyczne,* XVI, No. 1 (1968), 5–28.

Deals with literary consciousness during the Romantic movement. There are references to Byron.

43. Malins, Edward. *English Landscape and Literature, 1660–1840.* See K-SJ, XVII (1968), 5, XVIII (1969), No. 51.

Rev. by D. S. Bland in N&Q, CCXIII (Sept. 1968), 354–355.

44. Miyoshi, Masao. *The Divided Self: A Perspective on the Literature of the Victorians.* London: Univ. of London; New York: New York Univ. (1969).

Includes the Gothic novel and Romanticism in its first two chapters.

Rev. by Keith Cushman in *Library Journal,* 15 March 1969, p. 1148.

44a. Nichols, Stephen G., Jr., and Richard B. Vowles, eds. *Comparatists at Work: Studies in Comparative Literature.* Waltham, Mass.: Blaisdell, 1968.

This collection of essays includes Jean H. Hagstrum's "The Sister Arts: From Neoclassic to Romantic," pp. 161–194.

45. Osborne, John W. *William Cobbett, His Thought and His Times.* New Brunswick: Rutgers Univ., 1966.

Rev. by R. A. Lewis in *English Historical Review,* LXXXIII (July 1968), 629; by J. H. Plumb in *New York Review of Books,* 19 June 1969, pp. 36–37.

46. Palgrave, Francis Turner, ed. *The Golden Treasury of the Best Songs and Lyrical Poems in the English Language, With a Fifth Book Selected by John Press.* Fifth Edition. London and New York: Oxford Univ., 1964.

Selections from Byron, Keats, Moore, and Shelley are from Palgrave's original edition. Press's Fifth Book includes selections from Clare.

Rev. by Georg Seehase in *Zeitschrift für Anglistik und Amerikanistik,* XVI, No. 3 (1968), 309–312; by Klaus Oltman in *Die Neueren Sprachen,* XVII N.F. (Sept. 1968), 470–471.

47. Poteet, Lewis Jarrette. "Romantic Aesthetics in Oscar Wilde's Prose" [Doctoral dissertation, Minnesota, 1968], DA, XXIX (Sept. 1968), 907–A.

48. Poulet, Georges. *Etudes sur le temps humain.* IV: *Mesure de l'instant.* Paris: Plon, 1968.

"Les romantiques anglais," pp. 157–192.

49. Priestley, J. B. *The Prince of Pleasure and his Regency, 1811–1820.* London: Heinemann; New York: Harper & Row (1969).

Deals with the Byron scandal of 1816 and also alludes to other Romantics.

Rev. by A. E. Day in *Library Review,* XXII (Winter 1969), 218–219.

50. Rauber, D. F. "The Fragment as Romantic Form," MLQ, XXX (Jan. 1969), 212–221.
Views the fragment as "that form which more completely than any other embodies Romantic ideals."

51. Richardson, Joanna. "George IV: Patron of Literature," *Essays by Divers Hands*, XXXV (1969), 128–146.
Concludes that "Byron respected his taste and knowledge; Shelley and Hazlitt, who condemned him, knew little of his character."

51a. Rosen, Marvin S. "Authors and Publishers: 1750–1830," *Science and Society*, XXXII (Spring 1968), 218–232.
Refers to all of the major Romantic poets.

52. Schenk, H. G. *The Mind of the European Romantics: An Essay in Cultural History*. See K-SJ, XVII (1968), 6, XVIII (1969), 9.
Rev. by C. W. Parkin in *History*, LIII (Feb. 1968), 136–137; by J. F. Burnet in *English Historical Review*, LXXXIII (July 1968), 628; by Elinor Shaffer in MLR, LXIII (July 1968), 665–666; by Irene H. Chayes in ELN, VI, Supplement (Sept. 1968), 9–10; by Frederick Garber in CL, XX (1968), 357–359.

53. Scrimgeour, Gary James. "Drama and the Theatre in the Early Nineteenth Century" [Doctoral dissertation, Princeton, 1968], DA, XXIX (June 1969), 4469–A.

54. Scudder, Vida D. *Social Ideals in English Letters*. New York: Johnson, 1969.
A reprint of the 1898 edition with a new introduction by Martin Tucker.

54a. Seymour-Smith, Martin. *Poets Through Their Letters*. Vol. I: *Wyatt to Coleridge*. London: Constable; New York: Holt, Rinehart and Winston (1969).
One-third of the book is devoted to Wordsworth and Coleridge. References to Byron, Godwin, and Hazlitt are included.
Rev. by Anthony Burgess in Spec, 7 March 1969, pp. 306–307.

55. Smidt, Kristian. *Books and Men: A Short History of English and American Literature*. Oslo: J. W. Cappelen, 1967.
The second edition of a handbook first published in 1945. The Romantic poets are mentioned.

56. *Szenczi, Miklós. "La realtà ed i romantíci inglesi," in *Il Romanticismo: Atti del Sesto Congresso dell'Associazione internazionale per gli studi di lingua e letteratura italiana* (Budapest e Venezia, 10–17 Ottobre 1967), ed. Vittore Branca and Tibor Kardos (Budapest: Akadémiai Kiadó, 1968), pp. 83–90.

57. Talmon, J. L. *Romanticism and Revolt, Europe 1815–1848*. See K-SJ, XVIII (1969), No. 72.
Rev. in ELN, VI, Supplement (Sept. 1968), 7; by H. Hearder in *English Historical Review*, LXXXIII (Oct. 1968), 858; by H. G. Schenk in *History*, LIII (Oct. 1968), 448–449.

58. Thomas, Donald. *A Long Time Burning: The History of Literary Censorship in England*. London: Routledge and Kegan Paul; New York: Praeger (1969).
The travails of Byron, Hunt, and Shelley are given strong emphasis.
Rev. by Richard Haggart in *New Republic*, 13 June 1969, pp. 835–836.

59. *Tucker, Martin. *The Critical Temper*. Vol. II: *From Milton to Romantic Literature*. New York: F. Ungar, 1969.
Rev. by John R. Willingham in *Library Journal*, 15 March 1969, p. 1148.

60. Vinge, Louise. *The Narcissus Theme in Western European Literature up to the Early 19th Century*. See K-SJ, XVIII (1969), No. 74.
Rev. in *Forum for Modern Language Studies*, IV (Apr. 1968), 206; by J. Donovan in MLR, LXIII (Oct. 1968), 924–925; by Stephen Manning in *Speculum*, XLIV (Jan. 1969), 181; by Jean Seznec in *French Studies*, XXIII (Jan. 1969), 49–51.

61. Wellek, René. *A History of Modern Criticism*. See K-SJ, XVI (1967), 116, XVII (1968), 6–7, XVIII (1969), No. 76.
Rev. by George Nevin in *Poetry Review*, LIX (Winter 1968), 293–294; by Bernard Weinberg in JHI, XXX (Jan.–March 1969), 127–133; reply by René Wellek in JHI, XXX (Apr.–June 1969), 281–282.

62. *White, Reginald James. *The Age of George III*. London: Heinemann; New York: Walker (1968); New York: Doubleday, 1969.
Rev. in TLS, 26 Dec. 1968, p. 1451;

by Donald Greene in *Eighteenth Century Studies*, II (1969), 486–489; in *Choice*, VI (June 1969), 564–565.

62a. Winters, Yvor. *Forms of Discovery: Critical and Historical Essays on the Form of the Short Poem in English.* See K-SJ, XVIII (1969), 10.

Rev. by M. L. Rosenthal in *Poetry*, CXIV (May 1969), 116–118; by John Fraser in "Winters' Summa," *Southern Review*, V (Winter 1969), 184–202.

63. Woodring, Carl. "Recent Studies in the Nineteenth Century," SEL, VIII (Autumn 1968), 725–749.

A critical survey of books between June 1967 and June 1968.

63a. Wright, David, ed. *The Penguin Book of English Romantic Verse.* See K-SJ, XVIII (1969), 11.

Rev. by D.R.B. in *Unisa English Studies*, VI (Sept. 1968), 104.

II. BYRON

Works: Selected, Single, Translated

64. Bender, Robert M., and Charles L. Squier, eds. *The Sonnet: A Comprehensive Anthology of British and American Sonnets from the Renaissance to the Present.* New York: Trident, 1968.

A reprint of a book first published in 1965. See K-SJ, XVII (1968), 7.

65. *Byron: A Self-Portrait: Letters and Diaries, 1798–1824, with hitherto unpublished letters.* Ed. Peter Quennell. 2 vols. New York: Humanities, 1968.

A reprint of the 1950 volumes. See K-SJ, I (1952), 89.

66. *Byron Shishû.* [*Poetical Works.*] [Translated by] Kazuo Ogawa. Tokyo: Kadokawa shoten, 1964. [In Japanese.]

67. *Byron Shishû.* [*Poetical Works.*] ("Sekai no meishi," 13.) [Translated by] Kazuo Ogawa. Tokyo: Kôdansha, 1969. [In Japanese.]

68. *Byron Shishû.* [*Poetical Works.*] [Translated by] Shin'ichi Yoshida. Tokyo: Mikasa shobo, 1967. [In Japanese.]

69. *Don Juan* (1819). Ed. Brian Lee. London: Collins, 1969.

70. *Don Juan.* [Translated by] Tomas Vondrovic. Prague: Lyra pragensis, 1969. [In Czechoslovakian.]

70a. Kinsley, James, and James T. Boulton, eds. *English Satiric Poetry: Dryden to Byron.* See K-SJ, XVI (1967), 117.

Rev. by H.L.J. in *Unisa English Studies*, VI (June 1968), 94–95.

70b. *Lord Byron's "Cain": Twelve Essays and a Text with Variants and Annotations.* Ed. Truman Guy Steffan. Austin and London: Univ. of Texas, 1969.

Rev. by Paul F. Moran in *Library Journal*, 1 June 1959, p. 2234.

71. *Manfred: Ein Dramat Gedicht.* [*Manfred: A Dramatic Poem.*] Eds. Helmut Viebrock and Eileen Volhard. Translated by Otto Gildemeister. Frankfurt a. M.: Heinrich-Heine-Verl., 1969. [In German.]

72. *Poems.* Sel. Horace Gregory. New York: Crowell, 1969.

73. *Selected Poems and Letters.* Ed. William H. Marshall. Boston: Houghton Mifflin, 1968.

Books and Articles Relating to Byron and His Circle

73a. Adams, Robert Martin. *Nil: Episodes in the Literary Conquest of Void during the Nineteenth Century.* See K-SJ, XVII (1968), 9, XVIII (1969), 11.

Rev. by C. A. E. Jensen in *Mosaic*, II (Oct. 1968), 130–132.

74. Ashton, Thomas. "Peter Parker in Perry's Paper: Two Unpublished Byron Letters," K-SJ, XVIII (1969), 49–59.

Reproduces new letters from Byron to Perry of the *Morning Chronicle*. One letter, dated 7 Oct. 1814, includes verses by Byron which appeared in the *Chronicle* on the occasion of his cousin Peter Parker's death.

75. Barker, Kathleen M. D. "The First English Performance of Byron's *Werner*," MP, LXVI (May 1969), 342–344.

Details on the adaptation and performance by Macready in Bristol on 25 Jan. 1830.

76. Bate, Walter J. *Coleridge.* London: Weidenfeld and Nicolson; New York: Macmillan (1968).

In this short critical biography, Byron,

Hazlitt, Reynolds, and Shelley are mentioned.

Rev. in *Choice*, v (Oct. 1968), 948; by Lore Metzger in MLQ (Jan. 1969), 121–126; in TLS, 17 Apr. 1969, p. 411.

77. Batho, Edith C. *The Ettrick Shepherd.* New York: Greenwood, 1969.

Reprint of the 1927 edition.

78. Beaty, Frederick L. "Byron on Malthus and the Population Problem," K-SJ, XVIII (1969), 17–26.

"Byron . . . was receptive to Malthusian concepts, though not without serious theological and psychological misgivings."

79. Beaty, Frederick L. "Harlequin Don Juan," JEGP, LXVII (July 1968), 395–405.

The English pantomime as a literary antecedent for Byron's hero.

Ben-Israel, Hedva. See No. 10a.

79a. *Benton, Richard P. "Poe's 'Lionizing': A Quiz on Willis and Lady Blessington," *Studies in Short Fiction*, v (Spring 1968), 239–244.†

80. Berlioz, Hector. *The Memoirs of Hector Berlioz: Member of the French Institute, Including His Travels in Italy, Germany, Russia, and England, 1803–1865.* Ed. and trans. David Cairns. New York: Knopf; London: Gollancz (1969).

Berlioz mentions Byron twice in his memoirs (pp. 144, 166).

Rev. by Charles Reid in Spec, 7 March 1969, p. 312; by Hugh MacDonald in *Musical Times*, CX (May 1969), 487–488.

81. *Blakiston, Noel. "Byron, Shelley, e Trelawny a Pisa," in *Inghilterra e Toscana nell'Ottocento* (Florence: La Nuova Italia, 1968), pp. 65–69.

82. Blessington, Marguerite, Countess of. *Lady Blessington's Conversations of Lord Byron.* Ed. Ernest J. Lovell, Jr. Princeton: Princeton Univ., 1969.

83. Borst, William A. *Lord Byron's First Pilgrimage, 1809–1811.* Hamden, Conn.: Archon, 1969.

A reprint of a book first published in 1948. See K-SJ, I (1952), 90.

84. Bostetter, Edward E., ed. *Twentieth Century Interpretations of "Don Juan": A Collection of Critical Essays.* Englewood Cliffs, N.J.: Prentice-Hall, 1969.

85. Buxton, John. *Byron and Shelley: The History of a Friendship.* See KS-J, XVIII (1969), No. 132.

Rev. by John Lehmann in *London Magazine*, VIII (Jan. 1969), 90–97; by John D. Jump in RES, XXX (May 1969), 237–238.

86. Caruthers, Clifford Mack. "A Critical Study of the Plays of Lord Byron" [Doctoral dissertation, Temple, 1968], DA, XXIX (Oct. 1968), 1204-A.

See K-SJ, XVIII (1969), No. 139.

87. Chadbourne, Marc. "Melmoth and le pacte infernal," *Revue de Paris*, LXXV (Aug.–Sept. 1968), 8–14.

Mentions Byron's enthusiasm for Maturin's *Bertram.*

88. Childers, William. "Byron's *Waltz*: The Germans and their Georges," K-SJ, XVIII (1969), 81–95.

Byron's satire conveys "the anti-Germanic sentiments of an outraged English patriot."

89. Christensen, Allan Conrad. "Heroism in the Age of Reform: Byron, Goethe, and the Novels of Carlyle" [Doctoral dissertation, Princeton, 1968], DA, XXIX (July 1968), 254-A–255-A.

See K-SJ, XVIII (1969), No. 142.

89a. *Citron, Pierre. "Balzac, lecteur du *Don Juan* de Byron," *L'Année Balzacienne* (1967), pp. 342–344.

90. Clairmont, Claire. *The Journals of Claire Clairmont.* Ed. Marion Kingston Stocking, assisted by David Mackenzie Stocking. Cambridge, Mass.: Harvard Univ., 1968.

Rev. by Paul F. Moran in *Library Journal*, 15 Jan. 1969, p. 184; by Denis Donoghue in Li, 24 April 1969, p. 572; by Claire Tomalin in NS, 2 May 1969, p. 626; in *Choice*, VI (June 1969), 508.

91. Clark, Sir Kenneth. "The Worship of Nature," Li, 8 May 1969, pp. 643–648.

Several references to Byron in a discussion which deals, in part, with Wordsworth, Coleridge, and Romantic poetry.

92. Cline, Clarence L. *Byron, Shelley, and Their Pisan Circle.* London & New York: Russell and Russell, 1969.

A reprint of a book first published in 1952. See K-SJ, II (1953), 101, III (1954), 115, IV (1955), 115.

93. Clubbe, John. "Byron in Switzerland" [Letter], TLS, 6 Feb. 1969, p. 135.

Notes unpublished account of Byron in 1816, which is in the Hamilton Collection, Duke University Library.

94. Constable, John. *John Constable's Correspondence*. Vol. vi. *The Fishers*. Ed. R. B. Beckett. Ipswich: Suffolk Records Society, 1968.

Constable refers very disapprovingly to Byron in a letter of May 1824 to J. Fisher. Haydon is sympathetically mentioned on several occasions.

Rev. in TLS, 26 Sept. 1968, p. 1084; by D. S. Bland in N&Q, ccxiv (Feb. 1969), 78–79.

95. Cooke, Michael G. *The Blind Man Traces the Circle: On the Patterns and Philosophy of Byron's Poetry*. Princeton: Princeton Univ., 1969.

Rev. by Paul F. Moran in *Library Journal*, 1 June 1969, p. 2234.

96. Doherty, Francis M. *Byron*. London: Evans, 1968; New York: Arco, 1969.

97. Drinkwater, John. *The Pilgrim of Eternity: Byron, a Conflict*. Port Washington, N.Y.: Kennikat, 1969.

A reprint of the 1925 edition.

98. Elledge, W. Paul. *Byron and the Dynamics of Metaphor*. Nashville: Vanderbilt Univ., 1968.

99. Gerus-Tarnawecky, Iraida. "Literary Onomastics," *Names*, xvi (Dec. 1968), 312–324.

Frequent illustrations of the use of names in literature are drawn from Byron. Keats is also briefly mentioned.

100. Gleckner, Robert F. *Byron and the Ruins of Paradise*. See K-SJ, xviii (1969), No. 178.

Rev. by Brian Wilkie in JEGP, lxvii (July 1968), 526–529; by E. E. Bostetter in ELN, vi, Supplement (Sept. 1968), 23–24; in *Choice*, v (Sept. 1968), 776; in TLS, 5 Sept. 1968, p. 949; Peter L. Thorslev, Jr., in *Criticism*, x (Oct. 1968), 370–372; by William H. Marshall in SAQ, lxvii (Autumn 1968), 709–710; by Sister Thomas Becket in *Thought*, xiv (Spring 1969), 133–134; by John D. Jump in RES, xxx (May 1969), 238–239.

100a. Gower, Herschel. "Tennessee Writers Abroad, 1851: Henry Maney and Randal W. McGavock," *Tennessee Historical Quarterly*, xxvi (Winter 1967), 396–403.†

Both Maney and McGavock refer to Byron.

101. Grant, Douglas. "Byron: The Pilgrim and *Don Juan*," in *The Morality of Art: Essays Presented to G. Wilson Knight by His Colleagues and Friends*, ed. D. W. Jefferson (London: Routledge and Kegan Paul; New York: Barnes and Noble [1967]), pp. 175–184.

Indicates that *Don Juan* is overemphasized at the expense of Byron's earlier poetry.

102. Gunn, Peter. *My Dearest Augusta: A Biography of the Honourable Augusta Leigh, Lord Byron's Half-Sister*. London: Bodley Head, 1968. (Pub. as *My Dearest Augusta: A Biography of Augusta Leigh, Lord Byron's Half-Sister*. New York: Atheneum, 1968. See K-SJ, xviii [1969], No. 180.)

Rev. in TLS, 21 March 1968, p. 799; by Robert Halsband in SatR, 19 Oct. 1968, p. 34; by Katherine Gauss Jackson in *Harper's Magazine*, ccxxxvii (Nov. 1968), 162; by Anne Fremantle in NYT, 24 Nov. 1968, p. 48.

103. Gunn, Peter, "My Dearest Augusta" [Letter], TLS, 4 July 1968, p. 705. See also TLS, 25 July 1968, p. 799; 15 Aug. 1968, p. 881; 29 Aug. 1968, p. 921.

Gunn acknowledges his indebtedness to others for use of copyright material in writing *My Dearest Augusta*. Various responses are forthcoming.

104. Hagelman, Charles W., Jr., and Robert J. Barnes, eds. *A Concordance to Byron's "Don Juan."* See K-SJ, xvii (1968), 12, xviii (1969), No. 102.

Rev. by David V. Erdman in ELN, vi, Supplement (Sept. 1968), 24–25.

105. Hassett, Michael E. "Pope, Byron, and Satiric Technique," *Satire Newsletter*, vi (Fall 1968), 19–28.

Byron's satiric technique in *English Bards and Scotch Reviewers* is presented as patterned on Pope's style.

106. Hawkes, John, John Ashbery, and William Alfred, eds. *The American Literary Anthology*. New York: Farrar, Straus, and Giroux, 1968.

Includes Auden's "Byron: The Making of a Comic Poet," which first appeared in *New York Review of Books* in 1966. See K-SJ, xvii (1968), 9.

107. Hobhouse, John Cam. *Recollections of a Long Life*. 6 vols. New York: AMS, 1968.
A reprint of the 1910–1911 volumes.

108. Huscher, Herbert. "Thomas Hope, Author of *Anastasius*," KSMB, XIX (1968), 2–13.
Discusses the reactions of Byron, Hunt, Keats, and Shelley to Hope and his novel.

109. Jump, John D. "Byron's Letters," *Essays and Studies*, XXI. See K-SJ, XVIII (1969), No. 201.
Rev. in TLS, 28 Aug. 1968, p. 906.

110. Jump, John D. "Byron's *Vision of Judgment*," *Bulletin of the John Rylands Library*, LI (Autumn 1968), 122–136.
Discusses background of Byron's poems and compares it with Southey's *A Vision*.

111. Knight, G. Wilson. *Byron and Shakespeare*. See K-SJ, XVII (1968), 13, XVIII (1969), No. 207.
Rev. by Kurt Otten in *Erasmus*, XX (Oct. 1968), 603–604.

112. Knight, G. Wilson. "Byron and Spiritualism," *Light*, LXXXVI (Summer 1966), 52–57.
Spiritualism in *Childe Harold* and *Manfred*. An anonymous report of a lecture by G. Wilson Knight.

113. Kronenberger, Louis. "The Lady and the Lion," *Atlantic Monthly*, CCXXIII (Jan. 1968), 93, 98–100.
A review article on Peter Gunn's biography of Augusta Leigh, *My Dearest Augusta*. See No. 102.

114. Lauber, John. "*Don Juan* as Anti-Epic," SEL, VIII (Autumn 1968), 607–619.†
"*Don Juan* systematically parodies or attacks the major conventions of epic poetry as set forth by neoclassic criticism."

115. Lutyens, Mary. "The Murrays of Albemarle Street," TLS, 24 Oct. 1968, p. 1198.
Includes references to Byron.

116. McGann, Jerome J. "Byronic Drama in Two Venetian Plays," MP, LXVI (Aug. 1968), 30–44.†
Answers those critics who have found fault with the dramatic nature of Byron's plays by arguing that action in *Marino Faliero* and *The Two Foscari*, as in Aeschylus and Sophocles, is "dramatically symbolic revelation."

117. McGann, Jerome J. "Byron's First Tale: An Unpublished Fragment," KSMB, XIX (1968), 18–23.
Presents ten stanzas from an unfinished poem of Byron, entitled "Il diavolo inamorato—The Devil—A Tale."

118. McGann, Jerome J. *Fiery Dust: Byron's Poetic Development*. Chicago: Univ. of Chicago, 1968.
Rev. by Paul F. Moran in *Library Journal*, XCIII (15 Dec. 1968), 4656; in TLS, 1 May 1969, p. 471; by Ernest J. Lovell, Jr. in SAQ, LXVIII (Summer 1969), 428–430.

119. McGann, Jerome J. "Staging Byron's *Cain*," KSMB, XIX (1968), 24–27.
McGann recounts staging Byron's play at the University of Chicago in 1968.

*Maciejewski, Marian. See No. 42.

120. Madden, William A. *Matthew Arnold: A Study of the Aesthetic Temperament in Victorian England*. See K-SJ, XVIII (1969), No. 225.
Rev. by Edward Alexander in JEGP, LXVII (Oct. 1968), 532–537; by Paul Turner in RES, XIX (Nov. 1968), 330–331.

121. Manno, Fort Philip. "The Anti-Hero and the Anti-Heroic Mode: A Study in the Genesis and Development of the Victorian Poetical Protagonist" [Doctoral dissertation, Minnesota, 1968], DA, XXIX (Jan. 1969), 2219–A.
Chapter Three deals with the Byronic hero.

122. Marchand, Leslie A. *Byron's Poetry: A Critical Introduction*. Cambridge, Mass.: Harvard Univ., 1968.
A reissue of a book first published in 1965.
Rev. by John Clubbe in SAQ, LXVIII (Spring 1969), 272.

123. Marshall, William H. "The Davis Collection of Byroniana," K-SJ, XVIII (1969), 9–11.
Describes the collection at the University of Pennsylvania.

124. Maurois, André. *Don Juan ou La Vie de Byron*. Lausanne: Editions Rencontre, 1969.
A reprint of the 1952 edition of Byron's life. See K-SJ, III (1954), 116.

125. Mayfield, John S. "Byron's Vampyre Letter," *Hobbies*, LXXIII (Jan. 1969), 108–109.

Letter of 27 Apr. 1819, from Byron to M. Galignani, turns out to be a facsimile rather than an original. See K-SJ, XVII (1968), 11.

126. Michaels, Leonard. "Byron's *Cain*," *PMLA*, LXXXIV (Jan. 1969), 71–78.

In its treatment of human consciousness and in its use of paradox and irony, *Cain* resembles theatre of the absurd.

127. Moorman, Mary. *William Wordsworth: A Biography*. 2 vols. London and New York: Oxford Univ., 1968.

A paperback reprint of the original two-volume biography. See K-SJ, XVI (1967), 122.

128. Mortenson, Robert. "*Abel: A Mystery* by Philip Dixon Hardy; An Answer to Lord Byron's *Cain: A Mystery*," KSMB, XIX (1968), 28–32.

Answers Byron "by rewriting the drama from a different point of view."

129. Mortenson, Robert. "Byroniana: 'Remarks on *Cain*' Identified," *Harvard Library Bulletin*, XVI (July 1968), 237–241.†

Analyzes sources and contents of the unique copy of "Remarks on Cain" in the Houghton Library, Harvard University.

130. Mortenson, Robert. "The Copyright of Byron's *Cain*," *PBSA*, LXIII (Jan.–March 1969), 5–13.

Despite a lack of specific proof, it is unlikely that a jury trial ever took place; its copyright was thus never upheld.

131. Mortenson, Robert. "Lord Byron and Baron Lützerode: An Important Presentation Volume," K-SJ, XVIII (1969), 27–37.

Byron's presentation of his *Sardanapalus, The Two Foscari, and Cain* volume to Lützerode contains "unpublished autograph corrections of the text and several passages which appear in no other first editions of that volume."

132. Nielsen, Jørgen Erik. "Byroniana," N&Q, CCXIV (Feb. 1969), 56.

Traces back the report of a Byron anecdote to a Danish West Indian newspaper of 1825.

133. Nielsen, Jørgen Erik. "*Parga*: A Verse Tale Attributed to Byron," ES, L (1969), 397–405.

Information on a little-known imitation of Byron published in Sept. 1819.

134. Nordon, Pierre. "Alfred de Musset et l'Angleterre," *Les Lettres Romanes*, XXII (Feb. 1968), 3–19; (May 1968), 109–132.

The February article discusses Musset's attitude toward Byron before and after 1834. The May article measures Musset's debt to De Quincey against his debt to Byron and Shakespeare.

135. Nowell-Smith, Simon. "T. J. Wise as Bibliographer," *The Library*, XXIV (June 1969), 129–141.

Refers to Wise's work on Byron, Keats, and Shelley.

Palgrave, Francis Turner, ed. See No. 46.

Park, William, *et al.* See No. 4a.

136. P[arker], D[erek]. "The All-Night Don Juan," *Poetry Review*, LIX (Winter 1968), 312.

All-night reading of Byron's *Don Juan* raises funds for Byron Memorial appeal. See also "A Memorial Ceremony to Lord Byron" in *Poetry Review*, LX (Spring 1969), 61–62, "Byron Memorial Fund," LX (Spring 1969), 68, "Ceremony of Dedication," LX (Summer 1969), 131.

137. Parker, Derek. *Byron and His World.* London: Thames and Hudson; New York: Viking (1968).

Rev. in TLS, 23 Jan. 1969, p. 81.

138. Parks, Stephen. "Wraxall and Byron" [Letter], TLS, 19 Dec. 1968, p. 1433.

Record's Wraxall's comments on Byron in a MS collection of the former's unpublished memoirs and diaries.

139. Polidori, John. *The Vampyre: A Tale Written by Doctor Polidori*, with a biographical note by Donald K. Adams. Pasadena: Grant Dahlstrom, 1968.

140. Pollin, Burton R. "Byron, Poe, and Miss Matilda," *Names*, XVI (Dec. 1968), 390–414.

Takes note of "Byron's 1809 derogations of 'Rosa Matilda,' a Rosa with imputed characteristics of Anna Matilda but strongly and mistakenly identified with Rosa King."

141. Pollin, Burton R. "Lord Byron as Parodist of 'The Battle of Blenheim,' " BNYPL, LXXIII (Apr. 1969), 215–217.

Suggests that Byron, not Tom Moore as Geoffrey Carnall proposed, parodied Southey's poem in the *Morning Chronicle*.

142. Pollin, Burton R. "Poe's 'Sonnet – To Zante': Sources and Associations," *Comparative Literature Studies*, v (Sept. 1968), 303–315.†

The sources include Byron and Keats.

143. Potts, Abbie Findlay. *The Elegiac Mode: Poetic Form in Wordsworth and Other Elegists*. See K-SJ, xvii (1968), 16.

Rev. in TLS, 25 July 1968; by Kenneth T. Abrams in ELN, vi, Supplement (Sept. 1968), 42–43; by R. W. King in MLR, lxiv (Jan. 1969), 150–151; by R. E. C. Houghton in RES, xxx (May 1969), 235–237.

Priestley, J. B. See No. 49.

144. *Pujals, Esteban. "Lord Byron En Espana," *Atlántida*, vii, No. 37 (Jan.–Feb. 1969), 32–50.

145. *Pujals, Esteban. "Lord Byron y Dante," *Atlántida*, iii, No. 18 (Nov.–Dec. 1965), 649–658.

146. "Recent Acquisitions – Manuscripts," *Princeton Univ. Library Chronicle*, xxx (Autumn 1968), 60, 63.

Announces the acquisition of a letter from Teresa Guiccioli to Henry Wikoff and a single letter, manuscript, or paper, of Thomas Moore.

146a. *Rees, John. "Byron and Brooke" [Letter], TLS, 8 May 1969, p. 490.

Richardson, Joanna. See No. 51.

147. Ridenour, George M. *The Style of "Don Juan."* Hamden, Conn.: Archon, 1969.

A reprint of a book first published in 1960. See K-SJ, x (1961), 80, xi (1962), 119, xii (1963), 132, xiii (1964), 132.

148. Robinson, Charles E. "The Frustrated Dialectic of Byron and Shelley: Their Reciprocal Influences" [Doctoral dissertation, Temple, 1967], DA, xxix (July 1968), 237-A–238-A.

See K-SJ, xviii (1969), No. 255.

149. Robinson, Henry Crabb. *The Diary of Henry Crabb Robinson: An Abridgement*. Ed. Derek Hudson. See K-SJ, xvii (1968), 17, xviii (1969), No. 256.

Rev. in QQ, lxxv (Autumn 1968), 365; by R. W. King in MLR, lxiii (Oct. 1968), 946–947; by Geoffrey Carnall in N&Q, ccxiii (Nov. 1968), 439–440.

150. Robinson, Henry Crabb. *The London Theatre, 1811–1866: Selections from the Diary of Henry Crabb Robinson*. Ed. Eluned Brown. See K-SJ, xviii (1969), No. 257.

Rev. by Geoffrey Carnall in N&Q, (Nov. 1968), 439–440.

151. Robson, W. W. *Critical Essays*. New York: Barnes and Noble, 1969.

A reprint of a collection first published in 1966. See K-SJ, xvii (1968), 17, xviii (1969), No. 258.

152. Santucho, Oscar José. "A Comprehensive Bibliography of Secondary Materials in English: George Gordon, Lord Byron" [Doctoral dissertation, Baylor, 1968], DA, xxix (Jan. 1969), 2227-A.

See K-SJ, xviii (1969), No. 263.

153. Schmidtchen, Paul W. "Byron, the Don Juan, plus Shakespeare and Jonson," *Hobbies*, lxxiv (May 1969), 104–105, 127.

Schmidtchen mentions a copy of Jonson's works that the Byron family owned.

154. Serrano Poncela, Segundo. "Puschkin y Don Juan," *Revista Nacional de Cultura*, clxxxv (July–Sept. 1968), 80–94.

Reference is made to Byron's poem.

Seymour-Smith, Martin. See No. 54a.

155. Stanford, Raney. "The Romantic Hero and That Fatal Selfhood," *Centennial Review*, xii (Oct. 1968), 430–452.

Cites Byron as an example.

156. Steffan, T. G. "Byron's *Don Juan*," Exp, xxvii (Apr. 1969), Item 65.

"Byron made Haidée an ordinary girl in love as well as an ethereal paragon."

157. Stevens, H[arold] R[ay]. "Southey and the Satanic School of Poetry: the Apocalyptic Tradition in Byron's *Vision of Judgment*," *Unisa English Studies*, vi (Sept. 1968), 37–46.

Byron's main purpose was "to reverse Southey's indictment, and to prove that Southey—and not Byron—belongs to the Satanic school of poetry."

Thomas, Donald. See No. 58.

Trelawny, E. J. See No. 385.

158. Trousson, Raymond. *Le thème de Prométhée dans la littérature européenne*. See K-SJ, xv (1966), 153, xvi (1967), 124, xviii (1969), No. 282.

Rev. by Patrick Pollard in MLR, lxiii (July 1968), 661–662.

159. Trueblood, Paul G. *Lord Byron.* New York: Twayne, 1969.

160. "Vanishing Apparitions: A Poetry Recital," CLSB (Jan. 1969), p. 613.
Report of a poetry recital in which poems of Byron, Keats, and Shelley were included.

161. Viets, Henry R. "The London Edition of Polidori's *The Vampyre*," *PBSA*, LXIII (Apr.–June 1969), 83–103.
Discusses the false attribution to Byron.

162. *Voia, V. "Eminescu şi Byron. Un paralelism literar (I)," *Studia Universitatis Babes-Bolyai Series Philologica Cluj*, XVII (1968), 4. [In Rumanian.]

163. Wallach, Alan P. "Cole, Byron, and the 'Course of Empire,'" *Art Bulletin*, L (Dec. 1968), 375–379.†
Discusses Byron's concealed influences on Cole's technique in the five paintings.

164. Walsh, William. *Coleridge: The Work and the Relevance.* See K-SJ, XVII (1968), 18.
Rev. by Kenneth T. Abrams in ELN, VI, Supplement (Sept. 1968), 26–27; in QQ, LXXVI (Spring 1969), 128–130.

165. Watson, George. *Coleridge the Poet.* See K-SJ, XVII (1968), 18.
Rev. by William H. Marshall in ELN, VI, Supplement (Sept. 1968), 27–28.

165a. *Witt, Robert W. "'So We'll Go No More A-Roving,'" *Univ. of Mississippi Studies in English*, IX (1968), 69–84.

166. Woodcock, George. "The Deepening Solitude," *Malahat Review*, No. 5 (Jan. 1968), 45–62.†
In tracing the theme of the rebel in European literature, the author cites Byron's *Cain* and Godwin.

III. HUNT

Works: Selected, Single

167. **Autobiography of Leigh Hunt.* 2 vols. New York: AMS, 1968.
A reprint of Hunt's 1850 volumes.

168. **Autobiography of Leigh Hunt.* 2 vols. New York: Hofner, 1968.
Another reprint of Hunt's 1850 volumes.

169. Corrigan, Beatrice, ed. *Italian Poets and English Critics, 1755–1859: A Collection of Critical Essays.* Chicago: Univ. of Chicago, 1969.
Includes Hazlitt's "Sismondi and the Trecentisti," and Hunt's "Critical Notice of Dante's Life and Genius."

170. *Prefaces of Leigh Hunt, Mainly to His Periodicals.* Ed. R. B. Johnson. Port Washington, New York: Kennikat, 1968.
A reprint of Johnson's 1927 edition.

Books and Articles Relating to Hunt

Huscher, Herbert. See No. 108.

171. Nicholes, E[leanor] L. "Leigh Hunt's 'Feast of the Poets,' Boston 1813 Edition," BC, XVIII (Winter 1969), 515–518.

Park, William, *et al.* See No. 4a.

172. Scoggins, James. *Imagination and Fancy: Complementary Modes in the Poetry of Wordsworth.* See K-SJ, XVII (1968), 20.
Rev. by Karl Kroeber in ELN, VI, Supplement (Sept. 1968), 44.

173. Stewart, Jack F. "Romantic Theories of Humor Relating to Sterne," *Personalist*, XLIX (Autumn 1968), 459–473.†
Among others, examines Hazlitt's and Hunt's "notions of Humor" in relation to *Tristram Shandy.*

174. Tatchell, Molly. *Leigh Hunt and His Family in Hammersmith.* Hammersmith Local History Group, 1969.

Thomas, Donald. See No. 58.

175. Webby, Elizabeth. "Australian Literature and the Reading Public in the Eighteen-Twenties," *Southerly*, XXIX, No. 1, (1969), 17–42.
Mentions Leigh Hunt and the "Cockney School."

IV. KEATS

Works: Selected, Single, Translated

176. *Asakula.* [*Isabella.*] [Translated by] Kumaran Murkkottu. Second Edition. Kozhikode: P. K. Brothers, 1967. [In Malayalam.]

177. Foakes, R. A. *Romantic Criticism, 1800–1850.* See K-SJ, XVIII (1969), No. 327.
Rev. in TLS, 25 July 1968, p. 796; by

W. D. Maxwell-Mahon in *Unisa English Studies*, VII (March 1969), 98–99.

177a. *Gargaro, Francesco, ed. *Poeti inglesi*. Rome: Signorelli, 1968.

Poems of Keats and Clare are translated into Italian in this anthology.

178. **Gedichte*. [*Poems*.] [Translated by] Heinz Piontek. Stuttgart: Reclam, 1968. [In German.]

179. *George, A. G., ed. *Makers of Literary Criticism*, Vol. II. India: Asia Publishing House, 1967.

Includes selections from Keats's letters, Peacock's *Four Ages of Poetry*, and Shelley's *Defence of Poetry*.

Rev. by H. H. Anniah Gowda in *Literary Half-Yearly*, IX (July 1968), 117–118.

180. *Poems of 1820; and The Fall of Hyperion*. Ed. David G. Gillham. New York: Collins, 1969.

181. **Versuri*. [*Poetry*.] [Translated by] Aurel Covaci. Bucarest: Editura tineretului, 1969. [In Rumanian.]

Books and Articles Relating to Keats and His Circle

182. Albrecht, W. P. *Hazlitt and the Creative Imagination*. See K-SJ, XVI (1967), 126, XVII (1968), 22, XVIII (1969), No. 347.

Rev. by Geoffrey Carnall in MLR, LXIII (Oct. 1968), 947–948.

183. Atkinson, F. C. "Hardy's *The Woodlanders* and a Stanza by Keats," N&Q, CCXIII (Nov. 1968), 423.†

Traces a reference in Hardy's novel to Keats's lines beginning "In drear-nighted December."

184. Balslev, Thors, *pseud.* [Thora Balslev Blatt.] *Keats and Wordsworth: A Comparative Study*. Copenhagen: Munksgamid, 1967.

First published in 1962 by Munksgaard. See K-SJ, XIII (1964), 137, XV (1966), 156, XVIII (1969), 25.

Rev. by Herbert Foltinek in *Erasmus*, XX (Sept. 1968), 543–547.

Bate, Walter J. See No. 76.

185. Bate, Walter J. *John Keats*. See K-SJ, XIV (1965), 118, XV (1966), 156, XVI (1967), 126, XVII (1968), 22, XVIII (1969), No. 356.

Rev. by Miriam Allott in MLR, LXIII (Oct. 1968), 949–951.

186. Beaudry, Harry Richard. "The English Theatre and John Keats" [Doctoral dissertation, Duke, 1969], DA, XXIX (March 1969), 3090–A.

See K-SJ, XVIII (1969), 25.

187. Bell, Quentin. *Victorian Artists*. London: Routledge and Kegan Paul; Cambridge, Mass.: Harvard Univ. (1967).

Haydon is mentioned, and plates of "The Raising of Lazarus" and "Punch, or May Day" are included.

Rev. by Kenneth Garlick in *Victorian Studies*, XII (March 1969), 384–385; by Robert Peters in *Western Humanities Review*, XXIII (Spring 1969), 178–179.

188. Benchley, Nathaniel. *Welcome to Xanadu*. New York: Atheneum, 1968.

In this novel, Keats and Coleridge appear in a fantasy.

Rev. by Martin Levin in NYT, 21 July 1968, p. 33; by Katherine Gauss Jackson in *Harper's Magazine*, CCXXXVII (Aug. 1968), p. 78; by Elizabeth Easton in SatR, 10 Aug. 1968, p. 65.

Ben-Israel, Hedva. See No. 10a.

189. Blakiston, Noel. "Joseph Severn, Consul in Rome, 1861–1871," *History Today*, XVIII (May 1968), 326–336, 368.

A study of the last eighteen months of Severn's eleven years' consulship. Includes bibliography and portrait.

189a. Blanke, Gustav H. "Archibald MacLeish, 'Ars Poetica,'" *Jahrbuch für Amerikastudien*, No. 13 (1968), 236–245.†

Alludes to Keats's dislike for poetry "which has a palpable design upon us."

190. Booth, Michael R., ed. *English Plays of the Nineteenth Century*. Vol. I: *Drama, 1800–1850*. Oxford: Clarendon; New York: Oxford Univ. (1969).

Included is James Sheridan Knowles's *Virginius*, to which Reynolds wrote the Prologue.

191. Bornstein, George. "Keats's Concept of the Ethereal," K-SJ, XVIII (1969), 97–106.

Traces Keats's concept of ethereality in the letters and early poems, particularly in *Endymion*.

192. Brooks, Cleanth. *Modern Poetry and the Tradition*. Chapel Hill: Univ. of North Carolina, 1967.

A paperback reprint of a book first published in 1939. Keats and Shelley are compared.

193. Brown, Charles Armitage. *The Letters of Charles Armitage Brown*. Ed. Jack Stillinger. See K-SJ, XVI (1967), 127, XVII (1968), 23, XVIII (1969), No. 369.

Rev. by John L. Bradley in MLR, LXIII (July 1968), 682-683.

194. *Buchen, Irving H. "Keats's 'To Autumn': The Season of Optimum Form," *CEA Critic*, XXXI, No. 2 (1968), 11.

195. Bush, Douglas. *John Keats: His Life and Writings*. See K-SJ, XVII (1968), 23, XVIII (1969), No. 371.

Rev. by Irene H. Chayes in ELN, VI, Supplement (Sept. 1968), 32.

196. Chatterjee, Bhabatosh. "The Enchanted Castle in Keats's 'Epistle to Reynolds,'" N&Q, CCXIII (Sept. 1968), 334–335.†

Argues against those commentators who "see the intrusion of incongruity and malevolence" in Keats's passage on the Enchanted Castle (lines 26–66).

197. Clare, John. *Selected Poems and Prose of John Clare*. Ed. Eric Robinson and Geoffrey Summerfield. See K-SJ, XVII (1968), 10.

Rev. in TLS, 29 Feb. 1968, p. 198; by John D. Jump in N&Q, CCXIII (Sept. 1968), 353–354.

198. Clare, John. *The Wood is Sweet. Poems for Young Readers*. Chosen by David Powell; introd. Edmund Blunden. London: Bodley Head, 1966; New York: Watts, 1968.

199. *Clarke, Charles Cowden, and Mary C. Clarke. *Recollections of Writers*. Introd. Robert Gittings. London: Centaur, 1969.

A fascimile reprint of the 1878 edition.

Rev. by Martin Seymour-Smith in Spec, 25 Apr. 1969, pp. 550–551; letter by Katherine M. R. Kenyon in Spec, 2 May 1969, p. 598.

200. Clarke, Mary Cowden. *My Long Life: An Autobiographic Sketch*. St. Claire, Mich.: Scholarly Press, 1968.

A reprint of a book originally published in 1896.

201. Clubbe, John. *Victorian Forerunner: The Later Career of Thomas Hood*. Durham: Duke Univ., 1968.

For original dissertation see K-SJ, XVII (1968), 24.

Rev. in *Choice*, VI (March 1969), 52, 54; by Thomas L. Ashton in *Hartford Studies in Literature*, I (1969), 223–229.

201a. Columbo, John Robert. "Avison and Wevill," *Canadian Literature*, No. 34 (Autumn 1967), 72–76.†

The selflessness of Margaret Avison's poetry is compared with Keats's concept of "negative capability."

202. Colvin, Sir Sidney. *Keats*. New York: St. Martin's, 1968.

A paperback reprint of the 1889 edition. See K-SJ, XVIII (1969), No. 381.

203. *Colvin, Sir Sidney. *Keats*. New York: AMS, 1969.

A reprint of the 1889 edition.

Constable, John. See No. 94.

204. Copeman, W. S. C. *The Worshipful Society of Apothecaries of London: A History, 1617–1967*. Oxford: Pergamon, 1968.

Keats is included in a chapter on eminent apothecaries.

Rev. by Arthur S. MacNalty in *Medical History*, XIII (Apr. 1969), 202–203.

Corrigan, Beatrice, ed. See No. 169.

205. Cancelled.

206. D'Avanzo, Mario L. *Keats's Metaphors for the Poetic Imagination*. See K-SJ, XVII (1968), 24, XVIII (1969), No. 390.

Rev. by Miriam Allott in N&Q, CCXIV (Feb. 1969), 80; by Roland Hagenbüchle in *Erasmus*, XX (Oct. 1968), 600–602; by Walter H. Evert in K-SJ, XVIII (1969), 112–114.

207. Ehrenpreis, Anne Henry, ed. *The Literary Ballad*. See K-SJ, XVII (1968), 21.

Rev. by J. H. P. Pafford in MLR, LXIII (July 1968), 681–682.

208. Enscoe, Gerald E. *Eros and the Romantics: Sexual Love as a Theme in Coleridge, Shelley, and Keats*. See K-SJ, XVIII (1969), No. 394.

Rev. by Donald H. Reiman in K-SJ, XVIII (1969), 114–116.

209. Erdman, David V. and Ephim G. Fogel, eds. *Evidence for Authorship: Essays on Problems of Attribution*. See K-SJ, XVII (1968), 24.

Rev. by R. W. Dent in *Shakespeare Quarterly*, XX (Winter 1969), 99.

209a. Fandel, John. "Reading the Poem, Poetry," *Four Quarters*, XVIII (May 1969), 22–24.

Includes a brief discussion of "On First Looking into Chapman's Homer."

210. Ferguson, Oliver W. "Warton and Keats: Two Views of Melancholy," K-SJ, XVIII (1969), 12–15.

Cites parallel passages from the first edition of *Pleasures of Melancholy* (lines 171–190) and Keats's "Ode to a Nightingale."

211. Fogle, Richard H. "Beauty and Truth: John Middleton Murry on Keats," *D. H. Lawrence Review*, II (Spring 1969), 68–75.

Murry's "actual achievement is very substantial indeed."

212. Fusco, Robert J. "The Concrete Versus the Abstract in 'Ode on a Grecian Urn,'" *Massachusetts Studies in English*, II (Spring 1969), 22–28.

Suggests that Keats's conclusion in the Ode is based on a "metaphysical improbability."

213. George, Eric. *The Life and Death of Benjamin Robert Haydon, Historical Painter, 1786–1846.* See K-SJ, XVIII (1969), No. 401.

Rev. by D. S. Bland in N&Q, CCXIII (Sept. 1968), 351–352; by J. Mordaunt Crook in *English Historical Review*, LXXXIV (Apr. 1969), 405.

214. Gérard, Albert S. *English Romantic Poetry: Ethos, Structure, and Symbol in Coleridge, Wordsworth, Shelley, and Keats.* See K-SJ, XVIII (1969), No. 402.

Rev. by James A. Phillips in *Library Journal*, 15 Oct. 1968, p. 3787; in *Choice*, V (Nov. 1968), 1130; by M. K. Joseph in AUMLA, No. 30 (Nov. 1968), 249–250; in TLS, 21 Nov. 1968, p. 1304; by U. Laredo in *Unisa English Studies*, VII (March 1969), 97–98; by J. A. Appleyard in *Thought*, XLIV (Summer 1969), 297–299; by R. H. Fogle in K-SJ, XVIII (1969), 111–112.

Gerus-Tarnawecky, Iraida. See No. 99.

215. *Gibbs, A. M. *John Keats: Ode to a Nightingale; Ode on a Grecian Urn; To Autumn.* London: British Council, 1967. "Notes on Literature Series, 71."

216. Gittings, Robert. *John Keats.* See K-SJ, XVIII (1969), No. 403.

Rev. by Geoffrey Grigson in Li, LXXIX (25 Apr. 1968), 545; by Elinor Shaffer in *Cambridge Review*, LXXIX-A (7 June 1968), 553–554; by John R. Willingham in *Library Journal*, XCIII (Aug. 1968), 2853; by Joanna Richardson in NYT, 1 Sept. 1968, p. 4; by Harold Bloom in *New Republic*, 7 Sept. 1968, pp. 29–30; by Dorothy Tyler in *Detroit News*, 22 Sept. 1968, p. 3e; by George Nevin in *Poetry Review*, LIX (Autumn 1968), 202–203; by Hermann Peschmann in *English*, XVII (Autumn 1968), 104–105; in *Choice*, V (Nov. 1968), 1130; by G. M. Matthews in *New York Review of Books*, 7 Nov. 1968, pp. 28–30; by Louise Bogan in *New Yorker*, 28 Dec. 1968, p. 62; in *Studies in English Literature* (Japan), XLV (March 1969), 304–305; by Jack Stillinger in K-SJ, XVIII (1969), 107–111; in *Tamarack Review*, No. 4 (1969), pp. 81–85.

217. Goldberg, Milton A. *The Poetics of Romanticism: Toward a Reading of John Keats.* Yellow Springs, Ohio: Antioch, 1969.

218. Gomme, Andor H. *Attitudes to Criticism.* See K-SJ, XVII (1968), 25.

Rev. by Allan Rodway in N&Q, CCXIII (Sept. 1968), 355–357.

219. Grigson, Geoffrey. *Poems and Poets.* London: Macmillan, 1969.

Includes an essay on Shelley, "Proselytizer of the World" (pp. 57–61) and two on Clare, "John Clare" (pp. 71–88) and "Clare in Madness" (pp. 86–123).

Rev. in TLS, 13 March 1969, p. 259; by Rayner Heppenstall in *Sunday Times*, 16 March 1969, p. 60; by Campbell Black in Li, 20 March 1969, p. 60.

Halsted, John B., ed. See No. 29.

220. Harbage, Alfred. *Conceptions of Shakespeare.* See K-SJ, XVII (1968), 20.

Rev. by G. R. Hibbard in *Shakespeare Survey*, XXI (1968), 129.

221. Hardie, Martin. *Water-Colour Painting in Britain.* Vol. II: *The Romantic Period.* See K-SJ, XVII (1958), 26, XVIII (1969), No. 414.

Rev. by Walter J. Hipple, Jr., in JAAC, XXVII (Summer 1969), 469–470.

222. Haworth, Helen E. "Keats and the Metaphor of Vision," JEGP, LXVII (July 1968), 371–394.

Keats's visions are neither religious nor mystical, but "metaphors for the function of the poetical imagination."

223. Hayden, John O. "Hazlitt Reviews Hazlitt?", MLR, LXIV (Jan. 1969), 20–26.
Maintains that Hazlitt anonymously reviewed Hunt's *The Round Table* and his own *Characters of Shakespear's Plays* in the *Edinburgh Magazine* for Nov. 1817, pp. 352–361.

224. Hazlitt, Margaret. *The Journal of Margaret Hazlitt: Recollections of England, Ireland, and America.* Ed. Ernest J. Moyne. See K-SJ, XVIII (1969), No. 421.
Rev. in TLS, 29 Aug. 1968, p. 917: reply by D. A. N. Jones in TLS, 5 Sept. 1968, p. 945; in *Choice*, V (Oct. 1968), 1018.

225. Hazlitt, William. *An Essay on the Principles of Human Action, 1805.* Introd. John R. Nabholtz. Gainesville, Fla.: Scholars' Facsimiles and Reprints, 1969.
A reprint of Hazlitt's 1805 essay opposing materialistic philosophy.

226. *Hazlitt, William. *The Hazlitt Sampler: Selections from His Familiar Literature and Critical Essays.* Ed. Herschel H. Sikes. Gloucester, Mass.: Smith, 1969.
A reprint of a book first published in 1961. See K-SJ, XII (1963), 262.

227. Hazlitt, William. *Lectures on the English Comic Writers.* New York: Russell, 1969.
A reprint of Hazlitt's 1819 edition.

228. Hazlitt, William. *The Life of Thomas Holcroft.* Ed. Eldridge Colby. New York: Benjamin Blom, 1969.
A reprint of the 1925 edition.

229. Hazlitt, William. *A Reply to the Essay on Population by the Rev. T. R. Malthus.* New York: Augustus M. Kelley, 1968.
A reprint of Hazlitt's 1807 *Reply.*

230. Hill, Archibald A. "Some Points in the Analysis of Keats's 'Grecian Urn,' " in *Studies in Language, Literature, and Culture of the Middle Ages and Later,* ed. E. Bagby Atwood and Archibald A. Hill (Austin: Univ. of Texas, 1969), pp. 357–366.
Discusses and proposes answers to "imperfect" rhymes and problem lines, including "truth-beauty."

231. Hill, Douglas. *John Keats.* New York: Barnes and Noble, 1969.

232. Hinkel, Howard Hollis. "The Two Worlds of John Keats: A Study of His Poetry as Attempts to Reconcile the Disparity Between Intuited and Observed Reality" [Doctoral dissertation, Tulane, 1968], DA, XXIX (March 1969), 3098-A–3099-A.

233. Hood, Thomas. *Poems.* Ed. William Cole. New York: Crowell, 1968.

Huscher, Herbert. See No. 108.

234. Inglis, Fred. *Keats.* See K-SJ, XVI (1967), 129, XVII (1968), 27, XVIII (1969), No. 427.
Rev. by Miriam Allott in MLR, LXIII (Oct. 1968), 950–951.

235. Jack, Ian. *Keats and the Mirror of Art.* See K-SJ, XVII (1968), 27, XVIII (1969), No. 429.
Rev. by Irene H. Chayes in ELN, VI, Supplement (Sept. 1968), 32; by D. S. Bland in N&Q, CCXIII (Sept. 1968), 351–352; by Herbert Foltinek in *Erasmus,* XX (Sept. 1968), 543–547; by Miriam Allott in LXIII (Oct. 1968), 949–951; by Marcia Allentuck in *Art Journal,* XXVIII (Fall 1968), 122, 124.

236. *Jäger, Dietrich. "Über Zeit und Raum als Formen lyrischer Welterfahrung, besonders bei Eichendorff und Keats," *Literatur in Wissenschaft und Unterricht,* I (1968), 221–250.
The second half of a two-part essay. See K-SJ, XVIII (1969), No. 430.

237. Johnson, R. V. "Aesthetic Traits in Charles Lamb," *Southern Review* (Adelaide), III, No. 2 (1968), 151–158.
Refers to Pater's comparison of Keats with Lamb.

238. Jones, John. "Keats and 'The Feel of Not to Feel it,' " in *The Morality of Art: Essays Presented to G. Wilson Knight by His Colleagues and Friends,* ed. D. W. Jefferson (London: Routledge and Kegan Paul, 1969), pp. 185–194.
States that Keats knew exactly what he was doing when he wrote this disputed line from "In drear-nighted December."

239. Jones, Stanley. "Hazlitt, Cobbett, and the *Edinburgh Review,*" *Neophilologus,* LIII (Jan. 1969), 69–76.
Contrary to Hazlitt's belief, Cobbett did defend himself against attack in the *Edinburgh Review.*

240. Kane, Peter, "The Growth of Humanism in Keats," *Humanist* (London), LXXXIII (Aug. 1968), 233–235.

"His life was a living illustration of the courage and determination necessary for the self-creation of the mature humanist."

241. Kenney, Blair G. "Keats' 'Ode on a Grecian Urn,'" Exp, XXVII (May 1969), Item 69.

Argues that Keats's attitude is more one of playfulness than solemn pronouncement. "I believe it should be viewed as an experience rather than a pronouncement, a *jeu d'esprit* rather than a credo."

241a. *Kohli, Devindra. "Inner Resonance: A Note on the Odes of John Keats," *Quest*, No. 48 (Jan.–March 1966), 33–42.†

241b. Kroeber, Karl. *The Artifice of Reality: Poetic Style in Wordsworth, Foscolo, Keats, and Leopardi.* See K-SJ, XV (1966), 160, XVI (1967), 130, XVII (1968), 27, XVIII (1969), 30.

Rev. by Guido Almansi in *Giornale Storico Della Letteratura Italiana*, CXLV (1968), 429–436.

242. Leoff, Eve. "A Study of John Keats's *Isabella*" [Doctoral dissertation, Columbia, 1968], DA, XXIX (Sept. 1968), 874-A.

See K-SJ, XVIII (1969), No. 444.

243. Lowell, Amy. *John Keats.* 2 vols. Hamden, Conn.: Archon, 1969.

A reprint of a book first published in 1925.

243a. Lucie-Smith, Edward. "Dante Gabriel Rossetti," Li, LXXVII (15 June 1967), 788–790.†

Rossetti's unfinished poem "The Orchestra Pit" is representative of his debt to Keats.

244. McLuhan, Marshall. *The Interior Landscape: The Literary Criticism of Marshall McLuhan, 1934–1962.* Ed. Eugene McNamara. New York and Toronto: McGraw-Hill, 1969.

Includes an article on Keats's odes.

Madden, William A. See No. 39.

245. Mallaby, George. "Wordsworth and Hazlitt" [Letter], TLS, 25 July 1968, p. 789. See also David Lincoln, TLS, 1 Aug. 1968, p. 825; Michael Foot, TLS, 15 Aug. 1968, p. 873; Stanley Jones, 29 Aug. 1968, p. 928; Mary Moorman, 12 Sept. 1968, p. 997; Douglas Grant and Stanley Jones, 19 Sept. 1968, p. 1062.

Opens Pandora's box by asserting that the cause of Wordsworth's eventual hostility to Hazlitt was the result of a rape or attempted rape by Hazlitt of a peasant girl.

246. Marion, Sister Thomas. "An Exploration of 'Romantic' Elements in Some Shorter Poems of Matthew Arnold," *Greyfriar*, X (1968), 3–15.†

Concludes that as a result of his determination to alter Keats's Romantic aesthetic, Arnold became the lesser poet.

247. *Mathur, D. K. "The Concept of Suffering in Keats and Baudelaire," *Rajasthan University Studies in English* (1967–1968), 83–102.

248. Mathur, D. K. "The Meaning of 'Pure Poetry' in Keats and Baudelaire," *Quest*, LIX (Autumn 1968), 52–59.

Compares Keats and Baudelaire, who both "have a similar idea of the true poetical character."

249. Matthey, F. "Interplay of Structure and Meaning in the *Ode to a Nightingale*," ES, XLIX (Aug. 1968), 303–317.

Maintains that the carefully balanced symmetry of themes corresponds exactly to the pattern of verse in Keats's poem.

250. Mayhead, Robin. *John Keats.* See K-SJ, XVIII (1969), No. 452.

Rev. by R. H. Fogle in ELN, VI, Supplement (Sept. 1968), 32; by Ralph J. Miller, Jr., in *Poetry*, CXIII (Jan. 1969), 263.

251. Moler, Kenneth L. "'La Belle Dame sans Merci' and 'The Pleasures of Imagination,'" ES, XLIX (Dec, 1968), 539–540.

Sees an analogy Addison draws from *The Spectator*, No. 413, as a link with Keats's symbolic "knight at arms."

252. Motto, Anna Lydia, and John R. Clark. "Senecan Irony," *Classical Bulletin*, XLV (Nov. 1968), 6–7, 9–10.†

Contains a reference to Keats's concept of negative capability.

253. Murray, E. B. "Keats's 'Jack' Reynolds," N&Q, CCXIV (Feb. 1969), 57.

Answers Sallé's note of Sept. 1968 (see No. 271) and argues that a reference in a Keats letter of 17 Apr. 1817 to Reynolds is not to *The Rivals*, but to *1 Henry IV*.

254. Murry, John M. *John Clare and Other*

Studies. Milwood, N. Y.: Kraus Reprint Company, 1968.

A reprint of a book first published in 1950.

255. Murry, John M. *Keats*. Fourth Edition, rev. and enl. New York: Funk & Wagnalls, 1969.

A reprint of the 1955 edition. See K-SJ, v (1956), 130, vi (1957), 143, vii (1958), 126, viii (1959), 71, xii (1963), 140.

256. *Nagasawa, Jiro. "Endymion's Proem: Concerning When It Was Written," in *Maekawa Shunichi Kyoju Kanreki Kinenronbunshū* (Tokyo: Eihōsha, 1968), pp. 357–366.

257. Newton, J. M. "A Speculation about Landscape," *Cambridge Quarterly*, iv (Summer 1969), 273–282.

Refers to Keats's use of landscape in the Odes, *Endymion*, and "La Belle Dame sans Merci."

Nowell-Smith, Simon. See No. 135.

257a. "Notes on the Harvard Libraries," *Harvard Library Bulletin*, xvi (Oct. 1968), 402.

Notes an addition to the Keats collection "of a manuscript commonplace book kept by Georgiana Wylie Keats, the poet's sister-in-law. The manuscript of a sonnet addressed to her is included."

258. *Nuttall, Anthony D. *Two Concepts of Allegory*. London: Routledge and Kegan Paul; New York: Barnes and Noble (1967).

Keats's idea of the imagination as Adam's dream is mentioned.

Rev. by G. R. Hibbard in *Shakespeare Survey*, xxii (1969), 164–165.

259. *Ober, William B. "Drowsed with the Fume of Poppies: Opium and John Keats," *Bulletin of the New York Academy of Medicine*, xliv (July 1968), 862–881.

260. O'Brien, Veronica. "The Language of Poetry," *Studies*, lviii (Winter 1969), 415–426.

Includes a discussion of Keats's sonnet "When I have fears that I may cease to be."

261. O'Hara, J. D. "Hazlitt and Romantic Criticism of the Fine Arts," JAAC, xxvii (Fall 1968), 73–85.

Art critics of the Romantic period such as Hazlitt "possessed uncertain tastes and eclectic standards derived from literature and morality."

262. O'Neill, Judith, comp. *Critics on Keats*. Coral Gables, Fla.: Univ. of Miami, 1969.

A reprint of a collection first published in 1967. See K-SJ, xvii (1968), 29, xviii (1969), No. 465.

263. Ower, John. "The Epic Mythologies of Shelley and Keats," *Wascana Review*, iv, No. 1 (1969), 61–72.

Illustrates how Keats and Shelley fuse classical and biblical materials to create their epic framework in *Hyperion* and *Prometheus Unbound*.

Palgrave, Francis Turner, ed. See No. 46.

264. Park, Roy. "Coleridge and Kant: Poetic Imagination and Practical Reason," *British Journal of Aesthetics*, viii, No. 4 (Oct. 1968), 335–346.

Includes brief mention of Shelley and Keats.

265. Park, Roy. "Coleridge's Two Voices As a Critic of Wordsworth," *ELH*, xxxvi (June 1969), 361–381.

In part, Park compares Coleridge's critical view of Wordsworth with the views of Keats and Hazlitt toward the same poet.

266. Parsons, Coleman O. "Spenser's Braying Tiger," N&Q, ccxiv (Jan. 1969), 21–24.†

A line in the *Faerie Queene* (iv.x.46) may have influenced Keats in "The Poet."

267. Pevsner, Nikolaus. *Studies in Art, Architecture and Design*. 2 vols. New York: Walker; London: Thames and Hudson (1968).

Haydon is mentioned.

Rev. by David Piper in *Times* (London), 30 Nov 1968, p. 22-b.

268. Peyre, Henri. *The Failures of Criticism*. Ithaca: Cornell Univ., 1967.

This emended edition of *Writers and Their Critics* (1944) devotes part of its first chapter to a discussion of the critical reception of Keats and Shelley.

Rev. by Rémy G. Saisselin in JAAC, xxvii (Spring 1969), 360–362.

Pollin, Burton R. See No. 142.

269. Potter, Dennis. "Unread Classics: Wil-

liam Hazlitt," *Times* (London), 3 Aug. 1968, pp. 15, 18.
An appreciation.

Richardson, Joanna. See No. 51.

269a. *Rossetti, Dante Gabriel. *Letters of Dante Gabriel Rossetti*. Eds. Oswald Doughty and John Robert Wahl. Vols. III and IV. Oxford: Clarendon, 1967. See K-SJ, XVII (1967), 123, for Vols. I and II.
Includes correspondence with Harry Buxton Forman about Keats.
Rev. by Joan Rees in MLR, LXIV (Apr. 1969), 409–411.

270. *Sakata, Katsuzo. "Time and Eternity in 'Ode to a Nightingale' and 'Ode on a Grecian Urn,' " *Studies in English Literature* (Japan), XLV (Sept. 1968), 39–48. [In Japanese.]

271. Sallé, J.-C. "An Allusion to *The Rivals* in a Keats Letter," N&Q, CCXIII (Sept. 1968), 335–336.†
Found in Keats's letter of 17 Apr. 1817 to Reynolds.

271a. Sambrook, A. J. "*The Farmer's Boy*: Robert Bloomfield, 1766–1823," *English*, XVI (Summer 1967), 161–171.†
A precursor of John Clare.

272. Scott, Arthur F. *Close Readings: A Course in the Critical Appreciation of Poetry*. London: Heinemann, 1968.
Includes a discussion of Keats's "To Autumn."
Rev. by Shyamala Venkateswaran in *Literary Criterion*, VIII (Summer 1969), 85.

273. Scott, Nathan A., Jr. *Negative Capability: Studies in the New Literature and the Religious Situation*. New Haven: Yale Univ., 1969.
Keats's concept is discussed in the Preface and applied to the chapters that follow.

Seymour-Smith, Martin. See No. 54a.

274. Sheats, Paul D. "Keats's Second 'Hyperion' and the 'Purgatorio': Further Notes," N&Q, CCXIII (Sept. 1968), 336–338.†
Echoes of the *Purgatorio* in Keats's *The Fall of Hyperion* "further emphasize the independence with which he adapted the imagery and tone of *The Divine Comedy* to his own ends."

275. Sperry, Stuart M., Jr. "Richard Woodhouse's Interleaved and Annotated Copy of Keats's *Poems* (1817)," *Literary Monographs*, I. See K-SJ, XVIII (1969), No. 497.
Rev. by Barbara Hardy in N&Q, CCXIV (Jan. 1969), 40; by Leonidas M. Jones in K-SJ, XVIII (1969), 120–121.

Stewart, Jack F. See No. 173.

276. Stillinger, Jack. "Keats and Romance," SEL, VIII (Autumn 1968), 593–605.†
Reads Keats's *Isabella* as anti-romance.

277. Stillinger, Jack, ed. *Twentieth Century Interpretations of Keats's Odes: A Collection of Critical Essays*. Englewood Cliffs, N.J.: Prentice-Hall, 1968.

278. Stillinger, Jack. "The Order of Poems in Keats's First Volume," PQ, XLVIII (Jan. 1969), 92–101.
"There is a chartable progress from hesitancy to affirmation that explains both the order and relatedness of the poems."

279. Stillinger, Jack. "The Texts of Keats's 'Ode on Indolence,' " *Studies in Bibliography*, XXII (1969), 255–258.†
Maintains that Milnes was correct and Garrod incorrect in ordering the stanzas of this poem.

280. Storey, Mark. "Letters of John Clare, 1821: Revised Datings," N&Q, CCXIV (Feb. 1969), 58–64.
Proposes corrections of letters between Clare and his publishers preceding publication of *The Village Minstrel*.

281. Story, Patrick Lee. "Hazlitt's *Spirit of the Age*: A Facsimile Edition with Introduction and Textual Collations" [Doctoral dissertation, Northwestern, 1968], DA, XXIX (Jan. 1969), 2230-A.
See K-SJ, XVIII (1969), No. 501.

282. Swaminathan, S. R. "Keats and Benjamin West's *King Lear*," K-SJ, XVIII (1969,) 15–16.
Claims that West's painting, rather than Shakespeare's play, was the source for Keats's observation on the nature of intensity in art.

283. *Talbot, Norman. *The Major Poems of John Keats*. See K-SJ, XVIII (1969), No. 508.
Rev. in TLS, 27 March 1969, p. 331; by P. D. Sheats in K-SJ, XVIII (1969), 116–117.

"Vanishing Apparitions." See No. 160.

283a. Vickery, John B., ed. *Myth and Literature: Contemporary Theory and Practice.* See KS-J, XVI (1967), 133.

Rev. by Peter Ure in MLR, LXIV (Apr. 1969), 374–375.

284. Wasserman, Earl R. *The Finer Tone: Keats' Major Poems.* See K-SJ, XVII (1968), 32.

Rev. by Vivian de S. Pinto in *Critical Quarterly*, XI (1969), 90–91.

285. Wilbur, Richard. "Poetry and Happiness," *Shenandoah*, XX, No. 4 (Summer 1969), 3–23.

Includes references to Keats and Shelley. Wilbur argues that Frost's "Birches" is a reply to Shelley's neo-Platonic aspiration in *Adonais*.

286. Wycherley, H. Alan. "Keats: The Terminal Disease and Some Major Poems," *American Notes and Queries*, VII (Apr. 1969), 118–119.

Finds references to the symptoms of tuberculosis in Keats's Odes and in "La Belle Dame sans Merci."

V. SHELLEY

Works: Selected, Single, Translated

287. Cancelled.

288. Cancelled.

*George, A. G., ed. See No. 179.

Palgrave, Francis Turner, ed. See No. 46.

289. *Poems of Percy Bysshe Shelley.* Ed. Leo Gurko. New York: Crowell, 1968.

290. *Posthumous Poems of Shelley.* Ed. Irving Massey. Montreal: McGill-Queen's Univ., 1969.

291. *Shelley's Prometheus Unbound: A Variorum Edition.* Ed. Lawrence John Zillman. See K-SJ, IX (1960), 70.

Rev. by M. K. Joseph in AUMLA, XXXII (Nov. 1969), 251–253.

292. *Shelley's Prometheus Unbound: The Text and the Drafts: Toward a Modern Definitive Edition.* Ed. Lawrence John Zillman. See K-SJ, XVIII (1969), No. 541.

Rev. by James Phillips in *Library Journal*, 1 Oct. 1968, p. 3563; in TLS, 20 Feb. 1969, p. 181; in *Choice*, VI (Apr. 1969), 218.

293. *Shi No Bengo.* [*A Defence of Poetry.*] [Translated by] Kiyoshi Mori. Tokyo: Kenkyûsha, 1969. [In Japanese.]

Books and Articles Relating to Shelley and His Circle

294. Atkinson, Edmund. "The Shelleys," *Sussex Notes and Queries*, XVII (Nov. 1968), 62.

Information on the marriage of the poet's mother and father.

295. Bartel, Roland. "Shelley and Burke's Swinish Multitude," K-SJ, XVIII (1969), 4–9.

Traces the source for this opprobrious term from Burke to Shelley's ironic reference in *Oedipus Tyrannus.*

Bate, Walter J. See No. 76.

Ben-Israel, Hedva. See No. 10a.

296. Benoit, Raymond. "Shelley's Flying Saucer," *University Review*, XXXV (Dec. 1968), 139–143.

Sees the image of a flying saucer in *Prometheus Unbound* (IV.236–252) as representative of the final synthesis of opposites in Shelley's poetry.

297. Blackburn, Thomas. "Homage to Shelley," *Poetry Review*, LIX (Winter 1968), 238–239.

*Blakiston, Noel. See No. 81.

298. Bloom, Harold. *Shelley's Mythmaking.* Ithaca: Cornell Univ., 1969.

A reprint of a book first published in 1959. See K-SJ, IX (1960), 71, X (1961), 92, XI (1962), 133, XII (1963), 144, XIII (1964), 145.

299. Bloom, Harold. "Visionary Cinema," PR, XXXV (Fall 1968), 555–570.

In a favorable sense, Shelley's poetry makes "the visible a little hard to see."

300. Bowen, Catherine Drinker. "The Biographer and his Hero," *American Heritage*, XX (Dec. 1968), 16–17.

Quotes Maurois on the reason he wrote *Ariel*: he and Shelley both came from families they wished to escape.

301. Brailsford, H. N. *Shelley, Godwin, and Their Circle.* Hamden, Conn.: Archon, 1969.

A reprint of a book first published in 1913; second revised edition appeared in 1951. See K-SJ, III (1954), 121.

Brooks, Cleanth. See No. 192.

302. Butter, Peter H. *Shelley's Idols of the Cave.* New York: Haskell House, 1969.
A reprint of a book first published in 1954. See K–SJ, IV (1955), 122, V (1956), 132, VI (1957), 147, VII (1958), 129.

303. Carter, John, and John Sparrow. "Shelley, Swinburne, and Housman," TLS, 21 Nov. 1968, pp. 1318–19. Also see, P. S. Falla, TLS, 28 Nov. 1968, p. 1338.
A discussion of the disputed eighth line of Shelley's "A Lament." As Housman suspected, Swinburne's defense of the traditional text is shown to be incorrect.

304. Chernaik, Judith S. "The Figure of the Poet in Shelley," *ELH*, XXXV (Dec. 1968), 566–590.
The portrait of the poet was not self-indulgence on Shelley's part, but "an attempt to render dramatically the imaginative process which is the only escape from self."

305. Chernaik, Judith S. "Shelley's 'To Constantia': A Contemporary Printing Examined," TLS, 6 Feb 1969, p. 140. Also, see reply by Neville Rogers in TLS, 13 Feb. 1969, p. 159.
Discovers that the poem was published in a variant form in the *Oxford University and City Herald* of 31 Jan. 1818.

Cline, Clarence L. See No. 92.

306. Cowling, George H. *Shelley and Other Essays.* Freeport, N. Y.: Books for Libraries, 1968.
Reprint of 1936 edition.

307. Dawson, Carl. *Thomas Love Peacock.* See K–SJ, XVIII (1969), No. 566.
Rev. in *Choice*, V (Oct. 1968), 948.

308. de Beer, Gavin. "Shelley's House at Brunnen," KSMB, XIX (1968), 1.
Shelley, Mary, and Claire rented two rooms in this house on the Lake of Lucerne, in Aug. 1814.

309. DeRocco, Joseph. "Shelley's Empiricism" [Doctoral dissertation, Columbia, 1968], DA, XXIX (Sept. 1968), 867-A.
See K–SJ, XVIII (1969), No. 568.

309a. *Donaghy, Henry J. "Love and Mr. Wells: A Shelleyan Search for the Epipsyche," *Studies in Literary Imagination*, I (Oct. 1968), 41–50.†

309b. Duerksen, Roland A. "The Double Image of Beatrice Cenci in *The Marble Faun*," *Michigan Academician*, I (Spring 1969), 47–55.
"It appears likely that Hawthorne was well acquainted with the first full-scale literary treatment of the legendary story —Shelley's drama *The Cenci*."

310. Duerksen, Roland A. "Markings by Whitman in His Copy of Shelley's Works," *Walt Whitman Review*, XIII (Dec. 1968), 147–151.
Whitman's markings point to parallels between the prose and poetry of both men.

311. Duerksen, Roland A. *Shelleyan Ideas in Victorian Literature.* See K–SJ, XVII (1968), 36, XVIII (1969), No. 572.
Rev. by Jerome J. McGann in MP, LXVI (Feb. 1969), 280–281.

312. Dumas, Donald Gilbert. "William Godwin's *Caleb Williams*: Doctrine into Art" [Doctoral dissertation, California, Berkeley, 1968], DA, XXIX (June 1969), 4453-A–4454-A.

313. Eigner, Edwin M. *Robert Louis Stevenson and Romantic Tradition.* See K–SJ, XVIII (1969), No. 573.
Rev. by Travis R. Merritt in MP, LXVI (Aug. 1968), 87–89.

314. Ellis, Frederick S. *Lexical Concordance to the Political Works of Percy Bysshe Shelley.* New York: Burt Franklin, 1968.
A reprint of the 1892 edition. See K–SJ, XVIII (1969), No. 574.

315. Fairclough, Peter, ed. *Three Gothic Novels.* Baltimore: Penguin, 1968.
This paperback volume, with a Preface by Mario Praz, includes Mary Shelley's *Frankenstein.*
Rev. in *Times* (London), 5 Oct. 1968, p. 20.

316. Findlater, Richard, *pseud.* [Kenneth Bruce Findlater Bain.] *Banned! A Review of Theatrical Censorship in Britain.* See K–SJ, XVII (1968), 36.
Rev. by Paul O'Higgins in *Theatre Notebook*, XXIII (Winter 1968–69), 74–75.

Foakes, R. A. See No. 177.

317. Fuller, Jean Overton. *Shelley, A Biography.* See K–SJ, XVIII (1969), No. 579.
Rev. by George Nevin in *Poetry Review*, LIX (Autumn 1968), 202–203.

Gérard, Albert S. See No. 214.

318. *Godwin, William. *The Enquirer*. New York: Augustus M. Kelley, 1969.
A reprint of Godwin's 1797 volume.

319. Godwin, William. *Of Population*. New York: Augustus M. Kelley, 1964.
A reproduction of the London edition of 1820.

320. *Godwin, William. *Of Population . . . an Answer to Malthus*. New York: Burt Franklin, 1969.

321. Godwin, William. *Thoughts on Man, his Nature, Productions, and Discoveries*. New York: Augustus M. Kelley, 1969.
A reprint of the first edition of 1831.

322. Grabo, Carl H. *A Newton Among Poets: Shelley's Use of Science in* Prometheus Unbound. New York: Cooper Square; New York: Gordian (1968).
Reprint of a book first published in 1930.

323. Grabo, Carl H. Prometheus Unbound: *An Interpretation*. See K-SJ, XVIII (1969), No. 585.
Rev. in *Choice*, v (Feb. 1969), 1580.

Grigson, Geoffrey. See No. 219.

324. Cancelled.

325. Guinn, John Pollard. *Shelley's Political Thought*. Mouton Studies in English Literature, XLIV. The Hague and Paris: Mouton, 1969.

326. Hildebrand, W. H. "Shelley's Early Vision Poems," SIR, VIII (Summer 1969) 198–215.
Shelley achieves discovery of himself in *Alastor*, which stands as "a significant watershed" in his poetic development.

327. Howells, Coral Ann. "*Biographia Literaria* and *Nightmare Abbey*," N&Q, CCXIV (Feb. 1969), 50–51.
Mr. Flosky's discussion in Peacock's novel parallels Coleridge's attack on the Gothic melodrama in *Biographia Literaria* (Chapter XXIII).

328. *Hughes, Daniel. "Blake and Shelley: Beyond the Uroboros," in *William Blake: Essays for S. Foster Damon*, ed. Alvin H. Rosenfeld (Providence: Brown Univ., 1969), pp. 69–83.

329. Hunter, Parks C., Jr. "Undercurrents of Anacreontics in Shelley's 'To a Skylark' and 'The Cloud,' " SP, LXV (July 1968), 677–692.
Considers the influence of the Anacreontic odes "To a Cicada" and "Drinking" upon Shelley's two poems.

Huscher, Herbert. See No. 108.

330. Hume, Robert D. "Gothic versus Romantic: A Revaluation of the Gothic Novel," PMLA, LXXXIV (March 1969), 282–290.
Mary Shelley's *Frankenstein* is mentioned in this essay, which relates the Gothic novel to Romanticism at large.

331. Jeffrey, Lloyd N. " 'The Birds within the Wind': A Study in Shelley's Use of Natural History," K-SJ, XVIII (1969), 61–80.
"This examination of Shelley's bird imagery and symbology points to the need for a thorough reassessment of the poet's knowledge and use of natural history."

332. Kalim, Siddiq. "Robert Owen and Shelley," *Explorations*, I (Jan.–March 1969), 40–67.
Owen and Shelley knew each other personally and held each other in high esteem. It was *Queen Mab* that had greatest appeal to Owen.

333. Kinnaird, J. " 'But for Such Faith': A Controversial Phrase in Shelley's 'Mont Blanc,' " N&Q, CCXIII (Sept. 1968), 332–334.†
Proposes a new reading of these difficult lines that centers around the meaning of the word "faith."

Levine, Goerge, ed. See No. 39.

334. Levy, Robert Allen. "Shelley's Last Summer," *Journal of Historical Studies*, II (Winter 1968–69), 66–70.
An impressionistic description of Shelley's last day, culled from biographical sources.

335. Lund, Mary G. "Mary Shelley's Father," *Discourse*, XII (Winter 1969), 130–135.
Godwin's concepts of education and his relationship with Mary.

336. Lund, Mary Graham. "Shelley's Psychedelics," *University Review*, XXXV (Dec. 1968), 133–138.
"Shelley repeatedly sought a breakthrough into some apocalyptic revelation."

337. McTaggart, William Joseph. "A Textual Study of Percy Bysshe Shelley's 'A Ballad' Followed by a Brief Examination of Certain Sociological Problems Affecting

Church and State in Shelley's Day" [Doctoral dissertation, Ohio, 1968], DA, XXIX (Oct. 1968), 1211-A–1212-A.
See K-SJ, XVIII (1969), No. 606.

338. Madden, J. L. "Peacock, Tennyson, and Cleopatra," N&Q, CCXIII (Nov. 1968), 416–417.
The source for Tennyson's unflattering description of Cleopatra, from which Peacock draws in *Gryll Grange* (Chapter XXIII), is attributed to Shakespeare.

Madden, William A., ed. See No. 39.

339. Maniquis, Robert M. "The Puzzling *Mimosa*: Sensitivity and Plant Symbols in Romanticism," SIR, VIII (Spring 1969), 129–155.
Discusses the history of the *mimosa* and its use as a symbol by Romantic writers with particular emphasis on Shelley's "The Sensitive Plant."

340. *Marchi, Giovanni. "La tragedia dei Cenci nelle opere teatrali," *Nuova Antologia*, DIII (Aug. 1968), 530–547.

341. Massey, Irving. "Some Letters of Shelley Interest," KSMB, XIX (1968), 14–17.
Three fragmentary letters to John Addington Symonds are attributed to Mrs. Henrietta Hussey, a niece of Harriet Grove.

342. Matthews, G. M. "Shelley Lyrics," in *The Morality of Art: Essays Presented to G. Wilson Knight by His Colleagues and Friends*, ed. D. W. Jefferson (London: Routledge and Kegan Paul, 1969), pp. 195–209.
A more perceptive understanding of the intention of dramatic function of Shelley's lyrics is necessary.

343. Matthews, G. M. "The Triumph of Life," EC, XVIII (July 1968), 352–356.
Supports Kenneth Allott's traditional interpretation of lines 308–468 of the poem. (See K-SJ, X [1961], 91, for the Allott entry.)

344. *Maurois, André. *Ariel ou La vie de Shelley, Suivi de: Robert and Elizabeth Browning*. Lausanne: Editions Rencontre, 1969.
Reprints of well-known works.

344a. *Mauskopf, Charles. "Shelley's Dejection," *Xavier Univ. Studies*, VII, No. 13 (1968), 9–14.

345. Mays, Milton A. "*Frankenstein*, Mary Shelley's Black Theodicy," *Southern Humanities Review*, III (Spring 1969), 146–153.
Argues that the secret hero of the novel is "the Monster, a great Romantic rebel who . . . stands in most interesting relationship to Adam and Lucifer."

345a. Menen, Aubrey, and Clifton Fadiman. "Party of One—The Myth of English Literature," *Holiday*, XXVI (July 1959), 8, 10–14.†
Page numbers include Aubrey's attack on Scott and Shelley, and Fadiman's reply. Also see K-SJ, XV (1966), 168.

345b. Miller, Sara Mason. "Irony in Shelley's *The Cenci*," *Univ. of Mississippi Studies in English*, IX (1968), 23–25.
Shelley employs verbal, situational, thematic, and Socratic irony in his play, but at no time does dramatic irony appear.

346. Mills, Howard. *Peacock: His Circle and His Age*. Cambridge: Cambridge Univ., 1969.
Rev. in TLS, 22 May 1969, p. 555.

347. Murray, E. B. " 'Elective Affinity' in *The Revolt of Islam*," JEGP, LXVII (Oct. 1968), 570–585.
"Elective affinity best accounts for and explains the puzzling relationship among the major characters."

348. Murray, E. B. "Mont Blanc's Unfurled Veil," K-SJ, XVIII (1969), 39–48.
Defends Shelley's use of the word "unfurled" in Section III of the poem.

Nowell-Smith, Simon. See No. 135.

349. O'Malley, Glenn. *Shelley and Synesthesia*. See K-SJ, XV (1966), 168, XVI (1967), 138, XVII (1968), 39.
Rev. by Jerome J. McGann in MP, LXVI (Feb. 1969), 281–283.

350. *Orel, Harold. "Another Look at *The Necessity of Atheism*," *Mosaic*, II, No. 2 (1969), 27–37.

351. Otten, Terry. "Christabel, Beatrice, and the Encounter with Evil," *Bucknell Review*, XVII, No. 2 (May 1969), 19–31.
The affinities, especially among Geraldine, Christabel, and Beatrice, suggest that the authors shared a common view of evil and that they used similar techniques to expound it.

Ower, John. See No. 263.

Park, Roy. See No. 264.

352. *Peacock, Thomas Love. *Nightmare Abbey and Crotchet Castle*. Ed. Raymond Wright. Harmondsworth: Penguin, 1969.

A paperback edition of Peacock's two novels.

353. Peck, Walter E. *Shelley*. 2 vols. New York: Burt Franklin, 1968.

A reprint of the 1927 edition.

Peyre, Henri. See No. 268.

354. Pinkus, Phillip. "The Satiric Novels of Thomas Love Peacock," *Kansas Quarterly*, I (Summer 1969), 64–76.

Compares Peacock's novels with Augustan satire and finds both similarities and differences.

355. Pixton, William Hoover. "The Intellectual Movement of Shelley's Later Poetry" [Doctoral dissertation, North Carolina, 1968], DA, XXIX (June 1969), 4466-A–4467-A.

356. Cancelled.

357. Pollin, Burton R. *Godwin Criticism: A Synoptic Bibliography*. See K-SJ, XVIII (1969), No. 624.

Rev. by Kenneth Neill Cameron in *Institute for Computer Research in Humanities Newsletter*, IV (1968), 3–4; in PQ, XLVII (July 1968), 385; by David V. Erdman in ELN, VI, Supplement (Sept. 1968), 30–31; by Donald H. Reiman in JEGP, LXVII (Oct. 1968), 715–717; by Jack W. Marken in K-SJ, XVIII (1969), 117–120; by David McCracken in MP, LXVII (1969), 199–201; in TLS, 20 March 1969, p. 290; by C. B. Jones in MLR, LXIV (Apr. 1969), 403–404.

358. Pollin, Burton R. "Godwin's *Mandeville* in Poems of Shelley," KSMB, XIX (1968), 33–40.

Finds that Godwin's novel influenced Shelley in "Love's Philosophy" and "Ozymandias."

359. Power, Julia. *Shelley in America in the Nineteenth Century: His Relation to American Critical Thought and His Influence*. New York: Gordian, 1969.

Reprint of the 1940 edition.

360. Powers, H. M. "The Theatrical Criticism of Arthur Murphy, Leigh Hunt, and William Hazlitt" [Doctoral dissertation, Cornell, 1968], DA, XXIX (Dec. 1968), 1979-A.

361. Prance, Claude A. "Charles Lamb's Illustrators, 1796–1967," CLSB (July 1968), pp. 600–602; (Oct. 1968), pp. 604–609.

References to William Godwin in the July installment.

361a. *Praz, Mario. "Armida's Garden," CL, V (March 1968), 1–20.†

Tasso anticipates Shelley and other Romantics.

362. Press, John. *The Fire and the Fountain: An Essay on Poetry*. London: Methuen, 1966.

Mentions Shelley and his *Defence*.

Rev. by Georg Seehase in *Zeitschrift für Anglistik und Amerikanistik*, XVI, No. 4 (1968), 109–112.

363. Rader, Melvin. *Wordsworth: A Philosophical Approach*. See K-SJ, XVII (1968), 40.

Rev. by Karl Kroeber in ELN, VI, Supplement (Sept. 1968), 43; in QQ, LXXVI (Spring 1969), 124–125.

363a. Raine, Kathleen. *Blake and Tradition*. 2 vols. Princeton: Princeton Univ., 1968.

Contains references to Shelley and Mary Wollstonecraft Godwin.

Rev. by Morton D. Paley in ELN, VII (June 1970), 304–310.

364. Raine, Kathleen. *Defending Ancient Springs*. See K-SJ, XVIII (1969), 41.

Rev. by Douglas Barbour in QQ, LXXV (Winter 1968), 758–759.

365. *Rao, E. Nageswara. "The Significance of *Frankenstein*," *Triveni: A Cultural Journal*, XXXVII (Oct. 1968), 20–26.

366. Raynor, Henry. "Television Justice for Mrs. Shelley," *Times* (London), 12 Nov. 1968, p. 7.

Frankenstein adapted by Robert Muller as a television play.

367. Reiman, Donald H. *Percy Bysshe Shelley*. New York: Twayne, 1969.

368. Reiter, Seymour. *A Study of Shelley's Poetry*. See K-SJ, XVIII (1969), No. 638.

Rev. by Kenneth Neill Cameron in ELN, VI, Supplement (Sept. 1968), 37; by Jerome J. McGann in MP, LXVI (Feb. 1969), 280; by P. H. Butter in MLR, LXIV (Apr. 1969), 407–408.

Richardson, Joanna. See No. 51.

369. Rieger, James. *The Mutiny Within: The Heresies of Percy Bysshe Shelley*. See K-SJ, XVII (1968), 41, XVIII (1969), No. 639.

Rev. by P. H. Butter in MLR, LXIII (July 1968), 684–685; by Kenneth Neill Cameron in ELN, VI, Supplement (Sept. 1968), 37–38; by D. W. Harding in EC, XIX (Jan. 1969), 93–99.

Robinson, Charles E. See No. 148.

370. Rogers, Neville. *Shelley at Work: A Critical Inquiry*. Second Edition. See K-SJ, XVIII (1969), No. 640.

Rev. by P. H. Butter in MLR, LXIV (Jan. 1969), 151–152; by Jerome J. McGann in MP, LXVI (Feb. 1969), 283; by R. B. Woodings in *Studia Neophilologica*, XLI, No. 1 (1969), 195–196.

371. Rogers, Neville. "Shelley: Texts and Pretexts, the Case of First Editions," KSMB, XIX (1968), 41–46.

An uncritical acceptance of first editions can lead to a mechanical fundamentalism which ignores common sense.

372. Rubin, David. "A Study of Antinomies in Shelley's *The Witch of Atlas*," SIR, VII (Summer 1969), 216–228.

Examines fire and water imagery in order to understand Shelley's antinomian methods.

373. Ruff, James Lynn. "Image, Theme and Structure in *The Revolt of Islam*" [Doctoral dissertation, Northwestern, 1968], DA, XXIX (Jan. 1969), 2278-A.

See K-SJ, XVIII (1969), No. 645.

374. Russell, Bertrand. *The Autobiography of Bertrand Russell*. Vol. III: *1944–1967*. London: Allen and Unwin, 1969.

Russell speaks on more than one occasion of his admiration for Shelley.

Rev. by Iain Hamilton in ILN, 24 May 1969, pp. 42–43.

375. Salt, Henry S. *Percy Bysshe Shelley, Poet and Pioneer*. Port Washington, N. Y.: Kennikat, 1968.

A reprint of the 1887 edition.

376. Sanders, Mary K. "Shelley's Promethean Shadow on *Leaves of Grass*," *Walt Whitman Review*, XIII (Dec. 1968), 151–159.

Sees *Leaves of Grass* as a product of "Shelleyan inspiration."

377. Schulze, Earl J. *Shelley's Theory of Poetry: A Reappraisal*. See K-SJ, XVII (1968), 42; XVIII (1969), No. 651.

Rev. by Earl R. Wasserman in *Michigan Quarterly Review*, VII (Summer 1968), 219–221; by Donald H. Reiman in MP, LXVI (May 1969), 377–379.

Seymour-Smith, Martin. See No. 54a.

378. Shelley, Mary Wollstonecraft. *Frankenstein*. Adapted by Dale Carlson. New York: Golden, 1968.

Frankenstein adapted for children.

Rev. by Gloria Levitas in NYT (Juv.), 3 Nov. 1968, p. 52.

379. *Shelley, Mary Wollstonecraft. *Frankenstein* [Translated by] Christian Barth. Munich: Heyne, 1969. [In German.]

379a. *Shelley, Mary Wollstonecraft. *Frankenstein* [Translated by] K. B. Leder and Gert Leetz. Stuttgart: Europäischer Buch & Phonoklub, 1968. [In German.]

380. Shelley, Mary Wollstonecraft. *Frankenstein*. New York: Lancer, 1968.

380a. *Shelley, Mary Wollstonecraft. *Frankenstein: ovvero, Il Prometeo moderno*. [Translated by] Bruno Tasso. Milan: Sugar, 1968. [In Italian.]

381. Smith, Nelson Charles. "The Art of Gothic: Ann Radcliffe's Major Novels" [Doctoral dissertation, Washington, 1967], DA, XXIX (July 1968), 240-A–241-A.

Includes a brief discussion of *Frankenstein*.

382. Starling, Jeremiah Pelletier. "Shelley's Poetry of 1815–1816: *Alastor*, 'Hymn to Intellectual Beauty,' and 'Mont Blanc' " [Doctoral dissertation, North Carolina, 1968], DA, XXIX (June 1969), 4506-A–4507-A.

382a. *Strauss, P. "Escape from Nightmare Abbey?," *Theoria*, XXX (1968), 65–68.

383. Strong, Sir Archibald T. *Three Studies in Shelley and An Essay on Nature in Wordsworth and Meredith*. Hamden, Conn.: Archon, 1968.

A reprint of the 1921 edition.

384. Taylor, George Robert S. *Mary Wollstonecraft: A Study in Economics and Romance*. New York: Haskell, 1969.

A reprint of the 1911 edition.

Thomas, Donald. See No. 58.

385. Trelawny, E. J. *Records of Shelley, Byron, and the Author*. New York: Benjamin Blom, 1968.

A reprint of Trelawny's 1878 edition.

"Vanishing Apparitions." See No. 160.

386. Wade, Phil. "On the Occasion of the

150th Birthday of Frankenstein's Monster: Some Thoughts on His Parentage," *South Atlantic Bulletin*, XXXIV (Jan. 1969), 10.

States that Shelley's collaboration is clearly seen in Mary's novel.

387. Wardle, Ralph M., ed. *Godwin and Mary: Letters of William Godwin and Mary Wollstonecraft*. See K-SJ, XVII (1968), 43, XVIII (1969), No. 679.

Rev. by Lewis Patton in SAQ, LXVII (Autumn 1968), 708; in CLSB (Oct. 1968), p. 610.

388. Wasserman, Earl R. *Shelley's "Prometheus Unbound": A Critical Reading*. See K-SJ, XVI (1967), 142, XVII (1968), 43, XVIII (1969), No. 681.

Rev. by Anthea Morrison in MLR, LXIII (Oct. 1968), 948–949.

389. Weaver, Bennett. *Prometheus Unbound*. Hamden, Conn.: Archon, 1969.

A reprint of a book first published in 1957. See K-SJ, VII (1958), 132, VIII (1959), 78, IX (1960), 75.

390. Webb, Timothy. "Shelley's Sophocles: A Legend Re-examined," KSMB, XIX (1968), 47–52.

Notwithstanding Trelawny's and Lady Shelley's claims, Shelley did not have a copy of Sophocles with him when he drowned.

391. White, Robert L. " 'Rappaccini's Daughter,' *The Cenci*, and the Cenci legend," *Studi Americani*, XLV (1968), 63–86.

Proposes Shelley's play as the primary source for Hawthorne's story.

Wilbur, Richard. See. No 285.

392. Wittreich, Joseph Anthony, Jr. "The 'Satanism' of Blake and Shelley Reconsidered," SP, LXV (Oct. 1968), 816–833.

Explains that ultimately Blake and Shelley repudiate the view of Satan as the hero of *Paridise Lost*.

Woodcock, George. See No. 166.

393. Woodings, R. B., ed. *Shelley: Modern Judgements*. See K-SJ, XVIII (1969), No. 688.

Rev. in TLS, 1 Aug. 1968, p. 826.

394. Woodings, R. B. "Shelley's Sources for 'Charles the First,' " MLR, LXIV (Apr. 1969), 267–275.

Proposes that the major source for Shelley's play was Hume's *History of England*.

395. Woodings, R. B. "Shelley's Widow Bird," RES, N.S. XIX (Nov. 1968), 411–414.

This short ballad was intended as the basis for a longer personal love lyric.

395a. Wright, Celeste Turner. "Elinor Wylie: The Glass Chimaera and the Minotaur," *Twentieth Century Literature*, XII (Apr. 1966), 15–26.†

Shelley's poetry is suggested as one of many possible influences on her choice of imagery.

396. Zbierski, Henry K. "Some Notes on the Structure and Imagery of Shelley's 'Ode to the West Wind,' " *Studia Anglica Posnaniensia*, I, Nos. 1–2 (1968), 91–99.

VI. PHONOGRAPH RECORDINGS

Byron, Keats, Shelley

397. **Great Poems of English Literature*. CMS Records.

The last in this series of three records covers the nineteenth century.

398. **The Poetry of John Keats*. Read by Ralph Richardson. See K-SJ, IX (1960), 75, XI (1962), 139.

Rev. by Vashti Tyrrell in *Poetry Review*, LX (Spring 1969), 56–57.

399. *The Romantic Poets*. Vol. I. Read by Hurd Hatfield. Caedmon Records.

This recording, intended for grades 10–12, includes "Ode on a Grecian Urn" and the conclusion of *Adonais*.

Bibliography for July 1, 1969–June 30, 1971

VOLUME XX

Compiled by Lewis M. Schwartz, Robert A. Hartley, and G. Curtis Olsen

THIS bibliography, a regular department of the *Keats-Shelley Journal*, is a register of the literary interest in Keats, Shelley, Byron, and Hunt, and their circles from (approximately) July 1969 through June 1971.

The compilers are very grateful for their kind assistance to Williston R. Benedict; Gerald B. Kauvar of The City College of the City University of New York; Rae Ann Nager, editor of the *Keats-Shelley Journal*; Donald H. Reiman of The Carl H. Pforzheimer Library; Donald J. Ryan; and Carl R. Woodring of Columbia University. We also thank members of the library staffs of Columbia University, Hunter College and Kingsborough Community College of the City University of New York, and the New York Public Library.

Where a book has been issued by more than one publisher during the same year, the publication date appears at the end of the entry within parentheses. Two changes in style from previous years have been instituted: references to volume numbers in periodicals are now in Arabic rather than Roman numerals; citations to previous bibliographies of the journal are now to item rather than page number.

Each item that we have not seen is marked by an asterisk. Entries which have been abstracted in *Abstracts of English Studies* are marked with a dagger, but entries in previous bibliographies which were abstracted too late for notice have not been repeated. Entries which have been abstracted in *MLA Abstracts* are marked with a double dagger.

ABBREVIATIONS

ABC	American Book Collector
AL	American Literature
AN&Q	American Notes and Queries
ASNS	Archiv für das Studium der neuren Sprachen
AUMLA	Journal of the Australasian Universities Language and Literature Association
BA	Books Abroad
BC	Book Collector
BNYPL	Bulletin of the New York Public Library
CE	College English
CL	Comparative Literature
CLSB	C. L. S. Bulletin (Charles Lamb Society)
CR	Contemporary Review
DAI	Dissertation Abstracts International
EA	Etudes Anglaises
EC	Essays in Criticism
ELH	Journal of English Literary History
ELN	English Language Notes
ES	English Studies
Exp	Explicator
HLQ	Huntington Library Quarterly
ICS	L'Italia Che Scrive
ILN	Illustrated London News
JAAC	Journal of Aesthetics and Art Criticism
JEGP	Journal of English and Germanic Philology
JHI	Journal of the History of Ideas
KR	Kenyon Review
K-SJ	Keats-Shelley Journal
KSMB	Keats-Shelley Memorial Bulletin
LC	Library Chronicle
Li	Listener
LJ	Library Journal
MLN	Modern Language Notes
MLQ	Modern Language Quarterly
MLR	Modern Language Review
MP	Modern Philology
N&Q	Notes and Queries
NS	New Statesman
NYRB	New York Review of Books
NYT	New York Times Book Review
PBSA	Papers of the Bibliographical Society of America
PMLA	Publications of the Modern Language Association of America
PQ	Philological Quarterly
PR	Partisan Review
QQ	Queen's Quarterly
RES	Review of English Studies
RLC	Revue de Littérature Comparée
SAQ	South Atlantic Quarterly
SatR	Saturday Review
SEL	Studies in English Literature 1500–1900
SIR	Studies in Romanticism
SP	Studies in Philology
Spec	Spectator
SR	Sewanee Review
T&T	Time and Tide
TLS	Times Literary Supplement
UES	Unisa English Studies
UTQ	University of Toronto Quarterly
VQR	Virginia Quarterly Review
WC	Wordsworth Circle

Current Bibliography

I. GENERAL

Current Bibliographies

1. Arnott, James Fullarton, and John William Robinson. *English Theatrical Literature, 1559–1900: A Bibliography*. Incorporating Robert W. Lowe's *A Bibliographical Account of English Theatrical Literature*, published in 1888. London: Society for Theatre Research, 1970.

   Includes items by Byron, Hazlitt, and Hunt.

2. Blish, Mary. "A. C. Bradley: A Summary Account," PBSA, 62 (Oct.–Dec. 1968), 607–612.

   This bibliography of Bradley's works includes several items on Shelley and a few on Keats.

3. Brack, O. M., Jr., and Warner Barnes, eds. *Bibliography and Textual Criticism: English and American Literature, 1700 to the Present*. See K-SJ, 20 (1970), No. 1a.

   Rev. by Robert S. Fraser in LJ, 94 (1 Sept. 1969), 2906.

4. Cordasco, Francesco. *Eighteenth Century Bibliographies: Handlists of Critical Studies Relating to Smollett, Richardson, Sterne, Fielding, Dibdin, 18th Century Medicine, the 18th Century Novel, Godwin, Gibbon, Young, and Burke*. Metuchen, N.J.: Scarecrow, 1970.

   Reprints Godwin bibliography from Long Island Univ. Press, *18th Century Bibliographical Pamphlets*.

   Rev. in *Choice*, 7 (Oct. 1970), 1013–1014.

5. Erdman, David V., *et al.* "The Romantic Movement: A Selective and Critical Bibliography for 1968," ELN, 7, Supplement (Sept. 1969), 1–159.

6. Erdman, David V., *et al.* "The Romantic Movement: A Selective and Critical Bibliography for 1969," ELN, 8, Supplement (Sept. 1970), 1–158.

7. Freeman, Ronald E., ed. "Victorian Bibliography for 1969," *Victorian Studies*, 13 (June 1970), 467–531.

8. Freeman, Ronald E., ed. "Victorian Bibliography for 1970," *Victorian Studies*, 14 (June 1971), 473–539.

9. Cancelled.

10. Horden, John, and James B. Misenheimer, Jr., eds. "Nineteenth Century," *Annual Bibliography of English Language and Literature*, 42 (1969 [for 1967]), 303–414.

11. Horden, John, and James B. Misenheimer, Jr., eds. "Nineteenth Century," *Annual Bibliography of English Language and Literature*, 43 (1970 [for 1968]), 327–458.

12. Horden, John, and James B. Misenheimer, Jr., eds. "Nineteenth Century," *Annual Bibliography of English Language and Literature*, 44 (1971 [for 1969]), 337–471.

13. Howard-Hill, T. H. *Bibliography of British Literary Bibliographies*. Oxford: Oxford Univ., 1969.

    This first volume of a new three-volume *Index to British Literary Bibliography* contains entries of individual British authors from 1475 to the present.

    Rev. by Thomas J. Galvin in LJ, 94 (1 Sept. 1969), 2907.

14. Katona, Anna. "English Literature in Hungarian Translation, 1945–1965," *Angol Filólogiai Tanulmányok (Hungarian Studies in English)*, 3 (1967), 83–102.

    Lists translations into Hungarian of the works of Keats, Shelley, Byron, Charles and Mary Lamb, and Coleridge.

15. Lahiri, K. "A Classified List of Select Articles Published in *The Calcutta Review* (Series I, II, III) since 1844," *Calcutta Review*, N.S. 1 (Jan.–March 1970), 465–483.

    Includes many items on the Romantics.

16. Litto, Frederic M. *American Dissertations on the Drama and the Theatre: A Bibliography*. Kent, Ohio: Kent State Univ., 1969.

    Key-word index lists dissertations on Byron, Keats, Shelley, Hunt, and others.

17. Mészáros, Elsie. "Bibliography of Hungarian Writings on English Literature, 1957–1960," *Angol Filólogiai Tanulmányok (Hungarian Studies in English)*, 1 (1963), 123–131.

    Lists scholarly and critical articles on English literature published in Hungarian journals, 1957–1960. Many items on Byron, Keats, and Shelley.

18. Pady, Donald S. "Thomas Brower Peacock," *Bulletin of Bibliography*, 28 (Apr.–June 1971), 37–40.

    A collateral descendent of Thomas Love Peacock, this Peacock was an American journalist, writer, musician, and inventor who wrote an epic poem on Buffalo Bill. Lived 1852–1919. The article lists his works.

19. Park, William, *et al. National Library of Scotland: Catalogue of Manuscripts Acquired since 1925*. Vol. III: *Blackwood Papers, 1805–1900*. See K-SJ, 19 (1970), No. 4a.

    Rev. by Jenny Stratford in *Manuscripts*, 22 (Spring 1970), 131–132.

20. Schwartz, Lewis M., and Rae Ann Nager, with the assistance of Gerald B. Kauvar. "Current Bibliography," K-SJ, 19 (1970), 1–38.

21. Singer, Armand E. "Second Supplement to *The Don Juan Theme, Versions and Criticism: A Bibliography* (1965)," *Philological Papers*, 17 (June 1970), 102–170.

22. Vadon, Lehel, and Gabriella Zsuffa. "Bibliography of Hungarian Writings on English Literature, 1961–1965," *Angol Filólogiai Tanulmányok (Hungarian Studies in English)*, 3 (1967), 123–146.

    Lists scholarly and critical articles on English literature published in Hungarian journals. Many items on Byron, Keats, and Shelley.

23. Watson, George, ed. *The New Cambridge Bibliography of English Literature*. Vol. III: *1800–1900*. See K-SJ, 19 (1970), No. 6.

    Rev. in TLS, 11 Dec. 1969, p. 1432; by Alfred Owen Aldridge in *Comparative Literature Studies*, 7 (March 1970), 140; by Larry Earl Bone in LJ, 95 (1 Apr. 1970), 1354; by Howell J. Heaney in *Nineteenth Century Fiction*, 25 (Dec. 1970), 370–371; by Richard D. Altick in JEGP, 70 (Jan. 1971), 139–145. Also see No. 44.

24. Wilson, Edwin Graves, with the assistance of Robert G. Kirkpatrick. "Current Bibliography," K-SJ, 18 (1969), 1–55.

24a. Yarker, P. M., and Brian Lee. "The Nineteenth Century," in *The Year's Work in English Studies*, ed. C. G. Harlow and James Redmond, 48 (1969 [for 1967]), 279–315.

25. Yarker, P. M., and J. A. V. Chapple. "The Nineteenth Century," in *The Year's Work in English Studies*, ed. C. G. Harlow and James Redmond, 49 (1970 [for 1968]), 262–299.

Books and Articles Relating to English Romanticism

26. Aarsleff, Hans. *The Study of Language in England, 1780–1860*. See K-SJ, 18 (1969), No. 14.

    Rev. by Wolfgang Kühlwein in ASNS, 206 (March 1970), 371–372.

27. Abrams, M. H. *The Mirror and the Lamp: Romantic Theory and the Critical Tradition*. New York: Oxford Univ., 1971.

    A paperback reprint of a book first published in 1953. See K-SJ, 4 (1955), No. 11, 5 (1956), No. 10, 6 (1957), No. 12, 9 (1960), No. 13, 11 (1962), No. 17.

28. Abrams, M. H. *Natural Supernaturalism: Tradition and Revolution in Romantic Literature*. New York: Norton; London: Oxford Univ. (1971).

    Discusses most of the major Romantic poets.

    Rev. by Hubert F. Babinski in LJ, 96 (15 Feb. 1971), 640.

29. *Adams, Hazard. *The Interests of Criticism: An Introduction to Literary Theory*. New York: Harcourt, Brace and World, 1969.

    Discusses Romantic critics and criticism.

Rev. by Walter H. Clark, Jr., in JAAC, 29 (Fall 1970), 130–131.

30. Albert, Edward, and J. A. Stone, eds. *A History of English Literature*. 4th ed., rev. London: Harrap, 1971.

Paperback.

31. Aldridge, A. Owen, ed. *Comparative Literature: Matter and Method*. Urbana: Univ. of Illinois, 1969.

Includes a reprint of Lilian R. Furst's "Romanticism in Historical Prospective," pp. 61–89.

32. Allsop, Kenneth. "The Technicolor Wasteland: On Drugs and Literature," *Encounter*, 32 (March 1969), 64–72.

A review-article of Alethea Hayter's *Opium and the Romantic Imagination*. See K-SJ, 19 (1970), No. 34. Also see No. 88.

33. Ball, Patricia M. *The Central Self: A Study in Romantic and Victorian Imagination*. See K-SJ, 18 (1969), No. 16.

Rev. by H[orst]. O[ppel]. in *Neueren Sprachen*, N.F. 18 (Feb. 1969), 103 [in German], by Basil Willey in *Critical Quarterly*, 2 (Apr. 1969), 87–88; by Richard Harter Fogle in K-SJ, 19 (1970), 134–136; by Laurence Lerner in EC, 29 (Jan. 1970), 95–98; by D[avid]. V. E[rdman]. in ELN, 8, Supplement (Sept. 1970), 15; by Robert Langbaum in *Victorian Poetry*, 8 (Winter 1970), 356–358. Also see 109a.

34. Barfoot, C. C. "Current Literature 1969—II: Criticism and Biography," ES, 51 (Aug. 1970), 378–385.

This section deals with studies of the Romantics.

35. Barnes, T. R. *English Verse: Voice and Movement from Wyatt to Yeats*. See K-SJ, 18 (1969), No. 18.

Rev. by W. D. Maxwell-Mahon in UES, 7 (Sept. 1969), 113–114.

36. Bate, Walter Jackson, ed. *Criticism: The Major Texts*. New York: Harcourt Brace Jovanovich, 1970.

An enlarged edition of a book first published in 1952. See K-SJ, 3 (1954), No. 11.

37. *Bayley, John. *Pushkin: A Comparative Study*. Cambridge: Cambridge Univ., 1971.

Compares Pushkin with Byron, Keats, and other Romantic poets.

Rev. by Donald Davie in Li, 85 (17 June 1971), 789–790.

38. Bayley, John. *The Romantic Survival: A Study in Poetic Evolution*. London: Chatto and Windus, 1970.

A paperback reprint of a book first published in 1957. See K-SJ, 7 (1958), No. 23, 8 (1959), No. 18, 9 (1960), No. 19.

39. Beaty, Frederick L. *Light from Heaven: Love in British Romantic Literature*. DeKalb: Northern Illinois Univ., 1971.

40. Ben-Israel, Hedva. *English Historians on the French Revolution*. See K-SJ, 19 (1970), No. 10a.

Rev. by R. R. Palmer in *Victorian Studies*, 12 (1969), 476–477; by D[avid]. V. E[rdman]. in ELN, 7, Supplement (Sept. 1969), 6–7; by William Thomas in *English Historical Review*, 86 (Jan. 1971), 183–184.

40a. Bennett, Betty T. "British Poetry and the War with France, 1793–1815: An Edition" [Doctoral dissertation, New York Univ., 1970], DAI, 31 (June 1971), 6539–A.

Collects 400 war poems.

41. Berefelt, Gunnar. "On Symbol and Allegory," JAAC, 28 (Winter 1969), 201–212.

Deals with these two concepts in terms of Romantic aesthetics.

42. *Bewley, Marius, comp. *The English Romantic Poets: An Anthology with Commentaries*. New York: Modern Library, 1970.

43. Bloom, Harold. "First and Last Romantics," SIR, 9 (Fall 1970), 225–232.

A broad survey, appearing in an issue devoted to "The Concept of Romanticism."†

44. Bloom, Harold. "Recent Studies in the Nineteenth Century," SEL, 10 (Autumn 1970), 817–829.

An omnibus review. See K-SJ, 16 (1967), No. 116, 17 (1968), No. 168, 18 (1969), No. 206, 19 (1970), Nos. 6, 26, 33, 95. Also see Nos. 23, 46, 74, 87, 102, 234, 383, 584, 726, 766, 773, 788, 872, and 942.

45. Bloom, Harold. *The Ringers in the Tower: Studies in Romantic Tradition*. Chicago: Univ. of Chicago, 1971.

A collection of essays, including "Frankenstein, or the Modern Prometheus," "Keats and the Embarrassments of Poetic Tradition," and "The Unpastured Sea: An Introduction to Shelley."

46. Bloom, Harold, ed. *Romanticism and Consciousness: Essays in Criticism.* New York: Norton, 1970.

A collection of previously published essays on the Romantics and Romanticism, including W. J. Bate, "Negative Capability"; Alvin B. Kernan, "*Don Juan*: The Perspective of Satire"; and Harold Bloom, "The Unpastured Sea: An Introduction to Shelley."

See No. 44.

46a. Bloom, Harold. "To Reason with a Later Reason: Romanticism and the Rational," *Midway,* 11 (Summer 1970), 97–112.

"The polemic of Romantic poetry, which is to say, of the most vital modern poetry, is directed against inadequate accounts of reason, not against reason itself."

47. Bloom, Harold. *The Visionary Company: A Reading of English Romantic Poetry.* Ithaca and London: Cornell Univ., 1971.

A revised, enlarged edition of a book first published in 1961. See K-SJ, 12 (1963), No. 18, 13 (1964), No. 21, 14 (1965), No. 16. Also in paperback.

48. Bloom, Harold. *Yeats.* New York: Oxford Univ., 1970.

Yeats is viewed in the light of Shelley and the Romantic visionary tradition. Byron and Keats are also briefly considered.

Rev. by Thomas E. Luddy in LJ, 95 (1 June 1970), 2156; by Harry T. Moore in SR, 20 June 1970, pp. 37–39; by Ann Wordsworth in Spec, 225 (25 July 1970), 74; by James D. Boulger in *Thought,* 45 (Winter 1970), 620–623; by Sandra Siegel in *Diacritics,* 1 (Winter 1971), 35–38; by Kenneth Connelly in *Yale Review,* 60 (March 1971), 394–403; in TLS, 12 March 1971, p. 292; by William H. Pritchard in PR, 38 (Spring 1971), 107–112; by George P. Mayhew in BA, 45 (Spring 1971), 321–322.

49. Briggs, Asa, ed. *The Nineteenth Century: the Contradictions of Progress.* London: Thames and Hudson; New York: McGraw-Hill (1970).

This collection of essays on nineteenth-century art has references to Byron, Haydon, Hazlitt, and Shelley.

Rev. in TLS, 30 Oct. 1970, p. 1278; by Claire Nolte in LJ, 96 (1 Apr. 1971), 1262; in *Choice,* 8 (Apr. 1971), 272.

50. Burnshaw, Stanley. *The Seamless Web: Language-Thinking, Creature-Knowledge, Art-Experience.* New York: Braziller, 1970.

Has frequent references to the Romantics.

Rev. by Jonathan Raban in NS, 19 June 1970, pp. 893–894; in TLS, 28 Aug. 1970, p. 942; by D. C. Muecke in AUMLA, No. 35 (May 1971), 116–117.

51. Burton, Elizabeth. *The Pageant of Georgian England.* New York: Scribner's, 1967.

A few references to Byron, Keats, and Shelley.

Rev. by J. Jean Hecht in *Studies in Burke and His Time,* 11 (Fall 1969), 1365–1372.

52. Bush, Douglas. *Pagan Myth and Christian Tradition in English Poetry.* Philadelphia: American Philosophical Society, 1968. "Jayne Lectures for 1967."

Contains a section on "Romantic Hellenism," which refers to Keats and Shelley.

Rev. in *Choice,* 6 (Oct. 1969), 1010; by R. G. Lunt in RES, 21 (Feb. 1970), 65–66; by C. A. Patrides in MLR, 65 (Oct. 1970), 868–869.

53. Bush, Douglas. *Science and English Poetry: A Historical Sketch, 1590–1950.* London and New York: Oxford Univ., 1967.

Paperback edition of book published in 1950. Ch. iv: "The Romantic Revolt against Rationalsim."

Rev. by Colin A. Ronan, in *Annals of Science,* 25 (March 1969), 90–91; by J. V. P. in *Univ. of Edinburgh Journal,* 24 (Spring 1969), 77.

53a. Cevasco, G. A. "Slings and Arrows: A Consideration of Captious Literary Criticism," ABC, 20 (May 1970), 8–10.†

All the major Romantics are among those dealt with severely by critics.

54. Clarke, Colin. *River of Dissolution: D. H. Lawrence and English Romanticism*. London: Routledge and Kegan Paul; New York: Barnes and Noble (1969).

Rev. by Ralph Lawrence in *English*, 18 (Autumn 1969), 114–116; by Keith Cushman in LJ, 94 (1 Oct. 1969), 3449; in *Choice*, 17 (June 1970), 540; by Karen McLeod in RES, 21 (Nov. 1970), 521–523; by E. Delavenay in EA, 24 (Apr.–June 1971), 207–208.

54a. Coleman, William E. "On the Discrimination of Gothicisms" [Doctoral dissertation, City Univ. of New York, 1970], DAI, 31 (Dec. 1970), 2871–A.

Treats Byron's *Manfred*, Keats's "The Eve of St. Agnes," Shelley's *Cenci*, and Mary Shelley's *Frankenstein*.

55. Coleridge, Samuel Taylor. *The Collected Works of Samuel Taylor Coleridge*. IV: *The Friend*. 2 vols. Ed. Barbara E. Rooke, Princeton: Princeton Univ.; London: Routledge and Kegan Paul (1969). "Bollingen Series."

Refers to all of the major Romantic poets.

Rev. by I. A. Richards in Li, 82 (25 Sept. 1969), 423–424; in WC, 1 (Winter 1970), 27; by I[rene]. H. C[hayes]. in ELN, 8, Supplement (Sept. 1970), 33.

56. Cancelled.

57. Corrigan, Matthew. "Metaphor in William Blake: A Negative View," JAAC, 28 (Winter 1969), 187–199.

In the opening two pages of his article, the author discusses metaphor as it applies to the Romantic poets in general.

58. *Daiches, David. *A Critical History of English Literature*. Vol. IV: *The Romantics to the Present Day*. London: Secker & Warburg, 1968. Also in paperback.

Reprint in four volumes of a 1960 work in two volumes. See K–SJ, 11 (1962), No. 29.

59. Darvall, F. O. *Popular Disturbances and Public Order in Regency England*. Introduction by Angus Macintyre. London: Oxford Univ., 1970.

A reprint of the standard account of the Luddite disturbances and of the government's response to unrest in general.

60. Davie, Donald. "On Sincerity: From Wordsworth to Ginsberg," *Encounter*, 31 (Oct. 1968), 61–66.

Romanticism "permanently transformed the mental landscape, which in the 20th century we inhabit, however reluctantly."

61. Donohue, Joseph W., Jr. *Dramatic Character in the English Romantic Age*. Princeton: Princeton Univ., 1970.

References to Byron, Hunt, and Keats; chapters on Shelley's *Cenci*, pp. 157–186, and on Hazlitt, pp. 313–343.

Rev. by John Paul Russo in K-SJ, 20 (1971), 141–143; by Normand Berlin in *Massachusetts Review*, 12 (Spring 1971), 343–349.

62. Dorfman, Deborah. *Blake in the Nineteenth Century: His Reputation as a Poet from Gilchrist to Yeats*. New Haven: Yale Univ., 1969. "Yale Studies in English, 70."

References to the Romantics.

Rev. by W. H. Stevenson in EC, 20 (Apr. 1970), 250; by Mary Lynn Johnson in JEGP, 69 (July 1970), 525–528.

63. Downs, B. W. "Anglo-Swedish Literary Relations 1867–1900: The Fortunes of English Literature in Sweden," MLR, 65 (Oct. 1970), 829–852.

Refers, in part, to the Romantic poets.

64. Dyson, Henry Victor D., and John Butt. *Augustans and Romantics, 1689–1830*. London: Barrie and Jenkins, 1969. "Introductions to English Literature Series, Vol. 3."

Third revised edition of 1961, reissued in paperback. See K-SJ, 12 (1963), No. 26.

65. Elledge, W. Paul, and Richard L. Hoffman, eds. *Romantic and Victorian: Studies in Memory of William H. Marshall*. Cranbury, N.J.: Fairleigh Dickinson Univ., 1971.

A collection of essays which includes the following: Morse Peckham, "On the Historical Interpretation of Literature," pp. 21–25; Lionel Stevenson, "The Mystique of Romantic Narrative Poetry," pp. 26–42; Brian Wilkie, "Byron: Artistry and Style," pp. 129–146; Carl Woodring, "Nature, Art, Reason, and Imagination in *Childe Harold*," pp. 147–157; Robert D. Hume, "*The Island* and the Evolution of Byron's 'Tales,'" pp. 158–180; R. H. Fogle, "Byron and Nathaniel Hawthorne," pp. 181–197; Jerome J. McGann, "Shelley's Veils: A Thousand Images of Loveliness," pp. 198–218; Lewis G. Leary, "Leigh Hunt in Philadelphia," pp. 219–230; Jack Stillinger, "On the Interpretation of *Endymion*: The Comedian as the Letter E," pp. 250–263.

65a. *Fleissner, Robert F. " 'Pot Luck': Drugs and Romanticism," *English Association of Ohio Bulletin*, 11, iv (1970), 9–11.

66. Fletcher, Ian, ed. *Romantic Mythologies*. See K-SJ, 17 (1968), No. 28, 18 (1969), No. 29.

Rev. by Bernard Vannier in *Critique* (Paris), 25 (June 1969), 483–503.

67. *Foakes, R. A. *The Romantic Assertion: A Study in the Language of Nineteenth Century Poetry*. London: Methuen, 1970; New York: Barnes and Noble, 1971.

A reprint of a book first published in 1958. See K-SJ, 9 (1960), No. 27, 10 (1961), No. 24, 11 (1962), No. 31, 12 (1963), No. 28, 14 (1965), No. 20.

68. Fogle, Richard Harter. "Literary History Romanticized," *New Literary History*, 1 (Winter 1970), 237–247.

Discusses the relationship of Hawthorne to the English Romantic poets and to Byron in particular.

69. Foltinek, Herbert. *Vorstufen zum victorianischen Realismus: Der englische Roman von Jane Austen bis Charles Dickens* in *Wiener Beiträge zur englischen Philologie*. See K-SJ, 19 (1970), No. 24.

Rev. by Inga-Stina Ewbank in RES, 21 (May 1970), 231–232.

69a. Frosch, Thomas R. "The New Body of English Romanticism," *Soundings*, 54 (Winter 1971), 372–387.

Theme of mankind's renewal in the major Romantic poets.

70. Frye, Northrop. *The Stubborn Structure: Essays on Criticism and Society*. Ithaca: Cornell Univ., 1970.

Includes "The Drunken Boat: The Revolutionary Element in Romanticism," pp. 200–217, and "The Problem of Spiritual Authority in the Nineteenth Century," pp. 241–256.

71. Frye, Northrop. *A Study of English Romanticism*. See K-SJ, 18 (1969), No. 32.

Rev. by Ross Woodman in UTQ, 38 (July 1969), 371–373.

72. Furst, Lilian R. "Kafka and the Romantic Imagination," *Mosaic*, 3 (Summer 1970), 81–89.

"The Romantics saw the possibility of a world transformed by the imagination; Kafka confronts us with the reality of the accomplished transformation."

73. Furst, Lilian R. *Romanticism*. London: Methuen; New York: Barnes and Noble (1969). "The Critical Idiom."

Rev. by P. Mew in *Hermathena*, No. 110 (1970), pp. 107–108; in WC, 1 (Spring 1970), 76; by E. Pereira in UES, 8 (June 1970), 47–51; by Michael P. Gallagher in *Studies* (Dublin), 59 (Summer 1970), 218–219; in JAAC, 29 (Fall 1970), 144; in *Forum for Modern Language Studies*, 6 (Oct. 1970), 419; by Allan Rodway in *Durham Univ. Journal*, 63 (March 1971), 151–152.

74. Furst, Lilian R. *Romanticism in Perspective: A Comparative Study of Aspects of the Romantic Movements in England, France, and Germany*. See K-SJ, 19 (1970), No. 26.

Rev. in *Choice*, 7 (Oct. 1970), 1026, 1028; by Elinor Shaffer in MLR, 66 (Jan. 1971), 172–173; by Jacques Voisine in RLC, 45 (Apr.–June 1971), 280–284. Also see No. 44.

75. George, A. G. *Studies in Poetry*. London and New Delhi: Heinemann, 1971.

Essays on English poets ranging from the Renaissance to the Victorians. The major Romantics are all represented.

76. Gingerich, Solomon F. *Essays in the Romantic Poets*. New York: Octagon, 1969.

Reprint of 1924 edition. Essays on Byron and Shelley.

77. Gleckner, Robert F., and Gerald E. Enscoe, eds. *Romanticism: Points of View*. Second Edition. Englewood Cliffs, N.J.: Prentice-Hall, 1970.

This collection represents a revision of about half the original essays of 1962. See K-SJ, 12 (1963), No. 31, 13 (1964), No. 41.

78. Göller, Karl Heinz, ed. *Die Englische Lyrik: Von der Renaissance bis zur Gegen-*

wart. 2 vols. Düsseldorf: August Bagel, 1968.

An anthology of English lyrics, including the Romantics, with German translations and critical commentary.

Rev. by Thomas W. Ross in ASNS, 207 (Sept. 1970), 216–218.

79. Graham, Walter. *Tory Criticism in the Quarterly Review.* New York: AMS, 1970.

A reprint of a book first published in 1921.

80. *Grierson, Sir Herbert. *Lyrical Poetry of the Nineteenth Century.* New York: AMS, 1970.

Reprint of 1929 edition.

81. Gross, John. *The Rise and Fall of the Man of Letters: English Literary Life since 1800.* See K-SJ, 19 (1970), No. 28.

Rev. in TLS, 3 July 1969, pp. 717–718; by Burton Feldman in *Univ. of Denver Quarterly*, 4 (Sept. 1969), 105; by Iain Hamilton in ILN, 27 Sept. 1969, pp. 32–33; by Keith Cushman in LJ, 94 (15 Oct. 1969), 3648; by John Wain in *Encounter*, 33 (Nov. 1969), 75–87; by Arthur Mizener in *New Republic*, 3 Jan. 1970, pp. 30–32; by Seymour Betsky in *Univ. Quarterly*, 24 (Spring 1970), 216–222; by George Levine in PR, 37 (Spring 1970), 139–147; by Martin Lightfoot in EC, 20 (July 1970), 359–367.

82. Harris, R. W. *Romanticism and the Social Order 1780–1830.* See K-SJ, 19 (1970), No. 30.

Rev. by Frederick L. Beaty in K-SJ, 19 (1970), 138–140; in *Choice*, 7 (Nov. 1970), 1232.

83. Hartman, Geoffrey. *Beyond Formalism: Literary Essays, 1958–1970.* New Haven and London: Yale Univ., 1970.

Rev. by Keith Cushman in LJ, 95 (15 Nov. 1970), 3910; by Philip E. Lewis in *Diacritics*, 1 (Winter 1971), 2–6.

84. Hartman, Geoffrey. "Theories on the Theory of Romanticism," WC, 2 (Spring 1971), 51–56.

Makes suggestions about the course to pursue in the study of the "theory" of Romanticism in the 1970's. Originally delivered as a paper at the 1970 MLA convention.

85. Hassett, Michael E. "Compromised Romanticism in *Jude the Obscure*," *Nineteenth Century Fiction*, 25 (March 1971), 432–443.‡

Hardy "seems to deny the Romantics' faith in the power of a transcending or transforming imagination." There are references to Keats and Shelley.

86. Hayden, John O., ed. *Romantic Bards and British Reviewers: A Selected Edition of Contemporary Reviews of the Works of Wordsworth, Coleridge, Byron, Keats and Shelley.* Lincoln: Univ. of Nebraska; London: Routledge and Kegan Paul (1971).

87. Hayden, John O. *The Romantic Reviewers, 1802–1824: A Study of Literary Reviewing in the Early Nineteenth Century.* See K-SJ, 19 (1970), No. 33.

Rev. in TLS, 10 July 1969, p. 746; by Ian Fletcher in NS, 8 Aug. 1969, p. 194; by Ralph Lawrence in *English*, 18 (Autumn 1969), 114–116; by Nathan Comfort Starr in LJ, 95 (1 Jan. 1970), 68–69; by Leonidas M. Jones in K-SJ, 19 (1970), 133–134; in WC, 1 (Winter 1970), 27; in *Choice*, 7 (Feb. 1970), 1754; by Peter F. Morgan in JEGP, 69 (Apr. 1970), 318–321; by Nathaniel Teich in *Criticism*, 12 (Summer 1970), 255–256; by Donald H. Reiman in SAQ, 69 (Summer 1970), 413; by Seamus Deane in *Studies*, 59 (Summer 1970), 214–215; by Karl Kroeber in ELN, 7 (June 1970), 311–312; by R. Gordon Cox in N&Q, 215 (July 1970), 277–279; by I[rene]. H. C[hayes]. in ELN, 8, Supplement (Sept. 1970), 16. See also Nos. 44, 109a.

88. Hayter, Alethea. *Opium and the Romantic Imagination.* See K-SJ, 19 (1970), No. 34.

Paperback edition, 1970.

Rev. by Kenneth Allsop in *Encounter*, 32 (March 1969), 64–72; by Serge Fauchereau in *Critique* (Paris), 25 (July 1969), 629–638; by Douglas Hubble in MLR, 65 (Apr. 1970), 393–394; in *Times* (London), 24 June 1971, p. 11.

89. Hearn, L. *The English Romantic Poets.* Folcroft, Pa: Folcroft, 1970.

A reprint of the original (no date given), with chapters on Byron, Shelley, Wordsworth, and Keats.

90. Heffernan, James A. W. *Wordsworth's Theory of Poetry: The Transforming Imag-*

ination. Ithaca and London: Cornell Univ., 1969.

Includes a discussion of Wordsworth's letter of 1817, which compares stanzas on nature in *Childe Harold* with his own in "Tintern Abbey." Allusions also to other Romantics.

Rev. by Mark L. Reed in *Western Humanities Review*, 24 (Autumn 1970), 410–411.

91. *Hewitt, Barnard. *History of the Theatre from 1800 to the Present*. New York: Random House, 1970.

92. Hill, James L. "Defensive Strategies in Nineteenth- and Twentieth-Century Criticism," JAAC, 28 (Winter 1969), 177–185.

Discusses Romantic criticism.

93. Holloway, John, and Sir Peter Medawar. "A Reply to Sir Peter Medawar," *Encounter*, 33 (July 1969), 81–85; "A Rejoinder," 86–88.

Holloway replies to Medawar's article of Jan. 1969 (see No. 114), and Medawar responds.

93a. Huntley, Reid DeBerry. "Thomas Wolfe's Idea of the Imagination: Similarities to the Views of the Nineteenth Century English Romantic Poets and Critics" [Doctoral dissertation, North Carolina, 1969], DAI, 31 (July 1970), 390–A.

Discusses Keats, Shelley, and Hazlitt.

94. James, D. G. *Matthew Arnold and the Decline of English Romanticism*. See K-SJ, 11 (1962), No. 40, 12 (1963), No. 35, 13 (1964), No. 46.

Rev. by Paul Turner in ES, 51 (June 1970), 266–269.

95. *Keats-Shelley Memorial Bulletin*, 19 (1968).

Rev. by Prema Nandakumar in *Aryan Path*, 40 (Aug. 1969), 366–367.

96. *Kermode, Frank. *Romantic Image*. London: Fontana, 1971.

Paperback reprint of a book first published in 1957. See K-SJ 7 (1958), No. 46, 8 (1959), No. 36, 9 (1960), No. 42, 12 (1963), No. 40.

97. Knight, D. M. "The Physical Sciences and the Romantic Movement," *History of Science*, 9 (1970), 54–75.

Discusses both the influence of the Romantics upon the sciences and the impact of the sciences upon the Romantics.

98. Kreutz, Christian. *Das Prometheussymbol in der englischen Romantik*. See K-SJ, 14 (1965), No. 29, 17 (1968), No. 42.

Rev. by Roland Ball in CL, 21 (Winter 1969), 76–87.

99. Kroeber, Karl. "Constable and Wordsworth: the Ecological Movement of Romantic Art," *Journal of the Warburg and Courtauld Institutes*, 34 (1971), 377–386.

Compares landscape painting and landscape poetry in order to arrive at a definition of Romanticism which emphasizes its disparate and autonomous parts.

99a. Kroeber, Karl. "The Relevance and Irrelevance of Romanticism," SIR, 9 (Fall 1970), 297–306.‡

"Romanticism could be valuable today because it points to a radically different political aesthetics, one that defends, celebrates, and so sanctifies the surprising continuity that is life."

100. Kumar, Shiv K., ed. *British Victorian Literature: Recent Revaluations*. New York: New York Univ., 1969.

Includes an essay by L. A. Gottfried, "Between Two Worlds: Matthew Arnold and Romanticism: Excerpts from 'Matthew Arnold and the Romantics,' " pp. 435–456.

100a. *Kvič, R. "Translating English Romantic Poetry," in *The Nature of Translation: Essays on the Theory and Practice of Literary Translation*, ed. James S. Holmes (The Hague: Mouton, 1970), pp. 182–191. "Papers Presented to the International Conference on Translation as an Art, Bratislava, 1968."

101. Lambert, Byron C. "Paul Elmer More and the Redemption of History," *Modern Age*, 13 (Summer 1969), 277–278.

Refers to More's dislike of the Romantic movement.

102. Langbaum, Robert. *The Modern Spirit: Essays on the Continuity of Nineteenth- and Twentieth-Century Literature*. New York: Oxford Univ.; London: Chatto and Windus (1970).

Langbaum reprints and revises ten

miscellaneous essays. Passing references are made to Byron, Keats, and Shelley.

Rev. by Keith Cushman in LJ, 95 (July 1970), 2479; by Michael Cooke in *Yale Review*, 60 (Dec. 1970), 294–301; by Rainer Schulte in BA, 45 (Apr. 1971), 323. Also see No. 44.

103. Lean, E. Tangye. *The Napoleonists: A Study in Political Disaffection, 1760–1960.* New York: Oxford Univ., 1970.

Includes references to Byron, Godwin, Hazlitt, Hobhouse, and Hunt.

Rev. by Harold Kurtz in *History Today*, 21 (Feb. 1971), 146.

104. *Legouis, Emile, and Louis Cazamian. *A History of English Literature*. Book VII. Revised by Raymond Las Vergnas. London: J. M. Dent, 1964.

A new edition.

Rev. by A. J. Farmer in EA, 22 (Apr.–June 1969), 203.

105. Lévy, Maurice. *Le roman "Gothique" anglais, 1764–1824.* See K-SJ, 19 (1970), No. 40.

Rev. by J. M. S. Thompkins in RES, 21 (Aug. 1970), 367–368.

106. Longford, Elizabeth. *Wellington: The Years of the Sword.* Vol. I. New York: Harper and Row, 1969.

Includes references to Byron, Haydon, and Hobhouse.

Rev, in TLS, 13 Nov. 1969, pp. 1304–1305; by Sir Charles Petrie in ILN, 22 Nov. 1969, p. 22; by Richard L. Blanco in LJ, 95 (1 Jan. 1970), 62; by Harold Kurtz in *History Today*, 20 (Jan. 1970), 68; by J. H. Plumb in NYT, 1 March 1970, pp. 7, 44; by Richard A. Lingerman in *New York Times*, 11 March 1970, p. 45; by J. R. Western in *English Historical Review*, 86 (Jan. 1971), 68.

107. *Lucas, John, ed. *Literature and Politics in the Nineteenth Century.* London: Methuen; New York: Barnes and Noble (1971).

108. *Maar, Harko G. de. *A History of Modern English Romanticism.* New York: Haskell House, 1970.

Reprint of a 1924 book.

109. McGann, Jerome J. "The Dandy," *Midway*, 10, No. 1 (1969), 3–18.

Deals with Romanticism.

109a. MacGillivray, J. R. "New Editors and Critics of the English Romantics," UTQ, 40 (Fall 1970), 73–86.

An omnibus review. See K-SJ, 18 (1969), Nos. 16, 541, 19 (1970), Nos. 33, 90, 95, 217, 290, 292. Also see Nos. 33, 87, 228, 234, 562, 603, 743, 750, 773.

110. Mair, G. H. *Modern English Literature 1450–1959.* With additional chapters by A. C. Ward. Third Edition. London: Oxford Univ., 1969.

A paperback reprint of the 1960 edition. See K-SJ, 11 (1962), No. 50.

111. Margetson, Stella. *Leisure and Pleasure in the Nineteenth Century.* London: Cassell, 1969.

Includes references to Byron, Hunt, and Keats.

Rev. in ILN, 15 Feb. 1969, p. 34; by Katherine Tappert Willis in LJ, 13 (July 1969), 2608–2609; by W. J. Keith in *Canadian Forum*, 49 (Aug. 1969), 119.

112. Massey, Irving J. *The Uncreating World: Romanticism and the Object.* Bloomington and London: Indiana Univ., 1970.

Includes references to Byron, Godwin, and Shelley.

Rev. by Jean M. Perreault in LJ, 96 (15 Jan. 1971), 194; in *Choice*, 8 (May 1971), 380.

113. Mazlish, Bruce. "Autobiography and Psycho-analysis," *Encounter*, 35 (Oct. 1970), 28–37.

Defines modern autobiography as "a literary genre produced by romanticism."

114. Medawar, Sir Peter B. "Science and Literature," *Encounter*, 32 (Jan. 1969), 15–23.

Labels and confirms "the official Romantic view" that reason and imagination are antithetical. See No. 93 for reply and rejoinder.

115. Meller, Horst, *et al.*, eds. *British and American Classical Poems in Continuation of Herrig's "Classical Authors."* See K-SJ, 18 (1969), No. 54.

Rev. by Joachim-Konrad Meyer in *Zeitschrift für Anglistik und Amerikanistik*, 18, 1 (1970), 191–193.

116. Merivale, Patricia. *Pan the Goat-God: His Myth in Modern Times.* Cambridge, Mass.: Harvard Univ.; London: Oxford Univ. (1969). "Harvard Studies in Comparative Literature, No. 30."

Ch. ii, "Romantic Pan," includes material on Byron, Hunt, Keats, and Shelley.

Rev. by Ann Saddlemyer in *Canadian Literature*, No. 42 (Autumn 1969), pp. 96–98; by Howard W. Fulweiler in *Victorian Poetry*, 8 (Summer 1970), 172–175; by Ian Fletcher in MLR, 66 (Jan. 1971), 173–174. Also see No. 117.

117. Miller, J. Hillis. "Recent Studies in the Nineteenth Century," SEL, 9 (Autumn 1969), 737–753.‡

An omnibus review. See K-SJ, 18 (1969), Nos. 508, 541, 19 (1970), Nos. 37, 82, 90, 95, 98, 118, 122, 159, 217, 283, 292, 346. Also see Nos. 116, 211, 228, 234, 256, 314, 323, 405, 562, 704, 750, and 888.

118. Miyoshi, Masao. *The Divided Self: A Perspective on the Literature of the Victorians*. See K-SJ, 19 (1970), No. 44.

Rev. in *Choice*, 6 (Nov. 1969), 1224; in TLS, 18 Aug. 1970, p. 897; by Basil Willey in *Critical Quarterly*, 13 (Spring 1971) 94–95.

119. *Nethercot, Arthur H. *The Reputation of the Metaphysical Poets during the Age of Johnson and the Romantic Revival*. New York: Haskell House, 1969.

Reprint of a 1925 book.

120. Nicoll, Allardyce. *English Drama: A Modern Viewpoint*. New York: Barnes and Noble, 1968.

Ch. vi deals with the Romantics.

Rev. by M. D. Faber in *Modern Drama*, 12 (Sept. 1969), 215–217.

121. Ong, Walter J. *Rhetoric, Romance, and Technology: Studies in the Interaction of Expression and Culture*. Ithaca and London: Cornell Univ., 1971.

Includes a chapter on "Romantic Difference and the Poetics of Technology," pp. 255–283.

122. Orel, Harold, and George J. Worth, eds. *The Nineteenth Century Writer and His Audience: Selected Problems in Theory, Form, and Content*. Lawrence: Univ. of Kansas, 1969.

Included in this collection are W. P. Albrecht's "Hazlitt, Keats, and the Sublime Pleasure of Tragedy," pp. 1–30, and Harold Orel's "The Relationship between Three Poet-Dramatists and Their Public: Lord Byron, Thomas Talfourd, and Robert Browning," pp. 31–49.

123. Pace, Claire. "Claude the Enchanted: Interpretations of Claude in England in the Earlier Nineteenth-Century," *Burlington Magazine*, 111 (Dec. 1969), 733–740.

The Romantics, Hazlitt and Keats in particular, saw in Claude the theme of escape from the world.

124. Pearce, Roy Harvey. "The Burden of Romanticism," *Iowa Review*, 2 (Spring 1971), 109–128.

The author assesses the "burden" Romanticism has put upon certain types of subsequent poetry.

124a. Peckham, Morse. "On Romanticism: Introduction," SIR, 9 (Fall 1970), 217–224.

Discusses theories of Romanticism.

125. Peckham, Morse. *The Triumph of Romanticism: Collected Essays*. Columbia: Univ. of South Carolina, 1970.

Rev. by Christopher Ricks in NYRB, 20 May 1971, p. 44.

126. Pereira, E. "Romanticism Reviewed," UES, 8 (June 1970), 47–51.

An omnibus review. See K-SJ, 17 (1968), No. 44, 18 (1969), Nos. 42, 63, 19 (1970), Nos. 26, 29, 33, 38. Also see Nos. 74, 87.

127. Perkins, David, ed. *English Romantic Writers*. See K-SJ, 17 (1968), No. 51.

Rev. by W. D. Maxwell-Mahon in UES, 8 (Nov. 1970), 38–39.

128. Poynter, J. R. *Society and Pauperism: English Ideas on Poor Relief, 1795–1834*. London: Routledge and Kegan Paul; Toronto: Univ. of Toronto (1969). "Studies in Social History."

Many references to Godwin and Hazlitt; a few to Shelley.

Rev. in *International Review of Social History*, 14 (1969), 306; in *Choice*, 7 (Apr. 1970), 287.

129. *Prang, Helmut, ed. *Begriffsbestimmung der Romantik*. Darmstadt: Wissenschaftliche Buchgesellschaft, 1968.

Reprints twenty-two essays, written between 1911 and 1968, all seeking to define the term and concept "Romanticism."

Rev. by Lilian R. Furst in *German*

Life and Letters, 24 (Apr. 1971), 284–285.

130. *Preminger, Alex, Frank J. Warnke, and O. B. Hardison. *Encyclopedia of Poetry and Poetics*. Princeton: Princeton Univ., 1965.

Includes an article on "Romanticism."

Rev. by L[ouis]. C. B[onnerot]. in EA, 23 (Jan.–March 1970), 101–102.

131. Priestley, J. B. *The Prince of Pleasure and His Regency, 1811–1820*. See K-SJ, 19 (1970), No. 49.

Rev. by Raymond Mortimer in *Times* (London), 14 Sept. 1969, p. 61; by Sir Charles Petrie in ILN, 27 Sept. 1969, p. 32; in TLS, 6 Nov. 1969, p. 1275; by Edward J. Hundert in LJ, 94 (15 Dec. 1969), 4525; in *Choice*, 7 (Apr. 1970), 287.

132. Puppo, Mario. *Il Romanticism: Saggio Monografico con Antologia di Testi e della Critica*. Rome: Studium, 1967.

New edition of a 1951 book. See K-SJ, 3 (1954), No. 41.

133. Quennell, Peter. *Romantic England: Writing and Painting 1717–1851*. London: Weidenfeld and Nicolson; New York: Macmillan (1970).

Rev. by Harold Kurtz in *History Today*, 20 (1970), 825–826; by V. S. Pritchett in NS, 80 (1970), 378–380; in T&T, 51, No. 37 (1970), 10; by Cyril Connolly in the *Sunday Times* (London), 20 Sept. 1970, p. 31; by John Dixon Hunt in the *Times* (London), 24 Sept. 1970, p. 15; in *Connoisseur*, 176 (March 1971), 215.

134. *Rauter, Herbert. *Die Sprachauffassung der englischen Vorromantik in ihrer Bedeutung für die Literaturkritik und Dichtungstheorie der Zeit*. Bad Homburg, Berlin, Zurich: Gehlen, 1970. "Frankfurther Beiträge zur Anglistik und Amerikanstik."

134a. Ray, Ann Allen. "Romanticism: A Collection of Essays on Poetic Style" [Doctoral dissertation, Texas, 1969], DAI, 30 (Jan. 1970), 2977-A.

135. *Reizov, B. G. *Stendhal lecteur des romanciers anglais*. Lausanne: Editions du Grand-Chene, 1968.

136. Riese, Teut Andreas, and Dieter Riesner, eds. *Versdichtung der englischen Romantik: Interpretationen*. See K-SJ, 18 (1969), No. 64.

Rev. by P. Malekin in *Studia Neophilologica*, 42 (1970), 236–237; by Paul Goetsch in *Neuren Sprachen*, N.F. 19 (Nov. 1970), 586–588 [in German]: by Dieter Mehl in *Erasmus*, 23 (25 March 1971), 284–291.

137. Rosenfeld, Alvin H., ed. *William Blake: Essays for S. Foster Damon*. Providence: Brown Univ., 1969.

A collection of essays which includes Harold Bloom's "The Visionary Cinema of Romantic Poetry," pp. 18–35, and Daniel Hughes's "Blake and Shelley: Beyond the Uroboros," pp. 69–83. See K-SJ, 19 (1970), No. 328.

Rev. by Elizabeth Nelson in LJ, 94 (Aug. 1969), 2790.

138. Rubinstein, Annette T. *The Great Tradition in English Literature from Shakespeare to Shaw*. Vol. II. New York and London: Modern Reader Paperbacks, 1969.

A reprint of the 1953 edition. See K-SJ, 5 (1956), No. 44.

139. St. Clair, William. *Lord Elgin and the Marbles*. See K-SJ, 18 (1969), No. 65.

Rev. by John Clive in *Journal of Modern History*, 43 (March 1970), 140–141; by D. Dakin in *History* 55 (June 1970), 288–289.

140. Sampson, George, ed. *The Concise Cambridge History of English Literature*. Third Edition. Revised and enlarged by R. C. Churchill. Cambridge: Cambridge Univ., 1969.

Rev. by John R. Willingham in LJ, 94 (15 Oct. 1969), 3639; by David Glixon in SR, 16 May 1970, p. 39; by Basil Cottle in RES, 22 (May 1971), 174–178.

141. Schenk, H. G. *The Mind of the European Romantics: An Essay in Cultural History*. See K-SJ, 17 (1968), No. 58, 18 (1969), No. 67, 19 (1970), No. 52.

Rev. by Frederick Garber in CL, 20 (Fall 1968), 357–359; in *Choice*, 6 (Dec. 1969), 1378.

142. Schoenbaum, S[amuel]. *Shakespeare's Lives*. Oxford: Clarendon; New York: Oxford Univ. (1970).

Includes a chapter on the Romantics and their evaluation of Shakespeare.

143. Shea, F. X., S.J. "Religion and the Romantic Movement," SIR, 9 (Fall 1970), 285–296.‡

The Romantic Movement provides a "new departure for the human spirit," and allows for the revival of religion.

144. Singleton, Charles S., ed. *Interpretation: Theory and Practice*. Baltimore: Johns Hopkins, 1969.

Paul de Man in "The Rhetoric of Temporality," pp. 173–209, discusses Romanticism and the Romantic poets.

Rev. by Monroe C. Beardsley in JHI, 32 (Jan.–March 1971), 143–147.

145. *Smidt, Kristian. *Books and men. A short history of English and American Literature*. New Edition. Oslo: J. W. Cappelen forlag, 1971.

145a. Speirs, John. *Poetry towards Novel*. London: Faber, 1971.

The "poetic imaginativeness" of both novelists and poets of the 19th century, with Keats and Byron given considerable discussion.

146. Spender, Stephen, ed. *A Choice of English Romantic Poetry*. Freeport, N.Y.: Books for Libraries, 1969.

A reprint of the 1947 edition.

147. Spender, Stephen, and Donald Hall, eds. *The Concise Encyclopedia of English and American Poets and Poetry*. See K-SJ, 13 (1964), No. 72.

Rev. by L[ouis]. C. Bonnerot in EA, 23 (Jan.–March 1970), 100–101.

148. Steiner, George. "In Bluebeard's Castle. 1: The Great Ennui," Li, 85 (18 March 1971), 327–332.†

Twentieth-century chaos is a reaction to the ennui and frustration of the gifted Romantic writers.

149. Stillinger, Jack. "Refurbish or Perish," WC, 2 (Spring 1971), 46–50.

Recommends that the study of Romanticism in the 1970's concentrate on a historical approach, and that "graduate (and even undergraduate) courses" no longer be taught "as if all the students were going after Ph.D.'s." Originally delivered as a paper at the 1970 MLA convention.

149a. Subrahmanian, Krishnaswami. "The Theory of 'Suggestion' in Sanskrit Poetics, English Romanticism and French Symbolism" [Doctoral dissertation, Indiana, 1969], DAI, 30 (May 1970), 4957-A.

150. Sutherland, Donald. *On Romanticism*. New York: New York Univ., 1971.

Defines Romantic as a stylistic category. Ch. iii, "A Pard-like Spirit," is devoted to Shelley.

151. Swanson, Donald R. "Carlyle on the English Romantic Poets," *Lock Haven Review*, 11 (1969), 25–32.†

Discusses Byron, Keats, and Shelley.

152. Symons, Arthur. *The Romantic Movement in English Poetry*. New York: Phaeton, 1969.

A reprint of the 1909 edition.

153. Sypher, Wylie. *Literature and Technology: The Alien Vision*. New York: Random House, 1968.

A chapter, "Romantics and Aesthetics," discusses the affinity between the Romantic poets and science. Another portion of the book (pp. 146–151) compares the "materialism" of Keats and Marx.

Rev. by G. S. Rousseau in *Isis*, 60 (Fall 1969), 396–397.

154. *Talmon, J. *Romantisme et révolte: L'Europe entre 1815 et 1848*. Paris: Flammarion, 1968.

Translation of book originally in English. See K-SJ, 18 (1969), No. 72, 19 (1970), No. 57.

155. Thomas, Donald. *A Long Time Burning: The History of Literary Censorship in England*. See K-SJ, 19 (1970), No. 58.

Rev. by Dika Newlin in LJ, 94 (1 Sept. 1969), 2924; by Richard Bratset in *English Journal*, 59 (March 1970), 429–431.

156. Thorslev, Peter L., Jr. "Romantic Writers and the New Generation," WC, 2 (Spring 1971), 42–45.

Makes "a few tentative suggestions about Romantic studies in the next decade in view of the interests of our current generation of students." Originally delivered as a paper at the 1970 MLA convention.

156a. Tillotson, Geoffrey. "The Nineteenth Century and the Eighteenth," in *Eighteenth-Century Studies in Honor of Donald F. Hyde*, ed. William H. Bond (New York: Grolier Club, 1970), pp. 383–400.

Emphasizes continuities from eighteenth century in Victorian literature.

157. Trewin, J. C. "The Romantic Poets in the Theatre," KSMB, 20 (1969), 21–30.
Among others, discusses the dramatic efforts of Byron, Hunt, Keats, and Shelley.

158. *Van Tieghem, Paul. *Le romantisme dans la littérature européenne*. Paris: Michel, 1969.
First published in 1948.

159. Vinge, Louise. *The Narcissus Theme in Western European Literature up to the Early Nineteenth Century*. See K-SJ, 18 (1969), No. 74, 19 (1970), No. 60.
Rev. by Dietrich Briesemeister in ASNS, 205 (Aug. 1968), 202–204; by J. C. Meurs in ES, 50 (Dec. 1969), 614–618; by Manfred Beller in *Orbis Litterarum*, 24, No. 4 (1969), 315–320; by Alfred Foulet in *Romantic Review*, 61 (Feb. 1970), 45–50; by Raymond Trousson in *Studi Francesi*, 41 (May–Aug. 1970), 309–310; by Jef Barthels in *Revue des Langues Vivantes*, 36, No. 5 (1970), 553–554.

160. Vitoux, Pierre, ed. *La poésie romantique anglaise*. Paris: Librairie Armand Colin, 1971.
A general anthology, in English.

161. *Wain, John, ed. *Contemporary Reviews of Romantic Poetry*. Freeport, N.Y.: Books for Libraries, 1969. "Essay Index Reprint Series."
Reprint of 1953 edition. See K-SJ, 4 (1955), No. 66, 6 (1957), No. 51.

162. Watson, J[ohn]. R. *Picturesque Landscape and English Romantic Poetry*. London: Hutchinson, 1970.
Includes Chapters on Byron, Keats, and Shelley.
Rev. in *Times* (London), 4 Feb. 1971, p. 13; by John D. Jump in *Critical Quarterly*, 13 (Spring 1971), 87–88; by Hermann Peschmann in *English*, 20 (Summer 1971), 57–59.

163. *Watts-Dunton, Theodore. *Poetry and the Renascence of Wonder*. Port Washington, N.Y., and London: Kennikat, 1970.
Reprint of a 1916 book. Chapter on "Romanticism."

164. *Wedgwood, A. *Le Mouvement Romantique*. Adaptation française de O. Salway. Paris: Publications filmées d'art et d'histoire, 1969.
Includes a section on English Romanticism.
Rev. in *Studi Francesi*, 41 (May–Aug. 1970), 362.

165. *Wellek, René. *Storia della critica moderna* (1750–1950). Vol. III: *L'età di transizione*. Bologne: Soc. edit. Il. Mulino, 1969.
An Italian translation of Wellek's *A History of Modern Criticism*. Vol. III: *The Age of Transition*. See K-SJ, 16 (1967), No. 39, 17 (1968), No. 69, 18 (1969), No. 76, 19 (1970), No. 61.
Rev. by Giuseppe Carlo Rossi in ICS, 52 (June 1969), 111.

166. Wesling, Donald. "The Inevitable Ear: Freedom and Necessity in Lyric Form, Wordsworth and After," ELH, 36 (Sept. 1969), 544–561.
Argues for "the relevance of such criteria as movement, continuity, and transition" in reading Romantic and post-Romantic poetry.

166a. *Wheeler, Otis B. "The Sacramental View of Love in the Nineteenth and Twentieth Centuries," in *Essays in Honor of Esmond Linworth Marilla*, ed. Thomas A. Kirby and William J. Olive (Baton Rouge: Louisiana State Univ., 1970), pp. 342–354. "Louisiana State Univ. Studies, Humanities Series, 19."

167. Whitaker, Stephen P. *Imagination and Fancy in Nineteenth-Century Literature*. Folcroft, Pa.: Folcroft, 1970.
A reprint of the 1912 edition. All the major Romantics are represented.

168. White, Reginald James. *The Age of George III*. See K-SJ, 19 (1970), No. 62.
Rev. by Robert M. Calhoun in *Studies in Burke and His Time*, 12 (Winter 1970–1971), 1823–1826.

169. Williams, Raymond. "Ideas of Nature," TLS, 4 Dec. 1970, pp. 1419–1421.
Traces these ideas throughout history; brief mention of Wordsworth, Cobbett, Clare, and others.

170. Williams, Raymond, ed. *The Pelican Book of English Prose*. Vol. II: *From 1780 to the Present Day*. Harmondsworth: Penguin, 1970.
Rev. by J. Gury in RLC, 45 (Jan.–March 1971), 102.

171. Wimsatt, William K., Jr., and Cleanth Brooks. *Literary Criticism: A Short His-*

tory. 4 Vols. London: Routledge, 1970.

A paperback reprint of a book first published in 1957. See K-SJ, 7 (1958), No. 73, 8 (1959), No. 57, 9 (1960), No. 74, 10 (1961), No. 54.

172. *Wimsatt, W. K., Jr. *The Verbal Icon: Studies in the Meaning of Poetry.* London: Methuen, 1970.

First published in 1954. Discusses major Romantic poets.

173. Winters, Yvor. *Forms of Discovery: Critical and Historical Essays on the Forms of the Short Poem in English.* See K-SJ, 18 (1969), No. 81, 19 (1970), No. 62a.

Rev. by James McMichael in *Michigan Quarterly Review*, 9 (Spring 1970), 140–141.

174. *Wittreich, Joseph Anthony, Jr., ed. *The Romantics and Milton: Formal Essays and Critical Asides.* Cleveland: Case Western Reserve Univ., 1970.

Rev. in *Choice*, 8 (May 1971), 394.

175. Woodring, Carl. *Politics in English Romantic Poetry.* Cambridge, Mass.: Harvard Univ.; London: Oxford Univ. (1970).

Includes full chapters on Byron and Shelley, and comments on Keats and Hunt.

Rev. by Duane B. Schneider in LJ, 95 (15 Sept. 1970), 2920; by R. F. Storch in WC, 2 (Winter 1971), 32–37; by David V. Erdman in SIR, 10 (Winter 1971), 60–65; in *Choice*, 8 (May 1971), 394; by Harold Bloom in VQR, 47 (Summer 1971), 314–317.

II. BYRON

Works: Selected, Single, Translated

176. **Byron: Poetical Works.* Ed. Frederick Page. Third Edition, corrected by John Jump. London: Oxford Univ., 1970. "Oxford Standard Authors."

Previous edition published in 1945. Paperback.

177. **Byron.* Texts adapted by Laurence Lévi, Madeleine Œuvrard, and Christian Colombani. Paris: Paris-Match, 1970.

Selections of Byron's poetry in French.

178. *The Byronic Byron: A Selection from the Poems of Lord Byron.* Ed. Gilbert Phelps. Harlow, Essex: Longmans, 1971.

"Longman English Series."

179. **Le captif de Chillon (The Prisoner of Chillon); Le chevalier Harold, Chant* III *(Childe Harold, Canto* III*).* Translated by Paul Bensimon and Roger Martin. Paris: Flammarion, 1971. "Edition Montaigne."

Parallel English text and French translation.

Rev. in *Bulletin Critique du Livre Français*, 26 (1971), 669.

180. **Deltion Epistēmonikou Kai Philologikou Syllogou Ammochostou* (Cyprus) (1968 [for 1967]).

In Greek. Pages 37–53 include poetry of Byron.

181. Detz, Phyllis, Kermit M. Stover, and Betsy Schwartz, eds. *On This Day: An Anthology of Poetry and Prose for Every Day of the Year.* New York: Doubleday, 1970.

Includes selections from Byron, Hunt, Keats, and Shelley.

181a. **Don Juan,* Canto II. Translated by Kazuo Ogawa. *Oberon* (Tokyo), 29 (1968), 64–76; 30 (1968), 53–69.

182. **Don Zhuan.* [*Don Juan.*] Translation, Preface, and Epilogue by Tatyana Gnedich. [In Russian.]

Byron's poem adapted for the stage by N. P. Akimov. Played at the Leningrad State Theater, July 1966, but seems to date from 1963.

183. Flower, Desmond. *The Pursuit of Poetry.* Folcroft, Pa.: Folcroft, 1970.

Reprint of the 1939 edition, with letters from Byron to Murray and from Shelley to Hunt.

184. Kinsley, James and James T. Boulton, eds. *English Satiric Poetry: Dryden to Byron.* Columbia: Univ. of South Carolina, 1970.

An anthology.

Rev. by G[eorge]. A. T[est]. in *Satire Newsletter*, 8 (Spring 1971), 150.

185. **Lirikē.* [Translated by] Igor Krecu and Viktor Teleukē. Kišinev: Lumina, 1970. [In Moldavian.]

186. *Lord Byron's "Cain": Twelve Essays and a Text with Variants and Annotations.* Ed. Truman Guy Steffan. See K-SJ, 19 (1970), No. 70b.

Rev. in TLS, 13 Nov. 1969, p. 1298; in *Choice*, 7 (March 1970), 82; by Kenneth A. Bruffee in MP, 68 (Aug. 1970), 115; by E[dward]. E. B[ostetter]. in ELN, 8, Supplement (Sept. 1970), 29; by V. S. Pritchett in NYRB, 22 Oct. 1970, pp. 6, 8, 10; by Robert Mortenson in K-SJ, 20 (1971), 134–137; by J. Drummond Bone in N&Q, 216 (May 1971), 195–196.

187. **The Prisoner of Chillon*. Critical Text and Notes by Eugen Kölbing. Heidelburg: Carl Winter, n.d.

188. **The Prisoner of Chillon, and Other Poems, 1816*. Menston, Yorkshire: Scolar, 1969.
Facsimile reprint of first edition.

189. *Selected Poems and Letters*. Ed. William H. Marshall. See K-SJ, 19 (1970), No. 73.
Rev. by W. Paul Elledge in ELN, 7 (1969), 148–150; by Jerome J. McGann in MP, 67 (1969), 203–207; by J. Hillis Miller in SEL, 9 (1969), 737–749; in TLS, 8 Jan. 1970, p. 28; by E[dward]. E. B[ostetter]. in ELN, 8, Supplement (Sept. 1970), 28.

190. **Shih Chieh Ming Shih Hsüan I*. [*World Famous Poems Selected and Translated*.] Taipei: Hsien; Pan Ch'iao Chen: Hu P'o Pub. Ser. 294, 1970. [In Chinese.]
Includes translations of Byron's poems.

191. Turner, Michael R., comp. *Parlour Poetry: A Casquet of Gems*. New York: Viking, 1969.
Includes selections from Byron.
Rev. by John Hollander in *Harper's Magazine*, 239 (Dec. 1969), 152.

192. **Werner, A Tragedy*. A Facsimile of the Acting Version of William Charles Macready. Ed. Martin Spevack. Munich: W. Fink, 1970.

Yofyllis, Fot. See No. 753.

Books and Articles Relating to Byron and His Circle

193. Anderson, Patrick. *Over the Alps: Reflections on Travel and Travel Writing, with Special Reference to the Grand Tours of Boswell, Beckford and Byron*. London: Hart-Davis, 1969.

193a. *Aratani, Jiro. "L'influenza di Alfieri sulle tragedie byroniane," *Studi Italici* (Kyoto), 16 (1967), 23–33.

194. Arnold, Matthew. *Matthew Arnold's Essays in Criticism: First Series*. Ed. with Introduction and Notes by Sister Thomas Marion Hoctor, S.S.J. Chicago and London: Univ. of Chicago, 1968.
References by Arnold and the editor to Byron, Keats, and Shelley.
Rev. by F. W. Schulze in *Erasmus*, 22 (July 1970), Cols. 548–550.

195. Ashton, Thomas L. "Byron's Metrical Tales," BC, 19 (Autumn 1970), 384.
Queries location of holograph of Byron's *Parisina*.

196. Ashton, Thomas L. "Naming Byron's Aurora Raby," ELN, 7 (Dec. 1969), 114–120.
Suggests that the name is a combination of the dawn goddess and the Earl of Darlington's lesser title, Baron of Raby.

197. Avni, Abraham. "'Blue-Eyed Minerva': Byron and Pope," N&Q, 215 (Oct. 1970), 381.†
Sees Pope's influence in Byron's use of "blue-eyed" Athena in *Childe Harold*, II.i.

198. [Bain, Kenneth Bruce Findlater.] Findlater, Richard, *pseud. The Player Kings*. London: Weidenfeld and Nicolson, 1971.
Includes the careers of John Philip Kemble, Edmund Kean, and William Charles Macready. Contemporary estimates of these actors are made by Byron, Hazlitt, Hunt, and Keats.
Rev. by Louis A. Rachow in LJ, 96 (15 Apr. 1971), 1385.

199. *Baker, Harry J. *Biographical Sagas of Will Power*. New York: Vantage, 1970.
Byron included.

200. *Ball, Patricia. *Childe Harold's Pilgrimage, Cantos* III *and* IV, *and The Vision of Judgment*. Oxford: Blackwell, 1968. "Notes on English Literature, 32." Paperback.

201. Bank, George T. "The Auction Market," *Manuscripts*, 22 (Winter 1970), 62–63.
Notes the sale by auction at Sotheby's of "a single page Byron letter (published) of 1823," which "tells of his dog 'Lyon.'" Price: $912.

202. Bartlett, C. J. *Castlereagh*. See K-SJ, 17 (1968), No. 113, 19 (1970), No. 9.

Rev. by M. G. Brock in *History*, 55 (June 1970), 289.

203. Bate, Walter Jackson. *Coleridge*. See K-SJ, 19 (1970), No. 76.

Rev. by Bertram R. Davis in CLSB No. 204 (Oct. 1969), pp. 639–640.

203a. Baxter, Nancy Niblack. "Thomas Moore's Influence on 'Tamerlane,'" *Poe Newsletter*, 2 (Apr. 1969), 37.

Notes parallels with "The Veiled Prophet of Khorassan" in *Lalla Rookh*.

Bayley, John. See No. 37.

204. *Bekatoros, Spyr. ["A Hunting Party of Lord Byron in Cephalonia,"] *Kynegetika Nea*, No. 450 (1969). [In Greek.]

205. Bentley, G. E., Jr. "Byron, Shelley, Wordsworth, Blake, and *The Seaman's Recorder*," SIR, 9 (Winter 1970), 21–36.†‡

An "anonymous compendium" of some interest to students of the period.

206. Berlioz, Hector. *Memoires*. Ed. Pierre Citron. Paris: Garnier-Flammarion, 1969.

A French edition of Berlioz' *Memoirs*. For the English translation, see K-SJ, 19 (1970), No. 80.

Rev. in *Forum for Modern Language Studies*, 6 (Apr. 1970), 204.

207. Berlioz, Hector. *The Memoirs of Hector Berlioz: Member of the French Institute, Including His Travels in Italy, Germany, Russia, and England, 1803–1865*. Ed. and translated by David Cairns. See K-SJ, 19 (1970), No. 80.

Rev. By J. A. W. in *Music and Letters*, 50 (Oct. 1969), 502–503.

208. Bernard, Camille. "Some Aspects of Delacroix's Orientalism," *Bulletin of the Cleveland Museum of Art*, 58 (Apr. 1971), 123–127.

Discusses lifelong influence of Byron's *The Giaour* on Delacroix and reproduces three paintings of Delacroix inspired by the poem.

209. *Bewley, Marius. *Masks and Mirrors: Essays in Criticism*. New York: Atheneum, 1970.

Includes two essays on Byron: "The Colloquial Byron," pp. 50–76, and "The Romantic Imagination and the Unromantic Byron," pp. 77–103.

210. Blackstone, Bernard. *Byron*. Vol. I: *Lyric and Romance*; Vol. II: *Literary Satire, Humor and Reflexion*. Harlow, Essex: Longmans, for the British Council, 1970–1971. "Writers and Their Work, Nos. 215, 219."

Rev. in TLS, 11 June 1971, p. 682.

211. Blessington, Marguerite, Countess of. *Lady Blessington's Conversations of Lord Byron*. Ed. Ernest J. Lovell, Jr. See K-SJ, 19 (1970), No. 82.

Rev. by J. Hillis Miller in SEL, 9 (1969), 737–753; by Jerome J. McGann in MP, 67 (Nov. 1969), 205–206; by W. Paul Elledge in ELN, 8 (Dec. 1969), 148–150; by Edward E. Bostetter in K-SJ, 19 (1970), 129–133; in TLS, 8 Jan. 1970, p. 28; by Claire Tomalin in NS, 16 (Jan. 1970), 86–87; by Thomas L. Ashton in SAQ, 69 (Spring 1970); in *Choice*, 7 (May 1970), 384; by D[avid]. V. E[rdman]. in ELN, 8, Supplement (Sept. 1970), 28; by John Buxton in RES, 22 (Feb. 1971), 102–103. Also see No. 117.

Bloom, Harold, ed. See No. 46.

Bloom, Harold. See No. 48.

212. Blunden, Edmund. *Three Young Poets: Critical Sketches of Byron, Shelley, and Keats*. Folcroft, Pa.: Folcroft, 1970.

Reprint of a 1959 book.

213. Borst, William A. *Lord Byron's First Pilgrimage, 1809–1811*. See K-SJ, 1 (1952), No. 40, 19 (1970), No. 83.

Rev. in *Choice*, 6 (Dec. 1969), 1390, 1392.

214. Bostetter, Edward E., ed. *Twentieth Century Interpretations of "Don Juan": A Collection of Critical Essays*. See K-SJ, 19 (1970), No. 84.

Rev. by Joseph Anthony Wittreich, Jr., in K-SJ, 19 (1970), 143–144.

215. *Botsarēs, Notēs D. *Logoi kai Meletai*. Vol. II. Athens, 1967.

Includes an essay on Byron.

216. Boyd, Ernest. *Literary Blasphemies*. New York: Greenwood Press, 1969.

Reprint of the 1927 edition; includes an essay on Byron.

217. Brecknock, Albert. *Byron: A Study of the Poet in the Light of New Discoveries*. New York: Haskell House, 1967.

Reprint of a 1926 book.

Briggs, Asa, ed. See No. 49.

217a. *Brennecke, Detlef. "Die vier Übersetzungen Gottlieb Mohnikes aus dem

Englischen des Lord Byron," *Literatur in Wissenschaft und Unterricht* (Kiel), 3 (1970), 15–17,

218. Brilli, Attilio. *Il Gioco del Don Juan: Byron e la Satira*. Ravenna: A. Longo, 1971. "Biblioteca di Lettere e Arti, 35."

219. Brogan, Sir Dennis. "André Malraux: A Modern Byron," *Atlantic*, 227 (June 1971), 86–92.
A review of Pierre Galante's *Malraux*. Briefly mentions parallels.

220. Brombert, Victor. "Esquisse de la prison heureuse," *Revue d'Histoire Littéraire de la France*, 71 (March–Apr. 1971), 247–261.
Includes Byron among many writers on the subject.

221. Bruffee, Kenneth A. "Elegiac Romance," CE, 32 (Jan. 1971), 465–476.†
Discusses Byron's fragment of a novel as perhaps the first example of "elegiac romance," i.e., a work about a dead hero who had embarked on a quest, narrated by a character who is attempting to overcome the effect of the hero's loss.

Burton, Elizabeth. See No. 51.

222. Buxton, John. *Byron and Shelley: The History of a Friendship*. See K-SJ, 18 (1969), No. 132, 19 (1970), No. 85.
Rev. by Hermann Peschmann in *English*, 17 (Autumn 1968), 104–105; by John Lehmann in *London Magazine*, 8 (Jan. 1969), 90–97; in *Choice*, 6 (Sept. 1969), 812; by E[dward]. E. B[ostetter]. in ELN, 7, Supplement (Sept. 1969), 27–28; by James A. Phillips in LJ, 93 (15 Sept. 1969), 3140; by Stuart Curran in K-SJ, 20 (1971), 132–134.

223. Buxton, John. "The Poetry of Lord Byron," *Proceedings of the British Academy*, 56 (1970), 77–92.
Speaks of Byron's mind as a "conflict between Classical Sense and Romantic Sensibility."

224. "The Byron Fund Swells," *Times* (London), 31 Aug. 1969, p. 6h.
A fund to set up a plaque to Lord Byron in the Poets' Corner of Westminster Abbey.

225. Cheney, Thomas E. "Imagination and the Soul's Immensity," *Brigham Young Univ. Studies*, 9 (Summer 1969), 407–420.†
Among others who emphasized the "immensity of the soul of man," Byron, Keats, Shelley, Wordsworth, and Blake are mentioned. Shelley's pursuit of the ideal is defended.

226. *Chew, Samuel C. *Byron in England: His Fame and After-Fame*. St. Clair Shores, Mich.: Scholarly, 1970.
Reprint of a 1924 book.

227. "Chronique," *Cahiers Staëliens*, No. 12 (June 1971), 1–2.
Mentions talk given by Jean de Pange on Byron and Mme de Staël during Staël week in London, May 1971.

228. Clairmont, Claire. *The Journals of Claire Clairmont*. Ed. Marion Kingston Stocking, assisted by David Mackenzie Stocking. See K-SJ, 19 (1970), No. 90.
Rev. by R. Glynn Grylls in CLSB (July 1969), pp. 632–633; in TLS, 3 July 1969, p. 727: in Spec, 5 July 1969, pp. 17–18; by E[dward]. E. B[ostetter]. in ELN, 7, Supplement (Sept. 1969), 30; by Sylvan Barnet in K-SJ, 19 (1970), 140–141; by John Buxton in RES, 22 (Feb. 1971), 102–103. Also see Nos. 109a, 117.

229. Clarke, Isabel C. *Shelley and Byron: A Tragic Friendship*. New York: Haskell House, 1971.
Reprint of a 1934 book.

230. Clearman, Mary. "A Blueprint for *English Bards and Scotch Reviewers*: The First Satire of Juvenal," K-SJ, 19 (1970), 87–99.†
Byron used the first satire of Juvenal, initially as a blueprint and then as a guide, for his poem.

231. Cockshut, A[nthony]. O. J. *The Achievement of Walter Scott*. London: Collins; New York: New York Univ. (1969).
Includes references to Byron.
Rev. by Sir Charles Petrie in ILN, 26 July 1969, p. 29; by Edward J. Cutler in LJ, 95 (1 Apr. 1970), 1371; by K[enneth]. C[urry]. in ELN, 8, Supplement (Sept. 1970), 41–42.

Coleman, William E. See No. 54a.

232. *Collins, Philip. *Thomas Cooper, the Chartist: Byron and the "Poets of the Poor."* Nottingham: Univ. of Nottingham, 1969. "Nottingham Byron Lecture."

233. Colville, Derek. *Victorian Poetry and the*

Romantic Religion. Albany: State Univ. of New York, 1970.

The "Romantic Reformulation" of religious belief includes a discussion of Byron, Keats, and Shelley.

Rev. by F. X. Shea in SIR, 10 (Spring 1971), 153–154; by Karl Kroeber in *Victorian Studies*, 14 (June 1971), 462–463.

234. Cooke, Michael G. *The Blind Man Traces the Circle: On the Patterns and Philosophy of Byron's Poetry*. See K-SJ, 19 (1970), No. 95.

Rev. in TLS, 10 July 1969, p. 749; by W. Paul Elledge in K-SJ, 19 (1970), 125–127; by Kenneth A. Bruffee in MP, 68 (Aug. 1970), 115–117; in *Choice*, 7 (Sept. 1970), 840; by E[dward]. E. B[ostetter]. in ELN, 8, Supplement (Sept. 1970), 26–27. Also see Nos. 44, 109a, 117.

235. Cooper, Robert M. *Lost on Both Sides: Dante Gabriel Rossetti, Critic and Poet*. Athens, Ohio: Ohio Univ., 1970.

Includes references to Byron, Hunt, Keats, and Shelley.

Rev. by Keith Cushman in LJ, 96 (15 March 1971), 961.

236. Corrigan, Beatrice, ed. *Italian Poets and English Critics, 1755–1859: A Collection of Critical Essays*. See K-SJ, 19 (1970), No. 169.

Rev. by Karl Kroeber in *Italian Quarterly*, 13 (Summer 1969), 91–92; by Glauco Cambon in ELN, 7 (Dec. 1969), 146–148; by Daniel J. Donno in *Italica*, 48 (Autumn 1971), 390–391.

237. *Cozza, Andrea. "Il Byron di John Galt," *English Miscellany*, 22 (1971), 215–241.

238. Cramb, Isobel. "Francis Peacock 1723–1807: Dancing Master in Aberdeen," *Aberdeen Univ. Review*, 43 (Spring 1970), 251–261.

Cites Robert Anderson's *Aberdeen in Bygone Days* (Aberdeen, 1910) on the possibility that Byron may have resided in Francis Peacock's house.

239. Crozier, Alice C. *The Novels of Harriet Beecher Stowe*. New York: Oxford Univ., 1969.

Ch. vi, "Byron," describes Mrs. Stowe's "passionate involvement" with the life and works of Byron, who was "the single greatest literary and imaginative influence" on her writings.

Rev. in *Choice*, 7 (Oct. 1970), 1034, 1036; by Donald R. Noble, Jr., in *American Notes and Queries*, 9 (Dec. 1970), 61–62.

240. Cunningham, John M., Jr. "Byron's Poetics in *Don Juan*" [Doctoral dissertation, Duke, 1969], DAI, 30 (May 1970), 4979-A.

241. Curran, Stuart. "A New Byron Portrait," KSMB, 21 (1970), 1–2.

Discusses previously unrecorded pencil sketch of Byron, which is reproduced.

241a. Davenport, John A. "The Long Pilgrimage," *Intercollegiate Review*, 7 (Winter 1970–1971), 79–88.

Illustrated with pictures of Byron and Shelley, "who, long before the arrival of Eldridge Cleaver, were at war with established authority."

242. Day, Richard D., producer. "The Lord Byron Show."

A "half-dramatized reading" in Regents Park.

Rev. by Irving Wardle in *Times* (London), 5 Aug. 1970, p. 7.

243. de Beer, Sir Gavin. "Byron's French Passport," KSMB, 20 (1969), 31–36.

Despite assertions to the contrary, Byron never visited France. Reputed difficulties on his part in securing a passport are also in error and result from confusion with Shelley.

244. de Beer, Sir Gavin. "Maillons du Filet Byronien en Suisse," *Etudes de Lettres*, 3 (Apr.–June 1970), 110–129. Also see *Etudes de Lettres*, 4 (Jan.–March 1971), 59–65 for a letter by M. Pierre Meylan and de Beer's reply.

245. Diakonova, Nina. "Byron and the English Romantics," *Zeitschrift für Anglistik und Amerikanistik*, 18, No. 2 (1970), 144–167.†

Maintains that "in spite of furious controversy and mutual dislike, he and his brother poets can be regarded as participants in one and the same [Romantic] movement."

246. Dick, William. *Byron and His Poetry*. Folcroft, Pa.: Folcroft, 1969. "Poetry & Life Series."

Reprint of a 1913 book.

246a. *D'jakonova, N. Ja. "Bajron-poèt i Bajron-prozaik," *Vestnik Leningradskogo U. Ser. Istorii, Jazyka i Literatury*, 25, iv (1970), 99–109.
Summary in English.

247. *D'jakonova, N. Ja. "Russkÿ èpizod v poème Bajrona Don-Zuan," *Russko* (1968), pp. 256–263.

248. Dobrée, Bonamy. *Byron's Dramas*. Folcroft, Pa.: Folcroft, 1970.
Reprint of 1962 Byron Foundation Lecture. See K-SJ, 13 (1964), No. 141.

249. Dobrée, Bonamy. *Milton to Ouida: A Collection of Essays*. London: Frank Cuss; New York: Barnes and Noble (1970).
Includes essays on "Byron's Dramas," pp. 116–139, and "William Hazlitt," pp. 140–148.

250. Dodsworth, Martin, ed. *The Survival of Poetry: A Contemporary Survey, by Donald Davie [and Others]*. London: Faber, 1970.
The editor's essay on Thom Gunn begins and ends by comparing the poet to Byron.
Rev. by William H. Pritchard in EC, 21 (Apr. 1971), 211–220.

251. Doherty, Francis M. *Byron*. See K-SJ, 19 (1970), No. 96.
Rev. by Elaine Bender in LJ, 95 (15 Jan. 1970), 159; by D[avid]. V. E[rdman]. in ELN, 8 Supplement (Sept. 1970), 27; by Patrick Roberts in RES, 22 (Feb. 1971), 107–108.

Donohue, Joseph W., Jr. See No. 61.

252. Draffan, Robert A. "Jane Austen and Her Time," *History Today*, 20 (March 1970), 190–197.
Relates Jane Austen's achievement to some of her contemporaries, including Byron.

253. Du Bos, Charles. *Byron and the Need of Fatality*. Translated by Ethel Colburn Mayne. Folcroft, Pa.: Folcroft, 1969.
Reprint of a 1932 book.

254. Duke, David Carroll. "American Byronism: A Study in Twentieth Century Romanticism, Idealism, and Disillusionment" [Doctoral dissertation, Tennessee, 1970], DAI, 31 (March 1971), 4669-A.
"Byronism" is employed metaphorically; not a study of Byron's influence.

255. Earle, Kathleen. "Portrait of Margaret Lady Blessington," QQ, 77 (Summer 1970), 236–251.†
A brief description of her life, including her relationship with Byron and the genesis of her book *Conversations of Lord Byron with the Countess of Blessington*.

256. Elledge, W. Paul. *Byron and the Dynamics of Metaphor*. See K-SJ, 19 (1970), No. 98.
Rev. by Jerome J. McGann in MP, 67 (1969), 203–207; by E[dward]. E. B[ostetter]. in ELN, 7, Supplement (Sept. 1969), 28; by Ernest J. Lovell, Jr., in MLQ, 30 (Sept. 1969), 460–462; by M. K. Joseph in AUMLA, No. 32 (Nov. 1969), 251–253; by Brian Wilkie in JEGP, 68 (1969), 535–538; by Thomas L. Ashton in K-SJ, 19 (1970), 136–138; by John D. Jump in RES (Feb. 1970), 112–113; by Bernard Beatty in N&Q, 215 (May 1970), 197–198; by Robert F. Gleckner in *Criticism*, 12 (Winter 1970), 70–72. Also see No. 117.

257. Elledge, W. Paul. "Byron's Hungry Sinner: The Quest Motif in *Don Juan*," JEGP, 69 (Jan. 1971), 1–13.†‡
The quest centers on maternal oral gratification, a viewpoint consistent with the psychological theory that the traditional Don Juan seeks his mother in all women.

Elledge, W. Paul, and Richard L. Hoffman, eds. See No. 65.

258. Erdman, David V. "Byron's Mock Review of Rosa Matilda's Epic on the Prince Regent—A New Attribution," K-SJ, 19 (1970), 101–117.†
After a background discussion, Erdman reprints two installments of a mock review, entitled "The New Epic," which appeared in the *Morning Chronicle* of 2 and 12 Sept. 1812. The review is attributed to Byron.

259. Faulkner, Claude Winston. *Byron's Political Verse Satire*. Folcroft, Pa.: Folcroft, 1970.
Reprint of abstract (sic) of 1947 Univ. of Illinois dissertation.

Fogle, Richard Harter. See No. 65, 68.

260. Frank, Frederick S. "The Demon and the Thunderstorm: Byron and Madame de Staël," RLC, 43 (July–Sept. 1969), 320–343.

Their relationship was an "ambiguous emotion of detestation and delight."

261. Gál, István. "The British Travel-Diary of Sándor Bölöni Farkas, 1831," *Angol Filólogiai Tanulmányok (Hungarian Studies in English)*, 3 (1967), 23–47.
Farkas, a liberal nobleman, included Byron in his library. He attended the election to Parliament of Hobhouse and Burdett.

262. Gianakaris, C. J. "Tracking the Rebel in Literature," *Topic 18: A Journal of the Liberal Arts*, 9 (Fall 1969), 11–29.
Includes Byron's revolt against polite society.

263. *Giddey, Ernest. "Les Trahisons du Byronisme," *Etudes de Lettres*, 3 (Apr.–June 1970), 89–109.

Gingerich, Solomon F. See No. 76.

264. Glasgow, Eric. "Anglo-Greek Relations, 1800–1832," *Contemporary Review*, 216 (Apr. 1970), 184–188.
References to Byron.

265. Gleckner, Robert F. *Byron and the Ruins of Paradise*. See K-SJ, 18 (1969), No. 178, 19 (1970), No. 100.
Rev. by Bernard Beatty in MLR, 64 (July 1969), 655–656; by Hermann Peschmann in *English*, 17 (Autumn 1968), 104–105; by Jerome J. McGann in MP, 67 (Nov. 1969), 203–205.

266. *Goode, Clement Tyson. *Byron as Critic*. New York: Haskell House, 1964.
Reprint of 1920 Cornell dissertation.

267. Goodheart; Eugene. *The Cult of the Ego: The Self in Modern Literature*. Chicago and London: Univ. of Chicago, 1968.
References to Byron, Keats, and Shelley.

268. Grebanier, Bernard D. *The Uninhibited Byron: An Account of His Sexual Confusion*. New York: Crown; London: Owen (1970).
Rev. by Paul F. Moran in LJ, 95 (1 Oct. 1970), 3271; by Harvey Curtis Webster in SatR, 17 Oct. 1970, pp. 32–33; by V. S. Pritchett in NYRB, 22 Oct. 1970, pp. 6, 8, 10; by Harold Bloom in NYT, 22 Nov. 1970, p. 8; in *Choice*, 8 (June 1971), 551.

269. Greene, John. "Byron," *Revue des lettres modernes*, Nos. 234–237 (1970), pp. 7–14.
Byron's influence on d'Aurevilly is discussed.

270. Griffiths, Victor Segismundo. "Byron's Influence in Spanish America, 1830–1852" [Doctoral dissertation, Nebraska, 1970], DAI, 31 (Feb. 1971), 4119-A.

271. Guignard, Auguste. *Chillon: Notice Historique suivie du Poème de Byron sur Bonivard*. Lausanne: Editions La Tramontane, 1968.
Paperback.

272. Gunn, Peter. *My Dearest Augusta: A Biography of the Honourable Augusta Leigh, Lord Byron's Half-Sister*. See K-SJ, 18 (1969), No. 180, 19 (1970), No. 102.
Rev. by E[dward]. E. B[ostetter]. in ELN, 7, Supplement (Sept. 1969), 28.

273. Hagleman, Charles W., Jr., and Robert J. Barnes, eds. *A Concordance to Byron's "Don Juan."* See K-SJ, 17 (1968), No. 154, 18 (1969), No. 182, 19 (1970), No. 104.
Rev. by Jerome J. McGann in MP, 67 (Nov. 1969), 207.

274. Hamilton, George Heard. *19th and 20th Century Art: Painting-Sculpture-Architecture*. New York: Abrams, 1970.
Includes references to Byron. A color plate of Delacroix' *The Death of Sardanapalus* is included.
Rev. by Jacqueline Sisson in LJ, 96 (1 May 1971), 1600.

275. Hargreaves, Henry. "Dr. Robert Wilson: Alumnus and Benefactor of Marischal College—The Man and His Papers," *Aberdeen Univ. Review*, 43 (Autumn 1970), 374–384.
Wilson (b. 1787) kept journals (now in Aberdeen Univ.) of his extensive travels in Asia Minor and Europe. He claims to have been much in Byron's company at one time and comments on his "want of amiability."

276. Hargreaves-Mawdsley, W. N. *The English Della Cruscans and Their Time, 1783–1828*. The Hague: Martinus Nijhoff, 1967.
Traces signs of the Della Cruscan style in Byron, Hazlitt, Keats, and Shelley.
Rev. by Bernard Groom in *Forum for Modern Language Studies*, 5 (July 1969), 292–295; by J. F. Burnet in *English His-*

torical Review, 84 (July 1969), 615; by George E. Dorris in CL, 22 (Winter 1970), 75–77; by Mario Praz in ES, 52 (June 1971), 280–283.

277. Harson, Robert B. "Byron's 'Tintern Abbey,'" K-SJ, 20 (1971), 113–121.
The reference is to the "Epistle to Augusta," where Byron is "comparing his own peculiar circumstances and his relationship to his sister and to nature with experiences described by Wordsworth in 'Tintern Abbey.'"

278. Harvey, William R. "Charles Dickens and the Byronic Hero," *Nineteenth Century Fiction*, 24 (Dec. 1969), 305–316.‡
Examines Dickens' use of this popular romantic character type.

279. Hassan, M. A. "Who Was Harry Franklin?" N&Q, 216 (May 1971), 165–168.†
A favorable review of *Don Juan*, in the form of a letter from Harry Franklin to Christopher North, appeared in the Aug. 1821 number of *Blackwood's Magazine*. Hassan argues that Harry Franklin was John Gibson Lockhart.

Hayden, John O., ed. See No. 86.

Hearn, L. See No. 89.

280. Heath-Stubbs, John. *The Verse Satire*. London: Oxford Univ., 1969.
Ch. vii, "Regency Satire," includes Byron, Shelley, and Keats. Paperback.
Rev. in *Choice*, 7 (March 1970), 76.

Heffernan, James A. W. See No. 90.

281. Helmick, E. T. "Hellenism in Byron and Keats," KSMB, 22 (1971), 18–27.
Maintains that Keats's interest in Greek ideas, unlike Byron's, affected the substance of his poetry.

282. *Henley, V. W. "Trouble with Byron," *Fort Hare Papers*, 4 (Apr. 1970), 27–46.

283. Hewish, John. *Emily Brontë: A Critical and Biographical Study*. New York: St. Martin's; London: Macmillan (1969).
Treats influence of Byron, Shelley, and Keats.
Rev. in *Choice*, 7 (June 1970), 542.

283a. *Hibbard, Esther L. "Byron's View of Nature," *Essays and Studies in English Language and Literature* (Tohoku Gakuin Univ., Sendai, Japan), 55 (1969), 1–20.

284. Hirsch, E. D., Jr. *Validity in Interpretation*. See K-SJ, 18 (1969), No. 189.
Rev. by Henry W. Sams in *Journal of General Education*, 21 (Apr. 1969), 76–79; by E. N. Tigerstedy in *Studia Neophilologica*, 42 (1970), 483–485.

285. Hogg, James. *James Hogg: Selected Poetry*. Ed. Douglas S. Mack. Oxford: Clarendon, 1971.
Rev. by Douglas Dunn in NS, 16 Apr. 1971, pp. 553–554; in TLS, 14 May 1971, p. 557.

286. Hogg, James. *The Private Memoirs and Confessions of a Justified Sinner, Written by Himself, with a Detail of Curious Traditionary Facts and Other Evidence by the Editor*. Ed. John Carey. London: Oxford Univ., 1969. Paperback, 1970. "Oxford English Novels."
Rev. by Douglas S. Mack in *Library Review*, 22 (1969), 103–104; in *Choice*, 7 (June 1970), 542.

287. Hough, Graham. *Two Exiles: Lord Byron and D. H. Lawrence*. Folcroft, Pa.: Folcroft, 1970.
Reprint of 1956 Byron Foundation Lecture.

Hume, Robert D. See No. 65.

288. Jack, Adolphus Alfred. *Poetry and Prose*. Port Washington, N.Y.: Kennikat, 1969.
Reprint of the 1911 edition; includes a discussion of Byron's "oratorical poetry."

289. Jelistratowa, Anna A. "Byrons Verhältnis zu Shakespeare," *Shakespeare Jahrbuch*, 107 (1971), 72–84.†
Byron's measure of Shakespeare, compared with his estimates of Pope, Shelley, and others.

290. Johnson, Richard Colles. "'On John William Rizzo Hoppner,'" BC, 20 (Spring 1971), 104.
Reply to Walton (see No. 413) that Newberry Library has a copy of Byron's poem.

291. *Jones, Howard Mumford. *The Harp That Once: A Chronicle of the Life of Thomas Moore*. New York: Russell & Russell, 1970.
Reprint of a 1937 book.

292. *Kahn, Arthur D. "Byron's Single Difference with Homer and Virgil: The Redefinition of Epic in *Don Juan*," *Arcadia*, 5 (1970), 143–162.

293. Kahn, Arthur D. "Seneca and *Sardanapalus*: Byron, the Don Quixote of Neo-Classicism," SP, 66 (July 1969), 654–671.

Maintains that Seneca is the chief model and source for Byron's play.

294. Keating, L[ouis]. Clark. *André Maurois.* New York: Twayne, 1969.

References to Byron and Shelley, and to Maurois' lives of the two poets.

Rev. by Jack Kolbert in *French Review*, 43 (Dec. 1969), 332–333.

294a. Kelliher, W. Hilton. "Byron and Brooke" [Letter], TLS, 29 May 1969, p. 584.

On Byron's knowledge of a MS of Fulke Greville's.

295. Kelly, Larry Dennis. "Byron Biography: 1822–1830" [Doctoral dissertation, Pennsylvania, 1969], DAI, 31 (Sept. 1970), 1232-A.

Kelly, Linda. See No. 613.

Kernan, Alvin B. See No. 46.

296. Klein, H. M. " 'Sangrado'—Byron Before Scott," N&Q, 215 (May 1970), 174.†

The word "Sangrado" was first used in English by Byron in his maiden speech in the House of Lords.

297. Knight, Frida. *University Rebel: The Life of William Frend (1757–1841).* London: Gollancz, 1971.

As a private tutor, Anabella Milbanke was his favorite pupil, and he corresponded with her at the time of the separation from Byron.

298. Knight, G. Wilson. *The Burning Oracle: Studies in the Poetry of Action.* Folcroft, Pa.: Folcroft, 1971.

Reprint of the 1939 edition; includes "The Two Eternities: An Essay on Byron."

299. Knight, G. Wilson. *Byron and Shakespeare.* See K-SJ, 17 (1968), No. 169.

Rev. by Thomas B. Stroup in *Shakespeare Quarterly*, 21 (Spring 1970), 188–189.

299a. Knight, G. Wilson. "Herbert Read and Byron," *Malahat Review*, No. 9 (Jan. 1969), pp. 130–134.

A tribute to Sir Herbert Read, comparing him to Byron.

300. Knight, G. Wilson. *Neglected Powers: Essays on Nineteenth and Twentieth Century Literature.* London: Routledge and Kegan Paul; New York: Barnes and Noble (1971).

Includes "Colman and Don Leon," pp. 127–141, and "Herbert Read and Byron," pp. 481–490.

Rev. by Raleigh De Priest in LJ, 96 (1 June 1971), 1980; in *Choice*, 8 (June 1971), 551.

301. Kroeber, Karl, with Alfred and Theodora Kroeber. "Life against Death in English Poetry: A Method of Stylistic Definition," *Transactions of the Wisconsin Academy of Science, Arts and Letters*, 57 (1969), 29–40.

Keats, Shelley, and Byron are among the poets studied for the frequency of their use of "life" and "death" words.

302. Kronenberger, Louis. *The Polished Surface: Essays in the Literature of Worldliness.* New York: Knopf, 1969.

Includes a discussion of *Don Juan*, pp. 151–160.

Rev. by Frank N. Jones in LJ, 94 (15 Sept. 1969), 3067.

302a. Lambertson, C. L., ed. "Speaking of Byron," *Malahat Review*, No. 12 (Oct. 1969), pp. 18–42; No. 13 (Jan. 1970), pp. 24–46.†

Letters from Joanna Baillie to Sir Walter Scott dealing with Byron.

Langbaum, Robert. See No. 102.

303. *Langham-Carter, R. R. "Bartolini Busts in the South African Library," *Quarterly Bulletin of the South African Library*, 25 (Dec. 1970), 44–51.

Lean, E. Tangye. See No. 103.

304. Leggett, B. L. "Dante, Byron, and Tennyson's Ulysses," *Tennessee Studies in Literature*, 15 (1970), 143–159.†‡

Byron is named as an important influence upon the persona in Tennyson's poem.

305. *Leonard, William Ellery. *Byron and Byronism in America.* New York: Haskell House, 1964.

Reprint of a 1907 book.

306. *Lobet, Marcel. "Sur une traduction française des 'Journaux intimes de Byron,' " *Bulletin de l'Academie Royale de Langue et de Littérature française* (Bruxelles), 49 (1971), 67–95.

307. Lochhead, Marion. "John Galt," *Blackwood's Magazine*, 304 (Dec. 1968), 496–508.

References to Byron.

308. Lohf, Kenneth A. "Our Growing Collections," *Columbia Library Columns*, 18 (Feb. 1969), 29–44.

Notes Columbia Library's addition to its Thomas J. Wise Collection of letters and MSS relating to Wise's Byron *Bibliography*, including "miscellaneous page proofs bearing Wise's notes and corrections; portions of the text, made up of printed excerpts and holograph drafts, concerned with John Keats, Robert Southey, Allegra Byron, and other writers of the period; and a series of forty-three letters from the publisher Sir John Murray and eighteen from his son John Grey Murray."

Longford, Elizabeth. See No. 106.

309. *["Lord Byron Visits a Grotto in Attica,"] *Deltion Ellenikēs Spilaiologikēs Etairias*, 9 (1967), 50. [In Greek.]

310. Luke, K. McCormick. "Lord Byron's *Manfred*: A Study of Alienation from Within," UTQ, 40 (Fall 1970), 15–26.

Suggests that Manfred's character was "neither determined by Faustian motives nor tormented by the awareness of incestuous sin, but bound only by the unconscious confines of his own mind."

311. Lutz, Paul V. "Meet the Collector: Irving Wallace," *Manuscripts*, 22 (Spring 1970), 118–124.

In an interview, Wallace discusses his purchase in 1946 of a cancelled check of £50 from Shelley to Hunt, dated 25 Nov. 1817. He also indicates that he possesses letters and manuscripts of Byron.

312. McConnell, Frank D. "Byron's Reductions: 'Much Too Poetical,' " ELH, 37 (Sept. 1970), 415–432.

Byron's poetry is of undeniable power, but, "taken at its own self-evaluation, seems to deny many of our most basic tenets of belief in the nature and efficacy of creative language."

313. Cancelled.

314. McGann, Jerome J. *Fiery Dust: Byron's Poetic Development*. See K-SJ, 19 (1970), No. 118.

Rev. by W. Paul Elledge in JEGP, 68 (1969), 715–716; by E[dward]. E. B[ostetter]. in ELN, 7, Supplement (Sept. 1969), 29–30; by Donald H. Reiman in K-SJ, 19 (1970), 144–145; by Robert F. Gleckner in *Criticism*, 12 (Winter 1970), 70–72; by Gilbert Thomas in *English*, 19 (Autumn 1970), 105–106. Also see No. 117.

315. McGann, Jerome J. "Manuscripts of *Childe Harold's Pilgrimage*," *American Philosophical Society Yearbook* (1970), p. 653.

Work in progress towards a reproduction of the manuscripts and later a variorum edition of the poem.

McGann, Jerome J. See No. 65.

316. Mackiw, Theodore. *Prince Mazepa, Hetman of Ukraine, in Contemporary English Publications, 1687–1709*. Chicago: Ukrainian Research and Information Institute, 1967.

The historical figure behind Byron's *Mazeppa*.

Rev. by V. J. Kaye in *Canadian Slavonic Papers*, 10 (Summer 1968), 233–234.

317. *Makropoulos, Th. *Hē Polikeia kai hē Limnothalassa*. 1968.

Apparently, a book about Missolonghi with references to Byron.

318. Manners, G. S. "Byron on Job" [Letter], TLS, 2 Oct. 1969, p. 1132.

Byron wrote a poem, "On Job," which inadvertently was included in a volume of poetry by Henry Savile Shepherd.

319. Manning, Peter Jay. "Byron and the Stage" [Doctoral dissertation, Yale, 1968], DAI, 30 (Aug. 1969), 689-A.

320. Manning, Peter J. "Byron's *English Bards and Scotch Reviewers*: The Art of Allusion," KSMB, 21 (1970), 7–11.

Allusions by Byron to lines of Churchhill and Shakespeare show him manipulating a native tradition to his own satiric ends.

321. Manning, Peter J. "Byron's 'English Bards' and Shelley's 'Adonais': A Note," N&Q, 215 (Oct. 1970), 380–381.†

An echo of Byron's satire is found in *Adonais*.

322. Marchand, Leslie A. *Byron: A Portrait*. New York: Knopf, 1970; London: Murray, 1971.

A one-volume abridgement and revision of his three-volume 1957 work, *Byron: A Biography*. See K-SJ, 8 (1959),

No. 184, 9 (1960), No. 177, 10 (1961), No. 135, 12 (1963), No. 148.

Rev. by Paul F. Moran in LJ, 95 (1 Oct. 1970), 3271; by V. S. Pritchett in NYRB, 22 Oct. 1970, pp. 6, 8, 10; by Harold Bloom in NYT, 22 Nov. 1970, p. 8; by Michael Wood in *Times* (London), 8 Apr. 1971, p. 11; by Gabriel Pearson in Spec, 29 May 1971, pp. 733–736; in *Choice*, 8 (June 1971), 552.

323. Marchand, Leslie A. *Byron's Poetry: A Critical Introduction.* See K-SJ, 19 (1970), No. 122.

Rev. by Roland Bartel in CL, 22 (Winter 1970), 92–93. Also see No. 117.

324. Marchand, Leslie A. "The Letters of Lord Byron," *American Philosophical Society Yearbook* (1970), pp. 657–658.

Work in progress towards an edition of Byron's letters.

Margetson, Stella. See No. 111.

325. Marlowe, Derek. *A Single Summer with L. B.* London: Cape, 1969; New York: Viking, 1970.

A fictionalized account of the Byron and Shelley households during the summer of 1816. The Viking edition is entitled *A Single Summer with Lord B.*

Rev. by Maurice Capitanchik in Spec, 25 Oct. 1969, p. 551; by Thomas Lask in *New York Times*, 20 Jan. 1970, p. 41; by Harold Bloom in NYT, 15 Feb. 1970, p. 47; in *Choice*, 7 (Sept. 1970), 843.

326. Martin, L. C. *Byron's Lyrics.* Folcroft, Pa.: Folcroft, 1969.

Reprint of 1948 Byron Foundation Lecture.

Massey, Irving J. See No. 112.

326a. Mathaney, Margaret Heinen. "Baudelaire's Knowledge of English Literature," RLC, 44 (Jan.–March 1970), 98–117.

Byron.

327. Mather, J. Marshall. *Popular Studies of Nineteenth Century Poets.* Folcroft, Pa.: Folcroft, 1969.

A reprint of the 1892 edition, including studies of Shelley, Byron, and Hood.

328. *Maurice, Frederick D. *Sketches of Contemporary Authors, 1828.* Ed. A. J. Hartley. Hamden, Conn.: Shoe String, 1970.

Includes Byron and Shelley.

Rev. in Choice, 8 (March 1971), 67–68.

329. *Maurois, André. *Don Juan oder das Leben Byrons.* Translated by Hans Adolf Neunzig. Hamburg: Wegner, 1969.

330. *Maurois, André. *Don Juan, ou La vie de Byron.* Revised Edition. Paris: Grasset, 1969.

Another edition of the popular 1930 biography.

331. Maurois, André. *Memoirs: 1885–1967.* Translated from the French by Denver Lindley. New York: Harper, 1970.

Maurois discusses his lives of Byron and Shelley.

Rev. by Karen Horney in LJ, 95 (Aug. 1970), 2663–2664.

332. *Mayne, Ethel Colburn. *Byron.* Freeport, N.Y.: Books for Libraries, 1970.

Reprint of a 1924 book.

333. *Mayne, Ethel Colburn, *Byron.* New York: Barnes & Noble, 1969.

Reprint of a 1924 book.

Rev. in *Choice*, 7 (July–Aug. 1970), 686.

334. Mayne, Ethel Colburn. *The Life and Letters of Anne Isabella, Lady Noel Byron.* London: Dawsons; New York: Humanities (1969).

Reprint of a 1929 book.

335. Mehl, Dieter, ed. *Das englische Drama vom Mittelalter bis zur Gegenwart.* Vol. II. Düsseldorf: August Bagel, 1970.

Essays, in German, by various writers including Armin Geraths on *Manfred* and Wolfgang Riehle on *The Cenci.*

Merivale, Patricia. See No. 116.

Miller, Barnette. See No. 445.

336. Mitchell, Austin. *The Whigs in Opposition 1815–1830.* Oxford: Clarendon, 1967.

Many references to Hobhouse.

337. *Moller, Per Stig, ed. "La critique dramatique et litteraire de Malte-Brun," in *Det danske Sprog-og Litteraturselskab.* Copenhagen: Munksgaard, 1971.

Reviews of Byron's works in 1818.

338. *Moore, Thomas. *Tom Moore's Diary: A Selection.* Ed. and introduced by J. B. Priestley. St. Clair Shores, Mich.: Scholarly, 1970.

Reprint of 1925 edition.

339. Mordell, Albert, ed. *Notorious Literary Attacks.* Freeport, N.Y.: Books for Libraries, 1969.

A reprint of the 1926 edition. Attacks

upon Byron, Hazlitt, Hunt, and Shelley are included.

340. Morgan, Peter F. "Southey on Poetry," *Tennessee Studies in Literature*, 16 (1971), 77–89.†

Notes Southey's condemnation of Byron and the "Satanic school."

341. Morley, John. *Nineteenth-Century Essays.* Selected with an introduction by Peter Stansky. Chicago and London: Univ. of Chicago, 1970. "Classics of British Historical Literature."

Includes an essay on Byron first published in 1870.

342. Mortenson, Robert. "Byron and William Harness: Early Recollections of Lord Byron," PBSA, 65 (Jan.–March 1971), 53–65.†‡

An important early defender of Byron's reputation, Harness wrote two letters to *The True Patriot* in 1824. Scholarly study and partial texts of five Byron letters.

343. Mosier, John Friedel. "Byron's *Don Juan:* History as Epic" [Doctoral dissertation, Tulane, 1969], DAI, 30 (Dec. 1969), 2492-A.

344. Muecke, Douglas C. *The Compass of Irony.* London: Methuen; New York: Barnes and Noble (1969).

Includes references to Byron and Shelley.

Rev. in *Forum for Modern Language Studies*, 6 (Apr. 1970), 209–210.

345. *Murray, Sir John, IV. *Lord Byron and His Detractors.* New York: Haskell House, 1971.

Reprint of a 1906 book.

346. "News & Comment," BC, 19 (Winter 1970), 506.

Sale of two short Byron letters for £380 and autograph of sixteen lines of Keats's "Isabella" for £3200.

347. Nichol, John. *Byron.* New York: AMS, 1968. "English Men of Letters."

Reprint of an 1888 book.

348. Nicolson, Sir Harold. *Byron, the Last Journey, April 1823 – April 1824.* Hamden, Conn.: Archon, 1969.

Reprint of second edition (1948) of book first published in 1929.

349. Ogden, James. *Isaac D'Israeli.* Oxford: Clarendon, 1969.

Frequent allusions to Romantic figures, especially to Byron, whom D'Israeli knew well.

Rev. by J. W. Burrow in *Times* (London), 2 Aug. 1969, p. 21; in TLS, 2 Oct. 1969, p. 1119 (reply by Ogden, 30 Oct. 1969, p. 1259); by R. W. King in RES, 22 (Feb. 1971), 111–112.

350. Oliver, Richard A. "Romanticism and Opera," *Symposium*, 23 (Fall–Winter 1969), 325–331.

Refers to *Le Corsaire* and *Harold in Italy*, which were drawn from works by Byron.

351. Cancelled.

Orel, Harold, and George J. Worth, eds. See No. 122.

352. *Origo, Iris. *The Last Attachment: The Story of Byron and Teresa Guiccioli as Told in Their Unpublished Letters and Other Family Papers.* London: Murray, 1971.

Reprint of a 1949 book.

353. Osterberg, Oliver Sinclaire. "Proteus: Form and Idea in Three Metaphysical Dramas of George Gordon, Noel, Lord Byron" [Doctoral dissertation, Minnesota, 1970], DAI, 31 (Apr. 1971), 5567-A–5568-A.

On *Cain, Manfred,* and *The Deformed Transformed.*

354. Paananen, Victor N. "Byron and the Caves of Ellora," N&Q, 214 (Nov. 1969), 414–416.†

An explanation of Byron's footnote in *The Island*, IV.105–160.

355. Pack, Robert F. "Byron's Ode to Napoleon," *Journal of the Rutgers University Library*, 34 (June 1971), 43–45.

Discusses the background of this poem and describes a first edition recently acquired by the Rutgers University Library.

356. *Palacio, Jean de. "Un précurseur inattendu de Max Jacob: Lord Byron," RLC, 45 (Apr.–June 1971), 187–207.

357. Panichas, George A. "G. Wilson Knight: Interpreter of Genius," *English Miscellany*, 20 (1969), 291–312.†

Discusses Knight's strong interest in Byron.

358. *Papadopoulos, Nic. "George Gordon Byron," *Ēcho Ton Thatasson*, No. 348 (1968). [In Greek.]

359. Pearsall, Robert Brainard. "Chronological Annotations to 250 Letters of Thomas Moore," PBSA, 63 (Apr.-June 1969), 105–117.

A list of corrections and revisions of the dates of Moore's letters given by W. S. Dowden in his 1964 edition.

360. Peckham, Morse. *Beyond the Tragic Vision: The Quest for Identity in the Nineteenth Century*. New York: Braziller, 1970.

A paperback edition of a book first published in 1962. See K-SJ, 12 (1963), No. 171, 13 (1964), No. 212, 14 (1965), No. 143.

Rev. by Christopher Ricks in NYRB, 20 May 1971, p. 43.

361. "People," *Time*, 17 May 1968, p. 50.

Westminster Abbey agrees to Byron memorial plaque.

362. Perella, Nicolas J. "Night and the Sublime in Giacomo Leopardi," *Univ. of California Publications in Modern Philology*, 99 (1970), 1–151.

Compares Leopardi's literary theories with those of Byron, Shelley, and other Romantics.

363. Pinto, Vivian de Sola. *Byron and Liberty*. Folcroft, Pa.: Folcroft, 1969.

Reprint of 1944 Byron Foundation Lecture.

364. Piper, William B. *The Heroic Couplet*. Cleveland and London: Case Western Reserve Univ., 1969.

Includes Byron and Keats.

365. Plomer, William. "Byron in Westminster Abbey," *Cornhill Magazine*, No. 1060 (Summer 1969), pp. 309–312.†

Address at unveiling of Byron Memorial, 8 May 1969.

366. Pointon, Marcia B. *Milton and English Art*. Toronto: Univ. of Toronto, 1970.

Includes references to Byron, Godwin, Haydon, Hazlitt, and Shelley.

367. Pratt, John Marshall. "Byron and the Stream of Wit: Studies in the Development, Survival and Culmination of the Colloquial Mode in English Poetry" [Doctoral dissertation, Pennsylvania, 1969], DAI, 30 (Dec. 1969), 2495-A.

368. "The Price on Byron's Head," *Times* (London), 11 Feb. 1970, p. 15.

A lock of his hair and four letters to him by Augusta Leigh were sold at Sotheby's for £320 to H. P. Smith.

369. Pritchett, V. S. "The Craving Void," NYRB, 22 Oct. 1970, pp. 6, 8, 10.

A review article on Byron and on Truman Guy Steffan's *Lord Byron's "Cain"* (see No. 186), Bernard D. Grebanier's *The Uninhibited Byron* (see No. 268), and Leslie A. Marchand's *Byron: A Portrait* (see No. 321).

370. Prokosch, Frederic. *The Missolonghi Manuscript*. See K-SJ, 18 (1969), No. 251.

Rev. by E[dward]. E. B[ostetter]. in ELN, 7, Supplement (Sept. 1969), 30.

371. Pushkin, Alexander. *The Critical Prose of Alexander Pushkin, with Critical Essays by Four Russian Romantic Poets*. Ed. and translated by Carl R. Proffer. Bloomington and London: Indiana Univ., 1970.

Includes Pushkin's reflections on Byron's dramas.

Rev. by Robert P. Hughes in *The Russian Review*, 30 (Jan. 1971), 96–97; by Richard Gregg in *Slavic Review*, 30 (March 1971), 203–204.

372. Raimond, Jean. *Robert Southey: L'homme et son temps; L'oeuvre; Le rôle*. Paris: Didier, 1968. "Études Anglaises, No. 28."

Includes references to Byron, Hunt, Keats, Shelley, and their circles.

Rev. by Kenneth Curry in EA, 22 (Apr.-June 1969), 198–200.

373. Raymond, Dora Neill. *The Political Career of Lord Byron*. Folcroft, Pa.: Folcroft, 1970.

Reprint of a 1924 book.

374. *Reddy, D. V. Subba. *Byron's "Don Juan": A Study*. Tirupati, India: Malico, 1968.

375. Reiman, Donald H. "Byron's William Parry: Post-Postscript," K-SJ, 20 (1971), 21.

William St. Clair's account of William Parry (K-SJ, 19 [1970], 4–7) can be supplemented by an eyewitness account of Parry as a mental patient.

376. Reisner, Thomas A. "*Cain*: Two Romantic Interpretations," *Culture*, 31 (June 1970), 124–143.

Compares Byron's *Cain* and Blake's *The Ghost of Abel*.

377. Richards, Kenneth, and Peter Thomson,

eds. *Essays on Nineteenth Century British Theatre: The Proceedings of a Symposium Sponsored by the Manchester University Department of Drama.* London: Methuen; New York: Barnes and Noble (1971).

Includes William Ruddick's "Lord Byron's Historical Tragedies," pp. 83–94.

378. Ridenour, George M. "Byron and the Romantic Pilgrimage: A Critical Examination of the Third and Fourth Cantos of Lord Byron's *Childe Harold's Pilgrimage*" [Doctoral dissertation, Yale, 1955], DAI, 31 (June 1971), 6566–A.

379. Ridenour, George M. *The Style of "Don Juan."* New Haven: Archon, 1969.

A reprint of a book first published in 1960. See K-SJ, 10 (1961), No. 168, 11 (1962), No. 220, 12 (1963), No. 179, 13 (1964), No. 222.

380. Robinson, Charles E. "The Devil as Doppelgänger in *The Deformed Transformed*: The Sources and Meaning of Byron's Unfinished Drama," BNYPL, 74 (March 1970), 177–202.†‡

Emphasizes influence of Shelley and Byron's Faustian interpretation of Calderón.

Robinson, Charles E. See No. 920.

381. Robson, W. W. *Byron as Poet.* Folcroft, Pa.: Folcroft, 1969.

Reprint of 1957 Byron Foundation lecture.

382. Ross, William T. "Digressive Narrator and Narrative Technique in Byron's *Don Juan*" [Doctoral dissertation, Virginia, 1970], DAI, 31 (Apr. 1971), 5423–A.

383. Rutherford, Andrew, ed. *Byron: The Critical Heritage.* London: Routledge and Kegan Paul; New York: Barnes & Noble (1970). "The Critical Heritage Series."

Rev. in TLS, 28 May 1970, p. 662; reply by Alan Lang Strout in TLS, 18 June 1970, p. 662; by A. E. Dyson in *Critical Quarterly*, 12 (Autumn 1970), 284, 286; by Rowland Smith in *Dalhousie Review*, 50 (Winter 1970–1971), 561–563; by John H. Alexander in *Aberdeen Univ. Review*, 44 (Spring 1971), 73–74. Also see No. 44.

384. St. Clair, William. "Postscript to *The Last Days of Lord Byron*," K-SJ, 19 (1970), 4–7.†

From evidence presented in a libel suit against the *Examiner*, it appears the book was the joint production of William Parry and Thomas Hodgskin.

385. Savage, Catherine. "'Cette Prison Nommée La Vie': Vigny's Prison Metaphor," SIR, 9 (Spring 1970), 99–113.

Byron's influence is briefly noted.

386. Cancelled.

387. Schoenbaum, S[amuel]. "Dyce's Recollections of Wordsworth, Mrs. Siddons and Other Notable Persons," TLS, 22 Jan. 1971, pp. 101–102. Replies by Malcolm Elwin in TLS, 16 Apr. 1971, p. 449; by S[amuel]. Schoenbaum, 23 Apr. 1971, p. 476; by J. C. Maxwell, 30 Apr. 1971, p. 505; again by Malcolm Elwin, 21 May 1971, p. 594.

From a manuscript bequeathed to the South Kensington (Victoria and Albert) Museum in 1905. Recollections also of Lord and Lady Byron, Haydon, Hunt, and Keats.

388. Schwartz, Lewis M. "A New Review of Coleridge's *Christabel*," SIR, 9 (Spring 1970), 114–124.‡

The review referred to in the title is not new, but Schwartz's identification of Lamb as the reviewer is. The article also alludes to reviews of the poem by Moore and Hazlitt, and to Lamb's review of Keats's *Lamia* volume.

389. "Shade of Byron Disturbs Greek Tribute to Poet," *Times* (London), 22 March 1971, p. 2.

Wreath-laying ceremony is interrupted by an unnamed actor masquerading as the poet, in Hyde Park.

390. Shapiro, Harold I. "The Poetry of Architecture: Ruskin's Preparation for *Modern Painters*," *Renaissance and Modern Studies*, 15 (1971), 70–84.

Ruskin's early work includes references to Byron and Shelley; special mention of *The Cenci*.

391. Sheraw, C. Darrel. "Byron and the Course of Romantic Satire" [Doctoral dissertation, Ohio, 1970], DAI, 31 (Dec. 1970), 2940–A.

391a. *Sidorčenko, L. V. "Kommentarii Bajrona k *Vostočnym povestjam*," *Vestnik Leningradskogo U. Ser. Istorii, Jazyka i Literatury*, 25, iii (1970), 99–110.

On Byron's comments on Oriental Tales. Summary in English.

391b. *Šijaković, Miodrag. "Likovi Arbanasa u Bajronovim delima," *Gjurmime Albanologjike* (Prishtina), 1 (1962), 211–220.

Albanian characters in Byron's works. Summary in English.

392. *Simopoulos, Kyr. *Byron*. Athens: Editions Internationales, 1969. "Collection Les Grands Hommes de tous les temps, Vol. 21."

A profusely illustrated biography, possibly with selections from the poetry.

393. *Slingerland, H. "J. M. Heredia y José de Espronceda: ¿una conexión directa?" *Nueva Revista de Filología Hispánica*, 18, Nos. 3–4 (1970), 461–464.

Their common interest in Byron is discussed.

Speirs, John. See No. 145a.

394. Steffan, T. G. "Byron and Old Clothes: An Unpublished Letter," N&Q, 214 (Nov. 1969), 416–420.†

A letter of 28 Nov. 1822 from Byron to Captain Daniel Roberts.

395. *Stöhsel, Karl. *Lord Byrons Trauerspiel "Werner" und seine Quellen*. Amsterdam: Rodopi, 1970.

Reprint of an 1891 book.

Story, Patrick L. See No. 697.

396. *Stowe, Harriet Elizabeth. *Lady Byron Vindicated: A History of the Byron Controversy from Its Beginnings in 1816 to the Present Time*. New York: Haskell House, 1970.

Reprint of an 1870 book.

397. Cancelled.

398. Strauss, Walter A. *Descent and Return: The Orphic Theme in Modern Literature*. Cambridge, Mass.: Harvard Univ.; London: Oxford Univ. (1971).

References to Byron, Shelley, and Keats.

399. Stringham, Scott. "*I due Foscari*: From Byron's Play to Verdi's Opera," *West Virginia Univ. Philological Papers*, 17 (June 1970), 31–40.†‡

Discusses similarities and differences in Verdi's adaptation of Byron's play.

400. Sundell, Michael G. "The Development of 'The Giaour,' " SEL, 9 (Autumn 1969), 587–599.†‡

Byron's revisions of the poem in 1813 transformed it from a mere adventure story to one depicting "a mysterious and powerful character whose fate exemplifies humanity's."

Swanson, Donald R. See No. 151.

401. Szladits, Lola L. "New in the Berg Collection: 1962–1964," BNYPL, 73 (Apr. 1969), 227–252.

Godwin's *Imogen* (1784); Byron's MS of "Episode of Nisus and Euryalus."

401a. Talbot, Emile. "Considérations sur la définition stendhalienne du romantisme," *Stendhal Club*, 11 (July 1969), 327–336.

Byron was a principal influence on Stendhal's concept of Romanticism.

402. Thomas, P. G. *Aspects of Literary Theory and Practice 1550–1870*. Port Washington, N.Y.: Kennikat, 1970.

A reprint of the 1931 edition; includes chapters on Byron, Keats, and Shelley.

403. Trease, Geoffrey. *Byron: A Poet Dangerous to Know*. London: Macmillan; New York: Holt, Rinehart and Winston (1969).

Rev. in TLS, 4 Dec. 1969, p. 1391; by Polly Longsworth in NYT, 6 Sept. 1970, p. 16.

403a. *Trelawny, Edward John. *Recollections of the Last Days of Shelley and Byron*. Introduction by Edward Dowden. Freeport, N.Y.: Books for Libraries, 1971.

Reprint of 1906 edition.

Trewin, J. C. See No. 157.

404. Trousson, Raymond. *Le thème de Prométhée dans la littérature européenne*. See K-SJ, 15 (1966), No. 194, 16 (1967), No. 187, 18 (1969), No. 282, 19 (1970), No. 158.

Rev. by Roland Ball in CL, 21 (Winter 1969), 76–87.

405. Trueblood, Paul G. *Lord Byron*. See K-SJ, 19 (1970), No. 159.

Rev. by Joseph DeRocco in K-SJ, 19 (1970), 141–143; in *Choice*, 7 (May 1970), 388; by Frank McCambre in N&Q, 215 (May 1970), 199–200. Also see No. 117.

406. *Vernois, Paul, ed. *Le Réal dans la littérature et dans la langue*. Paris: Klincksieck, 1967.

Includes Miti Kataoka's "Le rôle du réal chez Goethe et chez Stendahl d'après leurs rapports parallèls avec Byron," p. 210.

407. Vickery, Walter N. "Byron's *Don Juan* and Pušhkińs *Evgenij Onegin*: The Question of Parallelism," *Indiana Slavic Studies*, 4 (1967), 181–191.

Sees parallels in plot, situations, characters, social commentary, and æsthetic impact in these two poems.

408. Viets, Henry R. "The Printings in America of Polidori's 'The Vampyre' in 1819," PBSA, 62 (July–Sept. 1968), 434–435.

Lack of magazine copyright allowed three American publishers to bring out editions of Polidori's short story by copying it from the *New Monthly Magazine* (London). Viets describes these editions.

409. *Voia, V. "Eminescu şi Byron. Un parallelism literar (II)," *Studia Universitatis Babes-Bolyai Series Philologica Cluj*, 14 (1969), 37–44.

410. Walker, Keith. "Byron," *New Society*, 13 Aug. 1970, pp. 280–282.

A general review of Byron's life, works, and radical propensities.

411. Wallace, Irving. "The Lovers," *Ladies Home Journal*, 88 (Feb. 1971), 127–133.

Excerpts from a forthcoming book, "The Nymphs and Other Maniacs." The article centers on Byron; Shelley is also mentioned.

412. Wallis, Bruce E. "Lord Byron's Critical Opinions" [Doctoral dissertation, Princeton, 1969], DAI, 30 (Sept. 1969), 1186-A.

413. Walton, Francis R. " 'On John William Rizzo Hoppner,' " BC, 19 (Autumn 1970), 384.

Requests location of copies of Byron's poem.

414. Watkin, David. *Thomas Hope, 1769–1831, and the Neo-Classical Idea.* London: John Murray, 1968.

Hope's novel *Anastasius*, published anonymously in 1819, was thought to be by Byron. Byron admired it and it may have influenced *Don Juan*. References to Haydon and Sir Bysshe Shelley.

Rev. by Ernle Money in *Contemporary Review*, 214 (Feb. 1969), 110–111; in *Choice*, 7 (July–Aug. 1970), 679.

414a. Watson, Harold Francis. *Coasts of Treasure Island: A Study of the Backgrounds and Sources for Robert Louis Stevenson's Romance of the Sea.* San Antonio, Tex.: Naylor, 1969.

Quotes passages from Frederick Chamier's autobiographical novel "The Life of a Sailor," serialized in the *Metropolitan*, May – Dec. 1831, describing Byron. Chamier was an officer on the *Salsette*, which carried Byron and Hobhouse from Malta to Greece in 1810. See pp. 35–38.

Watson, J[ohn]. R. See No. 162.

415. Weinstein, Mark A. *William Edmonstoune Aytoun and the Spasmodic Controversy.* See K-SJ, 18 (1969), No. 286.

Rev. by Erik Frykman in *Studia Neophilologica*, 42 (1970), 477–478.

416. Wellek, René. *Discriminations: Further Concepts of Criticism.* New Haven: Yale Univ., 1970.

Includes references to Byron, Hazlitt, Keats, and Shelley.

Rev. by Ben W. Fuson in LJ, 95 (15 Sept. 1970), 2920.

416a. West, William Edward. [Picture.] "Literary Portraits: II," *Library Chronicle* (Texas), N.S., No. 2 (Nov. 1970), pp. 46–47.

Reproduction of an 1822 oil portrait of Byron.

Wilkie, Brian. See No. 65.

417. Wilkins, Mary C. "Lord Byron Returns to Westminster," *Central Literary Magazine*, 40 (Spring 1970), 154–157.

Commemorates his being received into the Poets' Corner of Westminster Abbey on 8 May 1969.

417a. Wilkinson, Lise. "William Brockedon, F.R.S. (1787–1854)," *Notes and Records of the Royal Society of London*, 26 (June 1971), 65–72.

Writer, painter, inventor, Brockedon edited *Illustrations of the Life and Works of Lord Byron* (London 1833), which contained an engraving of a drawing he did of Teresa Guiccioli.

418. William, Misha, director. *Byron—The Naked Peacock.*

Drama on Byron, produced at the Young Vic.

Rev. by Irving Wardle in the *Times* (London), 7 Jan. 1971, p. 9.

419. Wolff, Tatiana, ed. *Pushkin on Literature*. London: Methuen, 1971.
References are made to Byron.
Rev. by Donald Davie in Li, 85 (17 June 1971), 789–790.

420. Woodberry, George E. *Makers of Literature*. Freeport, N.Y.: Books for Libraries; New York: Burt Franklin (1970).
Reprints of the 1900 edition; chapters on Byron and Shelley.

421. Woodhouse, C[hristopher]. M. "Byron and the First Hellenic Tourists," *Essays by Divers Hands*, 36 (1970), 147–166.†
Stresses Byron and Hobhouse's 1809 visit to Greece.

422. *Woodhouse, C[hristopher]. M. *The Philhellenes*. London: Hodder and Stoughton, 1969.
Discusses Byron in some detail. Keats, Shelley, and Trelawny are referred to as well.
Rev. by Sir Charles Petrie in ILN, 20 Sept. 1969, p. 26.

Woodring, Carl. See Nos. 65, 175.

423. Wordsworth, William, and Dorothy Wordsworth. *The Letters of William and Dorothy Wordsworth*. Vol. III: *The Middle Years. Part 2: 1812–1820*. Ed. Ernest De Selincourt. Second edition, revised by Mary Moorman and Alan G. Hill. Oxford: Clarendon, 1970.
Includes letters from William Wordsworth to Haydon, Hunt, and Reynolds. There are also references to Byron, Keats, and Shelley.
Rev. by W. J. B. Owen in MLR, 66 (Apr. 1971), 397–399.

424. Yarrow, P. J. "Three Plays of 1829, or Doubts about 1830," *Symposium*, 23 (Fall–Winter 1969), 373–383.
The subject and some of the details for Delavigné's *Marino Faliero* are taken from Byron's earlier work, but Yarrow concludes that Delavigné's "treatment is different and more dramatic."

425. *Zegger, R. E. "Greek Independence and the London Committee," *History Today*, 20 (Apr. 1970), 236–245.
Discusses Byron and Hobhouse.

426. *Zoras, G. *Ho Napoleon Bonapartēs kai hē synchronē Hellinikē Poiēsis*. Athens, 1969.
References to Byron.

III. HUNT

Works, Selected, Single

427. Coleman, Antony. "Leigh Hunt and Irish Politics," N&Q, 216 (March 1971), 88–90.
"Two unpublished letters of Leigh Hunt in the *Charles Gavan Duffy Papers* (National Library of Ireland MS. 5756) provide a modest addition to our knowledge of Hunt's political views."

Detz, Phyllis, Kermit M. Stover, and Betsy Schwartz, eds. See No. 181.

Flower, Desmond. See No. 183.

428. Jackson, James R. de J., ed. *Coleridge: The Critical Heritage*. London: Routledge and Kegan Paul, 1970.
Reviewers include Hunt and Hazlitt.
Rev. in TLS, 28 Aug. 1970, p. 946.

429. *Leigh Hunt's Letter on Hogg's Life of Shelley, with Other Papers*. Ed. Walter Edwin Peck. Folcroft, Pa.: Folcroft, 1969.
Reprint of 1927 edition.

430. Partridge, Eric, comp. *A Book of English Prose 1700–1914*. Freeport, N.Y.: Books for Libraries, 1970.
Reprint of the 1926 edition; includes Leigh Hunt's "A Chapter on Hats."

431. Reade, Brian, ed. *Sexual Heretics: Male Homosexuality in English Literature from 1850 to 1900*. London: Routledge and Kegan Paul, 1970.
Contains a selection, "Schooldays," from Leigh Hunt's *Autobiography*.
Rev. in *Times* (London), 19 Oct. 1970, p. 8; in TLS, 30 Oct. 1970, p. 1279.

432. Rowell, George, ed. *Victorian Dramatic Criticism*. London: Methuen, 1971.
Includes essays by Leigh Hunt, Lamb, and Hazlitt.
Rev. in TLS, 18 June 1971, p. 712.

433. *Six Letters of Leigh Hunt Adressed [sic] to W. W. Story, 1850–1856*. Folcroft, Pa.: Folcroft, 1969.
Reprint of 1913 edition. No editor given.

434. *Turner, James, ed. *Love Letters: An Anthology from the British Isles, 975–1944*. London: Cassell, 1970.
Includes letters from Hazlitt and Hunt.
Rev. in TLS, 6 Nov. 1970, p. 1296.

Books and Articles Relating to Hunt

Bain, Kenneth Bruce Findlater. See No. 198.

435. Blunden, Edmund. *Leigh Hunt: A Biography*. Hamden, Conn.: Archon, 1970.
A reprint of a book first published in 1930.

436. Brewer, Luther A. *My Leigh Hunt Library: The First Editions*. New York: Burt Franklin, 1970. "Bibliography & Reference Series, 326: Essays in Literature & Criticism, 58."
Reprint of a 1932 book.

437. Brewer, Luther A. *Some Lamb and Browning Letters to Leigh Hunt*. Folcroft, Pa.: Folcroft, 1969.
Reprint of a 1924 book.

Cooper, Robert M. See No. 235.

Donohue, Joseph W., Jr. See No. 61.

438. Duff, Gerald. "Leigh Hunt's Criticism of the Novel," *CLA Journal*, 13 (Dec. 1969), 109–118.
Though a great reader of novels, Hunt wrote little criticism of this form. His articles on novels fail to take into consideration the peculiar characteristics of this form, and instead apply critical criteria appropriate to drama. Though generally unsuccessful, such an approach sometimes yields insights.

Egbert, Donald D. See No. 794.

Elledge, W. Paul, and Richard L. Hoffman, eds. See No. 65.

439. Fenner, Theodore. "The Making of an Opera Critic: Leigh Hunt," *Musical Quarterly*, 45 (Oct. 1969), 439–463.†
His opera criticism for the *Examiner* from 1808 to 1822.

439a. Hudnall, Clayton E. "Leigh Hunt on Keats: Two New Poems," *Southern Humanities Review*, 4 (Fall 1970), 358–362.†‡
Reprints poems published in 1830 in *Mirror of Literature*, a London weekly.

440. *Johnson, Reginald Brimley. *Leigh Hunt*. New York: Haskell House, 1970.
Reprint of an 1896 book.

Kelly, Linda. See No. 613.

441. Kendall, Kenneth E. *Leigh Hunt's "Reflector."* The Hague and Paris: Mouton; New York: Humanities (1971).
Rev. by Louis Landré in EA, 24 (1971), 340–342.

Lean, E. Tangye. See No. 103.

Leary, Lewis G. See No. 65.

442. Levy, Robert H. "On the Pleasures of Forensic Rhetoric: Brougham and Gibbs in *Rex v. John and Leigh Hunt*," *Renaissance and Modern Studies*, 15 (1971), 85–102.
Rhetorical analysis of the speeches made by Brougham and Attorney General Vicary Gibbs at the Hunts' trial of 1811.

443. Lochhead, Marion. "Young Mr. Lockhart," *Blackwood's Magazine*, 304 (Sept. 1968), 213–224.
Discusses Lockhart's attacks on Hunt and Keats in *Blackwood's*.

Lutz, Paul V. See No. 311.

Margetson, Stella. See No. 111.

444. Masson, David I. "A Reminiscence of Clara Novello," *Music and Letters*, 50 (Oct. 1969), 481.
An addition to the Novello-Cowden Clarke Collection at the University of Leeds.

Merivale, Patricia. See No. 116.

445. Miller, Barnette. *Leigh Hunt's Relations with Byron, Shelley, and Keats*. Folcroft, Pa.: Folcroft, 1969.
Reprint of a 1910 book.

Mordell, Albert, ed. See No. 339.

446. Nowell-Smith, Simon. "Leigh Hunt as Bellman," TLS, 2 Apr. 1970, p. 367. Reply by Betty T. Bennett in TLS, 16 Apr. 1970, p. 430.
Bellman's verses, "demy broadsides embellished with a woodcut illustration of beadles or town-criers and with pictorial or ornamental woodcut borders," were sold door-to-door at Christmas time. Hunt wrote at least nine of these while under the apprenticeship of Henry Reynell.

447. Praz, Mario. *Mnemosyne: the Parallel between Literature and the Visual Arts*. The A. W. Mellon Lectures in the Fine Arts, 1967. Princeton: Princeton Univ., 1970. "Bollingen Series, 35, vol. 16."
References to Hazlitt, Hunt, and Keats.
Rev. in *Choice*, 7 (July–Aug. 1970), 674.

Raimond, Jean. See No. 372.

448. "Recent Acquisitions," *Books at Iowa*, No. 10 (Apr. 1969), pp. 35–38.
University of Iowa acquires Hunt and Hazlitt items.

449. "Recent Acquisitions," *Books at Iowa*, No. 12 (Apr. 1970), pp. 40–45.
University of Iowa acquires Hunt, Haydon, and B. W. Procter items.

Schoenbaum, S. See No. 387.

450. *Severn, Derek. "Leigh Hunt v. the Tories and the Prince Regent," *Cornhill Magazine*, No. 1066 (Winter 1970–1971), pp. 288–312.

451. Tatchell, Molly. *Leigh Hunt and His Family in Hammersmith*. See K-SJ, 18 (1970), No. 174.
Rev. by M. R. Huxstep in CLSB (Oct. 1969), pp. 637–638.

452. Tatchell, Molly. "Thornton Hunt," KSMB, 20 (1969), 13–20.
A biographical essay on Leigh Hunt's eldest son.

Trewin, J. C. See No. 157.

453. Williamson, Jane. *Charles Kemble: Man of the Theatre*. Lincoln: Univ. of Nebraska, 1970.
References to Hunt and Hazlitt.
Rev. in *Choice*, 7 (Sept. 1970), 861.

Woodring, Carl. See No. 175.

Wordsworth, William, and Dorothy Wordsworth. See No. 423.

IV. KEATS

Works: Collected, Selected, Single, Translated

454. Bond, W[illiam]. H. "Keats's Letter to Reynolds, 17 April 1818," K-SJ, 20 (1971), 17–19.
Reprinted for the first time from the original. The previously given date of 10 Apr. 1818 is corrected.

455. **A Choice of Keats's Verse*. Selected and introduced by C. Day Lewis. London: Faber, 1971.

456. **The Complete Works of John Keats*. Ed. H. Buxton Forman. 5 vols. New York: AMS, 1970.
Reprint of 1900–1901 edition.

Detz, Phyllis, Kermit M. Stover, and Betsy Schwartz, eds. See No. 181.

Downer, Arthur C. See No. 535.

457. Erzgräber, Willi, ed. *Englische Lyrik von Shakespeare bis Dylan Thomas*. Darmstadt: Wissenschaftliche Buchgesellschaft, 1969.
Includes Keats's "Ode to a Nightingale" and R. H. Fogle's article on it from PMLA (see K-SJ, 3 [1954], No. 147); Shelley's "Mont Blanc" and Earl R. Wasserman's essay on it from *The Subtler Language* (see K-SJ, 9 [1960], No. 500).

458. *Hartwig, Holger. *Traum und Umnachtung*. Berlin: G. Rump, 1968.
Includes poems by Keats.

Ikonomu, Mer. See No. 594.

459. **John Keats: A Thematic Reader*. Ed. Joseph Sendry and Richard Giannone. Glenview, Ill.: Scott, Foresman, 1971.

460. *Keats at Wentworth Place: Poems Written December 1818 to September 1820*. Introduction by Dorothy Hewlett. London: London Borough of Camden, 1971.
Paperback.
Rev. in TLS, 2 Apr. 1971, pp. 365–366.

461. **Lamia, Isabella, The Eve of St. Agnes, and Other Poems, 1820*. Menston, Yorkshire: Scolar, 1970.
Facsimile of first edition.

462. *Letters of John Keats: A New Selection*. Ed. Robert Gittings. London: Oxford Univ., 1970.
Paperback.

463. **Liriche scelte*. Second Edition. Ed. E. Buonpane. Milan: Dante Alighieri, 1969. [In Italian.]

464. **Meteora* (1968).
A journal of the arts, which includes Greek translations of poetry by Keats.

465. **Nea Hestia* (1969).
A Greek literary periodical, which includes translations of poetry by Keats.

466. *The Odes of Keats and Their Earliest Known Manuscripts*. Introduction, with notes, by Robert Gittings. London: Heinemann; Kent, Ohio: Kent State Univ. (1970).
Rev. by Charles W. Mann, Jr., in LJ, 95 (1 Sept. 1970), 2804; by Rodney G. Dennis in K-SJ, 20 (1971), 129; by Helen Vendler in SIR, 10 (Winter 1971), 65–69; in TLS, 2 Apr. 1971, pp. 365–366; in *Choice*, 8 (May 1971), 390.

467. *Poems and Selected Letters*. Ed. and introduced by Carlos Baker. New York: Scribners, 1970. "Scribner Library Lyceum Edition."
A paperback reprint of the 1962 edition.

468. *Poems by John Keats*. Illustrated by R. Anning Bell. London: Bell, 1971.
Reprinted from the *Endymion* series of illustrated poets, 1898.

469. *The Poems of John Keats*. Ed. Miriam Allott. London: Longman, 1970. "Longman Annotated English Poets."
Rev. by Jack Stillinger in K-SJ, 20 (1971), 122–129; in TLS, 2 Apr. 1971, pp. 365–366.

470. *The Poetical Works and Other Writings of John Keats*. Ed. with notes and appendices by H. Buxton Forman. Revised with additions by Maurice Buxton Forman. With an introduction by John Masefield. 8 vols. New York: Phaeton, 1970. "Hampstead Edition."
Reprint of 1939 edition.

471. **The Prelude to Poetry: The English Poets in Defence and Praise of Their Own Art*. Introduction by Ernest Rhys. London: Dent, 1971. "Everyman's Library."
This reissue, which first appeared in 1927, contains passages from Keats's letters.

472. **Selected Poems of John Keats*. Illustrated by Charles Mozley. New York: Watts, 1970.
An edition for young people.

473. *Selected Poetry and Letters*. Revised Edition. Ed. Richard Harter Fogle. New York: Holt, Rinehart and Winston, 1969.
A revision of the original 1951 edition. See K-SJ, 2 (1953), No. 66.

Yofyllis, Fot. See No. 753.

Books and Articles Relating to Keats and His Circle

474. *Abad, Gemino. "Imaginary Gardens with Real Toads: A Study of Keats' 'Poetics,' " *Diliman Review*, 13 (Oct. 1965), 407–419.†
On negative capability.

475. Abrams, M. H. "Coleridge, Baudelaire, and Modernist Poetics," in *Immanente Ästhetik–Ästhetische Reflexion: Lyrik als Paradigma der Moderne*, ed. W. Iser (Munich: Fink, 1966), pp. 113–138.
Mentions Keats, Shelley, Hazlitt.
Rev. by Richard Palmer in *Criticism*, 13 (Winter 1971), 95–102.

476. Abu-Shawareb, Hassan Muhammed Hassan. "Keats's Prescription for Man's Salvation: Theory and Practice" [Doctoral dissertation, South Carolina, 1970], DAI, 31 (Apr. 1971), 5347-A.

477. Adlard John. "John Clare: The Long Walk Home," *English*, 19 (Autumn 1970), 85–89.†
A general discussion of Clare and some of his works.

478. Albrecht, W. P. *Hazlitt and the Creative Imagination*. See K-SJ, 16 (1967), No. 214, 17 (1968), No. 303, 18 (1969), No. 347, 19 (1970), No. 182.
Rev. by Teut Andreas Riese in ASNS, 206 (Oct. 1969), 224–225.

Albrecht, W. P. See No. 122.

479. Cancelled.

480. *Albrecht, William P. *William Hazlitt and the Malthusian Controversy*. Port Washington, N.Y., and London: Kennikat, 1969.
Reprint of a 1950 book.

481. Allott, Miriam. "Keats and Wordsworth," KSMB, 22 (1971), 28–43.
Keats's poetry was influenced by Wordsworthian themes and preoccupations, particularly those "concerned with the nature of the poetic imagination and the successive stages of personal development."

482. Amis, Kingsley. *What Became of Jane Austen?, and Other Questions*. New York: Harcourt, Brace and World, 1971.
Refers to Keats, pp. 21–25.

483. Anderson, James Blakely, Jr. "Ambiguity and Paradox in the Poetry of Keats" [Doctoral dissertation, Tulane, 1969], DAI, 30 (Dec. 1969), 2474-A–2475-A.

484. Andrews, C. T. "Keats and Mercury," KSMB, 20 (1969), 37–43.
Argues that the available evidence does not suggest Keats took mercury in 1817 to treat a venereal disease.

485. Archibald, Douglas N. "Yeats's Encounters: Observations on Literary Influence and Literary History," *New*

Literary History, 1 (Spring 1970), 439–469.

Includes a brief discussion of Milton's "burdensome" influence on Keats's "Hyperion" poems.

Arnold, Matthew. See No. 194.

485a. *Bagchi, Krishna. "Keats' Sensuousness Re-Defined," *University of Rajastan Studies in English*, No. 4 (1969), 103–110.

Bain, Kenneth Bruce Findlater. See No. 198.

486. Bate, Walter Jackson. *The Burden of the Past and the English Poet*. Cambridge, Mass.: Harvard Univ., 1970.

An expansion of an essay that originally appeared in 1965. See K-SJ, 17 (1968), No. 13. Bate's survey of English writers between 1660 and 1830 includes Keats.

Rev. by Nathan Comfort Starr in LJ, 95 (15 March 1970), 1028–1029; in WC, 1 (Spring 1970), 75; in *Choice*, 7 (May 1970), 382; by Roger Sale in *Hudson Review*, 23 (Summer 1970), 364; by Benjamin Boyce in ELN, 8 (March 1971), 242–243; by George W. Nitchie in *Criticism*, 13 (Winter 1971), 107–108.

Bate, Walter Jackson. See No. 46.

Bayley, John. See No. 37.

487. Beall, Chandler. "Eugenio Montale's *Sarcofaghi*," in *Linguistic and Literary Studies in Honor of Helmut A. Hatzfeld*, ed. Allessandro S. Crisafulli. See K-SJ, 17 (1968), No. 312.

Rev. by Elio Gianturco in CL, 23 (Winter 1971), 60–66.

488. Beer, Gillian. "Aesthetic Debate in Keats's Odes," MLR, 64 (Oct. 1969), 742–748.†

Using Bate's observation that each of the odes presents "a miniature drama," the author suggests readings of "Ode to Psyche," "Ode to a Nightingale," and "Ode on a Grecian Urn."

489. Bell, Arthur H. "Madeline's House Is Not Her Castle," K-SJ, 20 (1971), 11–14.

The spatial dimensions and physical relationships that Keats took pains to establish in "The Eve of St. Agnes" suggest the poem is set in a medieval manor house rather than a castle.

490. Benvenuto, Richard. "La Belle Dame and the Pale Kings: Life's High Meed," *Michigan Academician*, 2 (Summer 1969), 57–62.†‡

The Knight cannot come to terms with death. "He stops living because he refuses to pay the price of living, which is death. He is left lifeless because he was afraid to die."

491. Beyer, Werner W. *Keats and the Daemon King*. New York: Octagon, 1969.

Reprint of a 1947 book.

491a. *Bidwell, Julie. "An Appreciation of Keats," *Nexus*, 1 (1967), 35–37.

492. *Birrell, Augustine. *William Hazlitt*. Westport, Conn.: Greenwood, 1970. "English Men of Letters."

Reprint of a 1902 book.

493. [Blatt, Thora Balslev.] Balslev, Thora. *Keats and Wordsworth: A Comparative Study*. Folcroft, Pa.: Folcroft, 1969.

Reprint of a 1962 book. See K-SJ, 13 (1964), No. 283, 15 (1966), No. 238, 18 (1969), No. 354, 19 (1970), No. 184.

Bloom, Harold, ed. See No. 46.

Bloom, Harold. See Nos. 45, 48.

494. *Blunden, Edmund. *John Clare: Beginner's Luck*. Waterbury, Kent: Bridge, 1971.

Limited edition of 250.

Blunden, Edmund. See No. 212.

495. Blunden, Edmund. *Shakespeare to Hardy: Short Studies of Characteristic English Authors*. Folcroft, Pa.: Folcroft, 1969.

Reprint of the 1948 edition; includes chapters on Keats, Peacock, and Shelley.

496. Blunden, Edmund. *Sons of Light: A Series of Lectures on English Writers*. Folcroft, Pa.: Folcroft, 1969.

Reprint of 1945 edition; contains an essay on John Clare.

497. Booth, Michael R., ed. *English Plays of the Nineteenth Century*. Vol. I: *Drama, 1800–1850*. See K-SJ, 19 (1970), No. 190.

Rev. in TLS, 24 July 1969, p. 829; by Marguerite McAneny in LJ, 14 (Aug. 1969), 2803; by William Angus in QQ, 76 (Winter 1969), 724–725; by Paul D. Herring in MP, 68 (Aug. 1970), 83–90; by Kurt Tetzeli v. Rosador in ASNS, 207 (Sept. 1970), 199–208; by Peter Davison in MLR, 65 (Oct. 1970), 884–886; by Robert Quentin in AUMLA, No. 34 (Nov. 1970), pp. 329–331; by George Rowell in RES, 21 (Nov. 1970), 31–32;

in *Choice*, 7 (May 1970), 400; by Sybil Rosenfeld in *Theatre Research*, 11 (1971), 61.

497a. Bowen, James K. "More on Hawthorne and Keats," *American Transcendental Quarterly*, 2 (Second Quarter 1969), 12.

A passage in Hawthorne's notebook apparently inspired by Keats's "Isabella."

Briggs, Asa, ed. See No. 49.

498. Brooks, Cleanth. *The Well Wrought Urn: Studies in the Structure of Poetry*. Revised Edition. London: Dobson, 1968.

First published in 1947. Contains an essay on "Ode on a Grecian Urn."

499. Brown, Charles Armitage. *Life of John Keats*. Ed. Dorothy Hyde Bodurtha and Willard Bissell Pope. Folcroft, Pa.: Folcroft, 1969.

Reprint of 1937 edition.

500. Bunn, James H. "Keats's *Ode to Psyche* and the Transformation of Mental Landscape," ELH, 37 (Dec. 1970), 581–594.

The poem's main purpose "is to represent retrospectively the process by which the poet's mind has become animated and transformed by Psyche."

500a. Bunn, James Harry, III. "The Palace of Art: A Study of Form in Retrospective Poems about the Creative Process" [Doctoral dissertation, Emory, 1969], DAI, 30 (Apr. 1970), 4400-A.

Keats's "Ode to Psyche" and "The Fall of Hyperion."

501. Burke, Kenneth. *Language as Symbolic Action. Essays on Life, Literature, and Method.* See K-SJ, 17 (1968), No. 321.

Rev. by Edward Engleberg in "For Interpretation," *Southern Review* (L.S.U.), N.S. 5 (Autumn 1969), 1260–1270.

Burnett, Joan N. See No. 772.

Burton, Elizabeth. See No. 51.

Bush, Douglas. See No. 52.

Cheney, Thomas E. See No. 225.

502. Clare, John. *Dwellers in the Wood: Two Poems*. Illustrated by Harold Goodwin. New York: Macmillan; London: Collier-Macmillan (1971).

Children's book, first published in 1967.

503. Clare, John. *The Letters of John Clare*. Ed. J. W. Tibble and Anne Tibble. London: Routledge and Kegan Paul; New York: Barnes and Noble (1970).

A reprint of a book first published in 1951.

504. *Clare, John. *The Poet Clare*. Pilgrim Cottage, Wilbarston, Market Harborough, Leicester: Pilgrim Publications, 1970.

505. Clare, John. *The Prose of John Clare*. Ed. J. W. Tibble and Anne Tibble. New York: Barnes and Noble, 1970.

A reprint of a book first published in 1951.

506. Clare, John. *Selected Poems*. Ed. Elaine Feinstein. London: University Tutorials, 1968.

507. *Clare, John. [Selections.] Harlow, Essex: Longmans, 1969. "Longmans Poetry Library."

507a. Clare, John. "Unpublished Poems by John Clare," ed. Eric Robinson and Geoffrey Summerfield, *Malahat Review*, No. 2 (Apr. 1967), pp. 106–120.

508. Clarke, Charles Cowden, and Mary C. Clarke. *Recollections of Writers*. See K-SJ, 19 (1970), No. 199.

Rev. in TLS, 24 July 1969, p. 839.

509. Clement, Peter William. "The Fine Isolated Versimilitudes of John Keats: A Sequential Study of the Letters" [Doctoral dissertation, Massachusetts, 1970], DAI, 31 (Nov. 1970), 2337-A.

510. Cancelled.

511. Clubbe, John. *Victorian Forerunner: The Later Career of Thomas Hood*. See K-SJ, 19 (1970), No. 201.

Rev. by Peter F. Morgan in JEGP, 68 (1969), 716–718; by Michael Slater in *Dickensian*, 66 (Jan. 1970), 59–60; by Barbara Dennis in *Durham Univ. Journal*, 62 (March 1970), 126; by Paul Turner in RES, 21 (May 1970), 249–250; by William G. Lane in MP, 68 (May 1971), 390–392.

512. Cohn, Robert Greer. "Keats and Mallarmé," *Comparative Literature Studies*, 7 (June 1970), 195–203.†‡

Argues that Keats and Mallarmé shared an essentially similar aesthetic outlook and that specific poems by Keats influenced specific works of Mallarmé.

Coleman, William E. See No. 54a.

513. *"Coleridge, Hazlitt and Romanticism," WC, 2 (Winter 1971), 23–25.

A survey of recent scholarship.

Colville, Derek. See No. 233.

514. Colvin, Sidney. *John Keats: His Life and Poetry; His Friends, Critics, and After-Fame*. New York: Octagon, 1970.
Reprint of 1917 work published by Scribner's.
Rev. in *Choice*, 7 (Dec. 1970), 1372.

515. Connolly, Paul Howard Thomas. "William Hazlitt: The Validity of Critical Impressionism" [Doctoral dissertation, Virginia, 1969], DAI, 30 (March 1970), 3938-A.

Cooper, Robert M. See No. 235.

516. Cancelled.

517. Cummings, Frederick, and Allen Staley. *Romantic Art in Britain: Paintings and Drawings, 1760–1860*. N.p.: Falcon, 1968.
Includes Haydon.
Rev. by Johannes L. Dewton in LJ, 95 (15 Jan. 1970), 147.

518. Danzig, Allan, ed. *Twentieth Century Interpretations of "The Eve of St. Agnes": A Collection of Critical Essays*. Englewood Cliffs, N.J.: Prentice-Hall, 1971.

519. Das, B. "Process and Reality in the Odes of Keats," *Indian Journal of English Studies*, 11 (1970), 17–33.
Keats's odes are "a progress from an awareness of death-in-life to that of life-in-death, an awareness of reality in the midst of process."

520. Das, Sisir Kumar. "Bright Star: An Attempt at Interpretation," *Bulletin of the Department of English (Calcutta Univ.)*, N.S. 4, No. 2 (1968–1969), 1–8.†
"Bright Star" integrates the height of mortal life with the desire for its continuation in a post mortal paradise.

520a. D'Avanzo, Mario L. "Frost's 'A Young Birch': a Thing of Beauty," *Concerning Poetry*, 3 (Fall 1970), 69–70.†
The poem is related to Keats's *Endymion*.

521. D'Avanzo, Mario L. "Keats' 'If by Dull Rhymes,' " *Research Studies*, 38 (March 1970), 29–35.
A close analysis of the language and form of this sonnet.

522. D'Avanzo, Mario L. *Keats's Metaphors for the Poetic Imagination*. See K-SJ, 17 (1968), No. 333, 18 (1969), No. 390, 19 (1970), No. 206.
Rev. by I[rene]. H. C[hayes]. in ELN, 8, Supplement (Sept. 1970), 37–38.

523. *Davis, F. "Talking about Sale-Rooms," *Country Life*, 149 (7 Jan. 1971), 11.
Includes reproduction of De Wint's "Cart Horses by a Tree."

524. Dawson, Leven Magruder. "Mutability and Irony in the Poetry of John Keats" [Doctoral dissertation, Rice, 1970], DAI, 31 (Dec. 1970), 2872-A.

525. "Day-Lewis Leads Tribute to Keats," *Times* (London), 24 Feb. 1971, p. 6.
Graveside memorial led by C. D. Lewis in Italy on 23 Feb. 1971.

526. DeFrees, Madeline. "Freshman Keats in an Un-Homeric Epoch," *College Composition and Communication*, 22 (May 1971), 175–176.
Not about Keats; satire on Freshman literature papers.

526a. Deguchi, Yasuo. "Keats to Catholicism," *Eigo Seinen: Rising Generation* (Tokyo), 115 (June 1969), 362–363. [In Japanese.]

527. *Delesalle, Jean-François. "Baudelaire et Keats," *Études Baudelairiennes*, 2 (1971), 189–195.

528. Del Re, Gabriele. "Sensibilità fisiologica e mito in John Keats," *English Miscellany*, 22 (1971), 155–172.

529. De Wint, Peter. ["A Cornfield," Picture.] *Country Life*, 147 (22 Jan. 1970), 181.
Reproduction of the 1815 painting.

530. De Wint, Peter. ["A Cornfield," Picture.] *Times* (London), 10 Feb. 1970, p. 9.
Part of an exhibition, "A Decade of English Naturalism, 1810–1820," at the Victoria and Albert Museum.

531. De Wint, Peter. An exhibition.
Sketches and watercolors; "Agnew's 98th annual exhibition of English watercolours and drawings."
Rev. by William Gaunt in *Times* (London), 21 Jan. 1971, p. 9.

531a. De Wint, Peter. ["La Moisson," Picture.] *Gazette des Beaux Arts*, 77 (Feb. 1971), Supplement, 125.
A black -and-white reproduction of a crayon sketch.

532. *D'Haen, Christine. "Verwantschap tussen Engelse poëzie en Gezelles poëzie,"

Gezellekroniek, 6 (Kapellen: Guido-Gezellegenootschap, 1970).

Keats and Shelley are among those compared with Gezelle.

533. Dickie, James. "The Grecian Urn: An Archaeological Approach," *Bulletin of the John Rylands Library, Manchester,* 52 (Autumn 1969), 96–114.†

Argues that Keats was influenced by several vases (especially the Borghese), by Claude, and by literary sources.

534. Dickstein, Morris. *Keats and His Poetry: A Study in Development.* Chicago and London: Univ. of Chicago, 1971.

Rev. by Thomas Lask in *New York Times,* 20 March 1971, p. 27; by Helen Vendler in NYT, 21 March 1971, pp. 5, 50; by Nathan Comfort Starr in LJ, 96 (15 May 1971) 1713,.

Dobrée, Bonamy. See No. 249.

Donohue, Joseph W. See No. 61.

535. Downer, Arthur C. *The Odes of Keats, with Notes and Analyses and a Memoir.* Folcroft, Pa.: Folcroft, 1969.

Reprint of an 1897 book.

536. Dube, Gunakar. "Autumn in Frost and Keats: A Study of Themes and Patterns," *Literary Criterion,* 9 (Summer 1971), 84–88.

"Keats was a Greek in spirit" and the four personifications of "To Autumn" "reveal his close 'affinity with the mythical imagination of the Greeks.' "

537. Duff, Gerald. "William Cobbett and the Prose of Revelation," *Texas Studies in Literature and Language,* 11 (Winter 1970), 1349–1365.‡

Hazlitt's description of Cobbett's prose style is included, and Hazlitt's own prose is compared with Cobbett's.

538. Duffin, H. C. "Beauty into Happiness at Rylestone," *The Aryan Path,* 40 (Aug. 1969), 343–346.

"Like Keats's nightingale the Doe is immortal. . . ."

538a. Eggenschwiler, David. "Nightingales and Byzantine Birds, Something Less Than Kind," ELN, 8 (March 1971), 186–191.

Keats compared to Yeats.

Elledge, W. Paul, and Richard L. Hoffman, eds. See No. 65.

539. Ende, Stuart Alan. "Vision and Consciousness in Keats's Poetry" [Doctoral dissertation, Cornell, 1970], DAI, 31 (June 1971), 6601-A–6602-A.

540. Enscoe, Gerald. *Eros and the Romantics: Sexual Love as a Theme in Coleridge, Shelley, and Keats.* See K-SJ, 18 (1969), No. 394, 19 (1970), No. 208.

Rev. by P. H. Butter in MLR, 64 (1969), 653–654; by D[avid]. V. E[rdman]. in ELN, 8, Supplement (Sept. 1970), 15.

541. *Evans. "Keats—the Man, Medicine and Poetry," *British Medical Journal,* 3 (5 July 1969), 7–11.

542. *Evans, B. Ifor. *Keats.* St. Clair Shores, Mich.: Scholarly, 1971. "Great Lives, 32."

Reprint of a 1934 book.

543. Faber, M. D. "Metaphor and Reality," *Dalhousie Review,* 49 (Winter 1969–1970), 497–504.

Because it eschews metaphor, the *haiku* reveals more about reality than Western poetry, represented by Shakespeare, Wordsworth, and Keats.

544. Farmer, Susan. "A Question about Keats" [Poem], *Meanjin Quarterly,* 28 (Sept. 1969), 348.

545. Feldman, Alan. "On Meeting Keats and Shelley in Rome, 1952" [Poem], *New American Review,* No. 13 (1971), pp. 165–166.

546. Fitzsimons, Raymund. *Barnum in London.* New York: St. Martin's, 1970.

Material on Benjamin Robert Haydon.

547. Fleissner, Robert F. "Frost's Response to Keats' Risibility," *Ball State Univ. Forum,* 11 (Winter 1970), 40–43.

The demonic creative impulse is a theme in both "Why did I laugh tonight?" and "The Demi-Urge's Laugh."

548. Foakes, R. A. *Romantic Criticism 1800–1850.* Columbia: Univ. of South Carolina, 1971.

A paperback reprint of a book first published in 1968. See K-SJ, 18 (1969), No. 327, 19 (1970), No. 177.

549. *Fogle, Richard Harter. *The Imagery of Keats and Shelley: A Comparative Study.* Chapel Hill: Univ. of North Carolina, 1969.

Paperback reprint of a 1949 book.

Fogle, Richard Harter. See No. 457.

550. Ford, Newell F. "Holy Living and Holy Dying in Keats's Poetry," K-SJ, 20 (1971), 37–61.

Discerns a pervasiveness of religious tone and imagery throughout Keats's poetry, emphasizing either imagined death and consequent salvation or celebrating holy life.

550a. Frascato, Gerald. "John Keats 'In Thrall,' " *Malahat Review*, No. 11 (July 1969), pp. 113–119.†

Biographical interpretation of "La Belle Dame sans Merci."

551. Fraser, G. S., ed. *John Keats: "Odes"—A Casebook*. London: Macmillan, 1971. "Casebook Series."

Paperback.

552. "From Corpses to Copses: John Keats and the Enjoyment of Life," TLS, 2 Apr. 1971, pp. 365–366. Replies by Robert Gittings in TLS, 9 Apr. 1971, p. 422; by Timothy Hewlett and Alan Osler, 16 Apr. 1971, p. 449; by George H. Ford, 23 Apr. 1971, p. 476.

An omnibus review. See Nos. 460, 466, 469.

553. Frosch, Thomas R. "The Descriptive Style of John Clare," SIR, 10 (Spring 1971), 137–149.†‡

The landscapes in Clare's poetry reveal the poet's attempt "to come to terms with the problematical experience of change."

553a. *Gabrielli, Vittorio. "Keats, la verità della bellezza," *Stampa*, 17 Feb. 1971, p. 3.

554. Gelfant, Blanche H. "Faulkner and Keats: The Ideality of Art in 'The Bear,' " *Southern Literary Journal*, 2 (Fall 1969), 43–65.

Describes the relevance of Keats's ideas and imagery to Faulkner's story.

555. George, A. "Bright Star: A Commentary on Keats's Sonnet," UES, 7 (Nov. 1969), 64–66.

Characterizes the sonnet as "a curious blend of objective writing and romantic confessional outpouring."

556. George, Eric. *The Life and Death of Benjamin Robert Haydon, Historical Painter, 1786–1846*. See K-SJ, 18 (1969), No. 401, 19 (1970), No. 213.

Rev. by Kenneth Garlick in *Apollo*, 91 (Feb. 1970), 168.

557. Gerard, Albert S. *English Romantic Poetry: Ethos, Structure, and Symbol in Coleridge, Wordsworth, Shelley, and Keats*. See K-SJ, 18 (1969), No. 402, 19 (1970), No. 214.

Rev. by Karl Kroeber in *Comparative Literature Studies*, 7 (March 1970), 117–119; by Jeanne Delbaere-Garant in *Revue des langues vivantes*, 37 (1971), 111.

558. Gittings, Robert. *John Keats*. See K-SJ, 18 (1969), No. 403, 19 (1970), No. 216.

Rev. by Sylva Norman in *Aryan Path*, 39 (Sept. 1968), 414–415; by U. Laredo in UES, 7 (Sept. 1969), 110–112; by I[rene]. H. C[hayes]. in ELN, 7, Supplement (Sept. 1969), 36–37; by James Kissane in SR, 78, No. 1 (1970), 203–211; by Kerry McSweeney in QQ, 77 (Spring 1970), 125–126.

559. *Gittings, Robert. *John Keats*. Boston: Atlantic Monthly, 1968. Paperback.

560. *Gittings, Robert. *John Keats*. Harmondsworth: Penguin, 1971.

Paperback edition of book published by Heinemann in 1968.

561. Gittings, Robert. "The Poetry of John Hamilton Reynolds," *Ariel*, 1 (Oct. 1970), 7–17.

A sketch of Reynolds' life and work, with emphasis on his family background as contributing to his lack of success.

562. Goldberg, Milton A. *The Poetics of Romanticism: Toward a Reading of John Keats*. See K-SJ, 19 (1970), No. 217.

Rev. in *Choice*, 6 (Sept. 1969), 816; in TLS, 18 Sept. 1969, p. 1021; by I[rene]. H. C[hayes]. in ELN, 8 Supplement (Sept. 1970), 38. Also see Nos. 109a, 117.

Goodheart, Eugene. See No. 267.

563. *Gray, Bennison. *Style: The Problem and Its Solution*. The Hague: Mouton, 1969.

Discusses two odes by Keats.

Rev. by M. Mincoff in MLR, 66 (Jan. 1971), 162–163.

564. Gribble, James. "Logical and Psychological Considerations in the Criticism of F. R. Leavis," *British Journal of Aesthetics*, 10 (Jan. 1970), 39–57.

Brief discussion of Leavis' criticism of Keats and Shelley.

565. Grigson, Geoffrey. *Poems and Poets.* See K-SJ, 19 (1970), No. 219.
Rev. by Janet Fletcher in LJ, 95 (1 Jan. 1970), 72; by Michael Mott in *Poetry*, 116 (1970), 46.

566. Groninger, Barbara Hutchison. "The Hyperion Poems: The Failure of Keats's Epic Ambitions" [Doctoral dissertation, Cornell, 1970], DAI, 31 (July 1970), 388-A.

566a. *Groot, H. B. de. "Albert Verweys, Keats en Matthew Arnold," *De Nieuwe Taalgids*, 61 (1968), 36–48.

567. Guilhamet, Leon M. "Keats's 'Negative Capability' and 'Disinterestedness': A Confusion of Ideals," UTQ, 40 (Fall 1970), 2–14.
A close study of Keats's use of these terms, with stress upon their troublesome relationship to each other.

568. Hamburger, Michael. *The Truth of Poetry: Tensions in Modern Poetry from Baudelaire to the 1960's.* London: Weidenfeld and Nicolson; New York: Harcourt, Brace and World (1970).
Includes references to Keats.
Rev. by John W. Charles in LJ, 95 (1 June 1970), 2158.

568a. Hamilton, James W. "Object Loss, Dreaming, and Creativity: The Poetry of John Keats," *The Psychoanalytic Study of the Child*, 24 (1969), 488–531.
Thesis is "that poetry represented for Keats an attempt to work through the mourning process [for death of his mother] and that dreaming was integrally related to his creative output."

Hargreaves-Mawdsley, W. N. See No. 276.

569. Harrison, Elizabeth. "John Keats, Dead one Hundred and Fifty Years, 23 February 1821" [Poem], QQ, 78 (Spring 1971), 18.

569a. Hartman, Geoffrey. "History-Writing as Answerable Style," *New Literary History*, 2 (Autumn 1970), 73–83.
Quotes Keats on the relationship between ideas and art.

570. Hartman, Geoffrey. "Toward Literary History," *Daedalus*, 99 (Spring 1970), 355–383.
Includes a phenomenological interpretation of "Hyperion," III.

Hassett, Michael E. See No. 85.

571. *Haworth, Helen E. "Arnold's Keats," *Revue de l'Université d'Ottawa*, 41 (Apr.–June 1971), 245–252.

572. Haworth, Helen E. "Emerson's Keats," HLB, 19 (Jan. 1971), 61–70.
Ignoring all else "Emerson took from Keats . . . a few lovely passages which represent the incredible beauty of the natural world and which on occasion express faith in the ultimate goodness and unity of man" with nature, art, and his culture.

573. Haworth, Helen E. "Keats's Copy of Lamb's *Specimens of English Dramatic Poets*," BNYPL, 74 (Sept. 1970), 419–427.‡
Keats's copy is in the Berg Collection of the New York Public Library.

574. Haworth, Helen E. "The Titans, Apollo, and the Fortunate Fall in Keats's Poetry," SEL, 10 (Autumn 1970), 637–649.†‡
"Hyperion," although a pagan narrative, echoes the Christian tradition of the Fortunate Fall apparent in the account of Adam and Eve, as well as Satan, in *Paradise Lost.*

575. Hayden, John O., ed. *Scott: The Critical Heritage.* London: Routledge and Kegan Paul, 1970. "The Critical Heritage Series."
Hazlitt's essay is included, as well as Peacock's "Mr. Chainmail and the Enchanter" from *Crotchet Castle.*
Rev. by Robert Alter in SR, 10 Oct. 1970, pp. 27–29; by Janet Adam Smith in *Times* (London) 2 Nov. 1970, p. 11; in TLS, 8 Jan. 1971, pp. 40–41.

Hayden, John O., ed. See No. 86.

576. Hazlitt, Margaret. *The Journal of Margaret Hazlitt: Recollections of England, Ireland, and America.* Ed. Ernest J. Moyne. See K-SJ, 18 (1969), No. 421, 19 (1970), No. 224.
Rev. by J[ohn]. E. J[ordan]. in ELN, 7, Supplement (Sept. 1969), 34–35; by Lodowick Hartley in *Studies in Burke and His Time*, 11 (Fall 1969), 1408–1409; by Rachel Trickett in N&Q, 214 (Dec. 1969), 480.

577. *Hazlitt, William. *Men and Manners: Sketches and Essays.* London: Ward Lock, 1970.

Reprint of first edition, 1852.

578. *Hazlitt, William. *Selected Essays.* Ed. John R. Nabholtz. New York: Appleton, 1970. "Crofts Classics."
A paperback.

579. Hazlitt, William, *Selected Writings.* Ed. and introduced by Ronald Blythe. Harmondsworth: Penguin, 1970.
A paperback.
Rev. by Dennis Potter in *Times* (London), 30 May 1970, p. 22; by D. A. N. Jones in *New Society,* 30 July 1970, pp. 206–207.

580. Hazlitt, William. *The Spirit of the Age; or, Contemporary Portraits.* Second edition, revised. Ed. E. D. Mackerness. London: Collins, 1969. "Collins Annotated Student Texts."
Also in paperback.

Hearn, L. See No. 89.

581. Heath-Stubbs, John. *The Ode.* London: Oxford Univ., 1969.
Ch. vi, "The Romantics," includes Keats and Shelley. Paperback.
Rev. in *Choice,* 7 (March 1970), 76.

Heath-Stubbs, John. See No. 280.

Helmick, E. T. See No. 281.

Hewish, John. See No. 283.

582. Hewlett, Dorothy. *A Life of John Keats.* Third edition, revised. New York: Barnes & Noble; London: Hutchinson (1970).
First edition published in 1937.
Rev. by John D. Jump in *Critical Quarterly,* 13 (Spring 1971), 87–88; in *Choice,* 8 (Apr. 1971), 224.

583. Hilton, Timothy. *Keats and His World.* London: Thames and Hudson; New York: Viking (1971).
Rev. by Thomas Lask in *New York Times,* 20 March 1971, p. 27; in TLS, 2 Apr. 1971, pp. 365–366.

584. Hood, Thomas. *Selected Poems of Thomas Hood.* Ed. John Clubbe. Cambridge, Mass.: Harvard Univ., 1970.
Rev. by Mary McBride in LJ, 95 (1 Oct. 1970), 3288; in *Choice,* 7 (Jan. 1971), 1510.

585. Hood, Thomas. *Whimsicalities and Warnings.* Ed. Julian Ennis. London: Panther, 1970.

586. *Hough, Graham. "Tra Keats e Leopardi," translated by D. Tippett Andalò, *Il Veltro,* 15 (1971), 187–200.

587. Housman, A. E. *The Letters of A. E. Houseman.* Ed. Henry Maas. Cambridge, Mass.: Harvard Univ., 1971.
Comments on Keats and Shelley.

588. Hudnall, Clayton E. "John Hamilton Reynolds, James Rice, and Benjamin Bailey in the Leigh Browne-Lockyer Collection," K-SJ, 19 (1970), 11–39.
Presents letters and poems from the collection relevant to Reynolds, Rice, and Bailey. Two unpublished letters of Reynolds to Mary Leigh appear as part of Appendix A.

589. Hudnall, Clayton E. "New Lines by Keats," ELN, 7 (Dec. 1969), 111–114.
Found in George Keats's notebook, and originally intended to come between stanzas 7 and 8 of *Isabella.*

Hudnall, Clayton E. See No. 439a.

590. Hudnall, Clayton E. "An Unpublished Memoir of Keats's Friend, Benjamin Bailey," N&Q, 215 (May 1970), 175–177.†
An account of Bailey's memoir of his years in Ceylon.

591. Hudson, William Henry. *Keats and His Poetry.* Folcroft, Pa.: Folcroft, 1969. "Poetry & Life Series."
Reprint of a 1911 book.

592. Hulton, Paul. "A Little-known Cache of English Drawings," *Apollo,* 89 (Jan. 1969), 52–55.
In the Royal Academy. Includes 100 sheets of anatomical drawings for *Macbeth* and *The Judgment of Solomon* by Haydon.

Huntley, Reid DeBerry. See No. 93a.

593. Hyder, Clyde Kenneth, and John Erskine Hankins. *Selected Nineteenth Century Essays.* Freeport, N.Y.: Books for Libraries, 1970.
Reprint of the 1938 edition; includes six essays by William Hazlitt.

594. *Ikonomou, Mer. *Ho Tzon Kēts kai tēn Hellada.* [*John Keats and Greece.*] Athens: Sideris, 1969. [In Greek.]
The book includes a brief biography, selected poems, and analyses.

595. "In Memory of Keats," *Times* (London), 16 Feb. 1971, p. 14.
Brief notice of a commemoration to

be held on 23 Feb. 1971 in Westminster Abbey.

596. Inglis, Fred. *Keats*. New York: Arco, 1969. "Arco Literary Critiques."

A reprint of a book first published by Evans Bros. in 1965. See K-SJ, 16 (1967), No. 262, 17 (1968), No. 367, 18 (1969), No. 427, 19 (1970), No. 234.

Rev. by Elaine Bender in LJ, 95 (15 Jan. 1970), 159; in *Choice*, 7 (March 1970), 76; by I[rene]. H. C[hayes]. in ELN, 8, Supplement (Sept. 1970), 38.

597. Jabbar, Abdul. "Keats's View of Poetry" [Doctoral dissertation, Case Western Reserve, 1969], DAI, 30 (March 1970), 3907-A–3908-A.

597a. Jack, Ian. *Keats and the Mirror of Art*. See K-SJ, 17 (1968), No. 369, 18 (1969), No. 429, 19 (1970), No. 235.

Rev. by George Whalley in *Malahat Review*, No. 7 (July 1968), pp. 123–129.

Jackson, James R. de J., ed. See No. 428.

598. Jarvis, A. W. "The Jennings Family," KSMB, 20 (1969), 44–46.

More information on Keats's maternal relatives. A water color sketch of the Rev. Midgley J. Jennings is included.

598a. Jaster, Frank. "Keats and the False Poets: Introduction to *Endymion*, Book III," *Southern Quarterly*, 9 (Jan. 1971), 213–221.†

Explains the role of Book III in terms of the work as a whole.

Jenkins, Elizabeth. See No. 846.

599. Jerome, Judson. "Dreaming of Death," *Writer's Digest*, 50 (May 1970), 14–19.

"Ode to a Nightingale" is not a poem of "self-indulgence and escapism," but rather indicates the poet's distrust of such posturing.

600. John, Brian. "Yeats and Carlyle," N&Q, 215 (Dec. 1970), 455.†

Includes Yeats's criticism of Keats.

601. Johnson, Richard Edward. "Settings of Innocence and Experience in the Poetry of Keats" [Doctoral dissertation, Tulane, 1968], DAI, 30 (Dec. 1969), 2487-A.

602. Jones, James Land. "Keats and the Last Romantics: Hopkins and Yeats" [Doctoral dissertation, Tulane, 1969], DAI, 30 (Dec. 1969), 2530-A.

603. Jones, John. *John Keats's Dream of Truth*. London: Chatto and Windus; New York: Barnes and Noble (1969).

Rev. by Christopher Ricks in the *Sunday Times* (London), 9 Nov. 1969, p. 54; in TLS, 18 Dec. 1969, p. 1446 (reply by Jones, 1 Jan. 1970, p. 12, and by Simon Nowell-Smith, 22 Jan. 1970, p. 85); in *Choice*, 7 (May 1970), 386; by Margaret Bottrall in *Critical Quarterly*, 12 (Autumn 1970), 286–287; by E. Pereira in UES, 9 (June 1971), 32–33. Also see 109a.

604. Jones, Leonidas M. "Reynolds and Rice in Defence of Patmore," KSMB, 21 (1970), 12–20.

Details of the legal defence and acquital of John Scott's second in the duel that cost Scott his life.

605. Jones, Stanley. "Dating Hazlitt's 'Essay' on Taste," EA, 22 (Jan.–March 1969), 68–71.

Dates original essay as 1815 or 1816; not 1828 as P. P. Howe had done.

605a. Jones, Stanley. "Howe's Edition of Hazlitt's Works: Two Notes," N&Q, 215 (May 1970), 174–175.†

Gives sources of five unidentified quotations and corrects a misdating.

605b. Kamijima, Kenkichi. "Kaette Kita Visionary," *Eigo Seinen: Rising Generation* (Tokyo), 114 (Aug. 1968), 514–515. [In Japanese.]

On "La Belle Dame sans Merci."

606. Kaplan, Charles, ed. *The Overwrought Urn*. New York: Pegasus, 1969.

Includes references by Robert Myers to "Promiscuous Unbound" and "Ode on a Greasy Urn."

607. Kaufman, Paul. " 'The Hurricane' and the Romantic Poets," *English Miscellany*, 21 (1970), 99–115.

Discusses "The Hurricane," a poem by William Gilbert, and its influence on, among others, Keats.

608. Kaufman, Paul. "James Rice, Friend of Keats: New Biographical Facts," N&Q, 216 (May 1971), 168–172.†

New information on a member of Keats's circle.

609. Kaufman, Paul. "A Keats Circle by the Sea," *English Miscellany*, 22 (1971), 173–213.

Further information on Brown, Reynolds, Rice, and the three Leigh sisters from the Leigh Brown-Lockyer Collection at the Keats Museum in Hampstead.

610. Kauvar, Gerald B. *The Other Poetry of Keats*. Rutherford, N.J.: Fairleigh Dickinson Univ., 1969.
Rev. by Nathan C. Starr in LJ, 95 (15 May 1970), 1884; in *Choice*, 7 (Dec. 1970), 1374.

611. "Keats, a Silhouette." [Picture.] Reproduced from *Hogg's Weekly Instructor* in TLS, 2 Apr. 1971, p. 366.

612. *Keller, Ulrich. *Der Augenblick als dicterische Form in der Lyrik von William Wordsworth und John Keats*. Bad Homburg, Berlin, Zurich: Gehlen, 1970. "Frankfurter Beiträge zur Anglistik und Amerikanstik, Vol. 4."

613. Kelly, Linda. *The Marvellous Boy: The Life and Myth of Thomas Chatterton*. London: Weidenfeld and Nicolson, 1971.
Includes a chapter on Keats and Chatterton. References to Shelley, Byron, and Hunt.

614. Kenyon, Katherine M. R. "When Did Keats Meet Fanny Brawne?" KSMB, 22 (1971), 53–58.
Suggests 19 Sept. 1819.

615. Kilgour, Norman. "At 'The Swan and Hoop,' " KSMB, 22 (1971), 52.
The original plan and the conveyance of the lease of "The Swan and Hoop" to Frances Keats in 1804 are reproduced, along with a brief introductory discussion.

616. *Knight, G. Wilson. *The Starlit Dome: Studies in the Poetry of Vision*. Introduction by W. F. Jackson Knight. London: Oxford Univ., 1971.
A paperback edition of a book originally published in 1941. Essays on Shelley and Keats.

617. Cancelled.

Kroeber, Karl, with Alfred and Theodora Kroeber. See No. 301.

618. Cancelled.

Langbaum, Robert. See No. 102.

Lean, E. Tangye. See No. 103.

619. Leavy, Stanley A. "John Keats's Psychology of Creative Imagination," *Psychoanalytic Quarterly*, 39 (Apr. 1970), 173–197.
Keats's theories of negative capability and the creative imagination prefigure psychoanalytic concepts.

620. Lee, A. E. " 'A Place in My Memory, Dearest,' " KSMB, 22 (1971), 44–51.
The author recalls his experiences since he took charge of the Keats Memorial House in Hampstead in Feb. 1945.

621. "Library Notes," WC, 1 (Autumn 1970), 171–172.
Announces acquisition of a letter from Elizabeth Barrett Browning to Haydon by the Keats-Shelley Memorial House, Rome. The text of the letter appears.

622. Lindenberger, Herbert. "Keats's 'To Autumn' and Our Knowledge of a Poem," CE, 32 (Nov. 1970), 123–134.†
Examines conflicting interpretations of "To Autumn" to argue that critics should discard the notion they are searchers after objective knowledge.

623. Little, Judy Ruth. "Large-Limbed Visions: Structure in the Long Poems of John Keats" [Doctoral dissertation, Nebraska, 1969], DAI, 30 (Jan. 1970), 2973-A–2974-A.

Lochhead, Marion. See No. 443.

Lohf, Kenneth A. See No. 308.

624. *Lombardo, Agostino. *Ritratto di Enobarbo: Saggi di letteratura inglese*. Pisa: Nistri-Lischi, 1971.
Includes an essay on Keats's poetry.

Longford, Elizabeth. See No. 106.

625. Lott, James. "Keats's 'To Autumn': The Poetic Consciousness and the Awareness of Process," SIR, 9 (Spring 1970), 71–81.†‡
The poem makes use of a "perceiver," or speaker, who reacts to the scene before him.

626. Low, Donald. "Hazlitt on Burns," WC, 2 (Summer 1971), 100.
A note on Hazlitt's lectures "On Burns and the Old English Ballads," delivered at the Surrey Institution and published in 1818.

627. Lowell, Amy. *John Keats*. Hamden, Conn.: Archon, 1969.
A reprint of a book first published in 1925.

628. Luke, David. "*The Eve of Saint Mark*: Keats's 'ghostly Queen of Spades' and the Textual Superstition," SIR, 9 (Summer 1970), 161–175.†‡
An analysis of the use Keats made of

the superstition upon which the poem is based.

628a. *Lund, Mary G. "Does *Endymion* Answer *Alastor*?" *Forum* (Houston), 7, ii (1969), 38–41.

629. Lyon, Harvey T. *Keats' Well-Read Urn: An Introduction to Literary Method.* Folcroft, Pa.: Folcroft, 1970.
Reprint of a 1958 book. See K-SJ, 8 (1959), No. 347, 10 (1961), No. 318.

630. Maas, Jeremy. *Victorian Painters.* London: Barrie and Kock; New York: Putnam (1969).
Includes Haydon and Severn.
Rev. by William J. Dane in LJ, 94 (1 Nov. 1969), 3996; by Phoebe Adams in *Atlantic Monthly* (Jan. 1970), p. 105; by J[ohn]. H[ollander]. in *Harper's Magazine*, 240 (Apr. 1970), 110.

631. McCall, Dan. " 'The Self-Same Song that Found a Path': Keats and *The Great Gatsby*," AL, 42 (Jan. 1971), 521–530.†
Explores the "complicated similarity" in theme, particularly the ambivalence of beauty. Compares attitudes towards permanence, death, wealth, beauty; stresses the search for ultimate truth through dreamer's heightened perceptions of the real world.

632. *MacEachen, Dugald B. *Keats & Shelley.* Lincoln, Neb.: Cliff's Notes, 1971.
Teaching aid.

633. MacKay, David. "Keats' 'Bright Star' Sonnet" [Letter], TLS, 3 July 1969, p. 731.
Reaffirms Robert Gittings' dating of the sonnet as Nov. 1818. See K-SJ, 18 (1969), No. 403, 19 (1970), No. 216.

634. McLuhan, Marshall. *The Interior Landscape: The Literary Criticism of Marshall McLuhan, 1943–1962.* See K-SJ, 19 (1970), No. 244.
Rev. by Keith Cushman in LJ, 95 (1 Feb. 1970), 497.

635. Maier, Rosemarie. "The Bitch and the Bloodhound: Generic Similarity in 'Christabel' and 'The Eve of St. Agnes,' " JEGP, 70 (Jan. 1971), 62–75.‡
Analyzes the poems as medieval gothic romances. Understood this way "the differences between them appear as variations on the same mythic theme."

Margetson, Stella. See No. 111.

636. Margolis, John D. "Keats's 'Men of Genius' and 'Men of Power,' " *Texas Studies in Literature and Language*, 11 (Winter 1970), 1333–1347.‡
Examines Keats's meaning of these terms as they appear in his letter to Benjamin Bailey in Nov. 1817.

637. Masson, David I. *Wordsworth, Shelley, Keats and Other Essays.* New York: Burt Franklin, 1970. "Research and Source Work Series, 489: Essays in Literature and Criticism, 68."
Reprint of the 1875 edition.

638. Matthews, G. M., ed. *Keats: The Critical Heritage.* London: Routledge and Kegan Paul; New York: Barnes & Noble (1971). "The Critical Heritage Series."

639. Mayhead, Robin. *John Keats.* See K-SJ, 18 (1969), No. 452, 19 (1970), No. 250.
Rev. by Anthea Morrison in *Durham Univ. Journal*, 61 (Dec. 1968), 49–50.

Merivale, Patricia. See No. 116.

640. Millar, Oliver. *The Later Georgian Pictures in the Collection of Her Majesty the Queen.* Vol. I: *Plates*; Vol. II: *Text.* London: Phaidon, 1969.
Haydon is included in this collection of works from the British School from 1768 to 1837.
Rev. by Ruth Bertrand in LJ, 94 (15 Dec. 1969); 4516.

Miller, Barnette. See No. 445.

641. Miller, Bruce E. "Form and Substance in 'Grecian Urn,' " K-SJ, 20 (1971), 62–70.
A reading of Keats's poem which focuses on reconciling the "beauty-truth" contradiction.

642. Mincoff, Marco. "Beauty is Truth—Once More," MLR, 65 (Apr. 1970), 267–271.†
Maintains that the last lines of "Ode on a Grecian Urn" do not present a conclusion based on a premise. Keats simply states "that on one occasion a work of art offered his imagination . . . a glimpse of that perfection which, we know from his letters, he believed did somehow exist somewhere in a Platonic world of being."

643. Minor, Mark George. "The Poet in His Joy: A Critical Study of John Clare's Poetic Development" [Doctoral dis-

sertation, Ohio State, 1970], DAI, 31 (March 1971), 4784-A.

644. Monteiro, George. "Dr. Williams' First Book," *Books at Brown*, 23 (1969), 85–88.

Describes William Carlos Williams' first book of poems (1909), which quoted Keats on title page. Williams described his first volume as "Bad Keats —nothing else."

644a. Montgomery, Neil. "Keats and Psychology," *Philosophical Journal*, 8 (Jan. 1971), 18–37.

A general discussion.

645. Muir, Kenneth. *John Keats: A Reassessment*. Second Edition. Liverpool: Liverpool Univ., 1969. "Liverpool English Texts and Studies, No. 5."

First published in 1958. See K-SJ, 9 (1960), No. 358, 10 (1961), No. 327, 11 (1962), No. 368.

646. Murray, E. B. "Ambivalent Mortality in the Elgin Marbles Sonnet," K-SJ, 20 (1971), 22–36.

Interprets Keats's sense of spiritual impotence in the poem not in the generally accepted meaning, but as a prologue to the larger and more important subject of art's mortality.

647. Murry, John Middleton. *Poetics, Critics, Mystics: A Selection of Criticisms Written between 1919 and 1955 by John Middleton Murry*. Ed. Richard Rees. Carbondale: Southern Illinois Univ.; London and Amsterdam: Feffer and Simons (1970).

Reprints an essay on Keats, pp. 27–34.

648. Nassar, Eugene Paul. *The Rape of Cinderella: Essays in Literary Continuity*. Bloomington: Indiana Univ., 1970.

Contains his essay "Keats: Bathos in *Hyperion*."

"News & Comment." See No. 346.

649. O'Brien, Veronica. "The Language of Poetry," *Studies*, 58 (Winter 1969), 415–426.

Includes a comparison of Milton's language to that of Keats.

650. O'Neill, Judith, comp. *Critics on Keats*. See K-SJ, 17 (1968), No. 401, 18 (1969), No. 465, 19 (1970), No. 262.

Rev. by I[rene]. H. C[hayes]. in ELN, 7, Supplement (Sept. 1969), 37; in *Choice*, 6 (Nov. 1969), 1224.

Orel, Harold, and George J. Worth, eds. See No. 122.

651. Origo, Iris. "Additions to the Keats Collection," TLS, 23 Apr. 1970, pp. 457–458. Replies by Park Honan in TLS, 14 May 1970, p. 539, and by M. D. George, 28 May 1970, p. 586.

A gift by Dr. Dallas Pratt to the Keats-Shelley Memorial House in Rome. Among the items contributed are a letter by Keats to his sister Fanny, 11 Sept. 1820; an unpublished autograph letter of Elizabeth Barrett Browning to Haydon, ca. Oct. 1842; an unpublished autograph letter of Haydon to Mrs. Browning; an autograph letter of E. B. Browning to R. H. Horne, 29 Dec. 1842; two sketches from Thomas Keats's notebook; an autograph letter of Oscar Wilde to Emily Speed; and other items.

651a. Osler, Alan. "Keats" [Letter], TLS, 16 Apr. 1971, p. 449.

Suggests lines 20–24 of the verse letter to Reynolds were inspired by two paintings of Claude depicting the arrival of Aeneas at the future site of Rome.

652. Osler, Alan. " 'On Seeing the Elgin Marbles,' " KSMB, 21 (1970), 32–34.

Suggests that the emendation "wings" for "winds" would correct an obscurity in the sonnet.

653. Ostle, Robin C. "Three Egyptian Poets of 'Westernization': ʿAbd al-Rahman Shukri, Ibrahim ʿAbd al-Qadir al Mazini, and Mahmud ʿAbdas al-ʿAqqad," *Comparative Literature Studies*, 7 (Sept. 1970), 354–373.†

Shukri, who lived during the early twentieth century, expressed his ideas on poetry in the language of Coleridge, Wordsworth, Keats, and Hazlitt.

Pace, Claire. See No. 123.

653a. *Paciosi, Filelfo. "Classicismo e romanticismo in Keats," *Dialoghi*, 16 (1968), 94–122.

654. Park, Roy. "Hazlitt and Bentham," JHI, 30 (Oct.–Dec. 1969), 369–384.

Discusses the importance of Hazlitt's criticism of Bentham's utilitarianism.

655. Park, Roy. *Hazlitt and the Spirit of the Age: Abstraction and Critical Theory*. Oxford: Clarendon, 1971.

656. Park, Roy. "The Painter as Critic: Haz-

litt's Theory of Abstraction," PMLA, 85 (Oct. 1970), 1072–1081.†‡

His theory of abstraction "as a process of individuation rather than generalization" was influenced by his early interest in painting and philosophy.

657. Park, Roy. " 'Ut Pictura Poesis': The Nineteenth-Century Aftermath," JAAC, 28 (Winter 1969), 155–164.

Includes a discussion of Hazlitt.

658. Patterson, Charles I., Jr. *The Daemonic in the Poetry of John Keats.* Urbana and London: Univ. of Illinois, 1970.

Rev. by Stuart M. Sperry, Jr. in JEGP, 70 (Jan. 1971), 171–172; by Robin Mayhead in *English*, 20 (Summer 1971), 59–62.

659. Pereira, E. "Aspects of English Romanticism with Special Reference to Keats," UES, 8 (June 1970), 35–40.

Sees the structural tensions of Keats's verse as characteristic of Romantic poetry.

660. Pereira, E. "John Keats: the Major Odes of 1819," UES, 7 (Nov. 1969), 49–63.

An analysis of "Ode to a Nightingale," "Ode on a Grecian Urn," and "To Autumn."

661. *Pereira, E. *John Keats: The Poet as Critic.* Pretoria: Univ. of South Africa, 1969.

662. Peter, Brother Baldwin. " 'The Eve of St. Agnes' and the Sleeping-Beauty Motif," KSMB, 22 (1971), 1–6.

"Porphyro's entrance, his waking of Madeline, and their marriage are roughly similar to the same narrative elements in Perrault's fairy tale," first published in London in 1729.

663. Pettet, E. C. *On the Poetry of Keats.* Cambridge: Cambridge Univ., 1970.

A reprint of the 1957 edition. See K-SJ, 7 (1958), No. 321, 8 (1959), No. 367, 9 (1960), No. 368, 10 (1961), No. 335, 11 (1962), No. 385, 14 (1965), No. 309.

664. Peyre, Henri. *The Failures of Criticism.* See K-SJ, 19 (1970), No. 268.

Rev. by John G. Clark in *French Studies*, 23 (July 1969), 320–323.

664a. Pinsky, Robert. " 'That Sweet Man, John Clare,' " in *The Rarer Action: Essays in Honor of Francis Fergusson*, ed. Alan Cheuse and Richard Koffler (New Brunswick, N.J.: Rutgers Univ., 1970), pp. 258–274.

Piper, William B. See No. 364.

665. Pitt, Valerie. "His Gift Knew What It Was: Reflections on William Wordsworth," *Church Quarterly*, 2 (Apr. 1970), 301–309.

Passing references to Hazlitt and Shelley's loss of interest in Wordsworth after the publication of *The Excursion*, and to Shelley's attribution of Wordsworth's later dullness to his political apostasy.

Pointon, Marcia B. See No. 366.

Poynter, J. R. See No. 128.

666. Praz, Mario. *The Romantic Agony.* Translated by Angus Davidson. Second edition, with a new foreword by Frank Kermode. London: Oxford Univ., 1970.

A reissue of the book originally published in 1951. See K-SJ, 7 (1958), No. 323.

Rev. by Barbara Hardy in Spec, 20 Feb. 1971, pp. 256–257.

Praz, Mario. See No. 447.

"Recent Acquisitions." See Nos. 448–449.

667. "Recent Acquisitions — Manuscripts," *Princeton Univ. Library Chronicle*, 31 (Autumn 1969), 66.

Between 1 July 1968 and 30 June 1969 the library acquired a single letter, manuscript, or paper of Joseph Severn.

668. Rees, Joan. *Bright Star: The Story of John Keats & Fanny Brawne.* London: Harrap, 1968.

A fictional account.

669. Reeves, James. *Commitment to Poetry.* New York: Barnes and Noble, 1969.

A compendium of Reeves's writings, including an essay on John Clare, and another on Keats's letters.

670. Reid, Benjamin L. *Tragic Occasions: Essays on Several Forms.* Port Washington, N.Y.: Kennikat, 1971.

Includes "Keats and the Heart's Hornbook," pp. 65–93.

671. Robertson, Margaret Y. "The Consistency of Keats's 'Ode on Indolence,' " *Style*, 4 (Spring 1970), 133–143.

Examines Keats's careful blending of such matters as words, images, and rhetorical techniques.

672. Rose, Alan. "The Impersonal Premise in Wordsworth, Keats, Yeats, and Eliot"

[Doctoral dissertation, Brandeis, 1969], DAI, 30 (Dec. 1969), 2547-A–2548-A.

673. Rosenmeyer, Thomas G. *The Green Cabinet: Theocritus and the European Pastoral Lyric*. Berkeley and Los Angeles: Univ. of California, 1969.
Discusses relevant passages in Keats.

674. Rossetti, Dante Gabriel. *Letters of Dante Gabriel Rossetti*. Vols. III and IV. Eds. Oswald Doughty and John Robert Wahl. See K-SJ, 20 (1970), No. 269a.
Rev. by Mireille Pagès in EA, 23 (July–Sept. 1970), 311–320.

675. *Rossetti, William Michael. *Life of John Keats*. New York: AMS, 1971.
Reprint of an 1887 book.

Rowell, George E., ed. See No. 432.

676. St. John-Stevas, Norman. "Walter Bagehot," *Essays By Divers Hands*, 36 (1970), 133–146.
Includes a discussion of Bagehot's treatment of Shelley and Keats.

676a. *Saito, Yuso. "Basho, Buson and Wordsworth, Shelley, Keats," in *Actes du Ve Congrès de l'Association Internationale de Littérature Comparée, Belgrade 1967*, ed. Nikola Banašević (Belgrade: Univ. of Belgrade; Amsterdam: Swets & Zeitlinger, 1969), pp. 419–425.

676b. Sakata, Katsuzo. "Keats No Dilemma," *Eigo Seinen: Rising Generation* (Tokyo), 114 (Feb. 1968), 82–83. [In Japanese.]
Keats's dilemma.

676c. *Sato, Kiyoshi. *Keats Kenkyu*. [*Study of Keats*.] Tokyo: Nanundo, 1968.

677. Schneider, Elisabeth. *The Aesthetics of William Hazlitt: A Study of the Philosophical Basis of his Criticism*. New York: Octagon, 1969.
Reprint of a 1933 book.

Schoenbaum, S. See No. 387.

678. Schwartz, Lewis M. "Keats's Reception by His English Contemporaries: A Collection of Reviews and Notices of the Poet for the Years 1816–1821" [Doctoral dissertation, New York, 1968], DAI, 30 (July 1969), 338-A–339-A.

Schwartz, Lewis M. See No. 388.

679. Scott, Nathan A., Jr. *Negative Capability: Studies in the New Literature and the Religious Situation*. New Haven: Yale Univ., 1969.
Discusses the background and meaning of Keats's concept in his Preface.
Rev. by William V. Spanos in JEGP, 69 (July 1970), 556–559; by John R. Willingham in LJ, 94 (15 Sept. 1969), 3068; by E. D. Mackerness in MLR, 65 (Oct. 1970), 859–860.

680. Scriven, Harvey. "Keats and the Shakespeare Anthology," KSMB, 22 (1971), 59–64.
Examines some extracts marked by Keats in his volumes of Shakespeare from the viewpoint of an anthologist.

681. "Section Meetings . . . English III." *South Atlantic Bulletin*, 35 (Jan. 1970), 20.
Theodore L. Huguelet's "Keats' 'To Autumn' as a Poem of Unalloyed Delight" was read at the 1969 meeting of SAMLA.

681a. Severn, Joseph. ["John Hamilton Reynolds," Picture.] *Connoisseur*, 170 (Jan. 1969), 36.
Reproduction of 1818 miniature.

682. Shackford, Martha Hale. *Studies of Certain Nineteenth Century Poets*. Natick, Mass.: Suburban, 1970.
A reprint of the 1946 edition, which includes a chapter on Keats's "Ode to a Nightingale."

683. *Sickels, Eleanor M. *The Gloomy Egoist: Moods and Themes of Melancholy from Gray to Keats*. New York: Octagon, 1969. "Columbia University Studies in English and Comparative Literature."
Reprint of a 1932 book.

684. Sinson, Janice C. *John Keats and the Anatomy of Melancholy*. London: Keats-Shelley Memorial Association, 1971.
Rev. by Joseph De Rocco in K-SJ, 20 (1971), 140–141.

685. Small, Thomas Edward. "John Keats's Cosmos: Images of Space and Time in the Poetry" [Doctoral dissertation, California, Berkeley, 1970], DAI, 31 (Jan. 1971), 3565-A.

686. Smith, Barbara H. *Poetic Closure: A Study of How Poems End*. Chicago: Univ. of Chicago, 1968.
Analyzes and reinterprets "Ode on a Grecian Urn," pp. 229–232.
Rev. by Robert W. Mayberry in *Journal of General Education*, 21 (Jan.

1970), 303–305; by John B. Bender in JAAC, 29 (Winter 1970), 270.

687. Solis, Gustavo Diaz. *Exploraciones Criticas.* Universidad Central de Venezuela, 1968.

A bilingual edition, including a chapter entitled "Six Odes of Keats."

Speirs, John. See No. 145a.

688. Sperry, Stuart M., Jr. "Keats and the Chemistry of Poetic Creation," PMLA, 85 (March 1970), 268–277.†‡

Deals with the influence of chemical theory on Keats's conception of the poetic process.

689. Sperry, Stuart M., Jr. "Keats's 'Epistle to John Hamilton Reynolds,' " ELH, 36 (Sept. 1969), 562–574.

Keats's references to paintings in this poem help him define aesthetic problems important to his development as a poet.

690. Sperry, Stuart M., Jr. "Romance as Wish-Fulfillment: Keats's *The Eve of St. Agnes,*" SIR, 10 (Winter 1971), 27–43.†‡

A new reading of the poem as the realization of dream and wish-fulfillment.

691. Spitzer, Leo. *Essays on English and American Literature.* See K-SJ, 13 (1964), No. 402, 17 (1968), No. 432.

Rev. by A. H. in *Univ. of Edinburgh Journal,* 24 (Spring 1969), 75.

692. [Sprigg, Christopher St. John.] Caudwell, Christopher, *pseud. Romance and Realism: A Study in English Bourgeios Literature.* Ed. Samuel Hynes. Princeton: Princeton Univ., 1970.

A Marxist interpretation of English literature with references to Keats and Shelley.

Rev. by William H. Magee in LJ, 96 (1 May 1971), 1613.

693. Stephen, Henry. "The Principles of Criticism as Applied to Poetry," *Calcutta Review,* N.S. 1 (July–Sept. 1969), 19–36.

Reprinted from *Calcutta Review* (May–June 1926). References to Keats, Shelley, Hazlitt.

694. Steward, Joyce S., and Eva M. Burkett, comps. *Introductory Readings in Literary Criticism.* Menlo Park, Calif., and London: Addison-Wesley, 1968.

A collection of reprints designed for the undergraduate. It includes Reuben A. Brower's "The Speaking Voice," pp. 293–302, which refers to Keats, Shelley, and the "Ode to the West Wind." This selection first appeared as a chapter in Brower's *The Fields of Light.* See K-SJ, 2 (1953), No. 74.

695. Stewart, I. "Mr. Keats is Gone to Scotland," *Country Life,* 148 (13 Aug. 1970), 382–384.

Illustrated, popularized account of Keats's Scottish trip in July 1818. Reproduces Severn's 1819 portrait of Keats.

696. Stillinger, Jack, ed. *Twentieth Century Interpretations of Keats's Odes: A Collection of Critical Essays.* See K-SJ, 19 (1970), No. 277.

Rev. by Joseph Anthony Wittreich, Jr., in K-SJ, 19 (1970), 143–144.

Stillinger, Jack. See No. 65.

696a. Storey, Mark. "Clare's 'Love and Beauty,' " Exp, 28 (March 1970), Item 60.

697. Story, Patrick L. "Byron's Death and Hazlitt's *Spirit of the Age,*" ELN, 7 (Sept. 1969), 42–46.†

Hazlitt's assertion that news of Byron's death moved him to break off composition of his essay on the poet "is a rhetorical anticipation of a popular outcry against the unsympathetic portrait, which had actually been completed for some time."

698. Story, Patrick L. "A Contemporary Continuation of Hazlitt's *Spirit of the Age,*" WC, 1 (Spring 1970), 59–65.†‡

By Sir William Allan, the Scottish historical painter and friend of Sir Walter Scott. Allan's fragments amount to a few hundred words.

699. Stouck, David. "The Modernity of Hazlitt's Familiar Essays," *Humanities Association Bulletin,* 21 (Spring 1970), 10–14.†

Hazlitt is modern in dealing with the experience of alienation, of homelessness, in "On Going a Journey" and other familiar essays.

699a. Straumann, Heinrich. "Keats und die glasërne Wand. Bemerkungen zu 'The Eve of St. Agnes,' " in *Festschrift Rudolf*

Stamm, ed. Eduard Kolb and Jörg Hasler (Bern and Munich: Francke, 1969), pp. 217–224.

Strauss, Walter A. See No. 398.

700. Suddard, S. J. Mary. *Keats, Shelley, and Shakespeare: Studies and Essays in English Literature*. Folcroft, Pa.: Folcroft, 1969.
Reprint of a 1912 book.

701. Swaminathan, S. R. "Keats's 'The Fall of Hyperion,' " KSMB, 20 (1969), 11–12.
A new interpretation of lines 16–18 of the poem.

Swanson, Donald R. See No. 151.

702. Swennes, Robert H. "Keats's Own Annotated Copy of *Endymion*," K-SJ, 20 (1971), 14–17.
Found in the William B. Wisdom Collection of the Tulane Univ. Library, it contains the poet's markings, which include some corrections not found in either the edition of the Formans or the edition of Garrod.

703. *Symonds, Emily Morse. *Little Memoirs of the Nineteenth Century*. Freeport, N.Y.: Books for Libraries, 1969. "Essay Index Reprint Series."
Reprint of a 1902 book. Includes essay on Benjamin Robert Haydon.

Sypher, Wylie. See No. 153.

704. Talbot, Norman. *The Major Poems of John Keats*. See K-SJ, 18 (1969), No. 508, 19 (1970), No. 283.
Rev. in *Choice*, 6 (July–Aug. 1969), 648–649. Also see No. 117.

705. Tatchell, Molly. "Charles Jeremiah Wells," KSMB, 22 (1971), 7–17.
A biographical essay on Keats's estranged friend.

706. Thomas, Edward. *Keats*. Folcroft, Pa.: Folcroft, 1970.
Reprint of a 1916 book.

707. Thomas, Edward. *A Literary Pilgrim in England*. Freeport, N.Y.: Books for Libraries, 1969.
A reprint of the 1917 edition; includes biographical sketches of John Clare, Keats, and Hazlitt.

Thomas, P. G. See No. 402.

708. Toliver, Harold E. *Pastoral Forms and Attitudes*. Berkeley: Univ. of California, 1971.
Ch. xi is entitled "Keats's Pastoral Alchemy as Therapy."

Trewin, J. C. See No. 157.

709. Troutman, Philip. "The Evocation of Atmosphere in the English Water-colour," *Apollo*, 88 (July 1968), 51–57.
Includes DeWint.

Turner, James, ed. See No. 434.

709a. *Tsukano, Ko. *Keats Kenkyu*. [*Study of Keats*.] Tokyo: Bunkahyoronsha, 1970.

710. Villard, Léonie. *The Influence of Keats on Tennyson and Rosetti*. Folcroft, Pa.: Folcroft, 1970.
Reprint of a 1914 book.

711. Viswanathan, S. "The Hymns of Sir William Jones, Part One," *Aryan Path*, 40 (Nov. 1969), 487–493; "Part Two," 40 (Dec. 1969), 543–550.
"The mythopoeic tendency in Jones's poetry is a forerunner of the myth-making trend in the poetry of Keats and Shelley."

712. Vogler, Thomas A. *Preludes to Vision: The Epic Venture in Blake, Wordsworth, Keats, and Hart Crane*. Berkeley: Univ. of California, 1971.

713. Waldoff, Leon. "From Abandonment to Scepticism in Keats," EC, 21 (Apr. 1971), 152–158.
Endymion "reflects the psychological origins of Keats's scepticism about dreams and permanence," which appears as a theme in the later poetry as well.

714. Wardle, Ralph M. *Hazlitt*. Lincoln: Univ. of Nebraska, 1971.

715. Wardle, Ralph M. "Hazlitt on *The Beggar's Opera*," SAQ, 70 (Spring 1971), 256–264.†
An early and enthusiastic review for the *Morning Chronicle*, in Oct. 1813.

Watkin, David. See No. 414.

716. Watson, J[ohn]. R. "Keats and the Pursuit of the Sublime," *Philosophical Journal*, 6 (July 1969), 112–126.
Discusses Keats's experience of sublime or picturesque landscape and its reflection in his poetry.

Watson, J[ohn]. R. See No. 162.

Wellek, René. See No. 416.

717. Whitridge, Arnold. "The English Language: A Musical Instrument and a Workaday Tool," BNYPL, 75 (Feb. 1971), 90–100.
Quotes Keats's "Ode to a Nightingale."

718. Wild, Reverend Patrick. "Address by the Reverend Patrick Wild," KSMB, 22 (1971), vii–ix.
Delivered at the Poets' Corner, Westminster Abbey, to commemorate the 150th anniversary of Keats's death.

719. *Wilde, Oscar. *The Artist as Critic: Critical Writings of Oscar Wilde*. Ed. Richard Ellmann, London: W. H. Allen, 1970.
Contains Wilde's "The Tomb of Keats," reprinted from the *Irish Monthly*.
Rev. by Cyril Connolly in the *Sunday Times* (London), 29 March 1970, p. 55; in TLS, 2 Apr. 1970, p. 354.

720. Williams, Porter, Jr. "Keats' 'On Sitting Down to Read *King Lear* Once Again,'" Exp, 29 (Nov. 1970), Item 26.‡

Williams, Raymond. See No. 169.

Williamson, Jane. See No. 453.

721. Withim, Philip. "The Psychodynamics of Literature," *Psychoanalytic Review*, 56, No. 4 (1969–1970), 556–581.
Keats's concept of negative capability is mentioned briefly.

Woodhouse, C[hristoper]. M. See No. 422.

Woodring, Carl. See No. 175.

Wordsworth, William, and Dorothy Wordsworth. See No. 423.

721a. *Yasunaga, Yoshio. "On Keats's *Lamia*: Dream and Reality," *Hiroshima Studies in English Language and Literature*, 16, i–ii (1969), 18–29. [In Japanese.]

V. SHELLEY

WORKS: COLLECTED, SELECTED, SINGLE, TRANSLATED

722. **Adonais e altre poesie*. Translated by Roberto Sanesi. Milan: Rusconi, 1970.

723. **Ai Yü Mêng*. [Translated by] Kuo Wen Ch'i. Tainan: Hua Ming Pub. Ser. 223, n.d. [In Chinese.]

724. *Alastor, and Other Poems; and Prometheus Unbound, with Other Poems; and Adonais*. Ed. Peter H. Butter. London: Collins, 1970. "Collins Annotated Student Texts."

725. Ashley, Leonard R. N., ed. *Nineteenth-Century British Drama: An Anthology of Representative Plays*. See K-SJ, 17 (1968), No. 456.
Rev. by Paul D. Herring in MP, 68 (Aug. 1970), 83–90.

726. *The Cenci*. Ed. Roland A. Duerksen. Indianapolis: Bobbs-Merrill, 1970. "Library of Liberal Arts."
In paperback.
Rev. in *Choice*, 7 (Feb. 1971), 1682.
Also see No. 44.

727. **The Cenci, a Tragedy in Five Acts, Given from the Poet's Own Editions*. Introduction by Alfred Forman and H. Buxton Forman, and a Prologue by John Todhunter. New York: Phaeton, 1970.
Reprint of 1886 edition.

728. **A Choice of Shelley's Verse*. Ed. Stephen Spender. London: Faber, 1971.
Paperback.

Detz, Phyllis, Kermit M. Stover, and Betsy Schwartz, eds. See No. 181.

729. "Domani" ["To-morrow"], *Ausonia*, 25 (Jan.–Feb. 1970), 19. [In Italian.]
Translator not identified.

730. *Epipsychidion, 1821, Together with Shelley's Manuscript Draft*. Menston, Yorkshire: Scolar, 1970.
Facsimile of the first edition and of Bodleian MS. Shelley d 1.

Erzgräber, Willi, ed. See No. 457.

731. **Essays and Letters*. Ed. with introductory note by Ernest Rhys. Freeport, N.Y.: Books for Libraries, 1971.
Reprint of 1887 edition.

731a. [Excerpt from *A Defence of Poetry*], *Aryan Path*, 39 (Nov. 1968), 487.
Filler.

Flower, Desmond. See No. 183.

732. **Gedichten*. [Poems.] [Translated by] Clara Eggink. Amsterdam: Contact, 1970. [In Dutch.]

733. *Harrison, Thomas Perrin, Jr., ed. *The Pastoral Elegy: An Anthology*. New York: Octagon, 1968.
Reprint of 1939 collection. Includes text of *Adonais* and notes.
Rev. in *Choice*, 7 (Apr. 1970), 227–228.

734. **Hellas: A Lyrical Drama. A Reprint of the Original Edition Published in 1822, with the Author's Prologue and Notes by Various Hands*. Ed. Thomas J. Wise. New York: Phaeton, 1970.
Reprint of 1886 edition.

735. "Invocazione alla Morte di Beatrice Cenci" [*Cenci* v.iv.101–119], translated

by Giuseppe Rigotti, *Ausonia*, 24 (Sept.–Dec. 1969), 38. [In Italian.]

736.**Italian Idylls*. Illustrated by Duine Campbell. Leicester: Offcut, 1968.

Limited edition of seventy numbered copies.

737. *Lefkēs, Giannēs. *Xena Tragoudia me tē dikē mou phonē*. Limassol, 1967.

Includes poetry by Shelley.

738. *Mám v duši more*. [Translated by] Ivan Mojik. Bratislava: Tatran, 1970. [In Czechoslovakian.]

739. *Pesme*. [Translated by] Ranka Kuić. Belgrade: Rad, 1969. [In Yugoslavian.]

740. Cancelled.

741. *Poetical Works*. Ed. Thomas Hutchinson. Second edition, corrected by G. M. Matthews. London: Oxford Univ., 1970. Paperback. "Oxford Standard Authors."

Hardcover edition, 1971.

742. **Political Writings, Including "A Defence of Poetry*." Ed. Roland A. Duerksen. New York: Appleton, 1970. Paperback. "Crofts Classics."

743. *Posthumous Poems of Shelley*. Ed. Irving Massey. See K-SJ, 19 (1970), No. 290.

Rev. by Kerry McSweeney in QQ, 76 (Winter 1969), 731–733; in TLS, 22 Jan. 1970, p. 74; by K[enneth]. N[eill]. C[ameron]. in ELN, 8, Supplement (Sept. 1970), 44; by Neville Rogers in RES, 21 (Nov. 1970), 514–515; by P. H. Butter in MLR, 66 (Apr. 1971), 401–402. Also see No. 109a.

744. **Prototypē Philologikē Epitheorēsis* (1969).

A Greek literary periodical, which includes some translations of poetry by Shelley.

745. **Selected Poems*. Ed. Elio Chinol. Milan: Mursia, 1968.

746. **Selected Poetry*. Ed. Neville Rogers. London: Oxford Univ., 1969.

British paperback edition of Houghton Mifflin "Riverside" edition. See K-SJ, 18 (1969), No. 538.

Rev. by D[onald]. H. R[eiman], in ELN, 7, Supplement (Sept. 1969), 42–43.

747. *The Shelley Notebook in the Harvard College Library*. Notes by George E. Woodberry. Folcroft, Pa.,: Folcroft, 1969.

Reprint of 1929 photo-facsimile of Shelley's notebook.

748. *Shelley's Critical Prose*. Ed. B. R. McElderry, Jr. See K-SJ, 17 (1968), No. 465, 18 (1969), No. 540.

Rev. by P. H. Butter in MLR, 64 (Oct. 1969), 887–888.

749. *Shelley's Literary and Philosophical Criticism*. Ed. John Shawcross. Folcroft, Pa.: Folcroft, 1969.

Reprint of 1909 edition.

750. *Shelley's "Prometheus Unbound": The Text and the Drafts*. Ed. Lawrence John Zillman. See K-SJ, 18 (1969), No. 541. 19 (1970), No. 292.

Rev. by R. B. Woodings in *Studia Neophilologica*, 41 (1969), 439–441; by Donald H. Reiman in JEGP, 68 (1969), 539–543; by K[enneth]. N[eill]. C[ameron]. in ELN, 7, Supplement (Sept. 1969), 45–46; by M. K. Joseph in AUMLA, No. 32 (Nov. 1969), pp. 251–253; by Kerry McSweeney in QQ, 76 (Winter 1969), 731–733; by E. B. Murray in K-SJ, 19 (1970), 119–125; by Neville Rogers in RES, 21 (Feb. 1970), 90–92; by Neville Rogers in MLR, 65 (Apr. 1970), 397–398; by Glenn O'Malley in MP, 68 (Feb. 1971), 308–310. Also see Nos. 109a, 117.

751. *Shelley's Prose; or, The Trumpet of a Prophecy*. Ed. David Lee Clark. See K-SJ, 17 (1968), No. 466, 18 (1969), No. 542.

Rev. by P. H. Butter in MLR, 64 (Oct. 1969), 887–888.

752. Cancelled.

753. *Yofyllis, Fot. *Xena Louloudia*. Athens, 1968.

A poetry anthology, including translations of eight poems by Shelley and one each by Byron and Keats.

Books and Articles Relating to Shelley and His Circle

754. *Able, Augustus Henry. *George Meredith and Thomas Love Peacock: A Study in Literary Influence*. New York: Phaeton, 1970.

Reprint of a 1933 book.

Abrams, M. H. See No. 475.

755. Allentuck, Marcia. "An Unpublished Account of Encounters with William Godwin in 1804," K-SJ, 20 (1971), 19–21.

Found in Joseph Carrington Cabell's diary of 1804.

756. Andrews, S. G. "Shelley, Medwin, and *The Wandering Jew*," K-SJ, 20 (1971), 78–86.

Contends that the poem should be restored to the Shelley canon because Medwin had confused it with a later poem of his own.

757. Antippas, Andy P. "The Structure of Shelley's *St. Irvyne*: Parallelism and the Gothic Mode of Evil," *Tulane Studies in English*, 18 (1970), 59–71.†‡

Shelley relies upon the structural principle of parallelism, "the variant repetition of narrative action and description."

758. Armstrong, Richard A. *Faith and Doubt in the Century's Poets*. Folcroft, Pa.: Folcroft, 1970.

Reprint of 1898 volume. Chapter on Shelley, "The Spirit of Revolt."

Arnold, Matthew. See No. 194.

759. Artaud, Antonin. *The Cenci*. Translated by Simon Watson Taylor. New York: Grove, 1969.

Largely based on Shelley's play.

Rev. by Richard M. Buck in LJ, 95 (1 May 1970), 1758; in *Choice*, 7 (Nov. 1970), 1244.

760. Artmann, H. C. *Frankenstein in Sussex. Fleis und Industrie*. Frankfurt: Suhrkamp, 1969.

Fiction.

761. *Axon, William Edward Armytage. *Shelley's Vegetarianism*. Read at a meeting of the Shelley Society, University College, Gower Street, London, 12 Nov. 1890. New York: Haskell House, 1971.

Reprint of an 1890 work.

762. Banerji, Jibon. "The Role of Godwinian Ideas in *The Borderers*," *Calcutta Review*, N.S. 1 (Jan.–March 1970), 419–422.

The Borderers tries to expose the ethical fallacies of *Political Justice*. The source of evil is in the individual, not in society. Hartman, whose thesis is similar, is not mentioned.

763. *Barker, Kathleen. "The Terrys and Godwin in Bristol," *Theatre Notebook*, 22 (Autumn 1967).

763a. Barnes, James J. "Galignani and the Publication of English Books in France: A Postscript," *Library*, 25 (Dec. 1970), 294–313.

Galignani was agent for "Bentley's Standard Novels Series," which included Godwin's *Fleetwood*.

764. Baskyar, D. D. "Beatrice of Shelley's Drama *The Cenci*," *Indian Journal of English Studies*, 12 (1971), 33–41.

"Shelley exalts the character of his heroine. . . . In his hands the historical Beatrice becomes an angel of innocence."

765. Bebbington, W. G. "Shelley's Cottage," N&Q, 216 (May 1971), 163–165.†

Discusses "the small house at Bishopsgate in Windsor Great Park which Shelley had leased, apparently for one year from 3 August 1815" and offers some conjectures about its possible present existence.

Bentley, G. E., Jr. See No. 205.

Bloom, Harold, ed. See Nos. 45, 46.

Bloom, Harold. See Nos. 45, 46, 48, 137.

Blunden, Edmund. See Nos. 212, 495.

766. Bornstein, George. *Yeats and Shelley*. Chicago and London: Univ. of Chicago, 1970.

Rev. by Peter A. Dollard in LJ, 95 (1 June 1970), 2156; in *Choice*, 7 (June 1970), 539; in TLS, 12 March 1971, p. 292; by Howard Sergeant in *English*, 20 (Spring 1971), 26–27. Also see No. 44.

767. Brailsford, H. N. *Shelley, Godwin and Their Circle*. Hamden, Conn.: Archon, 1969.

A reprint of a book first published in 1913.

768. Brew, Claude C. *Shelley and Mary in 1817: A Critical Study of the Text and Poetical Evolution of the 'Dedication' of "The Revolt of Islam," Based on a New Examination of the MSS and Including Hitherto Unpublished Material*. London: Keats-Shelley Memorial Association, 1971.

769. Brew, Claude Clifton. "An Examination, from the Manuscripts, of Percy Bysshe Shelley's 'Dedication' to *The Revolt of Islam*" [Doctoral dissertation, Ohio, 1969], DAI, 31 (Dec. 1970), 2868-A.

Briggs, Asa, ed. See No. 49.

770. Bright, Michael Helm. "The Nineteenth-Century English Pastoral Elegy" [Doc-

toral dissertation, Tulane, 1969], DAI, 30 (Apr. 1970), 4443-A.

Among other works, treats *Adonais.*

771. *Brophy, Robert J. " 'Tamar,' 'The Cenci,' and Incest," AL, 42 (May 1970), 241–244.†‡

Robinson Jeffers' poem was indebted to Shelley's play in structure, theme, and poetic vision.

771a. Bruns, Gerald L. "Poetry as Reality: The Orpheus Myth and Its Modern Counterparts," ELH, 37 (June 1970), 263–286.

Briefly discusses *Prometheus Unbound,* in which language is seen as a "formative process that mediates between the constructive mind and the 'senseless and shapeless' material."

772. Burnett, Joan N. "The Promethean Act," *Aryan Path,* 40 (Oct. 1969), 428–433.

The "Promethean act," interpreted as the "conquest of nature . . . divorced from spiritual finality," is contrasted to the Shelleyan and Aeschylean views of Prometheus. Passing mention of Keats.

Burton, Elizabeth. See No. 51.

Bush, Douglas. See No. 52.

773. Cameron, Kenneth Neill, ed. *Shelley and His Circle, 1773–1822.* The Carl H. Pforzheimer Library. Vols. III and IV. Cambridge, Mass.: Harvard Univ.; London: Oxford Univ. (1970).

Rev. by Richard H. Fogle in VQR, 46 (Summer 1970), 525–528; by John Holloway in Spec, 225, 29 Aug. 1970, p. 215; by John Clubbe in SAQ, 70 (Winter 1971), 122–125; in TLS, 23 Apr. 1971, p. 482; by Neville Rogers in BC, 20 (Autumn 1971), 400, 403–404, 407; in *Choice,* 7 (Dec. 1970), 1370, 1372. Also see Nos. 44, 109a.

774. Campbell, William Royce. "Shelley's Concept of Conscience," K-SJ, 19 (1970), 49–61.†

Ultimately, Shelley rejects conscience as a passive thing and searches for a more active basis in the imagination.

Cheney, Thomas E. See No. 225.

775. Chernaik, Judith. "A Systematic Search of Manuscripts of Shelley's Poems in British Libraries," *American Philosophical Society Yearbook* (1971), pp. 555–556.

776. Chernaik, Judith. "Textual Emendations for Three Poems by Shelley," K-SJ, 19 (1970), 41–48.†

The poems are "Mutability" ("The flower that smiles today"), a fragment beginning, "My dearest Mary," and "Hymn to Intellectual Beauty." Shelley's notebooks serve as the authority.

Clarke, Isabel C. See No. 229.

777. *Clarke, John Henry. *The God of Shelley and Blake.* New York: Haskell House, 1966.

Reprint of a 1903 book.

Coleman, William E. See No. 54a.

778. Collins, Ben L. "The Stanzaic Pattern of Shelley's 'Ode to the West Wind,' " K-SJ, 19 (1970), 7–8.†

Shelley used a sonnet form based on *terza rima.*

779. Colmer, John. "Godwin's *Mandeville* and Peacock's *Nightmare Abbey,*" RES, 21 (Aug. 1970), 331–336.

The influence of Godwin's novel upon *Nightmare Abbey.*

Colville, Derek. See No. 233.

780. Cone, Carl B. *The English Jacobins: Reformers in Late 18th Century England.* New York: Scribner's, 1968.

Discusses Godwin's defense of twelve members of London Corresponding Society and Society for Constitutional Information indicted for treason in 1794.

781. Cooper, Bryan. "Shelley's *Alastor*: The Quest for a Vision," K-SJ, 19 (1970), 63–76.†

Argues that the poem is "unified in a deeply symbolic way through the interweaving of motifs, each of which conveys multiple meanings."

Cooper, Robert M. See No. 235.

782. Cousins, James H. *The Work Promethean: Interpretations and Applications of Shelley's Poetry.* Port Washington, N.Y., and London: Kennikat, 1970.

Reprint of a 1938 book.

783. *Covi, C. "Shelley e Dante," in *Vita, cultura, scuola.* Trent: Temi, 1968.

784. Curran, Stuart. *Shelley's "Cenci": Scorpions Ringed with Fire.* Princeton: Princeton Univ., 1970.

Rev. by Joseph W. Donohue, Jr., in K-SJ, 20 (1971), 137–139; by Barton Wimble in LJ, 96 (1 Apr. 1971), 1286.

785. Curran, Stuart. "Shelley's Emendations to the *Hymn to Intellectual Beauty*," ELN, 7 (June 1970), 270–273.

These emendations to the printed version of the poem found in the *Examiner* of 19 Jan. 1817 are in Shelley's hand, and are found in the Silsbee notebook at Harvard University.

786. Curran, Stuart. "Shelley's Satiric Fragment on a Heavenly Feast: A Corrected Text," N&Q, 215 (Oct. 1970), 382.†

Edits lines 1–4.

787. D'Avanzo, Mario L. "Ahab, the Grecian Pantheon and Shelley's *Prometheus Unbound*: The Dynamics of Myth in *Moby Dick*," *Books at Brown*, 24 (1971), 19–44.

Argues that closing chapters of *Moby Dick* employ Shelley's symbolism in reverse to overthrow idealism; specific imagistic parallels between the two works are found.

Davenport, John A. See No. 241a.

788. Dawson, Carl. *His Fine Wit: A Study of Thomas Love Peacock*. London: Routledge and Kegan Paul; Berkeley: Univ. of California (1970).

Rev. by Angus Calder as "Booze vincit omnia" in NS, 10 Apr. 1970, p. 511; by Robert Nye in *Times* (London), 11 Apr. 1970, p. iv; in TLS, 23 Apr. 1970, p. 450; in *Choice*, 7 (June 1970), 540; by Rayner Heppenstall in *Encounter*, 34 (June 1970), 50–52; by John Cronin in *Studies*, 59 (Summer 1970), 219–221; by Michael Cooke in *Yale Review*, 60 (Dec. 1970), 294–301; by D. N. Gallon in RES, 22 (May 1971), 226–228; by John Epsey in *Nineteenth Century Fiction*, 26 (June 1971), 125–126; by Donald H. Reiman in K-SJ, 20 (1971), 130–132. Also see No. 44.

789. Dawson, Carl. *Thomas Love Peacock*. See K-SJ, 18 (1969), No. 566, 19 (1970), No. 307.

Rev. by Michael P. Gallagher in *Studies*, 59 (Summer 1970), 218–219; by Lionel Madden in *Victorian Studies*, 13 (June 1970), 435–437.

789a. *De Bartolomeis, Mariagrazia. "Il 'Prometeo liberato' di P. B. Shelley," *Rivista Letteraria per i Licei Classico, Scientifico, Artistico e per l'Istituto Magistrale*, 1 (1968–1969), 108–109.

de Beer, Sir Gavin. See No. 243.

790. *Del Litto, Vittorio. "Stendhal, Shelley et Marivaux," *Stendhal Club* (Lausanne), 11 (1968–1969), 72–73.

790a. Del Prado, Wilma. "The Philosophy of *Prometheus Unbound*," *Saint Louis University Research Journal* (Philippines), 1 (Dec. 1970), 716–722.

Undergraduate term paper.

D'Haen, Christine. See No. 532.

790b. Dobell, Robert J. "Bertram Dobell and T. J. Wise," BC, 19 (Autumn 1970), 348–355.

Dobell publishes excerpts from his grandfather's diary relating to Wise and the Shelley Society.

Donohue, Joseph W., Jr. See No. 61.

791. *Dowden, Edward. *Letters about Shelley, Interchanged by Three Friends—Edward Dowden, Richard Garnett, and William Michael Rossetti*. Ed. with introduction by R. S. Garnett. New York: AMS, 1971.

Reprint of a 1917 book.

792. Duncan-Jones, Katherine. "Miss Mitford and *Adonais*," RES, 22 (May 1971), 170–172.†

In a hitherto unpublished letter to Haydon, dated 14 Sept. 1821, she offers an unfavorable opinion of Shelley's poem.

792a. Edgar, Pelham. *A Study of Shelley, with Special Reference to His Nature Poetry*. New York: Haskell House, 1970.

Reprint of 1899 doctoral dissertation.

793. Edmunds, E. W. *Shelley and His Poetry*. Folcroft, Pa.: Folcroft, 1969. "Poetry and Life Series."

Reprint of a 1911 book.

794. Egbert, Donald D. *Social Radicalism and the Arts: Western Europe, a Cultural History from the French Revolution to 1968*. New York: Knopf, 1970.

Ch. vii, sec. 2: "Godwin and His Influence on Owen, Coleridge, Shelley, Leigh Hunt's Circle, etc."

795. *Elledge, W. Paul. "Good, Evil, and the Function of Art: A Note on Shelley," *Tennessee Studies in Literature*, 14 (1969), 87–92.‡

Elledge, W. Paul, and Richard L. Hoffman, eds. See No. 65.

796. Elton, Oliver. *Shelley*. Folcroft, Pa.:

Folcroft, 1969.

Reprint of a 1924 book.

797. Fain, John Tyree. "Peacock's Essay on Steam Navigation," *South Atlantic Bulletin*, 35 (May 1970), 11–15.

Peacock's review of the *Report from the Select Committee on the House of Commons, on Steam Navigation to India* has value, and should have been included in the Halliford Edition of his works.

798. *Fass, Barbara. "Shelley and St. Paul," *Concerning Poetry*, 4 (Spring 1971), 23–24.†

The mystical experience in "Hymn to Intellectual Beauty" resembles St. Paul's vision on the road to Damascus.

799. Faure, Georges. *Les Éléments du rythme poétique en anglais moderne: Esquisse d'une nouvelle analyse et essai d'application au "Prometheus Unbound" de P. B. Shelley.* The Hague and Paris: Mouton, 1970. "Studies in English Literature, 53."†

Rev. in *Bulletin Critique du Livre Français*, 26 (1971), 525.

Feldman, Alan. See No. 545.

800. *Finney, Ross Lee. *The Martyr's Elegy.* For high voice, chorus of mixed voices, and orchestra. Text from Shelley's *Adonais*. New York: C. F. Peters, 1967.

Piano-vocal score.

801. Firkins, Oscar W. *Power and Elusiveness in Shelley.* New York: Octagon, 1970.

Reprint of a 1937 book.

802. Flagg, John S. "Shelley and Aristotle: Elements of the *Poetics* in Shelley's Theory of Poetry," SIR, 9 (Winter 1970), 44–67.†‡

Aristotle's work, just as much as Plato's, may be viewed as a major source for the *Defence*.

803. Flax, Dorothy Ellin. "I Weep for Adonais" [Poem], *Aryan Path*, 42 (Feb. 1971), 71.

Fogle, Richard Harter. See No. 549.

804. Foxell, Nigel. *Ten Poems Analyzed.* See K-SJ, 18 (1969), No. 577.

Rev. by Karl Heinz Göller in ASNS, 206 (May 1969), 51–52.

805. French, Roberts W. "Shelley's *Adonais*, 36," Exp, 29 (Oct. 1970), Item 16.‡

Shelley's reference to Milton as "the third among the Sons of light" is after Enoch and Noah, not after Homer and Dante.

805a. Friedman, Barton R. "Under a Leprous Moon: Action and Image in *The King's Threshold*," *Arizona Quarterly*, 26 (Spring 1970), 39–53.

Yeats's play expresses Shelley's belief that the exercise of imagination, not calculation, should order human life.

806. Frye, Northrop. "The Critical Path: An Essay on the Social Context of Literary Criticism," *Daedalus*, 99 (Spring 1970), 268–342.

Discusses Peacock's *Four Ages of Poetry* and Shelley's *Defence of Poetry*.

807. Frye, Northrop. "Mythos and Logos," *Yearbook of Comparative and General Literature*, 18 (1969), 5–18.†

A thoroughgoing comparison of Shelley's *Defence* with Sidney's.

808. Fuller, Jean Overton. *Shelley: A Biography.* See K-SJ, 18 (1969), No. 579, 19 (1970), No. 317.

Rev. by K[enneth]. N[eill]. C[ameron]. in ELN, 7, Supplement (Sept. 1969), 41; by J. B. Beer in *Critical Quarterly*, 11 (Winter 1969), 382–383.

809. Fuller, Roy. "The Osmotic Sap," TLS, 14 May 1971, pp. 559–561. Replies by F. R. Leavis in TLS, 21 May 1971, p. 593; by Alexander Henderson, J. R. Prynne, Henning Krabbe, Walter Roberts, and Helen MacGregor, 28 May 1971, pp. 620–621; by Desmond King-Hele, 4 June 1971, p. 649; by Walter Roberts, 11 June 1971, p. 677; by Robert Ward, 18 June 1971, p. 707.

Discusses the relation of science to the poetic imagination, and juxtaposes Leavis' negative remarks about Shelley's "Ode to the West Wind" (in *Revaluations*) with Desmond King-Hele's view in *Shelley: His Thought and Work.*

810. Furtado, R. de Loyola. *Shelley: Concept of Nature.* Folcroft, Pa.: Folcroft, 1969.

Reprint of a 1958 book. See K-SJ, 9 (1960), No. 442.

811. Gallon, D. N. "T. L. Peacock's Later Years: The Evidence of Unpublished Letters," RES, 20 (Aug. 1969), 315–319. Reply by Peter A. Hawkins [Letter] in RES, 21 (Aug. 1970), 338.†

Peacock describes his unhappy later

life in letters to Hobhouse, 1839–1865. Hawkins takes issue with several statements by Gallon.

812. Gardner, John. "Frankenstein" [Poem], KR, 31, No. 4 (1969), 505–506.

812a. Garmon, Gerald Meredith. "Development of Tragic Realism in English Literature: 1720–1820" [Doctoral dissertation, Auburn, 1968], DA, 29 (Oct. 1968), 1207-A.

Godwin.

813. Garrett, John C. *Utopias in Literature since the Romantic Period.* Christchurch, N.Z.: Univ. of Canterbury, 1968. "The Macmillan Brown Lectures."

Shelley's poetry, particularly *Prometheus Unbound,* is extensively discussed.

Rev. in *Choice,* 7 (May 1970), 379.

814. George, Margaret. *One Woman's "Situation": A Study of Mary Wollstonecraft.* Urbana: Univ. of Illinois, 1970.

Rev. by Carl B. Cone in *American Historical Review,* 76 (Feb. 1971), 149.

815. Gerbner, George, *et al.*, ed. *The Analysis of Communication Contents: Developments in Scientific Theories and Computer Techniques.* New York: John Wiley, 1969.

Joseph Raben's "Content Analysis and the Study of Poetry," pp. 175–186, includes a comparison of *Paradise Lost* and *Prometheus Unbound.*

816. Gershman, Herbert S. "Romanticism Revisited," *Symposium,* 22 (Fall-Winter 1969), 241–254.

The Cenci is cited as an example of a play that illustrates the destructive but fascinating Romantic beauty of horror combined with eroticism.

Gingerich, Solomon F. See No. 76.

816a. Glimm, James York. "Five Essays on Mystical Experience in the Works of Wordsworth, Coleridge and Shelley" [Doctoral dissertation, Texas, 1969], DAI, 30 (Oct. 1969), 1525-A.

817. Godwin, William. *Caleb Williams.* Ed. David McCracken. London: Oxford Univ., 1970, "Oxford English Novels Series."

Rev. in TLS, 9 Apr. 1970, p. 381; in *Choice,* 7 (Feb. 1971), 1662.

818. Godwin, William. *Enquiry Concerning Political Justice.* Abridged and ed. K. Codell Carter. Oxford: Clarendon, 1971.

Rev. in TLS, 9 Apr. 1971, p. 427.

819. *Godwin, William. *Mary Wollstonecraft no omoide.* [*Memoirs of Mary Wollstonecraft*]. [Translated by] Shirai Atsushi and Shirai Takako. Tokyo: Miraisha, 1970. [In Japanese.]

820. *Godwin, William. *Memoirs of Mary Wollstonecraft.* Ed. with a preface, a supplement chronologically arranged and containing hitherto unpublished or uncollected material, and a bibliographical note, by W. Clark Durant. New York: Haskell House, 1969.

Reprint of 1927 edition.

821. *Godwin, William. ["Of Population"], in *Wirtschaftsfreiheit und Wirtschaftsgesetz in der englischen ökonomischen Klassik,* ed. Carl Brinkmann (Darmstadt: Wissenschaftliche Buchgesellschaft, 1968).

Reprint of 1948 edition.

822. *Godwin, William. *Godwin's "Political Justice"; Reprint of the Essay on "Property," from the Original Edition.* Ed. H. S. Salt. St. Clair Shores, Mich.: Scholarly, n.d. [ca. 1969].

Reprint of 1890 edition.

823. *Godwin, William. "Ricerca sulla giustizia politica e sulla sua influenza su morale e felicità," in *Gli Anarchi,* ed. Gian Mario Bravo. Turin: Unione Tipografico-Editrice Torinese, 1971.

Appears to be a translation of *Political Justice,* in whole or in part.

824. *Godwin, William. *Seiji no seigi.* [*Enquiry Concerning Political Justice* (VIII).] [Translated by] Hashimoto Yoshiharu. Tokyo: Barukansha, 1969. [In Japanese.]

Goodheart, Eugene. See No. 267.

824a. *Górski, Konrad. "The Reception of Shelley in Polish Literature," in *Gorski vijenic: A Garland of Essays Offered to Professor Elizabeth Mary Hill,* ed. R. Auty, L. R. Lewitter, and A. P. Vlasto (Cambridge: Modern Humanities Research Association, 1970), pp. 155–164.

824b. Goslee, Nancy Moore. "Mutual Amity: *Paradise Lost* and the Romantic Epic" [Doctoral dissertation, Yale, 1968], DAI, 30 (Aug. 1969), 723-A.

Treats *Prometheus Unbound* and the "Hyperion" fragments.

825. *Grabo, Carl. *The Meaning of "The*

Witch of Atlas." New York: Russell & Russell, 1971.

Reprint of a 1935 book.

826. Groot, H. B. de. "The Ouroboros and the Romantic Poets: A Renaissance Emblem in Blake, Coleridge, and Shelley," ES, 50 (Dec. 1969), 553–564.

The emblem is that of a snake which has curled itself round in a circle with its tail near or in its mouth. Shelley may have used this image in "The Dæmon of the World" and in *Prometheus Unbound.*

827. Gruman, Gerald J. *A History of Ideas about the Prolongation of Life: The Evolution of Prolongevity Hypotheses to 1800.* Philadelphia: American Philosophical Society, 1966. "Transactions of the American Philosophical Society, N.S. 56, pt. 9."

In Godwin there is a relationship between individual moral improvement and prolongevity, the mind being potentially omnipotent over the body.

828. *Grylls, R. Glynn. *Mary Shelley: A Biography*. New York: Haskell House, 1969.

Reprint of a 1938 book.

829. Guinn, John Pollard. *Shelley's Political Thought.* See K-SJ, 19 (1970), No. 325.

Rev. in *Choice*, 6 (Jan. 1970), 1574; by K[enneth]. N[eill]. C[ameron]. in ELN, 8, Supplement (Sept. 1970), 43.

830. Hall, James M. "The Spider and the Silkworm: Shelley's 'Letter to Maria Gisborne,' " KSMB, 20 (1969), 1–10.

The extended pair of similes of the spider and the silkworm in the first fourteen lines of this verse epistle reveal two of the poet's most important themes: "the nature of the poetic powers, and the problems a poet must face while living in a world hostile to poetry."

831. Hall, Jean Rogers. "The Transcendent Image: A Study of Shelley's Major Poetry" [Doctoral dissertation, California, Riverside, 1970], DAI, 31 (Feb. 1971), 4120-A.

832. Hall, Spencer. " 'With Nature Reconciled': A Study of Shelley's Visionary Humanism" [Doctoral dissertation, Stanford, 1970], DAI, 31 (May 1971), 6010-A.

Hargreaves-Mawdsley, W. N. See No. 276.

Hassett, Michael E. See No. 85.

833. Hawk, Susan Lee. "Shelley's Shadows: Studies in Analogy" [Doctoral dissertation, Yale, 1970], DAI, 31 (June 1971), 6610-A.

834. Haworth, Helen E. " 'Ode to the West Wind' and the Sonnet Form," K-SJ, 20 (1971), 71–77.

In this poem Shelley combines "the printed pattern and rhyme scheme of terza rima with the rhetorical pattern of the sonnet."

834a. Hawthorne, J. M. "The Strange Deaths of Sally, Ann, Lucy, and Others . . . ," *Trivium*, 7 (May 1971), 70–80.†

Shelley is among the Romantic writers using the imagined death of a loved one in their poems.

Hayden, John O., ed. See No. 86.

Hearn, L. See No. 89.

835. Heath-Stubbs, John. *The Pastoral.* London: Oxford Univ., 1969.

Includes Shelley.

Heath-Stubbs, John. See Nos. 280, 581.

Hewish, John. See No. 283.

836. Hewitt, Douglas. "Entertaining Ideas: A Critique of Peacock's *Crochet Castle*," EC, 20 (Apr. 1970), 200–212.†

Concludes that Peacock's unwillingness to take any ideas seriously is fatal to the effect of his novel.

837. Hildebrand, William H. "A Look at the Third and Fourth Spirit Songs: *Prometheus Unbound*, I," K-SJ, 20 (1971), 87–99.

The spirits are not ideas, but rather symbolic reflections of the metaphoric progression of the drama from dark to light.

838. Hoff, Peter Sloat. "Comedy and Satire in the Novels of Thomas Love Peacock" [Doctoral dissertation, Stanford, 1970], DAI, 31 (May 1971), 6058-A.

839. *Hogg, Thomas Jefferson. *The Life of Percy Bysshe Shelley*. Introduced by Edward Dowden. St. Clair Shores, Mich.: Scholarly, 1970.

Reprint of 1906 abridgment of a book first published in 1858.

840. Housman, A. E. *The Confines of Criticism: The Cambridge Inaugural, 1911.* The Complete Text, with Notes by John

Carter. Cambridge: Cambridge Univ., 1969.

Appended is an abridgment of "Shelley, Swinburne, and Housman" by Carter and John Sparrow from TLS; see K-SJ, 19 (1970), No. 303.

Rev. by William White in AN&Q, 8 (Jan. 1970), 66, 79–80, reply by John Carter, 8 (May 1970), 134; by John Colmer in AUMLA, No. 35 (May 1971), pp. 118–121.

Housman, A. E. See No. 587.

841. *Hughes, A. M. D. *The Nascent Mind of Shelley*. Oxford: Clarendon, 1971.

Reissue of 1947 book.

Hughes, Daniel. See No. 137.

842. Hughes, Daniel. "Shelley, Leonardo, and the Monsters of Thought," *Criticism*, 12 (Summer 1970), 195–212.†‡

Examines Shelley's expression of two archetypal creatures of thought, the "*demonic* avatars of obstruction and dismay" and the "benign *apocalyptic* images of sustenance and completion" in "On the Medusa of Leonardo da Vinci" and *Prometheus Unbound*, IV.

843. Hunter, Parks C., Jr. "Shelley's *Alastor*, 683," Exp, 29 (Jan. 1971), Item 40.‡

Finds a parallel between the *Alastor* poet and St. Leon in Godwin's novel of the same name.

Huntley, Reid De Berry. See No. 93a.

844. Jack, Adolphus Alfred. *Shelley: An Essay*. Port Washington, N.Y., and London: Kennikat, 1970.

Reprint of a 1904 book.

Jelistratowa, Anna A. See No. 289.

845. Jellicoe, Ann. "Shelley," *New Society*, 20 Aug. 1970, pp. 320–322.

A general review of his life, with emphasis on his revolutionary impact and his relevance to today's society.

846. Jenkins, Elizabeth. "Dr. Gully, Severn and an Experiment in Psychometry," KSMB, 21 (1970), 39–40.

Gully, a friend of Sir Percy Florence and Lady Shelley, confirms Lady Shelley's account of the spectral reappearance of the poet.

847. Kaminsky, Alice R. *George Henry Lewes as a Literary Critic*. Syracuse: Syracuse Univ., 1968.

Lewes admired Shelley, especially as a reformer, and much preferred him to the other Romantic poets.

Rev. by Kerry McSweeney in QQ, 76 (Winter 1969), 730–731.

Kaplan, Charles, ed. See No. 606.

Keating, L[ouis]. Clark. See No. 294.

Kelly, Linda. See No. 613.

848. Kendall, Lyle H., Jr. "On the Date of a Shelley Letter to Hogg," K-SJ, 19 (1970), 8–9.†

Shelley's letter to Hogg, beginning "am now at Grove's," can be correctly dated from its postmark as 20 Apr. 1818.

849. Kerenyi, C. *Prometheus: Archetypal Image of Human Existence*. Translated by Ralph Manheim. New York: Pantheon, 1963. "Bollingen Series, 65, vol. 1."

Brief discussion of Shelley's *Prometheus Unbound*.

850. King, Norman. " 'The Airy Form of Things Forgotten': Madame de Staël, l'Utilitarisme, et l'Impulsion Libérale," *Cahiers Staëliens*, No. 11 (Dec. 1970), pp. 6–26.

Mentions Godwin.

851. King-Hele, Desmond. *Shelley: His Thought and Work*. Second Edition. London: Macmillan; Teaneck, N.J.: Fairleigh Dickinson Univ. (1971).

First edition published in 1960. See K-SJ, 10 (1961), No. 414, 11 (1962), No. 486, 12 (1963), No. 426.

Knight, G. Wilson. See No. 616.

852. Kovačević, Ivanka. "William Godwin, The Factory Children and Dickens' *David Copperfield*," *Filološki Pregled* (Belgrade), 8, Nos. 3–4 (1970), 29–40.

Focuses on the Ruffigny episode in *Fleetwood* (Bk. I, Ch. xi–xiii), where a minor character recalls the hardships endured as an industrial child laborer. Comparisons are made with Dickens.

853. Kreutz, Christian. "Hartley Coleridges Prometheusbild," *Anglia*, 88 (June 1970), 196–221.

Brief mention of Shelley's influence.

854. Krnacik, John, Jr. "The Hero of Feeling in William Godwin's Fiction" [Doctoral dissertation, Michigan, 1968], DAI, 30 (July 1969), 284–A.

Kroeber, Karl, with Alfred and Theodora Kroeber. See No. 301.

855. Kuić, Ranka. *Revolucionarna Misao Per-*

sija Biša Šelija U Njegovim Proznim I Poetskim Delima: Njeni Izvori, Razvoj I Odnos Prema Idejama Viljema Godvina I Tomasa Peina. [*The Revolutionary Thought of Percy Bysshe Shelley; Its Roots, Its Development and the Relation It Bears to the Ideas of William Godwin and Thomas Paine.*] Belgrade: Univ. of Belgrade, 1968.†

856. Kurtz, Benjamin P. *The Pursuit of Death: A Study of Shelley's Poetry*. Folcroft, Pa.: Folcroft, 1969; St. Claire Shores, Mich.: Scholarly, 1971.
Reprints of a 1933 book.

857. *Kurtz, Benjamin P. *The Pursuit of Death: A Study of Shelley's Poetry*. New preface by James D. Hart. New York: Octagon, 1970.
Another reprint, but with a new preface.

858. La Cassagnère, C[hristian]. *La mystique du Prometheus Unbound de Shelley: Essai d'interprétation*. Paris: Lettres Modernes, 1970.
Rev. in *Bulletin Critique du Livre Français*, 25 (1970), 1229; by Bernard Brugière in *Langues Modernes*, 65 (March–Apr. 1971), 75.

859. Lane, Margaret. "Frances Wright (1795–1852): The Great Experiment," *Contemporary Review*, 218 (Jan. 1971), 7–14.
A radical social reformer in America, she became acquainted with Mary Shelley. Bibliography appended. Also see Kenneth Neill Cameron, *Shelley and His Circle*, III, 410.

Langbaum, Robert. See No. 102.

860. Lasky, Melvin J. "The Prometheans: On the Imagery of Fire and Revolution," *Encounter*, 31 (Oct. 1968), 22–32.†
Includes a discussion of *Prometheus Unbound*.

861. Lea, F. A. *Shelley and the Romantic Revolution*. Folcroft, Pa.: Folcroft, 1969; New York: Haskell House, 1971.†
Reprints of a 1945 book.

Lean, E. Tangye. See No. 103.

862. Lengeler, Rainer. "Shelleys Sonett Ozymandias," *Neueren Sprachen*, N.F. 18 (Nov. 1969), 532–539. [In German.]

862a. Lerner, Laurence. "An Essay on Pastoral," EC, 20 (July 1970), 275–297.†
Includes Shelley's *Epipsychidion*.

863. Lévy, Maurice. "Edgar Poe et la Tradition 'Gothique,' " *Caliban*, No. 5 (Jan. 1968), pp. 35–51.
Mentions Godwin's and Shelley's Gothic novels.

864. Lewis, C. S. *Selected Literary Essays, by C. S. Lewis*. Ed. Walter Hooper. London: Cambridge Univ., 1969.
Includes an essay on "Shelley, Dryden, and Mr. Eliot."

864a. Liebert, Herman W. "The Beinecke Library: Accessions 1970," *Yale Univ. Library Gazette*, 45 (Apr. 1971), 141–152.
More information on the editor of Shelley's *Poems and Sonnets*, "Charles Alfred Seymour." The name is a pseudonym for Thomas J. Wise, who employed the deception because of Lady Shelley's objection to having the poems published. See No. 915a.

Lund, Mary G. See No. 628a.

Lutz, Paul V. See No. 311.

865. McConnell, Frank D. "Shelleyan 'Allegory': *Epipsychidion*," K-SJ, 20 (1971), 100–112.
Shelleyan "allegory" is defined as "the intense awareness of the imaginative roots of poetic tradition, and the ability to transform these traditions into self-critical vehicles of the autonomous Romantic imagination."

866. McCracken, David. "Godwin's *Caleb Williams:* A Fictional Rebuttal of Burke," *Studies in Burke and His Time*, 11 (Winter 1969–1970), 1442–1452.
Argues that Falkland represents the pernicious Burkean principles of chivalry and that the novel is more political than has been thought.

867. McCracken, David. "Godwin's Literary Theory: The Alliance between Fiction and Political Philosophy," PQ, 49 (Jan. 1970), 113–133.‡
Contrary to many critics' belief, "Godwin the philosopher and Godwin the novelist were allies, not antagonists."

868. McCracken, David. "Godwin's Reading in Burke," ELN, 7 (June 1970), 264–270.
Godwin's reading of Burke "had an important and direct effect" on *Political Justice* and *Caleb Williams*.

869. McCrorie, Edward Pollitt. "Shelley's Style: From the Beginnings to 1819"

[Doctoral dissertation, Brown, 1970], DAI, 31 (June 1971), 6621-A.

870. MacDonald, Daniel J. *The Radicalism of Shelley and Its Sources.* New York: Phaeton, 1969.

Reprint of a 1912 book.

Rev. in *Choice*, 7 (Dec. 1970), 1376.

MacEachen, Dugald B. See No. 632.

871. Macey, Samuel L. "Shelley and the New Romantics," *Texas Quarterly*, 14 (Summer 1971), 91–95.

Shelley's work, although unpopular now, is particularly relevant to today's youth, and deserves another reading.

871a. *McNally, James. "Browning's Political Thought," QQ, 77 (1970), 578–590.‡

Notes Shelley's early influence.

872. McNiece, Gerald. *Shelley and the Revolutionary Idea.* Cambridge, Mass.: Harvard Univ.; London: Oxford Univ. (1969).

Rev. by Duane B. Schneider in LJ, 94 (15 Nov. 1969), 4146; by Melvin T. Solve in *Arizona Quarterly*, 26 (Summer 1970), 189–191; in TLS, 23 July 1970, p. 810; by K[enneth]. N[eill]. C[ameron]. in ELN, 8, Supplement (Sept. 1970), 45; by Gilbert Thomas in *English*, 19 (Autumn 1970), 105–106; by Donald H. Reiman in JEGP, 69 (Oct. 1970), 678–679. Also see No. 44.

873. McTaggart, William J. *England in 1819: Church, State and Poverty.* A study, textual and historical, of "A Ballad" by Shelley, formerly entitled "Young Parson Richards," including hitherto unpublished MS material. London: Keats-Shelley Memorial Association, 1970.

See K-SJ, 18 (1969), No. 606, 19 (1970), No. 337.

Rev. by Sylva Norman in *Aryan Path*, 41 (May 1970), 245; by Joseph DeRocco in K-SJ, 20 (1971), 140–141.

874. McTaggart, William J. "Some New Inquiries into Shelley's Platonism," KSMB, 21 (1970), 41–59.

Traces the development of Shelley's theme of Platonic love from *Alastor* to *Adonais*, with particular emphasis on *Prince Athanase.*

875. Madden, Lionel. "A Short Guide to Peacock Studies," *Critical Survey*, 4 (Summer 1970), 193–197.

A brief bibliography with critical comments.

876. Maddox, Donald L. "Shelley's *Alastor* and the Legacy of Rousseau," SIR, 9 (Spring 1970), 82–98.†‡

Rousseau's autobiographic works explain inconsistencies between *Alastor* and its preface, and provide insight into the figure of the Poet in the poem.

Manning, Peter J. See No. 321.

Marlowe, Derek. See No. 325.

877. *Marshall, Mrs. Julian [Florence A. Marshall]. *The Life & Letters of Mary Wollstonecraft Shelley.* 2 vols. New York: Haskell House, 1970.†

Reprint of an 1889 work.

878. Mason, Francis Claiborne. *A Study in Shelley Criticism: An Examination of the Principal Interpretations of Shelley's Art and Philosophy in England from 1818 to 1860.* Folcroft, Pa.: Folcroft, 1970.

Reprint of a 1937 book based on a 1929 doctoral dissertation.

Massey, Irving J. See No. 112.

Masson, David. See No. 637.

Mather, J. Marshall. See No. 327.

879. Mathews, James W. "Another Possible Origin of Howells's *The Shadow of a Dream*," *AL*, 42 (Jan. 1971), 558–562.†

"The Sensitive Plant" is a more likely source than *Endymion* for Howells's novel in terms of images, mood, and ending. As the lady exists as essence of divinity for the plant, so does Hermia for Faulkner; Faulkner has characteristics of the plant, and his degeneration and death are described in images similar to Shelley's.

880. Mathewson, George. "Matthew Arnold's 'Ineffectual Angel,' " KSMB, 21 (1970), 3–6.

Deals with the implications of Arnold's metaphor.

881. Matthews, G. M. *Shelley*. Harlow, Essex: Longmans, for the British Council, 1970. "Writers and Their Works, No. 214."†

Rev. in TLS, 21 Aug. 1970, p. 930; by R. A. Jones in UES, 9 (March 1971), 42.

Maurice, Frederick D. See No. 328.

882. *Maurois, André. *Ariel, ou La vie de Shelley*. Paris: Grasset, 1970.

Another edition of the popular 1923 biography.

Maurois, André. See No. 331.

883. Maxwell, J. C. "Arnold, Shelley and Joubert," N&Q, 215 (Jan. 1970) 24.

It was known as early as 1894 that Arnold's phrase "a beautiful and ineffectual angel" was an echo from Joubert.

883a. May, Leland C. "Parodies of the Gothic Novel" [Doctoral dissertation, Oklahoma State, 1969], DAI, 31 (Feb. 1971), 4128-A.

Includes Peacock's *Nightmare Abbey*.

884. *Mayor, Joseph Bickersteth. *A Classification of Shelley's Metres*. New York: Haskell House, 1971.

Reprint of an 1888 work.

885. Meadows, A. J. *The High Firmament: A Survey of Astronomy in English Literature*. Leicester: Leicester Univ., 1969.

Discusses Shelley's use of science.

Rev. by J. L. White in *Annals of Science*, 25 (Dec. 1969), 361–362; by William Powell Jones in *Isis*, 61 (Spring 1970), 121–122; by A. Armitage in *British Journal of the History of Science*, 5 (June 1970), 92.

886. *Medwin, Thomas. *The Life of Percy Bysshe Shelley: A New Edition Printed from a Copy Copiously Amended and Extended by the Author and Left Unpublished at His Death*. Introduction and commentary by H. Buxton Forman. St. Clair Shores, Mich.: Scholarly, 1971.

Reprint of 1913 edition.

Mehl, Dieter, ed. See No. 335.

Merivale, Patricia. See No. 116.

887. Mews, Hazel. *Frail Vessels: Women's Role in Women's Novels from Fanny Burney to George Eliot*. London: Athlone, 1969.

Includes a discussion of Mary Wollstonecraft Godwin's *Vindication of the Rights of Woman*.

Rev. by Sylvère Monod in EA, 23 (July–Sept. 1970), 345–346.

Miller, Barnette. See No. 445.

888. Mills, Howard. *Peacock: His Circle and His Age*. See K-SJ, 19 (1970), No. 346.

Rev. by David Gallon in *Cambridge Quarterly*, 4 (Summer 1969), 313–316; by Frederick L. Burwick in *Nineteenth Century Fiction*, 24 (Sept. 1969), 240–244; in *Choice*, 6 (Jan. 1970), 1576; by Alexander Welsh in ELN, 7 (March 1970) 225–226; by Lionel Madden in *Victorian Studies*, 13 (June 1970), 435–437; by J[ohn]. E. J[ordan]. in ELN, 8, Supplement (Sept. 1970), 40–41; by Gerald E. Enscoe in MLQ, 32 (June 1971), 226–229. Also see No. 117.

Mordell, Albert, ed. See No. 339.

889. Morton, A. L. *The English Utopia*. London: Lawrence & Wishart, 1969.

Includes references to Godwin and Shelley. First published in 1962.

Muecke, Douglas C. See No. 344.

890. Munro, Hector. "Coleridge and Shelley," KSMB, 21 (1970), 35–38.

No meeting ever occurred, but Coleridge desired it. Shelley, in turn, had great admiration for Coleridge.

891. Murphy, John Vincent. "Gothic Elements in Shelley's Canon" [Doctoral dissertation, Michigan, 1969], DAI, 30 (March 1970), 3913-A–3914-A.

891a. Murrin, Michael. *The Veil of Allegory: Some Notes toward a Theory of Allegorical Rhetoric in the English Renaissance*. Chicago and London: Univ. of Chicago, 1969.

Shelley's poetic theory is discussed, pp. 205–212.

892. Myers, Mitzi. "Aspects of William Godwin's Reputation in the 1790's" [Doctoral dissertation, Rice, 1969], DAI, 30 (Nov. 1969), 2034-A–2035-A.

893. "News & Comment," BC, 19 (Autumn 1970), 366.

Sale of *Queen Mab* (1813) for £1800.

894. *Nitchie, Elizabeth. *Mary Shelley, Author of "Frankenstein."* Westport, Conn.: Greenwood, 1970.

Reprint of a 1953 book. See K-SJ, 3 (1954), No. 223; 4 (1955), No. 254, 5 (1956), No. 289.

895. Nixon, Edna. "Mary Wollstonecraft, English Feminist," *History Today*, 20 (Sept. 1970), 655–662.

A general summary of her life and literary career.

896. Nixon, Edna. *Mary Wollstonecraft: Her Life and Times*. London: Dent, 1971.

897. Notopoulos, James A. *The Platonism of Shelley: A Study of Platonism and the Poetic Mind*. New York: Octagon, 1969.

Reprint of a book published in 1949.

See K-SJ, 1 (1952), No. 278; 2 (1953), No. 146.

897a. Orel, Harold. "Wordsworth's Repudiation of Godwinism," *Studies on Voltaire and the Eighteenth Century*, 57 (1967), 1123–1145.

Discusses Wordsworth's attraction to Enlightenment ideas, and his later rejection of them.

898. Pack, Robert Frederick. "Shelley and History: The Poet as Historian" [Doctoral dissertation, Pittsburgh, 1970], DAI, 31 (June 1971), 6564-A.

898a. Palacio, Jean de. "Encore du Nouveau sur Godwin," EA, 22 (Jan.–March 1969), 49–57. [In French.]

Examines Burton Pollin's recent contributions to Godwin scholarship.

899. Palacio, Jean de. *Mary Shelley dans son oeuvre: Contributions aux études shelleyennes*. Paris: Klincksieck, 1969.

Rev. in *Bulletin Critique du Livre Français*, 26 (1971), 31; by Jacques Voisine in RLC, 45 (Apr.–June 1971), 284–287.

900. Palacio, Jean de. "William Godwin, Ariosto, and the Grand Tour; or *Caleb Williams* Reconsidered," *Rivista di letterature moderne e comparate*, 23 (June 1970), 111–120.

Examines "the artistic motives and psychological aftermath of Falkland's Italian journey."

901. *Paul, C. Kegan. *William Godwin: His Friends and Contemporaries*. 2 vols. New York: AMS, 1970.

Reprint of an 1876 book.

902. Peacock, Thomas Love. *Memoirs of Shelley and Other Essays and Reviews*. Ed. Howard Mills. London: Hart-Davis; New York: New York Univ. (1970).

Also in paperback by Hart-Davis. Rev. by William Kean Seymour in *Contemporary Review*, 217 (Aug. 1970), 109–111; by Edward J. Cutler in LJ, 96 (15 Apr. 1971), p. 1370; by John Epsey in *Nineteenth Century Fiction*, 26 (June 1971), 125–126.

903. Peacock, Thomas Love. *Nightmare Abbey and Crotchet Castle*. Ed. Raymond Wright. See K-SJ, 19 (1970), No. 352.

Rev. by Angus Calder in NS, 10 Apr. 1970, p. 511.

904. Cancelled.

Perella, Nicolas J. See No. 362.

905. Pesta, John. "*Caleb Williams*: A Tragedy of Wasted Love," *Tennessee Studies in Literature* 16 (1971), 67–76.

Examines the "spiritual father-son relationship" existing between Falkland and Caleb Williams.

Pitt, Valerie. See. No 665.

906. Platzner, Robert L., and Robert D. Hume. "2. 'Gothic versus Romantic': A Rejoinder," PMLA, 86 (March 1971), 266–274.

A dialogue precipitated by Hume's earlier article in PMLA of 1969. See K-SJ, 19 (1970), No. 330.

Pointon, Marcia B. See No. 366.

907. Pollin, Burton R. *Discoveries in Poe*. Notre Dame, Ind.: Univ. of Notre Dame, 1970.

Includes a chapter on "Godwin and Poe," pp. 107–127.

908. Pollin, Burton R. "Godwin's Account of Shelley's Return in September 1814: A Letter to John Taylor," KSMB, 21 (1970), 21–31.

Discusses and publishes Godwin's letter of 8 Nov. 1814, which deals, in part, with the alliance of Shelley, Mary, and Claire Clairmont.

909. Pollin, Burton R. *Godwin Criticism: A Synoptic Bibliography*. See K-SJ, 18 (1969), No. 624, K-SJ, 19 (1970), No. 357.

Rev. by James T. Boulton in *Revue des Langues Vivantes*, 36, No. 2 (1970), 215–216; by Henri-François Imbert in RLC, 44 (July–Sept. 1970), 422–424.

910. Pollin, Burton R. " 'The World Is Too Much with Us': Two More Sources—Dryden and Godwin," WC, 1 (Spring 1970), 50–52.‡

Suggests that Godwin's *Pantheon* served "as [a] source or stimulus for lines 9–12" of Wordsworth's poem.

911. Posey, Horace G., Jr. "Shelley and Modern Aesthetics," *Bucknell Review*, 19 (Spring 1971), 97–114.†‡

Analyzes the Crocean and new critical modernity of the *Defence* and demonstrates its philosophic precision.

912. Power, Julia. *Shelley in America in the Nineteenth Century: His Relation to Amer-*

ican Critical Thought and His Influence. See K-SJ, 19 (1970), No. 359.†

Rev. in *Choice*, 7 (Apr. 1970), 234.

Poynter, J. R. See No. 128.

913. Rader Melvin. *Wordsworth: A Philosophical Approach.* See K-SJ 17 (1968), No. 564, 19 (1970), No. 363.

Rev. by H. A. Smith in MLR, 65 (July 1970), 605–606.

Raimond, Jean. See No. 372.

914. Raine, Kathleen. *Defending Ancient Springs.* See K-SJ, 18 (1969), No. 632, 19 (1970), No. 364.

Rev. by Vivian de Sola Pinto in MLR, 65 (Apr. 1970), 357–359; by K. P. S. Jochum in *Anglia*, 89 (Feb. 1971), 143–145.

915. Raitt, A. W. *Prosper Mérimée.* London: Eyre and Spottiswoode, 1970; New York: Scribners, 1971.

A biography of the 19th-century French Romantic figure who nearly married Mary Shelley. The Appendix includes Mary Shelley's article on Mérimée from the *Westminster Review* (Jan. 1829).

Rev. by William Beauchamp in NYT, 10 Jan. 1971, p. 6.

915a. "Recent Acquisitions," *Yale Univ. Library Gazette*, 45 (Oct. 1970), 81.

Yale acquired one of thirty copies of Shelley's *Poems and Sonnets*, ed. "Charles Alfred Seymour (Philadelphia 1887)." See No. 864a.

916. "Recent Acquisitions—Books," *Princeton Univ. Library Chronicle*, 31 (Winter 1970), 146.

Between 1 Jan. and 30 Nov. 1969 the library acquired a copy of *Shelley and Mary* (London 1882).

917. Reiman, Donald H. *Percy Bysshe Shelley.* See K-SJ, 19 (1970), No. 367.

Rev. by Joseph De Rocco in K-SJ, 19 (1970), 141–143; by K[enneth]. N[eill]. C[ameron]. in ELN, 8, Supplement (Sept. 1970), 45–46; by Richard Harter Fogle in SAQ, 69 (Autumn 1970), 548–549; by P. H. Butter in MLR, 65 (Oct. 1970), 882–883; by J. Drummond Bone in N&Q, 215 (Oct. 1970), 388–389.

918. Richards, George David. "Shelley's *Queen Mab*: A Critical Edition" [Doctoral dissertation, Duke, 1969], DAI, 30 (Jan. 1970), 2977-A–2978-A.

919. Robertson, Graham, ed. *Shelley.* London: Jackdaw Publications, 1971.

A folder of teaching aids, including facsimiles of *The Necessity of Atheism*, sample letters, and MSS.

Robinson, Charles E. See No. 137.

920. Robinson, Charles E. "The Shelley Circle and Coleridge's *The Friend*," ELN, 8 (June 1971), 269–274.

The source of Shelley's quotation on "Hope" in a letter of 8 Sept. 1816 to Byron is *The Friend* of 14 Sept. 1809.

921. Rogers, Neville. *Shelley at Work: A Critical Inquiry.* See K-SJ, 18 (1969), No. 640, 19 (1970), No. 370.

Rev. by Franz Wieselhufer in *Anglia*, 88 (Sept. 1970), 404–405.

922. Rosen, Frederick. "The Principle of Population as Political Theory: Godwin's *Of Population* and the Malthusian Controversy," JHI, 31 (Jan.–March 1970), 33–48.

Describes the background and issues of this controversy from 1798 to 1823.

Rosenfeld, Alvin H., ed. See No. 137.

923. Rossetti, William Michael. *A Memoir of Shelley.* With a fresh preface. New York: AMS, 1971.

Reprint of 1886 edition.

924. Ruoff, A. La Vonne, ed. "Landor's Letters to his Family: 1802–1825," *Bulletin of the John Rylands Library, Manchester*, 53 (Spring 1971), 465–500.†

Landor writes of his pleasure in meeting Thomas Jefferson Hogg in Florence in 1825. Hogg presented himself to Landor as a friend (as was Shelley) of William Lambe, M.D., who had succeeded to Landor's father's practice in Warwick.

925. Russell, Bertrand. *The Autobiography of Bertrand Russell.* Vol. II: *1914–1944*; Vol. III: *1944–1969*. See K-SJ, 18 (1969), No. 647, 19 (1970), No. 374.

Rev. by T. Corbishley in *The Month*, 228 (July–Aug. 1969), 96; in *International Review of Social History*, 14 (1969), 515; by E. Delavenay in EA, 23 (Jan.–March 1970), 98–99; by Dean Terrill in *Modern Age*, 14 (Spring 1970), 212–215.

St. John-Stevas, Norman. See No. 676.

Saito, Yuso. See No. 676a.

926. Salt, H. S. *A Shelley Primer*. Port Washington, N.Y., and London: Kennikat, 1969.
Reprint of an 1887 book.

926a. Sambrook, A. J. "The English Lord and the Happy Husbandman," *Studies on Voltaire and the Eighteenth Century*, 57 (1967), 1357–1373.
The influence of the pastoral ideal on Mary Wollstonecraft and Godwin.

926b. Sambrook, A. J. "An Essay on Eighteenth-Century Pastoral, Pope to Wordsworth," *Trivium*, 7 (May 1971), 103–115.†
Theories of Paine and Godwin were influential in the works of the later 18th-century poets.

927. Sambrook, James. "Some Heirs of Goldsmith: Poets of the Poor in the Late Eighteenth Century," *Studies in Burke and His Time*, 11 (Fall 1969), 1348–1361.
Mary Wollstonecraft and Godwin are included among those following the tradition of Goldsmith's *The Deserted Village*.

928. Scales, Luther Lee, Jr. "Miltonic Elements and the Humanization of Power in Shelley's Poetry, Culminating in Demogorgon's Song" [Doctoral dissertation, Drew, 1969], DAI, 30 (Nov. 1969), 2043-A.

929. Schultze, Earl J. *Shelley's Theory of Poetry: A Reappraisal*. See K-SJ, 17 (1968), No. 583, 18 (1969), No. 651, 19 (1970), No. 377.
Rev. by K[enneth]. N[eill]. C[ameron]. in ELN, 7, Supplement (Sept. 1969), 43–44.

930. Schwartz, Lewis M. "Two New Contemporary Reviews of Shelley's *Queen Mab*," K-SJ, 19 (1970), 77–85.
After summarizing the history of the poem's publication and reception, the author reprints two previously unknown reviews.

931. *Scott, Robert Pickett. *The Place of Shelley among the English Poets of His Time*. New York: Haskell House, 1971.
Reprint of an 1878 book.

932. Scott, Sir Walter. *Sir Walter Scott on Novelists and Fiction*. Ed. Ioan M. Williams. London: Routledge and Kegan Paul, 1968.
Includes Scott's reviews of Godwin's *Fleetwood* and Mary Shelley's *Frankenstein*.
Rev. by Thomas Crawford in RES, 21 (Aug. 1970), 385–386.

933. Sen, Amiyakumar. *Studies in Shelley*. Folcroft, Pa.: Folcroft, 1969.
Reprint of a 1936 book.

Shapiro, Harold I. See No. 390.

934. Shelley, Lady Jane, ed. *Shelley Memorials: From Authentic Sources; to Which is Added an Essay on Christianity by Percy Bysshe Shelley*. St. Clair Shores, Mich.: Scholarly, 1970.
Reprint of 1859 edition.

935. *Shelley, Mary Wollstonecraft. *Frankenstein*. Adapted and abridged by Marilyn Gillet. Paris: Hachette, 1970. "Facts and Fiction in Easy English Series."

936. *Shelley, Mary Wollstonecraft. *Frankenstein*. [Translated by] Friedrich Polakovics. Afterword by Hermann Ebeling. Munich: Hanser, 1970; Berlin, Darmstadt, Vienna: Deutsche Buch-Gemeinschaft, 1971.

937. *Shelley, Mary Wollstonecraft. *Frankenstein*. [Translated by] Hannah Betjeman. Preface and filmography by Michel Boujut. Levallois-Perret (Hauts-de-Seine): Cercle du bibliophile, n.d. [ca. 1969].

938. *Shelley, Mary Wollstonecraft. *Frankenstein*. [Translated by] K. B. Leder and Gert Leetz. Wien: Buchgemeinschaft Donauland, 1969.

939. *Shelley, Mary Wollstonecraft. *Frankenstein*. [Translated by] Tomáš Korbař. Prague: Lidové Nakladatelstvi, 1969.

940. *Shelley, Mary Wollstonecraft. *Frankenstein, čiže moderný Prometeus*. [Translated by] Pavel Vilikovský. Bratislava: Tatran, 1969.

941. *Shelley, Mary Wollstonecraft. *Frankenstein. El Moderno Prometeo*. [Translated by] E. Fariñas. Barcelona: Ferma, 1969.

942. Shelley, Mary W[ollstonecraft]. *Frankenstein; or The Modern Prometheus*. Ed. with an introduction by M. K. Joseph. London and New York: Oxford Univ., 1969.
Text based on 1831 edition. In paperback.
Rev. in TLS, 16 Oct. 1969, p. 1215; in

Choice, 7 (March 1970), 80; by Heinz Kosok in N&Q, 215 (Oct. 1970), 391–392; by Jennifer Gribble in AUMLA, No. 34 (Nov. 1970), pp. 328–329. Also see No. 44.

943. Shira, Atsushi. "The Impact on Japan of William Godwin's Ideas," *American Journal of Economics and Sociology*, 29 (Jan. 1970), 89–96.

His influence came relatively late, beginning with an 1877 translation of Thomas Malthus' *Essay on the Principle of Population*, for which Godwin is a major source.

944. Singh, Pratap. "Philosophical Interpretation of History in the Poetry of Shelley," *Calcutta Review*, N.S. 1 (Apr.–June 1970), 601–612.

For Shelley history is the process of realizing the spirit of liberty, which the Universal Soul accomplishes through man's efforts to perfect himself.

945. Spornick, Nickolas B. "The Satire in the Novels of Thomas Love Peacock" [Doctoral dissertation, Tennessee, 1969], DAI, 31 (Oct. 1970), 1814-A–1815-A.

Sprigg, Christopher St. John. See No. 692.

946. Stapp, Oneida. "A Shelley Handbook: Guide to Shelley and His Work" [Doctoral dissertation, East Texas State, 1970], DAI, 31 (March 1971), 4735-A.

947. Steffan, Truman Guy. "Seven Accounts of the Cenci and Shelley's Drama," SEL, 9 (Autumn 1969), 601–618.†‡

A comparative study. Shelley's modifications of the narrative appear superior to the others, both artistically and psychologically.

Stephen, Henry. See No. 693.

Steward, Joyce S., and Eva M. Burkett, comps. See No. 694.

947a. *Stock, A. G. "Shelley's Universe," *University of Rajastan Studies in English*, No. 4 (1969), pp. 1–5.

948. *Stovall Floyd. *Desire and Restraint in Shelley*. New York: Haskell House, 1970; St. Clair Shores, Mich.: Scholarly, 1971.

Reprints of a 1931 book.

949. Strachey, Lytton. *Biographical Essays*. New York: Harcourt, Brace and World, n.d. [ca. 1968].

Available in hardcover and paperback; includes an essay on Sir Timothy Shelley, "An Adolescent," first published in NS, 31 March 1917.

Strauss, Walter A. See No. 398.

Suddard, S. J. Mary. See No. 700.

Sutherland, Donald. See No. 150.

Swanson, Donald R., See No. 151.

Szladits, Lola L. See No. 401.

949a. Takahashi, Kiku. "Igirisu Romanshugi no Honyakukan," *Eigo Seinen: Rising Generation* (Tokyo), 116 (Oct. 1970), 587–589; (Nov. 1970), 644–646. [In Japanese.]

English Romantic's view of translation, with emphasis on Shelley.

950. *Taylor, G. R. Stirling. *Mary Wollstonecraft: A Study in Economics and Romance*. Westport, Conn.: Greenwood, 1969.

Reprint of a 1911 book.

Thomas, P. G. See No. 402.

951. *Thomsen, Christian W. "Die Verantwortung des Naturwissenschaftlers in Mary Shelley's *Frankenstein* und Heinar Kipphardt's *In der Sache J. Robert Oppenheimer*," *Literatur in Wissenschaft und Unterricht*, 4 (1971), 16–26.

952. Tomalin, Claire. "A Fallen Woman," NS, 21 May 1971, p. 712.†

Discusses Mary Wollstonecraft's letters to Gilbert Imlay and Godwin's decision to publish them.

953. Trawick, Leonard M., ed. *Backgrounds of Romanticism: English Philosophical Prose of the Eighteenth Century*. See K-SJ, 17 (1968), No. 599.

Rev. by Ralph Cohen in *Studies in Burke and His Time*, 11 (Fall 1969), 1403–1407.

Trelawny, Edward John. See No. 403a.

Trewin, J. C. See No. 157.

954. *Verkoren, Lucas. *A Study of Shelley's Defence of Poetry: Its Origin, Textual History, Sources, and Significance*. Folcroft, Pa.: Folcroft, 1969; New York: Haskell House, 1970.

Reprints of a 1937 book.

955. Viswanathan, S. "Eliot and Shelley: A Sketch of Shifts in Attitude," *Ariel*, 2 (Jan. 1971), 58–67.

Traces development of Eliot's views of Shelley, and argues that Eliot's "apparent hatred of Shelley was but the obverse of a fascination exercised by Shelley's poetry on him."

Viswanathan, S. See No. 711.

Wallace, Irving. See No. 411.

956. Wallace, Malcolm W., ed. *Studies in English.* Port Washington, N.Y.: Kennikat, 1969.

A reprint of the 1931 edition, which includes G. S. Brett's "Shelley's Relation to Berkeley and Drummond."

957. Walmsley, Robert. *Peterloo: The Case Reopened.* Manchester: Manchester Univ., 1969.

References to Shelley's poetic response to Peterloo, "The Mask of Anarchy."

Rev. in *International Review of Social History*, 14 (1969), 307; in *Choice*, 7 (Apr. 1970), 288.

Wasserman, Earl R. See No. 457.

958. Wasserman, Earl R. *Shelley: A Critical Reading.* Baltimore: Johns Hopkins Univ., 1971.

959. Waterlow, Sydney. *Shelley.* Port Washington, N.Y., and London: Kennikat, 1970.

Reprint of a 1913 book.

Watkin, David. See No. 414.

960. *Watson, George. *A New Rationale of Literary History.* London: Allen Lane, 1969.

Refers to Shelley's "To a Skylark."

Rev. by George Boas in JHI, 31 (Jan.–March 1970), 148–151.

Watson, J[ohn]. R. See No. 162.

961. Webb, Timothy. "Shelley's 'Hymn to Venus': A New Text," RES, 21 (Aug. 1970), 315–324.†‡

"The first attempt to restore what Shelley wrote in the light of the heavily corrected manuscript draft [Bodleian MS. Shelley adds. e. 12, pp. 210–205] and Hermann's (1806) edition of the Homeric Hymns. . . ."

Wellek, René. See No. 416.

962. Williams, Duncan. "Shelley's Demogorgon," *West Virginia Univ. Philological Papers*, 17 (June 1970), 25–30.†‡

Deals with the "enigma" of Demogorgon by accepting his own statement that he is "Eternity."

963. Wollstonecraft, Mary. *Letters to Imlay.* Ed. with a Memoir by C. Kegan Paul. New York: Haskell House, 1971.

Reprint of 1879 edition.

964. *Wollstonecraft, Mary. *Letters Written during a Short Residence in Sweden, Norway, and Denmark.* Introduction by Sylva Norman. Fontwell: Centaur, 1970. "The Regency Library."

Facsimile reprint of first edition, 1796, with new introduction.

965. *Wollstonecraft, Mary. *A Vindication of the Rights of Woman.* Second Edition. William Godwin. *Memoirs of the Author of "A Vindication of the Rights of Woman."* Farnborough: Gregg, 1970.

Facsimile reprints of editions of 1792 and 1798 respectively.

966. Woodberry, George E. *Literary Memoirs of the Nineteenth Century.* Port Washington, N.Y.: Kennikat, 1969.

A reprint of the 1921 edition; contains a chapter, "Remarks on Shelley."

Woodberry, George E. See No. 420.

967. Woodberry, George E. *The Torch.* Freeport, N.Y.: Books for Libraries, 1969.

A reprint of the 1905 edition; includes an essay on Shelley.

Woodhouse, C[hristopher]. M. See No. 422.

968. Woodings, R. B., ed. *Shelley: Modern Judgements.* See K-SJ, 18 (1969), No. 688, 19 (1970), No. 393.

Rev. by E. Pereira in UES, 7 (Sept. 1969), 114–115.

Woodring, Carl. See No. 175.

968a. Woolfson, Stanley G. "Dream Queen," Spec, 18 Oct. 1969, p. 525.

Claims last sentence in Peacock's *Four Ages of Poetry* to be longest in English literature.

Wordsworth, William, and Dorothy Wordsworth. See No. 423.

969. Wright, John W. *Shelley's Myth of Metaphor.* Athens: Univ. of Georgia, 1970.†

A paperback.

970. Wylie, Laura Johnson. *Shelley's Democracy.* Folcroft, Pa.: Folcroft, 1970.

Reprint of a chapter from a 1916 book, *Social Studies in English Literature.*

VI. PHONOGRAPH RECORDINGS

Byron, Keats, Shelley

971. *An Audio-Visual History of English Literature.* Educational Audio Visual.

This set of four records and eight color filmstrips, designed for the high school student, includes a section on "The Romantic Era."

Rev. by J[ohn]. R. S[earles]. in *English Journal*, 60 (Jan. 1971), 153–154.

972. *Early Victorian Poetry*. Read by Jill Balcon, Ian Holm, and others. Argo.

Poems by John Clare are included. Rev. by R. F. G[rady]. in LJ, 95 (15 Feb. 1970), 646.

973. *English Romantic Poetry*. Read by Claire Bloom, Anthony Quayle, Frederick Worlock, and Ralph Richardson. Caedmon.

Includes selections from Byron, Clare, Hood, Keats, Moore, Peacock, and Shelley.

974. *Enjoying Poetry*. Read by Bramwell Fletcher, Alexander Scourby, and Nancy Wickwire. Listening Library.

The first in this series of three records has Bramwell Fletcher reading from *The English Romantic Poets*. Selections from Byron, Keats, and Shelley are found here.

Rev. by Aaron L. Fessler in LJ, 95 (1 Jan. 1970), 54.

975. *Golden Treasury of English Poetry*. Read by Claire Bloom, Eric Portman, and John Neville. Caedmon, 1971.

This selection from Palgrave's anthology of English lyric poetry includes Byron, Keats, and Shelley.

976. *Hearing Poetry*. Vol 2. Introduced by Mark Van Doren. Readings by Hurd Hatfield, Jo Van Fleet, and Frank Silvera. Caedmon, 1971.

Includes poems by Byron, Keats, and Shelley.

977. *Lord Byron*. Read by Marius Goring and Margaretta Scott. Fontana.

Rev. in TLS, 13 Nov. 1970, p. 1337.

978. *The Poetry of George Gordon Byron*. Read by Tyrone Power. Caedmon, 1971.

Includes *Don Juan* (Canto I), "She Walks in Beauty," "On This Day I Complete My Thirty-Sixth Year," and *Childe Harold* (III, vv. 18–28, 68–75, 85–98, 113–118; IV, vv. 178–184).

979. *The Poetry of Percy Bysshe Shelley*. Read by Vincent Price. Caedmon, 1971.

Includes "When Soft Voices Die," "Ozymandias," "Ode to the West Wind," *Adonais*, and others.

980. *The Romantic Age in English Literature*. CMS Records.

Includes selections from Byron, Keats, and Shelley. Intended for the secondary grades, the package contains two records, two color filmstrips, and a *Teacher's Manual* published by Harcourt, Brace and World.

Rev. by J[ohn]. R. S[earles]. in *English Journal*, 58 (Nov. 1969), 1277.

Bibliography for July 1, 1971–December 31, 1972

VOLUMES XXI and XXII

Compiled by

ROBERT A. HARTLEY
Hunter College of the City University of New York

LEWIS M. SCHWARTZ
Kingsborough Community College of the City University of New York

with the assistance of G. Curtis Olsen

THIS bibliography, a regular department of the *Keats-Shelley Journal*, is a register of the literary interest in Keats, Shelley, Byron, Hunt, and their circles from (approximately) July 1971 through December 1972.

We take pleasure in acknowledging our gratitude to the following individuals for their generous assistance: Williston R. Benedict, who searched a number of periodicals; overseas contributors P. Bogomolova and L. Nikitina (M. E. Saltykov-Shchedrin State Public Library, Leningrad), D. H. Borchardt (La Trobe University, Melbourne), Jean de Palacio (Université de Lille), and K. Szymanowski (Instytutu Badań Literackich Polskiej Akademii Nauk, Poznań, Poland); Hubert F. Babinski (Columbia University), who translated a large number of Russian and Polish entries; Istvan Deak (Columbia University), who translated Hungarian entries; Mihai H. Handrea (The Carl H. Pforzheimer Library), who translated Romanian entries; Donald H. Reiman (The Carl H. Pforzheimer Library) and Carl Woodring (Columbia University), who read and corrected the manuscript, Rae Ann Nager (*Keats-Shelley Journal*), who provided editorial suggestions; and the library staffs of Columbia University, Hunter College and Kingsborough Community College of the City University of New York, and The New York Public Library.

Where a book has been issued by more than one publisher during the same year, the publication date appears at the end of the entry within parentheses. A change has been made in the cross reference system. Cross references (to item numbers) are now grouped together at the end of each section of the bibliography, rather than listed alphabetically by author throughout the bibliography as in previous issues.

Each item that we have not seen is marked by an asterisk. Entries which have been abstracted in *Abstracts of English Studies* are marked with a dagger, but entries in previous bibliographies which were abstracted too late for notice have not been repeated. Entries which have been (or will be) abstracted in *MLA Abstracts* are marked with a double dagger.

ABBREVIATIONS

ABC	American Book Collector
AL	American Literature
AN&Q	American Notes and Queries
ASNS	Archiv für das Studium der neuren Sprachen
AUMLA	Journal of the Australasian Universities Language and Literature Association
BA	Books Abroad
BC	Book Collector
BNYPL	Bulletin of the New York Public Library
CE	College English
CL	Comparative Literature
CLSB	C. L. S. Bulletin (Charles Lamb Society)
CR	Contemporary Review
DAI	Dissertation Abstracts International
EA	Etudes Anglaises
EC	Essays in Criticism
ELH	Journal of English Literary History
ELN	English Language Notes
ES	English Studies
Exp	Explicator
HLQ	Huntington Library Quarterly
ICS	L'Italia Che Scrive
ILN	Illustrated London News
JAAC	Journal of Aesthetics and Art Criticism
JEGP	Journal of English and Germanic Philology
JHI	Journal of the History of Ideas
KR	Kenyon Review
K-SJ	Keats-Shelley Journal
KSMB	Keats-Shelley Memorial Bulletin
LC	Library Chronicle
Li	Listener
LJ	Library Journal
MLN	Modern Language Notes
MLQ	Modern Language Quarterly
MLR	Modern Language Review
MP	Modern Philology
N&Q	Notes and Queries
NS	New Statesman
NYRB	New York Review of Books
NYT	New York Times Book Review
PBSA	Papers of the Bibliographical Society of America
PMLA	Publications of the Modern Language Association of America
PQ	Philological Quarterly
PR	Partisan Review
QQ	Queen's Quarterly
RES	Review of English Studies
RLC	Revue de Littérature Comparée
SAQ	South Atlantic Quarterly
SatR	Saturday Review
SEL	Studies in English Literature 1500–1900
SIR	Studies in Romanticism
SP	Studies in Philology
Spec	Spectator
SR	Sewanee Review
T&T	Time and Tide
TLS	Times Literary Supplement
UES	Unisa English Studies
UTQ	University of Toronto Quarterly
VQR	Virginia Quarterly Review
WC	Wordsworth Circle

Current Bibliography

I. GENERAL

Current Bibliographies

1. Bell, Inglis F., and Jennifer Gallup. *A Reference Guide to English, American, and Canadian Literature: An Annotated Checklist of Bibliographical and Other Reference Materials.* Vancouver: Univ. of British Columbia, 1971.

   Rev. by R. C. Ellsworth in QQ, 78 (Winter 1971), 634–635.

2. *Catalog of Books and Manuscripts at the Keats-Shelley Memorial House in Rome.* Boston: G. K. Hall, 1969.

   Reproduces the card catalog. Microfilms of all MS holdings are available in the Houghton Library at Harvard and in the Keats House at Hampstead.

3. Combs, Richard E. *Authors: Critical and Biographical References—a Guide to 4,700 Critical and Biographical Passages in Books.* Metuchen, N.J.: Scarecrow, 1971.

   Uses as its base approximately 500 relatively recent and in print books. References include Keats.

4. Dyson, A. E., ed. *English Poetry: Select Bibliographical Guides.* London: Oxford Univ., 1971.

   Includes bibliographies on Byron by John Jump, Keats by Robert Gittings, and Shelley by R. B. Woodings.

5. Erdman, David V., *et al.* "The Romantic Movement: A Selective and Critical Bibliography for 1970," ELN, 9, Supplement (Sept. 1971), 1–180.

6. Erdman, David V., *et al.* "The Romantic Movement: A Selective and Critical Bibliography for 1971," ELN, 10, Supplement (Sept. 1972), 1–215.

7. Freeman, Ronald E., ed. "Victorian Bibliography for 1971," *Victorian Studies,* 15 (June 1972), 507–584.

8. Horden, John, and James B. Misenheimer, Jr., eds. "The Nineteenth Century," *Annual Bibliography of English Language and Literature for 1970,* 45 (1972), 344–479.

9. Jordan, Frank, ed. *The English Romantic Poets: A Review of Research and Criticism.* Third Revised Edition. New York: Modern Language Association of America, 1972.

   A further revision of a guide first edited by T. M. Raysor in 1950. This edition includes revisions of Ernest Bernbaum's "The Romantic Movement" by Frank Jordan; Samuel C. Chew's "Byron" by Ernest J. Lovell, Jr.; Bennett Weaver's "Shelley" by Donald H. Reiman; and Clarence D. Thorpe's "Keats" by David Perkins.

10. Kennedy, Arthur G., and Donald B. Sands. *A Concise Bibliography for Students of English.* Fifth Edition. Revised by William E. Colburn. Stanford: Stanford Univ., 1972.

11. Munby, A. N. L., ed. *Sale Catalogues of Libraries of Eminent Persons.* Vols. I and II: *Poets and Men of Letters.* London: Mansell with Sotheby Parke-Bernet, 1971.

    Vol. I includes Byron, Hazlitt, and Peacock; Vol. II, Lady Blessington.

    Rev. by Eric Osborne in *Books and Bookmen,* 17 (Jan. 1972), 76; in **College and Research Libraries,* 33 (Jan. 1972), 39; in TLS, 18 Feb. 1972, p. 200; in **Library Review,* 23 (Spring 1972), 201; by Lionel Madden in *Victorian Studies,* 15 (Mar. 1972), 373–374; in **PBSA,* 66 (Oct. 1972), 457; in **Library,* 27 (Dec. 1972), 350.

12. Schwartz, Lewis M., Robert A. Hartley, and G. Curtis Olsen. "Current Bibliography [for July 1969 – June 1971]," K-SJ, 20 (1971), 1–87.

13. Vattamany, Viktoria. "Angol szépirodalom a magyar sajtóban, 1868–1872" ["English Literature in the Hungarian Press, 1868–1872"], *Angol Filológiai Tanulmányok: Hungarian Studies in English,* 5 (1969), 127–138.

Includes many items on Byron and Thomas Moore, and one on Shelley.

14. Ward, William S. *British Periodicals and Newspapers, 1789–1832: A Bibliography of Secondary Sources.* Lexington: Univ. of Kentucky, 1972.

Lists books and articles on periodicals and newspapers of the Romantic period.

15. Ward, William S., comp. *Literary Reviews in British Periodicals, 1798–1820: A Bibliography with a Supplementary List of General (Non-Review) Articles on Literary Subjects.* 2 vols. New York and London: Garland, 1972.

Companion volumes to Reiman's *The Romantics Reviewed.* See No. 118.

16. Watson, George, ed. *The New Cambridge Bibliography of English Literature.* Vol. III: *1800–1900.* See K-SJ, 19 (1970), No. 6, 20 (1971), No. 23.

Rev. by Donald J. Gray in *Victorian Studies,* 15 (Sept. 1971), 87–91; by Giuliano Pellegrini in *Rivista di letterature moderna e comparate,* 24 (Sept. 1971), 235–236.

17. Yarker, P. M., and J. A. V. Chapple. "The Nineteenth Century," in *The Year's Work in English Studies,* ed. Geoffrey Harlow, Elizabeth Brennan, and James Redmond, 50 (1971 [for 1969]), 285–331.

For additional CURRENT BIBLIOGRAPHIES see Nos. 343, 560.

BOOKS AND ARTICLES RELATING TO ENGLISH ROMANTICISM

18. Abrams, M. H. *Natural Supernaturalism: Tradition and Revolution in Romantic Literature.* See K-SJ, 20 (1971), No. 28.

Rev. by *P. C. Rule in *America,* 13 Nov. 1971, p. 409; in *AL, 43 (Nov. 1971), 506; by Robert Martin Adams in *Hudson Review,* 24 (Winter 1971–72), 687–693; by Graham Martin in Spec, 4 Mar. 1972, pp. 358–359; in *Choice,* 9 (Apr. 1972), 207; in **New Catholic World,* 215 (July 1972), 179; by Barry Westburg in JAAC, 31 (Fall 1972), 132; by A. R. Chisholm in *AUMLA,* No. 38 (Nov. 1972), pp. 279–280; by Herbert Lindenberger in ELN, 10 (Dec. 1972), 150–154; by E. D. Hirsch, Jr., in WC, 3 (Winter 1972), 17–20; by J. Hillis Miller in *Diacritics,* 2 (Winter 1972), 6–13; by Stuart M. Sperry, Jr., in *Yearbook of Comparative and General Literature,* No. 21 (1972), pp. 86–89. Also see Nos. 51, 82, 94.

19. Adams, Hazard. "Scholarship and the Idea of Criticism: Recent Writing on Yeats," *Georgia Review,* 26 (Fall 1972), 249–278.

An omnibus review. See K-SJ, 20 (1971), Nos. 48, 766. Also see Nos. 30, 571.

20. *Adburgham, Alison. *Women in Print: Writing Women and Women's Magazines from the Restoration to the Accession of Victoria.* London: Allen and Unwin, 1972.

Mentions, among others, Lady Blessington, Fanny Brawne, and Fanny Keats.

Rev. by Elizabeth Thomas in NS, 28 Apr. 1972, pp. 566–567; by Gillian Freeman in Spec, 29 Apr. 1972, p. 662; by Joanna Richardson in *History Today,* 22 (June 1972), 447.

21. Alvarez, A. *The Savage God: A Study of Suicide.* London: Weidenfeld and Nicolson, 1971; New York: Random House, 1972.

Mocks the indulgent excesses of Romantic suicide. References to Byron, Keats, and Shelley.

Rev. by Jonathan Raban in NS, 19 Nov. 1971, pp. 701–702; by Barbara Hardy in Spec, 18 Dec. 1971, pp. 890–891; by Ann Grace Mojtabai in LJ, 97 (1 Apr. 1972), 1325–26; by W. H. Auden in NYRB, 20 Apr. 1972, p. 3; by J. D. O'Hara in *New Republic,* 22 Apr. 1972, pp. 29–32; by Albert Rothenberg in SatR, 29 Apr. 1972, pp. 66–68; by William H. Gass in NYRB, 18 May 1972, pp. 3–4; by Eleanor Wilner in MLN, 87 (Dec. 1972), 998–1002.

22. Ball, Patricia M. *The Central Self: A Study in Romantic and Victorian Imagination.* See K-SJ, 18 (1969), No. 16, 20 (1971), No. 33.

Rev. by Francis Noel Lees in N&Q, 216 (Oct. 1971), 397–398; by [Klaus] Egbert Faas in *Anglia,* 90, No. 2 (1972), 251–254.

23. Ball, Patricia M. *The Science of Aspects:*

The Changing Role of Fact in the Work of Coleridge, Ruskin and Hopkins. London: Athlone, 1971.

References to Romanticism.

Rev. in TLS, 15 Oct. 1971, p. 1280; in *Choice*, 9 (Mar. 1972), 56; by Kenneth Allott in MLR, 67 (Apr. 1972), 404–405; by *R. L. Brett in RES, 23 (May 1972), 223–224; by P. Fontaney in EA, 25 (July–Sept. 1972), 441–442; by Roy Park in *British Journal of Aesthetics*, 12 (Summer 1972), 304–305. Also see No. 144.

24. Baum, Joan Mandell. "The Theatrical Compositions of the Major English Romantic Poets" [Doctoral dissertation, Columbia, 1969], DAI, 30 (Nov. 1969), 1976–A.

Treats the dramatic compositions of Byron, Shelley, and Keats.

25. Bayley, John. *Pushkin: A Comparative Study*. See K-SJ, 20 (1971), No. 37.

Rev. in TLS, 30 July 1971, p. 879; by V. S. Pritchett in NS, 6 Aug. 1971, pp. 180–181; by Nicholas Richardson in Spec, 7 Aug. 1971, p. 215; by Helen Muchnic in NYRB, 7 Oct. 1971, pp. 25–28; by George Gibian in *Slavic Review*, 31 (March 1972), 188; by Henry Gifford in EC, 22 (July 1972), 313–320; by J. G. Garrard in *Russian Review*, 31 (July 1972), 306–307; by Paul M. Austin in *Canadian Slavonic Papers*, 14 (Summer 1972), 391–392.

25a. Beaty, Frederick L. *Light from Heaven: Love in British Romantic Literature*. See K-SJ, 20 (1971), No. 39.

Rev. by Roger Howell, Jr., in *British Studies Monitor*, 3 (Fall 1972), 83; by James O. Hoge in *Georgia Review*, 26 (Winter 1972), 526–528. Also see No. 82.

26. Bereaud, Jacques G. A. "La Traduction en France à l'époque romantique," *Comparative Literature Studies*, 8 (Sept. 1971), 224–244.‡

Free translation gave way to the standard of fidelity to the original during the Romantic period. Translations of Godwin, Byron, and Scott are discussed.

27. *Bishop, Morris. *A Romantic Storybook.* Ithaca and London: Cornell Univ., 1971.

Examples of Romantic prose fiction.

28. Bloom, Harold. *The Ringers in the Tower: Studies in Romantic Tradition.* See K-SJ, 20 (1971), No. 45.

Rev. by Keith Cushman in LJ, 96 (July 1971), 2319; by Angus Fletcher in *Diacritics*, 1 (Fall 1971), 16–19; by Martin Lebowitz in *Nation*, 27 Sept. 1971, pp. 278–280; in *Choice*, 8 (Nov. 1971), 1172; by Diane Middlebrook in WC, 3 (Summer 1972), 184–185; by I[rene]. H. C[hayes]. in ELN, 10 Supplement (Sept. 1972), 11. Also see Nos. 51, 82, 94, 141.

29. Bloom, Harold. *The Visionary Company: A Reading of English Romantic Poetry*. See K-SJ, 20 (1971), No. 47.

Rev. in *Choice*, 8 (Sept. 1971), 828. Also see No. 562.

30. Bloom, Harold. *Yeats.* See K-SJ, 20 (1971), No. 48.

Rev. by Augustine Martin in *Studies* (Dublin), No. 237 (Spring 1971), pp. 98–102; by Marjorie G. Perloff in *Contemporary Literature*, 12 (Autumn 1971), 554–561; by Helen Vendler in JEGP, 70 (Oct. 1971), 691–696; by Norman Jeffares in RES, 22 (Nov. 1971), 514–517; Thomas Parkinson in ELN, 9 (Mar. 1972), 234–235; by Michael Sidnell in UTQ, 41 (Spring 1972), 263–273; in *MP, 70 (Nov. 1972), 168. Also see No. 19.

31. *Blunden, Edmund. *Reprinted Papers, Partly Concerning Some English Romantic Poets.* Folcroft, Pa.: Folcroft, 1971.

Reprint of a 1931 work, which includes material on Keats, Shelley, and Clare.

32. *Boker, Uwe. "Lyric der englische Romantik," in *Epochen der englischen Lyrik*, ed. Karl Heinz Göller (Düsseldorf: August Bagel, 1970), pp. 152–181.

33. Bradbury, Malcolm. *The Social Context of Modern English Literature*. New York: Schocken; Oxford: Blackwell (1971).

Romanticism is discussed.

Rev. by Richard Whittington-Egan in CR, 219 (Nov. 1971), 276–277; in *RES, 23 (May 1972), 245; in *Choice*, 9 (June 1972), 502; in **Canadian Forum*, 52 (Sept. 1972), 33; in **Social Forces*, 51 (Sept. 1972), 119.

34. Brumbaugh, Thomas B. "Walter Savage Landor as Romantic Classicist," *Topic*, No. 23 (Spring 1972), pp. 14–21.

A critical-biographical sketch with references to Byron, Shelley, and Hunt.

35. *Bryan, John Thomas Ingram. *The Interpretation of Nature in English Poetry.* Folcroft, Pa.: Folcroft, 1972.

Reprint of a 1932 work.

36. Burnshaw, Stanley. *The Seamless Web: Language-Thinking, Creature-Knowledge, Art-Experience.* See K-SJ, 20 (1971), No. 50.

Rev. by Calvin S. Brown in CL, 24 (Summer 1972), 277–279; by Michael Paul Gallagher in *Studies* (Dublin), 61 (Summer 1972), 193–196.

37. Buxton, John. "A Second Supplement to Toynbee's *Dante in English Literature,*" *Italian Studies,* 27 (1972), 41–43.

Lists allusions to Dante in Keats, Shelley, Mary Shelley, Maria Gisborne, Thomas Medwin, and Thomas Moore.

38. Carroll, David Barry. "Romantic Literary Theory and the Sublime" [Doctoral dissertation, Rice, 1971], DAI, 32 (Oct. 1971), 2051-A–2052-A.

Includes chapters on Keats, Shelley, and Byron.

39. Chiang, Oscar Ching-kuan. "Idealism in Plays Written By Early Nineteenth-Century Poets" [Doctoral dissertation, St. John's, 1972], DAI, 33 (Aug. 1972), 720-A–721-A.

Treats Byron, Shelley, and Keats.

40. Clarke, Colin. *River of Dissolution: D. H. Lawrence and English Romanticism.* See K-SJ, 20 (1971), No. 54.

Rev. by Miriam Allott in *Yearbook of English Studies,* 2 (1972), 327–333.

41. [Cooke, Michael G.] "The Editor's Lookout," SIR, 10 (Summer 1971), 157–158.

On the Romantics' view of the feminine.

42. *Courthope, William John. *The Liberal Movement in English Literature.* New York: AMS, 1972.

Reprint of an 1885 book.

43. Culler, A. Dwight. "Recent Studies in the Nineteenth Century," SEL, 11 (Autumn 1971), 763–782.‡

An omnibus review. See K-SJ, 20 (1971), Nos. 61, 175, 534, 784. Also see Nos. 48, 149, 400, 589.

44. Curran, Stuart. "The Mental Pinnacle: *Paradise Regained* and the Romantic Four-Book Epic," in *Calm of Mind: Tercentenary Essays on "Paradise Regained" and "Samson Agonistes" in Honor of John S. Diekhoff,* ed. Joseph Anthony Wittreich, Jr. (Cleveland and London: Case Western Reserve Univ., 1971), pp. 133–162.

Keats's *Endymion* and Shelley's *Prometheus Unbound* are discussed.

Rev. in *Choice,* 9 (May 1972), 367; in **Journal of General Education,* 24 (Oct. 1972), 188.

45. Daiches, David, ed. *The Penguin Companion to English Literature.* New York: McGraw-Hill, 1972. "Penguin Companions to World Literature."

Includes references to the Romantics.

Rev. by Charles R. Andrews in LJ, 97 (1 May 1972), 2077; by Richard Plant in NYT, 5 Nov. 1972, p. 31.

46. *Deugd, C. de. *Het metaphysisch grondpatroon van het romantische literaire denken, de fenomenologie van een geestesgesteldheid.* [*The Metaphysical Pattern of Romantic Criticism: A Phenomenology of the Romantic Mind.*] With a Summary in English. Second Edition. Groningen: Wolters-Noordhoff, 1971. [In Dutch.]

Considers the metaphysical aspects of Keats and Shelley.

Rev. by Cornelia Niekus Moore in *Yearbook of Comparative and General Literature,* No. 21 (1972), pp. 85–86.

47. *D'jakonova, N. Ja. *Londonskie romantiki i problemy anglijskogo romantizma.* [*The London Romantics and Problems of English Romanticism.*] Leningrad: Izd. Leningradskogo universiteta, 1970.

*Rev. by N. P. Mixal'skaja and G. V. Anikin in *Naučnye doklady vysšej školy filologičeskoj nauki,* No. 4 (1972), pp. 91–92.

48. Donohue, Joseph W., Jr. *Dramatic Character in the English Romantic Age.* See K-SJ, 20 (1971), No. 61.

Rev. in PQ, 50 (July 1971), 381; in *Choice,* 8 (Oct. 1971), 1037; by John I. Ades in *Educational Theatre Journal,* 23 (Oct. 1971), 353–356; by Charles Beecher Hogan in *Yale Review,* 61 (Autumn 1971), 137–139; by Bertrand Evans in MLQ, 32 (Dec. 1971), 444–445; by Joan Torgeson Knapp in ELN, 9 (Dec.

1971), 148–150; by Arnold Hare in *Theatre Research*, 12, No. 1 (1972), 93–95; by D[avid]. V. E[rdman]. in ELN, 10, Supplement (Sept. 1972), 26. Also see No. 43.

49. Duffy, Edward. "The Cunning Spontaneities of Romanticism," WC, 3 (Autumn 1972), 232–240.†‡

The major Romantic poets, Shelley included, use traditional verse forms as parody.

50. Edwards, Thomas R. *Imagination and Power: A Study of Poetry on Public Themes.* London: Chatto and Windus; New York: Oxford Univ. (1971).

Includes a chapter on the English Romantics and specific treatment of Shelley's "The Mask of Anarchy."

Rev. in **Christian Century*, 88 (10 Nov. 1971), 1333; in TLS, 19 Nov. 1971, p. 1438; by Denis Donoghue in Spec, 25 Dec. 1971, pp. 927–928; in *LJ, 97 (15 Jan. 1972), 199; by Morris Dickstein in NYT, 16 Jan. 1972, pp. 6, 10, 11, reply by William H. Pritchard, 4 Mar. 1972, p. 16; by Charles Molesworth in *Nation*, 31 Jan. 1972, pp. 151–152; by Jonathan Raban in NS, 4 Feb. 1972, pp. 148–149; in Li, 87 (9 Mar. 1972), 316; by Paul J. Korshin in PQ, 51 (July 1972), 608–609; by Patrick Cruttwell in *Hudson Review*, 25 (Autumn 1972), 469–474; in *AL, 44 (Nov. 1972), 533; in **National Review*, 24 (8 Dec. 1972), 1365.

51. Ehrstine, John W. "Romantic Theory: A Calling of the Wits Together," *Emerson Society Quarterly*, 18, No. 67 (1972), 186–196.‡

An omnibus review. See K-SJ, 20 (1971), Nos. 28, 45, 125, 150. Also see Nos. 18, 28, 110, 134.

52. *Eichner, Hans, ed. "*Romantic*" *and Its Cognates: The European History of a Word.* Toronto: Univ. of Toronto, 1972.

Includes George Whalley's "England: Romantic—Romanticism," pp. 157–262, which uses examples from Byron, Shelley, Keats, and others.

53. *Eitner, Lorenz. *Neoclassicism and Romanticism, 1750–1850.* Vol. I: *Enlightenment and Revolution.* Vol. II: *Restoration and Twilight Humanism.* Englewood Cliffs, N.J.: Prentice-Hall, 1970. "Sources and Documents in the History of Art Series."

Rev. by Jack J. Spector in *Art Bulletin*, 54 (Mar. 1972), 102–103; in **Burlington Magazine*, 114 (June 1972), 419.

54. Elledge, W. Paul, and Richard L. Hoffman, eds. *Romantic and Victorian: Studies in Memory of William H. Marshall.* See K-SJ, 20 (1971), No. 65.

See No. 82.

55. Fader, Daniel, and George Bornstein. *British Periodicals of the Eighteenth and Nineteenth Centuries.* Ann Arbor: University Microfilms, 1972.

56. *Fitzgerald, Robert D. "Diction and the Time Lag," *Southerly*, 31, No. 2 (1971), 144–154.

Brief references to Keats, to Francis Thompson's essay on Shelley, and (*passim*) to the Romantic period in England and its influence in Australia.

57. Forst, Graham Nicol. "Kant's 'Copernican Revolution' in Philosophy and the Romantic 'Revolution' in English Literature" [Doctoral dissertation, British Columbia, 1971], DAI, 32 (Nov. 1971), 2685-A.

58. Frese, John Jerome. "Four Voices: Studies in Consciousness and the Romantic Ode" [Doctoral dissertation, Iowa, 1972], DAI, 33 (Oct. 1972), 1681-A.

Shelley, Keats, Wordsworth, and Coleridge.

59. Frye, Northrop. *The Stubborn Structure: Essays on Criticism and Society.* See K-SJ, 20 (1971), No. 70.

Rev. by *Lorna Sage in NS, 80 (18 Dec. 1970), 844; in VQR, 47 (Summer 1971), cxii; by Wallace Jackson in SAQ, 70 (Summer 1971), 418–420; by Angel Capellán Gonzalo in *Filologia Moderna*, 12 (Nov. 1971 – Feb. 1972), 132–134 [in Spanish]; by Peter Faulkner in *Durham University Journal*, 64 (Mar. 1972), 177–180.

60. Frye, Northrop. *A Study of English Romanticism.* See K-SJ, 18 (1969), No. 32, 20 (1971), No. 71.

Rev. by Jon Lundin in *Studia Neophilologica*, 43, No. 2 (1971), 590–593.

61. Furst, Lilian R. *Romanticism.* See K-SJ, 20 (1971), No. 73.

Rev. by W. H. Stevenson in SIR, 11

(Summer 1972), 257–260; by Ronald Taylor in *German Life and Letters*, 25 (Oct. 1971), 62–63; by Evelio Echevarría in *Comparative Literature Studies*, 9 (Sept. 1972), 340–341.

62. Furst, Lilian R. *Romanticism in Perspective: A Comparative Study of Aspects of the Romantic Movements in England, France, and Germany*. See K-SJ, 19 (1970), No. 26, 20 (1971), No. 74.

Rev. by Thomas P. Saine in *Monatshefte*, 63 (July–Sept. 1971), 177–178; by Frederick Garber in CL, 24 (Spring 1972), 186–189.

63. Gérin, Winifred. *Emily Brontë: A Biography*. Oxford: Clarendon, 1971.

References to Byron, Shelley, and Keats.

Rev. in **Economist*, 241 (6 Nov. 1971), xii; by Douglas Dunn in NS, 82 (19 Nov. 1971), 704; in TLS, 17 Dec. 1971, p. 1596; by *Paul West in *Book World*, 5 Mar. 1972, p. 11; by Frank P. Riga in LJ, 97 (15 Apr. 1972), 1423; by Elizabeth Hardwick in NYRB, 18 (4 May 1972), 11; by *Shirley Chew in *Encounter*, 39 (Sept. 1972), 82; in *Choice*, 9 (Oct. 1972), 968; in **Yale Review*, 62 (Dec. 1972), xii.

64. *Gravil, R. I. "English Romantic Poets and 'Authentic Existence.' " (Doctoral dissertation, East Anglia, 1971.)

65. Hartman, Geoffrey H. *Beyond Formalism: Literary Essays, 1958–1970*. See K-SJ, 20 (1971), No. 83.

Rev. by Peter Tomlinson in EC, 22 (Apr. 1972), 206–215; by Richard Harter Fogle in *Yale Review*, 60 (Summer 1971), 618–620; in *Choice*, 8 (Jan. 1972), 1448; by Gerald Gillespie in *Comparative Literature Studies*, 9 (Dec. 1972), 455–458.

66. Hartman, Geoffrey H., ed. *New Perspectives on Coleridge and Wordsworth: Selected Papers from the English Institute*. New York: Columbia Univ., 1972.

Two essays in this volume contain comments on Keats and Shelley, Hartman's "Reflections on the Evening Star: Akenside to Coleridge," pp. 85–131, and Harold Bloom's "Coleridge: The Anxiety of Influence," pp. 247–267.

67. Hayden, John O., ed. *Romantic Bards and British Reviewers: A Selected Edition of Contemporary Reviews of the Works of Wordsworth, Coleridge, Byron, Keats and Shelley*. See K-SJ, 20 (1971), No. 86.

Rev. by Keith Cushman in LJ, 97 (1 May 1972), 1717–18; in *Choice*, 9 (Sept. 1972), 813–814. Also see Nos. 82, 119.

68. Hayden, John O. *The Romantic Reviewers, 1802–1824: A Study of Literary Reviewing in the Early Nineteenth Century*. See K-SJ, 19 (1970), No. 33, 20 (1971), No. 87.

Rev. by Derek Roper in RES, 22 (Aug. 1971), 362–364.

69. Hayter, Alethea. *Opium and the Romantic Imagination*. See K-SJ, 19 (1970), No. 34, 20 (1971), No. 88.

Rev. by I[rene]. H. C[hayes]. in ELN, 9, Supplement (Sept. 1971), 20–21.

70. *Herakly, T. G. "A Comparative Study of Periodical Criticism in the Romantic Age and the Theories of the Poets." (Doctoral dissertation, London Univ., 1969.)

71. Hoffman, Harland Lamont. "The Responses of High School Seniors to Nineteenth Century English Lyric Poetry" [Doctoral dissertation, Nebraska, 1971], DAI, 32 (Nov. 1971), 2529-A.

Among the six poems chosen as stimuli were Byron's "She Walks in Beauty" and Shelley's "Ozymandias."

72. *Hoffpauir, R. "The Theory and Practice of Epic (Especially Narrative and Character), with Special Reference to Southey, Landor, Wordsworth, Shelley, Keats, and Bryon." (Doctoral dissertation, London Univ., 1969.)

73. Hollander, John. *Images of Voice: Music and Sound in Romantic Poetry*. Cambridge: Heffer, 1970. "Churchill College Overseas Fellowship Lectures, No. 5."

Discusses the symbol of the shell in Keats and Shelley.

74. *Hope, A. D. "Henry Kendall: A Dialogue with the Past," *Southerly*, No. 3 (1972), pp. 163–173.

Shelley, Bryon, and Keats are mentioned briefly for their influence on Kendall.

75. Inkster, Ian. "A Note on Itinerant Science Lecturers, 1790–1850," *Annals of Science*, 28 (Apr. 1972), 235–236.

Inkster is accumulating material for a

study of this neglected subject, and requests information. The "influence of the lecturer in this period has been hitherto underrated."

76. Kaplan, Fred. *Miracles of Rare Device: The Poet's Sense of Self in Nineteenth Century Poetry*. Detroit: Wayne State Univ., 1972.
Concerned with Victorian poetry, but with many references to Keats, Shelley, and Byron.

77. *Keats-Shelley Memorial Bulletin*, 21 (1970).
Rev. by Prema Nandakumar in *Aryan Path*, 42 (Sept. 1971), 319–320.

78. *Keats-Shelley Memorial Bulletin*, 22 (1971).
Rev. by Prema Nandakumar in *Aryan Path*, 43 (Feb. 1972), 86.

79. *King-Hele, Desmond. "The Influence of Erasmus Darwin on Wordsworth, Coleridge, Keats and Shelley," in *Le Romantisme anglo-américain: Mélanges offerts à Louis Bonnerot*, [ed. Roger Asselineau *et al.*] (Paris. Didier, 1971), pp. 147–163.

80. *Klimenko, E. N. *Anglijskaya literatura pervoj poloviny XIX veka*. [*English Literature in the First Half of the 19th Century*.] Leningrad, 1971. "Leningradskij Gosudarstvennyj Universitet im. A. A. Ždanova."
An examination of the reception and evaluation of the French Revolution and national liberation movements, concepts of heroism, the destiny of national heritage, and reasons for the appeal to folklore sources.
*Rev. by B. Reizov in *Voprosy literatury*, No. 11 (1972), pp. 227–229.

81. Knight, D. M. "Chemistry, Physiology and Materialism in the Romantic Period," *Durham University Journal*, 64 (Mar. 1972), 139–145.
The Romantics sought to demonstrate that contemporary scientific theories refuted the mechanistic materialism of the French school.

82. Knoepflmacher, U. C. "Recent Studies in the Nineteenth Century," SEL, 12 (Autumn 1972), 801–824.
An omnibus review. See K-SJ, 20 (1971), Nos. 28, 39, 45, 65, 86, 145a, 712. Also see Nos. 18, 25a, 28, 54, 67, 128, 530, 547.

83. Kumar, Shiv K., ed. *British Romantic Poets: Recent Revaluations*. See K-SJ, 17 (1968), No. 44, 18 (1969), No. 42, 19 (1970), No. 38.
Rev. by C.T.P. in ABC, 20 (Sept. 1969), 4.

84. Landow, George P. "Shipwrecked and Castaway on the Journey of Life: An Essay towards a Modern Iconography," RLC, 46 (Oct.–Dec. 1972), 569–596.
"The image, the *situation*, of the man shipwrecked and castaway has compelled the Western imagination more than any other since the beginnings of Romanticism." There is a reference to Shelley.

85. Langbaum, Robert. *The Modern Spirit: Essays on the Continuity of Nineteenth- and Twentieth-Century Literature*. See K-SJ, 20 (1971), No. 102.
Rev. in **American Scholar*, 41 (Winter 1971–72), 146; by Peter Tomlinson in EC, 22 (Apr. 1972), 206–215; by Paul Veyriras in EA, 25 (Apr.–June 1972), 339 [in French]; by Park Honan in MLR, 67 (Oct. 1972), 874–875. Also see No. 86.

86. Lebowitz, Martin. "Historicism and Disorder," *Southern Review* (L.S.U.), 8 (Summer 1972), 696–703.
An omnibus review. See K-SJ, 20 (1971), Nos. 83, 102, 209. Also see Nos. 85, 179.

87. *Leedham-Green, E. "The Cult of the Horatian Ode in the Nineteenth Century." (Doctoral dissertation, Oxford, 1971.)

88. Lindenberger, Herbert. "The Idyllic Moment: On Pastoral and Romanticism," CE, 34 (Dec. 1972), 335–351.
Sees romantic pastoral as a state of mind rather than a period style, and defines it as an "island-experience."

89. Longford, Elizabeth. *Wellington*. Vol. I: *The Years of the Sword*. See K-SJ, 20 (1971), No. 106.
Rev. by Morton Ellis Goldstein in *Journal of Modern History*, 43 (Sept. 1971), 509–510.

90. Longford, Elizabeth. *Wellington*. Vol. II: *Pillar of State*. London: Weidenfeld and Nicolson, 1972.
References to Byron and Haydon.
Rev. by Paul Johnson in NS, 3 Nov.

1972, p. 640; by Philip Ziegler in Spec, 4 Nov. 1972, pp. 712–713.

91. Lucas, John, ed. *Literature and Politics in the Nineteenth Century*. See K-SJ, 20 (1971), No. 107.

Rev. by Jennifer Searle in *Cambridge Review*, 19 Nov. 1971, pp. 54–57; in *Choice*, 8 (Nov. 1971), 1179; by W. R. Ward in *Durham University Journal*, 64 (Mar. 1972), 167–169; by Paul Meier in EA, 25 (Apr.–June 1972), 336–338 [in French]; by Patrick Brantlinger in *Victorian Studies*, 16 (Sept. 1972), 106–107; by W. D. Maxwell-Mahon in UES, 10 (Sept. 1972), 76–77; by Sheila M. Smith in *Yearbook of English Studies*, 2 (1972), 304–305.

92. *Macchia, Giovanni. *I fantasmi dell'opera*. Milan: Mondadori, 1971.

On European and English Romanticism.

93. McConnell, Frank D. "Romanticism, Language, Waste: A Reflection on Poetics and Disaster," *Bucknell Review*, 20 (Winter 1972), 121–140.

Treats the revival in romantic criticism since the Second World War as a return to the main track of contemporary consciousness.

94. McFarland, Thomas. "Complex Acts of Invention: Six Studies in Romanticism," *Yale Review*, 61 (Winter 1972), 279–297.†

An omnibus review. See K-SJ, 20 (1971), Nos. 28, 45, 534, 583, 712. Also see Nos. 18, 28, 400, 438, 547.

95. Madden, Lionel, ed. *Robert Southey: The Critical Heritage*. London and Boston: Routledge, 1972. "The Critical Heritage Series."

Reviews and comments by Byron, Hunt, Hazlitt, Peacock, and Shelley are included.

96. *Marshall, Roderick. *Italy in English Literature, 1755–1815: Origins of the Romantic Interest in Italy*. Folcroft, Pa.: Folcroft, 1971.

Reprint of a 1934 work. Godwin, Hunt, Byron, Shelley, and Keats are discussed.

97. *Maynard, T. G. J. "The Literary Relevance of the Enclosed Garden as an Image in the Oriental Tale, 1704–1820." (Doctoral dissertation, London Univ., 1970.)

98. *Medawar, Sir Peter B. *The Hope of Progress*. London: Methuen, 1972.

Included in this collection are Medawar's "Science and Literature" and John Holloway's reply. See K-SJ, 20 (1971), Nos. 93, 114.

Rev. by John Kendrew in Spec, 29 Apr. 1972, p. 657; by John Naughton in NS, 5 May 1972, pp. 602–603.

99. Meredith, George. *The Letters of George Meredith*. Ed. C. L. Cline. 3 vols. Oxford: Clarendon, 1970.

References to Byron, Keats, and Shelley.

Rev. by John W. Morris in *Victorian Poetry*, 10 (Autumn 1972), 283–287.

100. Miller, James Whipple. "English Romanticism and Chinese Nature Poetry," CL, 24 (Summer 1972), 216–236.

101. *Mincoff, Marco. *A History of English Literature*. Part II: *1700–1832*. Sofia: Nauka i izkustvo, 1970.

Rev. by *A. Anikst in *Voprosy literatury*, No. 4 (1972), pp. 203–207.

102. Miyoshi, Masao. *The Divided Self: A Perspective on the Literature of the Victorians*. See K-SJ, 19 (1970), No. 44, 20 (1971), No. 118.

Rev. by Billie Andrew Inman in *Arizona Quarterly*, 27 (Autumn 1971), 273–275; by E. Pereira in UES, 9 (Dec. 1971), 72.

103. *Moščanskaja, O. L. "Tradicii narodnoj poezii v anglijskoj literature načala XIX veka" ["The Tradition of National Poetry in English Literature at the Beginning of the Nineteenth Century"], *Učennye zapiski Gorkogo universiteta*, Fascicle 154 (1971), pp. 111–119.

Optimism, equality, liberty, hatred of civil and church oppression, and humanism in national poetry are close to the revolutionary Romantics. They were attracted to the drama in folklore, and its lively action, simplicity, power, and freshness of feeling. The author discusses the national creativity which tended to democratize the poetry of Byron and Shelley. Shelley's "Sister Rosa: a Ballad" and "Ode to the West Wind," Byron's "Song for the Luddites," and Keats's "Robin Hood" are discussed.

104. *Neupokoeva, I. *Revoljucionno-romantičeskaja poema pervoj poloviny XIX veka.* [*The Revolutionary-Romantic Poem in the First Half of the Nineteenth Century.*] Moscow: Nauka, 1971.

A critical and historical analysis with examples from English and European Romanticism.

105. O'Keeffe, Timothy. "Ironic Allusion in the Poetry of Wilfred Owen," *Ariel*, 3 (Oct. 1972), 72–81.

Owen's disillusionment with the Romantic ideals that had early influenced him is expressed in his poetry through ironic references to Keats, Shelley, and their works.

106. *Omond, Thomas Stewart. *The Romantic Triumph.* Freeport, N.Y.: Books for Libraries, 1972.

Reprint of a 1900 book.

107. Oppel, Horst. *Englisch-deutsche Literaturbeziehungen.* Vol. II: *Von der Romantik bis zur Gegenwart.* Berlin: Erich Schmidt, 1971. "Grundlagen der Anglistik und Amerikanistik, Vol. 2."

Byron's influence on German literature is discussed. Many references to Shelley, Keats, Hazlitt, and Godwin.

108. Orel, Harold, and George J. Worth, eds. *The Nineteenth Century Writer and His Audience: Selected Problems in Theory, Form, and Content.* See K-SJ, 20 (1971), No. 122.

Rev. by Sheila M. Smith in MLR, 66 (Oct. 1971), 877–878.

109. Ower, John B. "Cosmic Aristocracy and Cosmic Democracy in Edith Sitwell," *Contemporary Literature*, 12 (Autumn 1971), 527–553.

Sees Edith Sitwell in the Romantic tradition of organicism, an example of which is Shelley's "The Cloud."

110. Peckham, Morse. *The Triumph of Romanticism: Collected Essays.* See K-SJ, 20 (1971), No. 125.

Rev. by Gerald McNiece in *Arizona Quarterly*, 28 (Winter 1972), 367–370. Also see No. 51.

111. Peterkiewicz, Jerzy. *The Other Side of Silence: The Poet at the Limits of Language.* London: Oxford Univ., 1970.

Many references to Byron, Keats, and Shelley.

112. Phillips, Steven R. "Johnson's *Lives of the English Poets* in the Nineteenth Century," *Research Studies* (Washington State University), 39 (Sept. 1971), 175–190.

Hazlitt's dismissal and Byron's praise of Johnson as critic are mentioned.

113. Poynter, J. R. *Society and Pauperism: English Ideas on Poor Relief, 1795–1834.* See K-SJ, 20 (1971), No. 128.

Rev. by R. A. Lewis in *English Historical Review*, 86 (Oct. 1971), 860; by R. G. Cowherd in *Journal of the History of Behavioral Sciences*, 8 (Jan. 1972), 151–152.

114. Prawer, Siegbert, ed. *The Romantic Period in Germany: Essays by Members of the London University Institute of Germanic Studies.* London: Weidenfeld and Nicolson; New York: Schocken (1970).

Brief references to the major English Romantics.

Rev. by Harold von Hofe in JEGP, 70 (Oct. 1971), 728–729.

115. Priestley, J. B. *The Prince of Pleasure and His Regency, 1811–1820.* See K-SJ, 19 (1970), No. 49, 20 (1971), No. 131.

Rev. by Patrick Anderson in Spec, 13 Dec. 1969, p. 839.

116. "Publication Projects," *British Studies Monitor*, 1 (Winter 1971), 46, 51.

Among projects announced are a "Dictionary of British Radicals" covering 1790–1914, with a request for scholarly contributions, and a multi-volumed "History of London," which will include George Rudé's *Hanoverian London, 1714–1808* and Francis Sheppard's *Mid-Victorian London, 1808–1870.*

117. *Quennell, Peter. *L'Angleterre romantique: Ecrivains et peintres, 1717–1851.* Editions du Chêne, 1972.

A French translation of a 1970 work. See K-SJ, 20 (1971), No. 133.

118. Reiman, Donald H., ed. *The Romantics Reviewed: Contemporary Reviews of British Romantic Writers.* 9 vols. New York and London: Garland, 1972.

A photo-facsimile of 900 periodical reviews (1793–1830) of the English Romantics. Also see No. 15.

119. "Reviewers and Their Victims," TLS, 19 May 1972, p. 573.

An omnibus review. See K-SJ, 20 (1971), Nos. 86, 638. Also see Nos. 67, 155, 476.

120. *Rieger, James. "Some Remarks on 'Structure,' " WC, 2 (1971), 107–109.†

Romanticism.

121. *Rosenbaum, S. P., ed. *English Literature and British Philosophy*. Chicago and London: Univ. of Chicago, 1971.

M. H. Abrams' "Mechanical and Organic Psychologies of Literary Invention" (pp. 136–167) has references to Hunt and Shelley, and Anne C. Bolgan's "The Philosophy of Bradley and the Mind and Art of Eliot" (pp. 251–277) refers to Keats.

Rev. by Frank P. Riga in LJ, 96 (15 Sept. 1971), 2775.

122. Ruoff, A. LaVonne. "Landor's Letters to His Family: 1826–1829," *Bulletin of the John Rylands Library, Manchester*, 54 (Spring 1972), 398–433.

Discusses Landor's relations with Hunt, Hazlitt, Charles Armitage Brown, Joseph Severn, and the Blessingtons, and his new enthusiasm for Keats and Shelley. Landor writes to his sister Ellen, "If you have not redd [*sic*] Keats and Shelley, read them."

123. Saradhi, K. P. "Browning and the Early 19th Century Theatre," *Osmania Journal of English Studies*, 8, No. 2 (1971), 19–30.

The dramas of Byron and Shelley are seen as poor theatre. Hunt's praise of William Macready's acting is noted.

124. Saxena, P. K. "Modern Assessment of the Romantic Poets: A Study in the Whirligig of Taste," *Bulletin of the Department of English* (Calcutta Univ.), N.S. 5, No. 2 (1969–70), 61–69.

Surveys the attacks on the English Romantics and the subsequent defenses.

125. Schmiefsky, Marvel. "Swinburne's Anti-Establishment Poetics," *Victorian Poetry*, 9 (Autumn 1971), 261–276.†

Discusses Swinburne's views on Keats, Shelley, and Byron.

126. *Sherwood, Margaret Pollock. *Undercurrents of Influence in English Romantic Poetry*. New York: AMS, 1971.

Reprint of a 1934 book.

127. Solomon, Stanley J. "Conflicting Sensibility in Death Poetry: 1740 to the Romantic Age," *Enlightenment Essays*, 2 (Summer 1971), 67–81.

128. Speirs, John. *Poetry towards Novel*. See K-SJ, 20 (1971), No. 145a.

Rev. in TLS, 16 July 1971, p. 828; by R. R. Davies in Li, 5 Aug. 1971, p. 185; by Joan Owen in LJ, 97 (1 June 1972), 2100; by John Beer in Spec, 24 July 1971, pp. 139–140; by Gilbert Thomas in *English*, 21 (Spring 1972), 27–29; in *Choice*, 9 (Sept. 1972), 818; by G. B. Tennyson in *Nineteenth Century Fiction*, 27 (Dec. 1972), 368–369. Also see No. 82.

129. Stavros, George. "Pater, Wilde, and the Victorian Critics of the Romantics" [Doctoral dissertation, Wisconsin, 1972], DAI, 33 (Nov. 1972), 2344-A.

130. Steiner, George. *In Bluebeard's Castle: Some Notes Towards the Redefinition of Culture*. London: Faber; New Haven: Yale (1971).

See K-SJ, 20 (1971), No. 148.

Rev. by Geoffrey Grigson in NS, 22 Oct. 1971, pp. 545–546; by Christopher Ricks in NYRB, 18 Nov. 1971, pp. 27–29; by Roy Fuller in *Encounter*, 37 (Dec. 1971), 47; by Barbara Hardy in Spec, 4 Dec. 1971, pp. 810–811; by Robert S. Picciotto in *Nation*, 10 Jan. 1972, pp. 53–54; in VQR, 48 (Spring 1972), lii.

131. *Stephens, Rosemary [Carswell]. "The Spirit of Romantic Poetry, Heritage of the Modern Poet," *South & West*, 9, No. 1 (1971), 24–25.

132. [Stevenson, W. H.] "The Editor's Lookout," SIR, 11 (Summer 1972), 169–170.

On the Romantics' search for the Universal.

133. [Stone, C. F., III.] "The Editor's Lookout," SIR, 11 (Spring 1972), 77–78.

On the problem of audience of the Romantics.

134. Sutherland, Donald. *On Romanticism*. See K-SJ, 20 (1971), No. 150.

Rev. by Hubert F. Babinski in LJ, 97 (1 Jan. 1972), 73; in PQ, 51 (July 1972), 634; by D[avid]. V. E[rdman]. in ELN,

10, Supplement (Sept. 1972), 15. Also see No. 51.

135. Sutton, Denys. "Romantics and Realists: The British Exhibition in Paris," *Apollo*, 95 (Mar. 1972), 232–235.

Illustrations include Benjamin Robert Haydon's "Wordsworth," Thomas Phillips' "Lady Caroline Lamb as Page," and John Martin's "Manfred on the Jungfrau."

136. Swingle, L. J. "On Reading Romantic Poetry," *PMLA*, 86 (Oct. 1971), 974–981.‡

Treats Romantic poetry as a poetry of question rather than doctrine. Includes references to the major Romantic poets.

137. *Tamura, Hidenosuke. "Roman-ha ni okeru 'Naimensei' to 'Gaimensei,' " *Oberon* (Tokyo), 34 (1971), 42–52. [In Japanese.]

Internality and externality in Romantic poets.

138. *Thomas, D. S. "The Political, Religious, and Moral Censorship of Literature in England from the Seventeenth to the Nineteenth Centuries." (Doctoral dissertation, London Univ., 1969.)

139. Thomas, Deborah Allen. "MLA Seminar 71: Dickens and the Romantic Tradition," *Dickens Studies Newsletter*, 3 (Mar. 1972), 4–6.

Account of panel discussion.

140. Thorlby, Anthony. *The Romantic Movement*. See K-SJ, 17 (1968), No. 64, 18 (1969), No. 73.

Rev. by Frederick Garber in CL, 24 (Spring 1972), 186–189.

141. Tobias, Richard C. "The Year's Work in Victorian Poetry: 1971," *Victorian Poetry*, 10 (Autumn 1972), 195–233.

An omnibus review. See K-SJ, 20 (1971), Nos. 45, 304. Also see No. 28.

142. Twitchell, James Buell. "The Romantic Psychodrama: An Interpretation of *The Rime of the Ancient Mariner*, *Manfred* and *Prometheus Unbound*, Act IV" [Doctoral dissertation, North Carolina, 1971], DAI, 32 (Mar. 1972), 5204-A–5205-A.

143. *Vaughan, Charles Edwyn. *The Romantic Revolt*. Folcroft, Pa.: Folcroft, 1971.

Reprint of a 1907 work.

144. Walsh, William. "Swains of Solyma, Advise," *Encounter*, 37 (Dec. 1971), 61–67.

An omnibus review. See K-SJ, 20 (1971), Nos. 145a, 486, 712, 728, 851, 958. Also see Nos. 23, 128, 371, 547, 555a, 648, 777.

145. Watson, J[ohn]. R. *Picturesque Landscape and English Romantic Poetry*. See K-SJ, 20 (1971), No. 162.

Rev. by Christopher Salvesen in RES, 23, (Feb. 1972), 89–90; by Gabriella Corradini Favati in *Rivista di letterature moderne e comparate*, 25 (Dec. 1972), 308–311.

146. *Watson, J[ohn]. R. "Turner and the Romantic Poets," in *Encounters: Essays on Literature and the Visual Arts*, ed. John Dixon Hunt (London: Studio Vista, 1971), pp. 96–123.

Rev. in TLS, 17 Sept. 1971, p. 1583; by Carol Burns in *Books and Bookmen*, 17 (May 1972), 84, 86.

147 Wilkie, Brian. *Romantic Poets and Epic Tradition*. See K-SJ, 15 (1966), No. 53, 16 (1967), No. 40, 17 (1968), No. 70, 18 (1969), No. 78.

Rev. by Mario Praz in MLR, 66 (July 1971), 670–672.

148. Wittreich, Joseph Anthony, Jr., ed. *The Romantics on Milton: Formal Essays and Critical Asides*. See K-SJ, 20 (1971), No. 174.

Rev. in TLS, 6 Aug. 1971, p. 953; by D[avid]. V. E[rdman]. in ELN, 9, Supplement (Sept. 1971), 22; by Andy P. Antippas in *Blake Newsletter*, No. 22 (Fall 1972), p. 55.

149. Woodring, Carl. *Politics in English Romantic Poetry*. See K-SJ, 20 (1971), No. 175.

Rev. by Brian Wilkie in JEGP, 70 (July 1971), 559–564; by C. J. Myers in *Dalhousie Review*, 51 (Summer 1971), 274–276; S[tuart]. C[urran]. in ELN, 9, Supplement (Sept. 1971), 22–23; by F. A. Whiting in CLSB, No. 212 (Oct. 1971), pp. 699–700; by Stephen R. Graubard in *American Historical Review*, 77 (Feb. 1972), 143–144; by Max F. Schulz in MLQ, 33 (Mar. 1972), 83–86; by John D. Jump in RES, 23 (May 1972), 214–216; by J. R. de J. Jackson in ELN, 10 (Sept. 1972), 53–54. Also see No. 43.

For additional BOOKS AND ARTICLES RELATING TO ENGLISH ROMANTICISM see Nos. 9, 14.

II. BYRON

WORKS: SELECTED, SINGLE, TRANSLATED

150. *Asimov's Annotated "Don Juan."* Text by Lord Byron. Notes by Isaac Asimov. Illustrated by Milton Glaser. Garden City, N.Y.: Doubleday, 1972.
Rev. by Frank P. Riga in LJ, 97 (1 Dec. 1972), 3912.

151. *Byron: Poems. Selected with an Introduction and Notes by Andrew Taylor. Melbourne: Cassell, 1970.

152. *Byron: Selected Poetry and Prose. Ed. Peter Gunn. Harmondsworth: Penguin, 1972. "Penguin English Library." Paperback.

153. *Byron: Selected Works.* Ed. Edward E. Bostetter. New York: Holt, Rinehart and Winston, 1972. "Rinehart Editions."
A revised and enlarged version of an edition first published in 1951 (see K-SJ, 2 [1953], No. 14). Includes *Cain*, *Beppo*, selections from *Don Juan* and Letters and Journals. Paperback.

154. *Byron's "Don Juan."* Ed. Truman Guy Steffan and Willis W. Pratt. Second Edition. 4 vols. Austin and London: Univ. of Texas, 1971.
See K-SJ, 7 (1958), No. 75.

155. *Byron's Hebrew Melodies.* Ed. Thomas L. Ashton. London: Routledge; Austin: Univ. of Texas (1972).
Includes a variorum text of *Hebrew Melodies.*
Rev. in *Times* (London), 2 Mar. 1972, p. 12; by Gilbert Thomas in *English*, 21 (Autumn 1972), 113–114; in *Choice*, 9 (Oct. 1972), 965. Also see No. 119.

156. *Don Juan (1819).* Ed. Brian Lee. See K-SJ, 19 (1970), No. 69.
Rev. by J. C. Maxwell in N&Q, 217 (Mar. 1972), 113–115.

157. *Fugitive Pieces. Reproduced from the First Edition. Bibliographical Note by Marcel Kessel. New York: Haskell House, 1972.
Reprint of the 1933 edition.

157a. Marchand, Leslie A. "An Unpublished Byron Poem," *Griffon* (Gennadius Library, Athens), No. 6 (Summer 1970), pp. 17–19.
Prints six *ottava rima* stanzas which Byron wrote on the flyleaves of a volume of sixteenth-century Italian poetry.

158. *Palomničestvo Čajl'd-Garol'da. Don-Žuan. [Childe Harold's Pilgrimage. Don Juan.] Moscow: Xudožestvennaya literatura, 1972. "Biblioteca vsemirnoj literatury. ser. 2, t. 67." ["The Library of World Literature, Series 2, Vol. 67."]
Included is a biographical and critical essay by A. [A.] Elistratova (pp. 5–24) and notes and commentary by O. Afonina, V. Rogov, and N. Ja. D'jakonova (pp. 791–862).

159. Steffan, T. G. "From Cambridge to Missolonghi: Byron Letters at the University of Texas," *Texas Quarterly*, 14 (Autumn 1971), 6–66.
Prints thirty-eight letters by Byron and three forgeries. Many "seem to be unpublished. . . ." Also see No. 160.

160. *Steffan, T. G., ed. *From Cambridge to Missolonghi: Byron Letters at the University of Texas.* Austin: Univ. of Texas, 1971.
See No. 159, of which this is a separate offprint.

161. *Werner, A Tragedy.* A Facsimile of the Acting Version of William Charles Macready. Ed. Martin Spevack. See K-SJ, 20 (1971), No. 192.
Rev. by Harold Orel in *Victorian Studies*, 15 (Sept. 1971), 93–95; by J. C. Trewin in *Theatre Notebook*, 26 (Autumn 1971), 45.

For additional WORKS BY BYRON see Nos. 95, 609.

BOOKS AND ARTICLES RELATING TO BYRON AND HIS CIRCLE

162. Allderidge, P. H. "Byron as a Vandal" [Letter], *Times* (London), 4 Aug. 1972, p. 13.
Concerns Byron's signature on a Greek column of Poseidon's temple. Reply by P. B. Waterfield, 7 Aug. 1972, p. 13.

163. Anderson, Howard. "The Manuscript of

M. G. Lewis's 'The Monk': Some Preliminary Notes," *PBSA*, 62 (July–Sept. 1968), 427–434.

The recently rediscovered holograph MS of the novel settles the question of which is the first edition, shows Lewis' original intentions regarding the conclusion, and provides the basis for a better printed text (now in preparation).

164. Arinshtein, Leonid M. "William Michael Rossetti als politischer Dichter," *Zeitschrift für Anglistik und Amerikanistik*, 19 (July 1971), 261–283. [In German.]

References to Byron and Shelley.

165. Ashton, Thomas L. "Byronic Lyrics for David's Harp: The Hebrew Melodies," SEL, 12 (Autumn 1972), 665–681.†‡

Because these poems do not suggest a religious inspiration they do "share in the essential unity of Byron's lyric corpus."

166. [Ashton, Thomas L.] Lombardi, Thomas William. "Byron's *Hebrew Melodies*" [Doctoral dissertation, Columbia, 1969], DAI, 33 (July 1972), 278-A–279-A.

167. Ashton, Thomas L. "The Censorship of Byron's *Marino Faliero*," HLQ, 36 (Nov. 1972), 27–44.‡

For performance at Drury Lane, Byron's play was subjected to extensive political censorship, which in effect destroyed it.

168. "Athenians Reminded of Byron's War," *Times* (London), 5 Nov. 1971, p. 8.

Describes an exhibition in Athens to mark the 150th anniversary of the Greek revolution.

169. Ayling, Stanley. *George the Third*. London: Collins; New York: Knopf (1972).

References to Byron.

Rev. by Sir Charles Petrie in ILN, 260 (June 1972), 73; by R. R. Rea in LJ, 97 (Aug. 1972), 2572; by John Raymond in NS, 22 (Sept. 1972), pp. 398–399; by Hugh Brogan in Spec, 14 Oct. 1972, p. 583; by J. H. Plumb in NYRB, 14 Dec. 1972, pp. 44–46.

170. *Babkina, G. "Rainis o Bajrone" ["Rainis on Byron"], *Učënnye zapiski Latviyskogo universiteta* (Riga), 174 (1972), 82–117.

In Latvian, with a summary in Russian.

171. [Bain, Kenneth Bruce Findlater.] Findlater, Richard, *pseud. The Player Kings*. See K-SJ, 20 (1971), No. 198.

Rev. in ILN, 27 March 1971, p. 16.

172. Balibé, Joseph-Marc. "Berlioz, Janin et les 'Impressions d'Italie,' " RLC, 45 (Oct.–Dec. 1971), 489–513.

Refers to Byron.

173. *Barratt, Glynn R. V. *I. I. Kozlov: The Translations from Byron*. Berne and Frankfurt: Lang, 1972. "Europäische Hochschulschriften: Reihe 16, Slav. Sprachen u. Literaturen, Bd. 1."

174. Barratt, G[lynn]. R. V. *Ivan Kozlov: A Study and a Setting*. Toronto: Hakkert, 1972.

The extensive influence of Byron on the Russian poet is discussed in detail.

175. "Bawdy Byron," *Times* (London), 13 May 1972, p. 14.

Reports that a new edition of Byron's letters edited by Leslie Marchand is to be published, including a "few letters . . . considered too indecent to be published before."

176. Beaty, Frederick L. "Byron's Longbow and Strongbow," SEL, 12 (Autumn 1972), 653–663.†‡

"The traditional identification of Longbow and Strongbow [in *Don Juan* XIII] with two of Byron's acquaintances has obscured the possibility that they symbolize considerably more than mere portraits from life."

177. Beaty, Frederick L. " 'With Verse Like Crashaw,' " N&Q, 217 (Aug. 1972), 290–292.†

Evidently Bryon considered Crashaw a bad versifier, hence his reference in *Don Juan* III.79.7–8.

178. Behler, Ernst. "Techniques of Irony in Light of the Romantic Theory," *Rice University Studies*, 57 (Fall 1971), 1–17.

Includes a paragraph on Byron's *Don Juan* as an example of Romantic irony.

179. Bewley, Marius. *Masks and Mirrors: Essays in Criticism*. See K-SJ, 20 (1971), No. 209.

Rev. by Clarence A. Brown in *Thought*, 46 (Spring 1971), 125–126. Also see No. 86.

180. Blackman, Maurice. "Gérard de Nerval et Thomas Moore: Note sur 'Stances

Élégiaques,' " *Revue d'Histoire Littéraire de la France*, 72 (May–June 1972), 428–431.

Discusses the influence of *Irish Melodies* on Nerval.

181. Blackstone, Bernard. *Byron*. Vol. III: *Social Satire, Drama, and Epic*. Harlow, Essex: Longman, for the British Council, 1971. "Writers and Their Work, No. 223."

182. Blackstone, Bernard. " 'The Loops of Time': Spatio-Temporal Patterns in 'Childe Harold,' " *Ariel*, 2 (Oct. 1971), 5–17.

"The fascination of *Childe Harold* lies here: in it we watch Byron living his personal present in the historic present and the historic past, and his personal past in the historic past and the historic present." Employing cybernetics vocabulary, Blackstone finds binary patterns in the poem.

183. *Blyth, Henry. *Caro: The Fatal Passion—The Life of Lady Caroline Lamb*. London: Hart-Davis, 1972.

184. Bosworth, C. E. "Some Correspondence in the John Rylands University Library of Manchester Concerning John Lewis Burckhardt and Lady Hester Stanhope's Physician," *Bulletin of the John Rylands University Library of Manchester*, 55 (Autumn 1972), 33–59.

Burckhardt, Swiss traveler and orientalist, mentions William John Bankes, oriental traveler and friend of Byron and Hobhouse.

185. *Brilli, Attilio. "Byron e Leopardi: il riso dei morti," *Studi Urbinati di Storia, Filosofia, e Letteratura*, 3 (1971), 1080–87.

186. Brogan, Howard O. "Byron's *Don Juan*, Canto II," Exp, 30 (Nov. 1971), Item 28.‡

Running through the whole episode is Byron's ironic use of religious allusion, employed "obviously to heighten the shock which he intends his readers to receive from his portrayal of the animal nature of man triumphing over his most sacred ideals in a time of maximum stress."

187. Brogan, Howard O. "Satirist Burns and Lord Byron," *Costerus*, 4 (1972), 29–47.

The emphasis is on Burns, whose satires are found similar to Byron's.

188. Bruffee, Kenneth A. "Elegiac Romance." See K-SJ, 20 (1971), No. 221.

Rev. by Claire Tomalin in NS, 16 Jan. 1970, pp. 86–87.

189. Büchi, Adolf. *Byrons "Manfred" und die historischen Dramen*. Bern: Francke, 1972. "Schweizer Anglistische Arbeiten: Swiss Studies in English, Vol. 68."

190. [Byron Society], *Times* (London), 28 Sept. 1971, p. 12.

An untitled item simply stating that a concert will be held to commemorate Byron.

191. [Byron Society], *Times* (London), 29 Feb. 1972, p. 14.

An untitled news item which announces a "dinner to mark 160th anniversary of Lord Byron's maiden speech in House of Lords."

192. [Byron Society], TLS, 14 Apr. 1972, p. 421.

An untitled notice of a lecture on Byron's letters to be given by Leslie Marchand at the Byron Society, 12 May 1972.

193. "Byronic," *Times* (London), 22 July 1971, p. 14.

Reports that a collection of letters will be returned to Newstead Abbey.

194. "Byron's 'Don Leon,' " TLS, 17 Dec. 1971, p. 1581.

Corrects an earlier impression (in TLS, 22 Oct. 1971, p. 1312) that *Don Leon* is not included in the British Museum's *General Catalogue of Printed Books*.

195. Carr, Wendell Robert. "James Mill's Politics: A Final Word," *Historical Journal*, 15 (June 1972), 315–320.

Mill supported John Cam Hobhouse's advocacy of extending the suffrage and of more frequent parliaments, in the Westminster election of 1819.

196. *Čavčanidze, D. "Bajron i russkie poety" ["Byron and Russian Poets"], *Literatura v škole*, No. 5 (1972), pp. 76–80.

Discusses the Byronic ear and the influence of Byron on Pushkin and Lermontov.

197. *Chambers, R[aymond]. W[itson]. *Ruskin (and others) on Byron*. New York: Haskell House, 1971.

Reprint of the "English Association Pamphlet, No. 62," 1925.

198. Cohane, Christopher B. "An Unincorporated Emendation to Byron's 'The Vision of Judgement,' " N&Q, 217 (Mar. 1972), 96.†

From the errata sheet of the first edition.

199. Colville, Derek. *Victorian Poetry and the Romantic Religion*. See K-SJ, 20 (1971), No. 233.

Rev. in *Choice*, 8 (Sept. 1971), 830.

200. Colvin, Christina, ed. *Maria Edgeworth: Letters from England, 1813–1844*. Oxford: Clarendon, 1971.

Byron is mentioned.

Rev. by D. A. Jones in Li, 86 (9 Sept. 1971), 341–342.

201. Corradini Favati, Gabriella. "I vagabondaggi italiani di un byroniano irlandese," *Rivista di letterature moderne e comparate*, 24 (Sept. 1971), 165–197; (Dec. 1971), 257–288.

On Charles Rolleston's grand tour, with many references to Byron.

202. Dénier, Renée. "L'Anglomanie de Stendhal," *Stendhal Club*, No. 55 (Apr. 1972), pp. 217–231.

Stendhal's dissatisfaction with the French translations of Byron's works led him to consult the originals.

203. De Pange, Victor, and Norman King. "La Bibliothèque Anglaise de Mme. de Staël," *Cahiers Staëliens*, 14 (Sept. 1972), 33–67.

De Staël's library included books by Byron, Godwin, Lewis, Moore, and Mary Wollstonecraft.

204. De Porte, Michael V. "Byron's Strange Perversity of Thought," MLQ, 33 (Dec. 1792), 405–419.‡

Byron's "own madness of heart" results from the metaphysical limits on man's freedom. Frequent references to *Childe Harold*.

205. Diakonova, Nina. "The Russian Episode in Byron's 'Don Juan,' " *Ariel*, 3 (Oct. 1972), 50–57.

Re-examines Byron's use of his sources and defends Byron's handling of the Russian episode as appropriate to the structure and theme of the poem as a whole. Briefly examines Byron's interest in Russia and speculates about his association with revolutionaries.

206.*Dick, William. *Byron and His Poetry*. New York: AMS, 1972. Reprint of a 1913 work in the "Poetry and Life Series."

207. *Dischner, Gisela. *Ursprunge der Rhineromantik in England: Zur Geschichte der romantischen Ästhetik*. Frankfurt am Main: Vittorio Klostermann, 1972.

Byron and Mary Shelley are discussed.

208. Diskin, Patrick. "The Gaelic Background to Anglo-Irish Poetry," *Topic*, 24 (Fall 1972), 37–51.

Thomas Moore's interest in Gaelic literature and his importance to the Anglo-Irish tradition are discussed.

209. *D'jakonova, N. Ja. "Zurnaly i pis'ma Bajrona" ["Letters and Journals of Byron"], *Ivestiya Akademii Nauk SSSR. Seriya literatury i yazyka*, 31, Fascicle 5 (1972), 430–443.

An analysis of the genre, language, style, and self-revelation of Byron's letters and journals.

210. Dobbs, Brian. *Drury Lane: Three Centuries of the Theatre Royal, 1663–1971*. London: Cassell, 1972.

Byron, Hunt, and Hazlitt are mentioned.

Rev. in *TLS, 18 Aug. 1972, p. 978; by Raymond Mander and Joe Mitchenson in *Books and Bookmen*, 17 (Aug. 1972), 88–89; in **Drama*, Fall 1972, p. 77.

211. *Dombrovskaya, E. Ya. "Bairon o Shekspire" ["Byron on Shakespeare"], *Moskovskii oblastnoi pedagogicheskii institut imeni N. K. Krupskoi* (Moscow), 220 (1970), 33–43.

212. England, Anthony Bertram. "The Rhetoric of 'Don Juan' and Some Aspects of Eighteenth-Century Literature" [Doctoral dissertation, Yale, 1969], DAI, 31 (Sept. 1970), 1270-A–1271-A.

213. Finley, Gerald E. "J. M. W. Turner and Sir Walter Scott: Iconography of a Tour," *Journal of the Warburg and Courtauld Institutes*, 35 (1972), 359–385.

Appendix includes extracts from the diary of Robert Cadell, Scott's publisher, who mentions reading an 1822 letter from Byron to Scott.

214. *Fox, Sir John Charles. *The Byron Mystery*. St. Clair Shores, Mich.: Scholarly, 1972.

Reprint of a 1924 book.

215. *Fuess, Claude M. *Lord Byron as a Satirist in Verse.* New York: Haskell House, 1972.

Reprint of a 1912 book.

216. Gahtan, Ellen Skorneck. "The Image of Greece in Byron's Works: No Common Muse" [Doctoral dissertation, Columbia, 1969], DAI, 33 (July 1972), 310-A–311-A.

217. Gans, Eric Lawrence. *The Discovery of Illusion: Flaubert's Early Works, 1835–1837.* Berkeley, Los Angeles, and London: Univ. of California, 1971. "University of California Publications in Modern Philology, Vol. 100."

Flaubert's brief portrait of Byron depicts him not as poet but as Romantic hero.

218. Gérin, Winifred. "Byron's Influence on the Brontës," *Essays by Divers Hands,* N.S. 37 (1972), 47–62.†

Byron's life and romantic works strongly influenced the early works of the Brontës.

219. Gilman, Sander L. "The Uncontrollable Steed: A Study of the Metamorphosis of a Literary Image," *Euphorion,* 66 (Mar. 1972), 32–54.

Includes discussion of Byron's *Mazeppa.* The presence of the image in *The Vision of Judgment, The Deformed Transformed,* and Shelley's *Prometheus Unbound* is noted.

220. *Godshalk, William Leigh. "Nabokov's Byronic *Ada*: A Note," *Notes on Contemporary Literature,* 2 (Mar. 1972), 2–4.†

221. Gose, Elliott B., Jr. *Imagination Indulged: The Irrational in the Nineteenth Century Novel.* Montreal and London: McGill-Queen's Univ., 1972.

Contains a chapter on M. G. Lewis' *The Monk* and comments on Byron and Shelley.

Rev. in *Choice,* 9 (Nov. 1972), 1129; by G. M. Harvey in *Dalhousie Review,* 52 (Summer 1972), 318–320.

222. Grebanier, Bernard D. *The Uninhibited Byron: An Account of His Sexual Confusion.* See K-SJ, 20 (1971), No. 268.

Rev. in **National Review,* 23 (9 Mar. 1971), 271; by E. B. Murray in *Contempora,* 1 (May–Aug. 1971), 47; by Douglas Dunn in NS, 2 July 1971, pp. 22–23; by Richard Newman in *Books and Bookmen,* 16 (July 1971), 48; in SAQ, 70 (Summer 1971), 437; by E. E. B[ostetter]. in ELN, 9 Supplement (Sept. 1971), 36.

223. Gruen, John. "Virgil Sings of 'Lord Byron,' " *New York Times,* Section 2 (Arts and Leisure), 9 Apr. 1972, pp. 17, 24.

A description of Virgil Thompson's opera on the poet (libretto by Jack Larson) to be given its world premiere at the Juilliard Theater on 20 April 1972.

224. Gurr, Andrew. "Don Byron and the Moral North," *Ariel,* 3 (Apr. 1972), 32–41.

Considers the influence of Byron's scandalous reputation on the creation of *Don Juan.* Byron's characterization of Juan, traditionally the seducer, as essentially innocent challenges the conventional morality that led to his own exile from England. Yet the poem also secretly vaunts Byron's sinfulness, just as in England Byron had contributed to his own reputation for dissoluteness.

225. Guthke, Karl S. *Die Mythologie der entgötterten Welt: Ein literarisches Thema von der Aufklärung bis zur Gegenwart.* Göttingen: Vandenhoeck and Ruprecht, 1971.

A sub-chapter is entitled "Byron: Der Gott Calvins als Revenant." There are also remarks on Shelley.

Rev. by Ludwig W. Kahn in *Yearbook of Comparative and General Literature,* No. 21 (1972), pp. 83–84.

226. Hagan, John. "Enemies of Freedom in 'Jane Eyre,' " *Criticism,* 13 (Fall 1971), 351–376.

Though a great admirer of Byron in her early career, Charlotte Brontë later repudiated him for his "moral flaws." Thus the unregenerate Rochester is depicted as a Byronic figure.

227. Hagelman, Charles W., Jr., and Robert J. Barnes, eds. *A Concordance to Byron's "Don Juan."* See K-SJ, 17 (1968), No. 154, 18 (1969), No. 182, 19 (1970), No. 104, 20 (1971), No. 273.

Rev. by Jürgen Schäfer in *Anglia,* 88, No. 4 (1970), 548–552.

228. *Haining, Peter, ed. *Gothic Tales of Terror: Classic Horror Stories from Great Brit-*

ain, Europe and the United States, 1765–1840. New York: Taplinger, 1972.

Works, or excerpts of works, by Byron and Mary Shelley appear in this anthology.

229. *Hamilton, Walter. *The Poets Laureate of England.* Detroit: Gale, 1968.

Reprint of an 1879 book. Byron's comments on H. J. Pye, Southey, and Wordsworth are quoted.

230. Hawes, Louis. "Turner's *Fighting Temeraire*," *Art Quarterly*, 35 (Spring 1972), 23–48.

Turner "harbored sombre doubts about the direction in which England, and humanity in general, was headed. . . . Reinforcing this apprehension was the ringing voice of Byron, the contemporary poet Turner read and admired most: *Childe Harold's Pilgrimage* (1812–18) put forth the similar moral that decadence follows upon imperial corruption and the curbing of individual freedom." Hawes sees this theme in Turner's painting, "The Fighting Temeraire Tugged to Her Last Berth to Be Broken Up."

231. Hayden, John O., ed. *Scott: The Critical Heritage.* See K-SJ, 20 (1971), No. 575.

Rev. by James Kinsley in MLR, 66 (July 1971), 672–673.

232. *Heine, Heinrich. *Werke.* Vol. III. Ed. Norbert and Rosemarie Altenhofer. Munich: Heimeran, 1972.

Includes Heine's comments on Byron.

233. Hewlett, Dorothy. "Preface," KSMB, 23 (1972), v–vi.

Refers to "*The Byron Society*, formed in London last year," and describes various events and commemorative services on the 150th anniversary of Shelley's death.

234. Hijiya, Yukihito. "Byron and the New Promethean Man" [Doctoral dissertation, New Mexico, 1972], DAI, 32 (May 1972), 6378-A.

235. Hogg, James. "*Memoir of the Author's Life*" *and* "*Familiar Anecdotes of Sir Walter Scott.*" Ed. Douglas S. Mack. Edinburgh: Scottish Academic Press, 1972.

The "Ettrick Shepherd" writes of Byron in his "Memoir," here reprinted from the version of 1832 with significant variations from other versions.

Rev. in *Blackwood's*, No. 1886 (Dec. 1972), pp. 571–572.

236. Holden, David. *Greece Without Columns.* London: Faber; New York: Lippincott (1972).

Includes frequent references to Byron.

Rev. in *Observer*, 14 May 1972, p. 37; in TLS, 19 May 1972, p. 564; in **Economist*, 20 May 1972, p. 77; by Mervyn Jones in NS, 83 (2 June 1972), 753–754; in **Kirkus Reviews*, 15 June 1972, p. 704; in **Publishers' Weekly*, 201 (19 June 1972), 54; in **Book World* (*Washington Post*), 23 July 1972, p. 1; in **Christian Science Monitor*, 2 Aug. 1972, p. 11; in *NYT, 1 Oct. 1972, p. 34; in *LJ, 97 (15 Oct. 1972), 3310; in **New Leader*, 55 (30 Oct. 1972), 18; in **America*, 18 Nov. 1972, p. 419.

237. "Houghton Library Acquisitions," *Harvard Library Bulletin*, 20 (Oct. 1972), 448–449.

Acquisition of Byron's "The Irish Avatar" (Paris, 1821), one of only two known copies extant; Keats's holograph MS of "Lamia"; and first edition of Shelley's *Oedipus Tyrannus.*

238. Hubbell, Jay B. "The Literary Apprenticeship of Edgar Allan Poe," *Southern Literary Journal*, 2 (Fall 1969), 99–105.

Mentions influence of Byron on Poe's "Tamerlane" and Poe's review of Hazlitt's *Characters of Shakespear's Plays.*

239. Hull, Gloria Thompson. "Women in Byron's Poetry: A Biographical and Critical Study" [Doctoral dissertation, Purdue, 1972], DAI, 33 (Dec. 1972), 2894-A.

240. *Huxley, H. H. "*Bos*, Bentley, and Byron," *Greece and Rome*, 19 (Oct. 1972), 187–189.

241. Inglis-Jones, Elisabeth. "A Pembrokeshire County Family in the Eighteenth Century, Part 2," *National Library of Wales Journal*, 17 (Summer 1972), 217–237.†

Quotes first-hand account of a conversation between Byron and Madame de Staël at an evening party given by Sir James Mackintosh.

242. Inglis-Jones, Elisabeth. "A Pembrokeshire County Family in the Eighteenth Century, Part 3," *National Library of*

Wales Journal, 17 (Winter 1972), 321–342.†

Quotes first-hand accounts of Teresa Guiccioli in Rome, 1827–28.

243. Isani, Mukhtar Ali. "The Naming of Fedallah in *Moby-Dick*," AL, 40 (Nov. 1968), 380–385.

Suggests Melville was influenced by Thomas Moore's *Lalla Rookh.*

244. Isani, Mukhtar Ali. "Zoroastrianism and the Fire Symbolism in *Moby-Dick*," AL, 44 (Nov. 1972), 385–397.

One source of Melville's knowledge of Zoroastrianism was Thomas Moore's *Lalla Rookh.*

245. Jeffrey, Lloyd N. "Homeric Echoes in Byron's *Don Juan*," *South Central Bulletin*, 31 (Winter 1971), 188–192.†‡

Without the influence of Homer, *Don Juan* would "lack some of its most entertaining and most powerful lines."

246. *Jenkins, Elizabeth. *Lady Caroline Lamb.* London: Sphere, 1972.

Revised edition of a 1932 book.

247. Johnson, Lee. "Delacroix and *The Bride of Abydos*," *Burlington Magazine*, 114 (Sept. 1972), 579–585.

Delacroix, who was strongly influenced by Byron's romantic works, did four paintings titled *Selim and Zuleika* inspired by *The Bride of Abydos.* Johnson compares the paintings to the relevant passages in the poem and to renderings by Géricault and Alexandre Colin. Beautifully illustrated.

248. Jump, John D. *Byron.* London and Boston: Routledge, 1972. "Routledge Author Guides."

Also in paperback.

Rev. in TLS, 17 Nov. 1972, p. 1398; by Robert Chapman in *Books and Bookmen*, 18 (Dec. 1972), 86–87.

249. *Karaiskakis, Sitsas. *Byron.* Gia ta 150 Chronia tou Xesikomou ton Hellinon (1821–1971). Athens: I. D. Kollaros, 1971.

250. Knight, G. Wilson. *Neglected Powers: Essays on Nineteenth and Twentieth Century Literature.* See K-SJ, 20 (1971), No. 300.

Rev. by Cyril Connolly in *Sunday Times* (London), 7 Feb. 1971, p. 27; in TLS, 1 Oct. 1971, p. 1171 (reply by Kiffin A. Rockwell, 15 Oct. 1971, p. 1273, and by John A. Brebner, 5 Nov. 1971, p. 1392); William Kean Seymour in CR, 219 (Oct. 1971), 221–222; by H. P. Collins in *Aryan Path*, 42 (Dec. 1971), 462–463; by F. F. Cannan in *Yearbook of English Studies*, 2 (1972), 325–327; by Idwal Jones in *Twentieth Century*, No. 1049 (1972), p. 57.

251. *Kortes, L. P. *Epoxa romantizma: Istoriya angliiskoi i amerikanskoi literatury; Stilisticheskie osobennost'prozy Bairona: Posobie po stilisticheskomu analizu khudozhestvennoi literatury.* [*The Epoch of Romanticism: A History of English and American Literature: Stylistic Features of Byron's Prose: A Textbook for the Stylistic Analysis of Literature.*] Minsk: Izd. Belorus. Univ., 1970.

252. *Krasnov, A. N. "Bajron v ocenke Gercena" ["Herzen's Estimate of Byron"], *Naučnye trudy Novosibirskogo pedagogičeskogo instituta*, Fascicle 65 (1971), pp. 219–231.

Byron is esteemed for his connection to the progressive social-political movements of his time. The revolutionary core of Byron's poetry is analyzed and his place in history assessed. Byron's reception and influence in Russia is discussed, and he is compared to Pushkin.

253. *Krasnov, A. N. "Russkaja kritika 10-x-načala 20-x godov XIX veka o Bajrone" ["Russian Criticism of Byron in the Second Decade of the Nineteenth Century to the Beginning of the Third"], *Naučnye trudy Novosibirskogo pedagogičeskogo instituta*, Fascicle 36 (1971), pp. 53–66.

Analyzes the views of the Russian intelligentsia on Byron's works, including those of Turgenev, P. A. Vyazemsky, K. N. Batyuskov, and Pushkin.

254. *Kushwaha, M. S. "Byron the Dramatist: A Reappraisal," *Punjab University Research Bulletin* (*Arts*), 3, No. 2 (1972), 113–120.

255. *Kuzik, D. M. "Nevidomij perespiv bajronovskoho *Prometja*" ["The Unnoticed Song in Byron's 'Prometheus'"], *Ukrainskaja literaturoznavstvo*, Fascicle 16 (1972), pp. 119–122.

About A. Navrocky's translation.

256. *Lamb, Lady Caroline. *Glenarvon* (*1816*).

Introd. James L. Ruff. Delmar, N.Y.: Scholars' Facsimiles and Reprints, 1972.

257. *Lambert, Cecily. "Fighting for Greece," *Adam: International Review*, 349–351 (1971), 74–77.
Byron, Shelley, and Keats are discussed.

258. Lanier, René Parks, Jr. "Aspects of Sublimity in the Poetry of Lord Byron" [Doctoral dissertation, Tennessee, 1972], DAI, 33 (Aug. 1972), 727-A.

259. Lee, C. Nicholas. "The Philosophical Tales of M. A. Aldanov," *Slavic and East European Journal*, 15 (Fall 1971), 273–292.
Discusses *For Thee the Best* (1940), a historical novel concerning the death of Byron.

260. Letzring, Monica. "Strangford's *Poems from the Portugese of Luis de Camoens*," CL, 23 (Fall, 1971), 289–311.‡
Discusses attitude of Byron (and others, including Moore, Medwin, Hobhouse, Southey) to Strangford's versions of the poems of Camoens and to his romantic portrayal of the Portugese poet.

261. Lohf, Kenneth A. "Our Growing Collections," *Columbia Library Columns*, 21 (Nov. 1971), 39.
Columbia receives gift of Byron first editions.

262. McGann, Jerome J. *Fiery Dust: Byron's Poetic Development*. See K-SJ, 19 (1970), No. 118, 20 (1971), No. 314.
Rev. by Kurt Otten in *Erasmus*, 23 (10 Aug. 1971), 747–748 [in German].

263. McKoski, Martin Michael. "Byron's *Childe Harold's Pilgrimage*: The Image of the Quest" [Doctoral dissertation, Florida State, 1972], DAI, 33 (Dec. 1972), 2943-A.

264. Marchand, Leslie A. *Byron: A Portrait*. See K-SJ, 20 (1971), No. 322.
Rev. in **Economist*, 239 (10 Apr. 1971), 60; by Doris Langley Moore in *Sunday Times* (London), 11 Apr. 1971, p. 30; by Douglas Dunn in NS, 2 July 1971, pp. 22–23; by E. E. B[ostetter]. in ELN, 9, Supplement (Sept. 1971), 36; in TLS, 22 Oct. 1971, p. 1312.

265. Maurice, Frederick D. *Sketches of Contemporary Authors, 1828*. Ed. A. J. Hartley. See K-SJ, 20 (1971), No. 328.
Rev. by Govind Narain Sharma in *Dalhousie Review*, 51 (Summer 1971), 301, 303, 305.

266. *Maurois, André. *Don Juan, ou La vie de Byron*. 2 vols. N.p., 1971.
Another edition of the popular biography.

267. Maxwell, J. C. "Byron and the Bishop of Clogher," N&Q, 217 (Mar. 1972), 96.†
Explains a sexual reference in *Don Juan* VIII.76.1–2.

268. *Mayne, Ethel Colburn. *Byron*. St. Clair Shores, Mich.: Scholarly, 1972.
Reprint of a 1924 book.

269. Merewether, John Armstrong. " 'The Burning Chain'—The Paradoxical Nature of Love and Women in Byron's Poetry" [Doctoral dissertation, Wayne State, 1969], DAI, 32 (Nov. 1971), 2699-A.

270. Middleton, William Shainline. "Early Medical Experience in Hawaii," *Bulletin of the History of Medicine*, 45 (Sept.–Oct. 1971), 444–460.
Byron's cousin and successor to his title, Captain George Byron, and his account, *Voyage of the H.M.S. Blonde to the Sandwich Islands* (London: Murray, 1826), are mentioned.

271. *Moore, Doris Langley. "Byronic Dress," *Costume*, No. 5 (1971), pp. 1–13.

272. *Moore, Thomas. *Lyrics and Satires from Tom Moore*. Selected by Sean O'Faolain. Shannon: Irish Univ. Press, 1971.
Reprint of a 1929 edition.

273. *Moore, Thomas. *Memoirs, Journal, and Correspondence of Thomas Moore*. Ed. Lord John Russell. 8 vols. St. Clair Shores, Mich.: Scholarly, 1971–72.
Reprint of the edition of 1853–56.

274. *Moore, Thomas. *Memoirs of the Life of the Rt. Hon. Richard Brinsley Sheridan*. 2 vols. Freeport, N.Y.: Books for Libraries, 1971.
Reprint of the 1858 edition.

275. Morse, J. I. "Byron's 'Ignis-Fatuus to the Mind,' " N&Q, 217 (Aug. 1972), 293–294.†
Finds source in the Earl of Rochester.

276. Murray, Roger. "A Case for the Study of Period Styles," CE, 33 (Nov. 1971), 139–148.
Supports argument with a discussion

of the use of interrogatives in the poetry of Byron and Shelley.

277. Nevo, Natan. "Don Gouan: Essai d'interprétation du 'Convive de pierre' de Pouchkine," *Comparative Literature Studies*, 9 (Sept. 1972), 283–290.
Mentions Byron's *Don Juan* as one influence on Pushkin's Don Juan in the "Stone Guest."

278. "News and Comment," BC, 21 (Spring 1972), 117–118.
Notes Sotheby's sale to Quaritch of Byron's five page letter to his tutor and Amelia Curran's portrait of William Shelley.

279. *Nicolson, Sir Harold George. *Byron: The Last Journey, April 1823 – April 1824.* St. Clair Shores, Mich.: Scholarly, 1972.
Reprint of a 1924 book.

280. Nielsen, Jørgen Erik. "Thomas Moore," N&Q, 217 (Jan. 1972), 27–28.
Requests information on two poems in Danish translation attributed to Moore. See No. 295.

281. *Noel, Roden. *Life of Lord Byron.* Port Washington, N.Y., and London: Kennikat, 1972.
Reprint of an 1890 work.

282. Norton, Rictor. "Aesthetic Gothic Horror," *Yearbook of Comparative and General Literature*, No. 21 (1972), pp. 31–40.
M. G. Lewis' *The Monk* is discussed.

283. Nurmi, Martin K. "A Thomas Moore Letter, October 30, 1831," *Serif*, 9 (Summer 1972), 42–43.†
To John Murray, concerning the MS of a pamphlet-letter by Byron in which he comments on Keats and others.

284. Origo, Iris. *The Last Attachment: The Story of Byron and Teresa Guiccioli as Told in Their Unpublished Letters and Other Family Papers.* See K-SJ, 20 (1971), No. 352.
Rev. in TLS, 16 July 1971, p. 836.

285. *Owsley, David T. "A New Bust of Byron," *Carleton Newsletter*, 44 (1970), 195–196.

286. *Patty, James S. "Byron and Nerval: Two Sons of Fire," in *Studies in Honor of Alfred G. Engstrom*, ed. Robert T. Cargo and Emanuel J. Mickel, Jr. (Chapel Hill: Univ. of North Carolina, 1972), pp. 99–115. "University of North Carolina Studies in the Romance Languages and Literatures, 124."

287. Perella, Nicolas J. "Night and the Sublime in Giacomo Leopardi." See K-SJ, 20 (1971), No. 362.
Rev. by R. O. J. Van Nuffel in RLC, 46 (July–Sept. 1972), 472–474.

288. Piper, William B. *The Heroic Couplet.* See K-SJ, 20 (1971), No. 364.
Rev. by Oliver F. Sigworth in *Arizona Quarterly*, 27 (Autumn 1971), 279–281.

289. Poenicke, Klaus. " 'Schönheit im Schosse des Schreckens': Raumgefüge und Menschenbild im englischen Schauerroman," ASNS, 207 (June 1970), 1–19.
Includes discussion of the horror novels of M. G. Lewis.

290. Porter, Laurence M. "Reflections on the World-View of Romantic Painting: Baudelaire's Critical Response to Delacroix's Painterly Style," *Centennial Review*, 16 (Fall 1972), 349–358.
"Revolt in Baudelaire's poetry knows no triumph. And as hopeless defiance, its major sources are Byronic."

291. "Publication Projects," *British Studies Monitor*, 2 (Spring 1972), 53–54.
Announces the new series, "Sale Catalogues of Libraries of Eminent Persons," which will include the sale catalogues of the libraries of Byron, Hazlitt, and Peacock. See No. 11.

292. Raimond, Jean. *Robert Southey: L'homme et sons temps; L'oeuvre; Le rôle.* See K-SJ, 20 (1971), No. 372.
Rev. by Geoffrey Carnall in MLR, 67 (Jan. 1972), 174–175.

293. *Raymond, Dora Neill. *The Political Career of Lord Byron.* New York: Russell and Russell, 1972.
Reprint of a 1924 book.

294. Reichley, Charley Ann Isom. "Lampoon: Archilochus to Byron" [Doctoral dissertation, Vanderbilt, 1971], DAI, 32 (Nov. 1971), 2703-A.

295. "Replies—Thomas Moore," N&Q, 217 (Aug. 1972), 305.
Replies to Nielsen (see No. 280) that poems were included in Galignani's 1827 edition of Moore's poetry.

296. "Replies—Thomas Moore: Quotations

in Letters," N&Q, 217 (Sept. 1972), 342.

An answer to a query (incorrectly cited).

297. Richards, Kenneth, and Peter Thomson, eds. *Essays on Nineteenth Century British Theatre: The Proceedings of a Symposium Sponsored by the Manchester University Department of Drama*. See K-SJ, 20 (1971), No. 377.

Rev. in TLS, 30 July 1971, p. 924 (reply by Stanley Wells, 6 Aug. 1971, p. 945); by George Rowell in RES, 23 (May 1972), 229–230; by Robertson Davies in *Victorian Studies*, 15 (June 1972), 488–490; by Stanley Wells in *Yearbook of English Studies*, 2 (1972), 307–308.

298. Robertson, James Michael. "Byron's *Don Juan* and the Aristocratic Tradition" [Doctoral dissertation, Duke, 1972], DAI, 33 (Dec. 1972), 2902-A–2903-A.

299. *Rousseau, George Sebastian, and Neil L. Rudenstine, eds. *English Poetic Satire: Wyatt to Byron*. New York: Holt, Rinehart and Winston, 1972. Paperback.

300. Ruprecht, Hans-George. " 'Weltliteratur' vue du Mexique en 1826," *Bulletin Hispanique*, 73 (July–Dec. 1971), 307–318.

References to Byron.

301. Rutherford, Andrew, ed. *Byron: The Critical Heritage*. See K-SJ, 20 (1971), No. 383.

Rev. by John Cronin in *Studies* (Dublin), No. 237 (Spring 1971), pp. 104–108; by E. E. B[ostetter]. in ELN, 9, Supplement (Sept. 1971), 37; by A. P. Robson in *Victorian Studies*, 15 (June 1972), 475–480; by J. Drummond Bone in N&Q, 217 (Aug. 1972), 314–315.

302. St. Clair, William L. *That Greece Might Still Be Free: The Philhellenes in the War of Independence*. London and New York: Oxford Univ., 1972.

Byron is discussed.

Rev. in *Guardian Weekly*, 106 (15 Jan. 1972), 19, and (17 June 1972), 23; by Mervyn Jones in NS, 2 June 1972, pp. 753–754; in **Economist*, 243 (3 June 1972), 61; in **Observer*, 11 June 1972, p. 28; by M. H. Ridgeway in LJ, 97 (July 1972), 2394; by M. I. Finley in Li, 31 Aug. 1972, pp. 277–279; in TLS, 1 Sept. 1972, p. 1024.

303. *Sakai, Yoshitaka. "Lord Byron One Hundred Sixty Years After," *English Literature and Language* (Tokyo), 8 (1971), 1–12. [In Japanese.]

304. Scott, Sir Walter. *The Journal of Sir Walter Scott*. Ed. W. E. K. Anderson. Oxford: Clarendon, 1972.

Here published in a newly edited and annotated version, Scott's *Journal* contains detailed references to Byron, some references to Haydon and Hunt, and passing mention of Hazlitt and Shelley.

Rev. by Richard Crossman in NS, 21 July 1972, pp. 96–97; in **Observer*, 13 Aug. 1972, p. 27; in **Books and Bookmen*, 17 (Sept. 1972), 62; in **Library Review*, 23 (Fall 1972), 302.

305. *Ševëlev, V. M. "Z istorii rossijs'kix perekladiv *Don Žuana* Bajrona" ["From the History of the Russian Translations of Byron's *Don Juan*"], *Vistnik Xar'kovs'koho universitetu*, No. 71, Philological Fascicle 7 (1972), pp. 87–92.

An appraisal of the translations of N. Žandra, V. Ljubovič-Romanovič, D. Min, D. D. Minaeva, P. A. Kozlov, G. Senegel, and T. Gnedič.

306. Sheraw, C. Darrel. "Coleridge, Shelley, Byron and the Devil," KSMB, 23 (1972), 6–9.

"The Devil's Thoughts," a satire by Coleridge and Southey which appeared in the *Morning Post* of 6 September 1799, inspired more radical imitations by Byron and Shelley.

307. Slethaug, Gordon E. "Patterns of Imagery in 'The Prisoner of Chillon,' " QQ, 78 (Autumn 1971), 449–455.

"Theme, imagery, and dialectical structure" suggest that the prisoner, rather than affirming the value of human freedom, has by the end of the poem accepted a condition of despair.

308. Smiehorowski, Astrid Scheper. "Byron's *Don Juan*: A Poet's Pessimistic Vision of Nature" [Doctoral dissertation, Brown, 1971], DAI, 32 (Mar. 1972), 5202-A.

309. "Societies and Conferences," *British Studies Monitor*, 3 (Fall 1972), 27–29.

Announces the revival of the Byron Society, lists events, and describes plans for an annual Byron journal.

310. *Sokolec', F. B. "Xudožni osoblivosti poemi D. G. Barjrona *Palomnictvo Cajl'd-Haral'da*" ["Byron's Artistically Personal Poem *Childe Harold's Pilgrimage*"], *Vistnik Kyivs'koho universitetu*, No. 5 (1971), pp. 83–86.

Byron was one of the first to use the theme of national liberation as an object of artistic representation, and the problems of presenting this theme determine the style of the poem, which is essentially speech in verse. The author discusses the varieties of artistic expression and poetical syntax as vehicles for oratory.

311. Speaight, Robert. "Sir Walter Scott," *Essays by Divers Hands*, N.S. 37 (1972), 108–121.

Scott is compared to Byron. Moore, Keats, Haydon, and Shelley are mentioned briefly.

312. Stafford, Barbara. " 'Medusa' or the Physiognomy of the Earth: Humbert de Superville's Cosmological Aesthetics," *Journal of the Warburg and Courtauld Institutes*, 35 (1972), 308–338.

A passing reference is made to Byron's interest in the theory that a race of giants existed before the creation of man.

313. Stine, Peter Wilfred. "The Changing Image of Mary Queen of Scots in Nineteenth-Century British Literature" [Doctoral dissertation, Michigan State, 1972], DAI, 33 (Aug. 1972), 733-A–734-A.

Includes some discussion of Byron's "The Prisoner of Chillon."

314. *Stockenström, G. *Ismael i öknen, Strindberg som mystiker*. Uppsala: Almqvist and Wiksell, 1972.

Includes comparisons between Dante's *Inferno* and Byron's *Cain*.

315. *Taborski, Boleslaw. *Byron and the Theatre*. Salzburg: Univ. of Salzburg, 1972. "Salzburg Studies in English: Poetic Drama, No. 1."

316. *Tarlinskaja, M. G. "Akcentnaja struktura i metr anglijskogo stixa (XIII–XIX vv.)" ["Accentual Structures and Meter of English Poetry from the Thirteenth Century to the Nineteenth"], *Voprosy Jazykoznanija*, No. 4 (1972), pp. 100–111.

Examples from Byron and Shelley are used.

317. *Thompson, B. Bussell. "Byron's *Cain* and Unamuno's *Abel Sanchez*: Two Faces of Heroic Anguish," in *Proceedings: Pacific Northwest Conference on Foreign Languages*, Vol. 22, ed. Walter C. Kraft (Corvallis: Oregon State Univ., 1971), 215–220.

318. Tillett, Margaret. *Stendhal: The Background to the Novels*. London: Oxford Univ., 1971.

References to Byron, Hazlitt, and Shelley.

Rev. by Liga Lusis in *AUMLA*, No. 38 (Nov. 1972), pp. 242–245.

319. Townsend, Richard Lee. "Lord Byron as Literary Chameleon: A Study in Literary Influence" [Doctoral dissertation, Michigan, 1971], DAI, 32 (May 1972), 6396-A–6397-A.

320. Trocard, Catherine. "A Propos de Byron et Stendhal: Du *Captif de Chillon* à *La Chartreuse de Parme* (1816–1839)," *Stendhal Club*, No. 54 (Jan. 1972), pp. 189–190.

Compares the reactions to imprisonment of Byron's and Stendhal's heroes.

321. Turney, Catherine. *Byron's Daughter: A Biography of Elizabeth Medora Leigh*. New York: Scribners, 1972.

Rev. in *Kirkus Reviews*, 40 (1 Mar. 1972), 313; in **Publishers' Weekly*, 201 (3 Apr. 1972), 64; in **Book World (Washington Post)*, 6 (12 Nov. 1972), 15; by Nancy E. Gwinn in LJ, 97 (15 Nov. 1972), 3703; in **Book World (Washington Post)*, 6 (24 Dec. 1972), 9.

322. *Vasiliu, Aurel. "Preromantism si romantism byronian la Eminescu si predecesori" ["Preromanticism and Byronic Romanticism with Eminescu and His Predecessors"], in *Romantismul românesc si romantismul european* [*Romanian Romanticism and European Romanticism*] (Bucarest: Societatea de Stiinte Filologice din Republica Socialistă România, 1970), pp. 153–166.

323. Vincent, E. R. *Byron, Hobhouse and Foscolo: New Documents in the History of a Collaboration*. New York: Octagon, 1972.

Reprint of a 1949 book.

324. *Wallace, Irving. *The Nympho and Other Maniacs*. New York: Simon and Schuster; London: Cassell (1971).

At least in part about Byron, with some reference to Shelley. See K-SJ, 20 (1971), No. 411.

Rev. in TLS, 10 Sept. 1971, p. 1092, reply by David Brown, 8 Oct. 1971, p. 1216.

325. Walling, William. "Tradition and Revolution: Byron's *Vision of Judgment*," WC, 3 (Autumn 1972), 223–231.†‡

Discusses Byron's reply to Southey's *Vision*, and "the various ways in which Byron accepted and modified what was for him the 'great' tradition of English poetry."

326. Wellek, René. *Discriminations: Further Concepts of Criticism*. See K-SJ, 20 (1971), No. 416.

Rev. by Jean-Louis Backès in RLC, 45 (July – Sept. 1971), 400–402 [in French]; in *JAAC, 30 (Spring 1972), 389.

327. Wickens, G. M. "*Lalla Rookh* and the Romantic Tradition of Islamic Literature in English," *Yearbook of Comparative and General Literature*, No. 20 (1971), pp. 61–66.‡

Discusses the bombastic "Romantic Orientalism" of Moore's poem and its pernicious influence on English translations of Arabic literature.

328. Wilson, James D. "Tirso, Molière, and Byron: The Emergence of Don Juan as Romantic Hero," *South Central Bulletin*, 32 (Winter 1972), 246–248.‡

"While Molière and Tirso portray the alienated libertine to expose the destructive evil of defying traditional social and religious order, Byron tells us about the vicissitudes of his young hero in order to satirize the rank corruption and hypocrisy permeating that same order."

329. Wittreich, Joseph Anthony, Jr. "Milton's Romantic Audience," *American Notes and Queries*, 10 (June 1972), 147–150.

Among others who lamented contemporary inattention to Milton, Byron is mentioned.

330. Wolff, Cynthia Griffin. "A Mirror for Men: Stereotypes of Women in Literature," *Massachusetts Review*, 13 (Winter – Spring 1972), 205–218.

Some comments on Byron and Mary Wollstonecraft.

331. Wolff, Tatiana, ed. *Pushkin on Literature*. See K-SJ, 20 (1971), No. 419.

Rev. by Christopher Ricks in *Sunday Times* (London), 27 June 1971, p. 28; by V. S. Pritchett in NS, 6 Aug. 1971, pp. 180–181; by Nicholas Richardson in Spec, 7 Aug. 1971, p. 215; by Helen Muchnic in NYRB, 7 Oct. 1971, pp. 25–28; by J. Thomas Shaw in *Slavic and East European Journal*, 16 (Spring 1972), 92–95; by Richard A. Gregg in *Slavic Review*, 31 (June 1972), 507; by Henry Gifford in EC, 22 (July 1972), 313–320; by Nikolai P. Poltoratzki in *Russian Review*, 31 (Oct. 1972), 424–425.

332. Woodhouse, C[hristopher]. M. *The Philhellenes*. Rutherford, N.J.: Fairleigh Dickinson Univ., 1971. See K-SJ, 20 (1971), No. 422 for the London edition.

Rev. by Patrick Anderson in Spec, 20 Sept. 1969, pp. 379–380; by Paul F. Moran in LJ, 21 (1 Dec. 1971), 4011; in *Choice*, 9 (June 1972), 569; by M. S. Anderson in *Journal of Modern History*, 44 (Dec. 1972), 616–617.

333. "Work in Progress," *American Philosophical Society Year Book* (1972), pp. 656–658.

Daniel Majdiak is working on a book on the influence of Byron on Stendhal.

334. Yax, Lawrence Donald. "Ocean and Other Water Imagery in Byron's Poetry" [Doctoral dissertation, Case Western Reserve, 1971], DAI, 32 (Sept. 1971), 1489-A.

335. Žirmunskij, V. M. *Bajron i Puškin*. Munich: Fink, 1970. "Slavische Propyläen: Texte in Neu-Und Nachdrucken, Vol. 72."

In Russian. Based on the editions of 1924 and 1937. Also see No. 336.

336. *Žirmunskij, V. [M]. *Bajron i Puškin. Iz istorii romanticeskoj poemy*. The Hague: Mouton, 1970. "Slavistic Printings and Reprintings, No. 138."

Reprint of Leningrad 1924 edition. Also see No. 335.

For additional Books and Articles Relating to Byron and His Circle see Nos. 4, 9, 11, 13, 20, 21, 24, 26, 34, 37, 38, 39, 52, 63, 67, 71, 72, 74, 76, 95, 96, 99, 103, 107, 111, 112,

114, 118, 122, 123, 125, 135, 142, 364, 419, 447, 449, 474, 518, 545, 594, 609, 638, 709, 722, 741, 787.

III. HUNT

Works: Collected, Selected

337. Rowell, George, ed. *Victorian Dramatic Criticism.* See K-SJ, 20 (1971), No. 432.
Rev. in *Shavian,* 4 (Spring 1972), 204; in *Choice,* 9 (Apr. 1972), 229; by Stanley Wells in *Yearbook of English Studies,* 2 (1972), 307–308.

338. **Tales, Now First Collected.* Preface by William Knight. Freeport, N.Y.: Books for Libraries, 1971.
Appears to be a reprint of the 1891 edition.

For additional Works by Hunt see No. 95.

Books and Articles Relating to Hunt

339. Brice, Alec W. "Reviewers of Dickens in the *Examiner*: Fonblanque, Forster, Hunt, and Morley," *Dickens Studies Newsletter,* 3 (Sept. 1972), 68–80.†
Using internal and external evidence, Brice attributes several reviews to Hunt.

340. Das, S[isir]. K[umar]. "Towards a Distinction Between Fancy and Imagination," *Bulletin of the Department of English* (Calcutta University), n.s. 5, No. 1 (1969–70), 41–61.
Quotes Hunt on the differences between fancy and imagination.

341. Fenner, Theodore. *Leigh Hunt and Opera Criticism: The "Examiner" Years, 1808–1821.* Lawrence: Univ. Press of Kansas, 1972.

342. Haight, Gordon S. "The George Eliot and George Henry Lewes Collections," *Yale University Library Gazette,* 46 (July 1971), 20–23.
The collection includes letters to Lewes from Leigh and Thornton Hunt.

343. *Ireland, A. *List of the Writings of William Hazlitt and Leigh Hunt.* New York: Burt Franklin, 1970.
Reprint of an 1868 work.

344. Kendall, Kenneth E. *Leigh Hunt's "Reflector."* See K-SJ, 20 (1971), No. 441.
Rev. by M. R. Huxstep in CLSB, No. 212 (Oct. 1971), p. 700; by Susie I. Tucker in RES, 23 (May 1972), 219–221; in *Choice,* 9 (Apr. 1972), 214.

345. *Landré, Louis. "Un hebdomadaire de contestation à l'époque du Romantisme: l'*Examiner,*" in *Le Romantisme anglo-américain: Mélanges offerts à Louis Bonnerot,* [ed. Roger Asselineau, *et al.*] (Paris: Didier, 1971), pp. 233–244.

346. Misenheimer, James B., Jr. "Leigh Hunt: A 'Great Introducer' in English Romanticism," *Yearbook of English Studies,* 1 (1971), 135–140.
On Hunt as journalist, anthologist, translator, and critic.

347. Praz, Mario. *Mnemosyne: The Parallel Between Literature and the Visual Arts.* See K-SJ, 20 (1971), No. 447.
Rev. by Arthur R. Evans, Jr., in *Yearbook of Comparative and General Literature,* No. 20 (1971), pp. 127–130; in TLS, 7 Jan. 1972, p. 13; in **Burlington Magazine,* 114 (May 1972), 345; by J. E. Chamberlin in *Hudson Review,* 25 (Winter 1972–73), 693–695.

348. "Recent Acquisitions," *Books at Iowa,* No. 16 (Apr. 1972), pp. 44–45.
University of Iowa acquires first edition of Hunt's *The Town: Its Memorable Characters and Events* (1848).

349. *Thomas, Donald. "Leigh Hunt's *Examiner,*" *Censorship* (London), 6 (Spring 1966), 38–42.

350. Welch, Jack. "The Leigh Hunt – William Moxon Dispute of 1836," *West Virginia University Philological Papers,* 18 (Sept. 1971), 30–41.
Presents heretofore unpublished correspondence between Hunt and Moxon owned by the University of Iowa Libraries. Moxon took "legal steps to secure a considerable sum which Hunt owed him," and "Hunt was literally forced to bargain for his own freedom."

351. Williamson, Jane. *Charles Kemble: Man of the Theatre.* See K-SJ, 20 (1971), No. 453.
Rev. by Peter Thomson in MLR, 66 (July 1971), 673–674; by S[tuart]. C[urran]. in ELN, 9, Supplement (Sept. 1971), 17.

352. Wilson, D. G. "Imagination and In-

sight," *Proceedings of the Royal Society of Medicine*, 64 (Aug. 1971), 811–818.

In this valedictory address, Wilson discusses Hunt, Hazlitt, and Lamb as examples of imaginative literary creators, and then advocates the application of imagination and insight in medical diagnosis.

For additional BOOKS AND ARTICLES RELATING TO HUNT see Nos. 34, 95, 96, 118, 121, 122, 123, 210, 304, 460, 467, 474, 496, 739.

IV. KEATS

WORKS: COLLECTED, SELECTED, SINGLE, TRANSLATED

353. **Anatomical and Physiological Note Book.* Printed from the Holograph in the Keats Museum, Hampstead. Ed. Maurice Buxton Forman. New York: Haskell House, 1970.

Reprint of a 1934 book.

354. *Cookson, Tommy, ed. *Keats.* Illustrated by George Gillespie. London: Edward Arnold, 1972. "The Portrait Series."

355. *"El Ha-stav." ["To Autumn." Trans.] Shimon Zandbank, Literary Supplement to *Haaretz*, 17 Nov. 1972. [In Hebrew.]

356. **The Keats Letters, Papers, and Other Relics.* Forming the Dilke Bequest in the Hampstead Public Library. Foreword by Theodore Watts-Dunton. Introd. H. Buxton Forman. Folcroft, Pa.: Folcroft, 1972.

Reprint of the 1914 edition.

357. *"La Belle Dame sans Merci." [Trans.] Shimon Zandbank, Literary Supplement to *Haaretz*, 17 Nov. 1972. [In Hebrew.]

358. **La Belle Dame Sans Merci (La Belle Dame Sans Merci. A Ballad).* [First and Second Versions. English Text and French Translation by] Henri Parisot. Paris: Editions de l'Heine, 1971. "Collection l'Envers."

359. *"Manuscripts, IV: *Otho the Great* by John Keats," *Library Chronicle* (Texas), No. 4 (Feb. 1972), pp. 58–59.

Reproduces two pages from the holograph at the University of Texas.

360. *The Odes of Keats and Their Earliest Known Manuscripts.* Introduction, with Notes, by Robert Gittings. See K-SJ, 20 (1971), No. 466.

Rev. by D[avid]. V. E[rdman]. in ELN, 9, Supplement (Sept. 1971), 46; by Jack Stillinger in JEGP, 71 (Apr. 1972), 263–267.

361. *Poems of 1820; and The Fall of Hyperion.* Ed. David G. Gillham. See K-SJ, 19 (1970), No. 180.

Rev. by J. C. Maxwell in N&Q, 217 (Mar. 1972), 113–115.

362. *The Poems of John Keats.* Ed. Miriam Allott. See K-SJ, 20 (1971), No. 469.

Rev. by R. W. King in RES, 22 (Nov. 1971), 504–506; by S[tuart]. M. S[perry]., [Jr.], in ELN, 10, Supplement (Sept. 1972), 50–51; by Jean-Claude Sallé in *Yearbook of English Studies*, 2 (1972), 301–302.

BOOKS AND ARTICLES RELATING TO KEATS AND HIS CIRCLE

363. Abbot, Dorothea M. "H. F. Cary: the Librarian Friend of Lamb and Coleridge," *Library Review*, 23 (Winter 1972), 326–330.

Brief references to Hazlitt and John Hamilton Reynolds as contributors to the *London Magazine*, to Cary's praise of a description in "Hyperion" in that periodical, and to the influence of Cary's translation of Dante on "Hyperion."

364. Ades, John I. "*Criticus Redivivus*: The History of Charles Lamb's Reputation as a Critic," CLSB, No. 215 (July 1972), pp. 1–6.

Byron's and, especially, Hazlitt's views of Lamb's criticism are discussed.

365. Amis, Kingsley. *What Became of Jane Austen?, and Other Questions.* See K-SJ, 20 (1971), No. 482.

Rev. by Eric Moon in LJ, 96 (15 Sept. 1971), 2773; by William H. Pritchard in *Hudson Review*, 24 (Winter 1971–72), 703–706; by Lawrence Graver in SatR, 15 Jan. 1972, pp. 43–44.

366. Antippas, A[ndy]. P. "Keats's Individual Talent and Tradition," *Tulane Studies in English*, 20 (1972), 87–95.‡

The author's argument, that the burden of past tradition convinced Keats of the relative meagerness of his talent, supports Bate and contradicts Bloom.

367. *Balotă, Nicolae. "Un poet modern—John Keats" ["A Modern Poet—John Keats"], in *Labirint* [*The Labyrinth*] (Bucarest: Editura Eminescu, 1970), pp. 277–282.

368. *Barfoot, C. C. "A Partial Grammar of Autumn," *Dutch Quarterly Review of Anglo-American Letters*, 2 (1972), 73–81.
Concerns Keats.

369. *Barrell, John. "The Idea of Landscape and the Sense of Place, 1730–1840: An Approach to the Poetry of John Clare." (Doctoral dissertation, Essex, 1971.)
Also see No. 370.

370. Barrell, John. *The Idea of Landscape and the Sense of Place, 1730–1840: An Approach to the Poetry of John Clare*. London: Cambridge Univ., 1972.
Also see No. 369.
Rev. in *Spec, 228 (25 Mar. 1972), 481; in TLS, 9 June 1972, p. 654; in *CR, 221 (Aug. 1972), 112; in **Connoisseur*, 181 (Oct. 1972), 139; by Barbara Lupini in *English*, 21 (Autumn 1972), 111–113.

371. Bate, Walter Jackson. *The Burden of the Past and the English Poet*. See K-SJ, 20 (1971), No. 486.
Rev. by Robert D. Hume in PQ, 50 (July 1971), 375; in TLS, 15 Sept. 1972, p. 1049. Also see No. 144.

372. Bebbington, W. G. "Jessie Pope and Wilfred Owen," *Ariel*, 3 (Oct. 1972), 82–93.
Briefly discusses biographical similarities between Owen and Keats.

373. Becker, Michael Gilbert. "A New Concordance to the Poetry of John Keats" [Doctoral dissertation, Wisconsin, 1971], DAI, 32 (Aug. 1971), 906-A.

374. "Benjamin Robert Haydon and his Circle," CLSB, No. 214 (Apr. 1972), p. 6.
Account of a talk given by Christine Morrison.

375. Benoit, Raymond. "In Dear Detail by Ideal Light: 'Ode on a Grecian Urn,' " *Costerus*, 3 (1972), 1–7.
A reading of the poem, in which Keats is seen as expressing both the full Apollonian-Dionysian balance of Greek civilization and our own alienation from it.

376. Benvenuto, Richard. " 'The Ballance of Good and Evil' in Keats's Letters and 'Lamia,' " JEGP, 71 (Jan. 1972), 1–11.‡
"Keats attacks the principle of moral classification," both in his letters and in "Lamia." Lamia "is a merger of contraries, making it impossible to classify her under the headings of conventional morality."

377. *Blunden, Edmund, ed. *Shelley and Keats, As They Struck Their Contemporaries*. New York: Haskell House, 1971.
Reprint of a 1925 work.

378. Bond, W. H. "Keats on Kean: An Early Version," *Harvard Library Bulletin*, 20 (Oct. 1972), 367–371.
Prints draft of a review which Keats wrote for the *Champion*, 28 Dec. 1817.

379. *Boulton, James T., ed. *Johnson: The Critical Heritage*. London: Routledge and Kegan Paul, 1971. "The Critical Heritage Series."
Includes Hazlitt's comments on Johnson.

380. *Bridges, Robert Seymour. *John Keats: A Critical Essay*. New York: Haskell House, 1972.
Reprint of an 1895 work.

381. Brisman, Leslie. " 'More Glorious to Return': Miltonic Repetition," *Yearbook of English Studies*, 1 (1971), 78–87.
On Miltonic echoes in Keats.

382. *"British Watercolors and Drawings from the Museum's Collection," *Rhode Island School of Design Bulletin*, 58 (Apr. 1972), 66–69.
Includes reproductions of Peter De Wint's "Lock Gate," "Richmond Park in Rain," "Welsh Estuary," "Landscape with Trees, near Lincoln," and "Dartmeet, Devonshire."

383. *Brock, Lord. *John Keats and Joseph Severn: The Tragedy of the Last Illness*. London: Keats-Shelley Memorial Association, 1972.

384. *Brown, Charles Armitage. *Shakespeare's Autobiographical Poems*. Being His Sonnets Clearly Developed with His Character Chiefly Drawn from His Works. New York: AMS, 1972.
Reprint of the London, 1838, edition.

385. Brown, Thomas H. "The Quest of Dante Gabriel Rossetti in 'The Blessed Damozel,' " *Victorian Poetry*, 10 (Autumn 1972), 273–277.

Discusses the influence of Keats's "Ode to a Nightingale."

386. Bunn, James. "Circle and Sequence in the Conjectural Lyric," *New Literary History*, 3 (Spring 1972), 511–526.

Passing references to Keats.

387. Bush, Elliott Jarvis. "The Poetry of John Clare" [Doctoral dissertation, Wisconsin, 1971], DAI, 32 (Dec. 1971), 3295-A.

388. Carroll, D. Allen. "The Road to Darien: Criticism as Play," *South Atlantic Bulletin*, 37 (Jan. 1972), 70.

An abstract of a paper on Keats's "On First Looking into Chapman's Homer," delivered at the 1971 S.A.M.L.A.

389. *Chatterjee, Bhabatosh. *John Keats: His Mind and Work*. New Delhi: Orient Longman, 1971.

Rev. by Gilbert Thomas in *English*, 21 (Autumn 1972), 113–114. Also see No. 504.

390. Chilcott, Tim. *A Publisher and His Circle: The Life and Work of John Taylor, Keats's Publisher*. London and Boston: Routledge, 1972.

Rev. by Richard Boston in NS, 12 May 1972, p. 648; by John Lehmann in *Books and Bookmen*, 17 (May 1972), 47; by Frank P. Riga in LJ, 97 (July 1972), 2382; by Basil Savage in CLSB, No. 215 (July 1972), p. 10; by Gilbert Thomas in *English*, 21 (Summer 1972), 72–73; in TLS, 27 Oct. 1972, p. 1270; in *Choice*, 9 (Oct. 1972), 966; in **AB Bookman's Weekly*, Yearbook (1972), Part 2, p. 32.

391. Clare, John. "The Gipsy Lass," *Journal of the Gypsy Lore Society*, 50 (July–Oct. 1971), 81.

Clare's poem is reprinted.

392. *Clare, John. *Poèmes et Proses de la Folie*. [Trans.] Pierre Leyris. Paris: Mercure de France, 1969.

English text with French translation.

393. Clubbe, John. *Victorian Forerunner: The Later Career of Thomas Hood*. See K-SJ, 19 (1970), No. 201, 20 (1971), No. 511.

Rev. by Carl H. Ketcham in *Arizona Quarterly*, 26 (Winter 1970), 367–369; by Angus Easson in N&Q, 216 (Nov. 1971), 424–425.

394. *Compton-Rickett, Arthur. *Personal Forces in Modern Literature*. New York: AMS, 1972.

Reprint of a 1906 work, which discusses Keats and Hazlitt.

395. Cordasco, Francesco. "Charles Wentworth Dilke, the Improvised Junius, and 'Papers Relating to the Authorship of Junius' in the British Museum," N&Q, 216 (Sept. 1971), 340–341.

Dilke on the identity of Junius.

396. D'Avanzo, Mario. "Keats's 'Ode on Melancholy,' the Cave of Spleen, and Belinda," *Humanities Association Bulletin* (Canada), 22 (Fall 1971), 9–11.†

Discusses influence of Pope's *The Rape of the Lock* on Keats's ode.

397. *Davidson, P. "A Study of Keats' Interest in the Theatre and Its Importance for His Work." (Doctoral dissertation, London Univ., 1971.)

398. DeLaura, David J. "Arnold and Hazlitt," ELN, 9 (June 1972), 277–283.†

Argues that Arnold's poem "The Voice" was inspired by Hazlitt's attitude toward Coleridge, and finds verbal echoes of Hazlitt in an essay passage.

399. De Wint, Peter. ["Winstay Park, Denbighshire," Picture.] *Apollo*, 95 (June 1972), 525.

Reproduction of watercolor painting acquired by the Victoria and Albert Museum.

400. Dickstein, Morris. *Keats and His Poetry: A Study in Development*. See K-SJ, 20 (1971), No. 534.

Rev. in *Choice*, 8 (Dec. 1971), 1329; by Jack Stillinger in JEGP, 71 (Jan. 1972), 150–152; by Walter H. Evert in *Criticism*, 14 (Spring 1972), 194–197; in TLS, 22 Sept. 1972, p. 1106; by S[tuart]. M. S[perry]., [Jr.], in ELN, 10, Supplement (Sept. 1972), 51–52. Also see Nos. 43, 94.

401. "Directory of Scholars Active," *Computers and the Humanities*, 7 (Nov. 1972), 118–119.

Describes work in progress on a "Computer Assisted Investigation of the Prosody of John Keats, and Gerard Manley Hopkins" by Robert Dilligan.

402. *Dodd, William N. "Keats's 'Ode to a

Nightingale' and 'Ode on a Grecian Urn': Two Principles of Organization," *Lingue e Stile* (Bologna), 6 (Aug. 1971), 241–261.

403. Dorment, Richard. "American Mythologies in Painting: Part 1, the Indian," *Arts Magazine*, 46 (Sept.–Oct. 1971), 46–49.

Includes reproduction of Benjamin Robert Haydon's painting, "Curtius Plunging into the Gulf."

404. Duncan-Jones, Katherine. "A Note on Tennyson's 'Claribel,'" *Victorian Poetry*, 9 (Autumn 1971), 348–350.

"The closest literary analog to 'Claribel' is . . . Keats's *Isabella*. . . ."

405. Eggers, J. Phillip. "Memory in Mankind: Keats's Historical Imagination," *PMLA*, 86 (Oct. 1971), 990–997.†‡

"History plays a major part in Keats's deepening acceptance of mortality and an accompanying affirmation of time and process through release from the fear of death," particularly in the Odes and two "Hyperion" poems.

406. Evans, David S. "Homage to Herschel," CR, 219 (Dec. 1971), 299–306.

William Herschel's discovery of Uranus in 1781 is alluded to in Keats's sonnet, "On First Looking into Chapman's Homer."

407. Evans, William Richard. "Mythology as Religion in Keats' Poetry" [Doctoral dissertation, Columbia, 1970], DAI, 32 (July 1971), 426-A–427-A.

408. *Fass, Barbara F. "A Biographical Approach to Keats's *Ode to Psyche*," *Humanities Association Bulletin* (Canada), 23 (1972), 23–29.†

409. Fass, Barbara F. "The Little Mermaid and the Artist's Quest for a Soul," *Comparative Literature Studies*, 9 (Sept. 1972), 291–302.†

The fairy tale of the mermaid's quest to become human has been taken by the artist as allegorical of his own quest to "wed aesthetics to ethics so that his art would serve humanity." Keats's struggle to distinguish the dreamer from the true poet embodies this theme.

410. Fields, Kenneth. "Postures of the Nerves: Reflections of the Nineteenth Century in the Poems of Wallace Stevens," *Southern Review* (L.S.U.), 7 (Summer 1971), 778–824.

"Keats writes to Shelley in the summer of 1820, 'My Imagination is a Monastery and I am its Monk.'" Stevens repeatedly rejects this idea in his poetry.

411. Fisher, Benjamin Franklin, IV. "Rossetti's 'William and Marie': Hints of the Future," ELN, 9 (Dec. 1971), 121–129.

Notes similarity of Rossetti's "Roderick and Rosalla" to Keats's "The Eve of St. Agnes."

412. Flower, Timothy Frank. "1. Forms of Re-creation in Nabokov's *Pale Fire*. 2. Charles Dickens and Gothic Fiction. 3. Making It New: Problems of Meaningful Form in the Sonnets of Sidney and Keats" [Doctoral dissertation, Rutgers, 1972], DAI, 32 (June 1972), 6927-A.

413. Forman, Maurice Buxton, ed. *Some Letters and Miscellanea of Charles Brown, the Friend of John Keats and Thomas Richards*. Folcroft, Pa.: Folcroft, 1969.

Reprint of 1937 edition.

414. Fraser, Angus M. "De Wint's Gypsy Paintings," *Journal of the Gypsy Lore Society*, 51 (Jan.–Apr. 1972), 47–49.

Lists De Wint's Gypsy paintings and requests information on their present locations.

415. Fraser, Angus M. "George Borrow and 'The Painter of the Heroic,'" N&Q, 216 (Oct. 1971), 380–386.†

Benjamin Robert Haydon.

416. Fraser, Angus [M]. "John Clare's Gypsies," *Journal of the Gypsy Lore Society*, 50 (July–Oct. 1971), 85–100.

Author presents a general summary of Clare's life, his interest in Gypsies, and extracts from relevant poems.

417. French, A. L. "Purposive Imitation: A Skirmish with Literary Theory," EC, 22 (Apr. 1972), 109–130.

Poses the question, "Can bad writing be made good by an appropriate context?" and concludes that it cannot. Discusses "Ode to a Nightingale" and alludes to Shelley's poems in this context.

418. Friedman, Martin B. "Hazlitt, Jerrold, and Horne: *Liber Amoris* Twenty Years After," RES, 22 (Nov. 1971), 455–462.†

A discussion of Douglas Jerrold's burlesque of Hazlitt's book and R. H. Horne's subsequent defense of it.

419. Gabrieli, Vittorio. *Il Mirto e l'Alloro: Studi sulla Poesia di Matthew Arnold.* Bari, Italy: Adriatica Editrice, 1961. "Biblioteca di Studi Inglesi, Vol. 1."

Many references to Keats, Shelley, and Byron.

420. Gérard, Albert S. *English Romantic Poetry: Ethos, Structure, and Symbol in Coleridge, Wordsworth, Shelley, and Keats.* See K-SJ, 18 (1969), No. 402, 19 (1970), No. 214.

Rev. by Elinor Shaffer in MLR, 66 (Oct. 1971), 874–875.

421. Gillin, Richard Lewis. "In That So Gentle Sky: A Study of John Clare's Sonnets" [Doctoral dissertation, Bowling Green, 1971], DAI, 32 (May 1972), 6374-A–6375-A.

422. Gittings, Robert. "A Draft of the Earliest Known Letter of Keats's Brother Tom," *Harvard Library Bulletin,* 19 (July 1971), 285–289.

Gittings deduces that the letter was to Richard Abbey, written from Margate between 4 and 24 July 1816, and that Keats joined Tom there "sometime after" 25 July 1816. The letter also provides evidence that Tom and Keats spent beyond their income.

423. Gittings, Robert. "Keats and Medicine," CR, 219 (Sept. 1971), 138–142.

Discusses Keats's medical training and interest in the profession.

424. Gittings, Robert. " 'This Living Hand,' " *Medical History,* 16 (Jan. 1972), 1–10.

"The second Keats Memorial Lecture, sponsored by the Royal College of Surgeons of England, the Society of Apothecaries, and Guy's Hospital, and delivered in the Royal College of Surgeons on 23 February 1971." Gittings discusses the period of Keats's illness and death.

425. Glenn, Priscilla Ray. "The Development of Keats's Mythic Understanding of the Function of the Poet" [Doctoral dissertation, North Texas State, 1971], DAI, 32 (Jan. 1972), 3950-A.

426. *Glenn, Priscilla R[ay]. "Keats's *Lamia*: The Imagination Brought Beyond Its Proper Bound," *Proceedings of the Conference of College Teachers of English of Texas,* 37 (1972), 34–40.

427. *Gorell, Ronald G. B. *John Keats: The Principle of Beauty.* New York: Haskell House, 1970.

Reprint of a 1948 book.

428. Gossman, Ann. "Love's Alchemy in the *Alexandria Quartet,*" *Critique: Studies in Modern Fiction,* 13, No. 2 (1971), 83–96.

Lawrence Durrell's *Justine* draws on Hazlitt's "On Imitation."

429. Gross, George C. "Mary Cowden Clarke, 'The Girlhood of Shakespeare's Heroines,' and the Sex Education of Victorian Women," *Victorian Studies,* 16 (Sept. 1972), 37–58.

Mrs. Clarke "spanned the nineteenth century and provided . . . an ideal model of Victorian womanhood at its most feminine yet most successful."

430. *Hanley, Evelyn A. "In the Garden of a Poet," *Home Garden and Flower Grower,* 59 (Feb. 1972), 58–59.

Concerns Keats. Illustrated.

431. Hart, Francis R. *Lockhart as Romantic Biographer.* Edinburgh: Edinburgh Univ.; Chicago: Aldine (1971).

Includes a comparison of the biographies of Napoleon by Scott, Hazlitt, and Lockhart.

Rev. by Alexander Welsh in SAQ, 71 (Summer 1972), 456–458; by John Henry Raleigh in *Victorian Studies,* 16 (Dec. 1972), 248–249.

432. *Harwell, Thomas Meade. *Keats and the Critics, 1848–1900.* Salzburg: Univ. of Salzburg, 1972. "Salzburg Studies in English: Romantic Reassessment Series, No. 2."

Reprint of a dissertation.

433. *Hazlitt, William. *Selected Writings.* Ed. Christopher Salvesen. New York: New American Library, 1972. "Signet Classics." Paperback.

434. Hazlitt, William. *The Spirit of the Age; or, Contemporary Portraits.* Second Edition, Revised. Ed. E. D. Mackerness. See K-SJ, 20 (1971), No. 580.

Rev. by J. C. Maxwell in N&Q, 217 (Mar. 1972), 113–115.

435. Hepburn, Ronald W. "Poetry and

'Concrete Imagination': Problems of Truth and Illusion," *British Journal of Aesthetics*, 12 (Winter 1972), 3–18.

Briefly considers "Ode on a Grecian Urn": "The urn image seems to express a universal human ideal; but trust in its coherence becomes undermined in the course of the poem."

436. *Heseltine, H. P. "Ripeness is all: the example of Keats," *Teaching of English*, No. 20 (June 1971), pp. 23–37.

Contrasts Keats's poetry and philosophy with Sylvia Plath's, and compares their responses and solutions to their anguish.

437. Hewlett, Dorothy. *A Life of John Keats*. Third Edition, Revised. See K-SJ, 20 (1971), No. 582.

Rev. by Neville Rogers in *Yearbook of English Studies*, 2 (1972), 302–303.

438. Hilton, Timothy. *Keats and His World*. See K-SJ, 20 (1971), No. 583.

Rev. in *Choice*, 9 (June 1972), 505. Also see No. 94.

439. Holmes, Richard. "That Marvellous Boy," *Books and Bookmen*, 16 (July 1971), 6–8, 10.

A review-article of books on Chatterton, with comments on Keats and Shelley.

440. *Hood, Thomas. *Letters of Thomas Hood*. Ed. Leslie Marchand. New York: Octagon, 1972.

Hood's letters to Charles and Maria Dilke. Reprint of a 1945 edition.

441. Hood, Thomas. *Selected Poems of Thomas Hood*. See K-SJ, 20 (1971), No. 584.

Rev. by S[idney]. L. H[all]. in CLSB, No. 210 (Apr. 1971), pp. 685–686; by J[ohn]. E. J[ordan]. in ELN, 9, Supplement (Sept. 1971), 45; by Jared R. Curtis in *Arizona Quarterly*, 27 (Autumn 1971), 285–287.

442. Houck, James Ashley. "An Examination of the Practical and Theoretical Literary Criticism of William Hazlitt" [Doctoral dissertation, Duquesne, 1971], DAI, 32 (Apr. 1972), 5740-A.

443. Housman, A. E. *The Letters of A. E. Housman*. Ed. Henry Maas. See K-SJ, 20 (1971), No. 587.

Rev. in **American Notes and Queries*, 10 (Jan. 1972), 78; in **Classical World*, 65 (Jan. 1972), 168; in *New Yorker*, 47 (19 Feb. 1972), 111; in *Choice*, 9 (Apr. 1972), 213; by Clyde K. Hyder in *Victorian Poetry*, 10 (Summer 1972), 185–194; in *VQR, 48 (Winter 1972).

444. *Hudson, William Henry. *Keats and His Poetry*. New York: AMS, 1972.

Reprint of a 1919 work in the "Poetry and Life Series."

445. Hulseberg, Richard Arnold. "The Validation of the Self in Wordsworth and Keats" [Doctoral dissertation, Illinois, 1971], DAI, 32 (Apr. 1972), 5791-A.

446. Huyler, Frank DeKlyn, III. "Keats and the Age of Sensibility: A Study of Keats' Development in Terms of Eighteenth Century Landscape and Sublime Poetry" [Doctoral dissertation, Tufts, 1971], DAI, 33 (Dec. 1972), 2937-A.

447. *Hyder, Clyde K., ed. *Swinburne as Critic*. London: Routledge and Kegan Paul, 1972.

Swinburne's comments on Keats and Byron are included.

448. Itzkowitz, Martin E. "Freneau's 'Indian Burying Ground' and Keats's 'Grecian Urn,' " *Early American Literature*, 6 (Winter 1971–72), 258–262.†‡

Keats and Freneau treat the same subject, but the former from the standpoint of "devout idealism" and the latter from "skeptical nominalism."

449. Jeffrey, Lloyd N. *Thomas Hood*. New York: Twayne, 1972. "Twayne English Authors Series, 137."

Byron, Keats, and Shelley are mentioned frequently.

450. Jones, John. *John Keats's Dream of Truth*. See K-SJ, 20 (1971), No. 603.

Rev. in *Studies in English Literature* (Japan), 47 (Aug. 1970), 78–83 [in Japanese].

451. *Jones, Stanley. "Hazlitt's Journal of 1823: Some Notes and Emendations," *Library*, 26, No. 4 (1971), 325–336.†

452. Jones, Stanley. "More Hazlitt Quotations: 'The Leman-Lake,' etc.," N&Q, 217 (Mar. 1972), 99.†

Sources for hitherto unidentified quotations in Hazlitt are provided.

453. Kauvar, Gerald B. *The Other Poetry of Keats*. See K-SJ, 20 (1971), No. 610.

Rev. by Donald E. Billiar in *Enlighten-*

ment Essays, 1 (Spring 1970), 49–51; by S[tuart]. M. S[perry]., [Jr.], in ELN, 10, Supplement (Sept. 1972), 53.

454. *Kearney, Colbert Joseph. "The Writings of Benjamin Robert Haydon." (Doctoral dissertation, Cambridge, 1972).

455. "Keats Letter and Poem in Manuscript for Sale," *Times* (London), 8 June 1972, p. 5.

The poem is "To Hope," and the letter is to his brothers and dated 1817. Reply by R. W. P. Cockerton, 26 June 1972, p. 13; reply to Cockerton by M. B. Hudson, 1 July 1972, p. 15; rejoinder by Cockerton, 5 July 1972, p. 13; reply by Oonagh Lahr, 21 July 1972, p. 13. See No. 545.

456. "Keats Poetry Prize Winners," *Times* (London), 25 Mar. 1972, p. 18.

Miss Noel Welch wins top prize in poetry competition commemorating the 150th anniversary of the death of Keats.

457. Kelly, Linda. *The Marvellous Boy: The Life and Myth of Thomas Chatterton.* See K-SJ, 20 (1971), No. 613.

Rev. by Bernard Jones in *Books and Bookmen*, 17 (Oct. 1971), 41; in TLS, 25 Aug. 1972, p. 988.

458. *Kestner, Joseph A., III. "Keats: The Solace of Space," *Illinois Quarterly*, 35, No. 1 (1972), 59–64.†

459. Kobler, J. F. "Lena Grove: Faulkner's 'Still Unravish'd Bride of Quietness,' " *Arizona Quarterly*, 28 (Winter 1972), 339–354.

An interpretation of *Light in August* which sees Keats's urn as equivalent to Faulkner's Lena Grove and the figures on the urn as equivalent to the other characters in the novel. Faulkner employs Keats's poem as a symbol in "a consistent, continuous, self-contained pattern."

460. Koch, June Q. "Politics in Keats's Poetry," JEGP, 71 (Oct. 1972), 491–501.‡

Argues that the opening lines of Book III of *Endymion* closely reflect condemnation of the legitimacy of the second Bourbon Restoration in 1815, as expressed in the *Examiner* by Haydon, Hazlitt, and Hunt. Concludes that a "clear relationship exists between these lines and the rest of Book III, and between Book III and the whole of *Endymion*."

461. Kramer, Lawrence Eliot. "Keats and the Structure of Consciousness" [Doctoral dissertation, Yale, 1972], DAI, 33 (Dec. 1972), 2896–A.

462. *Laffay, Albert. "Présence et absence du monde dans la poésie de Keats," in *Le Romantisme anglo-américain: Mélanges offerts à Louis Bonnerot*, [ed. Roger Asselineau, *et al.*] (Paris: Didier, 1971), pp. 165–179.

463. LaVia, John Thomas. "Johnson and the Romantics: The Continuity of Major English Shakespearean Criticism" [Doctoral dissertation, Duke, 1970], DAI, 31 (Nov. 1970), 2389–A–2390–A.

Hazlitt is discussed.

464. *Leoff, Eve. *A Study of John Keats's "Isabella."* Salzburg: Univ. of Salzburg, 1972. "Salzburg Studies in English: Romantic Reassessment, No. 17."

Reprint of a dissertation. See K-SJ, 19 (1970), No. 242.

465. LePage, Peter V. "Benjamin Britten's *Rejoice in the Lamb*," *Music Review*, 33 (May 1972), 122–137.

Mentions Keats, Shelley, and Clare as among the poets whose works Britten has set to music.

466. "Library Notes," *Princeton University Library Chronicle*, 33 (Winter 1972), 122.

An exhibition at the library included the autograph MS of Keats's "Ode on Melancholy," which is in the collection of Robert H. Taylor.

467. Lohf, Kenneth A. "Our Growing Collections," *Columbia Library Columns*, 22 (Nov. 1972), 41–42.

Columbia receives gift of forty-three editions of works by and about Keats, including an edition of Keats once owned by Hunt.

468. Luthra, Ram Lall. "Hazlitt's Evaluation of Contemporary Authors in *The Spirit of the Age*" [Doctoral dissertation, Oregon, 1971], DAI, 32 (Dec. 1971), 3259–A.

469. *McAleer, John J. "William Hazlitt—Shakespeare's 'Advocate and Herald,' " *Shakespeare Newsletter*, 22 (1972), 4.†

470. *McClain, William H. "Symbolic Extensions of the Hyperion-Myth," in *Traditions and Transitions:* Studies in

Honor of Harold Jantz, ed. Lieselotte Kurth, William H. McClain, and Holger Homann (Munich: Delp'sche Verlagsbuchhanglung KG, 1972), pp. 177–193.

471. McGaughey, Russell William, Jr. "The Philosophical Capability of John Keats" [Doctoral dissertation, Delaware, 1971], DAI, 33 (July 1972), 280-A.

472. McNeely, Trevor. "Matthew Arnold and the Vision of Sin: Underground Themes in the Poetry," *Mosaic*, 5, No. 1 (1971), 79–105.

Includes comments on Arnold's "Isolation" and Keats's *Endymion*.

473. McPherson, Sandra. "Homage to John Clare" [Poem], *Iowa Review*, 2 (Summer 1971), 18–19.

474. Margetson, Stella. *Regency London*. London: Cassell, 1971.

Ch. 7, "The Artists and the Writers," refers to Keats in some detail. The book includes references to Byron, Haydon, Hazlitt, and Hunt as well.

Rev. by Simon Harcourt-Smith in *History Today*, 22 (Feb. 1972), 149–150.

475. Masson, Louis Joseph. "The Fearful Vision: The Poetry of John Clare" [Doctoral dissertation, Syracuse, 1972], DAI, 33 (July 1972), 279-A.

476. Matthews, G. M., ed. *Keats: The Critical Heritage*. See K-SJ, 20 (1971), No. 638.

Rev. in **Booklist*, 69 (1 Sept. 1972), 22; *Choice*, 9 (Sept. 1972), 815. Also see No. 119.

477. Messier, Marta Haake. "From Sleep to Poetry: The Order of the Poems in Keats's *Lamia* Volume" [Doctoral dissertation, Illinois, 1971], DAI, 32 (Feb. 1972), 4572-A.

478. *Midzunoe, Yuichi. "The 'Favorite Speculation' of John Keats the Poet: Distinctive Ideas in His Quest for Wisdom," *Jimbun Kenkyu* (Chiba University, Japan), 1 (1972), 61–102.

479. Montgomery, Marion. "Keats's Journey Homeward to Habitual Self," *Southern Review* (L.S.U.), 8 (Spring 1972), 273–289.

Argues that "Keats's pursuit of impersonality as a poet" was a false track. "His greatest triumphs, such as the Odes, result from a return to the self after a brief flight . . . by . . . the imagination."

480. Montgomery, Marion. "Wordsworth's False Beatrice," *Arizona Quarterly*, 27 (Autumn 1971), 211–218.

Contains a brief argument that Wordsworth's disapproval of Keats and Shelley lies in his mature acceptance that dream cannot be reality.

481. More, Paul Elmer. *The Essential Paul Elmer More: A Selection of His Writings*. Ed. with Introduction and Notes by Byron C. Lambert. Foreword by Russell Kirk. New Rochelle, N.Y.: Arlington House, 1972.

An essay on Keats is included.

482. *Murry, John Middleton. *Studies in Keats*. New York: Haskell House, 1972.

Reprint of a 1930 book.

483. Nagarajan, M. S. "Chicago Critics and *King Lear*," *Indian Journal of English Studies*, 13 (1972), 161–172.

The views of Hazlitt, Keats, and Shelley on *King Lear* are briefly mentioned.

484. Nance, Guinevera Splawn. " 'A Recourse Somewhat Human': A Study of Poetry as Consolation in the Romantic Period" [Doctoral dissertation, Virginia, 1971], DAI, 32 (Feb. 1972), 4574-A.

Includes Keats.

485. Neiss, Douglas James. "Hazlitt and the Press. The Periodical Criticism in England and America, 1805–1905" [Doctoral dissertation, Case Western Reserve, 1972], DAI, 32 (June 1972), 6939-A.

486. "New and Notable," *Princeton University Library Chronicle*, 34 (Autumn 1972), 85.

A copy of Keats's *Poems* (1817) is given to the library.

487. *Novikova, M. "Kits—Maršak—Pasternak" ["Keats—Marshak—Pasternak"], in *Masterstvo perevoda* [*The Translator's Art*], Collection 8 (Moscow, 1971), pp. 28–54.

On individual translator style.

488. *Ogawa, Kazuo. "Full-Grown Lambs," *Eigo Seinen: Rising Generation* (Tokyo), 117 (1971), 408–412, 481–484, 541–545, 607–611. [In Japanese.]

On Keats.

489. *Owen, Frances Mary. *John Keats: A Study*. Folcroft, Pa.: Folcroft, 1972.

Reprint of an 1880 work.

490. Park, Roy. *Hazlitt and the Spirit of the*

Age: Abstraction and Critical Theory. See K-SJ, 20 (1971), No. 655.

Rev. by Ian Jack in CLSB, No. 213 (Jan. 1972), pp. 707–708; by W. P. Albrecht in WC, 3 (Spring 1972), 106–110; by Sybil Oldfield in *British Journal of Aesthetics*, 12 (Spring 1972), 207–208; by Gilbert Thomas in *English*, 21 (Spring 1972), 27–29; by R. W. King in RES, 23 (Aug. 1972), 370–371; by J[ohn]. E. J[ordan]. in ELN, 10, Supplement (Sept. 1972), 48–49; by L. A. Elioseff in JAAC, 31 (Winter 1972), 278.

491. Patterson, Charles I., Jr. *The Daemonic in the Poetry of John Keats*. See K-SJ, 20 (1971), No. 658.

Rev. by Miriam Allott in MLR, 66 (July 1971), 674–676; by Allan Rodway in RES, 22 (Aug. 1971), 387–388; by George M. Harper in *Georgia Review*, 25 (Winter 1971), 516–519; by Carolyn Sue Falk in *South Atlantic Bulletin*, 37 (Jan. 1972), 47–51; by Karl Kroeber in MP, 69 (Feb. 1972), 267–268; by S[tuart]. M. S[perry]., [Jr.], in ELN, 10 Supplement (Sept. 1972), 53–54.

492. Pereira, E. "John Keats: Three 1819 Odes," UES, 9 (Sept. 1971), 1–9.

Readings of "Ode to Psyche," "Ode on Melancholy," and "Ode on Indolence."

493. Péter, Ágnes. *Keats költészetelméletének fejlödése*. Budapest: ELTE soksz, 1971. "Angol és amerikai filólogiai értekezések: Theses on English and American Philology."

494. Pidgley, Michael. "An Englishman in Paris: Dawson Turner's Visits to David and Prud'hon," *Burlington Magazine*, 114 (Nov. 1972), 791–792.

A banker and a friend of Haydon, Turner's journal of his 1814 visit is now in the Norwich Castle Museum. His second visit (1815) is described in the catalog to his art collection, privately published in 1840.

495. Pinsker, Sanford. "The Unlearning of Ike McCaslin: An Ironic Reading of William Faulkner's 'The Bear,'" *Topic*, No. 23 (Spring 1972), pp. 35–51.

Briefly discusses the use of Keats's "Ode on a Grecian Urn" in Faulkner's story.

496. Pointon, Marcia R. "The Italian Tour of William Hilton R.A. in 1825," *Journal of the Warburg and Courtauld Institutes*, 35 (1972), 339–358.

Hilton was an artist and the brother-in-law of Peter De Wint. References to Hazlitt, Haydon, and Hunt.

497. Pope, Willard B[issell]. "Benjamin Robert Haydon" [Letter], CLSB, No. 215 (July 1972), p. 8.

On the location and condition of Haydon's grave.

498. Pope, Willard Bissell, ed. *Invisible Friends: The Correspondence of Elizabeth Barrett Barrett and Benjamin Robert Haydon, 1842–1845*. Cambridge, Mass.: Harvard Univ., 1972.

499. *Popescu, Nicolae, "John Keats a murit la Roma" ["John Keats Died in Rome"], *Luceafărul*, 14, No. 11 (Mar. 1971), 7.

500. Primeau, Ronald René. "Keats's Chaucer: Realism and Romanticism in the English Tradition" [Doctoral dissertation, Illinois, 1971], DAI, 32 (Feb. 1972), 4575-A.

501. Prince, Jeffrey Robert. "Havens of Intensity: Aestheticism in the Poetry of Keats, Tennyson and Yeats" [Doctoral dissertation, Virginia, 1971], DAI, 32 (Feb. 1972), 4629-A–4630-A.

502. Proudfoot, Christopher, and David Watkin. "A Pioneer of English Neo-Classicism: C. H. Tatham," *Country Life*, 151 (13–20 Apr. 1972), 918–921.

Includes a reproduction of Benjamin Robert Haydon's portrait of Tatham.

503. Pulleyn, Mary Margaret Buck. "Keats's View of Death" [Doctoral dissertation, Minnesota, 1972], DAI, 33 (July 1972), 324-A.

504. "Putting Facts Before Fairies," TLS, 30 June 1972, p. 741. Reply by J. C. Maxwell, 14 July 1972, p. 819.

An omnibus review. See Nos. 389, 530.

505. Rajiva, Stanley F. "Wordsworth and Beethoven as 'Romantic' Artists: Some Parallels," *Literary Criterion*, 10 (Winter 1971), 14–20.

Keats and Shelley were poets of the "pathetic fallacy," by which "the observed scene is made to originate the feelings of the observer." "Indolence" was Keats's term for the state of mind which occasioned such poetry.

506. Ravilious, C. P. "Thomas Hood, a Suggested Emendation," N&Q, 216 (Nov. 1971), 410.†
In line 27 of "The Lady's Dream," "spectres thin" perhaps should be the Keatsian "spectre-thin."

507. "Readings from Keats By Mrs. V. O. Anderson and Miss Ann Jones (Saturday, October 9th, 1971)," CLSB, No. 213 (Jan. 1972), p. 702.
Account of a Charles Lamb Society meeting.

508. Reid, Benjamin L. *Tragic Occasions: Essays on Several Forms.* See K-SJ, 20 (1971), No. 670.
Rev. in *AL, 43 (Jan. 1972), 680; in *Choice*, 8 (Jan. 1972), 1440; by Lodwick Hartley in *Georgia Review*, 26 (Spring 1972), 112–114.

509. Reid, John C. "Thamos [*sic*] Hood: Poetiser of the Commonplace," CLSB, No. 206 (Apr. 1970), pp. 653–654.
A brief biographical sketch.

510. Reid, Stephen A. "Keats's Depressive Poetry," *Psychoanalytic Review*, 58 (Fall 1971), 395–418.†
Keats and his poetry understood in terms of "the dynamics of the first half year of human life."

511. Reiman, Donald H. "Keats and the Humanistic Paradox: Mythological History in *Lamia*," SEL, 11 (Autumn 1971), 659–669.†‡
The poem, among other late poems of Keats, explores "the tragic implications of the mutability of all mortal existence, including the human imagination."

512. Riley, Sister Maria A., O.P. "John Keats, Liturgist of the Poetic Act: An Analysis of Keats's Use of Religious Imagery and Phraseology as a Vehicle for his Poetic Theory" [Doctoral dissertation, Florida State, 1971], DAI, 32 (May 1972), 6449-A.

513. Robinson, Jeffrey Cane. "Keats and the Waking Dream" [Doctoral dissertation, Brandeis, 1972], DAI, 32 (June 1972), 7001-A–7002-A.

514. *Rogers, Neville, comp. *Keats, Shelley, and Rome: An Illustrated Miscellany.* Postscript by Earl Wavell. Folcroft, Pa.: Folcroft, 1971.
Reprint of a 1949 book.

515. *Rogers, Robert. "The Dynamics of Metaphor: Modes of Mentation in Poetry," *Hartford Studies in Literature*, 3 (1971), 157–190.‡
Keats is discussed.

516. *Rollins, Hyder Edward, and Stephen Maxfield Parrish, eds. *Keats and the Bostonians.* New York: Russell and Russell, 1972.
Reprint of a 1951 work.

517. Rosebury, Theodor. *Microbes and Morals.* New York: Viking, 1971.
Mentions Keats's "case of syphilis."
Rev. by Marya Mannes in NYT, 10 Oct. 1971, pp. 31–32.

518. Ross, Robert N. " 'To Charm Thy Curious Eye': Erasmus Darwin's Poetry at the Vestibule of Knowledge," JHI, 32 (July–Sept. 1971), 379–394.
Likens Darwin's mental flexibility to Keats's "negative capability," and refers to Byron's attack on Darwin's poetry.

519. Sabbadini, Silvano. *Una Salvezza Ambigua: Studio sulla prima poesia di T. S. Eliot.* Bari, Italy: Adriatica Editrice, 1971. "Biblioteca di Studi Inglesi, Vol. 22."
Discusses Eliot's early interest in Keats.

520. Sallé, J[ean-].C[laude]. " 'Forlorn' in Milton and Keats," N&Q, 217 (Aug. 1972), 293.†
Sees Keats unconsciously recalling *Paradise Lost* IX.910, at conclusion of "Ode to a Nightingale."

521. Sallé, J[ean-].C[laude]. "Identification of Three Allusions in Hazlitt's Essays," N&Q, 217 (Mar. 1972), 99–100.†
Provides sources of previously unidentified allusions.

522. Sallé, Jean-Claude. "The Pious Frauds of Art: A Reading of the 'Ode on a Grecian Urn,' " SIR, 11 (Spring 1972), 79–93.‡
"Poetry, though erroneous, may be fine. Such is . . . the meaning of the 'Ode on a Grecian Urn.' "

523. Scott, Nathan A., Jr. *Negative Capability: Studies in the New Literature and the Religious Situation.* See K-SJ, 20 (1971), No. 679.

Rev. by H. T. Mason in N&Q, 217 (Sept. 1972), 350–351.

524. Sinson, Janice C. *John Keats and "The Anatomy of Melancholy."* See K-SJ, 20 (1971), No. 684.

Rev. by F. Seymour Smith in *Aryan Path*, 42 (Oct. 1971), 363–364.

525. *Søborg, Lotte. *John Keats. Den Keat'ske digterog digtopfattelse set i relation til samtidens økonomiske, politiske og sociale forhold.* Grena, Denmark: GMT, 1972.

526. [Sprigg, Christopher St. John.] Caudwell, Christopher, *pseud. Romance and Realism: A Study in English Bourgeois Literature.* Ed. Samuel Hynes. See K-SJ, 20 (1971), No. 692.

Rev. by George Woodcock in MLQ, 33 (March 1972), 88–90; in TLS, 28 Apr. 1972, p. 470.

527. Srivastava, Avadhesh K. "Aestheticism and Oscar Wilde's Style," *Indian Journal of English Studies*, 13 (1972), 59–75.

Discusses influence of Keats's "cult of beauty" on the Pre-Raphaelites and Wilde.

528. Stephens, Rosemary Carswell. "The Nymph Imagery of Keats and Shelley" [Doctoral dissertation, Mississippi, 1971], DAI, 32 (Jan. 1972), 3965-A.

529. Stevenson, Warren. "Lamia: A Stab at the Gordian Knot," SIR, 11 (Summer 1972), 241–252.†‡

Sees the poem as essentially ironic, Lamia being a predator, Lycius a sham poet-hero, and Apollonius an effective, but uncreative, destroyer of delusion.

530. Stillinger, Jack. *The Hoodwinking of Madeline and Other Essays on Keats's Poems.* Urbana, Chicago, London: Univ. of Illinois, 1971.

A collection of previously published essays.

Rev. by Frank P. Riga in LJ, 97 (15 Jan. 1972), 199; in *Choice*, 9 (July–Aug. 1972), 648; by S[tuart]. M. S[perry]., [Jr.], in ELN, 10, Supplement (Sept. 1972), 54–55; by Gilbert Thomas in *English*, 21 (Autumn 1972), 113–114. Also see Nos. 82, 504.

531. Storey, Mark. "Edwin Paxton Hood (Not the Reverend Romeo Elton) and John Clare," N&Q, 216 (Oct. 1971), 386–387.†

Reattribution of an article on Clare. See K-SJ, 18 (1969), No. 409.

532. *Strzetelski, Jerzy. "Dwa Sonety—Dwa Rodzaje Stylu" ["Two Sonnets—Two Types of Style"], *Pamiętnik Literacki*, No. 1 (1969), pp. 149–159.

Analyzes Keats's "On First Looking into Chapman's Homer" and D. G. Rossetti's "Pride of Youth."

533. *Strzetelski, Jerzy. *The English Sonnet: Syntax and Style.* Kraków, 1970. "Zeszyty Naukowe Uniwersytetu Jagiellońskiego, No. 213: Prace Językoznawcze, No. 27."

Concerns Keats.

Rev. by *Przemysław Mroczkowski in *Kwartalnik Neofilologiczny*, No. 4 (1970), pp. 446–452.

534. Stuart, William G., Jr. "Intramuralia: Books and People," HLQ, 34 (Aug. 1971), 368–369.

The Huntington Library has acquired a first edition of Lemprière's *Bibliotheca Classica* (1788). Keats probably used the 1788 edition to gain much of his knowledge of Latin and Greek mythology.

535. Swaminathan, S. R. "Virgil, Dryden and Yeats," N&Q, 217 (Sept. 1972), 328–330.

Mentions Yeats's quoting of *Endymion* in *A Vision.*

536. *Talbott, John Harold. *A Biographical History of Medicine: Excerpts and Essays on Men and Their Work.* New York: Grune and Stratton, 1970.

Includes Keats.

537. Tibble, J[ohn]. W[illiam]., and Anne Tibble. *John Clare: A Life.* New Edition, Revised by Anne Tibble. Totowa, N.J.: Rowman and Littlefield, 1972.

First edition published in 1932.

Rev. in TLS, 13 Oct. 1972, p. 1216.

538. Todd, Janet M. "In Adam's Garden: A Study of John Clare" [Doctoral dissertation, Florida, 1971], DAI, 33 (Aug. 1972), 768-A.

539. *Todd, Janet M. "Mary Joyce in the Poetry of John Clare," *Mary Wollstonecraft Newsletter*, 1, No. 1 (1972), 12–18.†

540. Toliver, Harold E. *Pastoral Forms and Attitudes.* See K-SJ, 20 (1971), No. 708.

Rev. in *Choice*, 9 (Apr. 1972), 208; by

Rosalie L. Colie in JEGP, 71 (July 1972), 447–448; in VQR, 48 (Spring 1972), lvi; by George deF. Lord in MLQ, 33 (Dec. 1972), 449–453.

541. *Travushkin, N. S. "Sotsial'no-oblichitel'nye stikhotvoreniya Tomasa Guda v Rossii" ["Thomas Hood's Socio-Accusatory Poetry in Russia"], *UZ Kazanskogo pedagogisheskogo instituta*, 85 (1971), 98–106.

542. *Tsukano, Tagayasu. "Chodatsu to shoso-Keats no sozoryoku" ["Transcendence and Impatience—Keats's Imagination"], *Eigo Seinen: Rising Generation* (Tokyo), 117 (1971), 88–89.

543. Udy, David. "The Neo-Classicism of Charles Heathcote Tatham," *Connoisseur*, 177 (Aug. 1971), 269–276.

Illustrated with Benjamin Robert Haydon's pastel portrait of Tatham.

544. Van Maanen, W. "Kean: From Dumas to Sartre," *Neophilologus*, 56 (Apr. 1972), 221–230.

Hazlitt is quoted.

545. "Ventes Publiques," *Bulletin du Bibliophile* (1972), pp. 370–371.

Notes sale in England of the following items on 27 June 1972: Byron's *A Sketch from Private Life* (original edition of a printed but unpublished poetic satire) for £2400 and *Fare thee well!* (a lyric pamphlet distributed to a few in 1816) for £2400; Keats's "To Hope" (the autograph MS of forty-eight lines) for £5800 and letter to his brothers (15 Apr. 1817) for £11,000; and an old copy of a letter, now lost, from Fanny Brawne (14 Feb. 1821) about Keats for £2600. See No. 455.

546. Viebrock, Helmut. "Geld und Traum: Scott Fitzgerald Zwischen Cole Porter und Keats," in *Festschrift für Edgar Mertner*, ed. Bernhard Fabian and Ulrich Suerbaum (Munich: Fink, 1969), pp. 293–313.

547. Vogler, Thomas A. *Preludes to Vision: The Epic Venture in Blake, Wordsworth, Keats, and Hart Crane*. See K-SJ, 20 (1971), No. 712.

Rev. by Brian Wilkie in JEGP, 71 (Apr. 1972), 255–260; by Karl Kroeber in ELN, 10 (Dec. 1972), 154–156. Also see Nos. 82, 94, 144.

548. *Voisine, Jacques. "William Hazlitt's Contribution to Romantic Criticism," in *Le Romantisme anglo-américain: Mélanges offerts à Louis Bonnerot*, [ed. Roger Asselineau, *et al.*] (Paris: Didier, 1971), pp. 211–232.

549. Wade, R. A. R. "An Introduction to John Clare," *Journal of the Gypsy Lore Society*, 50 (July–Oct. 1971), 82–85.

General biographical information is presented.

550. Wardle, Ralph M. *Hazlitt*. See K-SJ, 20 (1971), No. 714.

Rev. in *Choice*, 8 (Feb. 1972), 1588; by W. P. Albrecht in WC, 3 (Spring 1972), 106–110; in VQR, 48 (Spring 1972), lxi–lxii; by Lionel Stevenson in SAQ, 71 (Spring 1972), 268–269; by J[ohn]. E. J[ordan]. in ELN, 10, Supplement (Sept. 1972), 49; by J. H. Adamson in *Western Humanities Review*, 26 (Autumn 1972), 384–386; in TLS, 24 Nov. 1972, p. 1427.

551. Wesling, Donald. "The Dialectical Criticism of Poetry: An Instance from Keats," *Mosaic*, 5, No. 2 (1972), 81–96.†‡

A Marxist interpretation of "Ode to a Nightingale," which places the poem in the social context of England in 1819.

552. *Wigod, Jacob. *The Darkening Chamber: The Growth of Tragic Consciousness in Keats*. Salzburg: Univ. of Salzburg, 1972. "Salzburg Studies in English: Romantic Reassessment Series, No. 22."

553. *Xolmskaja, O. "Vstupitel'naja stat'ja k stixam D. Kitsa" ["Introductory Article on the Poetry of John Keats"], *Inostrannaya literatura*, No. 2 (1972), pp. 180–182.

A biographical sketch with characteristic translations of Keats into Russian.

554. *Yuan-Shu, Yen. " 'Biography of the White Serpent': A Keatsian Interpretation," *Tamkang Review*, 1 (Oct. 1970), 227–243.

For additional BOOKS AND ARTICLES RELATING TO KEATS AND HIS CIRCLE see Nos. 2, 3, 4, 9, 11, 20, 21, 24, 31, 37, 38, 39, 44, 46, 52, 56, 58, 63, 66, 67, 72, 73, 74, 76, 79, 95, 96, 99, 103, 105, 107, 111, 112, 114, 118, 121, 122, 125, 135, 210, 237, 238, 257, 283, 291, 304, 311, 318, 343, 352, 594, 628, 665, 668, 685, 691, 738, 741, 759.

V. SHELLEY

Works: Collected, Selected Single, Translated

555. **An Address to the Irish People*. New York: Oriole Editions, [ca. 1972]. "Oriole Chapbooks, 20." Available from Oriole Editions, 19 West 44th Street, New York, N.Y. 10036.
A facsimile reprint of the 1812 Dublin edition. Paperback.

555a. *A Choice of Shelley's Verse*. Ed. Stephen Spender. See K-SJ, 20 (1971), No. 728.
See No. 144.

556. *The Complete Poetical Works of Percy Bysshe Shelley*. Vol. I: *1802–1813*. Ed. Neville Rogers. Oxford: Clarendon, 1972.

557. **Selected Essays on Atheism*. New York: Arno, 1972.
Reprints "The Necessity of Atheism," "A Refutation of Deism," and "A Logical Objection to Christianity" [*sic*].

558. *Šelli. [Shelley.] *Pis'ma. Stat'i. Fragmenty*. [*Letters, Articles, Fragments*.] Ed. Z. E. Aleksandrova, A. A. Elistratova, and Ju.M. Kondrat'ev. Moscow: Nauka, 1972. "Akademija Nauk SSSR. Literaturnye pamjatniki."
The edition includes an essay by Elistratova on Shelley's prose (pp. 437–451), and notes and commentary by Kondrat'ev (pp. 452–518).
Rev. by *N. Ja. D'jakonova in *Inostrannaya literatura*, No. 10 (1972), pp. 265–267.

559. **The Sensitive Plant*. Illustrated by Laurence Housman. New York: Haskell House, 1972.
Reprint of the "Illustrated English Poems" edition of 1898.

For additional Works by Shelley see Nos. 95, 584, 609, 770.

Books and Articles Relating to Shelley and His Circle

560. Abdel-Hai, M. "Shelley and the Arabs: An Essay in Comparative Literature," *Journal of Arabic Literature*, 3 (1972), 72–89.
Stating that more poems of Shelley have been translated into Arabic than of any other nineteenth-century English poet, the author surveys the growth of Shelley's reputation in the Arab world and concludes with "A Tentative Bibliography of Arabic Translations of Shelley's Poems."

561. *Aichelburg, Wolf. "Der verlorene Engel. Zu Shelleys 150 Todestag," *Neuer Weg*, Nos. 7207–08 (July 1972), pp. 3–4.
A tribute to Shelley on the anniversary of his death.

562. "Anticipating the Anniversary," TLS, 24 Dec. 1971, p. 1603. Reply by Desmond King-Hele, 14 Jan. 1972, p. 41, and a rejoinder.
An omnibus review. See K-SJ, 20 (1971), Nos. 47, 851, 958. Also see Nos. 29, 648, 777.

563. Appasamy, S. P. "English Poetry as Religious Experience," *Aryan Path*, 42 (Nov. 1971), 399–405.
Quotes from Shelley's *Defence of Poetry*.

564. Artaud, Antonin, Roger Blin, and others. "Antonin Artaud's 'Les Cenci,'" *Drama Review*, 16 (June 1972), 90–145.
Preperformance block diagrams and reviews of Artaud's 1935 play, with its sources in Stendhal and Shelley.

565. *Arthur, Anthony R. "The Poet as Revolutionary in *The Revolt of Islam*," *Xavier University Studies*, 10, No. 2 (1971), 1–17.

565a. **Autographes et Documents historiques* [Bookseller's Catalogue], Librairie de l'Abbaye (Paris), Catalogue No. 207, Item 22.
A seven-line autograph letter from Barbey d'Aurevilly to Trébutien, 2 Jan. 1835, requesting the latter to inquire after William Godwin's works other than *Caleb Williams*.

566. Bandy, Melanie F. "The Idea of Evil in the Poetry of Blake and Shelley: A Comparative Study" [Doctoral dissertation, New Mexico, 1971], DAI, 32 (Mar. 1972), 5218-A.

567. *Ben, G. "Serdce iz serdec K. 180-letiju co dnja roždenija i k 150-letiju so dnja smerti Šelli" ["Heart of Hearts. For the 180th Anniversary of the Birth and

the 150th Anniversary of the Death of Shelley"], *Nauka i religija*, No. 7 (1972), pp. 85–88.

On Shelley's anti-religious views.

568. *Bland, D. E. "Population and Liberalism, 1770–1817," JHI, 34 (1972), 113–122.

Godwin is discussed.

569. Bloom, Harold. "*Clinamen*, or Poetic Misprision," *New Literary History*, 3 (Winter 1972), 373–391.

Quotes Shelley's *Defence of Poetry*.

570. Cancelled.

571. Bornstein, George. *Yeats and Shelley*. See K-SJ, 20 (1971), No. 766.

Rev. by D[avid]. V. E[rdman]. in ELN, 9, Supplement (Sept. 1971), 53; in *VQR, 47 (Winter 1971), xxvii; by Michael Sidnell in UTQ, 41 (Spring 1972), 263–273. Also see No. 19.

572. Boulger, James D. "Coleridge: The Marginalia, Myth-Making, and the Later Poetry," SIR, 11 (Fall 1972), 304–319.

Several references to Shelley as a myth-maker.

573. *Bouyxou, Jean-Pierre. *Frankenstein*. Lyon: Société d'études, recherches et documentation cinématographiques, 1969. "Collection Premier Plan, 51."

A filmography of the Frankenstein motif.

574. Brazell, James. *Shelley and the Concept of Humanity: A Study of His Moral Vision*. Salzburg: Univ. of Salzburg, 1972. "Salzburg Studies in English: Romantic Reassessment Series, No. 7."

575. Buxton, John. "A New Portrait of Jane Williams," KSMB, 23 (1972), 30.

Discusses accompanying reproduction of 1837 crayon drawing of Jane Williams by Alexander Blaikley.

576. Buxton, John. "On the Text of Some Letters by Shelley," *Bodleian Library Record*, 8 (June 1972), 338–342.

Buxton supplies a few corrections and additions to twelve letters of Shelley to Hookham (29 July 1812 to March 1813) in the Jones edition.

577. Buxton, John. "Shelley and the Tradition of the 'Progress Piece,' " KSMB, 23 (1972), 1–5.

Elements of "the long-established convention of the progress piece" are found in the "Ode to Liberty," *Defence of Poetry*, and *Hellas*.

578. Buxton, John. "Shelley's Neo-Classical Taste," *Apollo*, 96 (Oct. 1972), 276–281.

A discussion of Shelley's response to the fine arts. "For Shelley, this neo-classical requirement that a work of art should sustain the comparison with Antiquity was always the basis for aesthetic judgment." Shelley's neo-classical standards led him to prefer Raphael to Michelangelo and sculpture to painting. Buxton comments on Shelley's adaptation of the Hellenistic statue of "Niobe with Her Youngest Daughter" for *The Cenci* V.iv.159–164. He also comments on the affinities between the drawings of John Flaxman and the poetic style of Shelley, both influenced by the Classical ideal.

579. Caird, James B. "Charles Kirkpatrick Sharpe," *Library Review*, 23 (Autumn 1971), 75–80.

Cites Sharpe's comments on Shelley at Oxford as living "upon arsenic, aqua fortis and half an hour's sleep," and his subsequent opinion that Shelley had attempted to foster this impression at Oxford.

580. Callahan, Patrick J. "*Frankenstein*, Bacon, and the 'Two Truths,' " *Extrapolation*, 14 (Dec. 1972), 39–48.†

Sees the novel as a critique of Francis Bacon's theory that scientific discovery inevitably works to the good of mankind.

581. Cameron, Kenneth Neill, ed. *Shelley and His Circle, 1773–1822*. The Carl H. Pforzheimer Library. Vols. III and IV. See K-SJ, 20 (1971), No. 773.

Rev. by Carl Woodring in ELN, 9, Supplement (Sept. 1971), 53–54; by P. H. Butter in MLR, 66 (Oct. 1971), 876–877; by Neville Rogers in RES, 22 (Nov. 1971), 502–504.

582. *Campbell, Olwen Ward. *Thomas Love Peacock*. Freeport, N.Y.: Books for Libraries, 1971.

Reprint of a 1953 work.

583. *Carpenter, Edward, and George Barnefield. *The Psychology of the Poet Shelley*. New York: Haskell House, 1972.

Reprint of a 1925 book.

584. Chernaik, Judith. *The Lyrics of Shelley.* Cleveland and London: Case Western Reserve Univ., 1972.

A critical study which includes newly edited texts of several poems.

Rev. by Frank P. Riga in LJ, 97 (15 Oct. 1972), 3314.

585. Coats, Sandra Whitaker. "Gothic Elements in Shelley's *Prometheus Unbound*" [Doctoral dissertation, Texas A and M, 1971], DAI, 32 (Apr. 1972), 5732-A–5733-A.

585a. **Collection d'Autographes littéraires, Lettres et Manuscrits des XVIIè, XVIIIè, XIXè, XXè siècles* [Sale Catalogue], Hôtel Drouot (Paris), 26 Feb. 1969, Deuxième Partie, Lot 83.

Two letters, one from Pierre Louÿs to Paul Valéry, the other in reply, both of which quote from and comment on Shelley's *Epipsychidion.*

586. Cowan, Thomas Dale. "The Romantics as Therapists: Shelley and Keniston," SAQ, 71 (Summer 1972), 342–351.†

Relates the poet and the Yale psychologist to the contemporary youth movement.

587. Crompton, Margaret. "The Last Days of Shelley," CR, 221 (July 1972), 7–12.

A popularized account.

588. Cude, Wilfred. "Mary Shelley's Modern Prometheus: A Study in the Ethics of Scientific Creativity," *Dalhousie Review,* 52 (Summer 1972), 212–225.

The primary fault is not Frankenstein's for creating the monster, nor even for rejecting him once created, but rather society's for acting irresponsibly toward this product of scientific genius.

589. Curran, Stuart. *Shelley's "Cenci": Scorpions Ringed with Fire.* See K-SJ, 20 (1971), No. 784.

Rev. in *Choice,* 8 (Sept. 1971), 830; by K[enneth]. N[eill]. C[ameron]. in ELN, 9 Supplement (Sept. 1971), 54–55; by Harold Orel in *Victorian Studies,* 15 (Sept. 1971), 93–95; by John I. Ades in *Educational Theatre Journal,* 23 (Oct. 1971), 353–356; by Donald H. Reiman in JEGP, 70 (Oct. 1971), 682–684. Also see No. 43.

590. Dalsimer, Adele Mintz. "The Unappeasable Shadow: Shelley's Influence on Yeats" [Doctoral dissertation, Yale, 1971], DAI, 32 (June 1972), 6969-A–6970-A.

591. Damm, Robert F. "A Tale of Human Power: Art and Life in Shelley's Poetic Theory" [Doctoral dissertation, Miami Univ., 1970], DAI, 32 (July 1971), 385-A.

592. Davies, Phillips G. "The Attack on Shelley at Tanyrallt: A Suggestion," KSMB, 23 (1972), 40–43.

Considers the attack to be purely imaginary, but suggests "that a sensational murder committed in the immediate neighbourhood might well have turned Shelley's thoughts to the subject of violence and caused him to fear for his personal safety."

593. Dawson, Carl. *His Fine Wit: A Study of Thomas Love Peacock.* See K-SJ, 20 (1971), No. 788.

Rev. by J[ohn]. E. J[ordan]. in ELN, 9 Supplement (Sept. 1971), 49–50; by Sheila M. Smith in *Yearbook of English Studies,* 2 (1972), 298–299.

594. DeLaura, David J. "Ruskin and the Brownings: Twenty-five Unpublished Letters," *Bulletin of the John Rylands Library, Manchester,* 54 (Spring 1972), 314–356.

Ruskin confesses to reading little poetry, and then only the "most perfect," among which he includes Keats's. In another letter he rebuts Browning's disillusionment with Wordsworth and praise of Shelley in "The Lost Leader." In a derisive attack on Shelley, Ruskin calls him a "mere sick schoolboy" and parodies a scene from Canto I of *The Revolt of Islam* and "The Isle." But DeLaura notes that Ruskin's feelings about Shelley were actually complex and ambivalent. Some scattered references to Byron.

595. Delisle, Fanny. "A Study of Shelley's *A Defence of Poetry*" [Doctoral dissertation, New Hampshire, 1972], DAI, 33 (Nov. 1972), 2322-A.

596. Dickson, Keith. "In Defence of 'Comparative' Criticism," *German Life and Letters,* 25 (July 1972), 327–334.

Shelley's "The Mask of Anarchy" is mentioned in connection with Bertolt Brecht.

597. "Directory of Scholars Active," *Computers and the Humanities*, 6 (May 1972), 312.
Describes Burton R. Pollin's listing of 1250 musical works based on the poetry of Shelley.

598. Duerksen, Roland A. *Shelleyan Ideas in Victorian Literature*. See K-SJ, 17 (1968), No. 497, 18 (1969), No. 572, 19 (1970), No. 311.
Rev. by Heinz Bergner in *Anglia*, 88, No. 1 (1970), 150–152.

599. Duerksen, Roland A. "Shelleyan Witchcraft: The Unbinding of Brassbound," *Shaw Review*, 15 (Jan. 1972), 21–25.
Discusses the influence of *The Witch of Atlas* on Shaw's play, *Captain Brassbound's Conversion*.

600. Duffy, Edward Thomas. "The Image of Jean-Jacques Rousseau in the Work of Shelley and Other English Romantics" [Doctoral dissertation, Columbia, 1971], DAI, 33 (July 1972), 306-A.

601. Dyck, Sarah. "The Presence of that Shape: Shelley's *Prometheus Unbound*," *Costerus*, 1 (1972), 13–79.
Discusses "the three major images which form what can be considered the backbone of the poem," shape, empire, and heaven-hell.

602. Easton, A. ["Percy Bysshe Shelley," Portrait], KSMB, 23 (1972).
Frontispiece to KSMB is a version of the Curran portrait by A. Easton in the possession of Lord Abinger.

603. *Edmunds, Edward William. *Shelley and His Poetry*. New York: AMS, 1972.
Reprint of a 1912 work in the "Poetry and Life Series."

604. Edwards, Gwynne. "Calderón's *Los cabellos de Absalón*: a Reappraisal," *Bulletin of Hispanic Studies*, 48 (July 1971), 218–238.
Contests the view of Shelley and others that David is to be taken as a symbol of mercy and forgiveness.

605. Eggenschwiler, David. "Sexual Parody in 'The Triumph of Life,' " *Concerning Poetry*, 5 (Fall 1972), 28–36.‡
Shelley's parodic treatment of sexual love in the poem shows "how much natural experience had become for him an obstacle, rather than a means, to transcendent experience."

606. Faas, Klaus Egbert. "Die deskriptive Dichtung als Wegbereiter der romantischen Naturlyrik in England," *Germanisch-Romantische Monatsschrift*, 53, No. 2 (1972), 142–161.
Quotes Shelley's denial of the subject-object dualism.

607. Faulkner, Peter. "A Roman Camp in a Fourth Author?" N&Q, 217 (Oct. 1972), 381.
Touches on Peacock's *Crotchet Castle*.

608. Faure, Georges. *Les Éléments du rythme poétique en anglais moderne: Esquisse d'une nouvelle analyse et essai d'application au "Prometheus Unbound" de P. B. Shelley*. See K-SJ, 20 (1971), No. 799.
Rev. by Emerson R. Marks in JAAC, 30 (Spring 1972), 399–400.

609. *Fischer, Hermann, ed. *English Satirical Poetry from Joseph Hall to Percy B. Shelley*. Tübingen: Niemeyer, 1970.
Shelley and Byron.
Rev. by John R. Clark in *Satire Newsletter*, 9 (Fall 1971), 108.

610. Flagg, John Sewell. "*Prometheus Unbound* and *Hellas*: An Approach to Shelley's Lyrical Dramas" [Doctoral dissertation, Boston Univ., 1971], DAI, 32 (Oct. 1971), 2088-A.
See No. 611.

611. Flagg, John Sewell. *"Prometheus Unbound" and "Hellas": An Approach to Shelley's Lyrical Dramas*. Salzburg: Univ. of Salzburg, 1972. "Salzburg Studies in English: Romantic Reassessment Series, No. 14."
Reprint of a dissertation. See No. 610.

612. Flexner, Eleanor. *Mary Wollstonecraft: A Biography*. New York: Coward-McCann and Geoghegan, 1972.
Rev. in **Kirkus Reviews*, 1 July 1972, p. 766, and 15 July 1972, p. 812; in **Publishers' Weekly*, 10 July 1972, p. 42; by Barbara Abrash in LJ, 15 (1 Sept. 1972), 2720; in **Christian Science Monitor*, 13 Sept. 1972, p. 13; by Susan Brownmiller in NYT, 8 Oct. 1972, pp. 4, 18; in **Book World* (*Washington Post*), 8 Oct. 1972, p. 1, and 3 Dec. 1972, p. 5; in **Christian Century*, 89 (11 Oct. 1972), 1021; by *J. A. Seligmann in *Newsweek*, 80 (23 Oct. 1972), 105A; by *J. J. McAleer in *Best Sellers*, 32 (1 Nov. 1972),

351; by V. S. Pritchett in NYRB, 2 Nov. 1972, pp. 8–11.

613. Fogarty, Nancy Louise. "Shelley in the Twentieth Century: A Study of the Development of Shelley Criticism in England and America 1916–1971" [Doctoral dissertation, Nebraska, 1972], DAI, 33 (Dec. 1972), 2889-A–2890-A.

614. *Forman, Harry Buxton. *The Shelley Library*. New York: Haskell House, 1971.
Reprint of the 1886 work.

615. Frye, Northrop. *The Critical Path: An Essay on the Social Context of Literary Criticism*. Bloomington: Indiana Univ., 1971.
Peacock's *Four Ages of Poetry* and Shelley's *Defence* are mentioned in this expansion of an essay which first appeared in *Daedalus*. See K-SJ, 20 (1971), No. 806.
Rev. by Keith Cushman in LJ, 96 (15 May 1971), 1713; by David Bromwich in *Nation*, 20 Sept. 1971, pp. 247–248; in *CL, 24 (Winter 1972), 72.

616. Fullwood, Daphne. "The Early Poetry of W. B. Yeats," *Ariel*, 3 (July 1972), 80–90.
Notes the influence of Shelley, suggesting that Yeats was as much delighted by Shelley's lyricism as his Neoplatonic imagery. Discusses the resemblance of Yeats's "The Stolen Child" to Shelley's "To Jane: The Invitation" and "To Jane: The Recollection."

617. Garside, P. D. "Scott, the Romantic Past and the Nineteenth Century," RES, 23 (May 1972), 147–161.
Includes a discussion of the argument between Mr. Chainmail and Mr. MacQuedy on the Middle Ages, from Peacock's *Crotchet Castle*.

618. Gaylin, Willard. "The Frankenstein Myth Becomes a Reality—We Have the Awful Knowledge to Make Exact Copies of Human Beings," *New York Times Magazine*, 5 March 1972, pp. 12–13, 41, 43–44, 48–49.
New discoveries in genetics give Mary Shelley's novel "a relevance beyond its original time."

619. *Georgine, Sister. "Shelley's 'Adonais,'" *Indiana English Journal*, 4 (Spring 1970), 28–30, 39.

620. Gill, Stephen C. " 'Adventures on Salisbury Plain' and Wordsworth's Poetry of Protest 1795–97," SIR, 11 (Winter 1972), 48–65.†
Discusses similarities in outlook between Wordsworth's work and Godwin's *Caleb Williams*.

621. Godwin, William. *Caleb Williams*. Ed. David McCracken. See K-SJ, 20 (1971), No. 817.
Rev. by W. D. Maxwell-Mahon in UES, 8 (1970), 12–13; by Peter Faulkner in *Yearbook of English Studies*, 1 (1971), 276–277; by Rodney M. Baine in *Georgia Review*, 25 (Spring 1971), 113–116.

622. *Godwin, William. *De la justice politique*. [Benjamin Constant's Unpublished Translation of] *Enquiry Concerning Political Justice and Its Influence on General Virtue and Happiness*. Ed. with Introduction by Burton R. Pollin. Québec: Univ. Laval, 1972.
With varying title, also published by State University of New York Press, Albany.

623. Godwin, William. *Enquiry Concerning Political Justice*. Abridged and Ed. K. Codell Carter. See K-SJ, 20 (1971), No. 818.
Rev. by Jules Steinberg in PQ, 51 (July 1972), 684.

624. *Godwin, William. *Italian Letters; or The History of Count de St. Julian*. Ed. Burton R. Pollin. Lincoln: Univ. of Nebraska, 1972.
Reprint of an edition first published in 1965. See K-SJ, 16 (1967), No. 386.

625. Godwin, William. *St. Leon: A Tale of the Sixteenth Century*. Foreword by Devendra P. Varma. Introd. Juliet Beckett. New York: Arno, 1972.
A reprint of the London, 1831, "Standard Novels" edition, with a new foreword, introduction, and bibliography.

626. Grabo, Carl. *The Meaning of "The Witch of Atlas."* See K-SJ, 20 (1971), No. 825.
Rev. in *Choice*, 9 (Apr. 1972), 213.

627. *Hall, Spencer. " 'Doing' Shelley: An Essay Review," *Southern Humanities Review*, 6 (1972), 287–294.

628. Hamalian, Leo, and James V. Hatch. "How to Turn the Hip Generation on to Shelley and Keats," CE, 33 (Dec. 1971), 324–332.

Includes a description of a Shelley "happening" to be staged in class, in which a student plays Shelley and the teacher and class participate in re-enacting events in the poet's life relevant to the problems of today. Appropriate quotations from the poetry are employed.

629. Harding, Gunnar. "Fabulous Life of Percy Bysshe Shelley," translated from the Swedish by the author and Sydney B. Smith, *Ambit*, No. 47 (1971), pp. 7–9.

An impressionistic summary of some of the highlights of Shelley's life.

630. Hartley, Robert Arnold. "Images of Change in *The Revolt of Islam*" [Doctoral dissertation, Columbia, 1971], DAI, 32 (Dec. 1971), 3304-A.

631. Hascall, Dudley L. "Trochaic Meter," CE, 33 (Nov. 1971), 217–226.

Many illustrations from Shelley.

632. Hayden, Lucy Kelly. "A Rhetorical Analysis of Mary Wollstonecraft's *A Vindication of the Rights of Woman*" [Doctoral dissertation, Michigan, 1971], DAI, 32 (Mar. 1972), 5185-A.

633. Hildebrand, William. "Jupiter, Demogorgon, and Lear: A Note on the Source of *Prometheus Unbound* III.i.19," *Serif*, 8 (Sept. 1971), 11–13.

Finds source of Shelley's "the terror of the earth" in *King Lear* II.iv.284, "The terrors of the earth," and argues that Shelley intended the word "Demogorgon" to translate the former phrase.

634. Hoff, Peter S. "The Voices of *Crotchet Castle*," *Journal of Narrative Technique*, 2 (Sept. 1972), 186–198.‡

On the personas in Peacock's novel.

635. Hollis, Patricia. *The Pauper Press: A Study in Working-Class Radicalism of the 1830's*. London: Oxford Univ., 1970.

Hollis relates that Hetherington, a radical printer and bookseller, stocked the works of Shelley, along with Paine and Voltaire, in his shop.

Rev. in **English Historical Review*, 87 (Jan. 1972), 209; by James Hurst in *Science and Society*, 36 (Summer 1972), 242–244.

636. *Howells, C. A. "The Presentation of Emotion in the English Gothic Novels of the Late Eighteenth and Early Nineteenth Centuries, with Particular References to Ann Radcliffe's *Mysteries of Udolpho*, M. G. Lewis' *Monk*, Mary Shelley's *Frankenstein*, C. R. Maturin's *Melmoth the Wanderer*, Charlotte Brontë's *Jane Eyre*, and Works by the Minor Minerva Press Novelists Regina Maria Roche and Mary Anne Radcliffe." (Doctoral dissertation, London Univ., 1969.)

637. Hughes, Dean Thomas. "Romance and Psychological Realism in William Godwin's Novels" [Doctoral dissertation, Washington, 1972], DAI, 33 (Nov. 1972), 2330-A.

638. Irving, Washington. *Journals and Notebooks*. Vol. III: *1819–1827*. Ed. Walter A. Reichart. Madison, Milwaukee, London: Univ. of Wisconsin, 1970.

There are many references to Thomas Medwin, Shelley's relation and a friend of Irving, and some to Byron, Shelley, and Mary Shelley.

639. Jack, Ian. "Thomas Love Peacock: The Romantics' Aristophanes," CLSB, No. 207 (July 1970), pp. 655–656.

A brief biographical sketch.

640. *James, Henry Rosher. *Mary Wollstonecraft: A Sketch*. New York: Haskell House, 1971.

Reprint of a 1932 book.

641. Johnson, Betty F. "Shelley's *Cenci* and *Mrs. Warren's Profession*," *Shaw Review*, 15 (Jan. 1972), 26–34.

Traces a hitherto unnoticed relationship between the two plays.

642. Johnson, Diane. *The True History of the First Mrs. Meredith and Other Lesser Lives*. New York: Knopf, 1972.

Mary Ellen Meredith was the daughter of Thomas Love Peacock. Includes references to Harriet Shelley, Mary Shelley, and Shelley.

Rev. by S. R. Rounds in LJ, 97 (Aug. 1972), 2576; by V. S. Pritchett in NYRB, 2 Nov. 1972, pp. 8–11; in **New Republic*, 167 (11 Nov. 1972), 29; by *Phoebe Adams in *Atlantic*, 230 (Nov. 1972), 130; in **New Yorker*, 48 (16 Dec. 1972), 150; in *NYT, 31 Dec. 1972, p. 19.

643. *Jones, Beryl. "Shelley a Chymru" ["Shelley and Wales"], *Y Genhinen* [*The Leek*], 22 (Winter 1972), 29–30.

A review-article. See No. 782.

644. *Joukovsky, N. A. "A Critical Edition of Thomas Love Peacock's *Headlong Hall* and *Nightmare Abbey*, with Some Material for a Critical Edition of *Melincourt*." (Doctoral dissertation, Oxford, 1971.)

645. Juroe, James Glickson. "*St. Leon: A Tale of the Sixteenth Century* by William Godwin. A Critical and Annotated Edition" [Doctoral dissertation, Nebraska, 1971], DAI, 32 (Jan. 1972), 3954-A.

646. Justus, James H. "Arthur Mervyn, American," AL, 42 (Nov. 1970), 304–324.

A few references to the Godwinian beliefs of Charles Brockden Brown's hero.

647. Kiely, Robert. *The Romantic Novel in England.* Cambridge, Mass.: Harvard Univ., 1972.

Offers analyses of Godwin's *Caleb Williams*, Peacock's *Nightmare Abbey* and Mary Shelley's *Frankenstein*.

648. King-Hele, Desmond. *Shelley: His Thought and Work.* Second Edition. See K-SJ, 20 (1971), No. 851.

Rev. in *LJ, 97 (1 Jan. 1972), 61; by Neville Rogers in MLR, 67 (July 1972), 622–623; in *Choice*, 9 (July–Aug. 1972), 646. Also see Nos. 144, 562.

649. *Kramnick, Isaac. "On Anarchism and the Real World: William Godwin and Radical England," *American Political Science Review*, 66 (1972), 114–128.

650. Labelle, Maurice M. "Artaud's Use of Shelley's *The Cenci*: The Experiment in the 'Théâtre de la Cruauté,' " RLC, 46 (Jan.–Mar. 1972), 128–134.

Discusses the differences between Shelley's play and Artaud's. Shelley was "far more concerned with instructing the audience than Artaud."

651. LeBourgeois, John Y. "Some Unpublished Letters of Swinburne," N&Q, 217 (July 1972), 255–263.

Some references to Shelley in letters to Bertram Dobell.

652. Lees, Daniel Edward. "Shelley's Literary Reputation: 1950–1970" [Doctoral dissertation, Pennsylvania State, 1970], DAI, 32 (Aug. 1971), 923-A–924-A.

653. "Lerici 1972," KSMB, 23 (1972), vi–vii.

Description of a memorial weekend (8–10 July 1972) commemorating the 150th anniversary of Shelley's death.

654. Leslie, Margaret. "Mysticism Misunderstood: David Hartley and the Idea of Progress," JHI, 33 (Oct.–Dec. 1972), 625–632.

Refutes the common view that Hartley believed in the material progress of mankind, thus removing him as an antecedent of Helvetius, Godwin, and Priestley.

655. Levin, Beatrice. "Ghosts from an Enchanter Fleeing," *Ball State University Forum*, 12 (Summer 1971), 3–11.

A short story about a girl named after Shelley.

656. Lewis, C. S. *Selected Literary Essays, by C. S. Lewis.* Ed. Walter Hooper. See K-SJ, 20 (1971), No. 864.

Rev. by Henry Noel in *New Catholic World*, No. 1276 (July 1971), pp. 202–203.

657. Leyda, Seraphia DeVille. "*The Serpent Is Shut Out from Paradise*": *A Revaluation of Romantic Love in Shelley.* Salzburg: Univ. of Salzburg, 1972. "Salzburg Studies in English: Romantic Reassessment Series, No. 4."

Reprint of a dissertation. See K-SJ, 17 (1968), No. 531.

658. Lohf, Kenneth A. "Our Growing Collections," *Columbia Library Columns*, 21 (May 1972), 38.

Columbia receives gift of Godwin's *Deloraine*, 3 vols. (London 1833).

659. Ludlam, F. H. "The Meteorology of Shelley's Ode," TLS, 1 Sept. 1972, pp. 1015–16.

Reviews the controversy over Shelley's scientific accuracy in "Ode to the West Wind."

Reply by Desmond King-Hele and Peter Bradshaw, 22 Sept. 1972, p. 1105, and rejoinder by Ludlam, 29 Sept. 1972, p. 1157.

660. Lundin, Jon. "T. L. Beddoes at Göttingen," *Studia Neophilologica*, 43, No. 2 (1971), 484–499.

Beddoes' interest in science is compared to Shelley's.

661. Luria, Gina M. "Mary Hays: A Critical Biography" [Doctoral dissertation, New York Univ., 1972], DAI, 33 (Dec. 1972), 2898-A.

An examination of the life and work of

the feminist, with consideration of her relationship with Mary Wollstonecraft and William Godwin.

662. McGann, Jerome J. " 'Ave Atque Vale': An Introduction to Swinburne," *Victorian Poetry*, 9 (Spring–Summer 1971), 145–163.†‡

Shelley's *Adonais* is compared to Swinburne's poem.

663. McGann, Jerome J. "The Beauty of the Medusa: A Study in Romantic Literary Iconology," SIR, 11 (Winter 1972), 3–25.†

Discusses Shelley's "On the Medusa of Leonardo da Vinci in the Florentine Gallery," rebutting Mario Praz's contention that it represents the decadent fascination of the Romantics with horrible things. Rather, "Shelley's Medusa seeks to terrorize whatever in the observer is still committed to evil and to invigorate in him everything that strives for life."

664. McHaney, Thomas L. "An Early 19th Century Literary Agent: James Lawson of New York," *PBSA*, 64 (Apr.–June 1970), 177–192.

Lawson was acquainted with Thomas Colley Grattan, who was a friend of Thomas Medwin.

665. M[acksey]., R[ichard]. "In Memoriam: Earl Reeves Wasserman," MLN, 87 (Dec. 1972), 1013–1014.

In this tribute, Wasserman's works on Keats and Shelley are mentioned.

666. McNiece, Gerald. *Shelley and the Revolutionary Idea.* See K-SJ, 20 (1971), No. 872.

Rev. by Joan Rees in RES, 22 (Aug. 1971), 360–362; by Gerald Enscoe in ELN, 9 (Mar. 1972), 216–220; in *MP, 69 (May 1972), 358.

667. McQuade, Donald Anthony. "I. The Dramatic Functions of an Epilogue: A Study of the Final Speech of *The Tempest.* II. Convergences of Style: A Study of the Affinities Between Robert Frost and Ralph Waldo Emerson. III. The Exhausted Muse: Shelley's Imagination of Poetry" [Doctoral dissertation, Rutgers, 1972], DAI, 32 (June 1972), 6936-A–6937-A.

668. McSweeney, Kerry. "Swinburne's 'Thalassius,' " *Humanities Association Bulletin* (Canada), 22 (Winter 1971), 50–55.

Notes that "Thalassius" is "an allegory of the poet's soul in the manner of Shelley's 'Alastor' and Keats's 'Endymion.' "

669. McTaggart, William J. "The Design and Unity of Shelley's *Alastor* volume," KSMB, 23 (1972), 10–29.

The poems in this volume support the main idea of the title poem, that "the business of the poet . . . is to accept change on earth in all aspects of life, while remaining constantly aware of the immutability of the world of reality. . . ."

670. *Madden, J. L. "The Thought of Thomas Love Peacock: A Study of His Philosophical, Political, Social and Aesthetic Ideas." (Doctoral dissertation, Leicester, 1971.)

671. *Madigan, Francis V. "A Mirror of Shelley in Whitman," *Greyfriar*, 11 (1971), 3–19.

672. Massey, Irving. "Shelley's 'Dirge for the Year': The Relation of the Holograph to the First Edition," *Costerus*, 4 (1972), 99–104.

The substantial differences between Shelley's MS and the version in *Posthumous Poems* (1824), edited by Mary Shelley, raise questions about the relative contributions of the poet and the editor to the printed version.

673. *Matos, Hernandez Victor. "Proyección de la obra de Calderón en el mundo poético de Shelley." ["The Influence of the Work of Calderón on the Poetic World of Shelley."] (Doctoral dissertation, Madrid, 1971.)

674. Mattheisen, Paul F. "Uproar in the Echo: The Existential Aesthetic of Browning's *The Ring and the Book*," *Literary Monographs*, 3 (1970), 125–184, 216–221.

Browning's *Essay on Shelley* is discussed at length.

675. *Mays, Milton A. "*Frankenstein*, Mary Shelley's Black Theodicy," in *SF: The Other Side of Realism—Essays on Modern Fantasy and Science Fiction*, ed. Thomas Clareson (Bowling Green, Ohio: Bowling Green Univ. Popular Press, 1971), pp. 171–180.

Reprint of an article. See K-SJ, 19 (1970), No. 345.

676. "A Memorial to Shelley in Italy," CLSB, No. 216 (Oct. 1972), pp. 3–4.

Account of the ceremonies on the 150th Anniversary of Shelley's death at Casa Magni.

677. Mendel, Sydney. "Dissociation of Sensibility," *Dalhousie Review*, 51 (Summer 1971), 218–227.

Sees the loss of contact between head and heart as the predicament of modern man and attacks Godwin's emphasis on abstract reason.

678. Merritt, H. C. "Shelley's Influence on Yeats," *Yearbook of English Studies*, 1 (1971), 175–184.

Yeats's development from optimism to disillusion is traced through his changing attitudes to Shelley.

679. *Mikirtumova, E. "Pevec mira, svobody, bor'by" ["Singer of the Universe, Liberty, Struggle"], *Literaturnyj Azerbajdžan* (Baku), No. 8 (1972), pp. 140–143.

On Shelley.

680. Monteiro, George. "Edgar Poe and the New Knowledge," *Southern Literary Journal*, 4 (Spring 1972), 34–40.

Sees Poe's "Sonnet—To Science" in the tradition of the "success-in-failure" Romantic poem such as Shelley's "Ode to the West Wind."

681. Murry, John Middleton. *Heroes of Thought*. Freeport, N.Y.: Books for Libraries, 1971. "Essay Index Reprint Series."

Reprint of a 1938 book, which contains essays on Shelley, "Means and Ends," and Godwin, "The Independents' Dream."

682. Myers, Mitzi. "Godwin's Changing Conception of *Caleb Williams*," SEL, 12 (Autumn 1972), 591–628.†‡

Godwin's view of character and "morally ambivalent relationships" evolved during the actual composition of the book, which must not be isolated from his philosophical works.

683. Nethercot, Arthur H. "Who *Was* Eugene Marchbanks?" *Shaw Review*, 15 (Jan. 1972), 2–20.

Argues that Shelley was the chief model for Shaw's Eugene Marchbanks.

684. *Neupokoeva, I. "Perec svobody. K 150-letiju so dnja smerti anglijskogo poeta Persi Biši Šelli" ["Songs of Liberty. For the 150th Anniversary of the Death of the English Poet Percy Bysshe Shelley"], *Liternaturnaya Gazeyta*, No. 30 (26 July 1972), p. 15.

685. "News & Comment," BC, 20 (Summer 1971), 236.

Sale of Shelley's *Oedipus Tyrannus* (1820) for £4800, *Adonais* (1821), £2400, and *An Address to the Irish People* (1812), £1300; sale of Keats's own advance copy of *Endymion*, with four autograph corrections, for £6200.

686. *Nikol'skaja, L. I. "Iz istorii perevodov Šelli v Rossii" ["From the History of the Translation of Shelley into Russian"], *Russkaya Literatura*, No. 4 (1972), pp. 149–161.

Analysis of translations of "Ode to the West Wind," "Ozymandias," and excerpts from *Queen Mab*.

687. *Nikol'skaja, L. I. *Šelli v Rossii*. [*Shelley in Russia*.] Smolensk: Smolenskovj Gosudarstvennyj Pedagagičeskij Institut imeni K. Marksa, 1972. "Vzaimosvjazi literatur i problem perevoda." ["Interrelations of Literary and Translators' Problems."]

A textbook for philological students in special courses, which deals with the history of Russian translation of Shelley's lyrics. The analysis of the translations is concerned with the interrelations of the literary material, the art of translation, and the historical context of both.

688. Nixon, Edna. *Mary Wollstonecraft: Her Life and Times*. See K-SJ, 20 (1971), No. 896.

Rev. by Nancy Allum in *Books and Bookmen*, 17 (Feb. 1972), 76, 78; by Jane Aiken Hodge in *History Today*, 22 (Feb. 1972), 151–152; in TLS, 7 Apr. 1972, p. 388.

689. *Ogawa, Kazuo. "Destroyer and Preserver," *Eigo Seinen: Rising Generation* (Tokyo), 117 (1971), 2–5, 70–73, 139–142, 194–197, 268–271, 346–349. [In Japanese.]

690. *Oliver, R. C. B. "The Shelleys and Radnorshire," *Radnorshire Society Transactions*, 41 (1971), 8–21.

Shelley's uncle Thomas Grove had an estate in Radnorshire. Presumably the article concerns the frequent visits of the Shelleys.

691. Oras, Ants. "Notes on Introspection and Self-Analysis, Their Function and Imaginal Representation in Shelley," *Neuphilologische Mitteilungen*, 73 (June 1972), 275–283.

When inspired, Shelley transcends and obliterates his sense of self; when inspiration flags he is forced to introspection, and the image of self he sees is one of vulnerability. Oras contrasts this with Wordsworth's introspection, and to a lesser extent with Keats's.

692. Orel, Harold. "Shelley's *The Revolt of Islam*: the Last Great Poem of the English Enlightenment?" *Studies on Voltaire and the Eighteenth Century*, 89 (1972), 1187–1207.

Traces the development of Shelley's views on the reformation of society, seeing *The Revolt of Islam* as a transitional work in which, despite doubts, Shelley portrays the Enlightenment view that the power of human reason can lead to the establishment of the reign of love.

693. Ozolins, Aija. "The Novels of Mary Shelley: From *Frankenstein* to *Falkner*" [Doctoral dissertation, Maryland, 1972], DAI, 33 (Nov. 1972), 2389-A.

694. Palacio, Jean de. *Mary Shelley dans son oeuvre: Contributions aux études shelleyennes.* See K-SJ, 20 (1971), No. 899.

Rev. by *R. Las Vergnas in *Les Nouvelles Littéraires*, 24 (Dec. 1970); in **New French Books* (Second Quarter 1971), column 458; by *Marius Perrin in *Revue Belge de Philologie et d'Histoire*, 49, No. 4 (1971), 1418–1419; by *A. J. Farmer in *Les Livres*, No. 182 (Mar. 1972), p. 55; by *Simon Jeune in *Revue des Sciences Humaines*, No. 146 (Apr.–June 1972), pp. 322–323; by P. H. Butter in *Yearbook of English Studies*, 2 (1972), 300.

695. *Palacio, Jean de. "Shelley et D'Annunzio: motifs rapportés ou influence créatrice?" in *Le Romantisme anglo-américain: Mélanges offerts à Louis Bonnerot*, [ed. Roger Asselineau, *et al.*] (Paris: Didier, 1971), pp. 181–200.

696. Palmer, Chris. "Facts are Facts: Cobbett's *Rural Rides*," *Critical Review* (Melbourne), No. 15 (1972), pp. 105–112.

Evidently "even Shelley" was shocked at Cobbett's harsh references to Castlereagh after his suicide.

697. *"Paper Boats or the Hydra-Headed Woe," *Trace*, 67 (1968), 27–32.

On Shelley.

698. Parker, Ingrid J. "Landscape Imagery in Shelley's Major Poetry: The Forest and Related Settings" [Doctoral dissertation, New Mexico, 1971], DAI, 32 (May 1972), 6447-A.

699. Patterson, Kent. "A Terrible Beauty: Medusa in Three Victorian Poets," *Tennessee Studies in Literature*, 17 (1972), 111–120.

Comments on Shelley's "On the Medusa of Leonardo da Vinci in the Florentine Gallery." "In Shelley's hands, the Medusa becomes a symbol for the romantic aesthetic doctrine that the truly beautiful contains an element of the terrible."

700. *Peacock, Thomas Love. *Nightmare Abbey, The Misfortunes of Elphin, Crotchet Castle.* Ed. with Introduction and Notes by Charles B. Dodson. New York: Holt, Rinehart and Winston, 1971. Paperback.

Rev. in *Choice*, 9 (July–Aug. 1972), 647.

701. *Pearce, D. "The Riddle of Shelley's Cloud," *Yale Review*, 62 (Dec. 1972), 202–220.

702. Peart, Barbara. "Shelley and Shaw's Prose," *Shaw Review*, 15 (Jan. 1972), 39–45.

Discusses Shelley's considerable influence on Shaw's essays and prefaces to plays.

703. Peck, Mary Alice. "The Drama of Shelley and Browning: A Comparative Study" [Doctoral dissertation, Miami Univ., 1970], DAI, 32 (July 1971), 395-A.

704. Pénigault-Duhet, P. M. "Du Nouveau sur Mary Wollstonecraft: l'Oeuvre Littéraire de George Imlay," EA, 24 (July–Sept. 1971), 298–303.

Suggests that Helen Maria Williams, not Mary Wollstonecraft as suggested by Robert R. Hare (see K-SJ, 14 [1965], No. 407), collaborated with Imlay on *A*

Topographical Description of the Western Territory of North America.

705. "Personalia," *British Studies Monitor*, 2 (Spring 1972), 65–66.

Alice Fredman's critical biography of Mary Shelley is "progressing well."

706. Peterson, Carrol David. "The Development of William Godwin's Thought After 1793" [Doctoral dissertation, Arkansas, 1972], DAI, 33 (Nov. 1972), 2339-A.

707. Peterson, William S., and Fred L. Standley. "The J. S. Mill Marginalia in Robert Browning's *Pauline*: A History and Transcription," *PBSA*, 66 (Apr.–June 1972), 135–170.

This copy of *Pauline* contains not only Mill's annotations but Browning's replies to them. In one reply Browning explains that lines 141–143 refer to the late acknowledgment of Shelley's genius.

708. Pixton, William H. "Shelley's Commands to the West Wind," *South Atlantic Bulletin*, 37 (Nov. 1972), 70–73.

On the transition from supplication to command in the last eighteen lines of "Ode to the West Wind."

709. Platzner, Robert Leonard. "The Metaphysical Novel in England: The Romantic Phase" [Doctoral dissertation, Rochester, 1972], DAI, 33 (Nov. 1972), 2390-A.

Includes Mary Shelley's *Frankenstein* and M. G. Lewis' *The Monk.*

710. "The Poet of the Future," *Times* (London), 29 Apr. 1972, p. 8.

Prints extracts from Christopher Small's *Ariel Like a Harpy* (see No. 755).

711. "A Poetic Touch of the Present," *Times* (London), 6 July 1972, p. 11.

A notice of John Elliot's biographical drama about Shelley on BBC television marking the poet's 150th anniversary.

712. Pollin, Burton R. *Discoveries in Poe.* See K-SJ, 20 (1971), No. 907.

Rev. by *B. C. Bach in LJ, 95 (July 1970), 2480; in TLS, 22 Jan. 1971, p. 95; in *AL, 43 (Mar. 1971), 150; by S. L. Varnado in *Thought*, 46 (Spring 1971), 127–129; in *Choice*, 8 (Oct. 1971), 1020; by Joseph M. Flora in *Studies in Short Fiction*, 9 (Spring 1972), 211; in *RES, 23 (Nov. 1972), 530.

713. Pollin, Burton R. *Godwin Criticism: A Synoptic Bibliography.* See K-SJ, 18 (1969), No. 624, 19 (1970), No. 357, 20 (1971), No. 909.

Rev. by Johan Gerritsen in ES, 53 (Apr. 1972), 189; by Hans-Joachim Lang in *Anglia*, 90, No. 2 (1972), 249–251.

714. Pollin, Burton R. "Mary Hays on Women's Rights in the *Monthly Magazine*," EA, 24 (July–Sept. 1971), 271–282.

Pollin argues that the anonymous contributor to this controversy of 1796–97 is Mary Hays. Frequent mention of Mary Wollstonecraft and Godwin.

715. Pollin, Burton R. "The Significance of Names in the Fiction of William Godwin," *Revue des Langues Vivantes*, 37, No. 4 (1971), 388–399.†

The names are borrowed widely from history, literature, biography, and persons of Godwin's acquaintance.

716. "Publication Projects," *British Studies Monitor*, 1 (Summer 1970), 43.

Describes The Carl H. Pforzheimer Library's *Shelley and His Circle, 1773–1822* project.

717. Raine, Kathleen. *Defending Ancient Springs.* See K-SJ, 18 (1969), No. 632, 19 (1970), No. 364, 20 (1971), No. 914.

Rev. by Ants Oras in SR, 80 (Jan.–Mar. 1972), 200–211.†

718. Raisor, Philip. "The Failure of Browning's Childe Roland," *Tennessee Studies in Literature*, 17 (1972), 99–110.

Childe Roland reflects Browning's view of Shelley's character as expressed in his *An Essay on Shelley.*

719. Raitt, A. W. *Prosper Mérimée.* See K-SJ, 20 (1971), No. 915.

Rev. in **American Historical Review*, 77 (Feb. 1972), 157; by Spire Pitou in *Thought*, 47 (Spring 1972), 137–139.

720. Rasulis, Norman Alan. "Dreams and the Redemptive Vision in Shelley's Major Poetry" [Doctoral dissertation, Michigan State, 1970], DAI, 32 (July 1971), 397-A.

721. "Recent Acquisitions," *Yale University Library Gazette*, 46 (Oct. 1971), 120.

Six letters (1878–1880) from William Michael Rossetti to Trelawny and others concerning Shelley's tomb in Rome are acquired by Yale.

722. Reiman, Donald H. "Editing Shelley,"

in *Editing Texts of the Romantic Period.* Papers Given at the Conference on Editorial Problems, Univ. of Toronto, Nov. 1971, ed. John D. Baird (Toronto: Hakkert, 1972), pp. 27–45.

Describes the editorial principles guiding The Carl H. Pforzheimer Library's *Shelley and His Circle* series, and assesses recent editorial work on Shelley and Byron.

723. Reiman, Donald H. *Percy Bysshe Shelley.* See K-SJ, 19 (1970), No. 367, 20 (1971), No. 917.

Rev. by Alan Grob in JEGP, 71 (Apr. 1972), 261–263.

724. Reisner, Thomas Andrew. "Shelley's 'Fragment: A Face,' " N&Q, 217 (Mar. 1972), 96–97.†

Finds fragment was inspired by a painting Shelley saw in Bologna and described in a letter.

725. Richards, George. "Thomas Campbell and Shelley's *Queen Mab,*" *American Notes and Queries,* 10 (Sept. 1971), 5–6.

Campbell's *The Pleasures of Hope* "distinctly colors the style" of *Queen Mab.*

726. Ritter, Alan. "Anarchism and Liberal Theory in the Nineteenth Century," *Bucknell Review,* 19 (Fall 1971), 37–66.

Both liberals and anarchists recognize a need for a cohesive force in social relations, but liberals would rely on government and law, whereas anarchists would rely on social pressure. Godwin, representing the anarchist position, is discussed throughout.

727. *Ritz, Jean-Georges. "Le dynamisme prophétique de Shelley dans *Prometheus Unbound,*" in *Le Romantisme anglo-américain: Mélanges offerts à Louis Bonnerot,* [ed. Roger Asselineau, *et al.*] (Paris: Didier, 1971), pp. 201–209.

728. Roberts, Walter. "The Osmotic Sap" [Letter], TLS, 9 July 1971, p. 808.

See K-SJ, 20 (1971), No. 809. Roberts provides "the French original by André Chamois" on which the anonymous Cambridge poem about Shelley was based.

729. Robertson, Patricia R. "Shelley and Hawthorne: A Comparison of Imagery and Sensibility," *South Central Bulletin,* 32 (Winter 1972), 233–239.‡

Shelley and Hawthorne "were both visionary poets, whose attitudes toward poetry, life, truth, and reality were similar." Robertson discusses specific images and themes common to the two writers and concludes that "it is probable that Shelley influenced young Hawthorne even more than he was aware."

730. Roemer, Donald. "William Godwin's *Caleb Williams*: The Idealogue as Novelist" [Doctoral dissertation, Brandeis, 1971], DAI, 32 (Nov. 1971), 2705-A–2706-A.

731. Rogers, Neville. "Address by Dr. Neville Rogers (8 June 1972)," KSMB, 23 (1972), viii–x.

Centers on Shelley, the man and the poet.

732. Rogers, Neville. "The Editing of Shelley's Manuscripts," KSMB, 23 (1972), 44–53.

Opposes those who dismiss emended texts as too subjective. The label "Fundamentalist" is used pejoratively to describe the scholarly tendency to substitute "uncritical copying" for "critical reading."

733. *Rudolf, G. "Zur Psychologie der Horrorliteratur. Schizoides Körpererleben am Beispiel von Frankensteins Monster" ["Psychology of Horror Literature: Schizoid Body Experience on the Example of Frankenstein's Monster"], *Zeitschrift fur Psychsomatische Medizin und Psychoanalyse* (Göttingen), 18 (July–Sept. 1972), 205–219.

734. *Ruff, James Lynn. *Shelley's "The Revolt of Islam."* Salzburg: Univ. of Salzburg, 1972. "Salzburg Studies in English: Romantic Reassessment Series, No. 10."

Revision of a dissertation. See K-SJ, 19 (1970), No. 373.

735. *Saha, Kshetra Lal, *et al.* "Indian Study of English Poets: Shelley," *Indian Philosophy and Culture,* 15, No. 3 (1970), 18–23; 16, No. 1 (1971), 53–65.

736. Cancelled.

737. Schaubert, Else von. *Shelleys Tragödie "The Cenci" und Marlowes Doppeldrama "Tamburlaine."* See K-SJ, 16 (1967), No. 447, 18 (1969), No. 649.

Rev. by Robert Fricker in *Anglia,* 88, No. 1 (1970), 148–149.

738. Schilling, Hanna-Beate. "The Role of the Brothers Schlegel in American Literary Criticism as Found in Selected Periodicals, 1812–1833: A Critical Bibliography," AL, 43 (Jan. 1972), 563–579.
Includes articles by Godwin and Hazlitt which mention the Schlegels.

739. Schwartz, Lewis M. "Arthur Brooke, 'The Revolt of Islam' and the 'Man of Kent,' " N&Q, 216 (Oct. 1971), 379–380.†
Attributes an anonymous review of Shelley's poem (formerly attributed to Leigh Hunt) to John Chalk Claris, who wrote under the name "Arthur Brooke."

740. Scriven, Harvey. "An Unpublished Shelley Cheque," KSMB, 23 (1972), 38–39.
"The cheque now printed is a hitherto unpublished one," apparently intended to cover advertising expenses for *The Revolt of Islam*.

741. *Scudder, Vida Dutton. *The Life of the Spirit in the Modern English Poets*. Freeport, N.Y.: Books for Libraries, 1972.
Reprint of an 1895 work. Considerable discussion of Shelley, some of Byron and Keats.

742. "Sea Pilgrimage," *Times* (London), 8 July 1972, p. 5.
A wreath was thrown into the sea near Lerici, Italy, in memory of Shelley's death. A follow-up item appeared in the issue of 10 July 1972, p. 1.

743. *Sharp, Anthony. *Nightmare Abbey by Thomas Love Peacock*. Lexington, Mass.: Ginn, 1971.
A dramatization of Peacock's novel.

744. *Sharp, William. *Life of Percy Bysshe Shelley*. Port Washington, N.Y., and London: Kennikat, 1972.
Reprint of an 1887 work.

745. Shaw, George Bernard. "Art Corner," *Shaw Review*, 15 (Jan. 1972), 35–38.
Reprint of Shaw's review of Shelley's *The Cenci*.

746. Shaw, George Bernard. "Shaming the Devil about Shelley" [Excerpt], *Shaw Review*, 15 (Jan. 1972), 34.
Reprinted from *Albermarle Review*, Sept. 1892.

747. *Shelley, Mary Wollstonecraft. *Frankenstein*. [Trans.] Friedrich Polakovics. [Afterword by] Hermann Ebeling. Hamburg, Stuttgart, Munich: Deutscher Bücherbund, 1972.

748. *Shelley, Mary Wollstonecraft. *Frankenstein oder Der neue Prometheus*. [Trans.] Friedrich Polakovics. [Afterword by] Hermann Ebeling. Munich: Deutscher Taschenbuch, 1972.

749. *Shelley, Mary Wollstonecraft. *Frankenstein*. [Trans.] Raymonde de Gans. Geneva: Editions de la Hardière, 1968. [In French.]

750. "Shelley Museum in Italy to Be Enlarged," *Times* (London), 20 July 1972, p. 5.
An appeal to turn Casa Magni into a museum.

751. *Shirai, Atsushi. "The Position of Mary Wollstonecraft in the History of Feminist Thought," *Mita Gakkai Zasshi*, 62 (1969), 22–52. [In Japanese.]

752. Silverman, Edwin B. *Poetic Synthesis in Shelley's "Adonais."* The Hague and Paris: Mouton, 1972. "De Proprietatibus Litterarum. Series Practica, 36."

753. *Singh, Sheila Uttam. *Shelley and the Dramatic Form*. Salzburg: Univ. of Salzburg, 1972. "Salzburg Studies in English: Romantic Reassessment Series, No. 1."
Reprint of a dissertation.

754. Slater, John Frederick, "Edward Garnett: The 'Splendid Advocate,' 'Volpone' and 'Antony and Cleopatra': The Play of Imagination, Self-Concealment and Self-Revelation in Shelley's 'Epipsychidion' " [Doctoral dissertation, Rutgers, 1971], DAI, 32 (Dec. 1971), 3332-A–3333-A.

755. Small, Christopher. *Ariel Like a Harpy: Shelley, Mary and Frankenstein*. London: Gollancz, 1972.
Rev. by Graham Martin in Spec, 20 May 1972, pp. 773–774; in **Observer*, 21 May 1972, p. 37; in **Guardian Weekly*, 106 (3 June 1972), 22; by Piers Brendon in *Books and Bookmen*, 17 (Aug. 1972), 87.

756. *Solomon, Petre. "Shelley sau pasiunea ideilor" ["Shelley or the Passion for Ideas"], *Luceafărul* (Bucharest), 8 (July 1972), 7.

757. *Spark, Muriel, and Derek Stanford, eds. *My Best Mary: The Selected Letters of*

Mary Wollstonecraft Shelley. Folcroft, Pa.: Folcroft, 1972.

Reprint of the 1953 edition. See K-SJ, 3 (1954), No. 238, 4 (1955), No. 272, 10 (1961), No. 450.

758. Staves, Susan. "Don Quixote in Eighteenth-Century England," CL, 24 (Summer 1972), 193–215.

An example discussed is *The Infernal Quixote* by Charles Lucas (1800), a piece of anti-radical propaganda in the form of a novel. The satanic villain, Marauder, quotes and alludes to Godwin and Mary Wollstonecraft. The conception of Don Quixote as a sensitive romantic hero was developed in the novels of Mrs. Charlotte Smith, a friend of Godwin.

759. *Stephens, Sir Leslie. *Hours in a Library*. 4 vols. St. Clair Shores, Mich.: Scholarly, 1968.

Reprint of the 1904 edition. Contains essays on Hazlitt, Godwin, and Shelley.

760. Tausky, Thomas Edward. " 'To Rake the Moon From Out the Sea': Ideal Worlds in the Fiction of Thomas Love Peacock" [Doctoral dissertation, Yale, 1971], DAI, 32 (Jan. 1972), 3967-A.

761. *Tedford, Barbara W. "A Recipe for Satire and Civilization," *Costerus*, 2 (1972), 197–212.

Concerns Peacock.

762. *Thomson, James. *Biographical and Critical Studies*. Freeport, N.Y.: Books for Libraries, 1972. "Essay Index Reprint Series."

Reprint of an 1896 work, which includes three essays on Shelley.

763. Tillman-Hill, Iris. "Hardy's Skylark and Shelley's," *Victorian Poetry*, 10 (Spring 1972), 79–83.†

Hardy's "Shelley's Skylark" expresses the ambivalent feeling that the natural bird, which is Shelley's inspiration, is ordinary and mundane but that Shelley's extraordinary perception of the bird in "To a Skylark" is "self-justifying as well as immortal."

764. Tims, Margaret. "The Rights of Men—And Women," *Aryan Path*, 43 (Feb. 1972), 63–68.

On Mary Wollstonecraft, who advocated "not an equality of women with men" but "a search towards a supra-feminine and supra-masculine humanism, in which the self-interest of each is subordinated to a greater whole."

765. Tomkievicz, Shirley. "The First Feminist," *Horizon*, 14 (Spring 1972), 114–119.

General summary of Mary Wollstonecraft's life and works with references to Mary and Percy Shelley.

766. *Tótfalusi, István. *Shelley világa*. [*The World of Shelley*.] Budapest: Európa, 1971.

767. Turner, Justin G. " 'The Cenci': Shelley vs. the Truth," ABC, 22 (Feb. 1972), 5–9.

Compares Shelley's version (based on a biased account) to the actual events, and concludes that "a true and unbiased account of the Cenci and their associates would not have enlisted the sensitive Shelley's interest."

768. VanArsdel, Rosemary T. "The *Westminster Review*: Change of Editorship, 1840," *Studies in Bibliography*, 25 (1972), 191–204.

Mentions Peacock's introduction of Henry Cole to the Benthamite circle of liberals in the late 1820's.

769. Vaughan, Percy. *Early Shelley Pamphlets*. New York: Haskell House, 1972.

Reprint of a 1905 book on Shelley's early pamphlets.

770. *[Versek, Irta.] "E. Guillevic, Shelley, P. B., és Vasko Popa. Forditotta: Somlyó György, Bácski György" ["E. Guillevic, P. B. Shelley, and Vasko Popa, Translated by György Somlyó and György Bácski"], *Müvelödés*, 25 (June 1972).

771. Viebrock, Helmut. *Wer Ist Demogorgon? Versuch Einer Deutung von Shelleys "Prometheus Unbound*." Wiesbaden: Steiner, 1971. "Sitzungsberichte der Wissenschaftlichen Gesellschaft an der Johann Wolfgang Goethe-Universität Frankfurt am Main, 9, No. 4 (1970)."

772. Viswanathan, S. "Antiphonal Patterns in Shelley's 'Ode to the West Wind,' " *Papers on Language and Literature*, 8 (Summer 1972), 307–311.†‡

Finds "similarities of structure and motif as well as of tone and movement between Shelley's 'Ode to the West Wind' and the liturgical antiphons, especially the Greater and the Monastic O's. . . ."

773. Walling, William A. *Mary Shelley*. New York: Twayne, 1972. "Twayne English Authors Series, 128."

774. Walmsley, Robert. *Peterloo: The Case Reopened*. See K-SJ, 20 (1971), No. 957.
Rev. by Betty Kemp in *English Historical Review*, 86 (Oct. 1971), 863; by Richard Hawkins in *Historical Journal*, 15 (Sept. 1972), 588–590.

775. *Wardle, J. "Myth and Image in Three Romantics: A Study of Blake, Shelley and Yeats." (Doctoral dissertation, Queen's Univ., Belfast, 1971.)

776. *Warman, Christopher. "A Woman Who Made Room at the Top," *Times* (London), 7 Aug. 1972, p. 5.
On Mary Shelley.

777. Wasserman, Earl R. *Shelley: A Critical Reading*. See K-SJ, 20 (1971), No. 958.
Rev. by Frank P. Riga in LJ, 96 (Aug. 1971), 2510–11; by Gilbert Thomas in *English*, 21 (Spring 1972), 27–29; in VQR, 48 (Spring 1972), lvii; in *Choice*, 9 (May 1972), 372; by Stuart Curran in *Criticism*, 14 (Summer 1972), 295–298; by Gerald McNiece in *Arizona Quarterly*, 28 (Summer 1972), 189–192; by Richard E. Barbieri in *Thought*, 47 (Autumn 1972), 460–461; by S[tuart]. C[urran]. in ELN, 10 Supplement (Sept. 1972), 61; in **Yale Review*, 62 (Oct. 1972), vi; by Timothy Webb in RES, 23 (Nov. 1972), 511–514; by Kenneth Neill Cameron in MLQ, 33 (Dec. 1972), 463–466; by John S. Flagg in SIR, 11 (Winter 1972), 66–70; by *[Kerry McSweeney] in QQ, 79 (1972), 437. Also see Nos. 144, 562.

778. *Waten, Judah. "My two literary careers," *Southerly*, No. 7 (1971), pp. 83–92.
Waten refers to Shelley's influence on him.

779. Webb, Timothy. "Shelley and the Cyclops," KSMB, 23 (1972), 31–37.
Theorizes that Shelley translated Euripides' satyr play, *The Cyclops*, because of his interest "in the mentality of the outcast" who, like the Frankenstein Monster, was rejected by society for the wrong reasons.

780. *Webb, T[imothy]. "Shelley's Verse Translations from the Greek." (Doctoral dissertation, Oxford, 1969.)

781. Weissman, Judith. "Promethean Democracy: Studies in Shelley, Emerson, and Mill" [Doctoral dissertation, California, San Diego, 1972], DAI, 33 (Aug. 1972), 735-A.

782. *Williams, John Ellis. *Lle Bu'r Dwr.* [*Where There Once Had Been Water.*] Llandysul, Wales: Gwasg Gomer, 1970.
Includes discussion of Shelley's ties to Wales, presumably through his relatives the Groves and through his involvement with the Tremadoc Embankment project. See No. 643.

783. *Wollstonecraft, Mary. *Thoughts on the Education of Daughters*. Clifton, N.J.: A. M. Kelley, 1972.
Reprint of 1787 edition.

784. Wright, John W. *Shelley's Myth of Metaphor*. See K-SJ, 20 (1971), No. 969.
Rev. by S[tuart]. C[urran]. in ELN, 9, Supplement (Sept. 1971), 57–58; by Edna L. Steeves in *Georgia Review*, 26 (Summer 1972), 240–241; by P. H. Butter in *Yearbook of English Studies*, 2 (1972), 299.

785. Young, Arthur Paul. "Shelley and Nonviolence" [Doctoral dissertation, Miami Univ., 1971], DAI, 32 (Apr. 1972), 5755-A–5756-A.

786. Young, Kenneth. "The Literature of Politics," *Essays by Divers Hands*, N.S. 37 (1972), 134–152.
Includes a discussion of Shelley's "The Mask of Anarchy."

787. Zanco, Aurelio. *Saggi Inglesi*. Bari, Italy: Adriatica Editrice, 1967. "Biblioteca di Studi Inglesi, Vol. 8."
A collection of previously published essays, which includes: "L' 'Alfierismo' del Byron," pp. 247–267; "Appunti su Shelley," pp. 269–293 (see K-SJ, 4 [1955], No. 278); "*I Cenci* di P. B. Shelley e l'Imitazione di G. B. Niccolini," pp. 295–314.

788. *Zbierski, Henryk. "Metaforyka i kompozycja 'Ody do wiatru zachodniego' P. B. Shelleya" ["Metaphor and Composition in P. B. Shelley's 'Ode to the West Wind' "], *Sprawozdania Poznańskiego Towarzystwa Przyjaciół Nauk 1967*, No. 2 (1969), pp. 200–203.

789. Zimansky, Curt Richard. "This Proper Paradise: A Study of Shelley's Symbolism and Mythology" [Doctoral dissertation, Indiana, 1972], DAI, 33 (Aug. 1972), 771-A.

Alastor, The Revolt of Islam, Prometheus Unbound, and *Adonais* are discussed.

For additional BOOKS AND ARTICLES RELATING TO SHELLEY AND HIS CIRCLE see Nos. 2, 4, 9, 11, 13, 21, 24, 26, 31, 34, 37, 38, 39, 44, 46, 49, 50, 52, 56, 58, 63, 66, 67, 71, 72, 73, 74, 76, 79, 84, 95, 96, 99, 103, 105, 107, 109, 111, 114, 116, 118, 121, 122, 123, 125, 142, 164, 203, 207, 219, 221, 225, 228, 233, 237, 257, 260, 276, 278, 291, 304, 306, 311, 316, 318, 324, 330, 377, 410, 417, 419, 420, 439, 449, 465, 480, 483, 505, 528.

VI. PHONOGRAPH RECORDS

BYRON, KEATS, SHELLEY

790. **John Clare*. Argo ZPL 1166.

Readings of poems and letters.

Rev. by Margaret Willy in *English*, 21 (Autumn 1972), 102.

791. **Letters of the Romantic Poets*. Spoken Arts 1069.

792. **Nineteenth Century English Poetry*. Listening Library 3306.

793. **Nineteenth Century English Poetry*. Spoken Arts 860.

Also on cassette, SAC 7012.

794. **Poems of Byron*. Read by Frank Duncan, Peter Orr, and Richard Johnson. Directed by George Rylands. Argo PLP 1040/344.

Includes "She Walks in Beauty," and selections from *Beppo* and *Childe Harold*.

795. **Poems of Keats*. Read by Tony Church, Derek Godfrey, Richard Johnson, Margaretta Scott, and Gary Watson. Directed by George Rylands. Argo PLP 1043/341.

Includes "The Eve of St. Agnes," "Ode to a Nightingale," "Ode on a Grecian Urn," "Hyperion," and others.

796. **Shelley Treasury*. Spoken Arts 869.

Also on cassette, SAC 8026.

Bibliography for January 1, 1973–December 31, 1974

VOLUMES XXIII–XXV

Compiled by
ROBERT A. HARTLEY
New York, New York

ROBERT M. RYAN
Rutgers University – Camden

with the assistance of Clement Dunbar

THIS bibliography, a regular department of the *Keats-Shelley Journal*, is a register of the literary interest in Keats, Shelley, Byron, Hunt, and their circles from January 1973 through December 1974. We take pleasure in acknowledging our gratitude to the following individuals for their assistance: Hubert F. Babinski (Columbia University), Arthur Efron (S.U.N.Y. – Buffalo), Doucet D. Fischer (The Carl H. Pforzheimer Library), Marsha M. Manns (The Byron Society), Rae Ann Nager (*Keats-Shelley Journal*), Jean de Palacio (Université de Lille), Donald H. Reiman (The Carl H. Pforzheimer Library), Lewis M. Schwartz (Kingsborough Community College – C.U.N.Y.), Carl Woodring (Columbia University), and the library staffs of Columbia University, Lehman College (C.U.N.Y.), Library of Congress, New York Public Library, Rutgers University – Camden, and University of Pennsylvania.

We are especially grateful to Helen Manheim Hartley, who devoted a considerable amount of time to reading the proofs.

Where a book has been issued by more than one publisher during the same year, the publication date appears at the end of the entry within parentheses. Each item that we have not seen is marked by an asterisk. Entries which have been abstracted in *Abstracts of English Studies* are marked with a dagger, but entries in previous bibliographies which were abstracted too late for notice have not been repeated. Entries which have been (or will be) abstracted in *MLA Abstracts* are marked with a double dagger.

ABBREVIATIONS

ABC	American Book Collector
AL	American Literature
AN&Q	American Notes and Queries
ASNS	Archiv für das Studium der neuren Sprachen
AUMLA	Journal of the Australasian Universities Language and Literature Association
BA	Books Abroad
BC	Book Collector
BJ	Byron Journal
BNYPL	Bulletin of the New York Public Library
CE	College English
CL	Comparative Literature
CLB	Charles Lamb Bulletin, *supersedes* C.L.S. Bulletin (Charles Lamb Society)
CR	Contemporary Review
DAI	Dissertation Abstracts International
EA	Etudes anglaises
EC	Essays in Criticism
ELH	Journal of English Literary History
ELN	English Language Notes
ES	English Studies
Exp	Explicator
HLQ	Huntington Library Quarterly
ICS	L'Italia che scrive
ILN	Illustrated London News
JAAC	Journal of Aesthetics and Art Criticism
JEGP	Journal of English and Germanic Philology
JHI	Journal of the History of Ideas
K-SJ	Keats-Shelley Journal
KSMB	Keats-Shelley Memorial Bulletin
LC	Library Chronicle
Li	Listener
LJ	Library Journal
MLN	Modern Language Notes
MLQ	Modern Language Quarterly
MLR	Modern Language Review
MP	Modern Philology
MWN	Mary Wollstonecraft Newsletter, *and successor*, Mary Wollstonecraft Journal
N&Q	Notes and Queries
NS	New Statesman
NYRB	New York Review of Books
NYT	New York Times Book Review
PBSA	Papers of the Bibliographical Society of America
PMLA	Publications of the Modern Language Association of America
PQ	Philological Quarterly
PR	Partisan Review
QQ	Queen's Quarterly
RES	Review of English Studies
RLC	Revue de littérature comparée
SAQ	South Atlantic Quarterly
SatR	Saturday Review
SEL	Studies in English Literature 1500–1900
SIR	Studies in Romanticism
SP	Studies in Philology
Spec	Spectator
SR	Sewanee Review
T&T	Time and Tide
TLS	Times Literary Supplement
UES	Unisa English Studies
UTQ	University of Toronto Quarterly
VQR	Virginia Quarterly Review
WC	Wordsworth Circle

Current Bibliography

I. GENERAL

Current Bibliographies

1. Davies, Phillips G. "A Check List of Poems, 1593 to 1833, Entirely or Partly Written in the Spenserian Stanza," BNYPL, 77 (Spring 1974), 314–328.
   Byron, Godwin, Hunt, Keats, Peacock, Reynolds, and Shelley are on the list.
2. "English Literature, IX: Nineteenth Century," in *1971 MLA International Bibliography: Volume I*, comp. Harrison T. Meserole, Jayne K. Kribbs, *et al.* (1973), 77–97.
3. "English Literature, IX: Nineteenth Century," in *1972 MLA International Bibliography: Volume I*, comp. Harrison T. Meserole, Jayne K. Kribbs, *et al.* (1974), 86–106.
4. Erdman, David V., *et al.* "The Romantic Movement: A Selective and Critical Bibliography for 1972," ELN, 11, Supplement (Sept. 1973), 1–67.
5. Erdman, David V., *et al.* "The Romantic Movement: A Selective and Critical Bibliography for 1973," ELN, 12, Supplement (Sept. 1974), 1–70.
6. Frank, Frederick S. "The Gothic Novel: A Checklist of Modern Criticism," *Bulletin of Bibliography*, 30 (Apr.–June 1973), 45–54.
   Includes Byron, Keats, the Shelleys, Godwin, and Polidori.

6a. Hartley, Robert A., and Lewis M. Schwartz. "Current Bibliography [for July 1971 – Dec. 1972]," K-SJ, 21–22 (1972–73), 1–71.

7. Horden, John, and James B. Misenheimer, Jr., eds. "The Nineteenth Century," *Annual Bibliography of English Language and Literature for 1971*, 46 (1973), 364–515.
8. Knecht, Edgar. "Le myth du Juif errant: Esquisse de bibliographie raisonnée (1600–1844)," *Romantisme*, No. 8 (1974), pp. 103–116.
   In this bibliography of the Wandering Jew myth, works of Shelley and Bryon are included.
9. Ward, William S., comp. *Literary Reviews in British Periodicals, 1798–1820: A Bibliography with a Supplementary List of General (Non-Review) Articles on Literary Subjects*. See K-SJ, 21–22 (1972–73), No. 15.
   Rev. by Carl Woodring in K-SJ, 23 (1974), 141–142; by Leslie A. Marchand in BJ, No. 2 (1974), pp. 54–58. Also see No. 31.
10. Watson, J. R., and J. A. V. Chapple. "The Nineteenth Century," in *Year's Work in English Studies*, ed. Geoffrey Harlow *et al.*, 51 (1972 [for 1970]), 287–338.
11. Watson, J. R., and J. A. V. Chapple. "The Nineteenth Century," in *Year's Work in English Studies*, ed. Geoffrey Harlow *et al.*, 52 (1973 [for 1971]), 288–351.
12. Watson, J. R., B. E. Maidment, and J. A. V. Chapple. "The Nineteenth Century," in *Year's Work in English Studies*, ed. James Redmond *et al.*, 53 (1974 [for 1972]), 296–360.

For additional Current Bibliographies see Nos. 802, 803.

Books and Articles Relating to English Romanticism

13. Abrams, M. H. *Natural Supernaturalism: Tradition and Revolution in Romantic Literature*. See K-SJ, 20 (1971), No. 28; 21–22 (1972–73), No. 18.
    Rev. by P. H. Butter in MLR, 68 (Jan. 1973), 157–159; by Frederick Garber in MLQ, 34 (June 1973), 206–213; by Roger Sharrock in RES, 24 (Aug. 1973), 354–357; by David V. Erdman in ELN, 11, Supplement (Sept. 1973), 12; by Lee Sterrenburg in *Victorian Studies*,

17 (Mar. 1974), 332–334; by Morse Peckham in SIR, 13 (Fall 1974), 359–365.
Also see Nos. 29, 41, 57, 66.

14. Anderson, Erland Gregory. "Harmonious Madness: A Study of Musical Metaphors in the Poetry of Coleridge, Shelley and Keats" [Doctoral dissertation, Univ. of Washington, 1973], DAI, 34 (Jan. 1974), 4185-A.

15. Ardinger, Bruce James. "Reality and Romance: A Survey of English Romantic Verse Satire" [Doctoral dissertation, Kent State, 1974], DAI, 35 (Dec. 1974), 3668-A.

Shelley, Keats, and Hunt are discussed.

16. Asselineau, Roger, *et al.*, eds. *Le romantisme anglo-américain: Mélanges offerts à Louis Bonnerot.* See K-SJ, 21–22 (1972–73), Nos. 79, 345, 462, 548, 695, 727.

Rev. by Alastair Thomson in SIR, 12 (Winter 1973), 461–465; by Peter Genzel in *Zeitschrift für Anglistik und Amerikanistik*, 22, No. 1 (1974), 100–102 [in German].

17. Basa, Enikö Molnár. "*The Tragedy of Man* as an Example of the *Poème d'Humanité*: An Examination of the Poem by Imre Madách with Reference to the Relevant Works of Shelley, Byron, Lamartine and Hugo" [Doctoral dissertation, North Carolina, 1972], DAI, 33 (Feb. 1973), 4398-A.

18. Beaty, Frederick L. *Light from Heaven: Love in British Romantic Literature.* See K-SJ, 20 (1971), No. 39; 21–22 (1972–73), No. 25a.

See No. 29.

19. Bird, Clarence Thomas. "Unacknowledged Legislators: The Image of the Artist in Painting and Literature of the Romantic Era" [Doctoral dissertation, Florida State, 1973], DAI, 34 (Oct. 1973), 1849-A.

20. Bloom, Harold. *The Anxiety of Influence: A Theory of Poetry.* New York: Oxford Univ., 1973.

Numerous references to the Romantics.

Rev. by Reed Whittemore in *New Republic*, 10 Feb. 1973, pp. 36–39; by John Hollander in NYT, 4 Mar. 1973, pp. 27–28, 30; by Geoffrey H. Hartman in *Diacritics*, 3 (Spring 1973), 26–32; by Alison Heinemann in LJ, 98 (15 May 1973), 1583; by David J. Gordon in *Yale Review*, 62 (June 1973), 583–584; by John Hollander in *Poetry*, 122 (Aug. 1973), 298–303; by George Stade in PR, 40, No. 3 (1973), 495–500; by Paul Schwaber in CE, 35 (Oct. 1973), 86–89; by Kerry McSweeney in SIR, 13 (Winter 1974), 84–87; by Fred Moramarco in *Nation*, 218 (20 Apr. 1974), 503–505; by David Newton-DeMolina in *Cambridge Review*, 95 (May 1974), 169–171; by Paul de Man in CL, 26 (Sept. 1974), 269–275; by Daniel Hoffman in *American Scholar*, 43 (Autumn 1974), 658–671; by Sister Bernetta Quinn in *Thought*, 49 (Dec. 1974), 449–450.

21. Bloom, Harold. *The Ringers in the Tower: Studies in Romantic Tradition.* See K-SJ, 20 (1971), No. 45; 21–22 (1972–73), No. 28.

See Nos. 57, 66.

22. Bloom, Harold, and Lionel Trilling, eds. *Oxford Anthology of English Literature: Romantic Poetry and Prose.* New York: Oxford Univ., 1973.

Includes a general introduction, author introductions, introductions to individual works, and annotations.

23. *Borza, Eugene N. "Sentimental Philhellenism and the Image of Greece," in *Classics and the Classical Tradition: Essays Presented to Robert E. Dengler on the Occasion of His Eightieth Birthday*, ed. Eugene N. Borza and Robert W. Carrubba (University Park: Pennsylvania State Univ., 1973), pp. 5–25.

Deals with nineteenth-century English literature.

24. Brisman, Leslie. *Milton's Poetry of Choice and Its Romantic Heirs.* Ithaca: Cornell Univ., 1973.

Considerable material on Keats and Shelley.

Rev. by Herbert E. Shapiro in LJ, 98 (15 Feb. 1973), 546; by Joseph Anthony Wittreich, Jr., in JEGP, 73 (July 1974), 435–439; by David V. Erdman in ELN, 12, Supplement (Sept. 1974), 23.

25. Bullough, Geoffrey. "The Later History of Cockaigne," *Wiener Beiträge zur englischen Philologie*, 75 (1973), 22–35.

Briefly traces the concept of the kingdom of Cockaigne from the early fourteenth century to the modern era, noting Hunt, Keats, Shelley, and Byron.

26. *Caturvedī, S. P. *English Romantic Poets: Wordsworth, Coleridge, Keats, Shelley and Byron*. Bareilly, India: Prakash, 1972.
A critical study.

27. Clatanoff, Doris Ann Risch. "Poetry and Music: Coleridge, Shelley, and Keats and the Musical Milieu of Their Day" [Doctoral dissertation, Nebraska, 1973], DAI, 34 (Nov. 1973), 2551-A.

28. Clay, John D. "English Romantics and the Working Class," *Literature and Ideology*, No. 16 (1973), pp. 67–76.
Romanticism was anti-working class.

29. Clubbe, John. "Romanticism Today," *Mosaic* (Univ. of Manitoba), 7 (Spring 1974), 137–150.
An omnibus review. See Nos. 13, 18, 73.

30. Curnow, Wystan. "Romanticism and Modern American Criticism," SIR, 12 (Fall 1973), 777–799.‡
The attitudes of American literary critics to Keats, Shelley, and Byron are discussed.

31. Curran, Stuart. "Recent Studies in the Nineteenth Century," SEL, 14 (Autumn 1974), 637–668.
An omnibus review. See Nos. 9, 58, 79, 81, 100, 154, 219, 222, 229, 234, 317, 319, 356, 512, 590, 611, 635, 666, 739, 770.

32. Davis, Julie Sydney. "Creatures like Ourselves: The Romantic Criticism of Chaucer" [Doctoral dissertation, Case Western Reserve, 1972], DAI, 33 (Mar. 1973), 5118-A.
The views of Godwin, Hazlitt, and Hunt are examined.

33. Doggett, Frank. "Romanticism's Singing Bird," SEL, 14 (Autumn 1974), 547–561.
Shelley's "To a Skylark" and Keats's "Ode to a Nightingale" are discussed.

34. Donohue, Joseph W., Jr. *Dramatic Character in the English Romantic Age*. See K-SJ, 20 (1971), No. 61; 21–22 (1972–73), No. 48.
Rev. by Franz Zaic in *Anglia*, 91 (1973), 535–536.

35. Durning, Russell E. "Comparative Literature: An Essay in Definition," *Literary Half-Yearly*, 15 (Jan. 1974), 93–113.
Shelley and Keats contributed myth as poetic technique to Romantic poetry; Byron and Scott contributed influence and influence studies to comparative literature.

36. *Dutt, Sukumar. *The Supernatural in English Romantic Poetry, 1780–1830*. Folcroft, Pa.: Folcroft, 1972.
Reprint of the 1938 edition.

37. Eichner, Hans, ed. *"Romantic" and Its Cognates: The European History of a Word*. See K-SJ, 21–22 (1972–73), No. 52.
Rev. by Frank Jordan in QQ, 80 (Winter 1973), 642–643; by Lilian R. Furst in *Yearbook of Comparative and General Literature*, 23 (1974), 97–98; by Giuseppe Galigani in *Rivista di letterature moderne e comparate*, 27 (June 1974), 155–157 [in Italian]. Also see No. 47.

38. Fass, Barbara. *La Belle Dame Sans Merci and the Aesthetics of Romanticism*. Detroit: Wayne State Univ., 1974.
Treats Keats's "Lamia" and Peacock's *Rhododaphne*, and includes many references to Shelley.
Rev. by Alexander Gelley in LJ, 99 (1 June 1974), 1548.

39. Fogle, Richard Harter. "Nathaniel Hawthorne and the Great English Romantic Poets," K-SJ, 21–22 (1972–73), 219–235.‡
Fogle finds that Hawthorne was influenced by all five of the major poets but most frequently by Coleridge and "surprisingly often" by Shelley. Most of the article is concerned with "P's Correspondence," a witty sketch in which Hawthorne, through his protagonist, appraises each of the poets. Fogle finds that Hawthorne is genuinely Romantic in his faith in the imagination as the "organ of insight."

40. Fogle, Richard Harter. *The Permanent Pleasure: Essays on Classics of Romanticism*. Athens: Univ. of Georgia, 1974.
A collection of previously published essays, including "The Imaginal Design of Shelley's 'Ode to the West Wind,' " "Image and Imagelessness: A Limited Reading of *Prometheus Unbound*," "Dante and Shelley's *Adonais*," "Keats's 'Ode to a Nightingale,' " and "Beauty and

Truth: John Middleton Murry on Keats."

Rev. in VQR, 50 (Autumn 1974), cxxiv; in *Choice*, 11 (Nov. 1974), 1306.

41. Fogle, Richard Harter. "Romanticism Reconsidered," SR, 82 (Spring 1974), 383–392.

A review-article. See Nos. 13, 92, 100, 526.

42. Furst, Lilian R. *Romanticism in Perspective: A Comparative Study of Aspects of the Romantic Movements in England, France, and Germany*. See K-SJ, 19 (1970), No. 26; 20 (1971), No. 74; 21–22 (1972–73), No. 62.

Rev. by Rüdiger von Tiedemann in *Arcadia: Zeitschrift für vergleichende Literatur Wissenschaft*, 8, No. 1 (1973), 98–106 [in German].

43. Greene, D. Randolphe. "The Romantic Prometheus: Varieties of the Heroic Quest" [Doctoral dissertation, Wisconsin, 1973], DAI, 35 (July 1974), 403-A.

Discusses Byron and the Shelleys.

44. Grunes, Dennis Scott. "The Romantic Brother" [Doctoral dissertation, State Univ. of New York, Buffalo, 1974], DAI, 35 (Sept. 1974), 1623-A.

The Romantic search for a "soulmate"—an ideal brother or friend—can be seen in the works of Byron and the Shelleys.

45. Grunfeld, Frederic. "The Discovery of the Mediterranean," *Horizon*, 16 (Winter 1974), 97–103.

Byron and Shelley "discovered" it and "made it a focal point of European art, literature, and music."

46. Hagen, William Henry, Jr. "The Metaphysical Implications of Incest in Romantic Literature" [Doctoral dissertation, South Carolina, 1974], DAI, 35 (Oct. 1974), 2222-A.

47. Hamlin, Cyrus. "The Dilemma of Romanticism," UTQ, 44 (Fall 1974), 66–76.

A review-article. See No. 37.

48. *Hancock, Albert E. *The French Revolution and the English Poets: A Study in Historical Criticism*. Port Washington, N.Y.: Kennikat, 1967.

Reprint of the 1899 edition.

49. Hartman, Geoffrey H. *Beyond Formalism: Literary Essays, 1958–1970*. See K-SJ, 20 (1971), No. 83; 21–22 (1972–73), No. 65.

Rev. by Bertel Pedersen in *Arcadia: Zeitschrift für vergleichende Literatur Wissenschaft*, 8, No. 1 (1973), 116–120 [in German].

50. Haworth, Helen E. "'A Milk-White Lamb That Bleats'? Some Stereotypes of Women in Romantic Literature," *Humanities Association Review*, 24 (Fall 1973), 277–293.

Women are depicted as beautiful young virgins, submissive domestic wives, or "fallen" outcasts. Keats's early sonnets illustrate some of the stereotypes, while Byron and Shelley were (with Blake) the only poets who treated women as "fully adult sexual beings." Peacock and Wollstonecraft are also discussed.

51. Haworth, Helen E. "'The Virtuous Romantics': Indecency, Indelicacy, Pornography and Romantic Poetry," *Papers on Language and Literature*, 10 (Summer 1974), 287–306.

The Romantic period was at least as prudish as the Victorian; Romantic critics exhibited extreme puritanism in dealing with the works of Keats, Moore, and Byron. The novel of sensibility is probably responsible for such prudery because it had made fashionable the cultivation of shock and outraged sensitivity.

52. Hayden, John O., ed. *Romantic Bards and British Reviewers: A Selected Edition of Contemporary Reviews of the Works of Wordsworth, Coleridge, Byron, Keats and Shelley*. See K-SJ, 20 (1971), No. 86; 21–22 (1972–73), No. 67.

Rev. by Donald H. Reiman in K-SJ, 21–22 (1972–73), 264–266; by Duane Schneider in CLB, No. 1 (Jan. 1973), pp. 19–27. Also see No. 57.

53. Hayden, John O. *The Romantic Reviewers, 1802–1824: A Study of Literary Reviewing in the Early Nineteenth Century*. See K-SJ, 19 (1970), No. 33; 20 (1971), No. 87; 21–22 (1972–73), No. 68.

Rev. by Duane Schneider in CLB, No. 1 (Jan. 1973), pp. 19–27.

54. Heath, William W., ed. *Major British Poets of the Romantic Period*. New York: Macmillan, 1973.

55. Hibbert, Christopher. *George IV: Regent and King*. Vol. II: *1811–1830*. London: Lane, 1973.
 References to Byron, Hunt, Haydon, Keats, and Shelley.

56. *Hoffmeister, August W. *Die Blume in der Dichtung der englischen Romantik*. Berlin: Selbstverl, 1970.

57. Jackson, J. R. de J. "Some Recent Studies of the Romantic Period," UTQ, 42 (Spring 1973), 289–297.
 An omnibus review. See Nos. 13, 21, 52, 89, 95, 374, 403.

58. Jones, Howard Mumford. *Revolution and Romanticism*. Cambridge: Harvard Univ., 1974.
 Some discussion of Byron and Shelley.
 Rev. by Merrill D. Peterson in VQR, 50 (Summer 1974), 451–456; by Morse Peckham in SIR, 13 (Fall 1974), 359–365. Also see No. 31.

59. Joseph, Gerhard. "Recent Studies in the Nineteenth Century," SEL, 13 (Autumn 1973), 700–729.‡
 An omnibus review. See Nos. 215, 526, 568, 613, 621.

60. Jump, John D. *The Ode*. London: Methuen, 1974. "The Critical Idiom." Also in paperback.
 Keats and Shelley are included in the discussion.

60a. Kaplan, Fred. *Miracles of Rare Device: The Poet's Sense of Self in Nineteenth Century Poetry*. See K-SJ, 21–22 (1972–73), No. 76.
 Rev. by Robert F. Gleckner in *Blake Newsletter*, No. 24 (Spring 1973), pp. 99–101; by Park Honan in MLR, 68 (Oct. 1973), 895–897.

61. Kauvar, Gerald B., and Gerald C. Sorenson, comps. *Nineteenth-Century English Verse Drama*. Rutherford, N.J.: Fairleigh Dickinson Univ., 1973.
 Includes *The Cenci*, *Manfred*, and *Otho the Great*, each with an introduction by Gerald Kauvar.
 Rev. in *Choice*, 10 (Sept. 1973), 978.

62. Lister, Raymond. *British Romantic Art*. London: Bell, 1973.
 Numerous references to Keats, Shelley, and Byron.

63. Lohf, Kenneth A. "Our Growing Collections," *Columbia Library Columns*, 22 (Feb. 1973), 34–46.
 The George Dunlop Collection at Columbia contains autographs of Byron, Shelley, and Hunt.

64. *Maar, Harko G. de. *A History of Modern English Romanticism*. Folcroft, Pa.: Folcroft, 1974.
 Reprint of the 1924 edition.

65. McCreadie, Marsha Anne. "T. S. Eliot and the Romantic Poets: A Study of the Similar Poetic Themes and Methods Used by Eliot and Wordsworth, Coleridge, Keats, Byron, and Shelley" [Doctoral dissertation, Illinois, 1973], DAI, 34 (June 1974), 7713-A.

66. McGann, Jerome J. "Romanticism and the Embarrassments of Critical Tradition," MP, 70 (Feb. 1973), 243–257.†
 A review-article. See Nos. 13, 21, 95, 814.

67. *Newsome, David. *Platonism and English Romantic Thought*. London: Murray, 1974.

68. Onopa, Robert L. "The Idea of Literary Autonomy" [Doctoral dissertation, Northwestern, 1974], DAI, 35 (Dec. 1974), 3695-A.
 Discusses Romantic views on the subject.

69. Orel, Harold. "English Romantic Poets and the Enlightenment: Nine Essays on a Literary Relationship," *Studies on Voltaire and the Eighteenth Century*, 103 (1973), 7–210.
 Includes an essay on Keats, "Keats's Faith in Human Progress," and reprints essays on Shelley (see K-SJ, 19 [1970], No. 350; 21–22 [1972–73], No. 692), Byron (see K-SJ, 14 [1965], No. 135), and Godwin (see K-SJ, 20 [1971], No. 897a).
 Rev. in TLS, 21 Sept. 1973, p. 1090; by Pier Antonio Borgheggiani in *Rivista di letterature moderne e comparate*, 27 (Dec. 1974), 305–307 [in Italian].

70. Otten, Terry. *The Deserted Stage: The Search for Dramatic Form in Nineteenth-Century England*. Athens: Ohio Univ., 1972.
 Ch. 1: "Shelley's *The Cenci*"; ch. 2: "Byron's *Cain* and *Werner*."
 Rev. by Frank P. Riga in LJ, 98 (15

Jan. 1973), 168; in *Choice*, 10 (Sept. 1973), 982; by John Stokes in *Nineteenth Century Theatre Research*, 2 (Spring 1974), 39–41; by Stuart Curran in ELN, 12, Supplement (Sept. 1974), 24–25.

71. Pantůčková, Lidmilla. "W. M. Thackeray as a Critic of Literature," *Brno Studies in English*, 10–11 (1972), 1–447.

A monograph which includes considerable discussion of Thackeray's criticisms of Hazlitt, Byron, Hunt, Shelley, Keats, and Godwin.

72. Partridge, Monica. "Romanticism and the Concept of Communication in a Slavonic and a Non-Slavonic Literature," *Renaissance and Modern Studies*, 17 (1973), 62–82.†

A comparative study of the first generation of English Romantics, especially Wordsworth, and their Russian counterparts, especially Pushkin. Several references to Byron, a few to Shelley.

73. *Peyre, Henri. *Qu'est-ce-que le romantisme?* Paris: Presses universitaires de France, 1971.

Rev. by F. P. Bowman in *French Studies*, 27 (Jan. 1973), 74–75. Also see No. 29.

74. Potts, Abbie Findlay. *The Elegiac Mode: Poetic Form in Wordsworth and Other Elegists*. Ithaca: Cornell Univ., 1967.

Keats, Shelley, and Byron are discussed.

75. Prasad, S. K. "Sri Aurobindo on the Romantics," *Banasthali Patrika*, Nos. 17–18 (July 1971 – Jan. 1972), pp. 94–101.

References to Keats, Shelley, and Byron, all highly regarded by the Indian sage.

76. Quennell, Peter. *L'Angleterre romantique: Ecrivains et peintres, 1717–1851*. See K-SJ, 21–22 (1972–73), No. 117.

Rev. by Albert Delorme in *Revue de synthèse*, 73–74 (Jan.–June 1974), 193–194.

77. Rafroidi, Patrick. *L'Irlande et le romantisme: La littérature irlandaise-anglaise de 1789 à 1850 et sa place dans le mouvement occidental*. Paris: Editions universitaires, 1972. "Publications de l'Université de Lille."

Many references to Byron, Shelley, Keats, and Hunt.

78. *Reardon, Bernard M. G. "Religion and the Romantic Movement," *Theology*, 76 (Aug. 1973), 403–416.

79. Redpath, Theodore. *The Young Romantics and Critical Opinion, 1807–1824: Poetry of Byron, Shelley, and Keats as Seen by Their Contemporary Critics*. London: Harrap; New York: St. Martin's (1973). Also in paperback.

Rev. by J. B. Caird in *Library Review* (Glasgow), 24 (Winter 1973–74), 182; by Frank P. Riga in LJ, 99 (1 Apr. 1974), 1039; in *Choice*, 11 (May 1974), 439–440; by John O. Hayden in *Criticism*, 19 (Fall 1974), 342–344. Also see No. 31.

80. *Reed, Walter L. *Meditations on the Hero: A Study of the Romantic Hero in Nineteenth-Century Fiction*. New Haven: Yale Univ., 1974.

81. Reiman, Donald H., ed. *The Romantics Reviewed: Contemporary Reviews of British Romantic Writers*. See K-SJ, 21–22 (1972–73), No. 118.

Rev. in *Choice*, 10 (July–Aug. 1973), 744–747; by David V. Erdman in ELN, 11, Supplement (Sept. 1973), 17; by Peter F. Morgan in JEGP, 73 (Jan. 1974), 129–130; by Carl Woodring in K-SJ, 23 (1974), 139–141; by Leslie A. Marchand in BJ, No. 2 (1974), pp. 54–58. Also see No. 31.

82. *Ridenour, George M., ed. *Romantic Poetry*. Englewood Cliffs, N.J.: Prentice-Hall, 1973.

An anthology of poems, preceded by an introduction.

83. Rose, Michael Julius. "The Conquest of Time: A Study of the Lyric Poetry of Seven Romanticists: Eichendorff, Novalis, Wordsworth, Shelley, Keats, Lamartine, Hugo" [Doctoral dissertation, Michigan, 1973], DAI, 35 (July 1974), 414-A.

84. *Rozenberg, Paul. *Le romantisme anglais: Le défi des vulnérables*. Paris: Larousse, 1973.

Rev. by Claude Gervais in *Etudes littéraires*, 7 (1974), 320–322.

85. *Schubel, Friedrich. *Englische Literaturgeschichte der Romantik und des Viktorianismus*. 2nd ed. Berlin: de Gruyter, 1972.

86. Shaffer, E. [Omnibus review], *Journal of*

European Studies, 4 (Dec. 1974), 394–395.
An omnibus review of several titles in the "Salzburg Studies in English Literature: Romantic Reassessment Series." See Nos. 222, 356, 590, 754.

87. Skarda, Patricia Lyn. " 'The Music of His Mind': Gerard Manley Hopkins as Literary Critic and Theorist" [Doctoral dissertation, Texas, 1973], DAI, 34 (Nov. 1973), 2579-A.
Discusses Hopkins' evaluation of Byron, Shelley, and Keats.

88. Sparks, Leslie Wayne. "A Study of Romantic Melancholy" [Doctoral dissertation, Indiana, 1973], DAI, 34 (Mar. 1974), 5996-A.
Byron and Keats are considered.

89. Speirs, John. *Poetry towards Novel.* See K-SJ, 20 (1971), No. 145a; 21–22 (1972–73), No. 128.
Rev. by Irène Simon in *Revue des langues vivantes*, 39, No. 6 (1973), 569–570; by Stephen Gill in N&Q, 219 (May 1974), 194–195. Also see No. 57.

90. Sullivan, Mary Ann. "Worlds of Their Own: Space-Consciousness in the Works of Wordsworth, Byron, Shelley, and Keats" [Doctoral dissertation, Ohio State, 1973], DAI, 34 (Nov. 1973), 2581-A.

91. *Thompson, Gary R., ed. *The Gothic Imagination: Essays in Dark Romanticism.* Pullman: Washington State Univ., 1974.

92. Thorburn, David, and Geoffrey Hartman, eds. *Romanticism: Vistas, Instances, Continuities.* Ithaca: Cornell Univ., 1973. Also in paperback.
A collection of essays with references to Shelley, Byron, and Keats.
Rev. by Frank P. Riga in LJ, 98 (15 Oct. 1973), 3004–05; by Stuart A. Ende in WC, 5 (Summer 1974), 141–144. Also see No. 41.

93. *Viebrock, Helmut. "Die englische Romantik," in *Die europäische Romantik*, ed. Ernst Behler *et al.* (Frankfurt: Athenäum, 1972), pp. 333–405.

94. Wellek, René. "Poulet, Du Bos, and Identification," *Comparative Literature Studies*, 10 (June 1973), 173–191.
Discusses briefly the attitude of Charles Du Bos toward Byron, Shelley, and Keats.

94a. Wittreich, Joseph Anthony, Jr., ed. *The Romantics on Milton: Formal Essays and Critical Asides.* See K-SJ, 20 (1971), No. 174; 21–22 (1972–73), No. 148.
Rev. by Kenneth Muir in N&Q, 218 (Feb. 1973), 77–78.

95. Woodring, Carl. *Politics in English Romantic Poetry.* See K-SJ, 20 (1971), No. 175; 21–22 (1972–73), No. 149.
See Nos. 57, 66.

96. Woodward, A. G. "One View of 'Romanticism,' " *English Studies in Africa*, 16 (Mar. 1973), 1–7.
Emphasizes a feature common to both the Enlightenment and Romanticism, "adoration of the autonomy and freedom of the human spirit." Keats, Shelley, and Byron are cited.

97. Yetman, Michael G. "Emily Dickinson and the English Romantic Tradition," *Texas Studies in Literature and Language*, 15 (Spring 1973), 129–147.‡
Explores the "uniqueness as well as the traditional in Emily Dickinson's poetry" and discusses the influence of and aesthetic similarities to Wordsworth, Coleridge, Keats, and Shelley.

For additional Books and Articles Relating to English Romanticism see Nos. 261, 295, 322, 482, 484, 511, 549, 560, 563, 606, 607, 641, 642, 668, 738, 787, 793.

II. BYRON

Works: Collected, Selected, Single, Translated

98. **Beppo, racconto veneziano.* Ed. Attilio Brilli. Parma: Studium parmense, 1972.

99. *Byron's "Hebrew Melodies."* Ed. Thomas L. Ashton. See K-SJ, 21–22 (1972–73), No. 155.
Rev. by A. H. Elliott in RES, 24 (Aug. 1973), 353–354; by E. E. Bostetter in ELN, 11, Supplement (Sept. 1973), 36–37; by John D. Jump in *Yearbook of English Studies*, 3 (1973), 307–308; by Michael G. Cooke in K-SJ, 21–22 (1972–73), 256–258; by John Clubbe in SAQ, 72 (Spring 1973), 331–332; by Abraham Avni in ES, 55 (Apr. 1974), 166–169. Also see No. 125.

100. *Byron's Letters and Journals.* Ed. Leslie

Marchand. Vol. I: *1798–1810: "In My Hot Youth."* Vol. II: *1810–1812: "Famous in My Time."* Cambridge: Harvard Univ.; London: Murray (1973).

Rev. by Peter Conrad in NS, 86 (28 Sept. 1973), 430–432; by Philip Ziegler in Spec, 231 (29 Sept. 1973), 410–411; in TLS, 19 Oct. 1973, pp. 1265–66; by Joanna Richardson in *History Today*, 23 (Dec. 1973), 885–886; by Peter Grosvenor in *Publishers Weekly*, 14 Jan. 1974, p. 83; by Anthony Powell in *Apollo*, 99 (Jan. 1974), 71; by W. Clemons in *Newsweek*, 11 Feb. 1974, pp. 91–92; by C. Clarke in *Journal of European Studies*, 4 (Mar. 1974), 81–82; in *New Yorker*, 1 Apr. 1974, p. 123; by William K. Seymour in CR, 224 (Apr. 1974), 219–220; by Robert F. Gleckner in WC, 5 (Summer 1974), 133–138; by David V. Erdman in ELN, 12, Supplement (Sept. 1974), 40–41; by B. F. Fisher, IV, in ABC, 25 (Sept.–Oct. 1974), 4–5; by Ian Ferguson in UES, 12 (Sept. 1974), pp. 70–72; by Andrew Rutherford in *Aberdeen University Review*, 45 (Autumn 1974), 406–408; by Dewey R. Faulkner in *Yale Review*, 64 (Oct. 1974), 88–93; by Elma Dangerfield in BJ, No. 2 (1974), pp. 61–62. Also see Nos. 31, 41.

101. *Byron's Letters and Journals*. Ed. Leslie Marchand. Vol. III: *1813–1814: "Alas! the Love of Women!"* Cambridge: Harvard Univ.; London: Murray (1974).

Rev. by Philip Ziegler in Spec, 233 (3 Aug. 1974), 149; by P. Beer in Li, 92 (15 Aug. 1974), 221; by Elizabeth Longford in *Books and Bookmen*, 19 (Aug. 1974), 24–25; in TLS, 20 Sept. 1974, p. 992; by Joanna Richardson in *History Today*, 24 (Oct. 1974), 728; by Phoebe Adams in *Atlantic Monthly*, 234 (Nov. 1974), p. 123.

102. *Le captif de Chillon (The Prisoner of Chillon); Le chevalier Harold, chant III (Childe Harold, Canto III)*. Trans. Paul Bensimon and Roger Martin. See K-SJ, 20 (1971), No. 179.

Rev. by J. Drummond Bone in N&Q, 218 (Aug. 1973), 308–310.

103. **A Choice of Byron's Verse*. Selected and introd. Douglas Dunn. London: Faber, 1974. Paperback.

Rev. by Elizabeth Longford in *Books and Bookmen*, 19 (Aug. 1974), 24–25.

104. **Confessions of Lord Byron: A Collection of His Private Opinions of Men and of Matters*. Ed. W. A. Lewis Bettany. New York: Haskell, 1973.

Reprint of the 1905 edition of selections from Byron's letters and journals.

105. **Fugitive Pieces*. Ed. Marcel Kessel. Folcroft, Pa.: Folcroft, 1973.

Reprint of the 1933 edition.

106. *Lord Byron: Don Juan*. Ed. T. G. Steffan, E. Steffan, and W. W. Pratt. Harmondsworth: Penguin, 1973. "Penguin English Poets." Paperback.

Rev. in TLS, 18 May 1973, p. 558; by Thomas L. Ashton in ELN, 12, Supplement (Sept. 1974), 41–42; by Charles W. Hagelman, Jr., in *South Central Bulletin*, 34 (Oct. 1974), 136.

107. **Lord Byron in His Letters*. Selected by V. H. Collins. New York: Haskell, 1973.

Reprint of the 1927 edition.

108. **Sochineniia v trekh tomakh*. [Works in three volumes.] Trans. O. Afonina, M. Kurginian, and W. Levik. Moscow: Khudozh. lit-ra, 1974.

109. Steffan, T. G., ed. *From Cambridge to Missolonghi: Byron Letters at the University of Texas*. See K-SJ, 21–22 (1972–73), No. 160.

Rev. by E. E. Bostetter in ELN, 11, Supplement (Sept. 1973), 39.

110. **Verse Letter to John Murray*. London: Murray and Scolar Press, 1974.

Facsimile of Byron's ribald verse-letter of 8 Jan. 1818.

111. **The Vision of Judgement*. Introd. Lionel Madden. Menston: Scolar, 1973.

Facsimile of the text in the second issue of the first edition of *The Liberal*, No. 1, with a new introduction. Also in paperback.

112. *Werner: A Tragedy*. A Facsimile of the Acting Version of William Charles Macready. Ed. Martin Spevack. See K-SJ, 20 (1971), No. 192; 21–22 (1972–73), No. 161.

Rev. by J. Drummond Bone in N&Q, 218 (Feb. 1973), 73–75.

113. **Wybór poematów*. [Selected poems.] Wroclaw: Ossolineum, 1970. [In Polish.]

For additional WORKS BY BYRON see Nos. 61, 120, 223, 269, 735.

BOOKS AND ARTICLES RELATING TO BYRON AND HIS CIRCLE

114. *Aldridge, A. Owen. "The Vampire Theme: Dumas Père and the English Stage," in *Expression, Communication and Experience in Literature and Language,* Proceedings of the Twelfth Congress of the International Federation for Modern Languages and Literatures held at Cambridge Univ., 20–26 Aug. 1972, ed. Ronald G. Popperwell (London: Modern Humanities Research Association, 1973), pp. 285–286.

Abstract of a paper delivered at the congress. Concerns Polidori.

115. Allentuck, Marcia. "Byron and Goethe: New Unpublished References by Henry Gally Knight," PQ, 52 (Oct. 1973), 777–779.

After an 1824 visit with Goethe, Knight writes to William Sotheby: "His worship of Byron is even beyond the mark—He places him next to Shakespeare."

116. Allentuck, Marcia. "An Unremarked Drawing of Edward Trelawny," K-SJ, 23 (1974), 24–25.

The drawing by Edward Bird (1772–1819), which is now at McGill University, is reproduced.

117. Antonini, Giacomo. "Impact on Italian Opera," BJ, No. 1 (1973), pp. 21–24.

Byron's influence on Donizetti and Verdi.

118. Asfour, Mohammed Hassan. "The Crescent and the Cross: Islam and the Muslims in English Literature from Johnson to Byron" [Doctoral dissertation, Indiana, 1973], DAI, 34 (Jan. 1974), 4239-A.

119. Ashton, Thomas L. "*Marino Faliero*: Byron's '*Poetry* of Politics,' " SIR, 13 (Winter 1974), 1–13.

Stating that Romantic political poetry "synthesizes sexual and prophetic metaphor to embody political consciousness," Ashton demonstrates the Doge's final realization of his place in history as he "weds an *inevitable* sea to redeem sterile tyranny . . . with sweeping thoughts of freedom, seaweed, and waves of time." The interpretation is made concrete by references to the contemporary political situation in Italy and England and to the conflicts in our own time.

120. **Autographes et documents historiques* [Sale catalogue], Paris, Hôtel Drouot, 20 Feb. 1974, Lot 4.

A one-page letter of Byron, dated Little Hampton, 26 Aug. 1806, was sold for 1900 francs.

121. Babinski, Hubert F. "Ivan Mazeppa in European Romanticism" [Doctoral dissertation, Columbia, 1970], DAI, 33 (Jan. 1973), 3572-A.

122. Babinski, Hubert F. *The Mazeppa Legend in European Romanticism.* New York: Columbia Univ., 1974.

Rev. by Frank P. Riga in LJ, 99 (1 Sept. 1974), 2067; by Frank Mocha in *Polish Review*, 19, Nos. 3–4 (1974), pp. 191–200.

123. *Barber, Thomas G. *Byron—and Where He Is Buried.* Folcroft, Pa.: Folcroft, 1974.

Reprint of the 1939 edition.

124. Barrell, R. A. "Horace Walpole and France," *Humanities Association Bulletin*, 23 (Spring 1972), 33–40.

Byron was one of those whose praise helped to solidify Walpole's literary reputation.

125. Bateson, F. W. "Byron's Baby," NYRB, 20 (22 Feb. 1973), pp. 32–33.

An omnibus review. See Nos. 99, 215, 310.

126. Bauer, N. Stephen. "Byron's Doubting Cain," *South Atlantic Bulletin*, 39 (May 1974), pp. 80–88.

"Cain's tragedy, then, is that he had to sin in order to understand the world," and it is the tragedy of all men "who insist upon the primacy of self-experience. Cain's alternative was faith, to believe what he had heard—a luxury Byron refused him."

127. Bell, Michael Davitt. "The Glendinning Heritage: Melville's Literary Borrowings in *Pierre*," SIR, 12 (Fall 1973), 741–762.†‡

Includes a discussion of Pierre's development from the "submissive romanticism of Wordsworth to the dark, defiant romanticism of Byron."

128. Bergerolle, Claude. "Révolte sexuelle et liberté individuelle dans le *Don Juan*," *Romantisme*, No. 7 (1974), pp. 44–59.

An examination of certain images in *Don Juan* to show that Byron regarded sexual repression as the basis of political oppression and the right of the individual to choose for himself sexually as the basis of the freedom of the individual.

129. Berthier, Philippe. "Une vie 'en Byron': Le cas Barbey d'Aurevilly," *Romantisme*, No. 8 (1974), pp. 22–35.

The profound influence of Byron and his works on Barbey.

130. Blackstone, Bernard. "Byron and Islam: The Triple Eros," *Journal of European Studies*, 4 (Dec. 1974), 325–363.

An examination of the influence of Islamic culture on Byron's life and works. Blackstone argues that not only was this influence strong but that Byron had "an innate tendency" which made "Islam and its way of life enormously attractive to him." The "triple eros" is love, wisdom, and power, which Blackstone finds to be the theme both of Islamic thought and of Byron's life and poetry.

131. Blackstone, Bernard. "Byron and the Levels of Landscape," *Ariel*, 5 (Oct. 1974), 3–20.

Sees Byron as an "ecological poet," always conscious of the interaction between human civilization and the natural environment.

132. Blackstone, Bernard. "Byron's Greek Canto: The Anatomy of Freedom," *Yearbook of English Studies*, 4 (1974), 172–179.

A consideration of the themes and structure of *Childe Harold* II, showing that "Byron's world is an inner as well as an outer landscape."

133. Blyth, Henry. *Caro, the Fatal Passion: The Life of Lady Caroline Lamb*. New York: Coward, McCann and Geoghegan, 1973.

For London edition, see K-SJ, 21–22 (1972–73), No. 183.

Rev. by *Ann Freemantle in NYT, 18 Feb. 1973, p. 6; in *Choice*, 10 (July–Aug. 1973), 772; by E. E. Bostetter in ELN, 11, Supplement (Sept. 1973), 37–38; by Rosalie Mander [R. Glynn Grylls] in BJ, No. 1 (1973), pp. 31–32.

134. Boken, Julia Barbara. "Byron's Ladies: A Study of *Don Juan*" [Doctoral dissertation, Columbia, 1970], DAI, 33 (Apr. 1973), 5714-A.

135. "The Book by Byron's Bed at Missolonghi," BJ, No. 1 (1973), pp. 12–13.

Tasso's *Jerusalem Delivered*, trans. John Hoole, now owned privately in Portugal.

136. Bostetter, Edward E. "Masses and Solids: Byron's View of the External World," MLQ, 35 (Sept. 1974), 257–271.

"Byron was the only major Romantic poet to write within the Empirical tradition; the external world is the only reality for him."

137. Braddock, Joseph. *The Greek Phoenix*. London: Constable, 1972.

Considerable discussion of Byron and Greece.

Rev. by C. M. Woodhouse in BJ, No. 1 (1973), pp. 28–29.

138. Brand, C. P. "Byron and the Italians," BJ, No. 1 (1973), pp. 14–21.

Byron as an inspiration to Italian nationalists.

139. *Brent, Peter. *Lord Byron*. Introd. Elizabeth Longford. London: Weidenfeld and Nicolson, 1974. "Great Lives."

140. Brogan, Howard O. " 'Byron So Full of Fun, Frolic, Wit, and Whim,' " HLQ, 37 (Feb. 1974), 171–189.

Byron has suffered from the false legend of his bad manners, moodiness, and irritability; as the evidence of contemporaries shows, he was generally cheerful and fun-loving. Brogan reviews Byron's relations with Shelley, Mary, and Trelawny, and his remarks on Keats.

141. Brogan, Howard O. "Lady Byron: 'The Moral Clytemnestra of Her Lord,' " *Durham University Journal*, 66 (Mar. 1974), 146–155.

An indictment of Byron's wife on several counts of duplicity and treachery.

142. Brosse, Monique. "Byron et la mer," *Romantisme*, No. 7 (1974), pp. 60–76.

A discussion of sea imagery in Byron and its profound influence on French writers after him.

143. *Brouzas, Christopher G. *Byron's Maid*

of Athens: Her Family and Surroundings. Folcroft, Pa.: Folcroft, 1974.
Reprint of the 1949 edition.

144. Brown, Margaret. "Byron and Shelley: The Sea, a Shared Enthusiasm," BJ, No. 1 (1973), pp. 48–49.
An appreciation.

145. Burch, Francis F. "An Unpublished Letter of Thomas Moore," N&Q, 219 (Sept. 1974), 335–336.
The letter, dated 2 Oct. 1833, mentions Byron.

146. Burton, Anthony, and John Murdoch, comps. *Byron: An Exhibition to Commemorate the 150th Anniversary of His Death in the Greek War of Liberation, 19 April 1824.* London: Victoria and Albert Museum, 1974.
The exhibition at the Victoria and Albert Museum ran 30 May – 25 Aug. 1974. It was reviewed in **Apollo*, 99 (June 1974), 467; by Jonathan Raban in *Sunday Times* (London), 14 July 1974, p. 35; by Mollie Panter-Downes in *New Yorker*, 22 July 1974, pp. 68–72. Also see Nos. 162, 313.

147. "Byron and the Armenian in Graphics," *Armenian Review*, 27 (Summer 1974), 141–145.
Facsimile reprints of some pages from the Armenian-English Grammar on which Byron worked in 1816.

148. Cameron, Alan Harwood. "Byronism in Lermontov's *A Hero of Our Time*" [Doctoral dissertation, British Columbia, 1974], DAI, 35 (Dec. 1974), 3728-A.

149. Carr, Sherwyn T. "Bunn, Byron and *Manfred*," *Nineteenth Century Theatre Research*, 1 (Spring 1973), 15–27.
Discusses the first theatrical production of *Manfred* (by Alfred Bunn in 1834), focusing on the alterations in the text, which were major.

150. Cermakian, Marianne. "Byron chez Delécluze," *Romantisme*, No. 7 (1974), pp. 99–106.
The views of Etienne Delécluze, Stendhal, and Mérimée on Byron and his works.

151. *Chambers, R. W. *Ruskin (and Others) on Byron.* Folcroft, Pa.: Folcroft, 1974.
Reprint of the 1925 edition.

152. Churchill, K. G. "Byron and Italy," *Literary Half-Yearly*, 15 (July 1974), 67–86.
A retelling of Byron's associations with Italy; unlike Wordsworth, Byron could understand city life, and unlike most eighteenth-century travelers, he was not interested in the ruins and museums.

153. Clancy, Charles J. "Byron's *Don Juan*: A Comic Epic" [Doctoral dissertation, New York Univ., 1973], DAI, 34 (Feb. 1974), 5161-A.

153a. *Clancy, Charles J. *Lava, Hock and Soda-Water: Byron's "Don Juan."* Salzburg: Univ. of Salzburg, 1974. "Salzburg Studies in English: Romantic Reassessment Series, No. 41."

154. *Clancy, Charles J. "Review of *Don Juan* Criticism: 1900–1973," in *Salzburg Studies in English Literature: Romantic Reassessment, No. 40*, ed. James Hogg (Salzburg: Univ. of Salzburg, 1974), pp. 9–94.
See No. 31.

155. *Clayton, William. *The Byron Collection.* [Portfolio of prints.] Derby, England: Bemrose Editions, [*ca.* 1974].
A limited edition collection of full-color prints depicting Byron's personal effects painted by William Clayton.

156. Clogg, Richard, ed. *The Struggle for Greek Independence: Essays to Mark the 150th Anniversary of the Greek War of Independence.* London: Macmillan; Hamden, Conn.: Archon (1973).
Includes Robin Fletcher's "Byron in Nineteenth-Century Greek Literature" (pp. 224–247) and other essays with references to Byron.
Rev. by Ian Scott-Kilvert in BJ, No. 2 (1974), p. 62.

157. Clubbe, John. "After Missolonghi: Scott on Byron, 1824–1832," *Library Chronicle* (Univ. of Pennsylvania), 39 (Winter 1973), 18–33.‡
Three unpublished letters in the Univ. of Pennsylvania Library, from Scott to Tom Moore, discussing Byron.

158. Clubbe, John. "Byron and Scott," *Texas Studies in Literature and Language*, 15 (Spring 1973), 67–91.‡
An exploration of their friendship and its history: "it is chiefly for the quality of

their personal relationship . . . that their names deserved to be remembered together."

159. Clubbe, John. " 'The New Prometheus of New Men': Byron's 1816 Poems and *Manfred*," in *Nineteenth-Century Literary Perspectives: Essays in Honor of Lionel Stevenson*, ed. Clyde de L. Ryals *et al.* (Durham: Duke Univ., 1974), pp. 17–47.

160. *Collins, Joseph J. "Tennyson and the Spasmodics," *Victorian Newsletter*, No. 43 (Spring 1973), pp. 24–28.†

Notes Byronic traits in "Maud."

161. Connell, James Goodman, Jr. "Freedom and the Don Juan Tradition in Selected Narrative Poetic Works and *The Stone Guest* of Alexander Pushkin" [Doctoral dissertation, Ohio State, 1973], DAI, 34 (Nov. 1973), 2552-A.

162. Conrad, Peter. "Images of Byron," TLS, 31 May 1974, p. 584.

A consideration, prompted by the Byron Exhibition at the Victoria and Albert Museum, of the impossibility of reducing Byron to any fixed image because he was so much a symbol of his age and was so diversely depicted. Also see No. 146.

163. *Cooke, Sheila M., comp. *Byron Commemoration, 1974: Booklist*. Nottingham: Nottinghamshire County Library, 1974.

A pamphlet listing some items on Byron in the library.

164. Corner, Martin. "Text and Context in Arnold's Essays in Criticism," *Neophilologus*, 57 (Apr. 1973), 188–197.

Corner's argument is illustrated by examining Arnold's essay on Byron.

165. Corr, Thomas Joseph. "Views of the Mind (of Reason and Imagination) as Structural and Thematic Principles in the Works of Byron" [Doctoral dissertation, Duquesne, 1974], DAI, 35 (Sept. 1974), 1617-A.

166. Dakin, Douglas. *The Greek Struggle for Independence, 1821–1833*. Berkeley: Univ. of California, 1973.

Discusses Byron's role.

167. *Dalgado, D. G. *Lord Byron's Childe Harold's Pilgrimage to Portugal*. Folcroft, Pa.: Folcroft, 1974.

Reprint of the 1919 edition.

168. D'Ambruoso, Raphael R. "Byron's Development in the Use of the Satiric Verse Portrait" [Doctoral dissertation, New York Univ., 1973], DAI, 34 (Sept. 1973), 1275-A.

169. Driva, Ianna. "Byron in Greece," CR, 224 (Apr. 1974), 189–193.

There are qualities in the poet and in the poetry that appeal particularly to the Greek sensibility.

170. Dudley, Edward, and Maximillian E. Novak. *The Wild Man Within: An Image in Western Thought from the Renaissance to Romanticism*. Pittsburgh: Univ. of Pittsburgh, 1972.

Discusses Byron.

Rev. by Murray J. Leaf in *Journal of Modern History*, 46 (June 1974), 341–343.

171. *Edgcumbe, Richard. *Byron: The Last Phase*. New York: Haskell, 1972.

Reprint of the 1909 edition.

172. Eggenschwiler, David. "The Tragic and Comic Rhythms of *Manfred*," SIR, 13 (Winter 1974), 63–77.

Borrowing his critical terms from Suzanne K. Langer, Eggenschwiler discerns in the play a pattern of alternating comic and tragic rhythms, which accounts for a feeling of unity of theme.

173. Elledge, W. Paul. *Byron and the Dynamics of Metaphor*. See K-SJ, 19 (1970), No. 98; 20 (1971), No. 256.

Rev. by Charles I. Patterson, Jr., in *South Atlantic Bulletin*, 39 (May 1974), pp. 132–135.

174. Engelberg, Edward. *The Unknown Distance: From Consciousness to Conscience, Goethe to Camus*. Cambridge: Harvard Univ., 1972.

Ch. 2: "The Price of Consciousness: Goethe's *Faust* and Byron's *Manfred*." References also to Shelley and Keats.

Rev. by M. H. Parkinson in *Journal of European Studies*, 4 (Sept. 1974), 290.

175. *England, A. B. *Byron's "Don Juan" and Eighteenth-Century Literature: A Study of Some Rhetorical Continuities and Discontinuities*. Lewisburg, Pa.: Bucknell Univ., 1974.

176. Ennis, Julian. "The Death of Byron According to *The Bucks Gazette*, 1824," CR, 222 (Apr. 1973), 195–199.

An obituary and description of the funeral ceremonies.

177. Escarpit, Robert. "Byron, figure politique," *Romantisme*, No. 7 (1974), pp. 8–15.

Byron as an early advocate of national liberation movements.

178. *Evans, Constantine. "The Adventure of the Byronic Hero," *Baker Street Journal*, 23 (Sept. 1973), 140–146.†

A pastiche of Byronic and Holmesian elements, written in Spenserian stanzas.

179. Farrell, John P. "Arnold, Byron, and Taine," ES, 55 (Oct. 1974), 435–439.

Hippolyte Taine's influence was responsible for a dramatic change in Arnold's estimate of Byron.

179a. Fischer, Doucet D., and Donald H. Reiman, comps. *Byron on the Continent: A Memorial Exhibition, 1824–1974*. New York: The Carl H. Pforzheimer Library and New York Public Library, 1974.

Catalog with critical commentaries of the exhibition at the New York Public Library, Feb.–Apr. 1974.

Rev. in BNYPL, 77 (Summer 1974), 372.

180. Fisher, Alan S. "The Stretching of Augustan Satire: Charles Churchill's 'Dedication' to Warburton," JEGP, 72 (July 1973), 360–377.‡

Concludes with comparison of Churchill's satire and Byron's *Don Juan*.

181. *Fox, John Charles. *The Byron Mystery*. Folcroft, Pa.: Folcroft, 1974.

Reprint of the 1924 edition.

182. "From Missolonghi to Apsley House: A Reappraisal of Byron," Li, 91 (16 May 1974), 623–626.

Transcript of a BBC radio program on Byron, in which a number of Byron experts took part.

183. Garber, Frederick. "Byron's *Giaour* and the Mark of Cain," EA, 26 (Apr.–June 1973), 150–159.

Byron revised each new edition to suggest more clearly an interchangeable likeness between the Giaour and Hassan, both of whom bear the mark of Cain.

184. Goldstein, Stephen Leonard. "Byron in Radical Tradition: A Study in the Intellectual Backgrounds and Controversiality of *Cain*" [Doctoral dissertation, Columbia, 1970], DAI, 34 (Nov. 1973), 2560-A.

185. Gömöri, George. "The Myth of Byron in Norwid's Life and Work," *Slavonic and East European Review*, 51 (Apr. 1973), 231–242.

By a selective reading of Byron's life and works, Norwid came to see Byron as the type of the Romantic hero; Byron as an exiled political figure appealed to the Polish emigré who popularized Byron with Polish readers. Also see No. 186.

186. Gömöri, George. "The Myth of Byron in Norwid's Thought and Work," in *VII Międzynarodowy Kongres Slawistów w Warszawie 1973: Streszczenia referatów i komunikatów* (Warsaw: Pan, 1973), pp. 619–620.

An abstract in Polish of a paper delivered at the congress. For the full English text see No. 185.

187. *Goode, Clement T. *Byron as Critic*. New York: Burt Franklin, 1972.

Reprint of an edition, *ca.* 1923.

188. Gordon, Archie. "Byron's Gordon Ancestors," Li, 92 (19–25 Dec. 1974), 822–824.

On Byron's maternal ancestors and their castle at Gight.

189. *Gordon, Armistead C. *Allegra: The Story of Byron and Miss Clairmont*. New York: Haskell, 1973.

Reprint of the 1926 edition.

190. *Gordon, Cosmo. *Life and Genius of Lord Byron*. Folcroft, Pa.: Folcroft, 1974.

Reprint of the 1824 edition.

191. Gregory, Horace. *Spirit of Time and Place: Collected Essays of Horace Gregory*. New York: Norton, 1973.

A collection of previously published pieces, including "Lord Byron: The Poet as Letter Writer" and "The Sight of Nature in the Poetry of John Clare." Index lists many references to Keats, Shelley, and Byron, a few to Hunt.

192. *Grierson, Herbert. *Lord Byron: Arnold and Swinburne*. Folcroft, Pa.: Folcroft, 1974.

Reprint of the 1921 edition.

193. Grimble, Ian. "Byron," *New Humanist*, 90 (Aug. 1974), 122–123.

194. *Grimm, Gunter. "Die Byron-Übersetzungen Karl Wolfskehls," *Castrum Peregrini*, 107–109 (1973), pp. 39–66.

195. Grove, Gerald Robert, Sr. "John Neal: American Romantic" [Doctoral dissertation, Utah, 1974], DAI, 35 (Aug. 1974), 1045-A.

He was influenced by Byron and Shelley.

196. Grylls, R. Glynn. "Byron's Memoirs," TLS, 9 Feb. 1973, p. 153.

Corrects Gordon Haight (see No. 197) for wrongly blaming Tom Moore for the destruction of Byron's memoirs; Moore was the one man who protested the destruction.

197. Haight, Gordon. "To Whom It May Concern—and Others," TLS, 26 Jan. 1973, pp. 87–89.

A discussion of the publication of journals, memoirs, and letters not written for publication; mentions Byron's memoirs and their destruction. See No. 196.

198. Hannay, Prudence. "The Redoubtable Lady Holland," *History Today*, 23 (Feb. 1973), 94–104.

Byron and Moore were among those who "found the atmosphere of Holland House irresistible in spite of the domineering habits and tactics of their hostess."

199. *Harper, Henry H. *Byron's Malach Hamoves: A Commentary on Leigh Hunt's Work Entitled "Lord Byron and Some of His Contemporaries."* Revised ed. Folcroft, Pa.: Folcroft, 1973.

Reprint of the 1933 edition.

200. Harson, Robert R. "A Clarification Concerning John Polidori, Lord Byron's Physician," K-SJ, 21–22 (1972–73), 38–40.‡

Presents evidence that Byron was introduced to Polidori not by Sir Henry Halford but by Sir William Knighton.

201. *Henderson, Robert. "Phenomenon That Was Byron," *Daily Telegraph* (London), 15 June 1974, p. 13.

202. *Henson, Herbert H. *Byron*. New York: Haskell, 1974.

Reprint of the 1924 edition.

203. *Hillier, Bevis. "Byronic Attitudes," ILN, 262 (June 1974), 47–50.

204. Hinkel, Howard H. "The Byronic Pilgrimage to the Absurd," *Midwest Quarterly*, 15 (Summer 1974), 352–365.

In *Childe Harold's Pilgrimage* and *Don Juan*, Byron is an absurdist; progressively in his writing he abandons the wearying search for achievement in favor of growth and process.

205. Hoge, James O. "Lady Caroline Lamb on Byron and Her Own Wasted Life: Two New Letters," N&Q, 219 (Sept. 1974), 331–333.

One tentatively dated 1811, the second dated 21 May 1823, both addressed to Edward Bulwer. The first advises him not to read Byron, Scott, or Moore, and to keep to the "old poets"; the second is a self-pitying letter which alludes to her novel, *Glenarvon*.

206. *Hooker, Charlotte S. "Byron's Misadventures in Portugal," *McNeese Review*, 20 (1971–72), 47–51.

207. Howard, Ida Beth Heatly. "The Byronic Hero and the Renaissance Hero-Villain: Analogues and Prototypes" [Doctoral dissertation, North Texas State, 1973], DAI, 34 (Feb. 1974), 5176-A.

208. Howell, Margaret J. "Byron's Plays" [Letter], BJ, No. 1 (1973), p. 63.

Asks for information on nineteenth-century productions of Byron's plays.

208a. Howell, Margaret J. "*Sardanapalus*," BJ, No. 2 (1974), pp. 42–53.

On Charles Kean's 1853 production, which corrupted Byron's play on the problem of power into a scenic spectacle.

209. Humphreys, Arthur R. " 'The Genius of the Place': Turkey in English Letters," SAQ, 73 (Summer 1974), 306–323.

Byron is included.

210. *Jackson, Michael. "Lord Byron: 'A Gallant Spirit and Kind One,' " *Theology*, 77 (Nov. 1974), 578–582.

211. *Jackson-Stops, G. "Newstead Abbey, Nottinghamshire," *Country Life*, 155 (9 May 1974), 1122–25; (16 May 1974), 1190–93.

212. James, Clive. "Why Byron Won't Lie Down," *Observer*, 21 Apr. 1974, p. 15.

An appreciation inspired by the 150th anniversary of Byron's death: "What Byron changed, and goes on changing, was the course of English poetry. . . ."

213. Joannides, Paul. "A Byron Subject by Horace Vernet," *Burlington Magazine*, 116 (Nov. 1974), 668–669.

A painting inspired by *The Corsair*.

214. Jones, D. Walwin. "Byron-Inspired Music" [Letter], BJ, No. 1 (1973), p. 63.
Asks for contributions to a list of such works.

215. Jump, John D. *Byron*. See K-SJ, 21–22 (1972–73), No. 248.
Rev. by Mary McBride in LJ, 98 (15 Feb. 1973), 546; in *Choice*, 10 (May 1973), 458; by E. E. Bostetter in ELN, 11, Supplement (Sept. 1973), 39; by William Plomer in BJ, No. 1 (1973), pp. 30–31; by P. D. Fleck in *Humanities Association Review*, 25 (Spring 1974), 171–172. Also see Nos. 59, 125.

216. Jump, John D., ed. *Byron: "Childe Harold's Pilgrimage" and "Don Juan"—A Casebook*. London: Macmillan, 1973. Also in paperback.
Rev. by P. D. Fleck in *Humanities Association Review*, 25 (Spring 1974), 171–172; by Gilbert Phelps in BJ, No. 2 (1974), pp. 60–61.

217. Kahn, Arthur D. "The Pastoral Byron: Arcadia in *The Island*," *Arcadia. Zeitschrift für vergleichende Literatur Wissenschaft*, 8, No. 3 (1973), 274–283.
After discussing Byron's use of the Classical tradition of pastoral in *The Island*, Kahn concludes that Byron "attempts an objective analysis of the choice between nature and civilization and discovers that the appeal of the world is stronger than that of the pastoral dream."

218. Katkin, Wendy Freedman. "The Narrator of *Don Juan*: Byron's Last Hero" [Doctoral dissertation, State Univ. of New York, Buffalo, 1972], DAI, 33 (Mar. 1973), 5128-A.

219. *Kennelly, Laura B. "Satire and High Society: A Comparison of Byron's *Don Juan* and Wolfe's *Radical Chic*," in *Studies in Relevance: Romantic and Victorian Writers in 1972*, ed. Thomas Meade Harwell (Salzburg: Univ. of Salzburg, 1973), pp. 53–75. "Salzburg Studies in English: Romantic Reassessment Series, No. 32."
See No. 31.

220. *Kenworthy-Browne, John. "Byron Portrayed," *Antique Collector*, 45 (July 1974), 58–64.
On portraits of Byron. Illustrated.

221. King, Martha Jean. "The Influence of Byron on Italian Culture" [Doctoral dissertation, Wisconsin, 1973], DAI, 34 (May 1974), 7236-A.

222. Kirchner, Jane. *The Function of the Persona in the Poetry of Byron*. Salzburg: Univ. of Salzburg, 1973. "Salzburg Studies in English: Romantic Reassessment Series, No. 15."
Rev. in *Choice*, 11 (June 1974), 600. Also see Nos. 31, 86.

223. Kline, Richard B. "Byron's Boat, the Morat Bones, and Mr. St. Aubyn: A New Autograph Letter," K-SJ, 21–22 (1972–73), 33–38.‡
The letter, to Charles Hentsch, clarifies some biographical details.

224. Knight, G. Wilson. *Neglected Powers: Essays on Nineteenth and Twentieth Century Literature*. See K-SJ, 20 (1971), No. 300; 21–22 (1972–73), No. 250.
Rev. by Peter Milward in *Studies in English Literature* (Japan), 49, English Number (1973), 148–151; by J. Drummond Bone in N&Q, 219 (Oct. 1974), 379–381.

225. Knight, G. Wilson. "Reason for Ostracism" [Letter], BJ, No. 1 (1973), pp. 62–63.
Proposes that the rumors spread about Byron in 1816 may have been a Tory attempt to blackmail him into forsaking his liberal principles and political activities, and asks for research on the question.

226. Laffay, Albert. "Le donjuanisme de *Don Juan*," *Romantisme*, No. 7 (1974), pp. 32–43.
Byron in his life and Don Juan in the poem search in vain for their twin, the true object of their love. Such is the myth central to Byron's life and his works.

227. Lambert, Cecily. "Most Gorgeous Lady Blessington," KSMB, 25 (1974), 26–32.
A biographical sketch.

228. Levik, Wilhelm. "Byron in Russia," *Soviet Literature*, No. 10 (1974), pp. 159–163.
On Byron's popularity and translations of his works.

229. *Lim, Paulino M., Jr. *The Style of Lord Byron's Plays*. Salzburg: Univ. of Salz-

burg, 1973. "Salzburg Studies in English: Poetic Drama Series, No. 3."

See No. 31.

230. "List of Acquisitions, Dept. of Manuscripts, July 1970 to December 1972," *British Museum Quarterly*, 37 (Summer 1973), 73–77.

"Diaries, etc., of John Cam Hobhouse."

231. Little, William Thomas. "Don Juanism in Modern European Literature" [Doctoral dissertation, Washington Univ., 1973], DAI, 34 (Dec. 1973), 3410-A.

232. "The Living Byron: On the 150th Anniversary of the Poet's Death," trans. Peter Mann, *Soviet Literature*, No. 4 (1974), pp. 143–146.

233. Low, Donald A. "Byron and Europe," *Journal of European Studies*, 4 (Dec. 1974), 364–367.

An account of a symposium, "Byron's Influence on European Thought," held at Cambridge, 26 June – 1 July 1974.

234. *McCraw, Harry Wells. "Growing Up Absurd: Byron's *Don Juan*," in *Studies in Relevance: Romantic and Victorian Writers in 1972*, ed. Thomas Meade Harwell (Salzburg: Univ. of Salzburg, 1973), pp. 76–86. "Salzburg Studies in English: Romantic Reassessment Series, No. 32."

See No. 31.

235. McGann, Jerome J. "Editing Byron's Poetry," BJ, No. 1 (1973), pp. 5–10.

Reviews strengths and weaknesses of previous editions (noting, for example, that no "correct" edition of *Childe Harold* III, *Manfred*, or "The Prisoner of Chillon" has ever been published), and describes the goals of the "Oxford English Texts" Byron, which McGann is in the process of editing.

236. McGann, Jerome J. "Milton and Byron," KSMB, 25 (1974), 9–25.

After discussing the influence of Milton's Satan on the Byronic hero, McGann goes on to show that from 1816 on Byron "began to see a broad but clear parallel between the trials, betrayals, and goals of Milton's life and the similar circumstances of his own."

237. McGann, Jerome J. "Missing Manuscripts" [Letter], BJ, No. 1 (1973), p. 62.

Asks whereabouts of several Byron MSS for use in editing the "Oxford English Texts" Byron.

238. *Mackay, Charles. *Medora Leigh: A History and an Autobiography*. Introd. and commentary on the charges brought against Lord Byron by Mrs. Beecher Stowe. New York: AMS, 1973.

Reprint of the 1870 edition.

239. *Mackenzie, Harriet M. *Byron's Laughter: In Life and Poetry*. Folcroft, Pa.: Folcroft, 1973.

Reprint of the 1939 edition.

240. *Manganelli, Giorgio. "Byron e Stendhal alla tavola calda," *Giorno*, 22 Oct. 1973.

Both attended a dinner given by Ludovico di Breme, 16 Oct. 1816.

241. Manning, Peter J. "Edmund Kean and Byron's Plays," K-SJ, 21–22 (1972–73), 188–206.‡

Manning details the relationship between the two men and argues that Kean's portrayal of Shakespeare's tragic heroes influenced Byron's dramatic heroes. In particular, "Kean's interpretation of Richard [III] makes him not unlike the title figure of Byron's best play, *Sardanapalus*, with his undignified bearing and witty repartee."

242. Marchand, Leslie A. "Byron in His Letters and Journals," *Cornhill Magazine*, No. 1076 (Summer 1973), pp. 40–65.

Marchand's introduction to his *Byron's Letters and Journals*, with general remarks on style and content.

243. Marchand, Leslie A. "Byron's Letters," BJ, No. 1 (1973), pp. 34–46.

Byron's "tortured spirit" found expression in his poetry, rarely in his letters, which reflect, rather, his zest for life. The article is adapted from the introduction to Marchand's edition of *Byron's Letters and Journals*.

244. Martinez, L. "Liquidation du byronisme dans les romans de Dostoievski," in *VII Międzynarodowy Kongres Slawistów w Warszawie 1973: Streszczenia referatów i komunikatów* (Warsaw: PAN, 1973), pp. 642–644.

An abstract in Russian of a paper delivered at the congress.

245. *Mesrobian, Arpena. "Lord Byron at the Armenian Monastery on San Laz-

zaro," *Courier* (Syracuse Univ. Library), 11, No. 1 (1973), pp. 27–37.

See No. 246.

246. Mesrobian, Arpena. "Lord Byron at the Armenian Monastery of San Lazzaro," *Armenian Review*, 27 (Summer 1974), 131–140.

An account of his literary and linguistic collaboration with the monks. Also see No. 245.

247. Miller, Edmund. "Byron's *The Vision of Judgment*, Stanzas 48–51," Exp, 33 (Sept. 1974), Item 4.

In calling George III "Guelph" St. Peter is not only referring to the House of Hanover but also to the pro-papal party in medieval Italy (the two meanings of the word come from the same source), thus implying that the king's opposition to Catholic Emancipation is a betrayal of his heritage.

248. Montluzin, Emily Lorraine de. "Southey's 'Satanic School' Remarks: An Old Charge for a New Offender," K-SJ, 21–22 (1972–73), 29–33.

Southey's celebrated attack on Byron is shown to be largely a rehash of remarks made by Southey in an unsigned review of a work by Thomas Moore.

249. *Moore, Doris Langley. "Contrasting Memories of Byron," *Country Life*, 155 (30 May 1974), 1368–1369.

250. Moore, Doris Langley. *Lord Byron: Accounts Rendered.* London: Murray; New York: Harper and Row (1974).

Rev. by Christopher Ricks in *Sunday Times* (London), 19 May 1974, p. 35; by Phoebe Adams in *Atlantic Monthly*, 233 (June 1974), p. 115; by Jonathan Raban in NS, 88 (5 July 1974), 17–18; by Joanna Richardson in *History Today*, 24 (July 1974), 511–512; by Elizabeth Longford in *Books and Bookmen*, 19 (Aug. 1974), 24–25; in *Choice*, 11 (Nov. 1974), 1310.

251. *Moore, Thomas. *Life, Letters, and Journals of Lord Byron.* Ed. Sir Walter Scott. St. Clair Shores, Mich.: Scholarly, 1972.

Reprint of the 1920 edition.

252. Newton, K. M. "Byronic Egoism and George Eliot's *The Spanish Gypsy*," *Neophilologus*, 57 (Oct. 1973), 388–400.

Though George Eliot's novels suggest little interest in the Byronic hero, "Byronic figures emerge clearly in her poetry. . . ." Newton explores Eliot's critique of Byronic egoism by analyzing *The Spanish Gypsy*, particularly the Byronic Don Silva.

253. Nielson, Jorgen Erik. "Byron Apocrypha," N&Q, 218 (Aug. 1973), 291–292.†

Three poems attributed to Byron, discovered in English and Danish periodicals.

254. *Noel, Roden B. *Life of Lord Byron.* Folcroft, Pa.: Folcroft, 1973.

Reprint of the 1890 edition.

255. *Noel, Roden B. *Life of Lord Byron.* New York: AMS, 1973.

Reprint of the 1890 edition.

256. Ober, Kenneth H., and Warren U. Ober. "Žukovskij's Translation of 'The Prisoner of Chillon,' " *Slavic and East European Journal*, 17 (Winter 1973), 390–398.

Vasilij Andreevič Žukovskij (1783–1852) published his Russian translation in 1822. After a detailed comparison to the original, the authors conclude that the Russian is equal to Byron in his handling of the poem's themes, structure, and imagery.

257. Ogle, Robert B. "A Byron Contradiction: Some Light on His Italian Study," SIR, 12 (Winter 1973), 436–442.†‡

Attempts to resolve contradictory statements made by Byron about the origin of Italian comic epic by reference to two literary histories he is known to have read, Sismondi's *De la littérature du midi de l'Europe* and Pierre Louis Ginguene's *Histoire littéraire d'Italie*.

258. *Osborne, Keith, and Sheila M. Cooke, comps. *Lord Byron, 1788–1824.* Nottingham: Nottinghamshire County Library, 1974.

A portfolio of critical material.

259. Parker, David. "The Narrator of *Don Juan*," *Ariel*, 5 (Apr. 1974), 49–58.

Approaches the problem of multiple narrative voices by seeing the narrator as a traditional literary "rogue," discovering his identity through use of different disguises.

260. Pemberton, Richard R. "Ironie et tra-

gédie: Le *Sardanapale* de Byron," *Romantisme*, No. 7 (1974), pp. 16–31.

Discusses the relationship of tragedy to Romanticism, including recent scholarship on the subject, then examines *Sardanapalus* and finds it a true tragedy.

261. Pemberton, Richard R. "The Romantic Irony of Lord Byron" [Doctoral dissertation, California, Los Angeles, 1974], DAI, 35 (Nov. 1974), 3003-A.

262. Peters, John U. "Matthew Arnold: The Heroes of His Poetry" [Doctoral dissertation, Wisconsin, 1973], DAI, 35 (July 1974), 412-A.

Byron is one.

263. "Philhellenic Celebration," *Blackwood's Magazine*, 315 (Apr. 1974), 343–344.

Athens commemorates the 150th anniversary of Byron's death.

264. Pierssens, Michel. "Lautréamont et l'heritage du byronisme," *Romantisme*, No. 7 (1974), pp. 77–85.

Byronic elements in *Chants de Maldoror*.

265. Pistone, Danièle. "Byron et ses musiciens," *Romantisme*, No. 7 (1974), pp. 86–98.

Discusses musical settings of Byron's works, and includes a list of musical works inspired by Byron's poems.

266. Poenicke, Klaus. "Dark Sublime: Raum und Selbst in der amerikanischen Romantik," *Jahrbuch für Amerikastudien*, 36 (1972), 5–231.

A monograph with a number of references to Byron and Godwin.

267. *Polidori, John William. *The Vampyre: A Tale*. Introd. Russell Ash. Aylesbury, Bucks.: Shire, for Gubblecote Press, 1973.

Limited edition of 1000 copies.

268. Porter, Peter. "Byron and the Moral North: The Englishness of *Don Juan*," *Encounter*, 43 (Aug. 1974), 65–72.

Affectionate general comments on the poem, especially on the last (English) cantos.

269. *Pratt, Willis W. *Byron at Southwell: The Making of a Poet*. With new poems and letters from the rare book collection of the Univ. of Texas. New York: Haskell, 1973.

Reprint of the 1948 edition.

270. Price, Elizabeth. "Don Juan: A Chronicle of His Literary Adventures in Germanic Territory" [Doctoral dissertation, Washington Univ., 1974], DAI, 35 (Oct. 1974), 2291-A.

Byron's version aroused interest among German writers.

271. Pujals, Esteban. *Espronceda y lord Byron*. 2nd revised ed. Madrid: C.S.I.C., 1972.

272. *Quennell, Peter. *Byron*. Folcroft, Pa.: Folcroft, 1974.

Reprint of the 1934 edition in the "Great Lives" series.

273. *Quennell, Peter. *Byron*. New York: Haskell, 1974.

Reprint of the 1934 edition in the "Great Lives" series.

274. *Quennell, Peter. *Byron: The Years of Fame; Byron in Italy*. London: Collins, 1974.

Combined edition of works published in 1941 and 1967, with revisions of the latter.

275. *Quennell, Peter. "Lord Byron: Man and Legend," *Daily Telegraph Magazine* (London), 19 Apr. 1974, pp. 28–31, 33–34.

276. Cancelled.

277. *Rainwater, Frank. *Lord Byron: A Study of the Development of His Philosophy, with Special Emphasis upon the Dramas*. Folcroft, Pa.: Folcroft, 1974.

Reprint of a 1949 thesis summary.

278. *Reddy, D. V. Subba. *Byron's "Don Juan."* Folcroft, Pa.: Folcroft, 1974.

Reprint of the 1968 edition.

279. Redpath, Theodore. "Byron in Cambridge," BJ, No. 1 (1973), pp. 59–61.

Discusses Byron's attendance and lodgings.

280. Cancelled.

281. Rich, Douglas Denham. "Heroic Vision: A Study of Byron's Verse Tales" [Doctoral dissertation, Washington State, 1974], DAI, 35 (Dec. 1974), 3696-A.

282. Ridenour, George M. "My Poem's Epic," in *Parnassus Revisited: Modern Critical Essays on the Epic Tradition*, ed. Anthony C. Yu (Chicago: American Library Association, 1973), pp. 303–325.

Reprinted from *The Style of "Don Juan."*

283. Roberts, Cecil. "And Did Trelawny Lie?" *Books and Bookmen*, 19 (Oct. 1973), 62–66.

Yes, but he did it well. Includes an eyewitness account of the opening of Byron's grave.

284. Roberts, Steven V. "Byron Still Greek Hero 150 Years After He Died," *New York Times*, 19 Apr. 1974, p. 2.
Byron remains a symbol of liberty in Greece.

285. *Robson, H. L. "Byron, the Milbankes, and Seaham Village," *Antiquities of Sunderland*, 25 (1970–73), 1–25.

286. Rowse, A. L. "The Extraordinary Life Story of Byron's Cornish Grandmother," *Times* (London), 13 Apr. 1974, p. 12.
On Byron's paternal grandmother, Sophia Trevanion, a bluestocking friend of Mrs. Thrale, Fanny Burney, and Dr. Johnson.

286a. Rutherford, Andrew. "Byron: A Pilgrim's Progress," BJ, No. 2 (1974), pp. 4–26.
Byron's "whole career can be seen as a pilgrimage which culminates at Missolonghi—a pilgrimage in search of a poetic role compatible with his political ideals, and still more important to him, a political role compatible with his poetic imagination."

287. St. Clair, William. *That Greece Might Still Be Free: The Philhellenes in the War of Independence*. See K-SJ, 21–22 (1972–73), No. 302.
Rev. in *Slavic Review*, 32 (June 1973), 424; by David V. Erdman in ELN, 11, Supplement (Sept. 1973), 39; by Ian Scott Kilvert in BJ, No. 1 (1973), pp. 29–30; in *Choice*, 11 (June 1974), 596–597; by C. W. Crawley in *Historical Journal*, 17 (Mar. 1974), 199–200.

288. *Sainz de Robles, Federico C. "Byron y su trio de damas," *Vanguardia española* (Barcelona), 3 Dec. 1971.

289. Schroeder, Ronald Allan. "Byron and the New Romance: *Childe Harold's Pilgrimage* I–II and Medieval Tradition" [Doctoral dissertation, Northwestern, 1973], DAI, 34 (Mar. 1974), 5992-A.

290. Sheraw, C. Darrell. "*Don Juan*: Byron As Un-Augustan Satirist," *Satire Newsletter*, No. 19 (Spring 1973), pp. 25–33.†
"Little recognition today is given to the fact that Byron's role as satirist in *Don Juan*, as revealed through his satire technique, pose, and world view, is not only un-Augustan but actually modern."

291. *Sidorčenko, L. V. "O prototipax geroev 'Vostočnyx povestej' Bajrona (Lambros Kaconis i Žan Laffit)" [On the heroic prototypes in Byron's oriental tales (Lambros Kaconis and Jean Laffite)], *Izvestija Akademii Nauk S.S.S.R., Serija Literatury i Jazyka* (Moscow), 32 (1973), 121–126.

292. Simpson, Richard Hunt. "Sympathy as Value in Byron's Poetry" [Doctoral dissertation, Kent State, 1973], DAI, 35 (July 1974), 476-A.

292a. Singer, Eric. "Some Thoughts on Canto II of Byron's *Don Juan*," BJ, No. 2 (1974), pp. 64–78.
An appreciation of Byron's vitality.

293. Spence, G. W. "The Moral Ambiguity of *Marino Faliero*," *AUMLA*, 41 (May 1974), 6–17.
Faliero's motivation is not clear.

294. Spencer, Terence J. B. *Fair Greece! Sad Relic: Literary Philhellenism from Shakespeare to Byron*. New York: Octagon, 1973.
Reprint of the 1954 edition.

295. *Spender, Stephen. "The Romanticism of a Daemonic Temperament," *Daily Telegraph Magazine* (London), 19 Apr. 1974, pp. 37–39, 41.
On Byron.

296. Sperry, Stuart M. "Byron and the Meaning of *Manfred*," *Criticism*, 16 (Summer 1974), 189–202.
Manfred's confrontation with the fiend in the last scene dramatizes Byron's casting off of the persona of the Byronic hero.

297. Steffan, T. G. "Lord Henry's and Lady Adeline's Rank in Lord Byron's *Don Juan*," N&Q, 218 (Aug. 1973), 290–291.†
Evidence in the poem indicates that Lord Henry Amundeville was the younger son of a duke or marquess and that his wife outranked him.

298. Stephenson, William Alva, Jr. "Henry Fielding's Influence on Byron" [Doctoral dissertation, Texas Tech, 1973], DAI, 35 (July 1974), 478-A.

299. *Stevens, H. R. "Theme and Structure in Byron's *Manfred*: The Biblical Basis," UES, 11, No. 2 (1973), pp. 15–22.

300. Strickland, Margot. *The Byron Women.* London: Peter Owen, 1974.
Rev. in *TLS, 14 June 1974, p. 646; by A. L. Rowse in Spec, 230 (15 June 1974), 739; by Elizabeth Longford in *Books and Bookmen*, 19 (Aug. 1974), 24–25.

301. Taborski, Boleslaw. *Byron and the Theatre.* See K-SJ, 21–22 (1972–73), No. 315.
Rev. in *Choice*, 10 (Jan. 1974), 1722; in ELN, 12, Supplement (Sept. 1974), 42; by Margaret J. Howell in BJ, No. 2 (1974), pp. 59–60.

302. Tatchell, Molly. "Byron's 'Windsor Poetics,' " KSMB, 25 (1974), 1–5.
Discusses background and texts of an anti-Regent satirical poem prompted by the opening of a burial vault at Windsor.

303. Terzian, Aram. "George Gordon, Lord Byron: The Poet and the Legend," *Armenian Review*, 27 (Summer 1974), 115–131.
General remarks on the poet's life and work, with discussion of his influence on Armenian literature.

304. Thomson, Fred C. " 'With All Deliberate Speed': A Source in Scott," AN&Q, 11 (Nov. 1972), 38–40.
Byron also used the phrase.

304a. Train, Keith. "The Byron Family," BJ, No. 2 (1974), pp. 35–40.
1066–1974.

305. *Trelawny, Edward John. *Adventures of a Younger Son.* Ed. and introd. Edward Garnett. New York: AMS, 1973.
Reprint of the 1890 edition.

306. Trelawny, Edward John. *Adventures of a Younger Son.* Ed. and introd. William St. Clair. London: Oxford Univ., 1974. "Oxford English Novels."
Text collated with Harvard's recently purchased manuscript.

307. *Trelawny, Edward John. *Letters.* Ed. H. Buxton Forman. New York: AMS, 1973.
Reprint of the 1910 edition.

308. Trelawny, Edward John. *Records of Shelley, Byron, and the Author.* Ed. and introd. David Wright. Harmondsworth: Penguin, 1973. "Penguin English Library."
The 1878 edition of *Recollections of the Last Days of Shelley and Byron*, with a new introduction.
Rev. by William St. Clair in BJ, No. 2 (1974), pp. 58–59.

309. Trueblood, Paul G. "Byron's Political Realism," BJ, No. 1 (1973), pp. 50–58.
Finds Byron's political views and actions consistent throughout his career. Relevant episodes and literary works are discussed.

310. Turney, Catherine. *Byron's Daughter: A Biography of Elizabeth Medora Leigh.* London: Davies, 1974.
London edition of a 1972 book. See K-SJ, 21–22 (1972–73), No. 321.
Rev. in *Choice*, 10 (Mar. 1973), 99; by A. LaVonne Ruoff in *Western Humanities Review*, 27 (Summer 1973), 315–318, reply by Catherine Turney, 28 (Winter 1974), 102–103; by E. E. Bostetter in ELN, 11, Supplement (Sept. 1973), 39–40; by A. L. Rowse in Spec, 230 (15 June 1974), 739. Also see No. 125.

311. Tyler, Anthony Otis. "Byron's Use of Ancient History and Historians in *Childe Harold's Pilgrimage*, *Don Juan*, and *The Age of Bronze*" [Doctoral dissertation, Indiana, 1973], DAI, 34 (Oct. 1973), 1872-A.

312. "Unpublished Letter: From Mavrocordatos to Byron," BJ, No. 1 (1973), pp. 26–27.
The letter of Jan. 1824 (in French) is reproduced and translated. It urgently requests money to pay Greek soldiers.

313. *Victoria and Albert Museum. *Byron: An Exhibition Guide.* London: Victoria and Albert Museum, 1974.
The exhibition ran 30 May – 25 Aug. 1974. Also see No. 146.

314. Vitoux, Pierre. "Note sur Byron et la critique byronienne," *Romantisme*, No. 7 (1974), pp. 2–7.
Preface to an issue devoted to Byron.

315. *Vulliamy, C. E. *Byron, with a View of the Kingdom of Cant and a Dissection of the Byronic Ego.* Folcroft, Pa.: Folcroft, 1974.
Reprint of the 1948 edition.

316. *Vulliamy, C. E. *Byron, with a View of the Kingdom of Cant and a Dissection of the Byronic Ego.* New York: Haskell, 1974.
Reprint of the 1948 edition.

317. Wallis, Bruce. *Byron: The Critical Voice.* Vol. I: *Introduction and General Criticism.* *Vol. II: *Self-Criticism and Criticism of Individuals and Works.* Salzburg: Univ. of Salzburg, 1973. "Salzburg Studies in

English: Romantic Reassessment Series, Nos. 20–21."

Rev. in ELN, 12, Supplement (Sept. 1974), 42–43. Also see No. 31.

318. Walton, Francis R. "Byron's Lines *On John William Rizzo Hoppner*," K-SJ, 21–22 (1972–73), 40–42.‡

Presents evidence that Count Rizzo, the child's godfather, not Byron or the father, was responsible for the publication of Byron's lines and eleven translations.

319. Ward, Herman M. *Byron and the Magazines, 1806–1824*. Salzburg: Univ. of Salzburg, 1973. "Salzburg Studies in English: Romantic Reassessment Series, No. 19."

Rev. by David V. Erdman in ELN, 12, Supplement (Sept. 1974), 43. Also see No. 31.

320. Wesche, Ulrich Klaus. "Byron and Grabbe: A Comparative Study of Their Works and Their Relation to European Romanticism" [Doctoral dissertation, North Carolina, 1973], DAI, 34 (Mar. 1974), 5935-A.

321. Whitlock, William. "Byron and the Luddites," KSMB, 25 (1974), 6–8.

Byron's speech to the House of Lords against the frame-breaking bill is quoted, and the contemporary events which inspired it are briefly outlined.

322. Widdowson, Peter. "Emily Brontë: The Romantic Novelist," *Moderna Språk*, 66 (Feb.–Mar. 1972), 1–19.

Notes the influence of Byron and Shelley.

323. Wilson, Milton. "Travellers' Venice: Some Images for Byron and Shelley," UTQ, 43 (Winter 1974), 93–120.

An examination of received ideas about Venice, and the use of Venice, literally and symbolically, by Byron and Shelley.

324. Wood, Gerald Carl. "Byron's *Don Juan*: A Study in the Structure of Its Satire" [Doctoral dissertation, Florida, 1971], DAI, 35 (Dec. 1974), 3707-A.

325. *Wood, Pamela J., ed. *Byron*. Derby: English Life, 1974.

A pamphlet of critical material.

326. Zegger, Robert E. *John Cam Hobhouse: A Political Life, 1819–1852*. Columbia: Univ. of Missouri, 1973.

Rev. by Joanna Richardson in *History Today*, 23 (Dec. 1973), 885–886.

326a. Zulawski, Juliusz. "Byron's Influence in Poland," BJ, No. 2 (1974), pp. 28–34.

It was enormous, and political as well as literary.

For additional Books and Articles Relating to Byron and His Circle see Nos. 1, 6, 8, 17, 25, 26, 30, 35, 43–45, 50–52, 55, 58, 61–63, 65, 69, 70–72, 74, 75, 77, 79, 87, 88, 90, 92, 94, 96, 475, 610, 613, 672, 683, 693, 697, 735, 740, 799, 807.

III. HUNT

Works: Collected, Selected, Single

327. **The Correspondence*. Hildesheim: Olms, 1973.

Reprint of the 1862 edition, two volumes in one.

328. **Imagination and Fancy, with an Essay in Answer to the Question, "What is Poetry?"* New York: AMS, 1972.

Reprint of the 1844 edition.

329. **Leigh Hunt's Literary Criticism*. Ed. Lawrence and Carolyn Houtchens. With an essay in evaluation by Clarence D. Thorpe. New York: Octagon, 1973.

Reprint of the 1956 edition.

330. **Wit and Humour, Selected from the English Poets*. Folcroft, Pa.: Folcroft, 1972.

Reprint of the 1882 edition.

331. **Wit and Humour, Selected from the English Poets*. Norwood, Pa.: Norwood, 1973.

Reprint of the 1882 edition.

For additional Works by Hunt see Nos. 452, 575, 758.

Books and Articles Relating to Hunt

332. *Brack, O. M., Jr., and D. H. Stefanson, comps. *The Leigh Hunt Manuscripts in the University of Iowa Libraries*. Iowa City: Friends of the Univ. of Iowa Libraries, 1973.

333. *Brewer, Luther A. *Leigh Hunt and Charles Dickens: The Skimpole Caricature*. Folcroft, Pa.: Folcroft, 1973.

Reprint of 1930 book.

334. Ericksen, Donald H. "Harold Skimpole: Dickens and the Early 'Art for Art's Sake' Movement," JEGP, 72 (Jan. 1973), 48–59.

"Harold Skimpole seems meant to be more than á mere caricature of Leigh Hunt—but a portrait of a dilettante who is more vicious than amusing." Dickens' specific target was the current tendency to separate art and life, as represented by the Pre-Raphaelites and the "art for art's sake" movement.

335. Fenner, Theodore. *Leigh Hunt and Opera Criticism: The "Examiner" Years, 1808–1821*. See K-SJ, 21–22 (1972–73), No. 341.

Rev. by David R. Cheney in K-SJ, 21–22 (1972–73), 261–263; by Roy E. Aycock in *Musical Quarterly*, 59 (Apr. 1973), 314–320; by Karl Kroeber in WC, 4 (Summer 1973), 215; by David V. Erdman in ELN, 12, Supplement (Sept. 1974), 51–52.

336. *Johnson, R. Brimley. *Leigh Hunt*. Folcroft, Pa., Folcroft: 1973.

Reprint of the 1896 edition.

337. Kendall, Kenneth E. *Leigh Hunt's "Reflector."* See K-SJ, 20 (1971), No. 441; 21–22 (1972–73), No. 344.

Rev. by Leonidas M. Jones in K-SJ, 21–22 (1972–73), 263–264.

338. McCartney, Hunter P. "English Writer Leigh Hunt: Victim of Journalistic McCarthyism," *Journalism Quarterly*, 50 (Spring 1973), 92–96.

On the government's efforts to silence the *Examiner*.

339. Morpurgo, J. E. "Edmund Blunden: Poet of Community," CR, 225 (Oct. 1974), 192–198.

Several references to Hunt.

340. "Recent Acquisitions," *Books at Iowa*, 20 (Apr. 1974), 45–46.

University of Iowa has acquired seven autograph letters of Hunt and other memorabilia.

341. Short, Clarice. "The Composition of Hunt's *The Story of Rimini*," K-SJ, 21–22 (1972–73), 207–218.‡

On the basis of the manuscript evidence, "[a]t no point does it appear that the poetry came 'as naturally as leaves to a tree.' "

342. Stam, David H. "Leigh Hunt and *The True Sun*: A List of Reviews, August 1833 to February 1834," BNYPL, 77 (Summer 1974), 436–453.

Lists over 100 review articles by Hunt on politics, science, and the arts.

For additional Books and Articles Relating to Hunt see Nos. 1, 15, 25, 32, 55, 71, 77, 191, 199, 452, 461, 515, 521, 575, 613, 672, 758.

IV. KEATS

Works: Collected, Selected, Translated

343. *John Keats: The Complete Poems*. Ed. John Barnard. Harmondsworth: Penguin, 1973. "Penguin English Poets." Paperback.

Rev. in TLS, 16 Nov. 1973, p. 1409.

344. *Letters of John Keats: A New Selection*. Ed. Robert Gittings. See K-SJ, 20 (1971), No. 462.

Rev. by J. C. Maxwell in N&Q, 218 (Feb. 1973), 77; by Manfred Wojcik in *Zeitschrift für Anglistik und Amerikanistik*, 22, No. 1 (1974), 95–97 [in German].

345. **The Poems of John Keats*. Ed. Miriam Allott. Harlow, Essex: Longman; New York: Norton (1972). "Annotated English Poets."

Paperback reprint of the 1970 edition.

346. **Poesi: Odi e sonetti*. Trans. and introd. Eurialo de Michelis. Rome: Newton Compton italiana, 1973. Paperback.

347. **Selected Letters*. Ed. and introd. Robert Pack. New York: New American Library, 1974. Paperback.

348. **Three Odes of Keats*. Ed. E. L. Marilla. Folcroft, Pa.: Folcroft, 1974.

Reprint of the 1962 edition.

For additional Works by Keats see Nos. 61, 372, 531, 550.

Books and Articles Relating to Keats and His Circle

349. Anderson, Norman A. "Corrections to Amy Lowell's Reading of Keats's Marginalia," K-SJ, 23 (1974), 25–31.

Corrects misreadings, incorrect identifications, and omissions.

350. Antonelli, Edward Anthony. "The Pain of Truth: Keats's Struggle to Verify the Imaginative Experience" [Doctoral dissertation, Univ. of Washington, 1973], DAI, 34 (Nov. 1973), 2545-A.

351. Atkins, G. Douglas. " 'The Eve of St.

Agnes' Reconsidered," *Tennessee Studies in Literature*, 18 (1973), 113–132.‡

An attempt to delineate more precisely than have Wasserman, Stillinger, and Sperry the way in which romantic and realistic elements, as well as the mixture of affirmation and scepticism, come together to form the poem.

352. Baker, Carlos. "Robinson's Stoical Romanticism: 1890–1897," *New England Quarterly*, 46 (Mar. 1973), 3–16.

He was influenced by Wordsworth and Keats.

353. Barrell, John. *The Idea of Landscape and the Sense of Place, 1730–1840: An Approach to the Poetry of John Clare*. See K-SJ, 21–22 (1972–73), No. 370.

Rev. by David V. Erdman in ELN, 11, Supplement (Sept. 1973), 42; by Belinda Humphrey in *Anglo-Welsh Review*, 22, No. 1 (1973), 197–208; by Joanna E. Rapf in SIR, 13 (Winter 1974), 79–84.

354. Bate, Walter J. *John Keats*. See K-SJ, 14 (1965), No. 118; 15 (1966), No. 156; 16 (1967), No. 126; 17 (1968), No. 22; 18 (1969), No. 356; 19 (1970), No. 185.

Rev. by Manfred Wojcik in *Zeitschrift für Anglistik und Amerikanistik*, 21 (July 1973), 315–318 [in German].

355. *Bayley, John. *Keats and Reality*. Folcroft, Pa.: Folcroft, 1973.

Reprint of the 1962 edition of the British Academy Lecture.

356. *Beaudry, Harry R. *The English Theatre and John Keats*. Salzburg: Univ. of Salzburg, 1973. "Salzburg Studies in English: Poetic Drama Series, No. 13."

See Nos. 31, 86.

357. Bell, Arthur H. " 'The Depth of Things': Keats and Human Space," K-SJ, 23 (1974), 77–94.

Deals with "how, in Keats's view, a poem's spatial imagery is related to the reader's flow of thought as he reads or hears the poem," and argues that Keats's spatial images are not symbolic or allegorical but "regions of particular emotional and intellectual atmosphere." Discusses "The Eve of St. Agnes," in which the "pattern can be described as the gradual decreasing of space to a moment of constriction, and then a sudden release into 'wideness' "; "Lamia," in which there is a pattern of "spatial collapse"; "Ode to a Nightingale," in which "two spatial entities verge . . . upon becoming one"; and "The Fall of Hyperion," in which the "spatial surroundings of the poet in Moneta's temple are vast, but not entirely undefined."

358. Bernstein, Gene M. "Keats's 'Ode on a Grecian Urn': Individuation and the Mandāla," *Massachusetts Studies in English*, 4 (Spring 1973), 24–30.

A Jungian interpretation.

359. *Bhattacharya, Mohinimohan. *Keats and Spenser*. Folcroft, Pa.: Folcroft, 1973.

Reprint of the 1944 edition of the Benares Hindu Univ. Lecture.

360. Black, Michael. "Poetry as Original Language," *Critical Review*, 16 (1973), 3–18.‡

Linguists cannot explain in terms of grammar or syntax the unique verbal effects achieved by poets like Keats.

360a. Booth, James. "Keats: 'Ode on a Grecian Urn,' " *Critical Survey*, 6 (Summer 1973), 59–64.

A critical reading emphasizing the theme of human transience versus the immortality of art.

361. Boyar, Billy T. "Keats's 'Isabella': Shakespeare's *Venus and Adonis* and the Venus-Adonis Myth," K-SJ, 21–22 (1972–73), 160–169.‡

Finds "overwhelming evidence that Keats borrowed profusely" from Shakespeare's poem, and suggests that Keats "employs fertility myth, the language of love and life, to evince ironically the moral desolation of the age."

362. *Brandenburg, Albert J. [*pseud.* Erlande]. *The Life of John Keats*. Trans. Marion Robinson. Preface by John Middleton Murry. Folcroft, Pa.: Folcroft, 1973.

Reprint of the 1929 edition.

363. *Brightfield, Myron. *Scott, Hazlitt, and Napoleon*. Folcroft, Pa.: Folcroft, 1969.

Reprint of the 1943 edition.

364. *Brockbank, J. P. " 'Ode on a Grecian Urn': Reflections on a Masterpiece," *Delta*, No. 51 (Spring 1973), pp. 3–19.

365. Brogan, Howard O. "*The Cap and Bells*, or . . . *The Jealousies*?" BNYPL, 77 (Spring 1974), 298–313.

"Such satire as is to be found in the poem may be directed as much at Keats himself as at any of his contemporaries."

366. Brown, E. Carole. "The Matrix of the Dream: Poetry and Love in the Major Poems of Keats" [Doctoral dissertation, State Univ. of New York, Buffalo, 1973], DAI, 34 (Aug. 1973), 719-A.

367. *Brown, Leonard S. *The Genesis, Growth, and Meaning of "Endymion."* Folcroft, Pa.: Folcroft, 1974.

Reprint of the 1933 edition.

368. Bump, Jerome. "Hopkins and Keats," *Victorian Poetry*, 12 (Spring 1974), 33–43.

Discusses the early Hopkins' struggle to find his own voice against the domineering influence of Keats.

369. Burnby, J. G. L. *The Hammonds of Edmonton.* Edmonton: Edmonton Hundred Historical Society, 1973. "Occasional Paper, N.S., No. 26."

A short pamphlet about the Hammond dynasty of apothecaries and surgeons, one of whose members Keats was apprenticed to.

370. Cacciatore, Vera. *A Room in Rome.* Rome: Keats-Shelley Memorial Association, 1970.

Reprinted in 1973. Keats's room and the memories associated with it.

371. *Camden (London Borough), Libraries, Arts, and Recreation Department. *Keats House: A Guide.* 7th ed. London: London Borough of Camden, Director of Libraries and Arts, and Curator, 1974.

372. *Carmichael, Katherine K. *A Critical Edition of the Early Poems of John Keats.* With a philosophical supplement. Folcroft, Pa.: Folcroft, 1974.

Reprint of a 1944 thesis summary.

373. Cary, Richard. " 'The Clam-Digger: Capitol Island': A Robinson Sonnet Recovered," *Colby Library Quarterly*, 10, No. 8 (Dec. 1974), 505–511.

Robinson was influenced by Keats, whose sonnets he called "the greatest in the English language."

374. Chatterjee, Bhabatosh. *John Keats: His Mind and Work.* See K-SJ, 21–22 (1972–73), No. 389.

Rev. by Allan Rodway in RES, 24 (Nov. 1973), 504–505; by Stuart M. Sperry in ELN, 12, Supplement (Sept. 1974), 52–53; by Arthur H. Bell in K-SJ, 23 (1974), 149–151. Also see No. 57.

375. Chavis, Geraldine Giebel. "Dreams as Motif in John Keats's Works" [Doctoral dissertation, Syracuse, 1973], DAI, 34 (Apr. 1974), 6631-A.

376. Chilcott, Tim. *A Publisher and His Circle: The Life and Work of John Taylor, Keats's Publisher.* See K-SJ, 21–22 (1972–73), No. 390.

Rev. by John O. Hayden in K-SJ, 21–22 (1972–73), 266–268; by Raymond H. Shove in LJ, 43 (Jan. 1973), 78–80; by R. W. King in RES, 24 (May 1973), 225–226; by Richard D. Altick in *Comparative Literature Studies*, 10 (Sept. 1973), 270–272; by Roy Park in N&Q, 219 (Sept. 1974), 350–351; by Stuart M. Sperry in ELN, 12, Supplement (Sept. 1974), 53.

377. Church, Philip Dake. "That Disenchanted Harmony: The Nature and Mythological Poetry of George Meredith" [Doctoral dissertation, Michigan, 1972], DAI, 33 (May 1973), 6346-A.

Meredith's poetry and aesthetic is compared with Keats's.

378. Clare, John. *Birds Nest: Poems by John Clare.* Ed. Anne Tibble. Ashington: Mid Northumberland Arts Group, 1973.

379. *Clare, John. *Selected Poems.* Ed. J. W. and Anne Tibble. London: Dent, 1973. "Everyman's Library."

Reprint of the 1965 edition. Also in paperback.

380. Clare, John. *Selected Poems and Prose of John Clare.* See K-SJ, 17 (1968), No. 127.

Rev. by Wolfgang G. Müller in ASNS, 209 (Jan. 1973), 411–412.

381. *Clare, John. *Sketches in the Life of John Clare, Written by Himself.* Ed. Edmund Blunden. Folcroft, Pa.: Folcroft, 1974.

Reprint of the 1931 edition.

382. Clark, Eleanor. "Of Graves and Poets," *Commentary*, 58 (Nov. 1974), 61–73.

The history of the Protestant Cemetery in Rome, with particular reference to Keats and Shelley.

383. *Clarke, Charles Cowden. *Shakespeare-Characters, Chiefly Those Subordinate.* New York: AMS, 1974.

Reprint of the 1863 edition.

384. *Clarke, Mary Cowden. *The Girlhood of Shakespeare's Heroines: A Series of Fifteen Tales.* New York: AMS, 1974.

Reprint of the 1850–51 edition.

385. Clayborough, Arthur. " 'Negative Capability' and 'The Camelion Poet' in Keats's Letters: The Case for Differentiation," ES, 54 (Dec. 1973), 569–575.

Negative capability "means self-confidence, having the courage of one's vision"; this notion overlaps with but is not the same as the idea of the characterless poet.

386. Cockerton, R. W. P. "A Portrait of John Taylor (1781–1864)," KSMB, 24 (1973), 19.

A photograph of a water color, apparently by Joseph Severn.

387. Cognard, Anne Marie MacLeod. "The, Classical Affinity of Spenser and Keats: A Study of Time and Value" [Doctoral dissertation, Texas Christian, 1973], DAI, 34 (Mar. 1974), 5903-A.

388. *Colvin, Sidney. *Keats.* Folcroft, Pa.: Folcroft, 1973.

Reprint of a work first published in 1887.

389. Cooke, Michael G. "De Quincey, Coleridge, and the Formal Uses of Intoxication," *Yale French Studies*, No. 50 (1974), pp. 26–40.

Begins with "Ode to a Nightingale."

390. Corner, Martin. "Arnold, Lessing, and the Preface of 1853," JEGP, 72 (Apr. 1973), 223–235.‡

". . . Arnold recommends the *Laokoon* as part of his attack on the 'confused multitudinousness' of early Victorian poetry, for which Keats is held largely responsible."

391. *Corrington, John W. "Cassirer's Curse, Keats's Urn, and the Poem before the Poem," *Forum* (Houston), 10, No. 2 (1972), pp. 10–14.

392. Cottle, Basil. "Wordsworth and His Portraits: Two Unpublished Letters," N&Q, 218 (Aug. 1973), 285–286.†

The one he owned and the other he refused were both by Haydon.

393. Cumings, Alan J. "The Ritual of Ecstasy in the Poetry of John Keats" [Doctoral dissertation, Wisconsin, 1972], DAI, 33 (Jan. 1973), 3637-A.

394. Currier, Barbara. "The Gift of Personality: An Appraisal of 'Impressionist Criticism' " [Doctoral dissertation, Columbia, 1972], DAI, 33 (Apr. 1973), 5673-A.

Hazlitt is included.

395. Daalder, Joost. "W. H. Auden's 'The Shield of Achilles' and Its Sources," *AUMLA*, 42 (Nov. 1974), 186–198.

Keats is an important influence.

396. Danzig, Allan, ed. *Twentieth Century Interpretations of "The Eve of St. Agnes": A Collection of Critical Essays.* See K-SJ, 20 (1971), No. 518.

Rev. by Paul D. Sheats in K-SJ, 21–22 (1972–72), 255–256.

397. D'Avanzo, Mario L. " 'Ode on a Grecian Urn' and *The Excursion*," K-SJ, 23 (1974), 95–105.

A detailed comparison whose purpose is to show "how *The Excursion* underlies the general character of the Ode, in particular its thought, language, and tone."

398. *D'Avanzo, Mario L. "*Pierre* and the Wisdom of Keats's Melancholy," *Extracts* (Univ. of Pennsylvania), 16 (1973), 6–9.

399. Davis, Cynthia. "An Interview with Stanley Kunitz," CL, 15 (Winter 1974), 1–14.

Kunitz has been influenced by Keats.

400. Demmin, Julia Laker. "Myth and Mythmaking in Keats and Arnold" [Doctoral dissertation, Illinois, 1973], DAI, 34 (June 1974), 7701-A.

401. Dennehy, Frederick J. "The Broken Charm: A Study of John Clare's Poetry" [Doctoral dissertation, Virginia, 1973], DAI, 34 (Oct. 1973), 1854-A.

402. De Quincey, Thomas. *De Quincey as Critic.* Ed. John E. Jordan. London: Routledge, 1973. "Routledge Critics Series."

Essays on Keats, Hazlitt, and Clare are included.

403. Dickstein, Morris. *Keats and His Poetry: A Study in Development.* See K-SJ, 20 (1971), No. 534; 21–22 (1972–73), No. 400.

Rev. by Michael N. Stanton in K-SJ, 21–22 (1972–73), 253–255; by Paul Zietlow in PR, 40 (1973), 503–509; by Howard H. Hinkel in *Georgia Review*, 27 (Fall 1973), 432–435. Also see No. 57.

404. D'jakonova, Nina Ja. *Kits i ego sovremenniki.* [Keats and his contemporaries.] Moscow: Nauka, 1973.

405. Dunham, Larry Dean. "The Pleasure-

Pain Motif in the Poetry of John Keats" [Doctoral dissertation, Missouri, 1972], DAI, 34 (Sept. 1973), 1275-A.

406. Eagleton, T. "William Hazlitt: An Empiricist Radical," *New Blackfriars*, 54 (Mar. 1973), 108–117.

Observes in all Hazlitt's writing "a need to bind consciousness to concrete life without thereby denying its transformative creativity."

407. Ende, Stuart A. "Keats's Music of Truth," *ELH*, 40 (Spring 1973), 90–104.

Drawing on Yeats's theory that for each poet there is a single myth that "underlies his deepest meditations," Ende suggests that "we might consider Keats's poetic development in terms of the conflict between his desire for vision or imaginative apprehension and his powerful sense—in effect, a belief or myth of existence—of separation from such redeeming states." The conflict is traced in Keats's reaction to other poets and in *Endymion*.

408. Enderle, Dolores Ann. "The Evolution of Hazlitt's Prose Style" [Doctoral dissertation, Ball State, 1972], DAI, 33 (Mar. 1973), 5171-A.

409. England, George Eugene, Jr. "Beyond the Romantic Dilemma: A Study of the Poetry of Frederick Goddard Tuckerman" [Doctoral dissertation, Stanford, 1974], DAI, 35 (Sept. 1974), 1620-A.

Discusses the influence of Keats.

410. *Evans, B. Ifor. *Keats*. Folcroft, Pa.: Folcroft, 1974.

Reprint of the 1934 edition.

411. *Evans, B. Ifor. *Keats*. New York: Haskell, 1974.

Reprint of the 1934 edition.

412. Fairman, Patricia Shaw. "Macbeth and the Critics," *Filologia moderna*, 14 (Feb.–June 1974), 203–231.

Hazlitt is discussed.

413. Fleissner, Robert F. "Keats' Belle Ms.," *Unicorn*, 3, No. 1 (1974), 25–27.

The lady is "loveliness incarnate," not a female demon.

414. Fogle, R. H. "Keats's 'Lamia' as Dramatic Illusion," in *Nineteenth-Century Literary Perspectives: Essays in Honor of Lionel Stevenson*, ed. Clyde de L. Ryals *et al.* (Durham: Duke Univ., 1974), pp. 65–75.

415. Fritsche, Jo Ann M. "Visions of Action: John Keats's Major Narrative Poems of the 'Great Year' " [Doctoral dissertation, Case Western Reserve, 1972], DAI, 33 (Mar. 1973), 5121-A.

416. *Fujihara, Takeaki. "John Keats the Metapoet," *Studies in English Literature* (Japan), 50, No. 1 (1973), 29–45. [In Japanese.]

Keats is a poet whose constantly recurring theme is poetry itself, but he is not a pure metapoet for "his view of poetry is an integral part of his vision of life . . ." (from the English abstract, 50, English Number [1974], 225–226).

417. Gaunt, William. *The Restless Century: Painting in Britain, 1800–1900*. London: Phaidon; New York: Praeger (1972).

Discusses Haydon.

418. *Gelpi, Barbara Charlesworth. "The Image of the Anima in the Works of Dante Gabriel Rossetti," *Victorian Newsletter*, No. 45 (Spring 1974), pp. 1–7.

References to Keats.

419. Gilbert, Sandra. *Acts of Attention: The Poems of D. H. Lawrence*. Ithaca: Cornell Univ., 1972.

A number of references to Keats and Shelley.

420. Gittings, Robert. "John Keats, Physician and Poet," *Journal of the American Medical Association*, 224 (2 Apr. 1973), 51–55.

Medicine and poetry as rival attractions.

421. Glick, Robert Alan. "Imagery of Light and Darkness in Three Romantic Poets: Novalis, Keats and Wordsworth" [Doctoral dissertation, Indiana, 1972], DAI, 33 (May 1973), 6310-A.

422. Gordon, Catherine M. "Scott's Impact on Art," *Apollo*, 98 (July 1973), 36–39.

Quotes some remarks of Hazlitt on Scott and one of his illustrators.

423. *Gorell, Ronald B. *John Keats: The Principle of Beauty*. Folcroft, Pa.: Folcroft, 1973.

Reprint of the 1948 edition.

424. Goslee, Nancy M. " 'Under a Cloud in Prospect': Keats, Milton, and Stationing," PQ, 53 (Spring 1974), 205–219.

A reading of the "Hyperion" fragments in terms of Keats's use of Miltonic stationing.

425. Gradman, Barry Alan. "Dying into Life:

Metamorphosis in Keats's Poetry" [Doctoral dissertation, Brandeis, 1972], DAI, 33 (Jan. 1973), 3583-A.

426. *Grainger, Margaret, comp. *A Descriptive Catalogue of the John Clare Collection in Peterborough Museum and Art Gallery.* Peterborough: Peterborough Museum and Art Gallery, 1973.

Includes indexes to the poems in manuscript.

427. Griffith, Benjamin W. "Keats' 'On Seeing the Elgin Marbles,' " Exp, 31 (May 1973), Item 76.‡

The phrase "billowy main" must allude to the shipwreck of the statues in transit to England. Griffith also finds Platonic symbols in the last line.

428. Haley, Bruce E. "The Infinite Will: Shakespeare's *Troilus* and the 'Ode to a Nightingale,' " K-SJ, 21–22 (1972–73), 18–23.‡

"The tragedy of the romantic temperament is that it imagines and desires an ideal perfection which . . . is destroyed when grasped. Both Troilus and Keats's speaker attempt to renounce death and pain by renouncing that world in which these occur. The mind, desiring infinity, can conceptualize it, as Troilus does when he envisions a love sustained through the ages. But man is not content with an 'ideal' gratification; he must have one that richly satisfies the senses. . . . When the individual moves past pure will (desire and anticipatory idea) to execution, the idea is corrupted, thence becoming a slave to 'envious and calumniating time.' "

429. Hartman, Geoffrey H. "Poem and Ideology: A Study of Keats's 'To Autumn,' " in *Literary Theory and Structure: Essays in Honor of William K. Wimsatt*, ed. Frank Brady, John Palmer, and Martin Price (New Haven: Yale Univ., 1973), pp. 305–330.

430. Hartman, Geoffrey H. "Spectral Symbolism and the Authorial Self: An Approach to Keats's 'Hyperion,' " EC, 24 (Jan. 1974), 1–20.

In the two "Hyperion"s one can see Keats attempting to be an objective modern artist and yet being forced into a subjective role in order to protect and "nourish" failing divinities.

431. Harwell, Thomas Meade. *Keats and the Critics, 1848–1900.* See K-SJ, 21–22 (1972–73), No. 432.

Rev. in *Choice*, 10 (Apr. 1973), 619; by Wilfred S. Dowden in *CEA Critic*, 35 (May 1973), 33–34; by Stuart M. Sperry in ELN, 12, Supplement (Sept. 1974), 54.

432. Haworth, Helen E. " 'A Thing of Beauty is a Joy Forever'? Early Illustrated Editions of Keats' Poetry," *Harvard Library Bulletin*, 21 (Jan. 1973), 88–103.

A study of Keats's reputation in the Victorian era, as evidenced by the illustrations to his poems: "to an extraordinary extent they reflect and must have helped perpetuate the view of him as a poet revelling in luxurious images, a 'worshipper of beauty,' who was 'constitutionally melancholy,' 'physically frail,' and a 'myrial-hued [*sic*] fragile butterfly.' " Yet the number of these editions also attests to the popularity of Keats among the general reading public, in contrast to today.

433. *Haydon, Benjamin Robert. "Duke of Wellington" [Picture], *Apollo*, 98 (Sept. 1973), 169.

434. *Haydon, Benjamin Robert. "John Keats" [Detail of a drawing], *Art News*, 71 (Mar. 1972), 44.

435. *Haydon, Benjamin Robert. "Mrs. Haydon in Bed Nursing" [Drawing, 1823] and "William Wordsworth from Life" [Drawing], *Burlington Magazine*, 115 (Mar. 1973), xxxvii.

436. *Haydon, Benjamin Robert. "Self-Portrait" [Picture], *Apollo*, 98 (July 1973), 45.

437. *Hazlitt, William. *The Best of Hazlitt.* Comp. P. P. Howe. Freeport, N.Y.: Books for Libraries, 1972.

Reprint of the 1923 edition.

438. *Hazlitt, William. *Characteristics in the Manner of Rochefoucault's Maxims.* Introd. R. H. Horne. Folcroft. Pa.: Folcroft, 1973.

Reprint of the 1927 edition.

439. *Hazlitt, William. *The Fight.* Folcroft, Pa: Folcroft, 1974.

Reprint of the 1928 edition.

440. *Hazlitt, William Carew, ed. *Lamb and Hazlitt: Further Letters and Records Hith-*

erto Unpublished. Folcroft, Pa.: Folcroft, 1973.

Reprint of the 1900 edition.

441. *Hazlitt, William Carew, ed. *Lamb and Hazlitt: Further Letters and Records Hitherto Unpublished.* New York: AMS, 1973.

Reprint of the 1900 edition.

442. Hileman, William Peter. "The Bodily Vision: A Phenomenological Study of John Keats" [Doctoral dissertation, Illinois, 1973], DAI, 34 (Mar. 1974), 5971-A.

443. Hilles, Frederick W. "Reynolds among the Romantics," in *Literary Theory and Structure: Essays in Honor of William K. Wimsatt,* ed. Frank Brady, John Palmer, and Martin Price (New Haven: Yale Univ., 1973), pp. 267–283.

The views of Hazlitt and Haydon are discussed.

444. Holland, Norman N. *Poems in Persons: An Introduction to the Psychoanalysis of Literature.* New York: Norton, 1973.

Pp. 138–142 comment on Keats.

445. Hollander, John. "The Poem in the Ear," *Yale Review,* 62 (June 1973), 486–506.

Keats and Shelley are among the poets who most effectively exploit the sound value of poetry.

446. Hollingsworth, Keith. "The Nightingale Ode and Sophocles," K-SJ, 21–22 (1972–73), 23–27.‡

Suggests influence of *Oedipus at Colonus,* in which nightingales "are associated with preparations for a happy death."

447. Holstein, Michael Edward. "Poet, Hero, and Persona: A Study of the Personal and Poetic Identities of John Keats" [Doctoral dissertation, Minnesota, 1971], DAI, 33 (Jan. 1973), 3586-A.

448. Hood, Thomas. *The Letters of Thomas Hood.* Ed. Peter F. Morgan. Toronto: Univ. of Toronto, 1973.

Rev. by John Matthews in *Humanities Association Review,* 25 (Spring 1974), 174–176.

449. Hood, Thomas. *Selected Poems of Thomas Hood.* Ed. John Clubbe. See K-SJ, 20 (1971), No. 584; 21–22 (1972–73), No. 441.

Rev. by Peter F. Morgan in K-SJ, 23 (1974), 146–148.

450. *Horrocks, Sheila. "Through Clouds to Greatness," *Scotland's Magazine,* 70 (Apr. 1974), 35–37.

On Keats.

451. Houck, James Ashley. "Hazlitt on the Obligations of the Critic," WC, 4 (Autumn 1973), 250–258.†‡

Houck demonstrates Hazlitt's "reverential respect" for literature and its creators, and he shows that Hazlitt meant his critical views for his contemporary audience.

452. "Houghton Library Acquisitions," *Harvard Library Bulletin,* 21 (Oct. 1973), 449.

Papers of Joseph Severn, including a double letter about Keats from Hunt and Brown, 8–9 Mar. 1821.

453. *Howe, Percival P. *The Life of William Hazlitt.* Introd. Frank Swinnerton. Westport, Conn.: Greenwood, 1972.

Reprint of the 1947 edition.

454. Huang, Tsokan. "The Magazine Reviews of Keats' *Lamia* Volume (1820)" [Doctoral dissertation, Northwestern, 1972], DAI, 33 (Apr. 1973), 5726-A.

Also see No. 455.

455. Huang, Tsokan. *The Magazine Reviews of Keats's "Lamia" Volume (1820).* Salzburg: Univ. of Salzburg, 1973. "Salzburg Studies in English: Romantic Reassessment Series, No. 32."

Reprint of a dissertation. See No. 454.

456. *Ishii, Shonosuke. "John Clare no Shizen-shi" [John Clare's poems on nature], *Eigo Seinen: Rising Generation,* 119 (1973), 258–259, 332–333. [In Japanese.]

457. Jack, Ian. *Keats and the Mirror of Art.* See K-SJ, 17 (1968), No. 369; 18 (1969), No. 429; 19 (1970), No. 235; 20 (1971), No. 597a.

Rev. by Horst Höhne in *Zeitschrift für Anglistik und Amerikanistik,* 21 (Apr. 1973), 207–209 [in German].

458. Jäger, Dietrich. "Zwischen 'Universal Frame' und 'Melodious Plot': Musik und Gesang als Grundprinzipien der Welt in englischen Oden von Dryden bis Keats," *Kieler Beiträge zur Anglistik und Amerikanistik: Studien zur englischen und amerikanischen Sprache und Literatur,* 10 (1974), 224–248.

Discusses the use of music and song in the odes of Keats and Shelley.

459. Jeffrey, Lloyd N. *Thomas Hood*. See K-SJ, 21–22 (1972–73), No. 449.
Rev. by Lyle H. Kendall, Jr., in *South Central Bulletin*, 33 (May 1973), 57–58; by Peter F. Morgan in K-SJ, 23 (1974), 146–148.

460. "John's Other Life," *Scientific American*, 228 (June 1973), 40.
On Keats's medical training, summarized from an article by Robert Gittings (see No. 420).

461. Jones, Leonidas M. "Edward Holmes and Keats," K-SJ, 23 (1974), 119–128.
Identifies the writer of an anonymous letter on the death of Keats to the *Morning Chronicle* of 27 July 1821 as Edward Holmes, a schoolmate and mutual friend of Hunt.

462. Jones, Stanley. "Haydon and Northcote on Hazlitt: A Fabrication," RES, 24 (May 1973), 165–178.†
Haydon's diary entry of 3 Aug. 1826 is a fabrication in which Haydon's insulting remarks about Hazlitt are given false support by the supposed seconding of Northcote.

463. Jones, Stanley. "Hazlitt and the Walsh Porter Sale," EA, 26 (1973), 452–454.
Comment on a Hazlitt letter, with remarks on his taste in painting.

464. Jones, Stanley. "Howe's Edition of Hazlitt's *Complete Works*: A Correction," N&Q, 219 (Sept. 1974), 335.
Notes errors in the index concerning Johann Peter Salomon, violinist and concert manager.

465. Kinnaird, John. "Hazlitt as Poet: The Probable Authorship of Some Anonymous Verses on Wordsworth's Appointment as Stamp-Distributor," SIR, 12 (Winter 1973), 426–435.†‡
In the *Morning Chronicle*, 20 Apr. 1813. At the time, Hazlitt was Parliamentary reporter for this paper. The verses suggest that Wordsworth has betrayed his principles.

466. *Kirkup, James. "John Clare the Bird Watcher," *Eigo Seinen: Rising Generation*, 118 (1973), 634–637.

467. Knight, Joseph Elwood. "Hazlitt's Use of the Character Tradition, His Philosophy, and His Aesthetics in *The Spirit of the Age*" [Doctoral dissertation, Oregon, 1972], DAI, 33 (Mar. 1973), 5128-A.

468. Korenman, Joan S. "Faulkner's Grecian Urn," *Southern Literary Journal*, 7 (Fall 1974), 3–23.
An examination of Faulkner's use of Keats's ode in several works. Faulkner's attraction to the ode is owing to its similarity in the treatment of time and change to his own feelings on this theme.

469. Kronenberger, Louis. *The Last Word: Portraits of Fourteen Master Aphorists*. New York: Macmillan, 1972.
An essay on Hazlitt is included.

470. Kryger, King Chris. "The Aesthetics of Benjamin Robert Haydon" [Doctoral dissertation, Colorado, 1974], DAI, 35 (Oct. 1974), 2229-A.

471. Kudo, Naotaro. *The Life and Thoughts of Li Ho, the T'ang Poet*. Tokyo: Waseda Univ., n.d. [*ca.* 1970].
Compares Li Ho to Keats.

472. Lahr, Oonagh. "Greek Sources of 'Writ in Water,'" K-SJ, 21–22 (1972–73), 17–18.‡
"The bitter epitaph Keats devised for his own grave is sometimes supposed to derive from a line in Beaumont and Fletcher's *Philaster*, but 'to write in water, or on water' . . . is a proverbial expression in ancient Greek, and it is at least possible that Keats found it in reading the classics."

473. Lams, Victor J., Jr. "Ruth, Milton, and Keats's 'Ode to a Nightingale,'" MLQ, 34 (Dec. 1973), 417–435.‡
Lams seeks to show "Milton's presence as an antagonist to Keats in the poem." Keats's ultimate rejection of the consolation of Christianity represented by Milton is symbolized by the flight of the nightingale at the end of the poem.

474. Lawson, Margaret Ledford. "Sensation in the Poetry of Keats" [Doctoral dissertation, North Carolina, 1973], DAI, 34 (Nov. 1973), 2569-A.

475. Low, Donald A. "Byron and the 'Grecian Urn,'" TLS, 26 Oct. 1973, p. 1314.
Points to *Childe Harold* II as a major source.

476. Luke, David Beamer. "Shadow of a Magnitude: Toward a Theory of Fragmentation in the Poetry of John Keats"

[Doctoral dissertation, State Univ. of New York, Buffalo, 1974], DAI, 35 (Sept. 1974), 1627-A.

477. McClelland, John. "The Lexicon of *Les caves du Vatican*," *PMLA*, 89 (Mar. 1974), 256–267.

Includes a brief discussion of a quotation from "Ode to a Nightingale" in Gide's novel, and notes his love of Keats.

78. Mahoney, John L. "The Futuristic Imagination: Hazlitt's Approach to *Romeo and Juliet*," *British Journal of Aesthetics*, 14 (Winter 1974), 65–67.

The lovers live in an imagined world of future pleasure unrelated to their present or past experience.

79. Mathur, Durgalal. "Baudelaire a-t-il connu Keats?" *Bulletin baudelairien*, 8, No. 2 (9 Apr. 1973), p. 27.

What had been described as the sole allusion to Keats in Baudelaire is shown not to be one at all.

0. Matsuura, Tohru. "Devotees of Eternal Beauty: Kyukin and Keats," *Seijo-Bungei* (Seijo Univ.), No. 62 (1972), pp. 76–63 [*sic*].

1. Matthews, G. M., ed. *Keats: The Critical Heritage*. See K-SJ, 20 (1971), No. 638; 21–22 (1972–73), No. 476.

Rev. by Miriam Allott in *Yearbook of English Studies*, 3 (1973), 310–311; by Stuart M. Sperry in ELN, 11, Supplement (Sept. 1973), 51–52.

. May, Charles E. "Hardy's 'Darkling Thrush': The 'Nightingale' Grown Old," *Victorian Poetry*, 11 (Spring 1973), 62–65.†

Proposes that "Hardy purposely took Keats's romantic view of nature and inverted it to write an ironic rejection of such a view."

Messman, Frank J. "Richard Payne Knight and the Elgin Marbles Controversy," *British Journal of Aesthetics*, 13 (Winter 1973), 69–75.

B. R. Haydon's defense of the worth and authenticity of the marbles effectively destroyed Knight's reputation as a connoisseur of art.

Midzunoe, Yuichi. "The Spirital Cottager and Sapience: The Romantic Theory of Poetry in Keats," *Jimbun Kenkyu: The Journal of Humanities* (Chiba Univ.), No. 3 (1974), pp. 1–40.

485. *Monteiro, George. "James Gatz and John Keats," *Fitzgerald-Hemingway Annual* (1972), 291–294.

486. *Murry, John Middleton. *Studies in Keats, New and Old*. 2nd ed. Folcroft, Pa.: Folcroft, 1974.

Reprint of the 1939 edition.

487. Nichols, Olivia. "Keats and English 1013," CE, 35 (Oct. 1973), 50–51.

Whimsical remarks on "Sleep and Poetry" as it might strike a Freshman Composition teacher.

488. Nostrand, Sudie. "The Keats Circle: Further Letters" [Doctoral dissertation, New York Univ., 1973], DAI, 34 (Feb. 1974), 5115-A.

489. Ogawa, Kazuo. "Letters of John Keats: Notes and Digressions," *Bulletin of the Faculty of Humanities, Seikei University*, No. 10 (1974), pp. 1–33. [In Japanese.]

490. Ogden, James. "Henry Alford and Keats's Reputation," KSMB, 24 (1973), 8–11.

Alford is shown to be one of the early champions of Keats's poetry, though he emphasized Keats's unfulfilled promise as much as his achievement.

491. Osler, Alan. "Keats and the Classical Grasshopper," KSMB, 24 (1973), 25–26.

Sees influence of Thomas Moore's translation of an ode of Anacreon on Keats's "On the Grasshopper and Cricket," and particularly on the first line, "The poetry of earth is never dead."

492. Otten, Terry. "Macaulay's Secondhand Theory of Poetry," SAQ, 72 (Spring 1973), 280–294.†‡

He was influenced by Hazlitt and Peacock.

493. Paliwal, B. B. "Sri Aurobindo on Keats," *Banasthali Patrika*, Nos. 17–18 (July 1971–Jan. 1972), pp. 102–105.

The Indian sage considered Keats "an explorer of the soul" and an important philosophical thinker.

494. Palmberg, Adele Thornburn. "The Quest for Transcendence: The Contemplation of Death in the Lyric Poems of Novalis, Keats, and Shelley" [Doctoral dissertation, Illinois, 1974], DAI, 35 (Sept. 1974), 1631-A.

495. Pannill, Linda. "Keats's 'Lamia': A

'Knotty Problem,' " MWN, 1, No. 2 (Apr. 1973), pp. 17–24.†

"Both women and serpents . . . may be symbols of unformed Potentiality. So the Lamia . . . is an ideal object for the shaping power of the human mind. . . ."

496. Park, Roy. *Hazlitt and the Spirit of the Age: Abstraction and Critical Theory.* See K-SJ, 20 (1971), No. 655; 21–22 (1972–73), No. 490.

Rev. by John O. Hayden in *Yearbook of English Studies,* 3 (1973), 306–307; by Daniel Majdiak in JEGP, 72 (Oct. 1973), 572–576.

497. Parker, Patricia. "The Progress of Phaedria's Bower: Spenser to Coleridge," *ELH,* 40 (Fall 1973), 372–397.

Keats is included.

498. Patterson, Charles I., Jr. *The Daemonic in the Poetry of John Keats.* See K-SJ, 20 (1971), No. 658; 21–22 (1972–73), No. 491.

Rev. in *Studies in English Literature* (Japan), 48 (Oct. 1971), 135–140 [in Japanese]; by Helmut Viebrock in ASNS, 210 (1973), 416–417.

499. Perrine, Laurence. "The Poet and the Laboratory," *Southwest Review,* 58 (Autumn 1973), 285–292.

Mentions Keats and Shelley while discussing poets as discoverers and describers of the unknown, and affirming the need for poetry in an age of science.

500. Péter, Ágnes. *Keats költészetelméletének fejlödése.* See K-SJ, 21–22 (1972–73), No. 493.

Rev. by Miklosne Kretzoi in *Filológiai közlöny,* 19 (Jan.–June 1973), 202–205.

501. Peters, John U. "Jeffrey's Keats Criticism," *Studies in Scottish Literature,* 10 (Jan. 1973), 175–185.

An analysis of the critic's methodology, particularly his use of the subjective and objective modes. In defending Keats, he allowed his "individual" taste to overcome his "universal" taste.

502. Plambeck, Vernon Lewis. "Realism in Keats: A Study of Four Odes and Their Relationship to the Earlier Poems" [Doctoral dissertation, Nebraska, 1973], DAI, 34 (Nov. 1973), 2574-A.

503. Pointon, Marcia R. "Keats, Joseph Severn and William Hilton: Notes on a Dispute," N&Q, 218 (Feb. 1973), 49–54.†

Questions Severn's reliability in reporting Keats's attitude toward Hilton.

504. Pope, Willard Bissell, ed. *Invisible Friends: The Correspondence of Elizabeth Barrett Barrett and Benjamin Robert Haydon, 1842–1845.* See K-SJ, 21–22 (1972–73), No. 498.

Rev. in *Choice,* 10 (Mar. 1973), 87; by Leonidas M. Jones in K-SJ, 23 (1974), 148–149; by Stanley Jones in RES, 25 (Nov. 1974), 501–502.

505. Prance, Claude A. "*The Retrospective Review,*" ABC, 23 (July–Aug. 1973), 9–12.

J. H. Reynolds and C. W. Dilke were contributors to the *Review,* which was founded in 1820.

506. Price, James Ligon. "The Turn towards the Supernatural in Keats, Goethe, and Nerval" [Doctoral dissertation, Yale, 1973], DAI, 34 (May 1974), 7201-A.

507. Primeau, Ronald. "Chaucer's *Troilus and Criseyde* and the Rhythm of Experience in Keats's 'What Can I Do to Drive Away,' " K-SJ, 23 (1974), 106–118.

Keats "reproduces a rhythmic experience of pain passing into sweetness and sweetness into pain very like that found in Chaucer's poem and in his own major works of the time, the Odes."

508. Ready, Robert [John]. "Hazlitt: In and Out of 'Gusto,' " SEL, 14 (Autumn 1974), 537–546.

Denies that "gusto" is one of the major criteria of Hazlitt's literary criticism, but argues that "interest" is.

509. Ready, Robert John. "Sympathy: A Study of William Hazlitt" [Doctoral dissertation, Columbia, 1972], DAI, 33 (Apr. 1973), 5744-A.

510. Reynolds, John Hamilton. *The Letters of John Hamilton Reynolds.* Ed. Leonidas M. Jones. Lincoln: Univ. of Nebraska, 1973.

Includes letters to Keats.

Rev. in *Choice,* 10 (Nov. 1973), 1388; by John E. Jordan in ELN, 12, Supplement (Sept. 1974), 20.

511. Richards, Michael Reynard. "The Romantic Critics' Opinions of Elizabethan Non-Dramatic Literature" [Doctoral dissertation, Tennessee, 1972], DAI, 33 (Feb. 1973), 4361-A.

Hazlitt is discussed.

512. Ricks, Christopher. *Keats and Embarrassment*. Oxford: Clarendon, 1974.

Rev. by Patrick Swinden in *Critical Quarterly*, 16 (Winter 1974), 379–382; by John Bayley in Li, 91 (28 Mar. 1974), 410–411; by Jonathan Raban in NS, 87 (29 Mar. 1974), 446–448; by John Casey in Spec, 232 (13 Apr. 1974), 452–453; in *TLS, 26 Apr. 1974, p. 432; by Peter Conrad in *Encounter*, 43 (July 1974), 50–55; by Robert Nye in *Books and Bookmen*, 19 (Aug. 1974), 98–99; by Frank P. Riga in LJ, 99 (Aug. 1974), 1955; by Kenneth Grose in *English*, 23 (Autumn 1974), 115; by Karl Miller in NYRB, 3 Oct. 1974, pp. 35–37; in *Choice*, 11 (Oct. 1974), 1139; by C. Clarke in *Journal of European Studies*, 4 (Dec. 1974), 393. Also see No. 31.

513. *Robertson, Graham. *Keats*. London: Jackdaw, 1973.

A portfolio of teaching aids.

Rev. in TLS, 28 Sept. 1973, p. 1119.

514. Rosenfelt, Deborah Silverton. "Keats and Shelley: A Comparative Study of Their Ideas about Poetic Language and Some Patterns of Language Use in Their Poetry" [Doctoral dissertation, California, Los Angeles, 1972], DAI, 33 (Jan. 1973), 3669-A.

515. Ruoff, A. LaVonne. "The Publication of Landor's *Imaginary Conversations*: 1825–38," JEGP, 72 (Jan. 1973), 32–47.‡

Includes an account of Landor's break with John Taylor, his (and Keats's) publisher. Hunt and Hazlitt figure in the relationship between Landor and Taylor.

516. Russell, Charles Anthony. "Experience and Relationship: A Context for the Poetry of John Clare" [Doctoral dissertation, Pennsylvania, 1972], DAI, 33 (June 1973), 6883-A.

517. Ryan, Robert M. "Keats and the Truth of Imagination," WC, 4 (Autumn 1973), 259–266.†‡

Argues that Keats's statement about "the holiness of the Heart's affections and the truth of Imagination" was written in the context of religious speculation, not artistic creation.

518. Sanders, Charles Richard. "The Carlyle-Browning Correspondence and Relationship," *Bulletin of the John Rylands University Library of Manchester*, 57 (Autumn 1974), 213–246.

The two authors (and their wives) differed in their opinion of Keats.

519. *Šaxova, K. "Poezija nestrymnoho poryvu" [Poetry of uncontrollable passion], *Literaturna Ukrajina*, 25 (June 1968).

A review-article on Ukrainian translations of Keats's poems.

520. Schwartz, Lewis M. *Keats Reviewed by His Contemporaries: A Collection of Notices for the Years 1816–1821*. Metuchen, N.J.: Scarecrow, 1973.

An errata list can be obtained from Scarecrow Press, 52 Liberty St., Metuchen, N.J. 08840, or from Lewis M. Schwartz, 95 Kenmore St., Staten Island, N.Y. 10312.

Rev. by Frank P. Riga in LJ, 98 (July 1973), 2109; in TLS, 7 Sept. 1973, p. 1025; in *Choice*, 10 (Nov. 1973), 1390; by Stuart M. Sperry in ELN, 12, Supplement (Sept. 1974), 55–56; by John O. Hayden in K-SJ, 23 (1974), 142–143; by Kenyon C. Rosenberg in *American Reference Books Annual*, 5th ed. (1974), p. 524.

521. Schwartz, Lewis M. "Keats's Critical Reception in Newspapers of His Day," K-SJ, 21–22 (1972–73), 170–187.‡

Schwartz identifies John Wilson (Christopher North) as the author of two anonymous letters to the *Anti-Gallican Monitor*, 8 June and 16 July 1817, which attack the poetry of Keats and Hunt but praise the poetry of Reynolds and, especially, Shelley. But Schwartz also shows from other examples that "Keats was given an extraordinarily good reception in contemporary newspapers."

522. Smallwood, R. L. "The Occasion of Keats's 'Ode to a Nightingale,'" *Durham University Journal*, 67 (Dec. 1974), 49–56.

Knowledge of the precise time and circumstances of composition can be helpful in interpreting the poem.

523. Smith, Eric. *Some Versions of the Fall: The Myth of the Fall of Man in English Literature*. Pittsburgh: Univ. of Pittsburgh, 1973.

Keats's "Hyperion" is one version.

Rev. in *Choice*, 10 (Feb. 1974), 1869–70; by J. M. Evans in N&Q, 219 (Mar. 1974), 114–116; by Robert H. West in

Georgia Review, 28 (Summer 1974), 374–375; by Stephen Medcalf in RES, 25 (Aug. 1974), 365–366; in VQR, 50 (Winter 1974), xx.

524. Smith, Louise Z. "The Material Sublime: Keats and 'Isabella,'" SIR, 13 (Fall 1974), 299–311.

"In 'Isabella,' Keats presents a double view of the imagination as wisely passive and vainly struggling." Either way, he finds the imagination incapable of asserting the "material sublime" (a unity of dreaming and reality) "strongly enough to balance the disagreeables of the jostling world."

525. Snyder, Elliott Leslie. "The New Criticism and the Poetry of John Keats" [Doctoral dissertation, Connecticut, 1973], DAI, 34 (Nov. 1973), 2580-A.

526. Sperry, Stuart M. *Keats the Poet*. Princeton: Princeton Univ., 1973.

Rev. by Dorothy Sternlicht in LJ, 98 (Aug. 1973), 2301–02; in *Choice*, 10 (Oct. 1973), 1198; in TLS, 8 Feb. 1974, p. 130; by Richard Giannone in *Thought*, 49 (June 1974), 210–211; by Barry Gradman in *Criticism*, 16 (Summer 1974), 265–268; by Stuart Curran in ELN, 12, Supplement (Sept. 1974), 56; by Jack Stillinger in K-SJ, 23 (1974), 151–153. Also see Nos. 41, 59.

527. Stapleton, Laurence. *The Elected Circle: Studies in the Art of Prose*. Princeton: Princeton Univ., 1973.

Chapter on Hazlitt.

Rev. in *Choice*, 11 (Mar. 1974), 94; in VQR, 50 (Autumn 1974), cxxii.

528. Stefanik, Ernest C. "A Cursing Glory: John Berryman's *Love and Fame*," *Renascence*, 25 (Spring 1973), 115–127.†‡

Sees influence of Keats's "When I Have Fears."

529. Stephenson, William Curtis. "The Fall from Innocence in Keats's 'Lamia,'" *Papers on Language and Literature*, 10 (Winter 1974), 35–50.

Explores the dimensions of Lycius' tragic fall, and examines parallels with *Paradise Lost*.

530. Stillinger, Jack. *The Hoodwinking of Madeline and Other Essays on Keats's Poems*. See K-SJ, 21–22 (1972–73), No. 530.

Rev. by Paul D. Sheats in K-SJ, 21–22 (1972–73), 255–256; by Allan Rodway in RES, 24 (Nov. 1973), 504–505; by Miriam Allott in *Yearbook of English Studies*, 3 (1973), 314–315; by Helmut Viebrock in *Anglia*, 91 (1973), 537–540; by Roger Sharrock in N&Q, 219 (May 1974), 195–196.

531. Stillinger, Jack. *The Texts of Keats's Poems*. Cambridge: Harvard Univ., 1974.

532. Stone, William B. "Ike McCaslin and the Grecian Urn," *Studies in Short Fiction*, 10 (Winter 1973), 93–94.

Parallels between the Ode and Faulkner's "The Bear."

533. Storey, Mark, ed. *Clare: The Critical Heritage*. London: Routledge, 1973. "The Critical Heritage Series."

534. Storey, Mark. "A 'Missing' Letter from John Clare to John Taylor," N&Q, 218 (Feb. 1973), 54–57.

The letter, dated 7 Mar. 1821, expresses Clare's unhappiness over the cutting down of two elm trees.

535. Storey, Mark. *The Poetry of John Clare: A Critical Introduction*. London: Macmillan, 1974.

536. Storey, Mark. "Some Previously Unpublished Letters from John Clare," RES, 25 (May 1975), 177–185.

537. Swaminathan, S. R. "Keats's 'Epistle to Reynolds' and Scott's *Marmion*," N&Q, 219 (Sept. 1974), 333–334.

"Cuthbert de Saint Aldebrim" and other details derive from Scott.

538. Swennes, Robert Harvey, II. "John Keats's *Endymion*: A New Interpretation" [Doctoral dissertation, Indiana, 1973], DAI, 34 (Jan. 1974), 4220-A.

539. *Takahashi, Yushiro. *Keats Kenkyu: Jiga no Henyo to Riso-shugi*. [Study of Keats: evolution of ego and idealism.] Tokyo: Hokuseido, 1973.

540. Thekla, Sister. *The Disinterested Heart: The Philosophy of John Keats*. Newport Pagnell, Bucks.: Greek Orthodox Monastery of the Assumption, 1973. Paperback.

541. *Thomas, C. T. "The Metrical Structure of Keats's Odes of 1819," in *Literary Studies: Homage to Dr. A. Sivaramasubramonia Aiyer*, ed. K. P. K. Menon, M. Manuel, and K. Ayyappa Paniker (Trivandrum, India: St. Joseph's Press for the

Dr. A. Sivaramasubramonia Aiyer Memorial Committee, 1973), pp. 163–172.

542. Thompson, Leslie M. "Ritual Sacrifice and Time in 'Ode on a Grecian Urn,' " K-SJ, 21–22 (1972–73), 27–29.‡

Quoting Mircea Eliade on the time-annulling purpose of ritual sacrifice in primitive societies, Thompson suggests that the sacrificial procession in Keats's poem may have a similar significance.

543. Thurston, Norman. "Biography and Keats's Pleasure Thermometer," WC, 4 (Autumn 1973), 267–270.†‡

Discusses the "Pleasure Thermometer" passage in the letter to John Taylor "as a coherent and unified expression of Keats's attitude toward *Endymion*" at the time he wrote the letter.

544. Tibble, Anne. "John Clare and His Doctors," CLB, 4 (Oct. 1973), 77–81.

545. Tibble, J. W., and Anne Tibble. *John Clare: A Life*. Revised ed. See K-SJ, 21–22 (1972–73), No. 537.

Rev. by Joanna E. Rapf in SIR, 13 (Winter 1974), 79–84.

546. Tintner, Adeline R. "The Elgin Marbles and Titian's 'Bacchus and Ariadne': A Cluster of Keatsian Associations in Henry James," N&Q, 218 (July 1973), 250–252.†

The sculptures and painting are "joined in the *Princess Casamassima* as in Keats's life and poetry because James saw them as the two great heuristic experiences of his doomed poet manqué, Hyacinth, whose 'cockney vision' he modelled on the equally doomed great 'Cockney Poet,' Keats."

547. Tintner, Adeline R. "Keats and James and *The Princess Casamassima*," *Nineteenth Century Fiction*, 28 (Sept. 1973), 179–193.‡

The novel is filled with allusions to Keats's life and poetry.

548. Todd, Janet M. *In Adam's Garden: A Study of John Clare's Pre-Asylum Poetry*. Gainesville: Univ. of Florida, 1973. "University of Florida Humanities Monograph, No. 39."

549. Todd, Janet M. " 'Very Copys of Nature': John Clare's Descriptive Poetry," PQ, 53 (Jan. 1974), 84–99.

Clare's "descriptive" poetry (depicting nature without any explicit judgment or emotional response) is contrasted to the "Romantic" poetry (which depicts nature idealized and informed by the poet's emotional response) of Shelley and Keats.

550. Traub, George William. "Keats's 'Fall of Hyperion': A Textual and Critical Study" [Doctoral dissertation, Cornell, 1973], DAI, 34 (Sept. 1973), 1296-A.

551. Underhill, Hugh. "The 'Poetical Character' of Edward Thomas," EC, 23 (July 1973), 236–253.

Keats's influence.

552. Vendler, Helen. "The Experiential Beginnings of Keats's Odes," SIR, 12 (Summer 1973), 591–606.†‡

". . . [R]eflection on the experiences from which the odes may have originated, and on the residual presence of those experiences in the poems, can help define the shape and course of each ode as it completes itself into wholeness."

553. *Voisine, Jacques. "W. Hazlitt's Essay 'On the Prose Sytle of Poets,' a Comparatist's View," in *Expression, Communication and Experience in Literature and Language*, Proceedings of the Twelfth Congress of the International Federation for Modern Languages and Literatures held at Cambridge Univ., 20–26 Aug. 1972, ed. Ronald G. Popperwell (London: Modern Humanities Research Association, 1973), pp. 251–253.

An abstract of a paper delivered at the congress.

554. Wade, Stephen. "John Clare's Use of Dialect," CR, 223 (Aug. 1973), 81–84.

Clare used slang to "particularise" a work.

555. Walker, Carol Kyros. "The Longest Resonance: A Comparative Study of Keats and Stevens" [Doctoral dissertation, Illinois, 1972], DAI, 33 (Apr. 1973), 5695-A.

556. Wardle, Ralph M. *Hazlitt*. See K-SJ, 20 (1971), No. 714; 21–22 (1972–73), No. 550.

Rev. by Leonard M. Trawick in K-SJ, 21–22 (1972–73), 259–261; by D. G. Wilson in CLB, No. 2 (Apr. 1973), pp. 47–48; by Daniel Majdiak in JEGP, 72 (Oct. 1973), 572–576; by Stuart M. Tave in MP, 71 (Feb. 1974), 341–342.

557. White, H. W., and Neville Rogers. "The Vale of Tears in Keats, Shelley, and Others," KSMB, 24 (1973), 16–18.

Traces the origin and significance of the phrase.

558. Wigod, Jacob. *The Darkening Chamber: The Growth of Tragic Consciousness in Keats.* See K-SJ, 21–22 (1972–73), No. 552.

Rev. in *Choice,* 11 (Sept. 1974), 948.

559. Wilkes, John Edwin, III. "Aeolian Visitations and the Harp Defrauded: Essays on Donne, Blake, Wordsworth, Keats, Flaubert, Heine and James Wright" [Doctoral dissertation, California, Santa Cruz, 1973], DAI, 35 (Aug. 1974), 1129–A.

560. Wilkinson, Loren Earl. "Meaning, Man, and Earth: A Romantic Dilemma in Contemporary Thought" [Doctoral dissertation, Syracuse, 1973], DAI, 34 (Apr. 1974), 6609–A.

Discusses Keats's epistemology.

561. Wood, Harriet Harvey. "A Scorpion in the Post: J. G. Lockhart through His Letters," *Cornhill Magazine,* No. 1077 (Autumn 1973), pp. 114–132.

Discusses his involvement in *Blackwood*'s attack on Keats. Other references to John Murray and B. R. Haydon.

562. *Woodman, A. J. "Sleepless Poets: Catullus and Keats," *Greece and Rome,* 21 (Apr. 1974), 51–53.

563. Woodman, R. G. "Satan in the 'Vale of Soul-Making': A Survey from Blake to Ginsberg," *Humanities Association Review,* 25 (Spring 1974), 108–121.

Believing that the supernatural has its origin in the human mind, the early Romantic poets identified with Satan's rejection of divine authority. They saw such rebellion as virtuous—necessary for man's moral regeneration. Includes discussions of "Ode to Psyche" and *Prometheus Unbound.*

564. Wright, William C. "Hazlitt, Ruskin, and Nineteenth Century Art Criticism," JAAC, 32 (Summer 1974), 509–523.

"The relationship of Hazlitt's views [as a critic] of the fine arts to those held by Ruskin early in his career is the specific concern of this study."

565. Yakushigawa, Koichi. "What the Urn Said," *Doshisha Literature,* No. 27 (Nov. 1973), pp. 28–50.

An approach to the last two lines of "Ode on a Grecian Urn." These lines, "addressed to both the poet and the reader by the urn," allow them "to see the human world as it is without being attracted to euphoria by the fictitious world of the urn." The Nightingale Ode and "To Autumn" are discussed in this connection.

566. Zak, William Frank. "Keats and the Ideal of Disinterestedness: Aesthetic Distance and Control in the Major Poetry" [Doctoral dissertation, Michigan, 1972], DAI, 33 (Mar. 1973), 5208–A.

567. Zeff, Jacqueline Lupovich. "Narrative Technique in the Poetry of John Keats" [Doctoral dissertation, Pittsburgh, 1973], DAI, 35 (Aug. 1974), 1070–A.

For additional Books and Articles Relating to Keats and His Circle see Nos. 1, 6, 14, 15, 24–27, 30, 32, 33, 35, 38, 40, 50–52, 55, 60–63, 65, 69, 71, 74, 75, 77, 79, 83, 87, 88, 90, 92, 94, 96, 97, 140, 174, 191, 599, 646, 672, 693, 697, 763, 793, 799, 816, 829.

V. SHELLEY

Works: Collected, Selected, Single, Translated

568. *The Complete Poetical Works of Percy Bysshe Shelley.* Ed. Neville Rogers. Vol. I: *1802–1813.* See K-SJ, 21–22 (1972–73), No. 556.

Rev. in TLS, 2 Mar. 1973, p. 246, reply by Donald H. Reiman, 23 Mar. 1973, pp. 324–325, and reply to the review and Reiman by Neville Rogers, 4 May 1973, p. 501; by Gillian Beer in Spec, 19 May 1973, p. 620; by Kenneth Neill Cameron in SIR, 12 (Summer 1973), 693–699, reply by Neville Rogers, 13 (Summer 1974), 267–271, with rejoinder by Cameron, 271–274; in *Choice,* 10 (July–Aug. 1973), 778; by Stuart Curran in ELN, 11, Supplement (Sept. 1973), 59–60; by P. H. Butter in MLR, 69 (Apr. 1974), 383–384; by Donald H. Reiman in JEGP, 73 (Apr. 1974), 250–260; by Robert C. Casto in RES, 25 (May 1974), 225–228; by E. D. Mackerness in N&Q, 219 (Sept. 1974), 352–353. Also see No. 59.

569. **The Mask of Anarchy*. Foreword by Dennis Gould. 2nd ed. London: Kropotkin's Lighthouse Publications, 1973.
   Limited edition of 500 copies. Previous edition 1970.

570. **Original Poetry by Victor and Cazire*. Ed. Richard Garnett. Folcroft, Pa.: Folcroft, 1974.
   Reprint of the 1898 edition.

571. **Poems*. Selected and introd. Richard Church. Wood engravings by John Buckland-Wright. London: Folio, 1973.
   Reprint of the 1948 edition.

572. *[Poems]. Selected by Kathleen Raine. Harmondsworth: Penguin, 1973. "Poet to Poet."

573. *The Poems of Percy Bysshe Shelley*. Ed., selected, and introd. Stephen Spender. Illustrated by Richard Shirley Smith. New York: Heritage, 1974.

574. **Poesia*. Ed. Giuseppe Sardelli. Milan: Fabbi, 1970.

574a. Rogers, Neville. "An Unpublished Shelley Letter," KSMB, 24 (1973), 20–24.
   A humorous verse-letter to Edward Fergus Graham, dated Horsham, 7 June 1811. The humor is mostly at the expense of Sir Timothy Shelley.

575. **Shelley–Leigh Hunt: How Friendship Made History*. Ed. and introd. R. Brimley Johnson. New York: Haskell, 1972.
   Reprint of the 1929 edition. Includes some of Shelley's prose pamphlets and correspondence between Shelley and Hunt.

576. **Shelley: Poetry and Prose, with Essays by Browning, Bagehot, Swinburne, and Reminiscences by Others*. Introd. and notes by A. M. D. Hughes. Oxford: Clarendon, 1973. "Clarendon English Series." Paperback.
   Reprint of the 1931 edition.

577. **Shelley's "Defence of Poetry" and Blunden's Lectures on "Defence."* Folcroft, Pa.: Folcroft, 1973.
   Reprint of a 1948 book published in Japan.

578. **Shelley's Lost Letters to Harriet*. Ed. and introd. Leslie Hotson. Freeport, N.Y.: Books for Libraries, 1972.
   Reprint of the 1930 edition.

579. **Shelley's Lost Letters to Harriet*. Ed. and introd. Leslie Hotson. Folcroft, Pa.: Folcroft, 1974.
   Reprint of the 1930 edition.

580. **Shelley's Lost Letters to Harriet*. Ed. and introd. Leslie Hotson. New York: Haskell, 1974.
   Reprint of the 1930 edition.

581. **Verse and Prose from the Manuscripts of Percy Bysshe Shelley*. Ed. John C. E. Shelley-Rolls and Roger Ingpen. Folcroft, Pa.: Folcroft, 1974.
   Reprint of the 1934 edition.

For additional WORKS BY SHELLEY see Nos. 61, 604, 621, 635, 735, 753, 758.

BOOKS AND ARTICLES RELATING TO SHELLEY AND HIS CIRCLE

582. Abbey, Lloyd Robert. "Images of Interrelation in Shelley's Major Poetry" [Doctoral dissertation, Toronto, 1971], DAI, 34 (Feb. 1974), 5152-A.

583. Abbott, William Henry. "The Philosophy of History in Selected Works of Percy Bysshe Shelley" [Doctoral dissertation, Texas A&M, 1973], DAI, 34 (Jan. 1974), 4238-A.

584. Aldiss, Brian. "*The Billion Year Spree*: 1. Origin of the Species," *Extrapolation*, 14 (May 1973), 167–191.†
   Examination of the literary, scientific, and social context of *Frankenstein*, considered the first science-fiction novel. Chapter of a book. See No. 585.

585. Aldiss, Brian. *The Billion Year Spree: The True History of Science Fiction*. Garden City, N.Y.: Doubleday, 1973.
   Includes a chapter on Mary Shelley. Also see No. 584.
   Rev. in *Extrapolation*, 15 (Dec. 1973), 62.

586. Allsup, James Otis. "The Magic Circle: A Study of Shelley's Concept of Love" [Doctoral dissertation, Minnesota, 1973], DAI, 34 (May 1974), 7217-A.

587. *Angeli, Helen Rossetti. *Shelley and His Friends in Italy*. Ill. Maxwell Armfield. New York: Haskell, 1973.
   Reprint of the 1911 edition.

588. *Bailey, Ruth. *Shelley*. Folcroft, Pa.: Folcroft, 1974.
   Reprint of the 1934 edition.

589. Banerjee, Jibon. "Dramatic Writings of P. B. Shelley," *Bulletin of the Department*

of English (Calcutta Univ.), 9, No. 1 (1973–74), 1–8.

A sympathetic survey of the lyrical and stage dramas and dramatic fragments.

590. *Barton, Wilfred Converse. *Shelley and the New Criticism: The Anatomy of a Critical Misvaluation.* Salzburg: Univ. of Salzburg, 1973. "Salzburg Studies in English: Romantic Reassessment Series, No. 5."

See Nos. 31, 86.

591. Barzun, Jacques. [Letter], *Encounter*, 42 (Feb. 1974), 93; 42 (May 1974), 91.

Remarks on Mary Wollstonecraft.

592. *Bates, Ernest S. *A Study of Shelley's Drama "The Cenci."* Folcroft, Pa.: Folcroft, 1973.

Reprint of the 1908 edition.

593. Bean, John C. "The Poet Borne Darkly: The Dream-Voyage Allegory in Shelley's *Alastor*," K-SJ, 23 (1974), 60–76.

The "unifying theme of *Alastor* is not the poet's quest for love but his quest for spiritual knowledge and . . . the function of the dream-voyage is to define the limits of human knowledge by describing allegorically a poet's fate."

594. Bennett, James R. "*Prometheus Unbound*, Act I, 'The Play's the Thing,'" K-SJ, 23 (1974), 32–51.

Argues for the dramatic development of the character of Prometheus in Act I, emphasizing the psychological realism of Shelley's treatment. In terms of the play as a whole, the movement is from "psychological realism in Act I to apocalyptic vision and lyrical song in Act IV."

595. Berman, Ruth. "Teachers of English 121: The Romantic Period," *Kansas Quarterly*, 5 (Fall 1973), 50.

A short poem about teaching Romantic poetry, using Shelley and De Quincey as central images.

596. Bhalla, M. M. *Studies in Shelley*. Ed. Francine Ellison Krishna. New Delhi: Associated Publishing, 1973.

Has chapters on *Queen Mab*, *Alastor*, *The Revolt of Islam*, "Julian and Maddalo," *Prometheus Unbound*, *Adonais*, and *Hellas*.

597. Bloom, Harold. "How to Read a Poem: Browning's 'Childe Roland,'" *Georgia Review*, 28 (Fall 1974), 404–418.

". . . [T]he poem becomes Browning's interpretation of a poem like Shelley's 'Ode to the West Wind,' and perhaps all of Shelley's poetry."

598. *Blunden, Edmund. *Shelley: A Life Story*. Folcroft, Pa.: Folcroft, 1973.

Reprint of the 1946 edition.

599. *Blunden, Edmund, ed. *Shelley and Keats As They Struck Their Contemporaries*. Folcroft, Pa.: Folcroft, 1974.

Reprint of the 1925 edition.

600. Boe, Alfred Francis. "The Development of Shelley's Theory of the Mind" [Doctoral dissertation, Arizona, 1973], DAI, 34 (Dec. 1973), 3381-A.

601. Boos, Florence. "The Biographies of Mary Wollstonecraft," MWN, 1, No. 2 (Apr. 1973), pp. 6–10.†

A review-article. See Nos. 648, 650a, 813a.

602. Bosco, Ronald A. "On the Meaning of Shelley's 'Mont Blanc,'" *Massachusetts Studies in English*, 4 (Spring 1974), 37–55.

The poem is concerned with an "affirmation of the power of imagination" and "the discovery, investigation, and, ultimately, definition of Power as the principle of Permanence in the universe." Bosco opposes philosophical and epistemological approaches to the poem.

603. Bouquet, Robert Lawrence. "Obscure Syntax in Shelley's Visionary Poetry" [Doctoral dissertation, Columbia, 1971], DAI, 35 (Aug. 1974), 1040-A.

604. Boyar, Billy Thomas, Jr. "Shelley's 'The Magic Plant': Text, Interpretation, and Perspective" [Doctoral dissertation, Arizona State, 1973], DAI, 34 (Feb. 1974), 5092-A.

605. Brazell, James. *Shelley and the Concept of Humanity: A Study of His Moral Vision*. See K-SJ, 21–22 (1972–73), No. 574.

Rev. by P. H. Butter in MLR, 69 (July 1974), 624–625.

606. Breitinger, Eckard. *Der Tod im englischen Roman um 1800: Untersuchungen zum englischen Schauerroman*. Göppingen: Kümmerle, 1971. "Göppinger akademische Beiträge, 19."

Discusses Godwin's *Caleb Williams*, and has references to *Frankenstein* and Shelley's *Zastrozzi*.

Rev. by Horst Höhne in *Zeitschrift für*

Anglistik und Amerikanistik, 22, No. 1 (1974), 97–98 [in German].

607. Brogan, Howard O. "Romantic Classicism in Peacock's Verse Satire," SEL, 14 (Autumn 1974), 525–536.

Peacock's romantic Classicism is contrasted to the classical Romanticism of the major Romantic poets. "Peacock is thus to be seen as a man of his time, who, though sympathetic to the new literary currents of that time which we now label Romantic, embodied a criticism of the excesses of that literature, and of the broader aspects of life experience to which it was responding. . . ."

608. Brown, Lloyd W. "Jane Austen and the Feminist Tradition," *Nineteenth Century Fiction*, 28 (Dec. 1973), 321–338.‡

Some of Mary Wollstonecraft's ideas seem to be reflected in the novels.

609. Brown, Richard Elwood. "Images of the Self in Shelley's Poetry" [Doctoral dissertation, Cornell, 1972], DAI, 33 (Mar. 1973), 5165-A.

610. Bump, Jerome. " 'The Wreck of the Deutschland' and the Dynamic Sublime," *ELH*, 41 (Spring 1974), 106–129.

Discusses Shelley's concept of nature as powerfully creative *and* destructive in the context of the tradition of the "dynamic sublime," of which Hopkins' poem is a critique. Byron is also mentioned.

611. Cameron, Kenneth Neill. *Shelley: The Golden Years*. Cambridge: Harvard Univ., 1974.

Rev. in *New Yorker*, 15 July 1974, p. 87; by David Kwinn in LJ, 99 (Aug. 1974), 1952; in *Choice*, 11 (Oct. 1974), 1133; by Dewey R. Faulkner in *Yale Review*, 64 (Oct. 1974), 88–93. Also see Nos. 31, 626.

612. Cameron, Kenneth Neill. *The Young Shelley: Genesis of a Radical*. New York: Octagon, 1973.

Reprint of the 1950 edition.

613. Cameron, Kenneth Neill, ed. *Romantic Rebels: Essays on Shelley and His Circle*. Cambridge: Harvard Univ., 1973.

A collection of essays, reprinted from *Shelley and His Circle, 1773–1822*, Vols. I–IV, on Shelley, Mary Shelley, Godwin, Mary Wollstonecraft, Byron, Hunt, Peacock, and Harriet Shelley.

Rev. by Stuart Curran in ELN, 12, Supplement (Sept. 1974), 62; by Rae Ann Nager in K-SJ, 23 (1974), 160. Also see No. 59.

614. Cameron, Kenneth Neill, ed. *Shelley and His Circle, 1773–1822*. The Carl H. Pforzheimer Library. Vols. III and IV. See K-SJ, 20 (1971), No. 773; 21–22 (1972–73), No. 581.

Rev. by E. B. Murray in K-SJ, 21–22 (1972–73), 236–244.

615. Campbell, William Royce. "Shelley's Philosophy of History: A Reconsideration," K-SJ, 21–22 (1972–73), 43–63.‡

"These elements—dualism; progressivism, involving cycles; a distaste for man's past balanced by a hope for the triumph of Love in the future—were to become the main and stable components of Shelley's theory of history."

616. *Cappon, Alexander P. *The Scope of Shelley's Philosophical Thinking*. Folcroft, Pa.: Folcroft, 1974.

Reprint of the 1938 edition.

617. Carter, Gerald Charles. "Paradigms of Phenomenology in Three Romantic Poets" [Doctoral dissertation, Southern California, 1973], DAI, 34 (Mar. 1974), 5958-A.

Coleridge, Wordsworth, and Shelley.

618. Cary, Richard. "In Further Defense of Harriet Shelley: Two Unpublished Letters by Mark Twain," *Mark Twain Journal*, 16, No. 4 (Summer 1973), pp. 13–15.†‡

The letters affirm the position against Shelley taken in the essay seven years earlier.

619. *Chapman, John A. *Papers on Shelley, Wordsworth, and Others*. Folcroft, Pa.: Folcroft, 1974.

Reprint of the 1929 edition.

620. Chatterjee, Kalyan. "Marlow's Tragic Vision in *Lord Jim*," *Bulletin of the Department of English* (Calcutta Univ.), N.S., 8 (1972–73), 9–14.

Includes a suggestion that Marlow views Jim as a Shelleyan idealist seeking an obscure and elusive absolute truth.

621. Chernaik, Judith. *The Lyrics of Shelley*. See K-SJ, 21–22 (1972–73), No. 584.

Rev. in *Choice*, 9 (Jan. 1973), 1445; by Donald H. Reiman in JEGP, 72 (Apr.

1973), 244–246; by Kenneth Allott in N&Q, 218 (Aug. 1973), 311–312; by Stuart Curran in ELN, 11, Supplement (Sept. 1973), 57; by Timothy Webb in RES, 24 (Nov. 1973), 502–504; by *Arnold Ozra in *Criticism*, 15 (1973), 285–287; by Howard Sergeant in *English*, 22 (Summer 1973), 78–80; by Lawrence J. Zillman in MLQ, 34 (June 1973), 213–214; by P. H. Butter in *Yearbook of English Studies*, 4 (1974), 316–317. Also see No. 59.

622. *Clarke, John H. *The God of Shelley and Blake*. Folcroft, Pa.: Folcroft, 1973.
Reprint of the 1930 edition.

623. Cobb, Joann P. "Godwin's Novels and *Political Justice*," *Enlightenment Essays*, 4 (Spring 1973), 15–28.
"Godwin used the novels to illustrate the validity of the basic conclusions of *Political Justice*."

624. Cohn, Jan. "The Theory of Poetic Value in I. A. Richards' *Principles of Literary Criticism* and Shelley's *A Defence of Poetry*," K-SJ, 21–22 (1972–73), 95–111.‡
"The value theories of both Richards and Shelley are based on the effect poetry has on the mind. For Shelley the psychological process involves the stimulation and exercise of the imagination and the consequent development of love or sympathy. For Richards, poetry arouses and resolves more numerous and more complex sets of impulses than does an ordinary experience."

625. Collins, John. "Harry Buxton Forman and His Shelley Reprints," BC, 23 (Winter 1974), 506–517.
History of the editions, with remarks on Forman's involvement in the T. J. Wise forgeries.

626. Conrad, Peter. "The Transformations of Ariel," TLS, 9 Aug. 1974, pp. 846–848.
An omnibus review. See Nos. 611, 669.

627. Cores, Lucy Michaella. *Year of December: A Novel*. New York: McGraw-Hill, 1974.
Fiction based on the life of Claire Clairmont.

628. Crabbe, John Kenyon. "The Noblest Gift: Women in the Fiction of Thomas Love Peacock" [Doctoral dissertation, Oregon, 1973], DAI, 34 (Mar. 1974), 5904-A.

629. Crampton, Daniel Nicholas. "Shelley's Political Optimism: 'The Mask of Anarchy' to *Hellas*" [Doctoral dissertation, Wisconsin, 1973], DAI, 34 (Apr. 1974), 6585-A.

630. Curran, Stuart. *Shelley's "Cenci": Scorpions Ringed with Fire*. See K-SJ, 20 (1971), No. 784; 21–22 (1972–73), No. 589.
Rev. by A. H. Elliott in N&Q, 218 (Aug. 1973), 310–311.

631. Curran, Stuart, and Joseph Anthony Wittreich, Jr. "The Dating of Shelley's 'On the Devil, and Devils,'" K-SJ, 21–22 (1972–73), 83–94.‡
Argues that the essay was written in Nov. 1819.

632. Dalsimer, Adele M. "My Chief of Men: Yeats's Juvenilia and Shelley's *Alastor*," *Éire-Ireland*, 8, No. 2 (1973), pp. 71–90.†
A study of the *Alastor* theme in Yeats's early poems: "As Shelley did in *Alastor*, Yeats, in his earliest poems, sees the destruction of the poetic sensibility as inevitable. . . ."

633. Davies, Barrie. "Lampman and Religion," *Canadian Literature*, No. 56 (Spring 1973), pp. 40–60.
The Canadian poet Archibald Lampman's interest in Shelley, including his essay on *The Revolt of Islam*, is discussed.

634. Dawson, Leven M. "Jarrell's 'The Death of the Ball Turret Gunner,'" Exp, 31 (Dec. 1972), Item 29.†
"The paradoxical structure as well as the imagery . . . originates" in *Adonais*, st. 39.

635. Delisle, Fanny. *A Study of Shelley's "A Defence of Poetry": A Textual and Critical Evaluation*. 2 vols. Salzburg: Univ. of Salzburg, 1974. "Salzburg Studies in English: Romantic Reassessment Series, Nos. 27–28."
See No. 31.

636. *De Selincourt, Ernest. *Six Great Poets: Chaucer, Pope, Wordsworth, Shelley, Tennyson, the Brownings*. Folcroft, Pa.: Folcroft, 1973.
Reprint of the 1956 edition.

637. Des Pres, Terence George. "Visionary Experience in the Poems of Shelley" [Doctoral dissertation, Washington Univ., 1973], DAI, 33 (June 1973), 6905-A.

638. *Dowden, Edward. *Letters about Shelley, Interchanged by Three Friends, Edward Dowden, Richard Garnett, and Wm. Michael Rossetti*. Ed. and introd. R. S. Garnett. Folcroft, Pa.: Folcroft, 1973.

Reprint of the 1917 edition.

639. Duparc, Jean. *Shelley, imagination et révolution: A propos de "Prométhée délivré."* Paris: Centre d'Etudes et de Recherches Marxistes, 1973. "Cahiers du C.E.R.M., 106."

Available from the center at 64 Boulevard Auguste-Blanqui.

First part includes an analysis of recent scholarship by Cameron, Matthews, and Wasserman.

640. *Edwards, Anne. *Haunted Summer*. New York: Coward, McCann, 1972.

Fiction about Shelley and Mary.

641. Elliott, Barbara Lavelle Hill. "Shelley and the Romantic Reviewers: The Relevance of Poetry and Criticism in the Early Nineteenth Century" [Doctoral disseration, Rice, 1974], DAI, 35 (Oct. 1974), 2220-A.

642. Evans, Donald Wayne. "Thomas Hardy's Romanticism" [Doctoral dissertation, Southern Mississippi, 1972], DAI, 33 (Mar. 1973), 5120-A.

Hardy's view of nature is comparable to Shelley's.

643. Faure, Georges. *Les éléments du rythme poétique en anglais moderne: Esquisse d'une nouvelle analyse et essai d'application au "Prometheus Unbound" de P. B. Shelley*. See K-SJ, 20 (1971), No. 799; 21–22 (1972–73), No. 608.

Rev. by Jørgen Fafner in *Orbis Litterarum*, 29, No. 3 (1974), 286–287 [in German].

644. Fay, Janet Ann. "The Serious Satire of Thomas Love Peacock: A Critical Study of His Moral, Intellectual, and Aesthetic Opinions" [Doctoral dissertation, New York Univ., 1973], DAI, 34 (Sept. 1973), 1239-A.

645. Felton, Felix, *pseud.* [Robert Forbes]. *Thomas Love Peacock*. London: Allen and Unwin, 1973.

Rev. in TLS, 20 Apr. 1973, p. 443; by Bernard Jones in *Books and Bookmen*, 18 (July 1973), 24–25; by J. M. Aitken in *Library Review* (Glasgow), 24 (Summer 1973), 85–86; by Howard Mills in *Victorian Studies*, 17 (June 1974), 449–450; by *Gilbert Thomas in *English*, 22 (1974), 118; by D. N. Gallon in RES, 25 (May 1974), 223–224; by John E. Jordan in ELN, 12, Supplement (Sept. 1974), 59; by *Geoffrey Grigson in *Country Life*, 153 (1974), 1191.

646. Fennell, Francis L. "The Rossetti Collection at the Library of Congress: A Checklist," *Bulletin of Bibliography*, 30 (July–Sept. 1973), 132–136.

Includes a letter to B. R. Haydon and the MS of a sonnet on Shelley.

647. Flagg, John Sewell. *"Prometheus Unbound" and "Hellas": An Approach to Shelley's Lyrical Dramas*. See K-SJ, 21–22 (1972–73), No. 611.

Rev. by P. H. Butter in *Yearbook of English Studies*, 4 (1974), 314–316.

648. Flexner, Eleanor. *Mary Wollstonecraft: A Biography*. See K-SJ, 21–22 (1972–73), No. 612.

Rev. by Anne Firor Scott in SAQ, 72 (Autumn 1973), 608; in VQR, 49 (Winter 1974), xxviii. Also see No. 601.

649. Friedrich, Carl Joachim. "The Anarchist Controversy over Violence," *Zeitschrift für Politik*, 19, No. 3 (1972), 167–177.

Despite the more common association of anarchism with violence, major anarchist ideologists, Godwin among them, are radical pacifists who eschew violence totally. Violence belongs to the individual ideologist, not to the ideology.

650. Fuller, Roy. *Professors and Gods: Last Oxford Lectures on Poetry*. London: Deutsch; New York: St. Martin's (1973).

Attacks F. R. Leavis' evaluation of Shelley.

650a. George, Margaret. *One Woman's "Situation": A Study of Mary Wollstonecraft*. See K-SJ, 20 (1971), No. 814.

See No. 601.

651. Gerson, Noel B. *Daughter of Earth and Water: A Biography of Mary Wollstonecraft Shelley*. New York: Morrow, 1973.

Rev. by Susan Brownmiller in NYT, 11 Feb. 1973, pp. 10, 12; in *Choice*, 10 (Apr. 1974), 618; by Stuart Curran in ELN, 12, Supplement (Sept. 1974), 60; by Alice G. Fredman in K-SJ, 23 (1974), 136–138.

652. *Glasgow, Eric. "Shelley's Debt to

Greece," in *Salzburg Studies in English Literature: Romantic Reassessment, No. 11*, ed. James Hogg (Salzburg: Univ. of Salzburg, 1973), pp. 36–45.

653. Glut, Donald F. *The Frankenstein Legend: A Tribute to Mary Shelley and Boris Karloff.* Metuchen, N.J.: Scarecrow, 1973.

654. Godwin, William. *Caleb Williams.* Ed. David McCracken. See K-SJ, 20 (1971), No. 817; 21–22 (1972–73), No. 621.
Rev. by *Lloyd W. Brown in *Eighteenth Century Studies*, 6 (1973), 530–533.

655. Godwin, William. *Italian Letters; or The History of Count de St. Julian.* Ed. Burton R. Pollin. See K-SJ, 21–22 (1972–73), No. 624.
Rev. by David V. Erdman in ELN, 11, Supplement (Sept. 1973), 49.

656. *Godwin, William. *Life of Geoffrey Chaucer.* New York: AMS, 1974.
Reprint of the 1803 edition.

657. *Godwin, William. *Memoirs of Mary Wollstonecraft.* Ed. W. Clark Durant. New York: Gordon, 1972.
Reprint of the 1927 edition.

658. *Godwin, William. *Memoirs of the Author of "A Vindication of the Rights of Woman."* Introd. Gina Luria. New York: Garland, 1974. "The Feminist Controversy in England, 1788–1810."
Reprint of the 1798 edition, with a new introduction.

659. Godwin, William. *St. Leon: A Tale of the Sixteenth Century.* Foreword by Devendra P. Varma. Introd. Juliet Beckett. See K-SJ, 21–22 (1972–73), No. 625.
Rev. by Parks C. Hunter, Jr., in SIR, 12 (Winter 1973), 469–474.

660. *Godwin, William. *St. Leon: A Tale of the Sixteenth Century.* Introd. Gina Luria. New York: Garland, 1974. "The Feminist Controversy in England, 1788–1810."
Reprint of the 1799 edition, with a new introduction.

661. *Gribble, Francis H. *The Romantic Life of Shelley and the Sequel.* New York: Haskell, 1972.
Reprint of the 1911 edition.

662. *Grylls, R. Glynn. *William Godwin and His World.* Folcroft, Pa.: Folcroft, 1974.
Reprint of the 1953 edition.

663. Hall, Spencer. "Shelley's 'Mont Blanc,'" SP, 70 (Apr. 1973), 199–221.‡
"Like much of Shelley's poetry, 'Mont Blanc' is not a totally unified work, either formally or conceptually." Hall finds that the poem exhibits a basic, unresolved problem of Shelley's thought: the concept of Power is represented as an "independent ontological reality, instead of as a symbolic projection which cannot be separated from the self-conscious activity of the poet's mind"; yet the latter is what is taking place in the poem.

664. Hartley, Robert A. "Phosphorescence in Canto I of *The Revolt of Islam*," N&Q, 218 (Aug. 1973), 293–294.†
Here (I.53.1–5) and elsewhere in Shelley, the latency of light is "an image of the eclipse but eventual resurgence of the Spirit of Good."

665. Hartley, Robert A. "The Uroboros in Shelley's Poetry," JEGP, 73 (Oct. 1974), 524–542.
An examination of the circular serpent and its sources for Shelley in the revolutionary tradition and the works of Sir William Drummond. Includes discussion of *The Revolt of Islam* and *Prometheus Unbound*, particularly the relationship of the *uroboros* to Necessity and Demogorgon.

666. *Hildebrand, William H. *Shelley's Polar Paradise: A Reading of "Prometheus Unbound."* Salzburg: Univ. of Salzburg, 1974. "Salzburg Studies in English: Romantic Reassessment Series, No. 18."
See No. 31.

667. *Hogg, Thomas Jefferson. *Shelley at Oxford.* Introd. R. A. Streatfeild. Folcroft, Pa.: Folcroft, 1974.
Reprint of the 1904 edition.

668. Höhne, Horst. "Mary Shelley's *Frankenstein*: Komplexität eines poetischen Bildes und das ideologische Dilemma romantischer Dichtung," *Zeitschrift für Anglistik und Amerikanistik*, 22, No. 3 (1974), 266–289.

669. Holmes, Richard. *Shelley: The Pursuit.* London: Weidenfeld and Nicolson, 1974.
Rev. by Lorna Sage in NS, 88 (2 Aug. 1974), 156–157; by Richard Luckett in Spec, 233 (3 Aug. 1974), 146. Also see No. 626.

670. Hunter, Parks C., Jr. "The Equivocal Cain Images in Shelley's *Adonais*," KSMB, 24 (1973), 12–15.

The Cain image in *Adonais*, st. 34, "connotes protection for the poet and expresses the idea of the poet being worthy of special consideration."

671. Hunter, Parks C., Jr. "William Godwin's Lengthy Preoccupation with *Antonio*," K-SJ, 23 (1974), 21–24.
Chronicles Godwin's composition of the tragedy and shows that "Alonzo," thought to be a different work, is actually just an earlier name for *Antonio*.

672. Irvine, William, and Park Honan. *The Book, the Ring, and the Poet: A Biography of Robert Browning*. New York: McGraw-Hill, 1974.
Ch. 2: "To Shelley's School." Index lists many references to Byron and Keats, a few to Hunt.

673. Jackel, David. "Jane Austen and 'Thorough Novel Slang,'" N&Q, 218 (Feb. 1973), 46–47.†
Finds phrase "vortex of dissipation," disliked by Austen, in Godwin's *St. Leon*, among other novels.

674. Jeffrey, Lloyd N. "'Beasts of the Woods and Wildernesses' in the Poetry of Shelley," K-SJ, 21–22 (1972–73), 64–82.‡
Though "Shelley's mammalian world is generally that of the literary man and not of the naturalist," he is "always ready to confound our generalities." This survey of mammalian images concentrates on sources.

675. *Johnson, Charles F. *Three Americans and Three Englishmen*. Folcroft, Pa.: Folcroft, 1973.
Reprint of the 1886 edition. Shelley is included.

676. Joukovsky, Nicholas A. "The First Printing of Peacock's 'The Pool of the Diving Friar,'" N&Q, 219 (Sept. 1974), 334–335.
The poem was published in the *New Monthly* magazine five years before it appeared in *Crotchet Castle*.

677. *Kalim, M. Siddiq. *The Social Orpheus: Shelley and the Owenites*. Lahore, Pakistan: Research Council, Government College, 1973.

678. Keenan, Richard C. "Browning and Shelley," *Browning Institute Studies*, 1 (1973), 119–145.
Revises the generally accepted thesis that the later Browning shed the influence of Shelley. Keenan finds that "Browning's interest in Shelley continued to surface periodically throughout his lifetime."

679. Keenan, Richard C. "Shelley's Influence on the Poetry of Robert Browning" [Doctoral dissertation, Temple, 1974], DAI, 35 (Dec. 1974), 3686-A.

680. Kiely, Robert. *The Romantic Novel in England*. See K-SJ, 21–22 (1972–73), No. 647.
Rev. in *Choice*, 10 (Mar. 1973), 94.

681. Kilgour, Norman. "A New Portrait of Shelley?" KSMB, 24 (1973), 1–2.
The question is left unanswered, but two possible sources of the picture are suggested.

682. King-Hele, Desmond. *Shelley: His Thought and Work*. 2nd. ed. See K-SJ, 20 (1971), No. 851; 21–22 (1972–73), No. 648.
Rev. by Joseph DeRocco in K-SJ, 21–22 (1972–73), 252–253.

683. Klapper, Molly. "The German Literary Influence on Shelley and Byron with Special Reference to Goethe" [Doctoral dissetration, New York Univ., 1974], DAI, 35 (Aug. 1974), 1048-A.

684. Klein, Mary Ann. "Conceptual and Artistic Limits of Eight Nineteenth-Century British Literary Utopias" [Doctoral dissertation, Marquette, 1973], DAI, 35 (Aug. 1974), 1048-A.
Mary Shelley's *The Last Man* is discussed.

685. Klotz, Günther. "Funktionswandel des englischen Romans im letzten Jahrzehnt des 18. Jahrhunderts," *Zeitschrift für Anglistik und Amerikanistik*, 22, No. 3 (1974), 229–250.
Caleb Williams is discussed.

686. Kramnick, Isaac. "On Anarchism and the Real World: William Godwin and Radical England." See K-SJ, 21–22 (1972–73), No. 649.
Replies by Thomas Hone, *American Political Science Review*, 66 (Dec. 1972), 1316, by Terry M. Perlin, 1316–17, and by Bruce Gillespie, 67 (June 1973), 576–577.

687. Kroeber, Karl. "Experience as History:

Shelley's Venice, Turner's Carthage," *ELH*, 41 (Fall 1974), 321–339.

Kroeber explicates passages in "Lines Written among the Euganean Hills" to exemplify his thesis that the "Romantic identifies individual experience with historical process." Thus, "for Shelley, the immediate experience, what he sees from the hill, would not be complete (nor accurately represented) did not his imagination encompass within his sensory perceptions the history (past and future) invisibly *in* his perceiving."

688. Lees, Daniel E. "Shelley's 'Medusa' and Hegelian Synthesis," UES, 12 (Sept. 1974), pp. 1–3.

Thesis (st. 1–2): stasis and death; antithesis (st. 3–4): life; synthesis (st. 5): life-in-death.

689. Leighton, Margaret. *Shelley's Mary: A Life of Mary Godwin Shelley*. New York: Farrar, Strauss, 1973.

Juvenile literature.

690. Lentz, Vern B., and Douglas D. Short. "Hardy, Shelley, and the Statues," *Victorian Poetry*, 12 (Winter 1974), 370–372.

"There can be little doubt that Hardy was indebted to Shelley's 'Ozymandias' in creating 'The Children and Sir Nameless'; indeed the one is perhaps best thought of as the prototype for the other." But the differences between the poems illustrate the "transition from the Romantic to the modern temperament."

691. Leo, John Robert. "Visualized Triumph Patterns in Shelley: A Phenomenological Reading" [Doctoral dissertation, Northwestern, 1973], DAI, 34 (Dec. 1973), 3347-A.

692. *Levine, George. "*Frankenstein* and the Tradition of Realism," *Novel*, 7 (Fall 1973), 14–30.†

693. Lewis, Hanna B. "Hoffmannsthal, Shelley, and Keats," *German Life and Letters*, 27 (Apr. 1974), 220–234.

Hoffmannsthal was influenced by Shelley, Keats, and Byron. Yet he was not attracted by the revolutionary, the passionate, or the ironic, but by "the aesthetic philosophy, the poet's role in life, the mystical aspects of genius, and the penetrative view of nature."

694. Leyda, Seraphia DeVille. "*The Serpent Is Shut Out from Paradise*": *A Revaluation of Romantic Love in Shelley*. See K-SJ, 21–22 (1972–73), No. 657.

Rev. by P. H. Butter in *Yearbook of English Studies*, 4 (1974), 314–316.

695. McCurdy, Harold G. "Shelley and the Assassins," *Georgia Review*, 27 (Summer 1973), 182–193.‡

A psychoanalytic study of Shelley inspired by the prose fragment *The Asssasins*, which McCurdy takes to be a statement of Shelley's view that love should be pursued at any cost. McCurdy argues that Shelley, in his repeated attempts to pursue love, destroyed those who stood in his way and thus incurred an ever-growing burden of guilt feelings.

696. Macey, Patricia Gale Dunfield. "The World's Slow Stain: A Study of Darkness and Light and Life and Death in Selected Poems by Percy Bysshe Shelley" [Doctoral dissertation, Indiana, 1973], DAI, 34 (July 1973), 280-A.

697. McGann, Jerome J. *Swinburne: An Experiment in Criticism*. Chicago: Univ. of Chicago, 1972.

Includes considerable discussion of the influence of Shelley, Byron, and Keats.

Rev. by Lionel Stevenson in JEGP, 72 (Apr. 1973), 249–252.

698. McGavran, Margaret Ross. "Mary and Margaret: The Triumph of Woman" [Doctoral dissertation, Cornell, 1973], DAI, 34 (Sept. 1973), 1248-A.

Mary Wollstonecraft and Margaret Fuller.

699. McNiece, Gerald. "Shelley, John Stuart Mill, and the Secret Ballot," *Mill News Letter*, 8 (Spring 1973), pp. 2–7.†

Both distrusted it, but for different reasons.

700. Manogue, Ralph Anthony. "A Critical Edition of Robert Southey's *Wat Tyler*" [Doctoral dissertation, New York Univ., 1971], DAI, 33 (Mar. 1973), 5131-A.

Demonstrates the influence of William Godwin.

701. Matthewson, George. "Claire Clairmont on Shelley's Circle," N&Q, 218 (Feb. 1973), 48–49.†

James Thomson (B.V.) recorded in his diary a conversation with Captain

Silsbee, reporting Claire's reminiscences of many of her early acquaintances.

702. *Maurois, André. *Ariel; ou La vie de Shelley*. Paris: Club des amis du livre, 1971.

Another edition of the perennial best-seller.

703. Mayer, Elsie Francis. "Form and Meaning in Shelley's Poetic Fragments" [Doctoral dissertation, Wayne State, 1973], DAI, 34 (Dec. 1973), 3350-A.

704. *Mayfield, John S. "Swinburne in Miniature," *Courier* (Syracuse Univ. Library), 11 (July 1974), 38–39.

A newly discovered Swinburne notebook contains a poem entitled "Shelley," a portion of which is reproduced. Also see No. 791.

705. *Medwin, Thomas. *The Life of Percy Bysshe Shelley*. Revised ed. Introd. and commentary by H. Buxton Forman. Folcroft, Pa.: Folcroft, 1973.

Reprint of the 1913 edition.

706. Miller, Betty. *Robert Browning: A Portrait*. New York: Scribner's, n.d. [1973].

Considerable treatment of Shelley's influence.

707. Milne, Fred LaFaye. "The Center and the Circumference: A Study of Shelley's Philosophic Development" [Doctoral dissertation, Massachusetts, 1973], DAI, 34 (Apr. 1974), 6599-A.

708. Minami, Akira. " 'Ashes and Sparks': The Role of the West Wind," *Studies in English Literature* (Japan), 49 (Mar. 1973), 199–210.

"Ode to the West Wind" read in terms of Shelley's personal life and political prophesying. "We have understood the function of 'ashes and sparks' in three ways: (1) as a defiant expression to the [*sic*] tyranny and death, (2) to figure volcanic action, and (3) as bringing forth an association of fertilizing effect."

709. Mirarchi, Margaret J. Klett. "A Study of the Grotesque in the Works of Thomas Lovell Beddoes" [Doctoral dissertation, Pennsylvania, 1973], DAI, 34 (June 1974), 7714-A.

Discusses the influence of Shelley.

710. Monro, D. H. "Godwin, Oakeshott, and Mrs. Bloomer," JHI, 35 (Oct.–Dec. 1974), 611–624.

"The institution-lover [Oakeshott] is just as likely to misunderstand and distort social facts as the institution-hater [Godwin]."

711. Cancelled.

712. Neal, Shirley Winifred Zwoyer. "Family Relationships in *The Revolt of Islam*" [Doctoral dissertation, Illinois, 1973], DAI, 34 (June 1974), 7716-A.

713. Neumann, Bonnie Rayford. "Mary Shelley" [Doctoral dissertation, New Mexico, 1972], DAI, 33 (Apr. 1973), 5689-A.

714. Noel-Bentley, Peter Charles. "The Religious Poetry of James Thomson (B.V.)" [Doctoral dissertation, Toronto, 1972], DAI, 34 (Sept. 1973), 1250-A.

Shelley was an important influence.

715. *O'Brien, H. J. "Francis Stuart's Cathleen Ni Houlahan," *Dublin Magazine*, 8 (Summer 1971), 48–54.†

Shelley's dome image as a recurrent symbol in Stuart's "The Coloured Dome."

716. Origo, Iris. "Three Exhibits at Casa Magni," KSMB, 24 (1973), 3–7.

"An address given at the opening of the Shelley Memorial Rooms at Casa Magni, 9th July, 1972."

717. Ousby, Ian. " 'My Servant Caleb': Godwin's *Caleb Williams* and the Political Trials of the 1790's," UTQ, 44 (Fall 1974), 47–55.

The novel was born in a political milieu of government spying on the radical opposition. "Godwin chose to call Caleb a 'spy' at a time when radicals were hyper-conscious of the presence of political spies in their midst," a point fundamental to our interpretation of the novel.

718. Palacio, Jean de. "Godwin et la tentation de l'autobiographie (William Godwin et J. J. Rousseau)," EA, 27 (Apr. 1974), 143–157.

Comparison of Godwin's autobiographical writing in Essay 18 of *Thoughts on Man* with Rousseau's *Confessions*.

719. Palacio, Jean de. *Mary Shelley dans son oeuvre: Contributions aux études shelleyennes*. See K-SJ, 20 (1971), No. 899; 21–22 (1972–73), No. 694.

Rev. by Béatrice Micha in *Arcadia: Zeitschrift für vergleichende Literatur Wissenschaft*, 8, No. 2 (1973), 228–230; by

Alice G. Fredman in K-SJ, 23 (1974), 129–133.

720. *Peacock, Thomas L. *The Plays of Thomas Love Peacock, Published for the First Time.* Ed. A. B. Young. Folcroft, Pa.: Folcroft, 1974.

Reprint of the 1910 edition.

721. *Peck, Walter E. *Shelley: His Life and Work.* 2 vols. Folcroft, Pa.: Folcroft, 1973.

Reprint of the 1927 edition.

722. *Pennell, Elizabeth R. *Mary Wollstonecraft Godwin.* Folcroft, Pa.: Folcroft, 1974.

Reprint of the 1885 edition in the "Eminent Women" series.

723. Perrin, Jean. *Les structures de l'imaginaire shelleyen.* Grenoble: Presses universitaires de Grenoble, 1973.

724. *Pixton, William H. " 'The Sensitive Plant': Shelley's Acquiescence to Agnosticism," *Ball State University Forum,* 14, No. 4 (1973), pp. 35–44.‡

". . . Shelley indicates that life and man's mental activity are ultimately beyond human comprehension" (quoted from the abstract).

725. Pollin, Burton R. " 'Alastors' in the Works of Coryatt, Heywood, Southey, and Shelley," ES, 55 (Oct. 1974), 428–434.

Notes the appearance of the word in ancient and medieval literature and in three English works earlier than Shelley's poem.

726. Pollin, Burton R. "Charles Lamb and Charles Lloyd as Jacobins and Anti-Jacobins," SIR, 12 (Summer 1973), 633–647.†‡

Traces the change in their view of Godwinism in their published works.

727. Pollin, Burton R. "Godwin's *Memoirs* as a Source of Shelley's Phrase 'Intellectual Beauty,' " K-SJ, 23 (1974), 14–20.

Argues for a Godwinian rather than Platonic explanation of Shelley's phrase.

728. Pollin, Burton R. "Permutations of Names in *The Borderers,* or Hints of Godwin, Charles Lloyd, and a Real Renegade," WC, 4 (Winter 1973), 31–35.‡

Sources of the names in the drafts and final version of Wordsworth's play.

729. *[Portrait thought to be of Shelley], T&T, 55 (Oct. 1974), p. 4.

730. Poston, Carol Hoaglan. "Mary Wollstonecraft's *A Vindication of the Rights of Woman*: A Critical and Annotated Edition" [Doctoral dissertation, Nebraska, 1973], DAI, 34 (Nov. 1973), 2575-A.

730a. Poston, Carol H[oaglan], and Janet M. Todd. "Some Textual Variations in the First Two Editions of *A Vindication of the Rights of Woman,*" MWN, 2 (May 1974), 27–29.

The changes are minor, but they do reveal "growing assurance in her own unconventional opinions."

731. Powers, Katherine Richardson. "The Influence of William Godwin on the Novels of Mary Shelley" [Doctoral dissertation, Tennessee, 1972], DAI, 33 (Feb. 1973), 4359-A.

732. Prance, Claude. "The Laughing Philosopher—Some Thoughts on Thomas Love Peacock," ABC, 24 (Mar.–Apr. 1974), 21–25.

Observations on some of the characters and the libraries that appear in the novels, along with speculation on Peacock's relationship with Charles Lamb.

733. Priestley, F. E. L. "The Central Paradox in Browning," *Humanities Association Review,* 24 (Spring 1973), 87–97.†

Discusses Browning's attitude toward Shelley.

734. Priestman, Donald G. "*The Borderers*: Wordsworth's Addenda to Godwin," UTQ, 44 (Fall 1974), 56–65.

Oswald is Godwin's malevolent man, but Wordsworth supplements Godwin by showing that nature can help replace malevolence with benevolence. Marmaduke is Godwin's benevolent man, but here Wordsworth rejects the Godwinian notion that faith can be founded on rationalism and shows instead that it must be based on "a love of and receptivity to nature."

735. Rapin, René. "Byron et Shelley: Dialogue et commentaire sur Hamlet," *Etudes de lettres,* 6 (Jan.–Mar. 1973), 3–24.

Rapin translates into French the conversation on the character of Hamlet attributed to Shelley and Byron, and in introductory comments he suggests that the recorder was Trelawny, not Medwin.

736. Rayan, Krishna. *Suggestion and Statement*

in Poetry. London: Univ. of London, 1972.
Numerous references to Shelley.

737. Reese, Theodore Irving, III. "The Character and Role of Guinevere in the Nineteenth Century" [Doctoral dissertation, Brandeis, 1972], DAI, 33 (Mar. 1973), 5138-A.
Peacock is included.

738. Reiman, Donald H. "Editing Shelley," in *Editing Texts of the Romantic Period*, ed. John D. Baird. See K-SJ, 21–22 (1972–73), No. 722.
Rev. by Peter Davison in *Library*, 27 (Dec. 1973), 358–361; by Jack Stillinger in K-SJ, 23 (1974), 144.

739. Reiman, Donald H., ed. *Shelley and His Circle, 1773–1822*. The Carl H. Pforzheimer Library. Vols. V and VI. Cambridge: Harvard Univ., 1973.
Rev. in *Choice*, 11 (May 1974), 436; by Stuart Curran in ELN, 12, Supplement (Sept. 1974), 63–64; by G. M. Matthews in TLS, 6 Sept. 1974, p. 948. Also see No. 31.

740. Reisner, Thomas A. "Echo of Byron in Shelley," N&Q, 219 (Sept. 1974), 333.
Epipsychidion 17–26 and *Childe Harold* III.xxxiii.289–297.

741. Reisner, Thomas A. "Some Scientific Models for Shelley's Multitudinous Orb," K-SJ, 23 (1974), 52–59.
Finds analogies between *Prometheus Unbound* IV.236–279 and descriptions of planetary rotation in Newton, Laplace, and Euler.

742. Reisner, Thomas A. "Tabula Rasa: Shelley's Metaphor of the Mind," *Ariel*, 4 (Apr. 1973), 90–102.‡
The mind is formed by internal inspiration as well as by external sensation.

743. Richards, George D. "Shelley's Urn of Bitter Prophecy," K-SJ, 21–22 (1972–73), 112–125.‡
Tracing the "erosion of Shelley's youthful confidence" from *Queen Mab* to "The Triumph of Life," Richards argues that "not until his ardor turned to dejection and doubt did he fully mature as an artist."

744. Richards, I. A. *Beyond*. New York: Harcourt Brace Jovanovich, 1974.
Includes a discussion of *Prometheus Unbound*.
Rev. by Keith Cushman in LJ, 99 (1 Mar. 1974), 659; by Dudley Young in NYT, 26 May 1974, pp. 15–16.

745. *Richpense, Albertine de. " 'Je meurs, je faille, je tombe'; ou Analyse de l'orgasme shelleyenne," *Etudes littéraires de l'Afrique belge de nord*, 2, No. 1 (1973), 31–35.

746. *Rickert, Alfred E. "Two Views of *The Cenci*: Shelley and Artaud," *Ball State University Forum*, 14, No. 1 (1973), pp. 31–35.‡
". . . Shelley's play is found to be a prototype for Artaud's conception of the theatre of cruelty" (quoted from the abstract).

747. *Roe, Ivan. *Shelley: The Last Phase*. Folcroft, Pa.: Folcroft, 1973.
Reprint of the 1953 edition.

748. *Roe, Ivan. *Shelley: The Last Phase*. New York: Cooper Square, 1973.
Reprint of the 1953 edition.

749. Rogers, Stephen. *Classical Greece and the Poetry of Chenier, Shelley, and Leopardi*. Notre Dame, Ind.: Univ. of Notre Dame, 1974.
Rev. by David Kwinn in LJ, 99 (1 June 1974), 1549.

750. *Rossi, Alice S., comp. *The Feminist Papers: From Adams to de Beauvoir*. New York: Columbia, 1973; Bantam, 1974.
Includes Mary Wollstonecraft.

751. Ruff, James Lynn. *Shelley's "The Revolt of Islam."* See K-SJ, 21–22 (1972–73), No. 734.
Rev. by P. H. Butter in *Yearbook of English Studies*, 4 (1974), 314–316.

752. Russell, Herb. "Masters' 'Alfred Moir,' 14," Exp, 31 (Mar. 1973), Item 54.†‡
Evidence that the unnamed book which Moir claims to have been the primary influence on his life is an edition of Shelley.

753. Ryan, Donald J. "Percy Bysshe Shelley's *Laon and Cythna*: A Critical Edition of the Manuscripts in the Bodleian Library" [Doctoral dissertation, New York Univ., 1972], DAI, 33 (May 1973), 6324-A.

754. *Salama, Adel. *Shelley's Major Poems: A Re-Interpretation*. Salzburg: Univ. of Salzburg, 1973. "Salzburg Studies in English: Romantic Reassessment Series, No. 9."
Rev. by P. H. Butter in MLR, 69 (July 1974), 625; in *Choice*, 11 (July–Aug. 1974), 763. Also see No. 86.

755. Scales, Luther L., Jr. "The Poet as Miltonic Adam in *Alastor*," K-SJ, 21–22 (1972–73), 126–144.‡
Sees the quest of the *Alastor* poet as "refracting" the pattern of the creation, fall, and redemption of Man in *Paradise Lost* and *Paradise Regained*.

756. Schier, Donald. "A Contemporary French Critique of *Caleb Williams*," RLC, 47 (July–Sept. 1973), 412–418.
By Abbé André Morellet, whose critique Schier contrasts to modern interpretations.

757. Schulze, Earl J. *Shelley's Theory of Poetry: A Reappraisal*. See K-SJ, 17 (1968), No. 583; 18 (1969), No. 651; 19 (1970), No. 377; 20 (1971), No. 929.
Rev. by Martin Seletzky in *Anglia*, 91 (1973), 124–127.

758. *Scott, W. S., ed. *The Athenians, Being Correspondence between Thomas Jefferson Hogg and His Friends, Thomas Love Peacock, Leigh Hunt, Percy Bysshe Shelley, and Others*. Folcroft, Pa.: Folcroft, 1973.
Reprint of the 1943 edition.

759. Scrivener, Michael H. "Bostetter's Case Against Shelley," *Paunch* (State Univ. of N.Y., Buffalo), No. 38 (Mar. 1974), pp. 40–50.
Concedes the substance of Bostetter's case, but argues that there are redeeming features which Bostetter ignored.

760. Seeber, Laurian. "Shelley's Relation to Rousseau" [Doctoral dissertation, North Carolina, 1973], DAI, 34 (Nov. 1973), 2655-A.

761. *Sharp, William. *Life of Percy Bysshe Shelley*. Folcroft, Pa.: Folcroft, 1973.
Reprint of the 1887 edition.

762. Shaw, George Bernard. *Collected Letters*. Ed. Dan H. Laurence. Vol. I: *1874–1897*. Vol. II: *1898–1910*. New York: Dodd, Mead, 1972.
A number of references to Shelley.

763. Shaw, George Bernard. *Nondramatic Literary Criticism*. Ed. Stanley Weintraub. Lincoln: Univ. of Nebraska, 1972.
Includes the essays, "Shaming the Devil about Shelley" and "Keats."

764. Shealy, Ann E. *Journey through the Unapparent: A Reading of Shelley's "The Triumph of Life."* Hicksville, N.Y.: Exposition, 1974.

765. Shealy, Ann E. "The Shattered Lamp: A Study of Annihilation in the Poetry of Shelley" [Doctoral dissertation, Case Western Reserve, 1972], DAI, 33 (Mar. 1973), 5141-A.

766. *Shelley, Mary. *The Choice: A Poem on Shelley's Death*. Ed. H. Buxton Forman. Folcroft, Pa.: Folcroft, 1973.
Reprint of the 1876 edition.

767. *Shelley, Mary. *Frankenstain; ē Synchronos Promētheus*. Trans. Rozita Sōkou. Athens: Galaxias, 1971.

768. Shelley, Mary. *Frankenstein*. Directed by John Whale. Screenplay by Garrett Fort and Francis Edwards Farogh. Ed. Richard J. Anobile. London: Macmillan; London: Pan; New York: Universe (1974). "The Film Classics Library."
Photographs and dialogue from a film version.

769. *Shelley, Mary. *Frankenstein: A Gothic Thriller in Two Acts*. Adapted by David Campton. London: Miller, 1973. Paperback.

770. Shelley, Mary. *Frankenstein; or The Modern Prometheus*. The 1818 text, ed. with variant readings, an introd., and notes by James Rieger. Indianapolis: Bobbs-Merrill, 1974. Also in paperback.
Rev. in *Choice*, 11 (June 1974), 603; by Donald Newlove in *Village Voice*, 25 July 1974, p. 25. Also see No. 31.

771. *Shelley, Mary. *Frankenstein; or The Modern Prometheus*. London: Arrow, 1973. Paperback.

772. *Shelley, Mary. *Frankenstein; ovvero Il Prometeo moderno*. Trans. Bruno Tasso. Milan: Club degli editori, 1973.

773. *Shelley, Mary. *Frankenstein: The True Story*. Adapted by Christopher Isherwood and Bachardy. London: Avon, 1974.
Script of a television play.
Rev. by W. I. Scobie in *London Magazine*, 14, No. 1 (Apr.–May 1974), 107–110.

774. *Shelley, Mary. *Frankeştayn*. Trans. Giovanni Scognamillo. Istanbul: Milliyet Yayin, 1971.

775. *Shelley, Mary. *Letters of Mary W. Shelley*. Introd. Henry H. Harper. Folcroft, Pa.: Folcroft, 1972.
Reprint of the 1918 edition.

776. *Shelley, Mary. *Proserpine and Midas: Two Unpublished Mythological Dramas.* Ed. and introd. A. H. Koszul. Folcroft, Pa.: Folcroft, 1973.
Reprint of the 1922 edition.

777. *Shelley, Mary. *The Story of Frankenstein.* Adapted by Carol Christian. London: Macmillan, 1974.
Secondary school text.

778. Silverman, Edwin B. *Poetic Synthesis in Shelley's "Adonais."* See K-SJ, 21–22 (1972–73), No. 752.
Rev. by Donald H. Reiman in K-SJ, 23 (1974), 144–146.

779. *Simon, Brian, ed. *The Radical Tradition in Education in Britain: A Compilation of Writings by William Godwin* [*et al.*]. London: Lawrence and Wishart, 1972.

780. Simpson, Leo. *The Peacock Papers.* Toronto: Macmillan of Canada, 1974.
Satirical novel in which T. L. Peacock is a leading character.

781. Singh, Sheila Uttam. *Shelley and the Dramatic Form.* See K-SJ, 21–22 (1972–73), No. 753.
Rev. by P. H. Butter in *Yearbook of English Studies*, 4 (1974), 314–316.

782. Small, Christopher. *Mary Shelley's "Frankenstein": Tracing the Myth.* Pittsburgh: Univ. of Pittsburgh, 1973.
American edition of *Ariel like a Harpy: Shelley, Mary and Frankenstein.* See K-SJ, 21–22 (1972–73), No. 755.
Rev. by Frank P. Riga in LJ, 98 (Aug. 1973), 2301; in *Choice*, 11 (July–Aug. 1974), 764; by Stuart Curran in ELN, 12, Supplement (Sept. 1974), 61–62; by Alice G. Fredman in K-SJ, 23 (1974), 135–136.

783. Smith, Carolyn Wendel. "Time and Eternity in Shelley's Major Poetry" [Doctoral dissertation, Brown, 1972], DAI, 33 (Feb. 1973), 4364-A.

784. *Smith, George B. *Shelley: A Critical Biography.* Folcroft, Pa.: Folcroft, 1974.
Reprint of the 1877 edition.

785. *Smith, James, and Horace Smith. *Rejected Addresses; or The New Theatrum Poetarum.* Introd. Andrew Boyle. Folcroft, Pa.: Folcroft, 1974.
Reprint of the 1924 edition.

786. Stamper, Rexford. "*Caleb Williams*: The Bondage of Truth," *Southern Quarterly*, 12 (Oct. 1973), 39–50.
"Caleb does learn about the truth, but what he learns is that he can never know the truth. The portion, or vision, of it which he does discover serves to exclude him from society and leads to his moral destruction."

787. *Stephenson, William. "Romanticism and Modern Science," in *Studies in Relevance: Romantic and Victorian Writers in 1972*, ed. Thomas Meade Harwell (Salzburg: Univ. of Salzburg, 1973), pp. 4–16. "Salzburg Studies in English: Romantic Reassessment Series, No. 32."
Shelley is discussed.

788. Stillians, Bruce. "Frost's 'To the Thawing Wind,'" Exp, 31 (Dec. 1972), Item 31.†
". . . Frost's critique of poetic pretense in Shelley's 'Ode to the West Wind.'"

789. Story, Patrick. "Pope, Pageantry, and Shelley's 'Triumph of Life,'" K-SJ, 21–22 (1972–73), 145–159.
Finds (1) thematic and structural parallels between the procession in Shelley's poem and the conclusion of Pope's *Epilogue to the Satires*; and (2) parallels between Shelley's chariot and its passenger and Pope's *Dunciad.* Concludes with suggested sources for Shelley's four-visaged charioteer.

790. Svaglic, Martin J. "Shelley and King Lear," in *Nineteenth-Century Literary Perspectives: Essays in Honor of Lionel Stevenson*, ed. Clyde de L. Ryals *et al.* (Durham: Duke Univ., 1974), pp. 49–63.

791. *Swinburne, Algernon C. *Shelley.* Preface by John S. Mayfield. Worcester, Mass.: Achille St. Onge, 1973.
A limited edition of newly discovered poem by Swinburne entitled "Shelley." Available from Achille St. Onge, 7 Arden Road, Worcester, Mass. 01606. Also see No. 704.

792. Swinden, Patrick. "Shelley: 'Ode to the West Wind,'" *Critical Survey*, 6 (Summer 1973), 52–58.
Demonstrates Shelley's grasp on the actual in spite of his soaring aspiration.

793. Swingle, L. J. "Frankenstein's Monster and Its Romantic Relatives: Problems of Knowledge in English Romanticism," *Texas Studies in Literature and Language*, 15 (Spring 1973), 51–66.‡

"Mary Shelley's novel is a study of the mind in the process of trying to come to terms with the Stranger. . . . Here the human mind does not merely encounter the Stranger; instead it creates it." Tragedy arises out of "tension between opposing claims about what is true," which offers a means of placing Mary Shelley's novel in the literary context of the period. Swingle compares the monster with Keats's Porphyro in "The Eve of St. Agnes."

794. *Szenczi, Miklós, Tibor Szobotka, and Anna Katona. *Az angol irodalom története.* [A history of English literature.] Budapest: Gondolat, 1972.

Includes a chapter on Shelley.

Rev. by Zoltán Abádi-Nagy in *Angol filológiai tanulmányok: Hungarian Studies in English,* 8 (1974), 102–106; by Lászlo Orszagh in *Zeitschrift für Anglistik und Amerikanistik,* 22, No. 2 (1974), 209–211 [in English].

795. Tetreault, Ronald Richard. "A Modest Creed: Scepticism and Prophecy in Shelley" [Doctoral dissertation, Cornell, 1974], DAI, 35 (Aug. 1974), 1124-A.

796. Thompson, E. P. "Solitary Walker," *New Society,* 19 Sept. 1974, pp. 749–751.

A review-article. See No. 804.

797. *Thompson, Francis. *Shelley.* Introd. George Wyndham. Folcroft, Pa.: Folcroft, 1973.

Reprint of the 1909 edition.

798. Thorn, Arline R. "Shelley's *The Cenci* as Tragedy," *Costerus,* 9 (1973), 219–228.†

"In *The Cenci,* Shelley's tragic universe is pervaded by the sense of evil at the heart of things, even in the seat of divine power." After illustrating the genuinely tragic themes of the play, Thorn rebuts F. R. Leavis' criticism of it.

799. Thorsen, W. B. "Hanzel Joyce Sale Brings $896,265," ABC, 24 (Sept.–Oct. 1973), 13–15.

Among the items in the collection of David Gage Joyce, sold in Chicago in Sept. 1973, were Byron's farewell message to his wife, Shelley's MS of "Prince Athanase," and a first edition of Keats's 1820 volume.

800. Thurman, William Richard, Jr. "Letters about Shelley from the Richard Garnett Papers, University of Texas" [Doctoral dissertation, Texas, 1972], DAI, 33 (Mar. 1973), 5145-A.

801. Todd, Janet M. "The Language of Sex in *A Vindication of the Rights of Woman,*" MWN, 1, No. 2 (Apr. 1973), pp. 10–17.†

On the use of "man" to denote "humanity" and its sexist implications.

802. Todd, Janet M., and Florence Boos. "Check List for Mary Wollstonecraft," MWN, 1, No. 2 (Apr. 1973), pp. 1–5.†

Also see No. 803.

803. Todd, Janet M., and Madeleine Marshall. "Biographical Notes," MWN, 2, No. 1 (Dec. 1973), pp. 27–33.†

Includes a supplement to the Mary Wollstonecraft checklist. See No. 802.

804. Tomalin, Claire. *The Life and Death of Mary Wollstonecraft.* London: Weidenfeld and Nicholson; New York: Harcourt Brace Jovanovich (1974).

Rev. by Patricia Beer in Li, 92 (5 Sept. 1974), 314–315; by Richard Cobb in TLS, 6 Sept. 1974, pp. 941–944; by J. H. Plumb in NS, 88 (6 Sept. 1974), 320; by Margaret Drabble in Spec, 233 (14 Sept. 1974), 338–339; by Joanna Richardson in *History Today,* 24 (Nov. 1974), 806–807; by Lorna Sage in *Encounter,* 43 (Dec. 1974), 67–72. Also see No. 796.

805. *Tomkievicz, Shirley. "Mary Wollstonecraft, 1759–1797," in *Makers of Modern Thought,* ed. Bruce Mazlish (New York: American Heritage, 1972), pp. 249–259.

806. Torres, Augusto M. "Complejo de Frankenstein," *Cuadernos hispanoamericanos,* 291 (Sept. 1974), 702–707.

807. Tropp, Martin. "Mary Shelley's 'Monster': A Study of *Frankenstein*" [Doctoral dissertation, Boston Univ., 1973], DAI, 34 (Oct. 1973), 1871-A.

Includes discussion of Byron.

808. Tsur, Reuven. "Articulateness and Requiredness in Iambic Verse," *Style,* 6 (Spring 1972), 123–148.

Remarks on prosody in "Ode to the West Wind."

809. Ullman, James R. *Mad Shelley.* New York: Gordian, 1974.

Reprint of the 1930 edition.

810. Van Luchene, Stephen Robert. "Essays in Gothic Fiction: From Horace Walpole

to Mary Shelley" [Doctoral dissertation, Notre Dame, 1973], DAI, 34 (Jan. 1974), 4220-A.

811. Veninga, Catherine Williams. "Shelley and the Idealist Tradition: A Study of *Prometheus Unbound*" [Doctoral dissertation, Rice, 1973], DAI, 34 (Sept. 1973), 1259-A.

812. Wagner, Vern. "The Offense of Poetry," CE, 34 (May 1973), 1045–59.‡

Supports Peacock's critique against Shelley's *A Defence of Poetry*.

813. Walling, William A. *Mary Shelley*. See K-SJ, 21–22 (1972–73), No. 773.

Rev. in *Choice*, 10 (Sept. 1973), 986; by Alice G. Fredman in K-SJ, 23 (1974), 133–135.

813a. Wardle, Ralph. *Mary Wollstonecraft: A Critical Biography*. See K-SJ, 17 (1968), No. 43; 18 (1969), No. 680.

See No. 601.

814. Wasserman, Earl R. *Shelley: A Critical Reading*. See K-SJ, 20 (1971), No. 958; 21–22 (1972–73), No. 777.

Rev. by Ross Woodman in K-SJ, 21–22 (1972–73), 244–252; by James Rieger in JEGP, 72 (Jan. 1973), 147–149; by Milton Wilson in ELN, 11 (1973), 64–68; by P. H. Butter in *Yearbook of English Studies*, 3 (1973), 308–310. Also see No. 66.

815. *Waterlow, Sydney. *Shelley*. Folcroft, Pa.: Folcroft, 1973.

Reprint of the 1913 edition.

816. Westerbeck, Colin Leslie, Jr. "The Dancer and the Statue: A Reading of the Poetry of Shelley, Keats and Yeats in Terms of Friedrich Nietzsche's *The Birth of Tragedy*" [Doctoral dissertation, Columbia, 1973], DAI, 34 (Nov. 1973), 2664-A.

817. White, Harry Steven. "The Opposition of Power and Will in Shelley's Thought" [Doctoral dissertation, Northwestern, 1972], DAI, 33 (Apr. 1973), 5696-A.

818. *White, Newman Ivey. *Shelley*. 2 vols. New York: Octagon, 1972.

Reprint of the 1940 edition.

819. Williams, Dennis Alfred. "William Godwin's Struggle for Autonomy, 1791–1797" [Doctoral dissertation, Kentucky, 1974], DAI, 35 (Sept. 1974), 1582-A.

820. *Wilson, Milton. *Shelley's Later Poetry: A Study of His Prophetic Imagination*. Westport, Conn.: Greenwood, 1974.

Reprint of the 1959 edition.

821. Winegarten, Renee. "Literary Terrorism," *Commentary*, 57 (Mar. 1974), 58–65.

Shelley exemplifies Romantic fascination with pain and terror.

822. *Wollstonecraft, Mary. *The Love Letters of Mary Wollstonecraft to Gilbert Imlay*. Preface by Roger Ingpen. Folcroft, Pa.: Folcroft, 1974.

Reprint of the 1908 edition.

823. *Wollstonecraft, Mary. *Mary: A Fiction*. Introd. Gina Luria. New York: Garland, 1974. "The Feminist Controversy in England, 1788–1810."

Reprint of the 1788 edition, with a new introduction.

824. *Wollstonecraft, Mary. *Posthumous Works*. Ed. William Godwin. Introd. Gina Luria. New York: Garland, 1974. "The Feminist Controversy in England, 1788–1810."

Reprint of the 1798 edition, with a new introduction.

825. *Wollstonecraft, Mary. *Posthumous Works of the Author of "A Vindication of the Rights of Woman."* Clifton, N.J.: Kelley, 1972.

Reprint of the 1798 edition.

826. *Wollstonecraft, Mary. *Thoughts on the Education of Daughters, with Reflections on Female Conduct in the More Important Duties of Life*. Introd. Gina Luria. New York: Garland, 1974. "The Feminist Controversy in England, 1788–1810."

Reprint of the 1787 edition, with a new introduction.

827. *Wollstonecraft, Mary. *A Vindication of the Rights of Woman, with Strictures on Political and Moral Subjects*. Introd. Gina Luria. New York: Garland, 1974. "The Feminist Controversy in England, 1788–1810."

Reprint of the 1792 edition, with a new introduction.

828. Woshinsky, Barbara. "Olymphe de Gouges' *Declaration of the Rights of Women* (1791)," MWN, 2, No. 1 (Dec. 1973), pp. 1–6.†

Questions whether Gouges and Mary Wollstonecraft knew one another.

829. Wright, George T. "The Lyric Present: Simple Present Verbs in English Poems," *PMLA*, 89 (May 1974), 563–579.

Many of the illustrations are from Shelley, a number from Keats. An appendix considers the frequency of progressive forms, again with examples from Shelley.

830. Zirker, Joan McTigue. "The Gothic Tradition in English Fiction, 1764–1824" [Doctoral dissertation, Indiana, 1974], DAI, 35 (July 1974), 422-A.

Discusses Mary Shelley.

For additional BOOKS AND ARTICLES RELATING TO SHELLEY AND HIS CIRCLE see Nos. 1, 6, 8, 14, 15, 17, 24–27, 30, 32, 33, 35, 38–40, 43–45, 50, 52, 55, 58, 60–63, 65, 69–72, 74, 75, 77, 79, 83, 87, 90, 92, 94, 96, 97, 140, 144, 174, 191, 195, 266, 322, 323, 382, 419, 445, 458, 492, 494, 499, 514, 521, 557, 563.

Index

This index is alphabetized according to the "letter-by-letter" system, in which each letter is considered up to the first mark of punctuation, and spaces and hyphens are ignored; for example, "To Autumn," Tobias, "To Chillon." Likewise, names beginning with "Mac" and "Mc" are in letter-by-letter alphabetical order, not grouped together.

References consist of a boldface Roman numeral representing the annual bibliography volume number, which will be found at the top of each right-hand page in the bibliography portions of this book, and an Arabic number representing the item number within that particular annual bibliography.

For more information on the use, contents, and scope of the index, see "How to Use This Book," p. ix.

Errata

XIII, 371: *For* Euralio *read* Eurialo
XVI, 141: *For* Merimée *read* Mérimée
XVI, 249: *For* Alistair *read* Alastair
XVI, 362: *For* Edwin G. *read* Edwin B.
XVII, 137: *For* A. W. Galignani *read* A. and W. Galignani
XVIII, 219: *For* Pauline *read* Paulino
XVIII, 318: *Insert* [*sic*] *after* Salemo; *actually* Salerno
XVIII, 596: *For* Mary Allen *read* Mary Ellen
XIX, 46: *For* Oltman *read* Oltmann
XIX, 226: *For* Herschel H. *read* Herschel M.
XIX, 250: *For* Miller *read* Mills
XIX, 396: *For* Henry K. *read* Henryk
XX, 100a: Kvič: *is a variation of* Kuić
XX, 174: For *The Romantics and Milton* read *The Romantics on Milton*
XX, 277: *For* Robert B. *read* Robert R.
XX, 366: *For* Marcia B. *read* Marcia R.
XX, 405: *For* Frank McCambre *read* J. Drummond Bone
XX, 405: *For* (May 1970), 199–200 *read* (May 1970), 198–200
XX, 487: *For* Allessandro *read* Alessandro
XX, 501: *For* Engleberg *read* Engelberg
XX, 553a: *For* Gabrielli *read* Gabrieli
XX, 566a: *For* Verweys *read* Verwey
XX, 576: *For* Lodowick *read* Lodwick
XX, 614: *For* Katherine *read* Katharine
XX, 764: *For* Baskyar *read* Baskiyar
XXI–XXII, 80: *For* Klimenko, E. N. *read* Klimenko, E. I.
XXI–XXII, 125: *For* Schmiefsky *read* Shmiefsky
XXI–XXII, 704: *Insert* [*sic*] *after* George Imlay; *actually* Gilbert Imlay
XXIII–XXV, 133: *For* Ann Freemantle *read* Anne Fremantle
XXIII–XXV, 253: *For* Nielson, Jorgen Erik *read* Nielsen Jørgen Erik
XXIII–XXV, 290: *For* Darrell *read* Darrel
XXIII–XXV, 590: *For* Wilfred *read* Wilfrid
XXIII–XXV, 693: *For* Hoffmannsthal *read* Hofmannsthal *(in title and annotation)*
XXIII–XXV, 701: *For* Matthewson *read* Mathewson